ベルサイユのばら

THE ROSE OF VERSAILLES

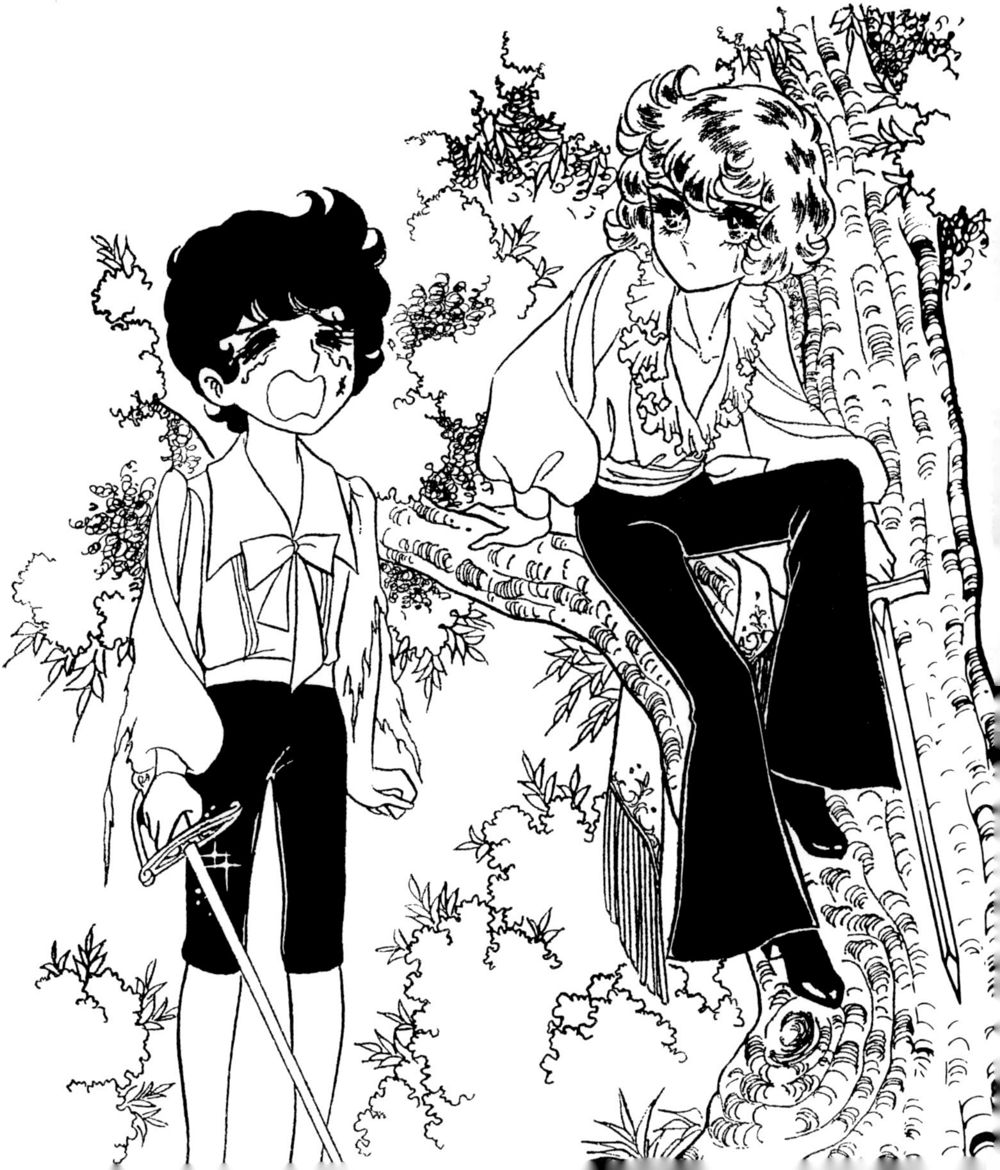

Episode 67

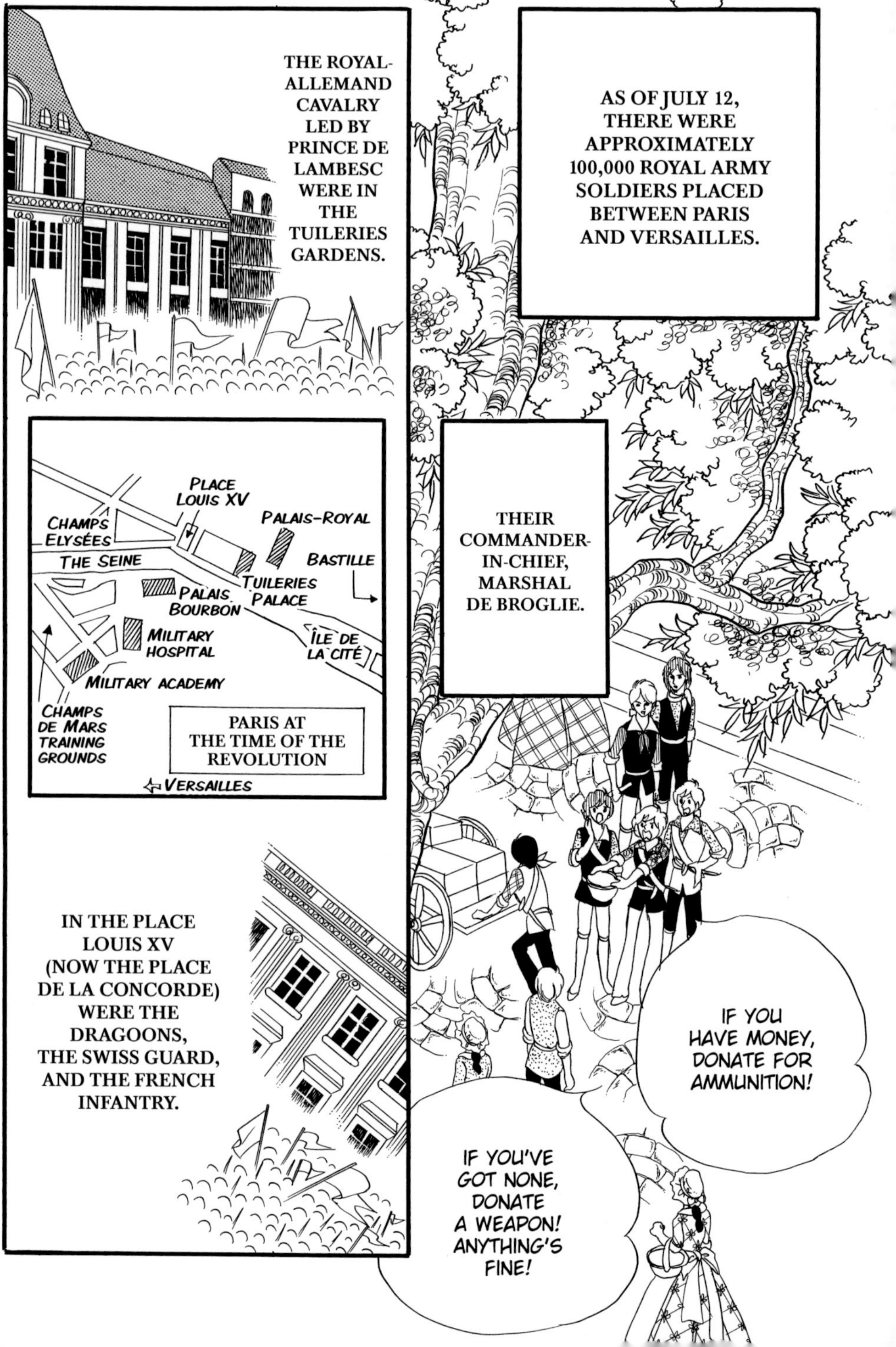

AS OF JULY 12, THERE WERE APPROXIMATELY 100,000 ROYAL ARMY SOLDIERS PLACED BETWEEN PARIS AND VERSAILLES.
THEIR COMMANDER-IN-CHIEF, MARSHAL DE BROGLIE.
IF YOU HAVE MONEY, DONATE FOR AMMUNITION!
IF YOU'VE GOT NONE, DONATE A WEAPON! ANYTHING'S FINE!
THE ROYAL-ALLEMAND CAVALRY LED BY PRINCE DE LAMBESC WERE IN THE TUILERIES GARDENS.
PLACE LOUIS XV
PALAIS-ROYAL
CHAMPS ELYSÉES
BASTILLE
THE SEINE
TUILERIES PALACE
PALAIS BOURBON
MILITARY HOSPITAL
ÎLE DE LA CITÉ
MILITARY ACADEMY
CHAMPS DE MARS TRAINING GROUNDS
PARIS AT THE TIME OF THE REVOLUTION
VERSAILLES
IN THE PLACE LOUIS XV (NOW THE PLACE DE LA CONCORDE) WERE THE DRAGOONS, THE SWISS GUARD, AND THE FRENCH INFANTRY.

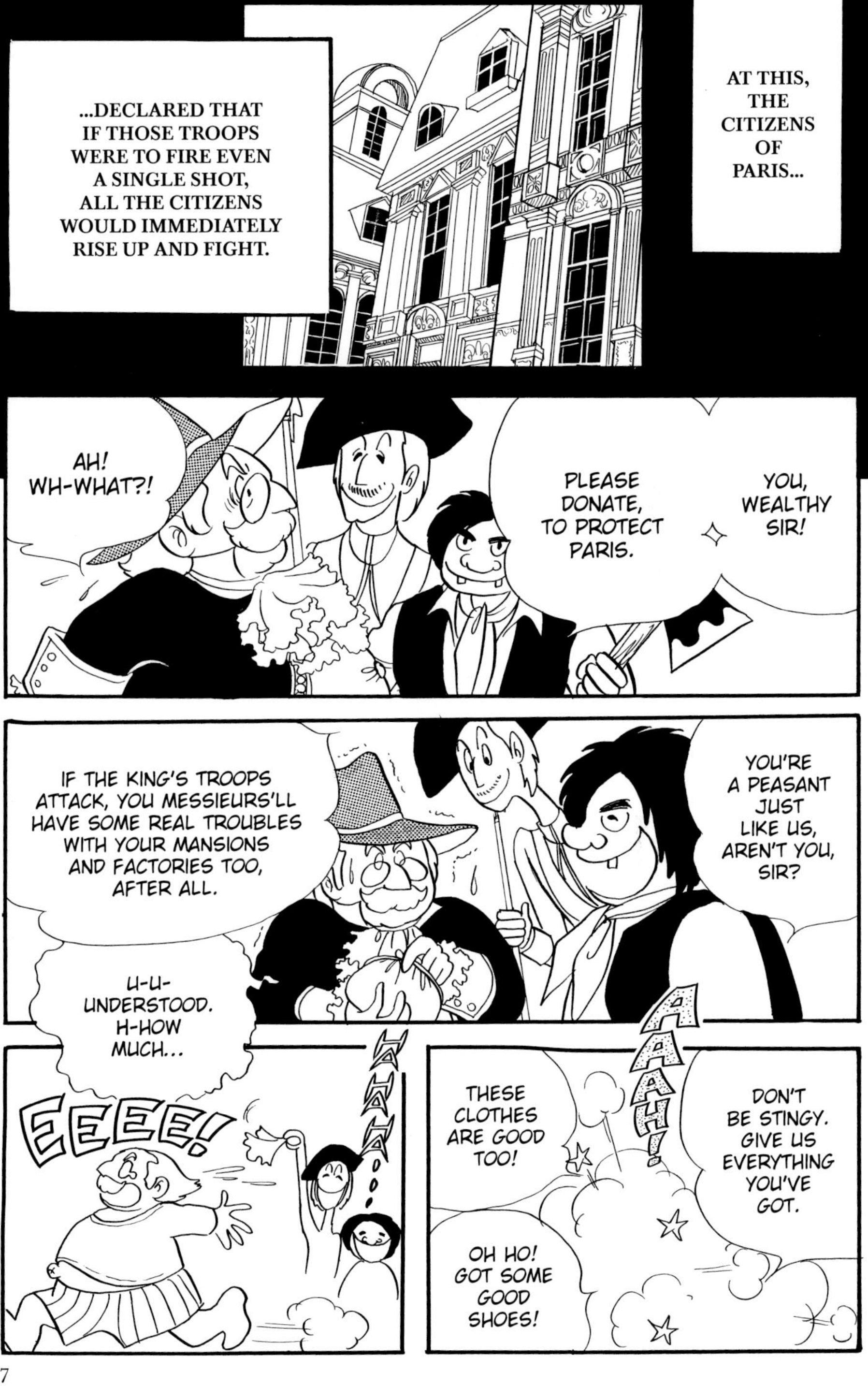
AT THIS, THE CITIZENS OF PARIS...
...DECLARED THAT IF THOSE TROOPS WERE TO FIRE EVEN A SINGLE SHOT, ALL THE CITIZENS WOULD IMMEDIATELY RISE UP AND FIGHT.
YOU, WEALTHY SIR!
PLEASE DONATE, TO PROTECT PARIS.
AH! WH-WHAT?!
YOU'RE A PEASANT JUST LIKE US, AREN'T YOU, SIR?
IF THE KING'S TROOPS ATTACK, YOU MESSIEURS'LL HAVE SOME REAL TROUBLES WITH YOUR MANSIONS AND FACTORIES TOO, AFTER ALL.
U-U-UNDERSTOOD. H-HOW MUCH...
AAAAH!
DON'T BE STINGY. GIVE US EVERYTHING YOU'VE GOT.
THESE CLOTHES ARE GOOD TOO!
OH HO! GOT SOME GOOD SHOES!
HAHAHA...
EEEE!

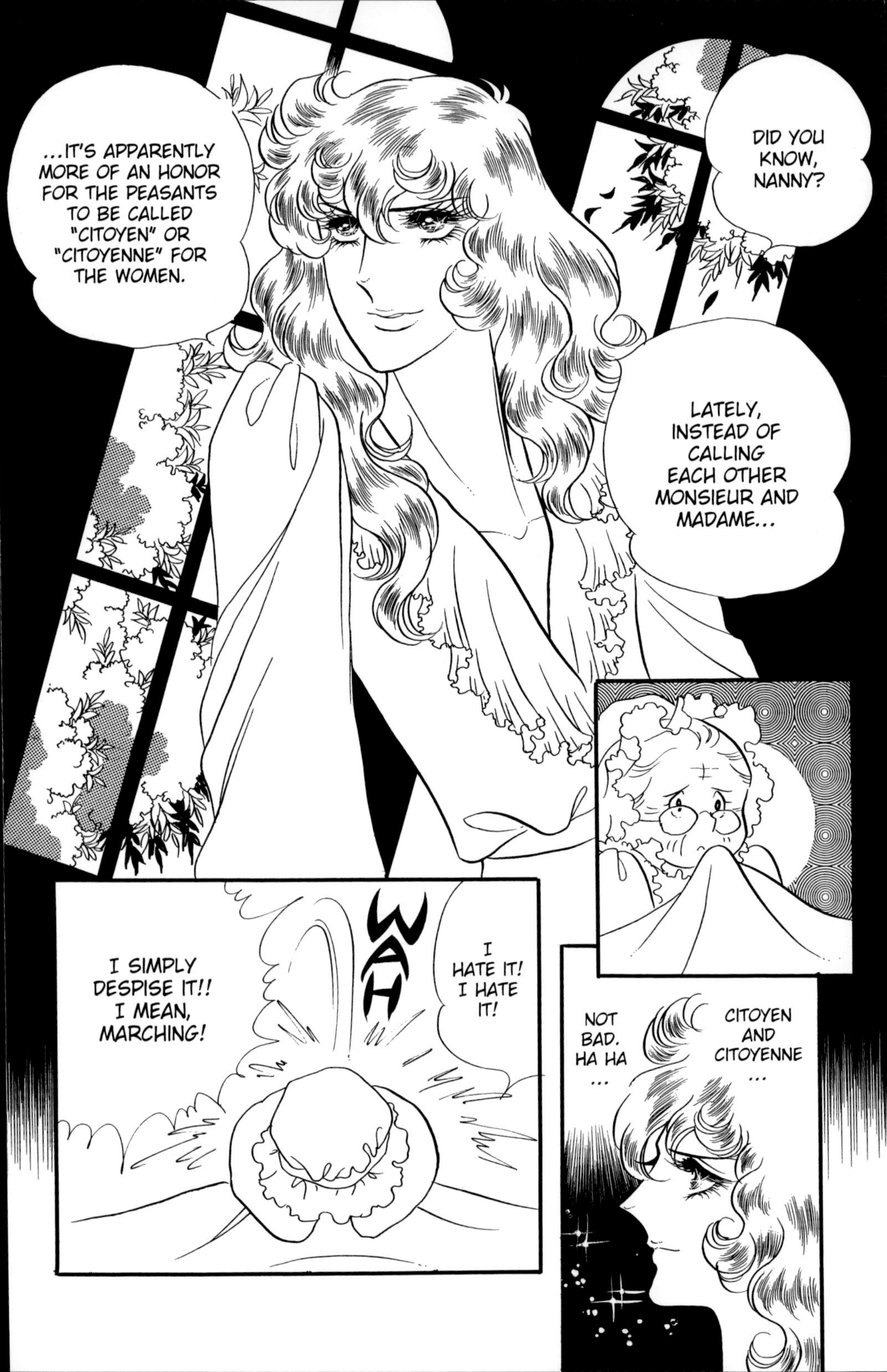
DID YOU KNOW, NANNY?
LATELY, INSTEAD OF CALLING EACH OTHER MONSIEUR AND MADAME...
...IT'S APPARENTLY MORE OF AN HONOR FOR THE PEASANTS TO BE CALLED "CITOYEN" OR "CITOYENNE" FOR THE WOMEN.
CITOYEN AND CITOYENNE ...
NOT BAD. HA HA ...
I HATE IT! I HATE IT!
WAH
I SIMPLY DESPISE IT!! I MEAN, MARCHING!

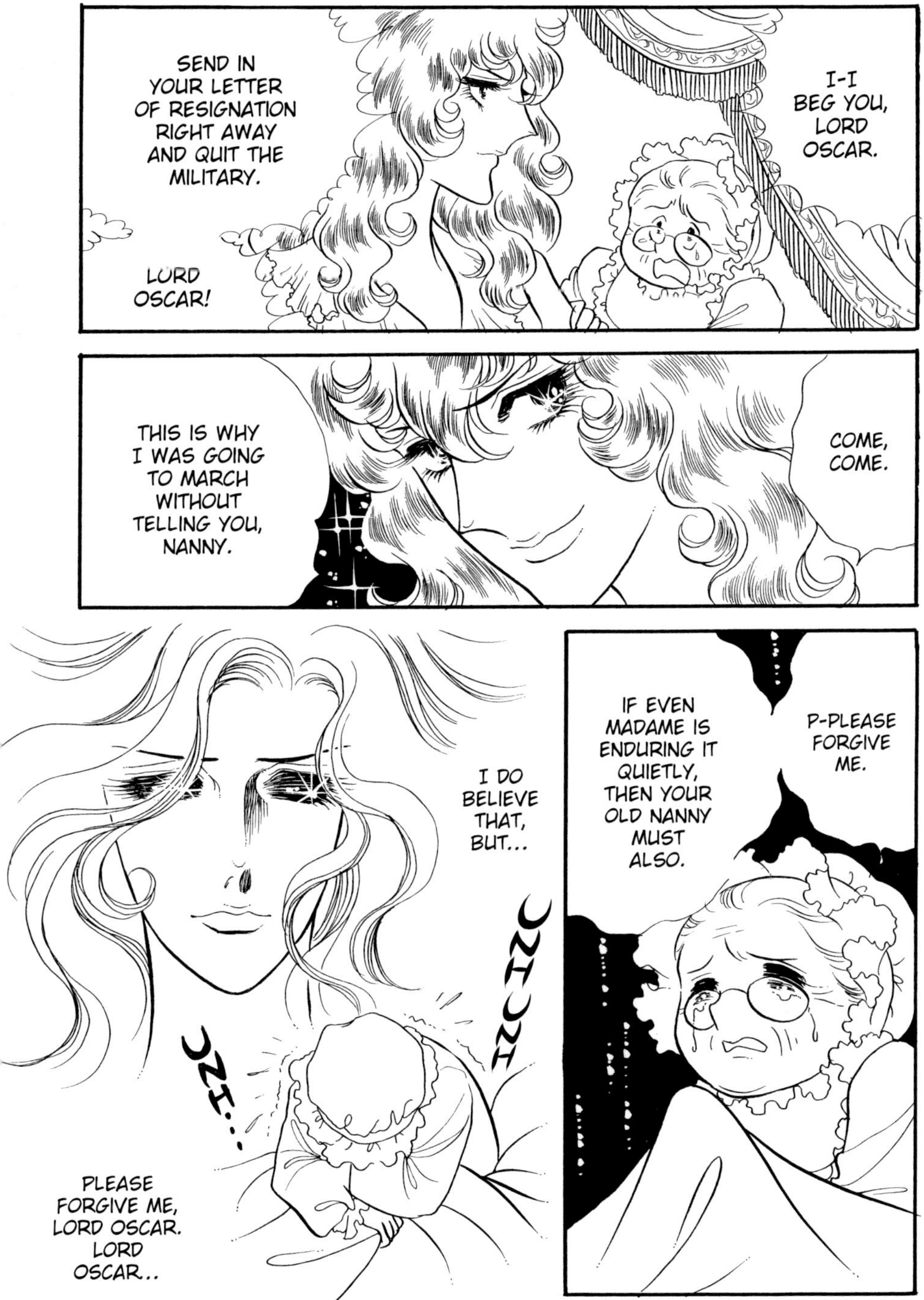
I-I BEG YOU, LORD OSCAR.
SEND IN YOUR LETTER OF RESIGNATION RIGHT AWAY AND QUIT THE MILITARY.
LORD OSCAR!
COME, COME.
THIS IS WHY I WAS GOING TO MARCH WITHOUT TELLING YOU, NANNY.
P-PLEASE FORGIVE ME.
IF EVEN MADAME IS ENDURING IT QUIETLY, THEN YOUR OLD NANNY MUST ALSO.
I DO BELIEVE THAT, BUT...
PLEASE FORGIVE ME, LORD OSCAR. LORD OSCAR...

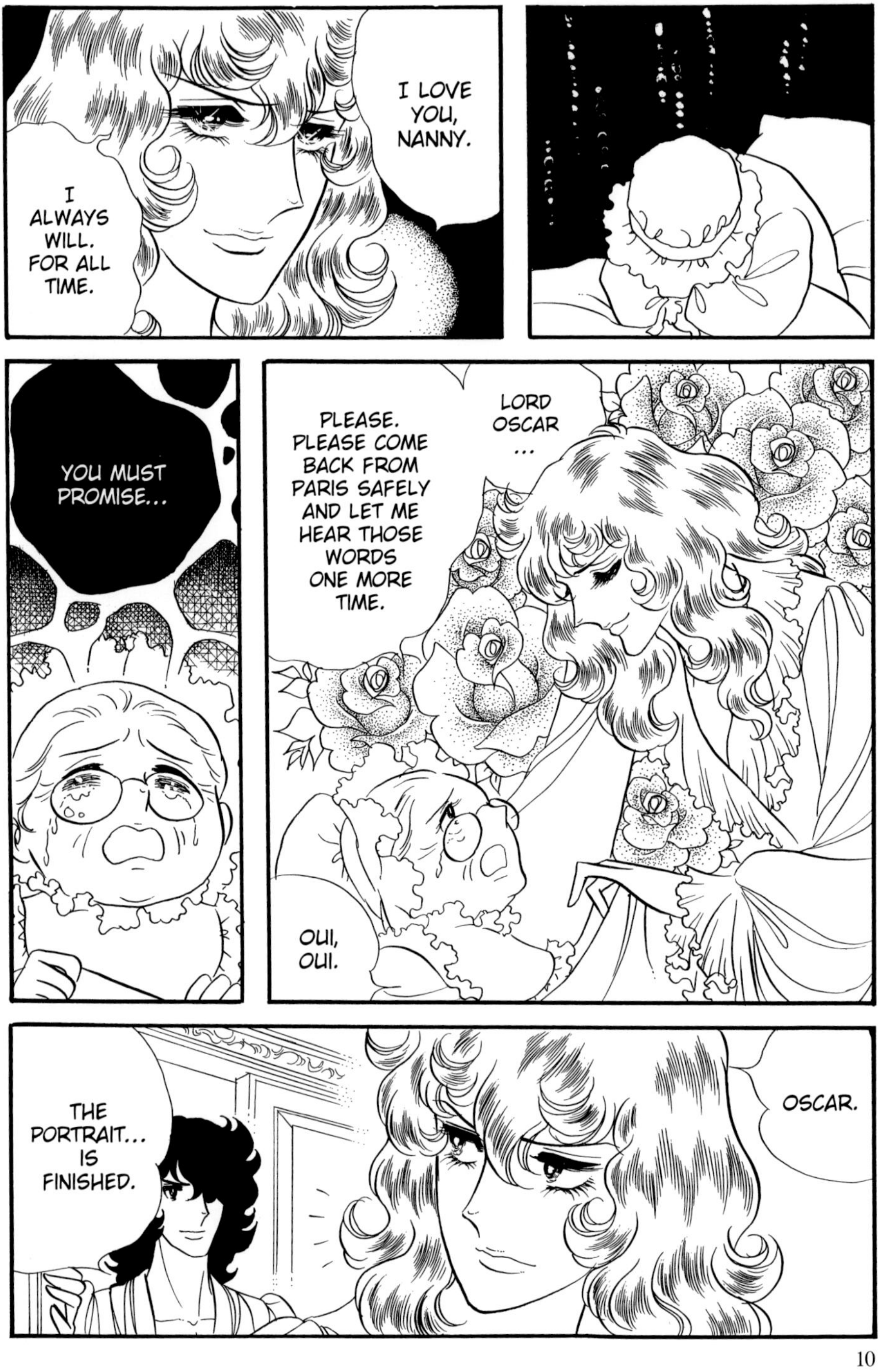
I LOVE YOU, NANNY.
I ALWAYS WILL. FOR ALL TIME.
LORD OSCAR ...
PLEASE. PLEASE COME BACK FROM PARIS SAFELY AND LET ME HEAR THOSE WORDS ONE MORE TIME.
OUI, OUI.
YOU MUST PROMISE...
OSCAR.
THE PORTRAIT... IS FINISHED.

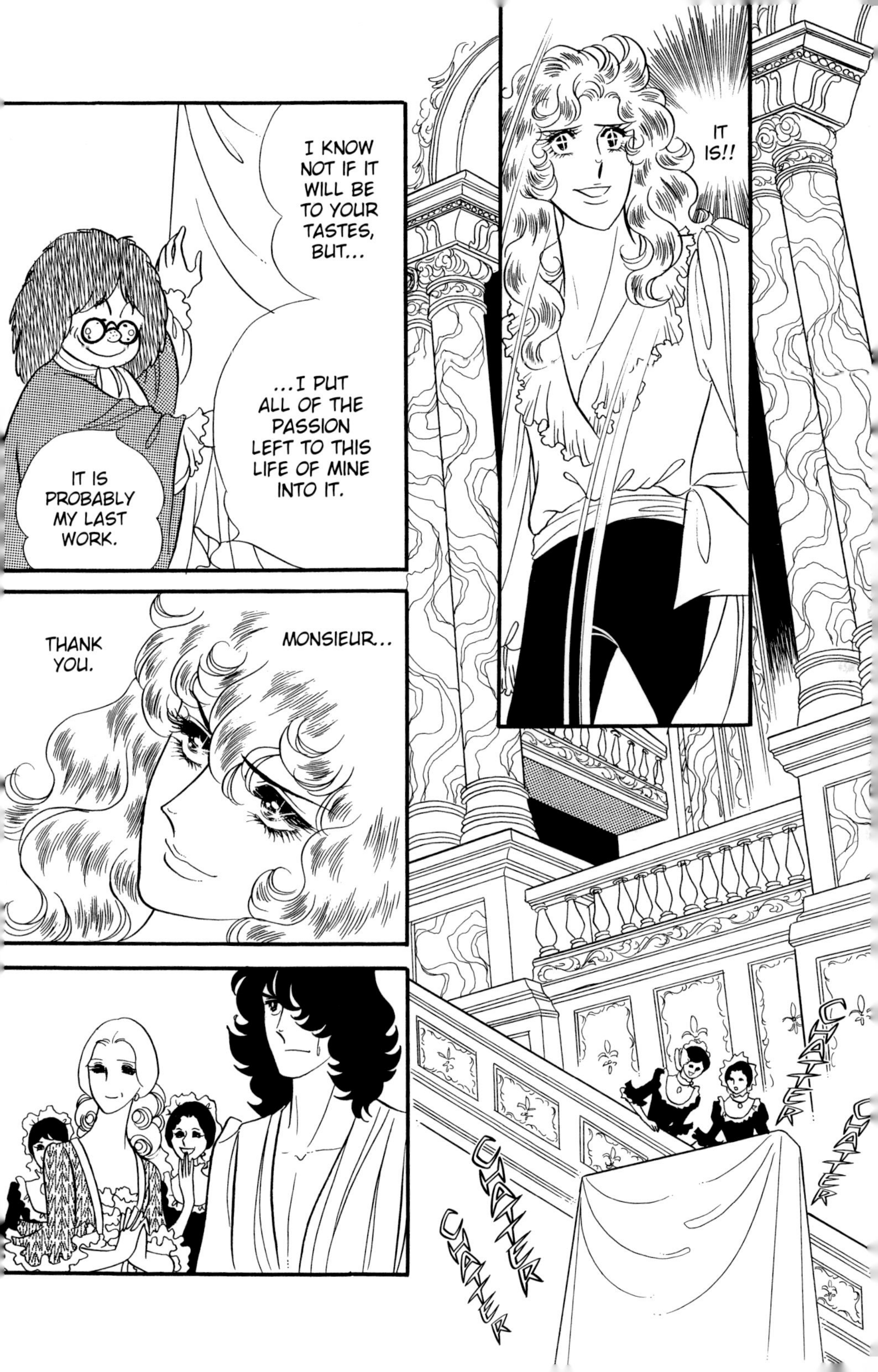
IT IS!!
CHATTER
CHATTER
CHATTER
CHATTER
I KNOW NOT IF IT WILL BE TO YOUR TASTES, BUT...
...I PUT ALL OF THE PASSION LEFT TO THIS LIFE OF MINE INTO IT.
IT IS PROBABLY MY LAST WORK.
MONSIEUR...
THANK YOU.

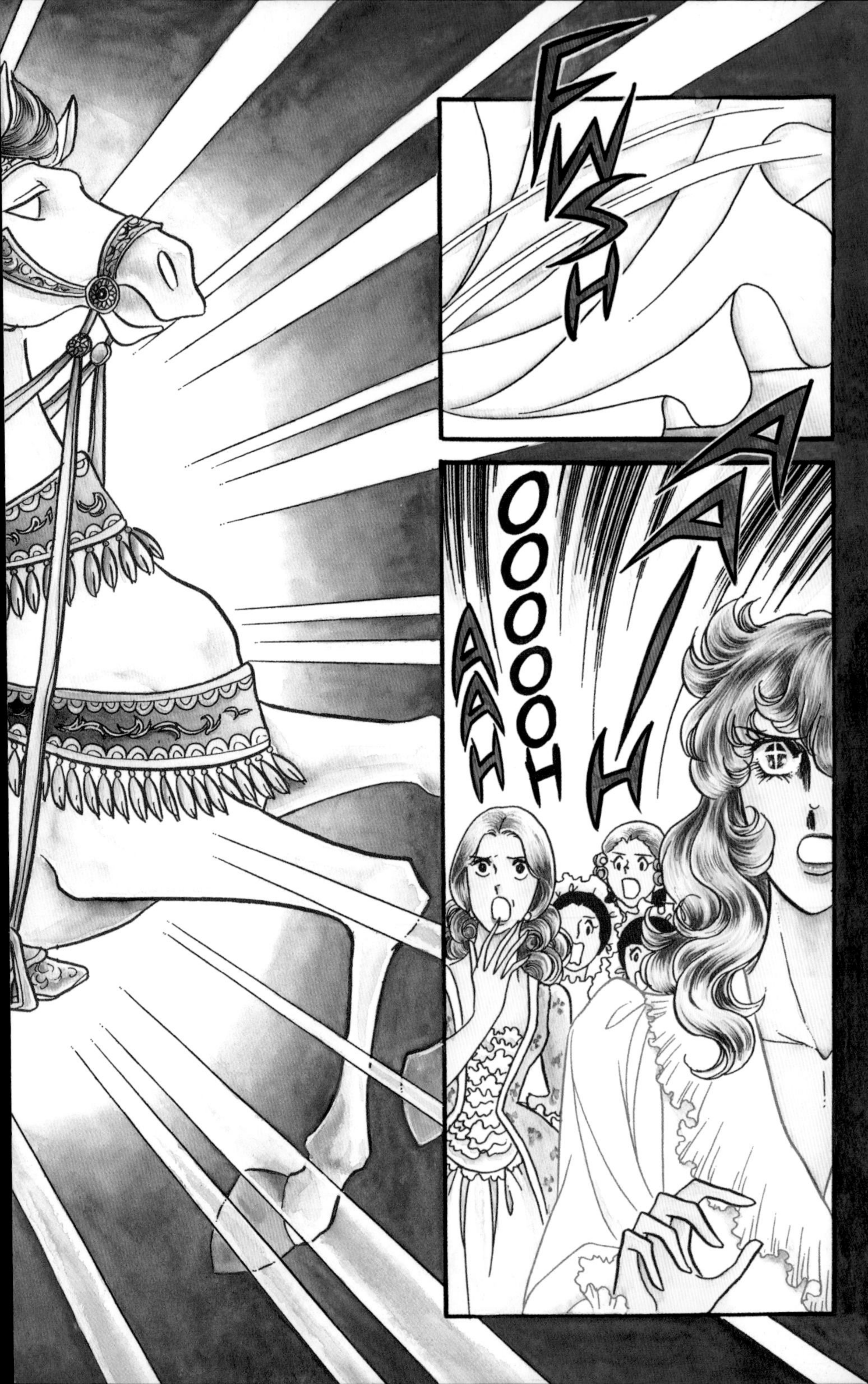
FWSH
AAAHH
OOOOOOOH
AAAH

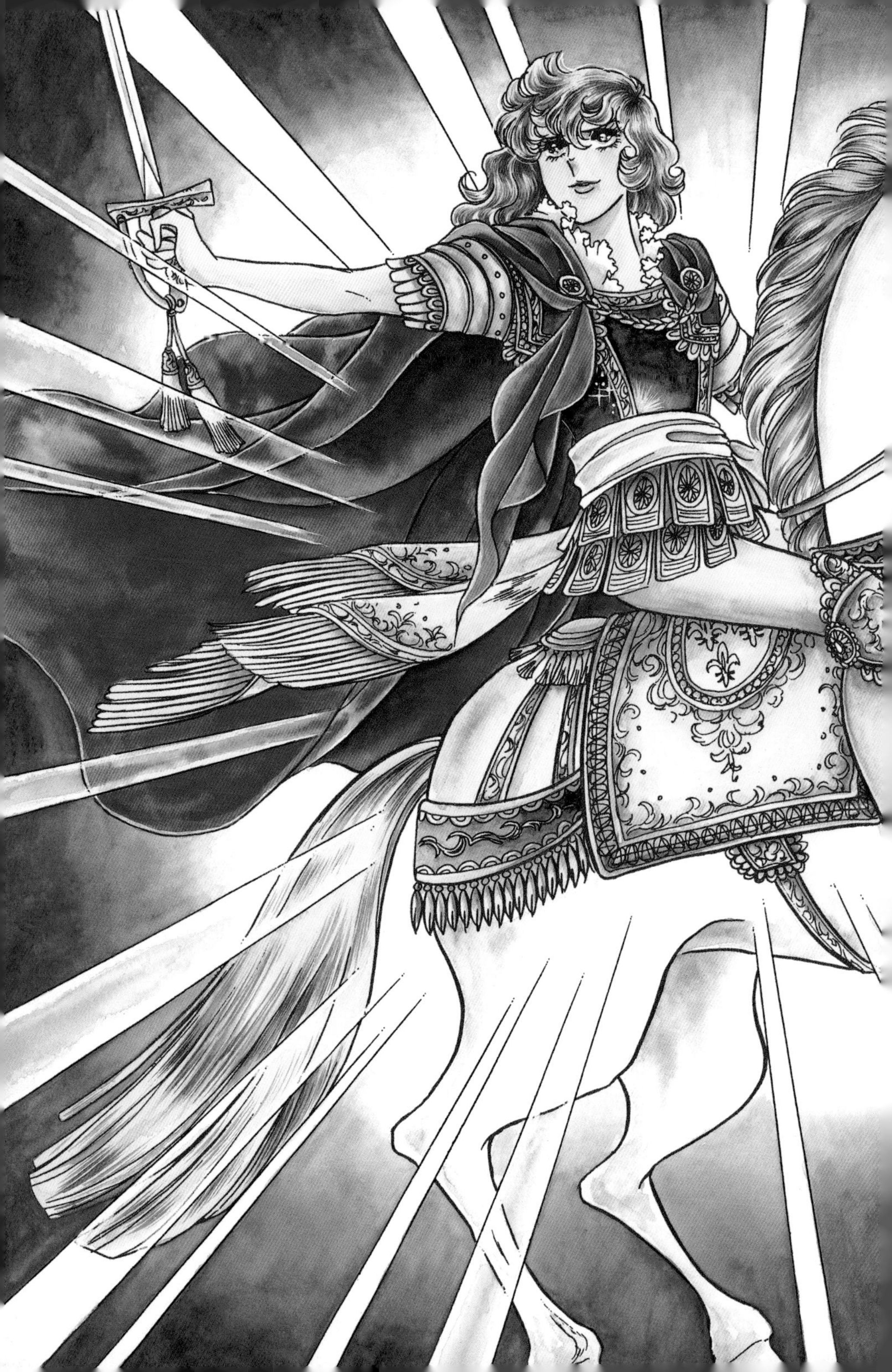

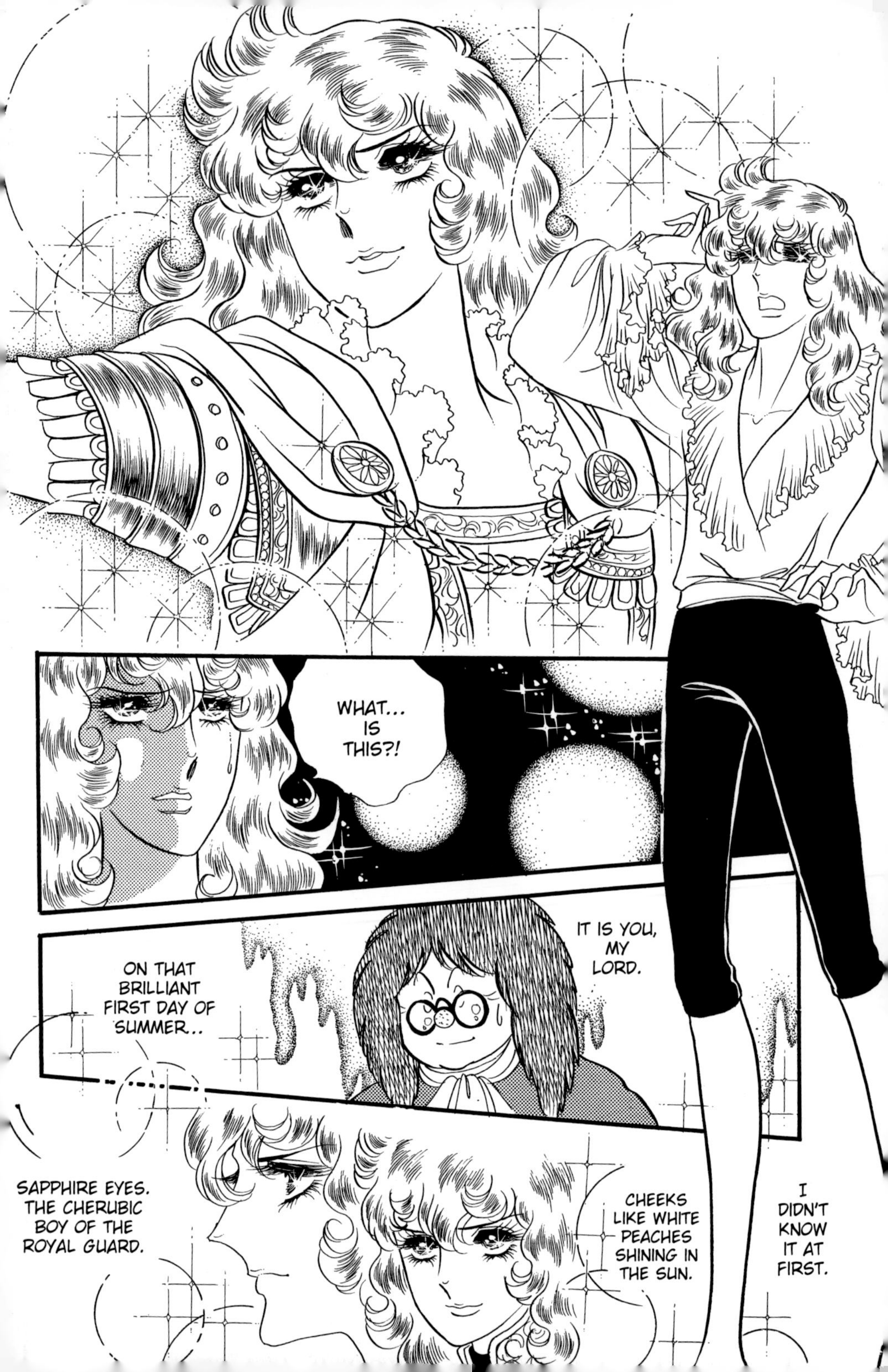
WHAT... IS THIS?!
IT IS YOU, MY LORD.
ON THAT BRILLIANT FIRST DAY OF SUMMER...
I DIDN'T KNOW IT AT FIRST.
CHEEKS LIKE WHITE PEACHES SHINING IN THE SUN.
SAPPHIRE EYES. THE CHERUBIC BOY OF THE ROYAL GUARD.

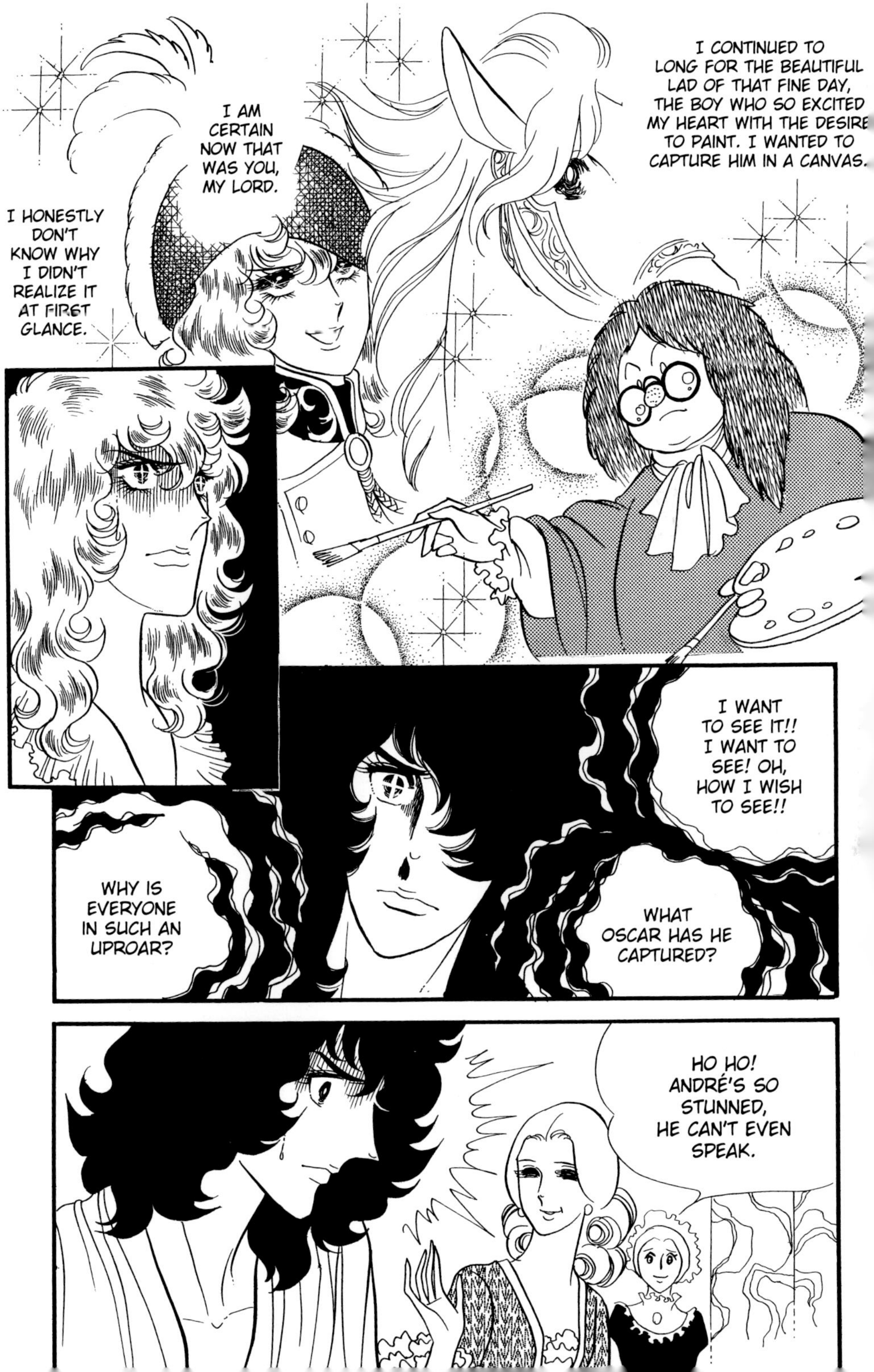
I CONTINUED TO LONG FOR THE BEAUTIFUL LAD OF THAT FINE DAY, THE BOY WHO SO EXCITED MY HEART WITH THE DESIRE TO PAINT. I WANTED TO CAPTURE HIM IN A CANVAS.
I AM CERTAIN NOW THAT WAS YOU, MY LORD.
I HONESTLY DON'T KNOW WHY I DIDN'T REALIZE IT AT FIRST GLANCE.
I WANT TO SEE IT!! I WANT TO SEE! OH, HOW I WISH TO SEE!!
WHAT OSCAR HAS HE CAPTURED?
WHY IS EVERYONE IN SUCH AN UPROAR?
HO HO! ANDRÉ'S SO STUNNED, HE CAN'T EVEN SPEAK.

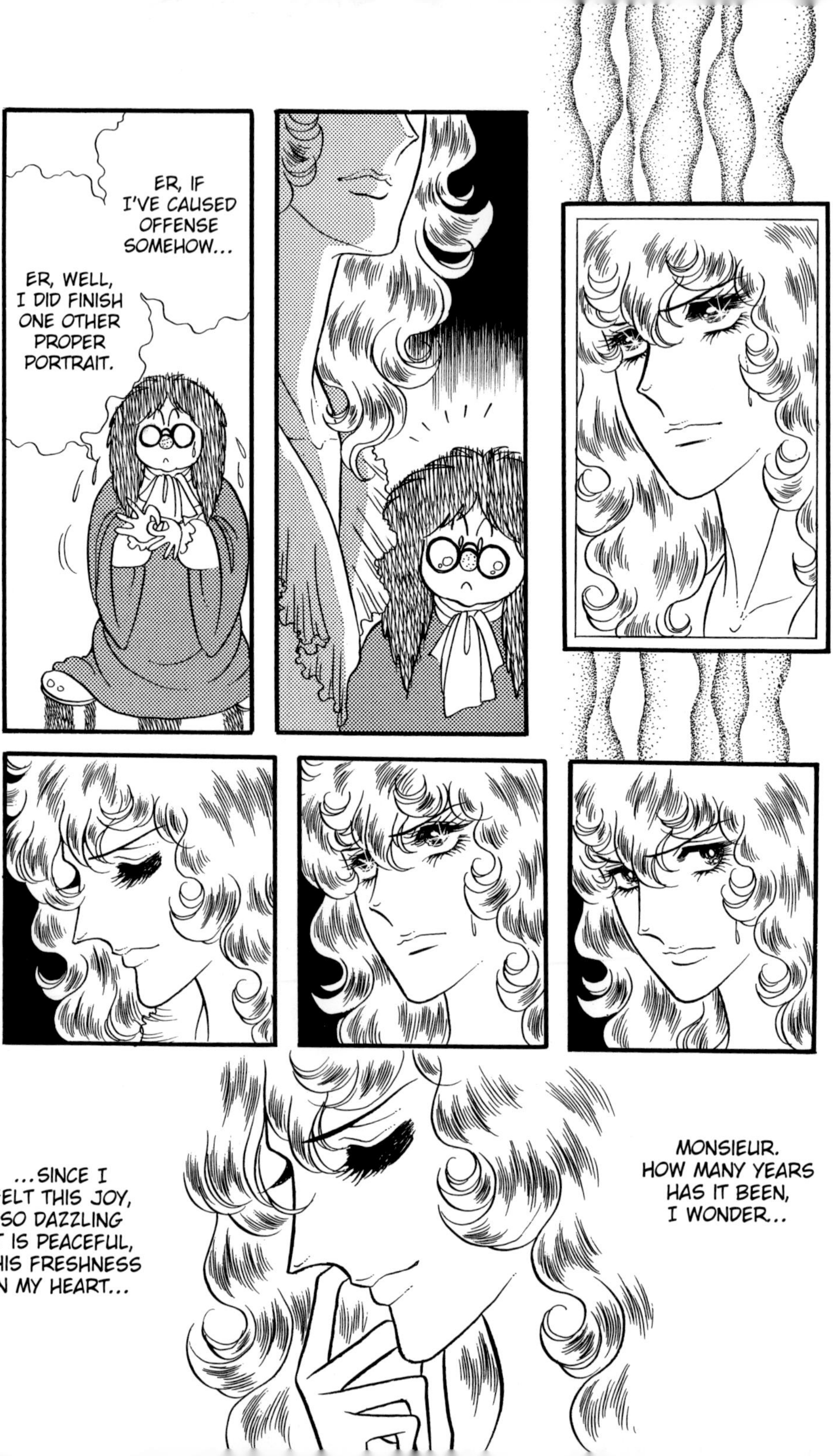
ER, IF I'VE CAUSED OFFENSE SOMEHOW...
ER, WELL, I DID FINISH ONE OTHER PROPER PORTRAIT.
MONSIEUR. HOW MANY YEARS HAS IT BEEN, I WONDER...
...SINCE I FELT THIS JOY, SO DAZZLING IT IS PEACEFUL, THIS FRESHNESS IN MY HEART...

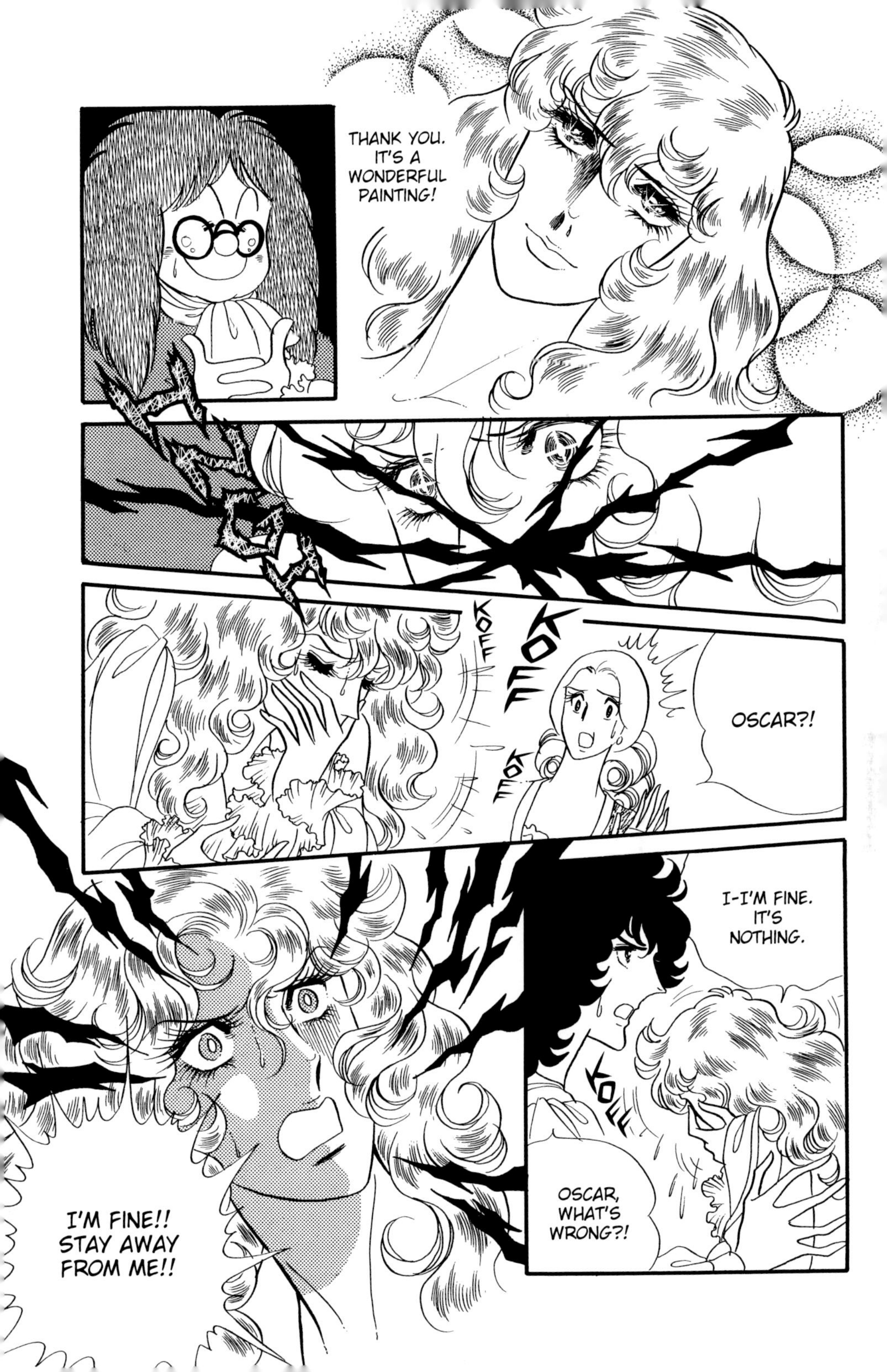
THANK YOU. IT'S A WONDERFUL PAINTING!
OSCAR?!
KOFF
KOFF
KOFF
I-I'M FINE. IT'S NOTHING.
KOFF
OSCAR, WHAT'S WRONG?!
I'M FINE!! STAY AWAY FROM ME!!

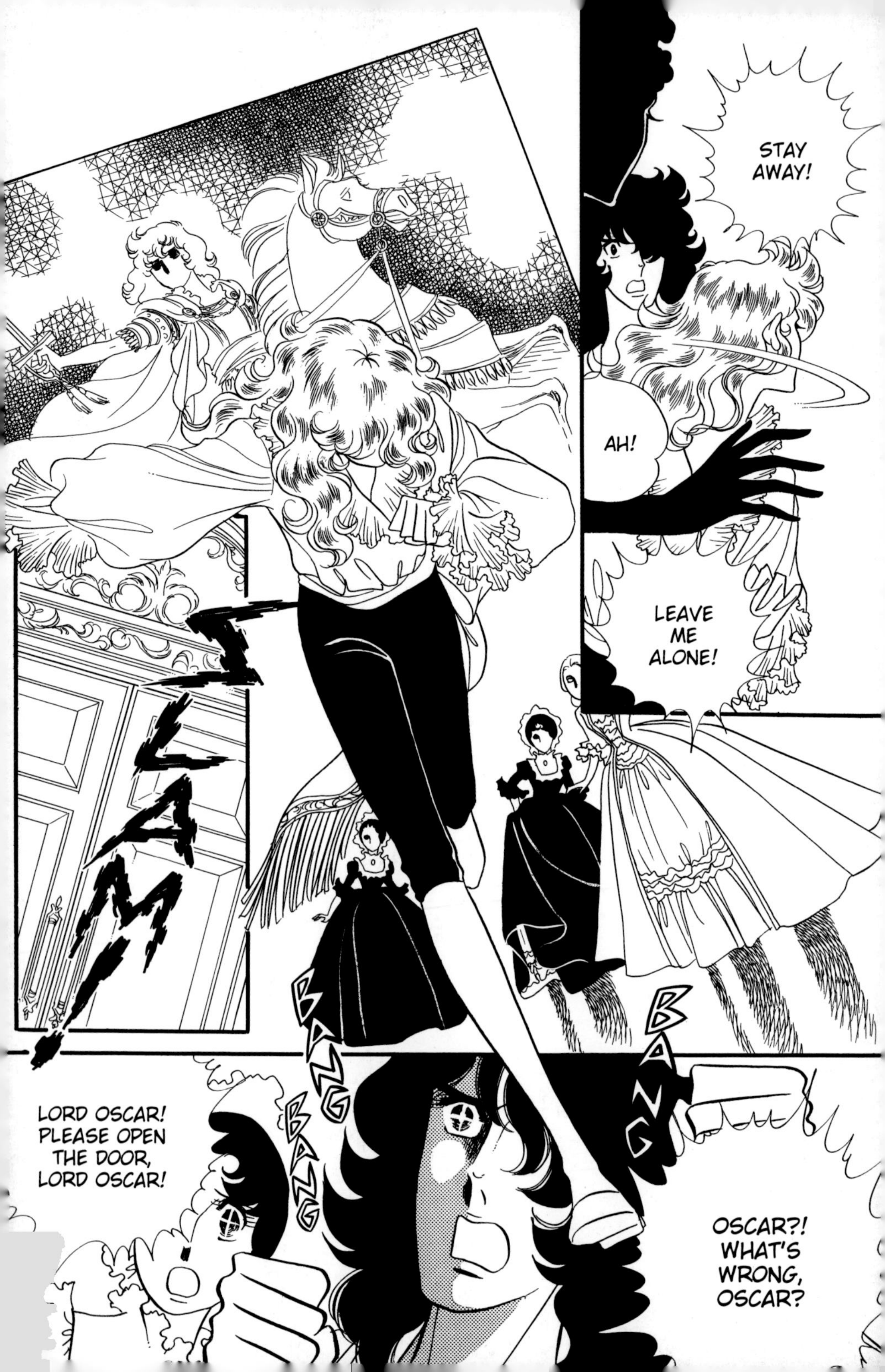
STAY AWAY!
AH!
LEAVE ME ALONE!
SLAM
BANG
BANG
BANG
BANG
OSCAR?! WHAT'S WRONG, OSCAR?
LORD OSCAR! PLEASE OPEN THE DOOR, LORD OSCAR!

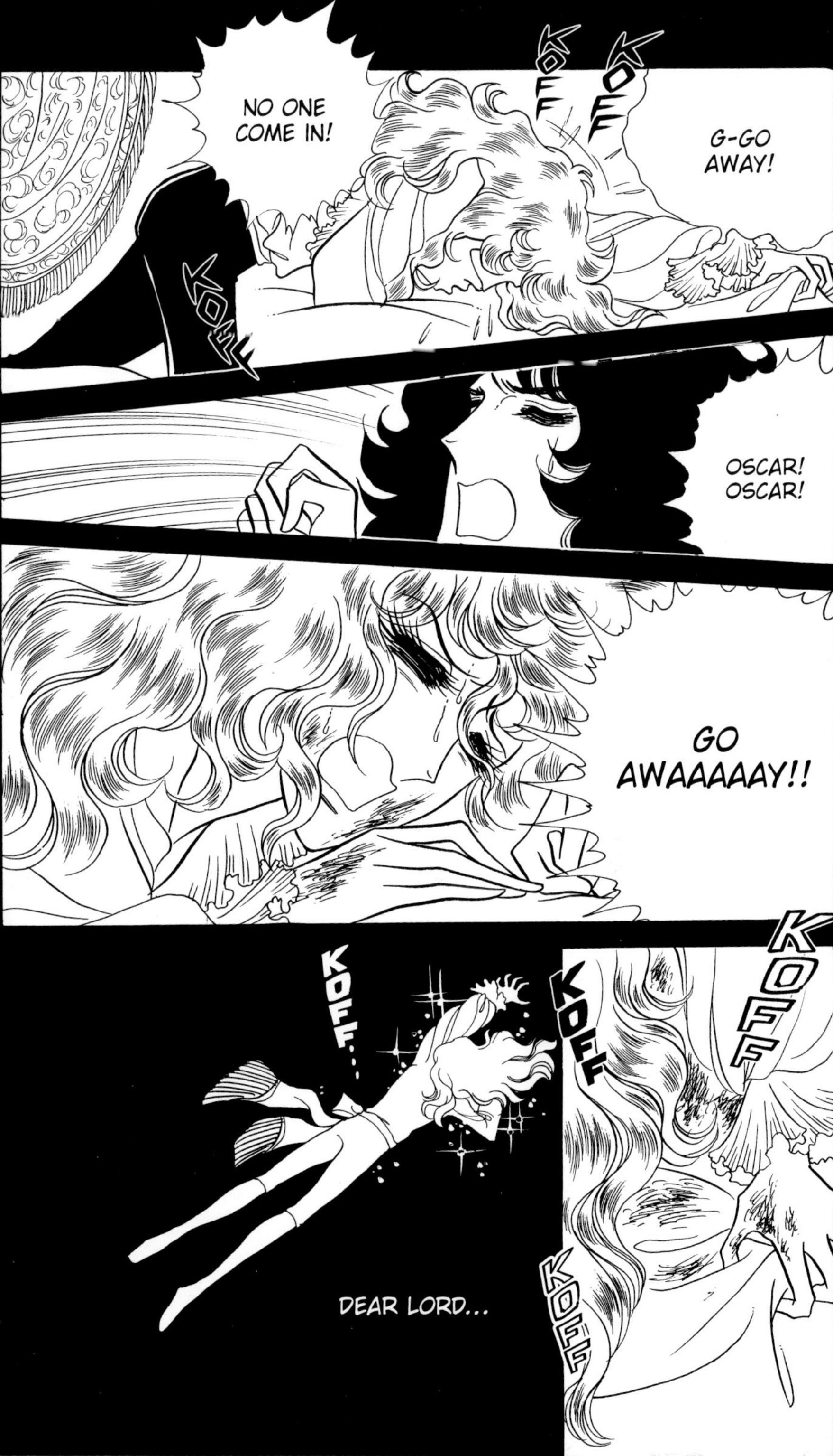
G-GO AWAY!
KOFF
KOFF
NO ONE COME IN!
KOFF
OSCAR! OSCAR!
GO AWAAAAAY!!
KOFF
KOFF
KOFF
KOFF...
DEAR LORD...

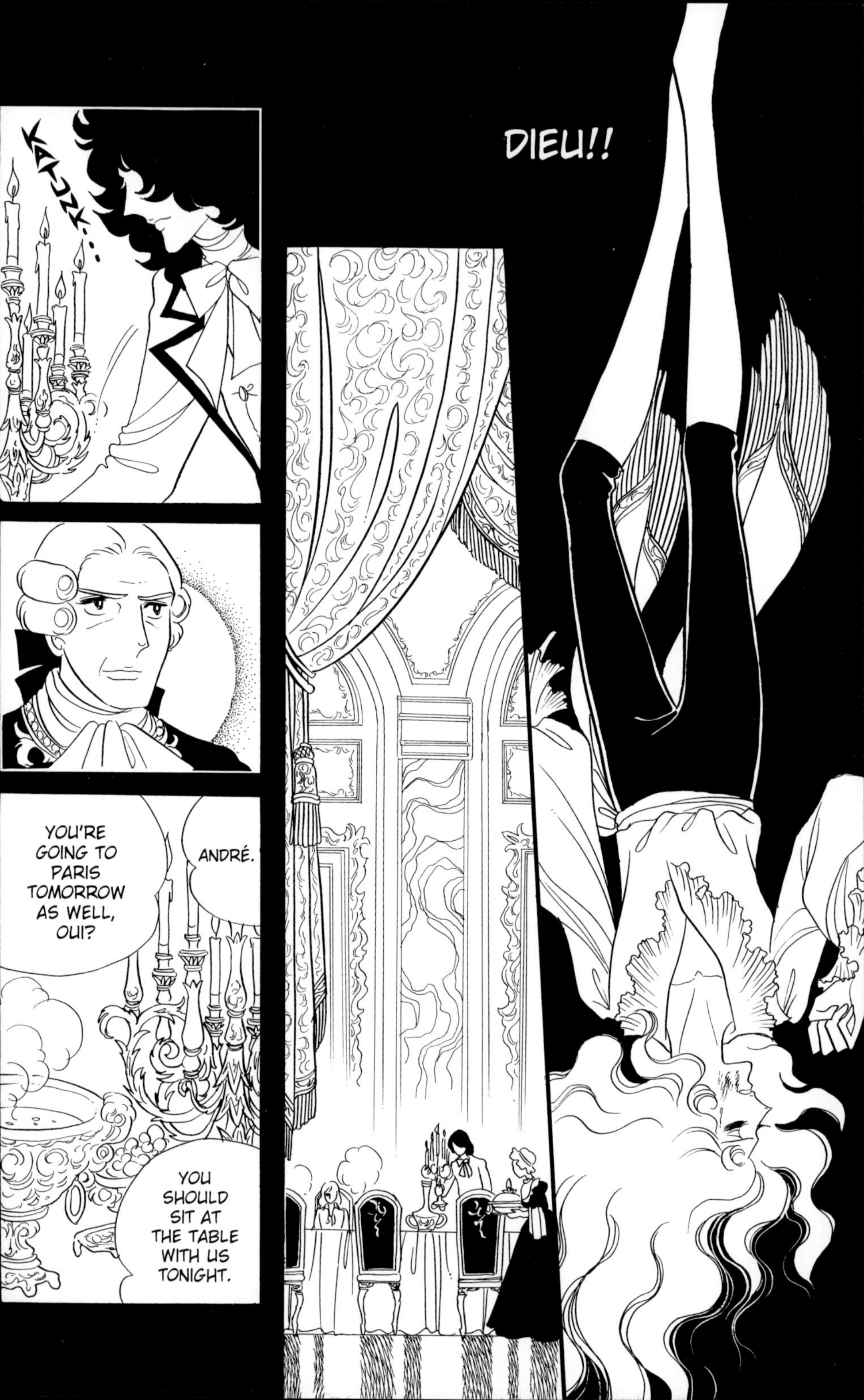
DIEU!!
KATUNK...
ANDRÉ.
YOU'RE GOING TO PARIS TOMORROW AS WELL, OUI?
YOU SHOULD SIT AT THE TABLE WITH US TONIGHT.

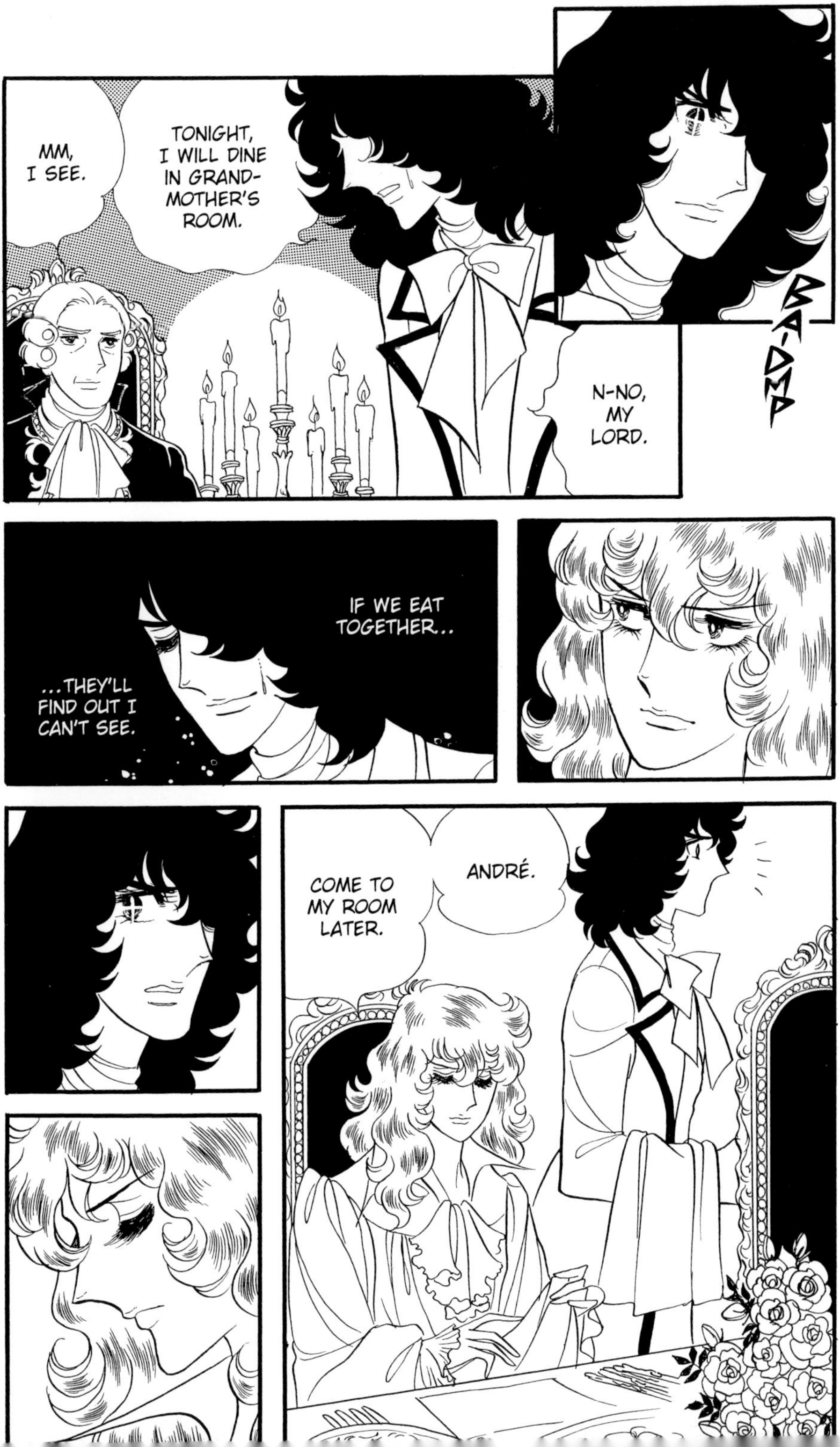
TONIGHT, I WILL DINE IN GRAND-MOTHER'S ROOM.
MM, I SEE.
BA-DMP
N-NO, MY LORD.
IF WE EAT TOGETHER...
...THEY'LL FIND OUT I CAN'T SEE.
ANDRÉ.
COME TO MY ROOM LATER.

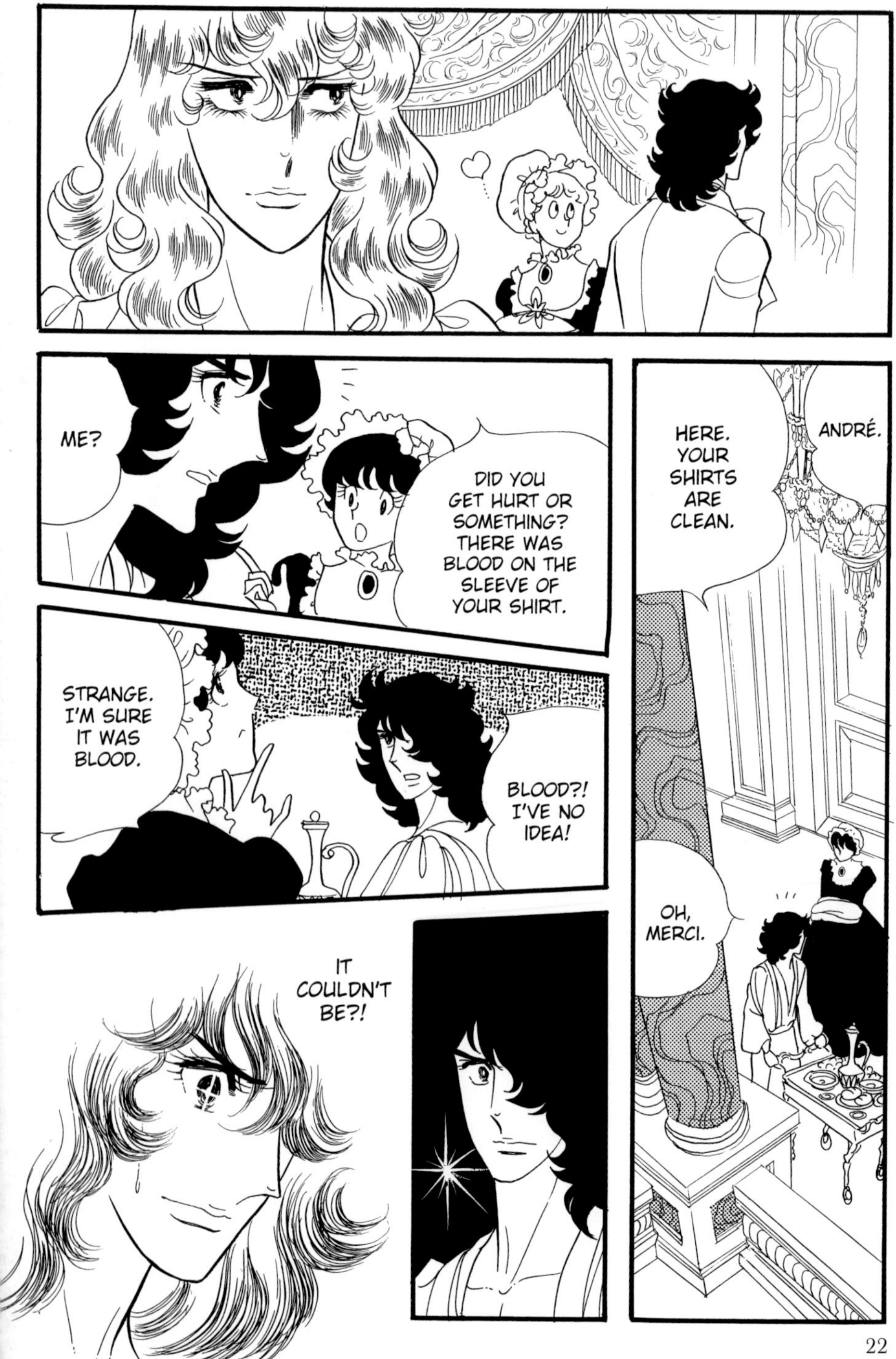
ANDRÉ.
HERE. YOUR SHIRTS ARE CLEAN.
OH, MERCI.
DID YOU GET HURT OR SOMETHING? THERE WAS BLOOD ON THE SLEEVE OF YOUR SHIRT.
ME?
BLOOD?! I'VE NO IDEA!
STRANGE. I'M SURE IT WAS BLOOD.
IT COULDN'T BE?!

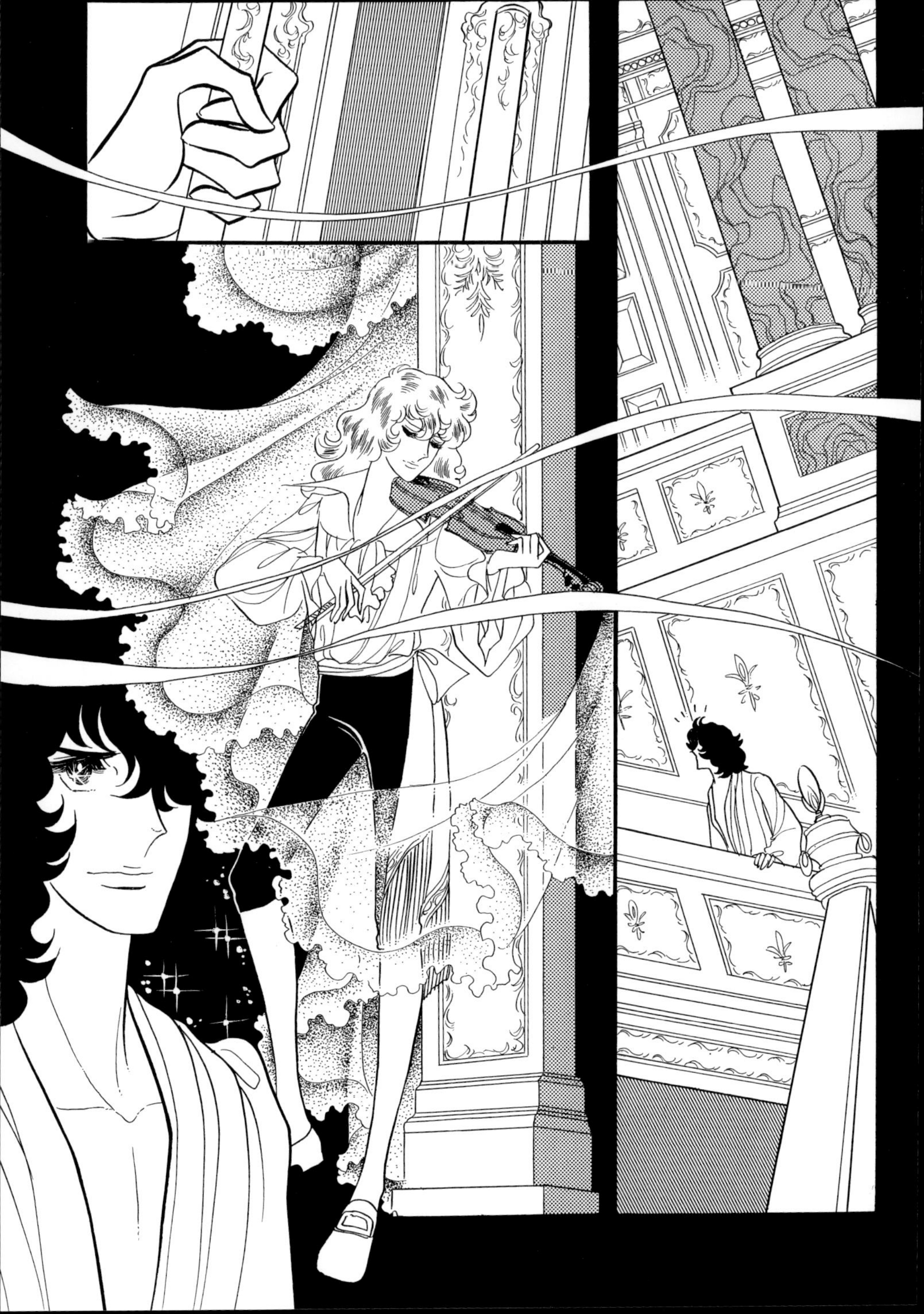

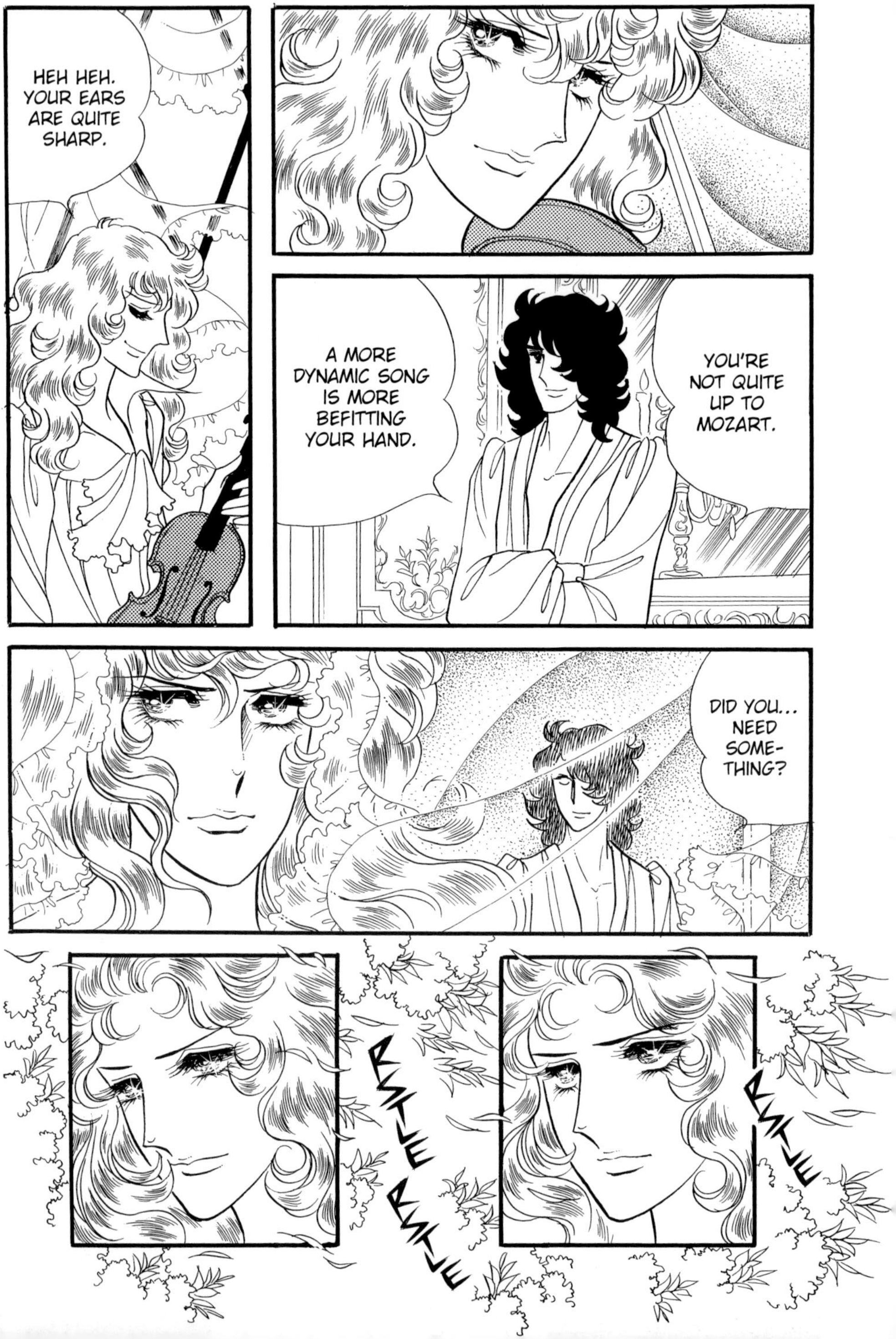
YOU'RE NOT QUITE UP TO MOZART.
A MORE DYNAMIC SONG IS MORE BEFITTING YOUR HAND.
HEH HEH. YOUR EARS ARE QUITE SHARP.
DID YOU... NEED SOME-THING?
RUSTLE
RUSTLE RUSTLE

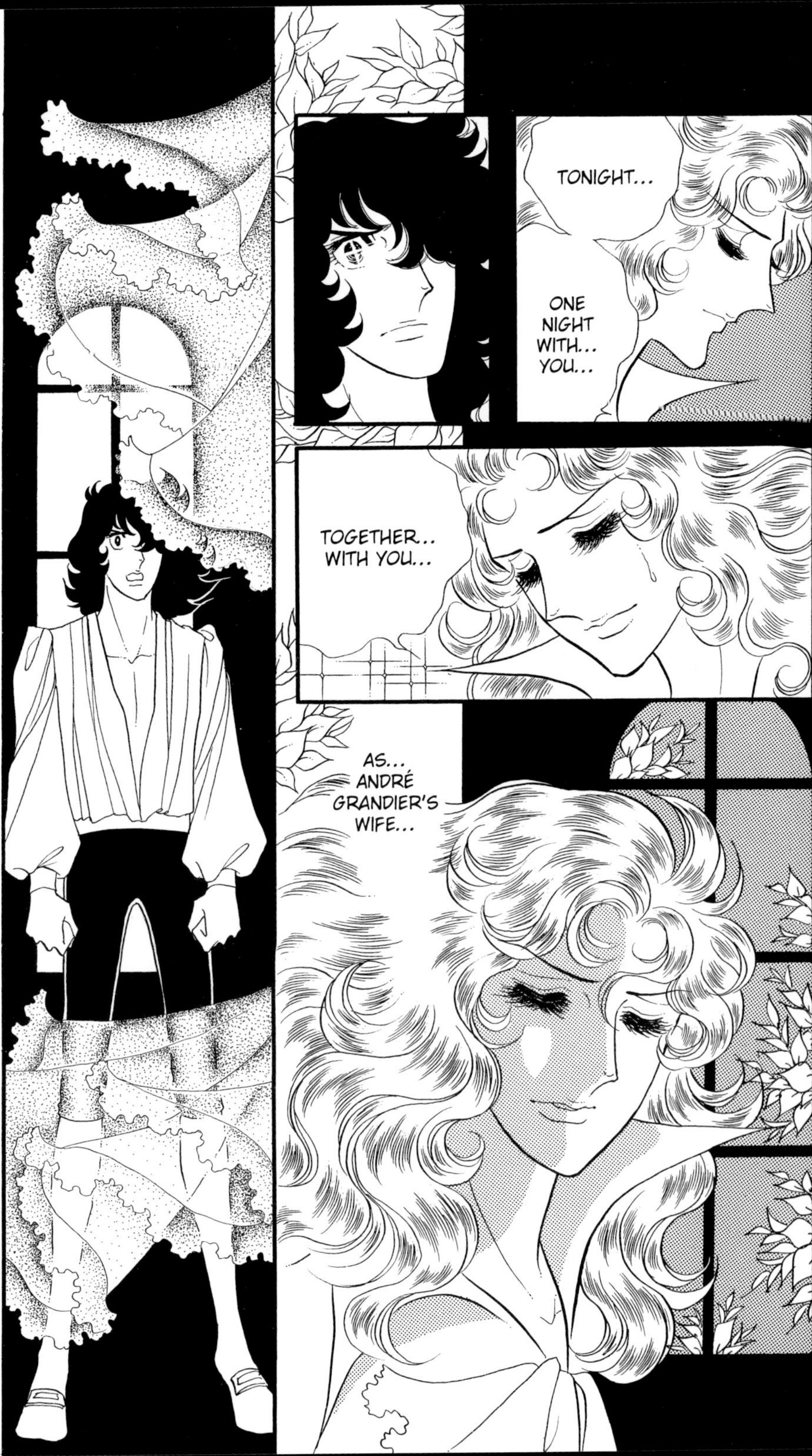

TONIGHT...
ONE NIGHT WITH... YOU...
TOGETHER.. WITH YOU...
AS... ANDRÉ GRANDIER'S WIFE...

THE ROSE OF VERSAILLES

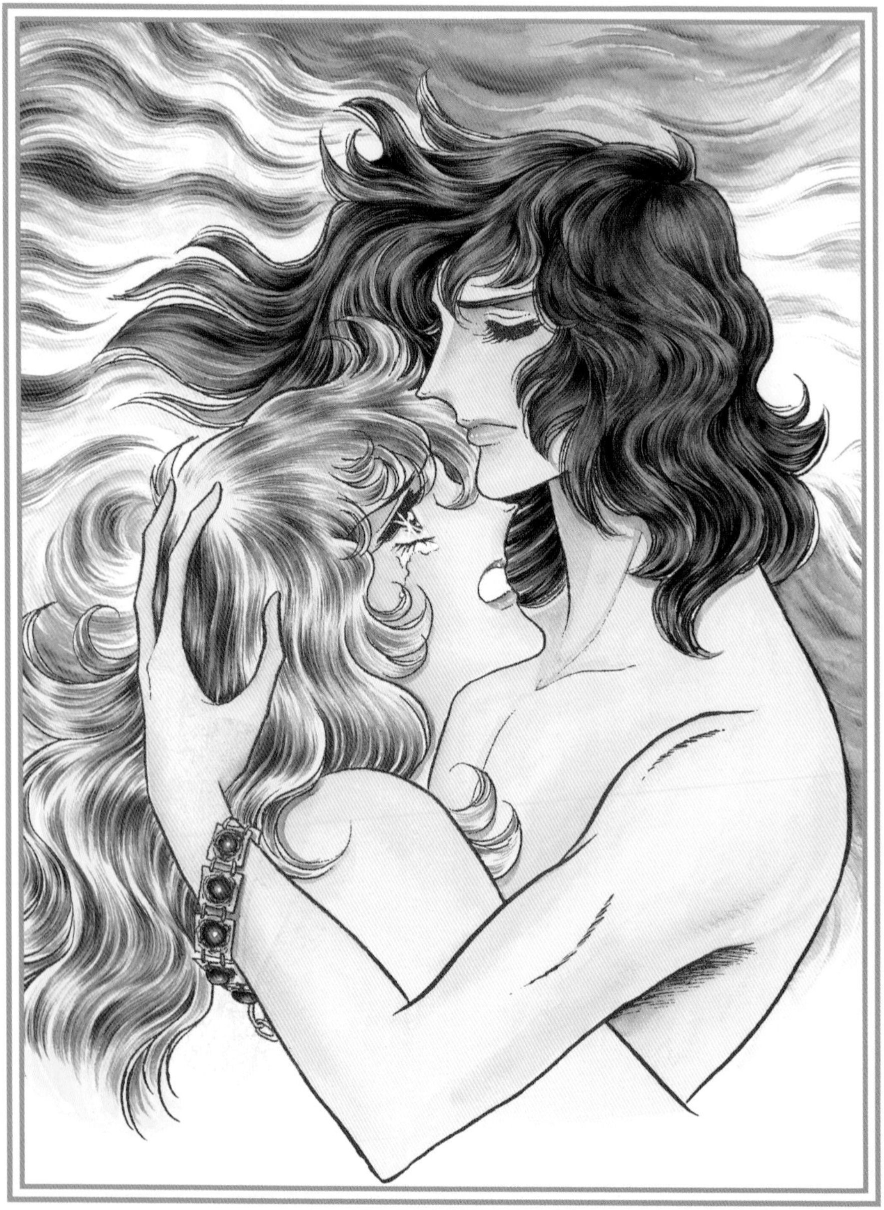

1973 WEEKLY MARGARET MAGAZINE ISSUE 40 COVER PAGE
(SPECIAL COLORIZED VERSION)

◆ THE ROLLERCOASTER ROMANCE TO THRILL THE HEART AND EXCITE THE SOUL
♥ OSCAR AND ANDRÉ NOW BOUND TOGETHER?!

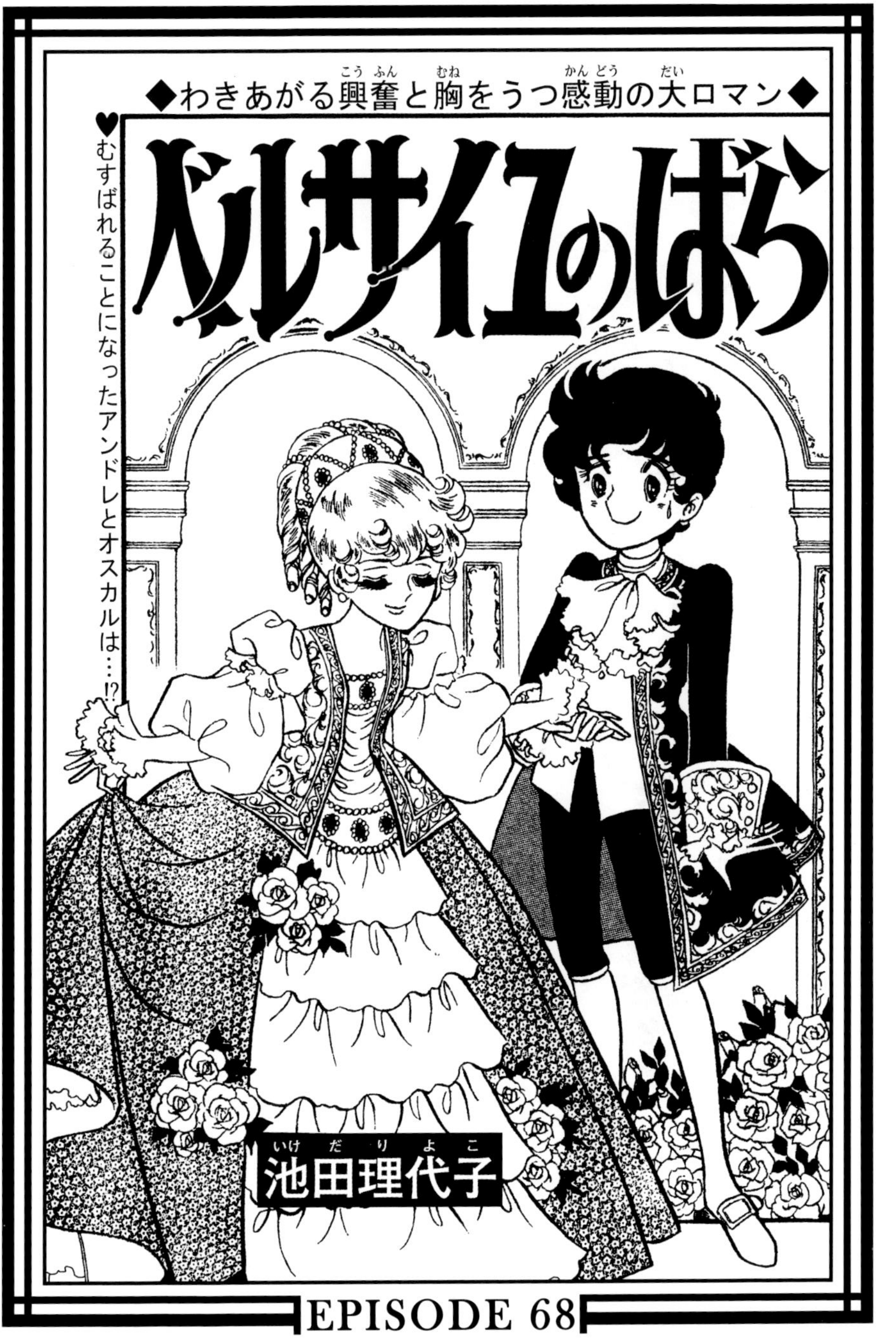
◆わきあがる興奮と胸をうつ感動の大ロマン◆
ベルサイユのばら
♥むすばれることになったアンドレとオスカルは…!?
池田理代子
EPISODE 68

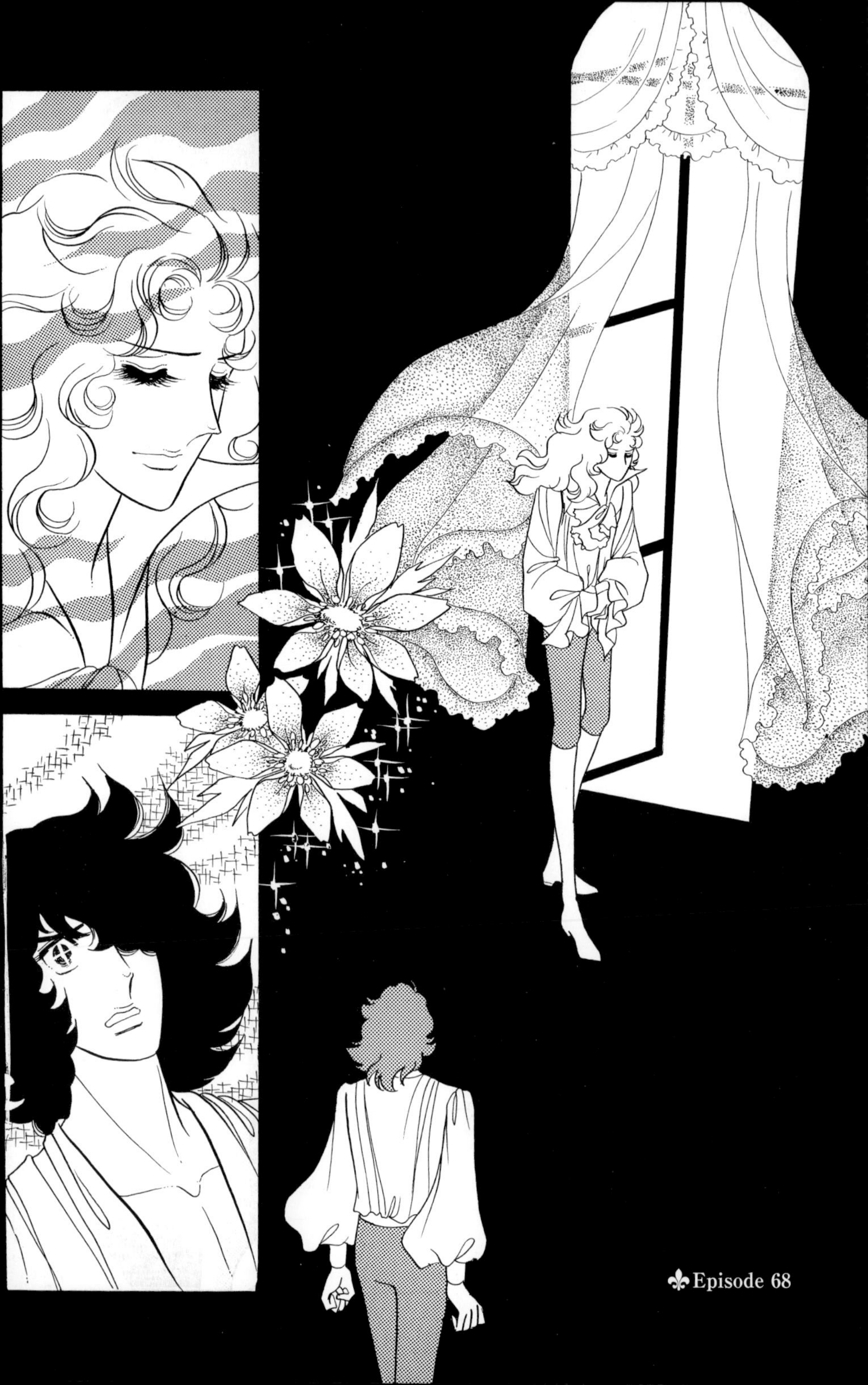

⚜ Episode 68

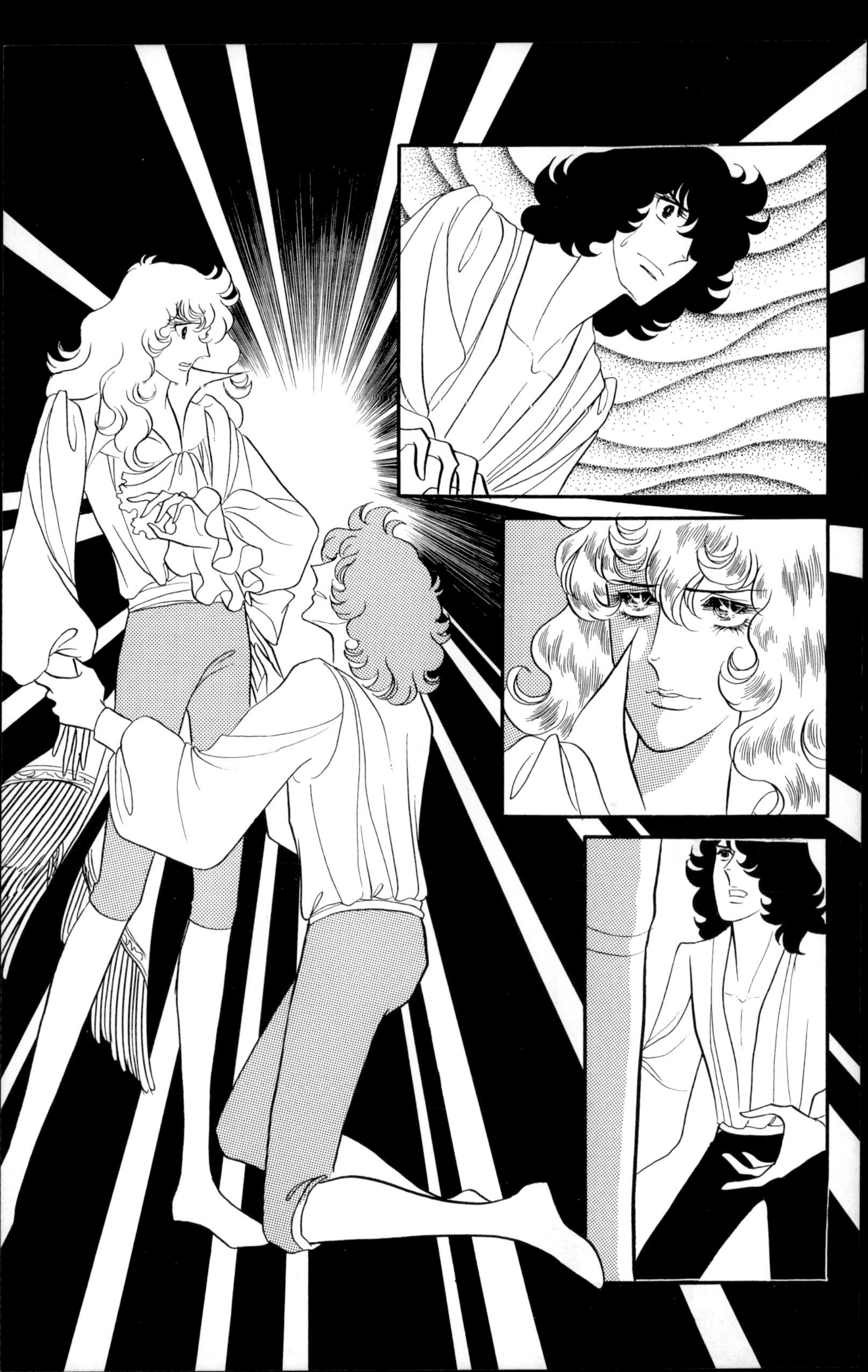

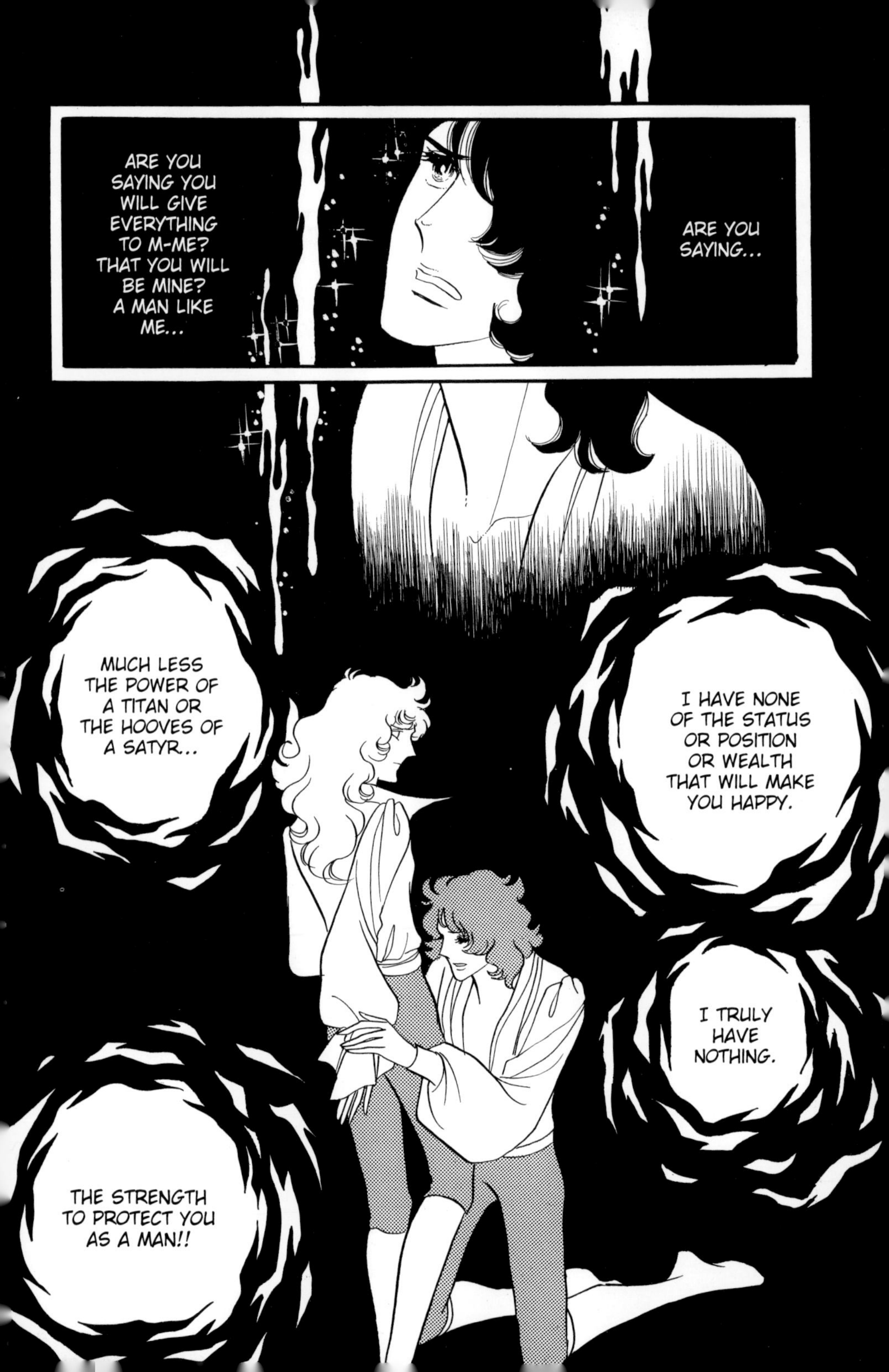
ARE YOU SAYING...
ARE YOU SAYING YOU WILL GIVE EVERYTHING TO M-ME? THAT YOU WILL BE MINE? A MAN LIKE ME...
I HAVE NONE OF THE STATUS OR POSITION OR WEALTH THAT WILL MAKE YOU HAPPY.
I TRULY HAVE NOTHING.
MUCH LESS THE POWER OF A TITAN OR THE HOOVES OF A SATYR...
THE STRENGTH TO PROTECT YOU AS A MAN!!

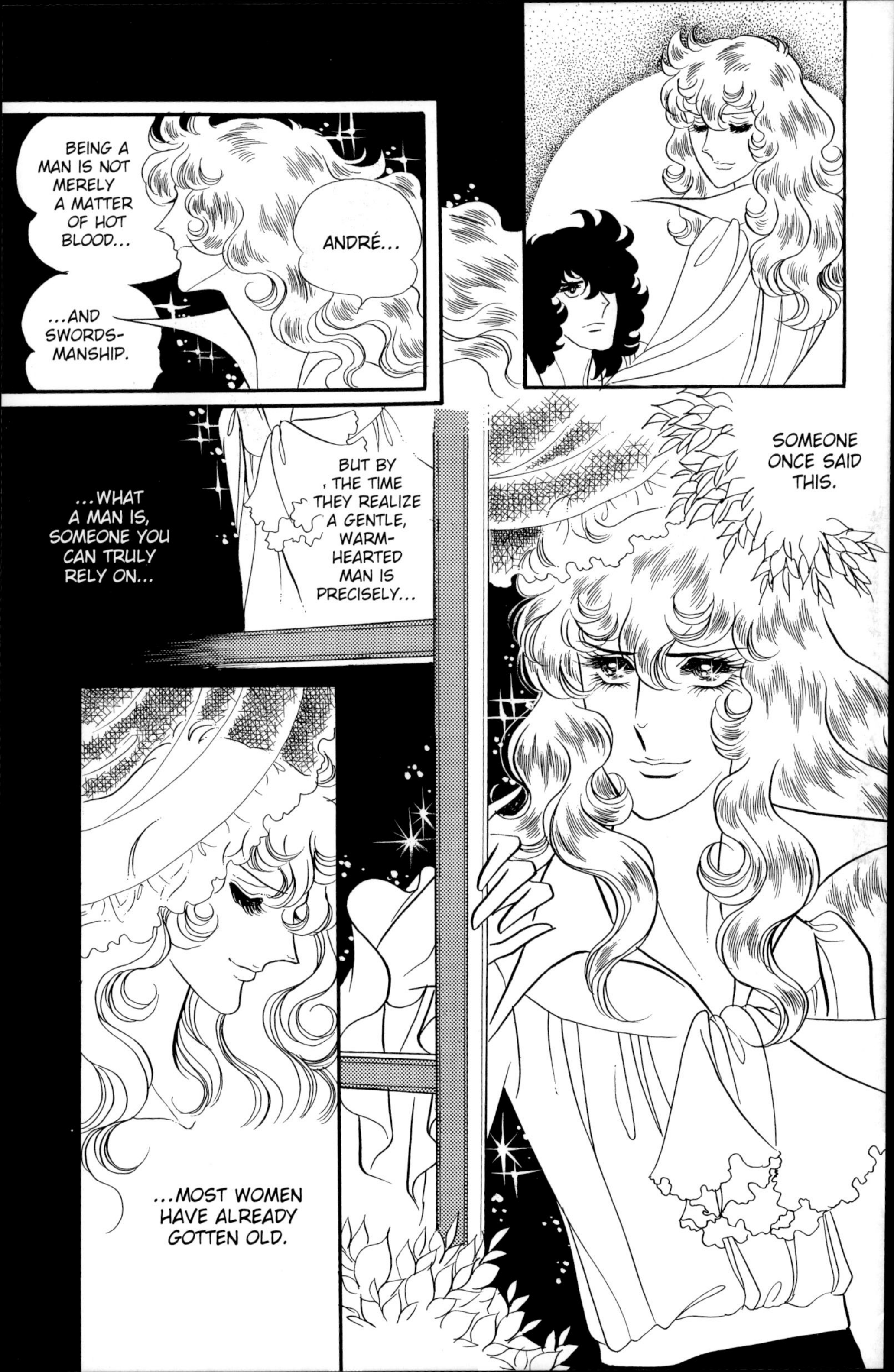
ANDRÉ...
BEING A MAN IS NOT MERELY A MATTER OF HOT BLOOD...
...AND SWORDSMANSHIP.
SOMEONE ONCE SAID THIS.
BUT BY THE TIME THEY REALIZE A GENTLE, WARM-HEARTED MAN IS PRECISELY...
...WHAT A MAN IS, SOMEONE YOU CAN TRULY RELY ON...
...MOST WOMEN HAVE ALREADY GOTTEN OLD.

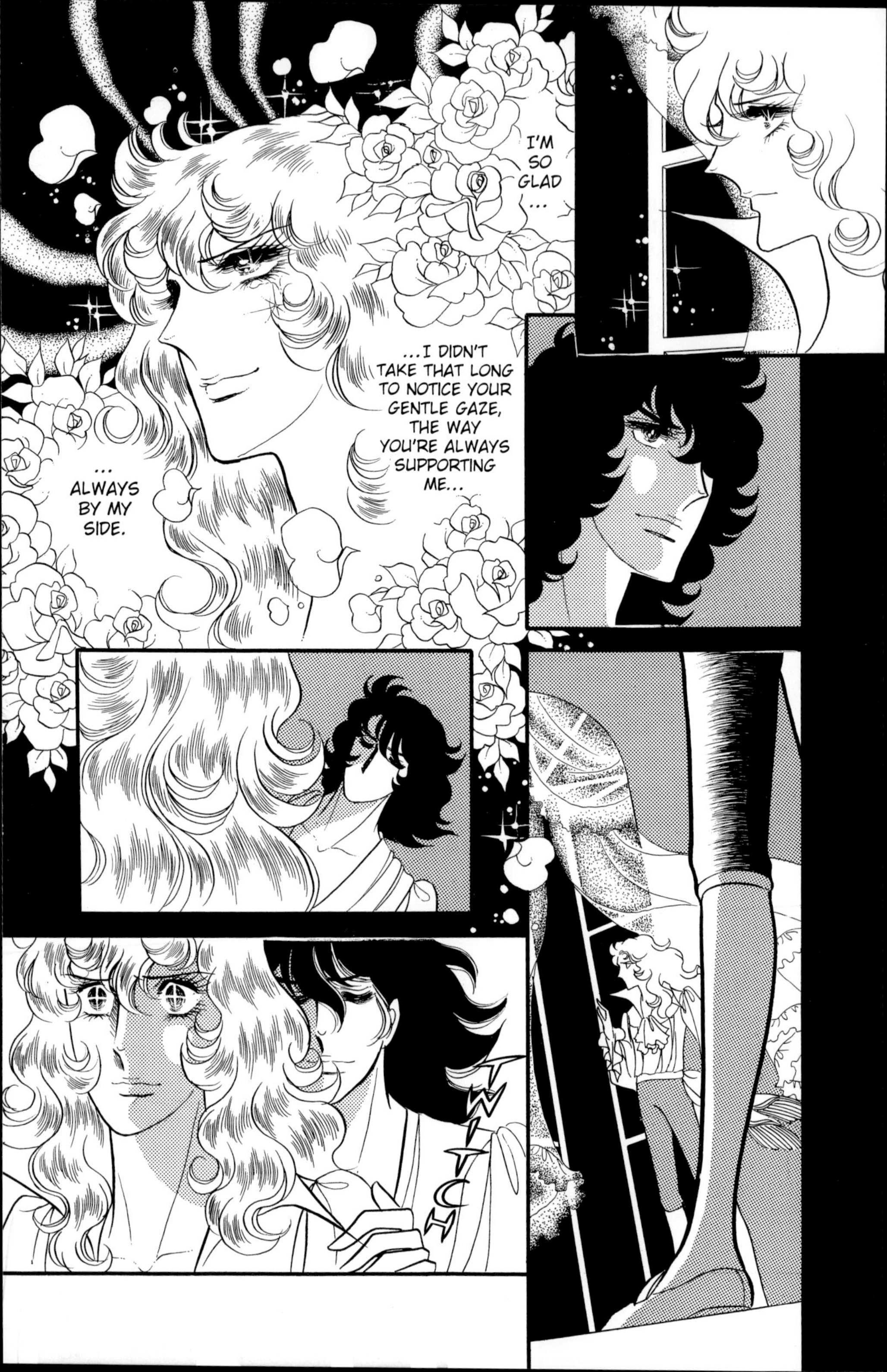
I'M SO GLAD...
...I DIDN'T TAKE THAT LONG TO NOTICE YOUR GENTLE GAZE, THE WAY YOU'RE ALWAYS SUPPORTING ME...
...ALWAYS BY MY SIDE.
TWITCH

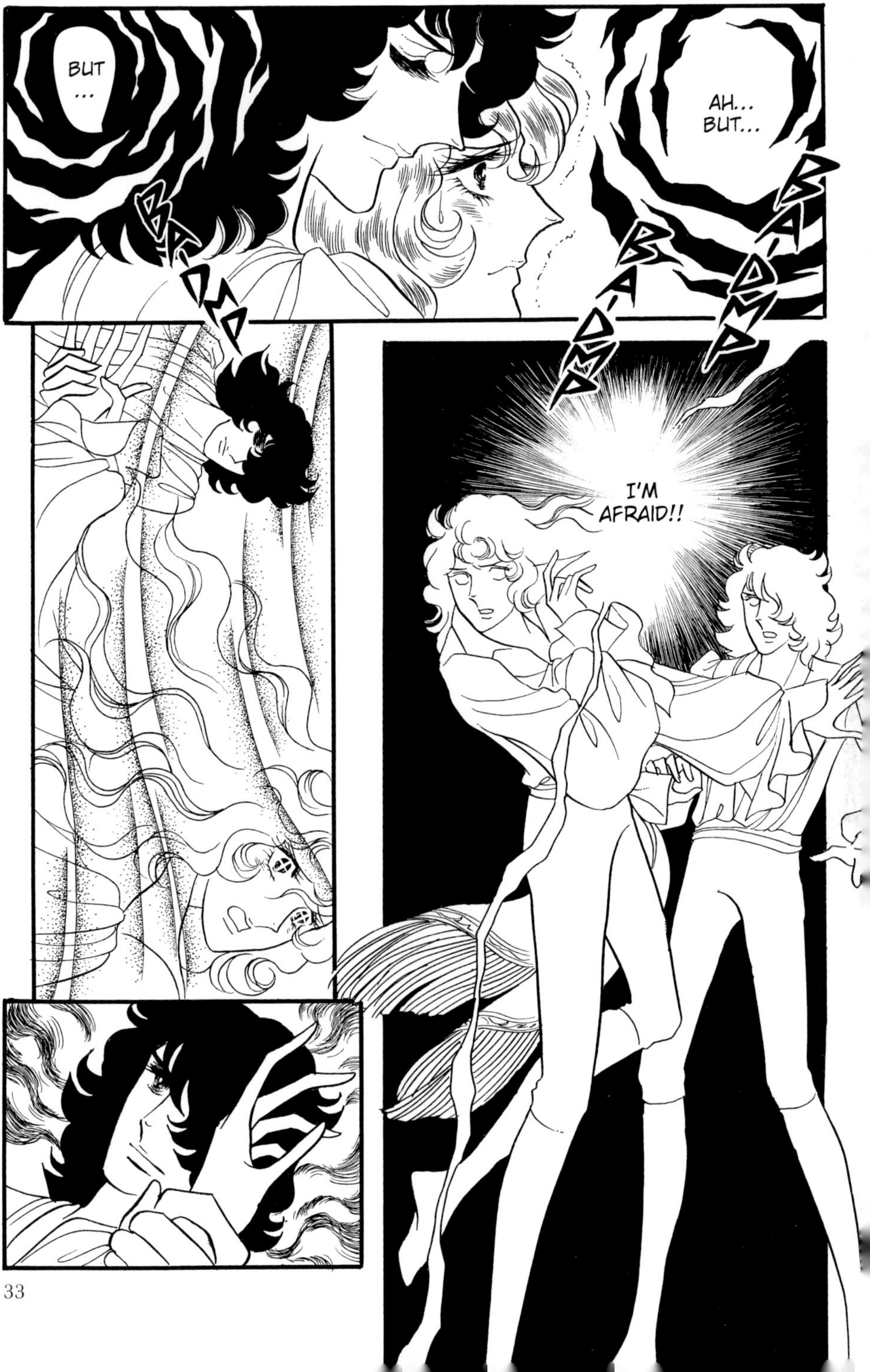
AH... BUT...
BA-DMP
BA-DMP
BUT ...
BA-DMP
I'M AFRAID!!

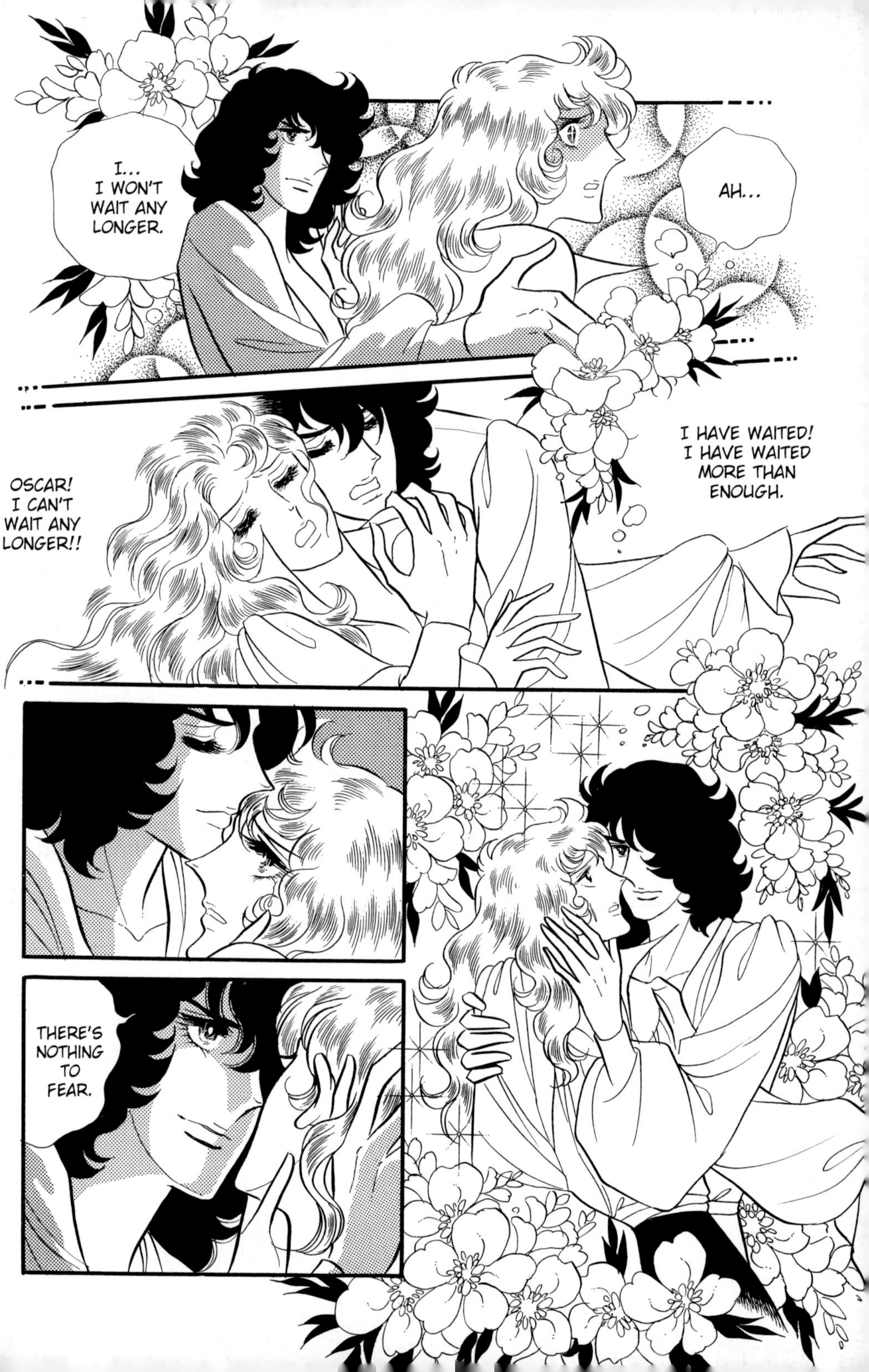
AH...
I... I WON'T WAIT ANY LONGER.
I HAVE WAITED! I HAVE WAITED MORE THAN ENOUGH.
OSCAR! I CAN'T WAIT ANY LONGER!!
THERE'S NOTHING TO FEAR.

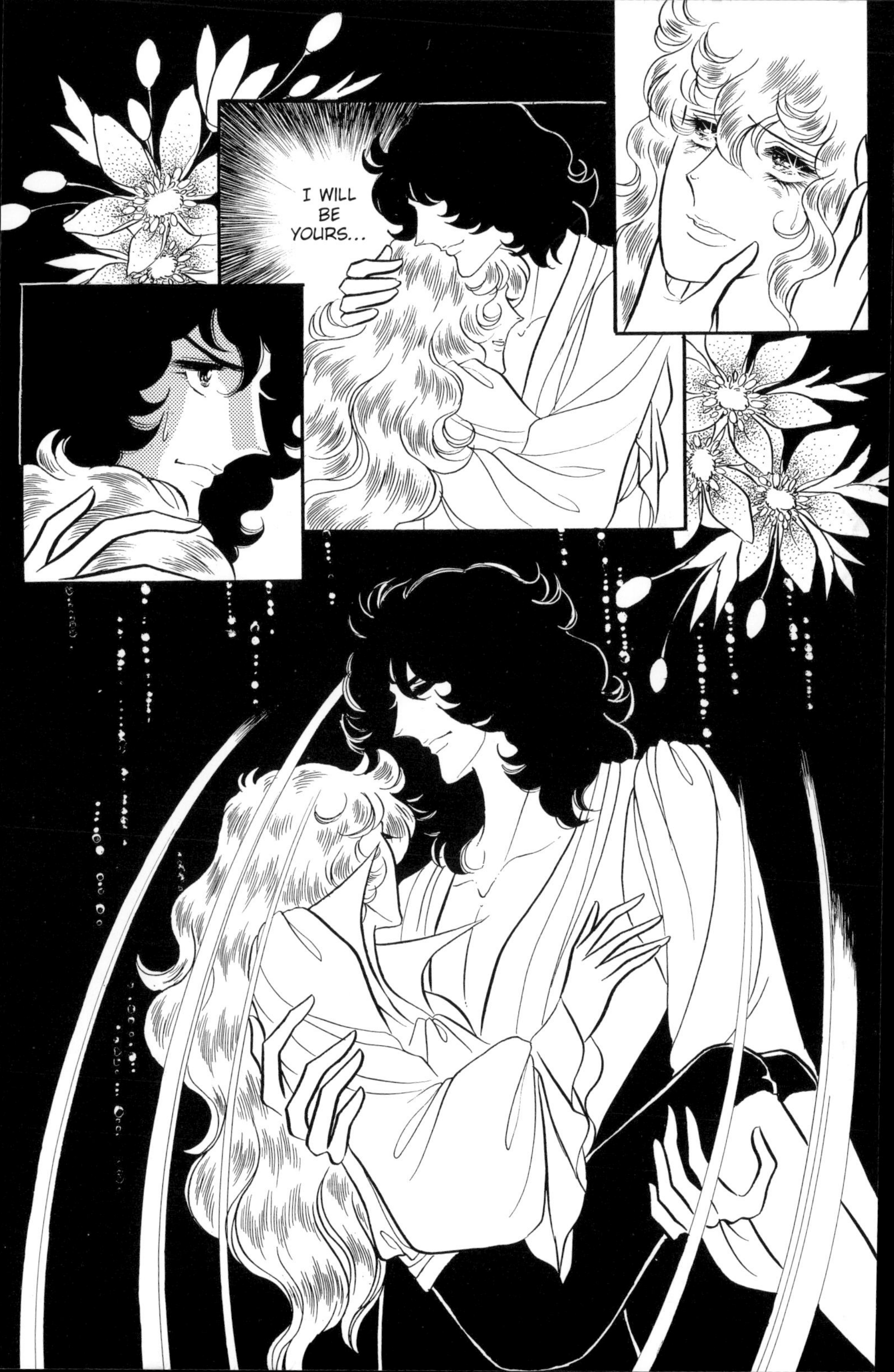
I WILL BE YOURS...

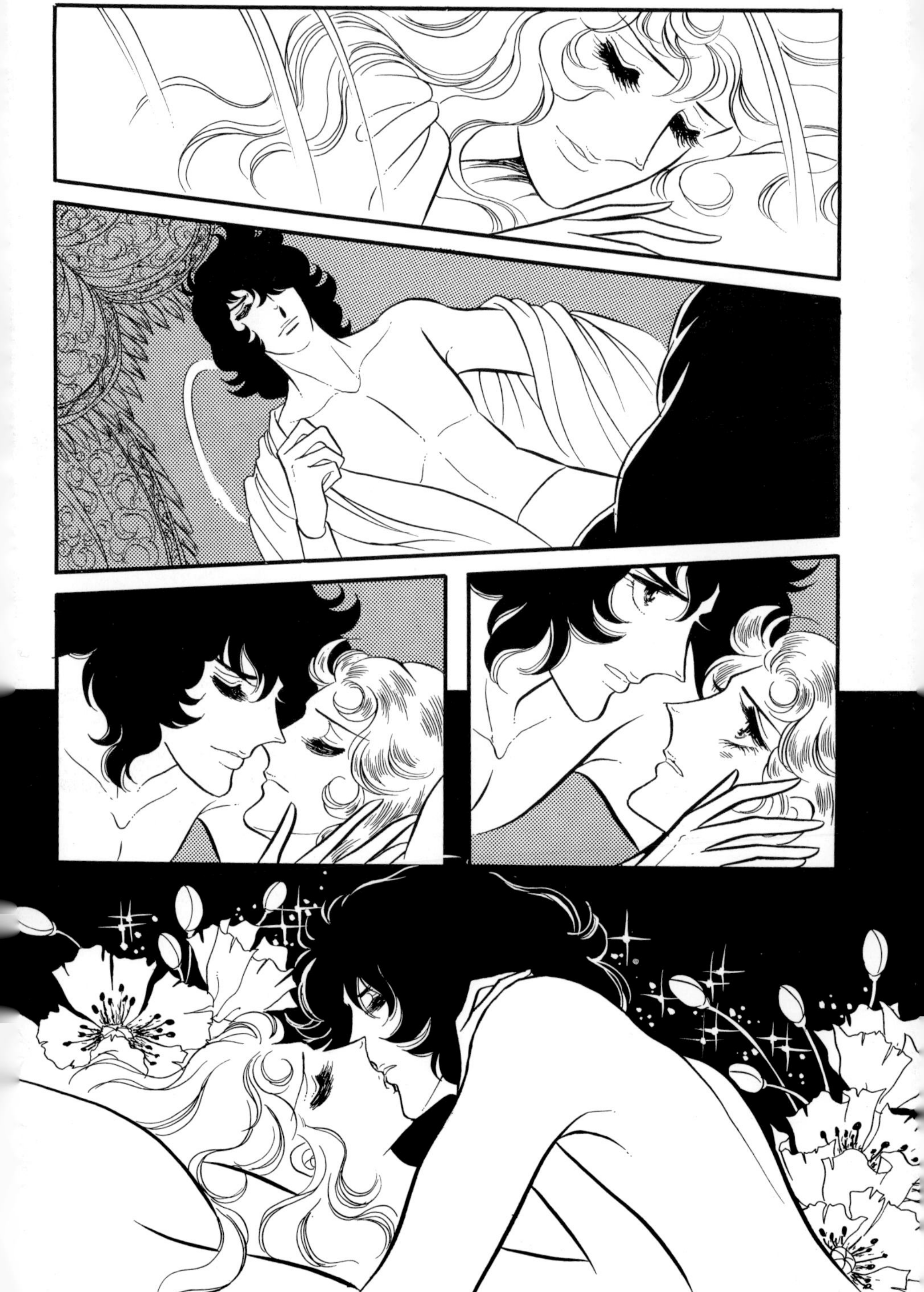

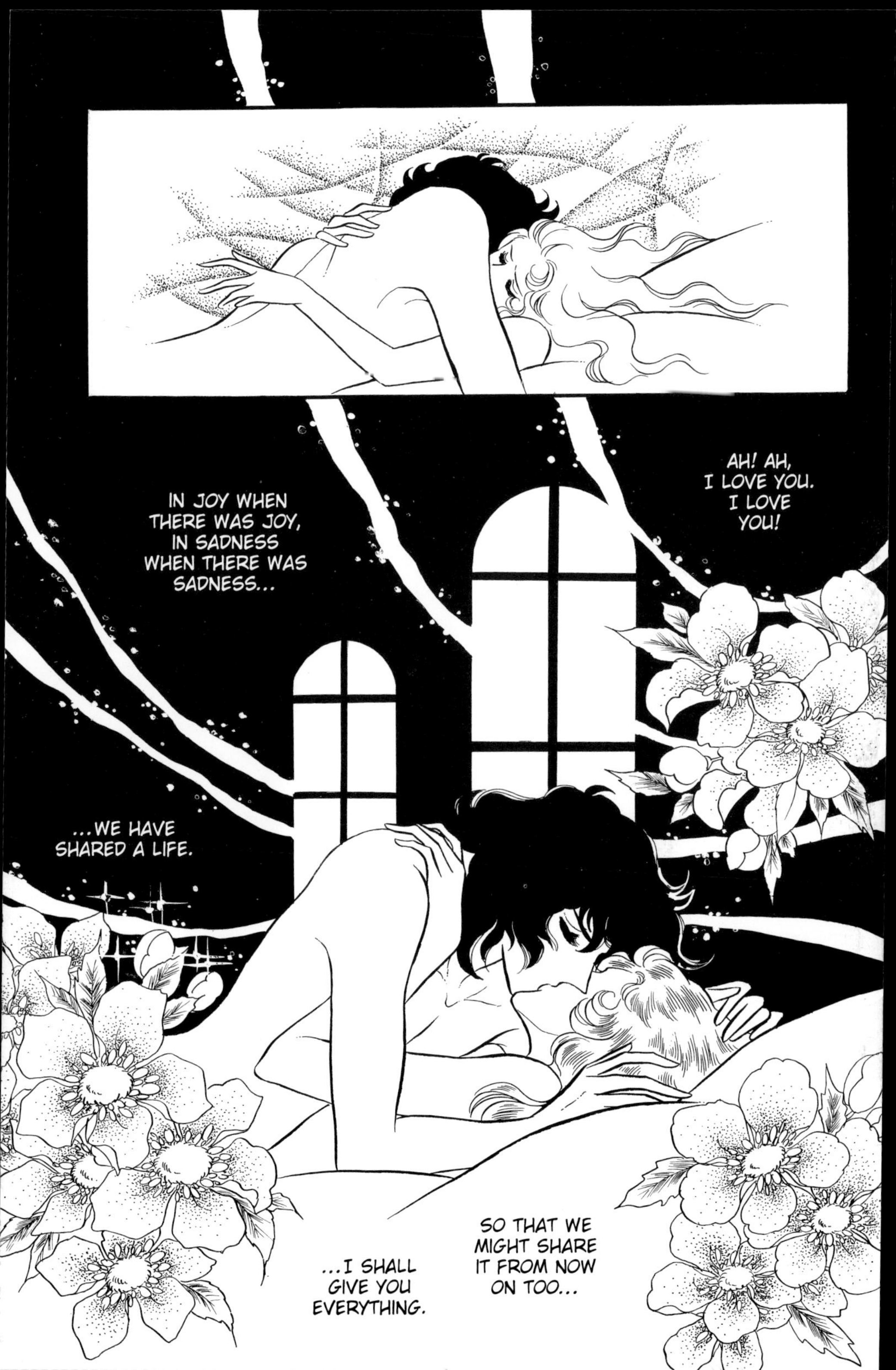
AH! AH, I LOVE YOU. I LOVE YOU!
IN JOY WHEN THERE WAS JOY, IN SADNESS WHEN THERE WAS SADNESS...
...WE HAVE SHARED A LIFE.
SO THAT WE MIGHT SHARE IT FROM NOW ON TOO...
...I SHALL GIVE YOU EVERYTHING.

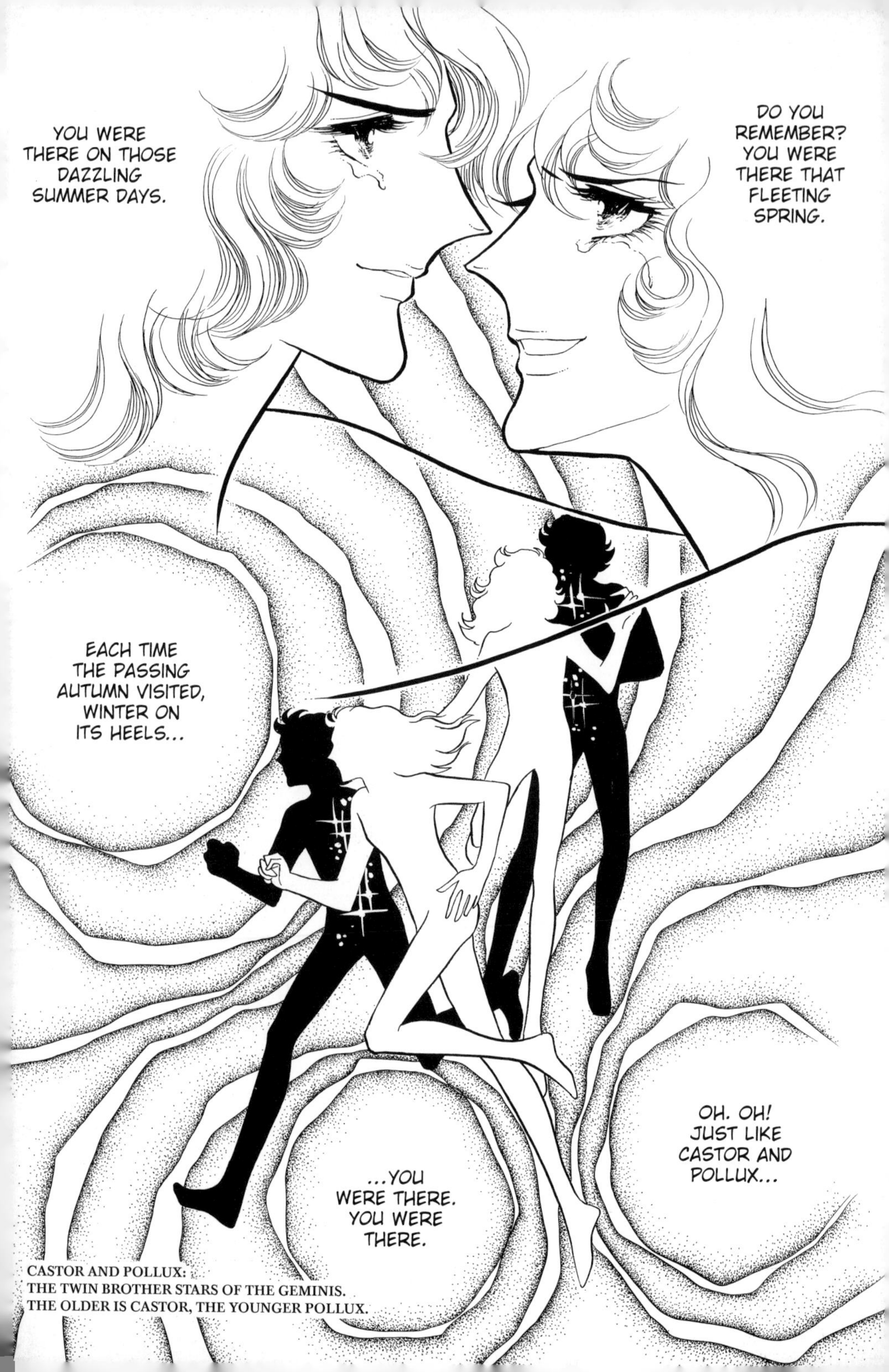
DO YOU REMEMBER? YOU WERE THERE THAT FLEETING SPRING.
YOU WERE THERE ON THOSE DAZZLING SUMMER DAYS.
EACH TIME THE PASSING AUTUMN VISITED, WINTER ON ITS HEELS...
...YOU WERE THERE. YOU WERE THERE.
OH. OH! JUST LIKE CASTOR AND POLLUX...
CASTOR AND POLLUX:
THE TWIN BROTHER STARS OF THE GEMINIS.
THE OLDER IS CASTOR, THE YOUNGER POLLUX.

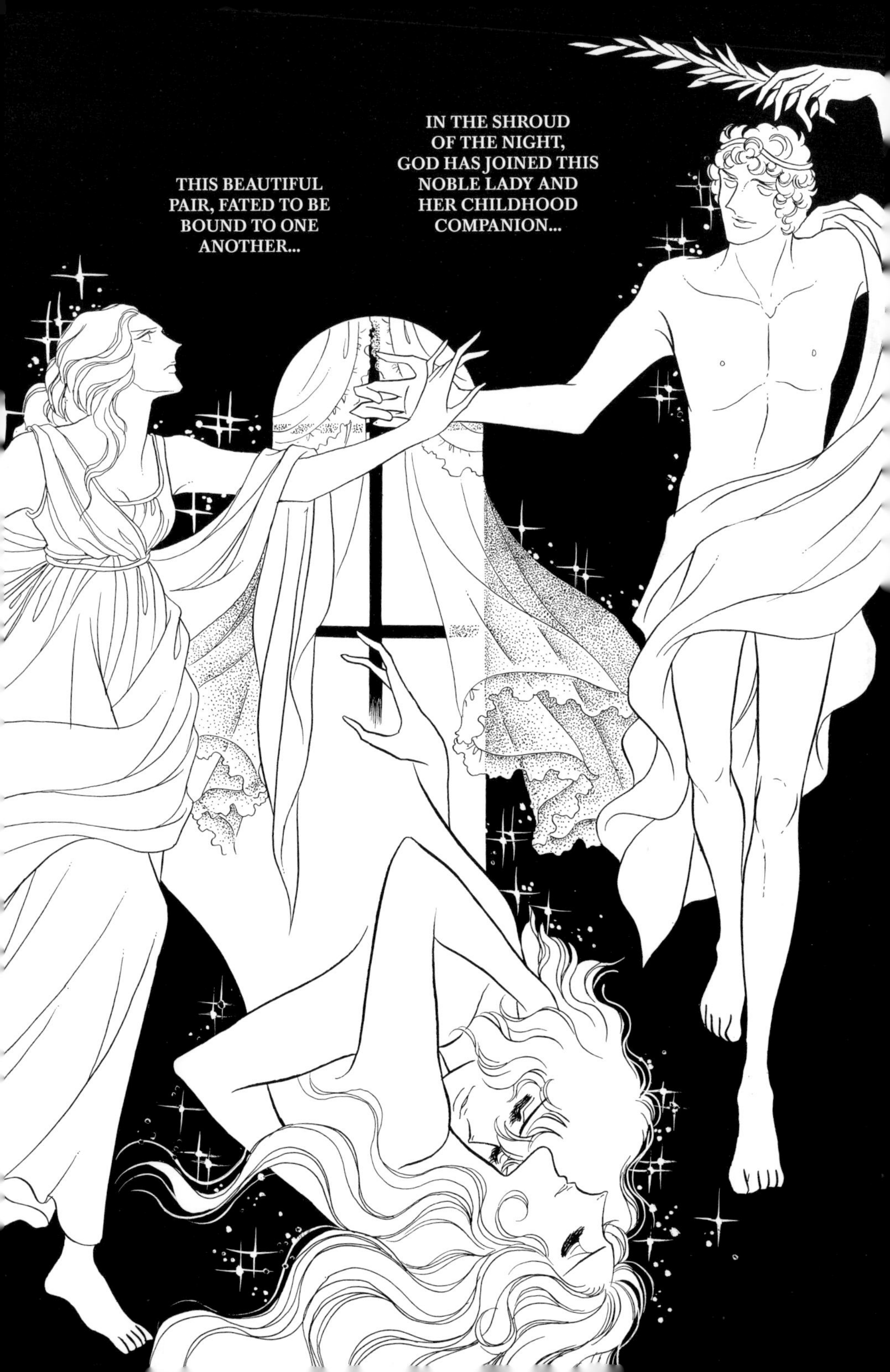
IN THE SHROUD OF THE NIGHT, GOD HAS JOINED THIS NOBLE LADY AND HER CHILDHOOD COMPANION...
THIS BEAUTIFUL PAIR, FATED TO BE BOUND TO ONE ANOTHER...

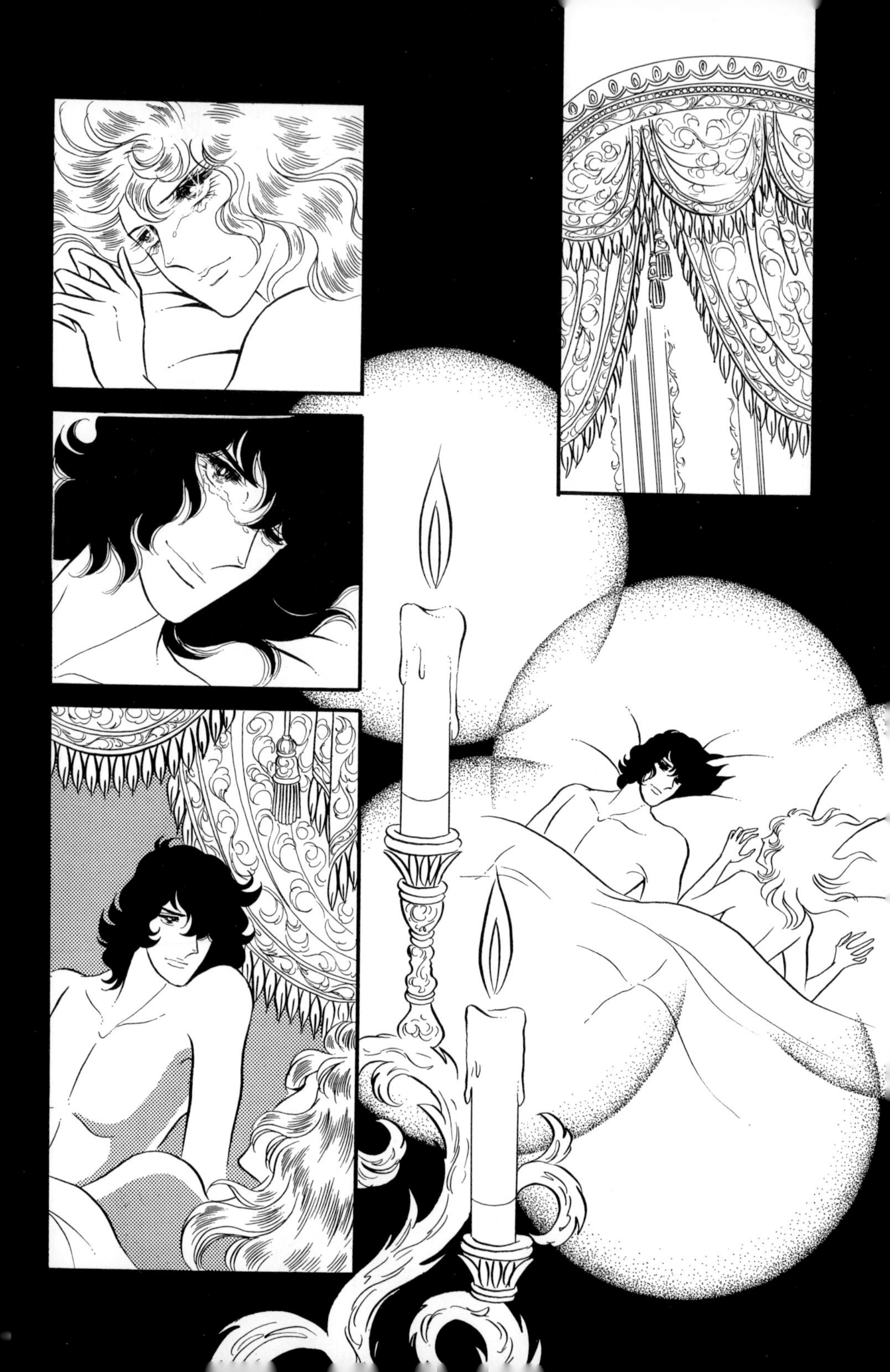

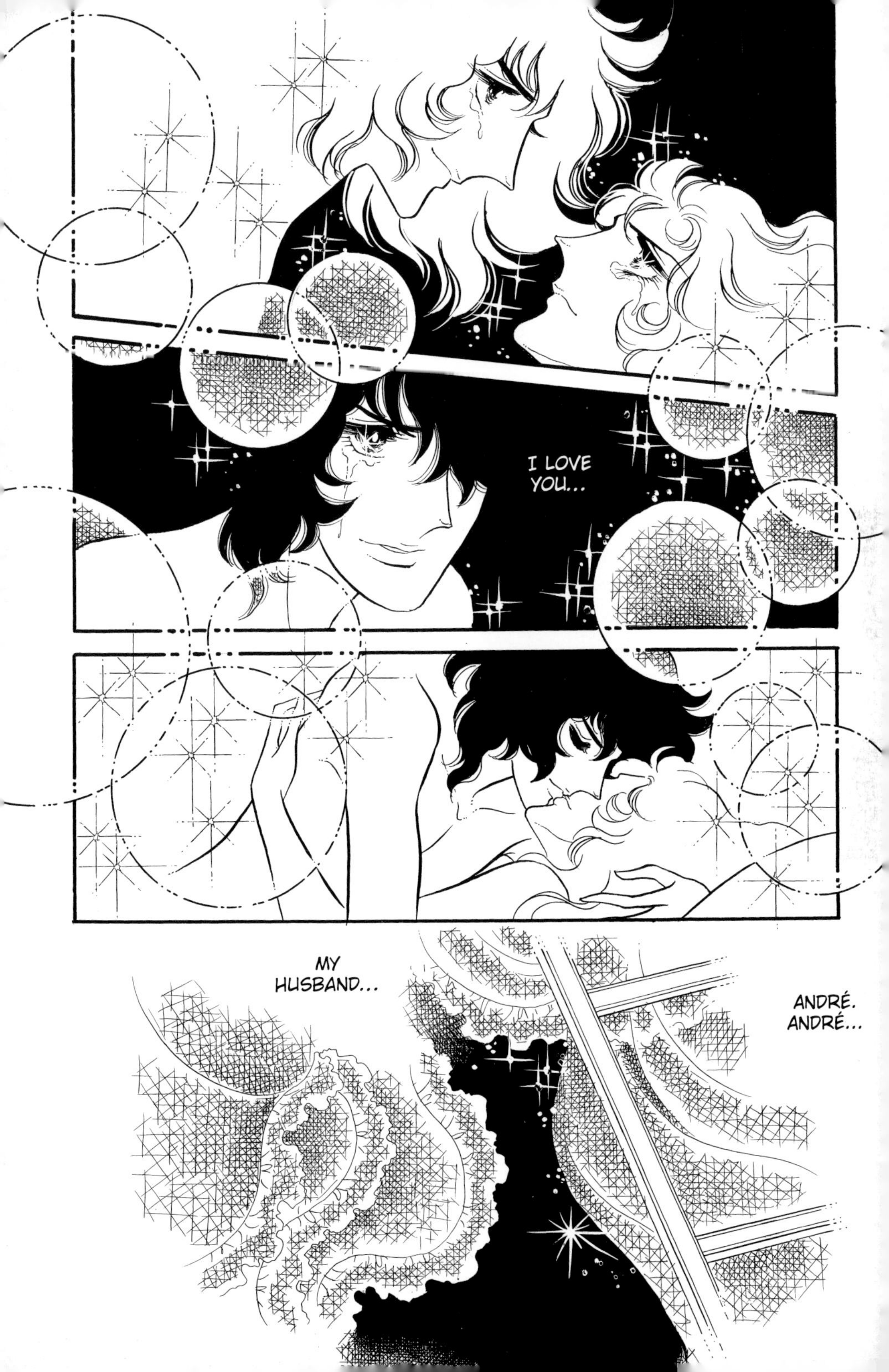
I LOVE YOU...
ANDRÉ. ANDRÉ...
MY HUSBAND...

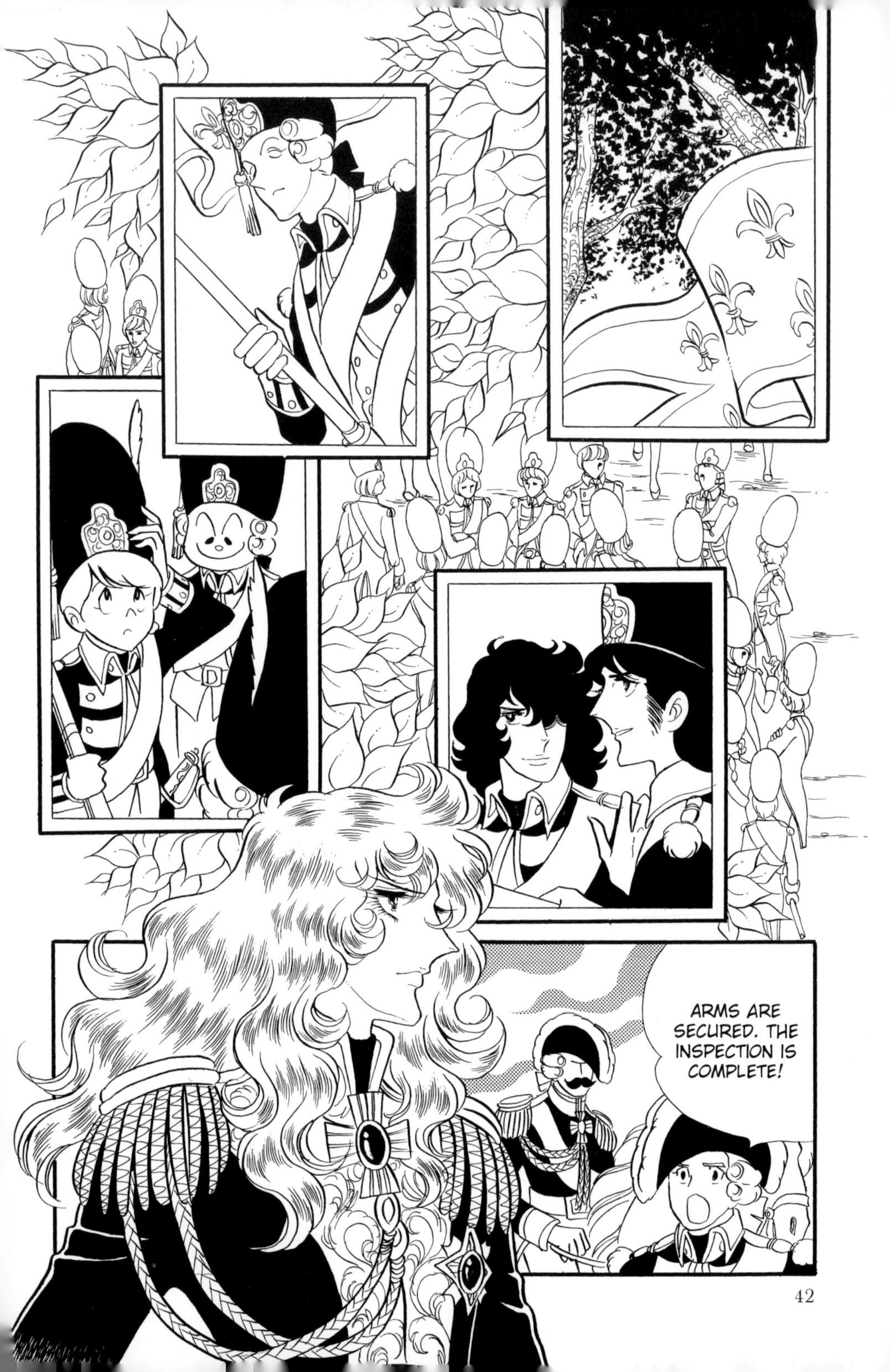
ARMS ARE SECURED. THE INSPECTION IS COMPLETE!

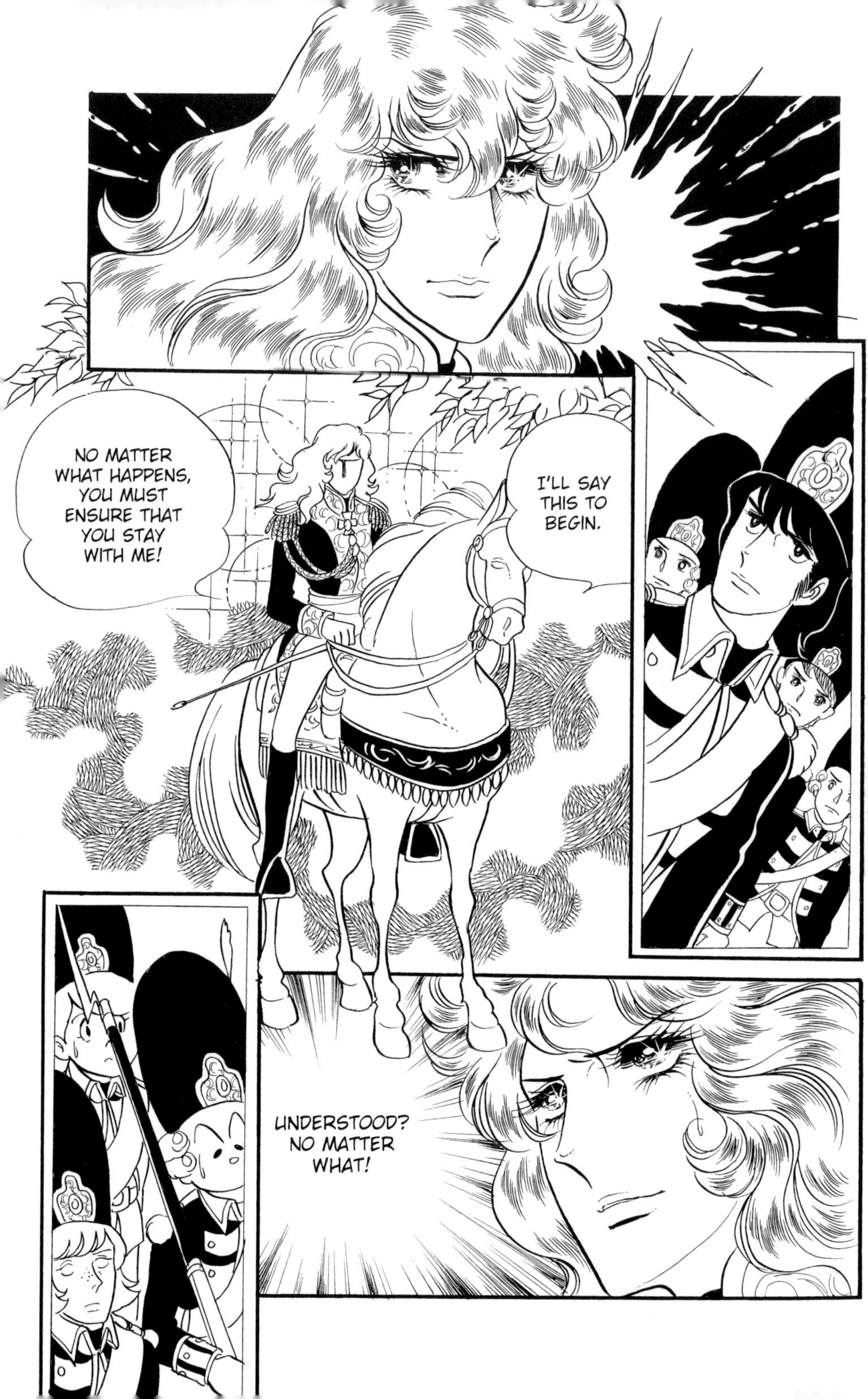
I'LL SAY THIS TO BEGIN.
NO MATTER WHAT HAPPENS, YOU MUST ENSURE THAT YOU STAY WITH ME!
UNDERSTOOD? NO MATTER WHAT!

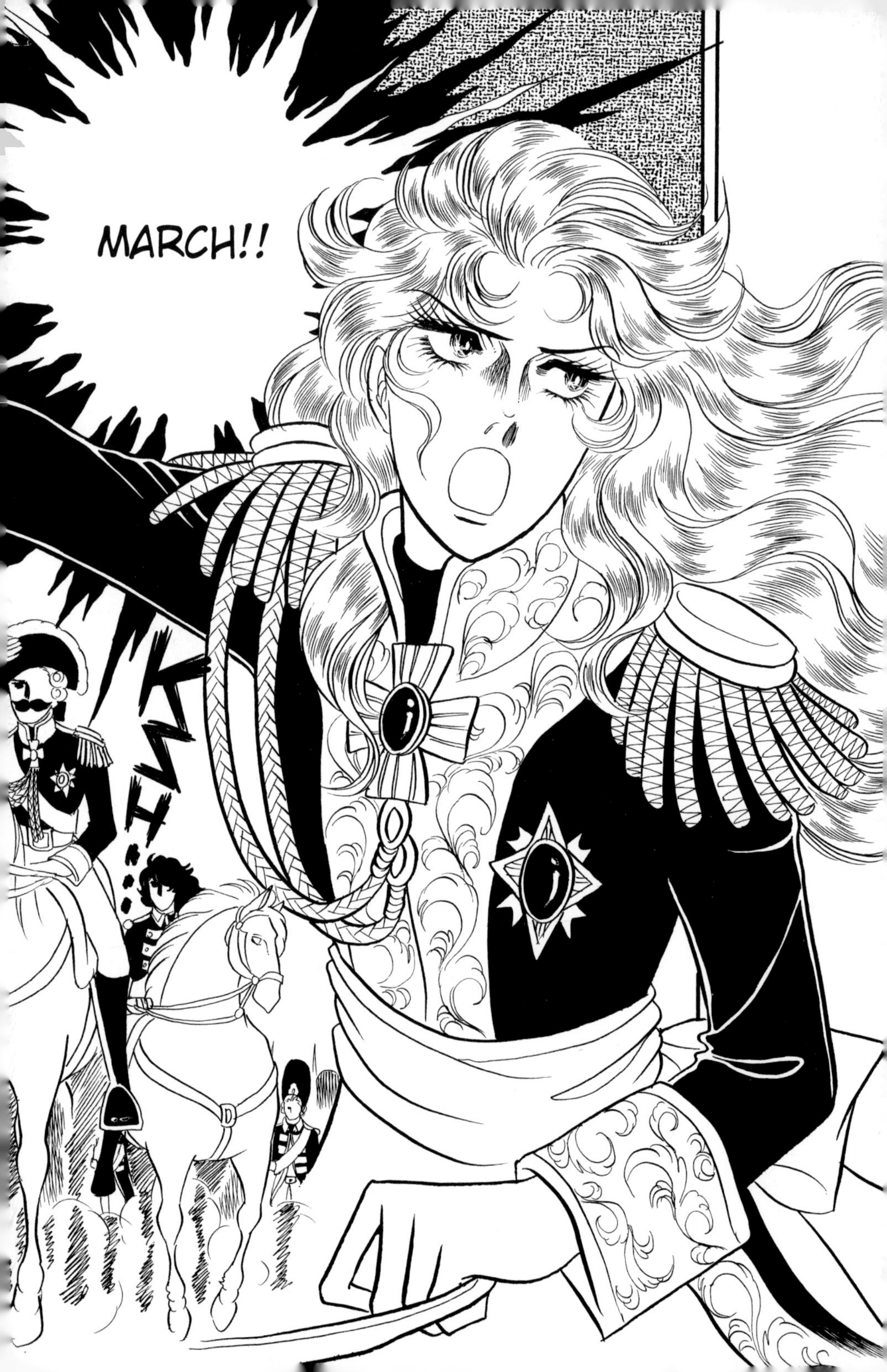
MARCH!!

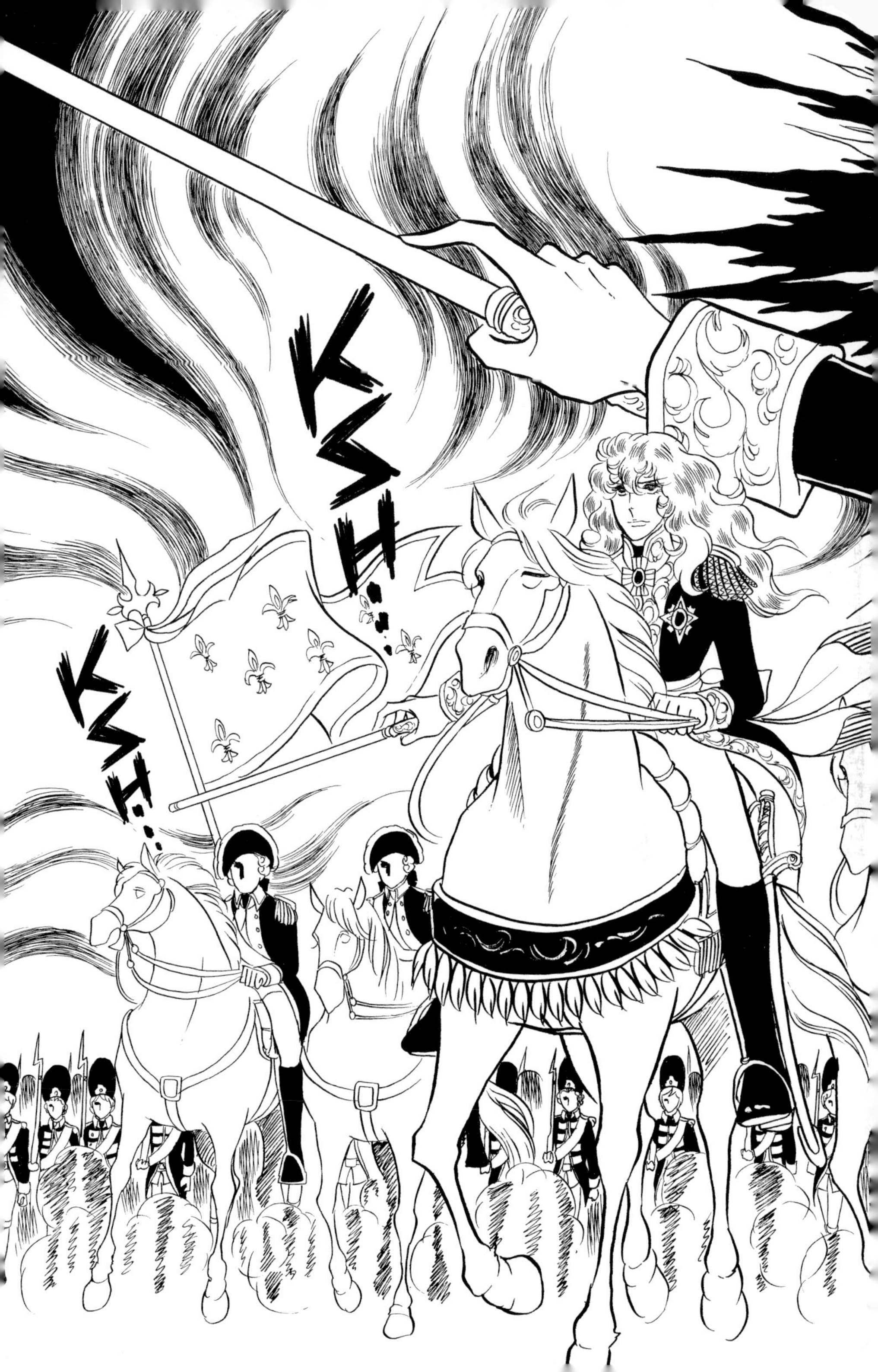
KSHH...
KSHH...

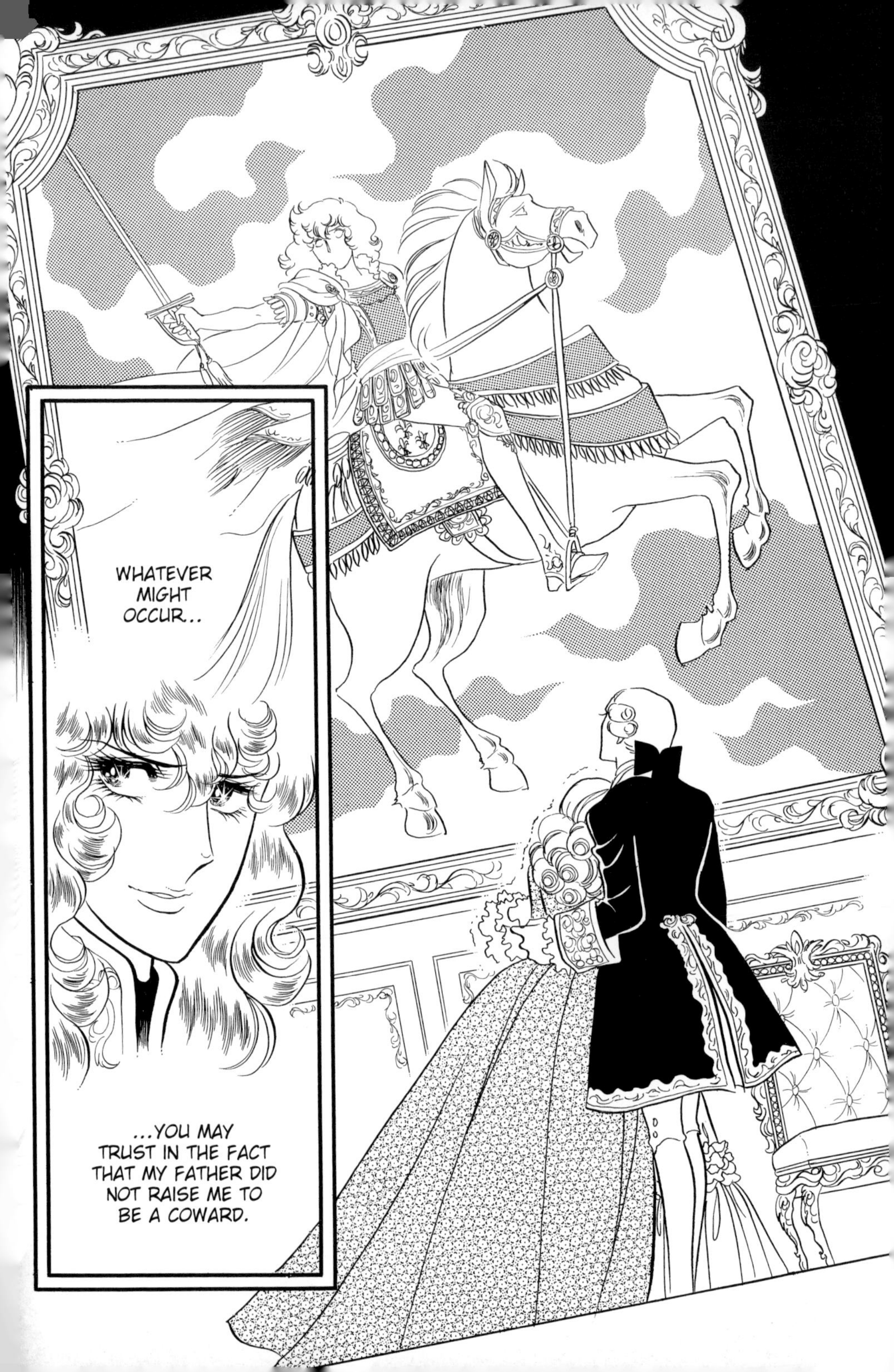
WHATEVER MIGHT OCCUR..
...YOU MAY TRUST IN THE FACT THAT MY FATHER DID NOT RAISE ME TO BE A COWARD.

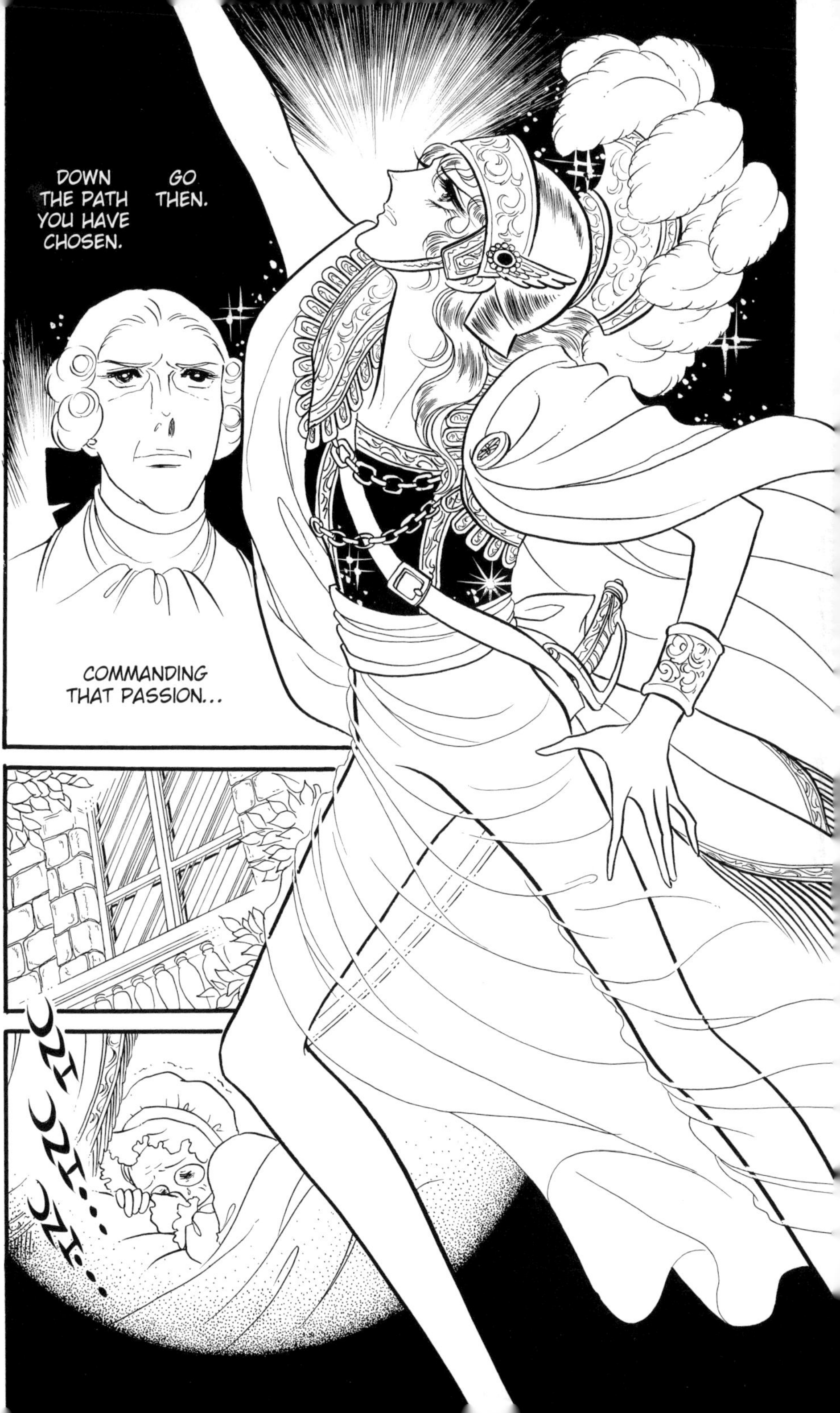
GO THEN.
DOWN THE PATH YOU HAVE CHOSEN.
COMMANDING THAT PASSION...

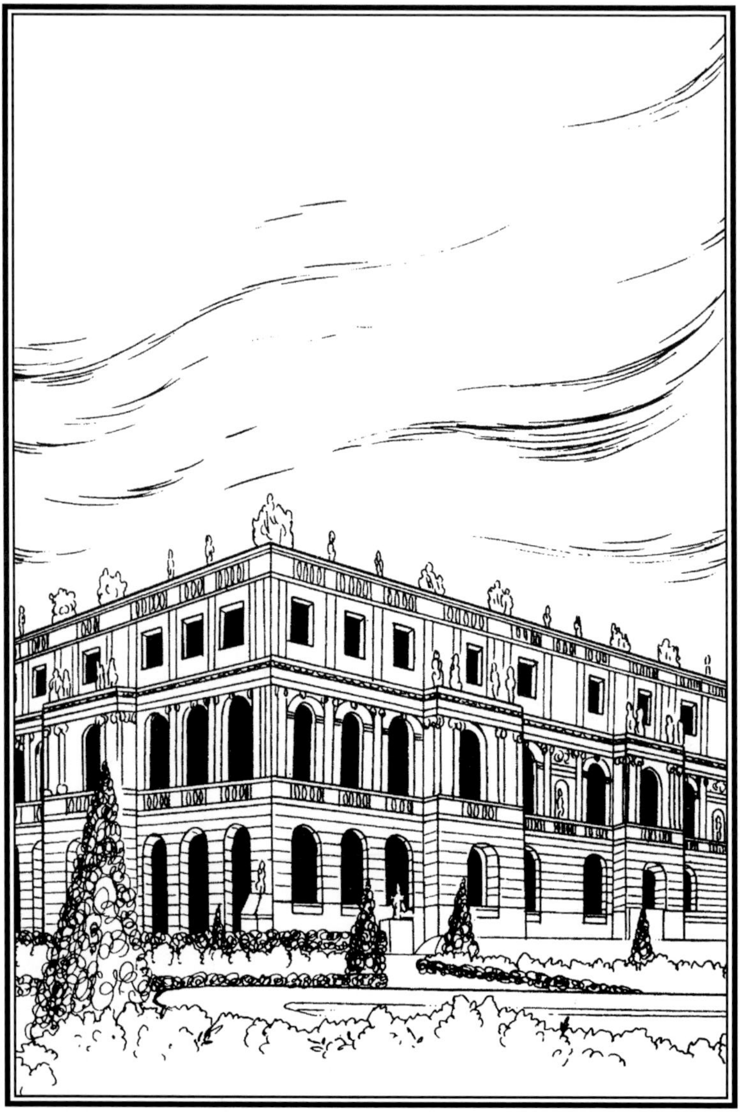

1974 MARGARET COMICS TRADE PAPERBACK
VOLUME 8 INSERT ART

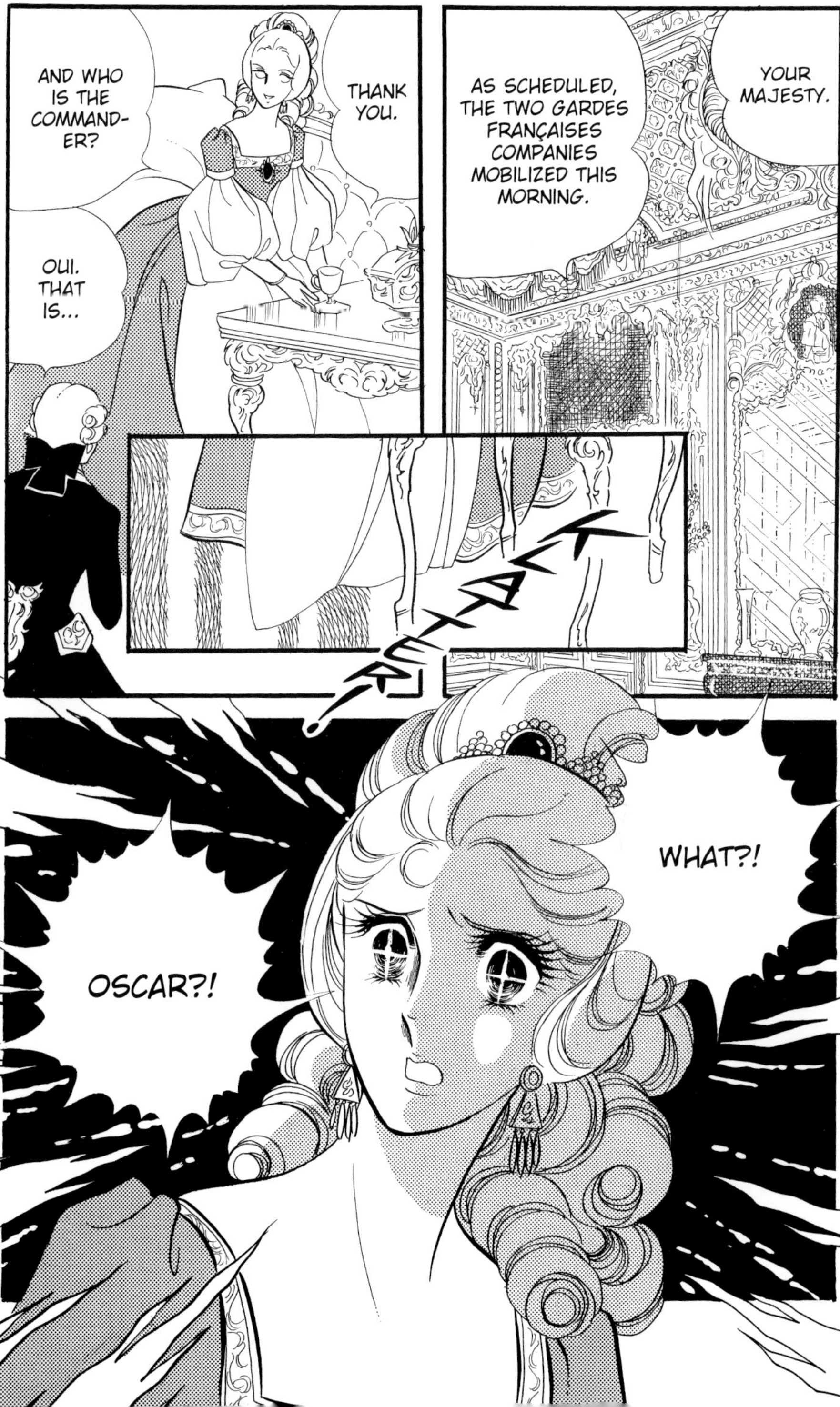
YOUR MAJESTY.
AS SCHEDULED, THE TWO GARDES FRANÇAISES COMPANIES MOBILIZED THIS MORNING.
THANK YOU.
AND WHO IS THE COMMANDER?
OUI. THAT IS...
KLATTER!
WHAT?!
OSCAR?!

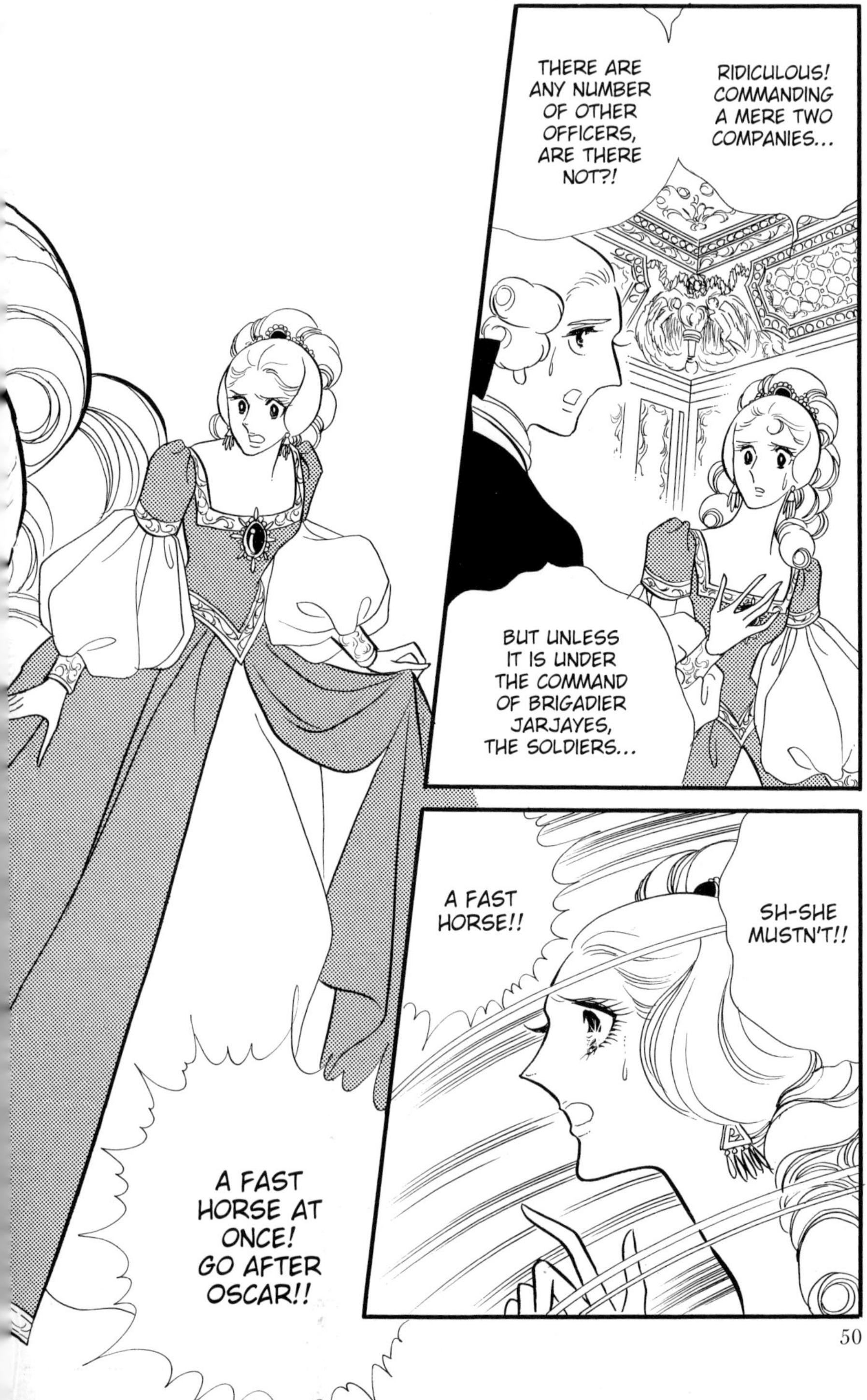
RIDICULOUS! COMMANDING A MERE TWO COMPANIES...
THERE ARE ANY NUMBER OF OTHER OFFICERS, ARE THERE NOT?!
BUT UNLESS IT IS UNDER THE COMMAND OF BRIGADIER JARJAYES, THE SOLDIERS...
SH-SHE MUSTN'T!!
A FAST HORSE!!
A FAST HORSE AT ONCE! GO AFTER OSCAR!!

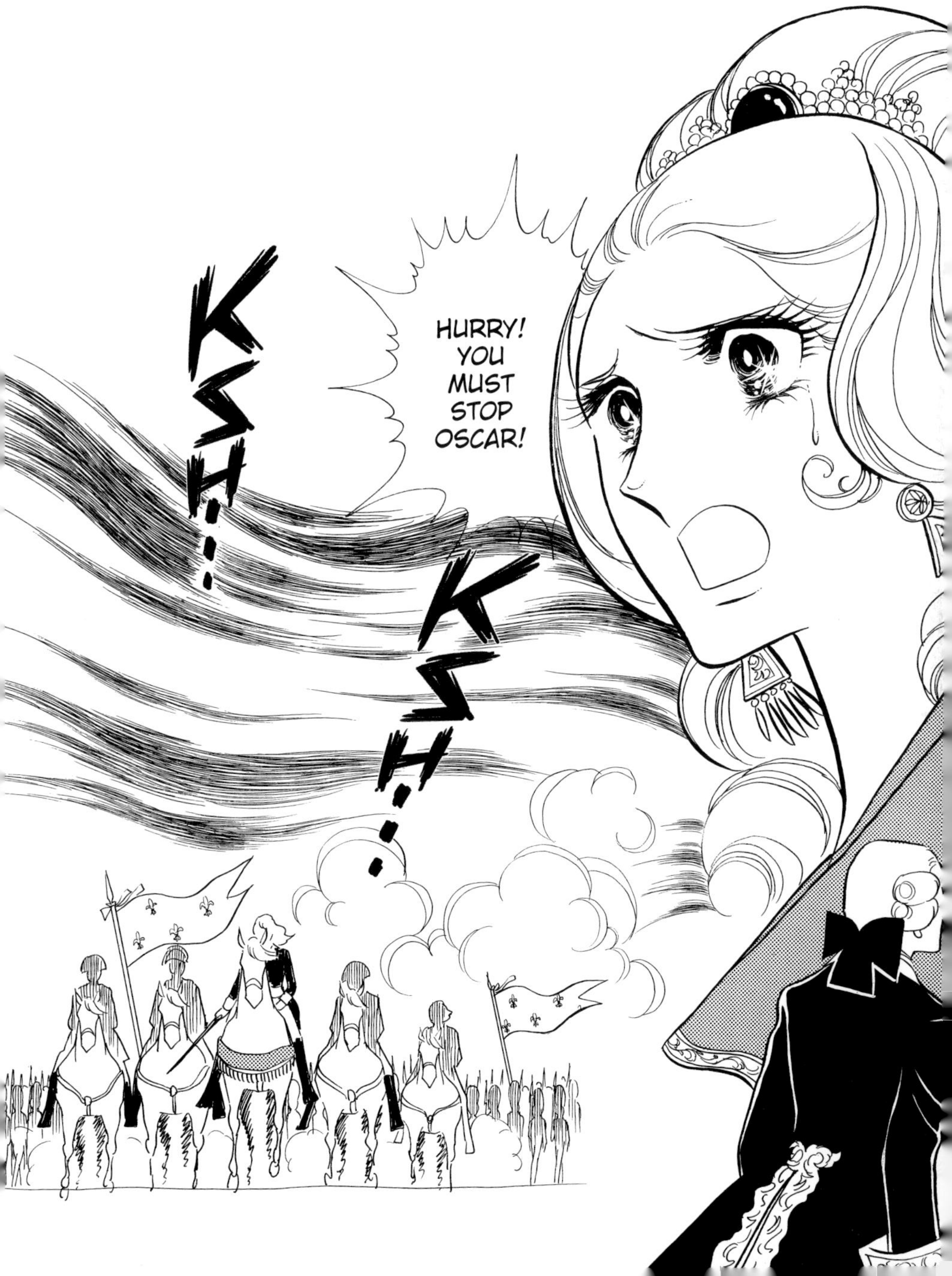
HURRY! YOU MUST STOP OSCAR!
KSSH...
KSSH...

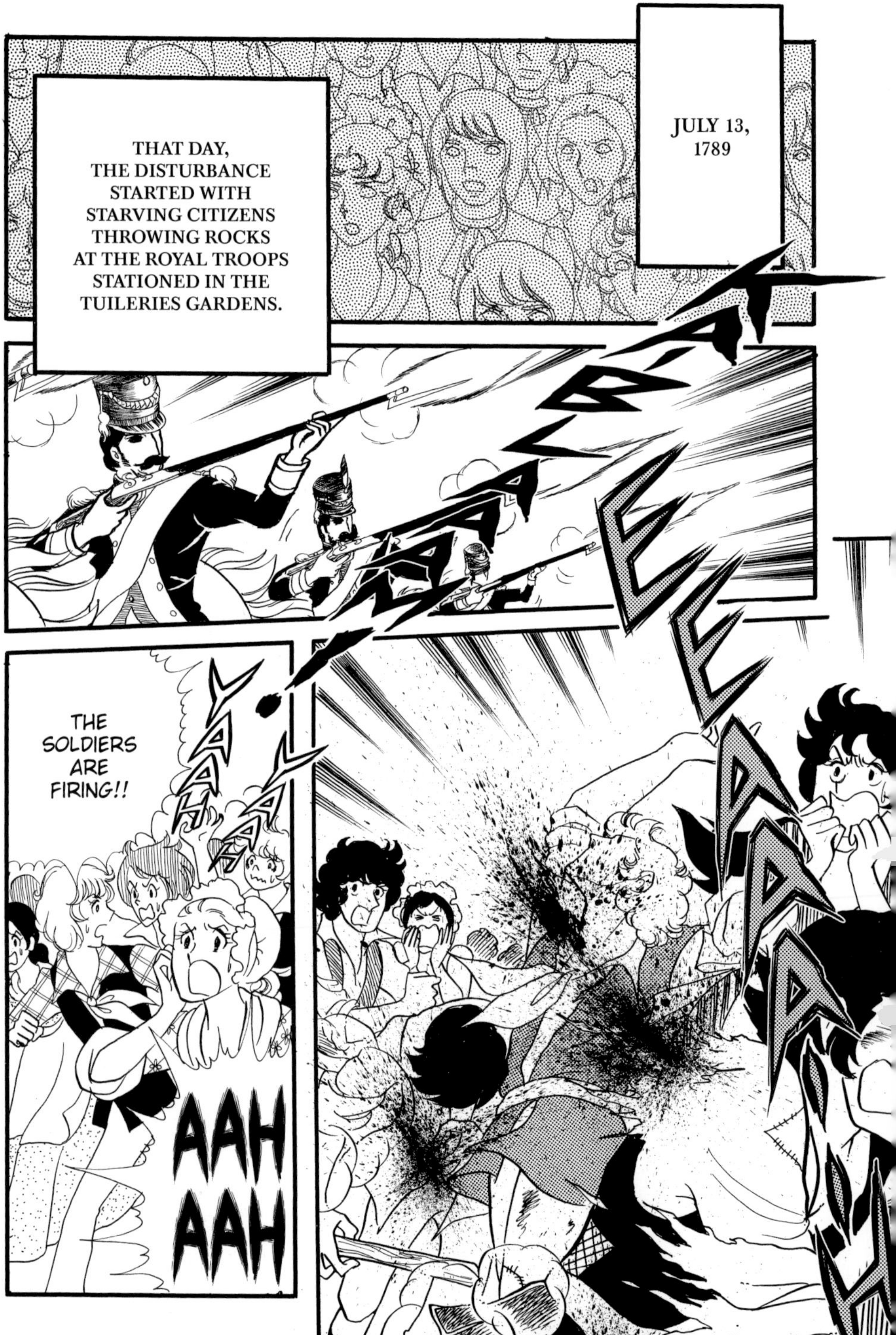
JULY 13, 1789
THAT DAY, THE DISTURBANCE STARTED WITH STARVING CITIZENS THROWING ROCKS AT THE ROYAL TROOPS STATIONED IN THE TUILERIES GARDENS.
YAAH
YAAAH
THE SOLDIERS ARE FIRING!!
AAH AAH

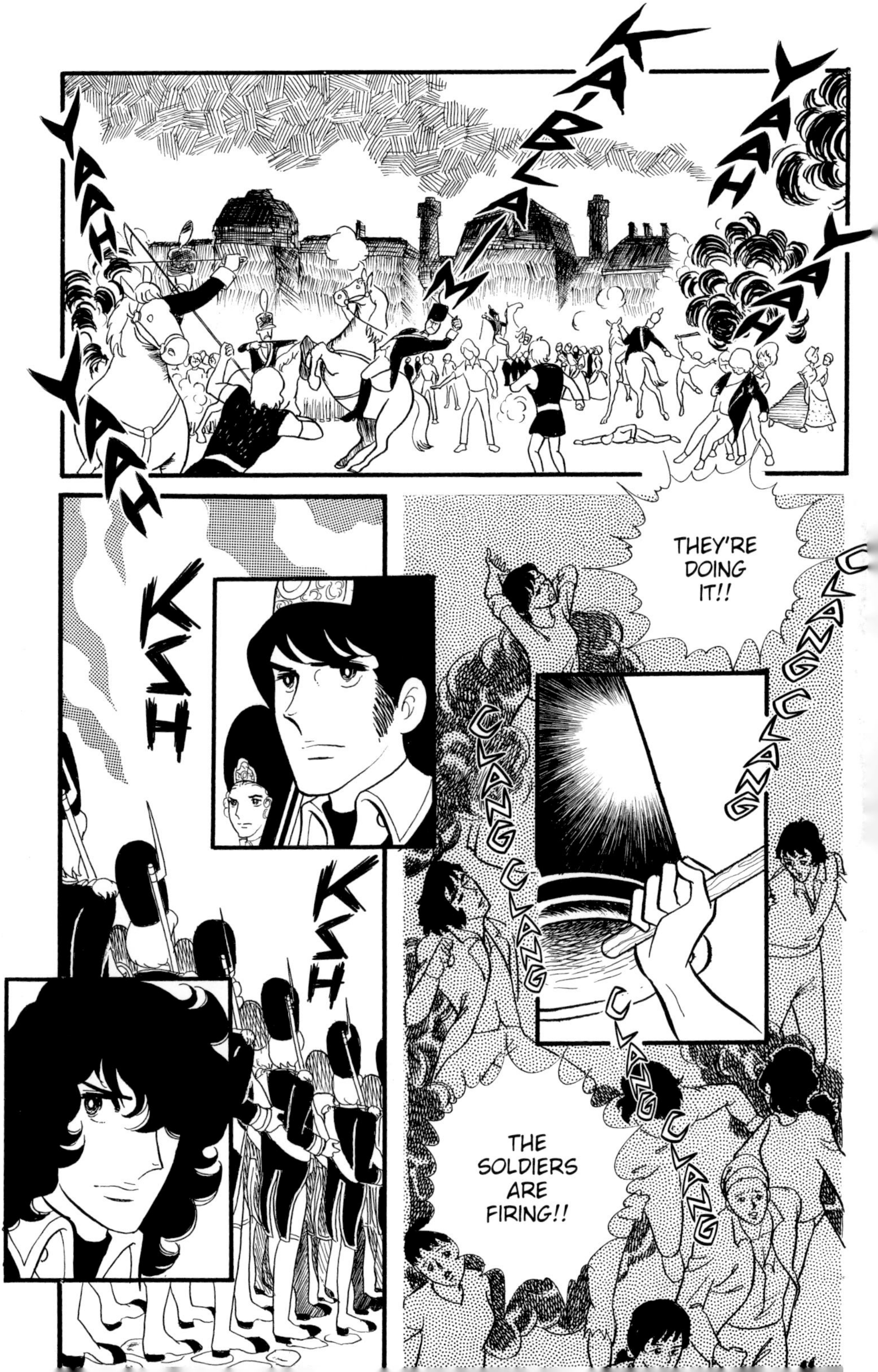
YAAH
YAAH
KA-BLAM
YAAH
YAAH
THEY'RE DOING IT!!
CLANG CLANG CLANG
CLANG CLANG
CLANG CLANG
THE SOLDIERS ARE FIRING!!
KSSH
KSSH

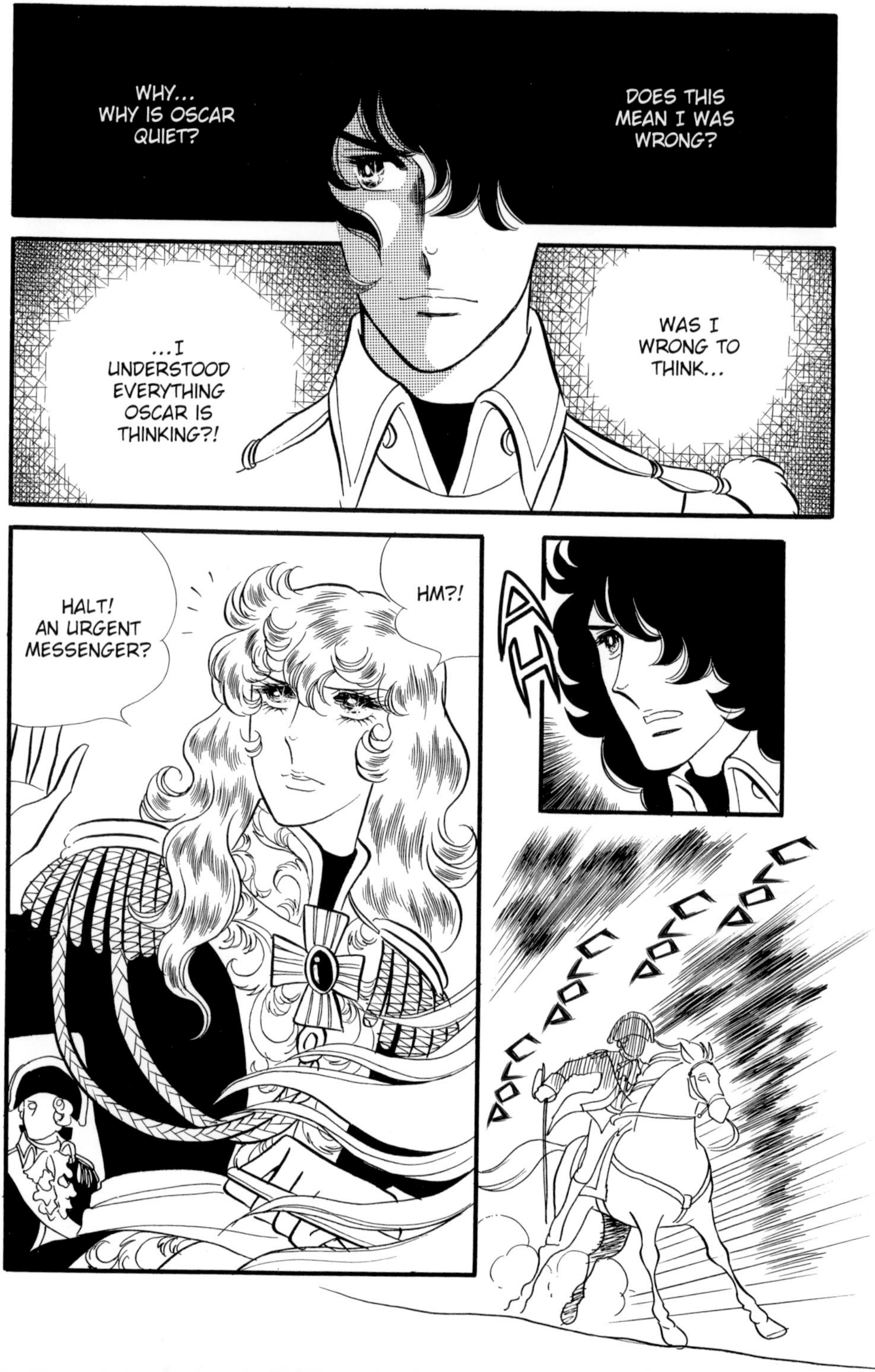
DOES THIS MEAN I WAS WRONG?
WHY... WHY IS OSCAR QUIET?
WAS I WRONG TO THINK...
...I UNDERSTOOD EVERYTHING OSCAR IS THINKING?!
AH
HM?!
HALT! AN URGENT MESSENGER?

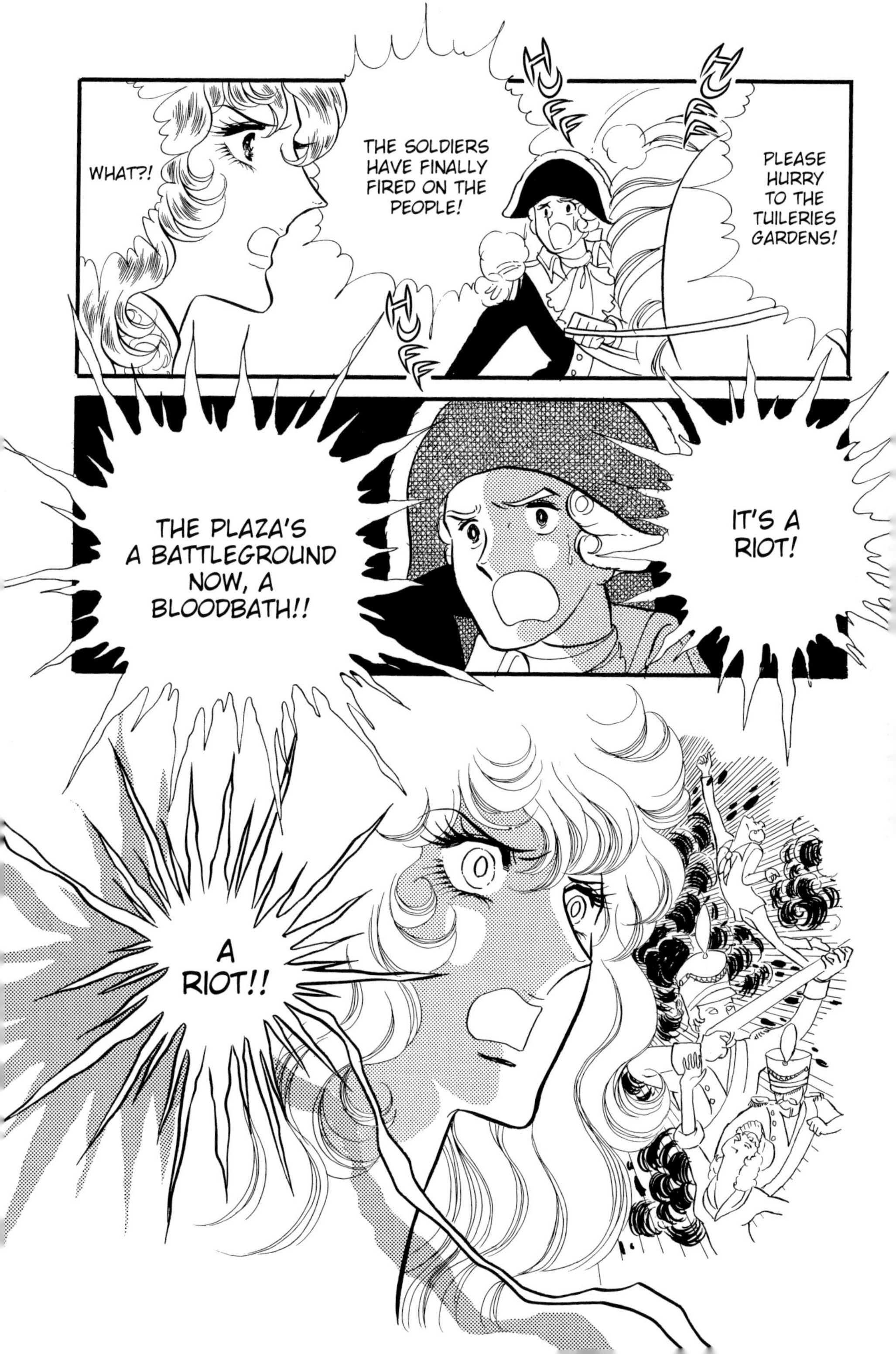
HUFF
HUFF
PLEASE HURRY TO THE TUILERIES GARDENS!
THE SOLDIERS HAVE FINALLY FIRED ON THE PEOPLE!
HUFF
WHAT?!
IT'S A RIOT!
THE PLAZA'S A BATTLEGROUND NOW, A BLOODBATH!!
A RIOT!!

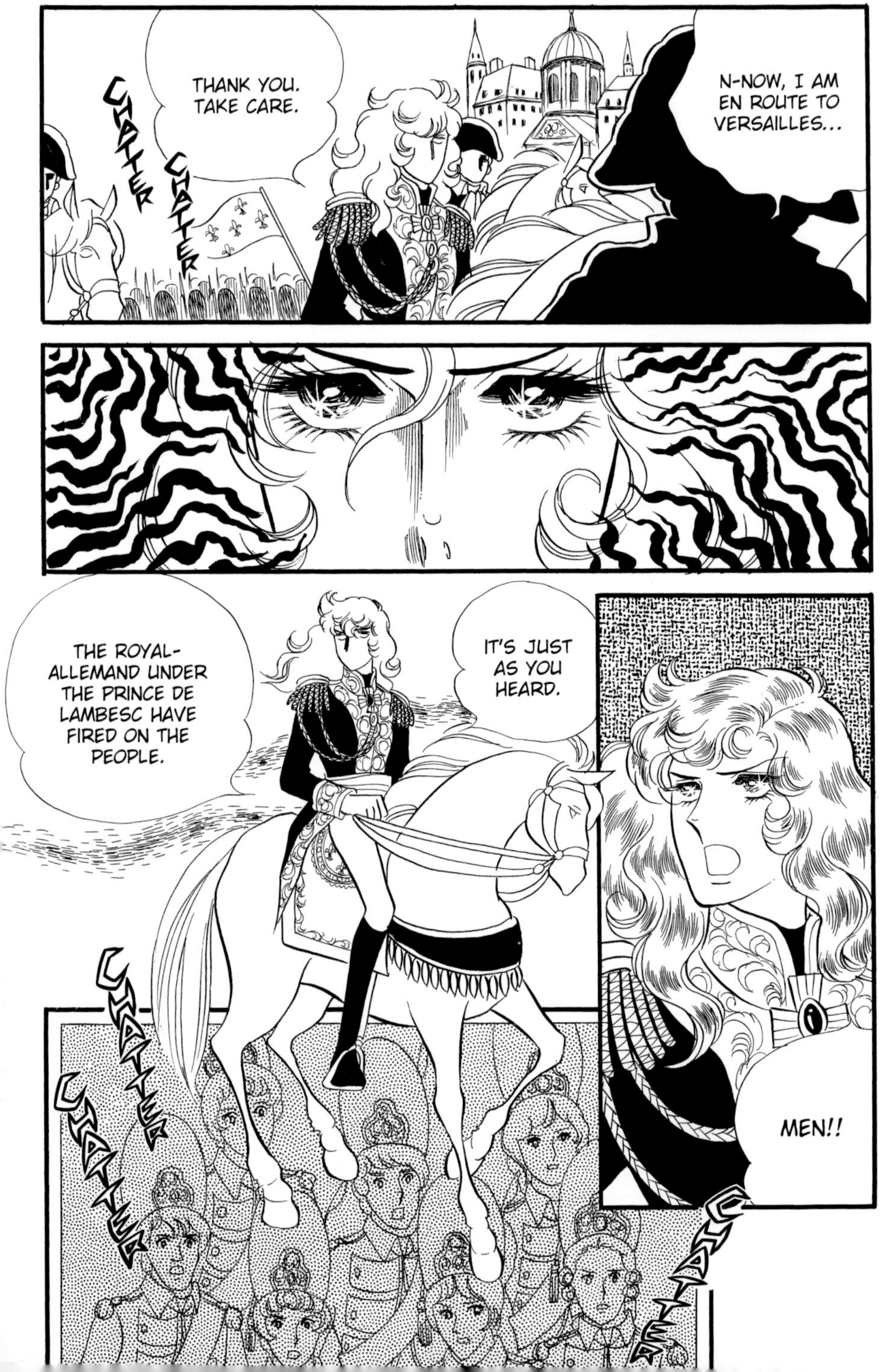
N-NOW, I AM EN ROUTE TO VERSAILLES...
THANK YOU. TAKE CARE.
CHATTER CHATTER
MEN!!
CHATTER
IT'S JUST AS YOU HEARD.
THE ROYAL-ALLEMAND UNDER THE PRINCE DE LAMBESC HAVE FIRED ON THE PEOPLE.
CHATTER CHATTER

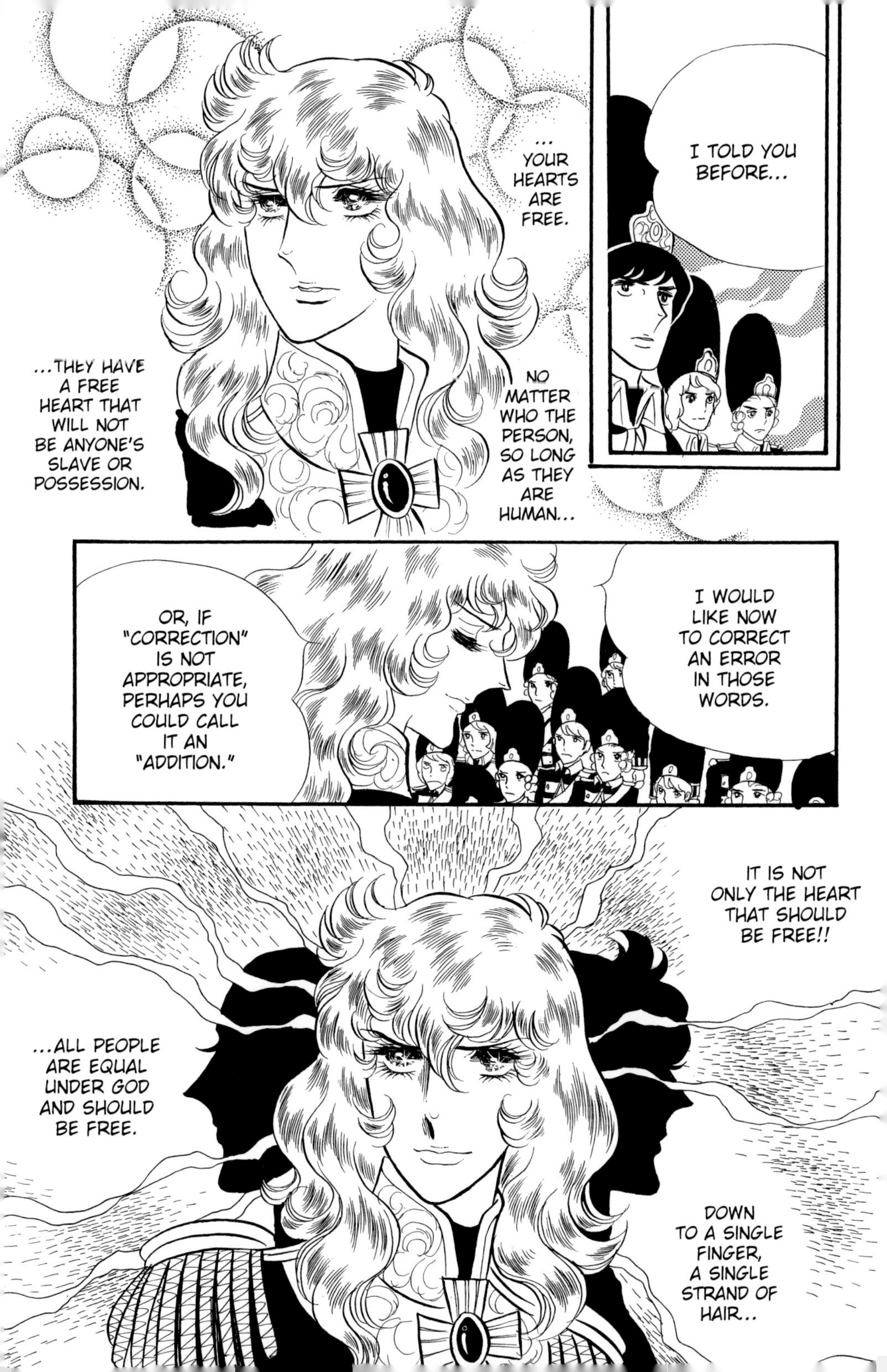
I TOLD YOU BEFORE...
... YOUR HEARTS ARE FREE.
NO MATTER WHO THE PERSON, SO LONG AS THEY ARE HUMAN...
...THEY HAVE A FREE HEART THAT WILL NOT BE ANYONE'S SLAVE OR POSSESSION.
I WOULD LIKE NOW TO CORRECT AN ERROR IN THOSE WORDS.
OR, IF "CORRECTION" IS NOT APPROPRIATE, PERHAPS YOU COULD CALL IT AN "ADDITION."
IT IS NOT ONLY THE HEART THAT SHOULD BE FREE!!
...ALL PEOPLE ARE EQUAL UNDER GOD AND SHOULD BE FREE.
DOWN TO A SINGLE FINGER, A SINGLE STRAND OF HAIR...

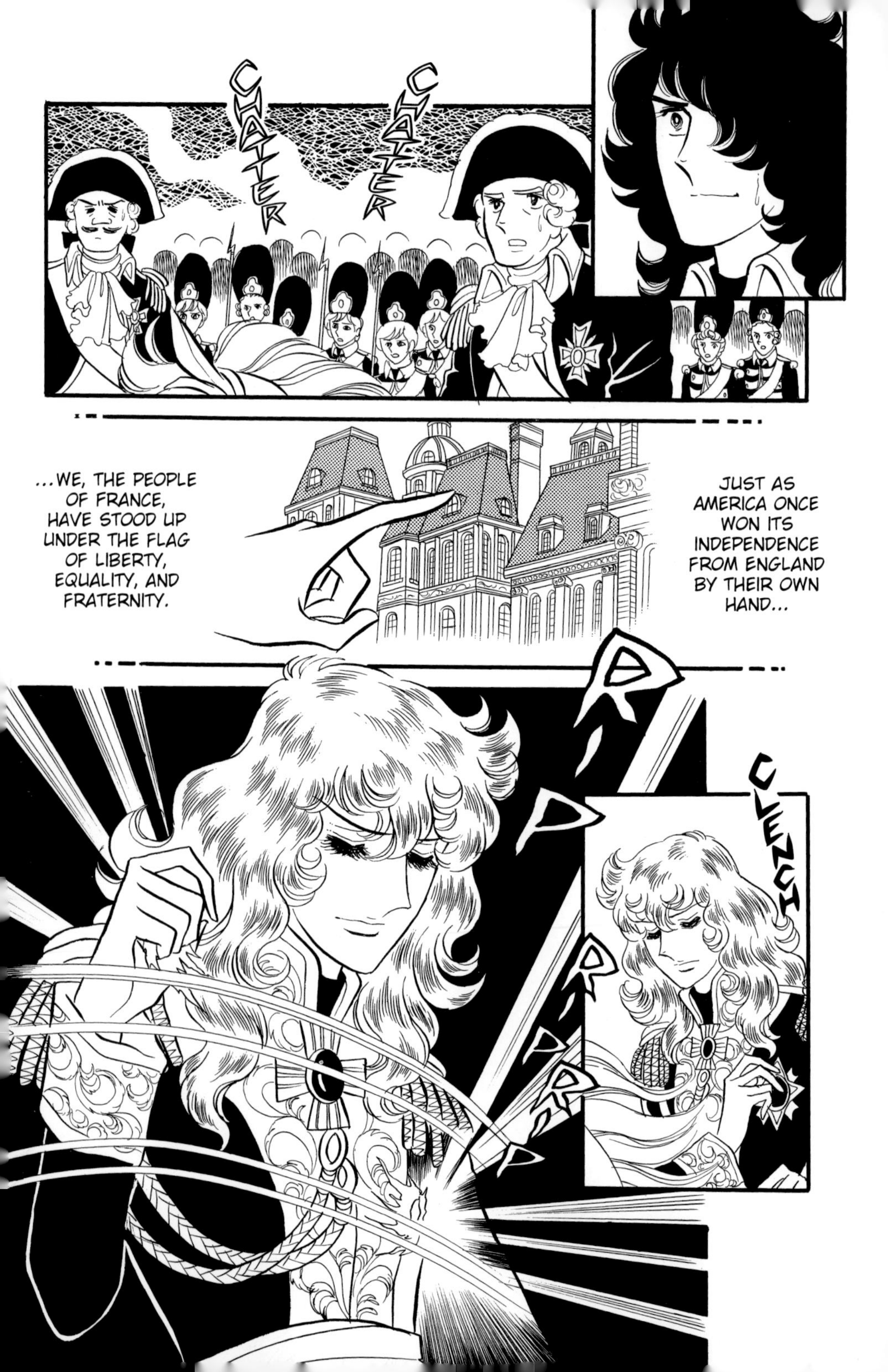
CHATTER
CHATTER
JUST AS AMERICA ONCE WON ITS INDEPENDENCE FROM ENGLAND BY THEIR OWN HAND...
...WE, THE PEOPLE OF FRANCE, HAVE STOOD UP UNDER THE FLAG OF LIBERTY, EQUALITY, AND FRATERNITY.
CLENCH

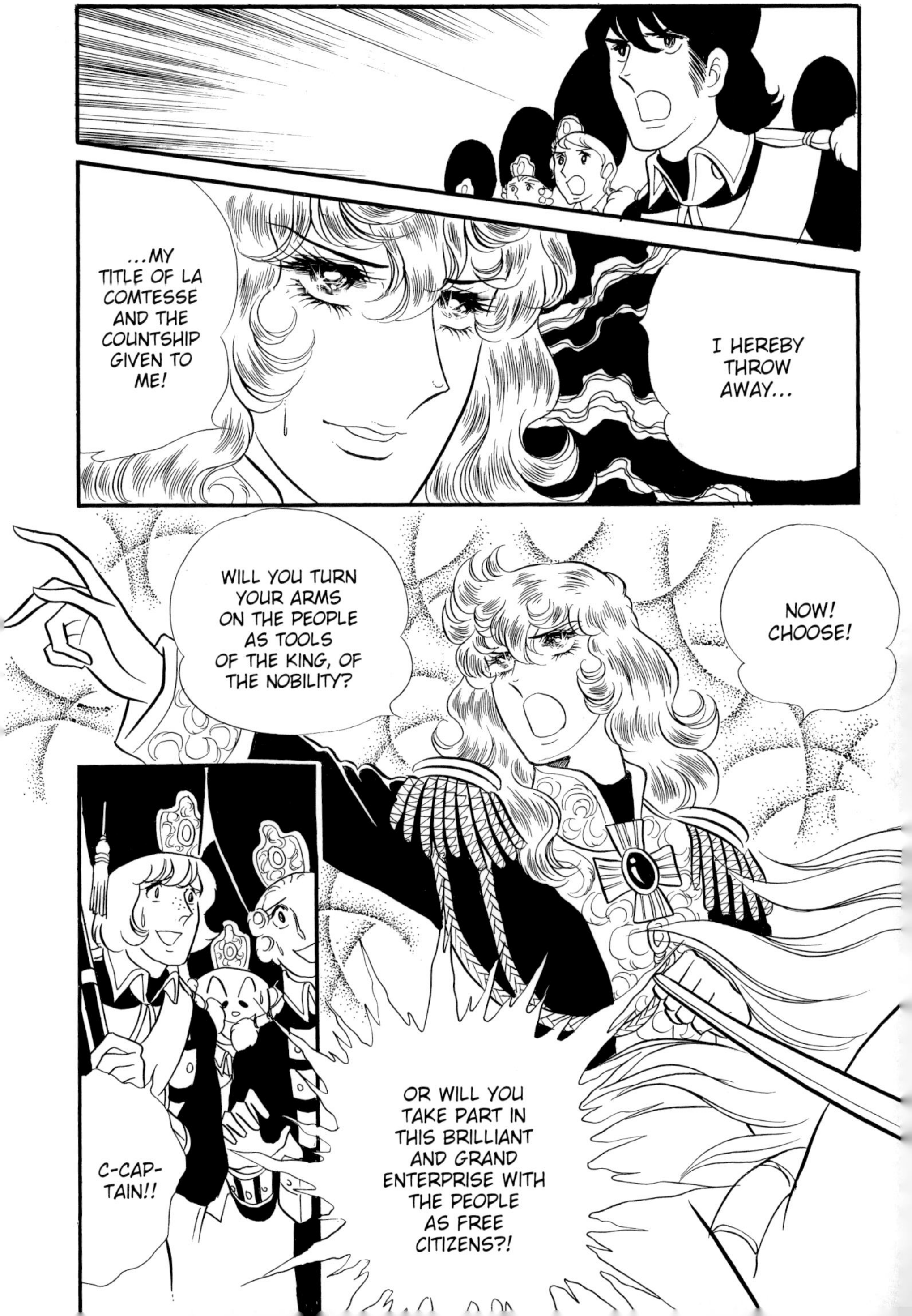
I HEREBY THROW AWAY...
...MY TITLE OF LA COMTESSE AND THE COUNTSHIP GIVEN TO ME!
NOW! CHOOSE!
WILL YOU TURN YOUR ARMS ON THE PEOPLE AS TOOLS OF THE KING, OF THE NOBILITY?
OR WILL YOU TAKE PART IN THIS BRILLIANT AND GRAND ENTERPRISE WITH THE PEOPLE AS FREE CITIZENS?!
C-CAP-TAIN!!

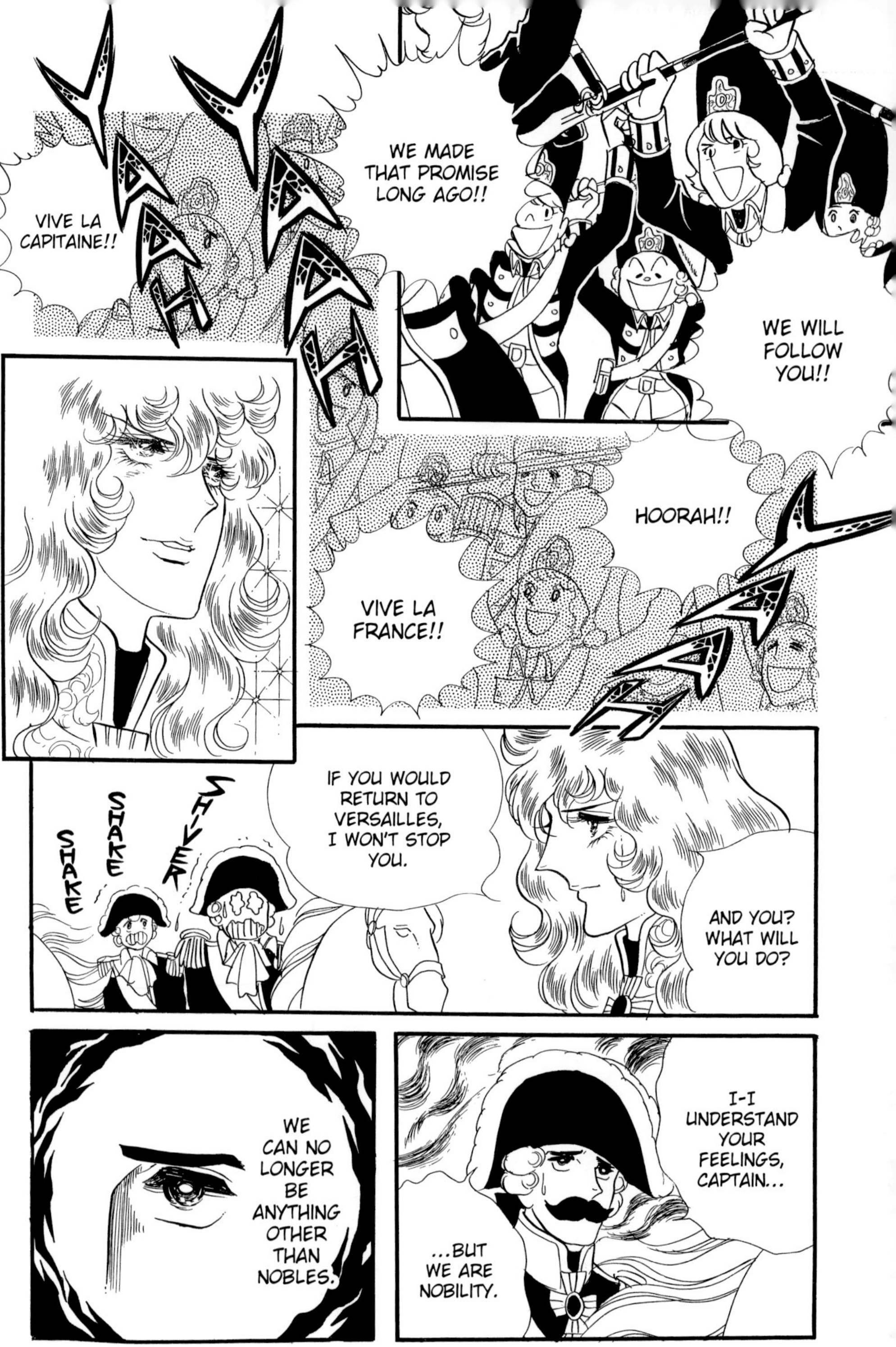
WE WILL FOLLOW YOU!!
WE MADE THAT PROMISE LONG AGO!!
VIVE LA CAPITAINE!!
HOORAH!!
VIVE LA FRANCE!!
IF YOU WOULD RETURN TO VERSAILLES, I WON'T STOP YOU.
AND YOU? WHAT WILL YOU DO?
SHIVER
SHAKE
SHAKE
I-I UNDERSTAND YOUR FEELINGS, CAPTAIN...
...BUT WE ARE NOBILITY.
WE CAN NO LONGER BE ANYTHING OTHER THAN NOBLES.

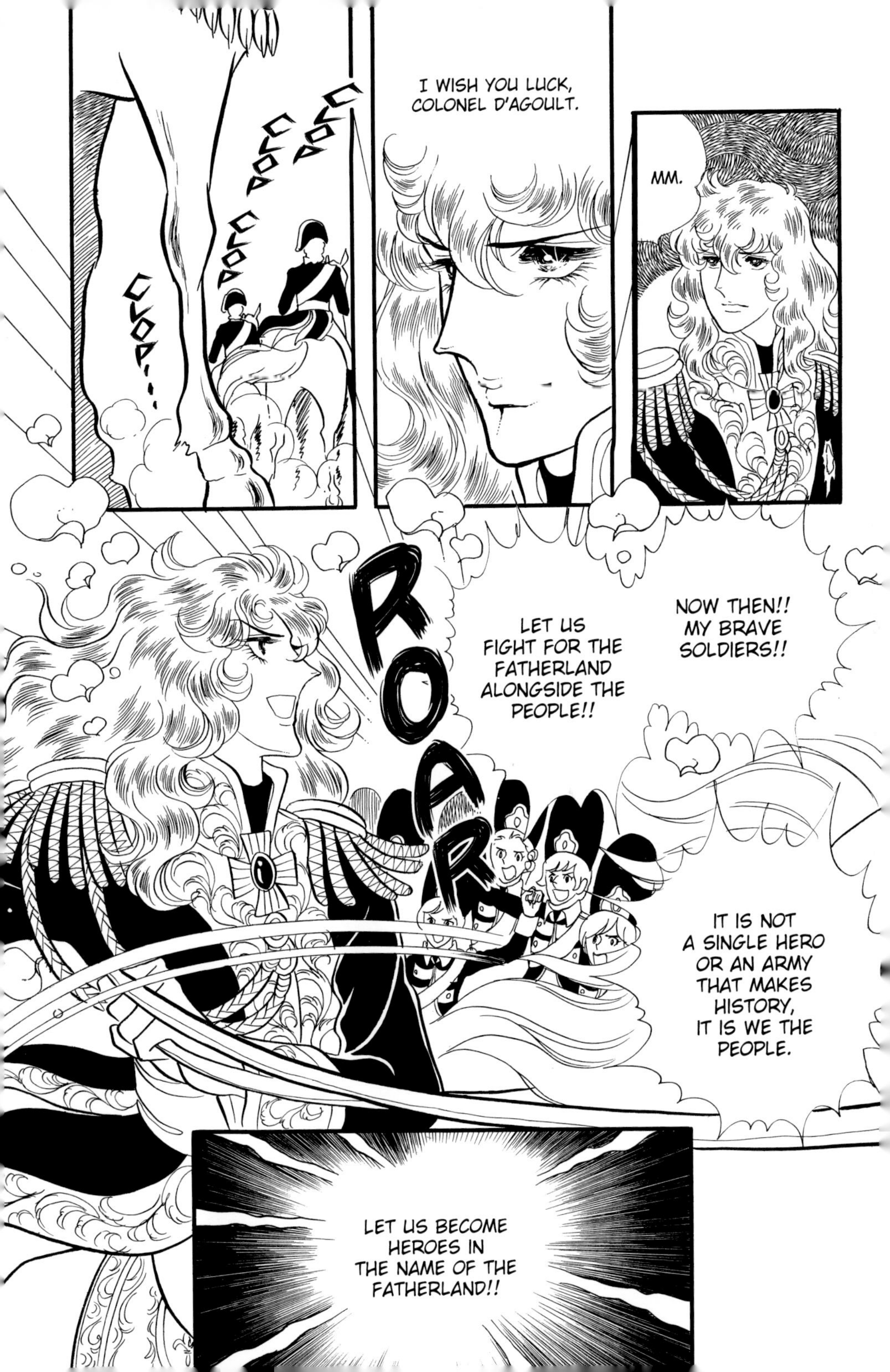
MM.
I WISH YOU LUCK, COLONEL D'AGOULT.
CLOP
CLOP
CLOP
CLOP
CLOP...
NOW THEN!! MY BRAVE SOLDIERS!!
LET US FIGHT FOR THE FATHERLAND ALONGSIDE THE PEOPLE!!
ROAR
IT IS NOT A SINGLE HERO OR AN ARMY THAT MAKES HISTORY, IT IS WE THE PEOPLE.
LET US BECOME HEROES IN THE NAME OF THE FATHERLAND!!

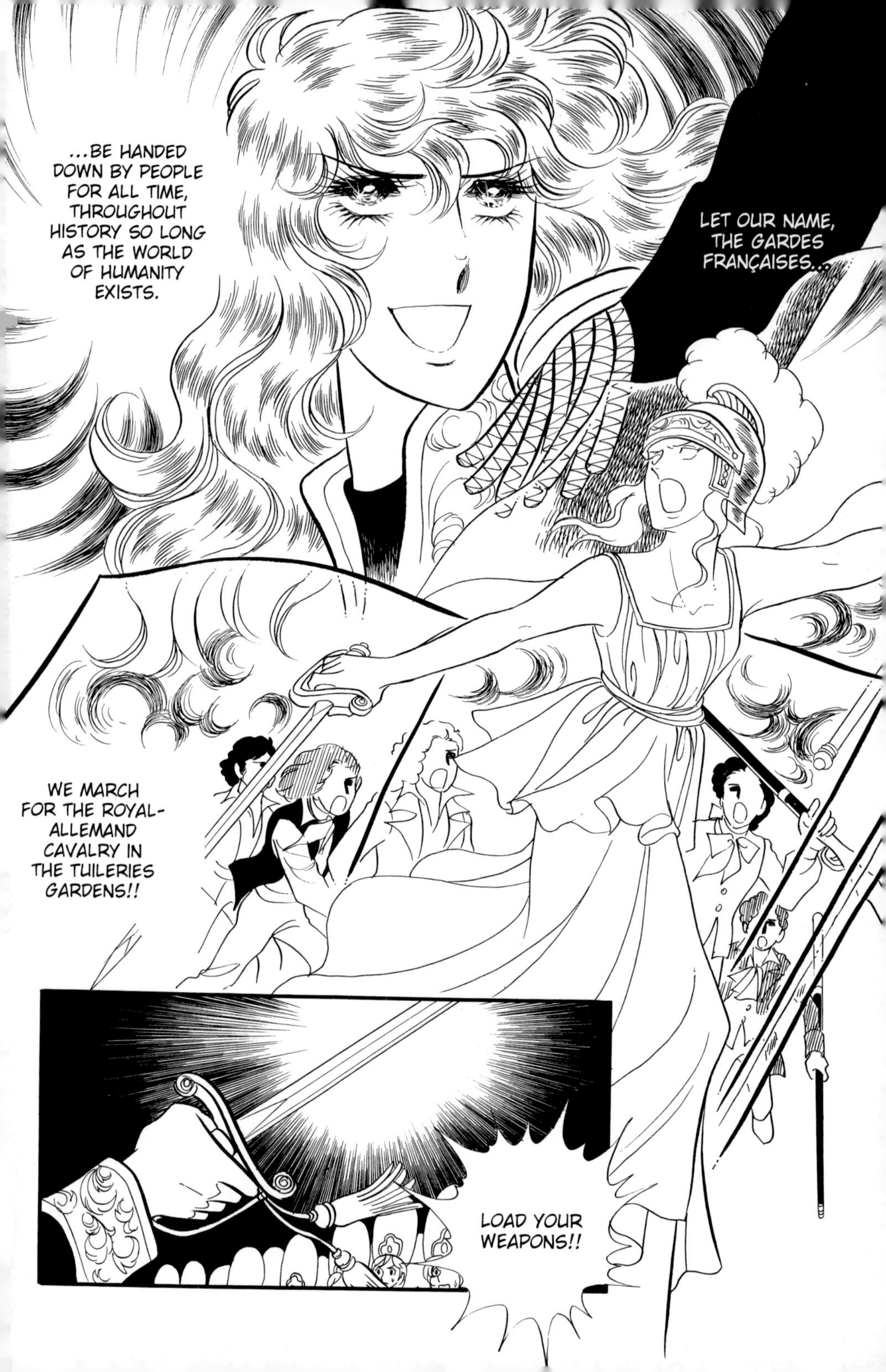
LET OUR NAME, THE GARDES FRANÇAISES...
...BE HANDED DOWN BY PEOPLE FOR ALL TIME, THROUGHOUT HISTORY SO LONG AS THE WORLD OF HUMANITY EXISTS.
WE MARCH FOR THE ROYAL-ALLEMAND CAVALRY IN THE TUILERIES GARDENS!!
LOAD YOUR WEAPONS!!

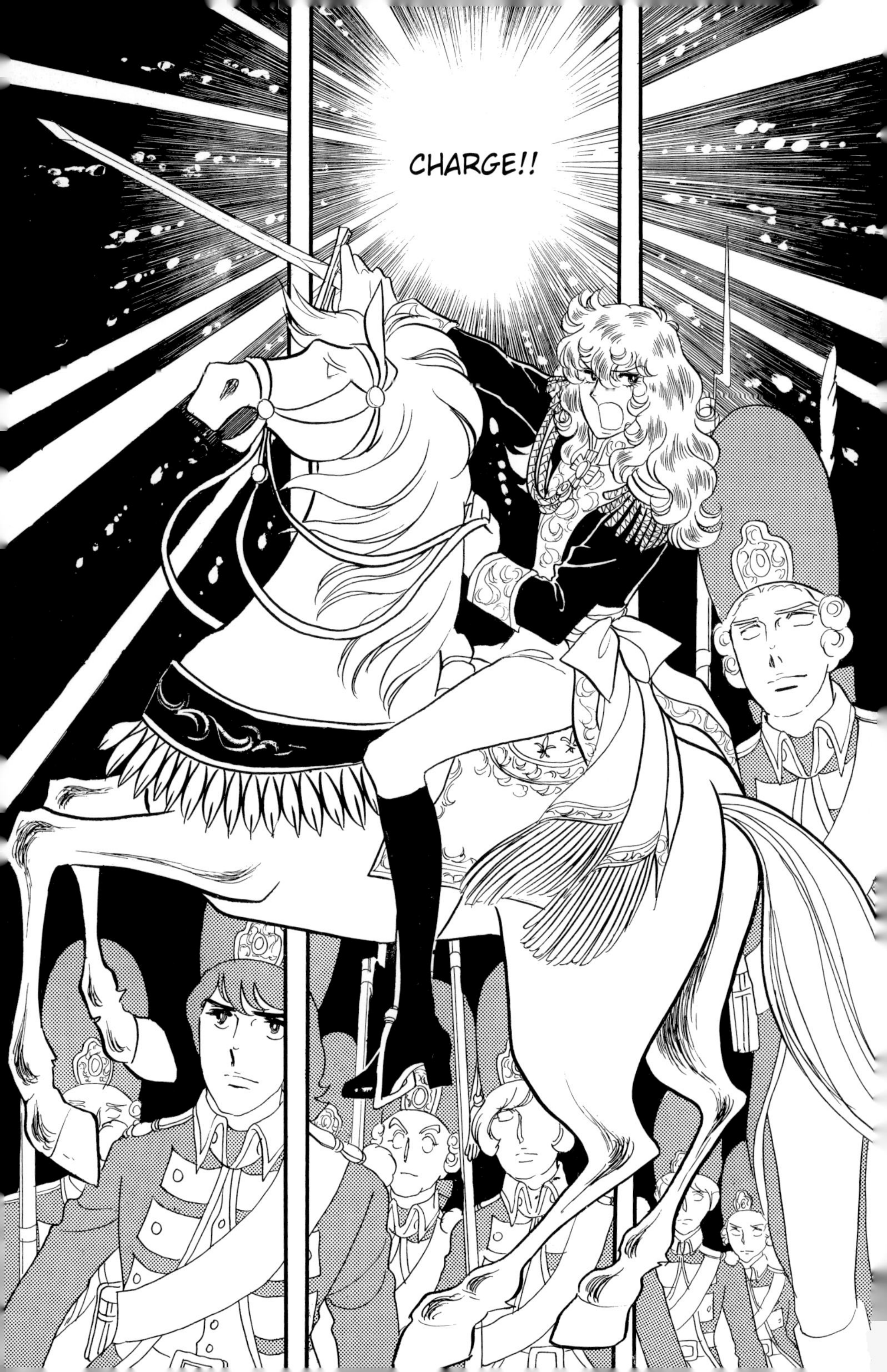
CHARGE!!

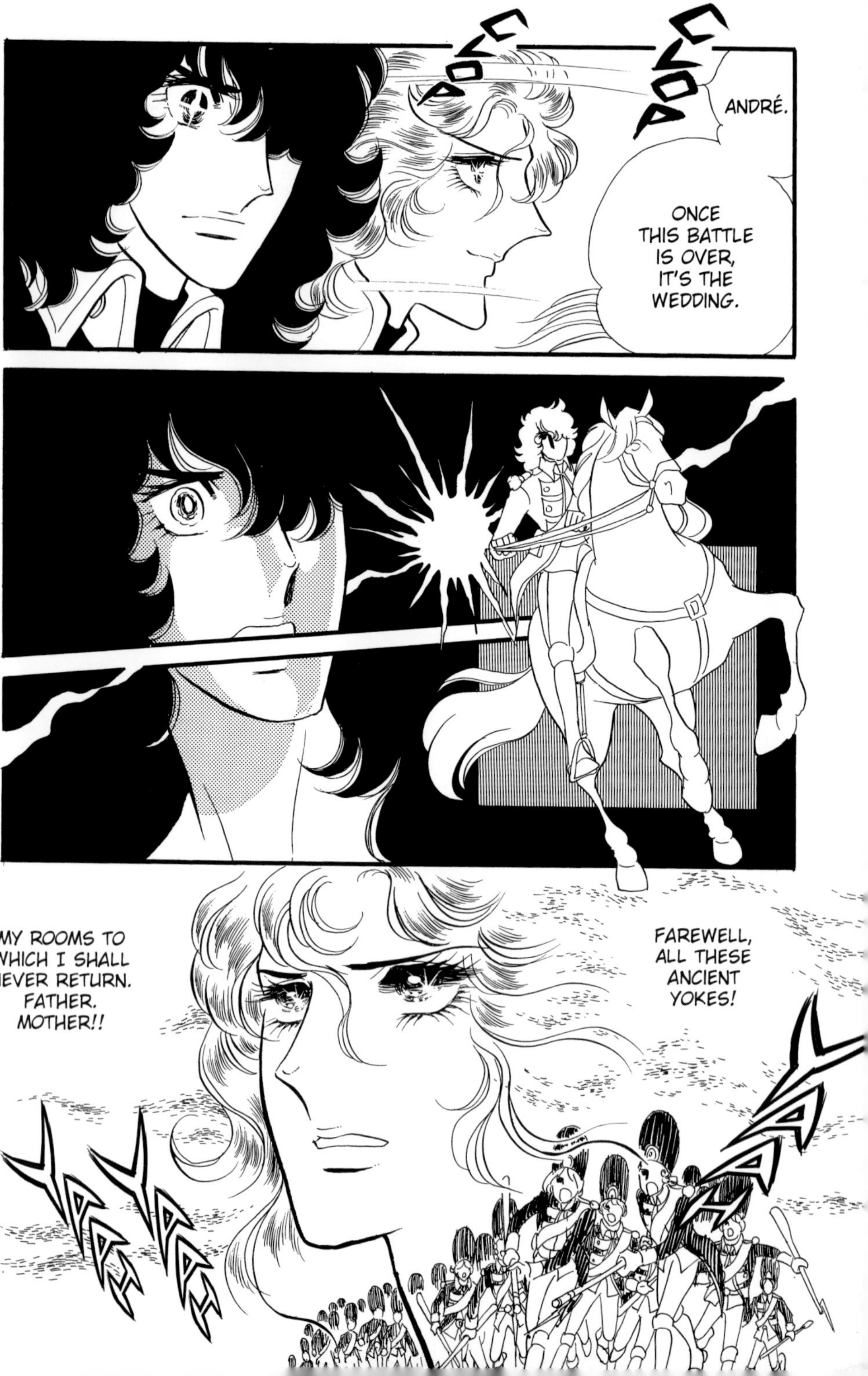
CLOP
CLOP
ANDRÉ.
ONCE THIS BATTLE IS OVER, IT'S THE WEDDING.
FAREWELL, ALL THESE ANCIENT YOKES!
MY ROOMS TO WHICH I SHALL NEVER RETURN. FATHER. MOTHER!!

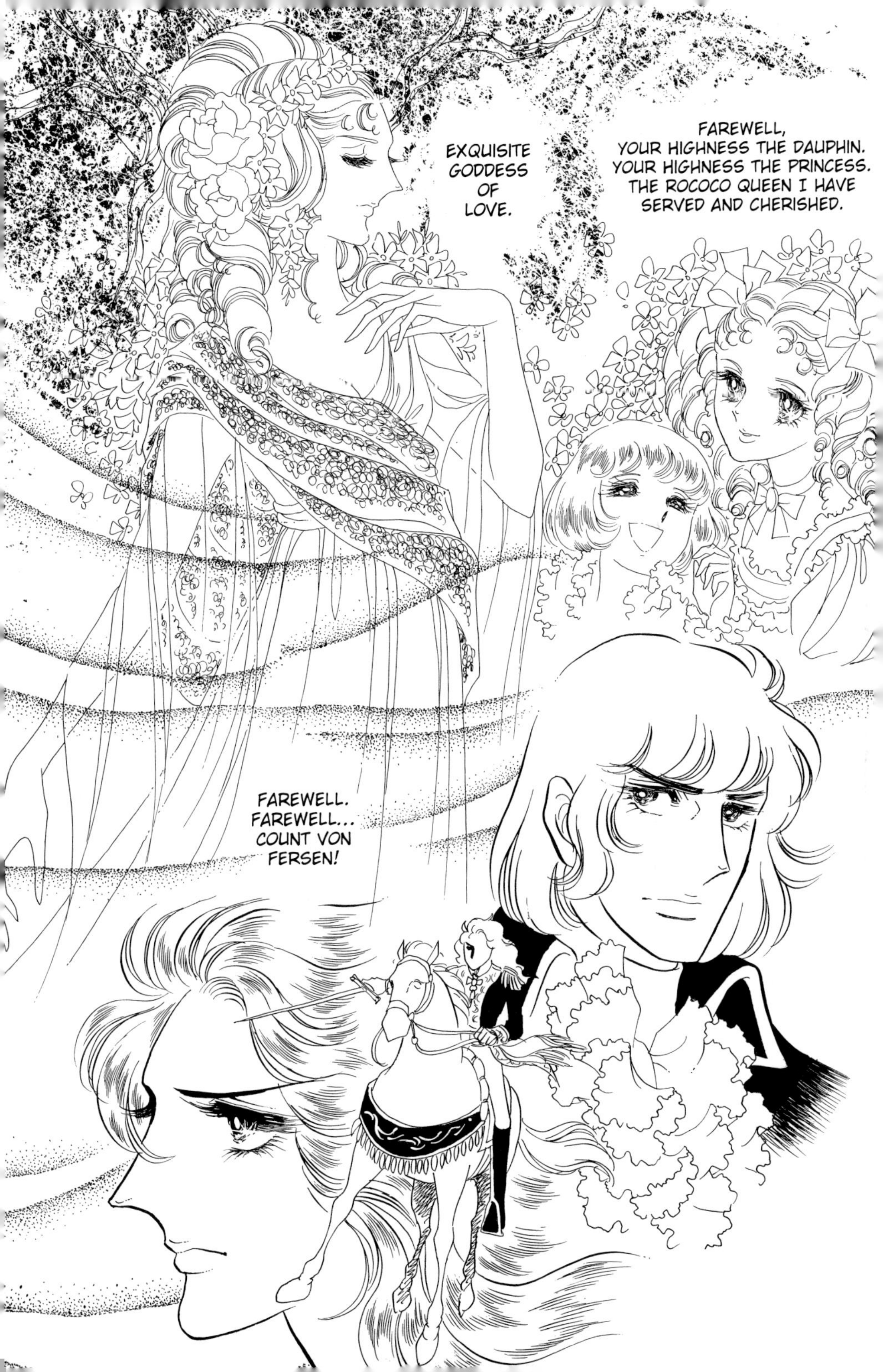
FAREWELL, YOUR HIGHNESS THE DAUPHIN. YOUR HIGHNESS THE PRINCESS. THE ROCOCO QUEEN I HAVE SERVED AND CHERISHED.
EXQUISITE GODDESS OF LOVE.
FAREWELL. FAREWELL... COUNT VON FERSEN!

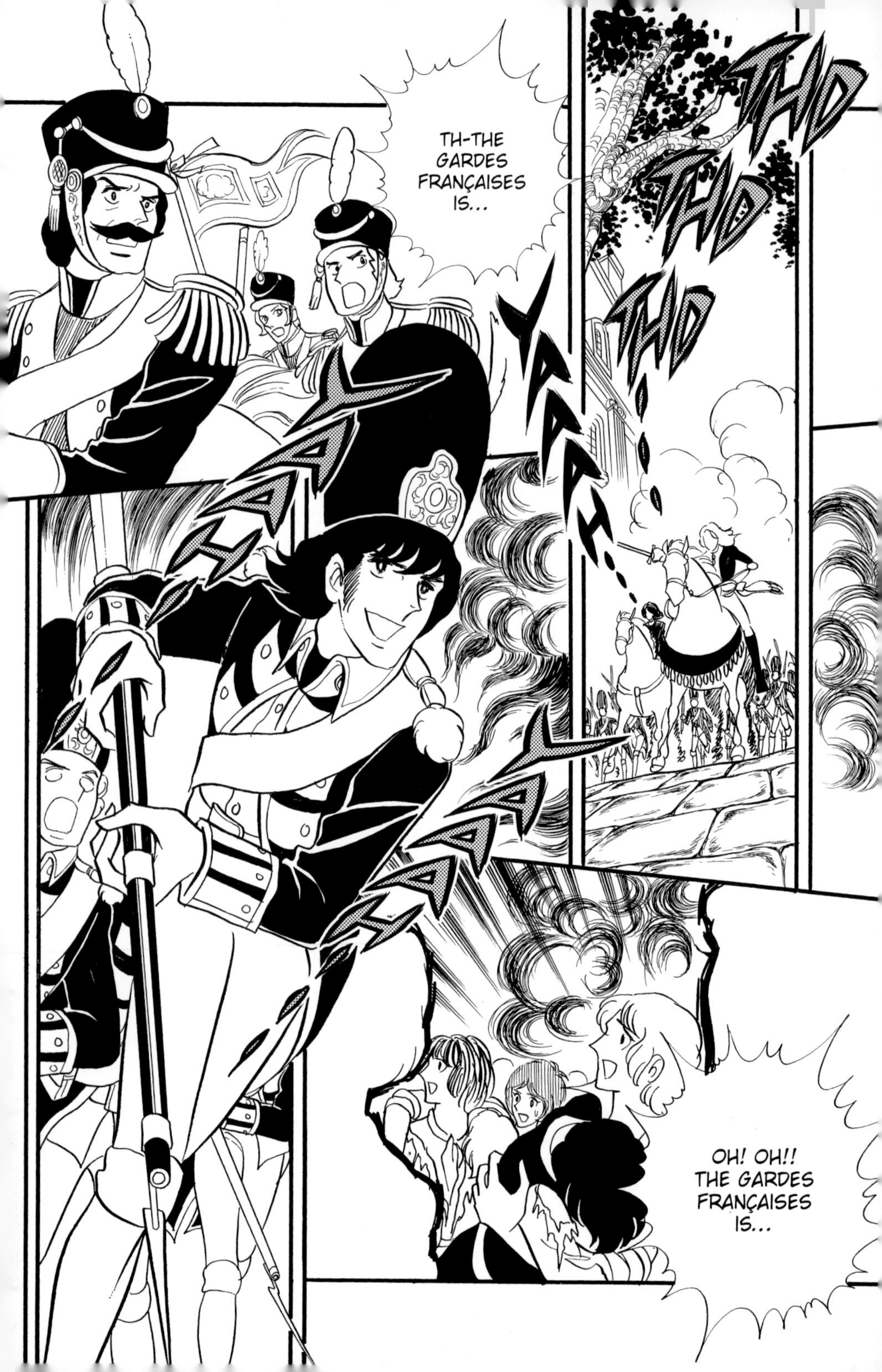
THD THD THD
YAAAH...
TH-THE GARDES FRANÇAISES IS...
YAAAH
YAAAAH
OH! OH!! THE GARDES FRANÇAISES IS...

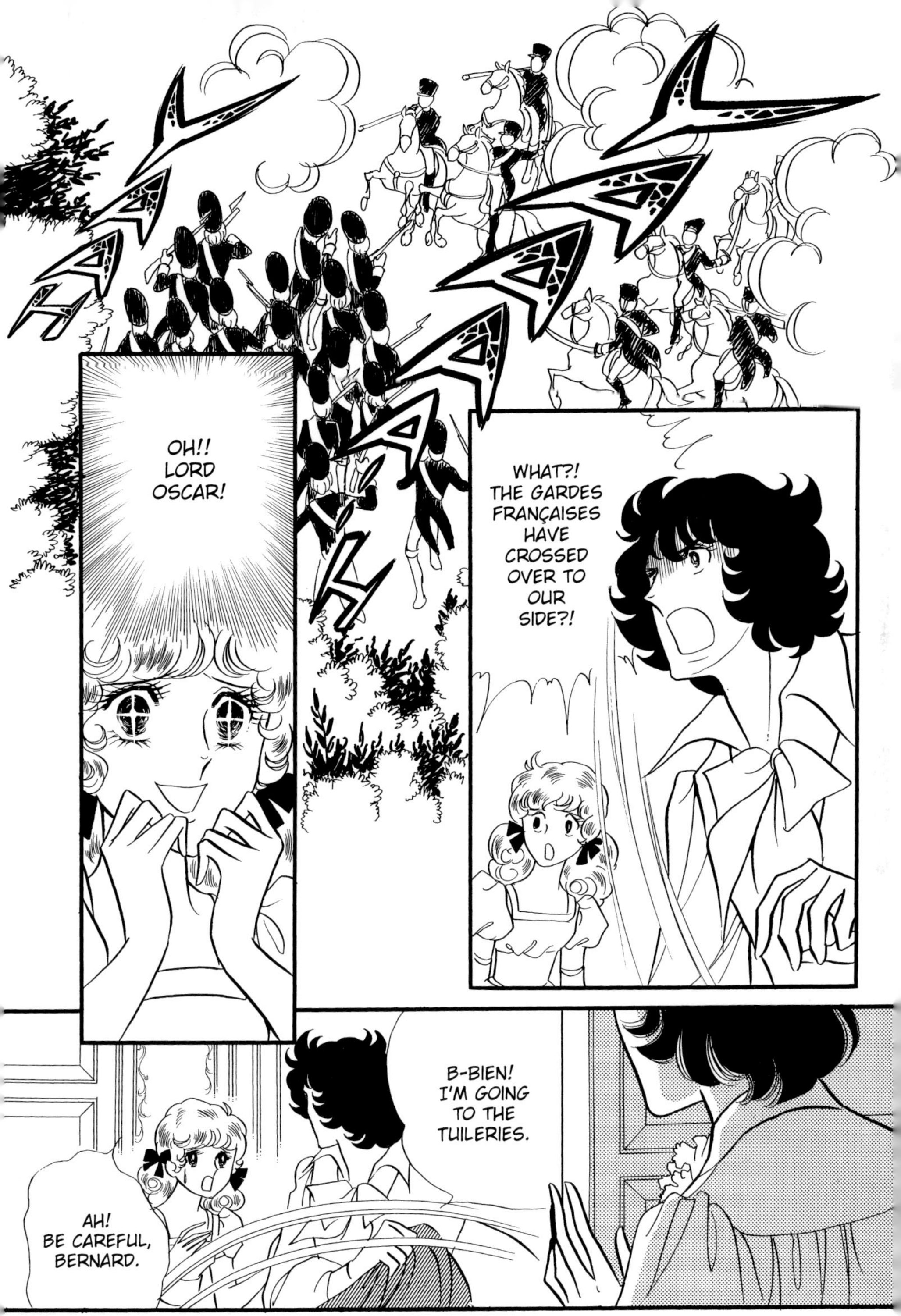
WHAT?! THE GARDES FRANÇAISES HAVE CROSSED OVER TO OUR SIDE?!
OH!! LORD OSCAR!
B-BIEN! I'M GOING TO THE TUILERIES.
AH! BE CAREFUL, BERNARD.

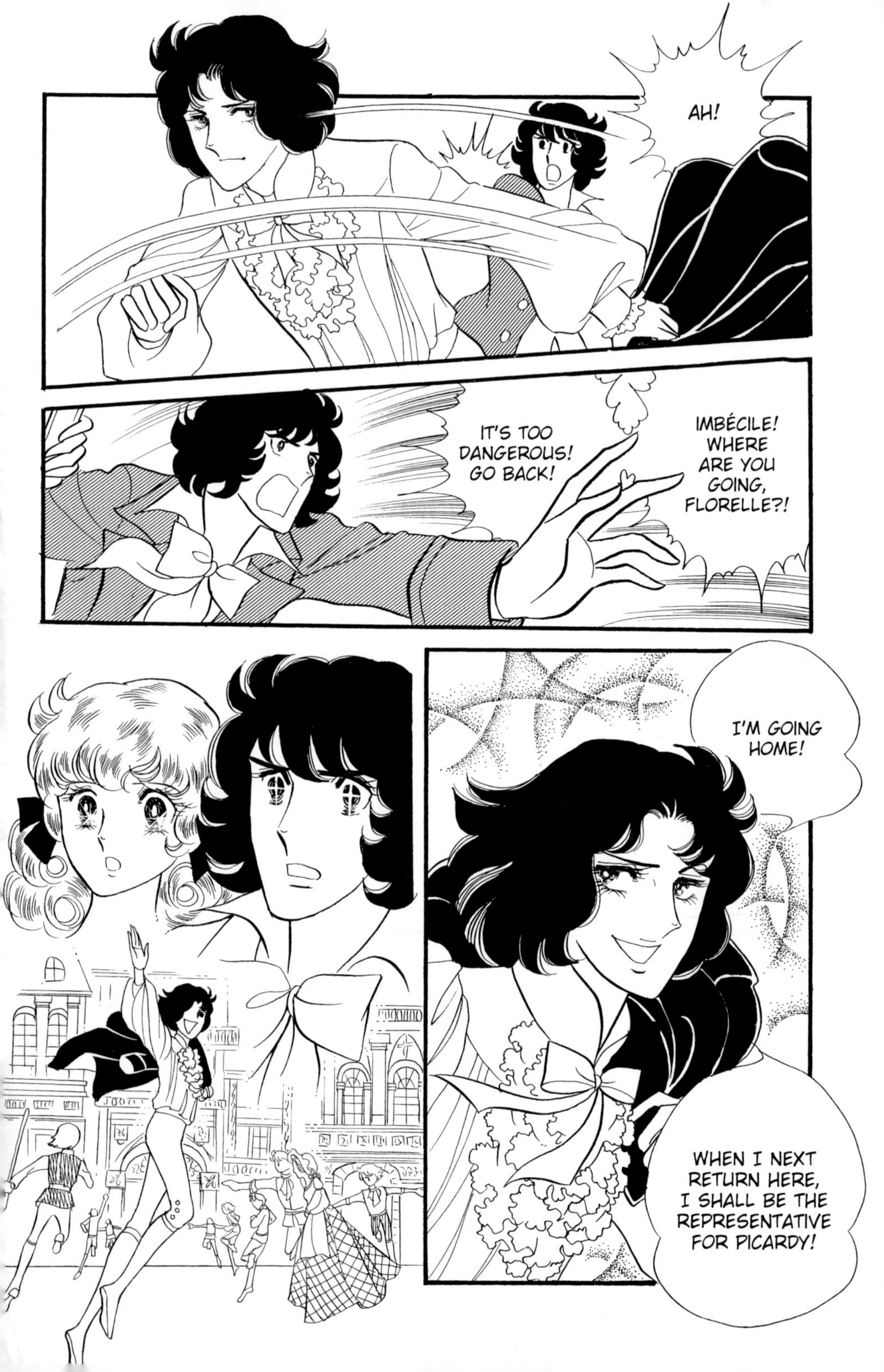
AH!
IMBÉCILE! WHERE ARE YOU GOING, FLORELLE?!
IT'S TOO DANGEROUS! GO BACK!
I'M GOING HOME!
WHEN I NEXT RETURN HERE, I SHALL BE THE REPRESENTATIVE FOR PICARDY!

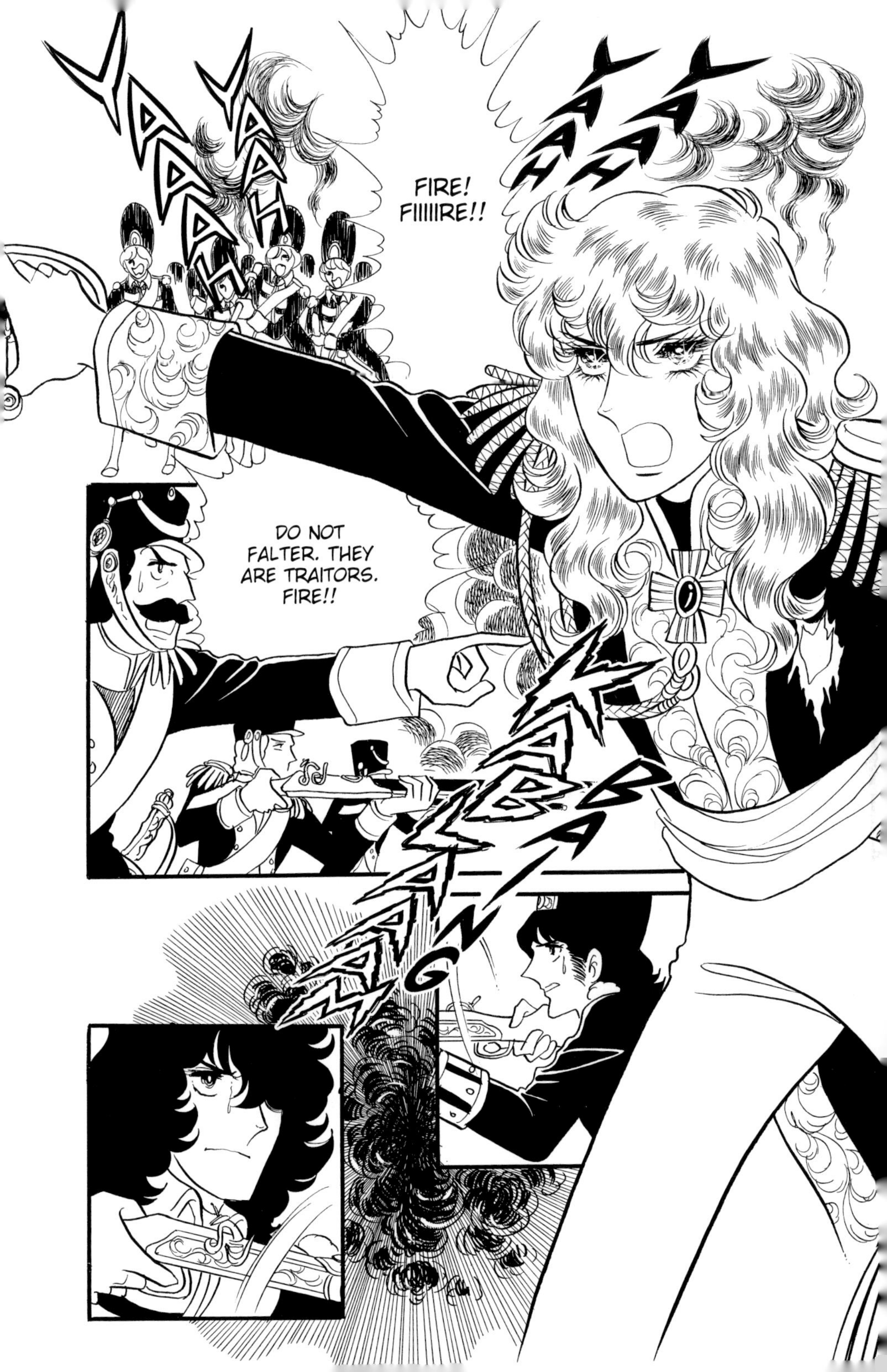
YAAAH
FIRE! FIIIIRE!!
YAAAH
DO NOT FALTER. THEY ARE TRAITORS. FIRE!!
BANG
KABLAAAM

1974 WEEKLY
MARGARET MAGAZINE
COMBINED ISSUE 02-03
BONUS STICKER ART

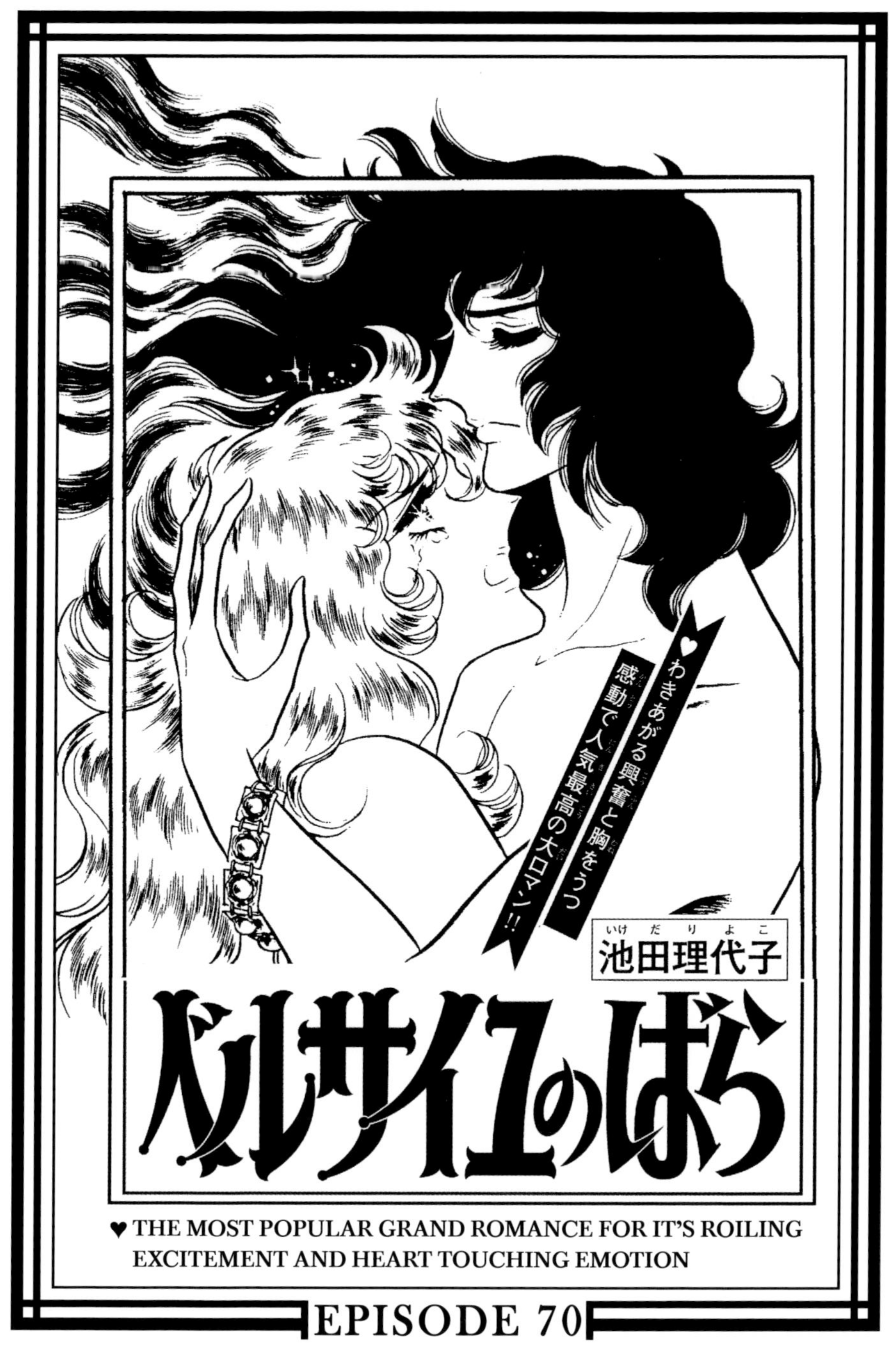
♥わきあがる興奮と胸をうつ
感動で人気最高の大ロマン!!
池田理代子
ベルサイユのばら

♥ THE MOST POPULAR GRAND ROMANCE FOR IT'S ROILING EXCITEMENT AND HEART TOUCHING EMOTION

EPISODE 70

Episode 70

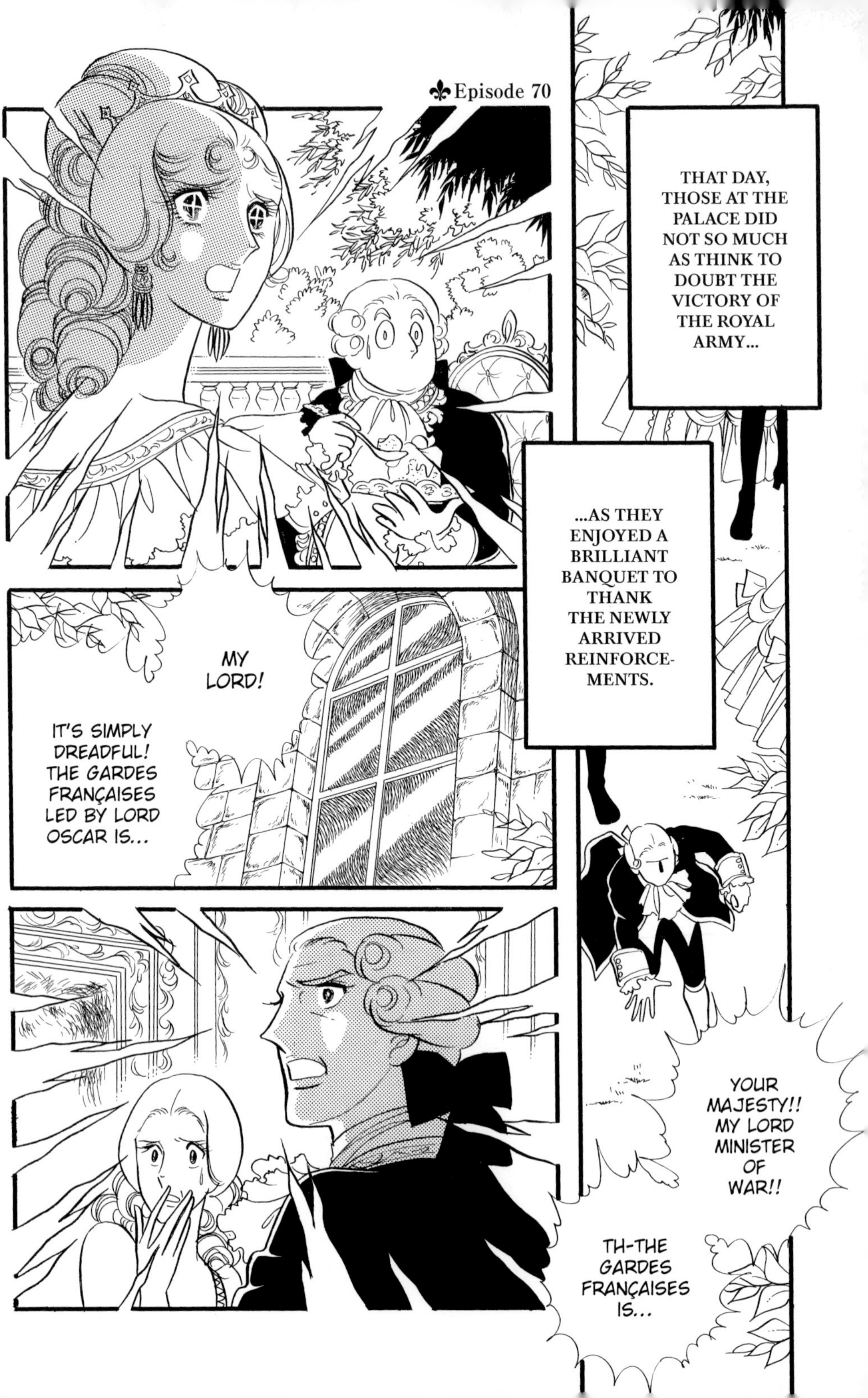

THAT DAY, THOSE AT THE PALACE DID NOT SO MUCH AS THINK TO DOUBT THE VICTORY OF THE ROYAL ARMY...
...AS THEY ENJOYED A BRILLIANT BANQUET TO THANK THE NEWLY ARRIVED REINFORCE-MENTS.
YOUR MAJESTY!! MY LORD MINISTER OF WAR!!
TH-THE GARDES FRANÇAISES IS...
MY LORD!
IT'S SIMPLY DREADFUL! THE GARDES FRANÇAISES LED BY LORD OSCAR IS...

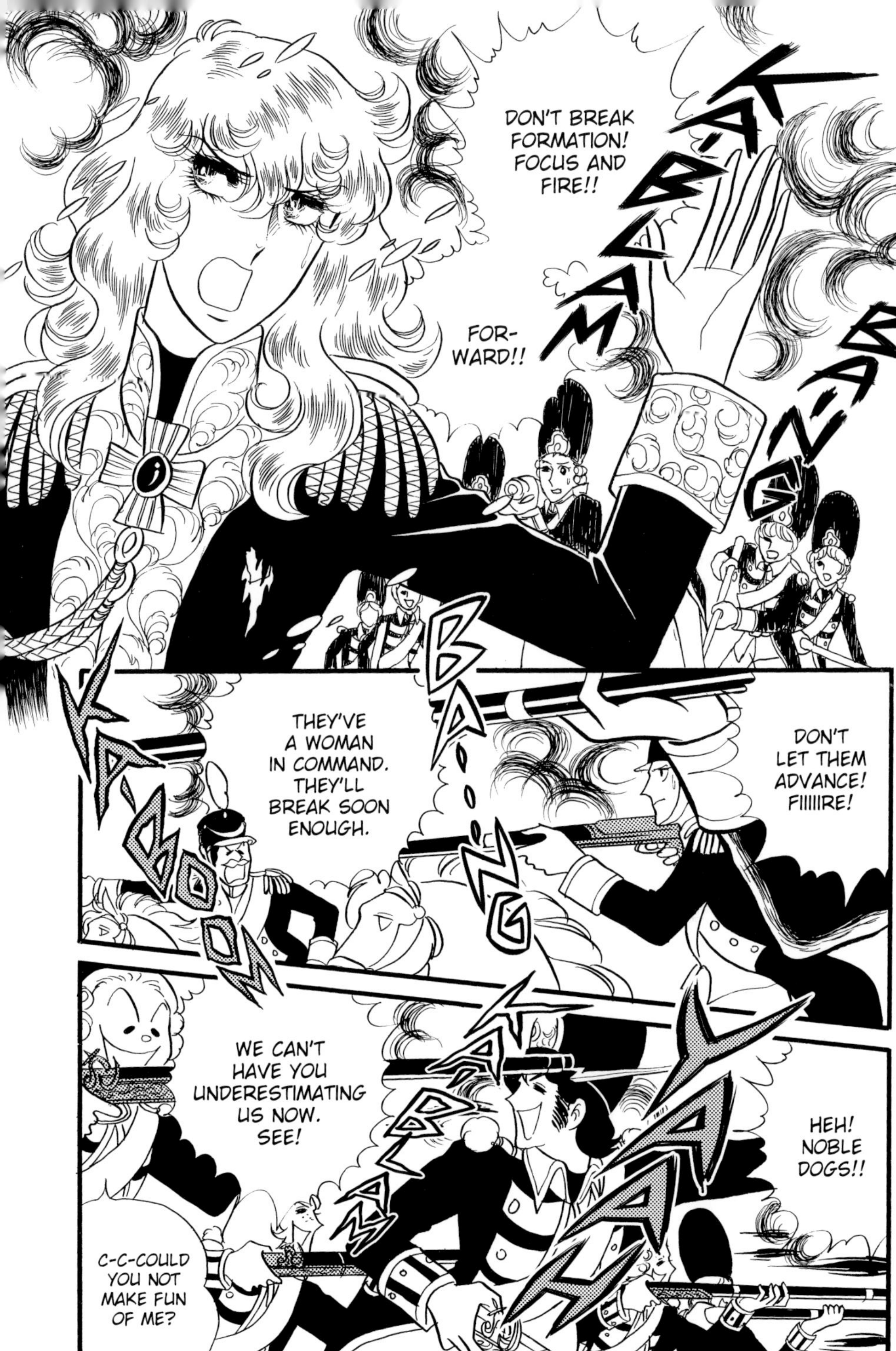
DON'T BREAK FORMATION! FOCUS AND FIRE!!
KA-BLAM
BANG
FOR-WARD!!
DON'T LET THEM ADVANCE! FIIIIRE!
BANG
THEY'VE A WOMAN IN COMMAND. THEY'LL BREAK SOON ENOUGH.
KA-BOOM
HEH! NOBLE DOGS!!
YAAAH
KA-BLAM
WE CAN'T HAVE YOU UNDERESTIMATING US NOW. SEE!
C-C-COULD YOU NOT MAKE FUN OF ME?

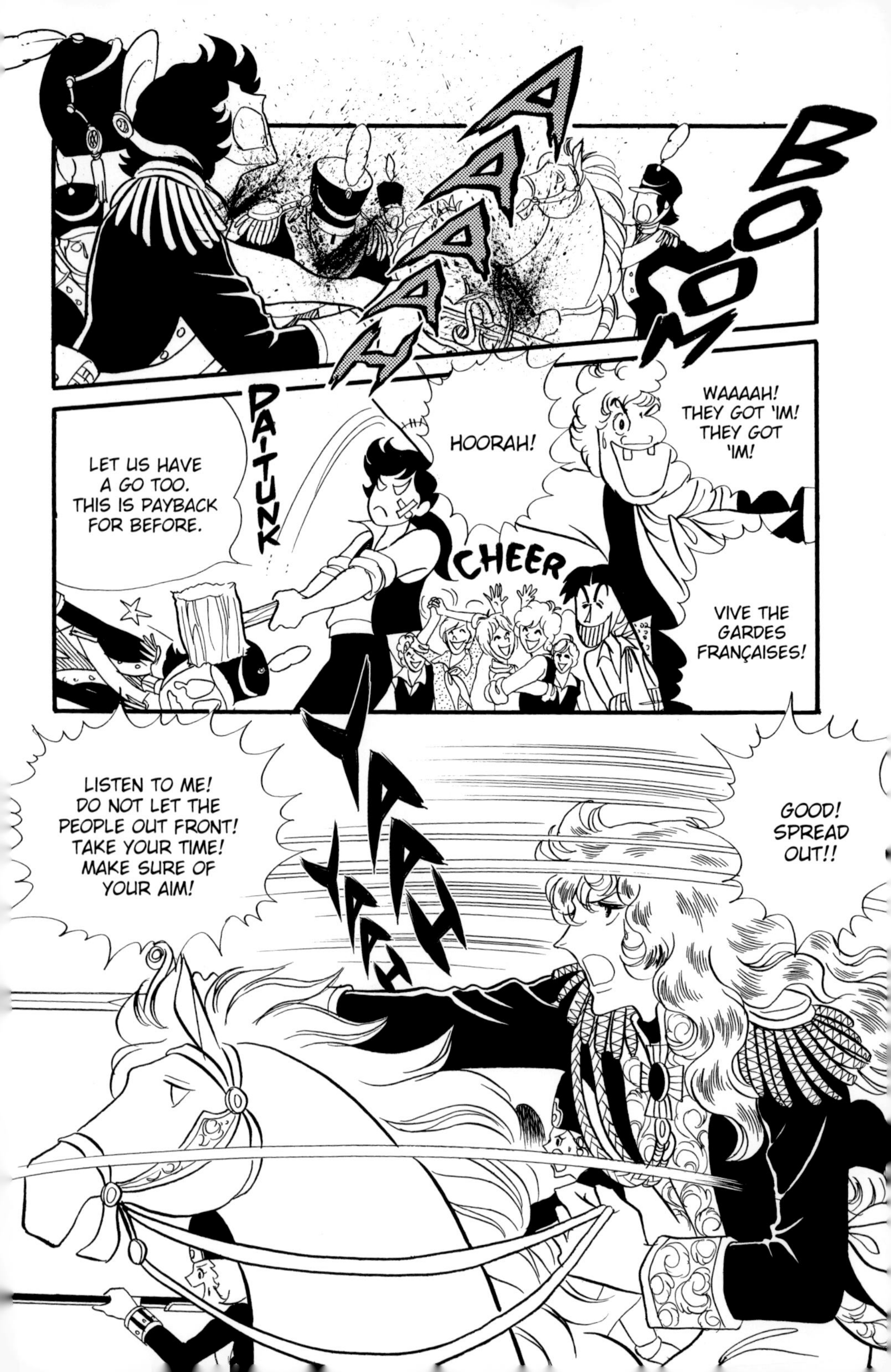
BOOM
AAAAAH
WAAAAH! THEY GOT 'IM! THEY GOT 'IM!
VIVE THE GARDES FRANÇAISES!
HOORAH!
CHEER
PATUNK
LET US HAVE A GO TOO. THIS IS PAYBACK FOR BEFORE.
GOOD! SPREAD OUT!!
YAAAH
YAAAH
LISTEN TO ME! DO NOT LET THE PEOPLE OUT FRONT! TAKE YOUR TIME! MAKE SURE OF YOUR AIM!

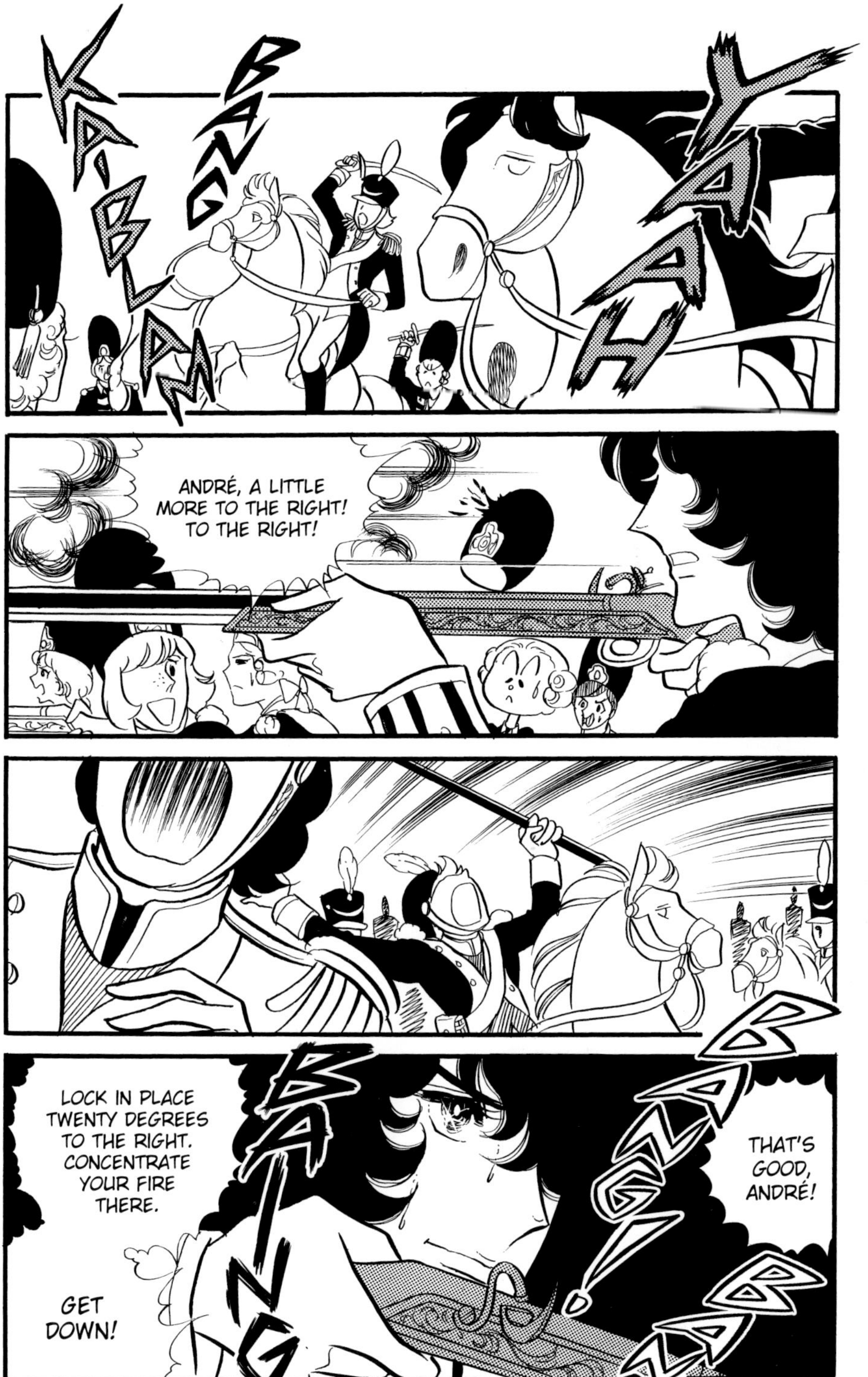
YAAH
BANG
KABLAM
ANDRÉ, A LITTLE MORE TO THE RIGHT! TO THE RIGHT!
THAT'S GOOD, ANDRÉ!
BANG! BANG
LOCK IN PLACE TWENTY DEGREES TO THE RIGHT. CONCENTRATE YOUR FIRE THERE.
BANG
GET DOWN!

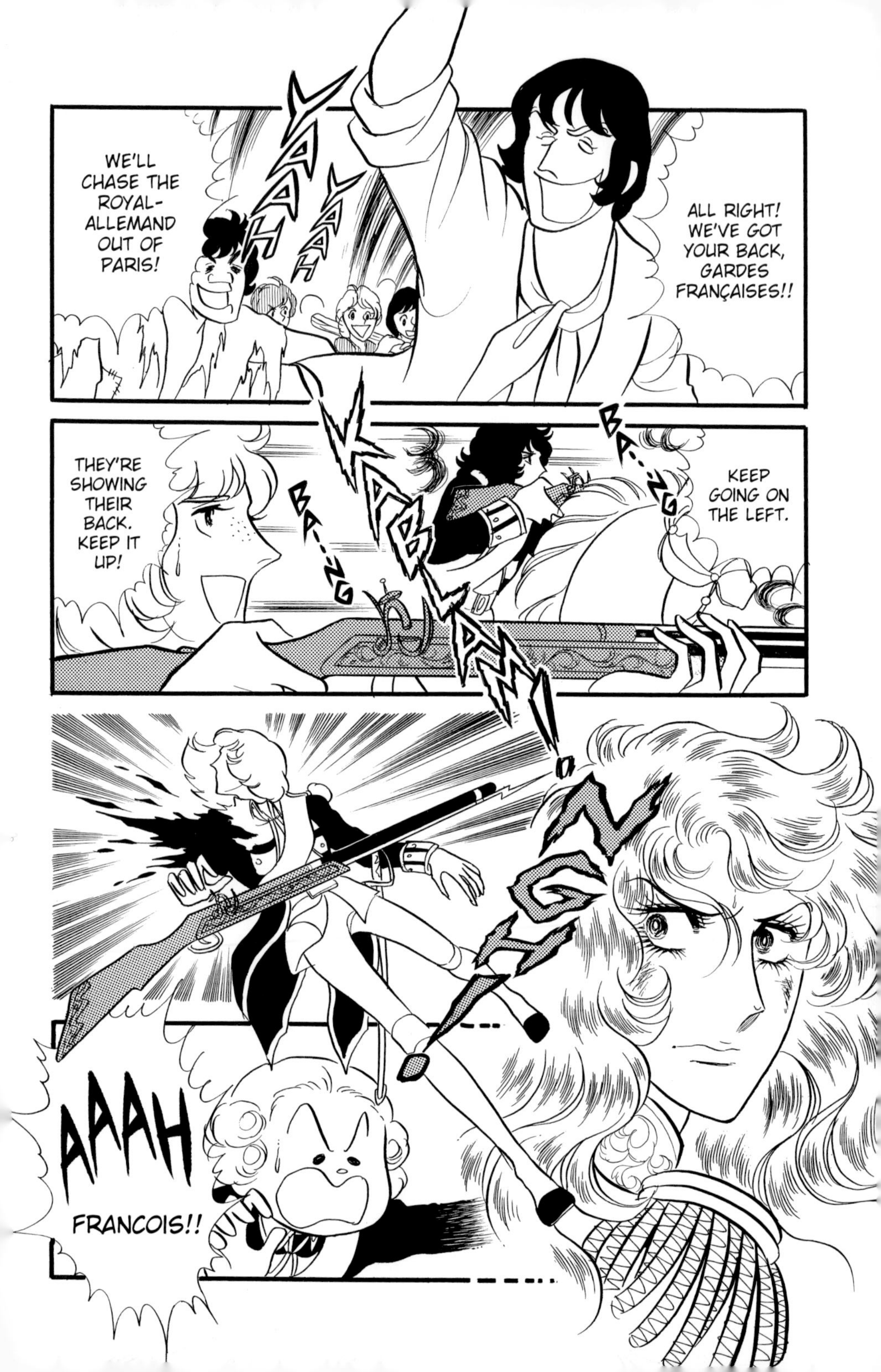

ALL RIGHT! WE'VE GOT YOUR BACK, GARDES FRANÇAISES!!
WE'LL CHASE THE ROYAL-ALLEMAND OUT OF PARIS!
KEEP GOING ON THE LEFT.
BA...NG
BA...NG
THEY'RE SHOWING THEIR BACK. KEEP IT UP!
KABLAM!!
AAAH
FRANCOIS!!

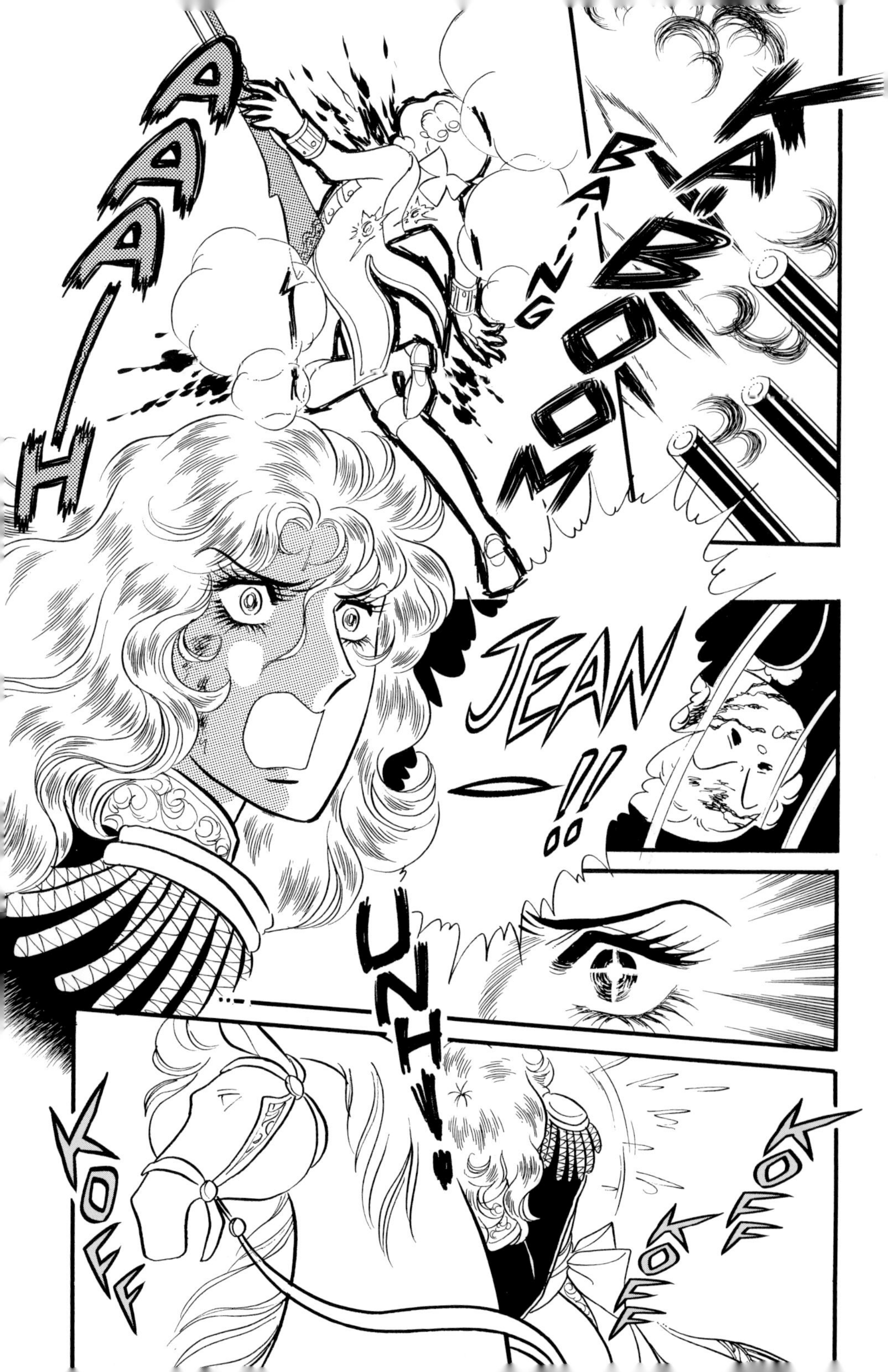
KABOOM
BANG
AAAA—H
JEAN—!!
UNH...!!
KOFF KOFF
KOFF

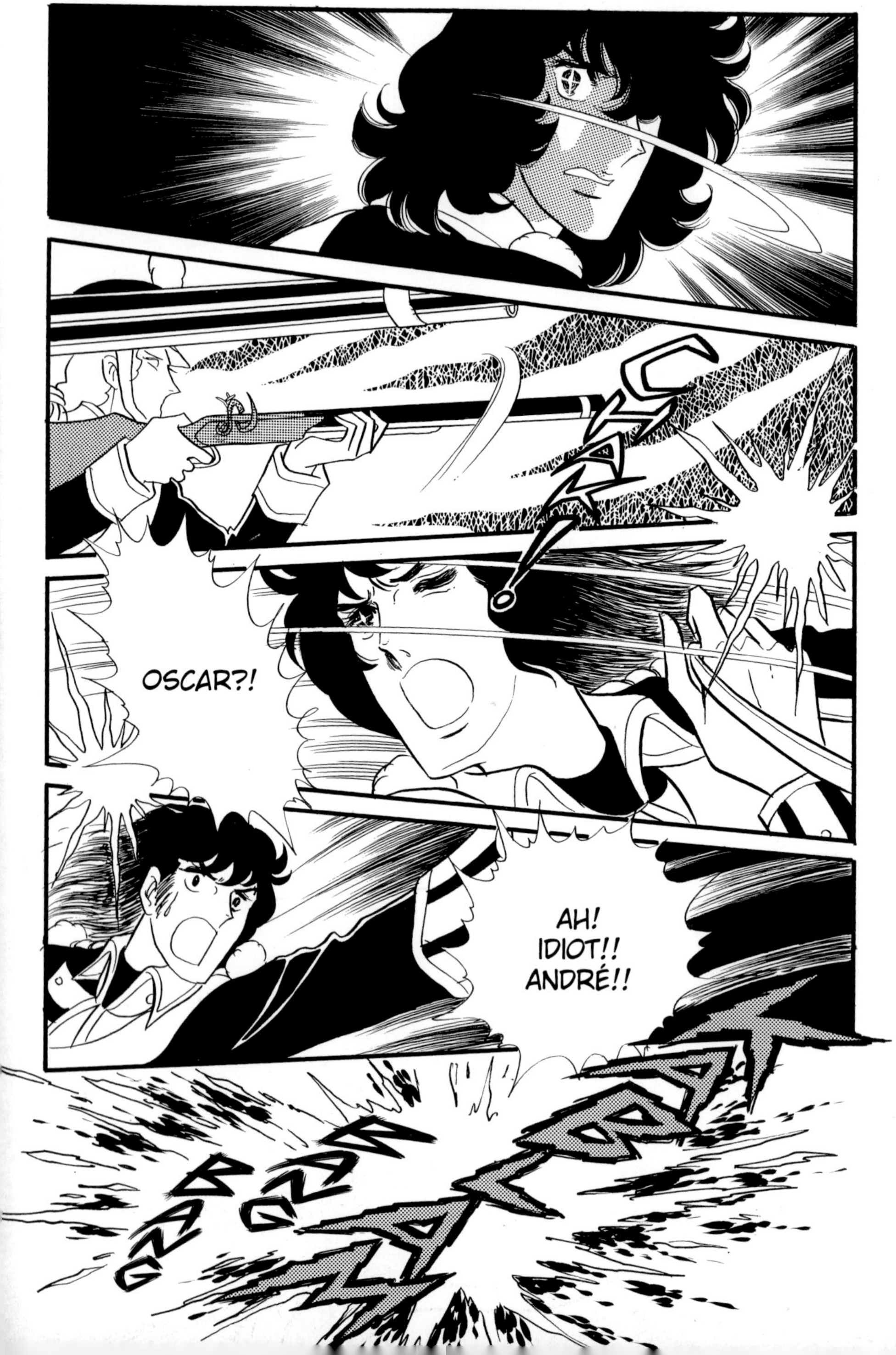
CRACK!
OSCAR?!
AH!
IDIOT!!
ANDRÉ!!

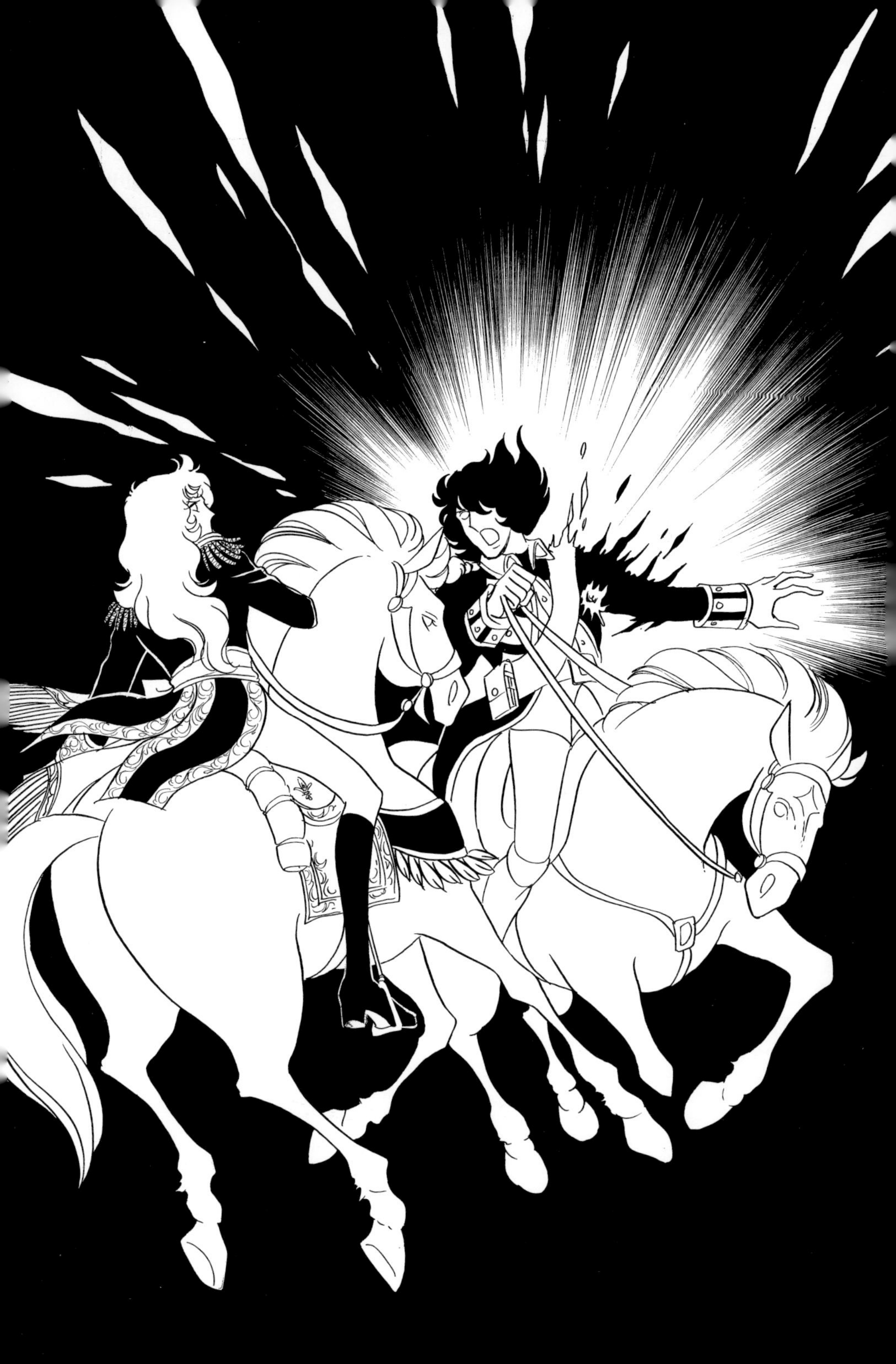

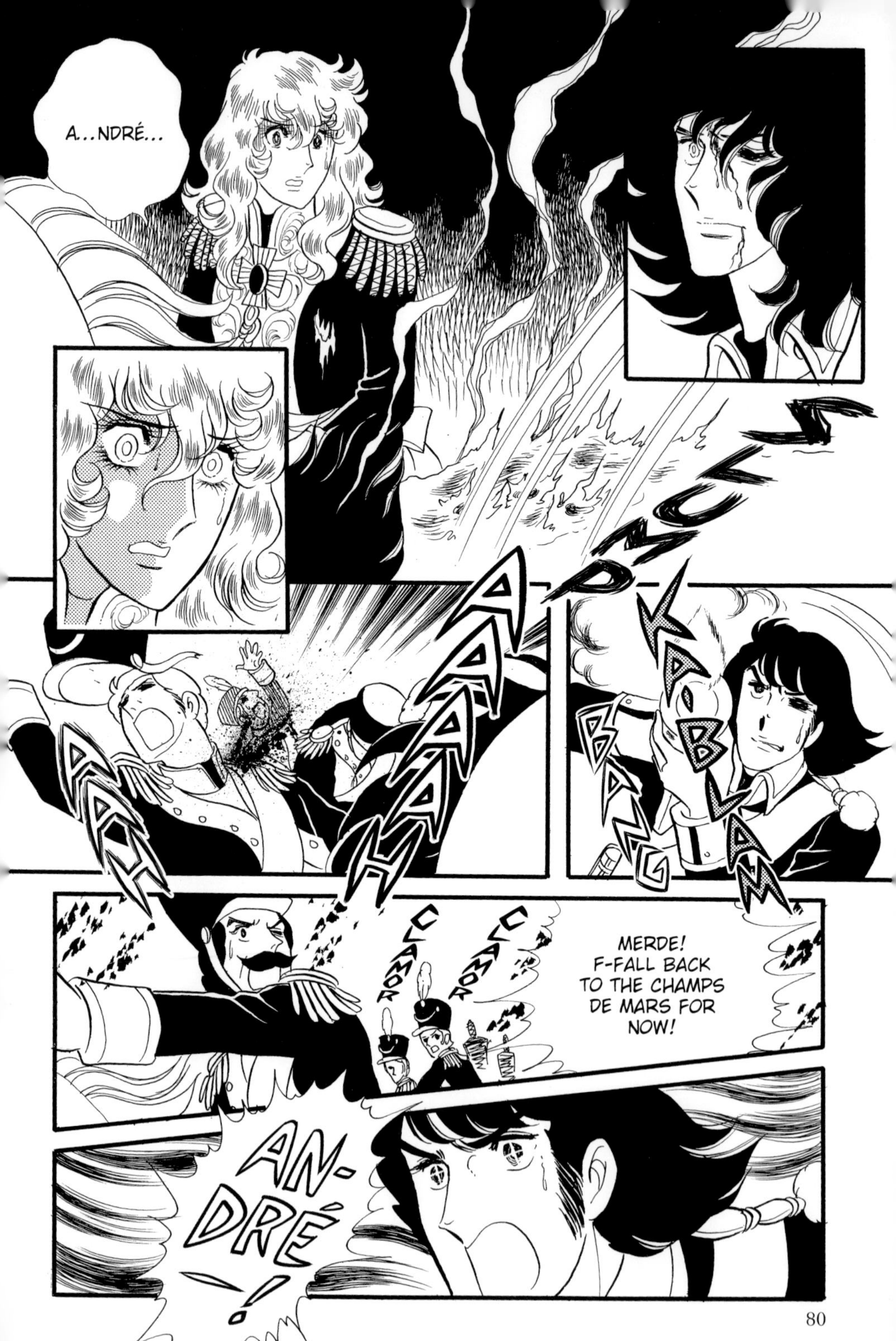
A...NDRÉ...
KABLAM
BANG
AAAAAAH
AAAH
MERDE! F-FALL BACK TO THE CHAMPS DE MARS FOR NOW!
CLAMOR
CLAMOR
AN-DRÉ—!

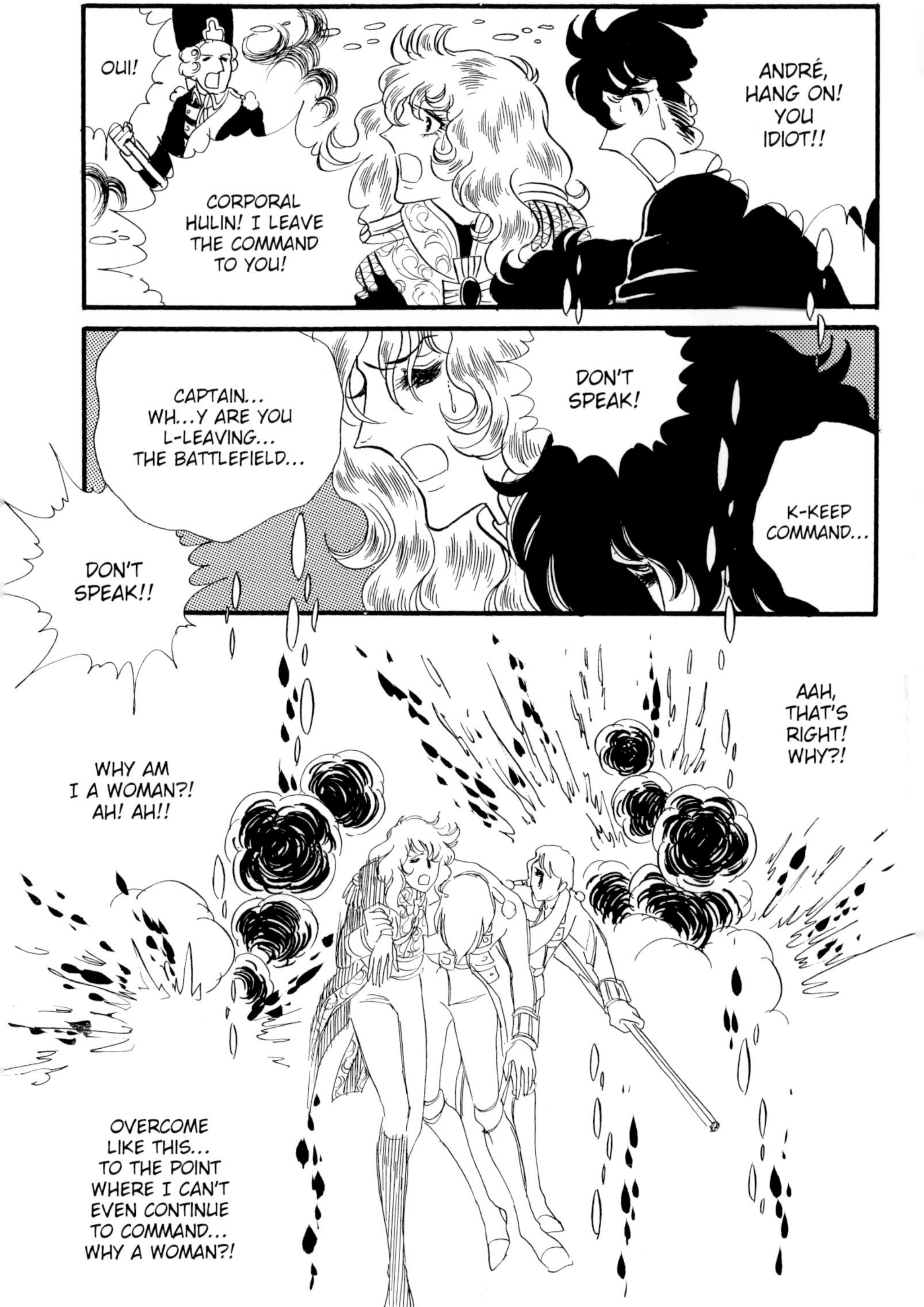
ANDRÉ, HANG ON! YOU IDIOT!!
CORPORAL HULIN! I LEAVE THE COMMAND TO YOU!
OUI!
DON'T SPEAK!
K-KEEP COMMAND...
CAPTAIN... WH...Y ARE YOU L-LEAVING... THE BATTLEFIELD...
DON'T SPEAK!!
AAH, THAT'S RIGHT! WHY?!
WHY AM I A WOMAN?! AH! AH!!
OVERCOME LIKE THIS... TO THE POINT WHERE I CAN'T EVEN CONTINUE TO COMMAND... WHY A WOMAN?!

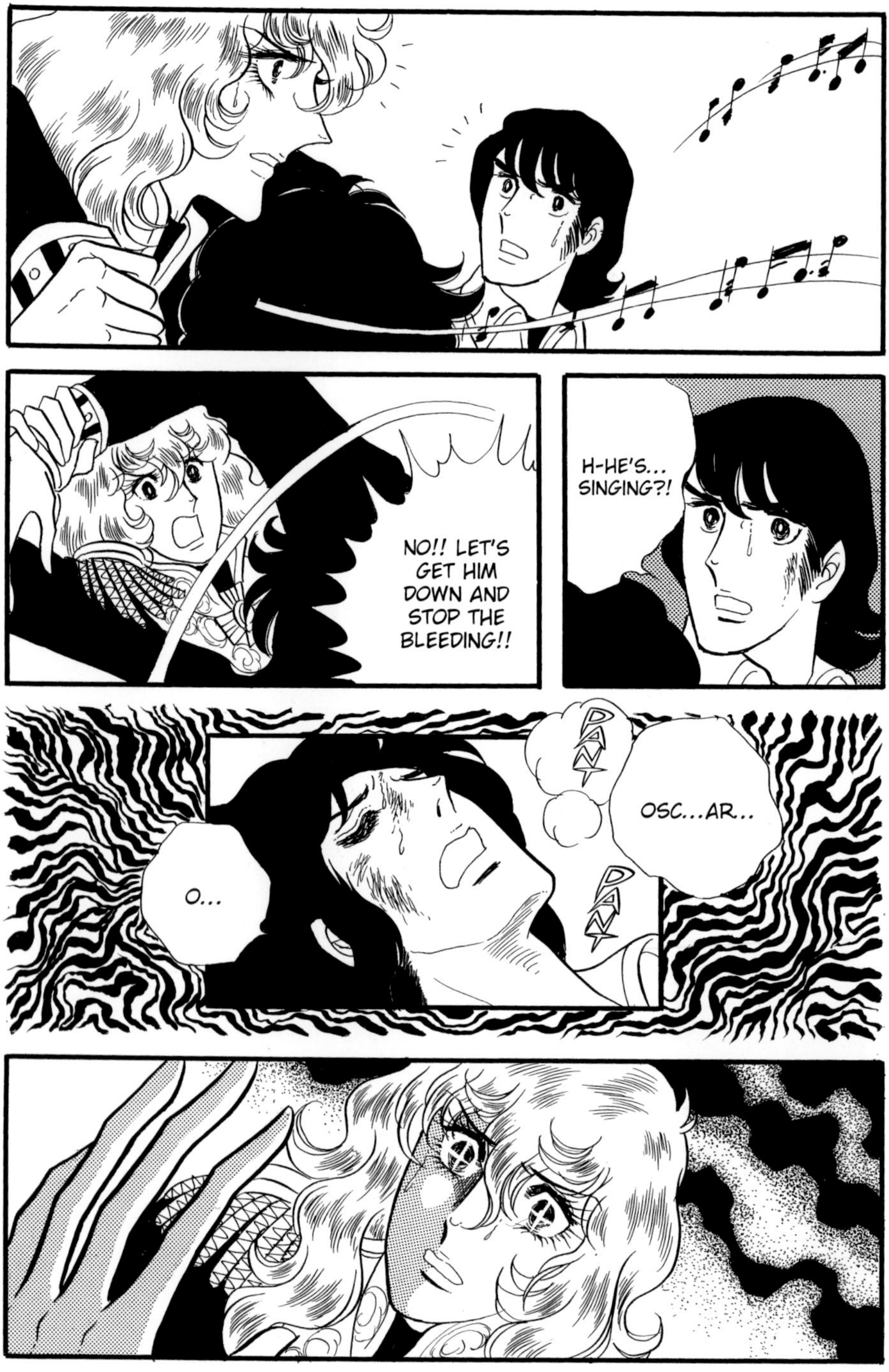
H-HE'S... SINGING?!
NO!! LET'S GET HIM DOWN AND STOP THE BLEEDING!!
PANT
OSC...AR...
PANT
O...

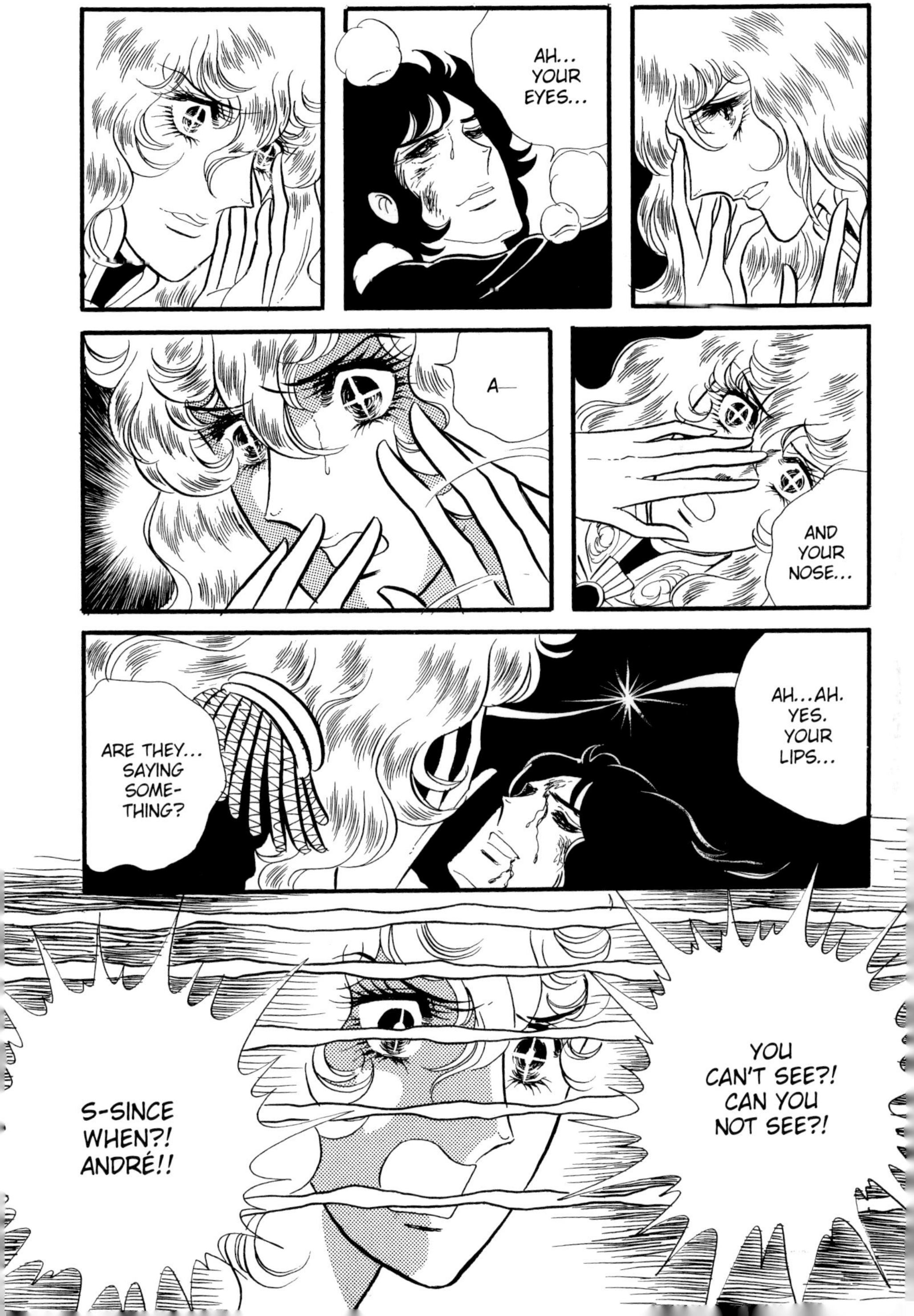
AH... YOUR EYES...
AND YOUR NOSE...
A—
AH...AH. YES. YOUR LIPS...
ARE THEY... SAYING SOME-THING?
YOU CAN'T SEE?! CAN YOU NOT SEE?!
S-SINCE WHEN?! ANDRÉ!!

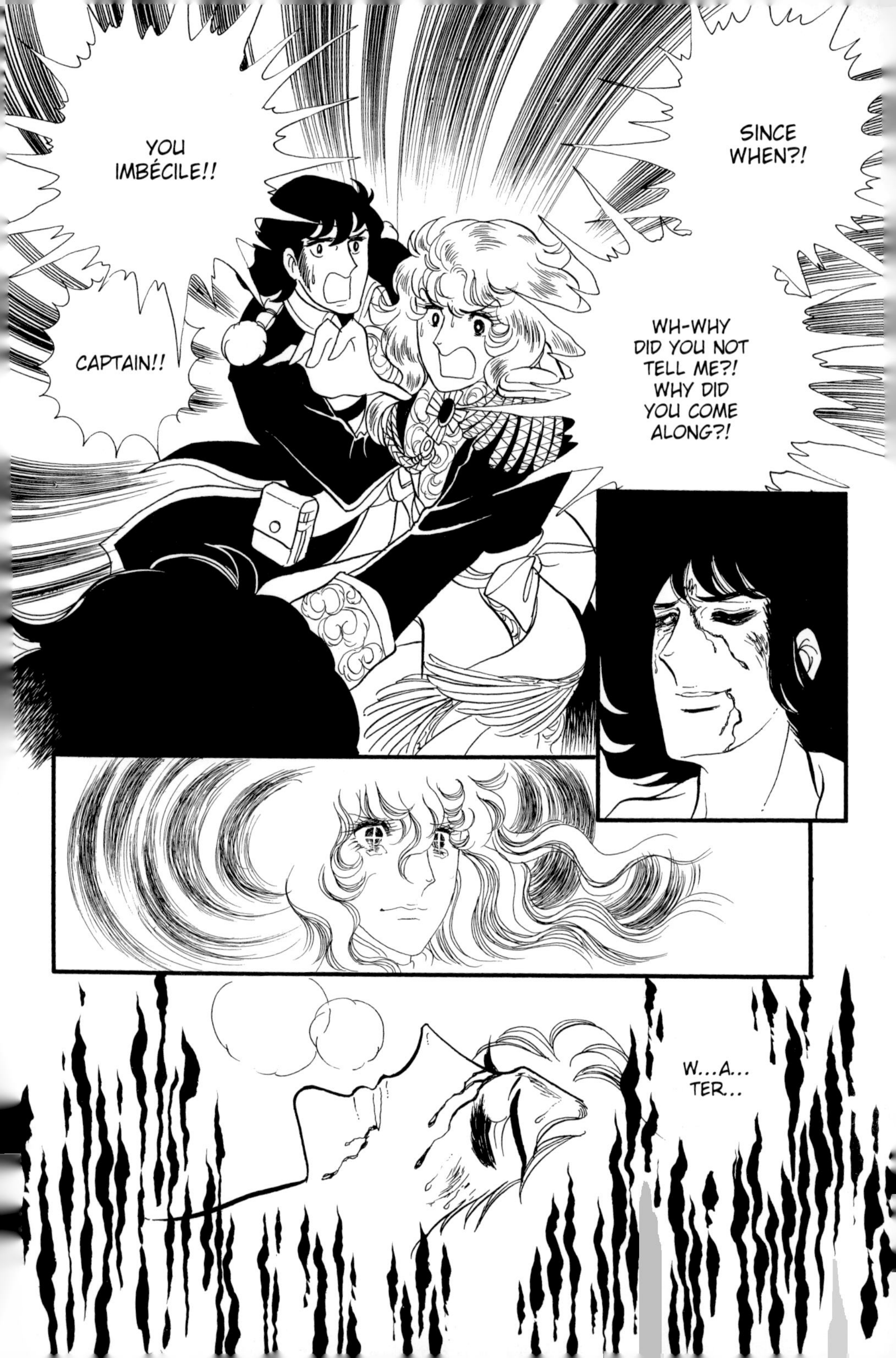
SINCE WHEN?!
WH-WHY DID YOU NOT TELL ME?! WHY DID YOU COME ALONG?!
YOU IMBÉCILE!!
CAPTAIN!!
W...A... TER...

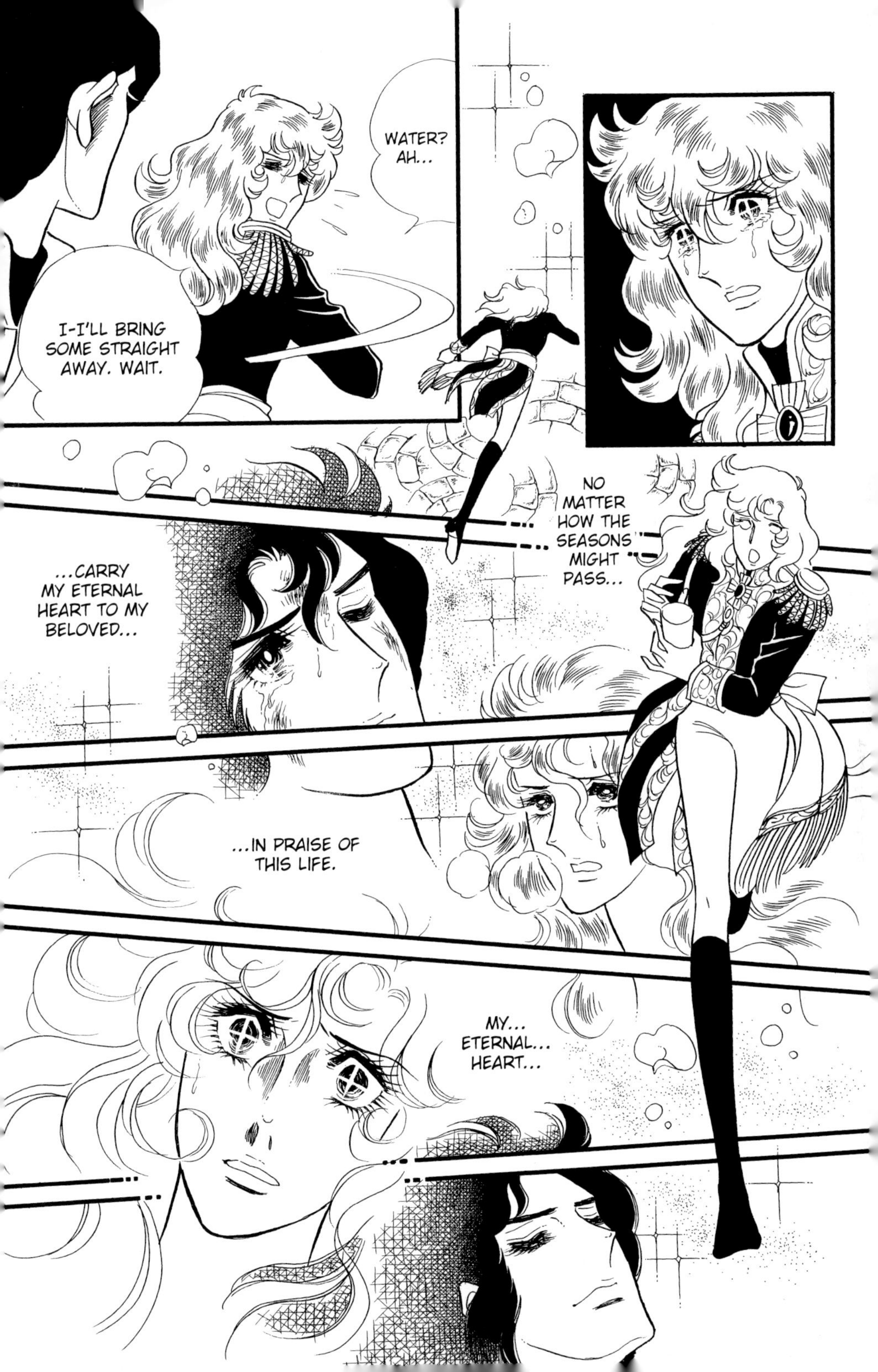
WATER? AH...
I-I'LL BRING SOME STRAIGHT AWAY. WAIT.
NO MATTER HOW THE SEASONS MIGHT PASS...
...CARRY MY ETERNAL HEART TO MY BELOVED...
...IN PRAISE OF THIS LIFE.
MY... ETERNAL... HEART...

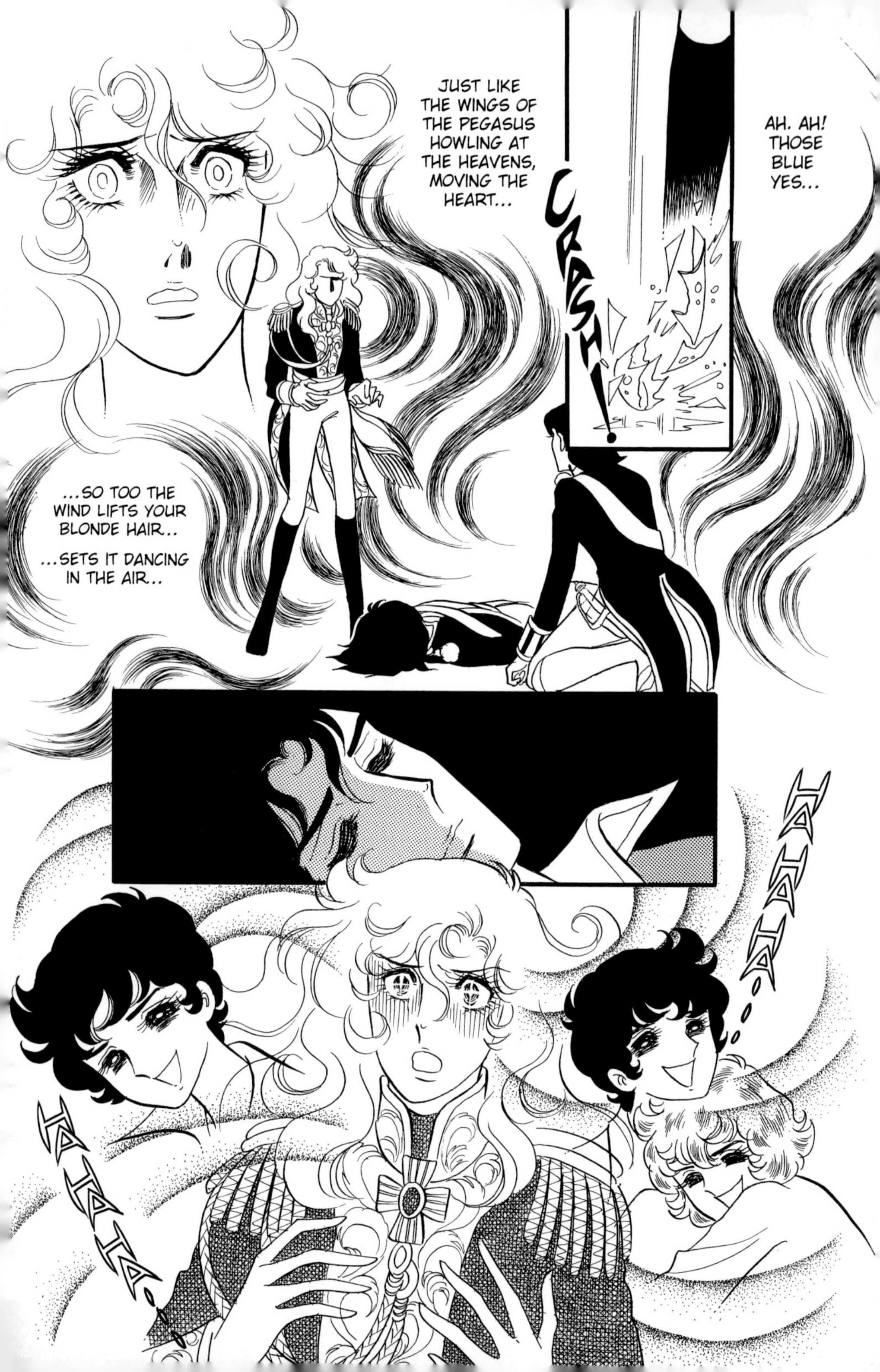
AH. AH! THOSE BLUE YES...
CRASH!
JUST LIKE THE WINGS OF THE PEGASUS HOWLING AT THE HEAVENS, MOVING THE HEART...
...SO TOO THE WIND LIFTS YOUR BLONDE HAIR...
...SETS IT DANCING IN THE AIR...
HAHAHAHA...
HAHAHAHA...

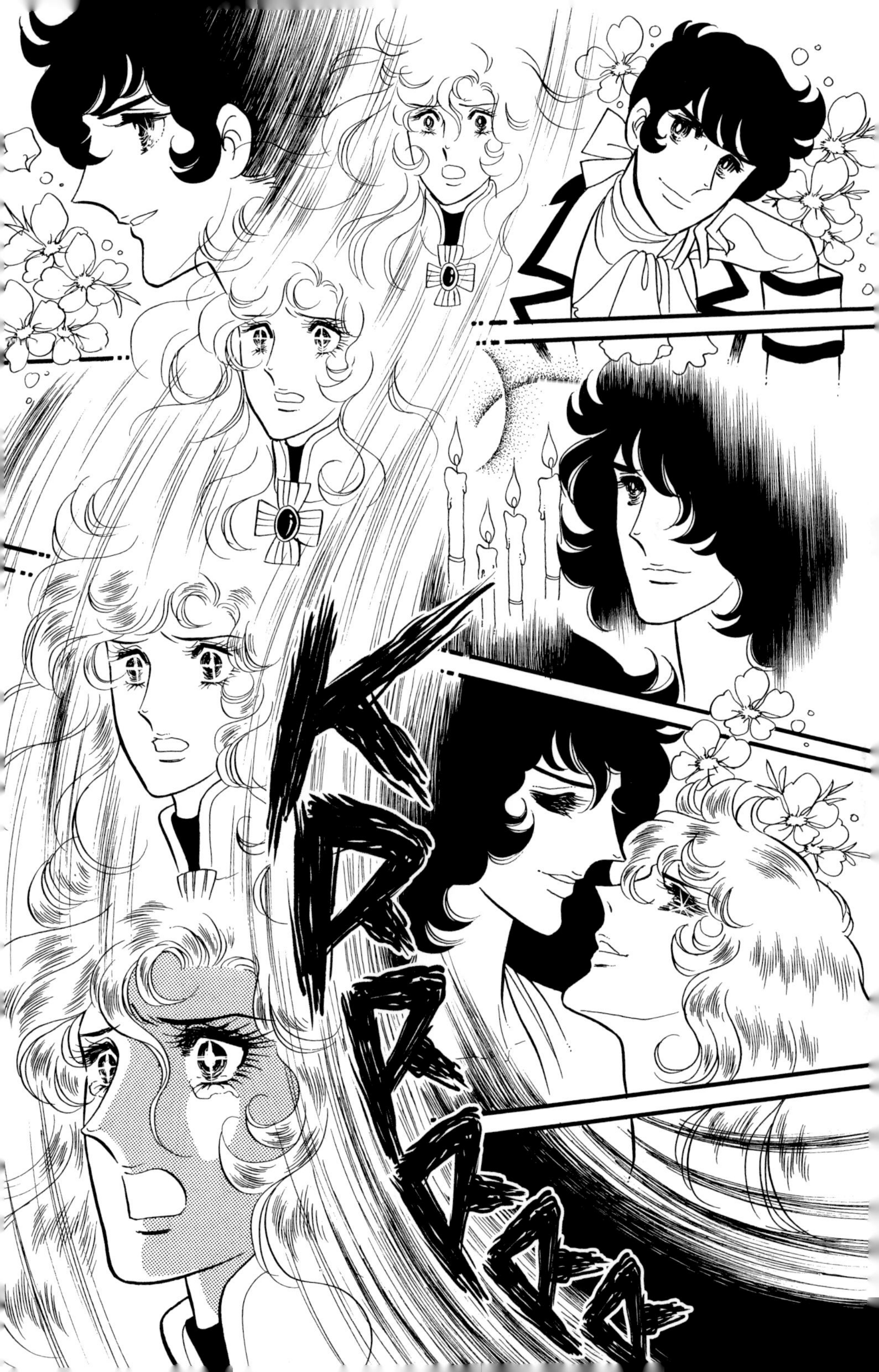
KRRRRRR

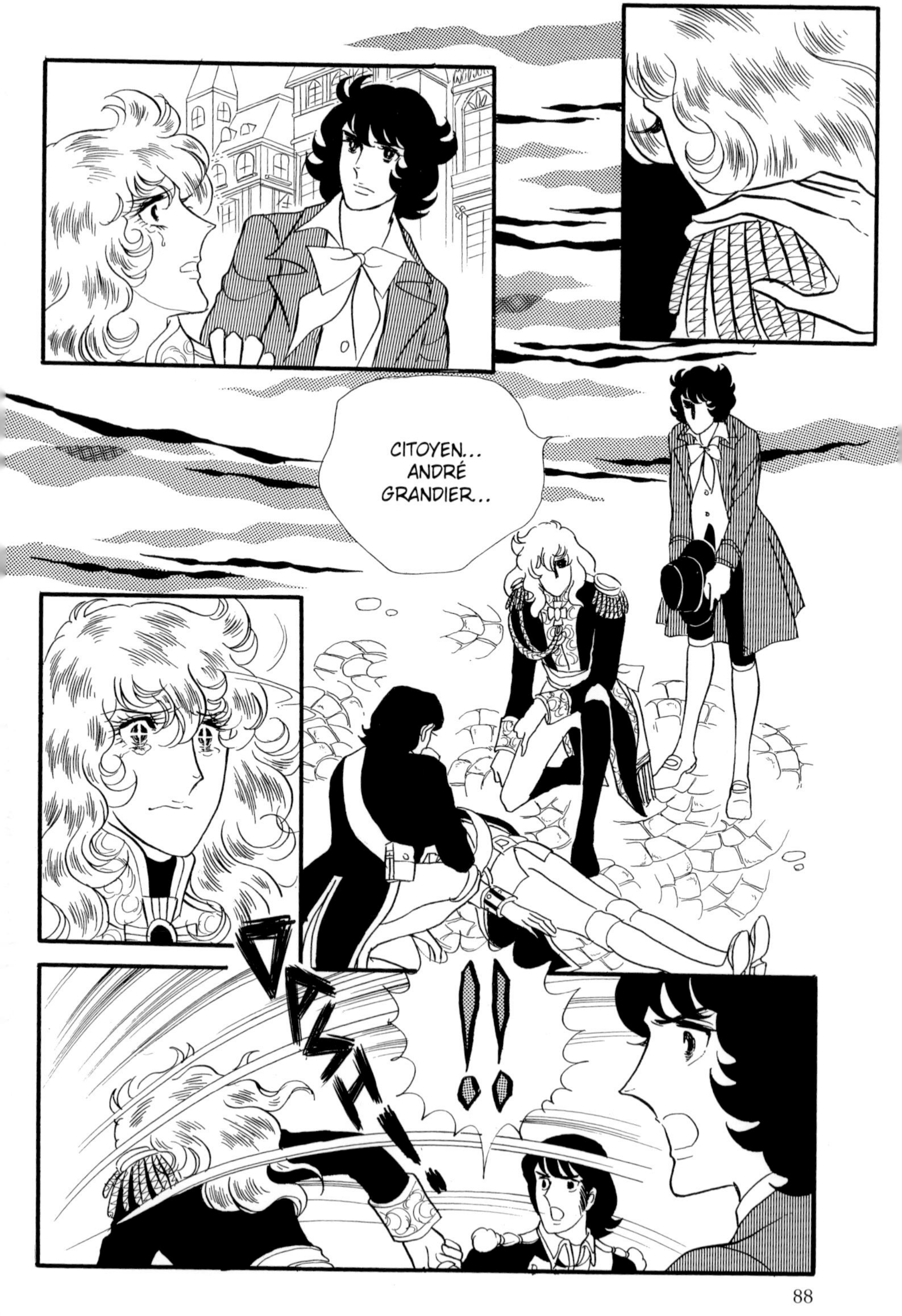
CITOYEN... ANDRÉ GRANDIER...
DASH!!

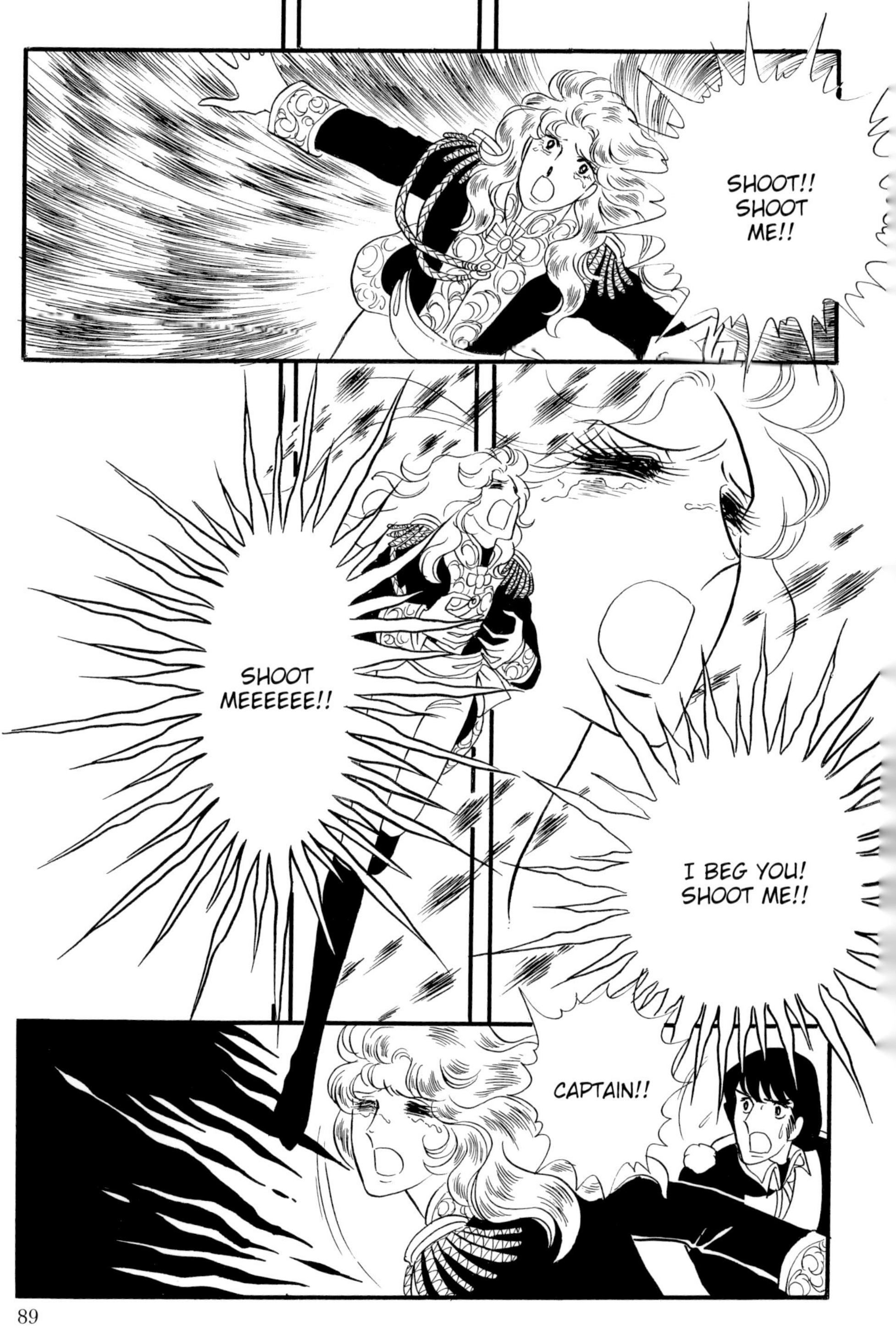
SHOOT!! SHOOT ME!!
I BEG YOU! SHOOT ME!!
SHOOT MEEEEEE!!
CAPTAIN!!

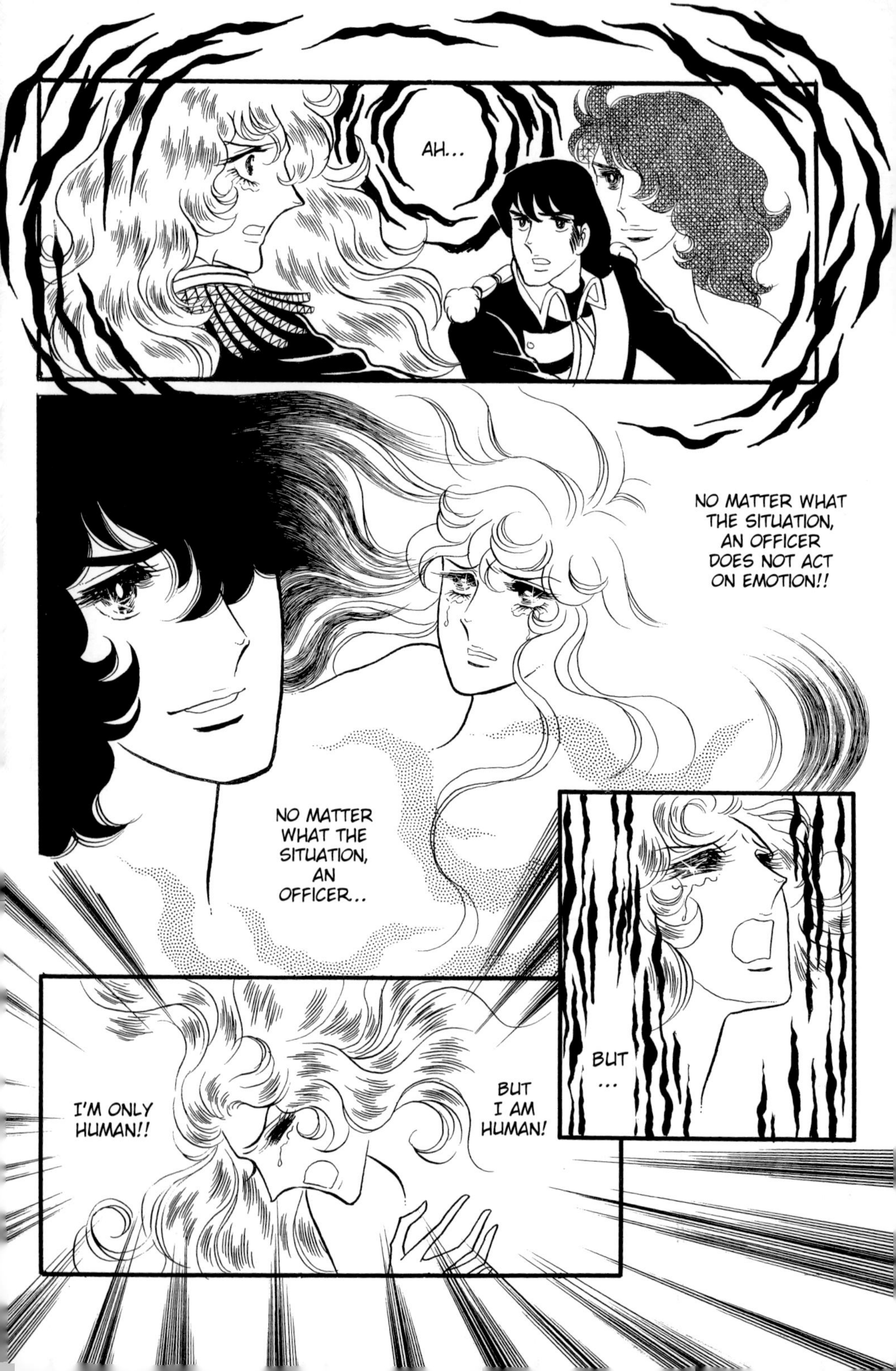
AH...
NO MATTER WHAT THE SITUATION, AN OFFICER DOES NOT ACT ON EMOTION!!
NO MATTER WHAT THE SITUATION, AN OFFICER..
BUT ...
BUT I AM HUMAN!
I'M ONLY HUMAN!!

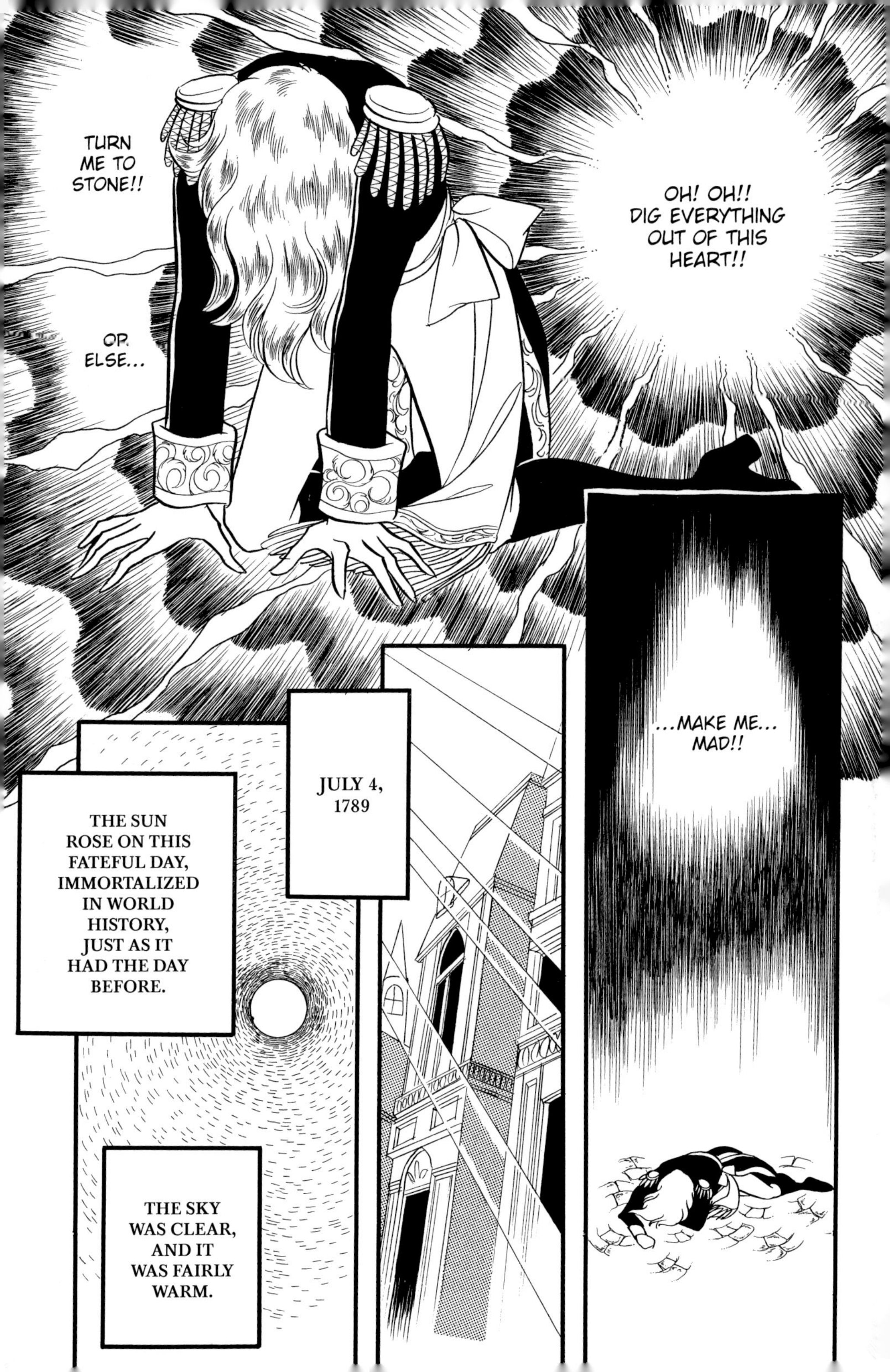
OH! OH!! DIG EVERYTHING OUT OF THIS HEART!!
TURN ME TO STONE!!
OR ELSE...
...MAKE ME... MAD!!
JULY 4, 1789
THE SUN ROSE ON THIS FATEFUL DAY, IMMORTALIZED IN WORLD HISTORY, JUST AS IT HAD THE DAY BEFORE.
THE SKY WAS CLEAR, AND IT WAS FAIRLY WARM.

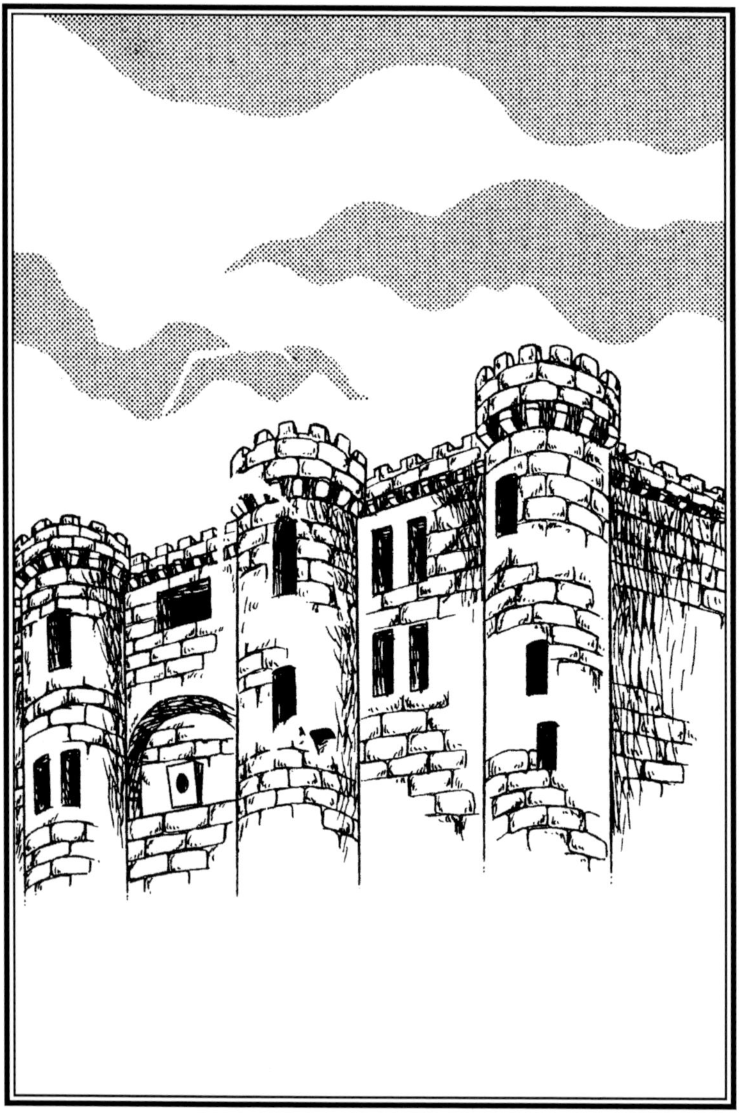

1974 MARGARET COMICS TRADE PAPERBACK
VOLUME 8 INSERT ART

THE BASTILLE WAS BUILT AS A FORTRESS ON THE RIGHT BANK OF THE SEINE LONG AGO, IN 1383, OVER A PERIOD OF THIRTEEN YEARS...

...TO PROTECT THE HÔTEL SAINT-POL, THE RESIDENCE OF CHARLES V, THE KING AT THE TIME.

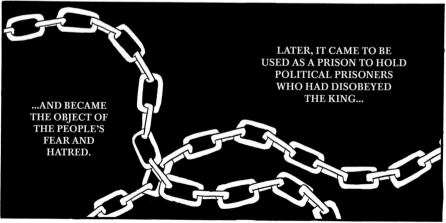

LATER, IT CAME TO BE USED AS A PRISON TO HOLD POLITICAL PRISONERS WHO HAD DISOBEYED THE KING...

...AND BECAME THE OBJECT OF THE PEOPLE'S FEAR AND HATRED.

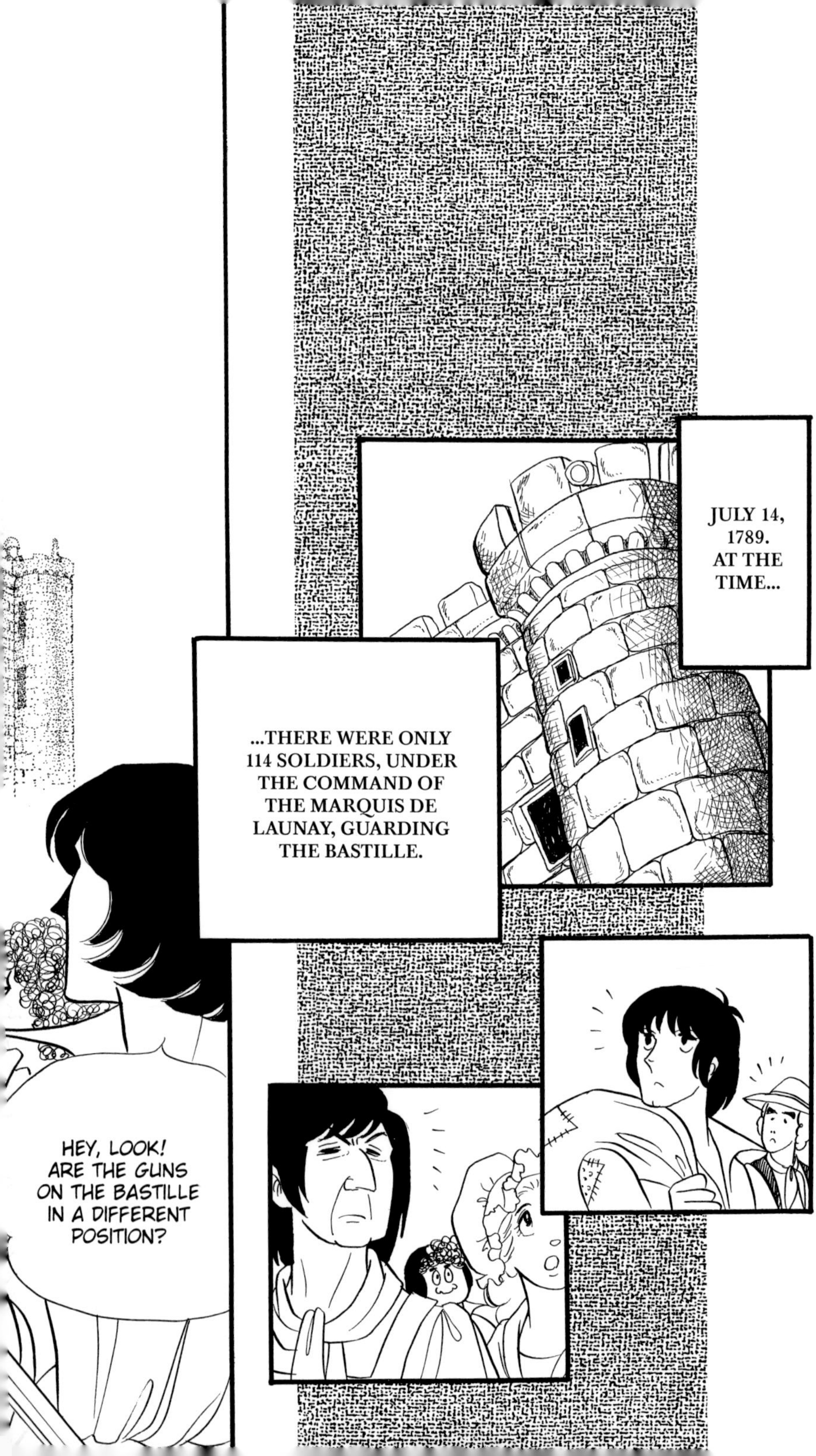
JULY 14, 1789. AT THE TIME...
...THERE WERE ONLY 114 SOLDIERS, UNDER THE COMMAND OF THE MARQUIS DE LAUNAY, GUARDING THE BASTILLE.
HEY, LOOK! ARE THE GUNS ON THE BASTILLE IN A DIFFERENT POSITION?

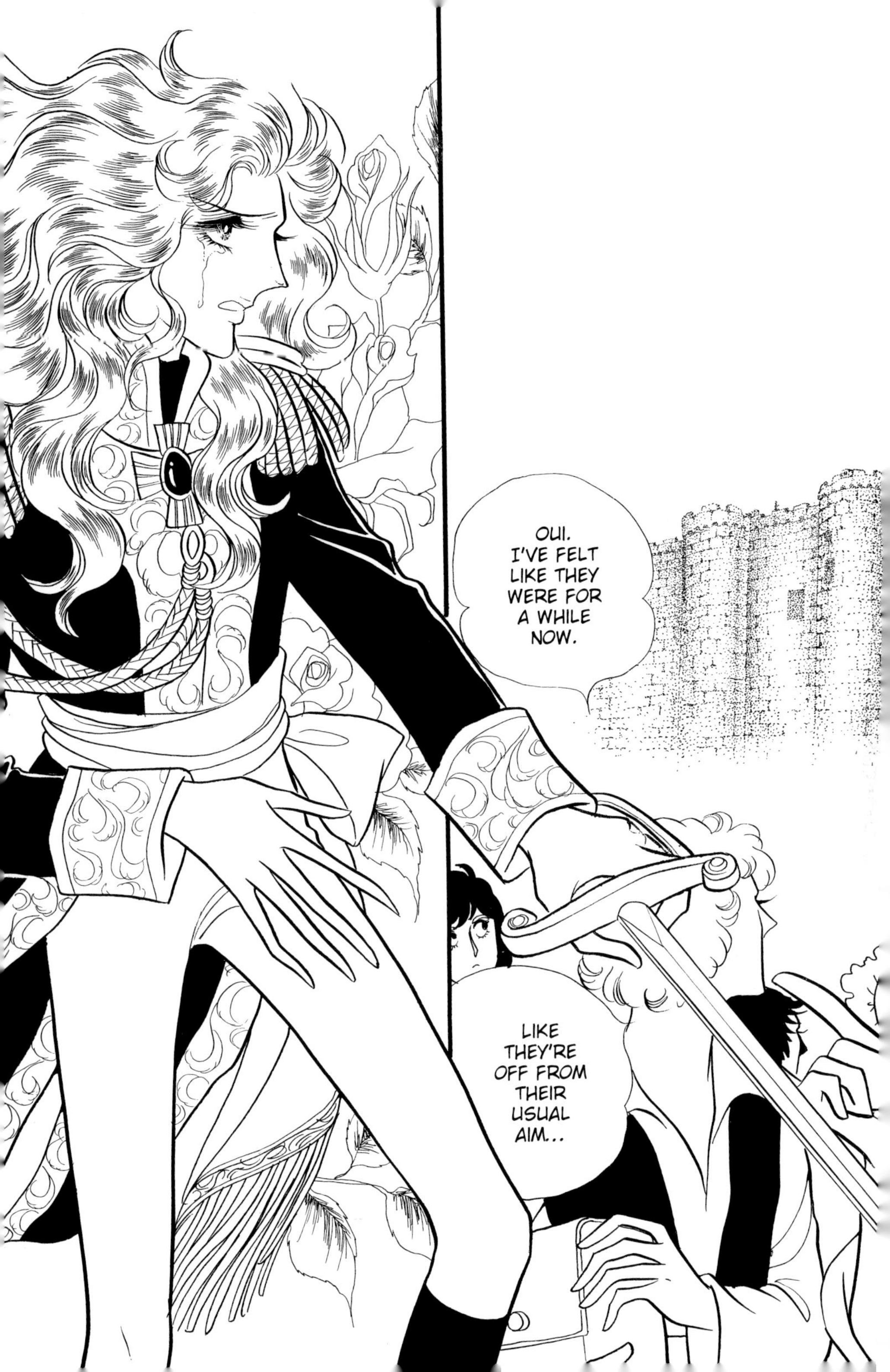
OUI. I'VE FELT LIKE THEY WERE FOR A WHILE NOW.
LIKE THEY'RE OFF FROM THEIR USUAL AIM...

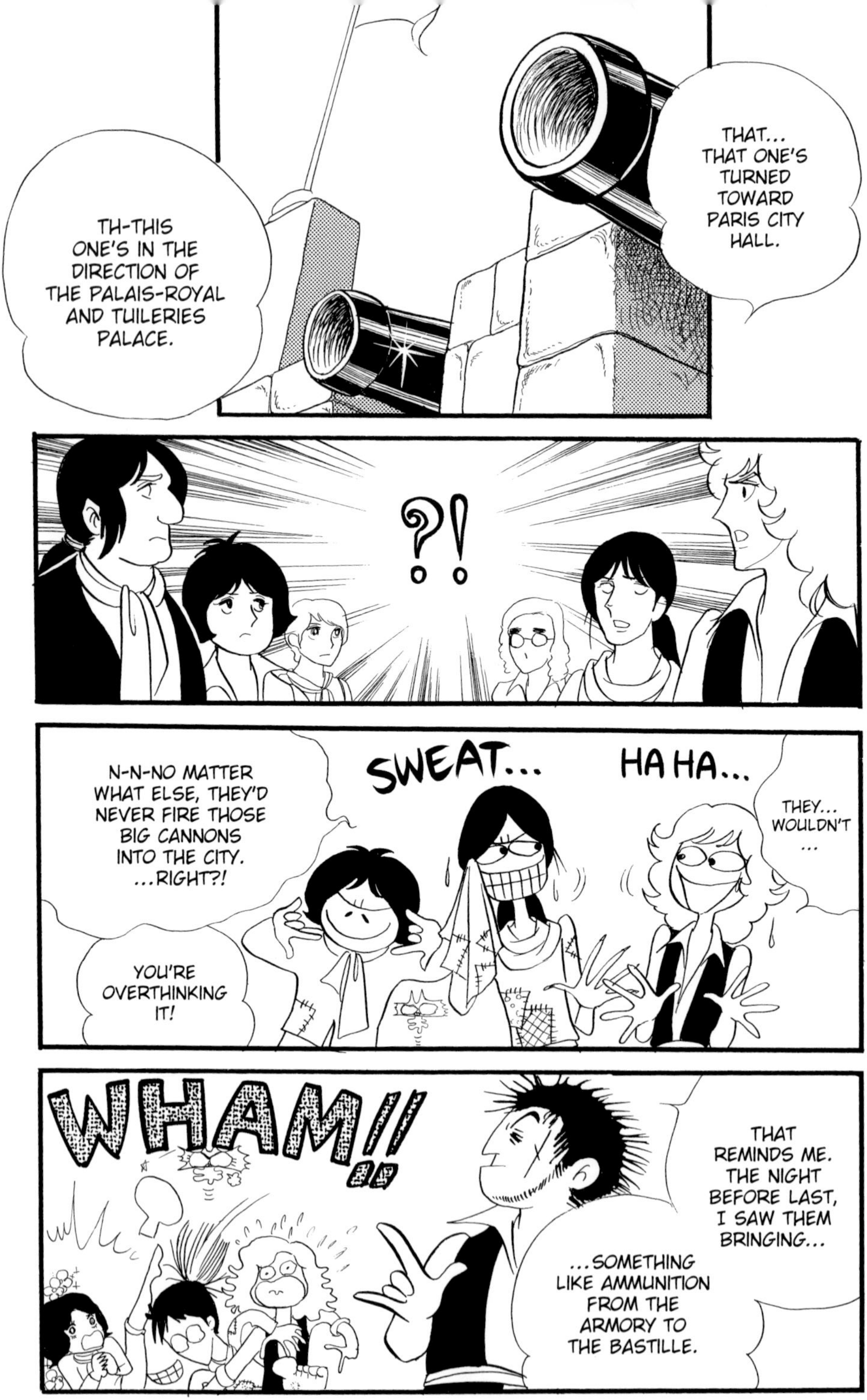
THAT... THAT ONE'S TURNED TOWARD PARIS CITY HALL.
TH-THIS ONE'S IN THE DIRECTION OF THE PALAIS-ROYAL AND TUILERIES PALACE.
?!
THEY... WOULDN'T ...
HA HA...
SWEAT...
N-N-NO MATTER WHAT ELSE, THEY'D NEVER FIRE THOSE BIG CANNONS INTO THE CITY. ...RIGHT?!
YOU'RE OVERTHINKING IT!
THAT REMINDS ME. THE NIGHT BEFORE LAST, I SAW THEM BRINGING...
...SOMETHING LIKE AMMUNITION FROM THE ARMORY TO THE BASTILLE.
WHAM!!

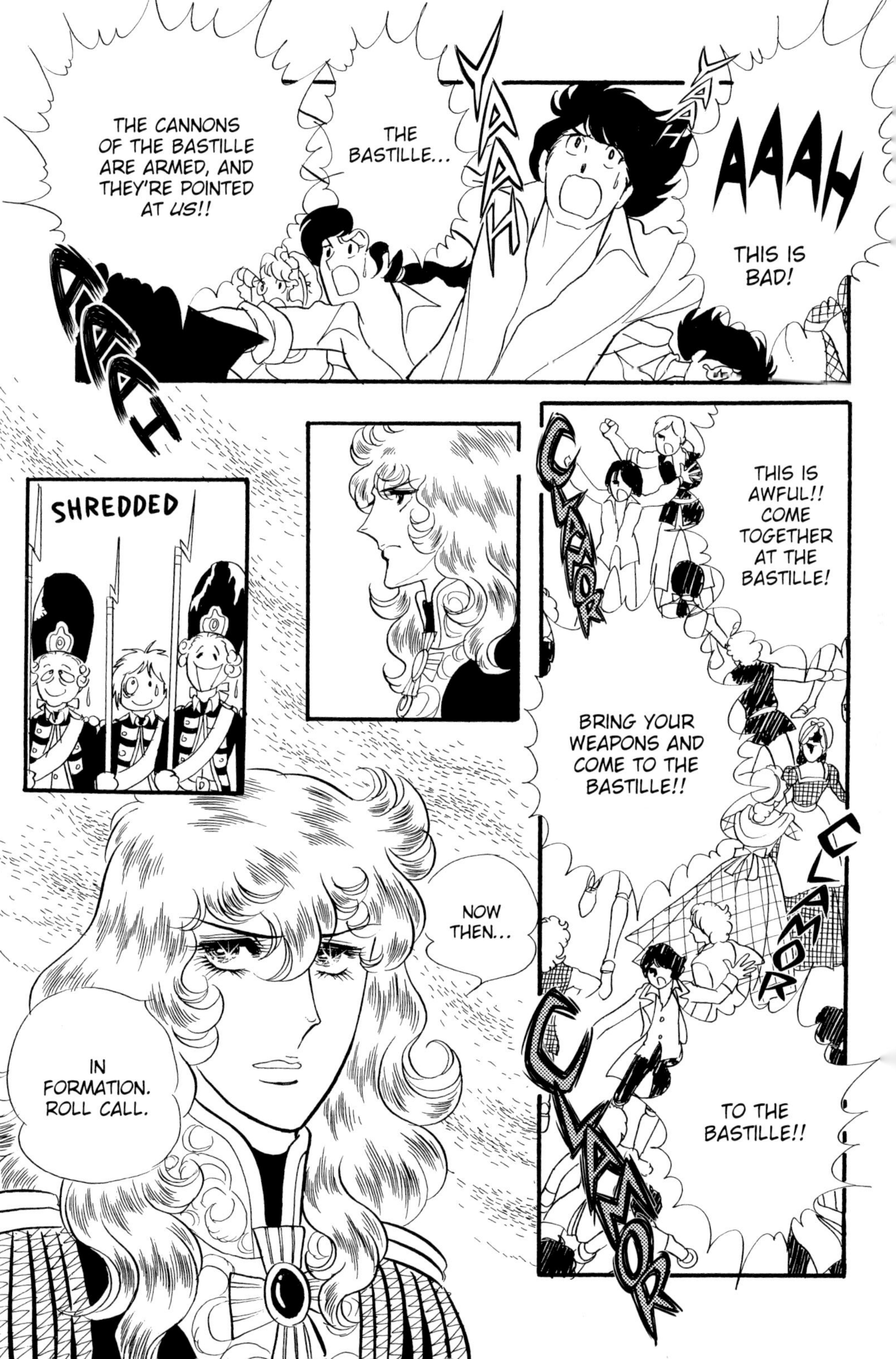

AAAH
THIS IS BAD!
THE BASTILLE...
THE CANNONS OF THE BASTILLE ARE ARMED, AND THEY'RE POINTED AT US!!
CLAMOR
THIS IS AWFUL!! COME TOGETHER AT THE BASTILLE!
BRING YOUR WEAPONS AND COME TO THE BASTILLE!!
CLAMOR
TO THE BASTILLE!!
CLAMOR
SHREDDED
NOW THEN...
IN FORMATION. ROLL CALL.

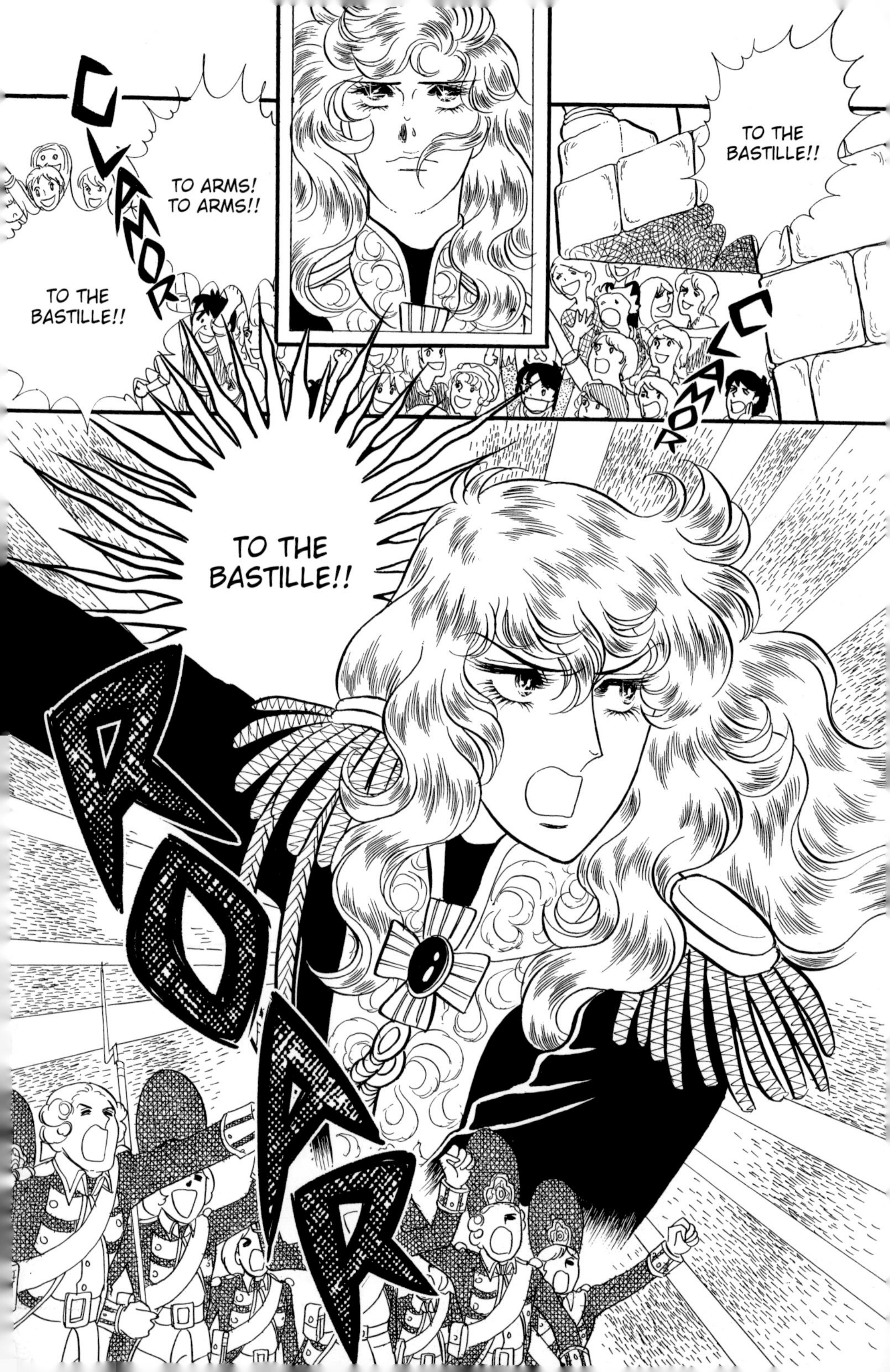
TO THE BASTILLE!!
CLAMOR
TO ARMS! TO ARMS!!
CLAMOR
TO THE BASTILLE!!
TO THE BASTILLE!!
ROAR

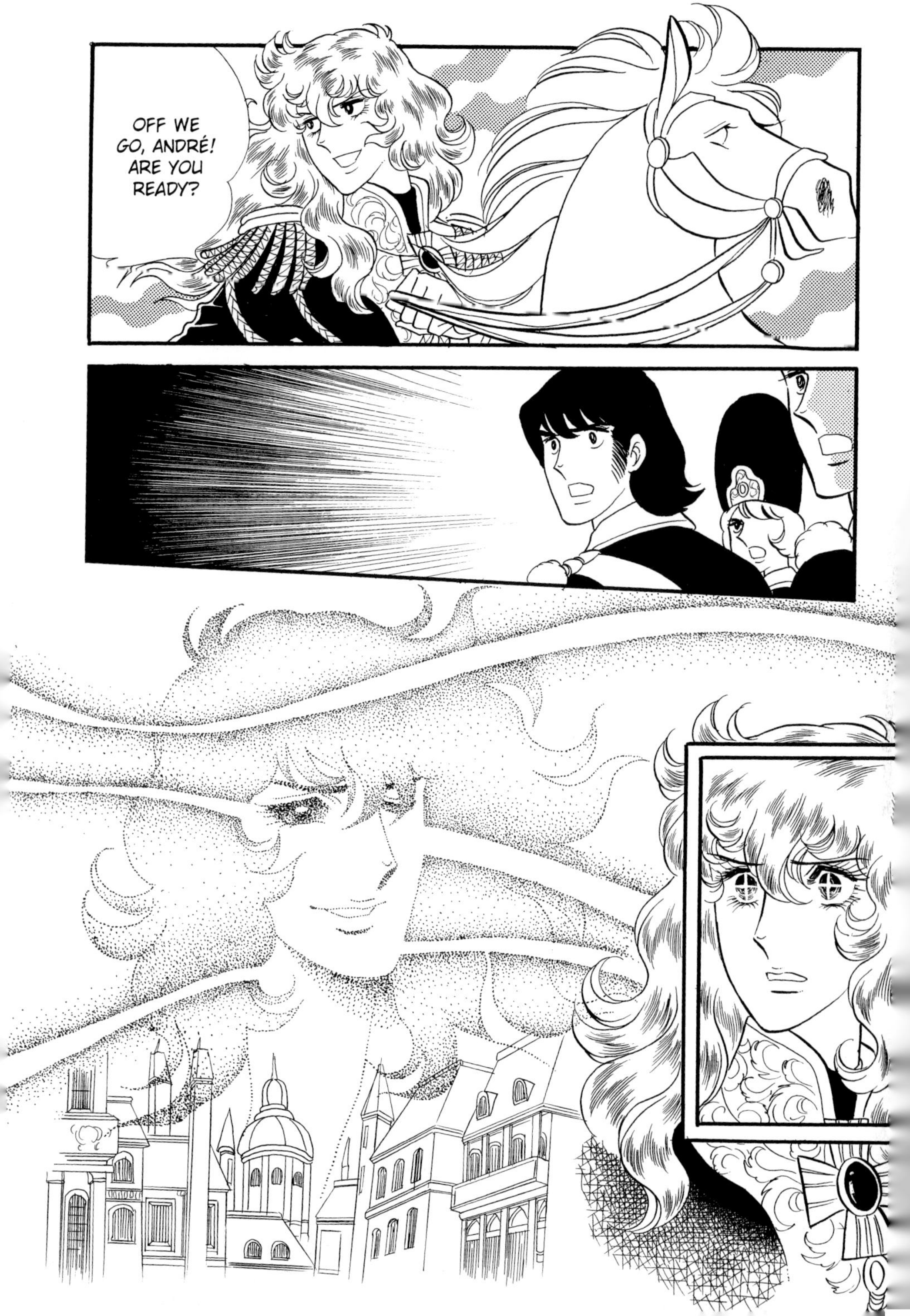
OFF WE GO, ANDRÉ! ARE YOU READY?

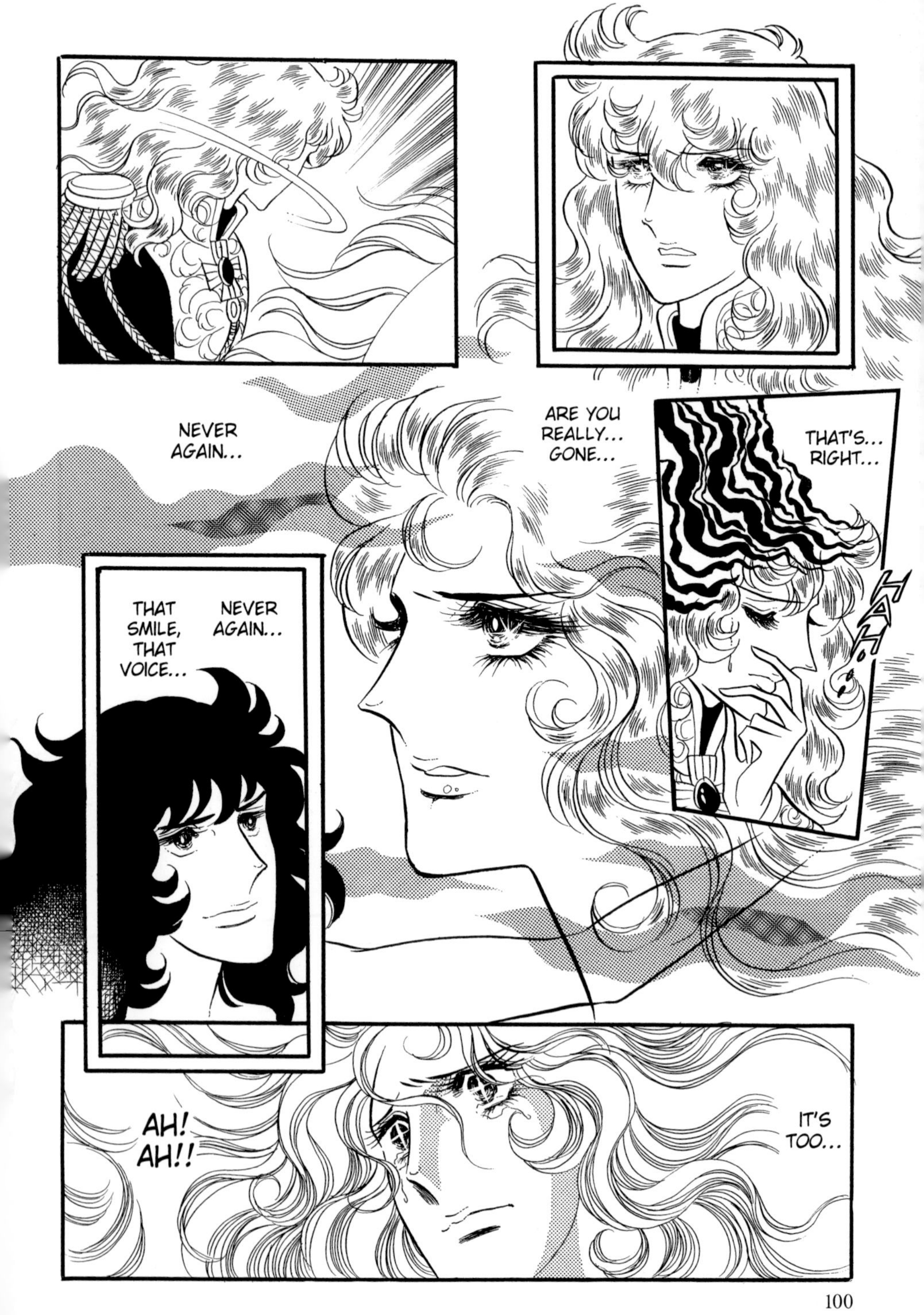
THAT'S... RIGHT...
HAH!
ARE YOU REALLY... GONE...
NEVER AGAIN...
NEVER AGAIN...
THAT SMILE, THAT VOICE...
IT'S TOO...
AH! AH!!

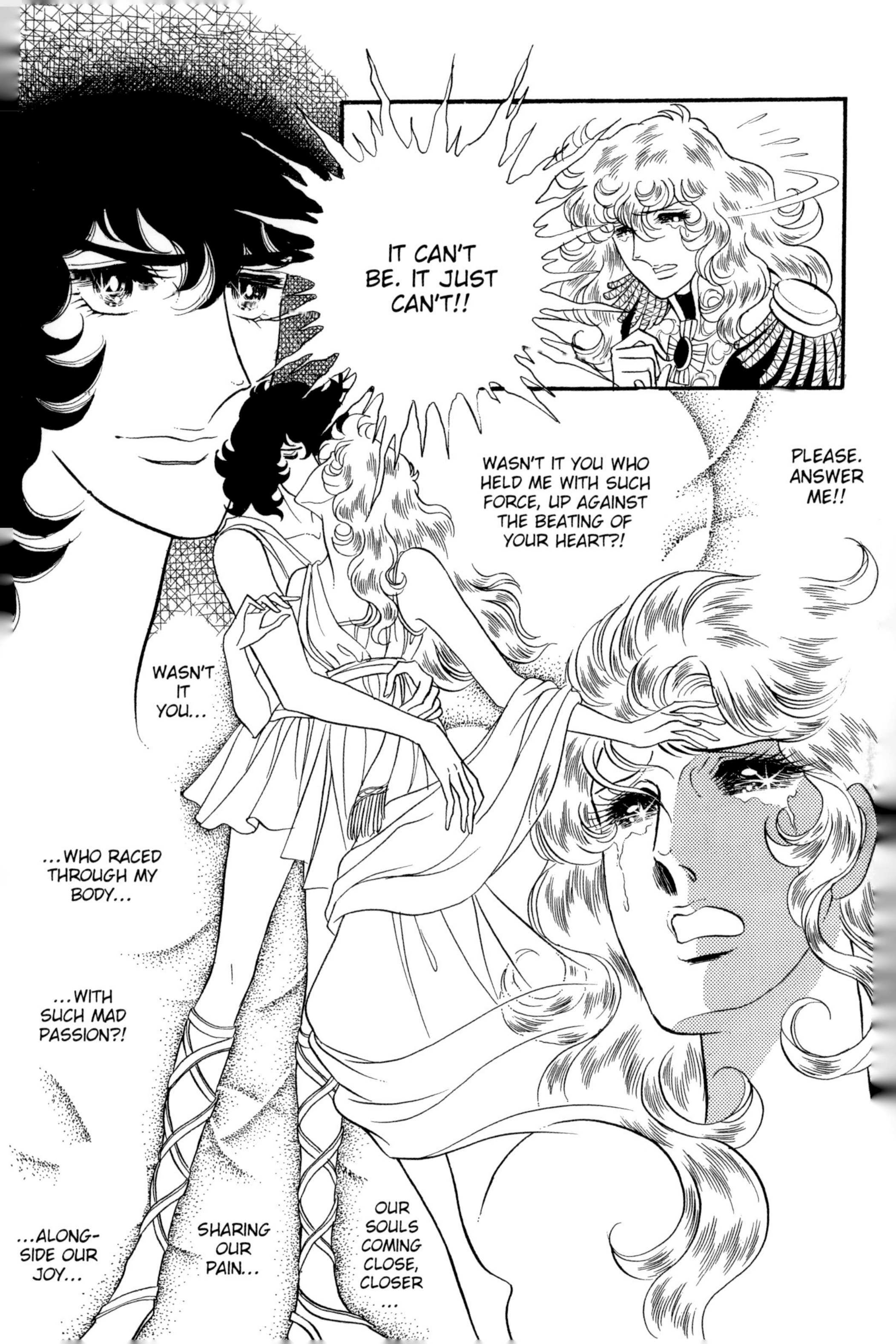
IT CAN'T BE. IT JUST CAN'T!!
PLEASE. ANSWER ME!!
WASN'T IT YOU WHO HELD ME WITH SUCH FORCE, UP AGAINST THE BEATING OF YOUR HEART?!
WASN'T IT YOU...
...WHO RACED THROUGH MY BODY...
...WITH SUCH MAD PASSION?!
OUR SOULS COMING CLOSE, CLOSER ...
SHARING OUR PAIN...
...ALONG-SIDE OUR JOY...

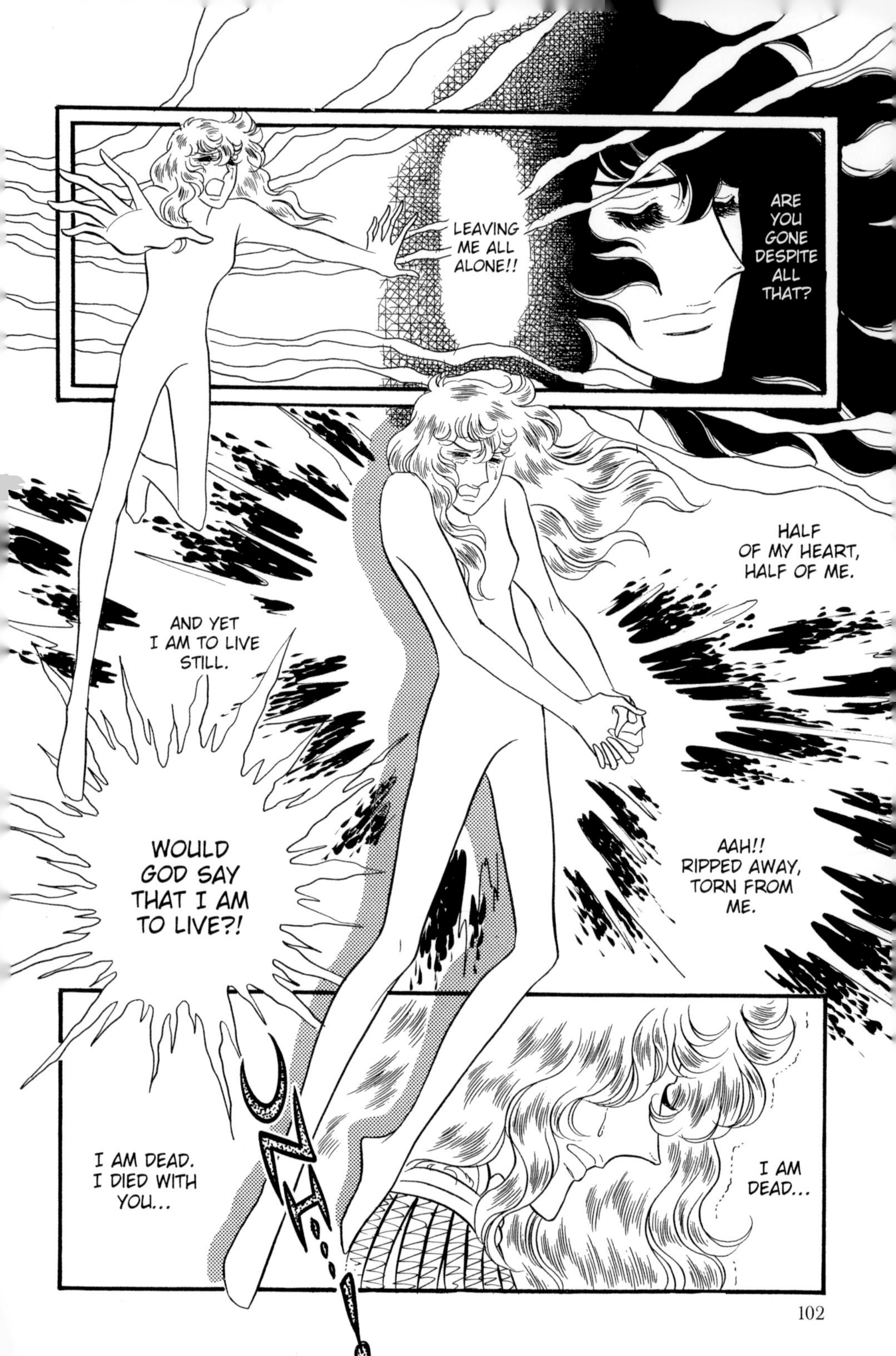
ARE YOU GONE DESPITE ALL THAT?
LEAVING ME ALL ALONE!!
HALF OF MY HEART, HALF OF ME.
AAH!! RIPPED AWAY, TORN FROM ME.
AND YET I AM TO LIVE STILL.
WOULD GOD SAY THAT I AM TO LIVE?!
I AM DEAD...
I AM DEAD. I DIED WITH YOU...

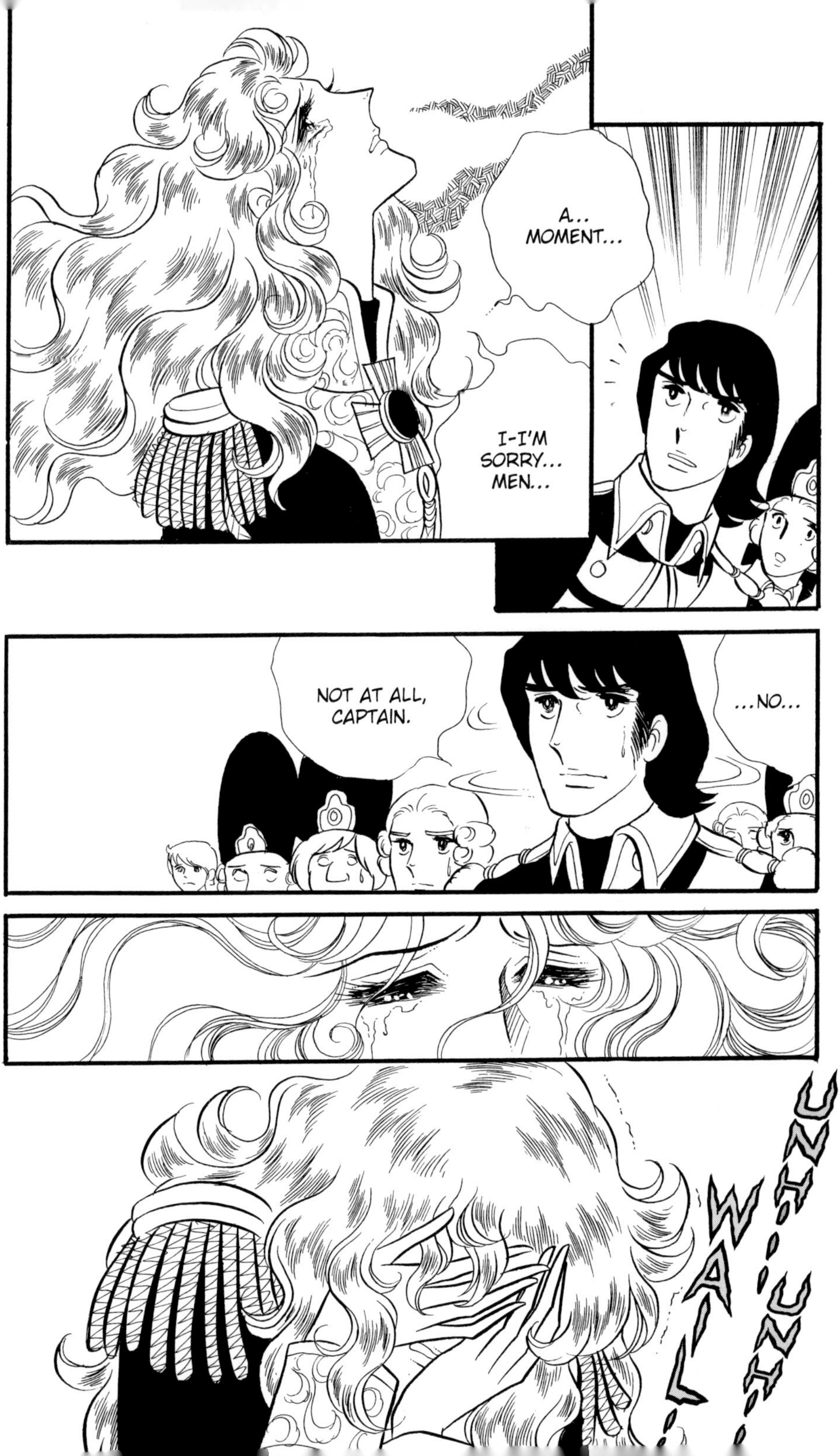
A... MOMENT...
I-I'M SORRY... MEN...
...NO...
NOT AT ALL, CAPTAIN.
UNH... UNH...
WAIL!!

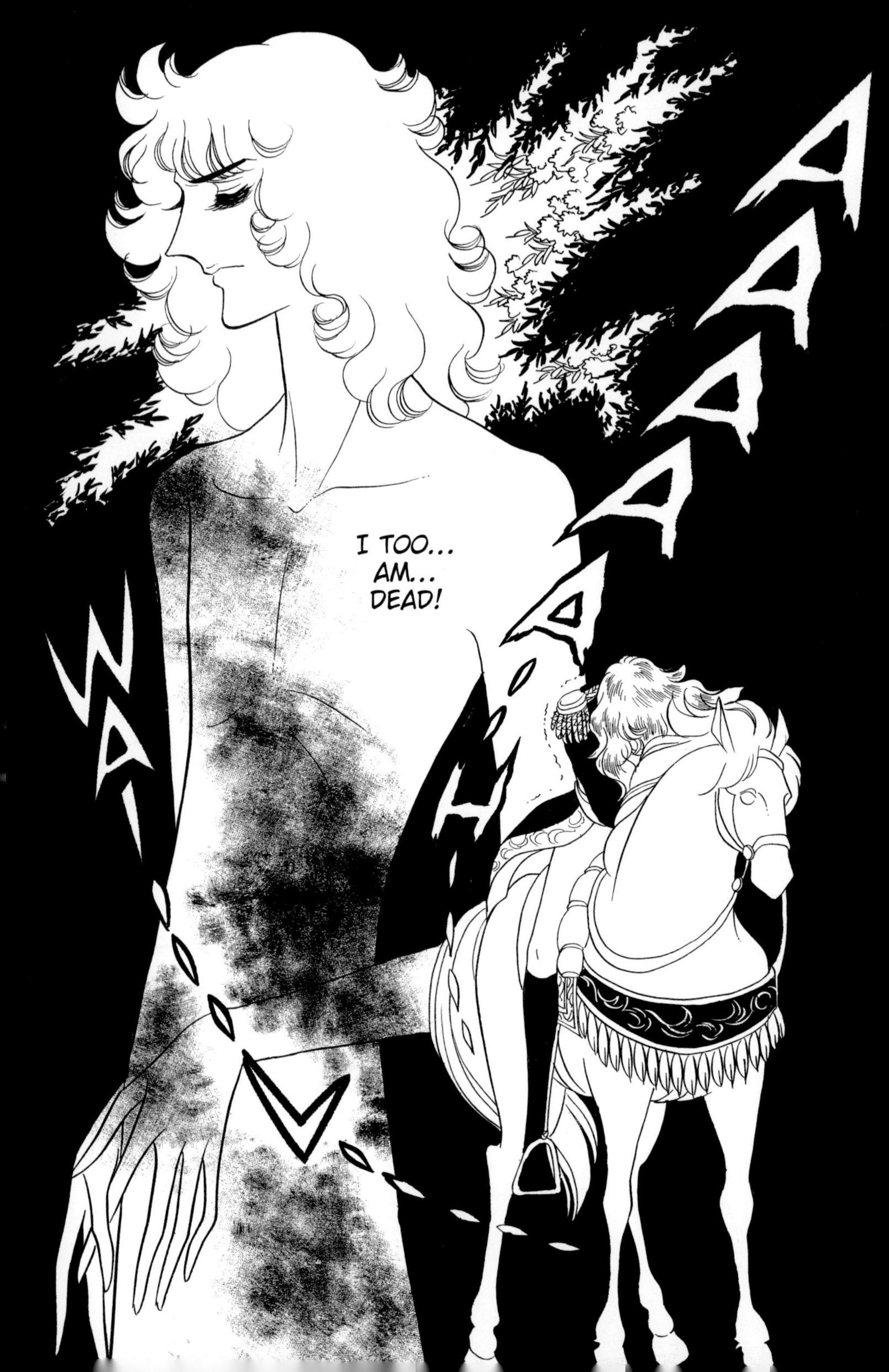
I TOO... AM... DEAD!

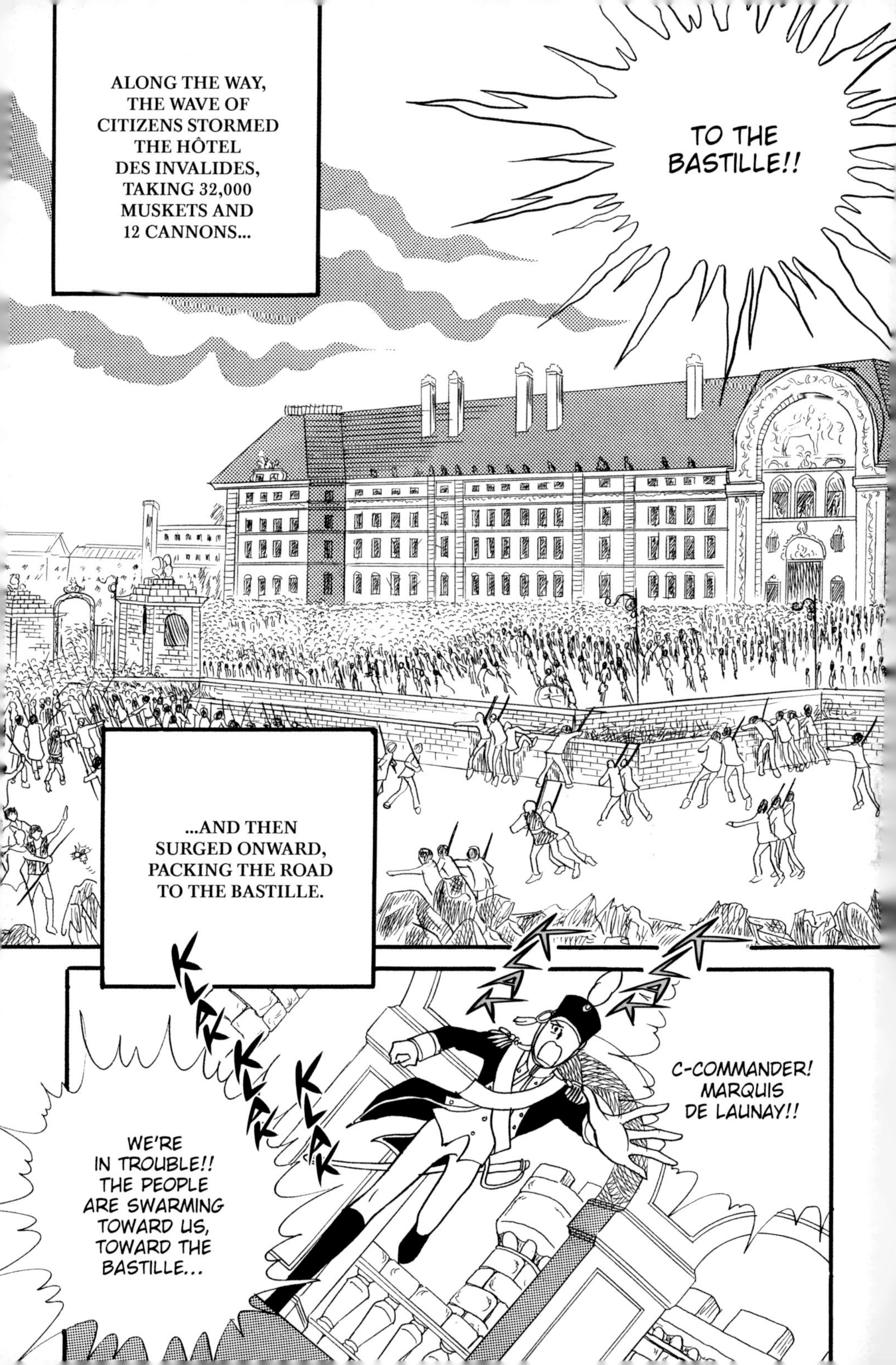
TO THE BASTILLE!!
ALONG THE WAY, THE WAVE OF CITIZENS STORMED THE HÔTEL DES INVALIDES, TAKING 32,000 MUSKETS AND 12 CANNONS...
...AND THEN SURGED ONWARD, PACKING THE ROAD TO THE BASTILLE.
C-COMMANDER! MARQUIS DE LAUNAY!!
KLAK KLAK KLAK
WE'RE IN TROUBLE!! THE PEOPLE ARE SWARMING TOWARD US, TOWARD THE BASTILLE...

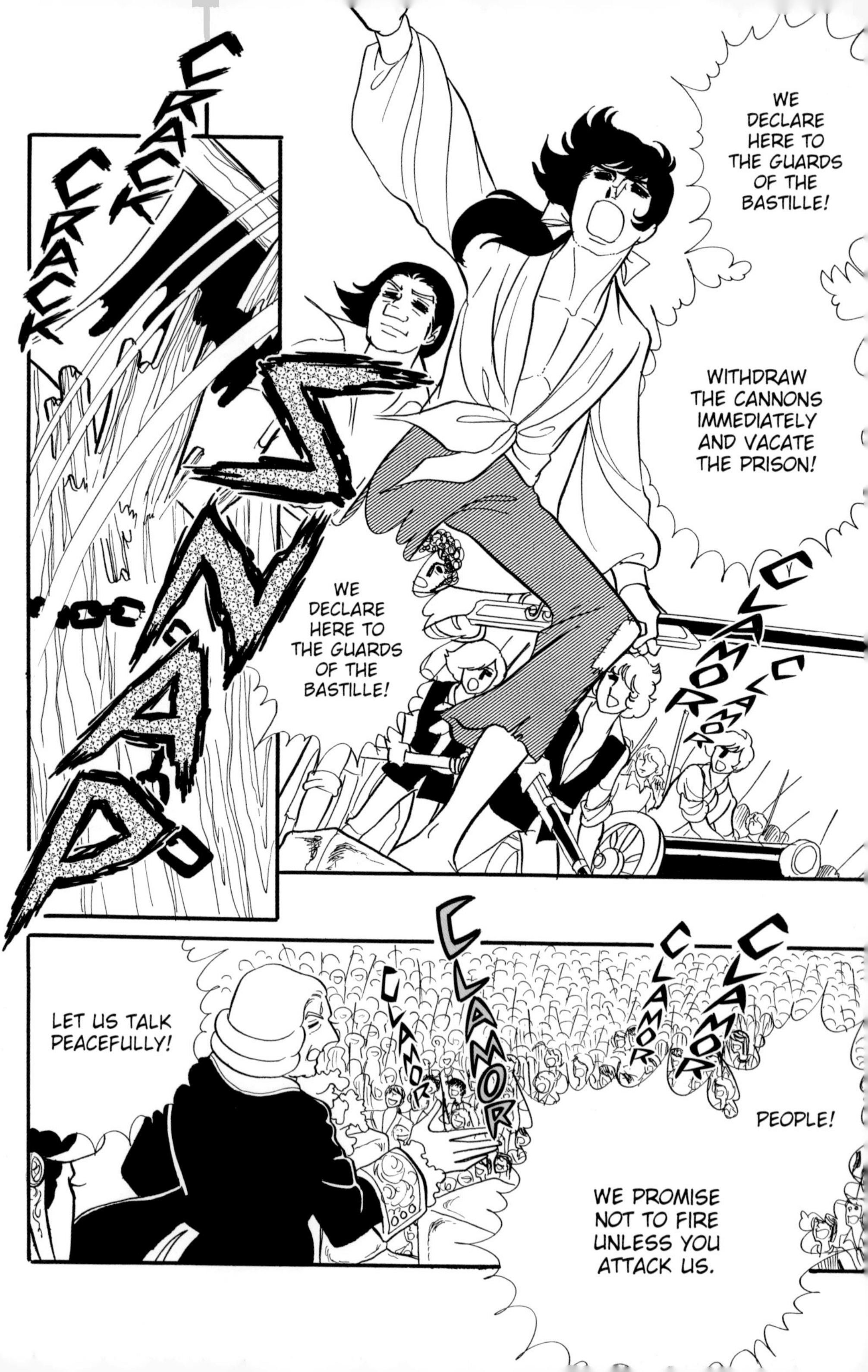
WE DECLARE HERE TO THE GUARDS OF THE BASTILLE!
WITHDRAW THE CANNONS IMMEDIATELY AND VACATE THE PRISON!
CLAMOR
CLAMOR
WE DECLARE HERE TO THE GUARDS OF THE BASTILLE!
CRACK
CRACK
ZAP
PEOPLE!
WE PROMISE NOT TO FIRE UNLESS YOU ATTACK US.
CLAMOR
CLAMOR
CLAMOR
CLAMOR
LET US TALK PEACEFULLY!

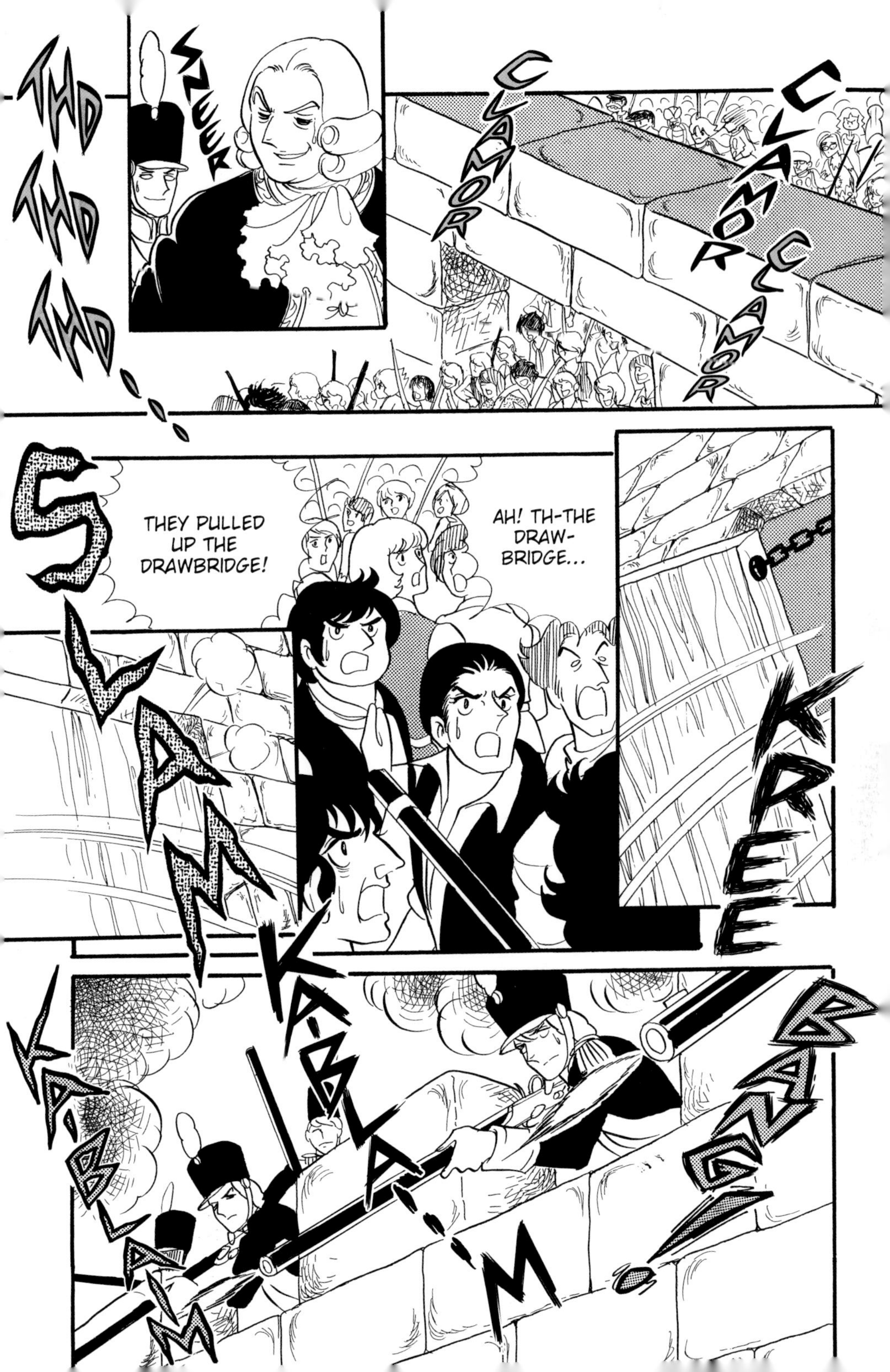
CLAMOR CLAMOR
CLAMOR
SNEER
!
THUD THUD THUD...
KREEEE
AH! TH-THE DRAW-BRIDGE...
THEY PULLED UP THE DRAWBRIDGE!
SLAM
BANG!
KA-BLA-M
KA-BLAM

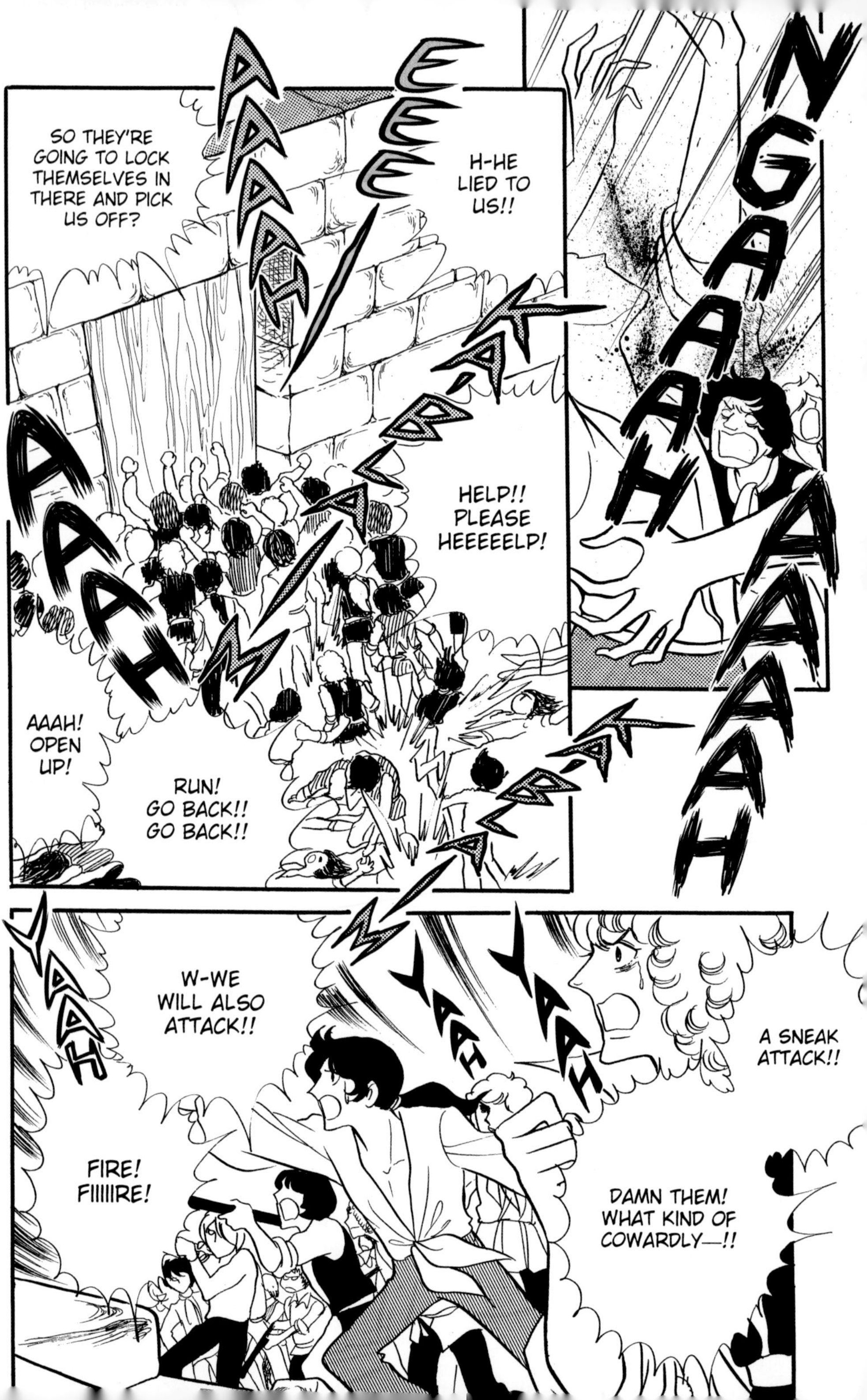

NGAAAAAAH
AAAAAAH
H-HE LIED TO US!!
SO THEY'RE GOING TO LOCK THEMSELVES IN THERE AND PICK US OFF?
AAAAAH!
EEEE
KABLAM!
HELP!! PLEASE HEEEEELP!
AAAAH
KABLAM!
RUN! GO BACK!! GO BACK!!
AAAH! OPEN UP!
A SNEAK ATTACK!!
YAAAH
YAAAH
W-WE WILL ALSO ATTACK!!
YAAAH
DAMN THEM! WHAT KIND OF COWARDLY—!!
FIRE! FIIIIRE!

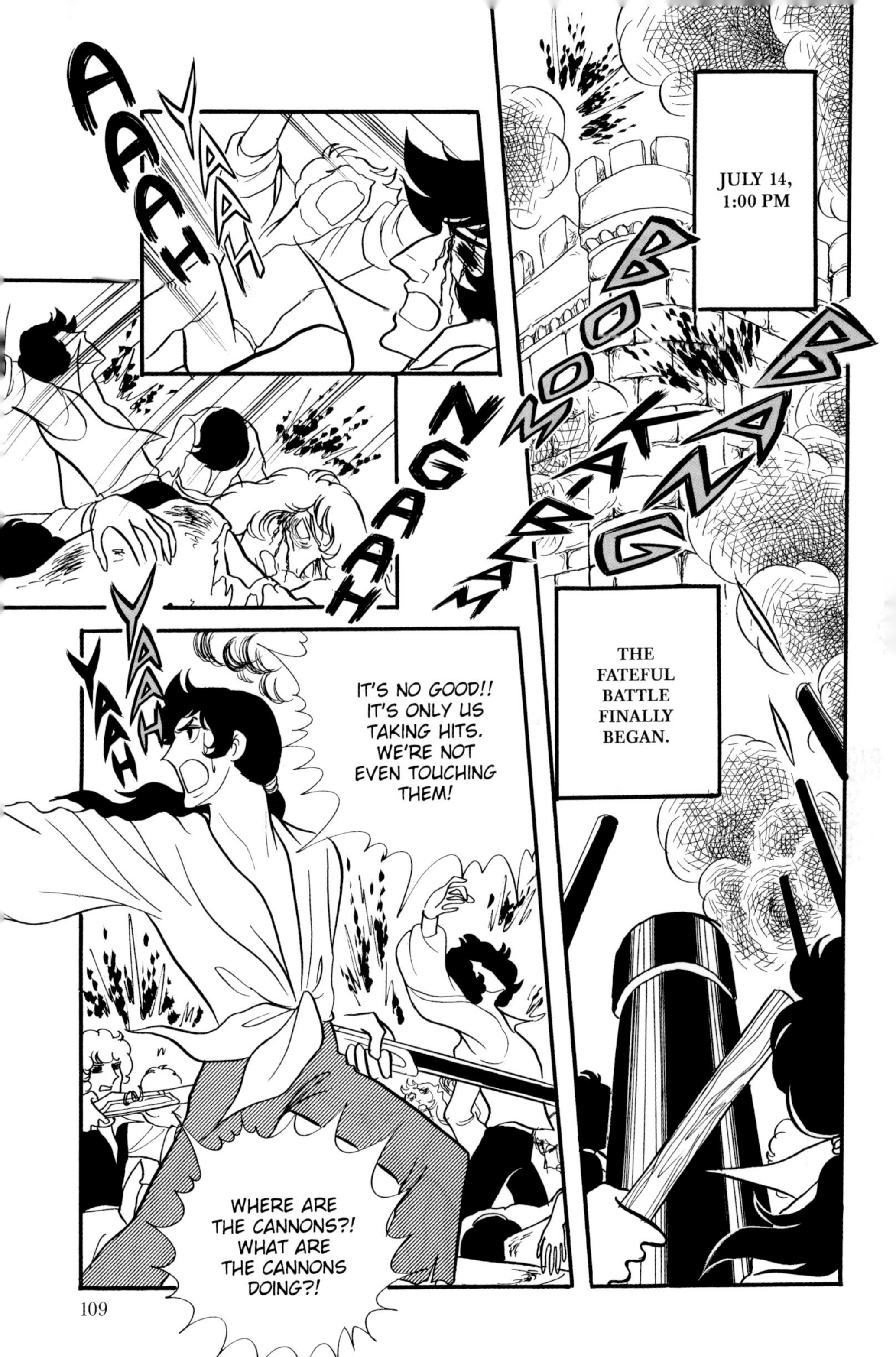
JULY 14, 1:00 PM
BOOM
BANG
KABLAM
THE FATEFUL BATTLE FINALLY BEGAN.
AAAH
YAAAH
NGAAAH
YAAAH
YAAH
IT'S NO GOOD!! IT'S ONLY US TAKING HITS. WE'RE NOT EVEN TOUCHING THEM!
WHERE ARE THE CANNONS?! WHAT ARE THE CANNONS DOING?!

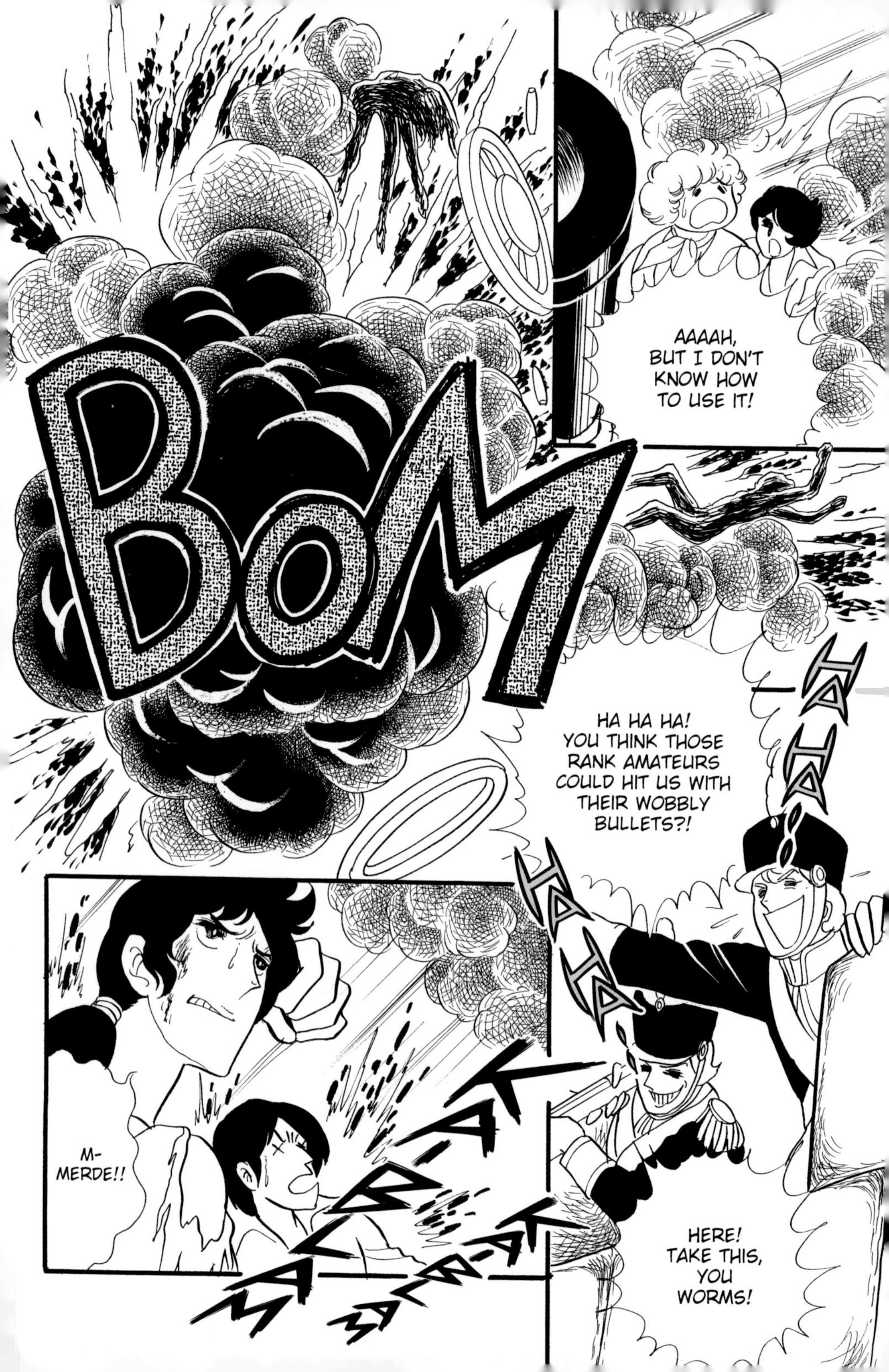
AAAAH, BUT I DON'T KNOW HOW TO USE IT!
BOM
HA HA HA! YOU THINK THOSE RANK AMATEURS COULD HIT US WITH THEIR WOBBLY BULLETS?!
HERE! TAKE THIS, YOU WORMS!
M-MERDE!!

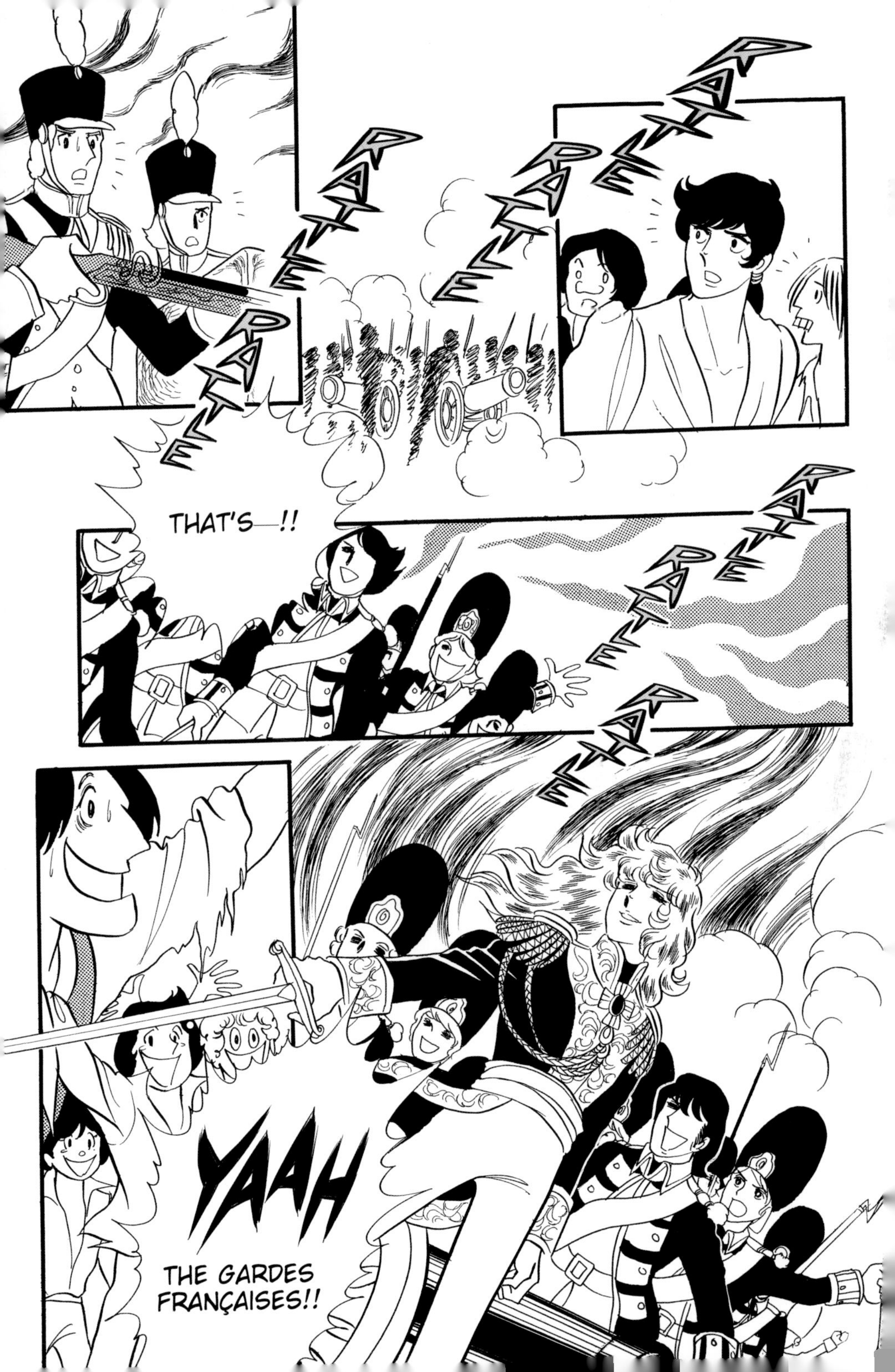
RATTLE
RATTLE
RATTLE
RATTLE
THAT'S—!!
RATTLE
RATTLE
RATTLE
YAAH
THE GARDES FRANÇAISES!!

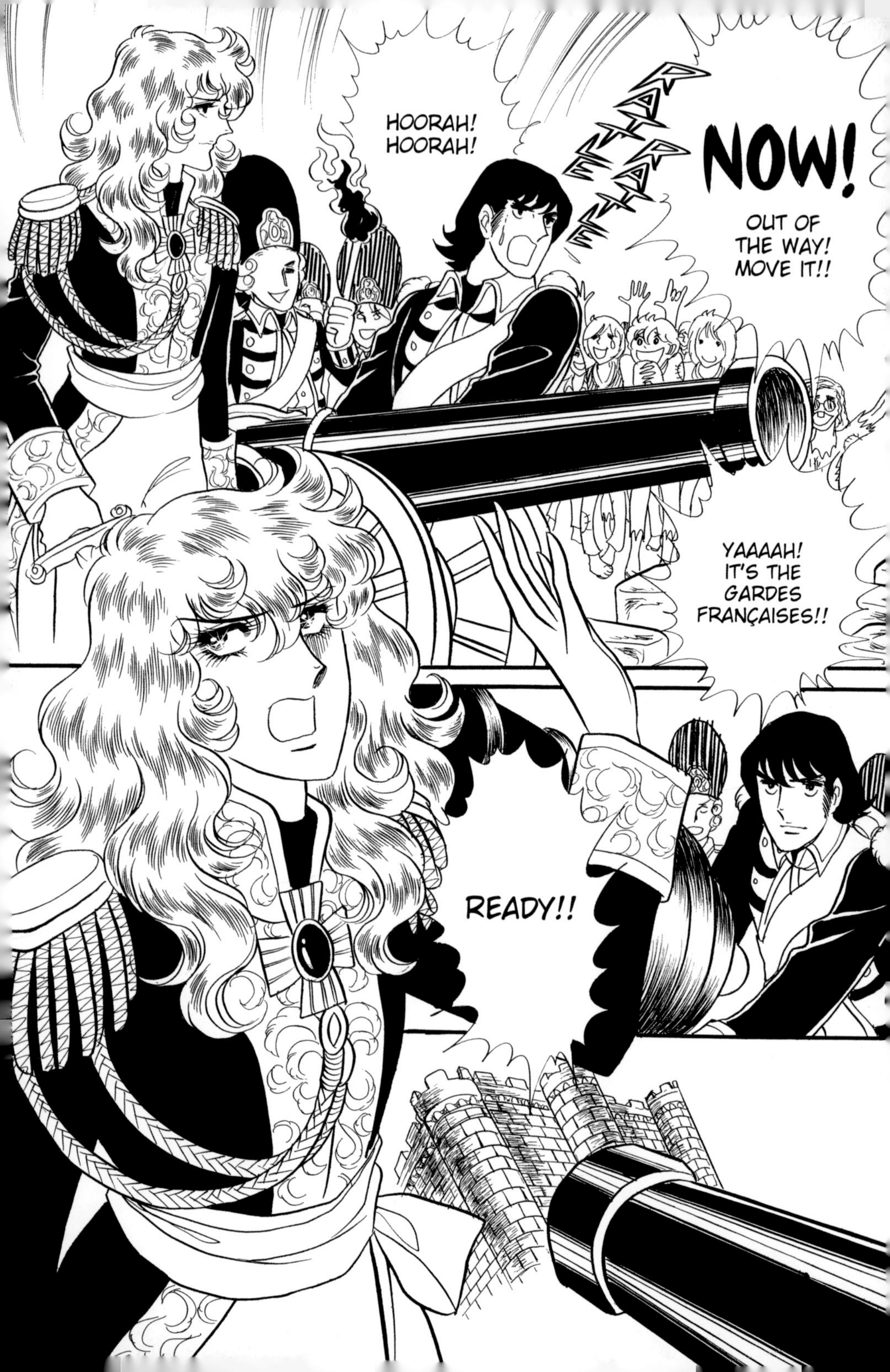
NOW!
OUT OF THE WAY! MOVE IT!!
RATTLE RATTLE
HOORAH! HOORAH!
YAAAAH! IT'S THE GARDES FRANÇAISES!!
READY!!

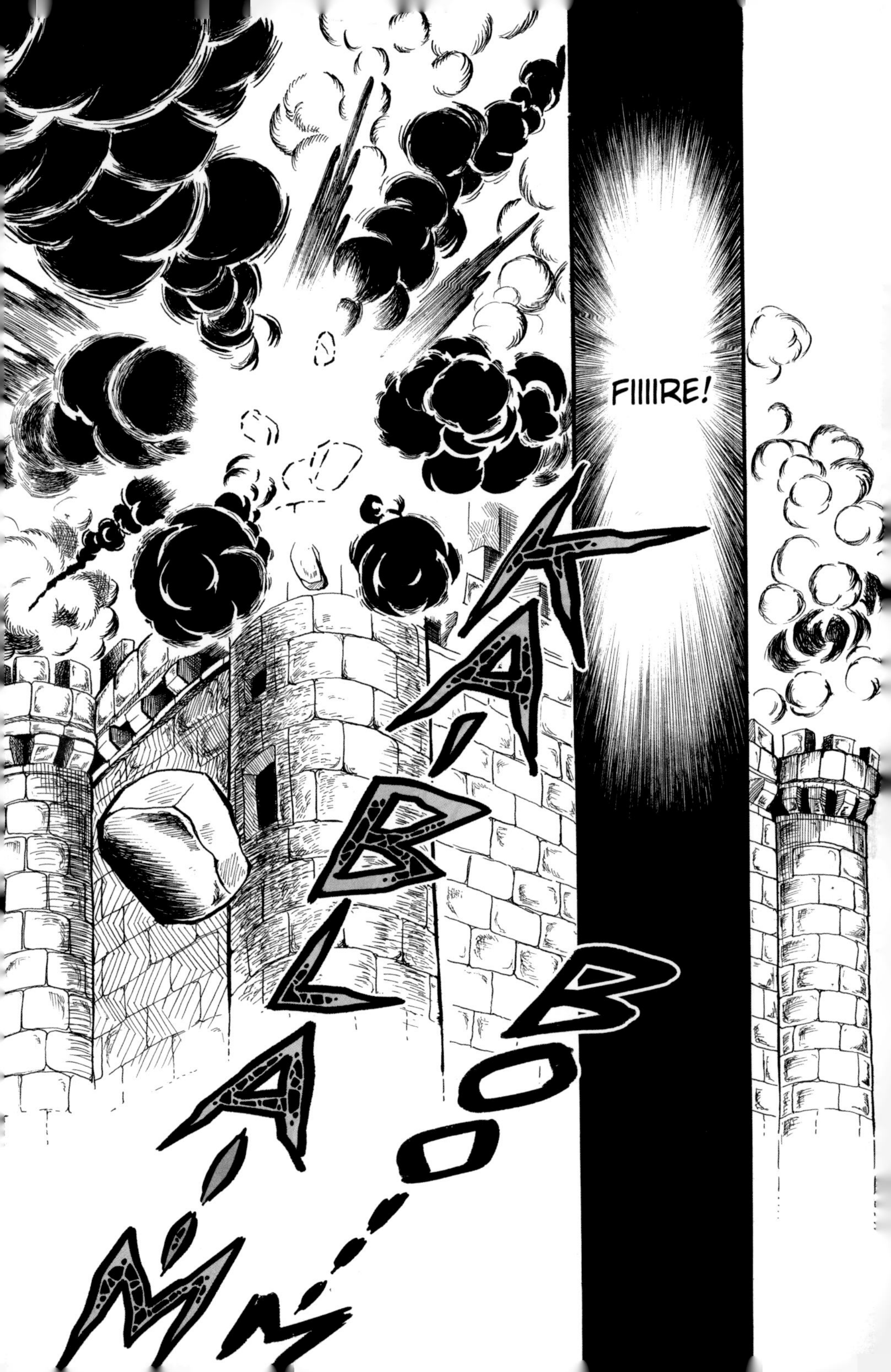
FIIIIRE!
KABLAM
BOOM

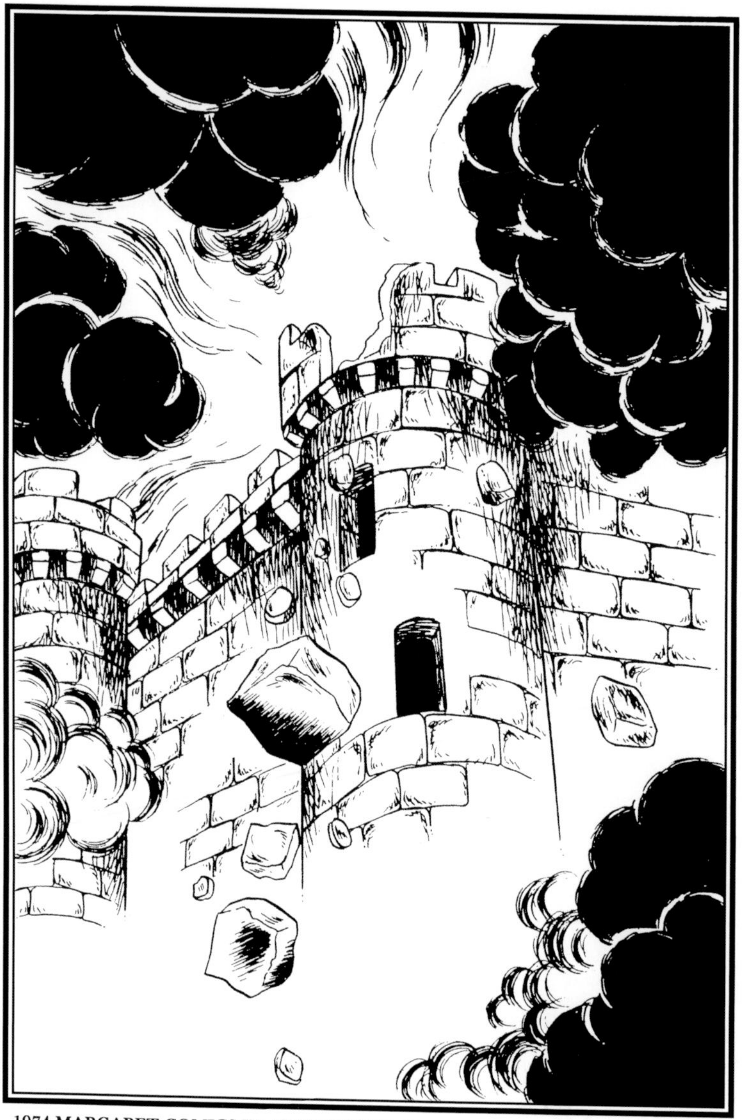

1974 MARGARET COMICS TRADE PAPERBACK
VOLUME 8 INSERT ART

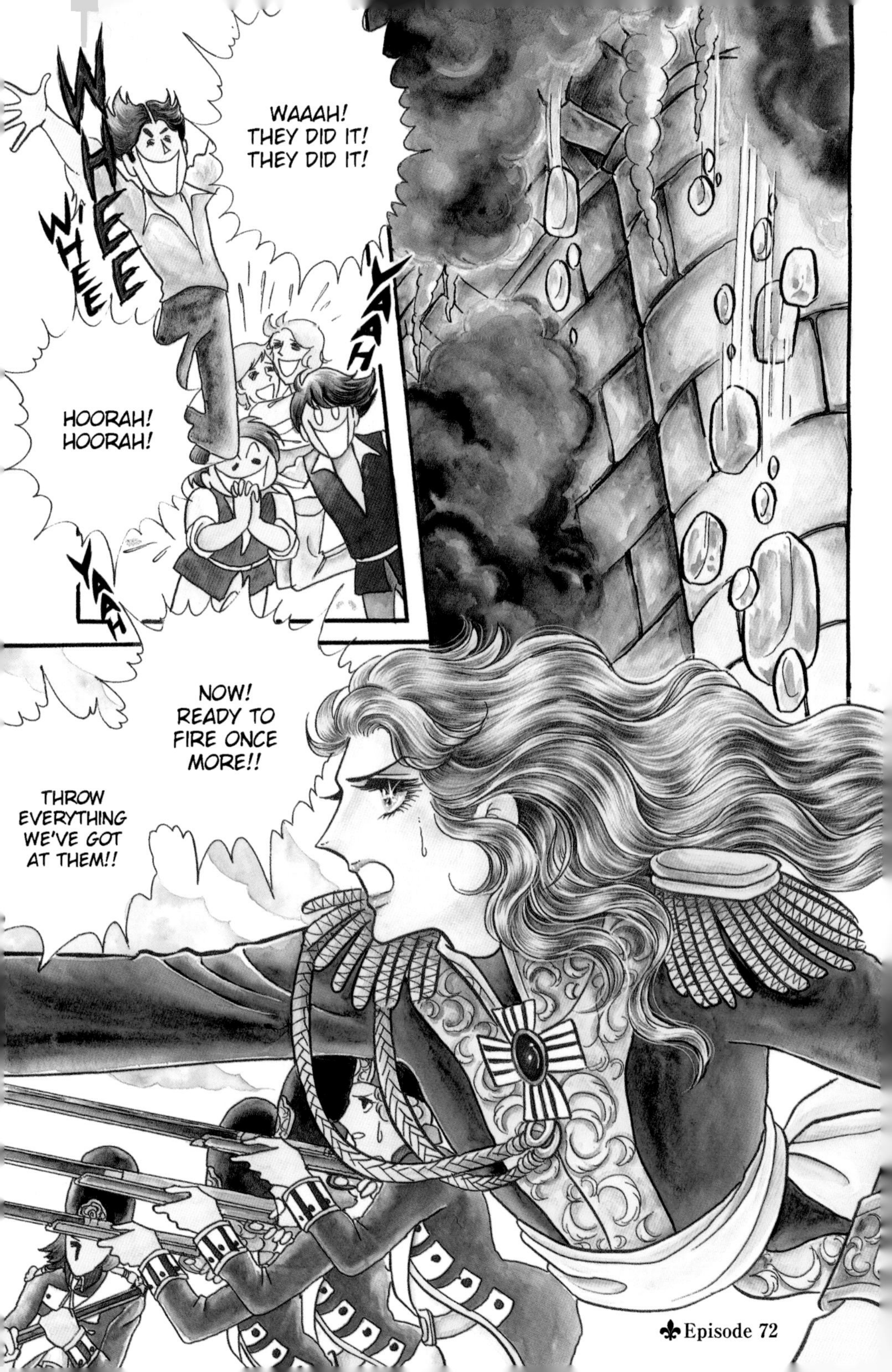
YAAAH
WAAAH! THEY DID IT! THEY DID IT!
WHEEE
WHEE
HOORAH! HOORAH!
YAAAH
NOW! READY TO FIRE ONCE MORE!!
THROW EVERYTHING WE'VE GOT AT THEM!!

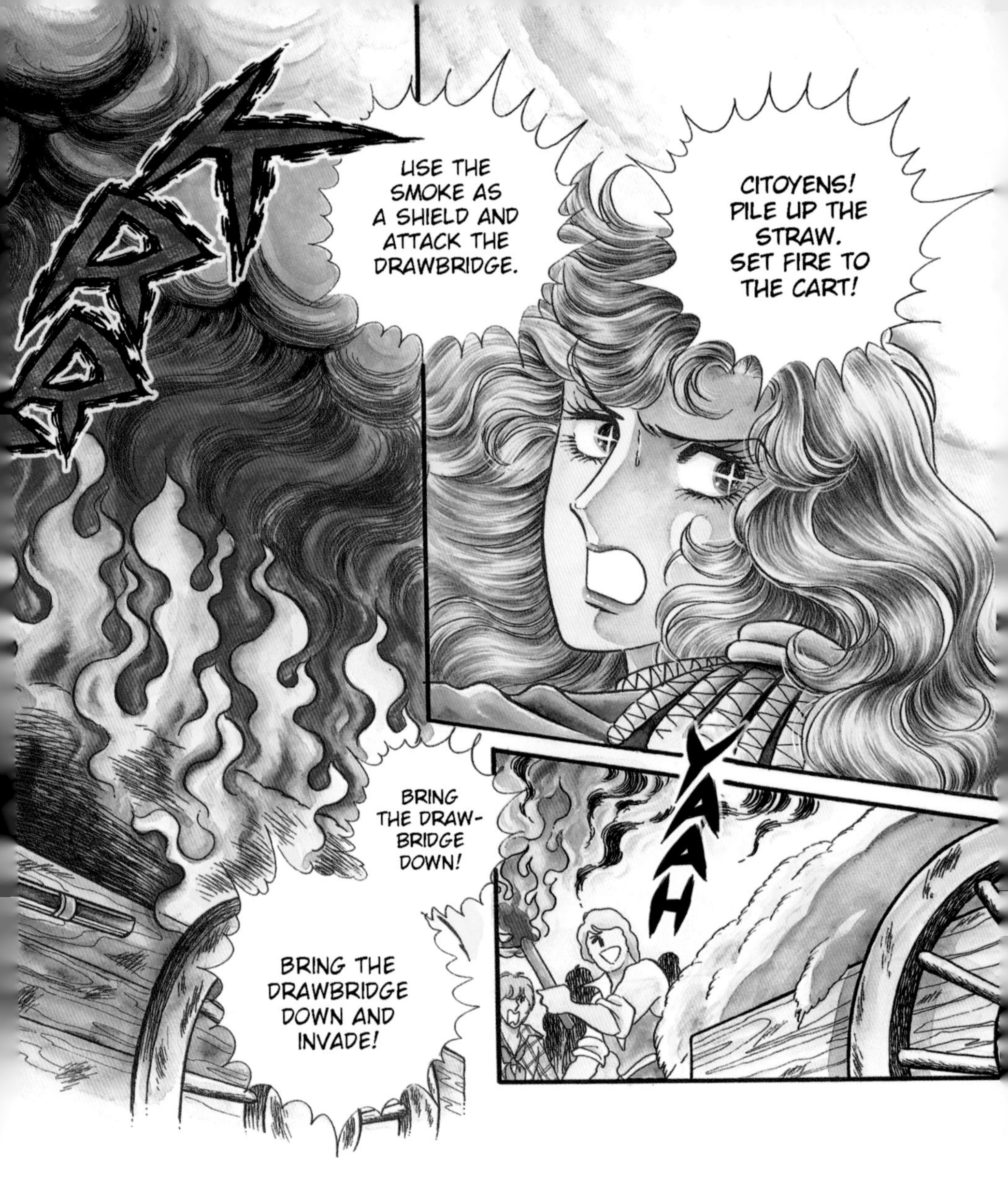
CITOYENS! PILE UP THE STRAW. SET FIRE TO THE CART!
USE THE SMOKE AS A SHIELD AND ATTACK THE DRAWBRIDGE.
YAAH
BRING THE DRAW-BRIDGE DOWN!
BRING THE DRAWBRIDGE DOWN AND INVADE!

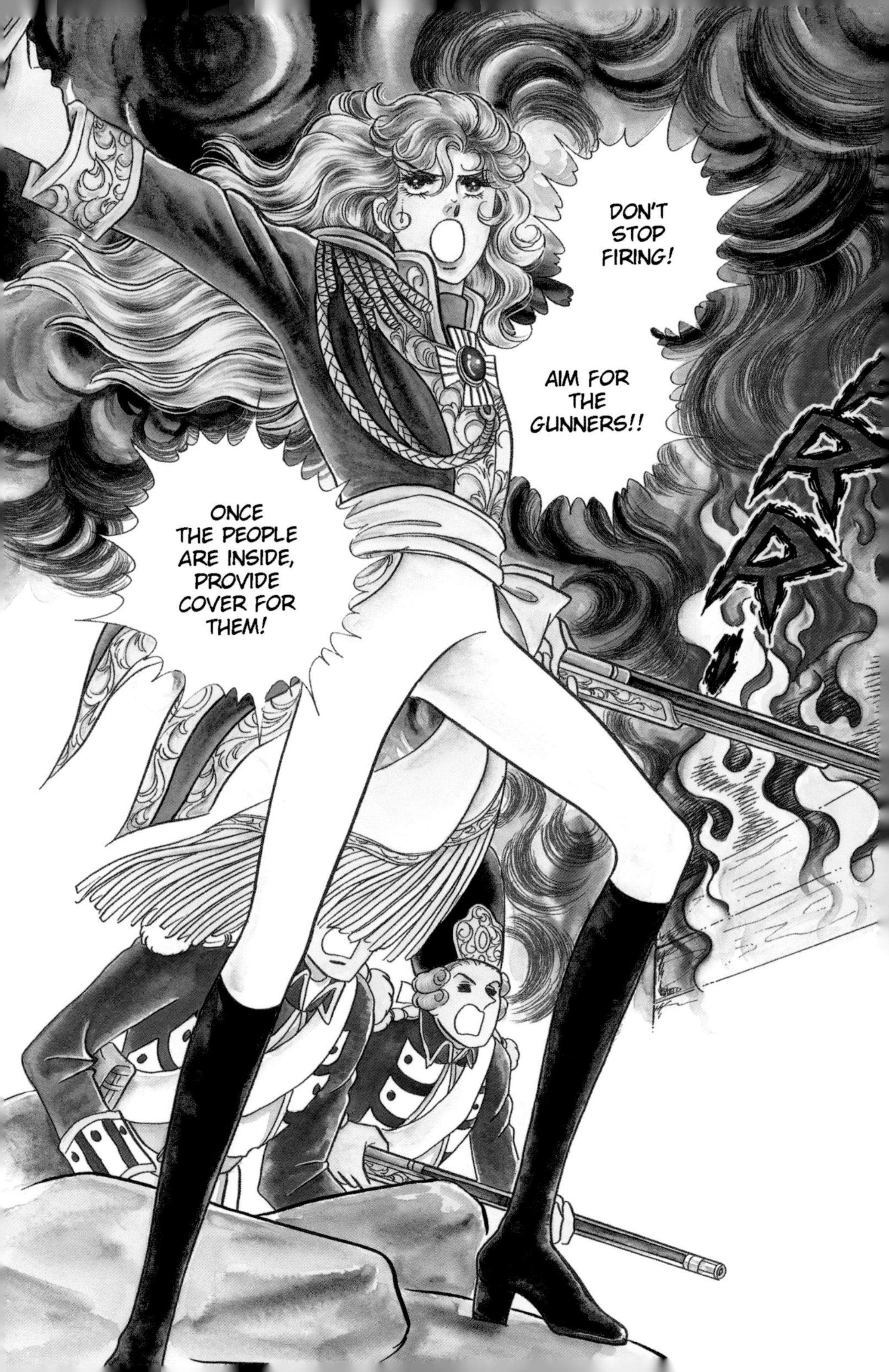
DON'T STOP FIRING!
AIM FOR THE GUNNERS!!
ONCE THE PEOPLE ARE INSIDE, PROVIDE COVER FOR THEM!

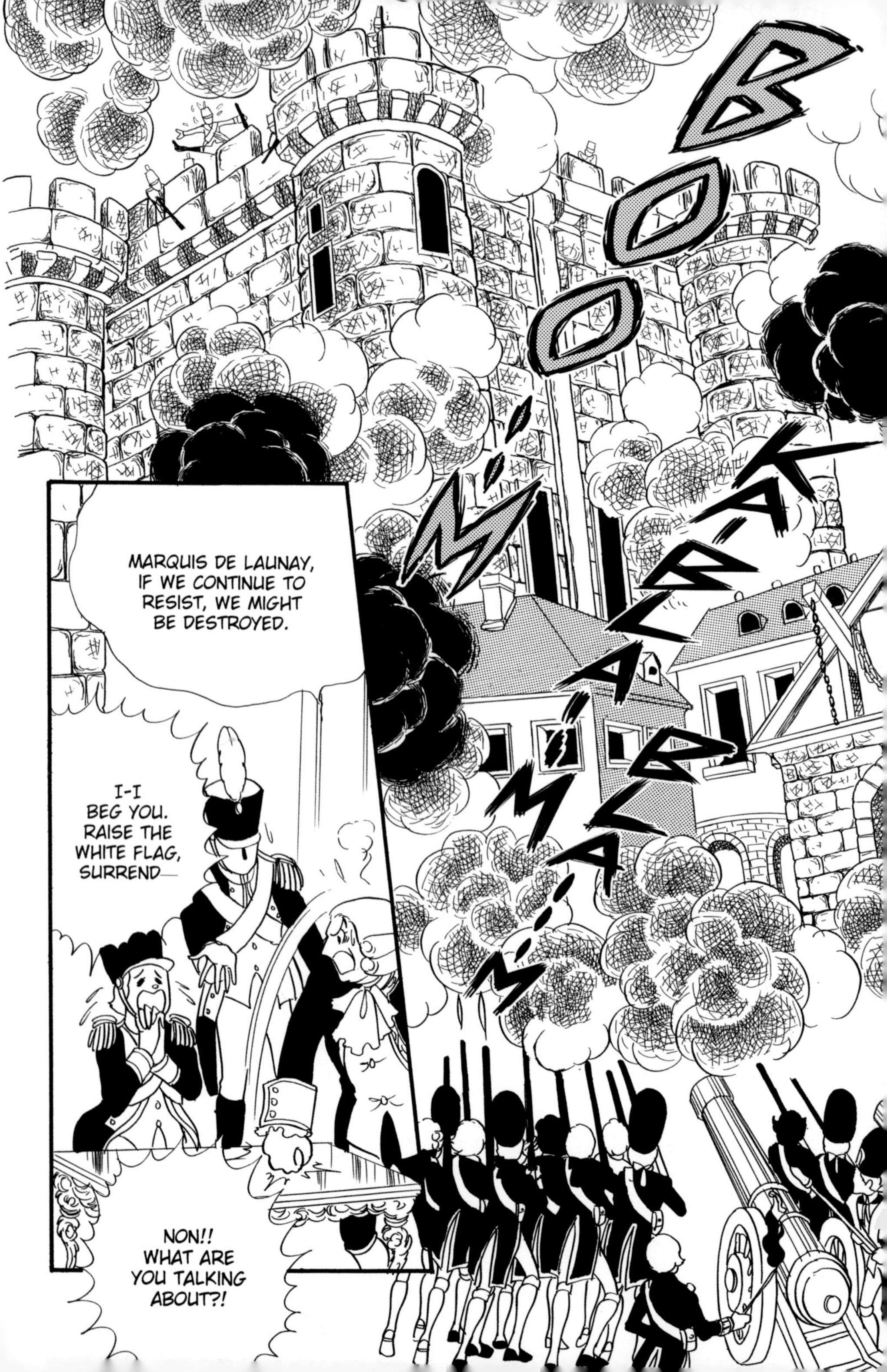
BOOM!!
KABLAM!! BLAM!!
MARQUIS DE LAUNAY, IF WE CONTINUE TO RESIST, WE MIGHT BE DESTROYED.
I-I BEG YOU. RAISE THE WHITE FLAG, SURREND—
NON!! WHAT ARE YOU TALKING ABOUT?!

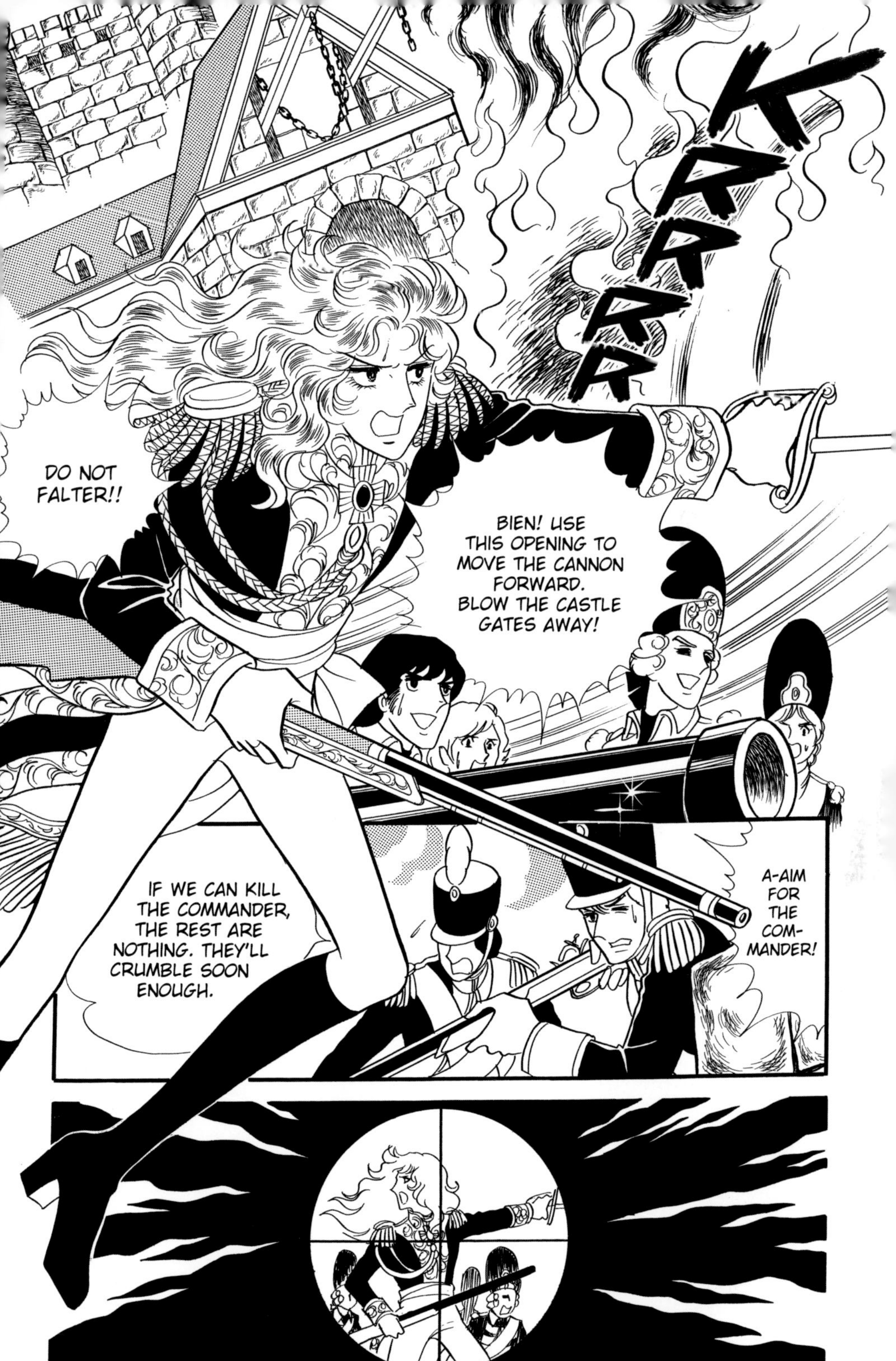
KRRRRR
BIEN! USE THIS OPENING TO MOVE THE CANNON FORWARD. BLOW THE CASTLE GATES AWAY!
DO NOT FALTER!!
A-AIM FOR THE COM-MANDER!
IF WE CAN KILL THE COMMANDER, THE REST ARE NOTHING. THEY'LL CRUMBLE SOON ENOUGH.

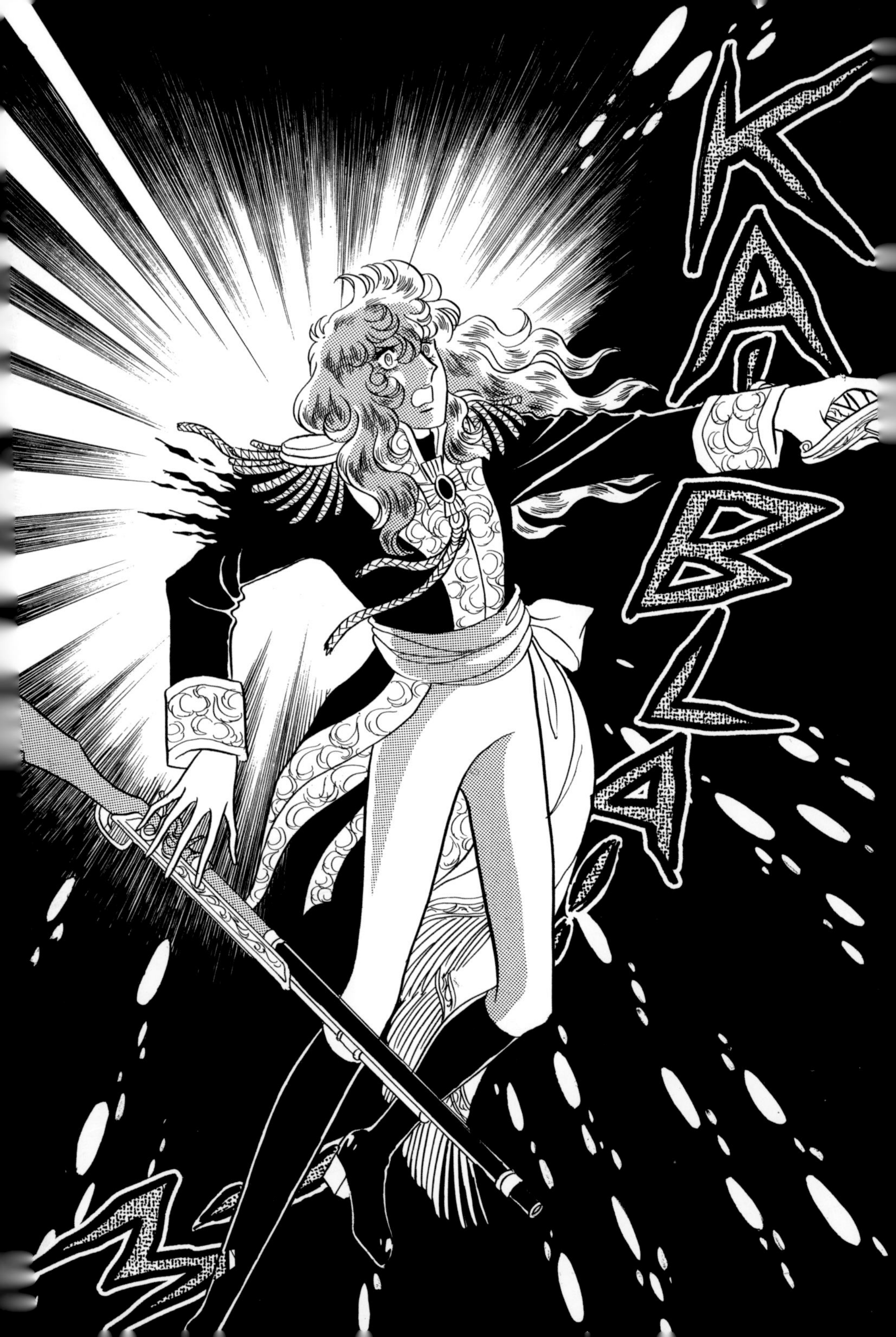
KABLAM

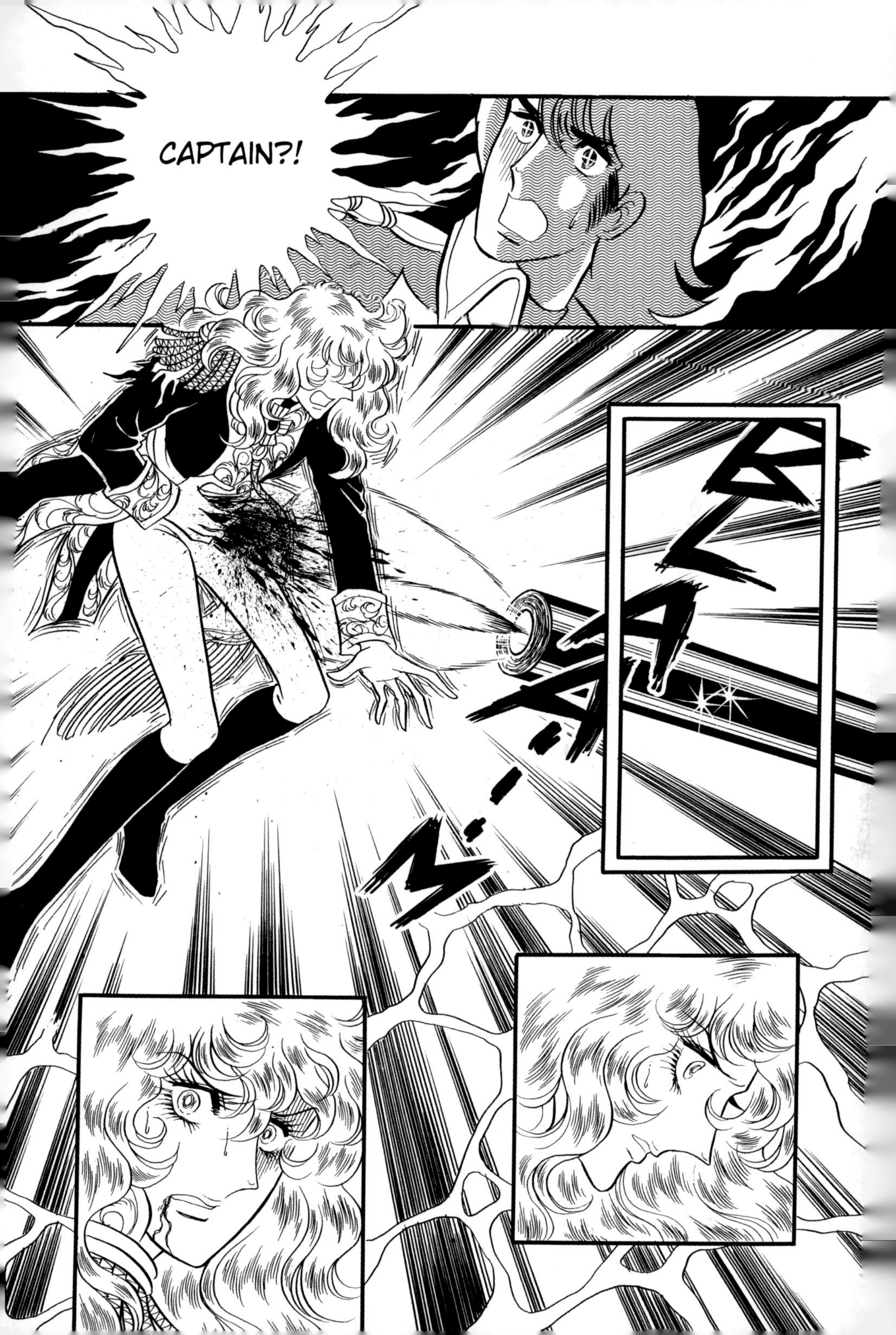
CAPTAIN?!
BLAAM

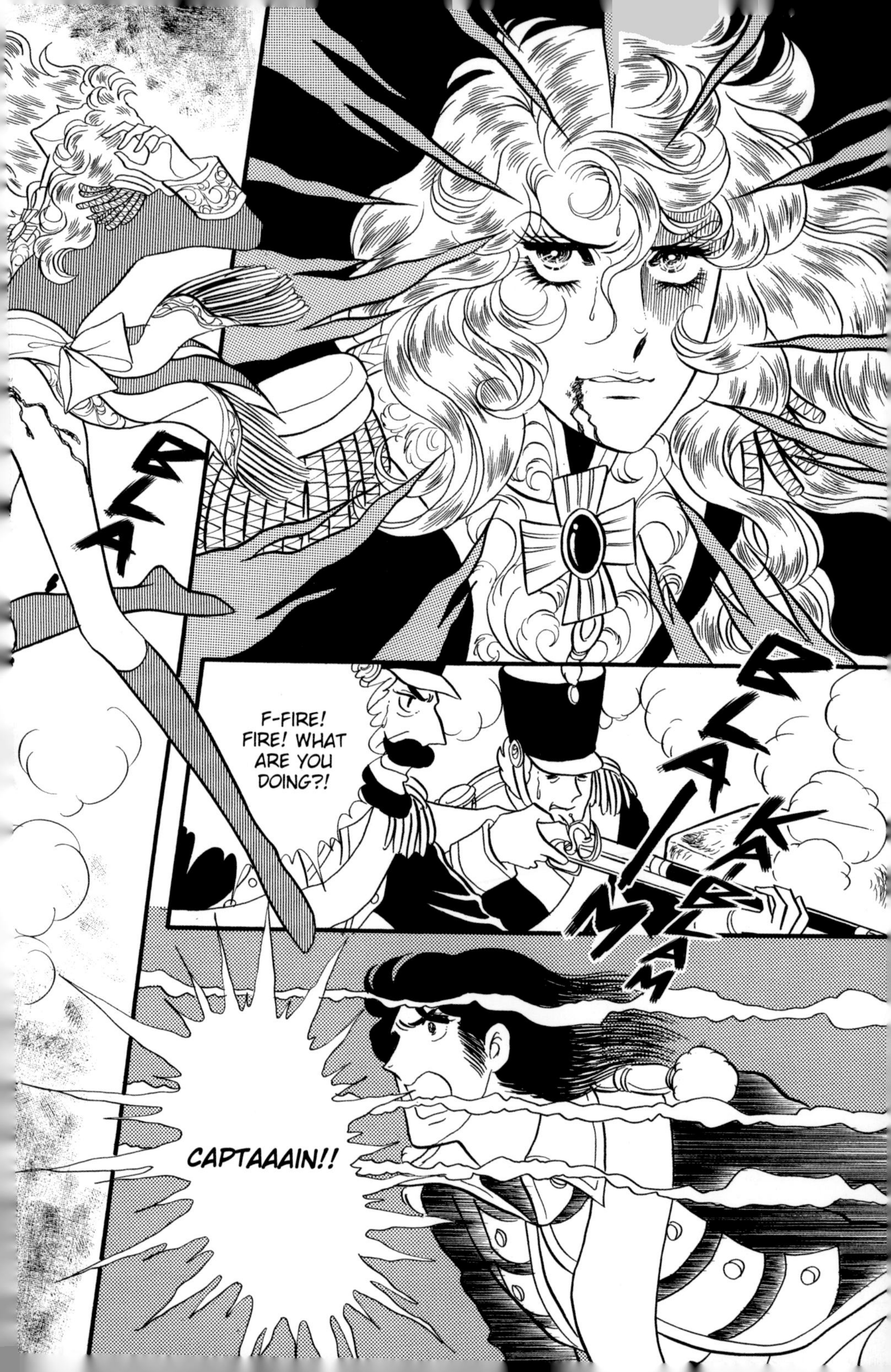
BLAM
KABLAM
F-FIRE! FIRE! WHAT ARE YOU DOING?!
CAPTAAAIN!!
BLA

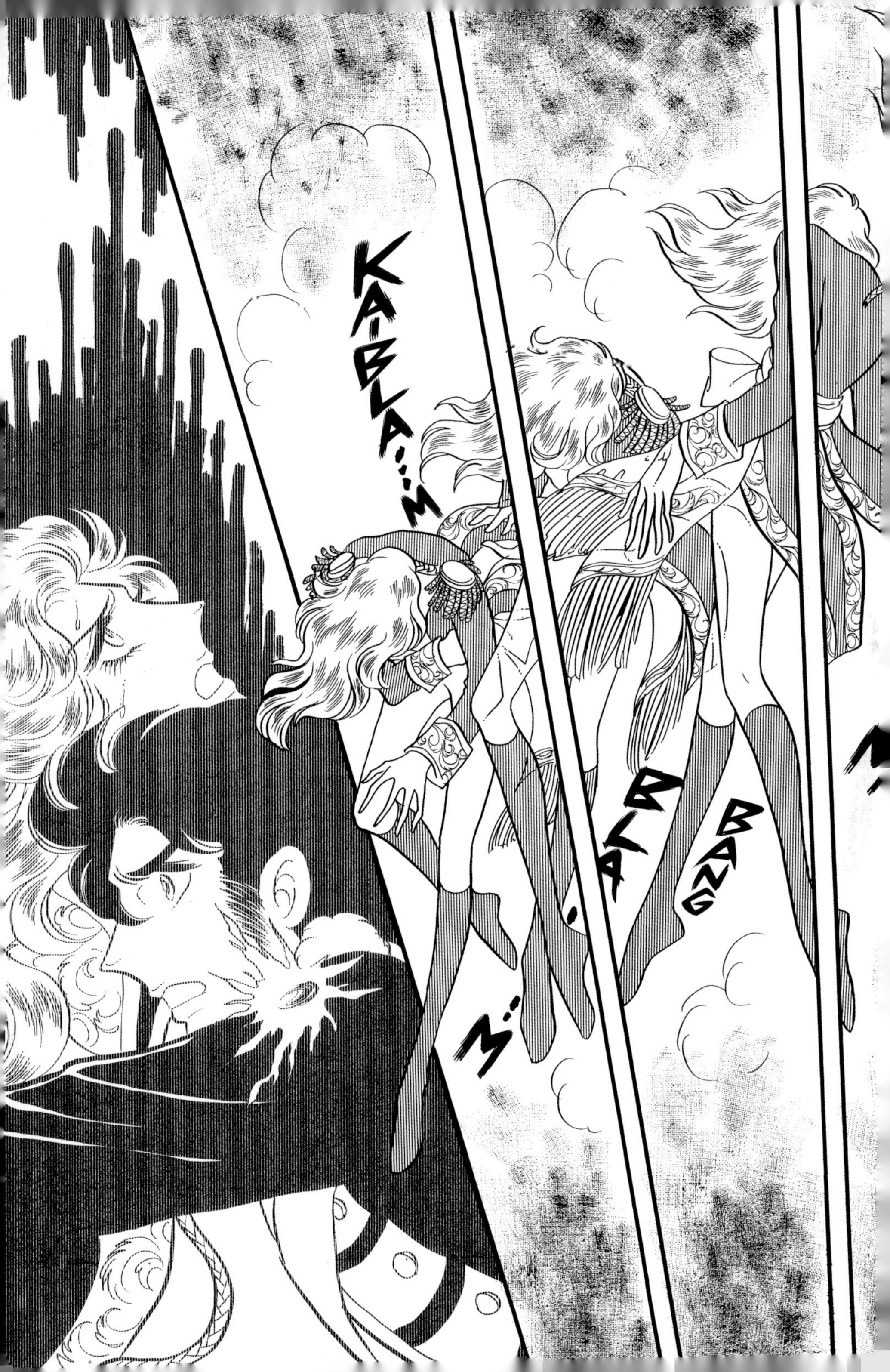
BANG
BLA...
M...
KA-BLA...M

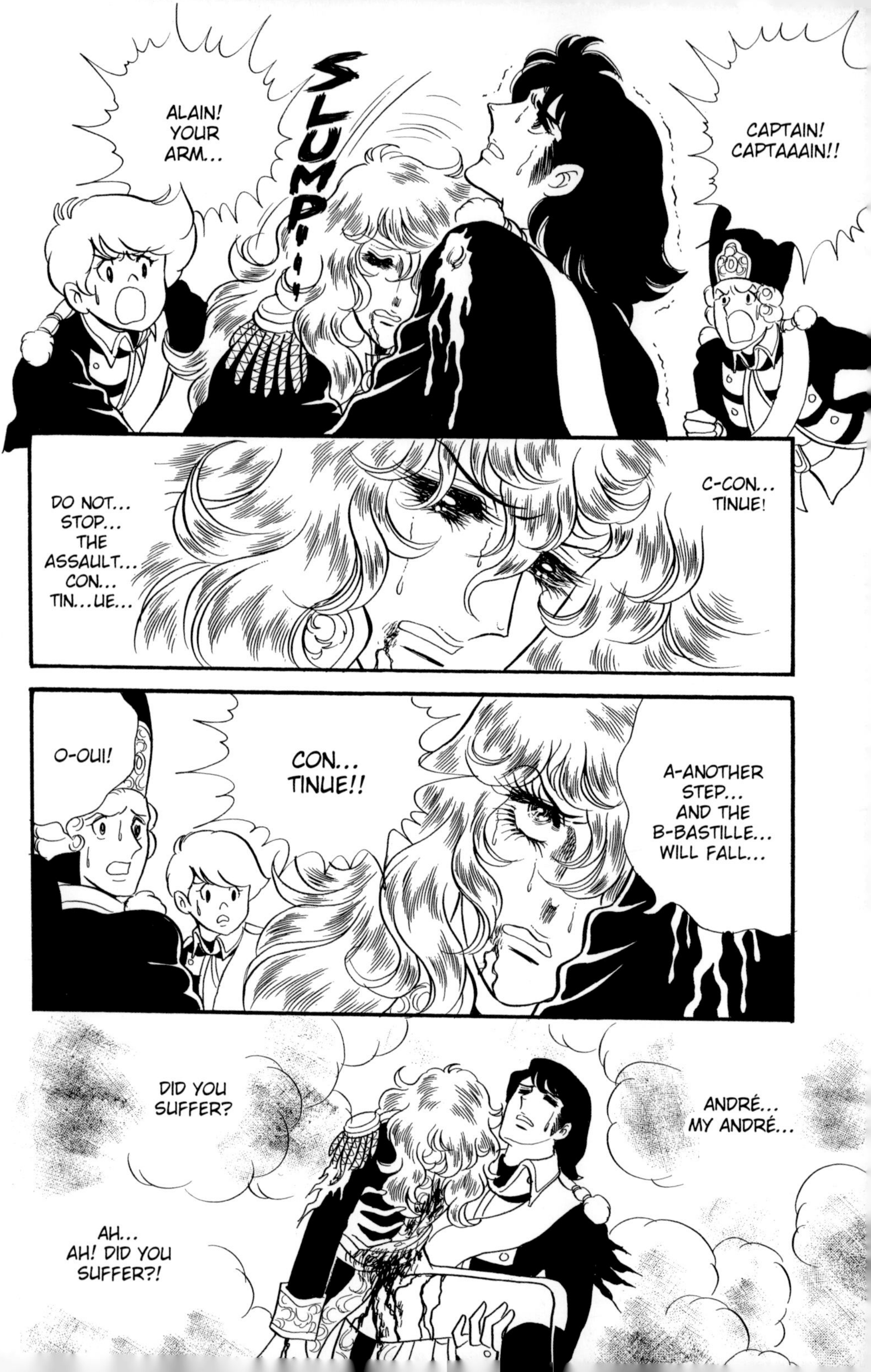

CAPTAIN! CAPTAAAIN!!
SLUMP!!!
ALAIN! YOUR ARM...
C-CON... TINUE!
DO NOT... STOP... THE ASSAULT... CON... TIN...UE...
A-ANOTHER STEP... AND THE B-BASTILLE... WILL FALL...
CON... TINUE!!
O-OUI!
ANDRÉ... MY ANDRÉ...
DID YOU SUFFER?
AH... AH! DID YOU SUFFER?!

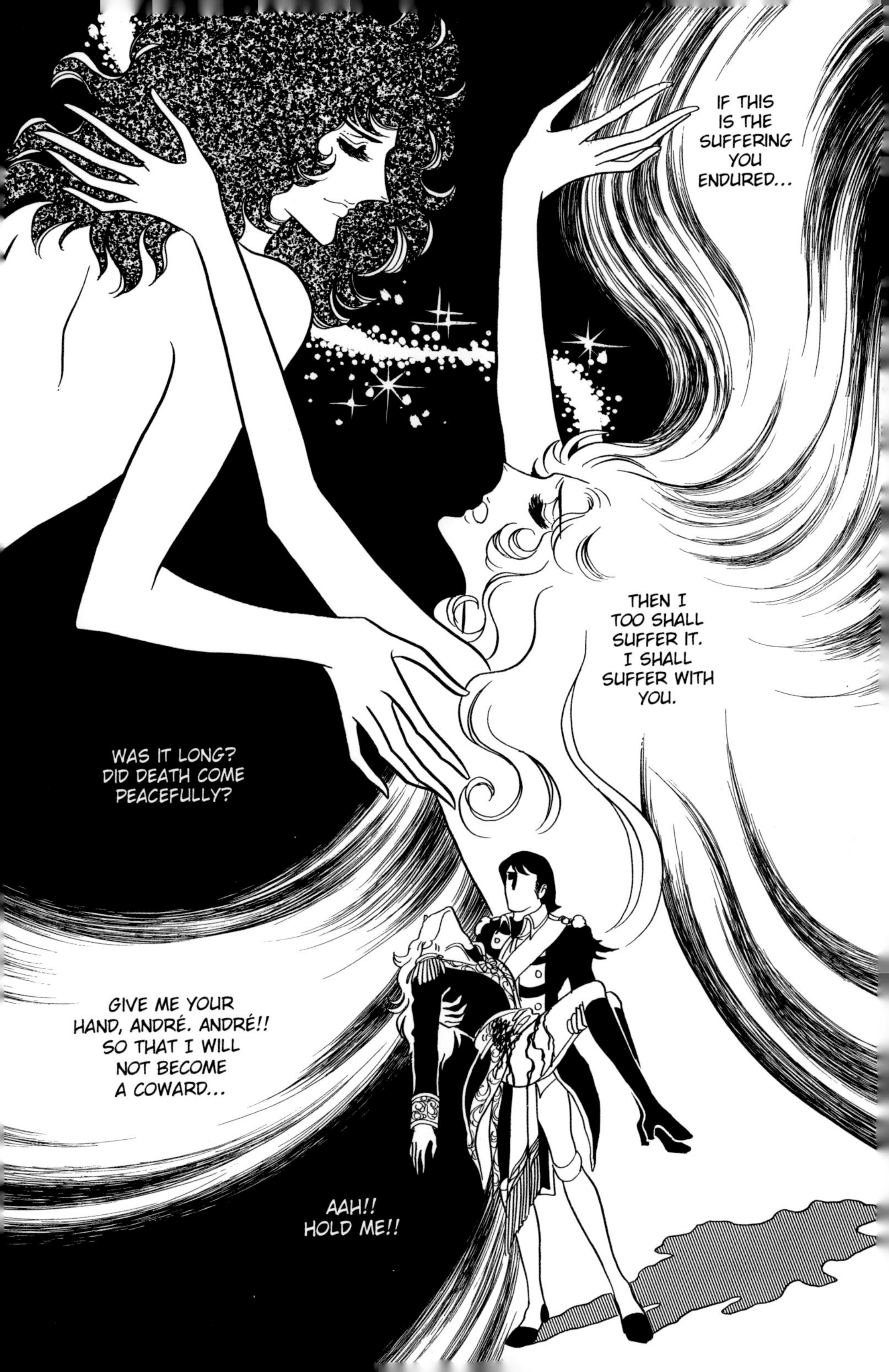
IF THIS IS THE SUFFERING YOU ENDURED...
THEN I TOO SHALL SUFFER IT. I SHALL SUFFER WITH YOU.
WAS IT LONG? DID DEATH COME PEACEFULLY?
GIVE ME YOUR HAND, ANDRÉ. ANDRÉ!! SO THAT I WILL NOT BECOME A COWARD...
AAH!! HOLD ME!!

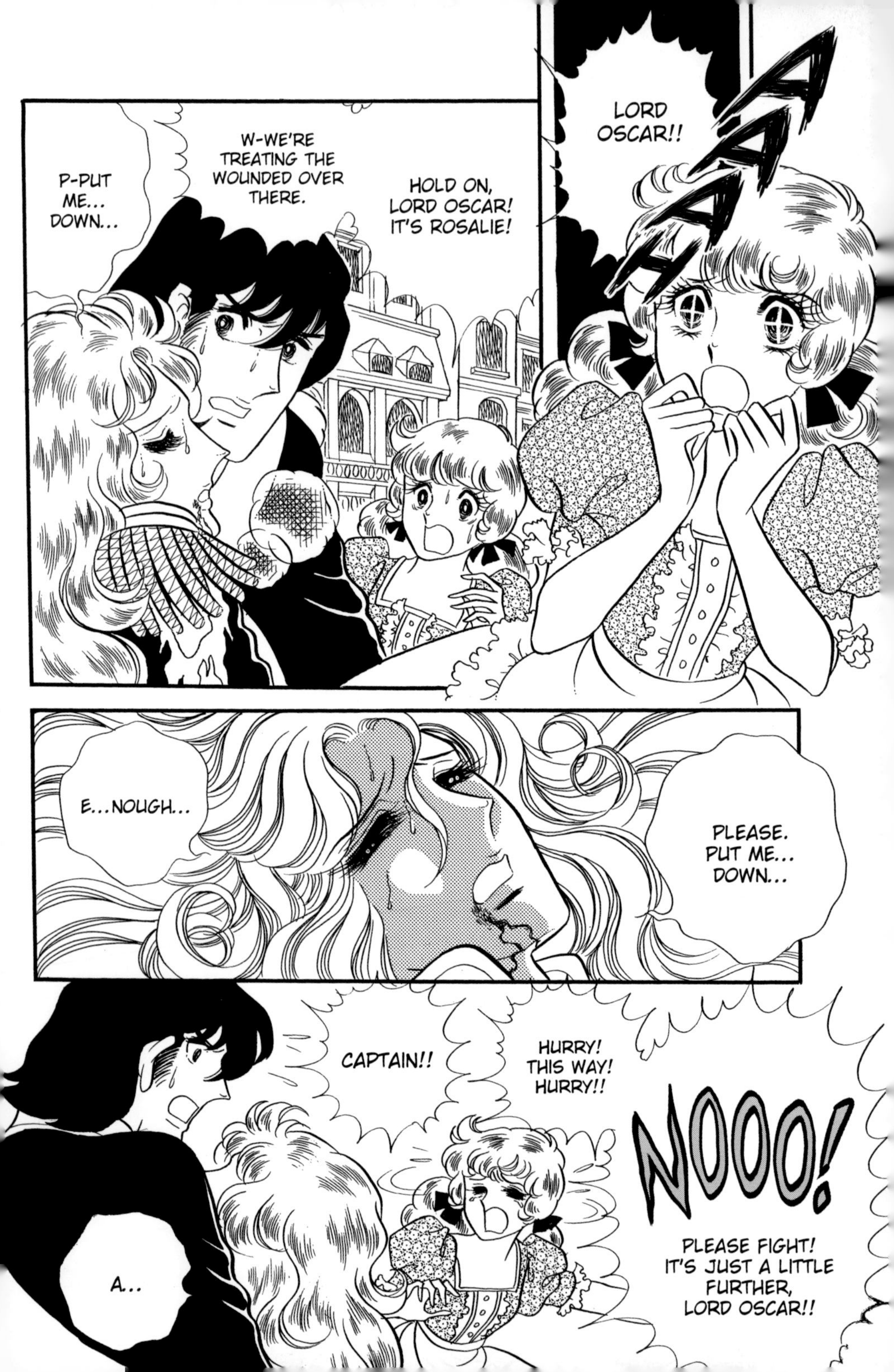
LORD OSCAR!!
HOLD ON, LORD OSCAR! IT'S ROSALIE!
W-WE'RE TREATING THE WOUNDED OVER THERE.
P-PUT ME... DOWN...
PLEASE. PUT ME... DOWN...
E...NOUGH...
NOOO!
PLEASE FIGHT! IT'S JUST A LITTLE FURTHER, LORD OSCAR!!
HURRY! THIS WAY! HURRY!!
CAPTAIN!!
A...

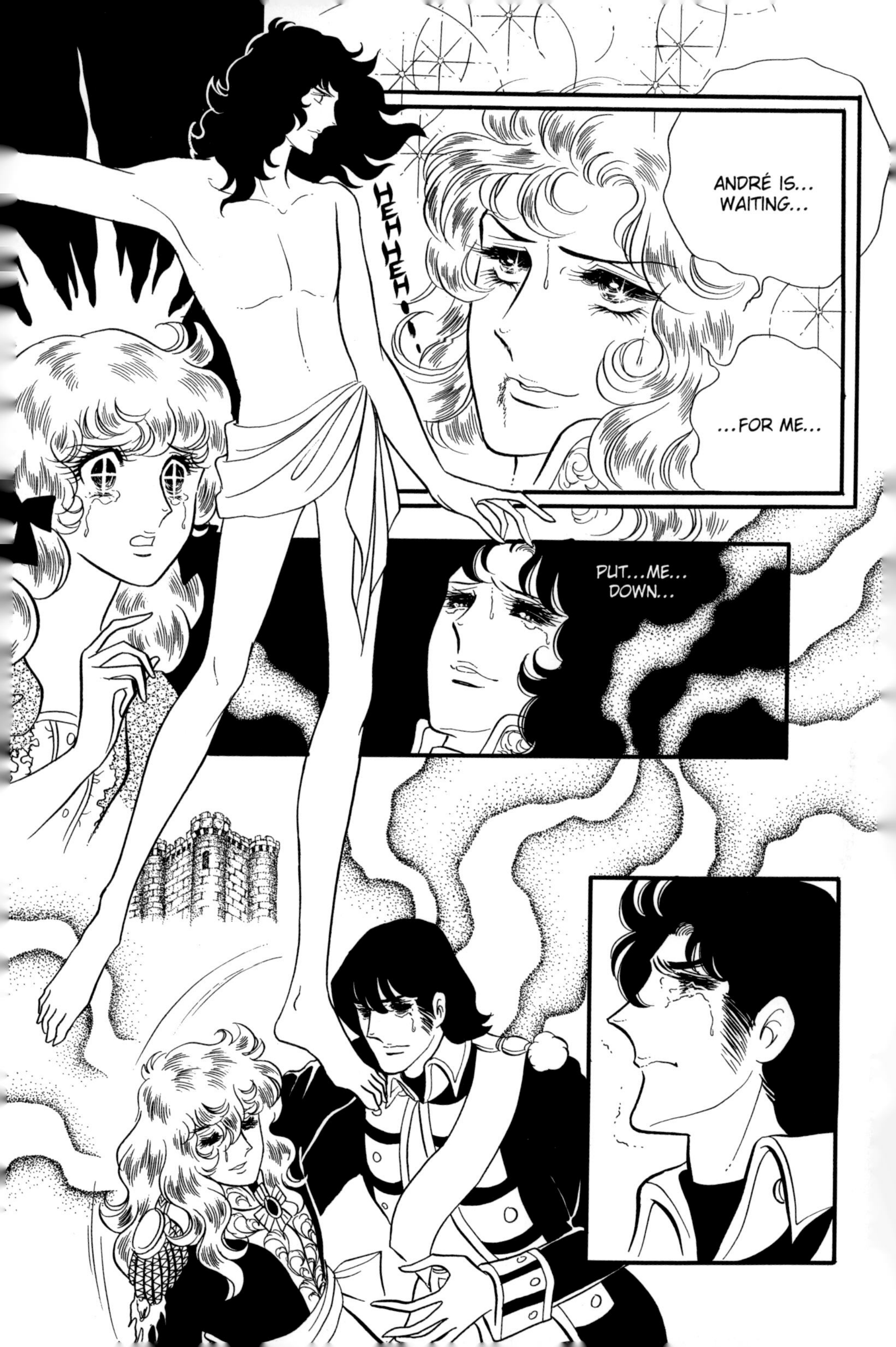
ANDRÉ IS... WAITING...
...FOR ME...
HEH HEH...
PUT...ME... DOWN...

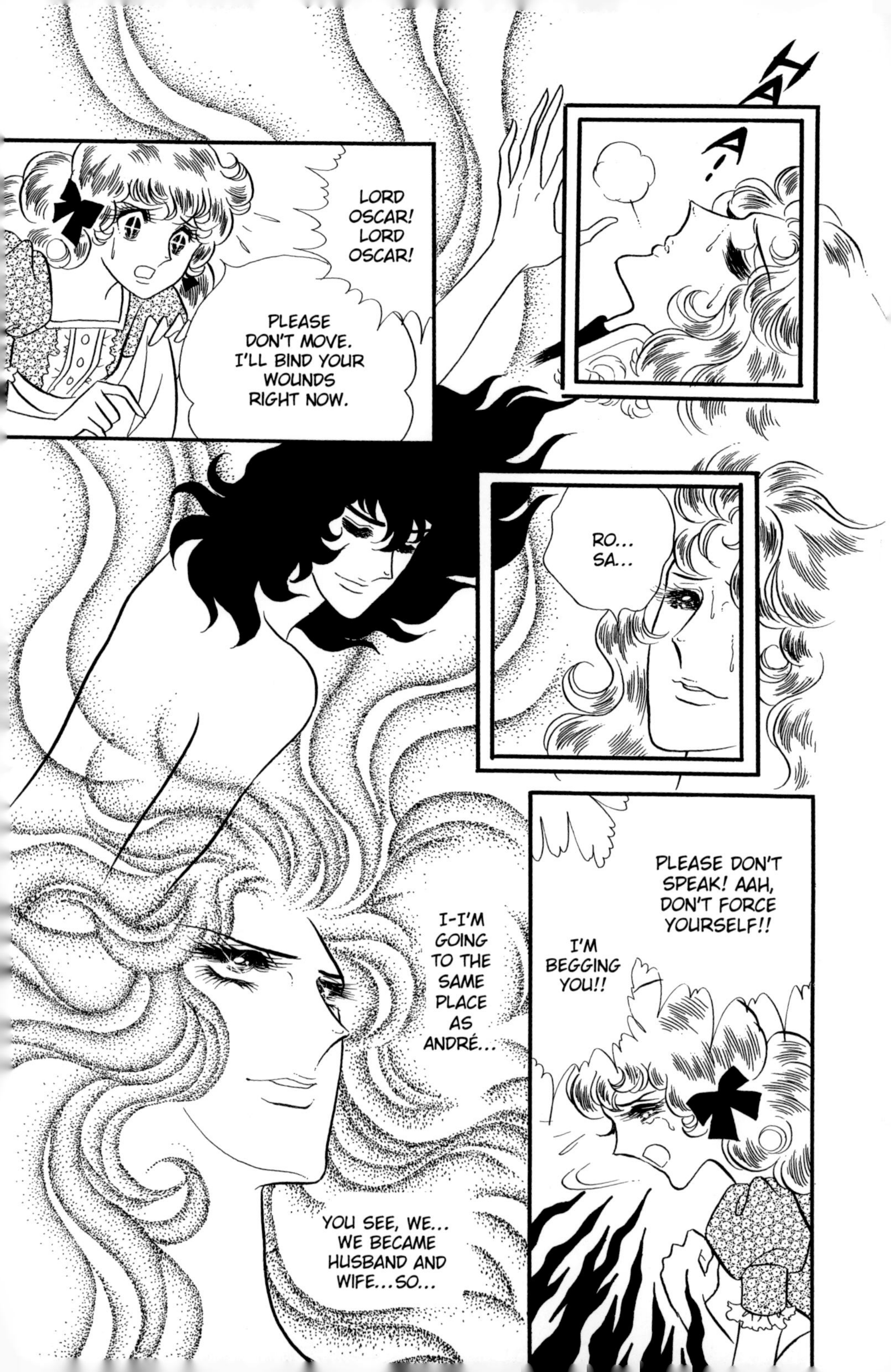
HA
A
LORD OSCAR! LORD OSCAR!
PLEASE DON'T MOVE. I'LL BIND YOUR WOUNDS RIGHT NOW.
RO... SA...
PLEASE DON'T SPEAK! AAH, DON'T FORCE YOURSELF!!
I'M BEGGING YOU!!
I-I'M GOING TO THE SAME PLACE AS ANDRÉ...
YOU SEE, WE... WE BECAME HUSBAND AND WIFE...SO...

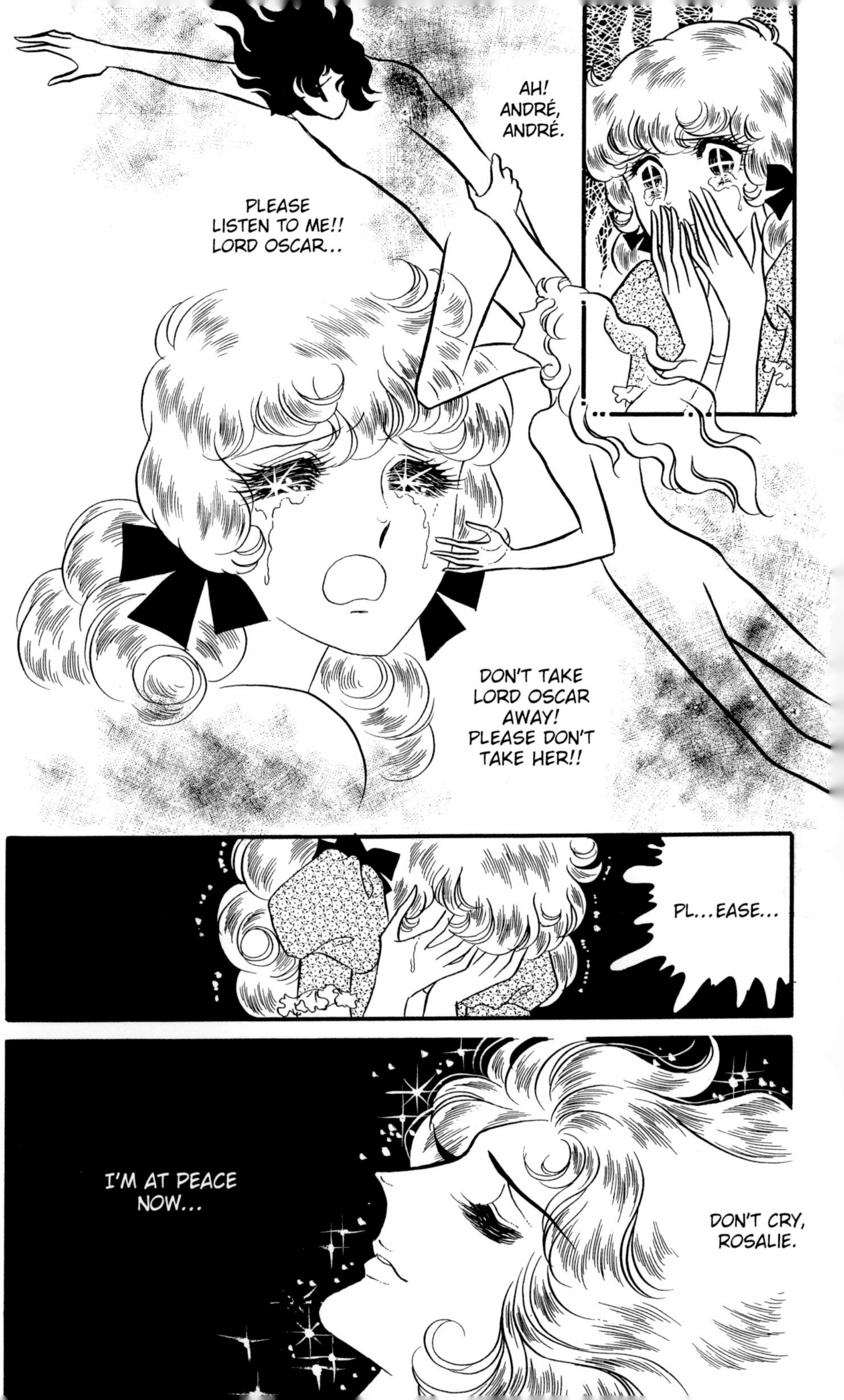
AH! ANDRÉ, ANDRÉ.
PLEASE LISTEN TO ME!! LORD OSCAR...
DON'T TAKE LORD OSCAR AWAY! PLEASE DON'T TAKE HER!!
PL...EASE...
DON'T CRY, ROSALIE.
I'M AT PEACE NOW...

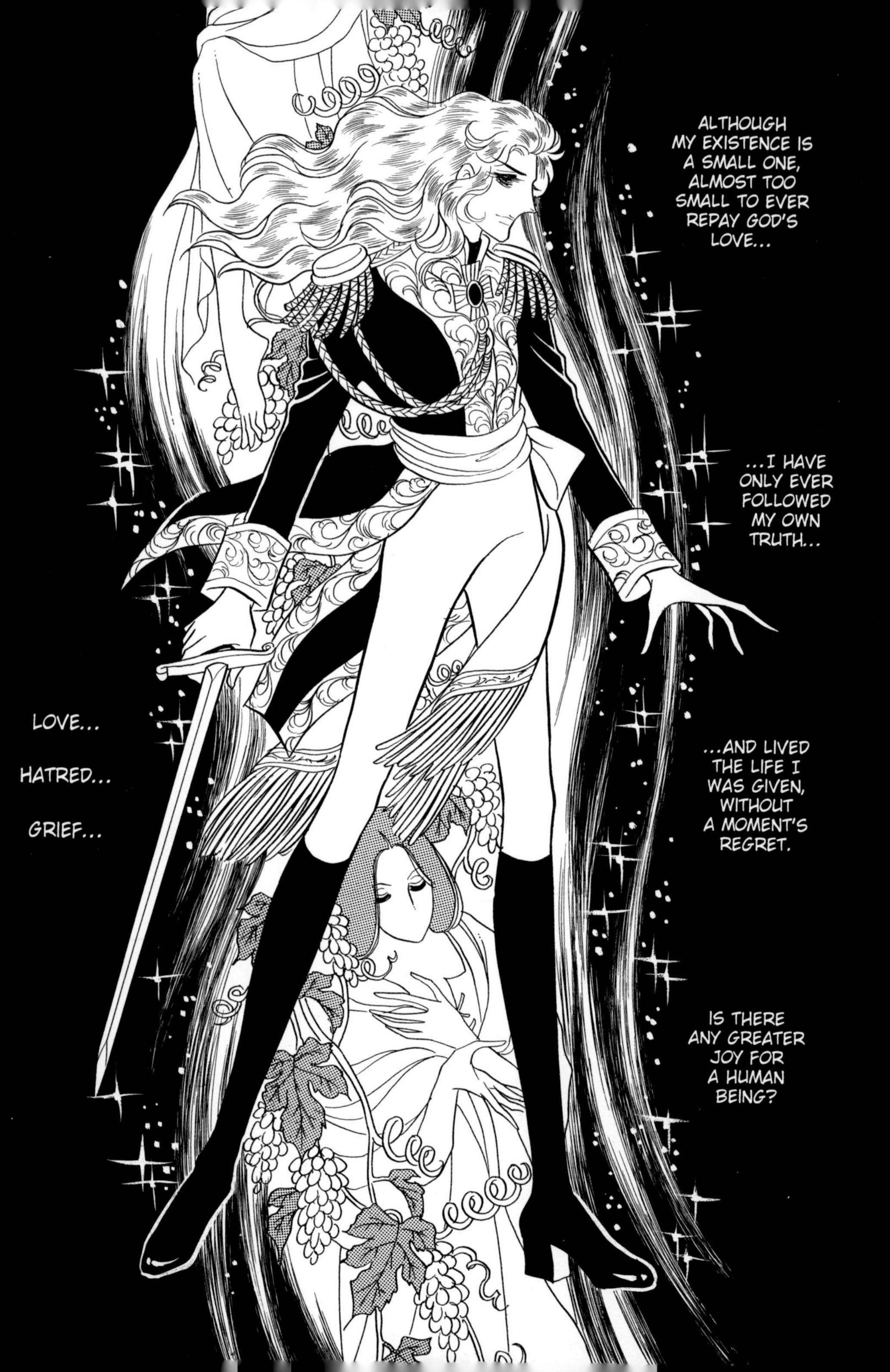
ALTHOUGH MY EXISTENCE IS A SMALL ONE, ALMOST TOO SMALL TO EVER REPAY GOD'S LOVE...
...I HAVE ONLY EVER FOLLOWED MY OWN TRUTH...
...AND LIVED THE LIFE I WAS GIVEN, WITHOUT A MOMENT'S REGRET.
IS THERE ANY GREATER JOY FOR A HUMAN BEING?
LOVE...
HATRED...
GRIEF...

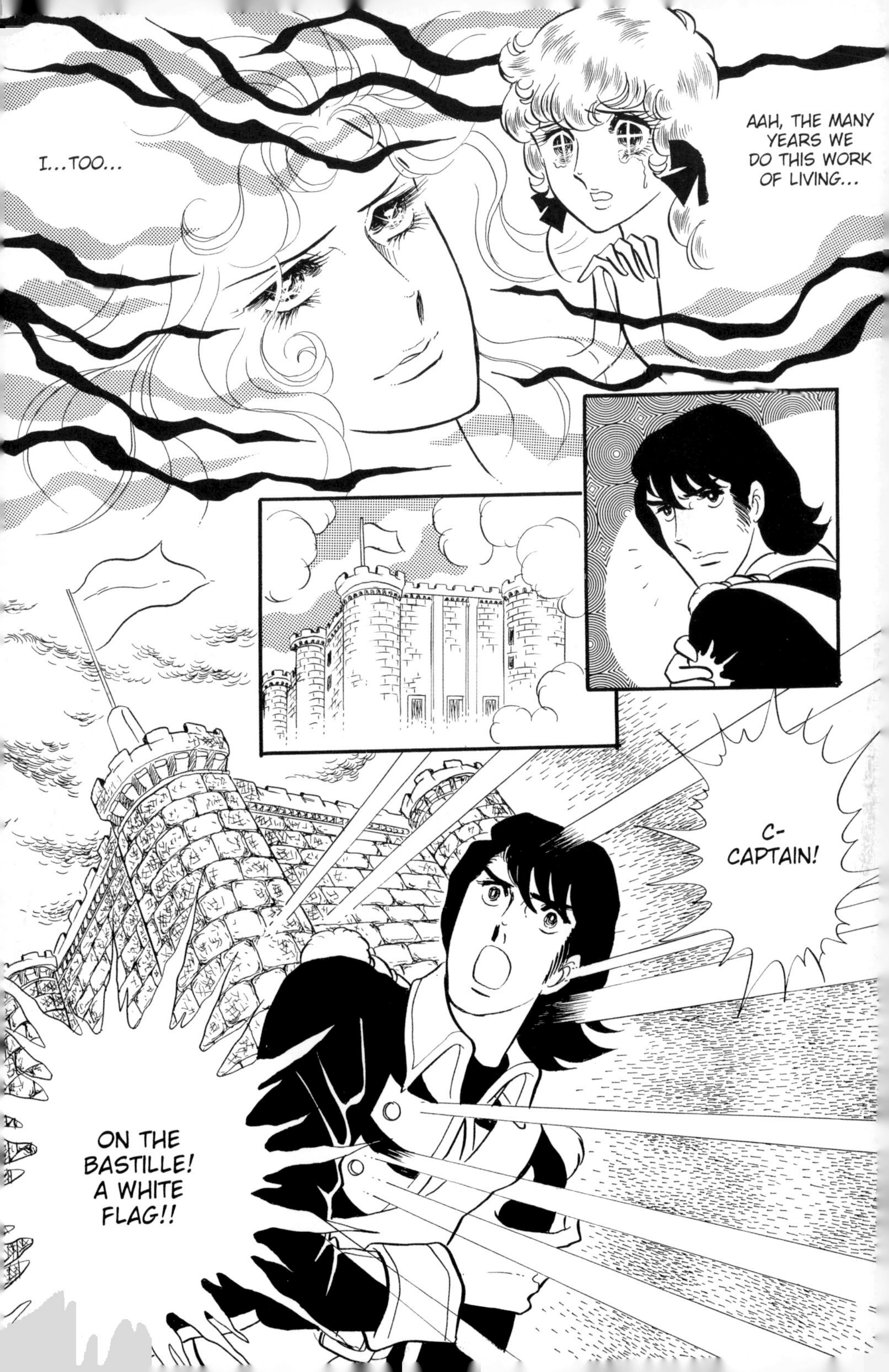
AAH, THE MANY YEARS WE DO THIS WORK OF LIVING...
I...TOO...
C-CAPTAIN!
ON THE BASTILLE! A WHITE FLAG!!

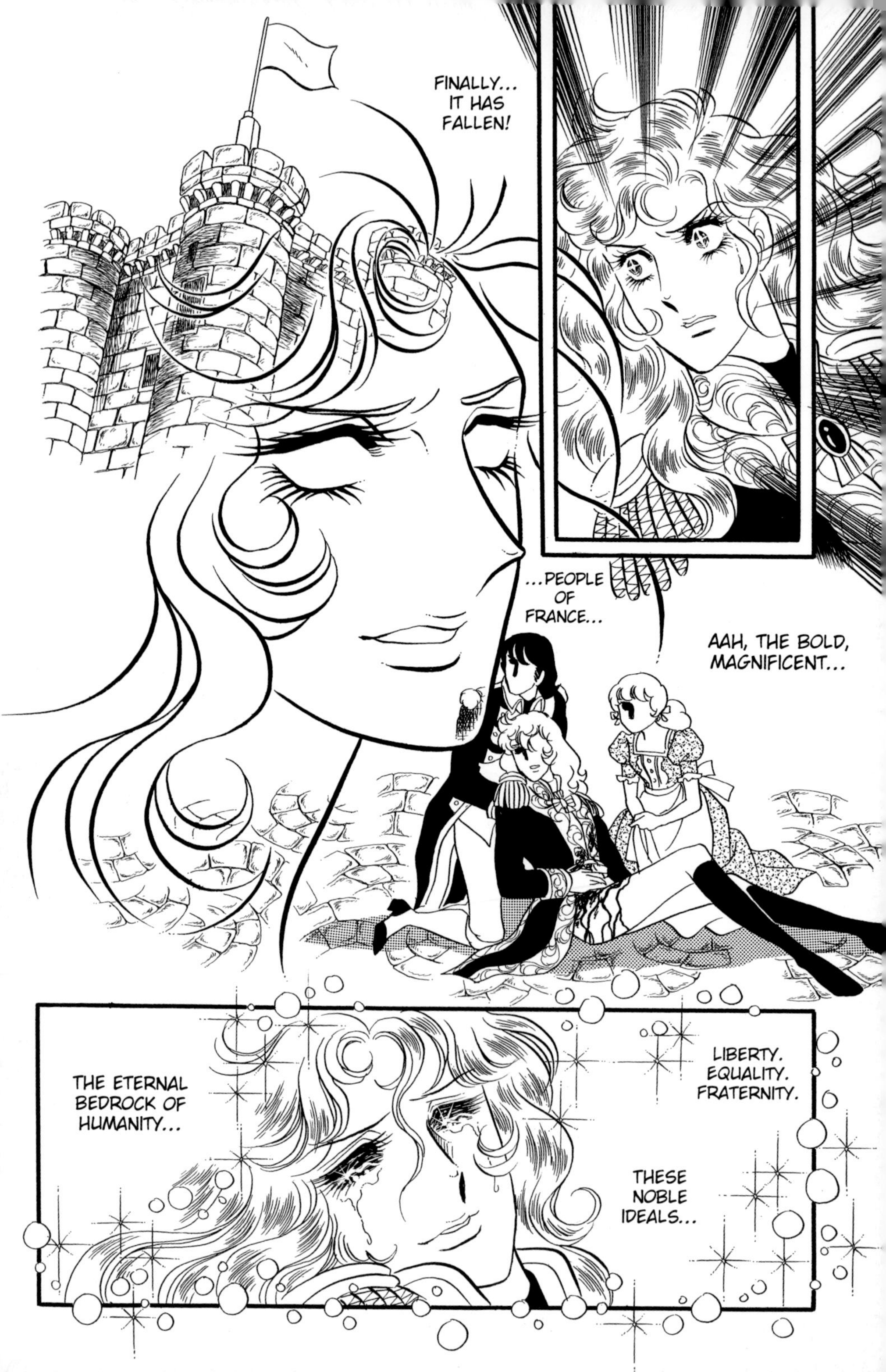
FINALLY... IT HAS FALLEN!
AAH, THE BOLD, MAGNIFICENT...
...PEOPLE OF FRANCE...
LIBERTY. EQUALITY. FRATERNITY.
THESE NOBLE IDEALS...
THE ETERNAL BEDROCK OF HUMANITY...

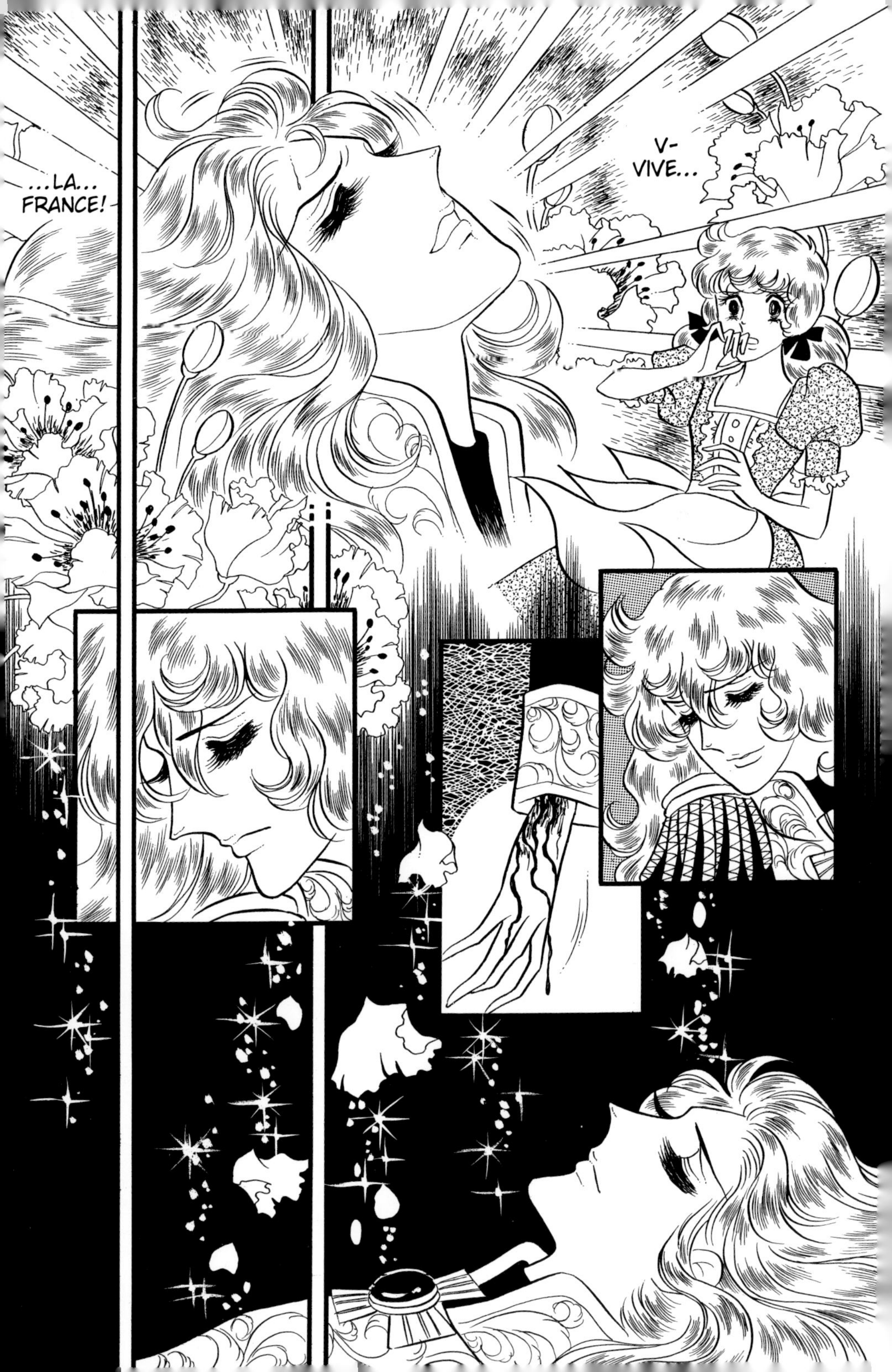
V- VIVE...
...LA... FRANCE!

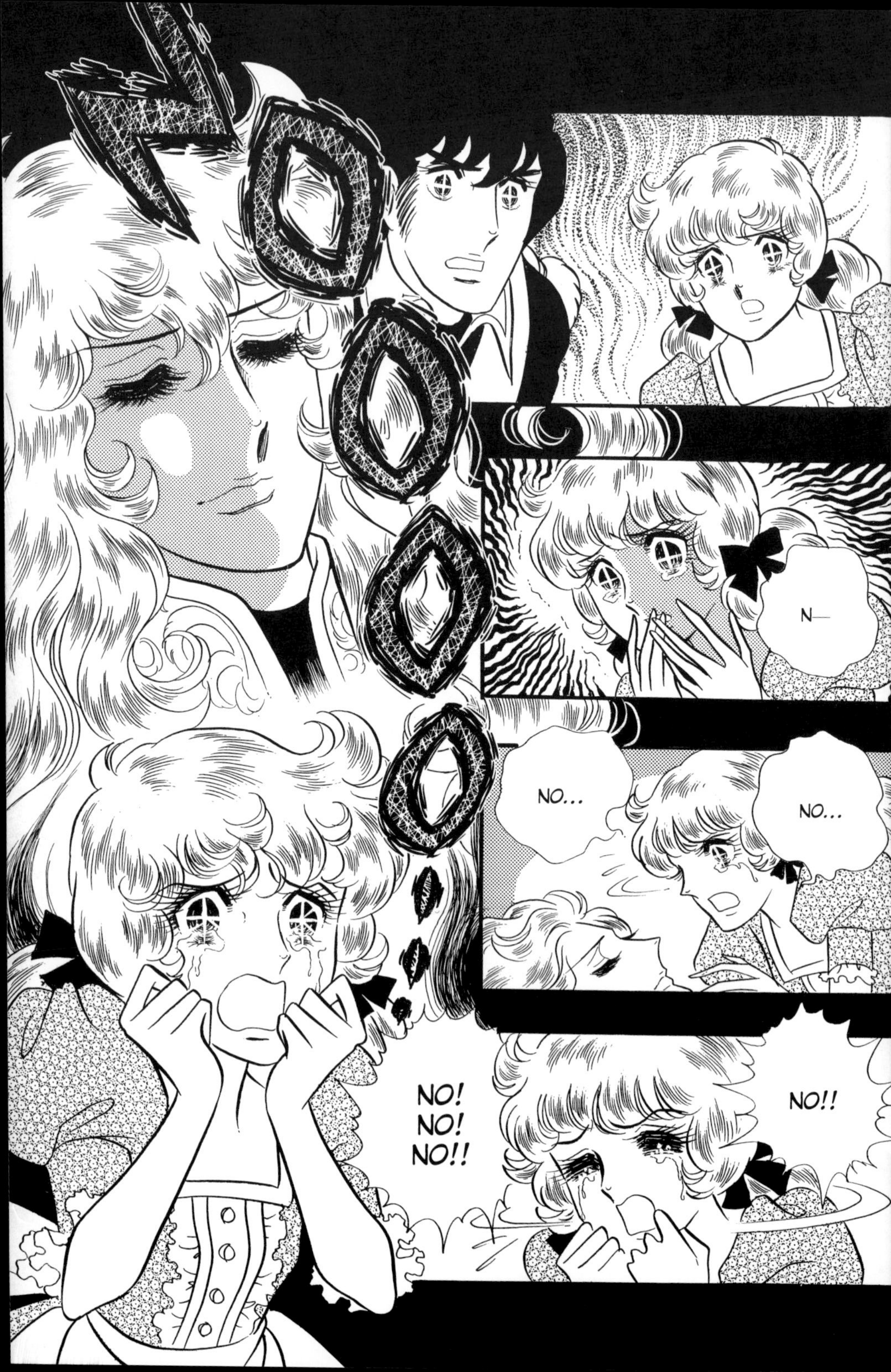
N—
NO...
NO...
NO!!
NO!
NO!
NO!!

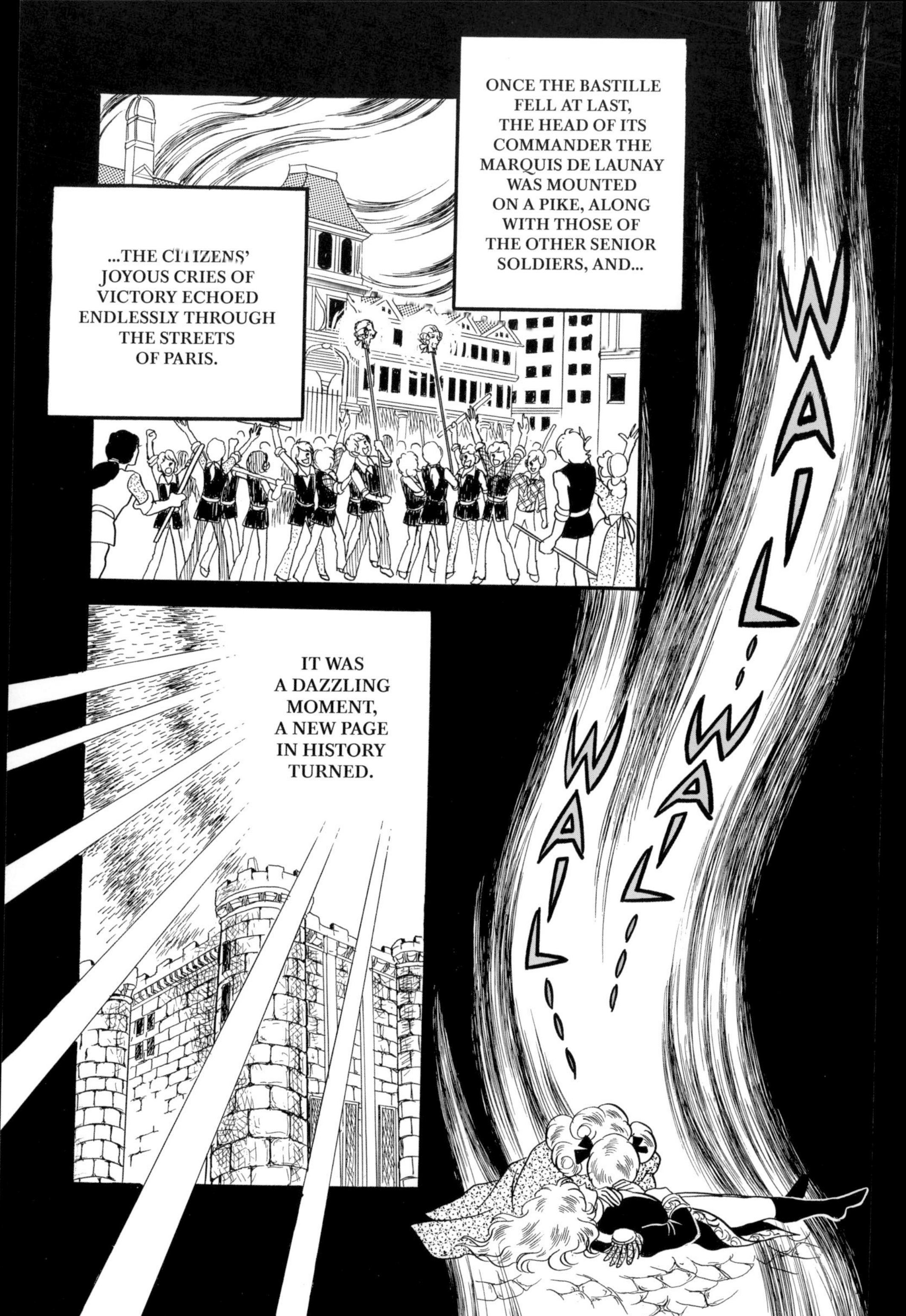
ONCE THE BASTILLE FELL AT LAST, THE HEAD OF ITS COMMANDER THE MARQUIS DE LAUNAY WAS MOUNTED ON A PIKE, ALONG WITH THOSE OF THE OTHER SENIOR SOLDIERS, AND...
...THE CITIZENS' JOYOUS CRIES OF VICTORY ECHOED ENDLESSLY THROUGH THE STREETS OF PARIS.
IT WAS A DAZZLING MOMENT, A NEW PAGE IN HISTORY TURNED.
WAIL... WAIL...
WAIL...

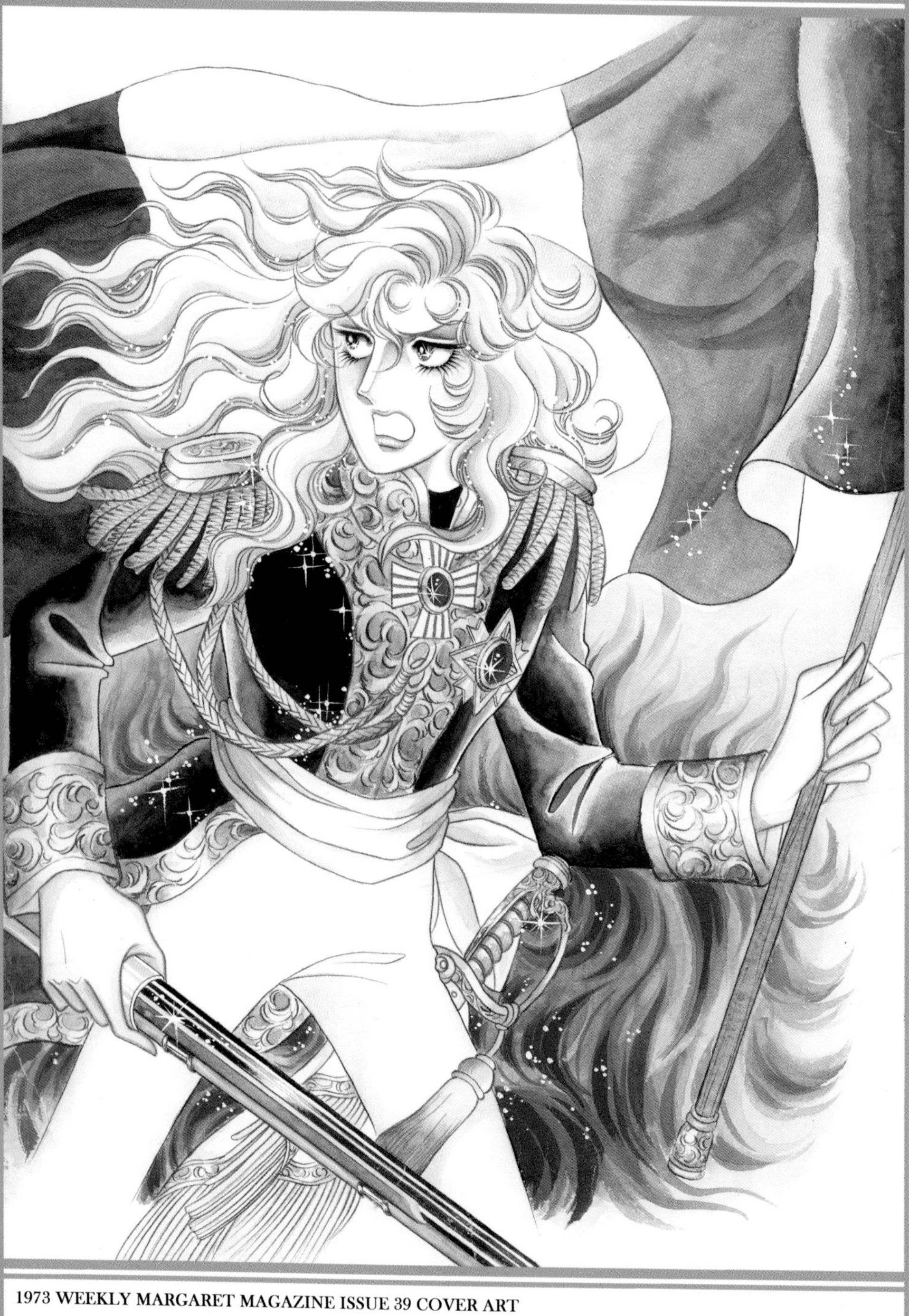

1973 WEEKLY MARGARET MAGAZINE ISSUE 39 COVER ART

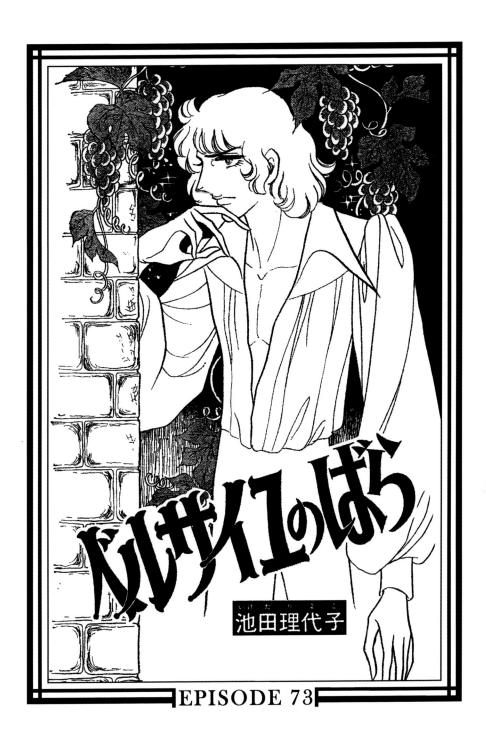

ベルサイユのばら

池田理代子

EPISODE 73

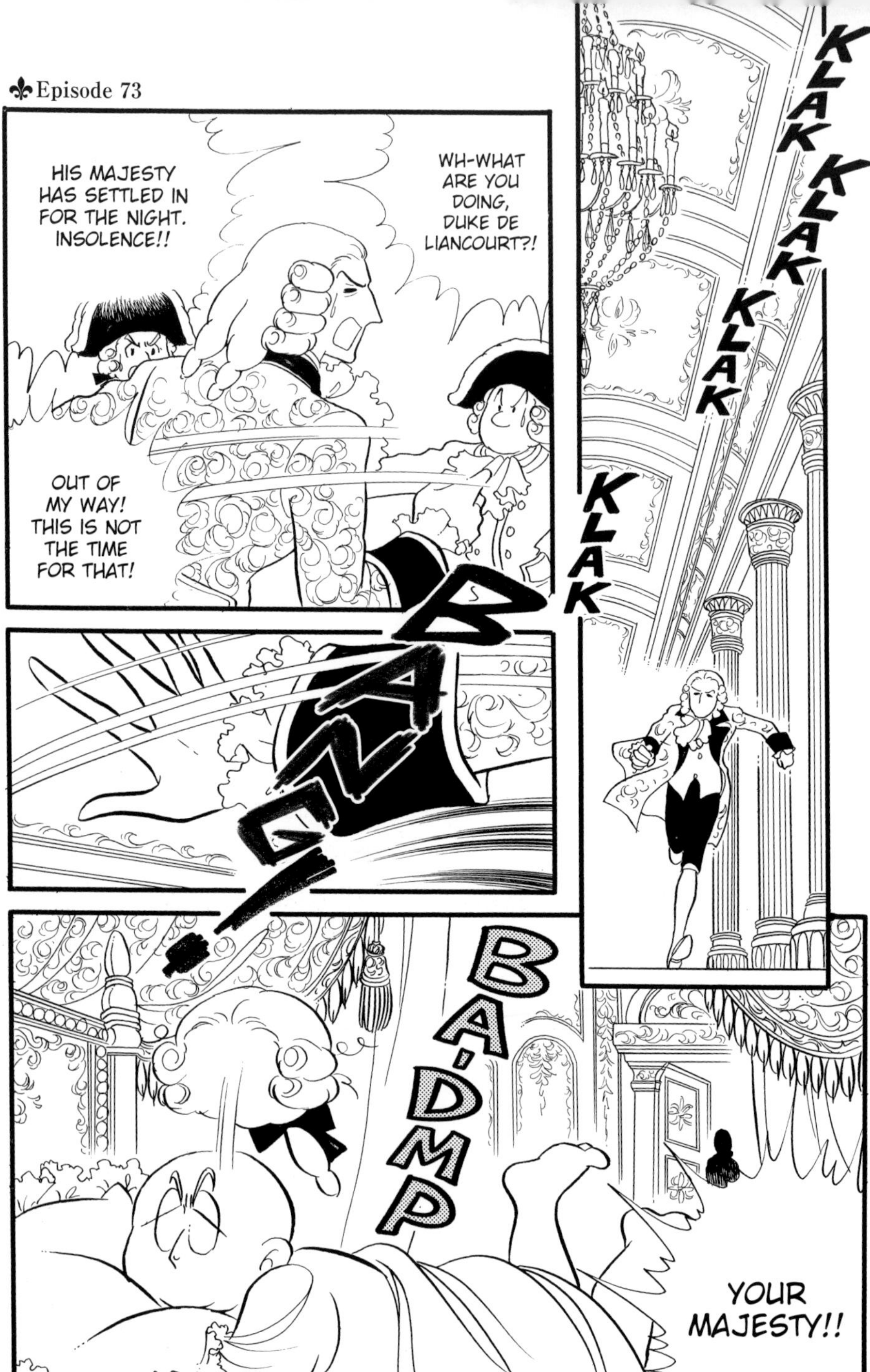
KLAK
KLAK
KLAK
KLAK
WH-WHAT ARE YOU DOING, DUKE DE LIANCOURT?!
HIS MAJESTY HAS SETTLED IN FOR THE NIGHT. INSOLENCE!!
OUT OF MY WAY! THIS IS NOT THE TIME FOR THAT!
BANG!
BA-DMP
YOUR MAJESTY!!

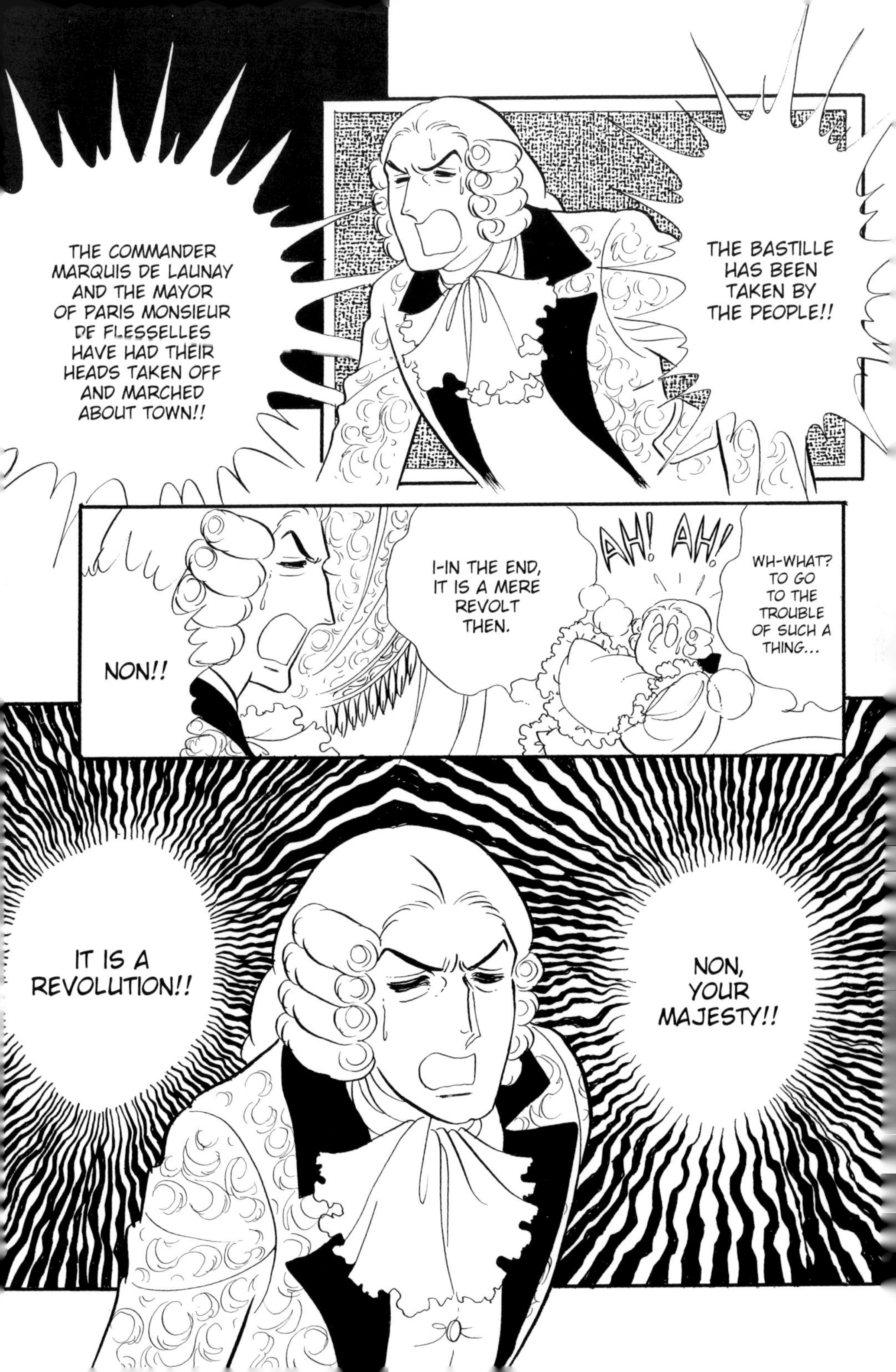
THE BASTILLE HAS BEEN TAKEN BY THE PEOPLE!!
THE COMMANDER MARQUIS DE LAUNAY AND THE MAYOR OF PARIS MONSIEUR DE FLESSELLES HAVE HAD THEIR HEADS TAKEN OFF AND MARCHED ABOUT TOWN!!
WH-WHAT? TO GO TO THE TROUBLE OF SUCH A THING...
AH! AH!
I-IN THE END, IT IS A MERE REVOLT THEN.
NON!!
NON, YOUR MAJESTY!!
IT IS A REVOLUTION!!

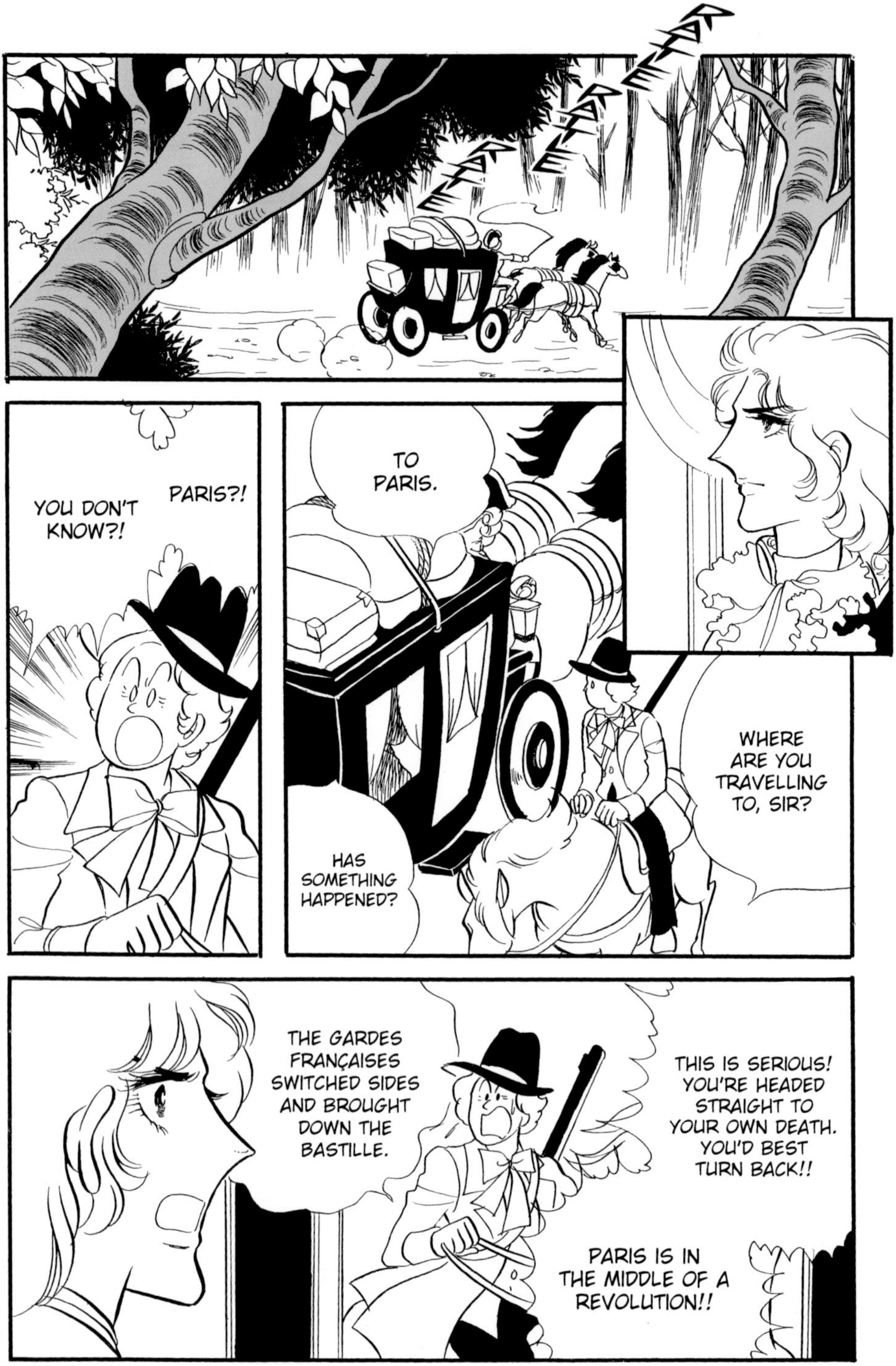

RATTLE
RATTLE
RATTLE
WHERE ARE YOU TRAVELLING TO, SIR?
TO PARIS.
HAS SOMETHING HAPPENED?
PARIS?!
YOU DON'T KNOW?!
THIS IS SERIOUS! YOU'RE HEADED STRAIGHT TO YOUR OWN DEATH. YOU'D BEST TURN BACK!!
PARIS IS IN THE MIDDLE OF A REVOLUTION!!
THE GARDES FRANÇAISES SWITCHED SIDES AND BROUGHT DOWN THE BASTILLE.

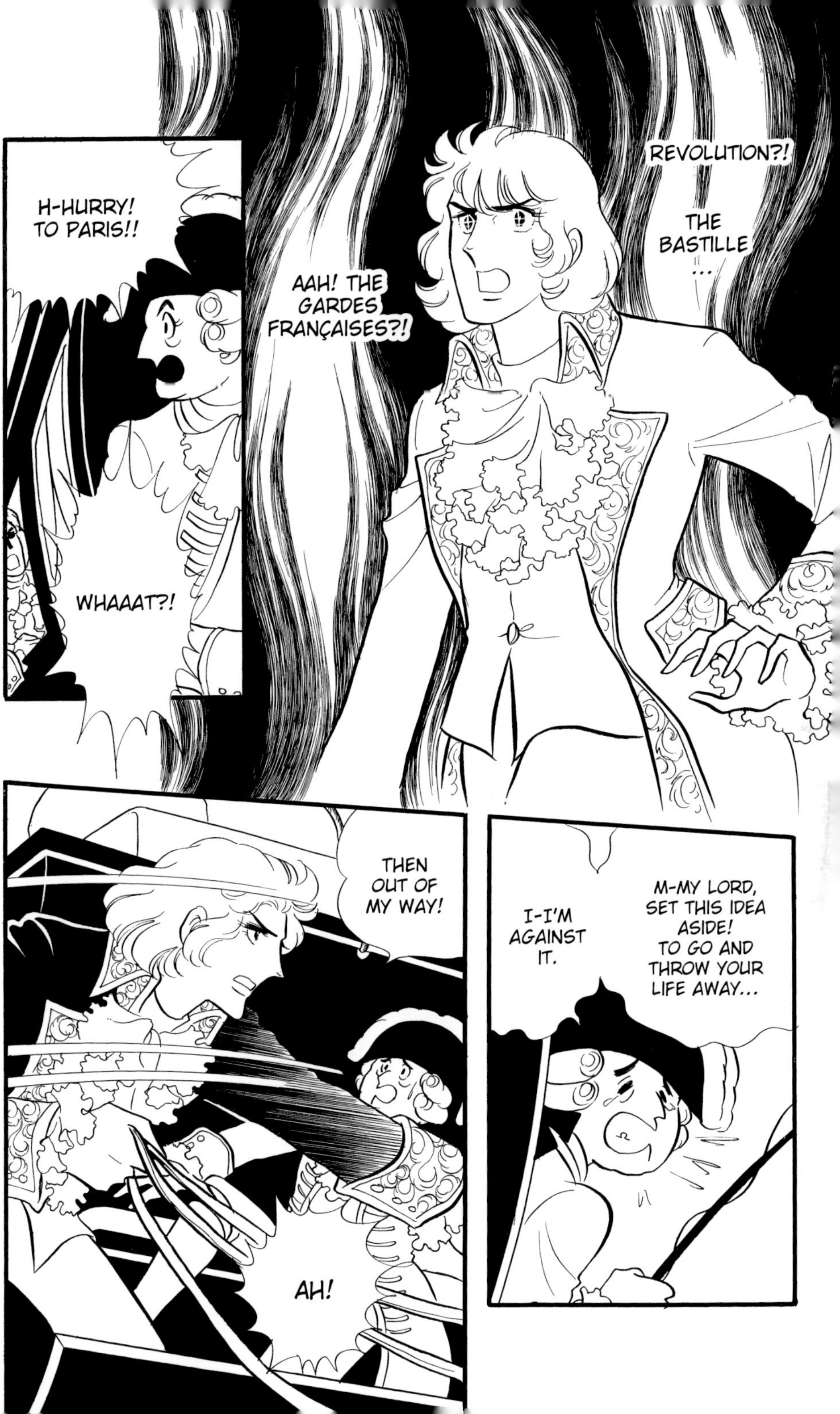

REVOLUTION?!
THE BASTILLE ...
AAH! THE GARDES FRANÇAISES?!
H-HURRY! TO PARIS!!
WHAAAT?!
M-MY LORD, SET THIS IDEA ASIDE! TO GO AND THROW YOUR LIFE AWAY...
I-I'M AGAINST IT.
THEN OUT OF MY WAY!
AH!

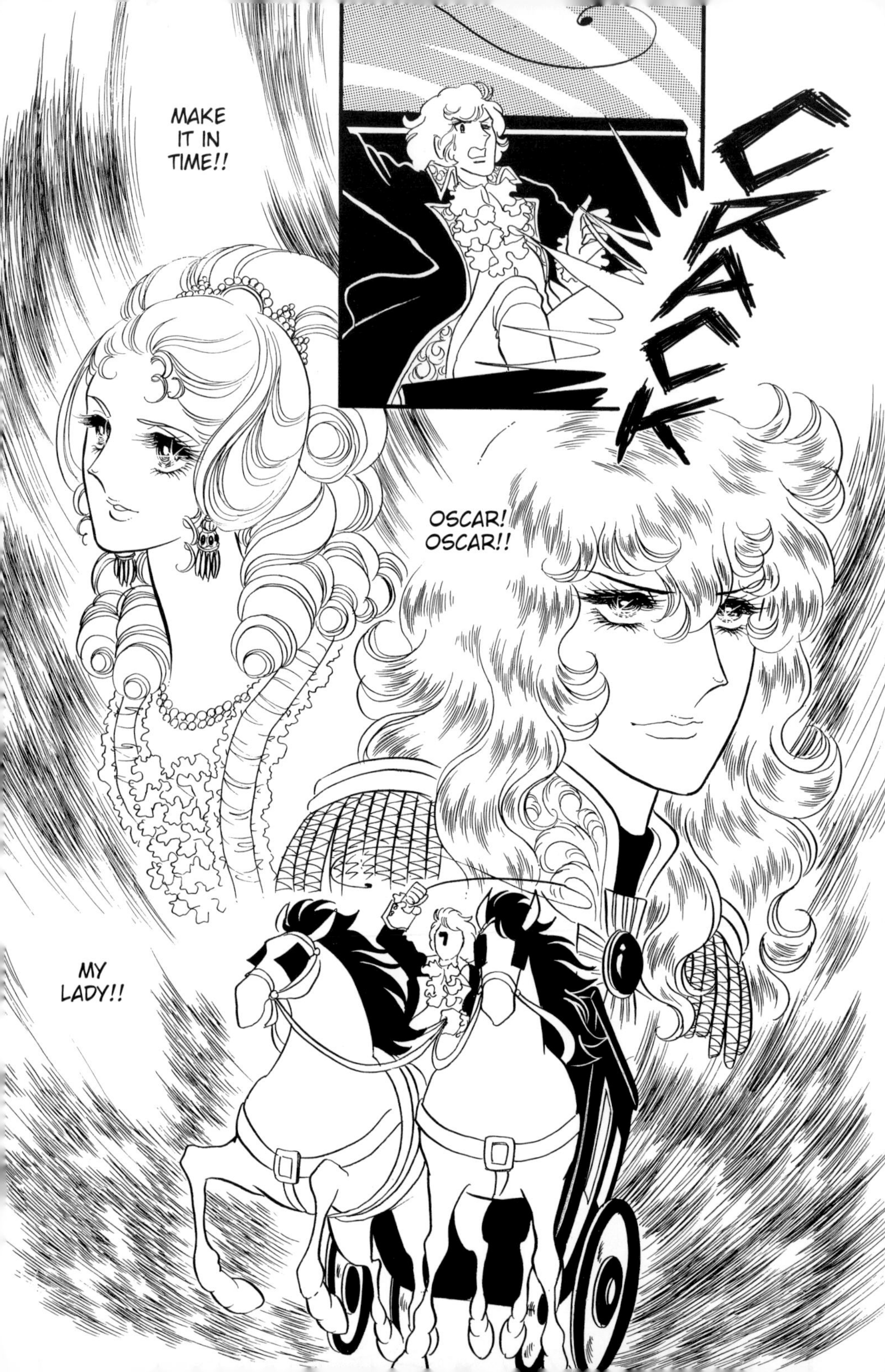
CRACK
MAKE IT IN TIME!!
OSCAR! OSCAR!!
MY LADY!!

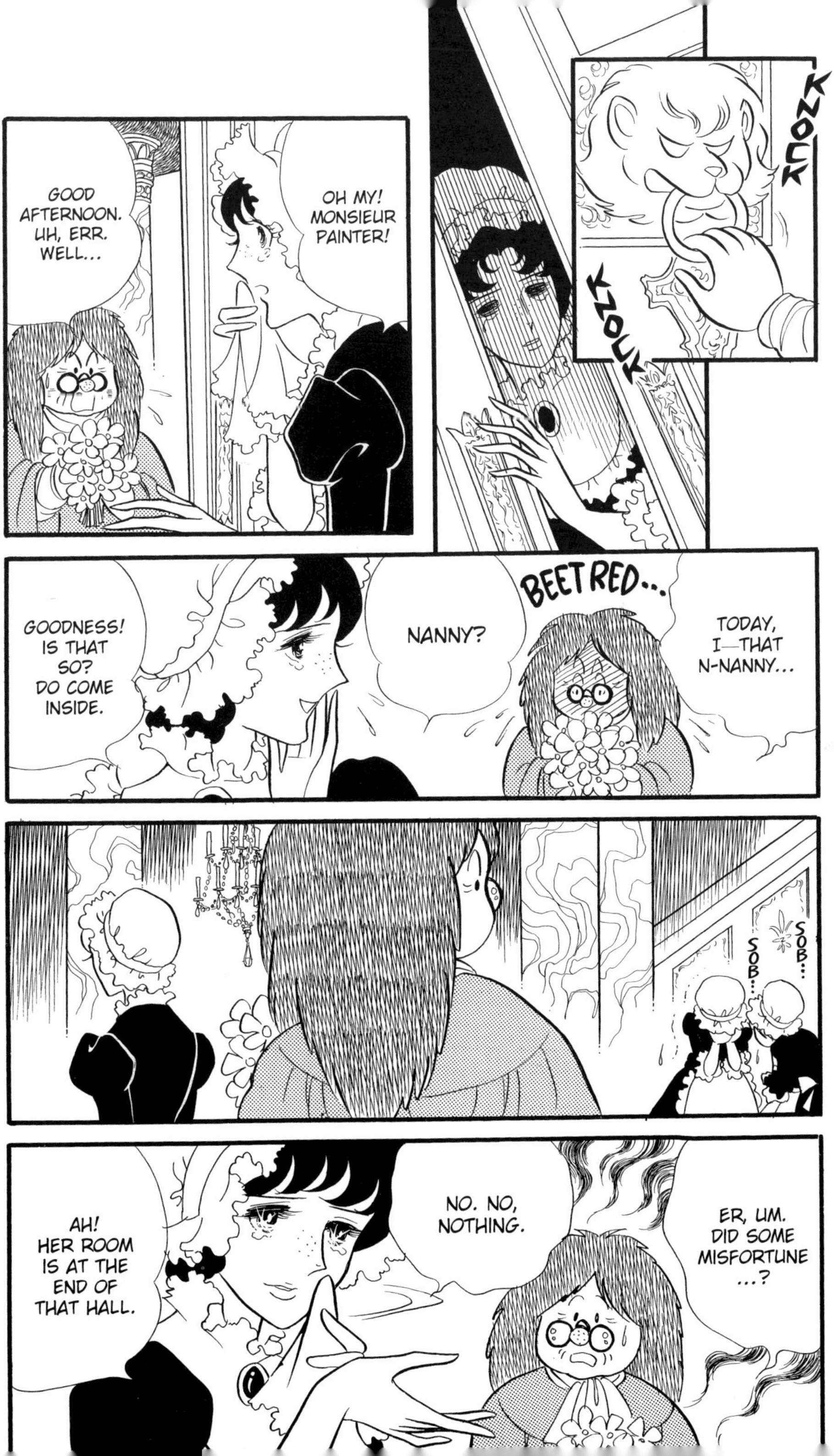
KNOCK
KNOCK
OH MY! MONSIEUR PAINTER!
GOOD AFTERNOON. UH, ERR. WELL...
TODAY, I—THAT N-NANNY...
BEETRED...
NANNY?
GOODNESS! IS THAT SO? DO COME INSIDE.
SOB...
SOB...
ER, UM. DID SOME MISFORTUNE ...?
NO. NO, NOTHING.
AH! HER ROOM IS AT THE END OF THAT HALL.

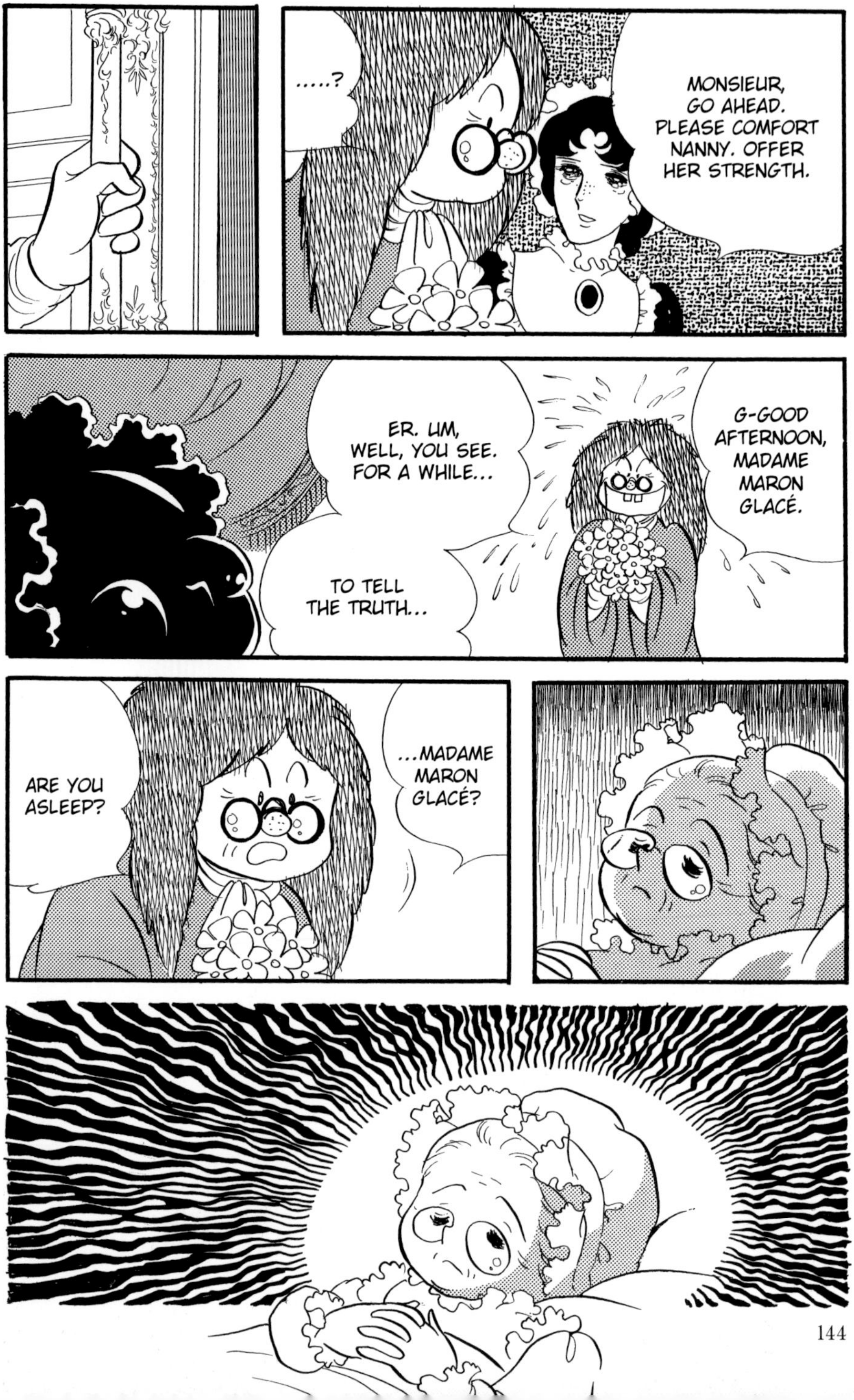
MONSIEUR, GO AHEAD. PLEASE COMFORT NANNY. OFFER HER STRENGTH.
.....?
G-GOOD AFTERNOON, MADAME MARON GLACÉ.
ER. UM, WELL, YOU SEE. FOR A WHILE...
TO TELL THE TRUTH...
...MADAME MARON GLACÉ?
ARE YOU ASLEEP?

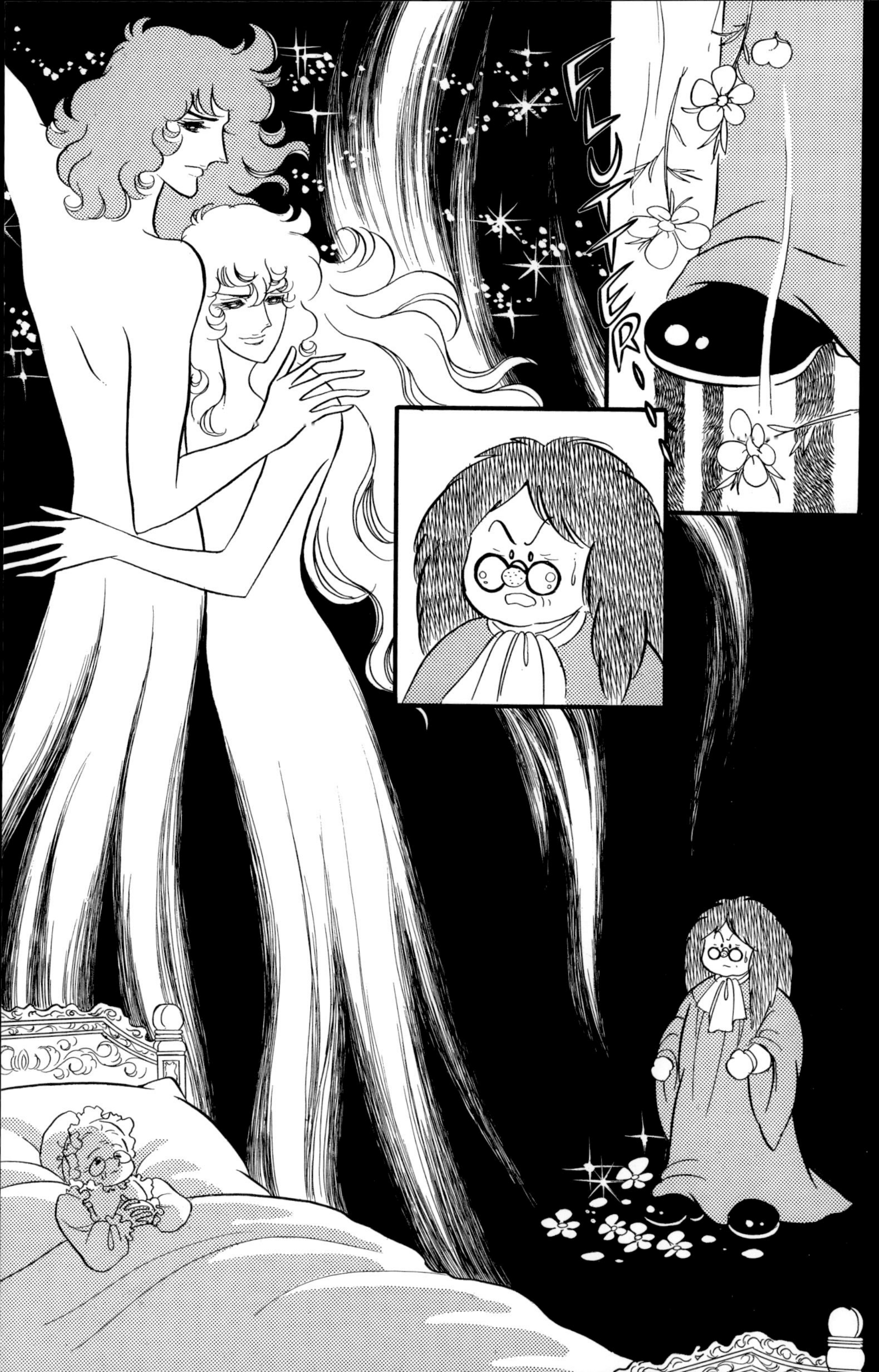
FLUTTER...

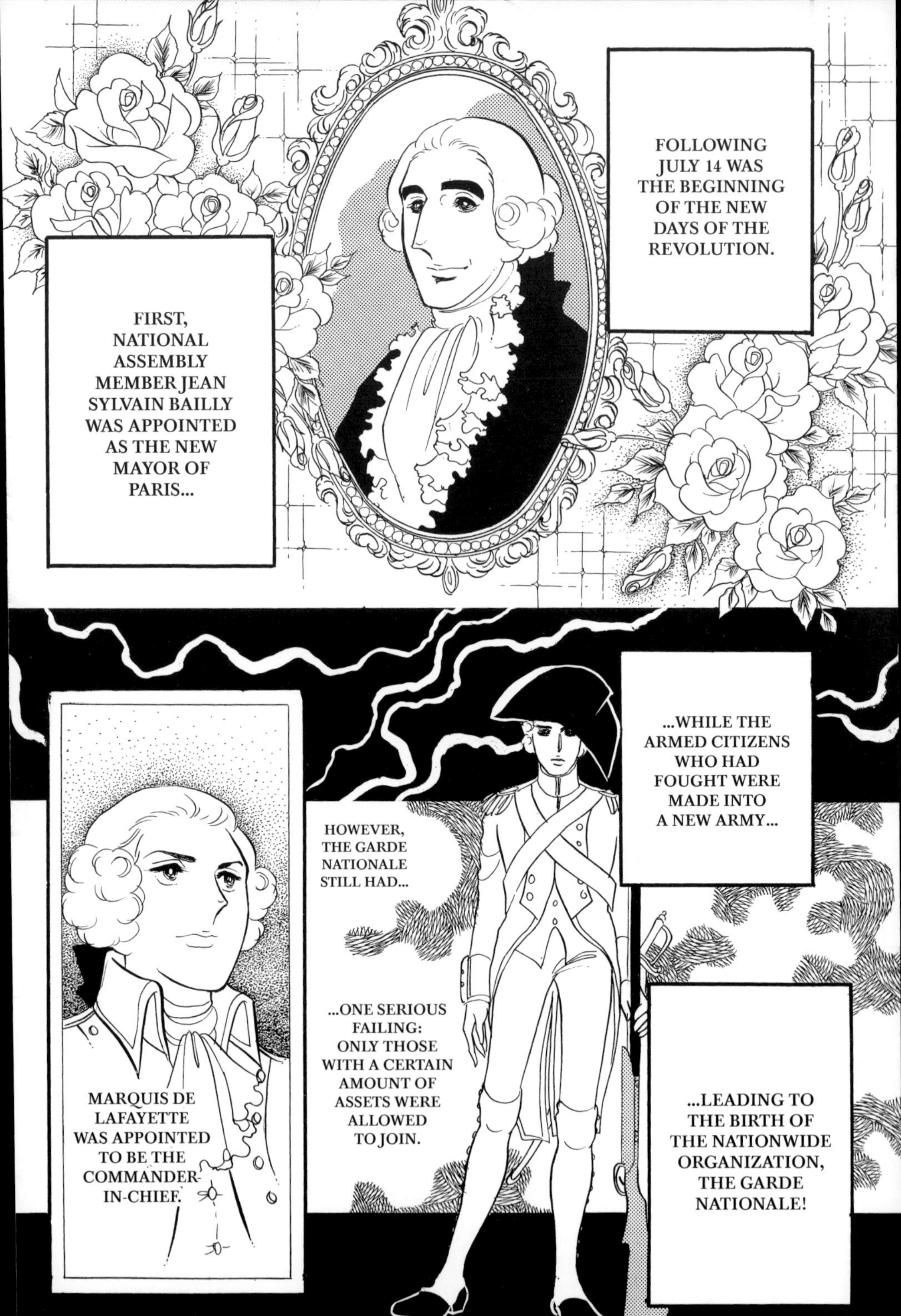
FOLLOWING JULY 14 WAS THE BEGINNING OF THE NEW DAYS OF THE REVOLUTION.
FIRST, NATIONAL ASSEMBLY MEMBER JEAN SYLVAIN BAILLY WAS APPOINTED AS THE NEW MAYOR OF PARIS...
...WHILE THE ARMED CITIZENS WHO HAD FOUGHT WERE MADE INTO A NEW ARMY...
...LEADING TO THE BIRTH OF THE NATIONWIDE ORGANIZATION, THE GARDE NATIONALE!
HOWEVER, THE GARDE NATIONALE STILL HAD...
...ONE SERIOUS FAILING: ONLY THOSE WITH A CERTAIN AMOUNT OF ASSETS WERE ALLOWED TO JOIN.
MARQUIS DE LAFAYETTE WAS APPOINTED TO BE THE COMMANDER-IN-CHIEF.

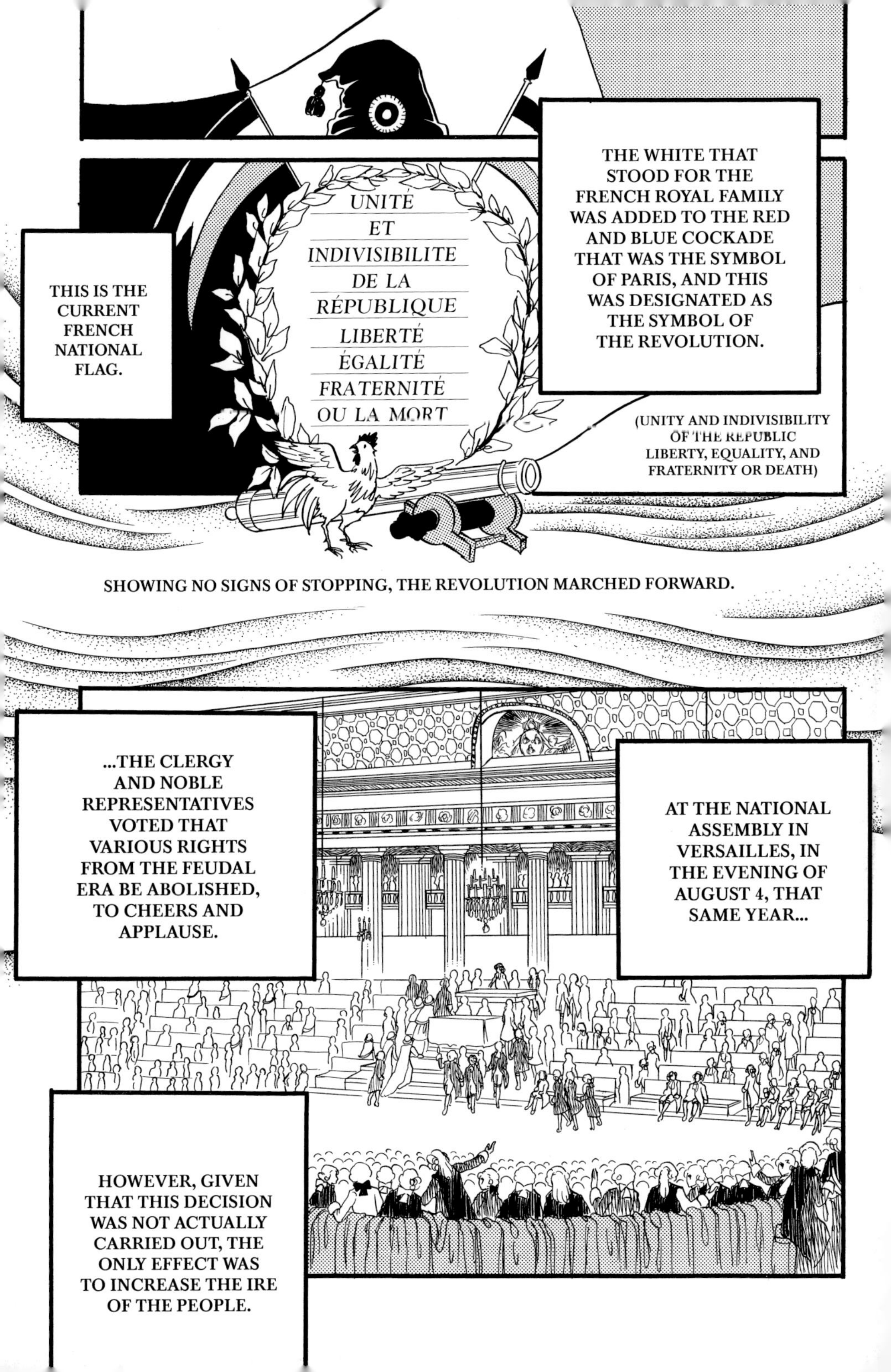
THE WHITE THAT STOOD FOR THE FRENCH ROYAL FAMILY WAS ADDED TO THE RED AND BLUE COCKADE THAT WAS THE SYMBOL OF PARIS, AND THIS WAS DESIGNATED AS THE SYMBOL OF THE REVOLUTION.
UNITÉ ET INDIVISIBILITE DE LA RÉPUBLIQUE LIBERTÉ ÉGALITÉ FRATERNITÉ OU LA MORT
(UNITY AND INDIVISIBILITY OF THE REPUBLIC LIBERTY, EQUALITY, AND FRATERNITY OR DEATH)
THIS IS THE CURRENT FRENCH NATIONAL FLAG.
SHOWING NO SIGNS OF STOPPING, THE REVOLUTION MARCHED FORWARD.
AT THE NATIONAL ASSEMBLY IN VERSAILLES, IN THE EVENING OF AUGUST 4, THAT SAME YEAR...
...THE CLERGY AND NOBLE REPRESENTATIVES VOTED THAT VARIOUS RIGHTS FROM THE FEUDAL ERA BE ABOLISHED, TO CHEERS AND APPLAUSE.
HOWEVER, GIVEN THAT THIS DECISION WAS NOT ACTUALLY CARRIED OUT, THE ONLY EFFECT WAS TO INCREASE THE IRE OF THE PEOPLE.

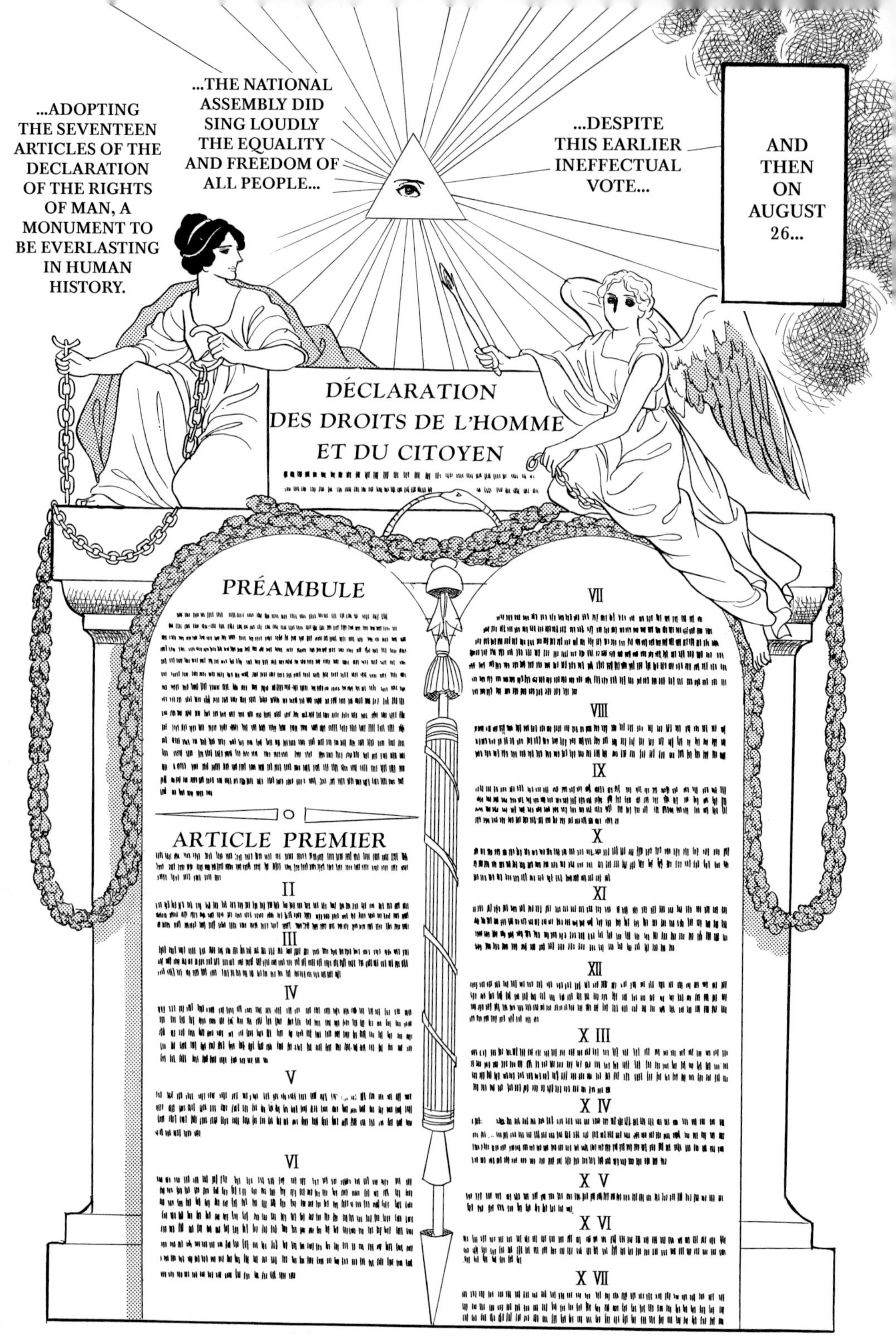
AND THEN ON AUGUST 26...
...DESPITE THIS EARLIER INEFFECTUAL VOTE...
...THE NATIONAL ASSEMBLY DID SING LOUDLY THE EQUALITY AND FREEDOM OF ALL PEOPLE...
...ADOPTING THE SEVENTEEN ARTICLES OF THE DECLARATION OF THE RIGHTS OF MAN, A MONUMENT TO BE EVERLASTING IN HUMAN HISTORY.
DÉCLARATION DES DROITS DE L'HOMME ET DU CITOYEN
PRÉAMBULE
ARTICLE PREMIER
II
III
IV
V
VI
VII
VIII
IX
X
XI
XII
XIII
XIV
XV
XVI
XVII

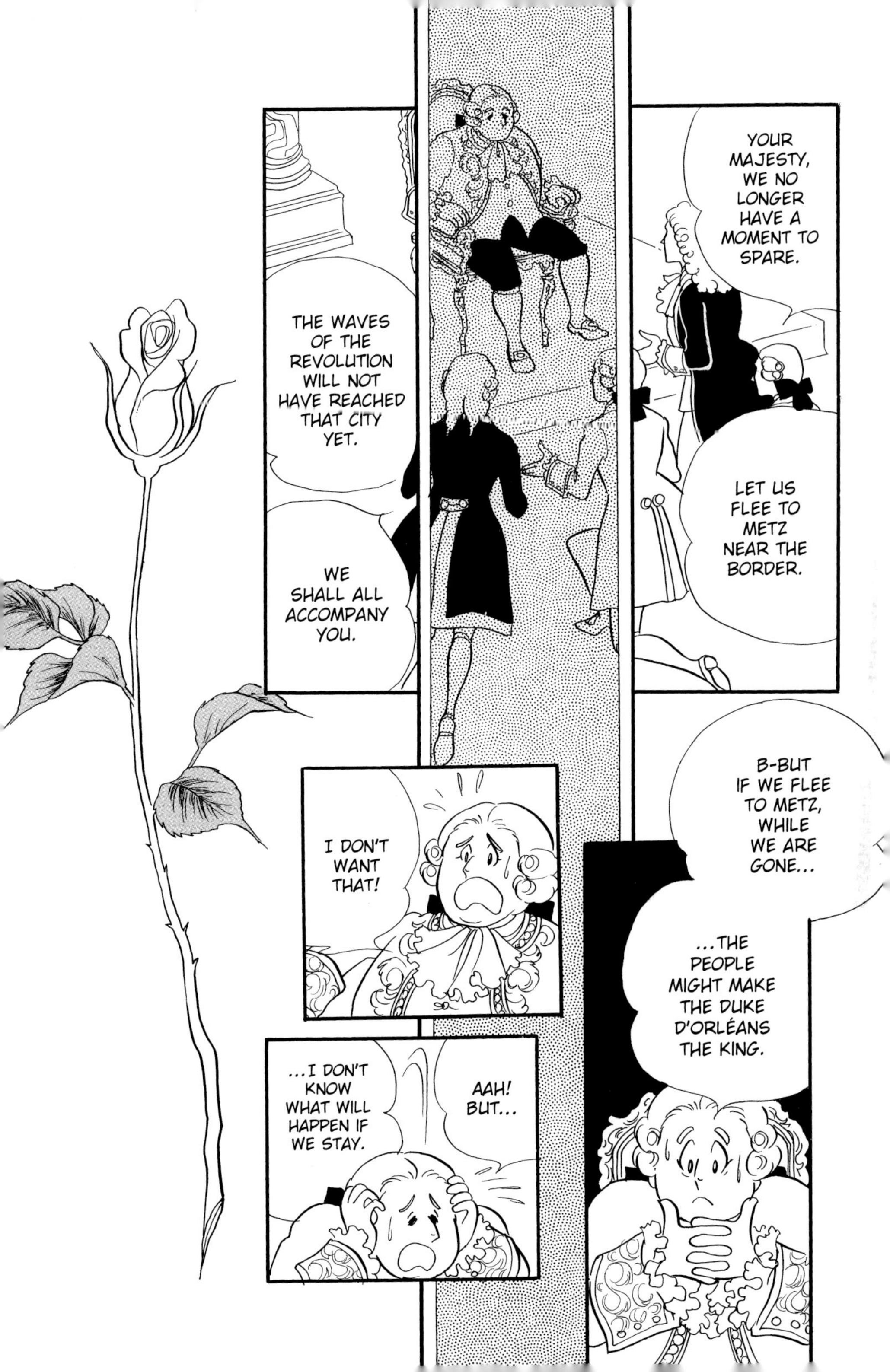
YOUR MAJESTY, WE NO LONGER HAVE A MOMENT TO SPARE.
LET US FLEE TO METZ NEAR THE BORDER.
THE WAVES OF THE REVOLUTION WILL NOT HAVE REACHED THAT CITY YET.
WE SHALL ALL ACCOMPANY YOU.
B-BUT IF WE FLEE TO METZ, WHILE WE ARE GONE...
...THE PEOPLE MIGHT MAKE THE DUKE D'ORLÉANS THE KING.
I DON'T WANT THAT!
AAH! BUT...
...I DON'T KNOW WHAT WILL HAPPEN IF WE STAY.

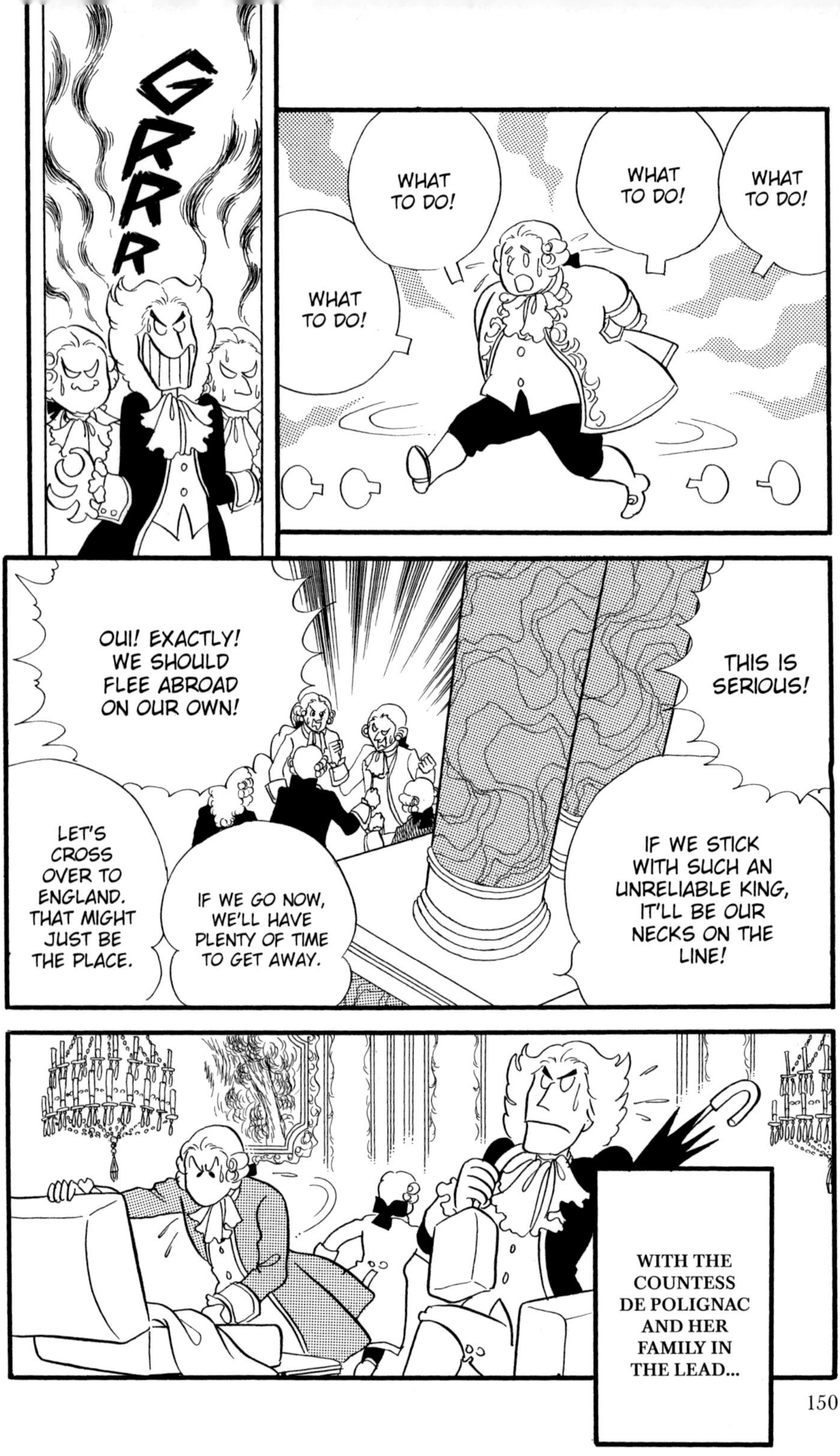
WHAT TO DO!
WHAT TO DO!
WHAT TO DO!
WHAT TO DO!
GRRR
THIS IS SERIOUS!
OUI! EXACTLY! WE SHOULD FLEE ABROAD ON OUR OWN!
IF WE STICK WITH SUCH AN UNRELIABLE KING, IT'LL BE OUR NECKS ON THE LINE!
IF WE GO NOW, WE'LL HAVE PLENTY OF TIME TO GET AWAY.
LET'S CROSS OVER TO ENGLAND. THAT MIGHT JUST BE THE PLACE.
WITH THE COUNTESS DE POLIGNAC AND HER FAMILY IN THE LEAD...

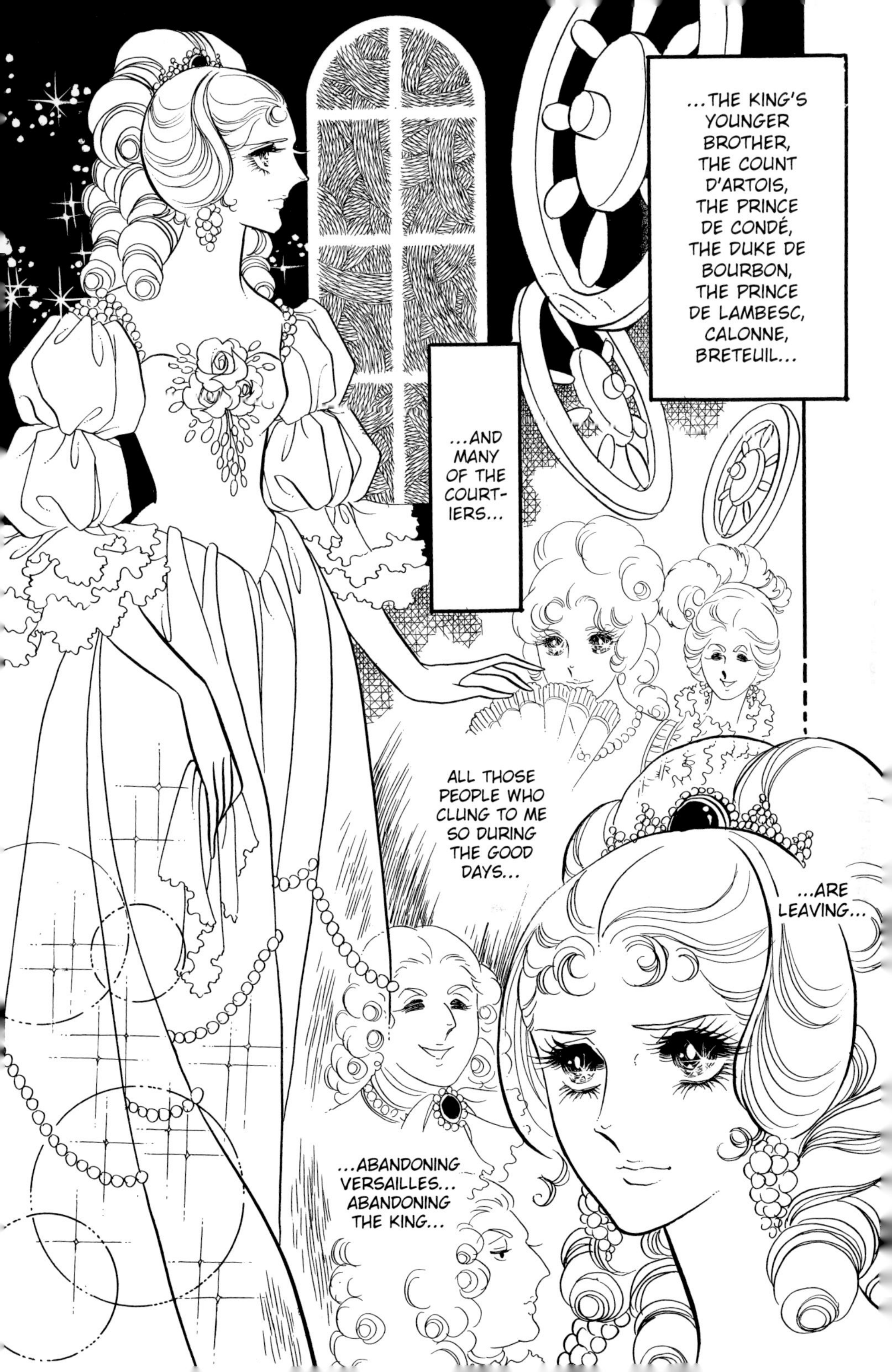
...THE KING'S YOUNGER BROTHER, THE COUNT D'ARTOIS, THE PRINCE DE CONDÉ, THE DUKE DE BOURBON, THE PRINCE DE LAMBESC, CALONNE, BRETEUIL...
...AND MANY OF THE COURT-IERS...
ALL THOSE PEOPLE WHO CLUNG TO ME SO DURING THE GOOD DAYS...
...ARE LEAVING...
...ABANDONING VERSAILLES... ABANDONING THE KING...

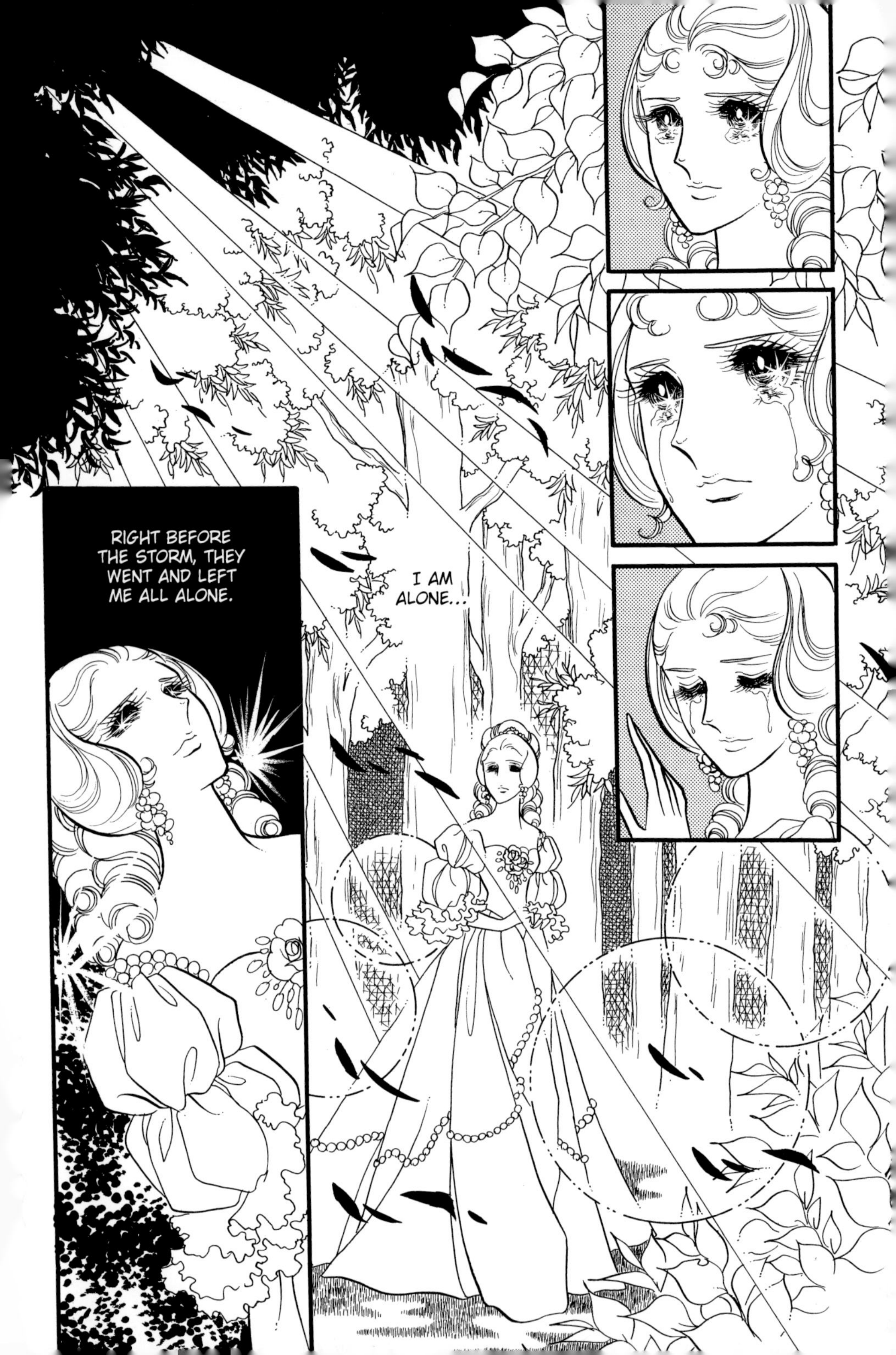
I AM ALONE...
RIGHT BEFORE THE STORM, THEY WENT AND LEFT ME ALL ALONE.

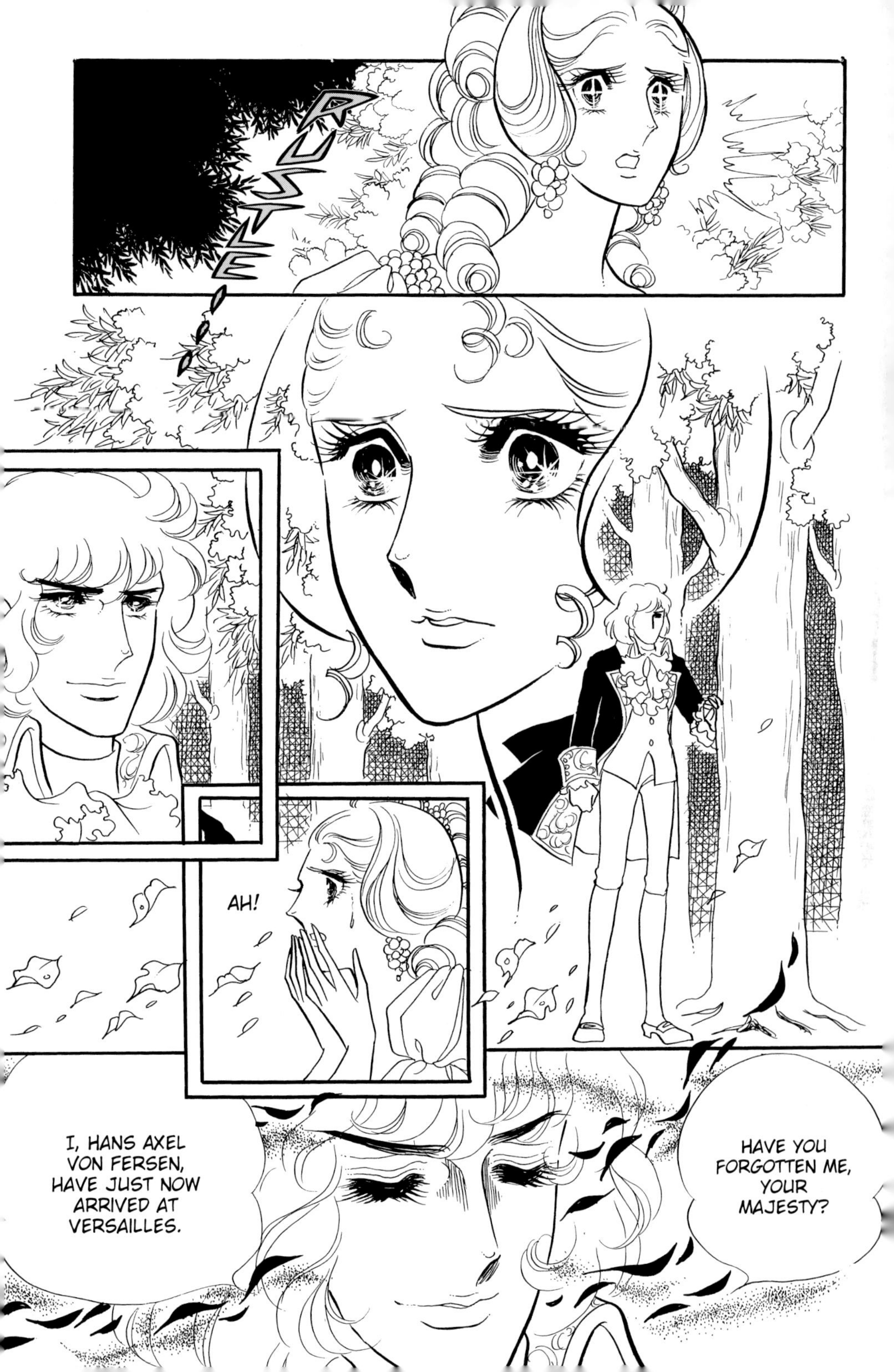
RUSTLE
AH!
HAVE YOU FORGOTTEN ME, YOUR MAJESTY?
I, HANS AXEL VON FERSEN, HAVE JUST NOW ARRIVED AT VERSAILLES.

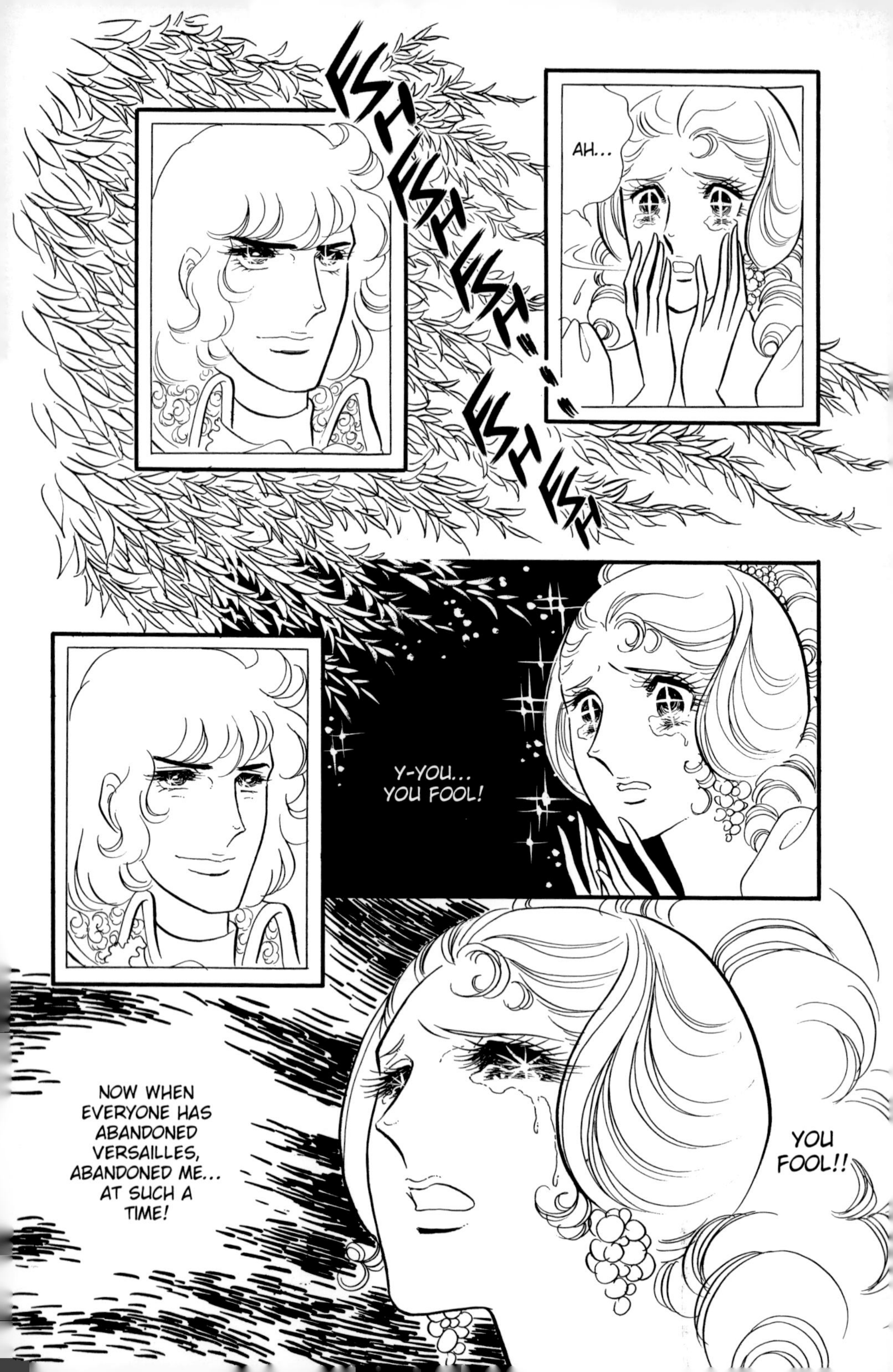

AH...
FSH FSH FSH FSH... FSH FSH FSH
Y-YOU... YOU FOOL!
YOU FOOL!!
NOW WHEN EVERYONE HAS ABANDONED VERSAILLES, ABANDONED ME... AT SUCH A TIME!

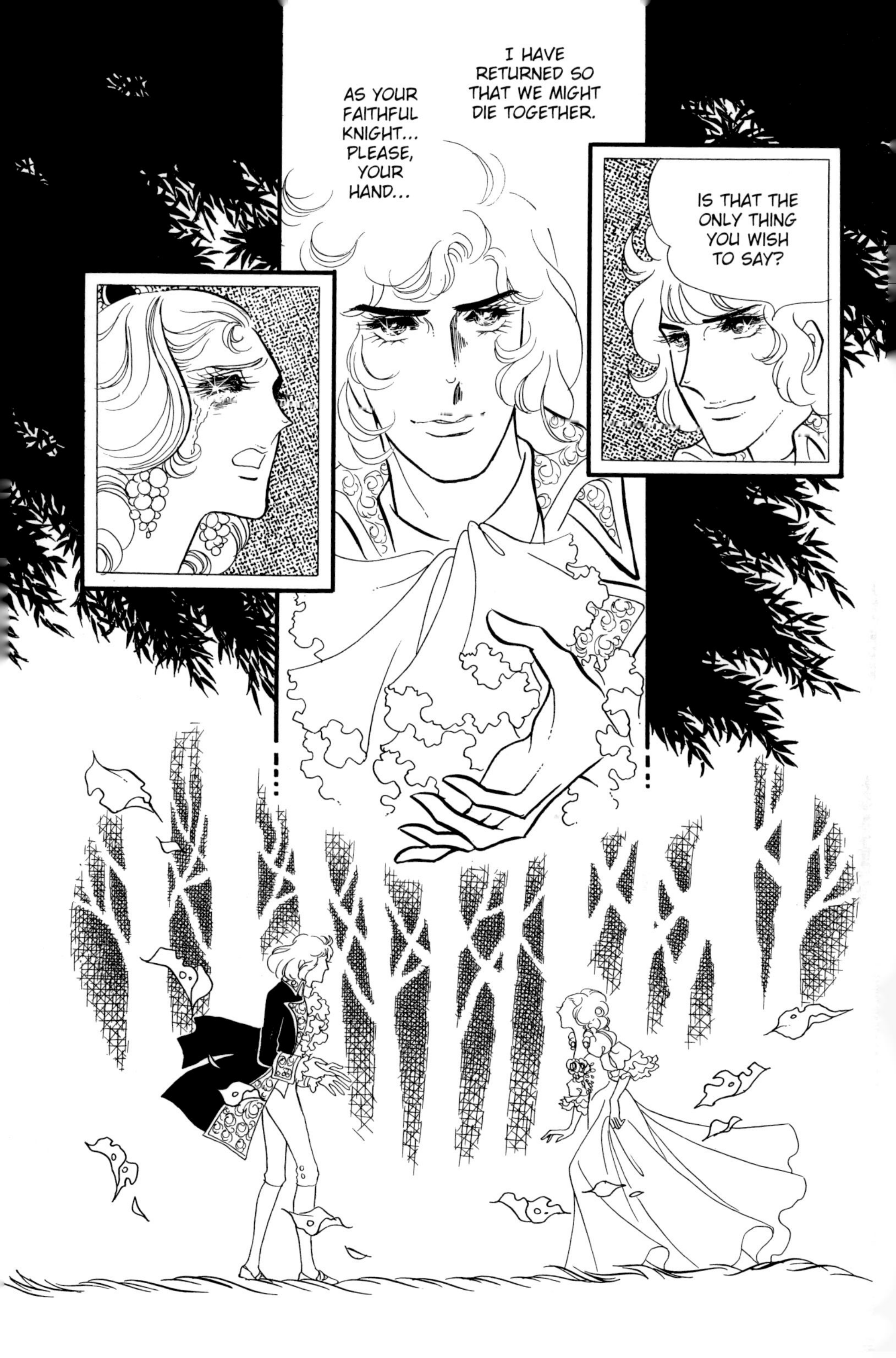

IS THAT THE ONLY THING YOU WISH TO SAY?
I HAVE RETURNED SO THAT WE MIGHT DIE TOGETHER.
AS YOUR FAITHFUL KNIGHT... PLEASE, YOUR HAND...

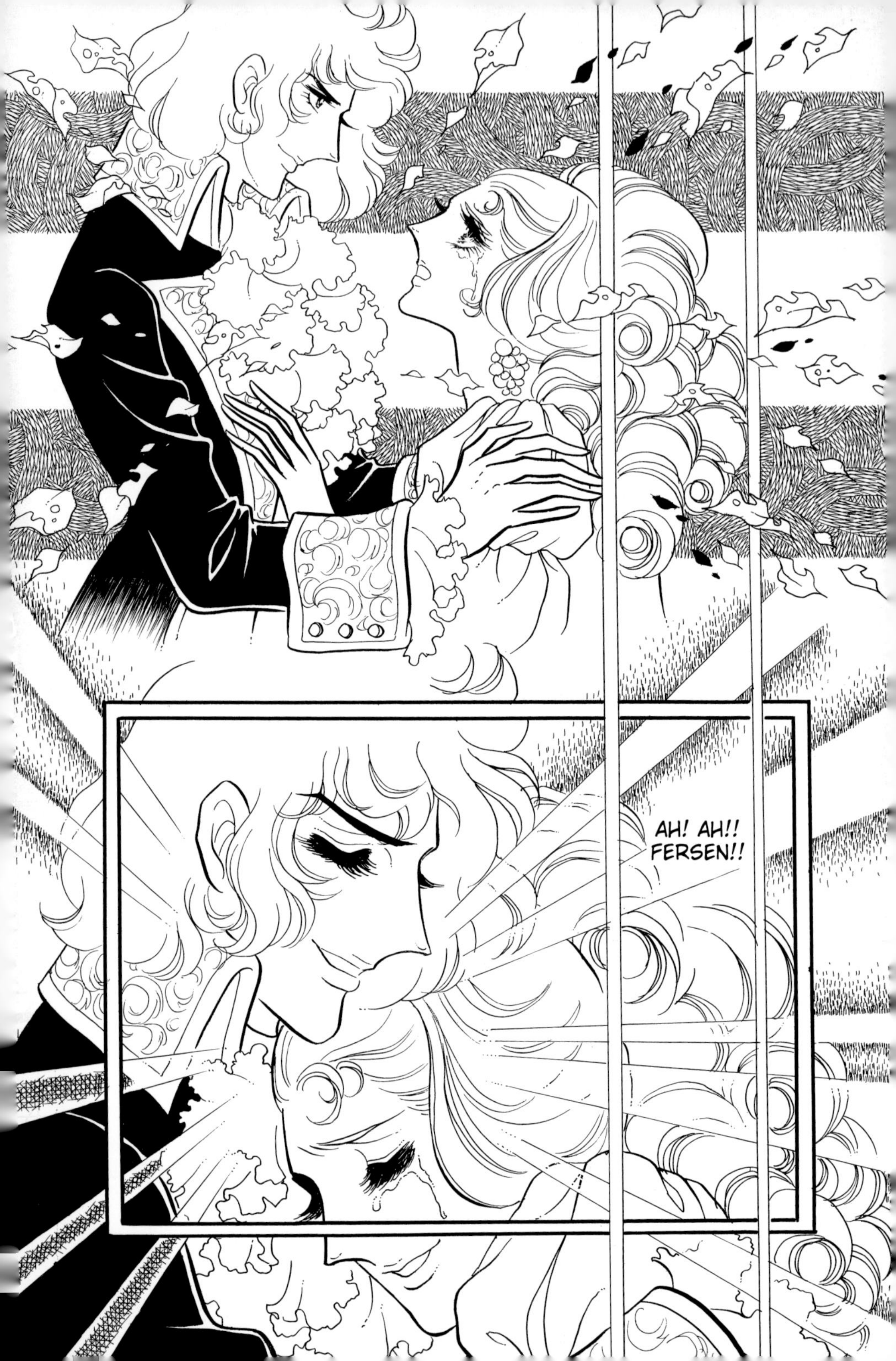
AH! AH!! FERSEN!!

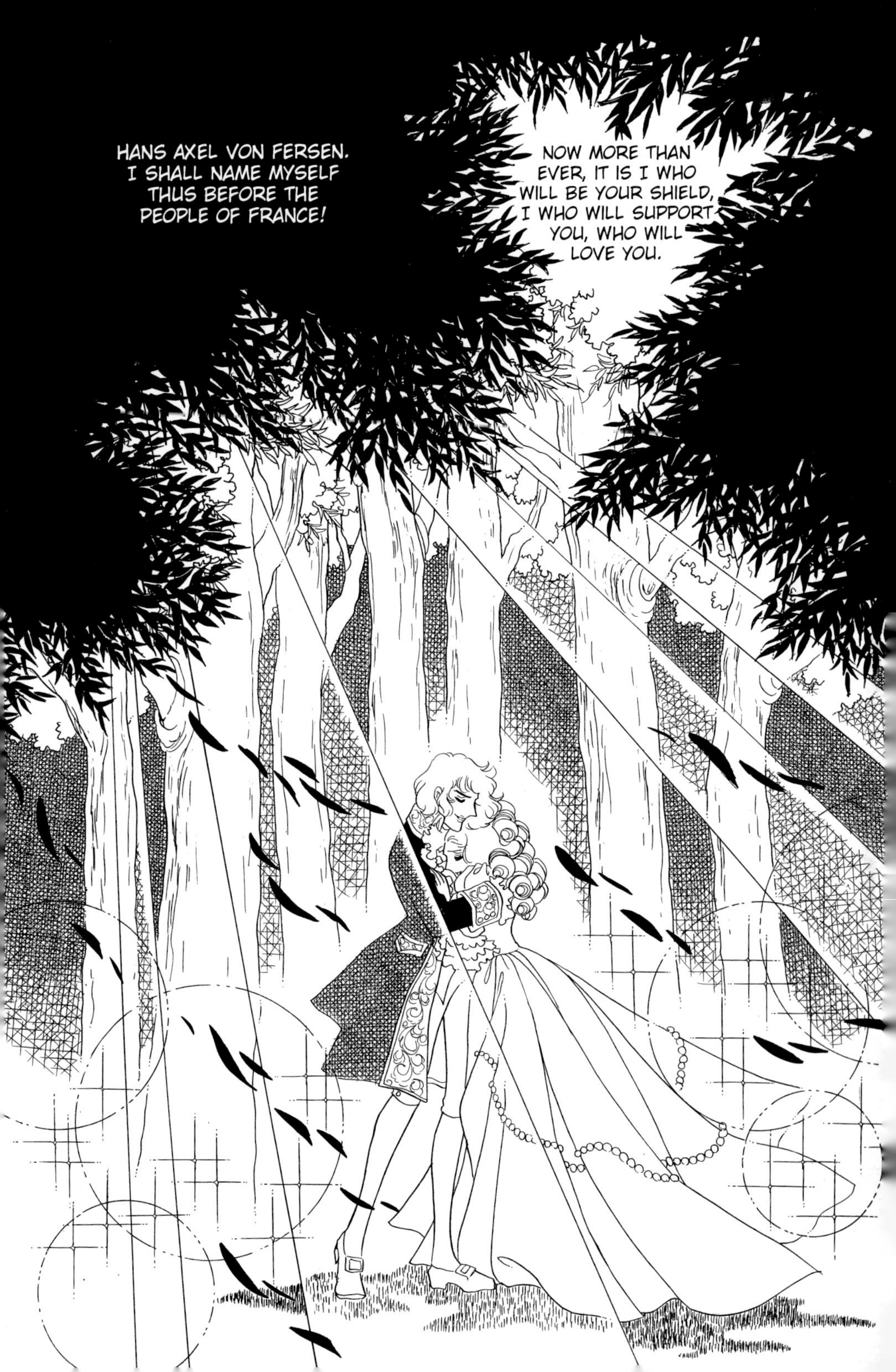
NOW MORE THAN EVER, IT IS I WHO WILL BE YOUR SHIELD, I WHO WILL SUPPORT YOU, WHO WILL LOVE YOU.
HANS AXEL VON FERSEN. I SHALL NAME MYSELF THUS BEFORE THE PEOPLE OF FRANCE!

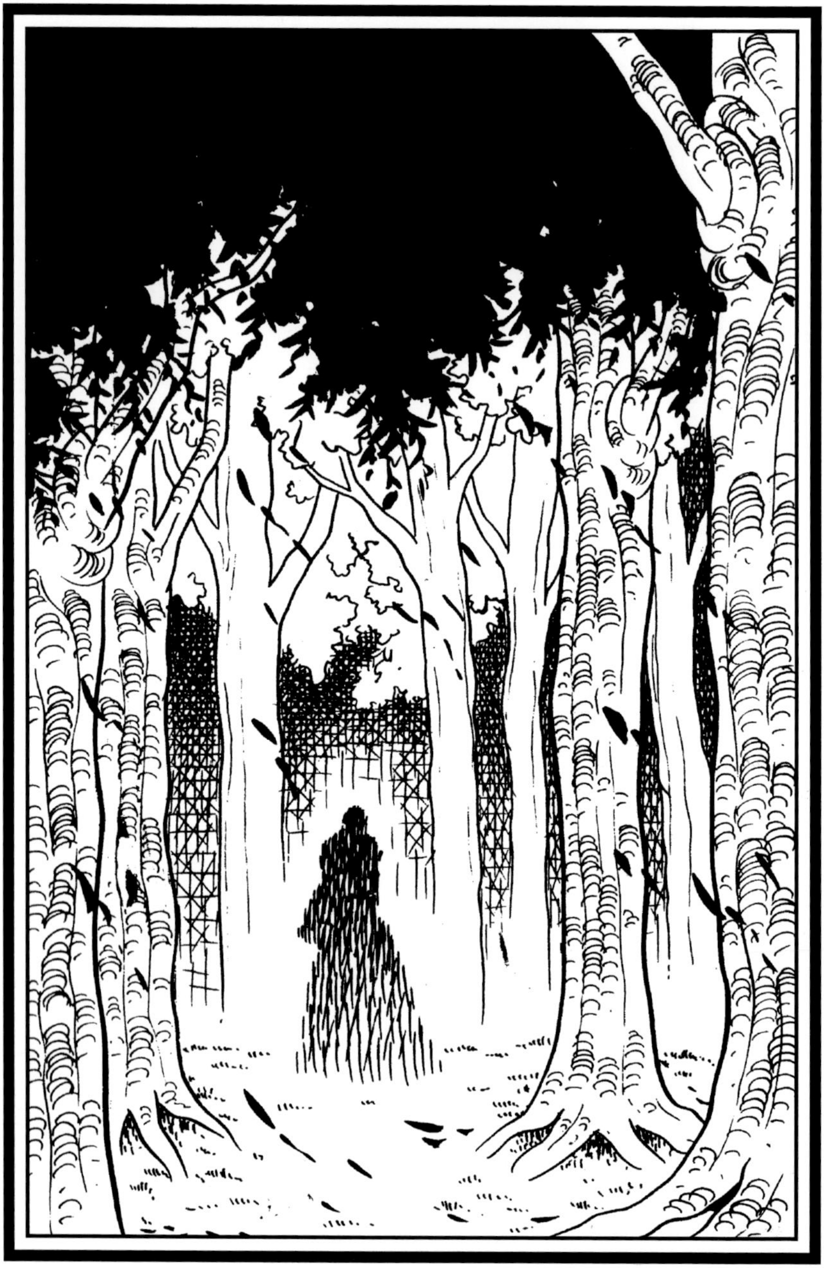

1974 MARGARET COMICS TRADE PAPERBACK VOLUME 8 INSERT ART

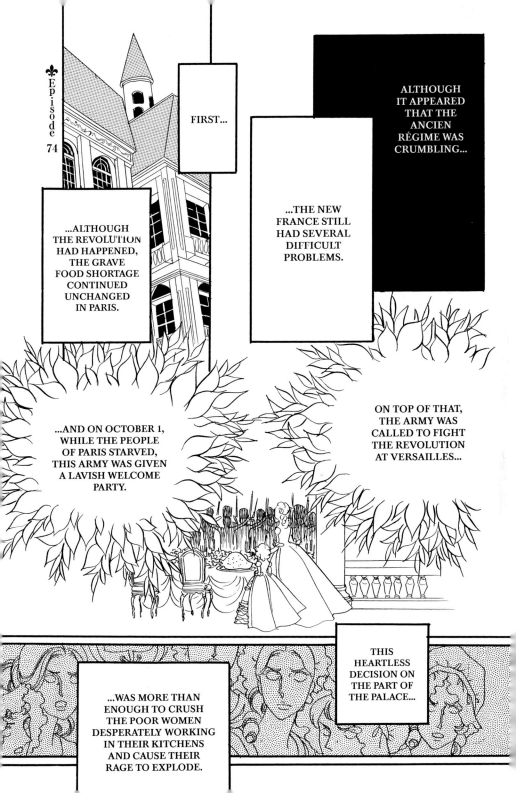

FIRST...

ALTHOUGH IT APPEARED THAT THE ANCIEN RÉGIME WAS CRUMBLING...

...THE NEW FRANCE STILL HAD SEVERAL DIFFICULT PROBLEMS.

...ALTHOUGH THE REVOLUTION HAD HAPPENED, THE GRAVE FOOD SHORTAGE CONTINUED UNCHANGED IN PARIS.

ON TOP OF THAT, THE ARMY WAS CALLED TO FIGHT THE REVOLUTION AT VERSAILLES...

...AND ON OCTOBER 1, WHILE THE PEOPLE OF PARIS STARVED, THIS ARMY WAS GIVEN A LAVISH WELCOME PARTY.

THIS HEARTLESS DECISION ON THE PART OF THE PALACE...

...WAS MORE THAN ENOUGH TO CRUSH THE POOR WOMEN DESPERATELY WORKING IN THEIR KITCHENS AND CAUSE THEIR RAGE TO EXPLODE.

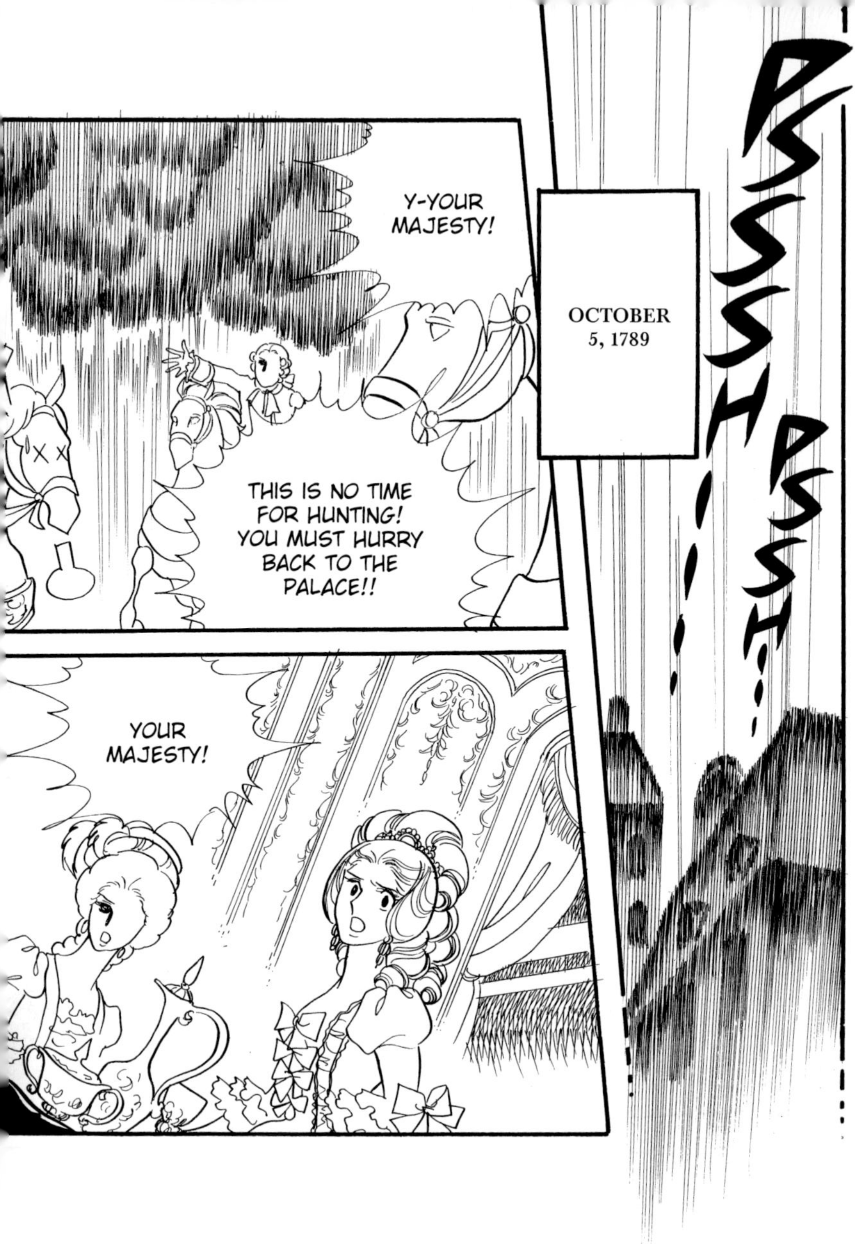
PSSSH...
PSSH...
OCTOBER 5, 1789
Y-YOUR MAJESTY!
THIS IS NO TIME FOR HUNTING! YOU MUST HURRY BACK TO THE PALACE!!
YOUR MAJESTY!

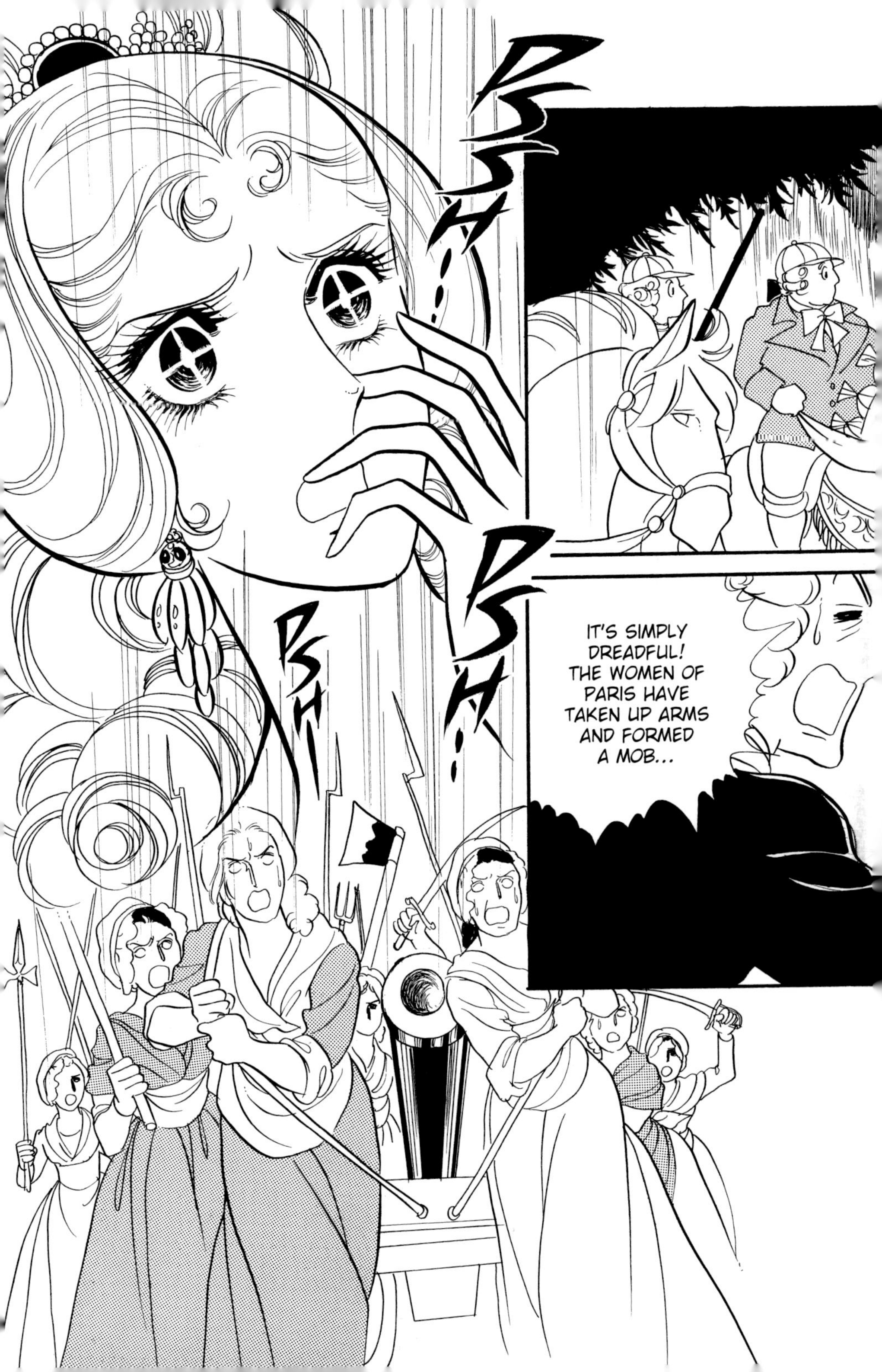
IT'S SIMPLY DREADFUL! THE WOMEN OF PARIS HAVE TAKEN UP ARMS AND FORMED A MOB...
BSH...!
BSH..!
BSH

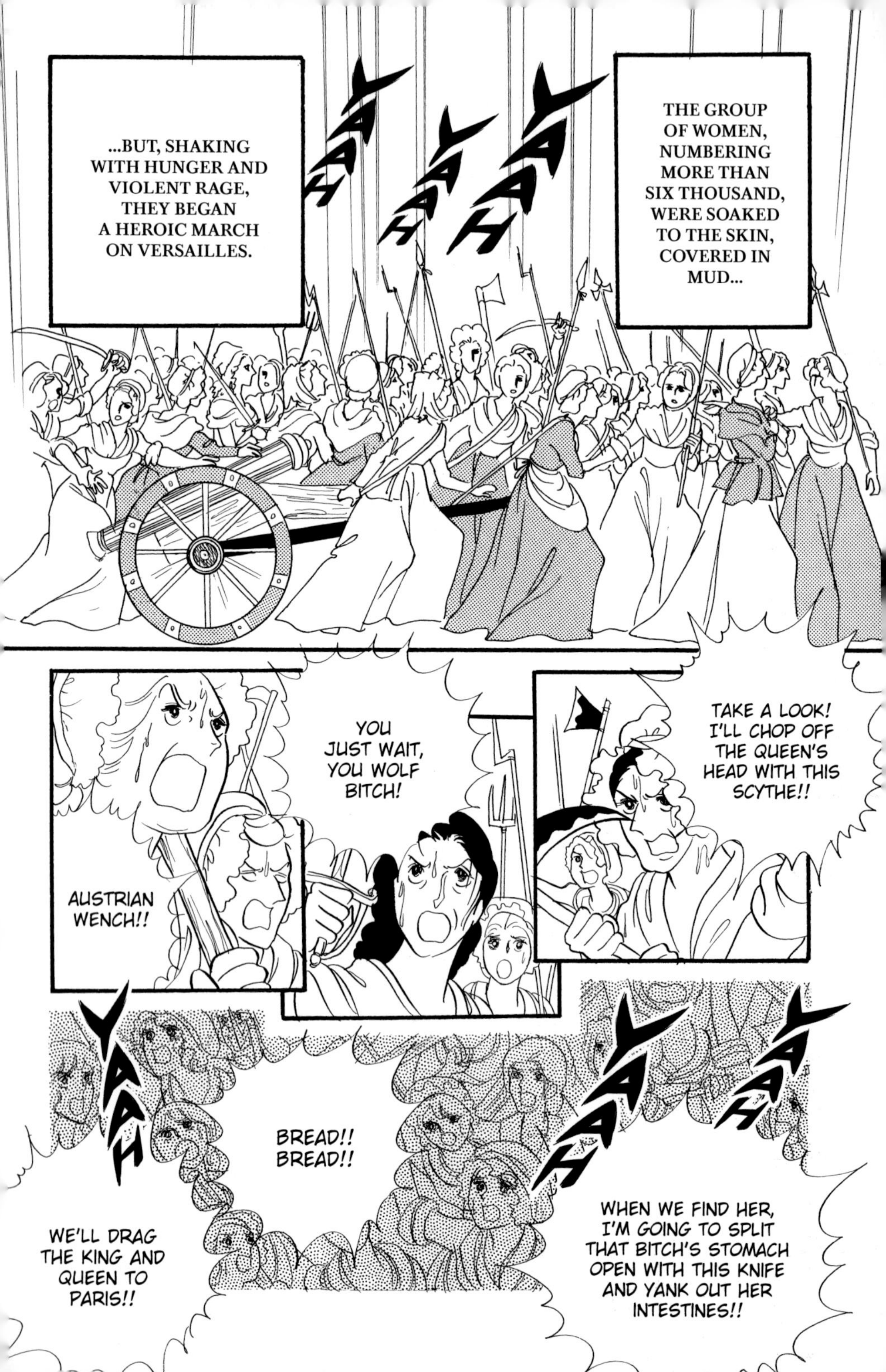

THE GROUP OF WOMEN, NUMBERING MORE THAN SIX THOUSAND, WERE SOAKED TO THE SKIN, COVERED IN MUD...
YAAH
YAAH
YAAH
...BUT, SHAKING WITH HUNGER AND VIOLENT RAGE, THEY BEGAN A HEROIC MARCH ON VERSAILLES.
TAKE A LOOK! I'LL CHOP OFF THE QUEEN'S HEAD WITH THIS SCYTHE!!
YOU JUST WAIT, YOU WOLF BITCH!
AUSTRIAN WENCH!!
YAAH
YAAH
WHEN WE FIND HER, I'M GOING TO SPLIT THAT BITCH'S STOMACH OPEN WITH THIS KNIFE AND YANK OUT HER INTESTINES!!
BREAD!! BREAD!!
YAAH
WE'LL DRAG THE KING AND QUEEN TO PARIS!!

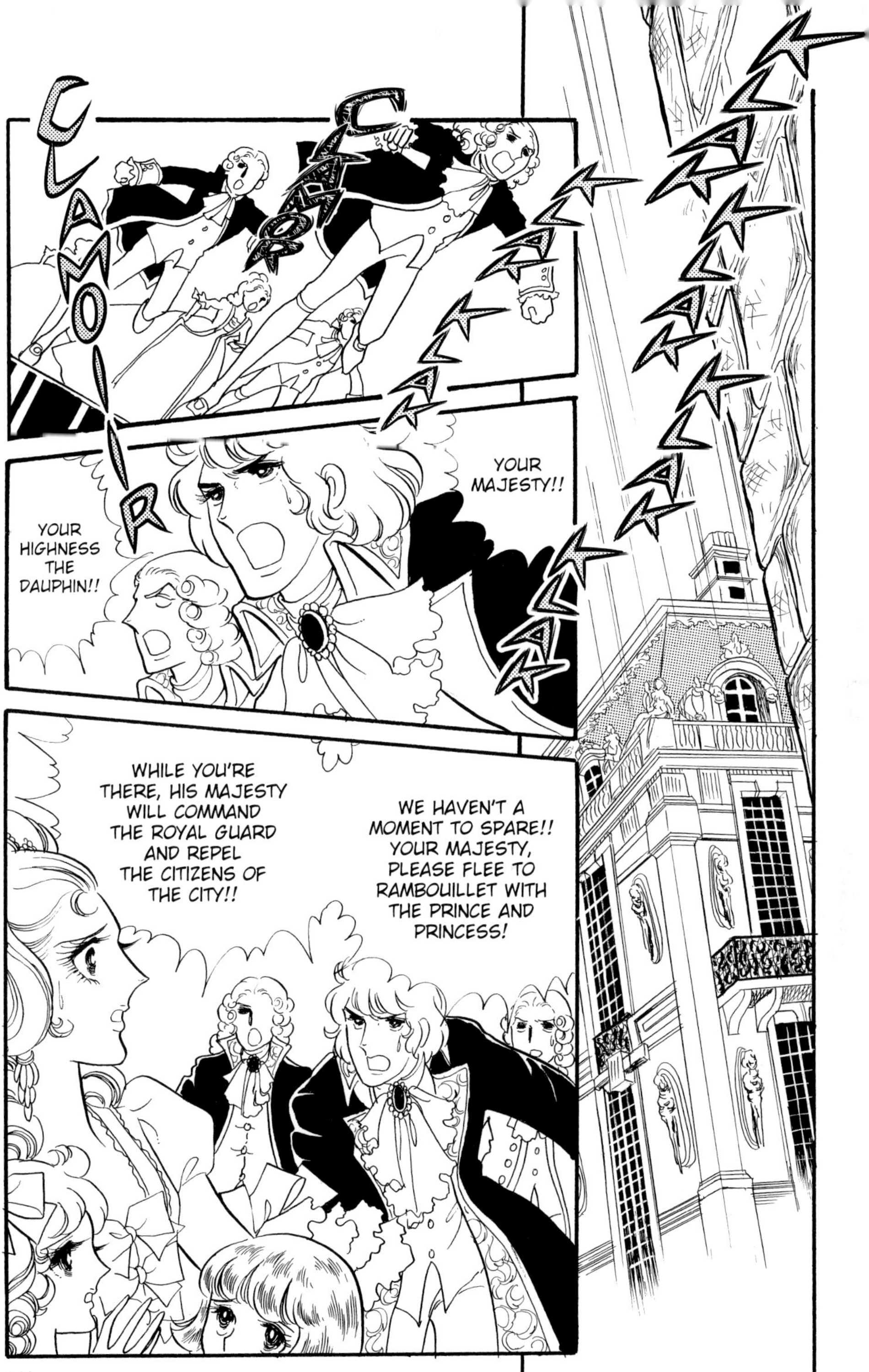
CLACK CLACK CLACK
CLACK CLACK CLACK
CLAMOR
CLAMOR
YOUR MAJESTY!!
YOUR HIGHNESS THE DAUPHIN!!
WE HAVEN'T A MOMENT TO SPARE!! YOUR MAJESTY, PLEASE FLEE TO RAMBOUILLET WITH THE PRINCE AND PRINCESS!
WHILE YOU'RE THERE, HIS MAJESTY WILL COMMAND THE ROYAL GUARD AND REPEL THE CITIZENS OF THE CITY!!

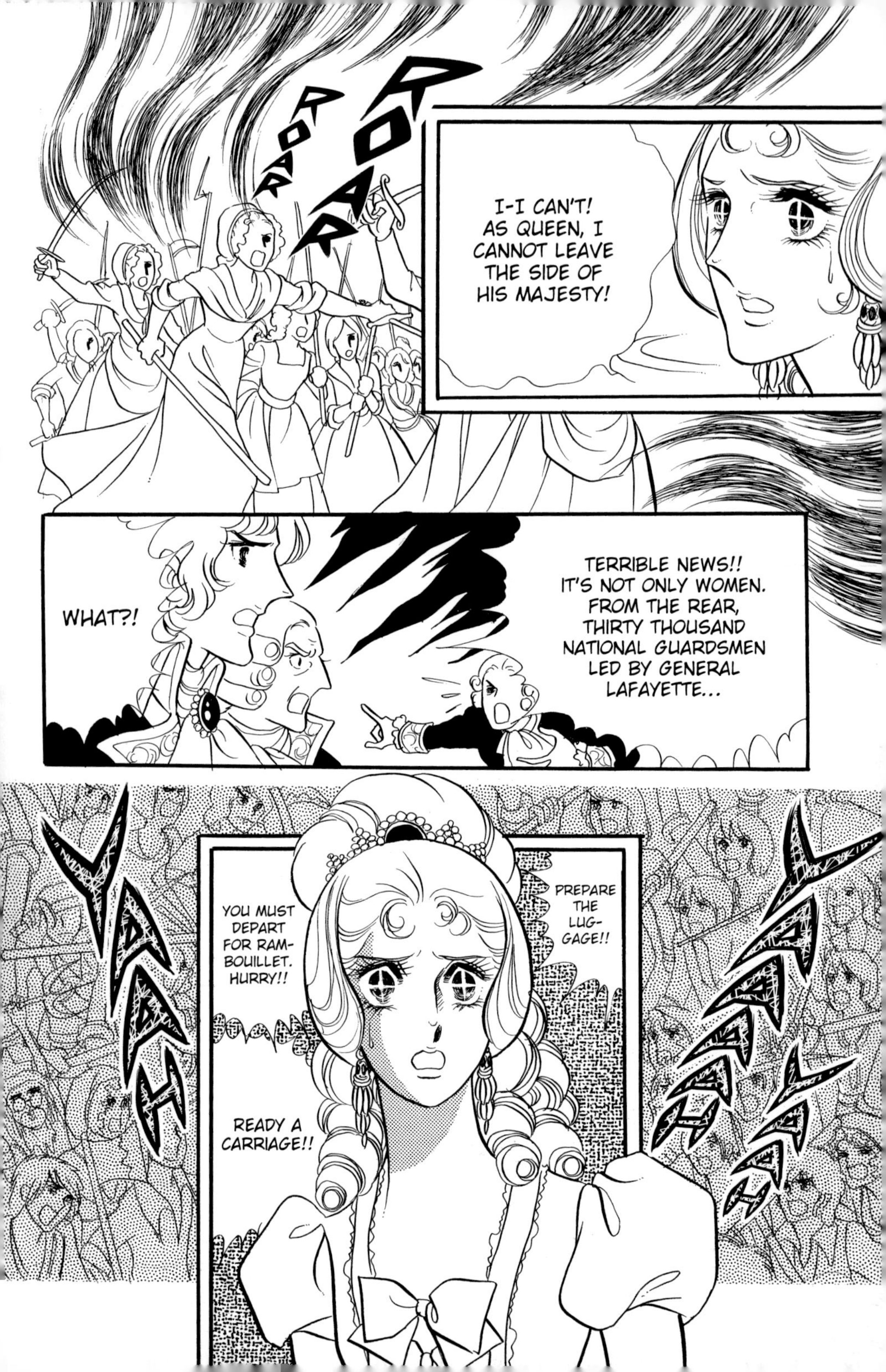
I-I CAN'T!
AS QUEEN, I CANNOT LEAVE THE SIDE OF HIS MAJESTY!
ROAR
ROAR
TERRIBLE NEWS!! IT'S NOT ONLY WOMEN. FROM THE REAR, THIRTY THOUSAND NATIONAL GUARDSMEN LED BY GENERAL LAFAYETTE...
WHAT?!
YAAAAH
YAAH
PREPARE THE LUG-GAGE!!
YOU MUST DEPART FOR RAM-BOUILLET. HURRY!!
READY A CARRIAGE!!
YAAH

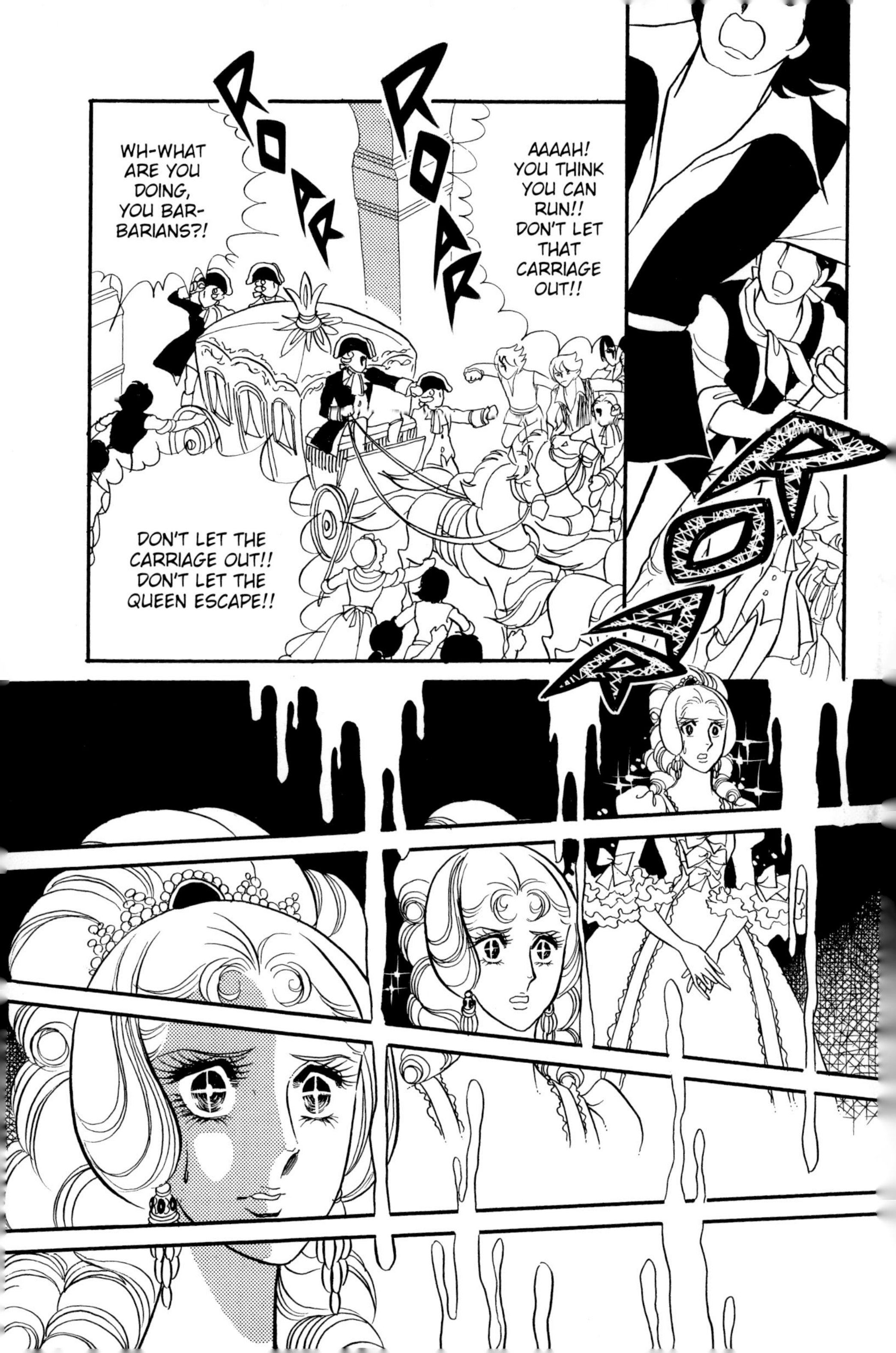
ROAR
AAAAH! YOU THINK YOU CAN RUN!! DON'T LET THAT CARRIAGE OUT!!
ROAR
ROAR
WH-WHAT ARE YOU DOING, YOU BAR-BARIANS?!
DON'T LET THE CARRIAGE OUT!! DON'T LET THE QUEEN ESCAPE!!

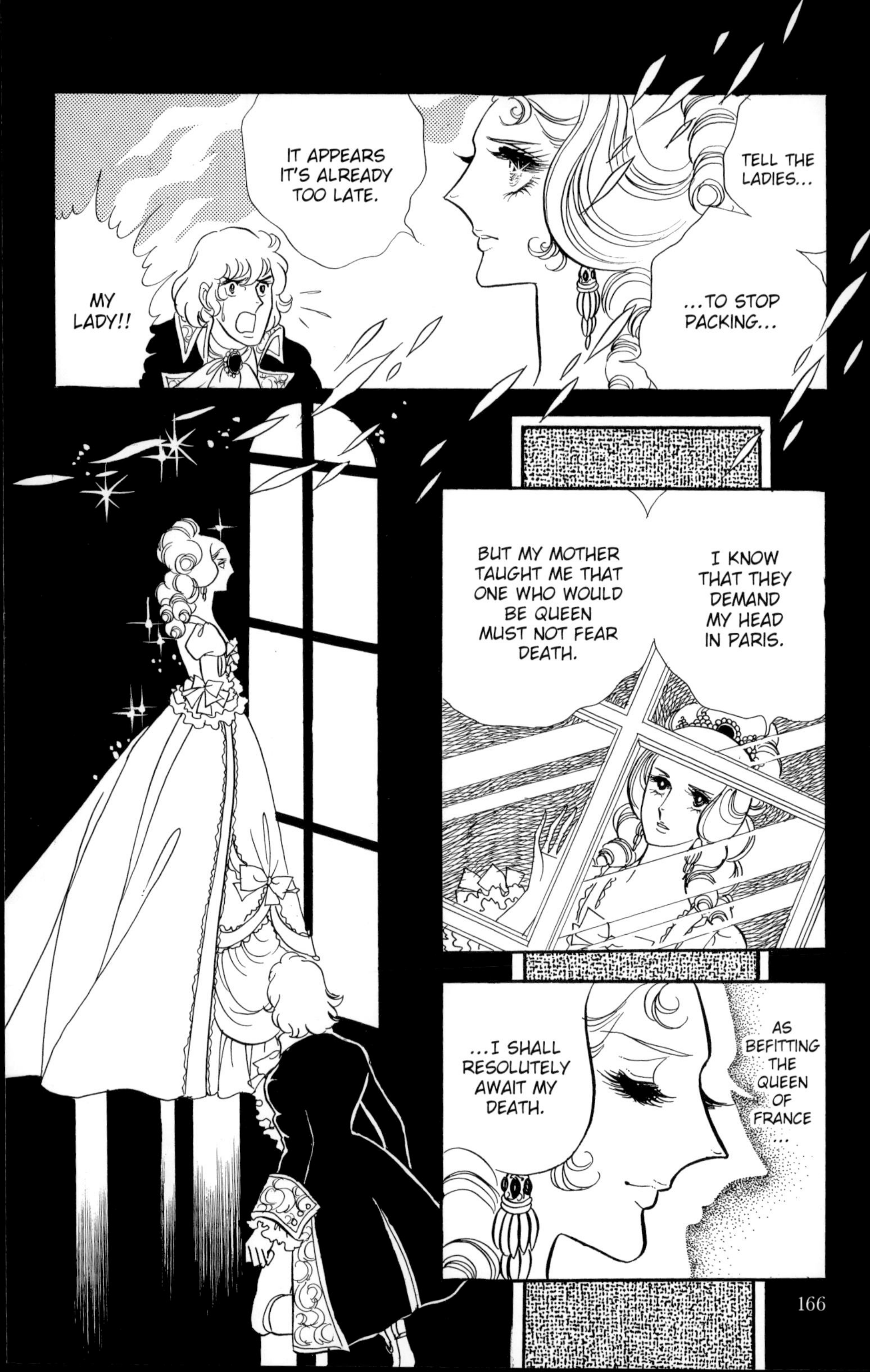

TELL THE LADIES...
...TO STOP PACKING...
IT APPEARS IT'S ALREADY TOO LATE.
MY LADY!!
I KNOW THAT THEY DEMAND MY HEAD IN PARIS.
BUT MY MOTHER TAUGHT ME THAT ONE WHO WOULD BE QUEEN MUST NOT FEAR DEATH.
AS BEFITTING THE QUEEN OF FRANCE...
...I SHALL RESOLUTELY AWAIT MY DEATH.

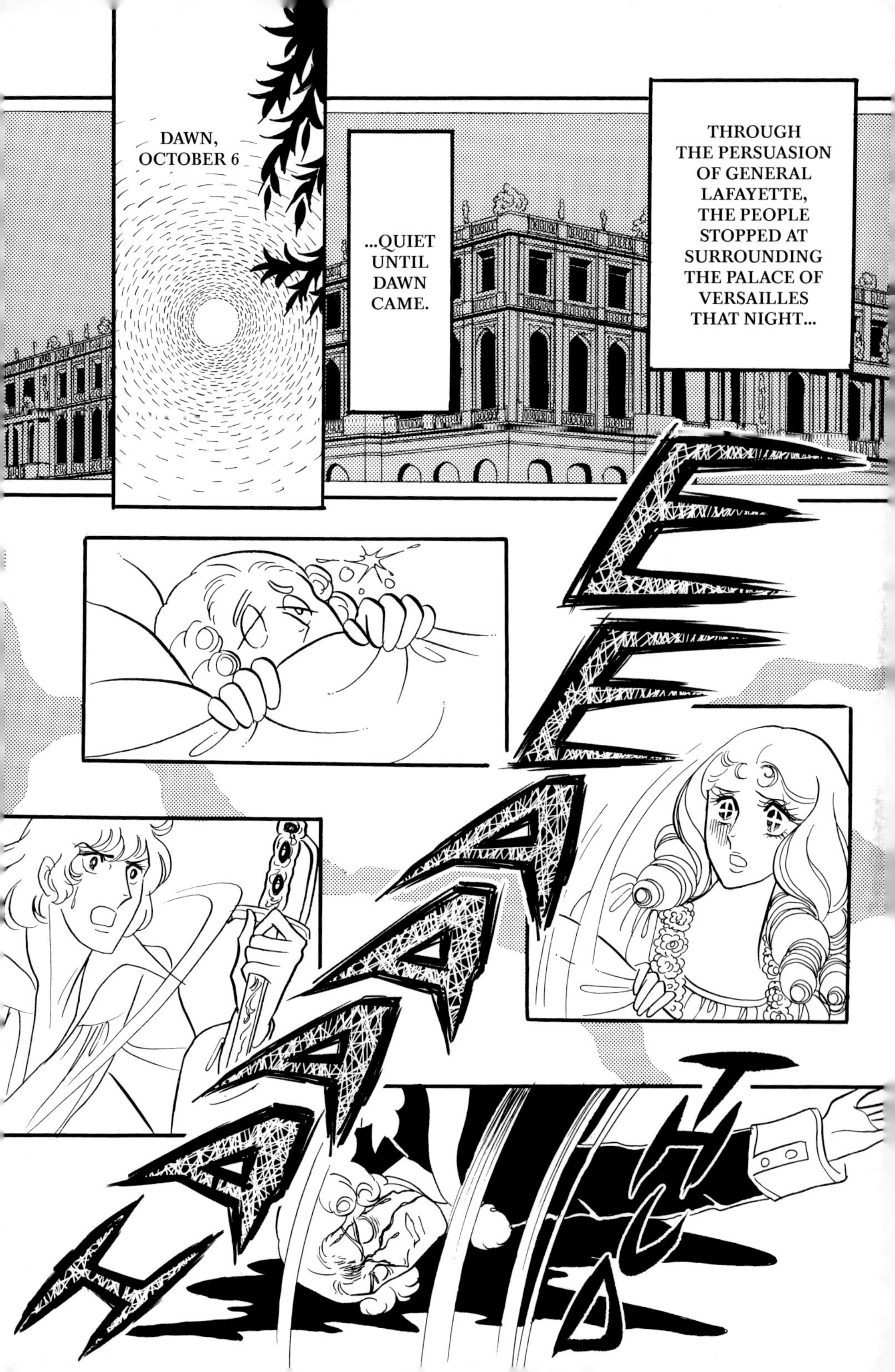
THROUGH THE PERSUASION OF GENERAL LAFAYETTE, THE PEOPLE STOPPED AT SURROUNDING THE PALACE OF VERSAILLES THAT NIGHT...
...QUIET UNTIL DAWN CAME.
DAWN, OCTOBER 6
EEEAAAAH

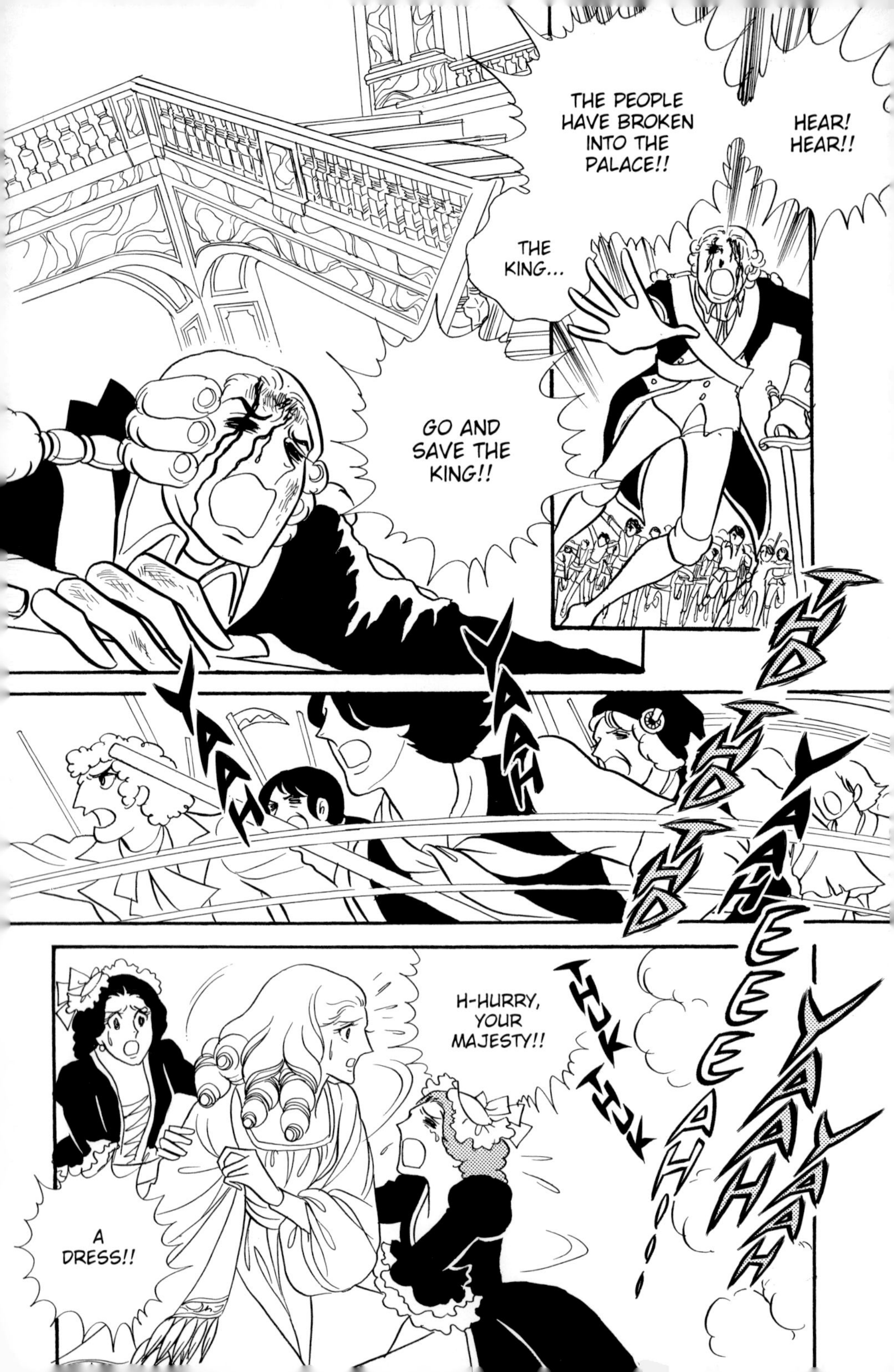
HEAR! HEAR!!
THE PEOPLE HAVE BROKEN INTO THE PALACE!!
THE KING...
GO AND SAVE THE KING!!
THUD THUD THUD THUD
YAAAH
YAAH
YAAHEEEEAAH!!!
YAAAAAAH
THUK THUK
H-HURRY, YOUR MAJESTY!!
A DRESS!!

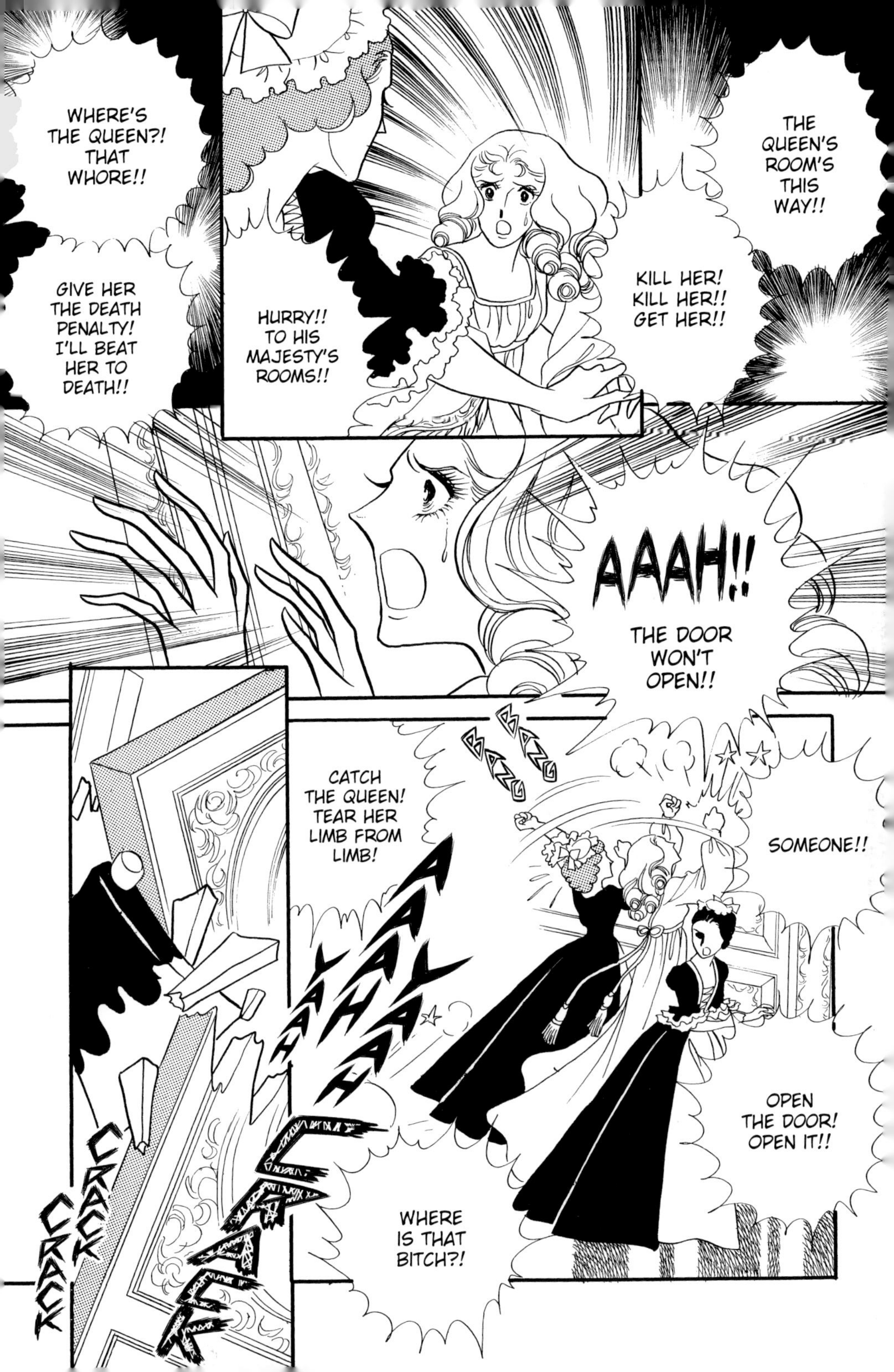
THE QUEEN'S ROOM'S THIS WAY!!
KILL HER! KILL HER!! GET HER!!
HURRY!! TO HIS MAJESTY'S ROOMS!!
WHERE'S THE QUEEN?! THAT WHORE!!
GIVE HER THE DEATH PENALTY! I'LL BEAT HER TO DEATH!!
AAAH!!
THE DOOR WON'T OPEN!!
BANG BANG
SOMEONE!!
OPEN THE DOOR! OPEN IT!!
CATCH THE QUEEN! TEAR HER LIMB FROM LIMB!
WHERE IS THAT BITCH?!
CRACK
CRACK CRACK

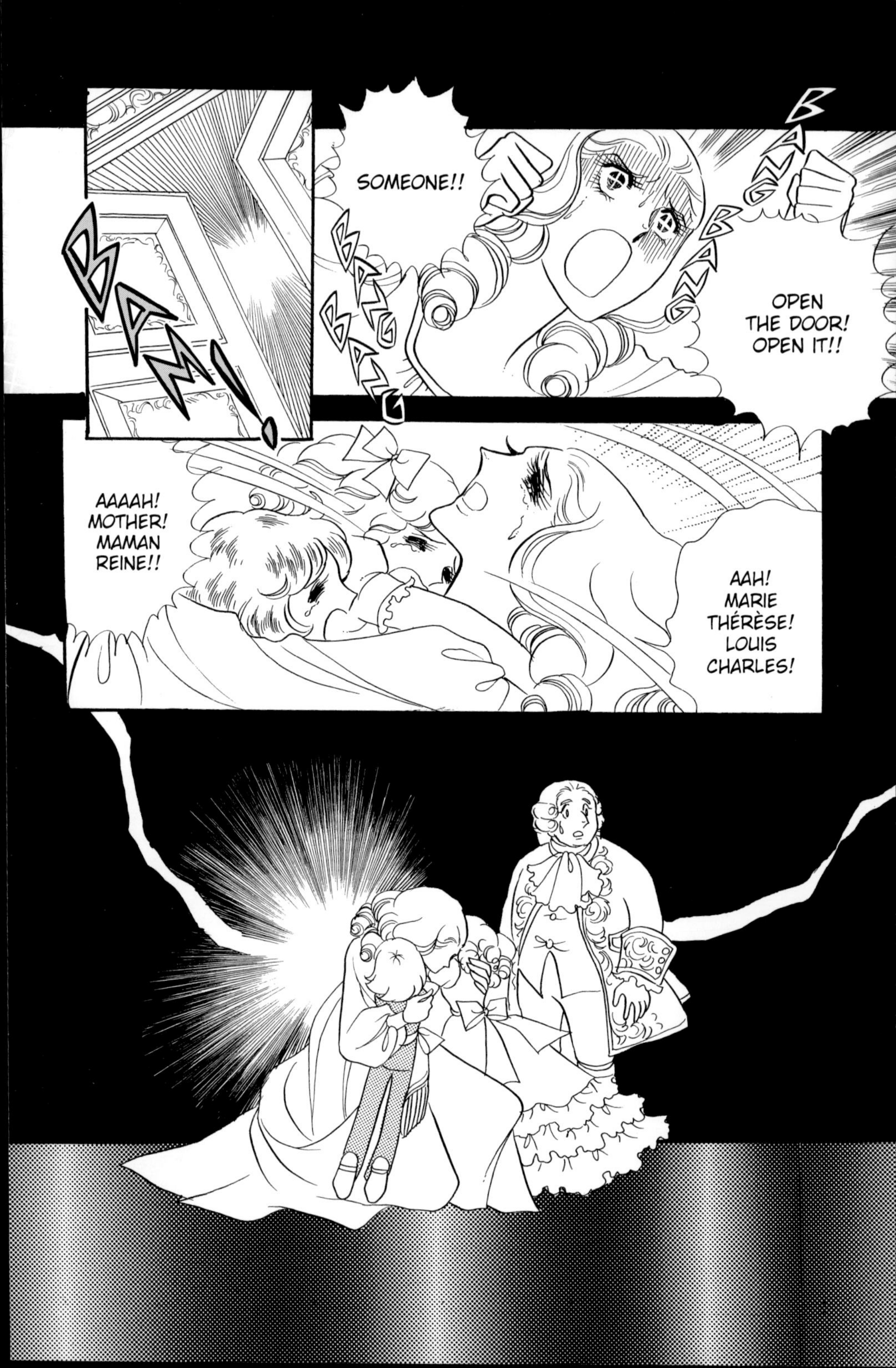
BANG BANG
OPEN THE DOOR! OPEN IT!!
SOMEONE!!
BANG BANG
BAM!
AAH! MARIE THÉRÈSE! LOUIS CHARLES!
AAAAH! MOTHER! MAMAN REINE!!

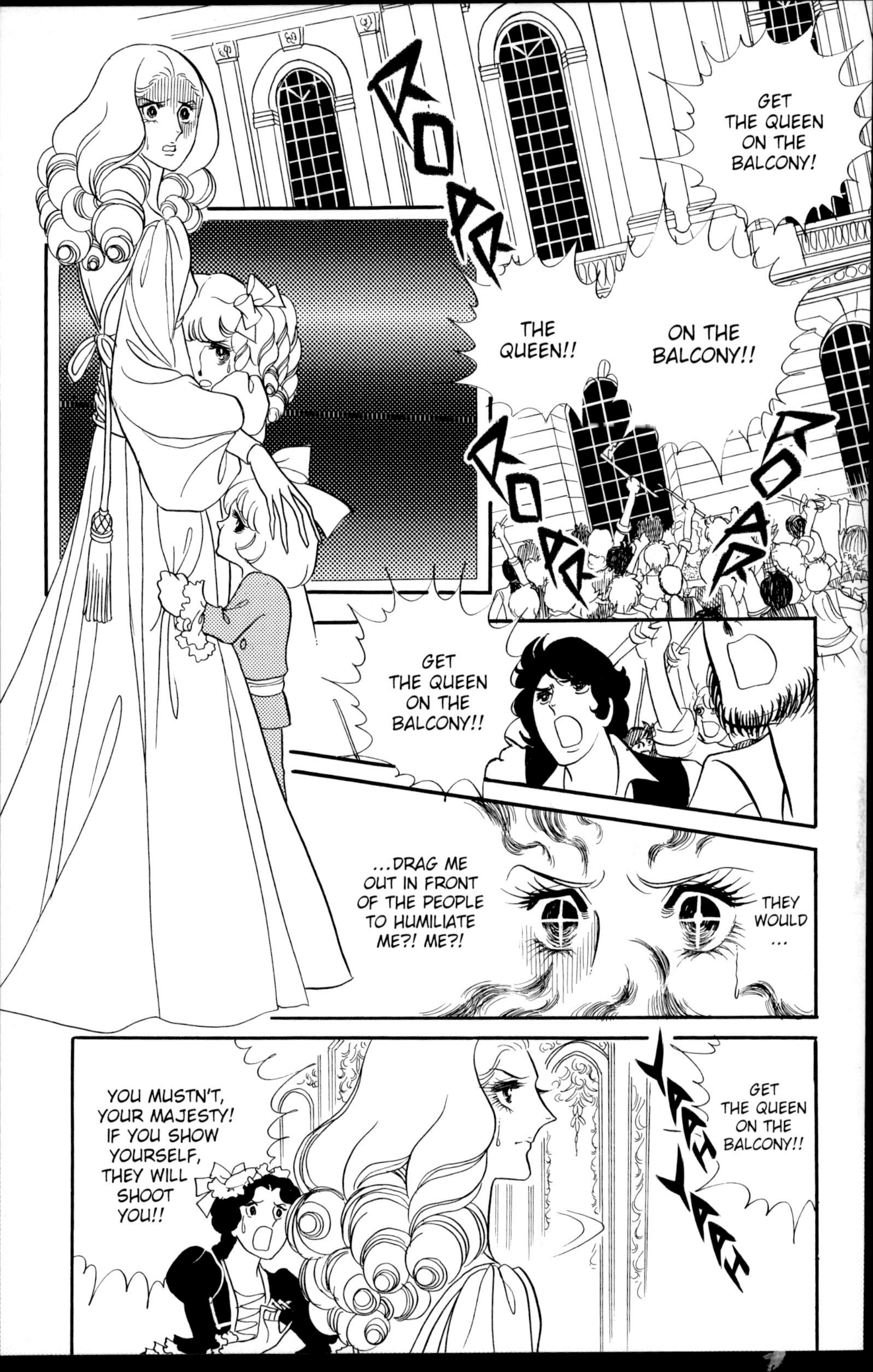
GET THE QUEEN ON THE BALCONY!
ROAR
ON THE BALCONY!!
THE QUEEN!!
ROAR
ROAR
GET THE QUEEN ON THE BALCONY!!
THEY WOULD ...
...DRAG ME OUT IN FRONT OF THE PEOPLE TO HUMILIATE ME?! ME?!
GET THE QUEEN ON THE BALCONY!!
YAAH YAAH
YOU MUSTN'T, YOUR MAJESTY! IF YOU SHOW YOURSELF, THEY WILL SHOOT YOU!!

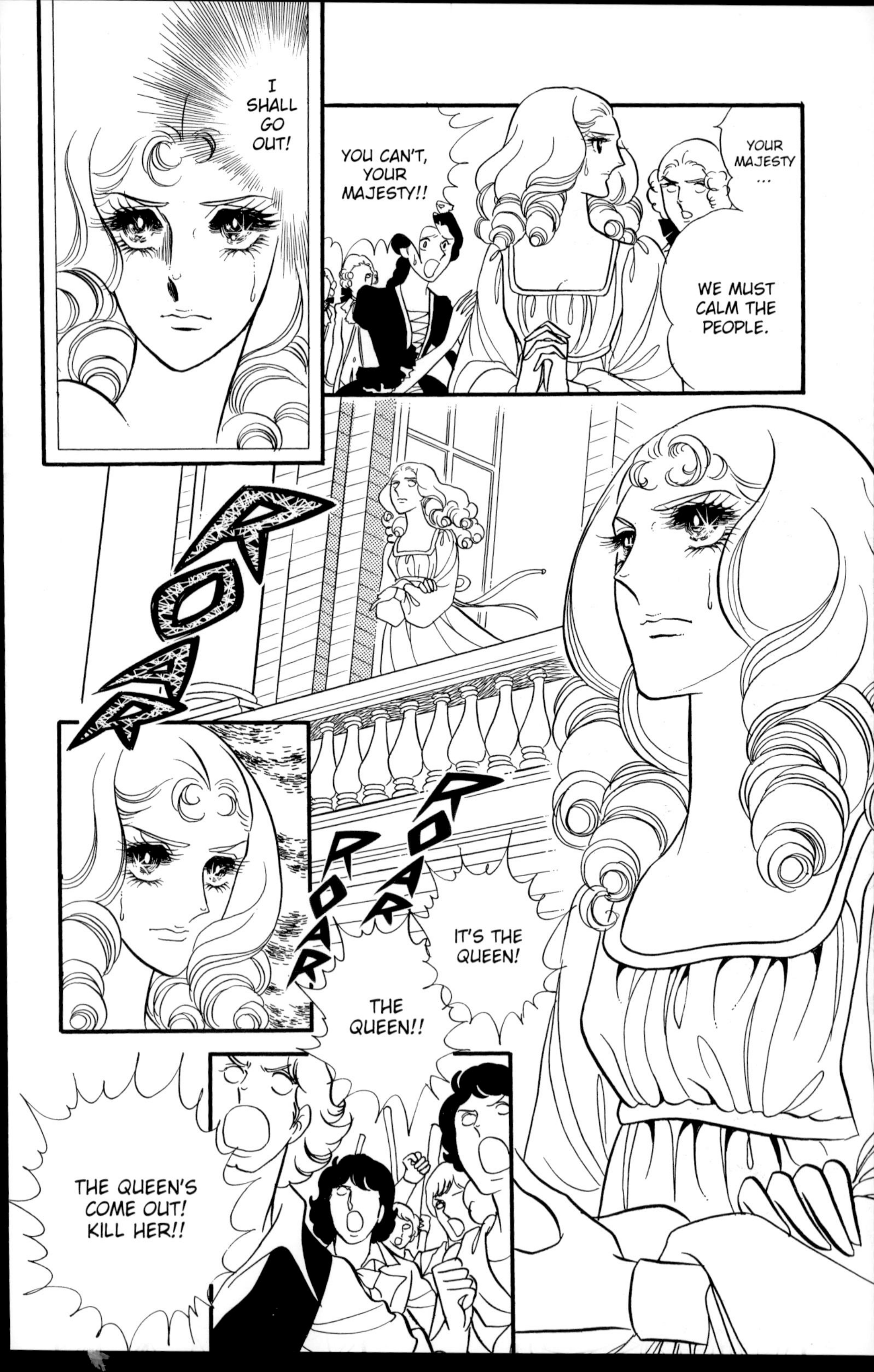
YOUR MAJESTY ...
WE MUST CALM THE PEOPLE.
YOU CAN'T, YOUR MAJESTY!!
I SHALL GO OUT!
ROAR
ROAR
ROAR
IT'S THE QUEEN!
THE QUEEN!!
THE QUEEN'S COME OUT! KILL HER!!

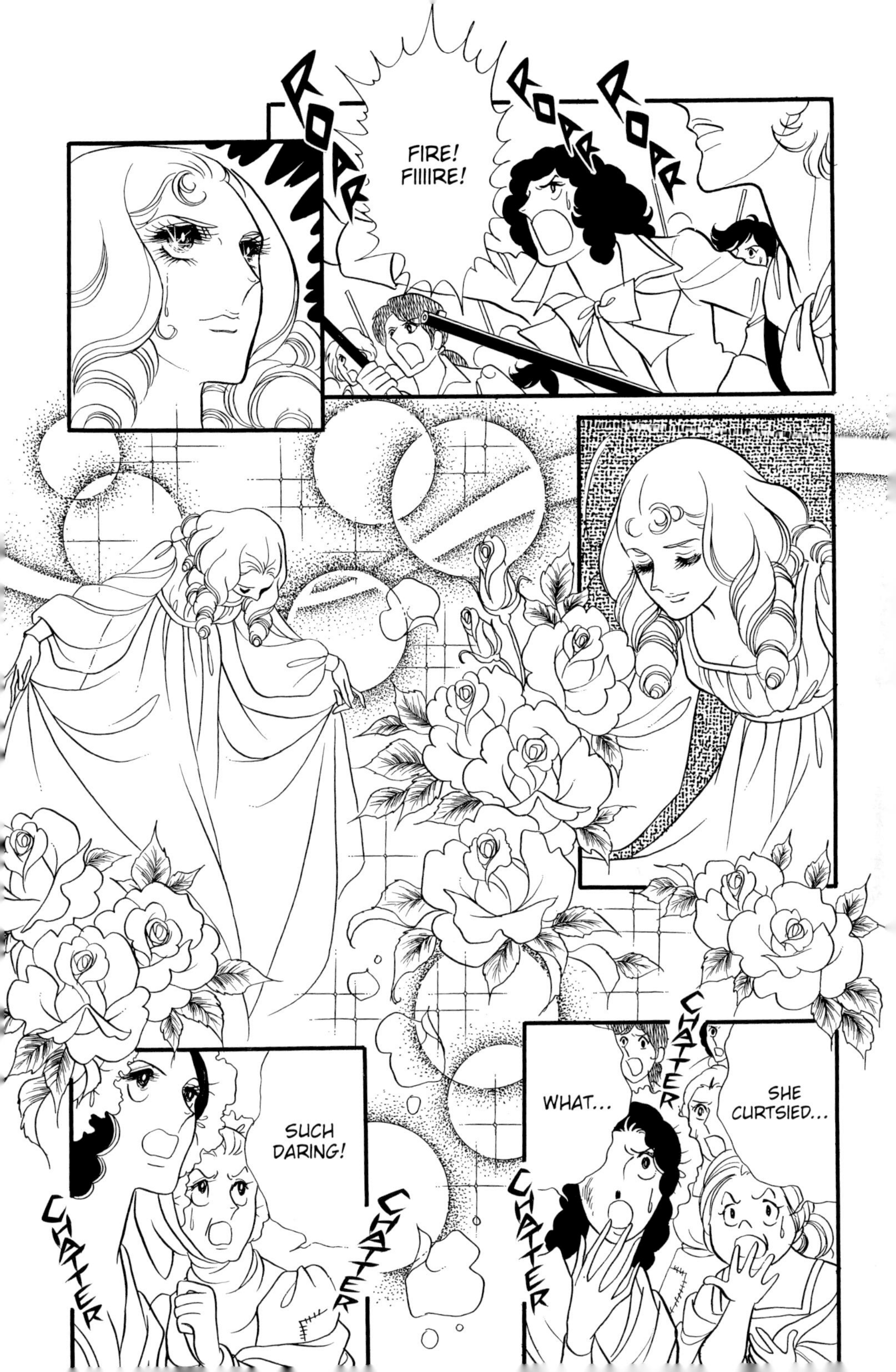
ROAR
ROAR
FIRE! FIIIRE!
ROAR
SHE CURTSIED...
CHATTER
WHAT...
CHATTER
SUCH DARING!
CHATTER
CHATTER

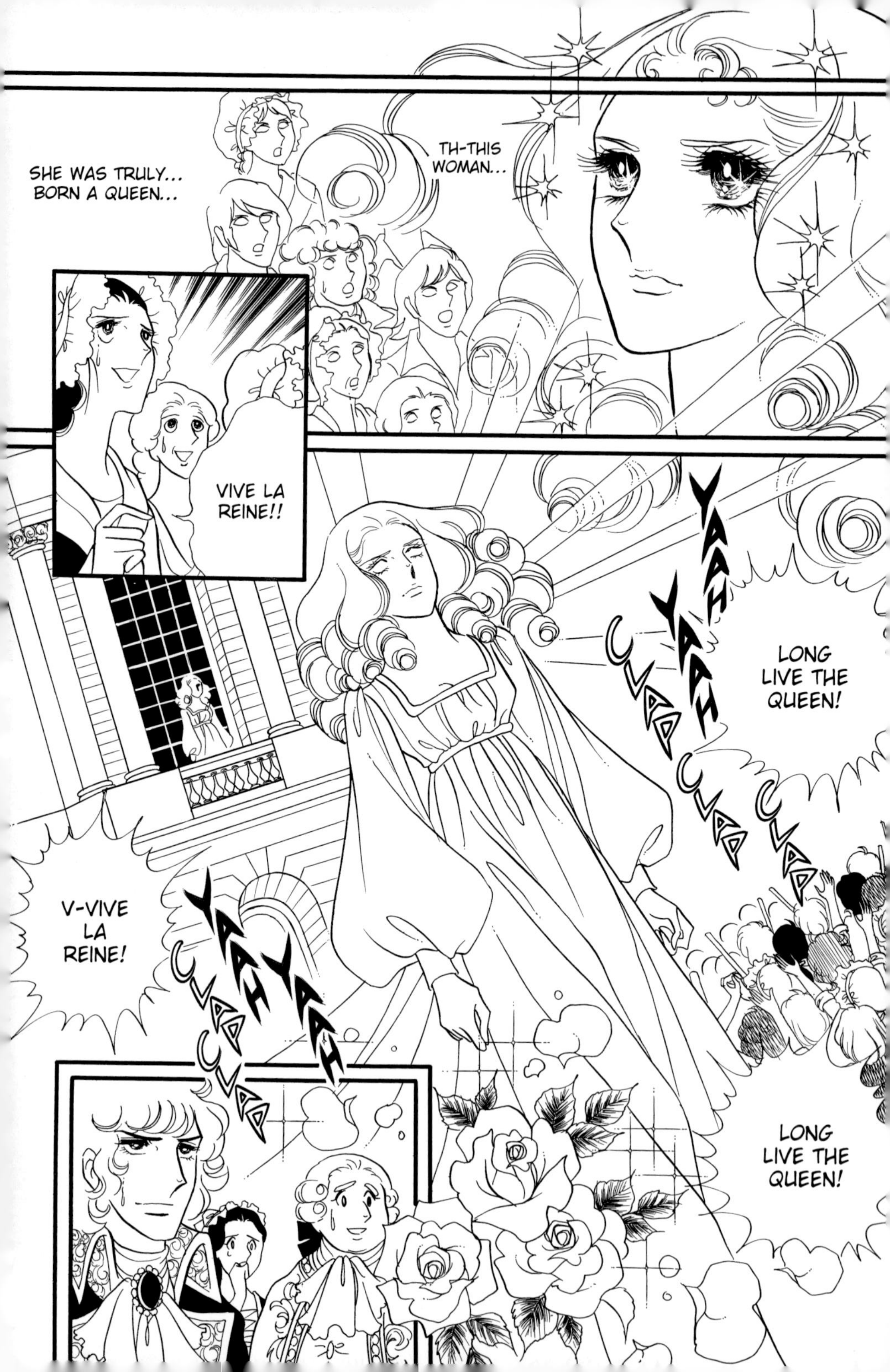
TH-THIS WOMAN...
SHE WAS TRULY... BORN A QUEEN...
VIVE LA REINE!!
YAAH YAAH
CLAP CLAP CLAP
LONG LIVE THE QUEEN!
LONG LIVE THE QUEEN!
V-VIVE LA REINE!
YAAH YAAH
CLAP CLAP

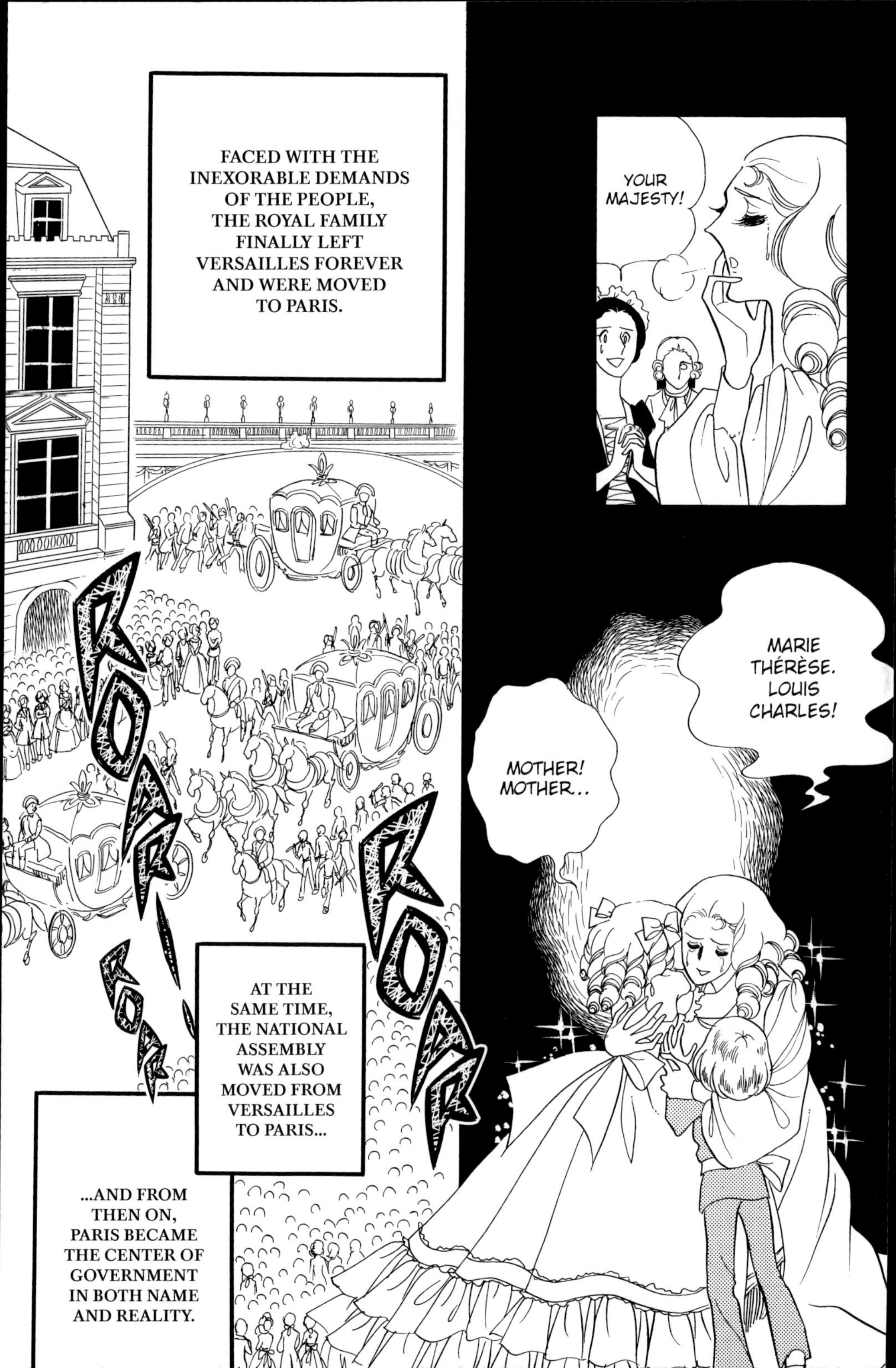
YOUR MAJESTY!
MARIE THÉRÈSE. LOUIS CHARLES!
MOTHER! MOTHER..
FACED WITH THE INEXORABLE DEMANDS OF THE PEOPLE, THE ROYAL FAMILY FINALLY LEFT VERSAILLES FOREVER AND WERE MOVED TO PARIS.
ROAR
ROAR
ROAR
AT THE SAME TIME, THE NATIONAL ASSEMBLY WAS ALSO MOVED FROM VERSAILLES TO PARIS...
...AND FROM THEN ON, PARIS BECAME THE CENTER OF GOVERNMENT IN BOTH NAME AND REALITY.

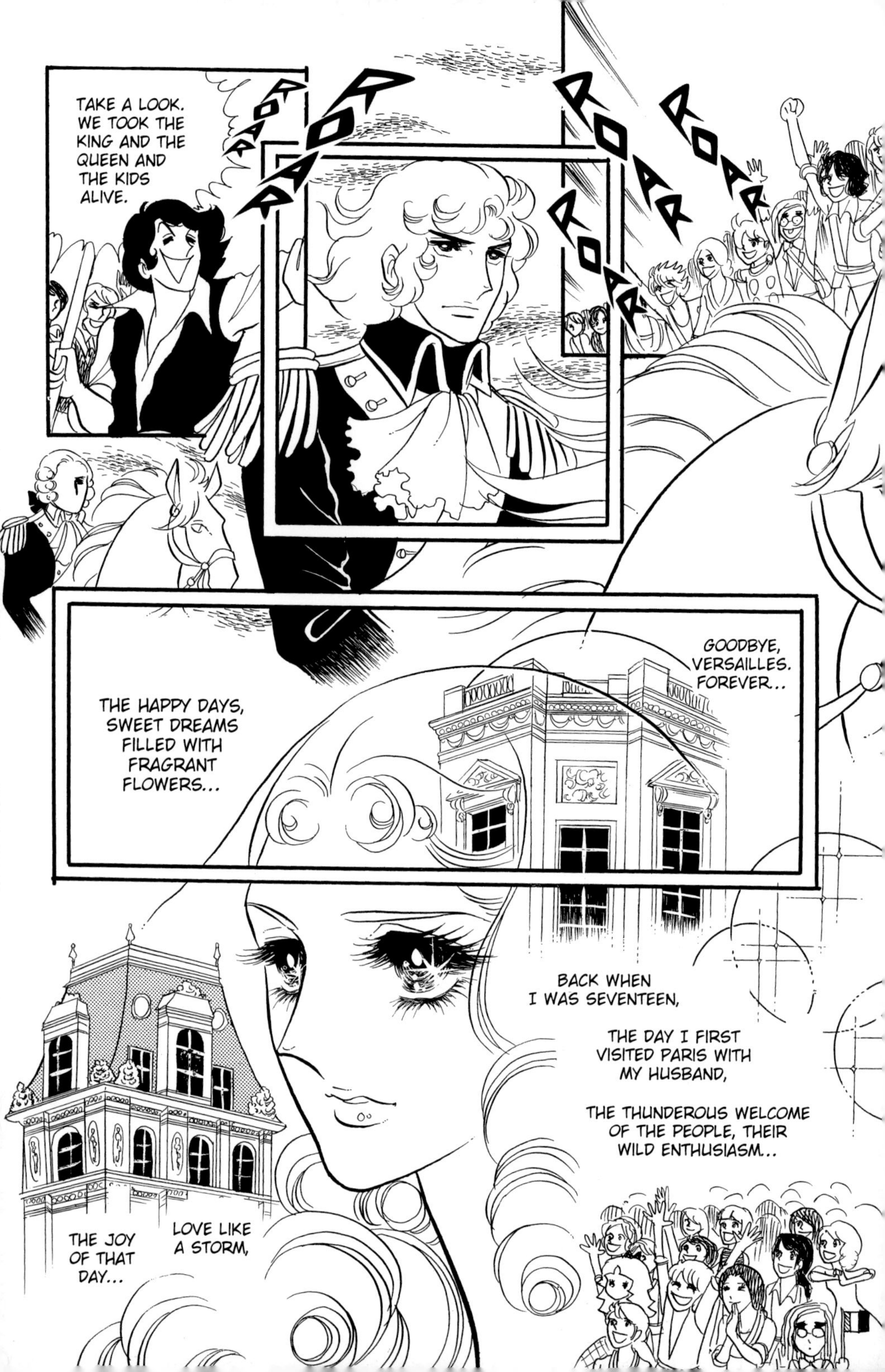
ROAR
ROAR
ROAR
ROAR
ROAR
TAKE A LOOK. WE TOOK THE KING AND THE QUEEN AND THE KIDS ALIVE.
GOODBYE, VERSAILLES. FOREVER...
THE HAPPY DAYS, SWEET DREAMS FILLED WITH FRAGRANT FLOWERS...
BACK WHEN I WAS SEVENTEEN,
THE DAY I FIRST VISITED PARIS WITH MY HUSBAND,
THE THUNDEROUS WELCOME OF THE PEOPLE, THEIR WILD ENTHUSIASM...
LOVE LIKE A STORM,
THE JOY OF THAT DAY...

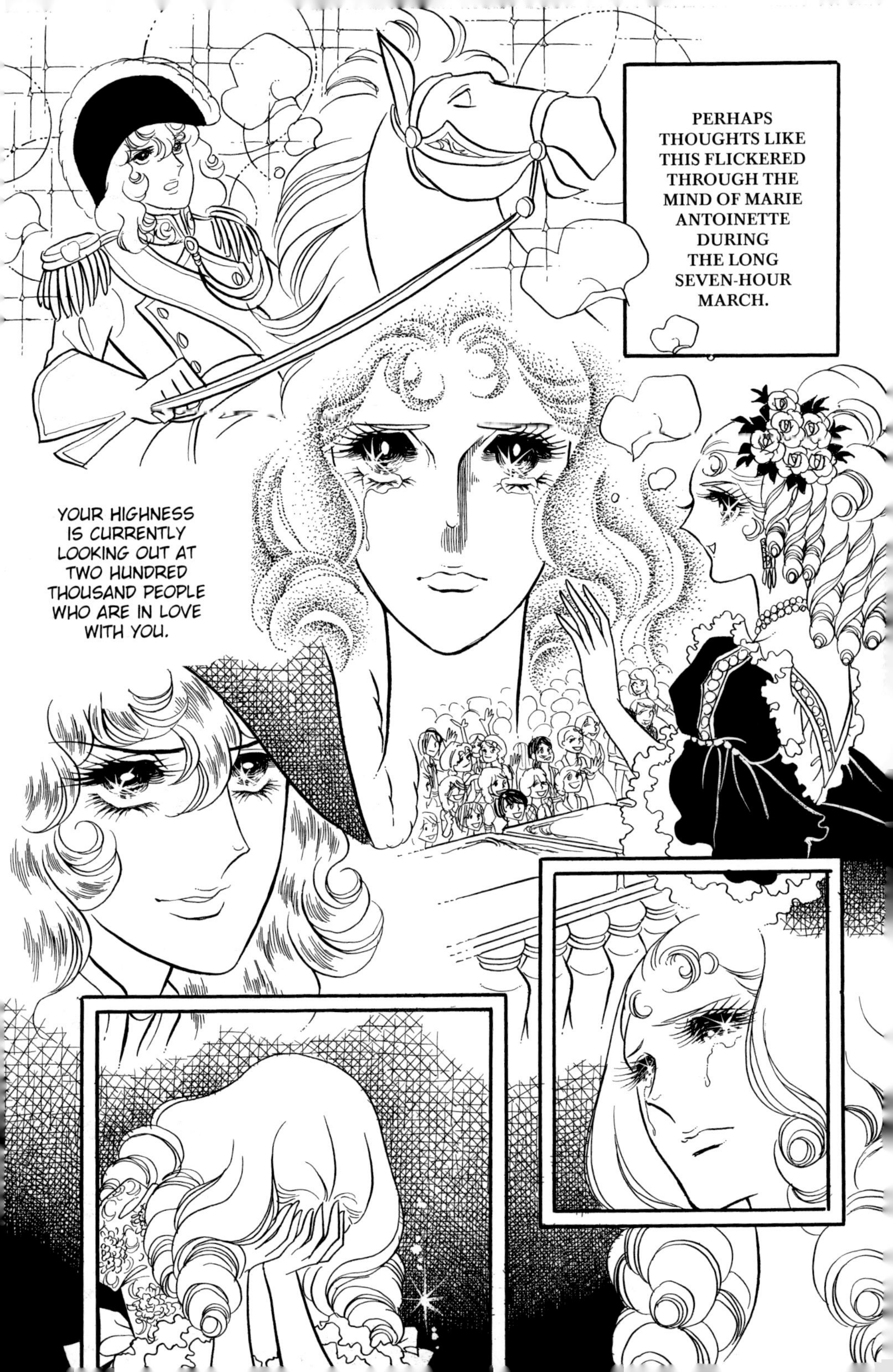
PERHAPS THOUGHTS LIKE THIS FLICKERED THROUGH THE MIND OF MARIE ANTOINETTE DURING THE LONG SEVEN-HOUR MARCH.
YOUR HIGHNESS IS CURRENTLY LOOKING OUT AT TWO HUNDRED THOUSAND PEOPLE WHO ARE IN LOVE WITH YOU.

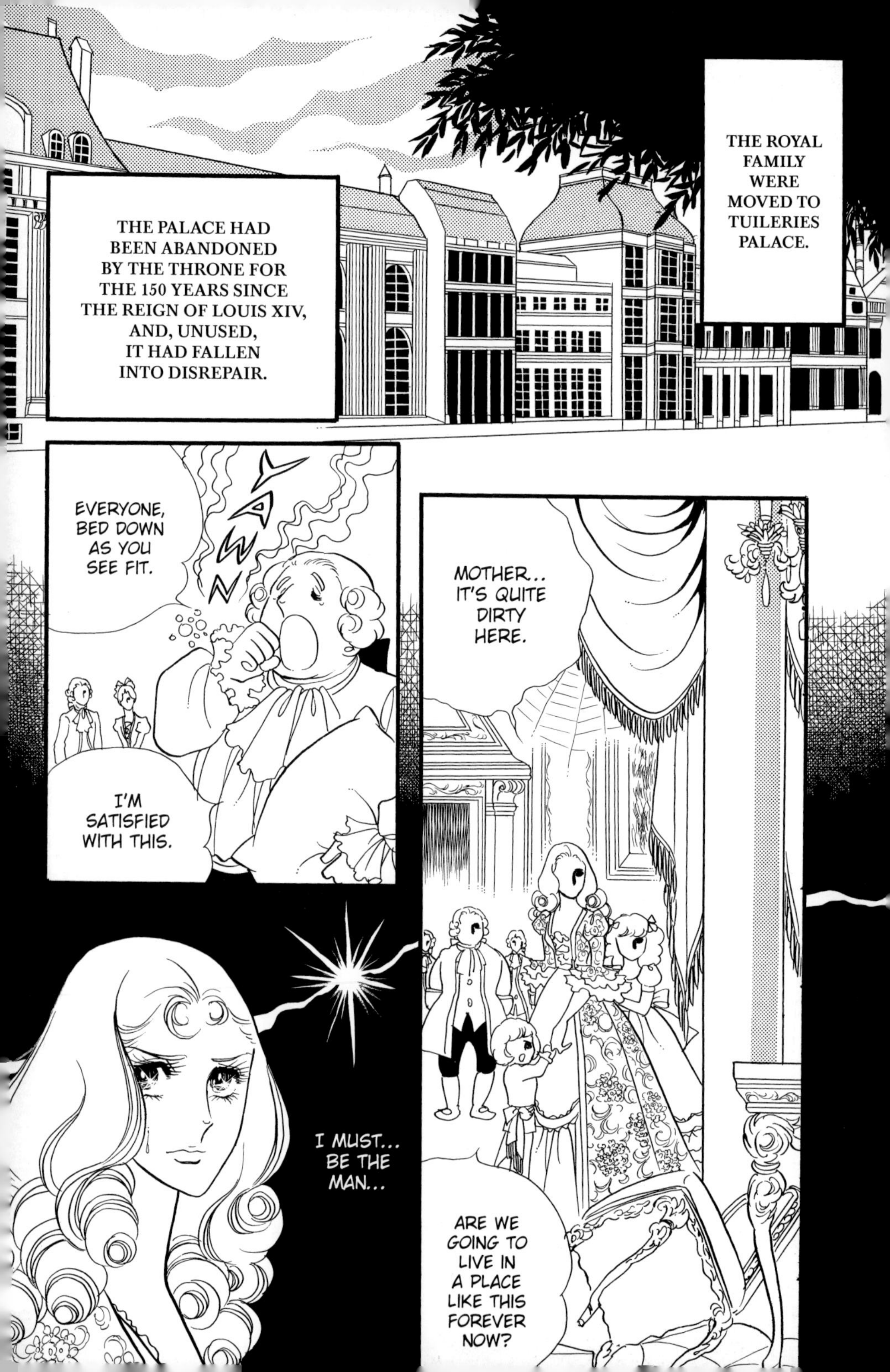
THE ROYAL FAMILY WERE MOVED TO TUILERIES PALACE.
THE PALACE HAD BEEN ABANDONED BY THE THRONE FOR THE 150 YEARS SINCE THE REIGN OF LOUIS XIV, AND, UNUSED, IT HAD FALLEN INTO DISREPAIR.
MOTHER... IT'S QUITE DIRTY HERE.
ARE WE GOING TO LIVE IN A PLACE LIKE THIS FOREVER NOW?
YAWN
EVERYONE, BED DOWN AS YOU SEE FIT.
I'M SATISFIED WITH THIS.
I MUST... BE THE MAN...

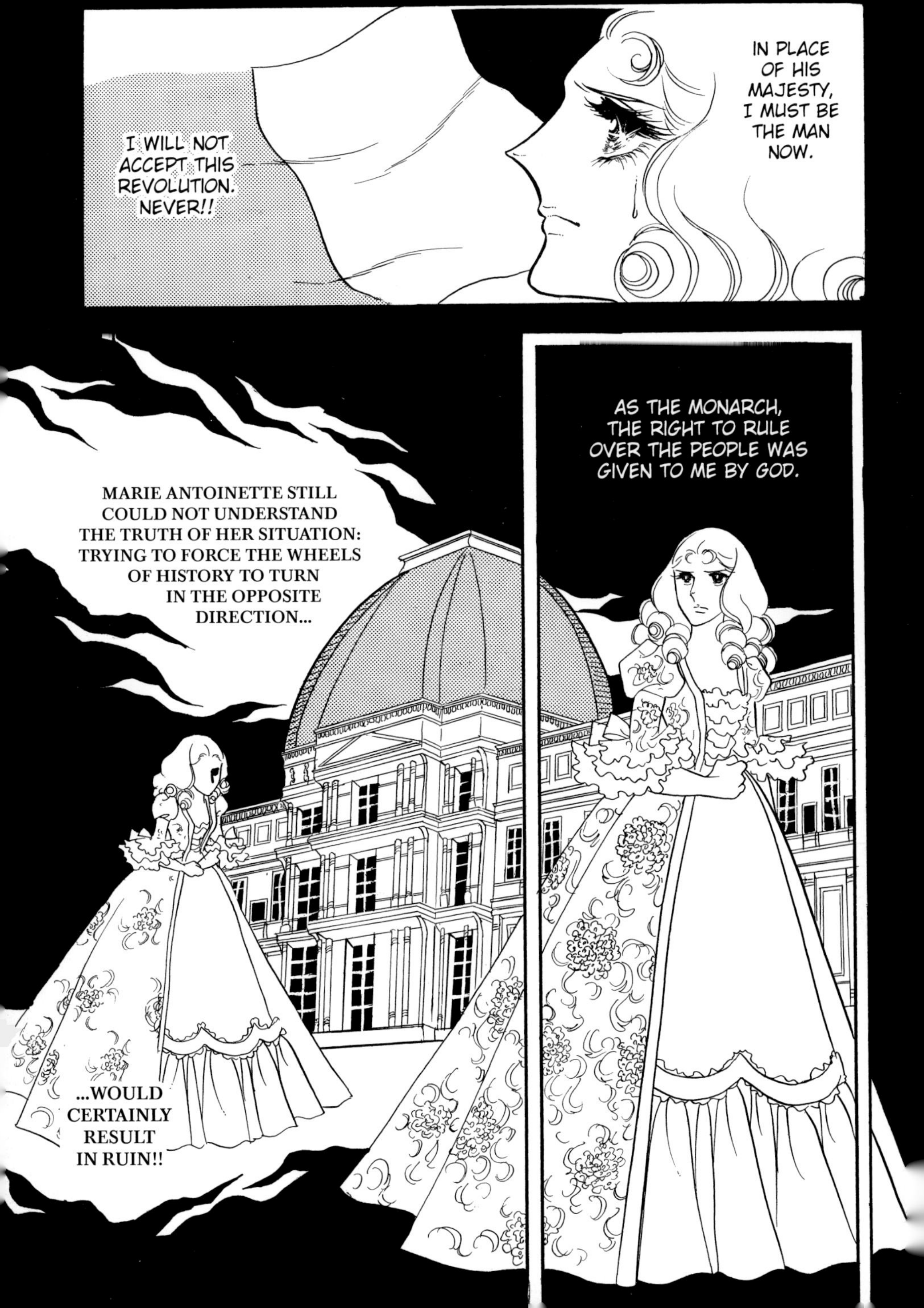
IN PLACE OF HIS MAJESTY, I MUST BE THE MAN NOW.
I WILL NOT ACCEPT THIS REVOLUTION. NEVER!!
AS THE MONARCH, THE RIGHT TO RULE OVER THE PEOPLE WAS GIVEN TO ME BY GOD.
MARIE ANTOINETTE STILL COULD NOT UNDERSTAND THE TRUTH OF HER SITUATION: TRYING TO FORCE THE WHEELS OF HISTORY TO TURN IN THE OPPOSITE DIRECTION...
...WOULD CERTAINLY RESULT IN RUIN!!

1974 MARGARET COMICS TRADE PAPERBACK
VOLUME 8 COVER

♥ THE UNCONTAINABLE EXCITEMENT!!
♥ AN INCREDIBLY MOVING GRAND ROMANCE!!

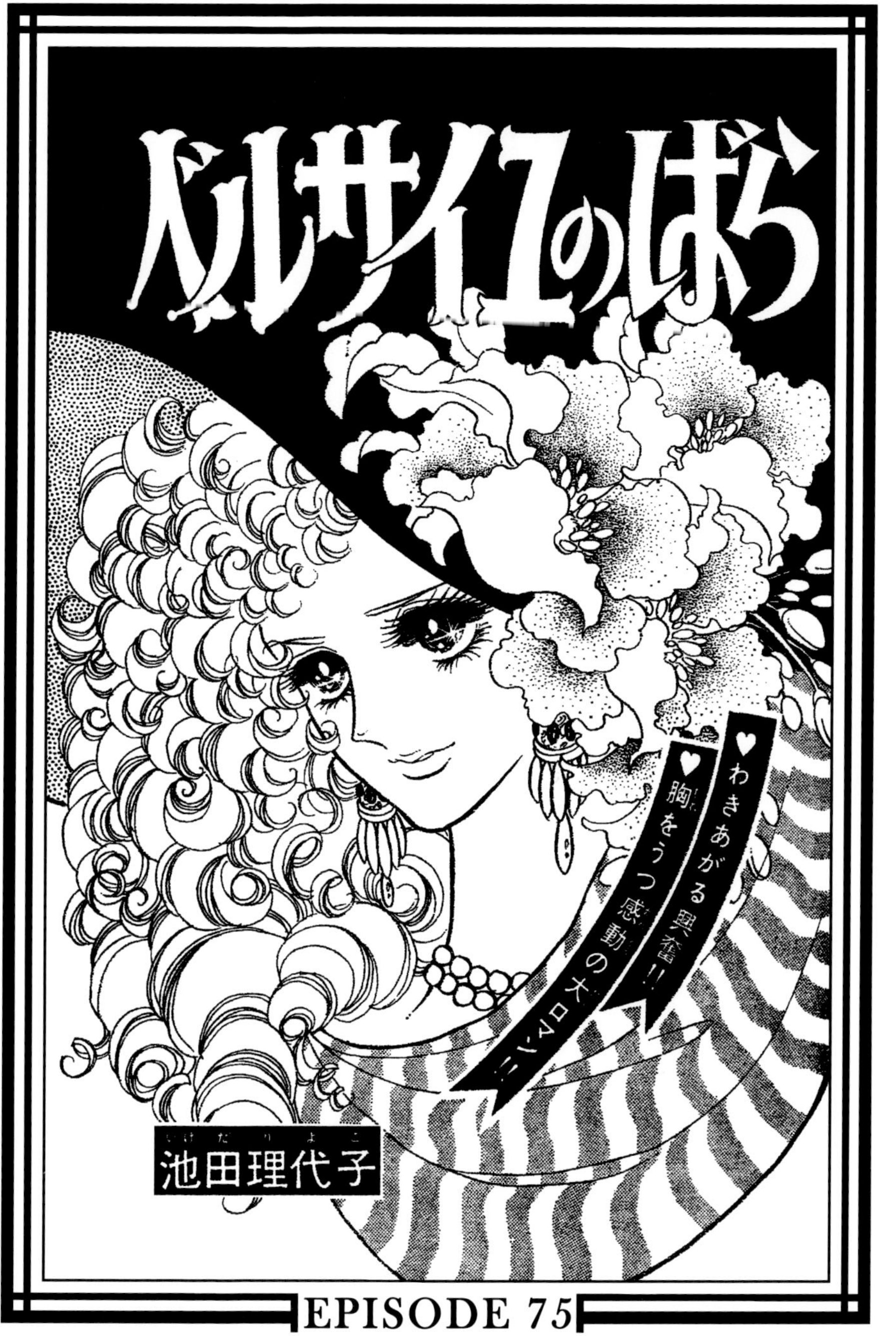
ベルサイユのばら
♥わきあがる興奮!!
♥胸をうつ感動の大ロマン!!
池田理代子

EPISODE 75

⚜Episode 75

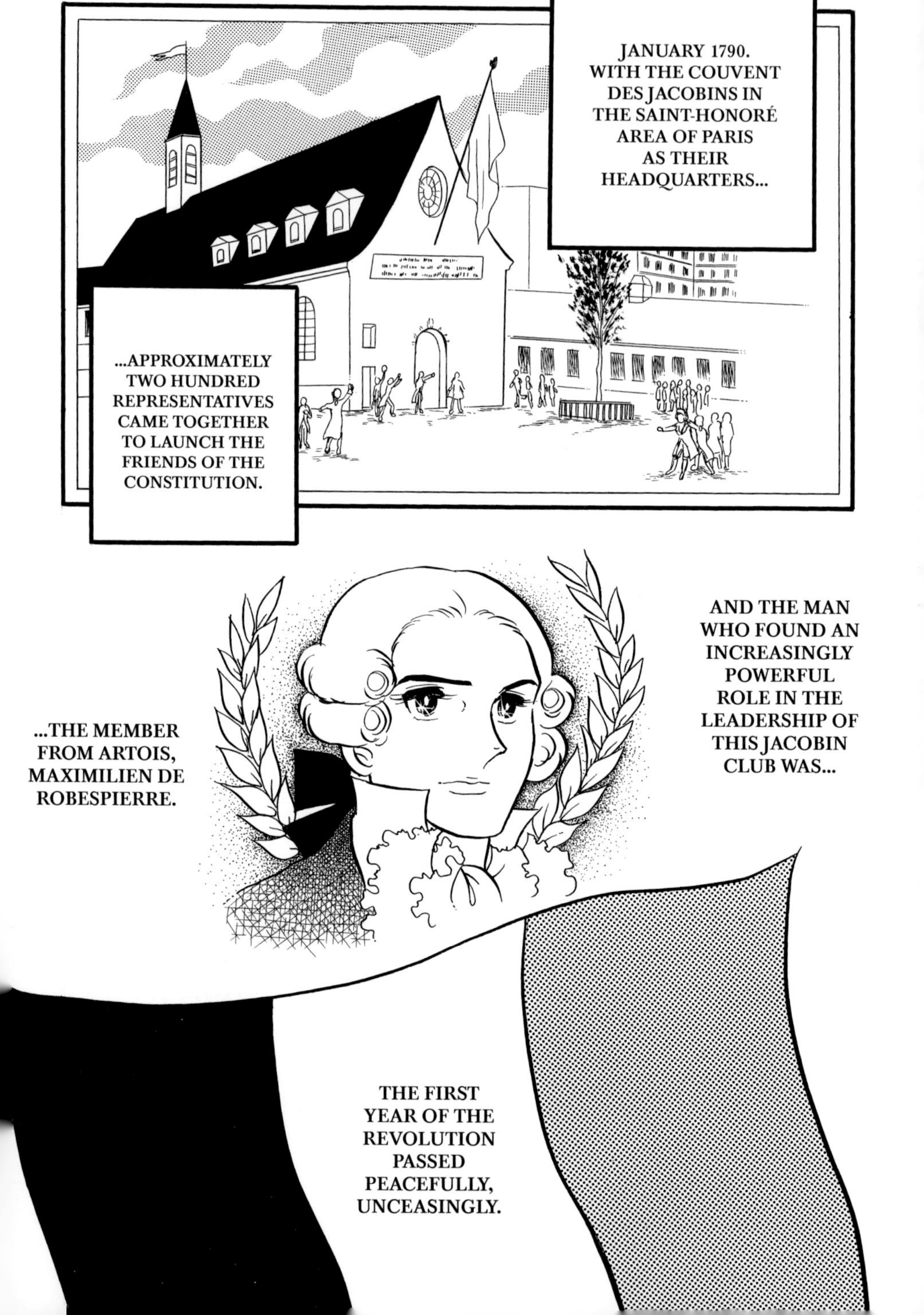
JANUARY 1790. WITH THE COUVENT DES JACOBINS IN THE SAINT-HONORÉ AREA OF PARIS AS THEIR HEADQUARTERS...
...APPROXIMATELY TWO HUNDRED REPRESENTATIVES CAME TOGETHER TO LAUNCH THE FRIENDS OF THE CONSTITUTION.
AND THE MAN WHO FOUND AN INCREASINGLY POWERFUL ROLE IN THE LEADERSHIP OF THIS JACOBIN CLUB WAS...
...THE MEMBER FROM ARTOIS, MAXIMILIEN DE ROBESPIERRE.
THE FIRST YEAR OF THE REVOLUTION PASSED PEACEFULLY, UNCEASINGLY.

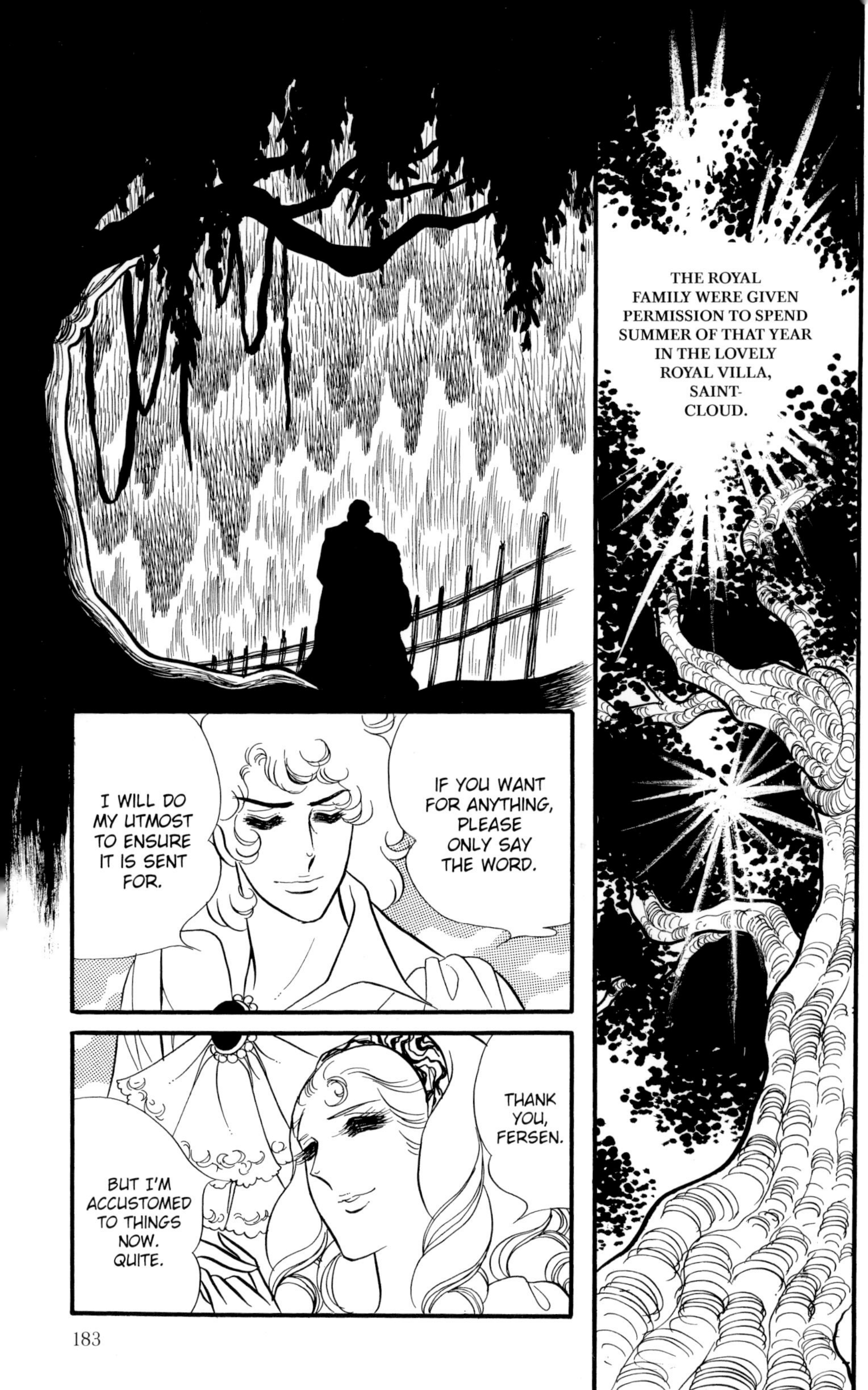
THE ROYAL FAMILY WERE GIVEN PERMISSION TO SPEND SUMMER OF THAT YEAR IN THE LOVELY ROYAL VILLA, SAINT-CLOUD.
IF YOU WANT FOR ANYTHING, PLEASE ONLY SAY THE WORD.
I WILL DO MY UTMOST TO ENSURE IT IS SENT FOR.
THANK YOU, FERSEN.
BUT I'M ACCUSTOMED TO THINGS NOW. QUITE.

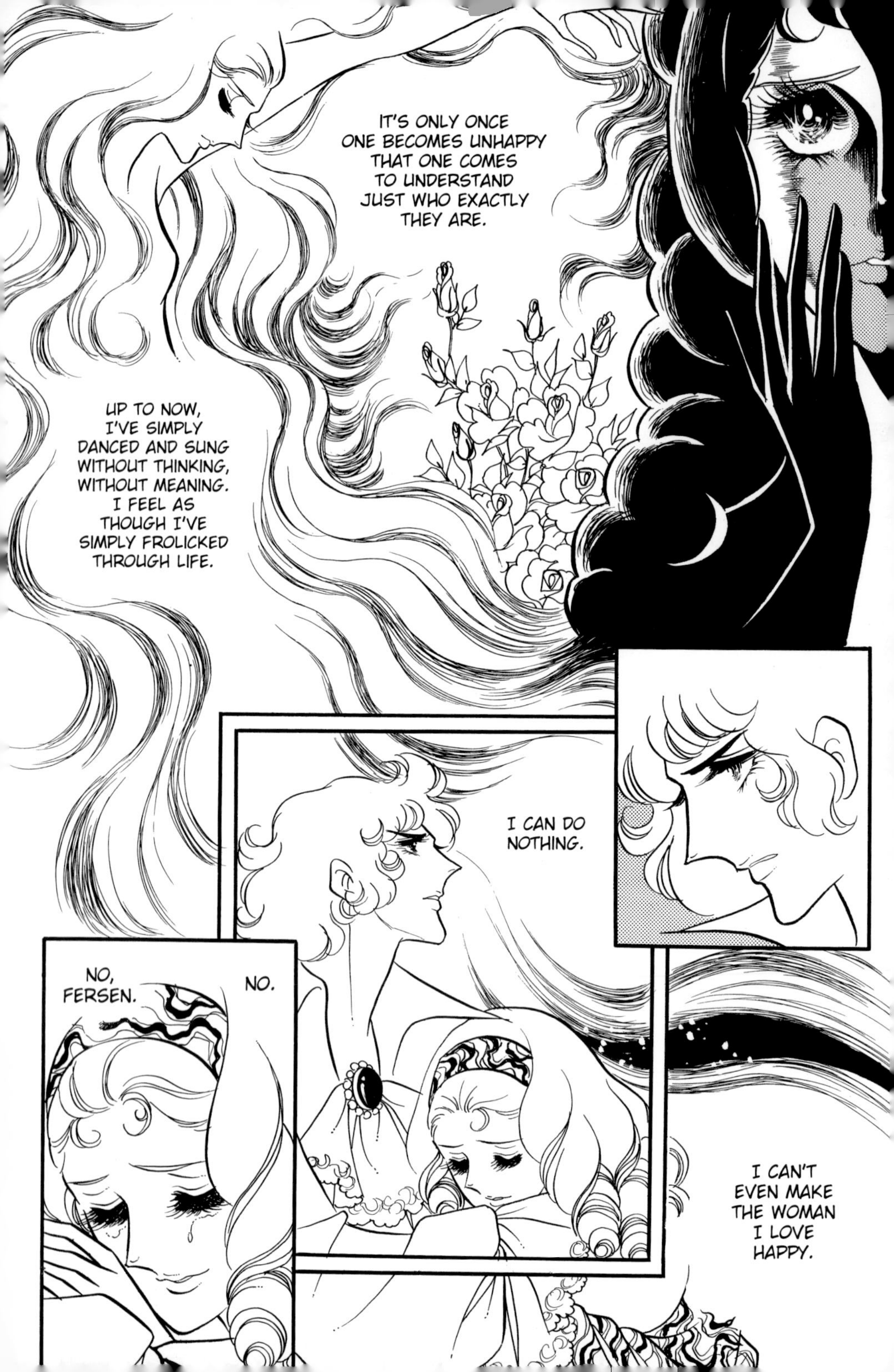
IT'S ONLY ONCE ONE BECOMES UNHAPPY THAT ONE COMES TO UNDERSTAND JUST WHO EXACTLY THEY ARE.
UP TO NOW, I'VE SIMPLY DANCED AND SUNG WITHOUT THINKING, WITHOUT MEANING. I FEEL AS THOUGH I'VE SIMPLY FROLICKED THROUGH LIFE.
I CAN DO NOTHING.
I CAN'T EVEN MAKE THE WOMAN I LOVE HAPPY.
NO.
NO, FERSEN.

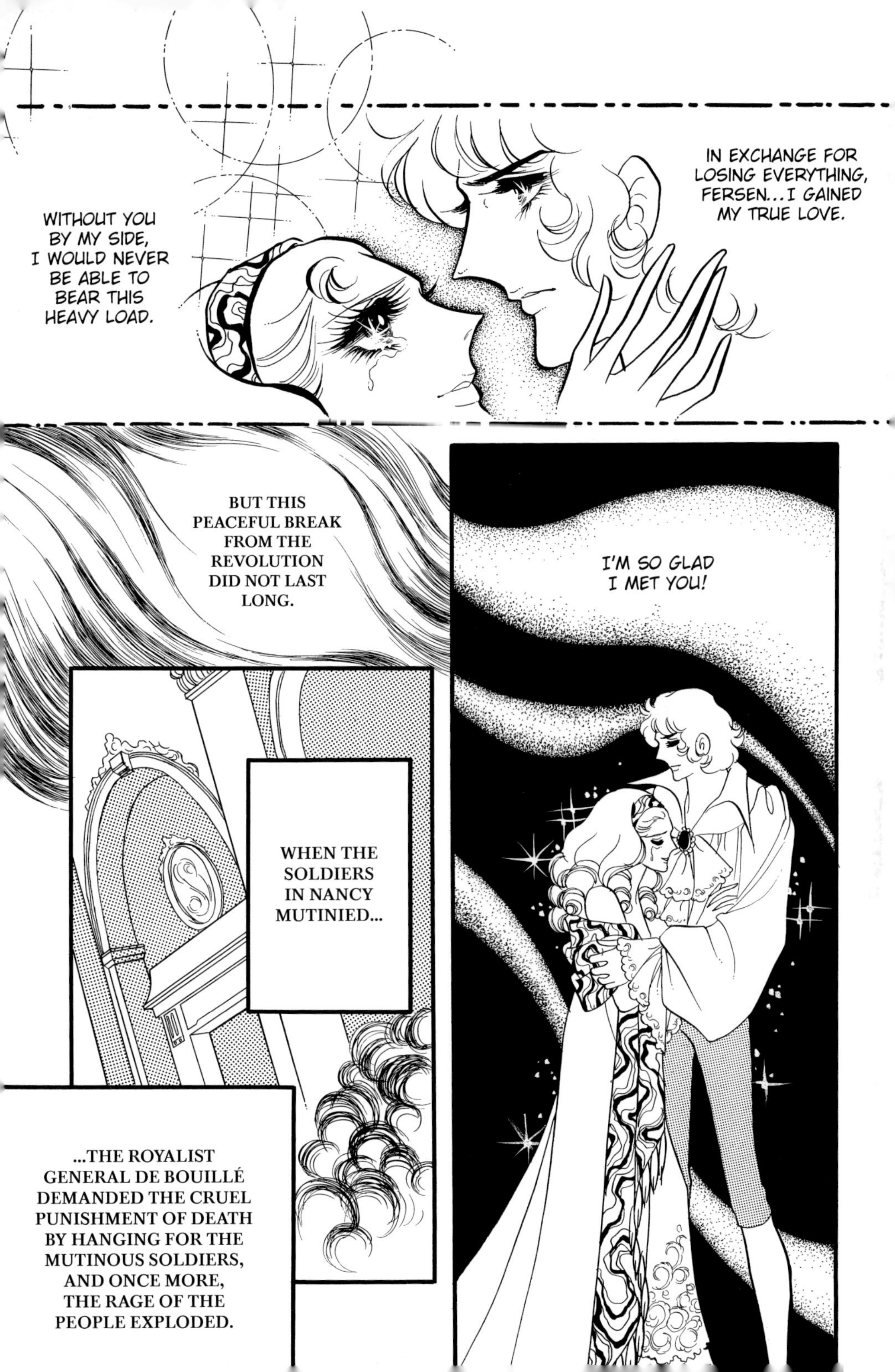
IN EXCHANGE FOR LOSING EVERYTHING, FERSEN...I GAINED MY TRUE LOVE.
WITHOUT YOU BY MY SIDE, I WOULD NEVER BE ABLE TO BEAR THIS HEAVY LOAD.
I'M SO GLAD I MET YOU!
BUT THIS PEACEFUL BREAK FROM THE REVOLUTION DID NOT LAST LONG.
WHEN THE SOLDIERS IN NANCY MUTINIED...
...THE ROYALIST GENERAL DE BOUILLÉ DEMANDED THE CRUEL PUNISHMENT OF DEATH BY HANGING FOR THE MUTINOUS SOLDIERS, AND ONCE MORE, THE RAGE OF THE PEOPLE EXPLODED.

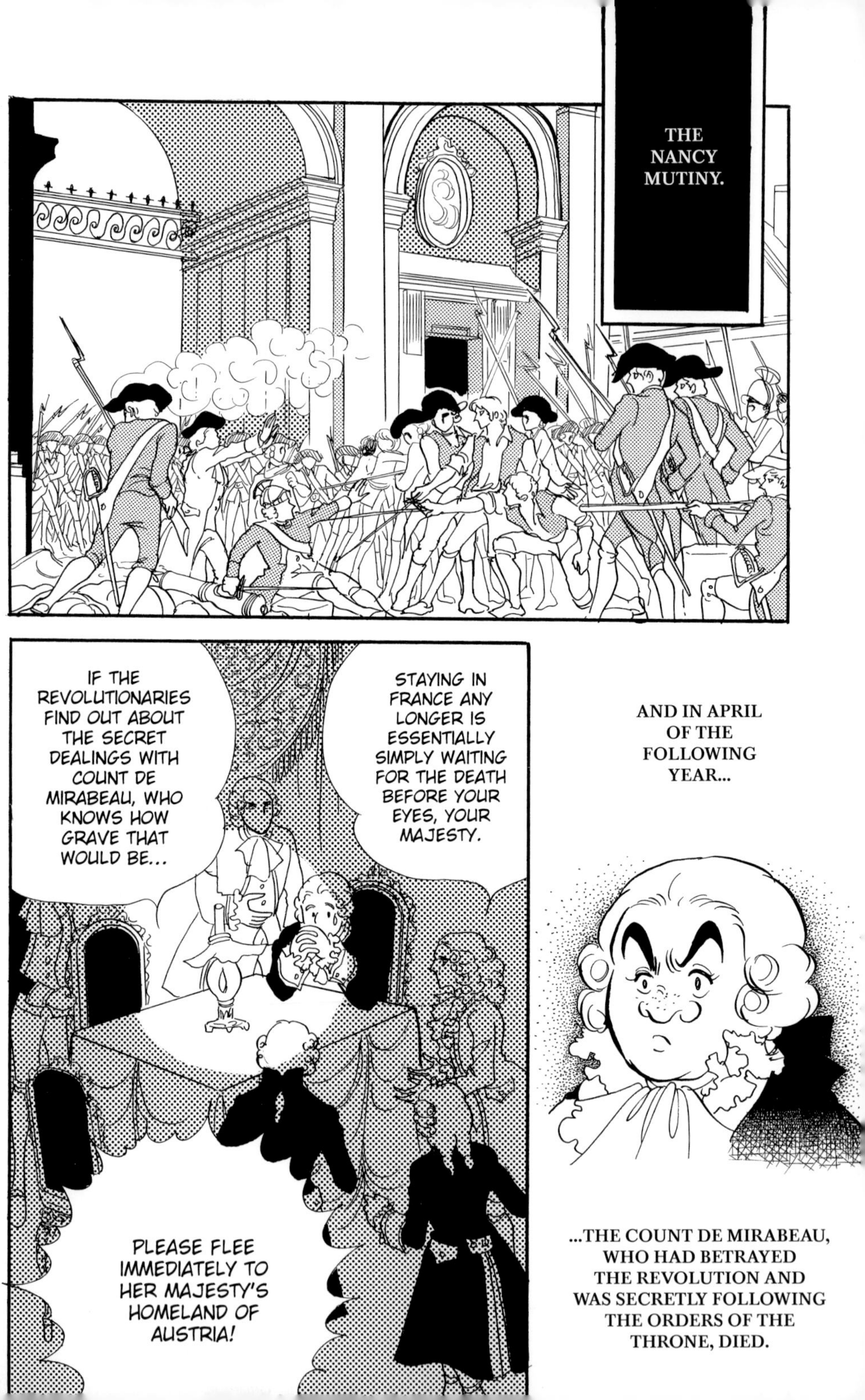
THE NANCY MUTINY.
AND IN APRIL OF THE FOLLOWING YEAR...
...THE COUNT DE MIRABEAU, WHO HAD BETRAYED THE REVOLUTION AND WAS SECRETLY FOLLOWING THE ORDERS OF THE THRONE, DIED.
STAYING IN FRANCE ANY LONGER IS ESSENTIALLY SIMPLY WAITING FOR THE DEATH BEFORE YOUR EYES, YOUR MAJESTY.
IF THE REVOLUTIONARIES FIND OUT ABOUT THE SECRET DEALINGS WITH COUNT DE MIRABEAU, WHO KNOWS HOW GRAVE THAT WOULD BE...
PLEASE FLEE IMMEDIATELY TO HER MAJESTY'S HOMELAND OF AUSTRIA!

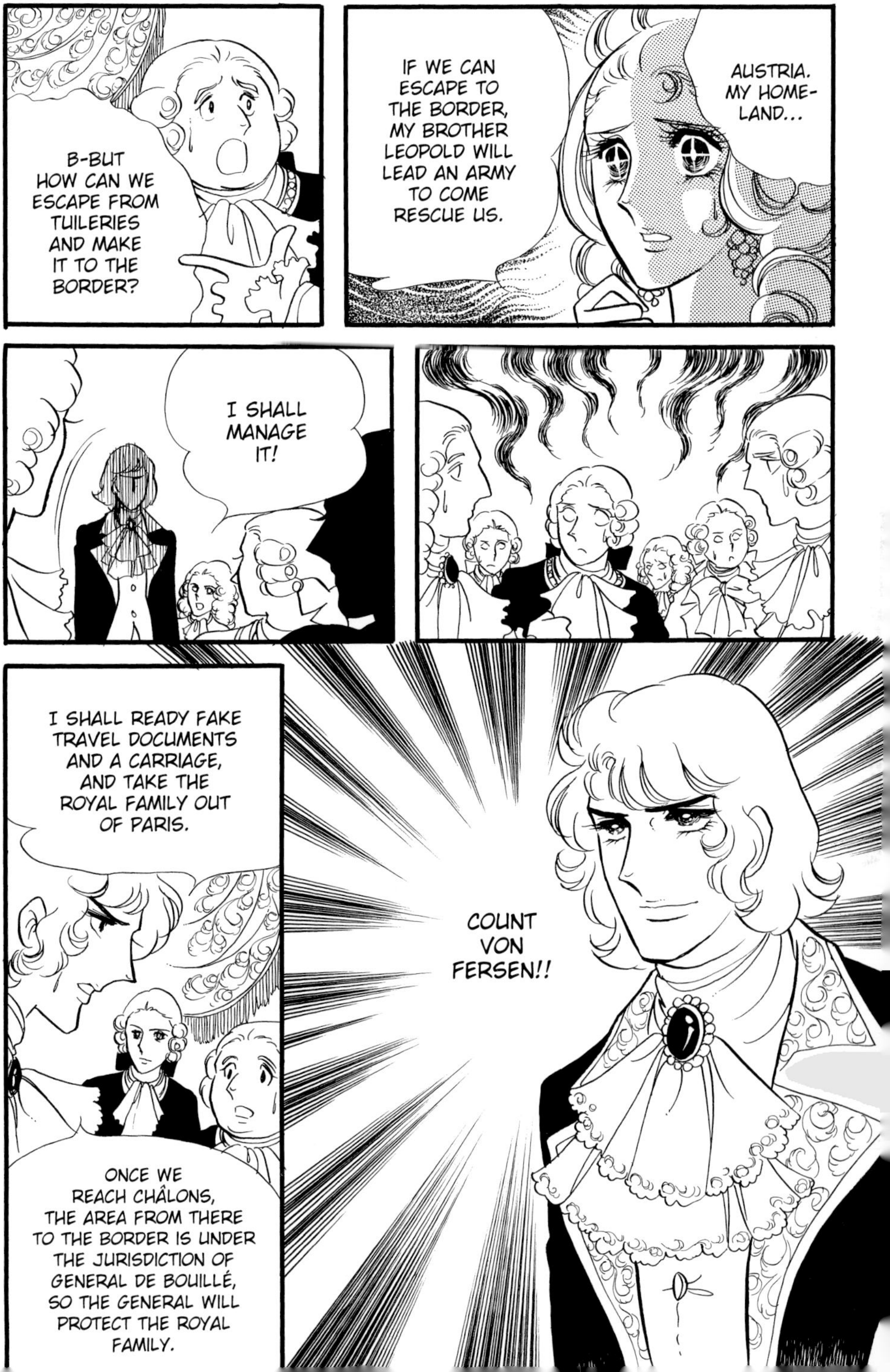
AUSTRIA. MY HOME-LAND...
IF WE CAN ESCAPE TO THE BORDER, MY BROTHER LEOPOLD WILL LEAD AN ARMY TO COME RESCUE US.
B-BUT HOW CAN WE ESCAPE FROM TUILERIES AND MAKE IT TO THE BORDER?
I SHALL MANAGE IT!
COUNT VON FERSEN!!
I SHALL READY FAKE TRAVEL DOCUMENTS AND A CARRIAGE, AND TAKE THE ROYAL FAMILY OUT OF PARIS.
ONCE WE REACH CHÂLONS, THE AREA FROM THERE TO THE BORDER IS UNDER THE JURISDICTION OF GENERAL DE BOUILLÉ, SO THE GENERAL WILL PROTECT THE ROYAL FAMILY.

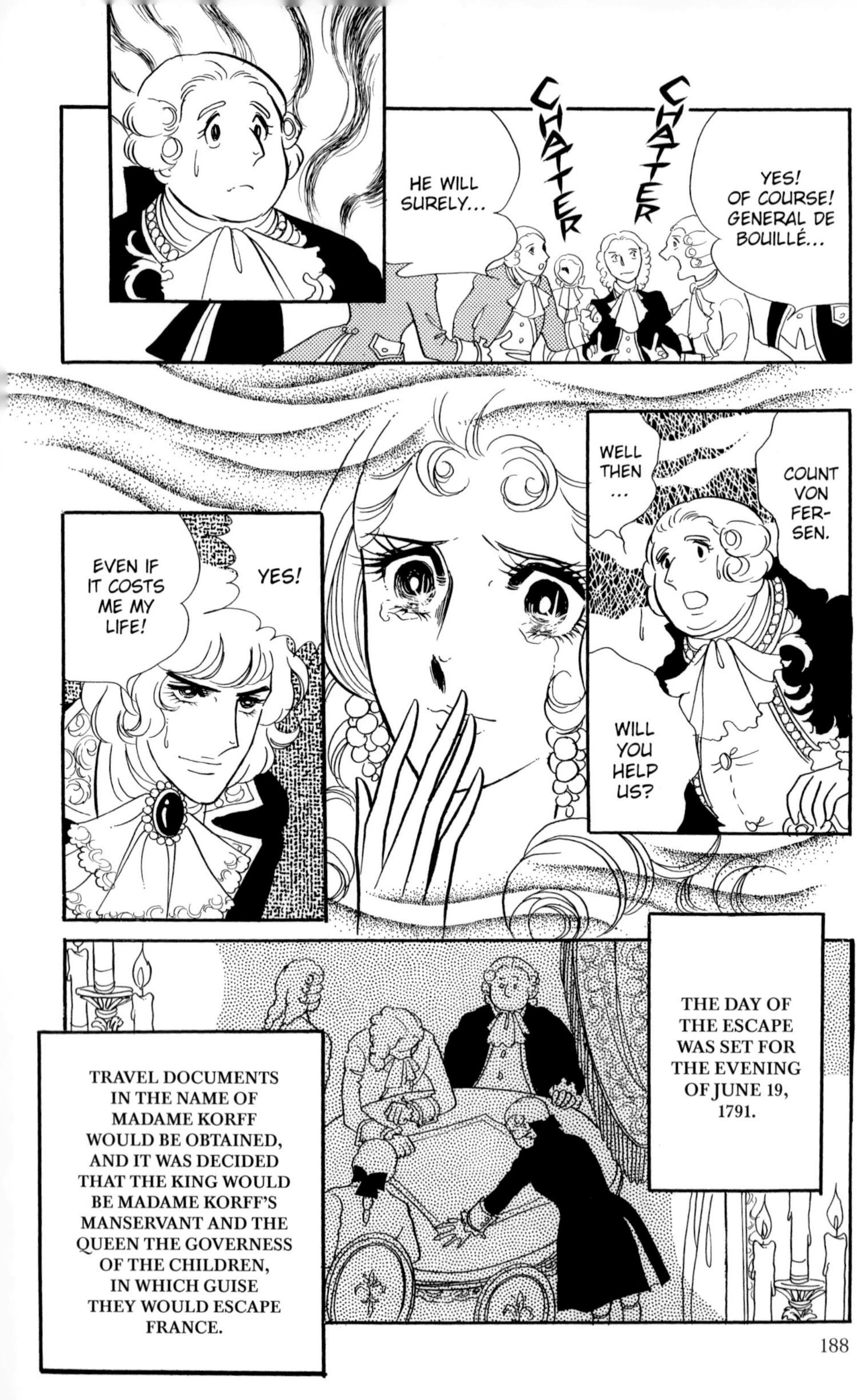
YES! OF COURSE! GENERAL DE BOUILLÉ...
CHATTER
CHATTER
HE WILL SURELY...
COUNT VON FER-SEN.
WELL THEN ...
WILL YOU HELP US?
YES!
EVEN IF IT COSTS ME MY LIFE!
THE DAY OF THE ESCAPE WAS SET FOR THE EVENING OF JUNE 19, 1791.
TRAVEL DOCUMENTS IN THE NAME OF MADAME KORFF WOULD BE OBTAINED, AND IT WAS DECIDED THAT THE KING WOULD BE MADAME KORFF'S MANSERVANT AND THE QUEEN THE GOVERNESS OF THE CHILDREN, IN WHICH GUISE THEY WOULD ESCAPE FRANCE.

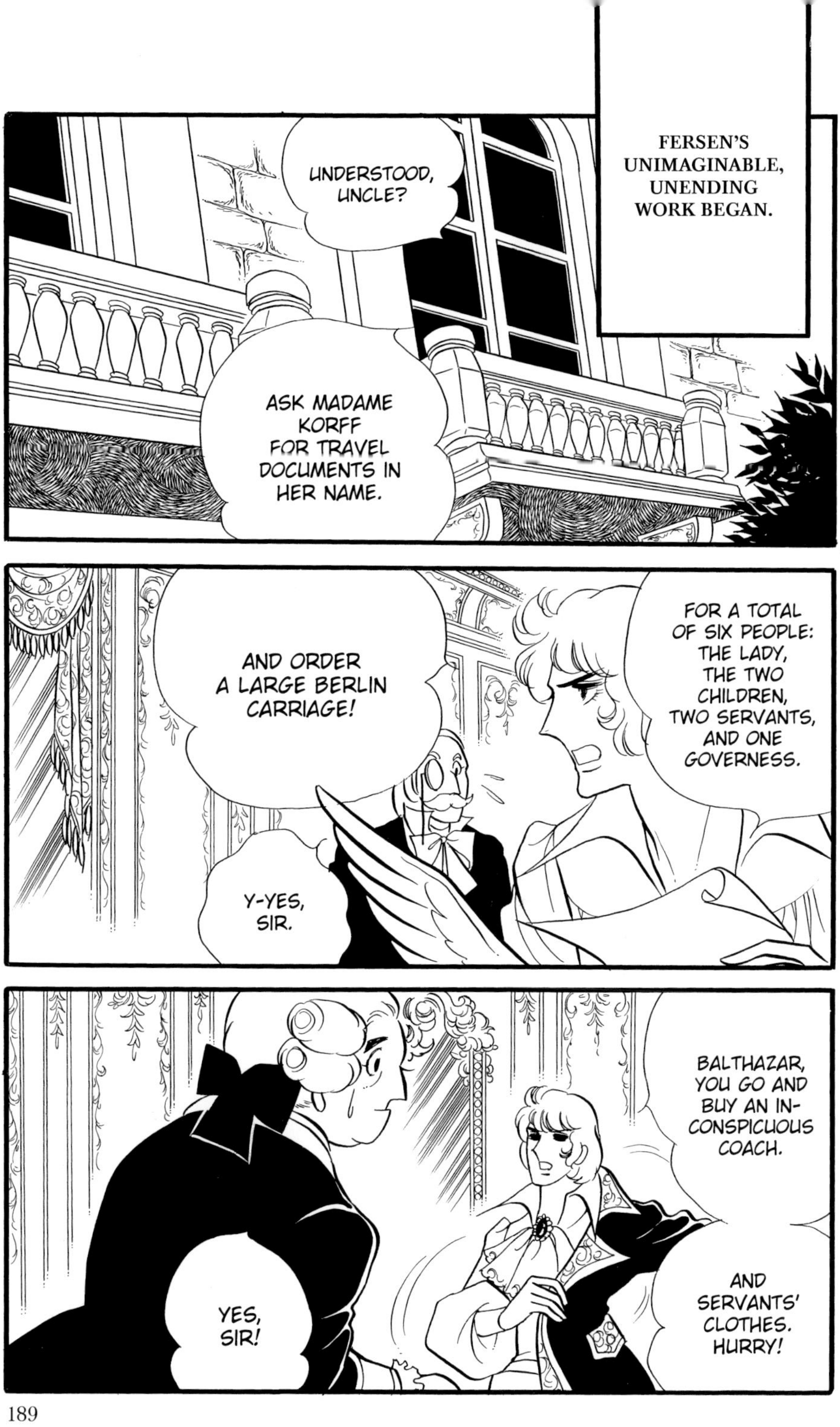
FERSEN'S UNIMAGINABLE, UNENDING WORK BEGAN.
UNDERSTOOD, UNCLE?
ASK MADAME KORFF FOR TRAVEL DOCUMENTS IN HER NAME.
FOR A TOTAL OF SIX PEOPLE: THE LADY, THE TWO CHILDREN, TWO SERVANTS, AND ONE GOVERNESS.
AND ORDER A LARGE BERLIN CARRIAGE!
Y-YES, SIR.
BALTHAZAR, YOU GO AND BUY AN IN-CONSPICUOUS COACH.
AND SERVANTS' CLOTHES. HURRY!
YES, SIR!

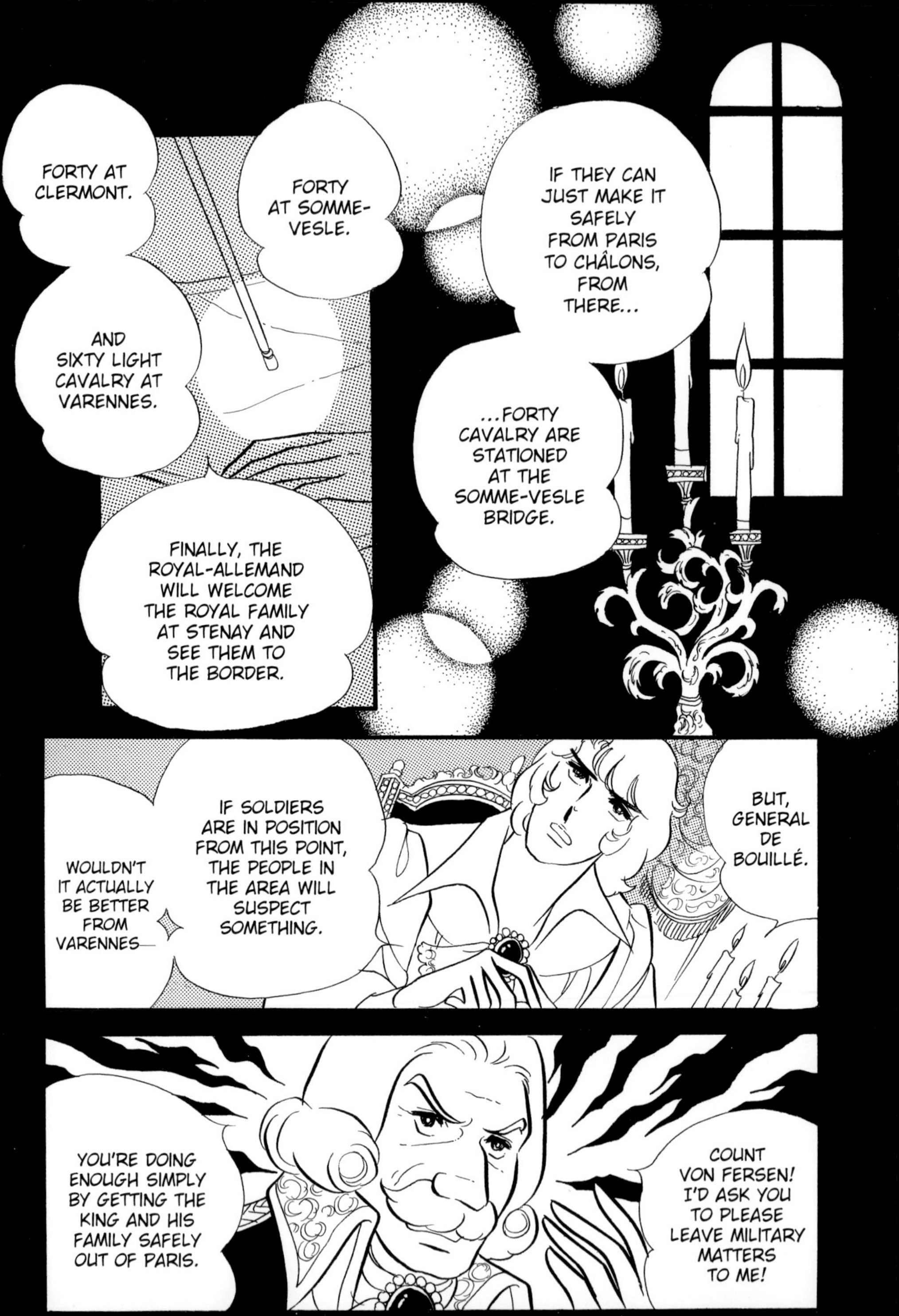
IF THEY CAN JUST MAKE IT SAFELY FROM PARIS TO CHÂLONS, FROM THERE...
...FORTY CAVALRY ARE STATIONED AT THE SOMME-VESLE BRIDGE.
FORTY AT SOMME-VESLE.
FORTY AT CLERMONT.
AND SIXTY LIGHT CAVALRY AT VARENNES.
FINALLY, THE ROYAL-ALLEMAND WILL WELCOME THE ROYAL FAMILY AT STENAY AND SEE THEM TO THE BORDER.
BUT, GENERAL DE BOUILLÉ.
IF SOLDIERS ARE IN POSITION FROM THIS POINT, THE PEOPLE IN THE AREA WILL SUSPECT SOMETHING.
WOULDN'T IT ACTUALLY BE BETTER FROM VARENNES—
COUNT VON FERSEN! I'D ASK YOU TO PLEASE LEAVE MILITARY MATTERS TO ME!
YOU'RE DOING ENOUGH SIMPLY BY GETTING THE KING AND HIS FAMILY SAFELY OUT OF PARIS.

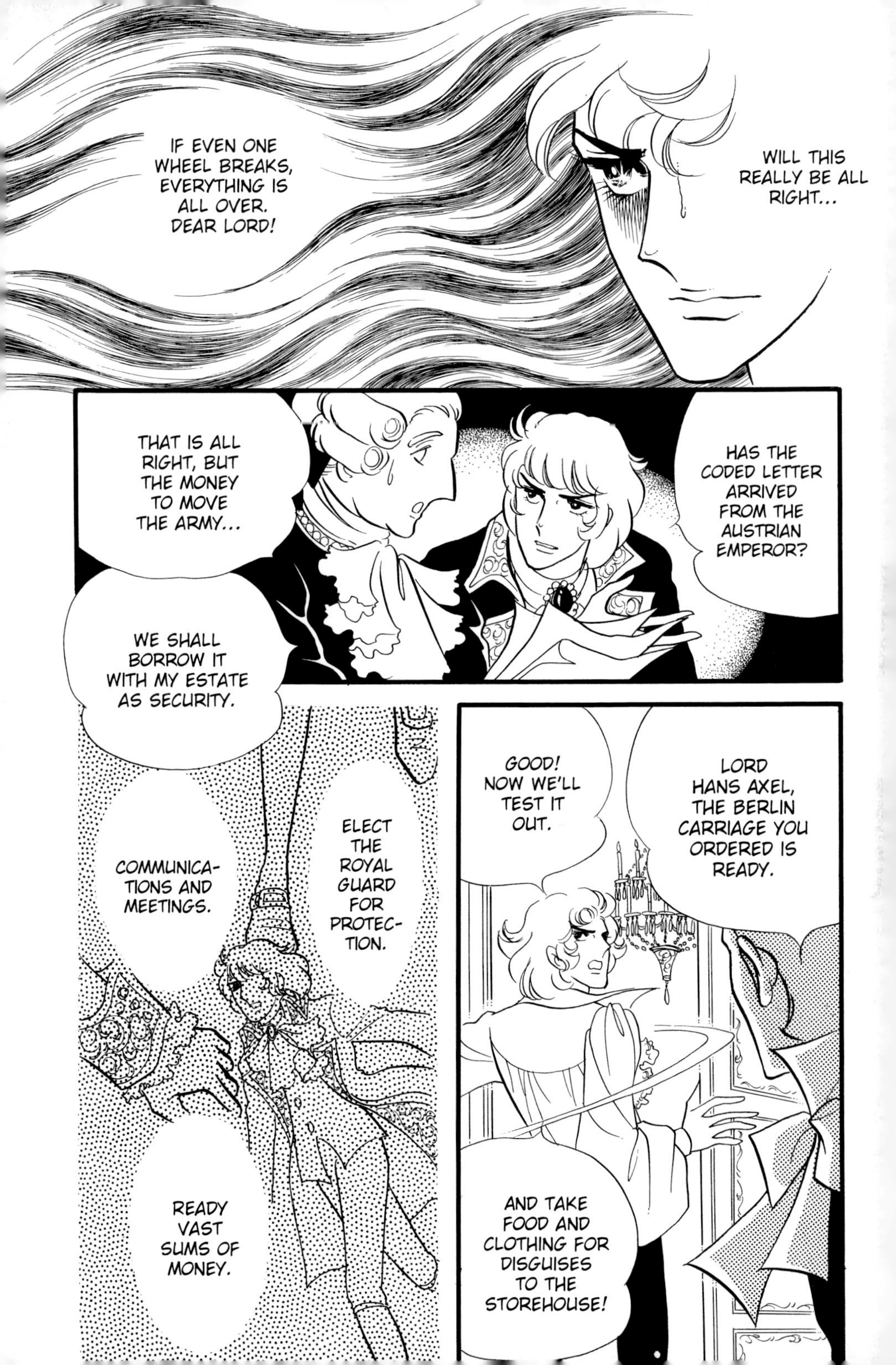
WILL THIS REALLY BE ALL RIGHT...
IF EVEN ONE WHEEL BREAKS, EVERYTHING IS ALL OVER. DEAR LORD!
HAS THE CODED LETTER ARRIVED FROM THE AUSTRIAN EMPEROR?
THAT IS ALL RIGHT, BUT THE MONEY TO MOVE THE ARMY...
WE SHALL BORROW IT WITH MY ESTATE AS SECURITY.
LORD HANS AXEL, THE BERLIN CARRIAGE YOU ORDERED IS READY.
GOOD! NOW WE'LL TEST IT OUT.
AND TAKE FOOD AND CLOTHING FOR DISGUISES TO THE STOREHOUSE!
ELECT THE ROYAL GUARD FOR PROTEC-TION.
COMMUNICA-TIONS AND MEETINGS.
READY VAST SUMS OF MONEY.

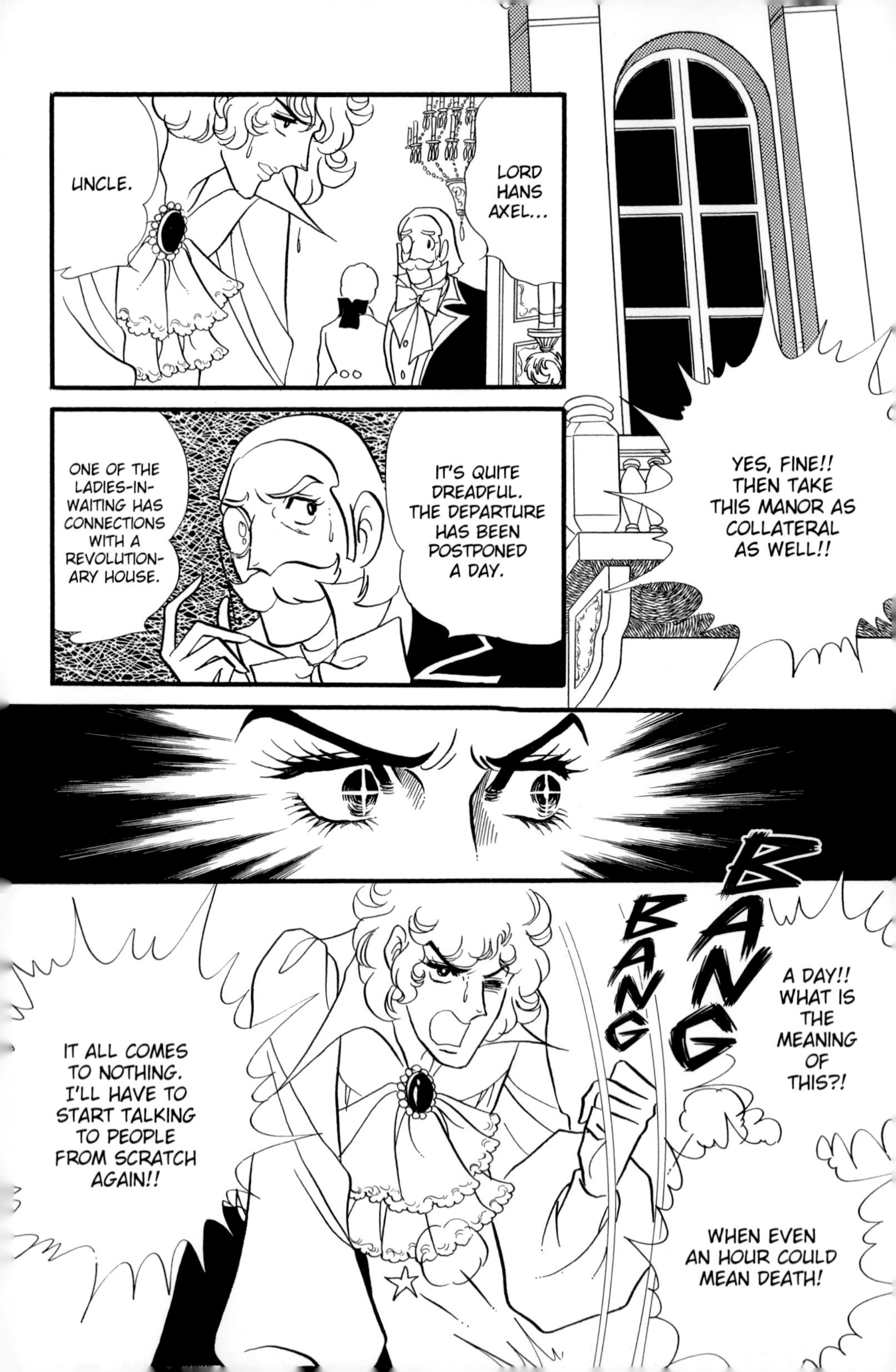
YES, FINE!! THEN TAKE THIS MANOR AS COLLATERAL AS WELL!!
LORD HANS AXEL...
UNCLE.
IT'S QUITE DREADFUL. THE DEPARTURE HAS BEEN POSTPONED A DAY.
ONE OF THE LADIES-IN-WAITING HAS CONNECTIONS WITH A REVOLUTIONARY HOUSE.
BANG
BANG
A DAY!! WHAT IS THE MEANING OF THIS?!
WHEN EVEN AN HOUR COULD MEAN DEATH!
IT ALL COMES TO NOTHING. I'LL HAVE TO START TALKING TO PEOPLE FROM SCRATCH AGAIN!!

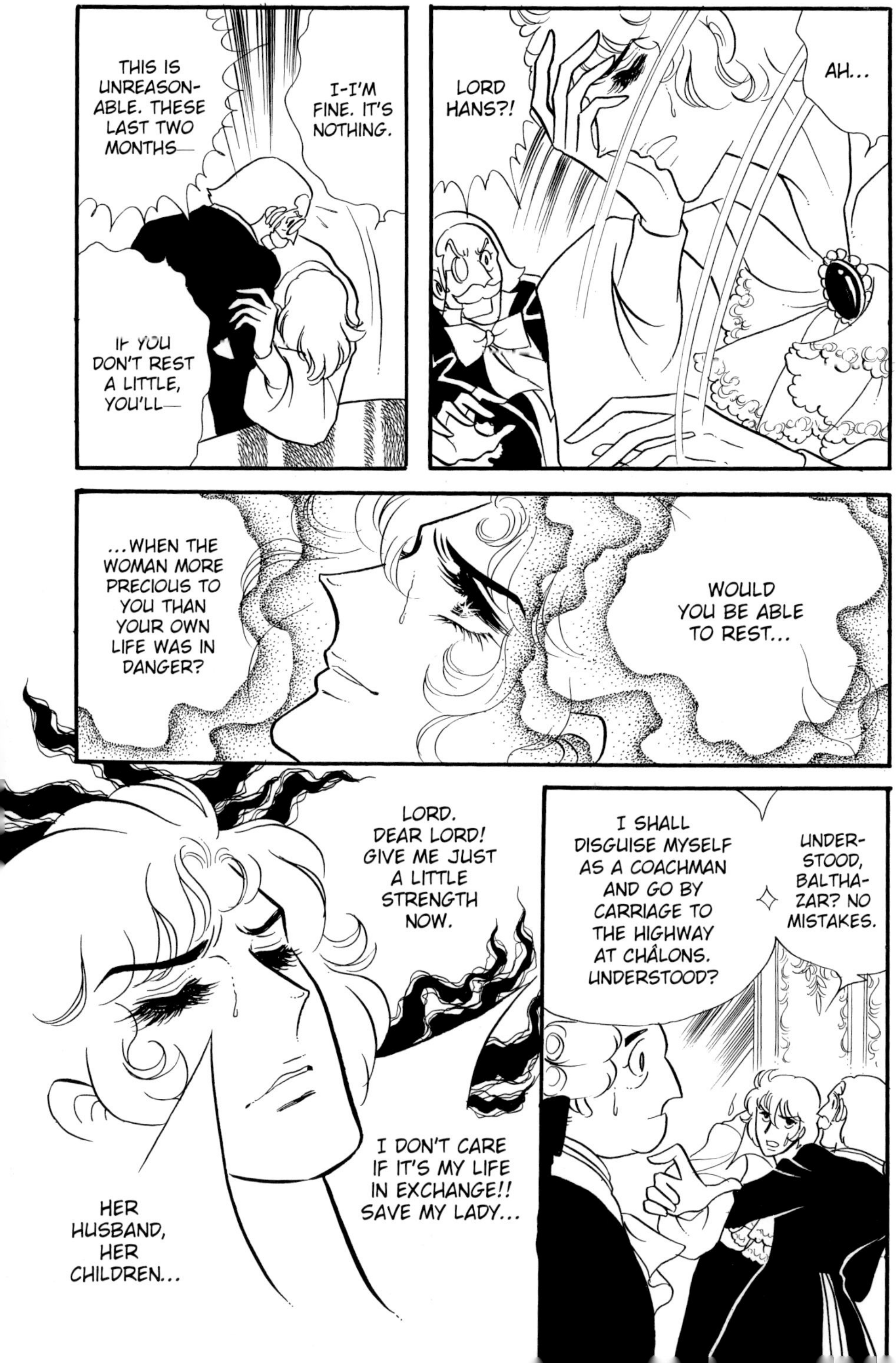
AH…
LORD HANS?!
I-I'M FINE. IT'S NOTHING.
THIS IS UNREASON-ABLE. THESE LAST TWO MONTHS—
IF YOU DON'T REST A LITTLE, YOU'LL—
WOULD YOU BE ABLE TO REST…
…WHEN THE WOMAN MORE PRECIOUS TO YOU THAN YOUR OWN LIFE WAS IN DANGER?
UNDER-STOOD, BALTHA-ZAR? NO MISTAKES.
I SHALL DISGUISE MYSELF AS A COACHMAN AND GO BY CARRIAGE TO THE HIGHWAY AT CHÂLONS. UNDERSTOOD?
LORD. DEAR LORD! GIVE ME JUST A LITTLE STRENGTH NOW.
I DON'T CARE IF IT'S MY LIFE IN EXCHANGE!! SAVE MY LADY…
HER HUSBAND, HER CHILDREN…

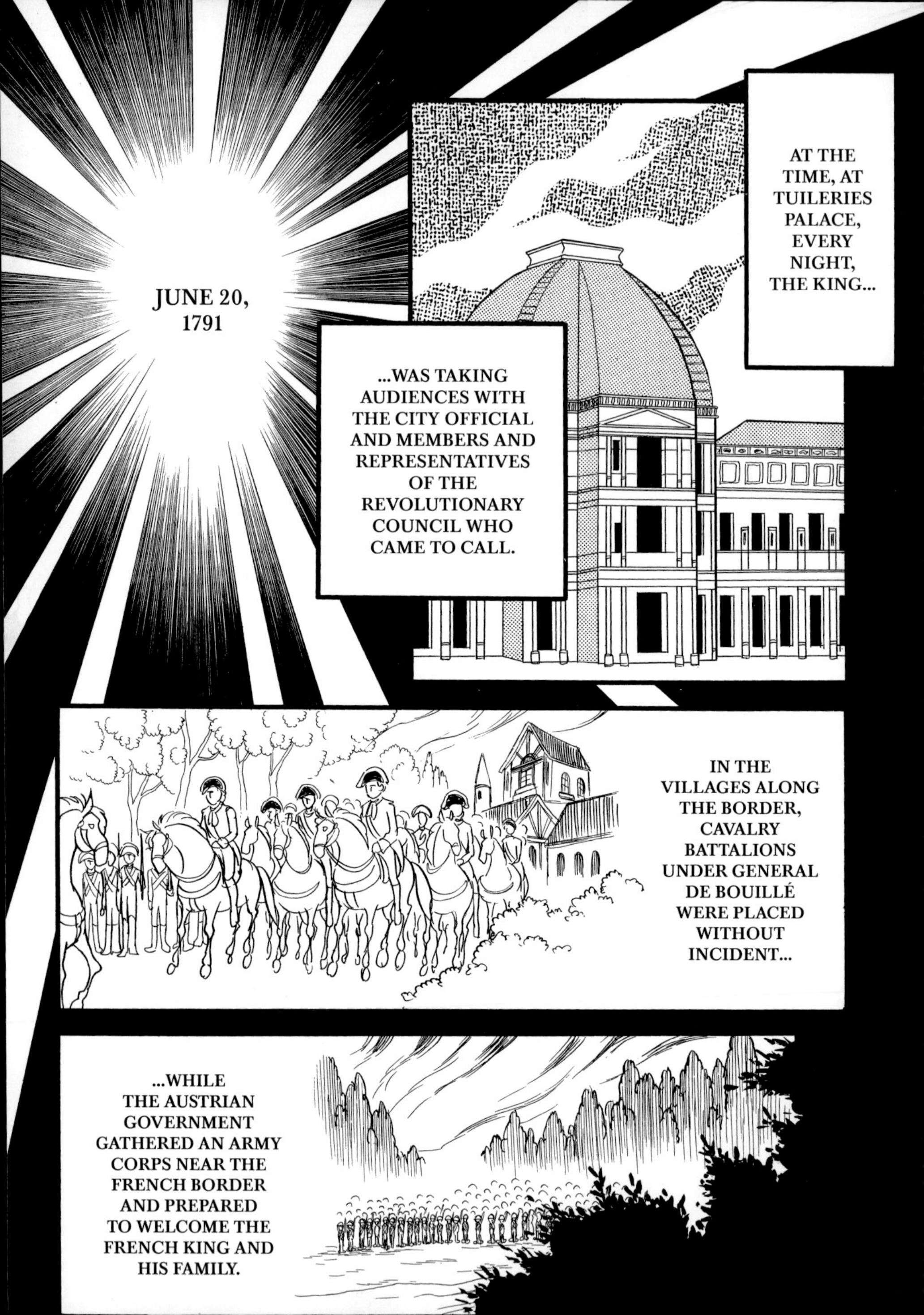
AT THE TIME, AT TUILERIES PALACE, EVERY NIGHT, THE KING...
...WAS TAKING AUDIENCES WITH THE CITY OFFICIAL AND MEMBERS AND REPRESENTATIVES OF THE REVOLUTIONARY COUNCIL WHO CAME TO CALL.
JUNE 20, 1791
IN THE VILLAGES ALONG THE BORDER, CAVALRY BATTALIONS UNDER GENERAL DE BOUILLÉ WERE PLACED WITHOUT INCIDENT...
...WHILE THE AUSTRIAN GOVERNMENT GATHERED AN ARMY CORPS NEAR THE FRENCH BORDER AND PREPARED TO WELCOME THE FRENCH KING AND HIS FAMILY.

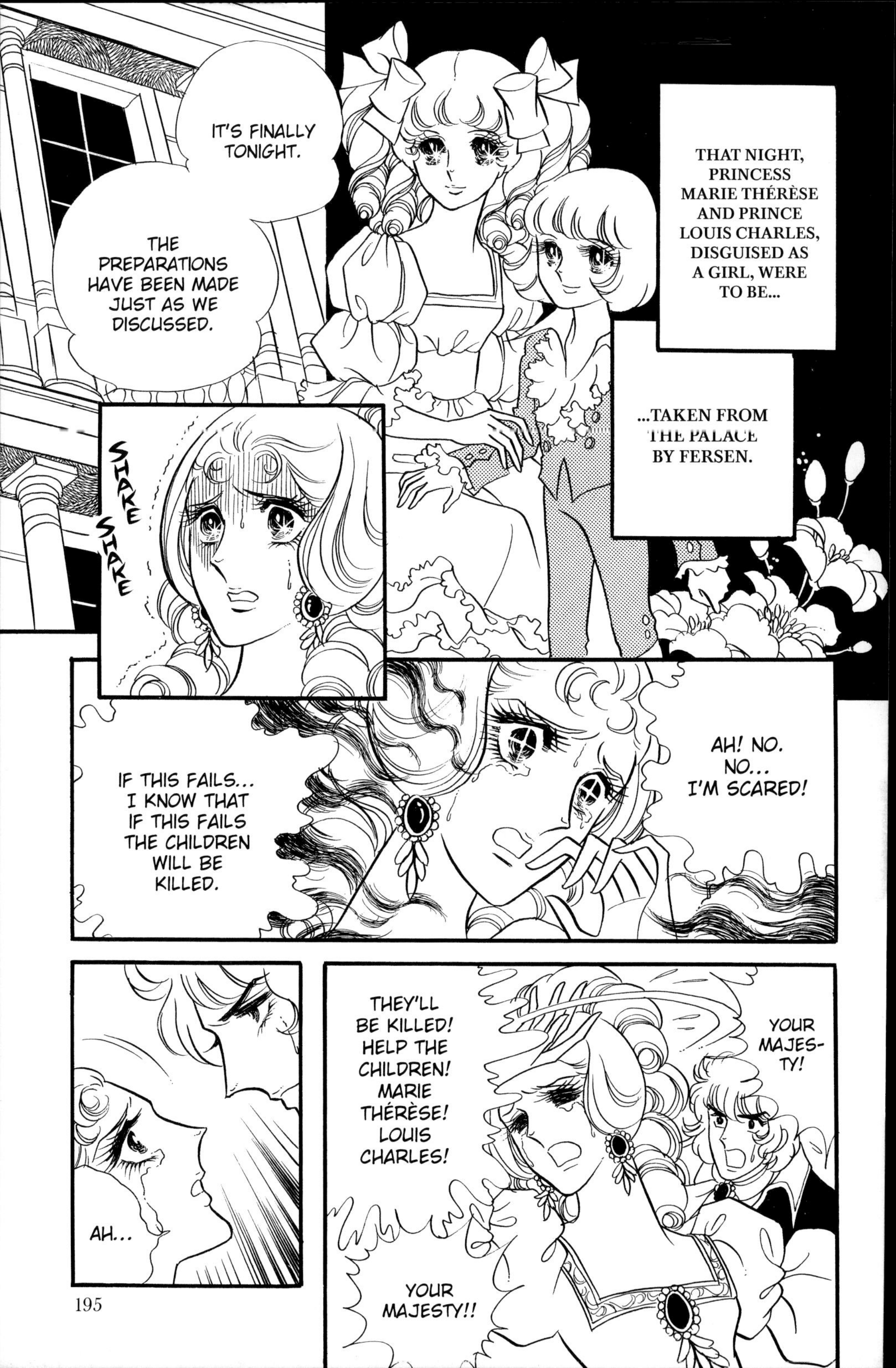
THAT NIGHT, PRINCESS MARIE THÉRÈSE AND PRINCE LOUIS CHARLES, DISGUISED AS A GIRL, WERE TO BE...
...TAKEN FROM THE PALACE BY FERSEN.
IT'S FINALLY TONIGHT.
THE PREPARATIONS HAVE BEEN MADE JUST AS WE DISCUSSED.
SHAKE SHAKE
AH! NO. NO... I'M SCARED!
IF THIS FAILS... I KNOW THAT IF THIS FAILS THE CHILDREN WILL BE KILLED.
YOUR MAJESTY!
THEY'LL BE KILLED! HELP THE CHILDREN! MARIE THÉRÈSE! LOUIS CHARLES!
YOUR MAJESTY!!
AH...

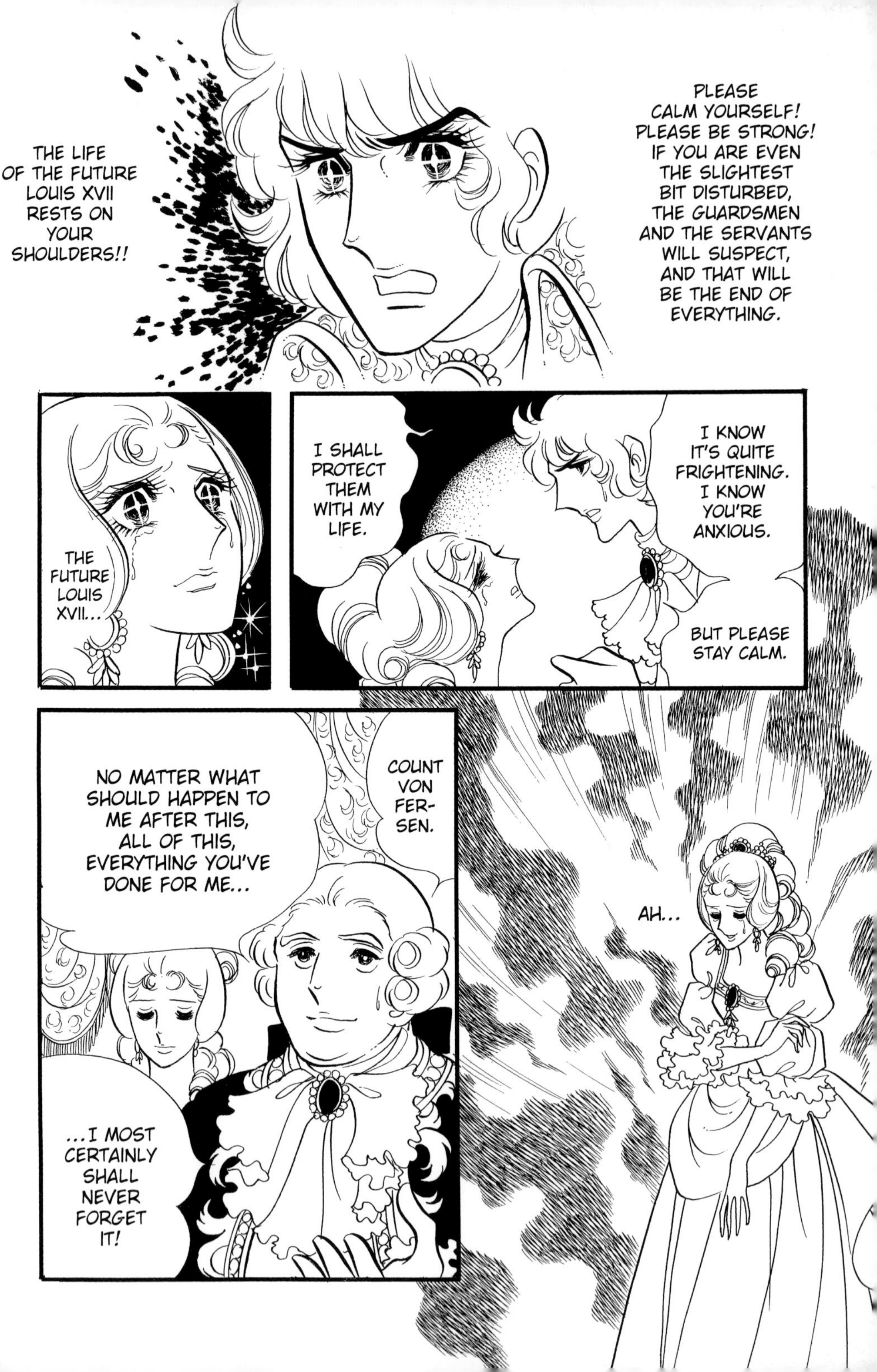
PLEASE CALM YOURSELF! PLEASE BE STRONG! IF YOU ARE EVEN THE SLIGHTEST BIT DISTURBED, THE GUARDSMEN AND THE SERVANTS WILL SUSPECT, AND THAT WILL BE THE END OF EVERYTHING.
THE LIFE OF THE FUTURE LOUIS XVII RESTS ON YOUR SHOULDERS!!
I KNOW IT'S QUITE FRIGHTENING. I KNOW YOU'RE ANXIOUS.
I SHALL PROTECT THEM WITH MY LIFE.
BUT PLEASE STAY CALM.
THE FUTURE LOUIS XVII...
AH...
COUNT VON FER-SEN.
NO MATTER WHAT SHOULD HAPPEN TO ME AFTER THIS, ALL OF THIS, EVERYTHING YOU'VE DONE FOR ME...
...I MOST CERTAINLY SHALL NEVER FORGET IT!

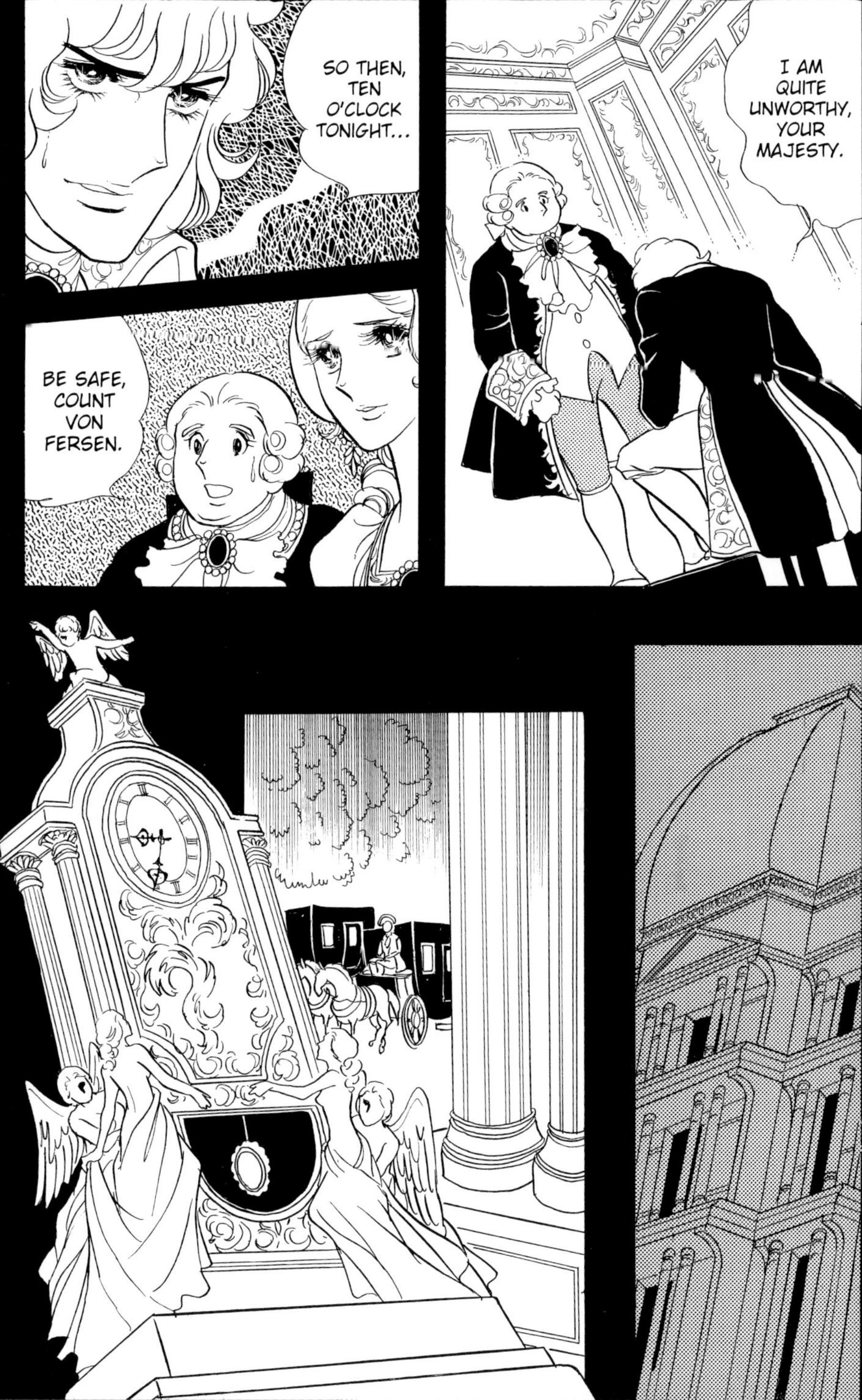
I AM QUITE UNWORTHY, YOUR MAJESTY.
SO THEN, TEN O'CLOCK TONIGHT...
BE SAFE, COUNT VON FERSEN.

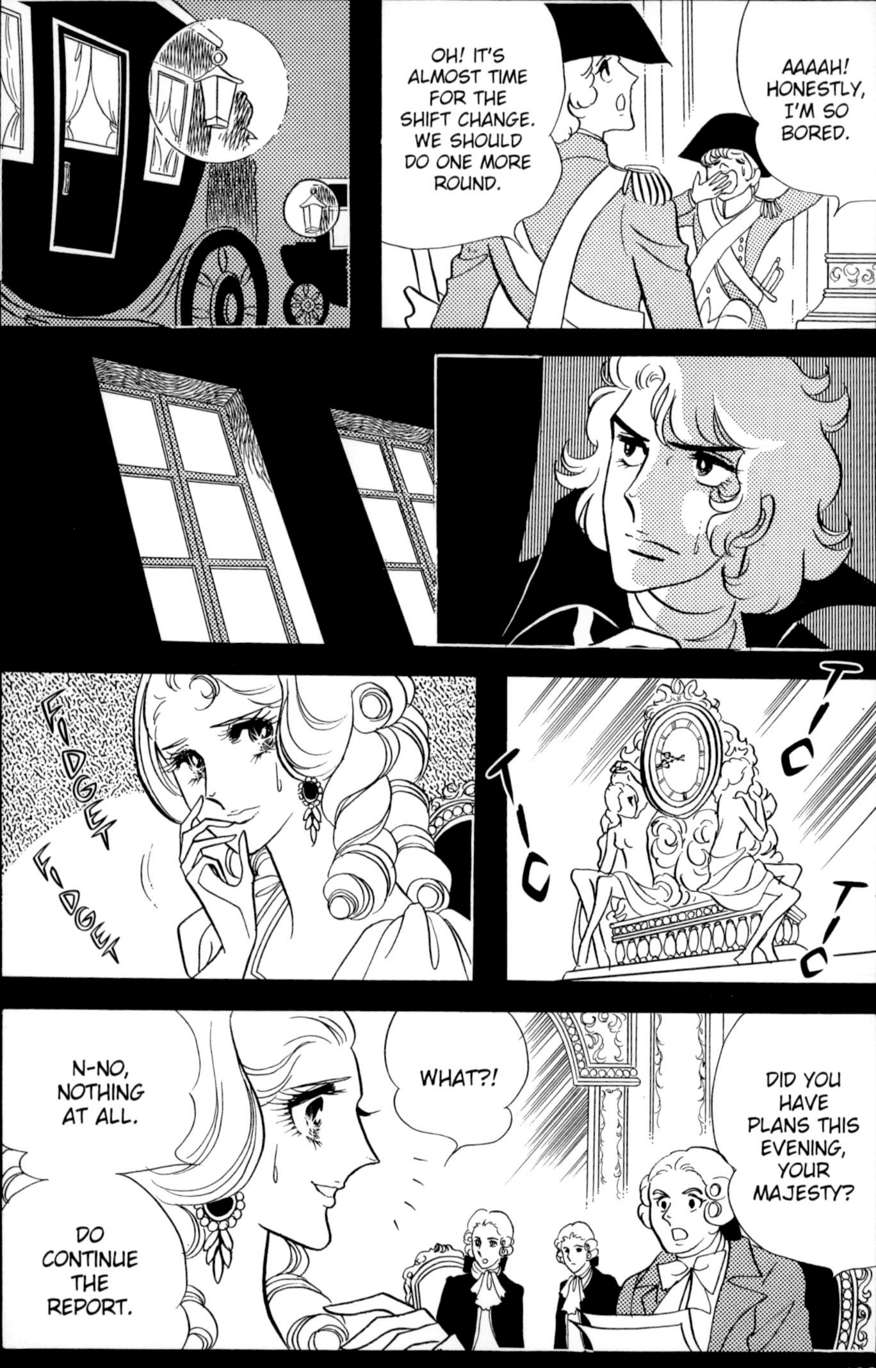
AAAAH! HONESTLY, I'M SO BORED.
OH! IT'S ALMOST TIME FOR THE SHIFT CHANGE. WE SHOULD DO ONE MORE ROUND.
TIC
TIC
TIC
FIDGET
FIDGET
DID YOU HAVE PLANS THIS EVENING, YOUR MAJESTY?
WHAT?!
N-NO, NOTHING AT ALL.
DO CONTINUE THE REPORT.

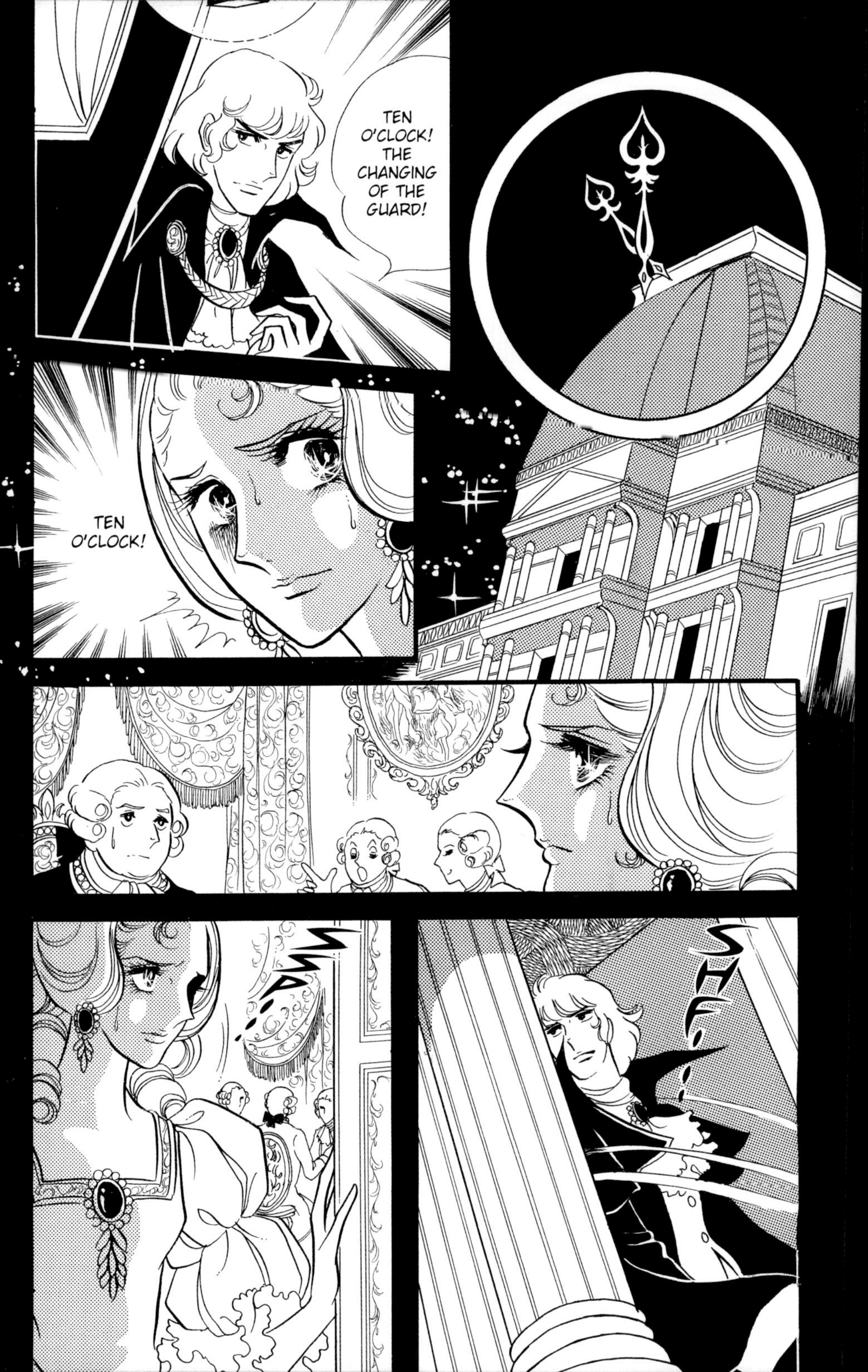

TEN O'CLOCK! THE CHANGING OF THE GUARD!
TEN O'CLOCK!
SHF...!
SWP...!

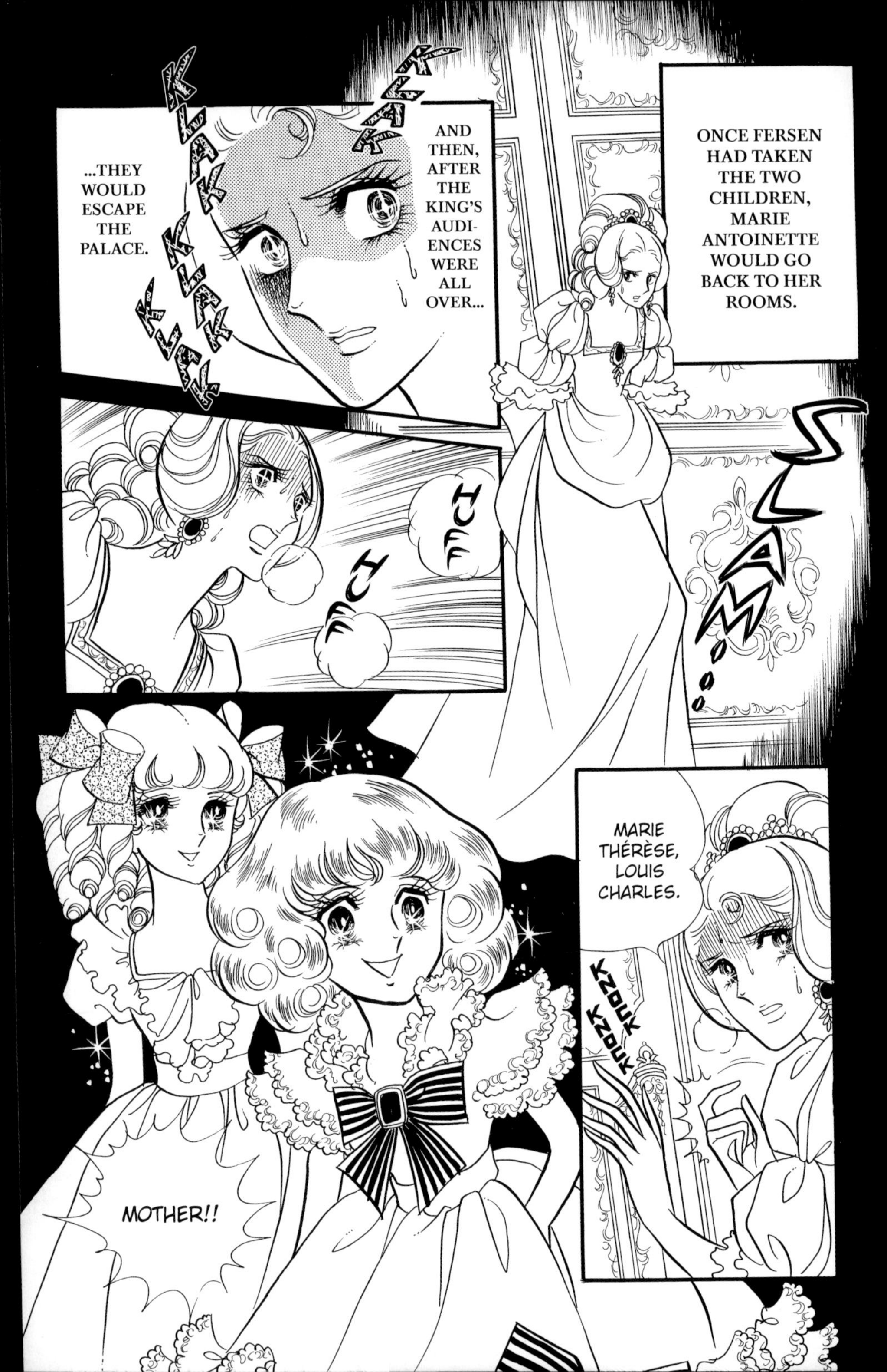
ONCE FERSEN HAD TAKEN THE TWO CHILDREN, MARIE ANTOINETTE WOULD GO BACK TO HER ROOMS.
SLAM...
AND THEN, AFTER THE KING'S AUDIENCES WERE ALL OVER...
KLAK KLAK KLAK
...THEY WOULD ESCAPE THE PALACE.
HUF HUF
MARIE THÉRÈSE, LOUIS CHARLES.
KNOUK KNOUK
MOTHER!!

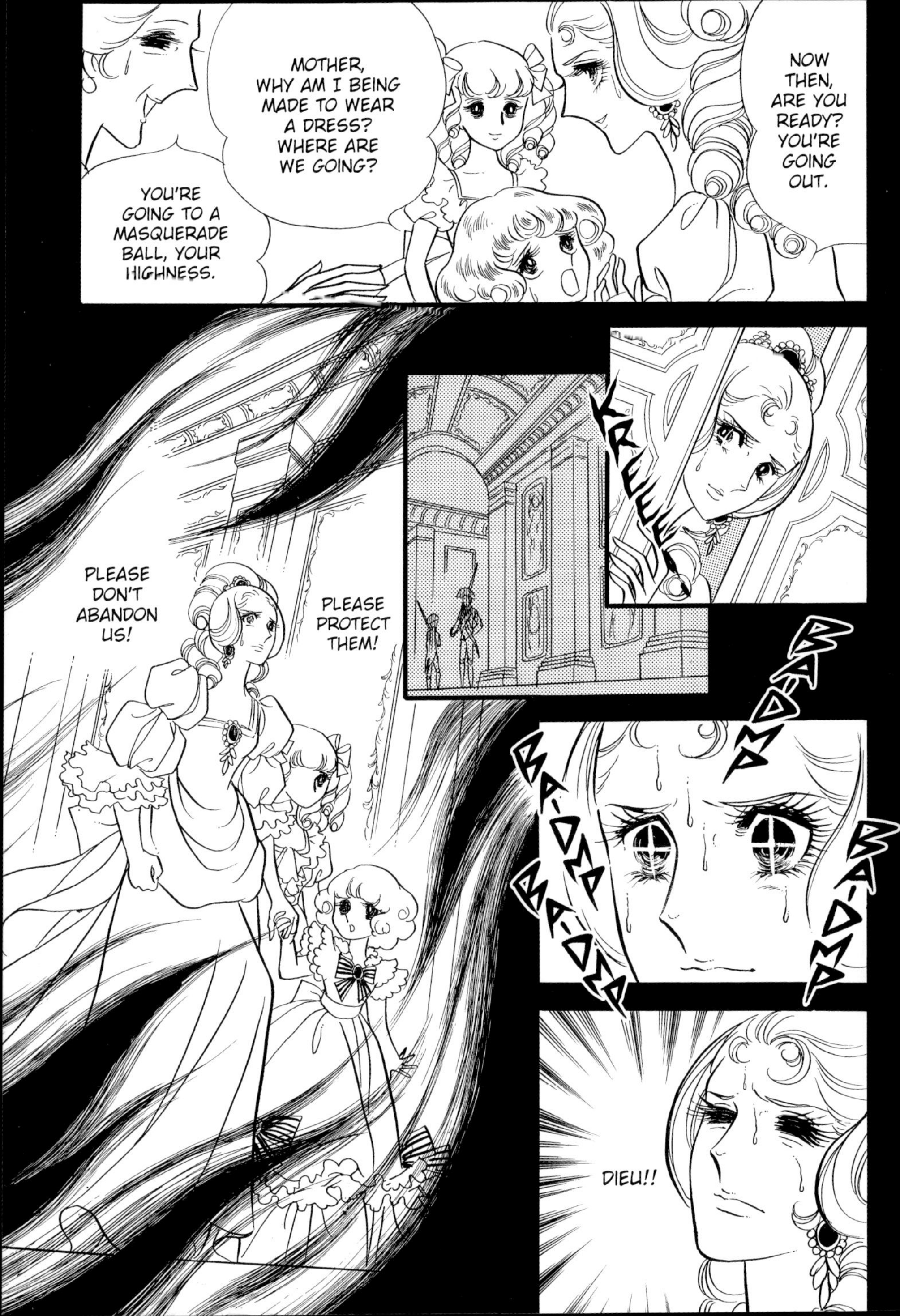
NOW THEN, ARE YOU READY? YOU'RE GOING OUT.
MOTHER, WHY AM I BEING MADE TO WEAR A DRESS? WHERE ARE WE GOING?
YOU'RE GOING TO A MASQUERADE BALL, YOUR HIGHNESS.
KREEE
BA-DMP
BA-DMP
BA-DMP
BA-DMP
DIEU!!
PLEASE PROTECT THEM!
PLEASE DON'T ABANDON US!

1974 WEEKLY
MARGARET MAGAZINE
COMBINED ISSUE 04-05
COVER INSERT ART

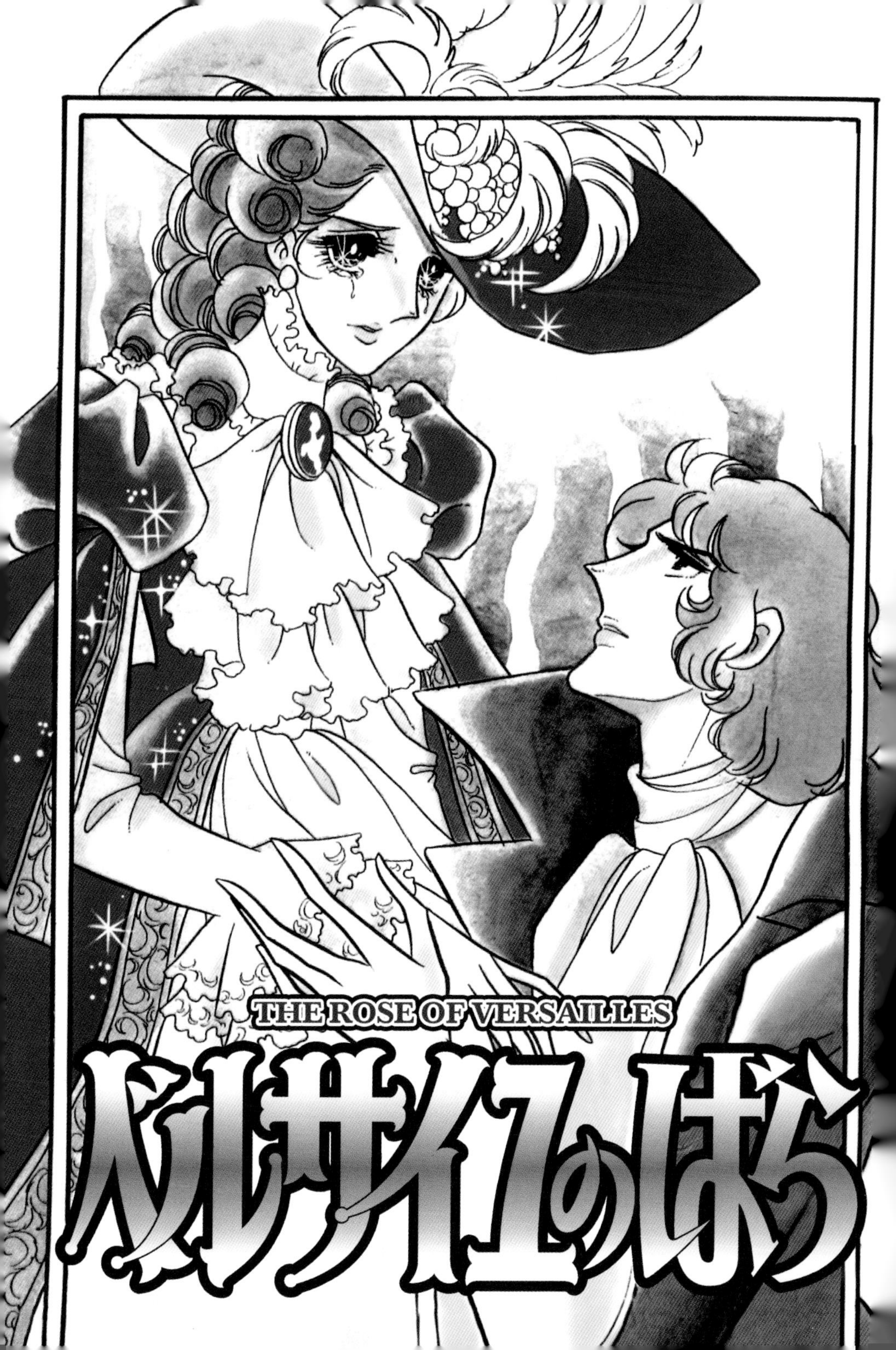
THE ROSE OF VERSAILLES
ベルサイユのばら

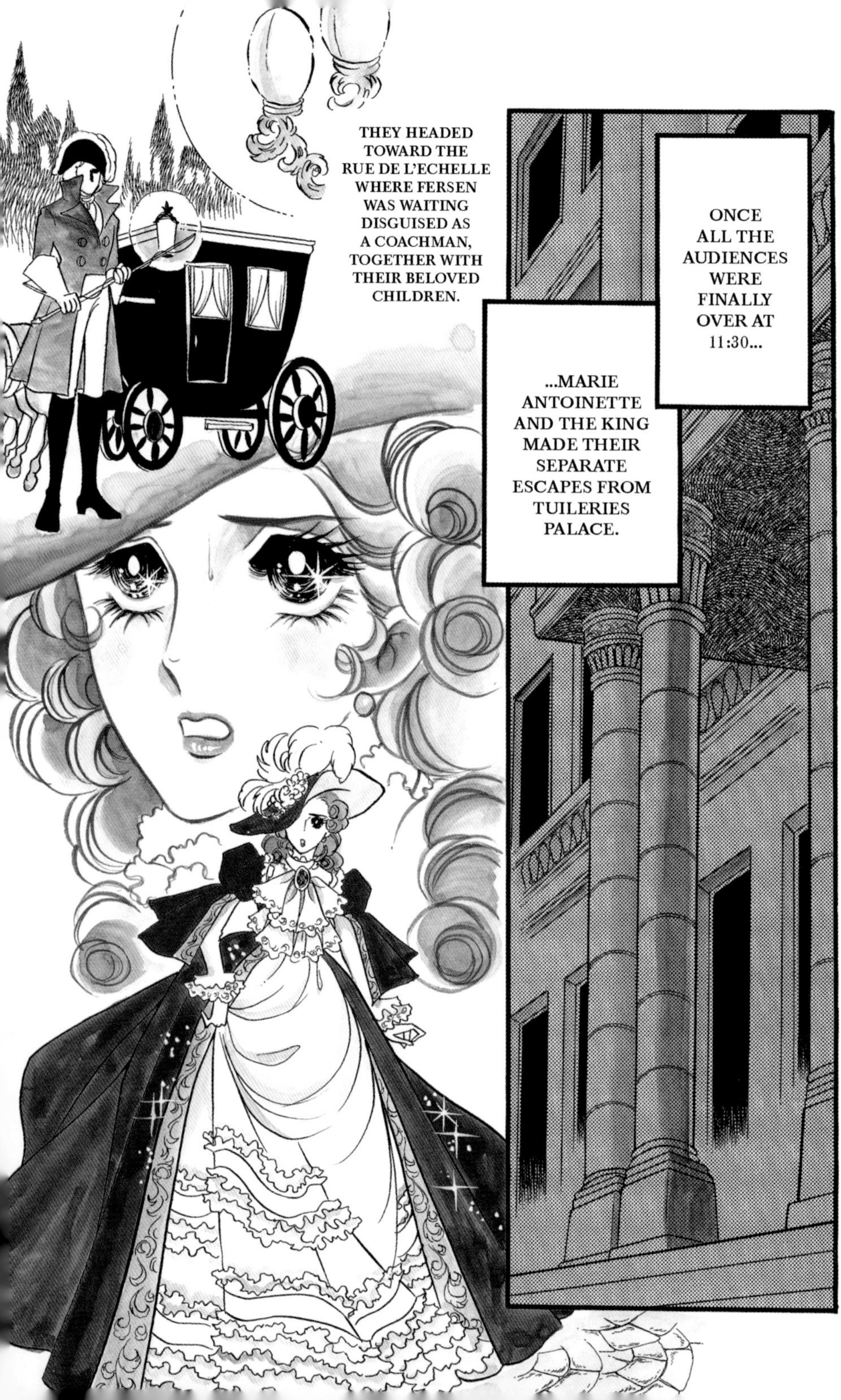
ONCE ALL THE AUDIENCES WERE FINALLY OVER AT 11:30...
...MARIE ANTOINETTE AND THE KING MADE THEIR SEPARATE ESCAPES FROM TUILERIES PALACE.
THEY HEADED TOWARD THE RUE DE L'ECHELLE WHERE FERSEN WAS WAITING DISGUISED AS A COACHMAN, TOGETHER WITH THEIR BELOVED CHILDREN.

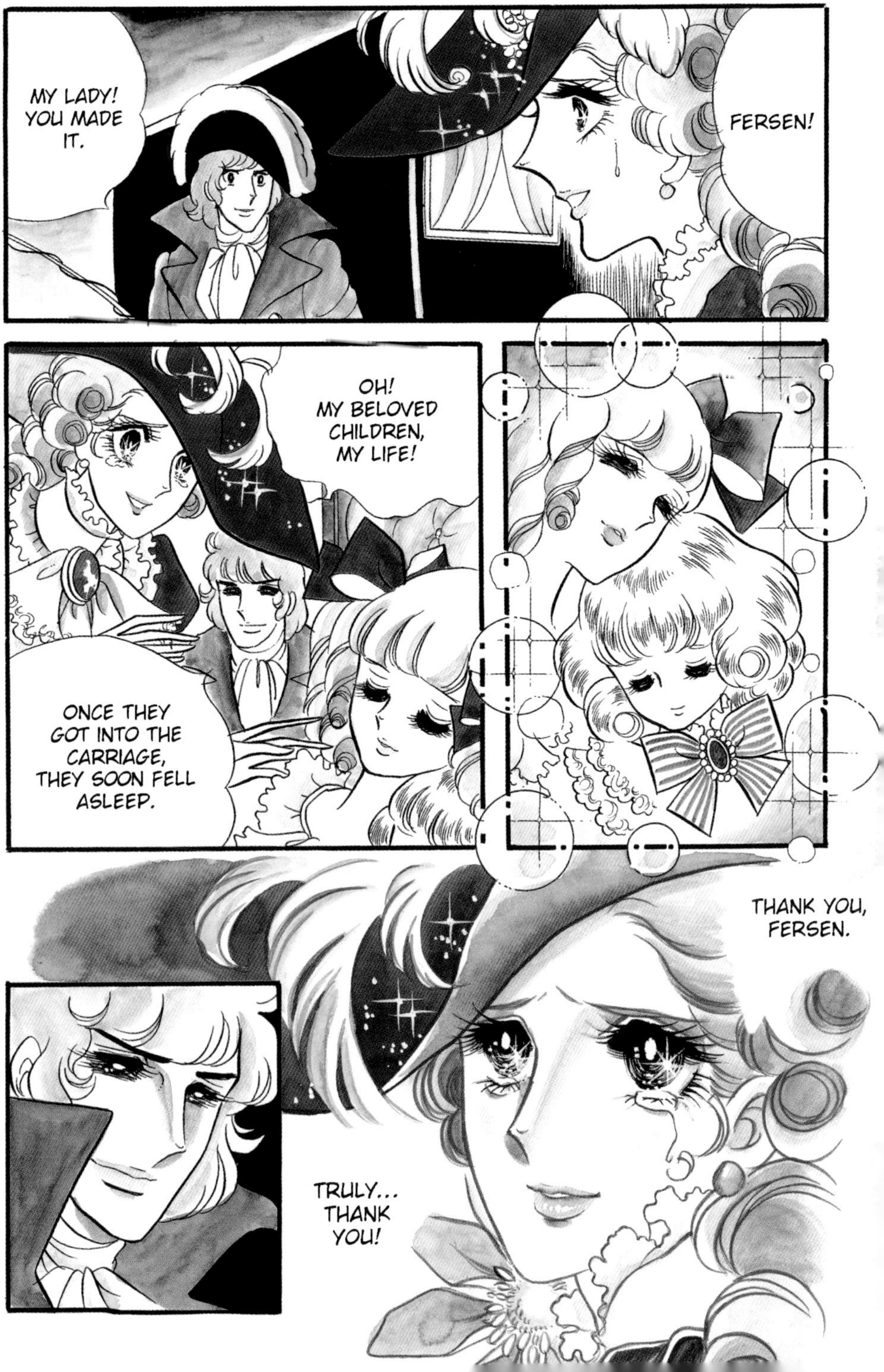
FERSEN!
MY LADY! YOU MADE IT.
OH! MY BELOVED CHILDREN, MY LIFE!
ONCE THEY GOT INTO THE CARRIAGE, THEY SOON FELL ASLEEP.
THANK YOU, FERSEN.
TRULY... THANK YOU!

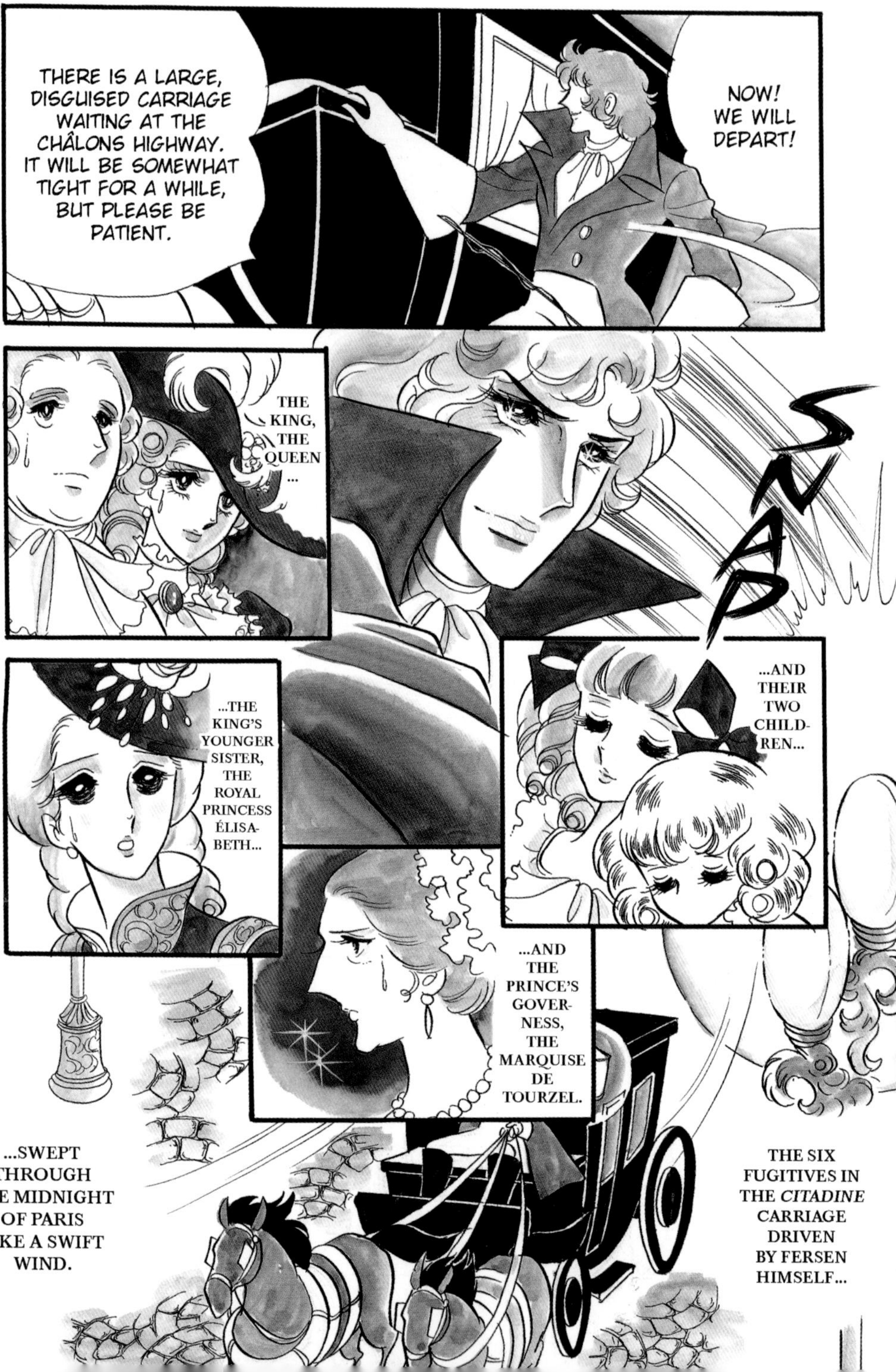
NOW! WE WILL DEPART!
THERE IS A LARGE, DISGUISED CARRIAGE WAITING AT THE CHÂLONS HIGHWAY. IT WILL BE SOMEWHAT TIGHT FOR A WHILE, BUT PLEASE BE PATIENT.
SNAP
THE KING, THE QUEEN...
...AND THEIR TWO CHILDREN...
...THE KING'S YOUNGER SISTER, THE ROYAL PRINCESS ÉLISABETH...
...AND THE PRINCE'S GOVERNESS, THE MARQUISE DE TOURZEL.
THE SIX FUGITIVES IN THE *CITADINE* CARRIAGE DRIVEN BY FERSEN HIMSELF...
...SWEPT THROUGH THE MIDNIGHT OF PARIS LIKE A SWIFT WIND.

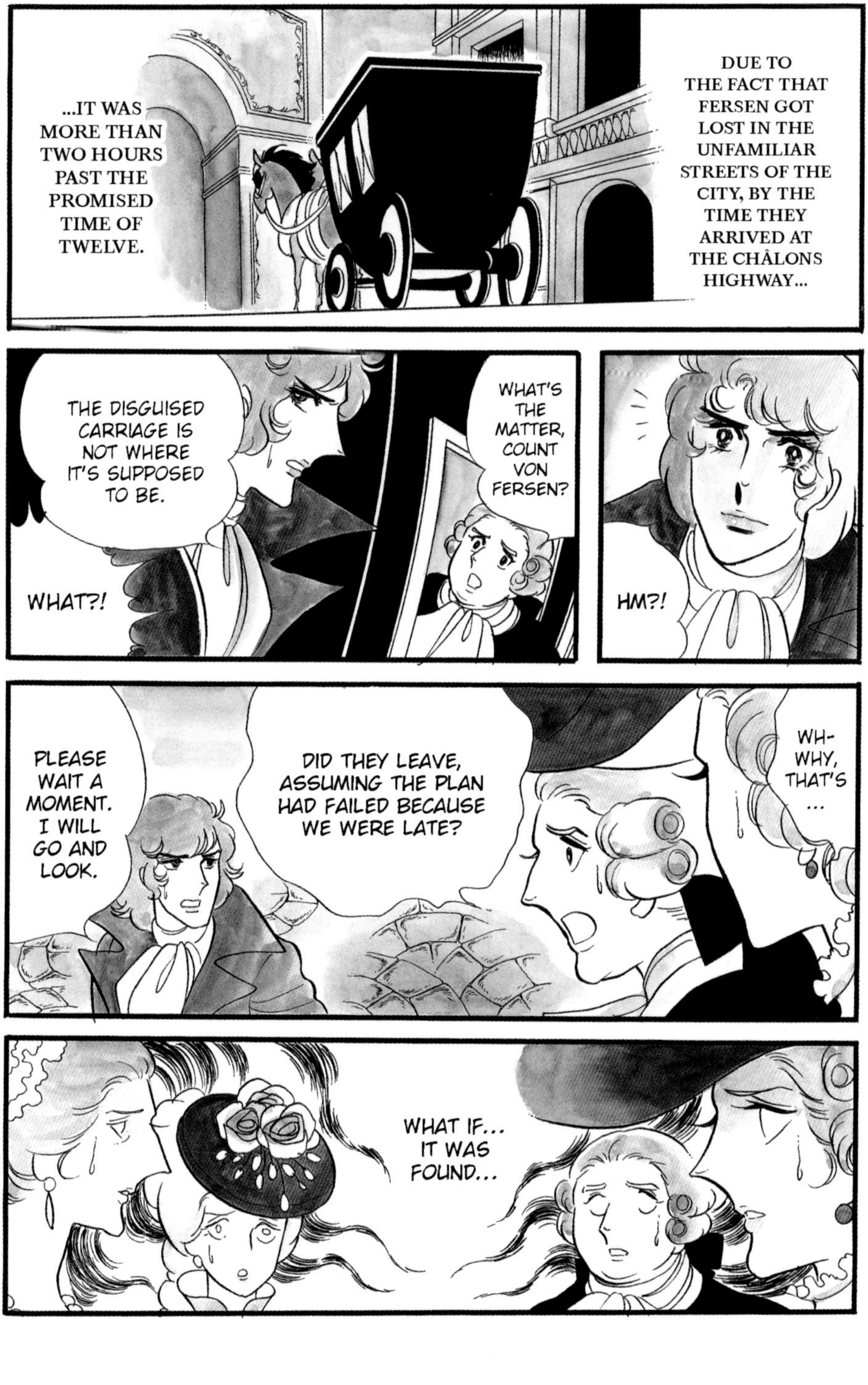
DUE TO THE FACT THAT FERSEN GOT LOST IN THE UNFAMILIAR STREETS OF THE CITY, BY THE TIME THEY ARRIVED AT THE CHÂLONS HIGHWAY...
...IT WAS MORE THAN TWO HOURS PAST THE PROMISED TIME OF TWELVE.
HM?!
WHAT'S THE MATTER, COUNT VON FERSEN?
THE DISGUISED CARRIAGE IS NOT WHERE IT'S SUPPOSED TO BE.
WHAT?!
WH- WHY, THAT'S ...
DID THEY LEAVE, ASSUMING THE PLAN HAD FAILED BECAUSE WE WERE LATE?
PLEASE WAIT A MOMENT. I WILL GO AND LOOK.
WHAT IF... IT WAS FOUND...

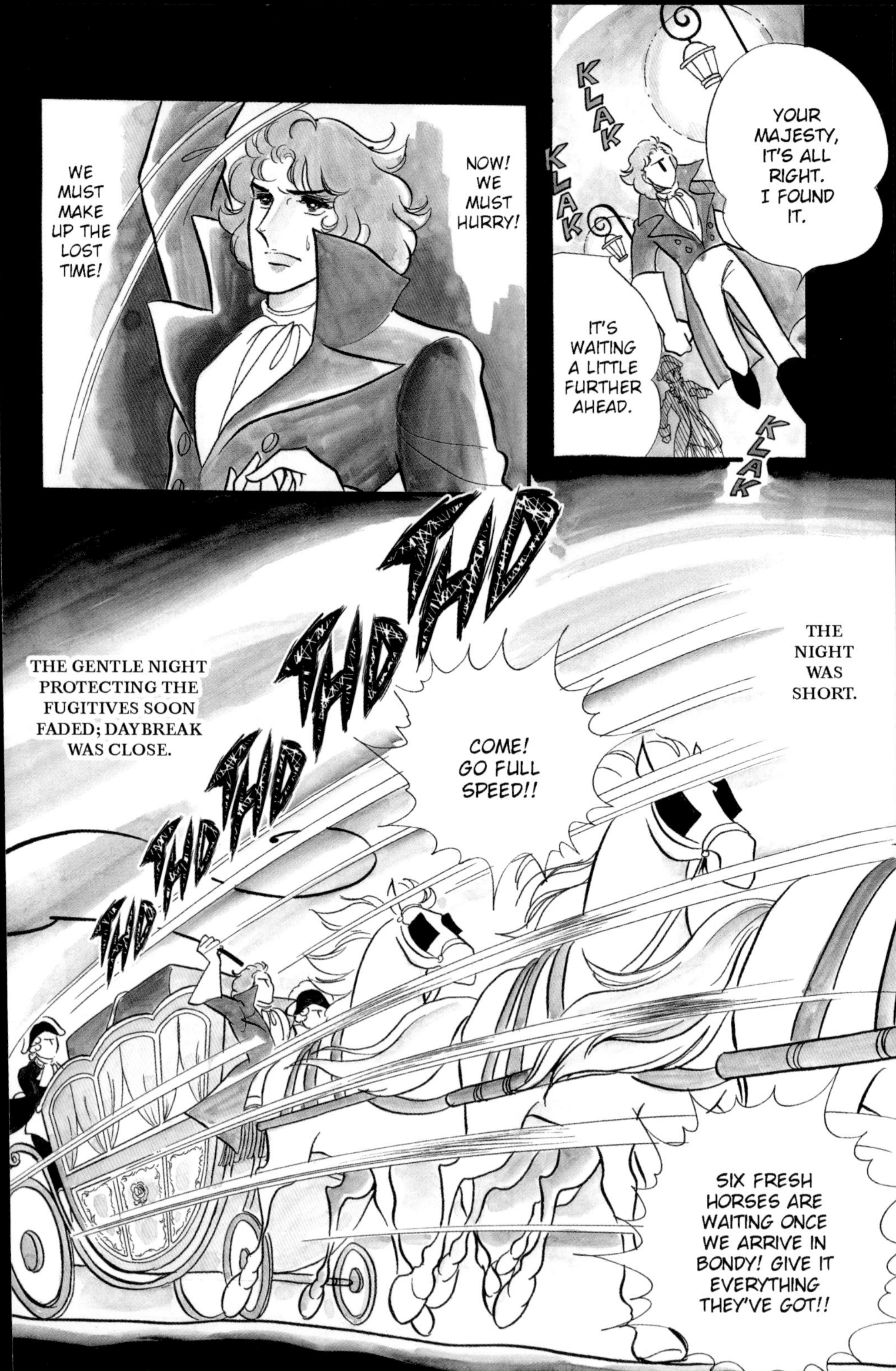
YOUR MAJESTY, IT'S ALL RIGHT. I FOUND IT.
KLAK
KLAK
IT'S WAITING A LITTLE FURTHER AHEAD.
KLAK
NOW! WE MUST HURRY!
WE MUST MAKE UP THE LOST TIME!
THE NIGHT WAS SHORT.
THE GENTLE NIGHT PROTECTING THE FUGITIVES SOON FADED; DAYBREAK WAS CLOSE.
COME! GO FULL SPEED!!
THD THD THD THD THD
SIX FRESH HORSES ARE WAITING ONCE WE ARRIVE IN BONDY! GIVE IT EVERYTHING THEY'VE GOT!!

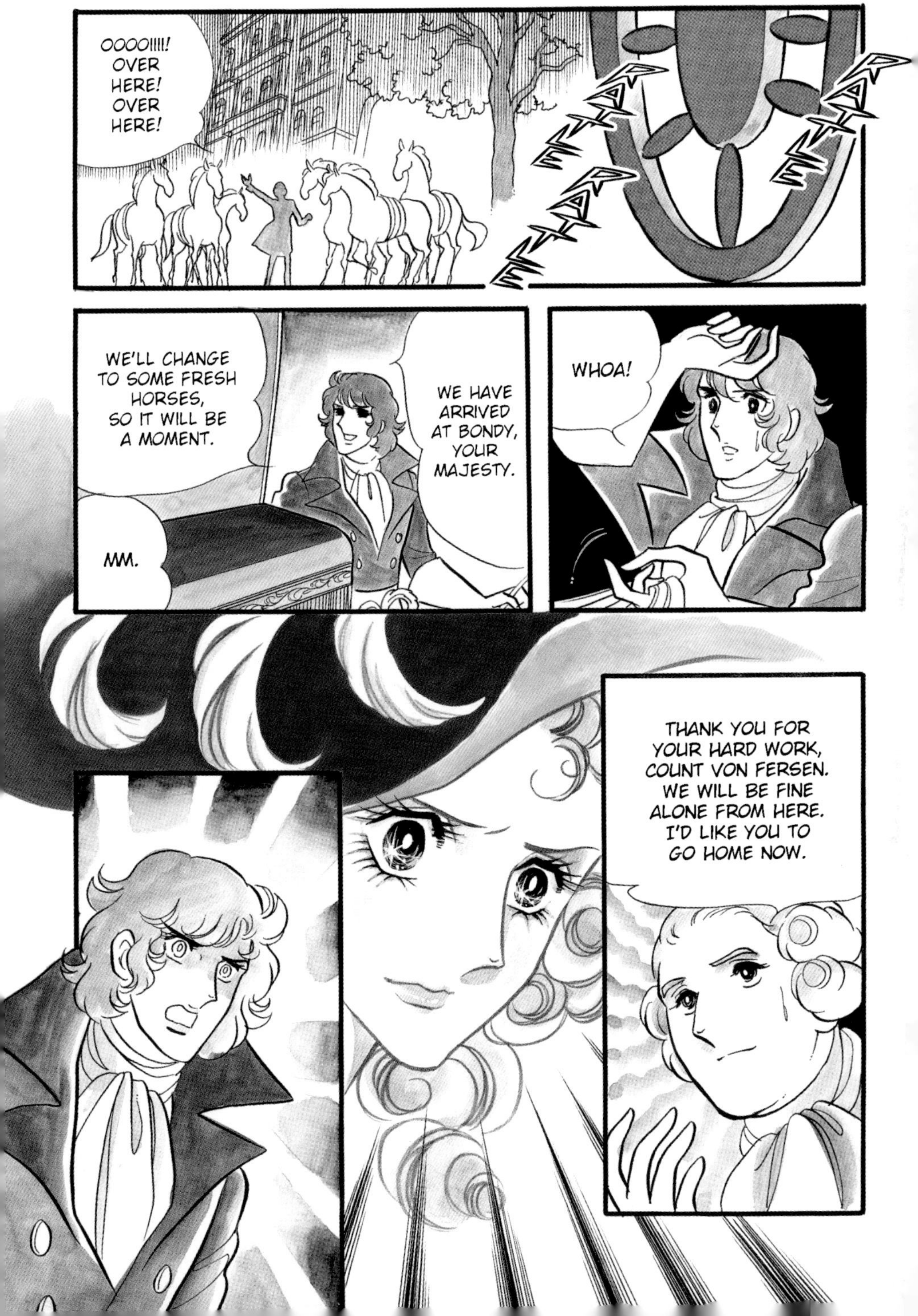
RATTLE
RATTLE
RATTLE
OOOOIIII! OVER HERE! OVER HERE!
WHOA!
WE HAVE ARRIVED AT BONDY, YOUR MAJESTY.
WE'LL CHANGE TO SOME FRESH HORSES, SO IT WILL BE A MOMENT.
MM.
THANK YOU FOR YOUR HARD WORK, COUNT VON FERSEN. WE WILL BE FINE ALONE FROM HERE. I'D LIKE YOU TO GO HOME NOW.

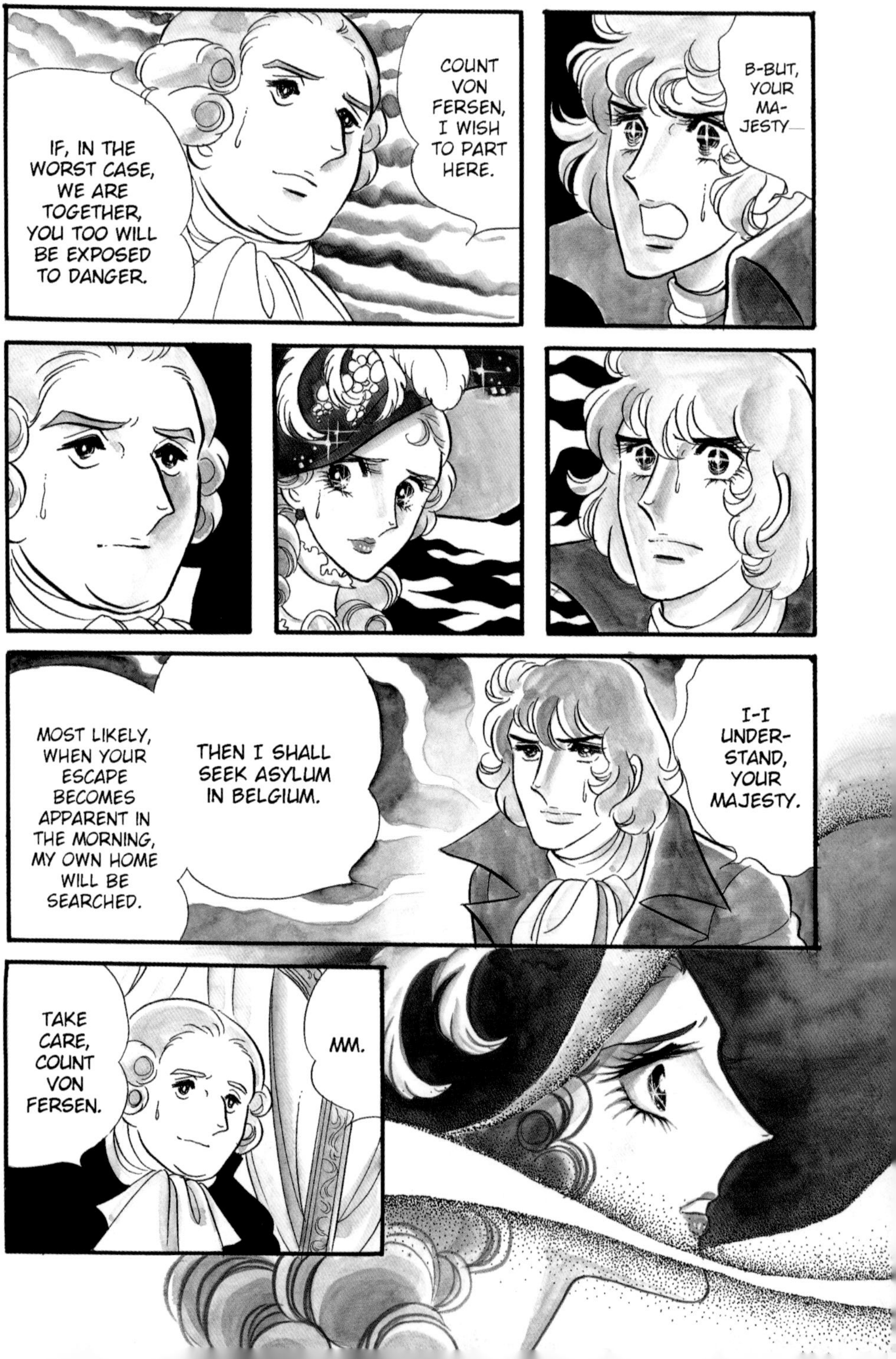
B-BUT, YOUR MAJESTY—
COUNT VON FERSEN, I WISH TO PART HERE.
IF, IN THE WORST CASE, WE ARE TOGETHER, YOU TOO WILL BE EXPOSED TO DANGER.
I-I UNDERSTAND, YOUR MAJESTY.
THEN I SHALL SEEK ASYLUM IN BELGIUM.
MOST LIKELY, WHEN YOUR ESCAPE BECOMES APPARENT IN THE MORNING, MY OWN HOME WILL BE SEARCHED.
MM.
TAKE CARE, COUNT VON FERSEN.

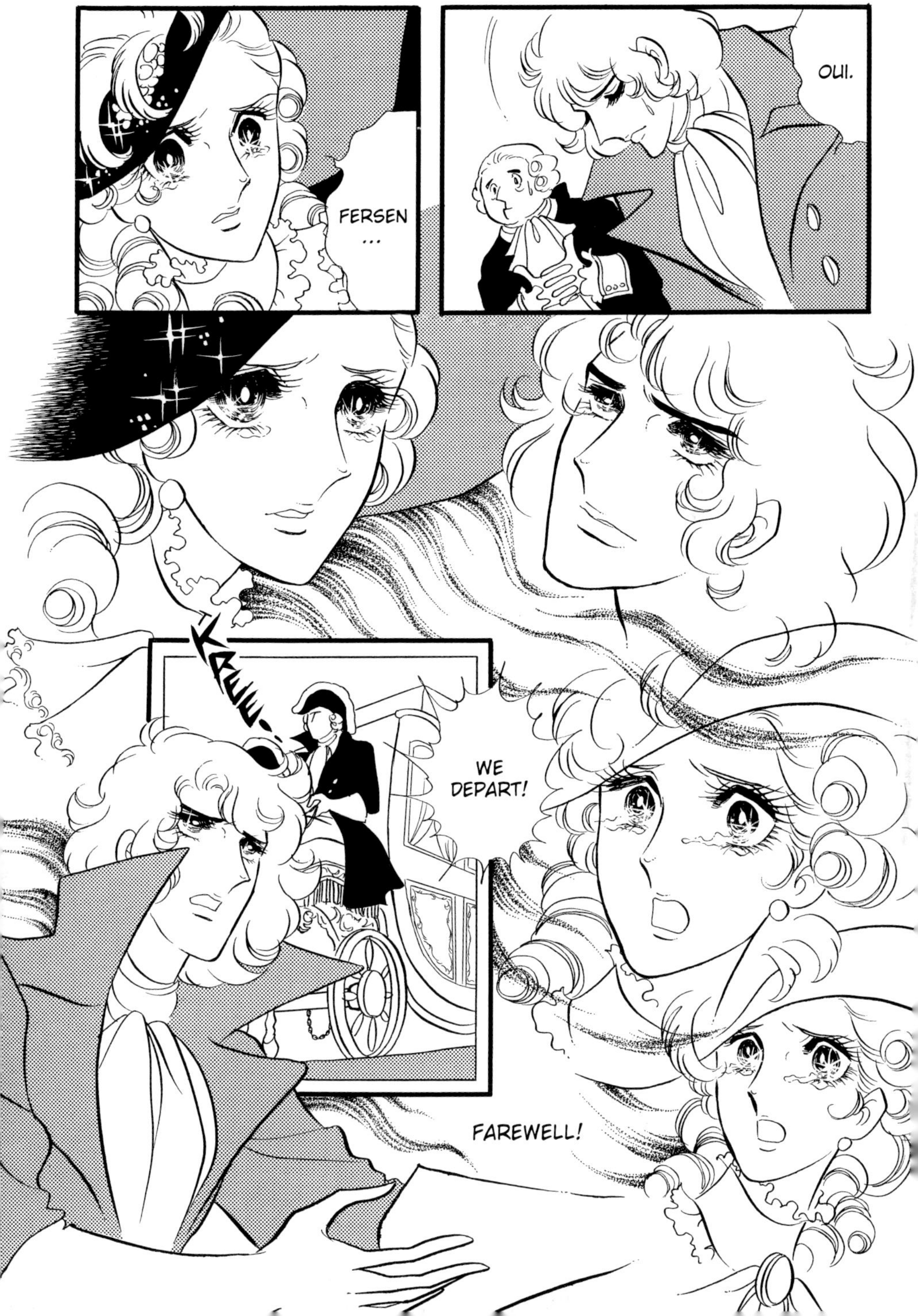
OUI.
FERSEN ...
KREEE..
WE DEPART!
FAREWELL!

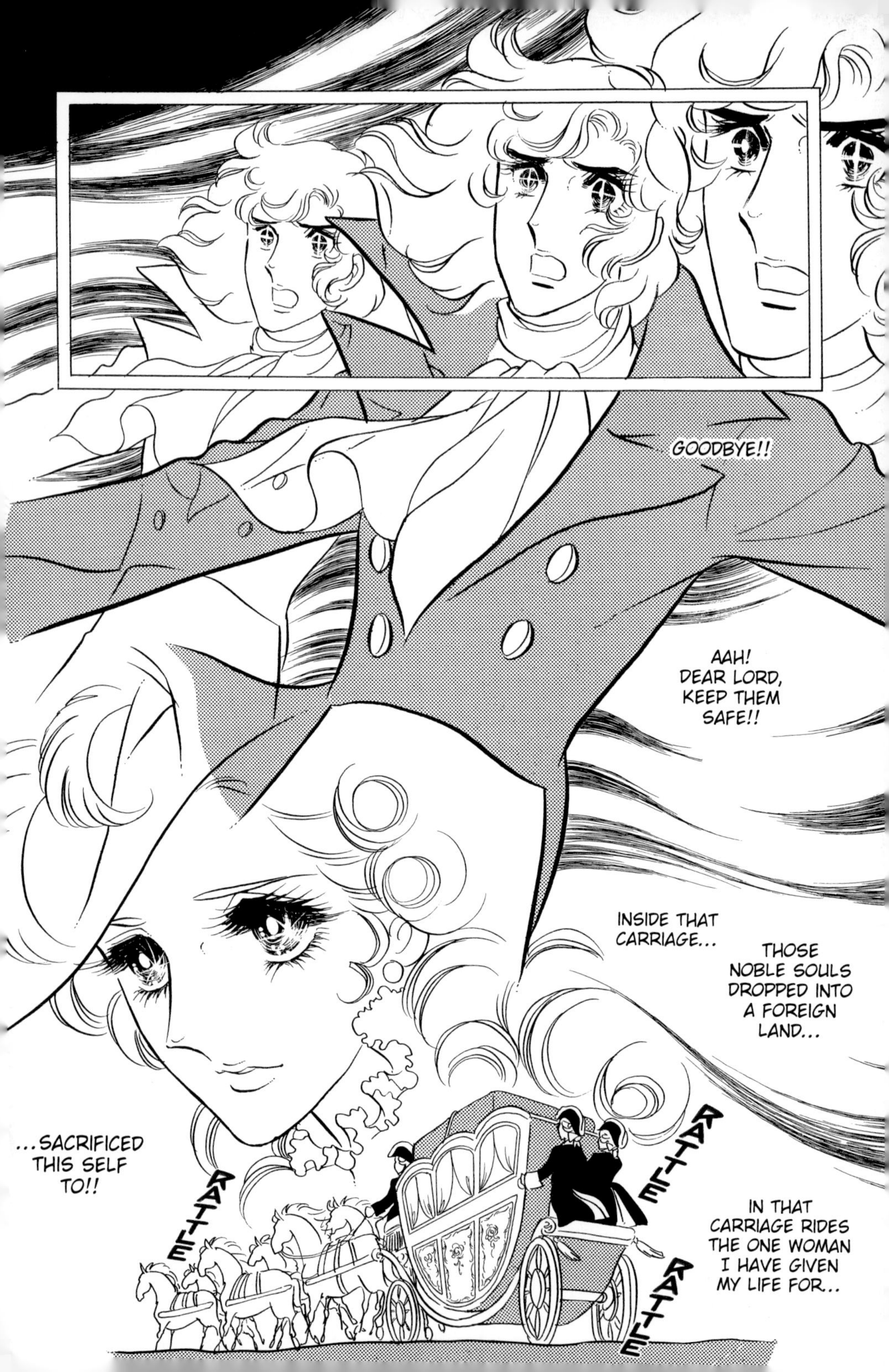
GOODBYE!!
AAH! DEAR LORD, KEEP THEM SAFE!!
INSIDE THAT CARRIAGE...
THOSE NOBLE SOULS DROPPED INTO A FOREIGN LAND...
RATTLE
IN THAT CARRIAGE RIDES THE ONE WOMAN I HAVE GIVEN MY LIFE FOR...
RATTLE
RATTLE
...SACRIFICED THIS SELF TO!!

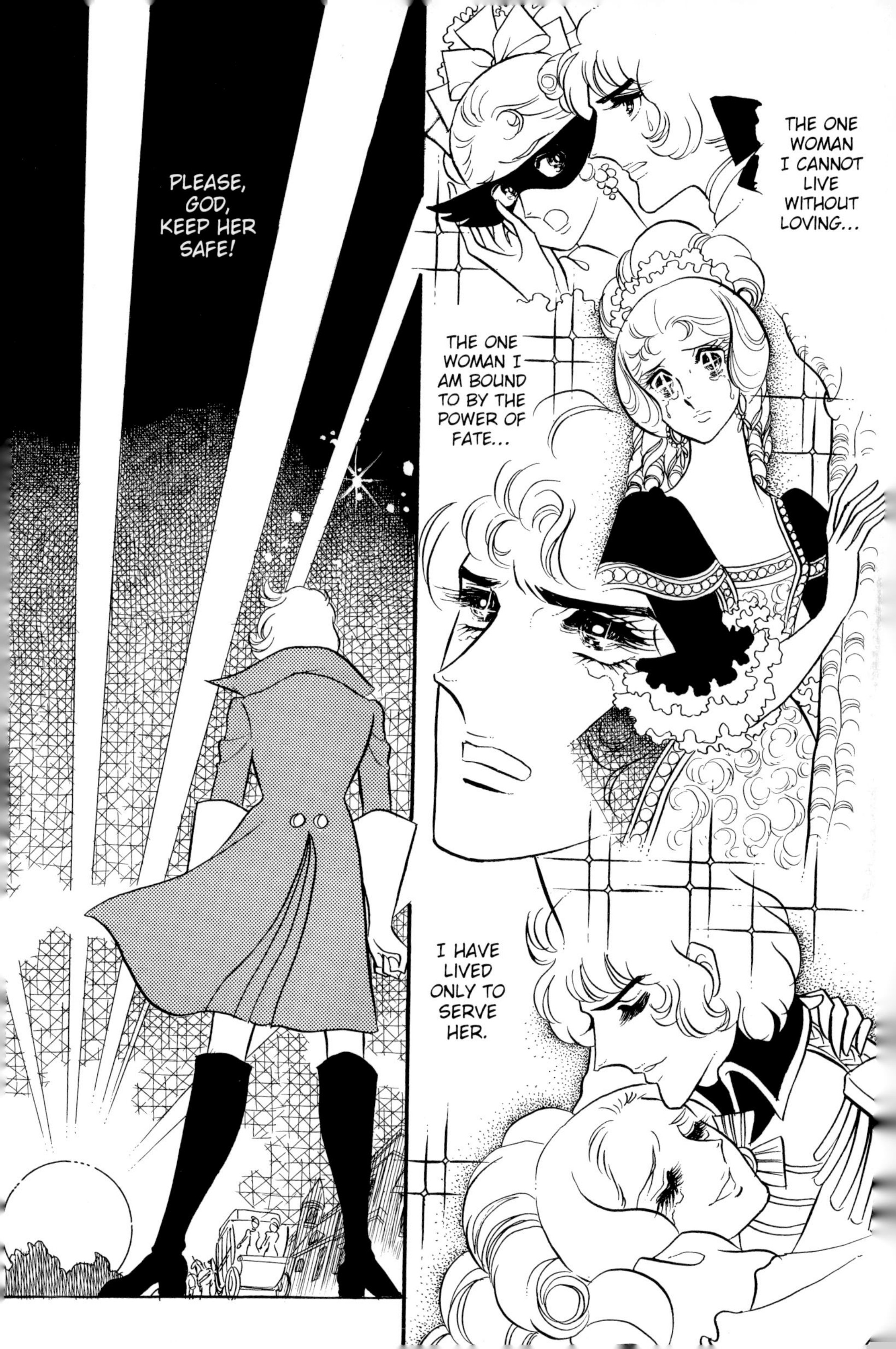
THE ONE WOMAN I CANNOT LIVE WITHOUT LOVING...
THE ONE WOMAN I AM BOUND TO BY THE POWER OF FATE...
I HAVE LIVED ONLY TO SERVE HER.
PLEASE, GOD, KEEP HER SAFE!

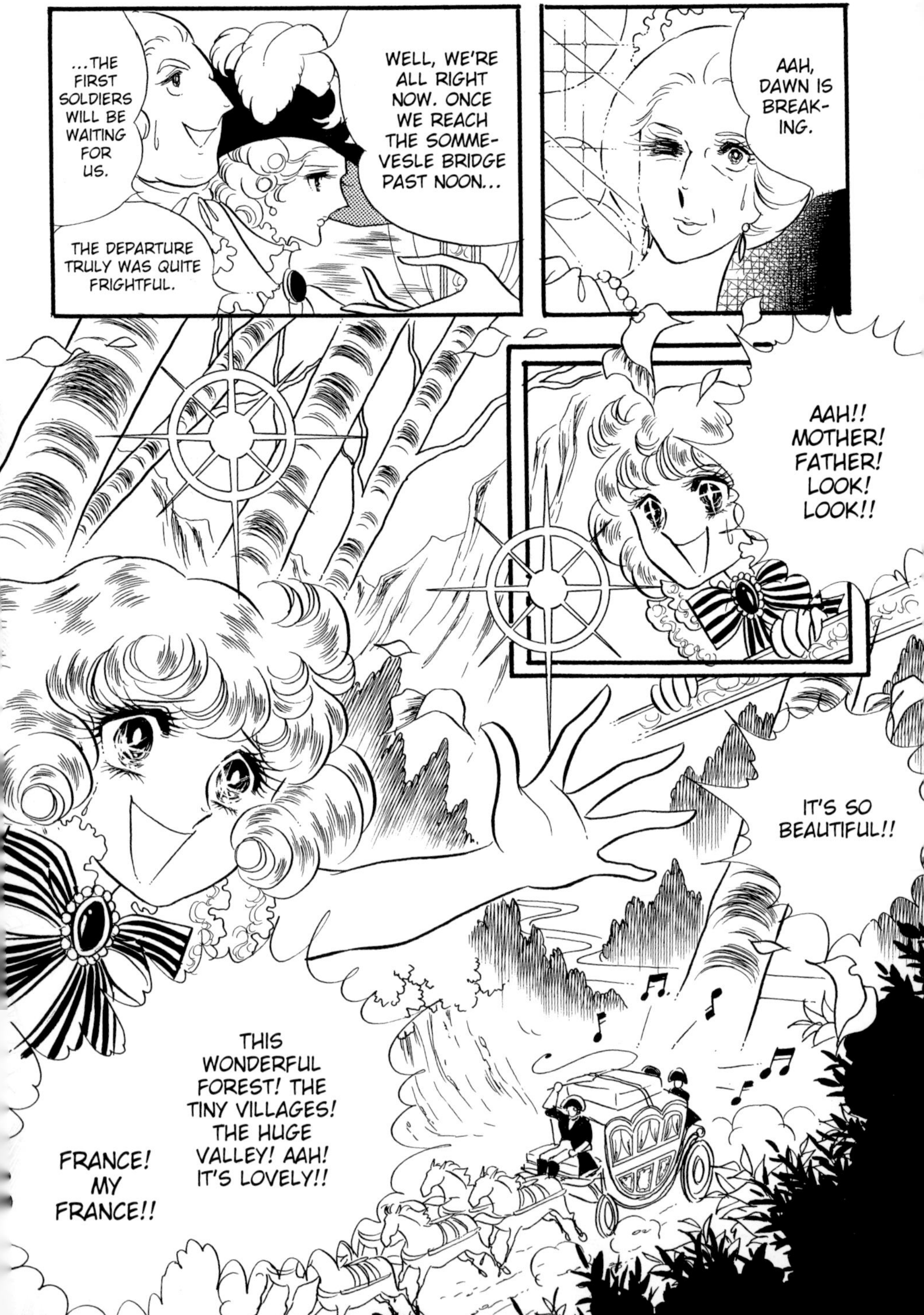
AAH, DAWN IS BREAKING.
WELL, WE'RE ALL RIGHT NOW. ONCE WE REACH THE SOMMEVESLE BRIDGE PAST NOON...
...THE FIRST SOLDIERS WILL BE WAITING FOR US.
THE DEPARTURE TRULY WAS QUITE FRIGHTFUL.
AAH!! MOTHER! FATHER! LOOK! LOOK!!
IT'S SO BEAUTIFUL!!
THIS WONDERFUL FOREST! THE TINY VILLAGES! THE HUGE VALLEY! AAH! IT'S LOVELY!!
FRANCE! MY FRANCE!!

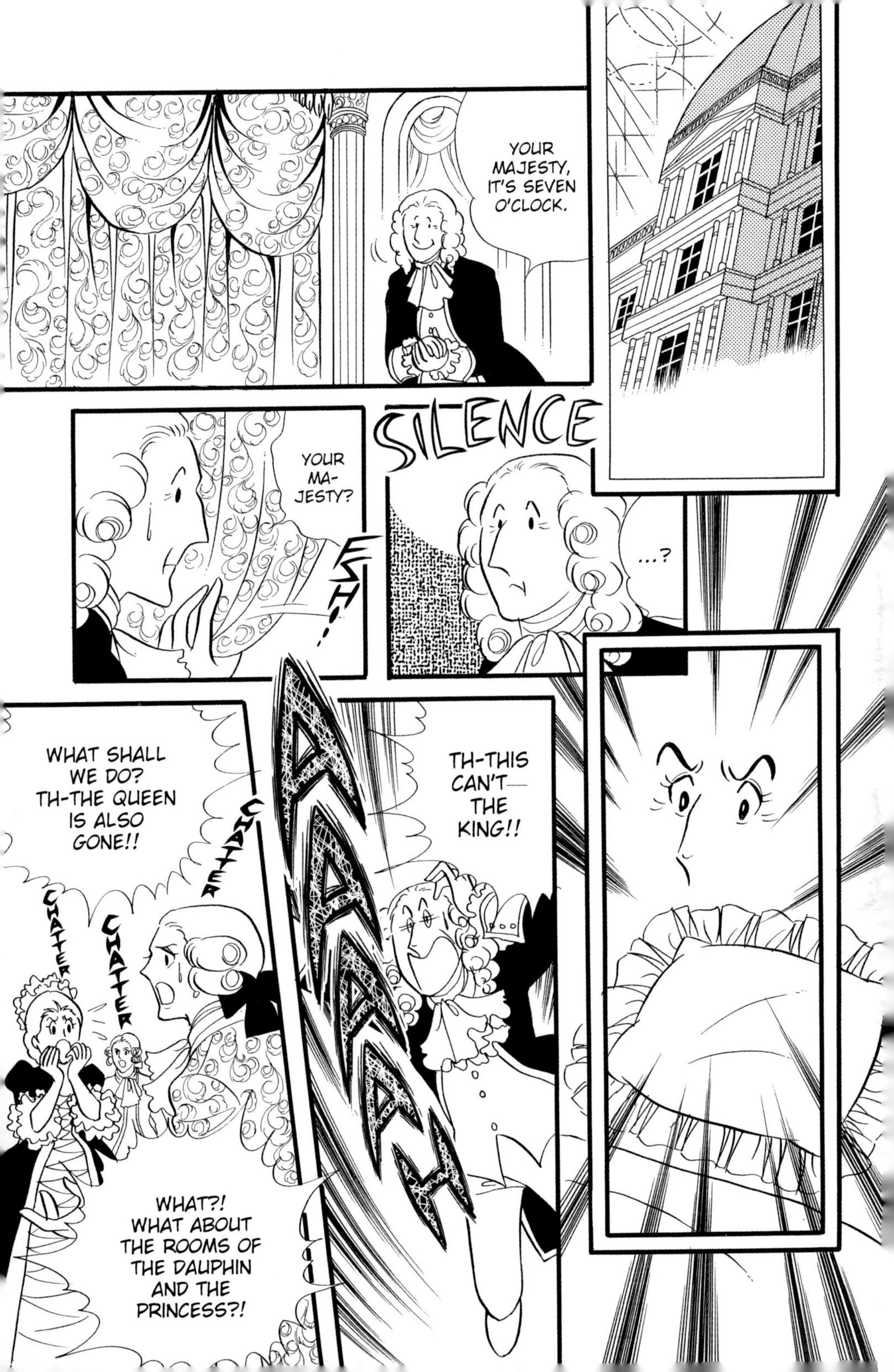
YOUR MAJESTY, IT'S SEVEN O'CLOCK.
SILENCE
...?
YOUR MAJESTY?
FSH!!
TH-THIS CAN'T— THE KING!!
AAAAAH
WHAT SHALL WE DO? TH-THE QUEEN IS ALSO GONE!!
CHATTER
CHATTER
CHATTER
WHAT?! WHAT ABOUT THE ROOMS OF THE DAUPHIN AND THE PRINCESS?!

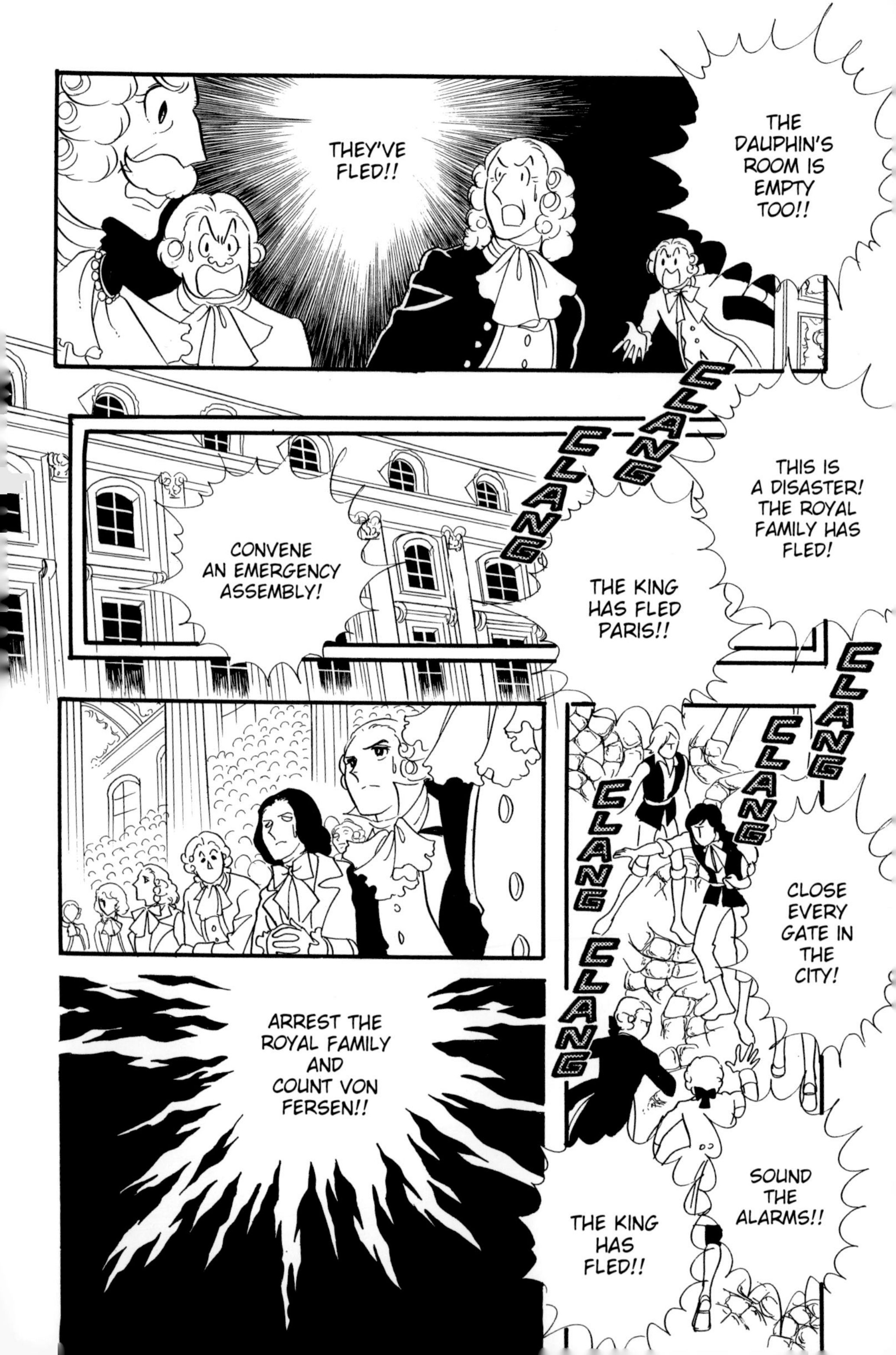
THE DAUPHIN'S ROOM IS EMPTY TOO!!
THEY'VE FLED!!
CLANG
CLANG
THIS IS A DISASTER! THE ROYAL FAMILY HAS FLED!
THE KING HAS FLED PARIS!!
CONVENE AN EMERGENCY ASSEMBLY!
CLANG
CLANG
CLANG
CLOSE EVERY GATE IN THE CITY!
CLANG
SOUND THE ALARMS!!
THE KING HAS FLED!!
ARREST THE ROYAL FAMILY AND COUNT VON FERSEN!!

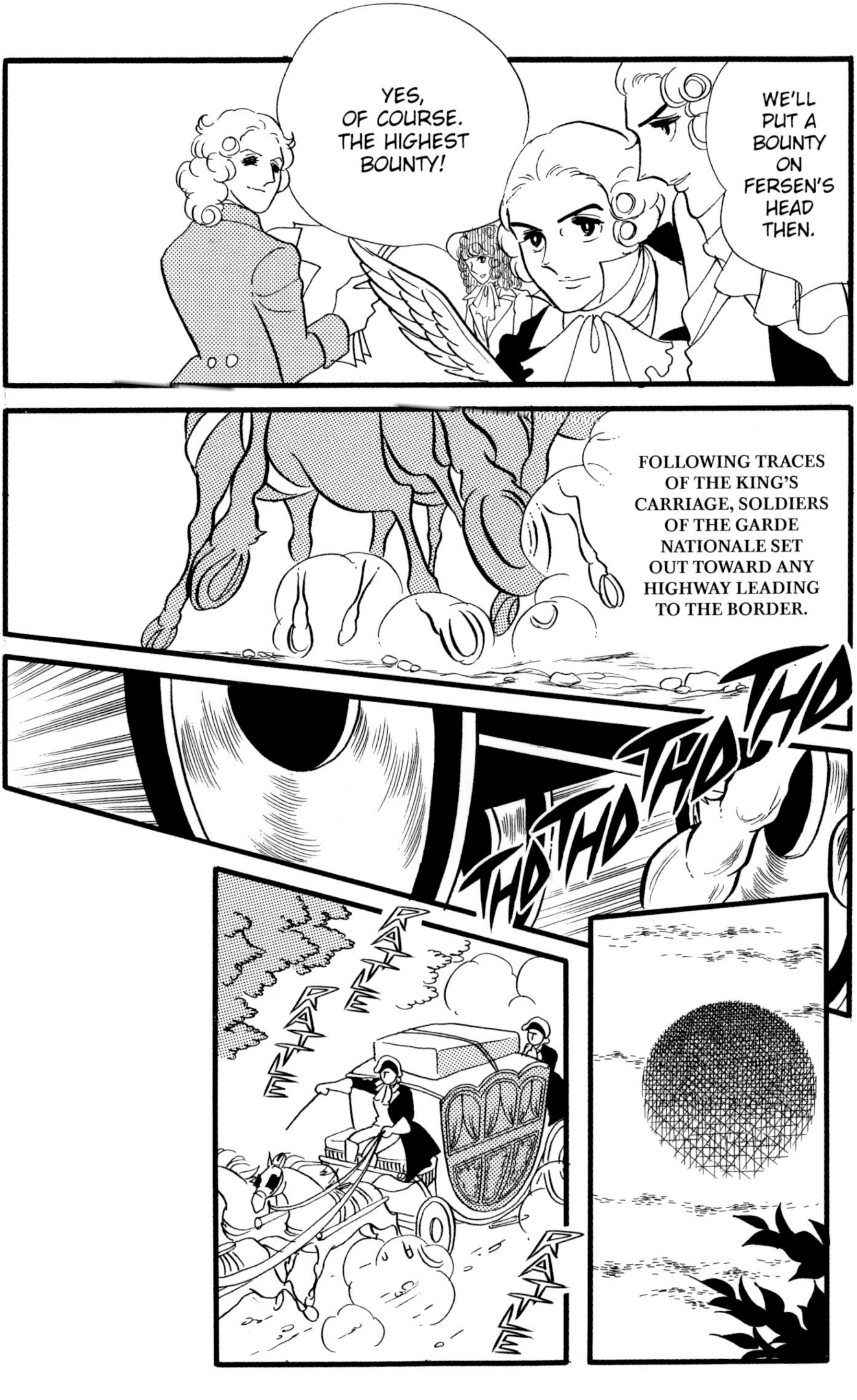
WE'LL PUT A BOUNTY ON FERSEN'S HEAD THEN.
YES, OF COURSE. THE HIGHEST BOUNTY!
FOLLOWING TRACES OF THE KING'S CARRIAGE, SOLDIERS OF THE GARDE NATIONALE SET OUT TOWARD ANY HIGHWAY LEADING TO THE BORDER.
THD THD THD THD
RATTLE
RATTLE
RATTLE

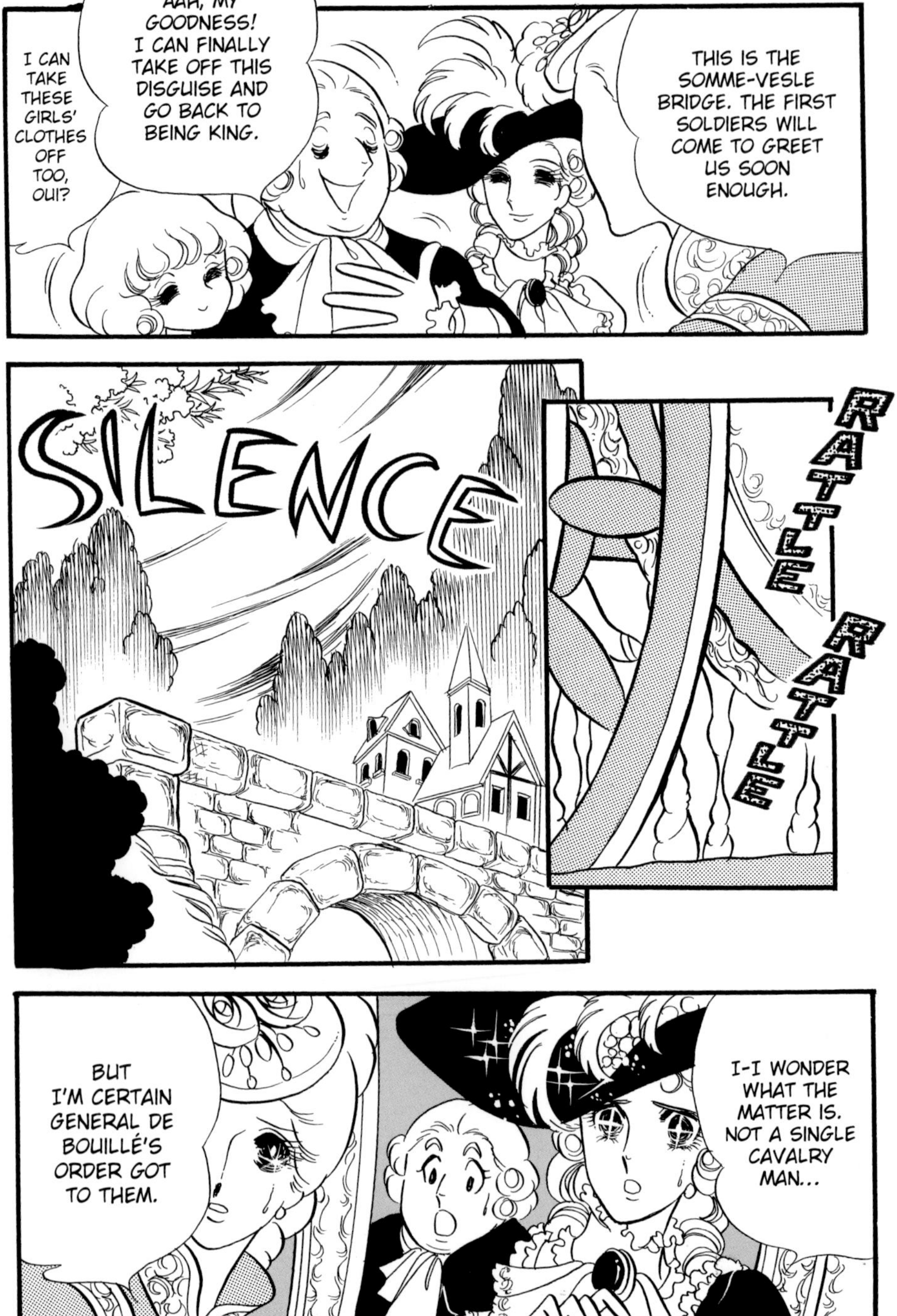
THIS IS THE SOMME-VESLE BRIDGE. THE FIRST SOLDIERS WILL COME TO GREET US SOON ENOUGH.
AAH, MY GOODNESS! I CAN FINALLY TAKE OFF THIS DISGUISE AND GO BACK TO BEING KING.
I CAN TAKE THESE GIRLS' CLOTHES OFF TOO, OUI?
RATTLE RATTLE
SILENCE
I-I WONDER WHAT THE MATTER IS. NOT A SINGLE CAVALRY MAN...
BUT I'M CERTAIN GENERAL DE BOUILLÉ'S ORDER GOT TO THEM.

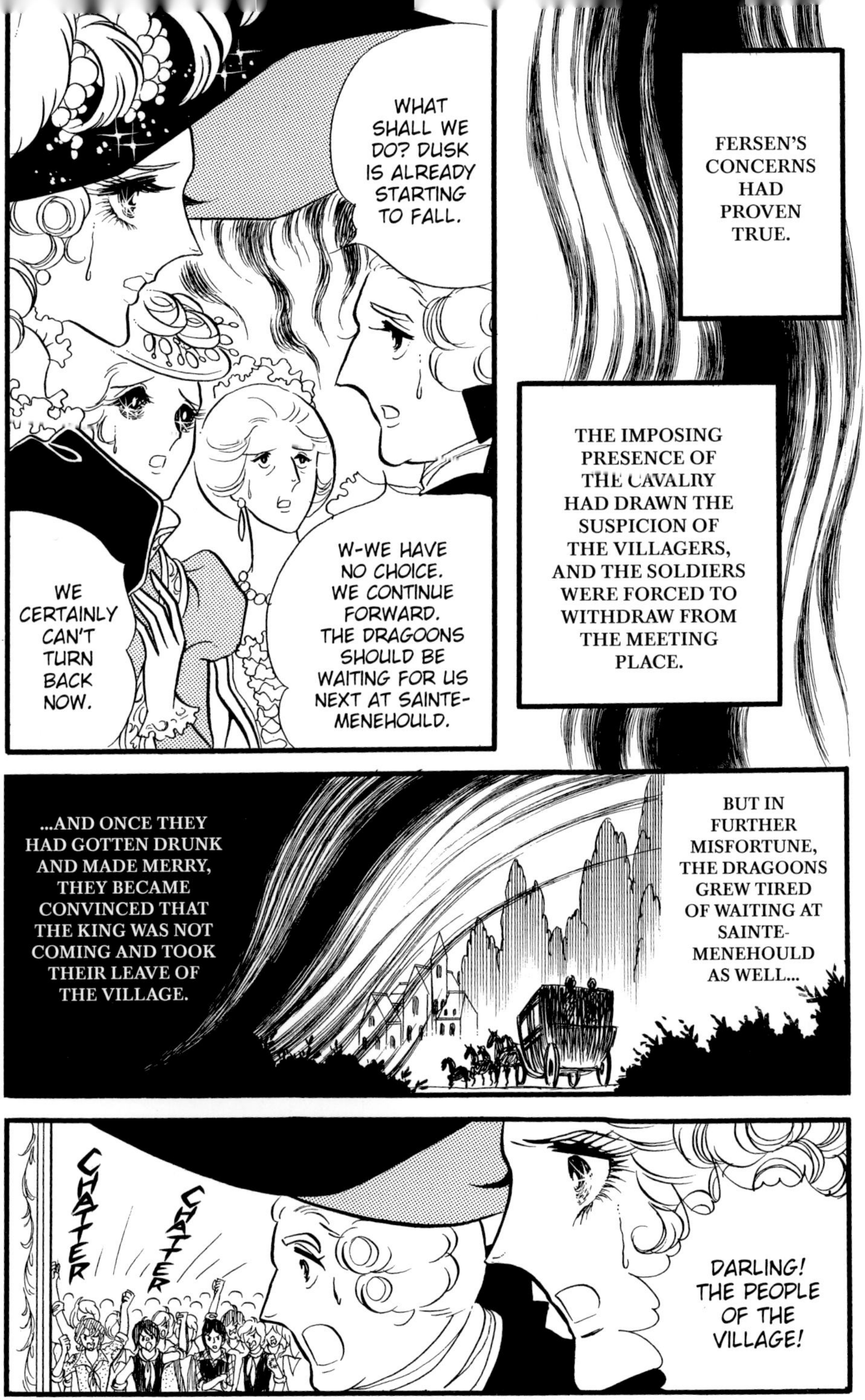
FERSEN'S CONCERNS HAD PROVEN TRUE.
THE IMPOSING PRESENCE OF THE CAVALRY HAD DRAWN THE SUSPICION OF THE VILLAGERS, AND THE SOLDIERS WERE FORCED TO WITHDRAW FROM THE MEETING PLACE.
WHAT SHALL WE DO? DUSK IS ALREADY STARTING TO FALL.
W-WE HAVE NO CHOICE. WE CONTINUE FORWARD. THE DRAGOONS SHOULD BE WAITING FOR US NEXT AT SAINTE-MENEHOULD.
WE CERTAINLY CAN'T TURN BACK NOW.
BUT IN FURTHER MISFORTUNE, THE DRAGOONS GREW TIRED OF WAITING AT SAINTE-MENEHOULD AS WELL...
...AND ONCE THEY HAD GOTTEN DRUNK AND MADE MERRY, THEY BECAME CONVINCED THAT THE KING WAS NOT COMING AND TOOK THEIR LEAVE OF THE VILLAGE.
DARLING! THE PEOPLE OF THE VILLAGE!
CHATTER
CHATTER

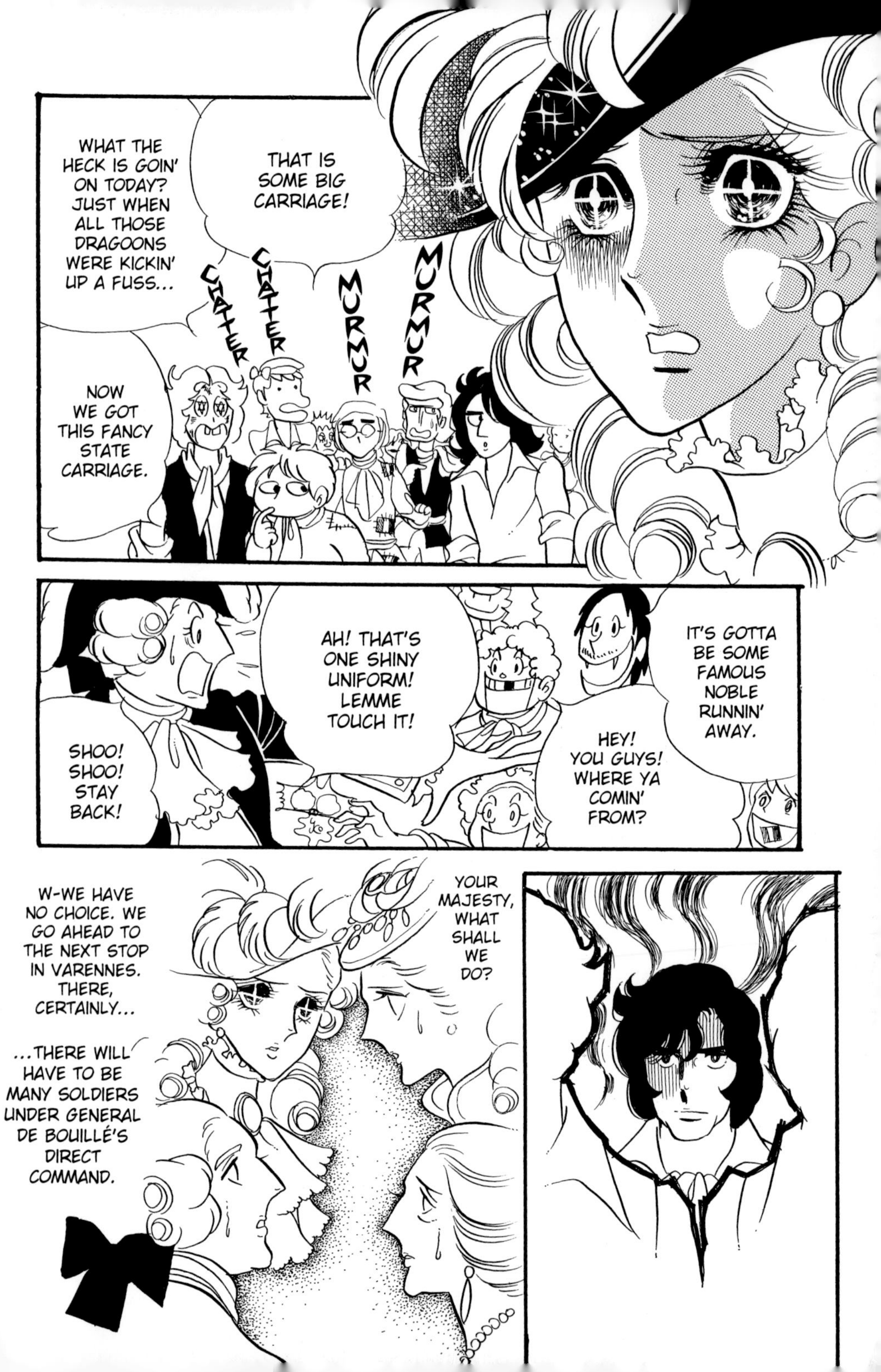
THAT IS SOME BIG CARRIAGE!
WHAT THE HECK IS GOIN' ON TODAY? JUST WHEN ALL THOSE DRAGOONS WERE KICKIN' UP A FUSS...
MURMUR
MURMUR
CHATTER
CHATTER
NOW WE GOT THIS FANCY STATE CARRIAGE.
IT'S GOTTA BE SOME FAMOUS NOBLE RUNNIN' AWAY.
HEY! YOU GUYS! WHERE YA COMIN' FROM?
AH! THAT'S ONE SHINY UNIFORM! LEMME TOUCH IT!
SHOO! SHOO! STAY BACK!
YOUR MAJESTY, WHAT SHALL WE DO?
W-WE HAVE NO CHOICE. WE GO AHEAD TO THE NEXT STOP IN VARENNES. THERE, CERTAINLY...
...THERE WILL HAVE TO BE MANY SOLDIERS UNDER GENERAL DE BOUILLÉ'S DIRECT COMMAND.

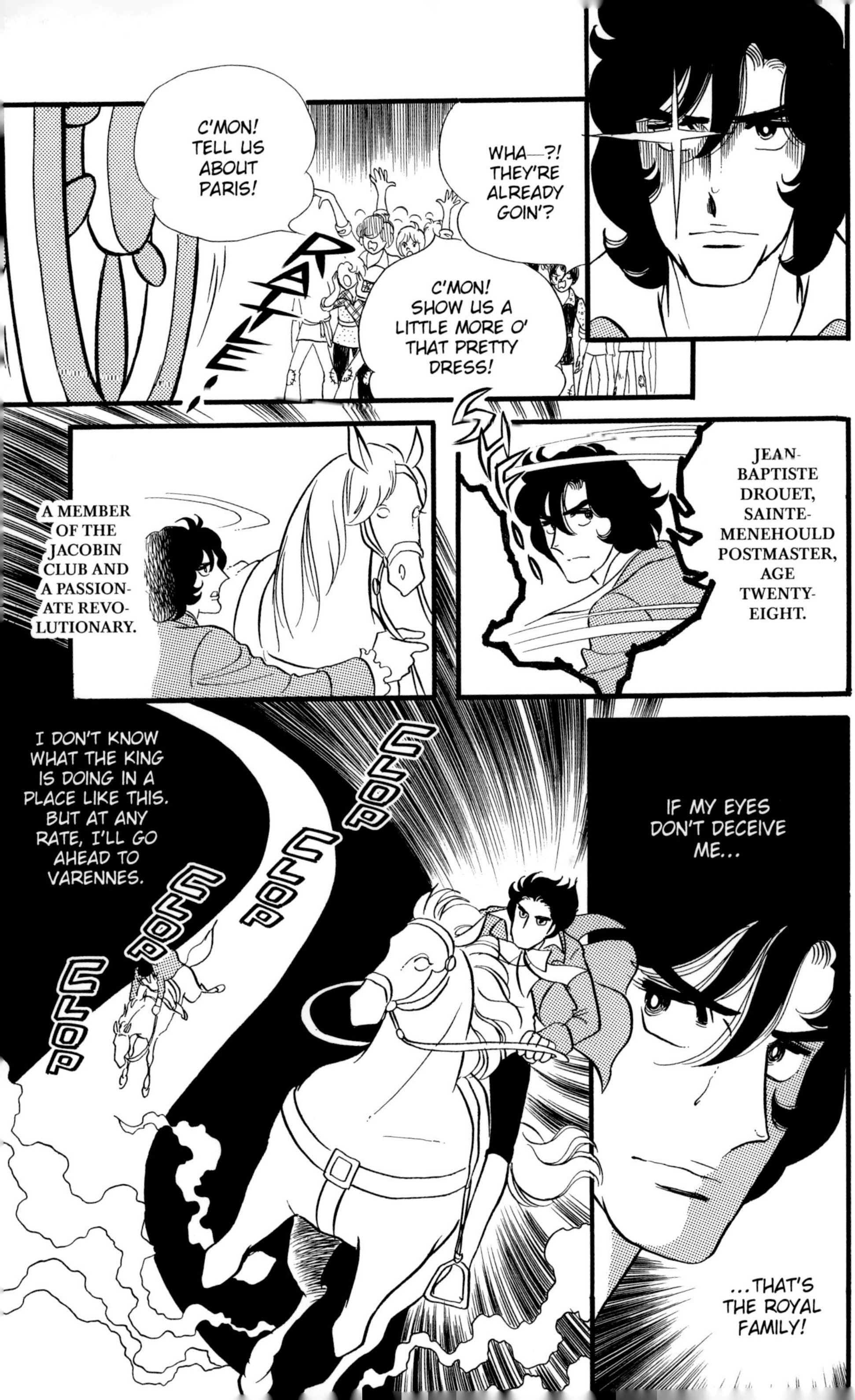
WHA—?! THEY'RE ALREADY GOIN'?
C'MON! TELL US ABOUT PARIS!
C'MON! SHOW US A LITTLE MORE O' THAT PRETTY DRESS!
RATTLE...
JEAN-BAPTISTE DROUET, SAINTE-MENEHOULD POSTMASTER, AGE TWENTY-EIGHT.
A MEMBER OF THE JACOBIN CLUB AND A PASSIONATE REVOLUTIONARY.
IF MY EYES DON'T DECEIVE ME...
...THAT'S THE ROYAL FAMILY!
I DON'T KNOW WHAT THE KING IS DOING IN A PLACE LIKE THIS. BUT AT ANY RATE, I'LL GO AHEAD TO VARENNES.
CLOP CLOP
CLOP CLOP

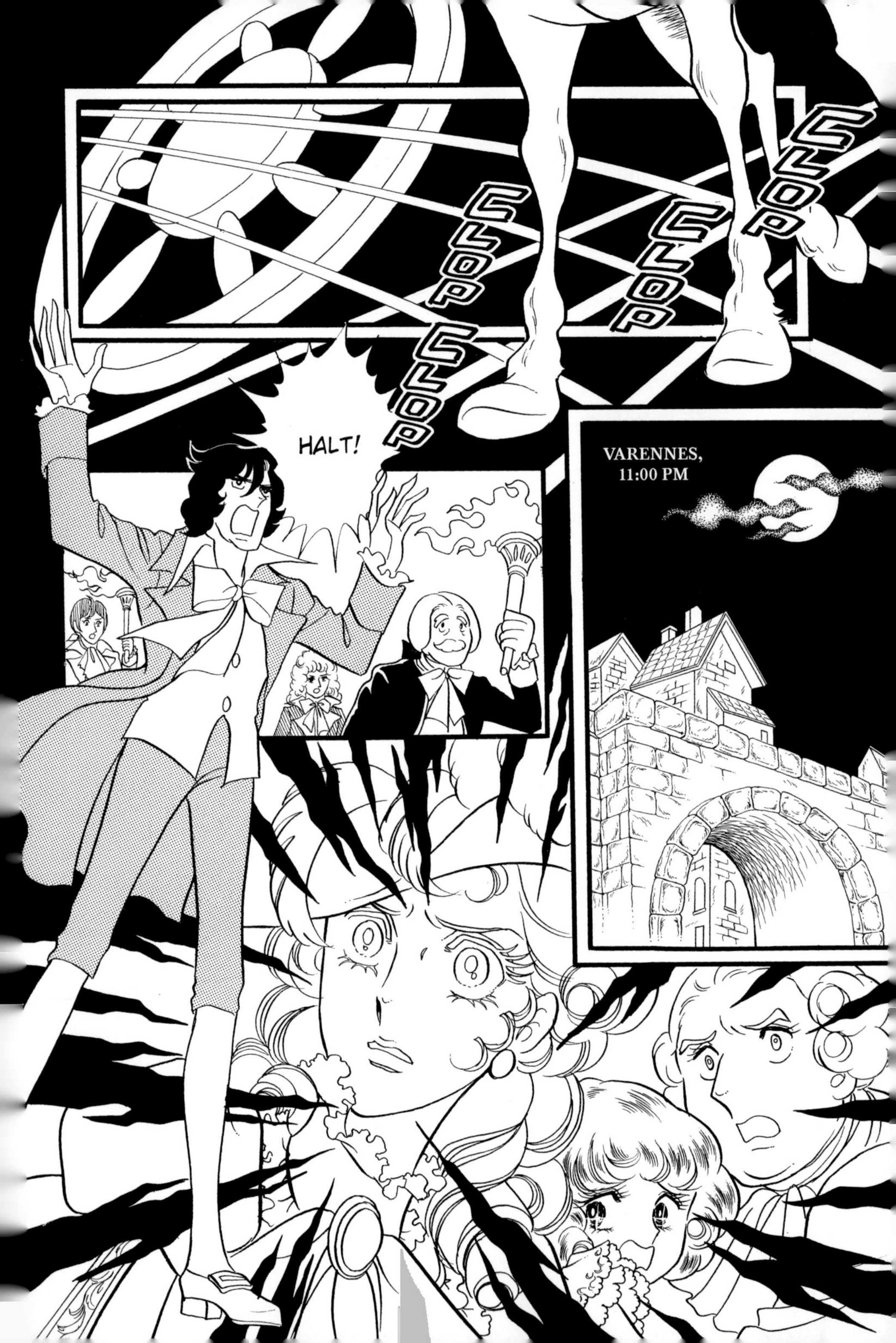
CLOP
CLOP
CLOP CLOP
VARENNES, 11:00 PM
HALT!

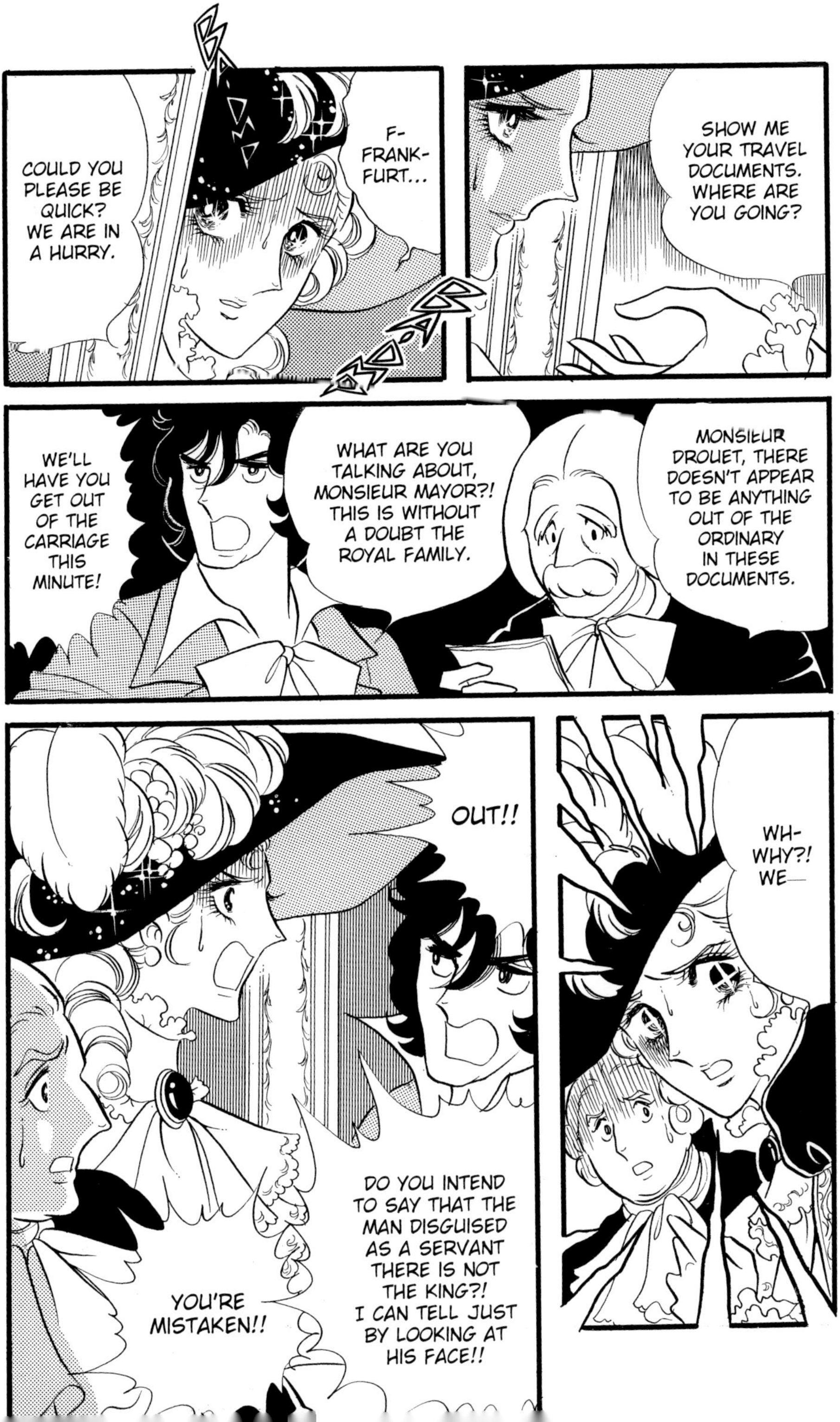

SHOW ME YOUR TRAVEL DOCUMENTS. WHERE ARE YOU GOING?
BA-DMP
BA-DMP
F-FRANK-FURT...
COULD YOU PLEASE BE QUICK? WE ARE IN A HURRY.
MONSIEUR DROUET, THERE DOESN'T APPEAR TO BE ANYTHING OUT OF THE ORDINARY IN THESE DOCUMENTS.
WHAT ARE YOU TALKING ABOUT, MONSIEUR MAYOR?! THIS IS WITHOUT A DOUBT THE ROYAL FAMILY.
WE'LL HAVE YOU GET OUT OF THE CARRIAGE THIS MINUTE!
WH-WHY?! WE—
OUT!!
DO YOU INTEND TO SAY THAT THE MAN DISGUISED AS A SERVANT THERE IS NOT THE KING?! I CAN TELL JUST BY LOOKING AT HIS FACE!!
YOU'RE MISTAKEN!!

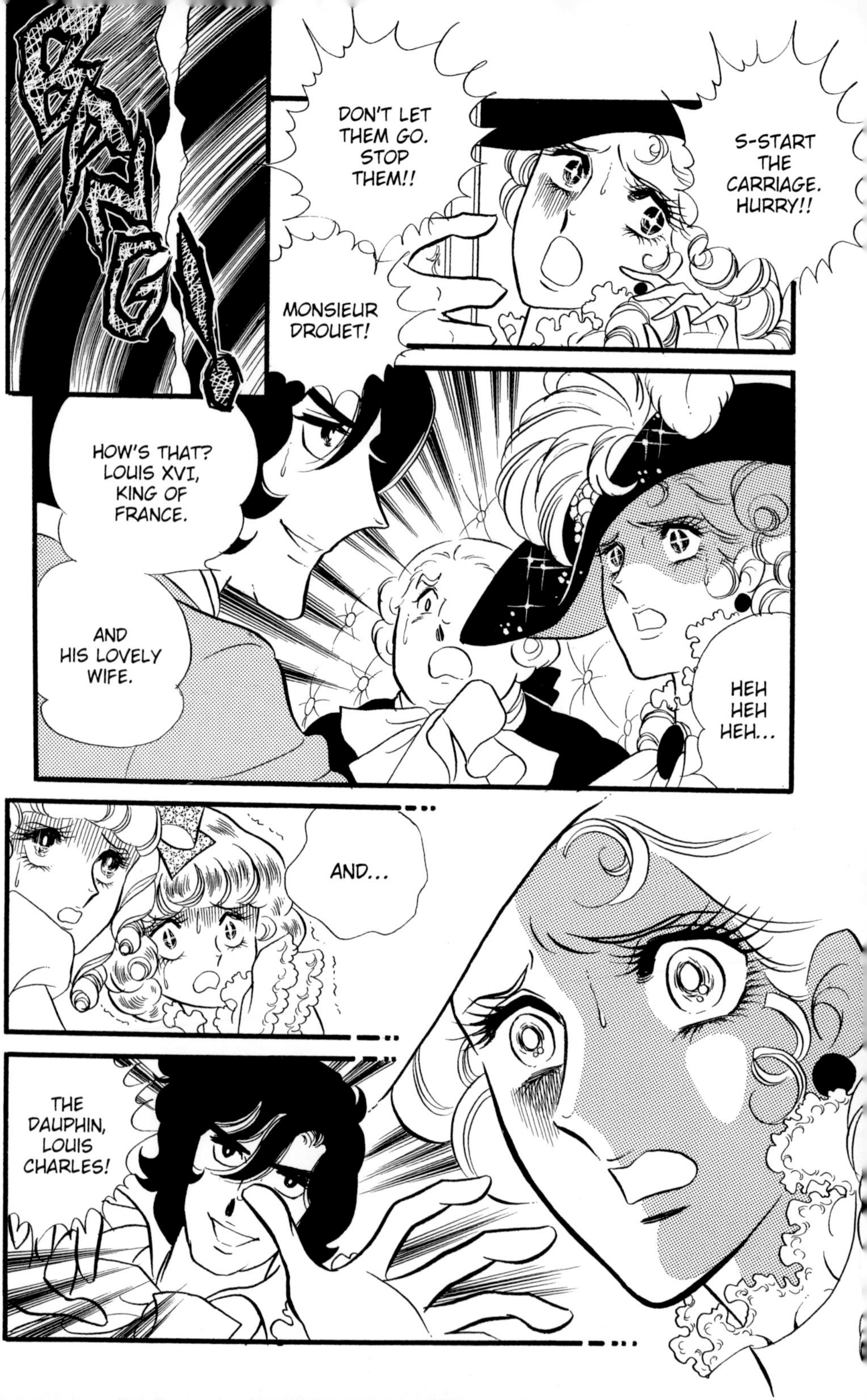
S-START THE CARRIAGE. HURRY!!
DON'T LET THEM GO. STOP THEM!!
MONSIEUR DROUET!
BANG!
HOW'S THAT? LOUIS XVI, KING OF FRANCE.
AND HIS LOVELY WIFE.
HEH HEH HEH...
AND...
THE DAUPHIN, LOUIS CHARLES!

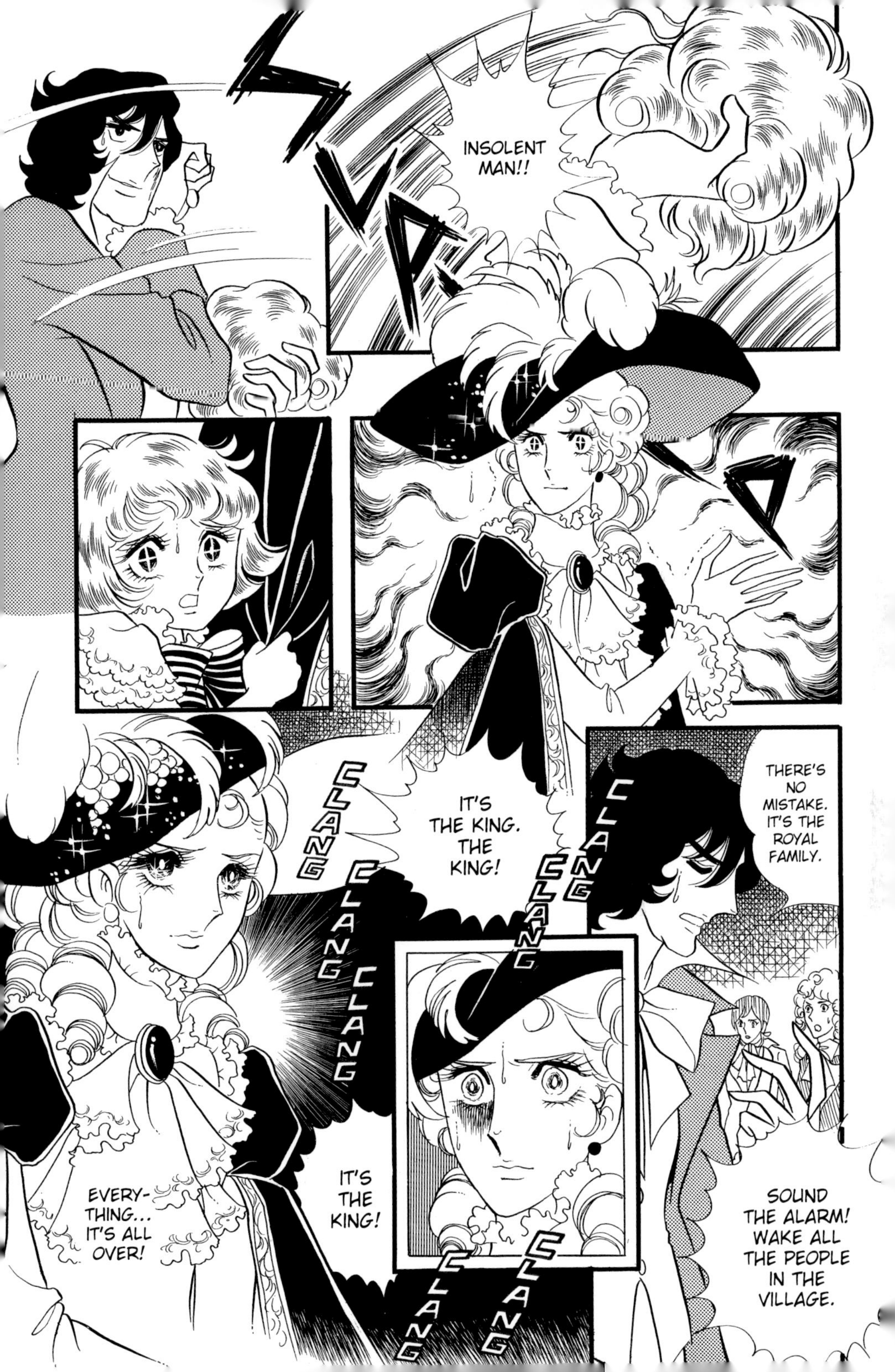

INSOLENT MAN!!
THERE'S NO MISTAKE. IT'S THE ROYAL FAMILY.
CLANG
CLANG
IT'S THE KING. THE KING!
CLANG
CLANG
SOUND THE ALARM! WAKE ALL THE PEOPLE IN THE VILLAGE.
CLANG
CLANG
IT'S THE KING!
EVERY-THING... IT'S ALL OVER!

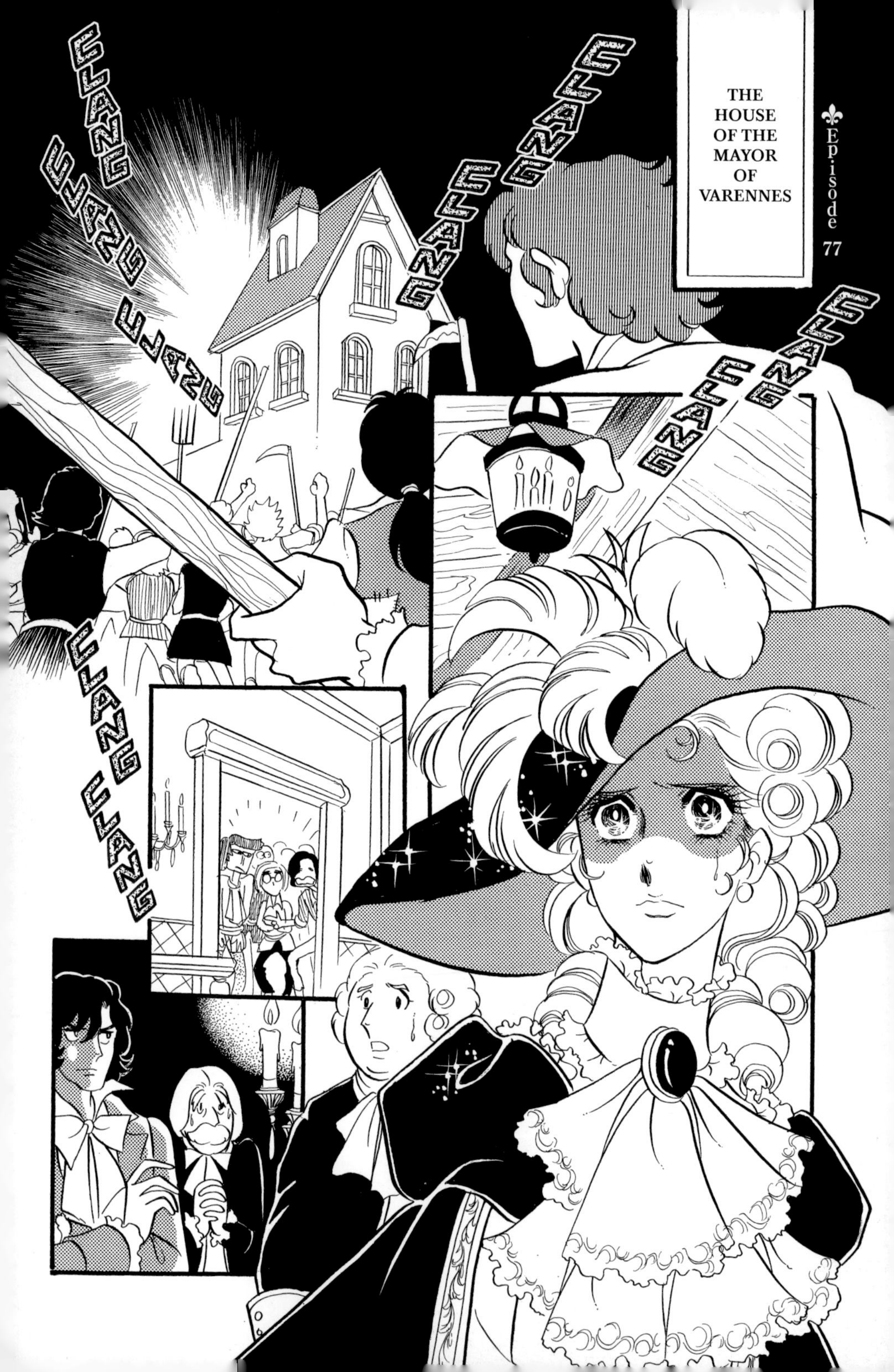

Episode 77
THE HOUSE OF THE MAYOR OF VARENNES
CLANG CLANG
CLANG CLANG
CLANG CLANG
CLANG CLANG

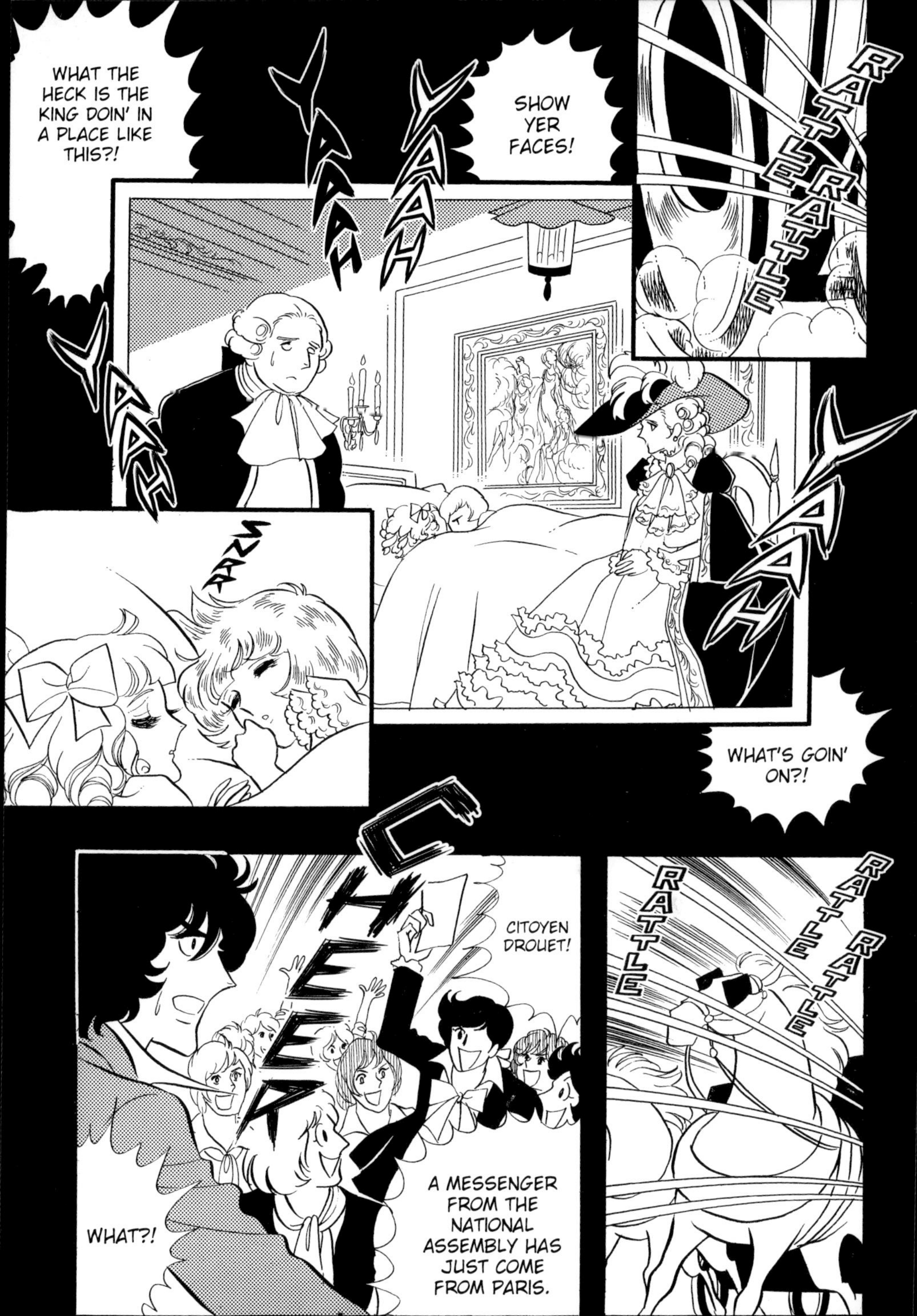
RATTLE RATTLE
SHOW YER FACES!
YAAAH YAAAH
WHAT THE HECK IS THE KING DOIN' IN A PLACE LIKE THIS?!
YAAAH
YAAAH
SNRR
WHAT'S GOIN' ON?!
RATTLE RATTLE RATTLE
CITOYEN DROUET!
A MESSENGER FROM THE NATIONAL ASSEMBLY HAS JUST COME FROM PARIS.
WHAT?!

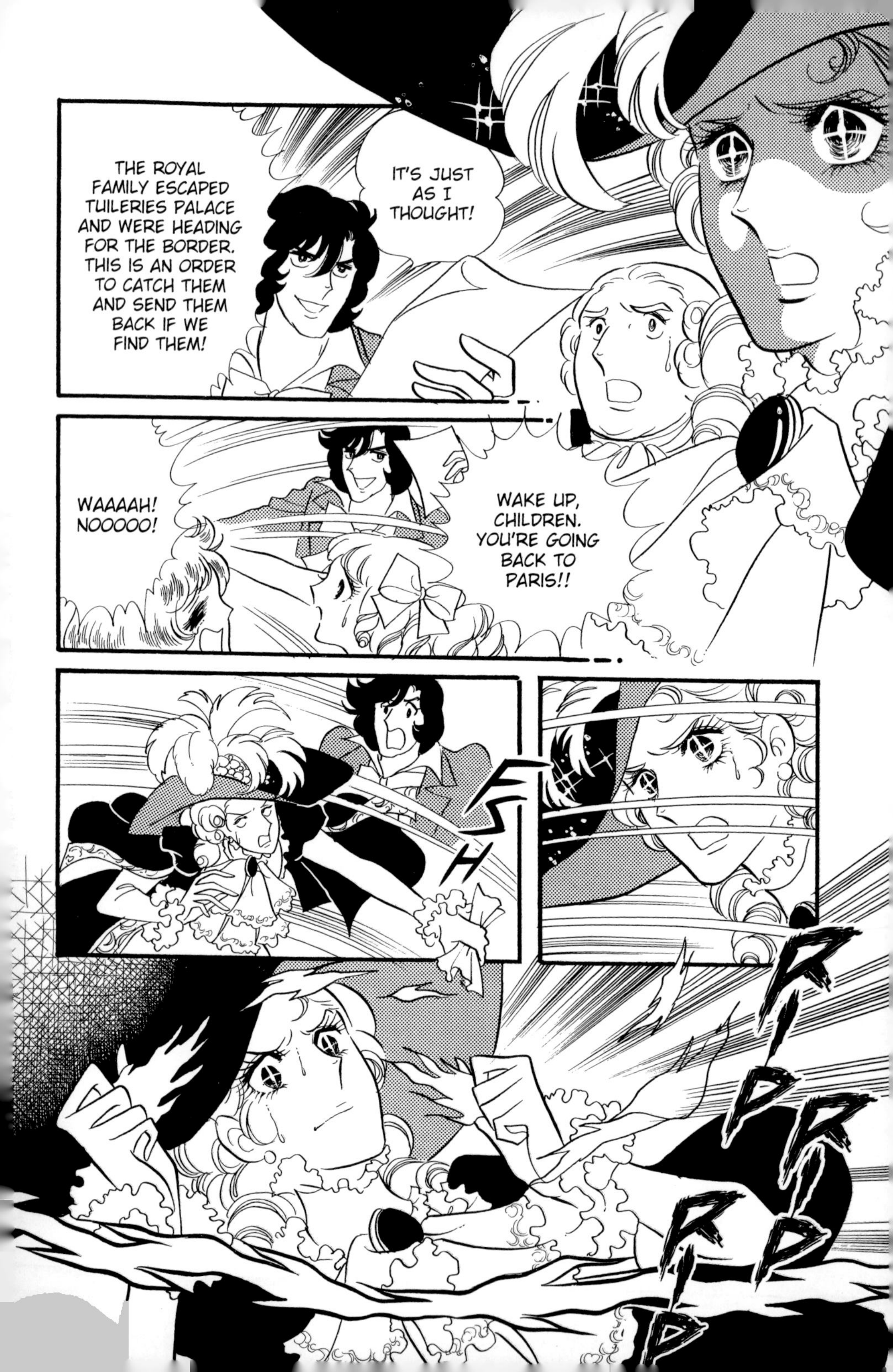
IT'S JUST AS I THOUGHT!
THE ROYAL FAMILY ESCAPED TUILERIES PALACE AND WERE HEADING FOR THE BORDER. THIS IS AN ORDER TO CATCH THEM AND SEND THEM BACK IF WE FIND THEM!
WAKE UP, CHILDREN. YOU'RE GOING BACK TO PARIS!!
WAAAAH! NOOOOO!
FSH
RIP
RIP
RIP

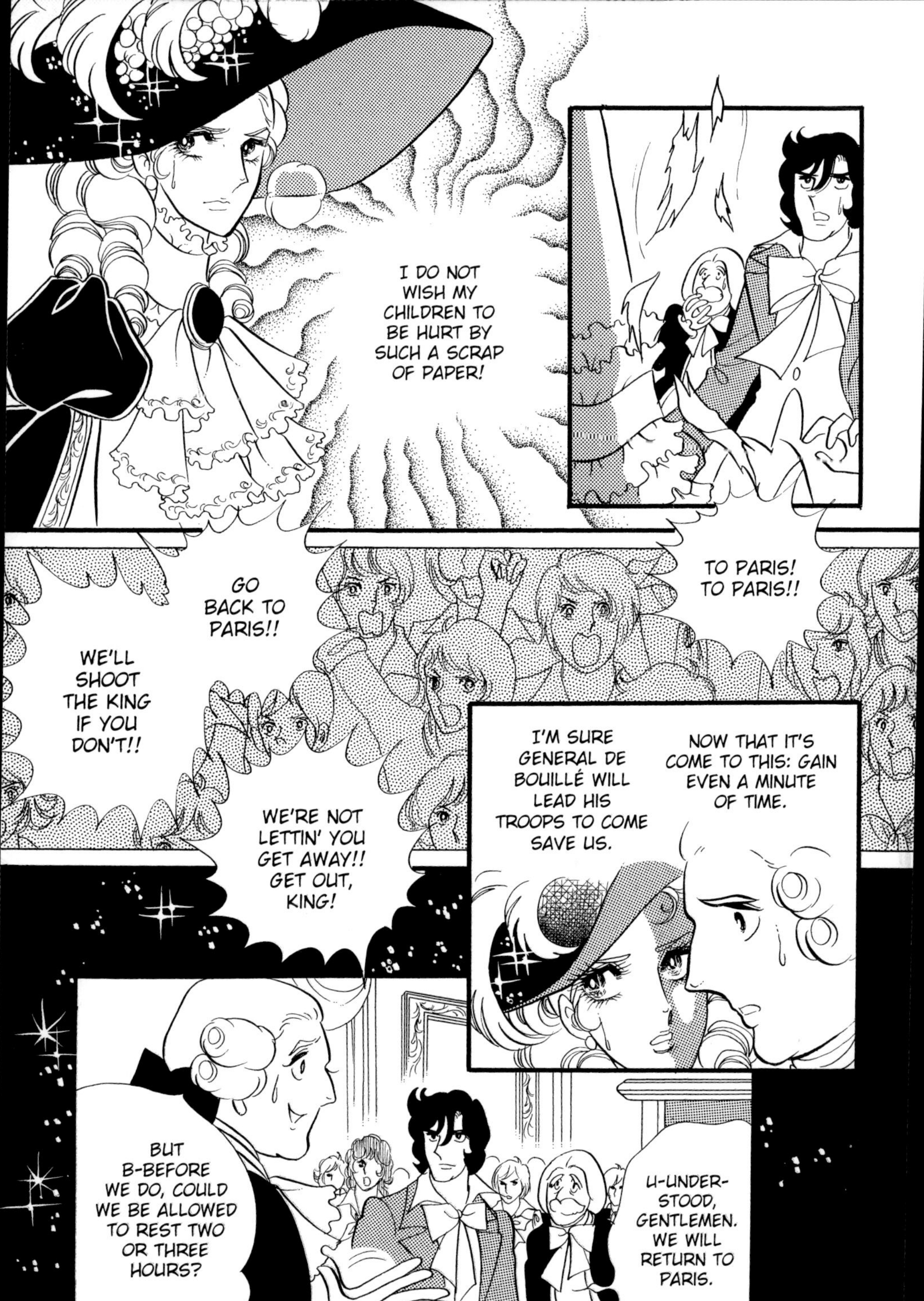
I DO NOT WISH MY CHILDREN TO BE HURT BY SUCH A SCRAP OF PAPER!
TO PARIS! TO PARIS!!
GO BACK TO PARIS!!
WE'LL SHOOT THE KING IF YOU DON'T!!
WE'RE NOT LETTIN' YOU GET AWAY!! GET OUT, KING!
NOW THAT IT'S COME TO THIS: GAIN EVEN A MINUTE OF TIME.
I'M SURE GENERAL DE BOUILLÉ WILL LEAD HIS TROOPS TO COME SAVE US.
U-UNDER-STOOD, GENTLEMEN. WE WILL RETURN TO PARIS.
BUT B-BEFORE WE DO, COULD WE BE ALLOWED TO REST TWO OR THREE HOURS?

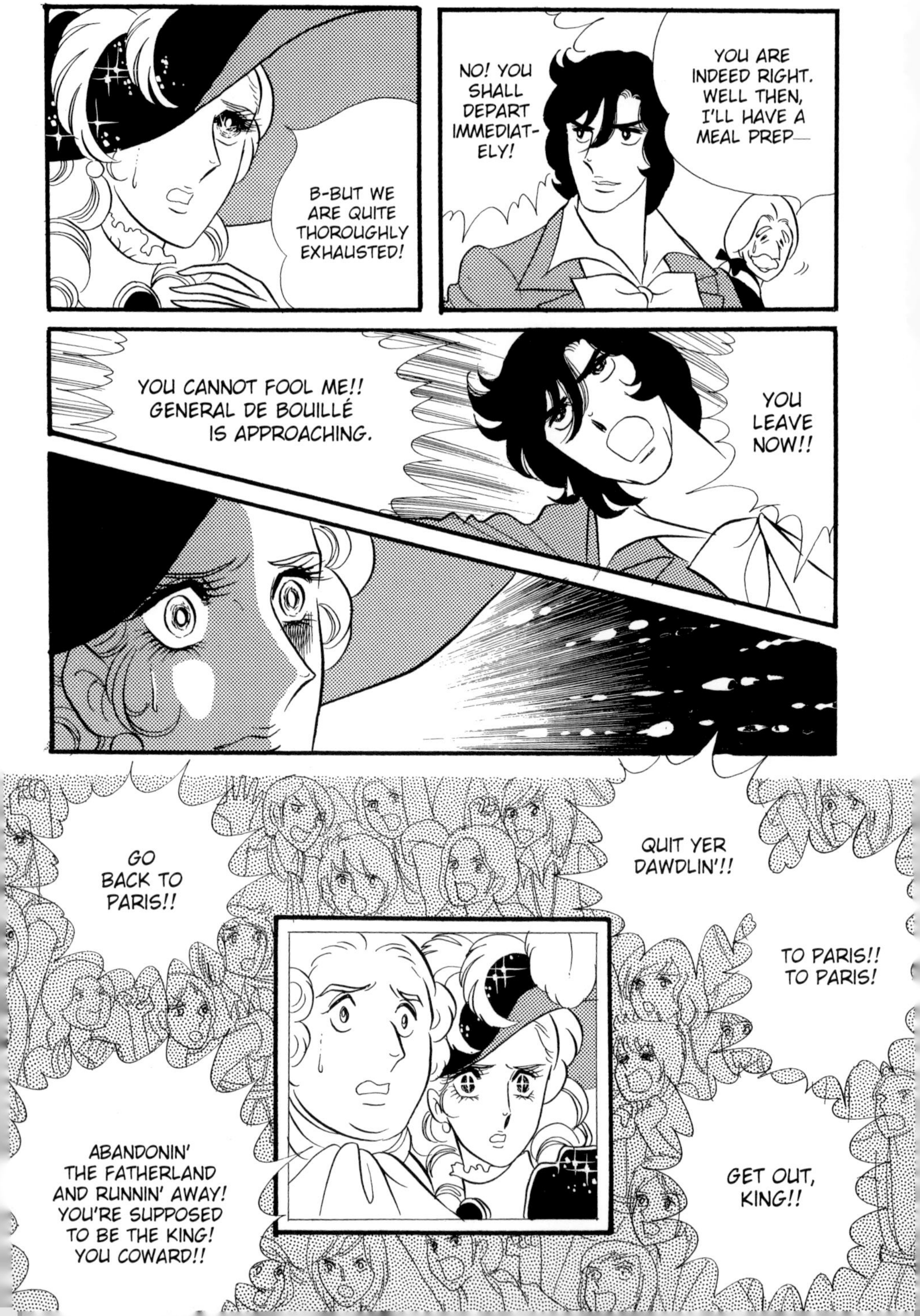
YOU ARE INDEED RIGHT. WELL THEN, I'LL HAVE A MEAL PREP—
NO! YOU SHALL DEPART IMMEDIAT-ELY!
B-BUT WE ARE QUITE THOROUGHLY EXHAUSTED!
YOU LEAVE NOW!!
YOU CANNOT FOOL ME!! GENERAL DE BOUILLÉ IS APPROACHING.
QUIT YER DAWDLIN'!!
GO BACK TO PARIS!!
TO PARIS!! TO PARIS!
GET OUT, KING!!
ABANDONIN' THE FATHERLAND AND RUNNIN' AWAY! YOU'RE SUPPOSED TO BE THE KING! YOU COWARD!!

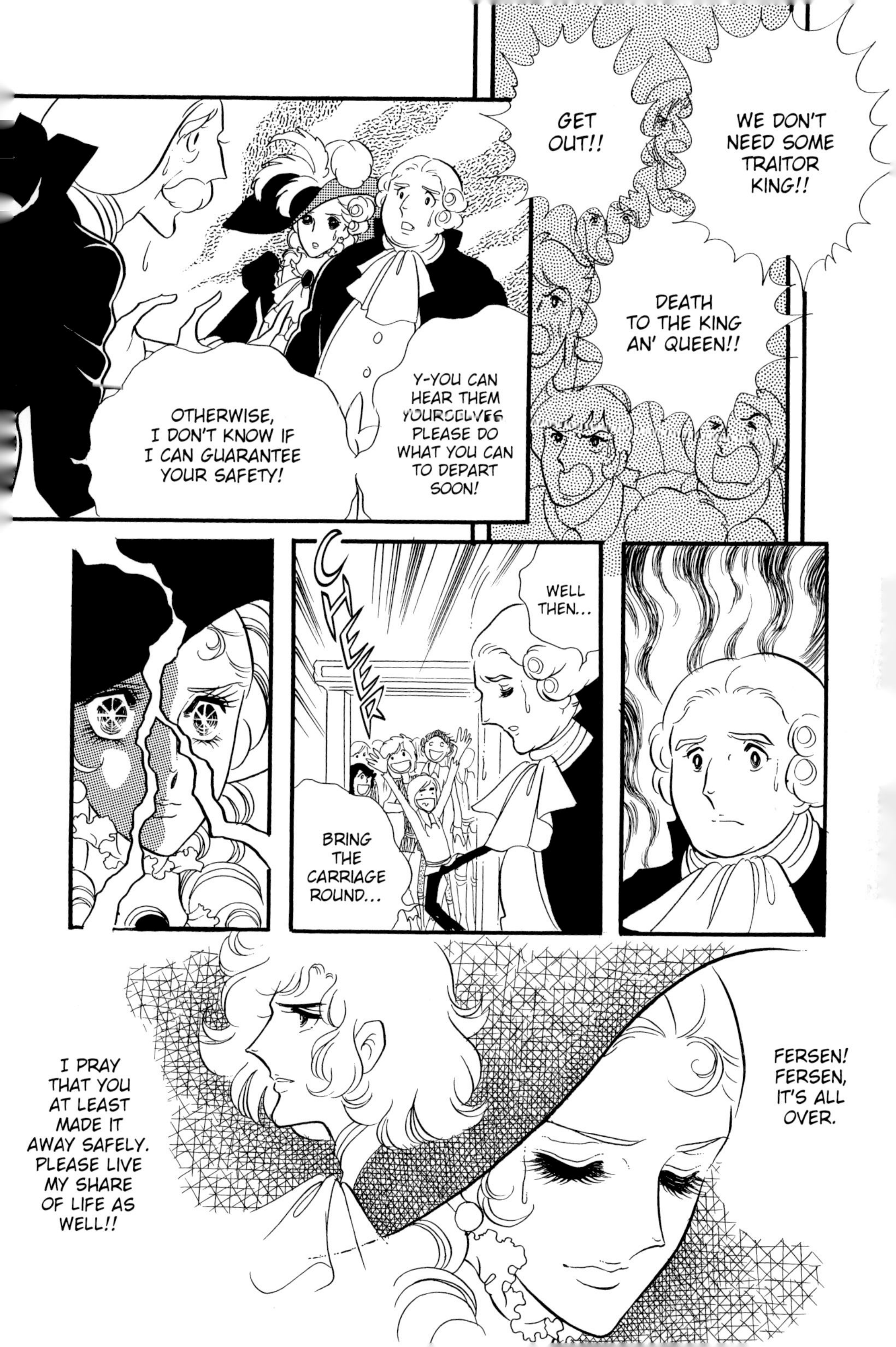
WE DON'T NEED SOME TRAITOR KING!!
GET OUT!!
DEATH TO THE KING AN' QUEEN!!
Y-YOU CAN HEAR THEM YOURSELVES PLEASE DO WHAT YOU CAN TO DEPART SOON!
OTHERWISE, I DON'T KNOW IF I CAN GUARANTEE YOUR SAFETY!
WELL THEN...
CHEER
BRING THE CARRIAGE ROUND...
FERSEN! FERSEN, IT'S ALL OVER.
I PRAY THAT YOU AT LEAST MADE IT AWAY SAFELY. PLEASE LIVE MY SHARE OF LIFE AS WELL!!

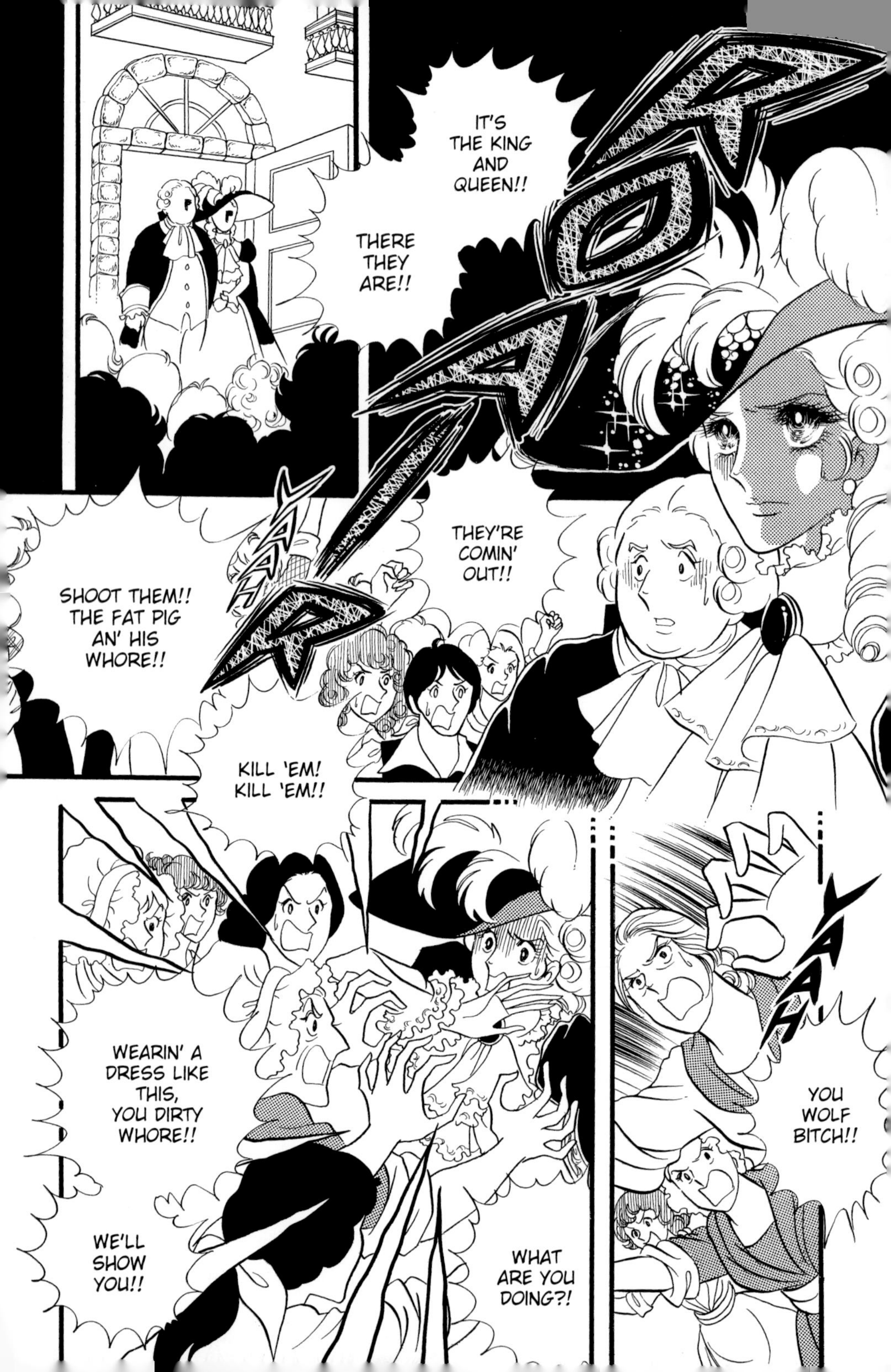
IT'S THE KING AND QUEEN!!
THERE THEY ARE!!
THEY'RE COMIN' OUT!!
SHOOT THEM!! THE FAT PIG AN' HIS WHORE!!
KILL 'EM! KILL 'EM!!
YAAH
YOU WOLF BITCH!!
WHAT ARE YOU DOING?!
WEARIN' A DRESS LIKE THIS, YOU DIRTY WHORE!!
WE'LL SHOW YOU!!

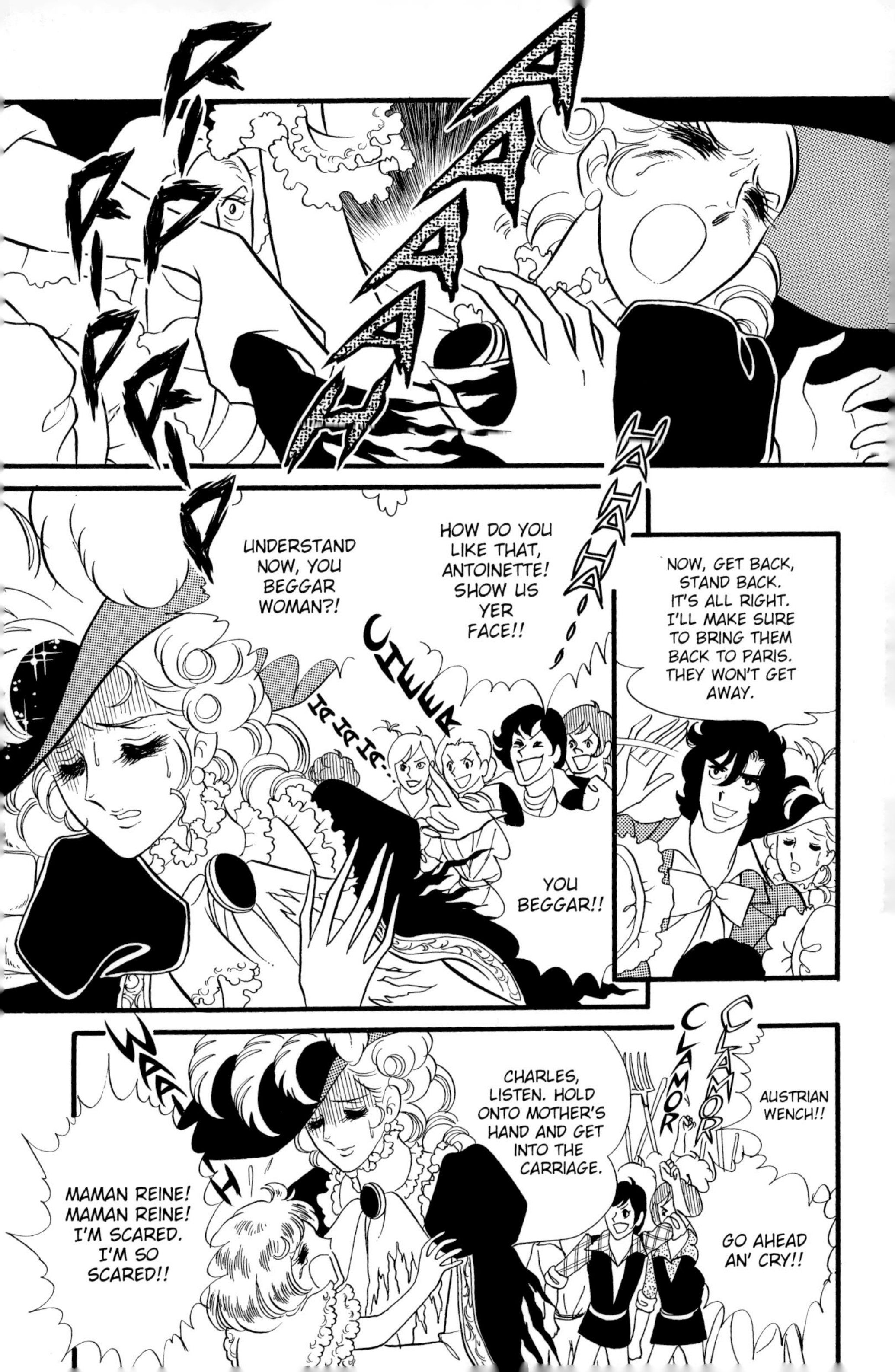

NOW, GET BACK, STAND BACK. IT'S ALL RIGHT. I'LL MAKE SURE TO BRING THEM BACK TO PARIS. THEY WON'T GET AWAY.
HOW DO YOU LIKE THAT, ANTOINETTE! SHOW US YER FACE!!
UNDERSTAND NOW, YOU BEGGAR WOMAN?!
YOU BEGGAR!!
CLAMOR
CLAMOR
AUSTRIAN WENCH!!
GO AHEAD AN' CRY!!
CHARLES, LISTEN. HOLD ONTO MOTHER'S HAND AND GET INTO THE CARRIAGE.
MAMAN REINE! MAMAN REINE! I'M SCARED. I'M SO SCARED!!

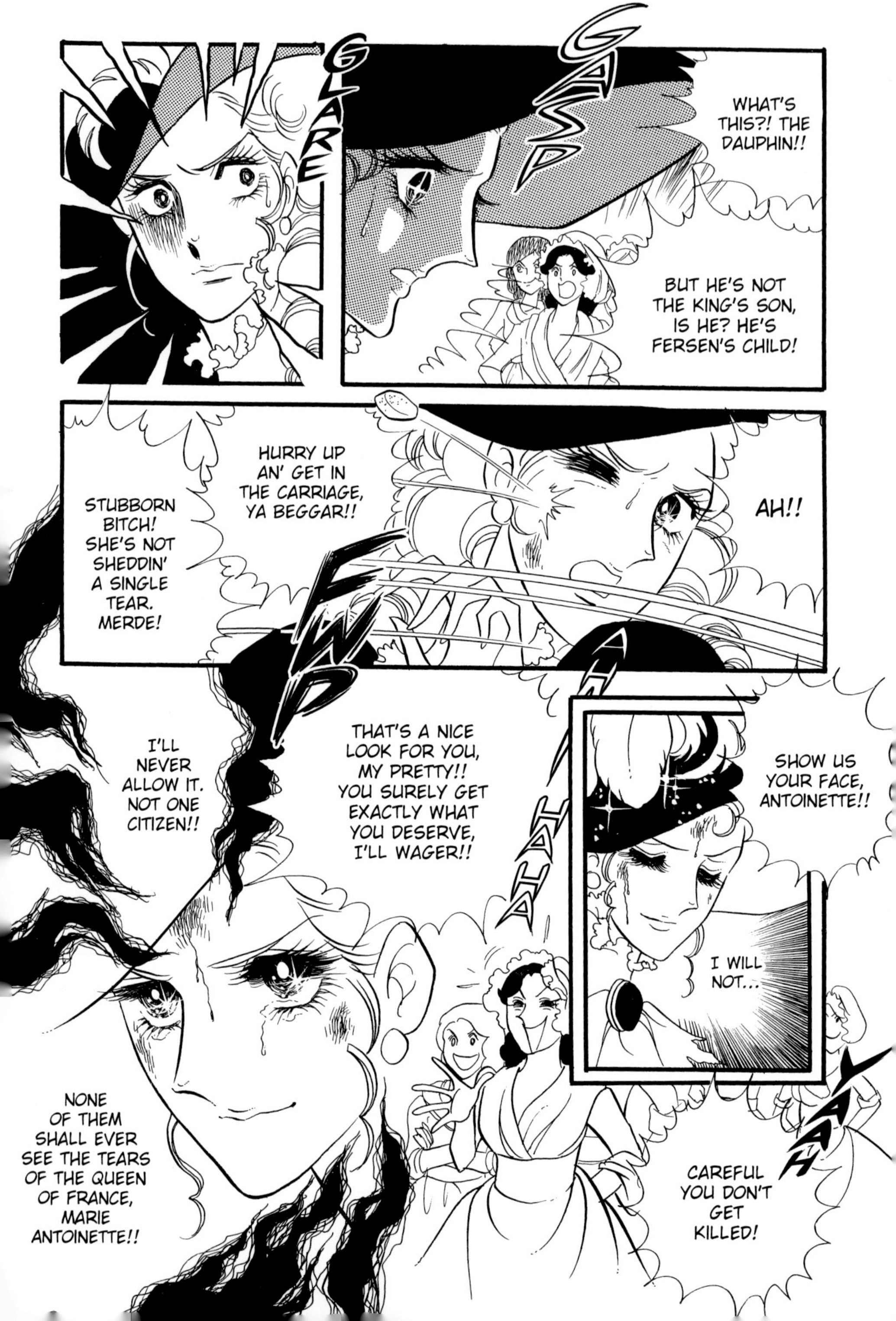
GASP
WHAT'S THIS?! THE DAUPHIN!!
BUT HE'S NOT THE KING'S SON, IS HE? HE'S FERSEN'S CHILD!
GLARE
AH!!
HURRY UP AN' GET IN THE CARRIAGE, YA BEGGAR!!
STUBBORN BITCH! SHE'S NOT SHEDDIN' A SINGLE TEAR. MERDE!
SHOW US YOUR FACE, ANTOINETTE!!
I WILL NOT...
YAAH
CAREFUL YOU DON'T GET KILLED!
AHAHAHA
THAT'S A NICE LOOK FOR YOU, MY PRETTY!! YOU SURELY GET EXACTLY WHAT YOU DESERVE, I'LL WAGER!!
I'LL NEVER ALLOW IT. NOT ONE CITIZEN!!
NONE OF THEM SHALL EVER SEE THE TEARS OF THE QUEEN OF FRANCE, MARIE ANTOINETTE!!

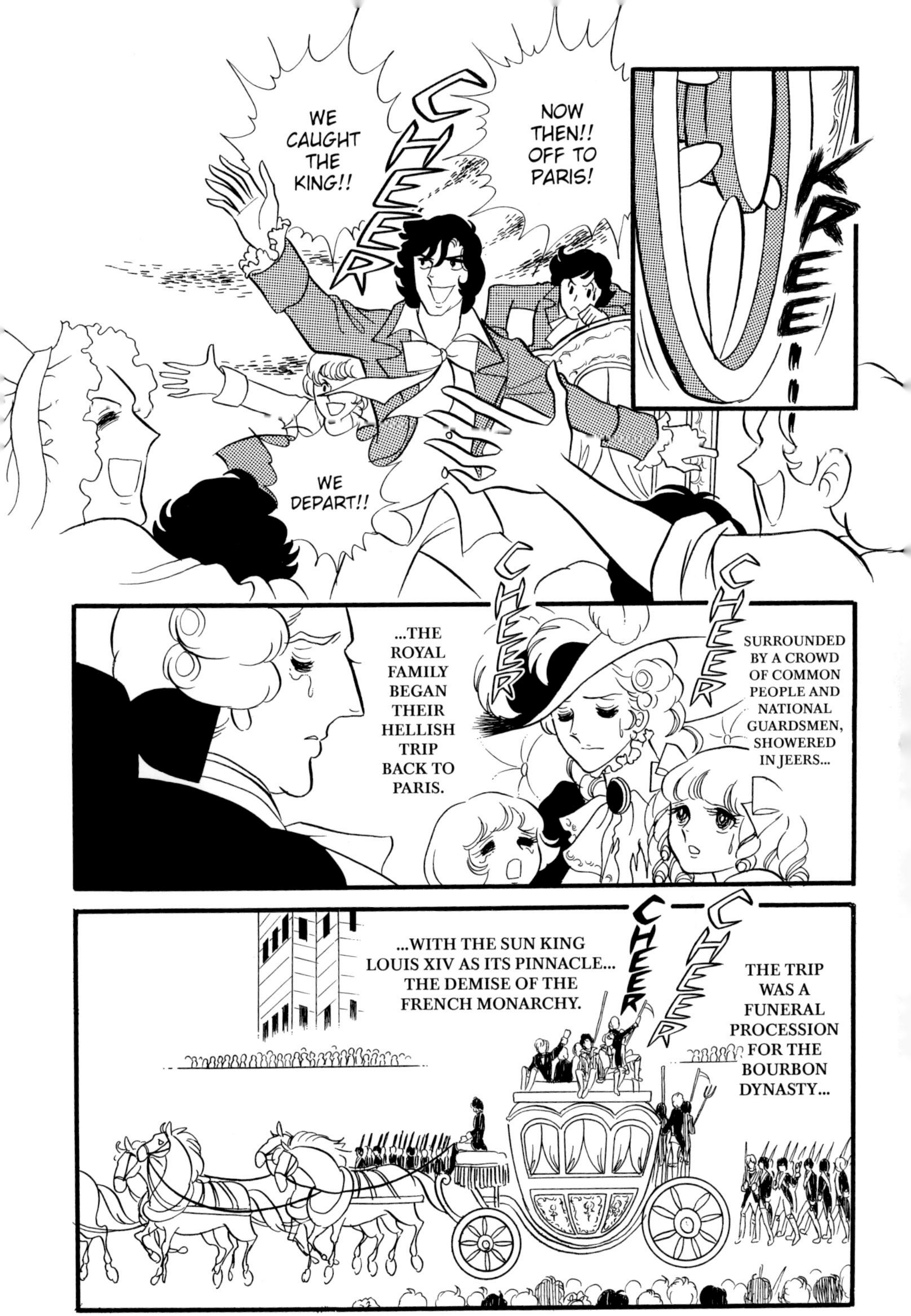
KREE!!!
NOW THEN!! OFF TO PARIS!
CHEER
WE CAUGHT THE KING!!
WE DEPART!!
CHEER
CHEER
CHEER
SURROUNDED BY A CROWD OF COMMON PEOPLE AND NATIONAL GUARDSMEN, SHOWERED IN JEERS...
...THE ROYAL FAMILY BEGAN THEIR HELLISH TRIP BACK TO PARIS.
CHEER
CHEER
THE TRIP WAS A FUNERAL PROCESSION FOR THE BOURBON DYNASTY...
...WITH THE SUN KING LOUIS XIV AS ITS PINNACLE... THE DEMISE OF THE FRENCH MONARCHY.

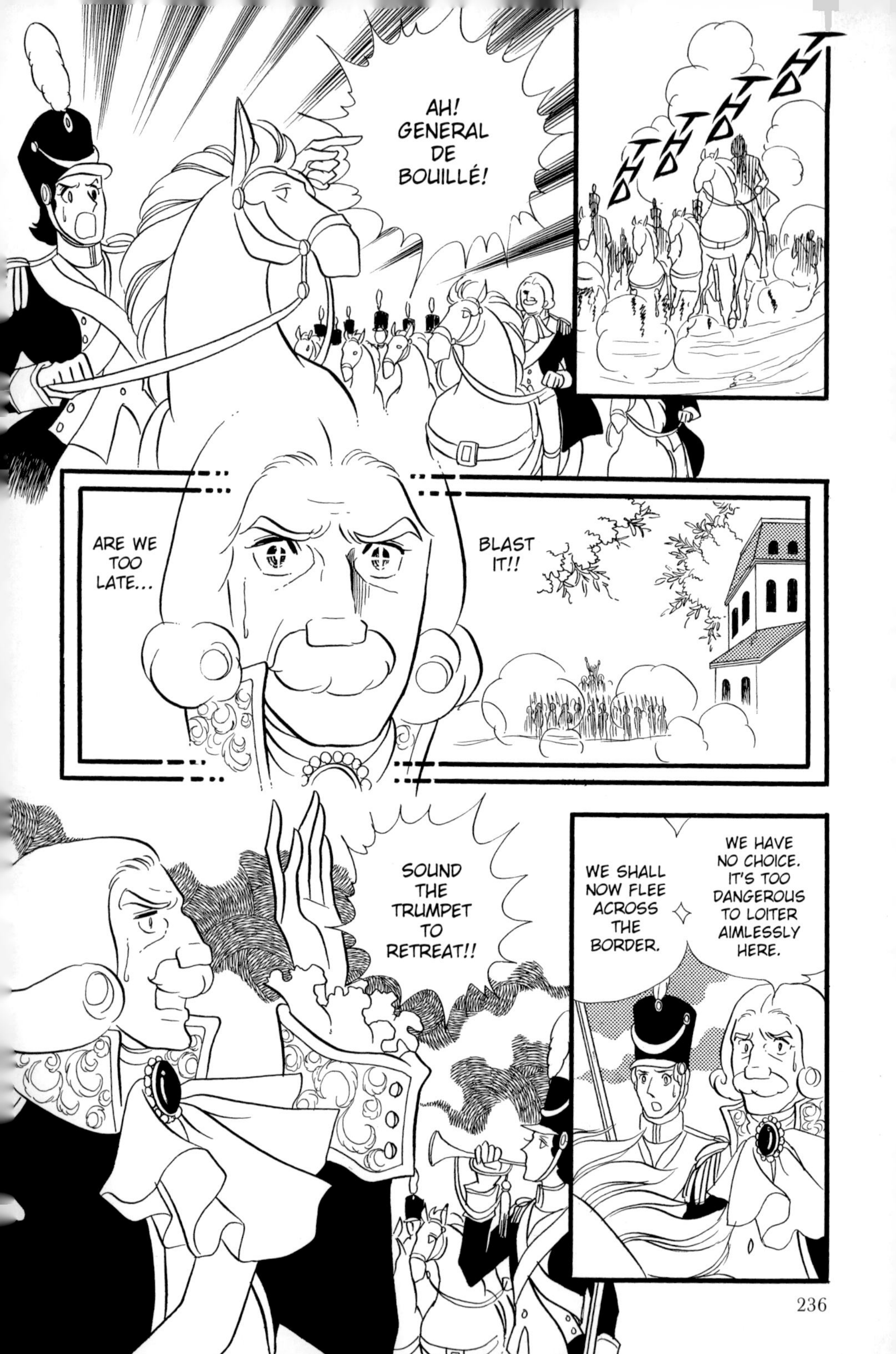
THD THD THD THD
AH! GENERAL DE BOUILLÉ!
BLAST IT!!
ARE WE TOO LATE...
WE HAVE NO CHOICE. IT'S TOO DANGEROUS TO LOITER AIMLESSLY HERE.
WE SHALL NOW FLEE ACROSS THE BORDER.
SOUND THE TRUMPET TO RETREAT!!

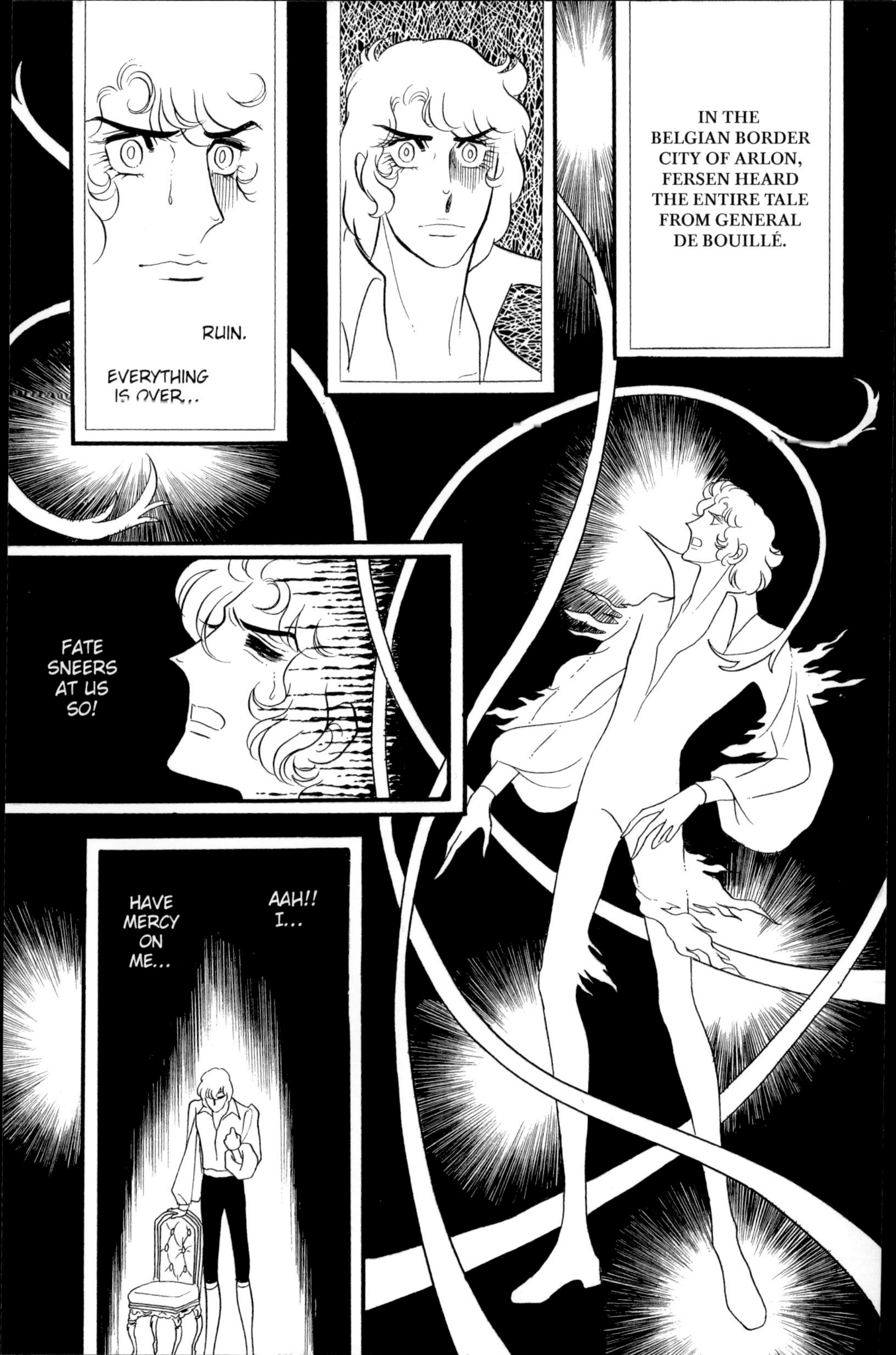

IN THE BELGIAN BORDER CITY OF ARLON, FERSEN HEARD THE ENTIRE TALE FROM GENERAL DE BOUILLÉ.
RUIN.
EVERYTHING IS OVER...
FATE SNEERS AT US SO!
AAH!! I...
HAVE MERCY ON ME...

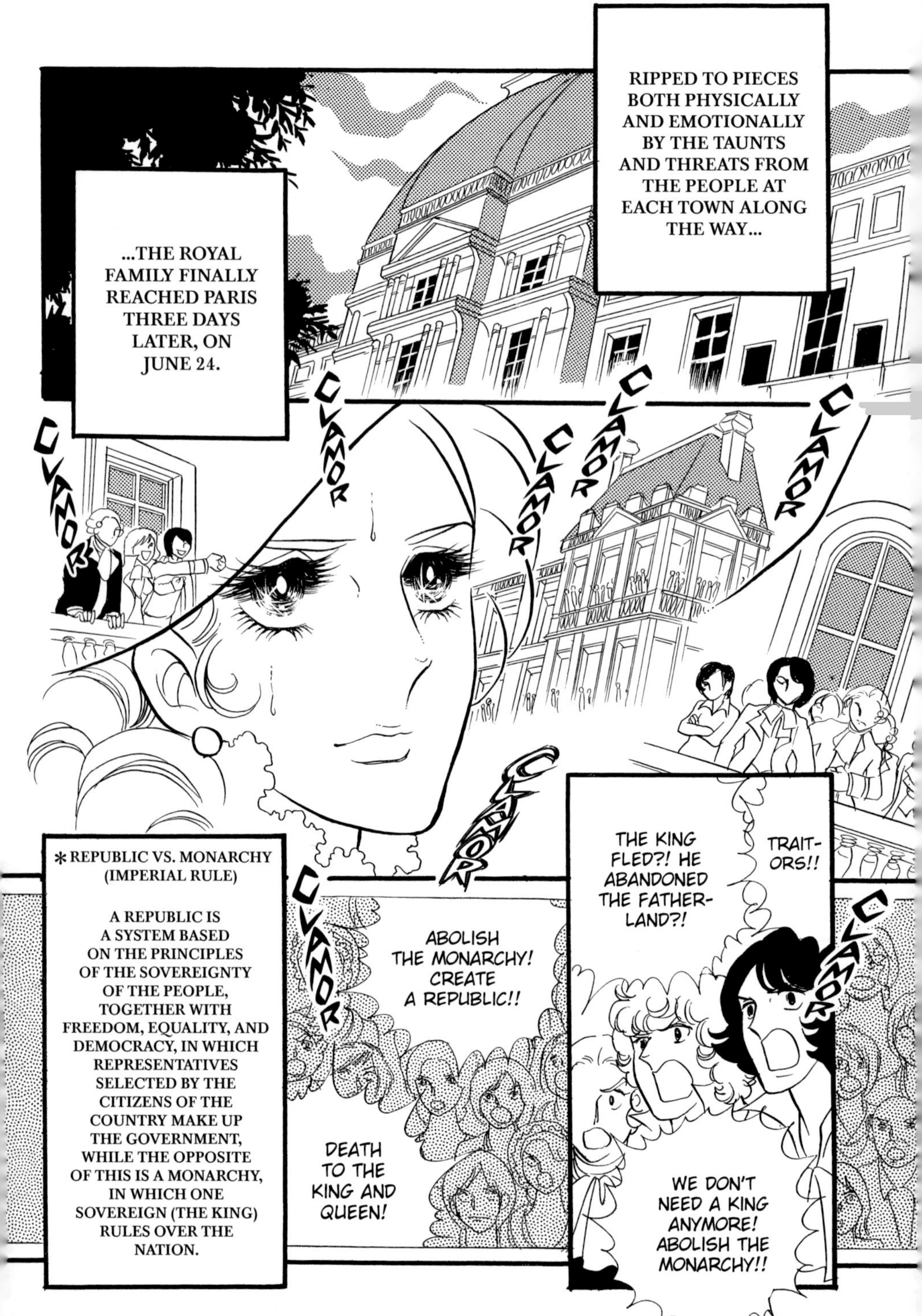
RIPPED TO PIECES BOTH PHYSICALLY AND EMOTIONALLY BY THE TAUNTS AND THREATS FROM THE PEOPLE AT EACH TOWN ALONG THE WAY...
...THE ROYAL FAMILY FINALLY REACHED PARIS THREE DAYS LATER, ON JUNE 24.
CLAMOR
CLAMOR
CLAMOR
CLAMOR
CLAMOR
CLAMOR
TRAIT-ORS!!
THE KING FLED?! HE ABANDONED THE FATHER-LAND?!
CLAMOR
WE DON'T NEED A KING ANYMORE! ABOLISH THE MONARCHY!!
ABOLISH THE MONARCHY! CREATE A REPUBLIC!!
CLAMOR
DEATH TO THE KING AND QUEEN!

*REPUBLIC VS. MONARCHY (IMPERIAL RULE)

A REPUBLIC IS A SYSTEM BASED ON THE PRINCIPLES OF THE SOVEREIGNTY OF THE PEOPLE, TOGETHER WITH FREEDOM, EQUALITY, AND DEMOCRACY, IN WHICH REPRESENTATIVES SELECTED BY THE CITIZENS OF THE COUNTRY MAKE UP THE GOVERNMENT, WHILE THE OPPOSITE OF THIS IS A MONARCHY, IN WHICH ONE SOVEREIGN (THE KING) RULES OVER THE NATION.

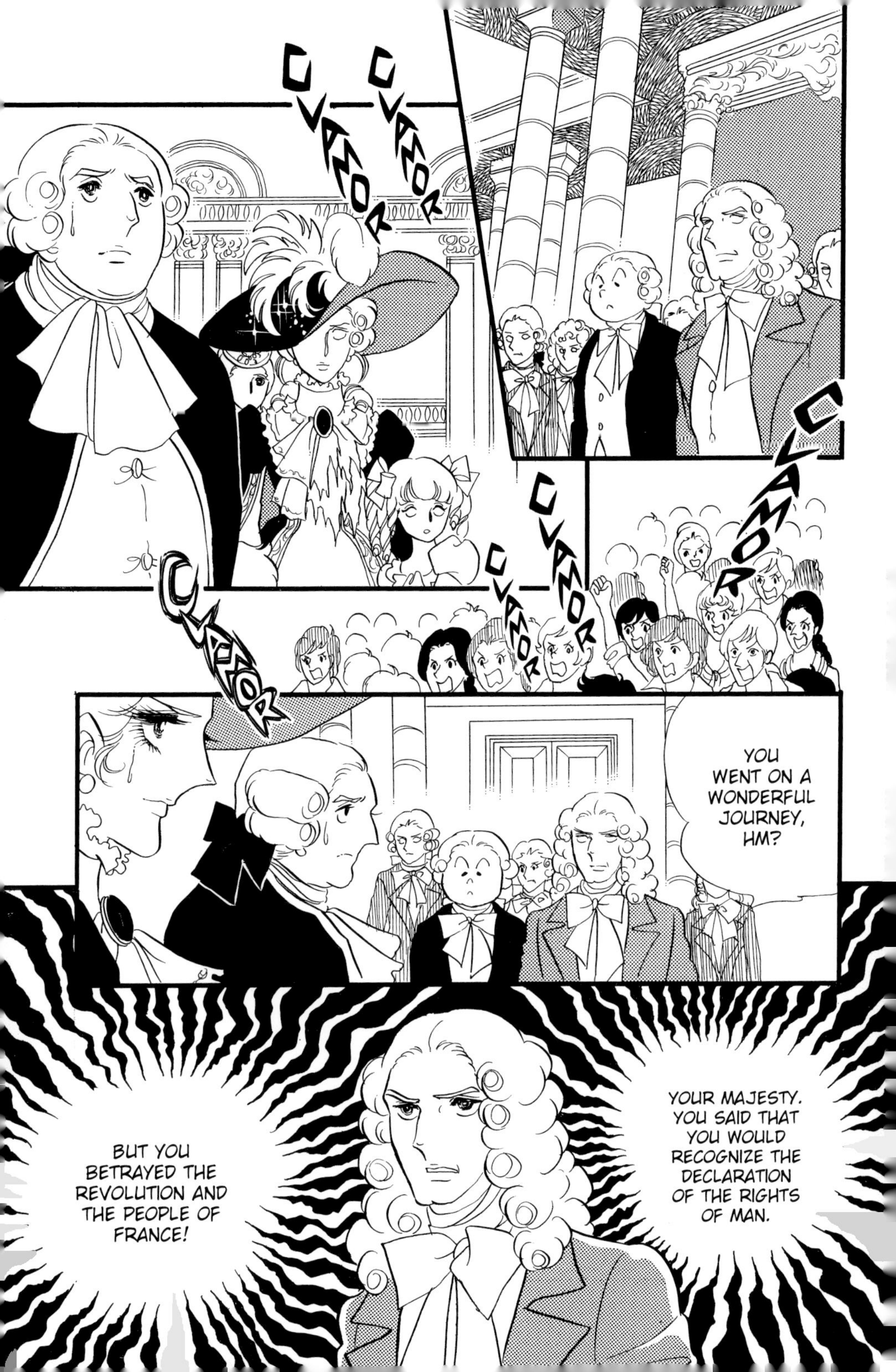
CLAMOR
CLAMOR
CLAMOR
CLAMOR
CLAMOR
CLAMOR
YOU WENT ON A WONDERFUL JOURNEY, HM?
YOUR MAJESTY. YOU SAID THAT YOU WOULD RECOGNIZE THE DECLARATION OF THE RIGHTS OF MAN.
BUT YOU BETRAYED THE REVOLUTION AND THE PEOPLE OF FRANCE!

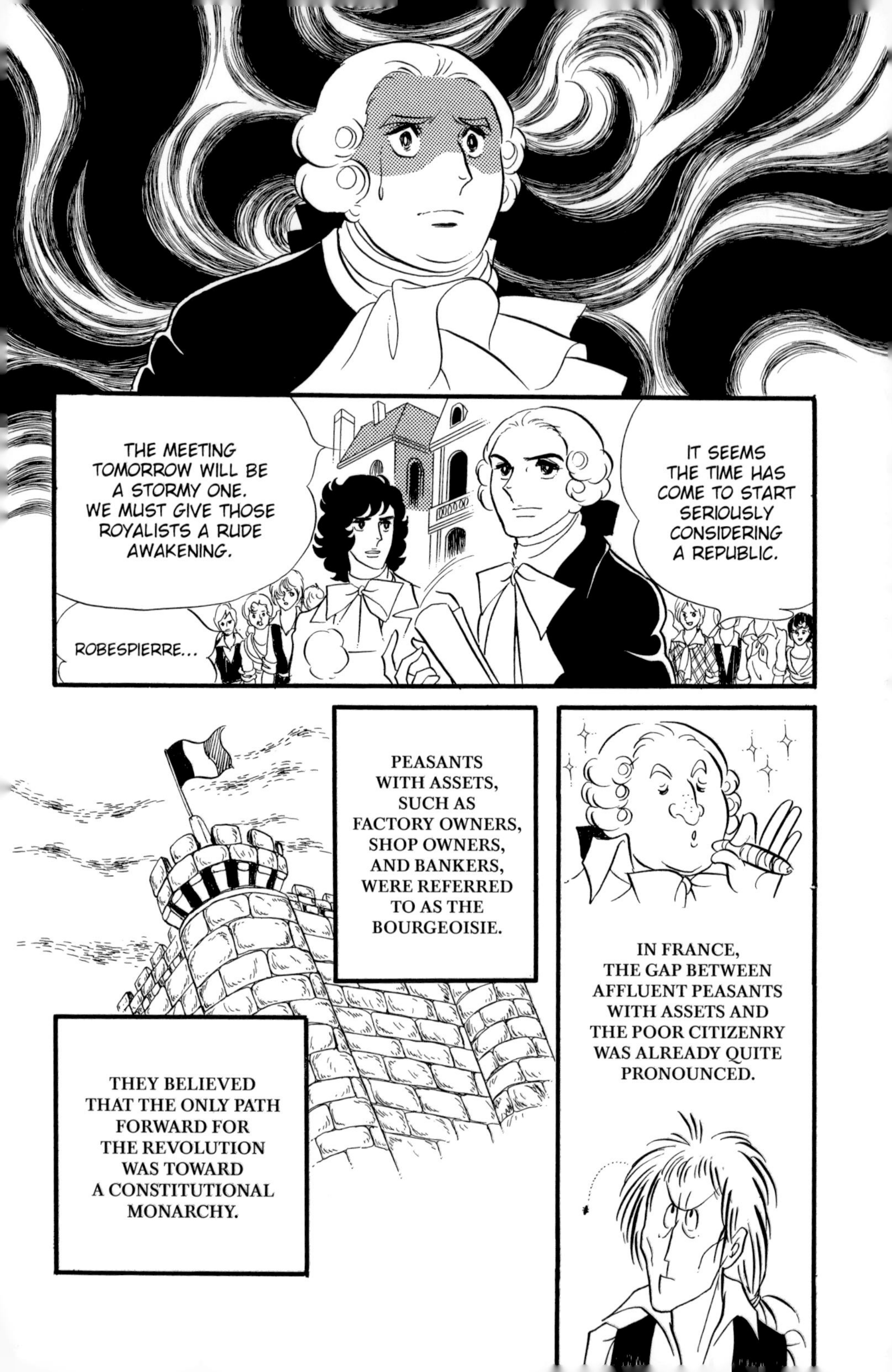
IT SEEMS THE TIME HAS COME TO START SERIOUSLY CONSIDERING A REPUBLIC.
THE MEETING TOMORROW WILL BE A STORMY ONE. WE MUST GIVE THOSE ROYALISTS A RUDE AWAKENING.
ROBESPIERRE...
IN FRANCE, THE GAP BETWEEN AFFLUENT PEASANTS WITH ASSETS AND THE POOR CITIZENRY WAS ALREADY QUITE PRONOUNCED.
PEASANTS WITH ASSETS, SUCH AS FACTORY OWNERS, SHOP OWNERS, AND BANKERS, WERE REFERRED TO AS THE BOURGEOISIE.
THEY BELIEVED THAT THE ONLY PATH FORWARD FOR THE REVOLUTION WAS TOWARD A CONSTITUTIONAL MONARCHY.

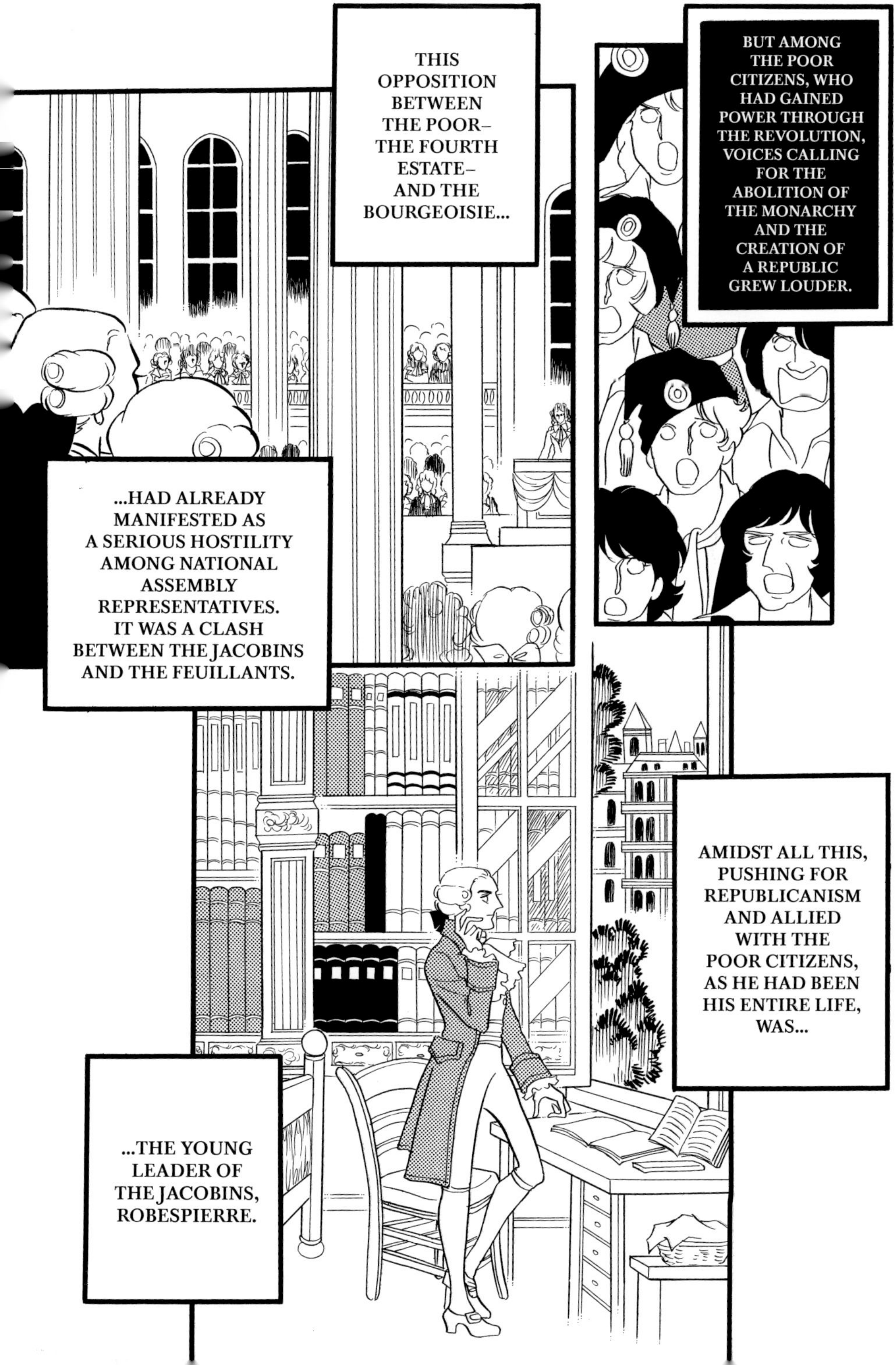
BUT AMONG THE POOR CITIZENS, WHO HAD GAINED POWER THROUGH THE REVOLUTION, VOICES CALLING FOR THE ABOLITION OF THE MONARCHY AND THE CREATION OF A REPUBLIC GREW LOUDER.
THIS OPPOSITION BETWEEN THE POOR–THE FOURTH ESTATE–AND THE BOURGEOISIE...
...HAD ALREADY MANIFESTED AS A SERIOUS HOSTILITY AMONG NATIONAL ASSEMBLY REPRESENTATIVES. IT WAS A CLASH BETWEEN THE JACOBINS AND THE FEUILLANTS.
AMIDST ALL THIS, PUSHING FOR REPUBLICANISM AND ALLIED WITH THE POOR CITIZENS, AS HE HAD BEEN HIS ENTIRE LIFE, WAS...
...THE YOUNG LEADER OF THE JACOBINS, ROBESPIERRE.

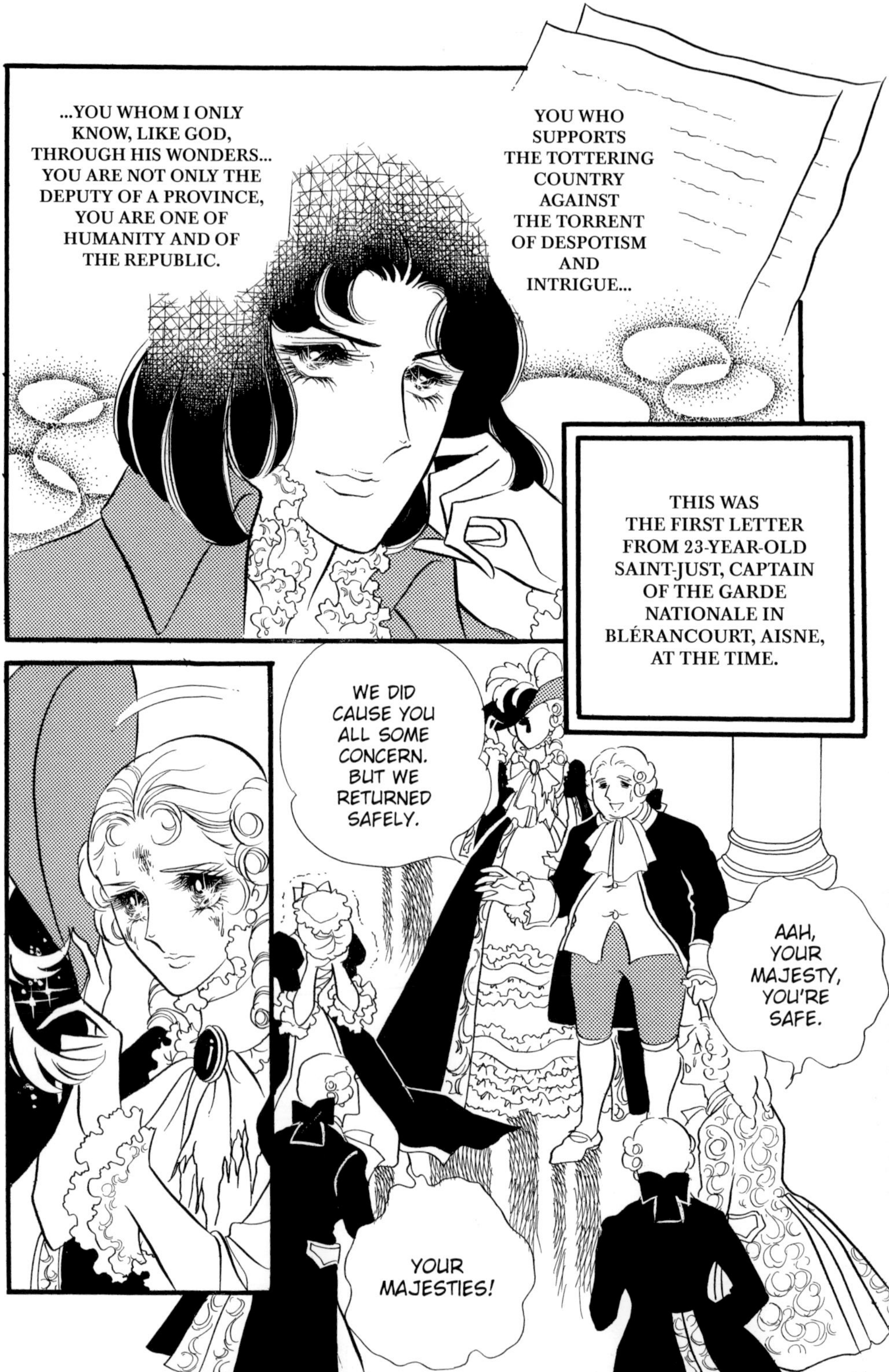
YOU WHO SUPPORTS THE TOTTERING COUNTRY AGAINST THE TORRENT OF DESPOTISM AND INTRIGUE...
...YOU WHOM I ONLY KNOW, LIKE GOD, THROUGH HIS WONDERS... YOU ARE NOT ONLY THE DEPUTY OF A PROVINCE, YOU ARE ONE OF HUMANITY AND OF THE REPUBLIC.
THIS WAS THE FIRST LETTER FROM 23-YEAR-OLD SAINT-JUST, CAPTAIN OF THE GARDE NATIONALE IN BLÉRANCOURT, AISNE, AT THE TIME.
WE DID CAUSE YOU ALL SOME CONCERN. BUT WE RETURNED SAFELY.
AAH, YOUR MAJESTY, YOU'RE SAFE.
YOUR MAJESTIES!

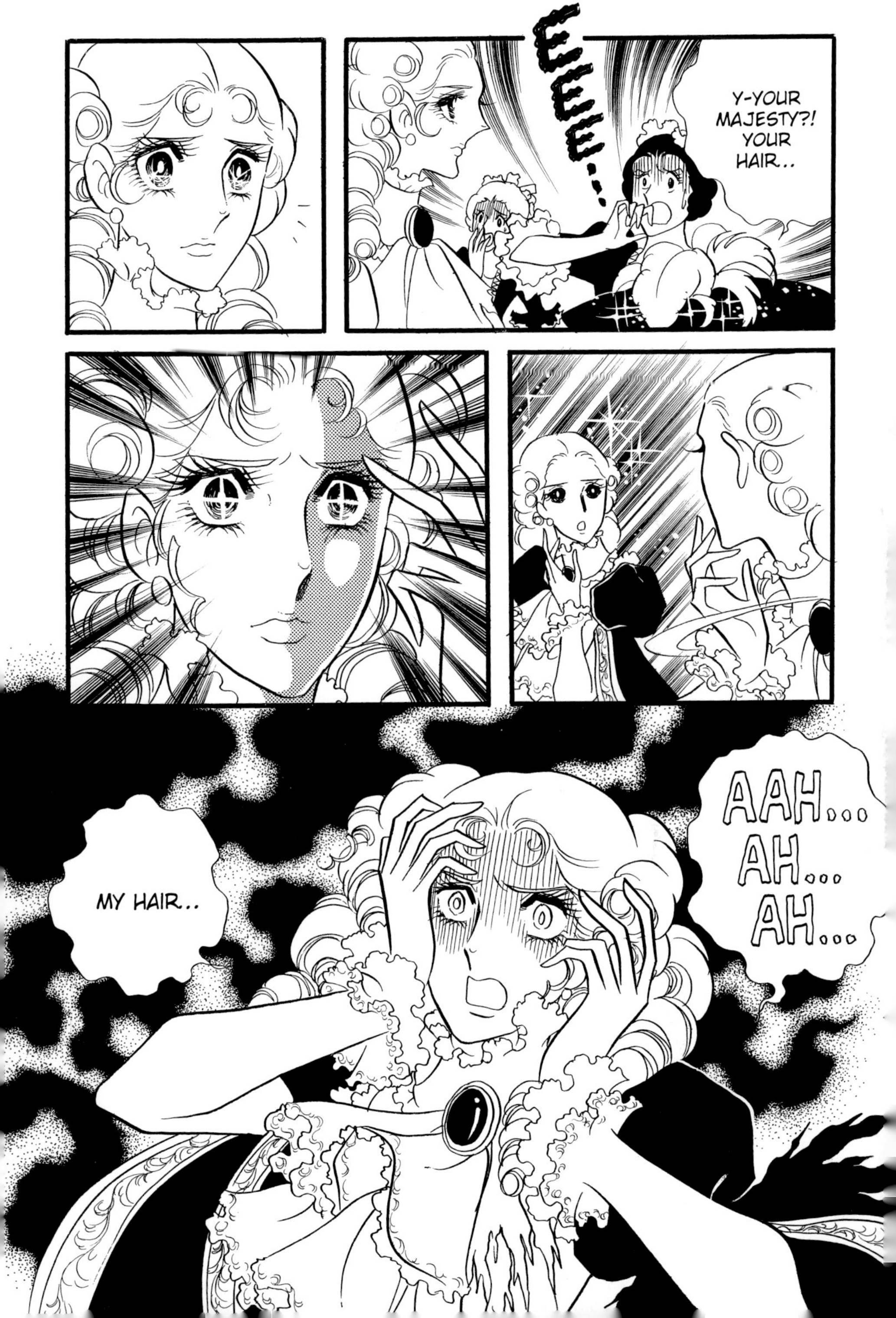
EEE...
Y-YOUR MAJESTY?! YOUR HAIR..
AAH... AH... AH...
MY HAIR..

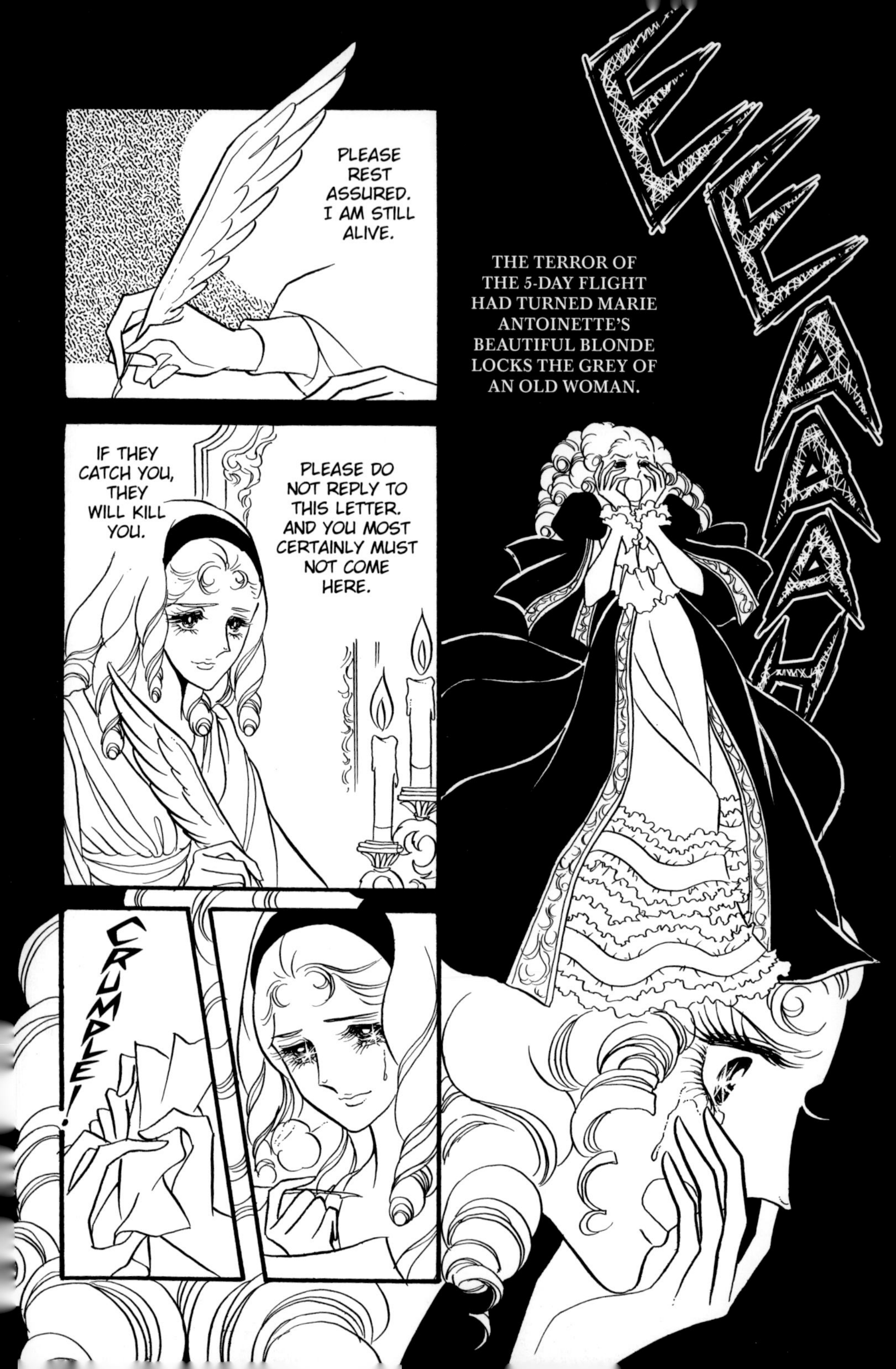
EEAAAH
THE TERROR OF THE 5-DAY FLIGHT HAD TURNED MARIE ANTOINETTE'S BEAUTIFUL BLONDE LOCKS THE GREY OF AN OLD WOMAN.
PLEASE REST ASSURED. I AM STILL ALIVE.
PLEASE DO NOT REPLY TO THIS LETTER. AND YOU MOST CERTAINLY MUST NOT COME HERE.
IF THEY CATCH YOU, THEY WILL KILL YOU.
CRUMPLE!

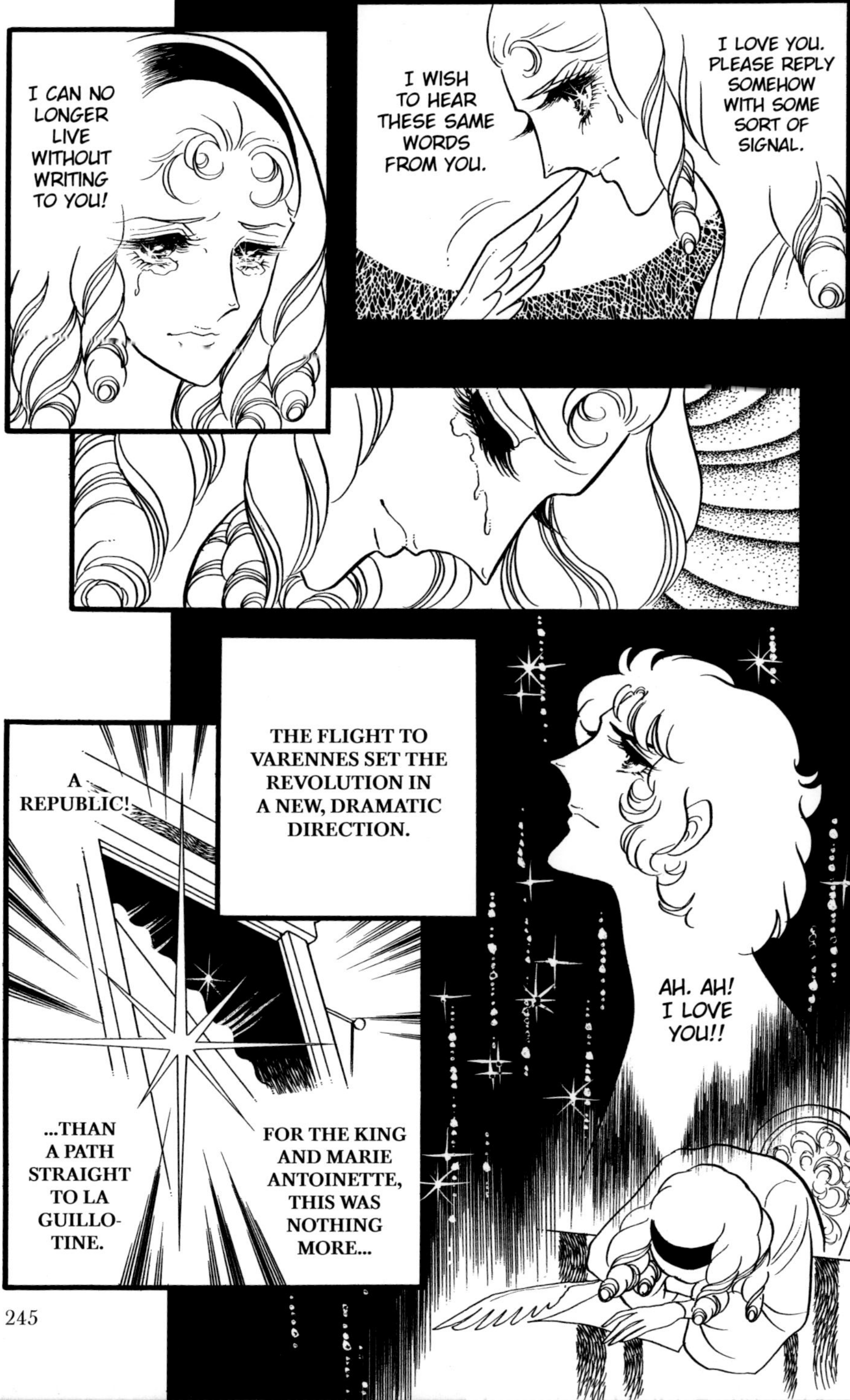
I LOVE YOU. PLEASE REPLY SOMEHOW WITH SOME SORT OF SIGNAL.
I WISH TO HEAR THESE SAME WORDS FROM YOU.
I CAN NO LONGER LIVE WITHOUT WRITING TO YOU!
AH. AH! I LOVE YOU!!
THE FLIGHT TO VARENNES SET THE REVOLUTION IN A NEW, DRAMATIC DIRECTION.
A REPUBLIC!
FOR THE KING AND MARIE ANTOINETTE, THIS WAS NOTHING MORE...
...THAN A PATH STRAIGHT TO LA GUILLO-TINE.

♥ IDENTITY EXPOSED, THE ROYAL FAMILY FAILED TO FLEE TO AUSTRIA. WHAT SEVERE FATE AWAITS THEM ...?

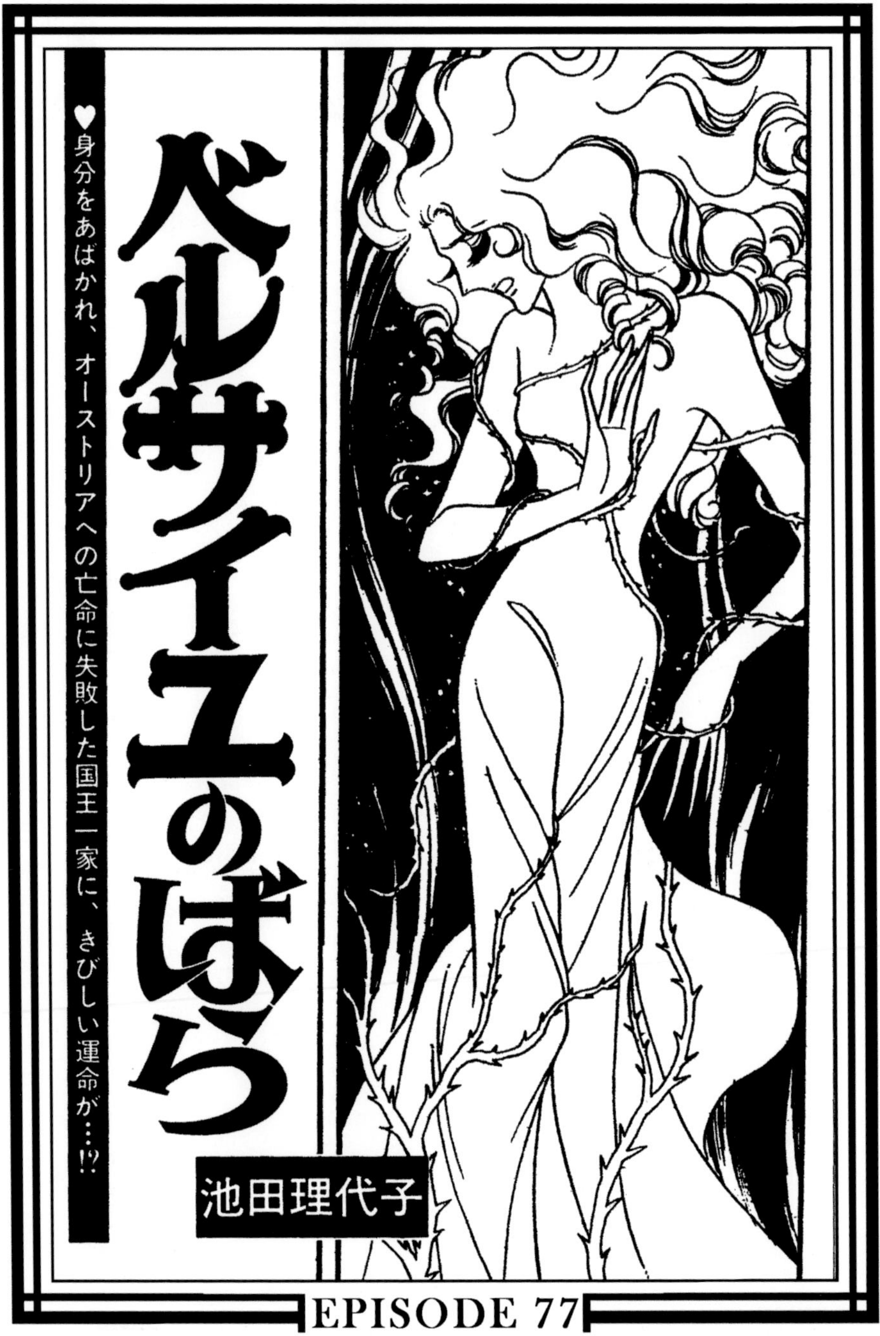
♥身分をあばかれ、オーストリアへの亡命に失敗した国王一家に、きびしい運命が……!?
ベルサイユのばら
池田理代子

EPISODE 77

This is the title page of the previous chapter. It is placed at the end here due to pagination.

THE ROSE OF VERSAILLES

ベルサイユのばら

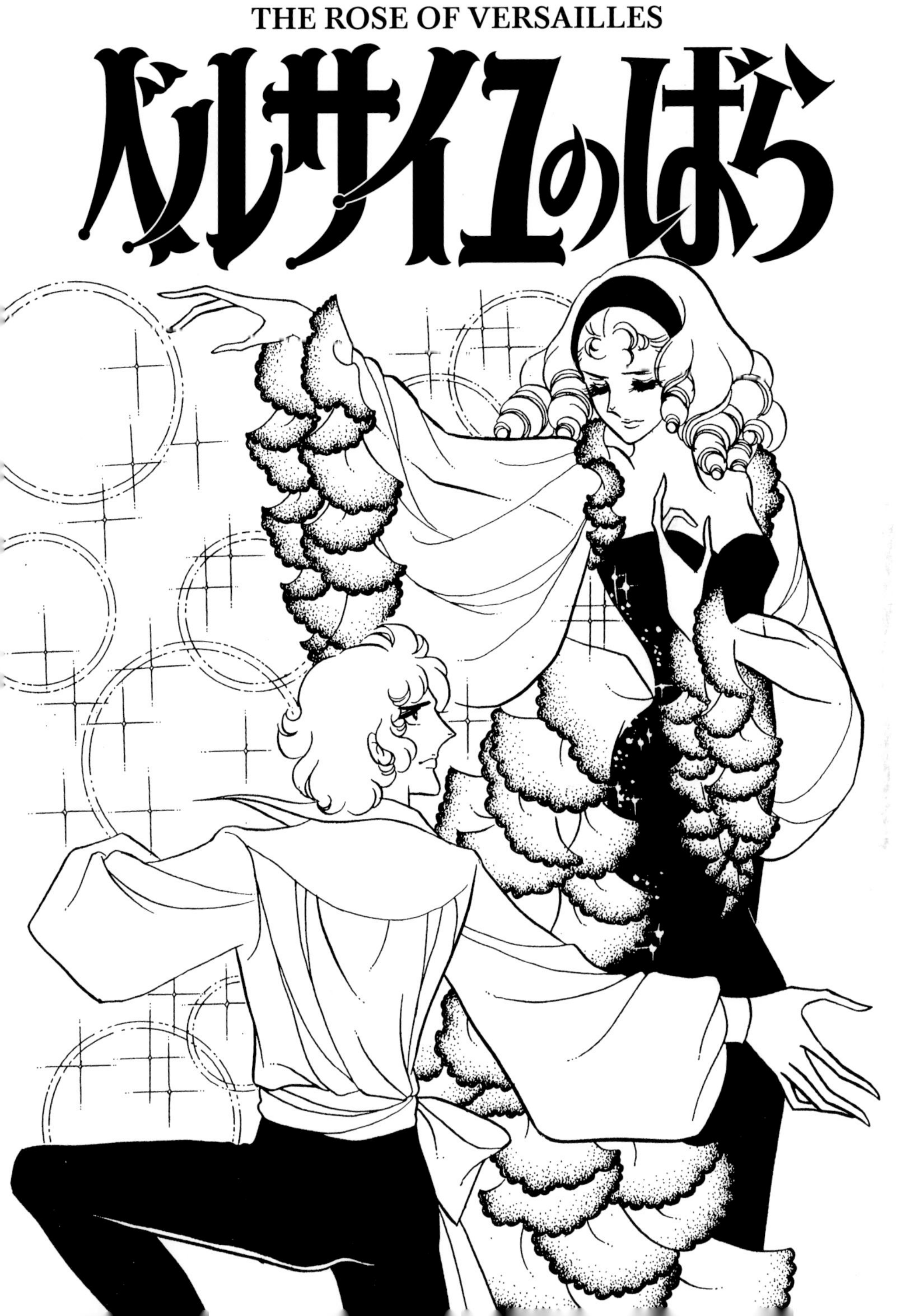

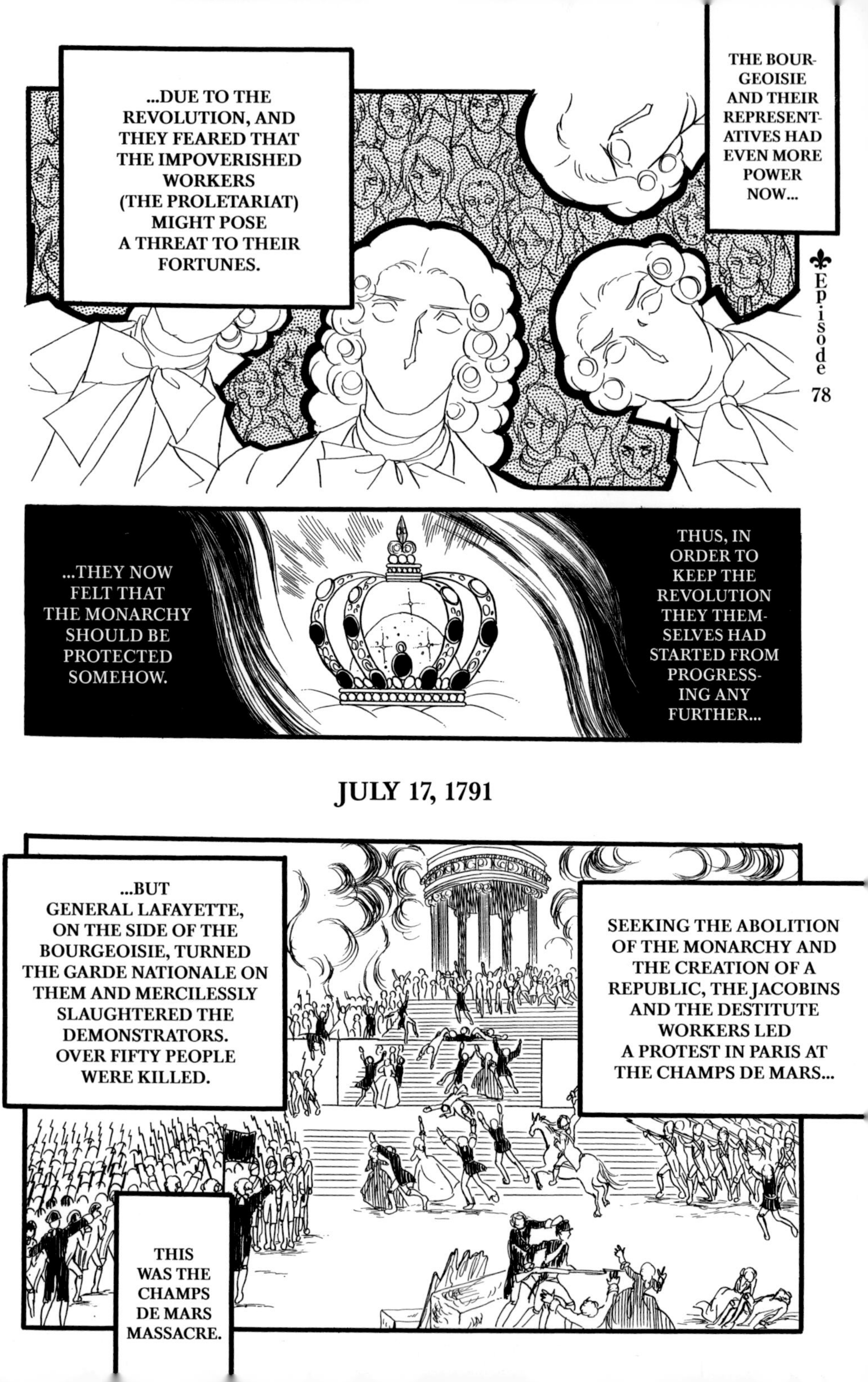
THE BOURGEOISIE AND THEIR REPRESENTATIVES HAD EVEN MORE POWER NOW...
...DUE TO THE REVOLUTION, AND THEY FEARED THAT THE IMPOVERISHED WORKERS (THE PROLETARIAT) MIGHT POSE A THREAT TO THEIR FORTUNES.
THUS, IN ORDER TO KEEP THE REVOLUTION THEY THEMSELVES HAD STARTED FROM PROGRESSING ANY FURTHER...
...THEY NOW FELT THAT THE MONARCHY SHOULD BE PROTECTED SOMEHOW.
JULY 17, 1791
SEEKING THE ABOLITION OF THE MONARCHY AND THE CREATION OF A REPUBLIC, THE JACOBINS AND THE DESTITUTE WORKERS LED A PROTEST IN PARIS AT THE CHAMPS DE MARS...
...BUT GENERAL LAFAYETTE, ON THE SIDE OF THE BOURGEOISIE, TURNED THE GARDE NATIONALE ON THEM AND MERCILESSLY SLAUGHTERED THE DEMONSTRATORS. OVER FIFTY PEOPLE WERE KILLED.
THIS WAS THE CHAMPS DE MARS MASSACRE.

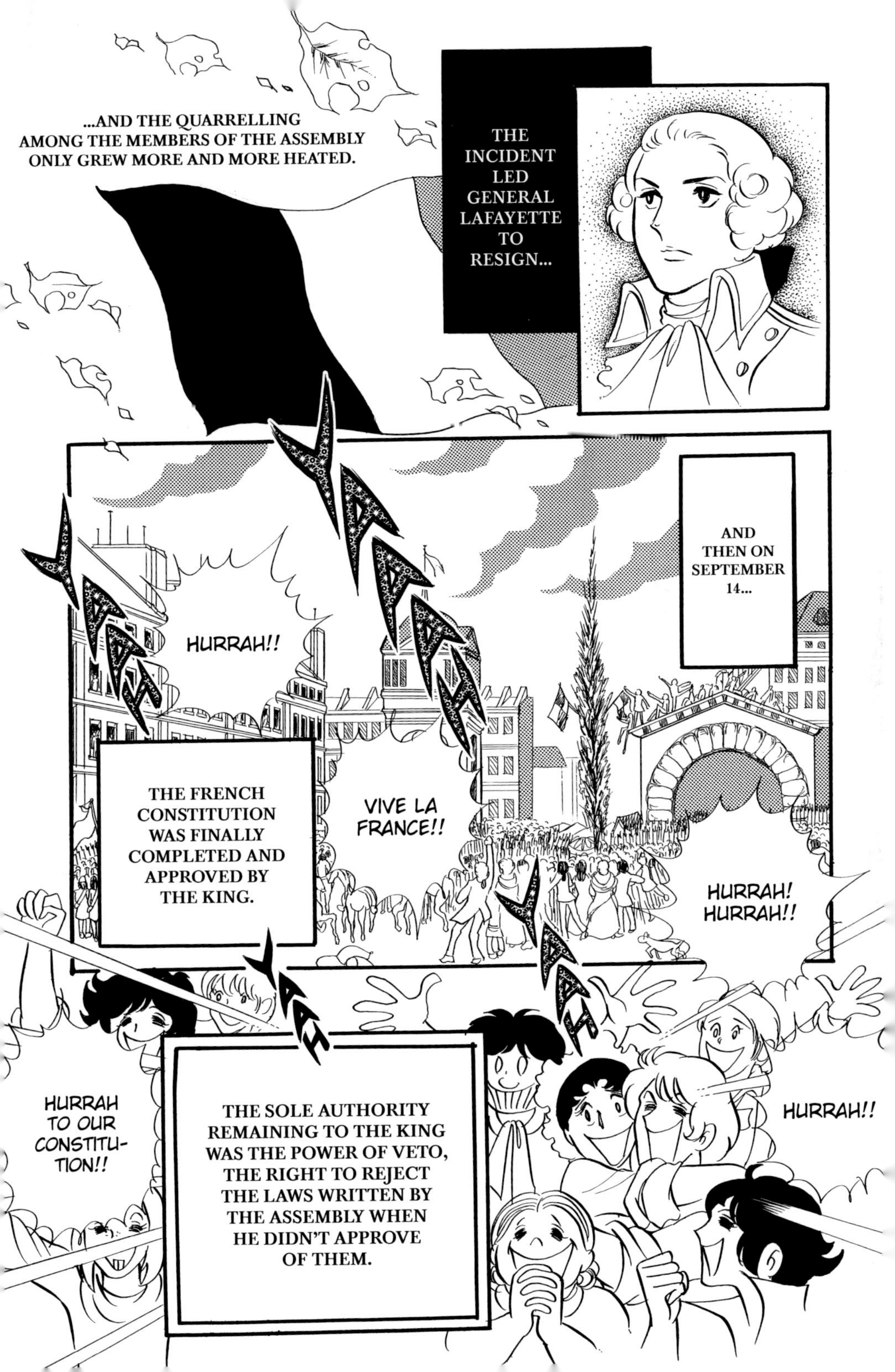

THE INCIDENT LED GENERAL LAFAYETTE TO RESIGN...
...AND THE QUARRELLING AMONG THE MEMBERS OF THE ASSEMBLY ONLY GREW MORE AND MORE HEATED.
AND THEN ON SEPTEMBER 14...
HURRAH!!
THE FRENCH CONSTITUTION WAS FINALLY COMPLETED AND APPROVED BY THE KING.
VIVE LA FRANCE!!
HURRAH! HURRAH!!
HURRAH!!
THE SOLE AUTHORITY REMAINING TO THE KING WAS THE POWER OF VETO, THE RIGHT TO REJECT THE LAWS WRITTEN BY THE ASSEMBLY WHEN HE DIDN'T APPROVE OF THEM.
HURRAH TO OUR CONSTITU-TION!!

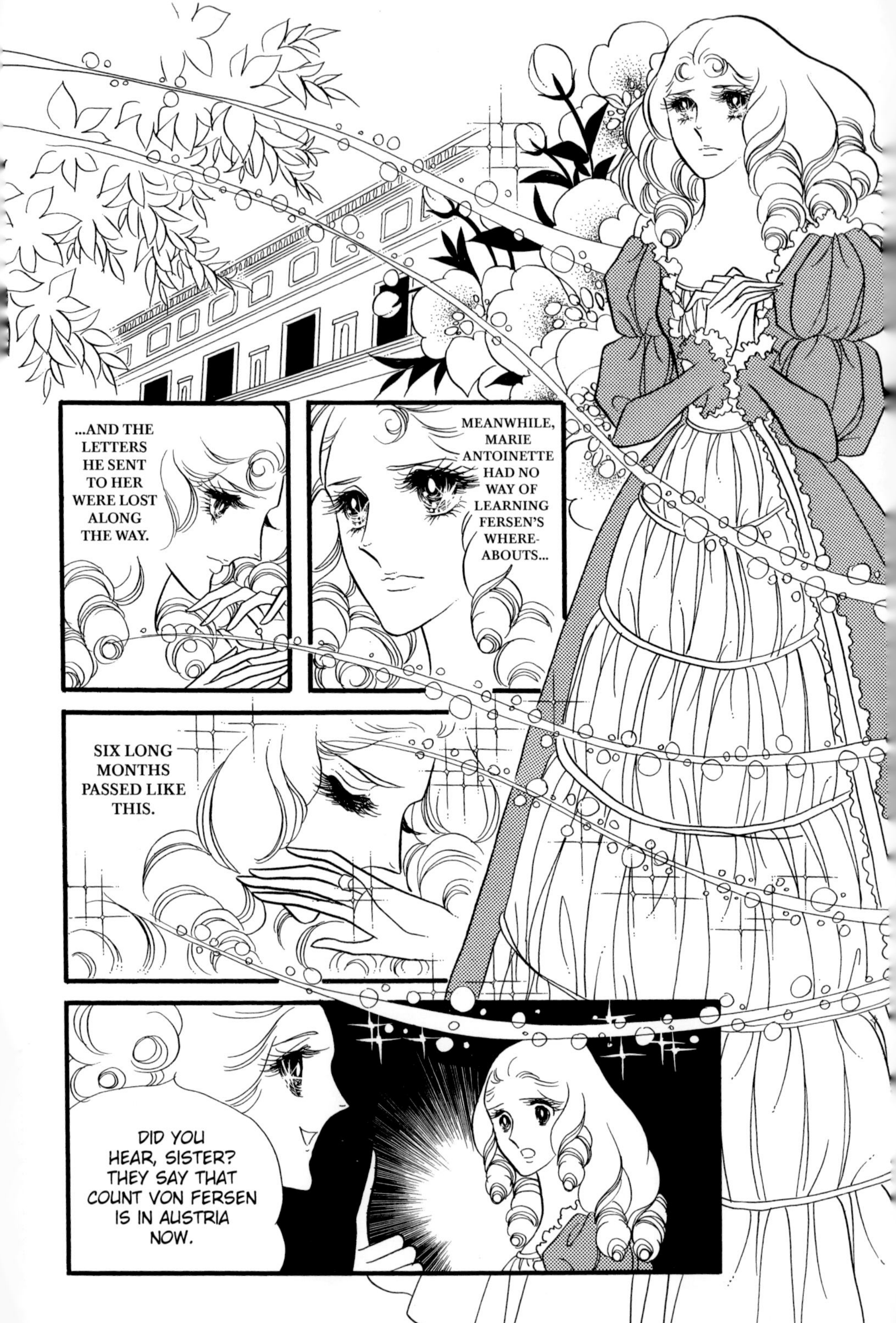
MEANWHILE, MARIE ANTOINETTE HAD NO WAY OF LEARNING FERSEN'S WHERE-ABOUTS...
...AND THE LETTERS HE SENT TO HER WERE LOST ALONG THE WAY.
SIX LONG MONTHS PASSED LIKE THIS.
DID YOU HEAR, SISTER? THEY SAY THAT COUNT VON FERSEN IS IN AUSTRIA NOW.

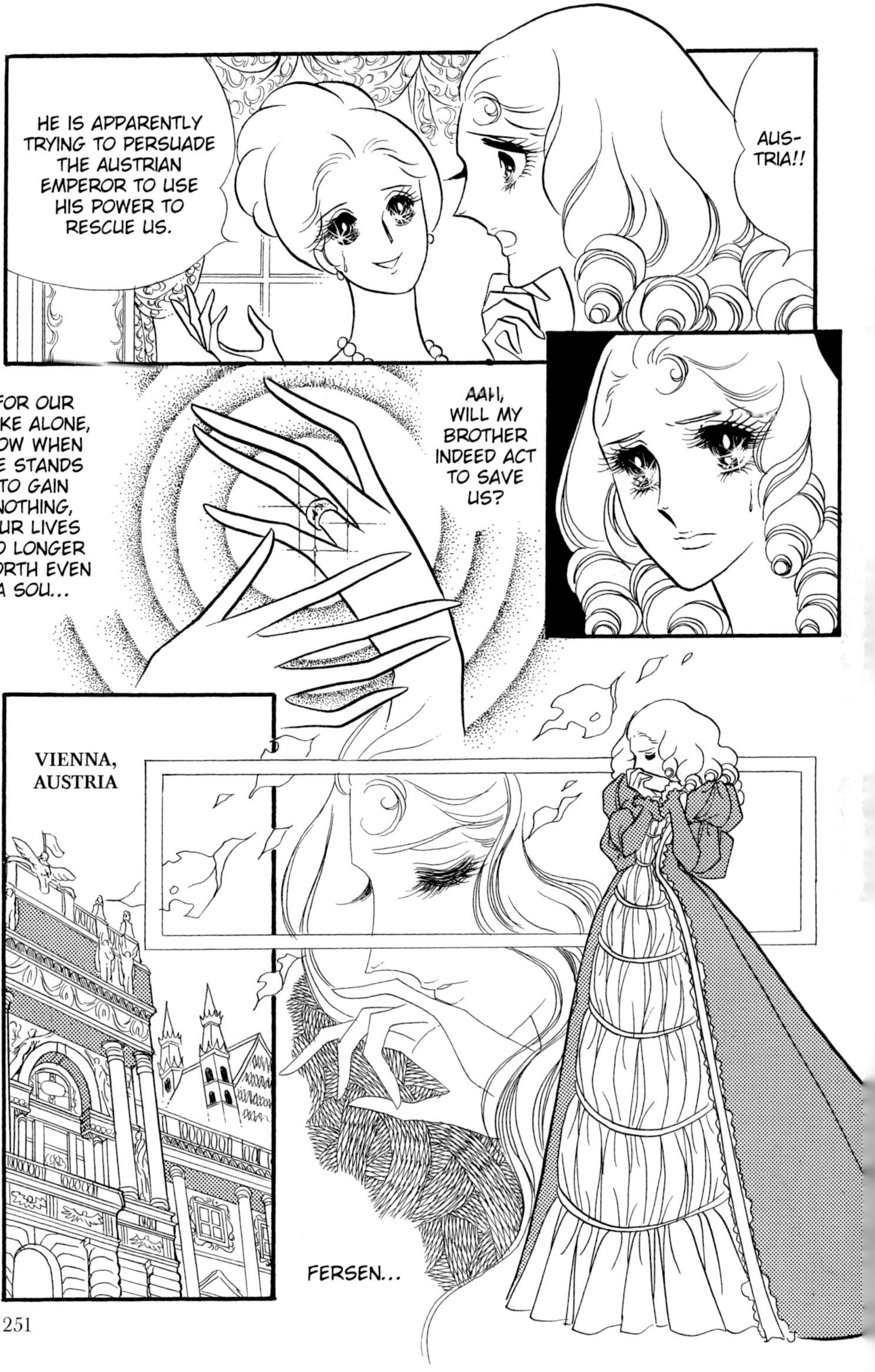
AUS-
TRIA!!
HE IS APPARENTLY TRYING TO PERSUADE THE AUSTRIAN EMPEROR TO USE HIS POWER TO RESCUE US.
AAH, WILL MY BROTHER INDEED ACT TO SAVE US?
FOR OUR SAKE ALONE, NOW WHEN HE STANDS TO GAIN NOTHING, OUR LIVES NO LONGER WORTH EVEN A SOU...
FERSEN...
VIENNA, AUSTRIA

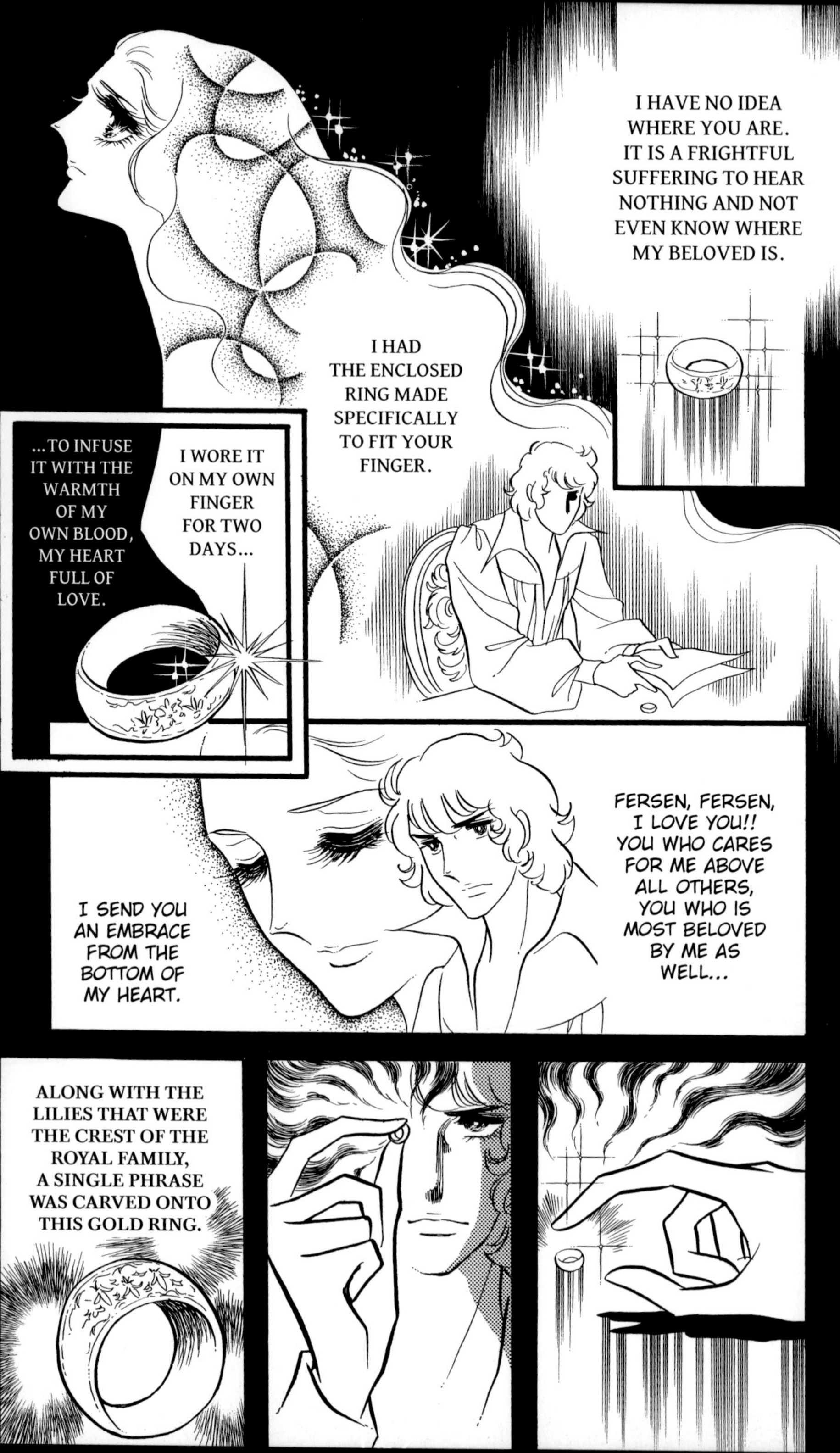
I HAVE NO IDEA WHERE YOU ARE. IT IS A FRIGHTFUL SUFFERING TO HEAR NOTHING AND NOT EVEN KNOW WHERE MY BELOVED IS.
I HAD THE ENCLOSED RING MADE SPECIFICALLY TO FIT YOUR FINGER.
I WORE IT ON MY OWN FINGER FOR TWO DAYS...
...TO INFUSE IT WITH THE WARMTH OF MY OWN BLOOD, MY HEART FULL OF LOVE.
FERSEN, FERSEN, I LOVE YOU!! YOU WHO CARES FOR ME ABOVE ALL OTHERS, YOU WHO IS MOST BELOVED BY ME AS WELL...
I SEND YOU AN EMBRACE FROM THE BOTTOM OF MY HEART.
ALONG WITH THE LILIES THAT WERE THE CREST OF THE ROYAL FAMILY, A SINGLE PHRASE WAS CARVED ONTO THIS GOLD RING.

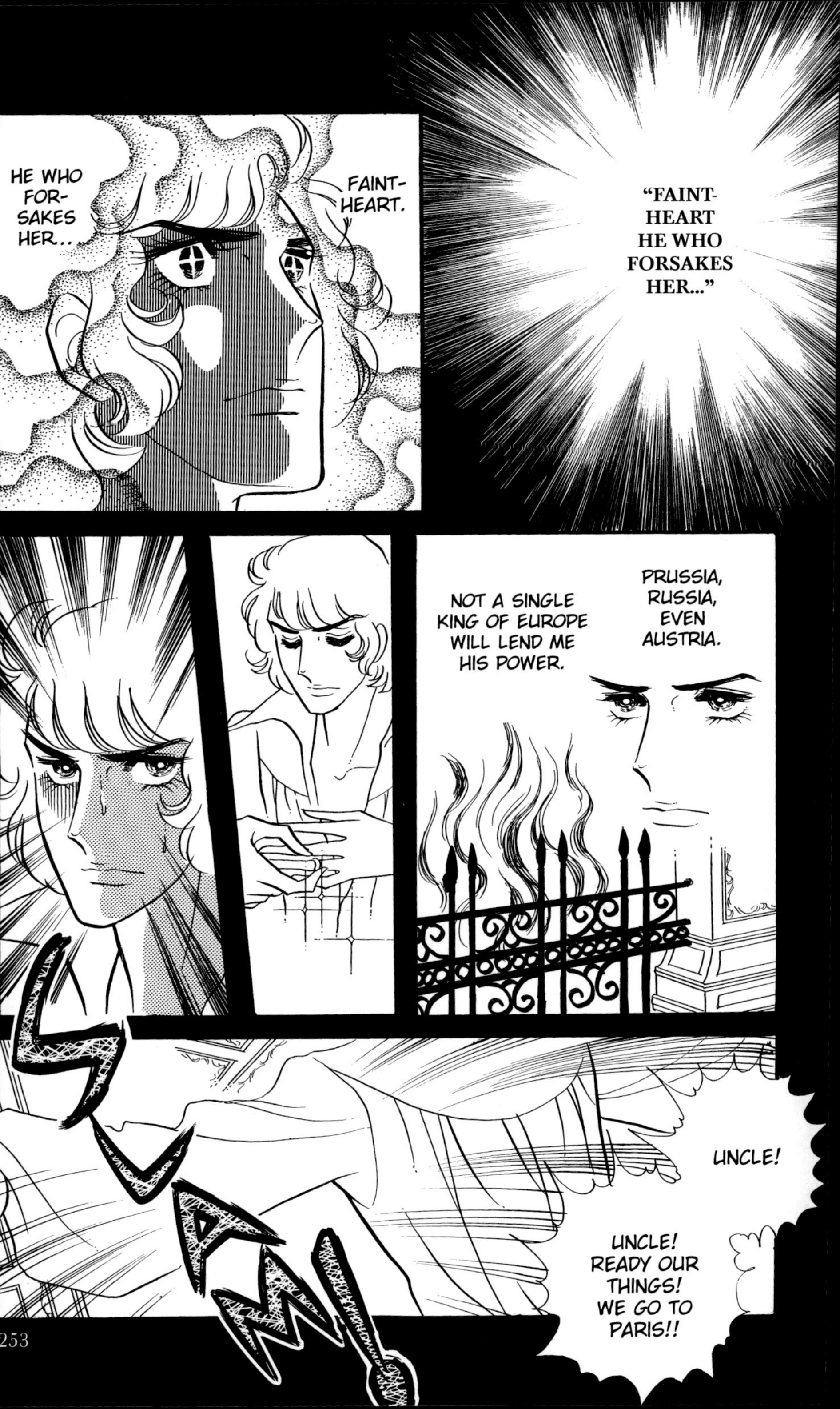
"FAINT-HEART HE WHO FORSAKES HER..."
FAINT-HEART.
HE WHO FOR-SAKES HER..
PRUSSIA, RUSSIA, EVEN AUSTRIA.
NOT A SINGLE KING OF EUROPE WILL LEND ME HIS POWER.
UNCLE!
UNCLE! READY OUR THINGS! WE GO TO PARIS!!
SLAM!

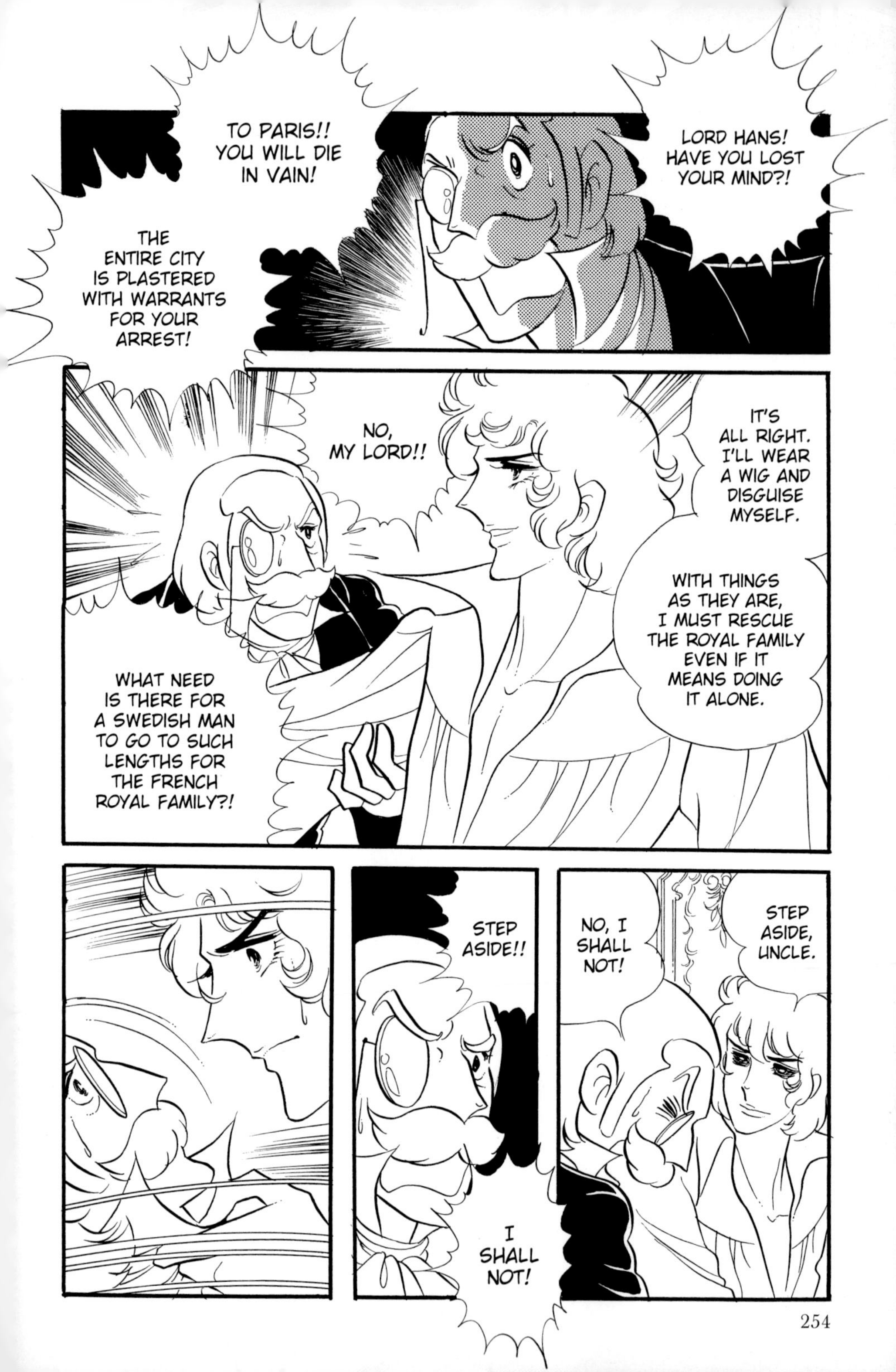
LORD HANS! HAVE YOU LOST YOUR MIND?!
TO PARIS!! YOU WILL DIE IN VAIN!
THE ENTIRE CITY IS PLASTERED WITH WARRANTS FOR YOUR ARREST!
IT'S ALL RIGHT. I'LL WEAR A WIG AND DISGUISE MYSELF.
WITH THINGS AS THEY ARE, I MUST RESCUE THE ROYAL FAMILY EVEN IF IT MEANS DOING IT ALONE.
NO, MY LORD!!
WHAT NEED IS THERE FOR A SWEDISH MAN TO GO TO SUCH LENGTHS FOR THE FRENCH ROYAL FAMILY?!
STEP ASIDE, UNCLE.
NO, I SHALL NOT!
STEP ASIDE!!
I SHALL NOT!

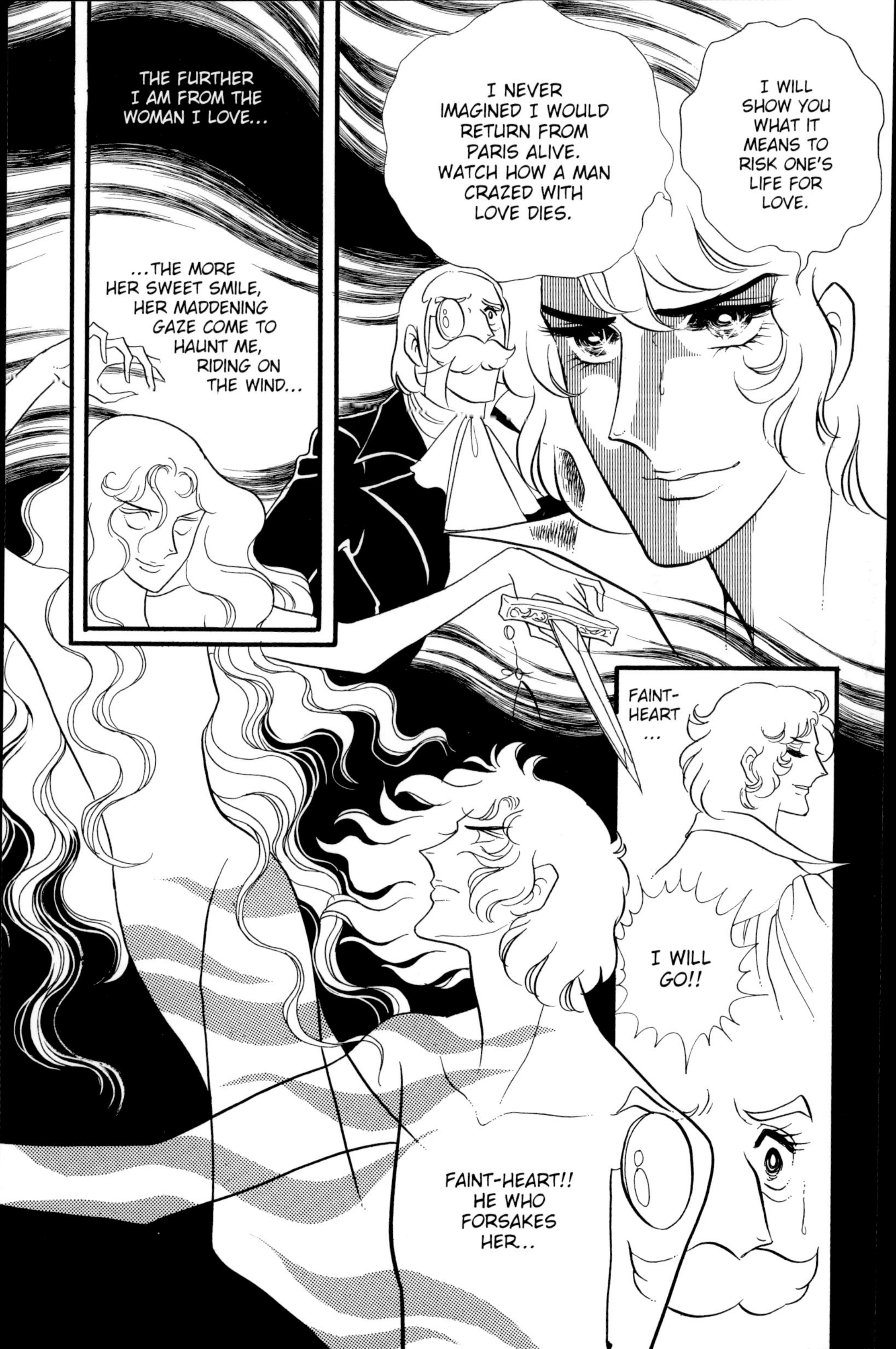
I WILL SHOW YOU WHAT IT MEANS TO RISK ONE'S LIFE FOR LOVE.
I NEVER IMAGINED I WOULD RETURN FROM PARIS ALIVE. WATCH HOW A MAN CRAZED WITH LOVE DIES.
THE FURTHER I AM FROM THE WOMAN I LOVE...
...THE MORE HER SWEET SMILE, HER MADDENING GAZE COME TO HAUNT ME, RIDING ON THE WIND...
FAINT-HEART...
I WILL GO!!
FAINT-HEART!! HE WHO FORSAKES HER..

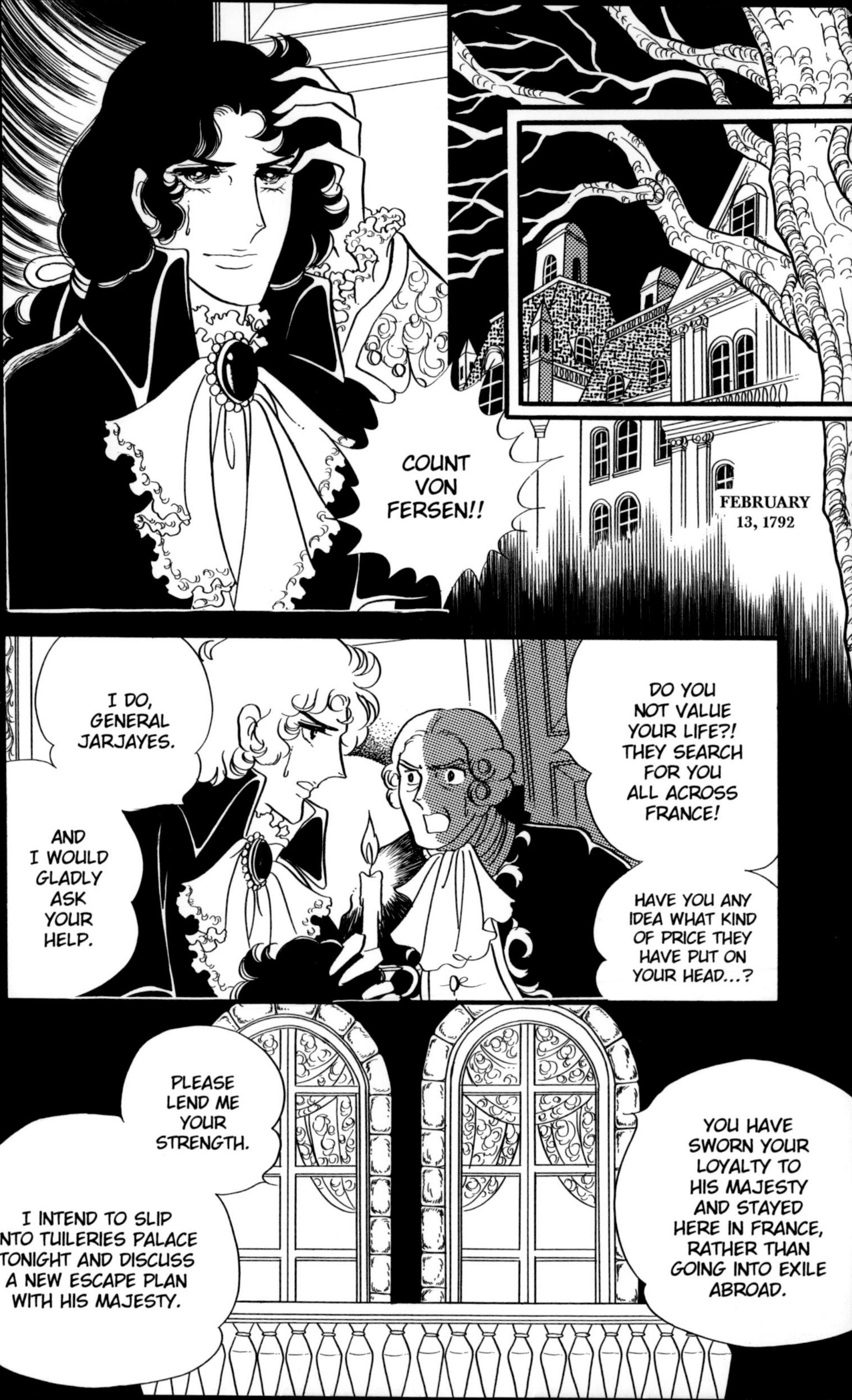
FEBRUARY 13, 1792
COUNT VON FERSEN!!
DO YOU NOT VALUE YOUR LIFE?! THEY SEARCH FOR YOU ALL ACROSS FRANCE!
HAVE YOU ANY IDEA WHAT KIND OF PRICE THEY HAVE PUT ON YOUR HEAD...?
I DO, GENERAL JARJAYES.
AND I WOULD GLADLY ASK YOUR HELP.
YOU HAVE SWORN YOUR LOYALTY TO HIS MAJESTY AND STAYED HERE IN FRANCE, RATHER THAN GOING INTO EXILE ABROAD.
PLEASE LEND ME YOUR STRENGTH.
I INTEND TO SLIP INTO TUILERIES PALACE TONIGHT AND DISCUSS A NEW ESCAPE PLAN WITH HIS MAJESTY.

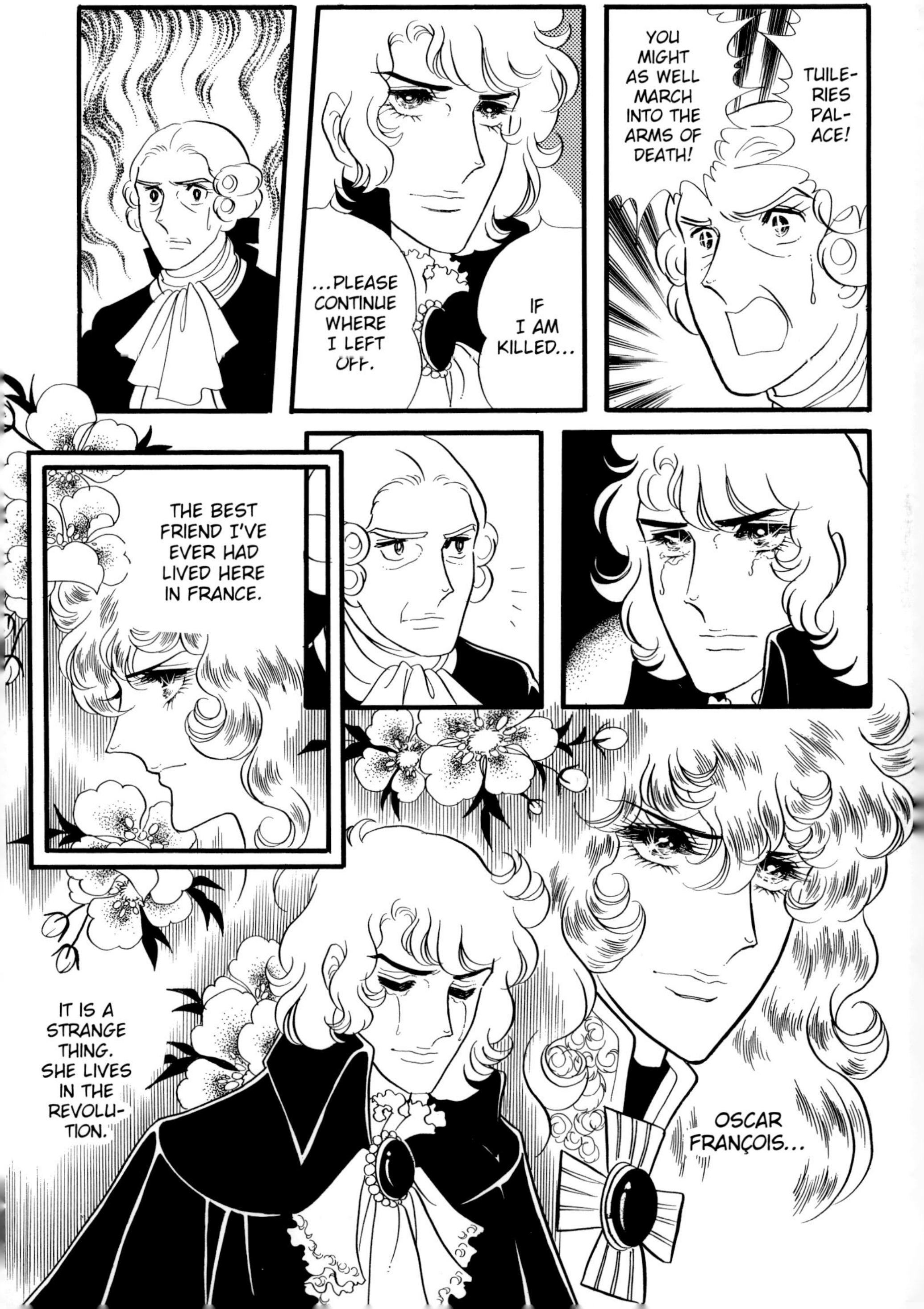
TUILERIES PALACE!
YOU MIGHT AS WELL MARCH INTO THE ARMS OF DEATH!
IF I AM KILLED...
...PLEASE CONTINUE WHERE I LEFT OFF.
THE BEST FRIEND I'VE EVER HAD LIVED HERE IN FRANCE.
OSCAR FRANÇOIS...
IT IS A STRANGE THING. SHE LIVES IN THE REVOLUTION.

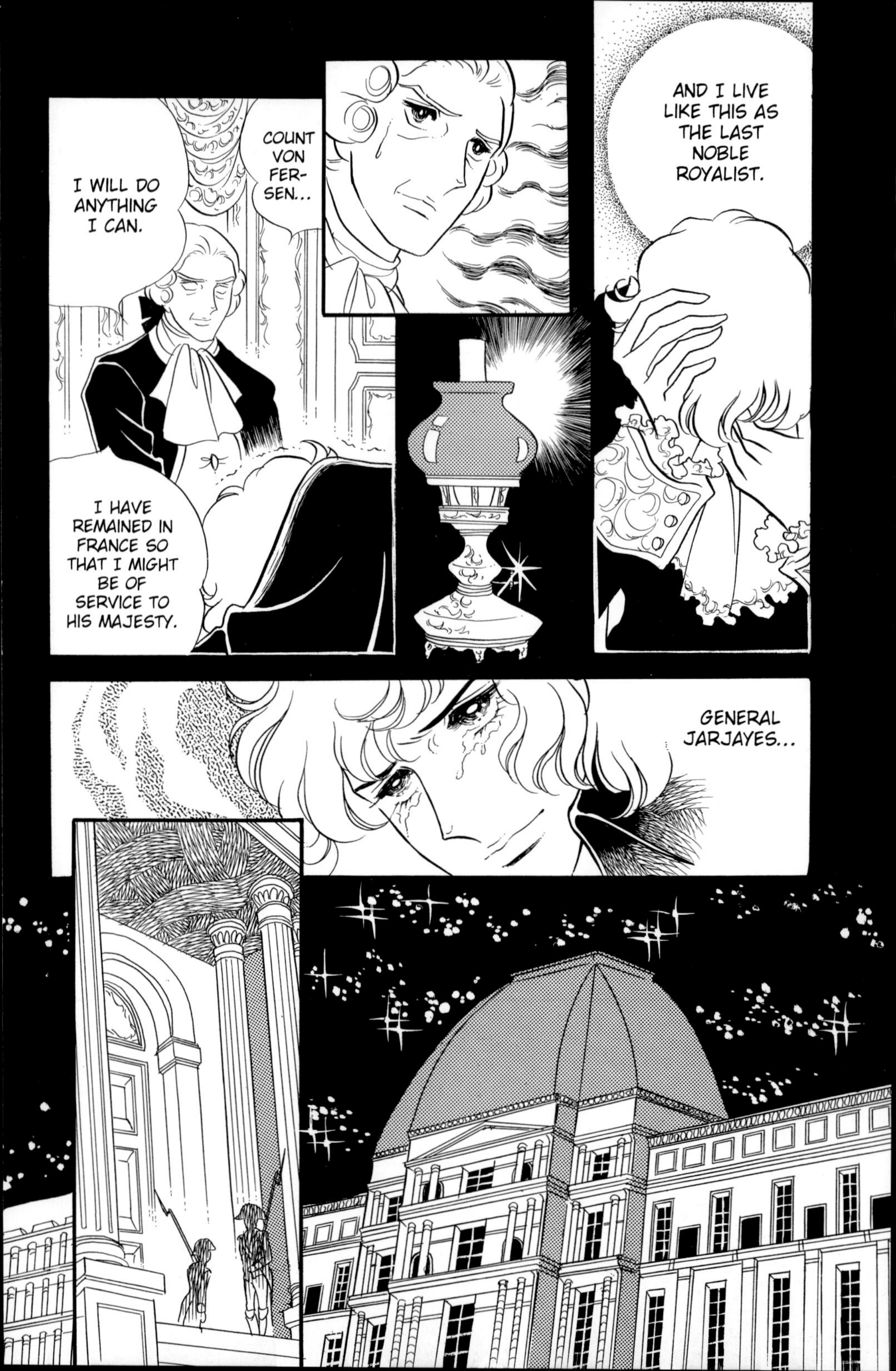
AND I LIVE LIKE THIS AS THE LAST NOBLE ROYALIST.
COUNT VON FER-SEN...
I WILL DO ANYTHING I CAN.
I HAVE REMAINED IN FRANCE SO THAT I MIGHT BE OF SERVICE TO HIS MAJESTY.
GENERAL JARJAYES...

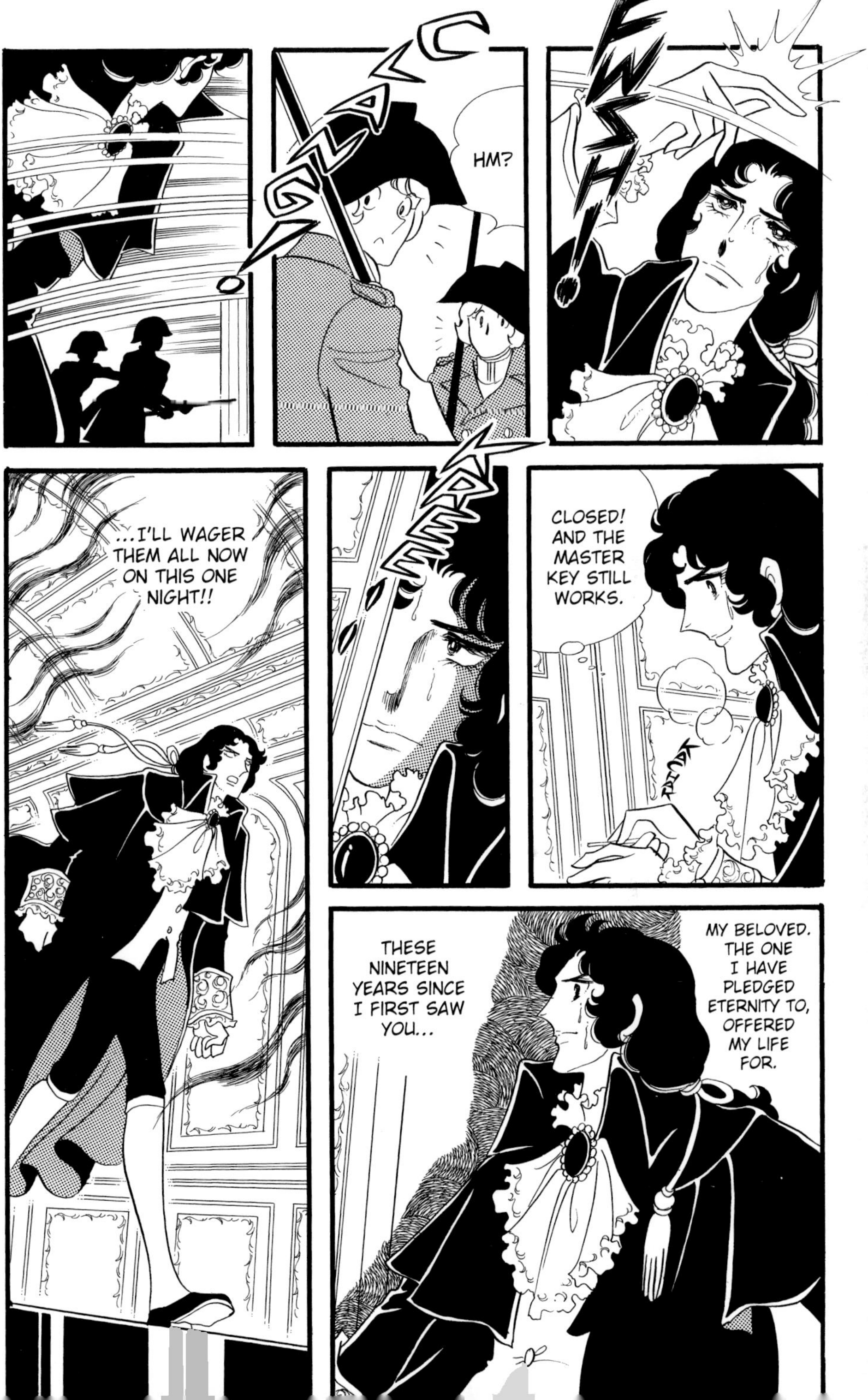
CLANG!
HM?
FWSH!
...I'LL WAGER THEM ALL NOW ON THIS ONE NIGHT!!
KREE...
CLOSED! AND THE MASTER KEY STILL WORKS.
THESE NINETEEN YEARS SINCE I FIRST SAW YOU...
MY BELOVED. THE ONE I HAVE PLEDGED ETERNITY TO, OFFERED MY LIFE FOR.

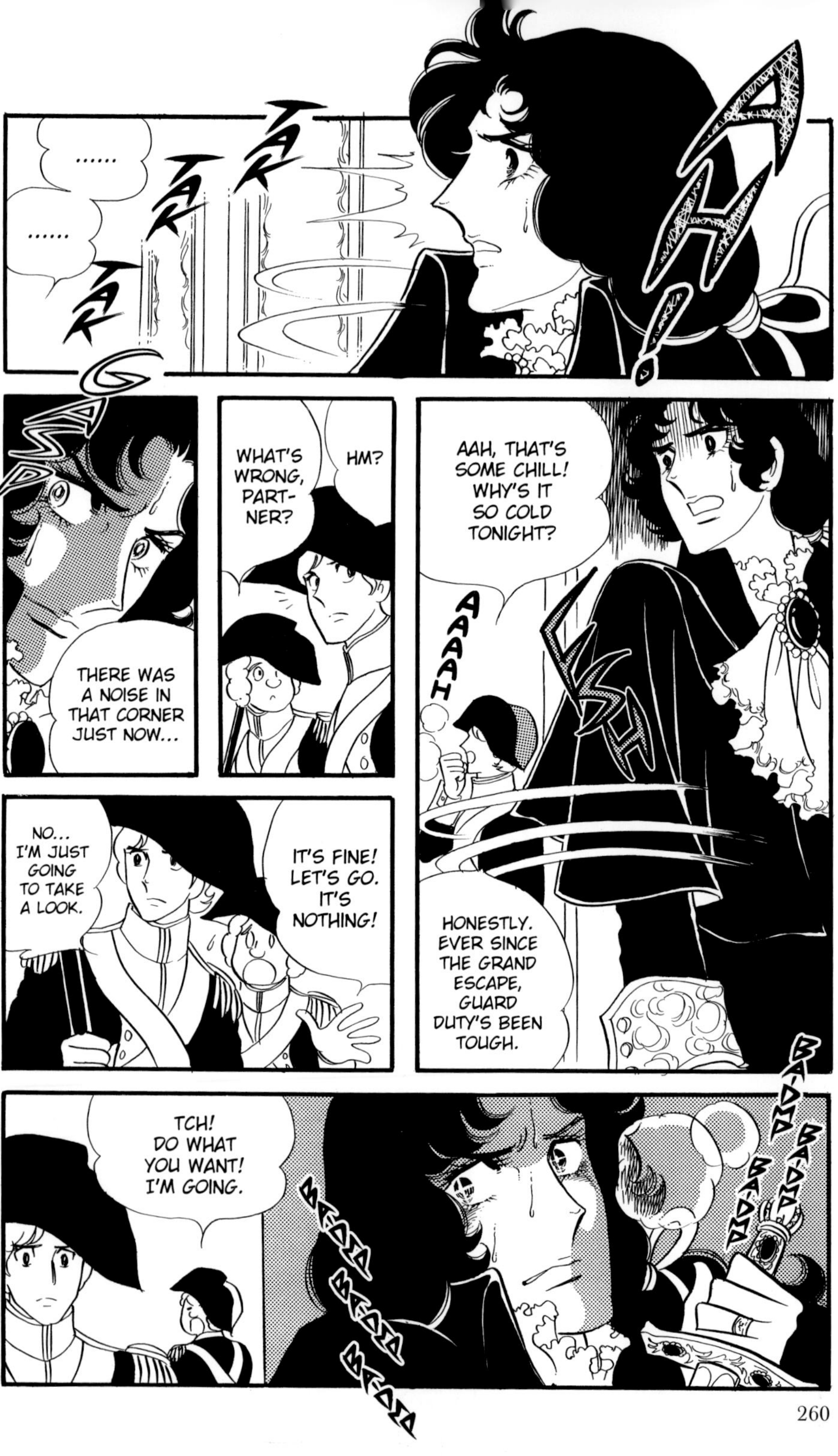
AH!?
TAK
TAK
TAK
......
......
GASP
HM?
WHAT'S WRONG, PARTNER?
THERE WAS A NOISE IN THAT CORNER JUST NOW...
IT'S FINE! LET'S GO. IT'S NOTHING!
NO... I'M JUST GOING TO TAKE A LOOK.
AAH, THAT'S SOME CHILL! WHY'S IT SO COLD TONIGHT?
AAAAH
HONESTLY. EVER SINCE THE GRAND ESCAPE, GUARD DUTY'S BEEN TOUGH.
BA-DMP
BA-DMP
BADMP
TCH! DO WHAT YOU WANT! I'M GOING.

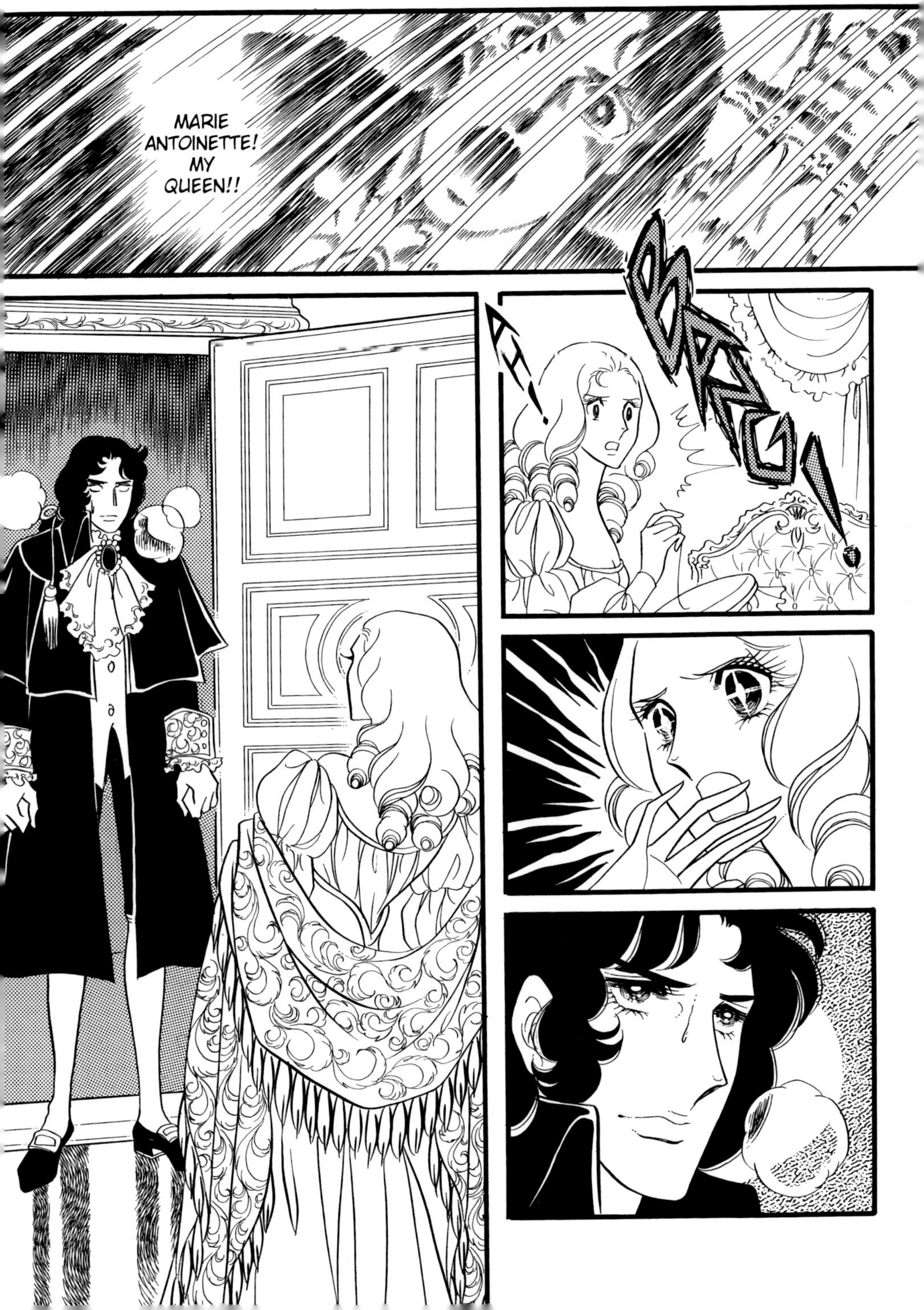
MARIE ANTOINETTE! MY QUEEN!!
BANG!
AH!

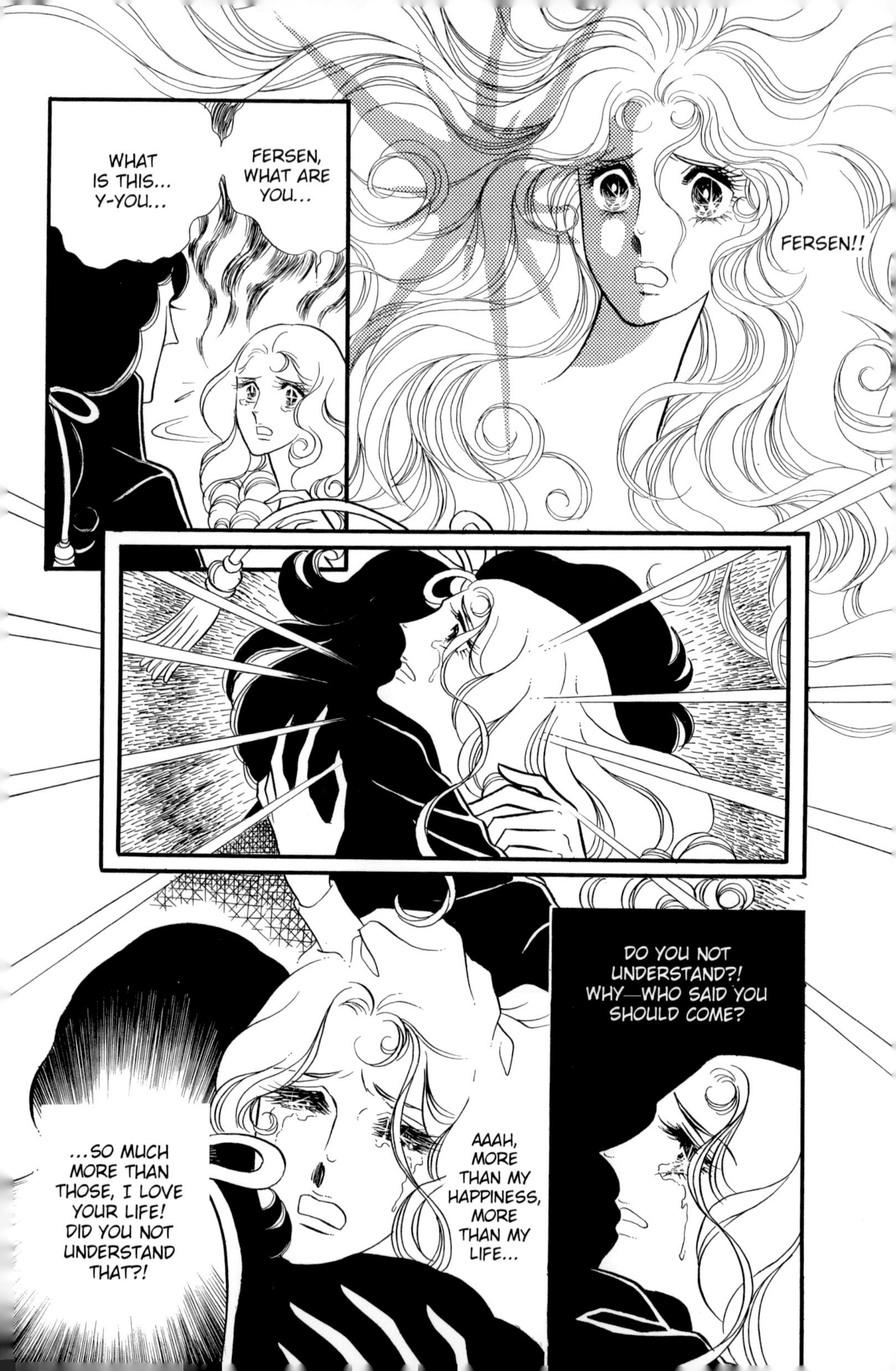
FERSEN!!
FERSEN, WHAT ARE YOU...
WHAT IS THIS... Y-YOU...
DO YOU NOT UNDERSTAND?! WHY—WHO SAID YOU SHOULD COME?
AAAH, MORE THAN MY HAPPINESS, MORE THAN MY LIFE...
...SO MUCH MORE THAN THOSE, I LOVE YOUR LIFE! DID YOU NOT UNDERSTAND THAT?!

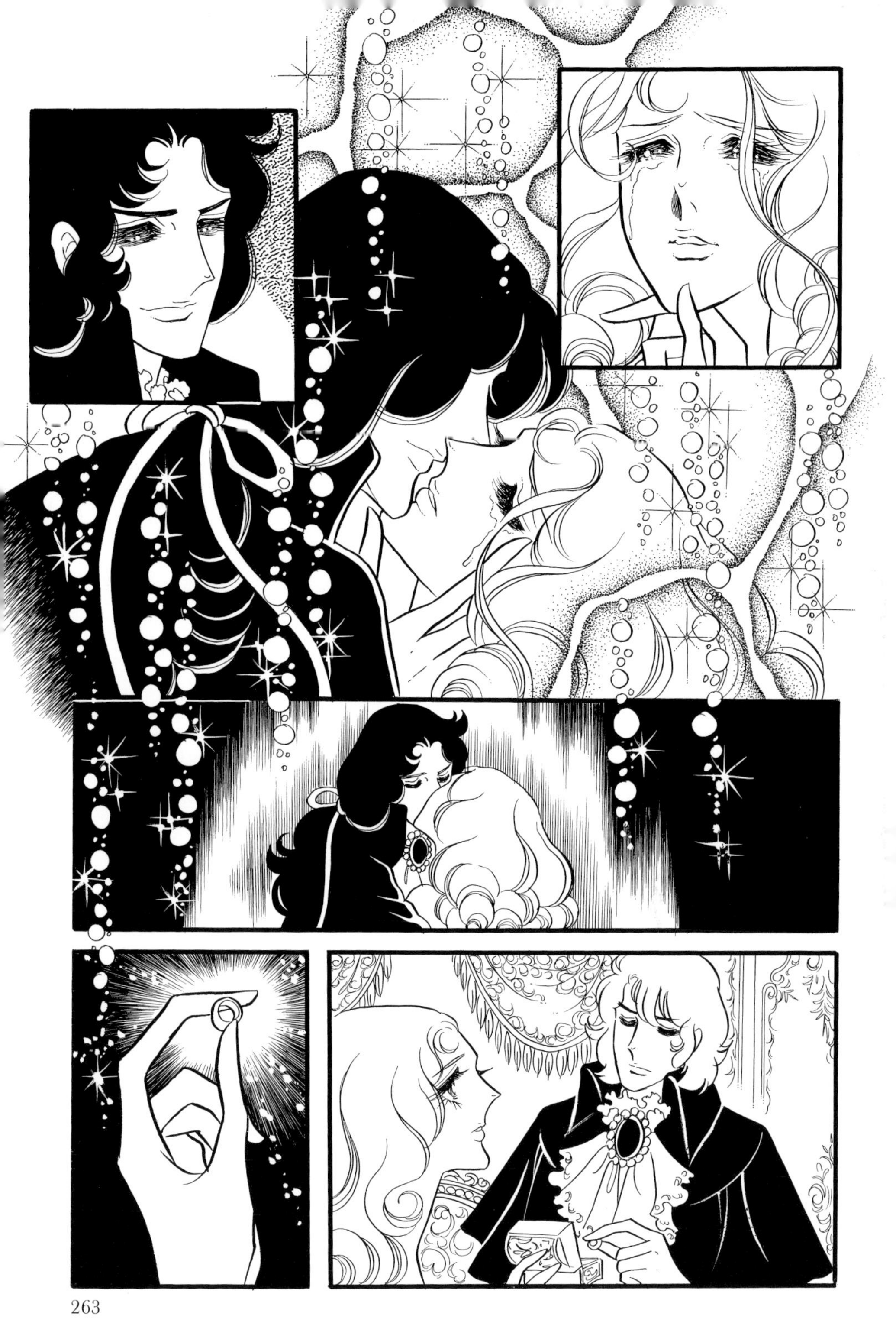

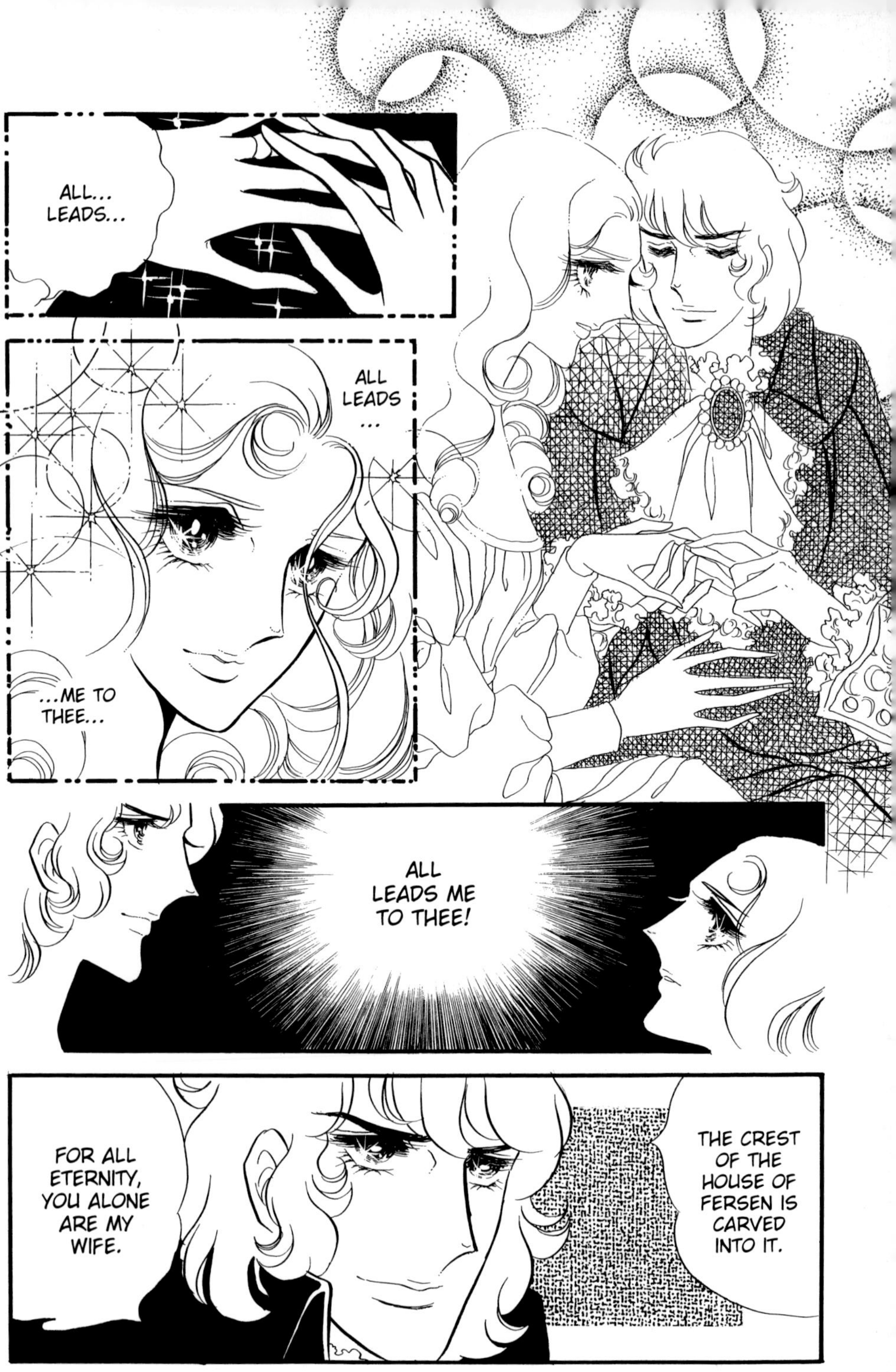
ALL... LEADS...
ALL LEADS ...
...ME TO THEE...
ALL LEADS ME TO THEE!
THE CREST OF THE HOUSE OF FERSEN IS CARVED INTO IT.
FOR ALL ETERNITY, YOU ALONE ARE MY WIFE.

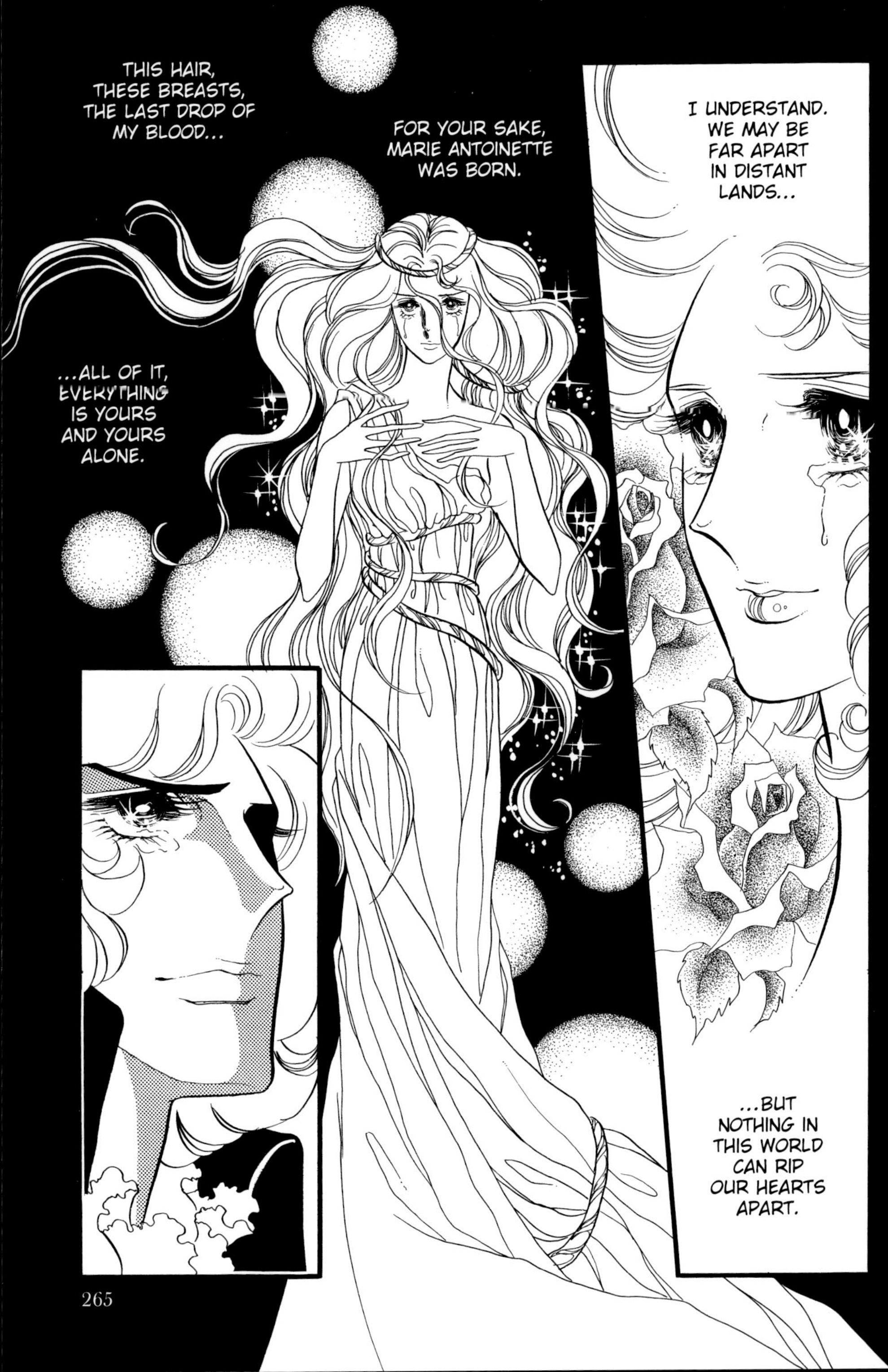
I UNDERSTAND. WE MAY BE FAR APART IN DISTANT LANDS...
...BUT NOTHING IN THIS WORLD CAN RIP OUR HEARTS APART.
FOR YOUR SAKE, MARIE ANTOINETTE WAS BORN.
THIS HAIR, THESE BREASTS, THE LAST DROP OF MY BLOOD...
...ALL OF IT, EVERYTHING IS YOURS AND YOURS ALONE.

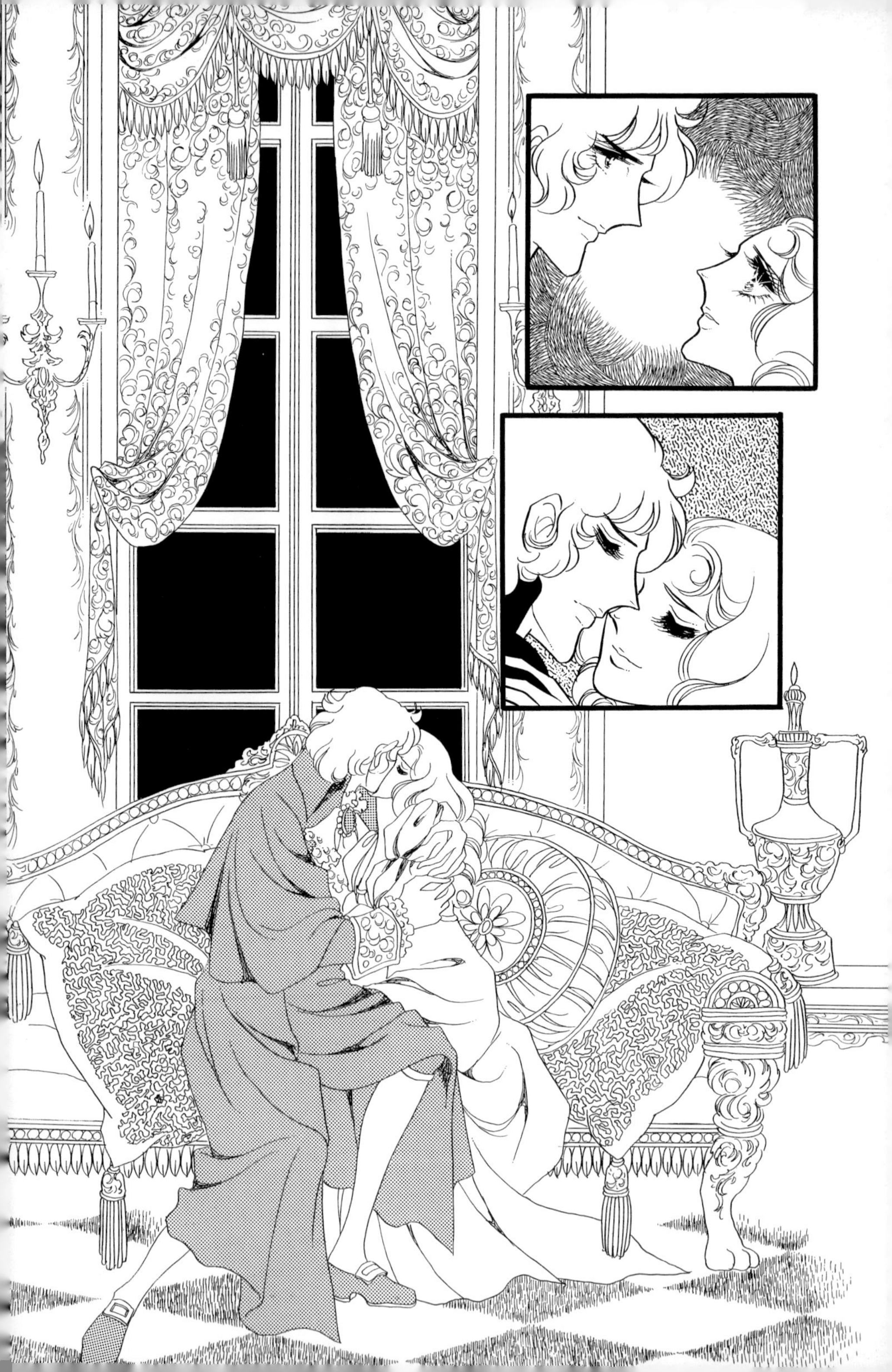

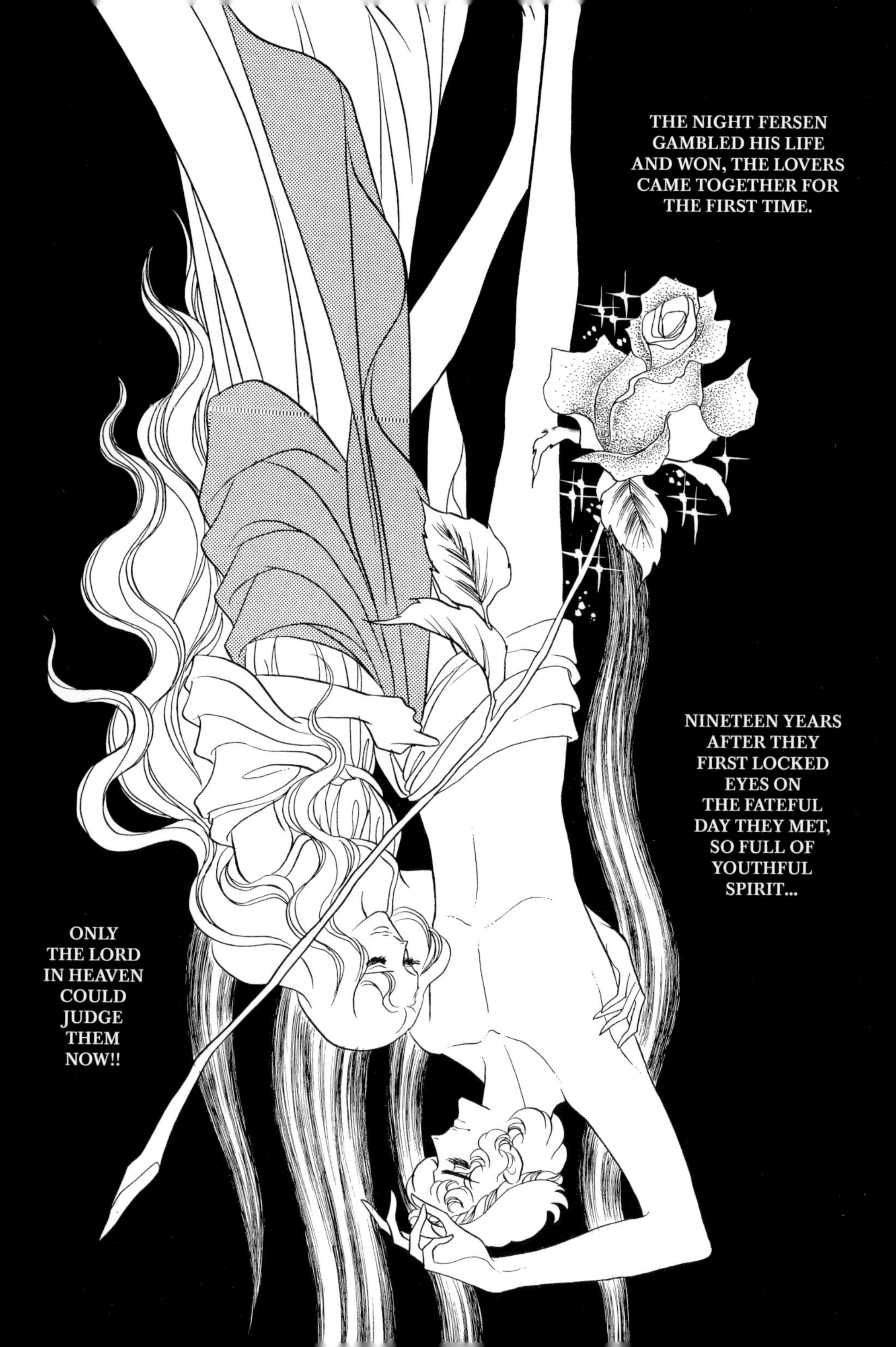
THE NIGHT FERSEN GAMBLED HIS LIFE AND WON, THE LOVERS CAME TOGETHER FOR THE FIRST TIME.
NINETEEN YEARS AFTER THEY FIRST LOCKED EYES ON THE FATEFUL DAY THEY MET, SO FULL OF YOUTHFUL SPIRIT...
ONLY THE LORD IN HEAVEN COULD JUDGE THEM NOW!!

1974 MARGARET COMICS TRADE PAPERBACK
VOLUME 9 COVER

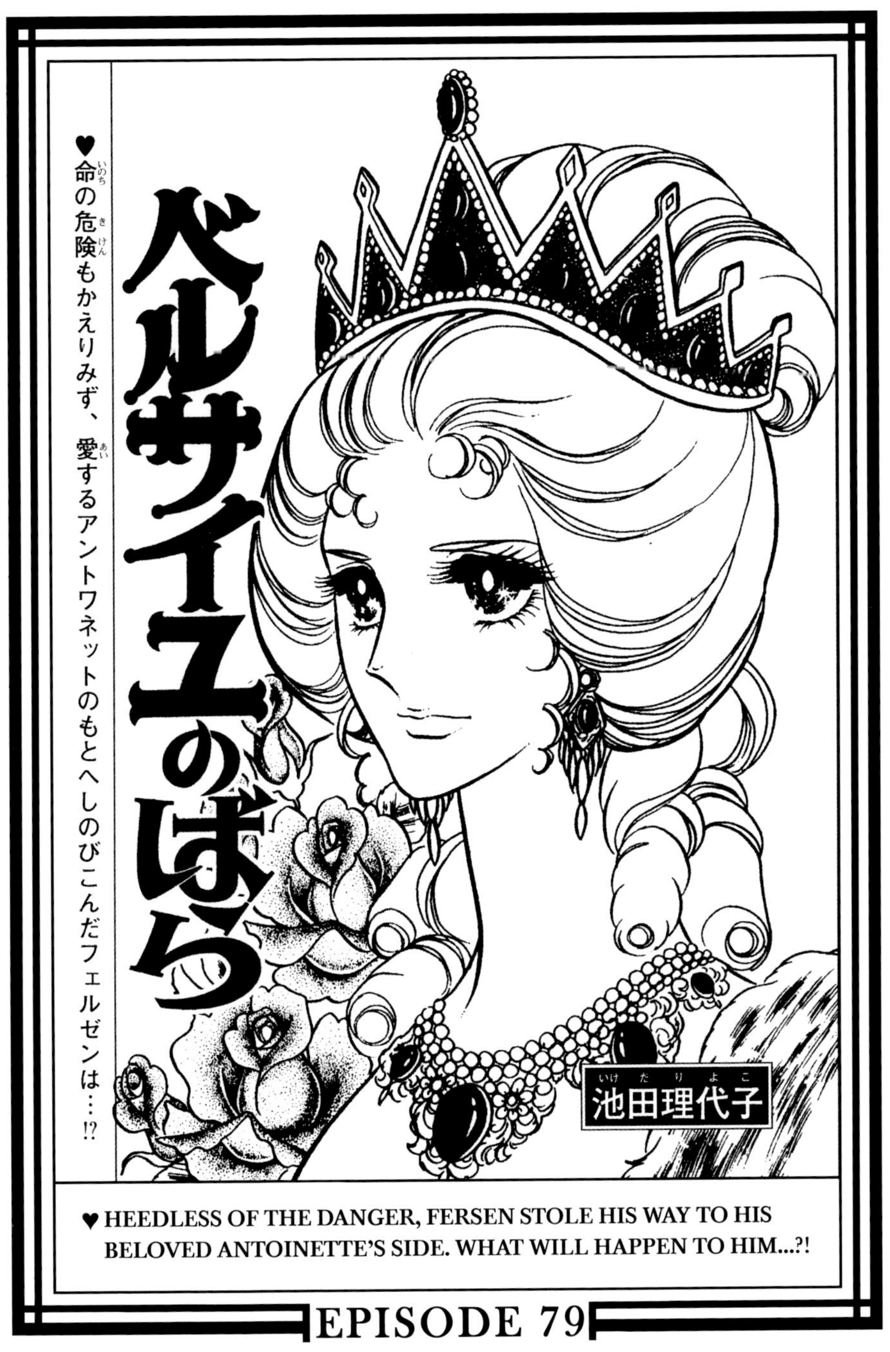
ベルサイユのばら
♥命の危険もかえりみず、愛するアントワネットのもとへしのびこんだフェルゼンは…!?
池田理代子

♥ HEEDLESS OF THE DANGER, FERSEN STOLE HIS WAY TO HIS BELOVED ANTOINETTE'S SIDE. WHAT WILL HAPPEN TO HIM...?!

EPISODE 79

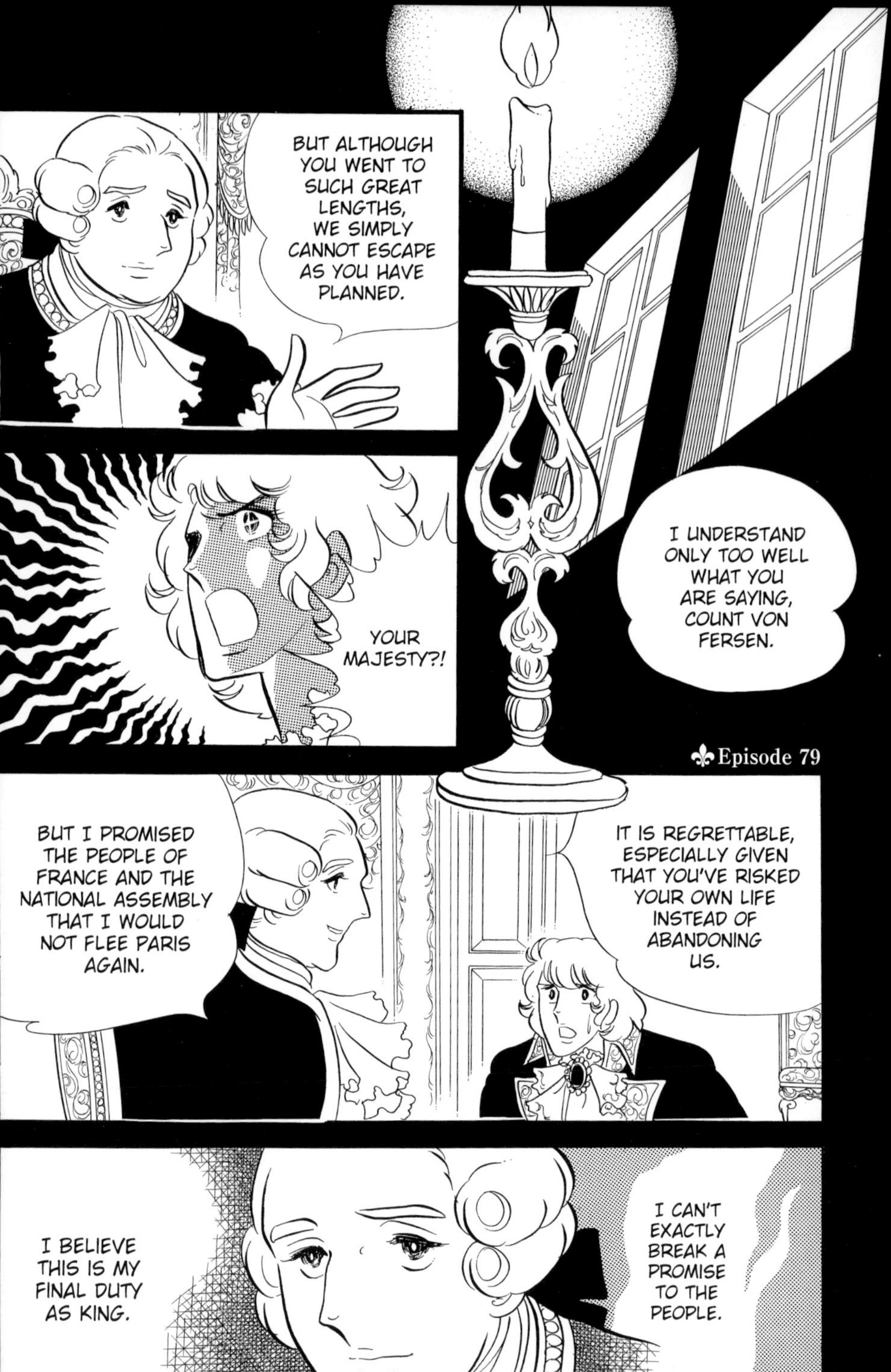
I UNDERSTAND ONLY TOO WELL WHAT YOU ARE SAYING, COUNT VON FERSEN.
BUT ALTHOUGH YOU WENT TO SUCH GREAT LENGTHS, WE SIMPLY CANNOT ESCAPE AS YOU HAVE PLANNED.
YOUR MAJESTY?!
IT IS REGRETTABLE, ESPECIALLY GIVEN THAT YOU'VE RISKED YOUR OWN LIFE INSTEAD OF ABANDONING US.
BUT I PROMISED THE PEOPLE OF FRANCE AND THE NATIONAL ASSEMBLY THAT I WOULD NOT FLEE PARIS AGAIN.
I CAN'T EXACTLY BREAK A PROMISE TO THE PEOPLE.
I BELIEVE THIS IS MY FINAL DUTY AS KING.

⚜ Episode 79

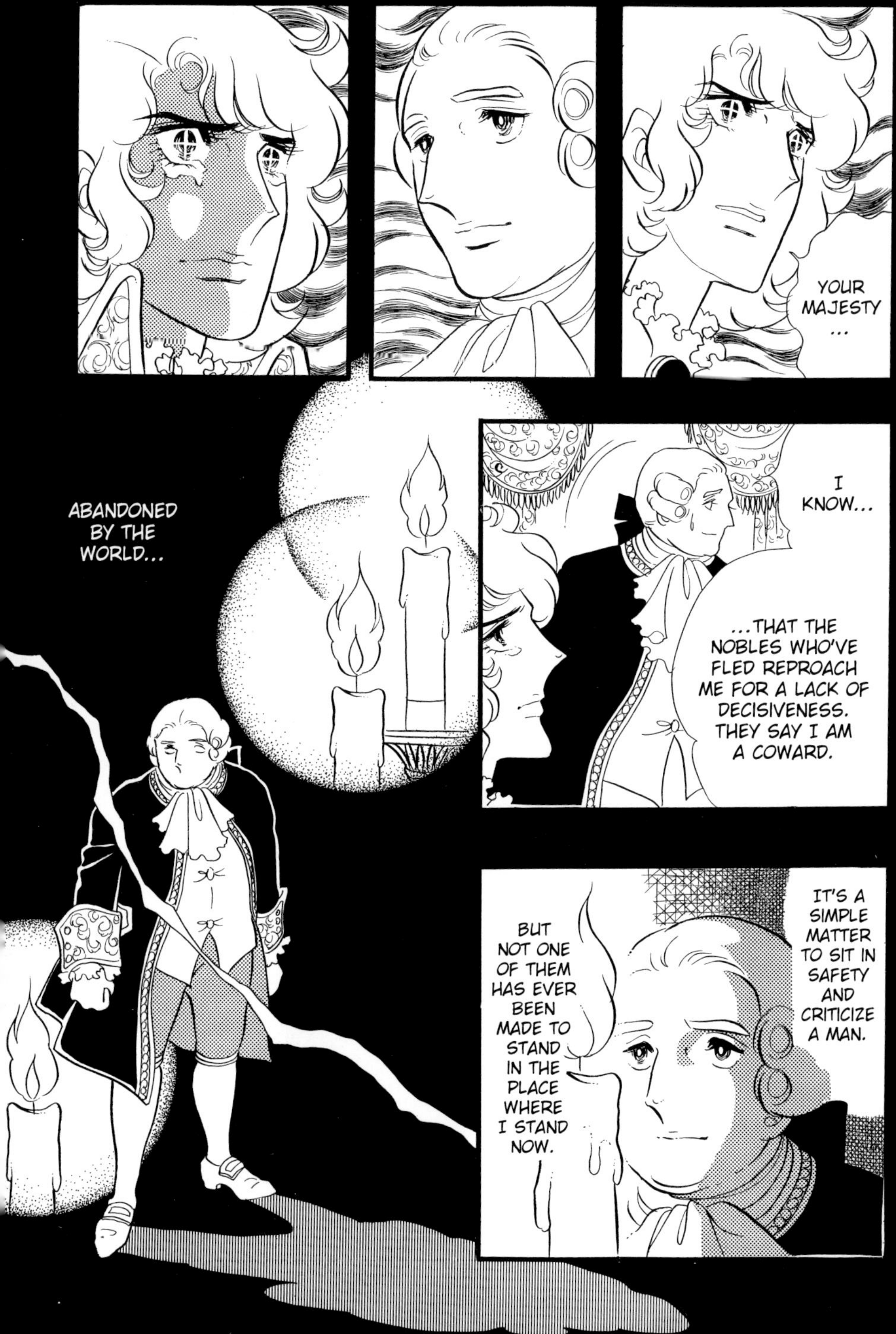
YOUR MAJESTY ...
I KNOW...
...THAT THE NOBLES WHO'VE FLED REPROACH ME FOR A LACK OF DECISIVENESS. THEY SAY I AM A COWARD.
IT'S A SIMPLE MATTER TO SIT IN SAFETY AND CRITICIZE A MAN.
BUT NOT ONE OF THEM HAS EVER BEEN MADE TO STAND IN THE PLACE WHERE I STAND NOW.
ABANDONED BY THE WORLD...

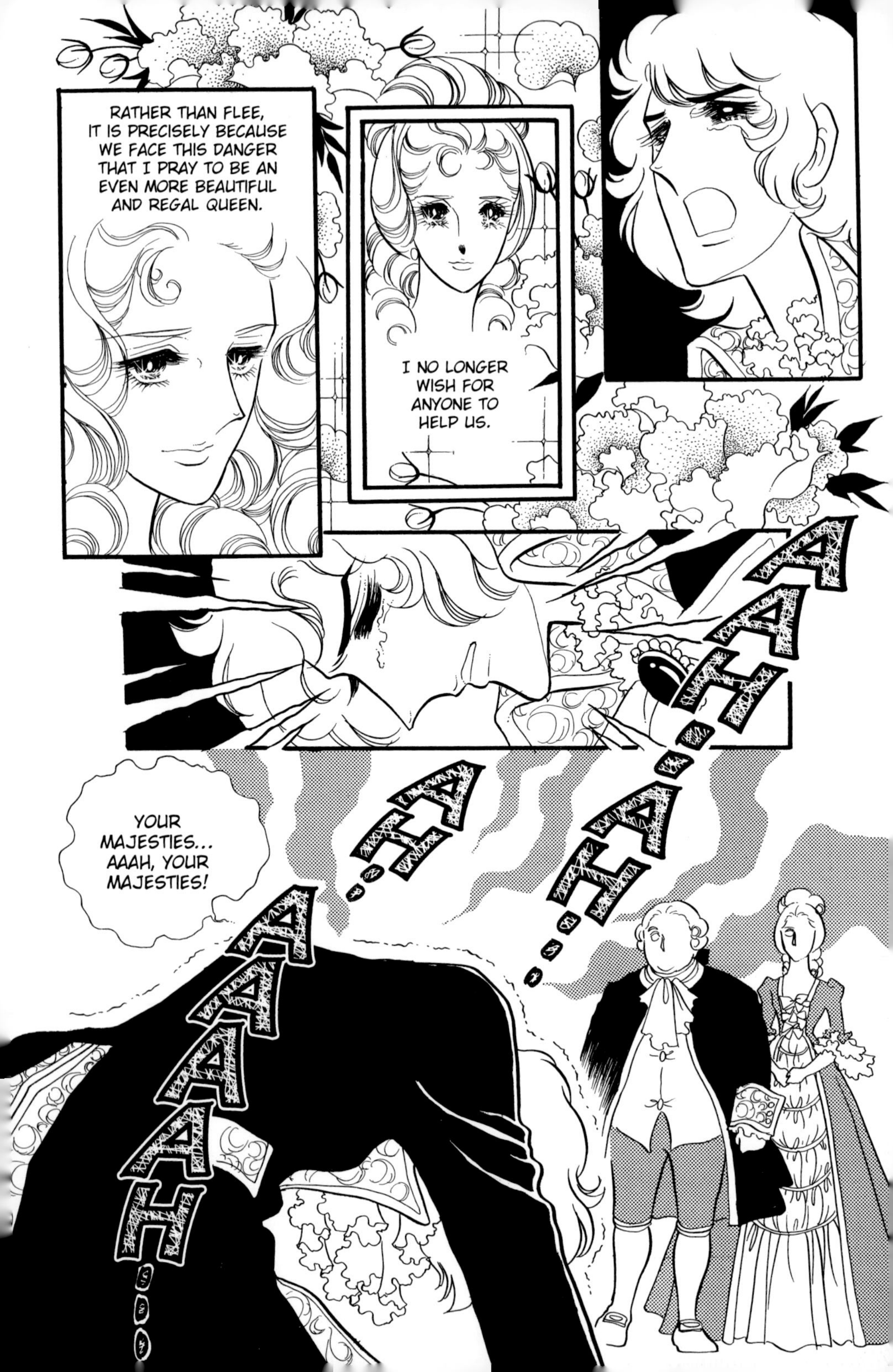
I NO LONGER WISH FOR ANYONE TO HELP US.
RATHER THAN FLEE, IT IS PRECISELY BECAUSE WE FACE THIS DANGER THAT I PRAY TO BE AN EVEN MORE BEAUTIFUL AND REGAL QUEEN.
AAH!
AH..
AH..
YOUR MAJESTIES... AAAH, YOUR MAJESTIES!
AAAAAH...

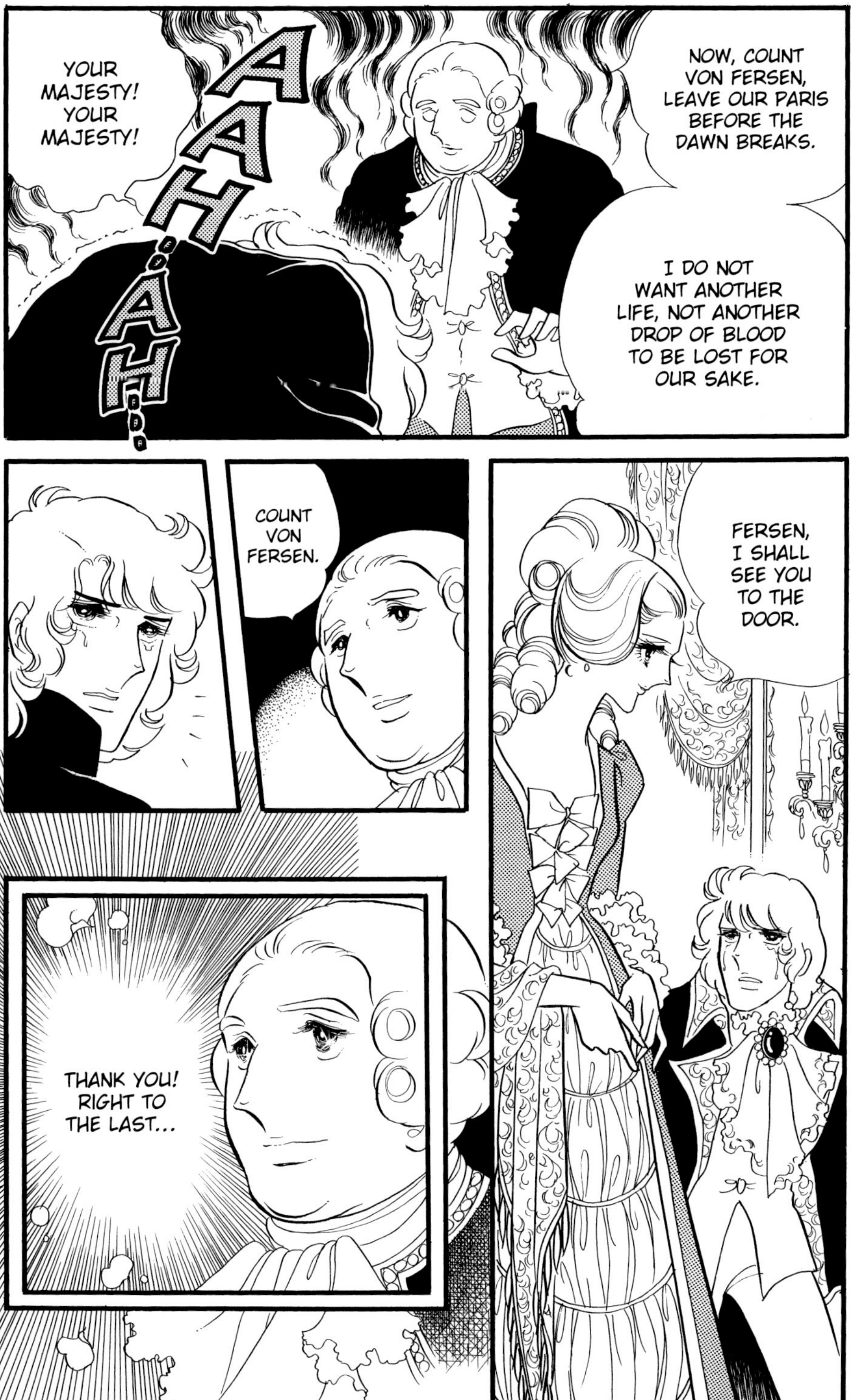
NOW, COUNT VON FERSEN, LEAVE OUR PARIS BEFORE THE DAWN BREAKS.
I DO NOT WANT ANOTHER LIFE, NOT ANOTHER DROP OF BLOOD TO BE LOST FOR OUR SAKE.
AAH... AAH...
YOUR MAJESTY! YOUR MAJESTY!
FERSEN, I SHALL SEE YOU TO THE DOOR.
COUNT VON FERSEN.
THANK YOU! RIGHT TO THE LAST...

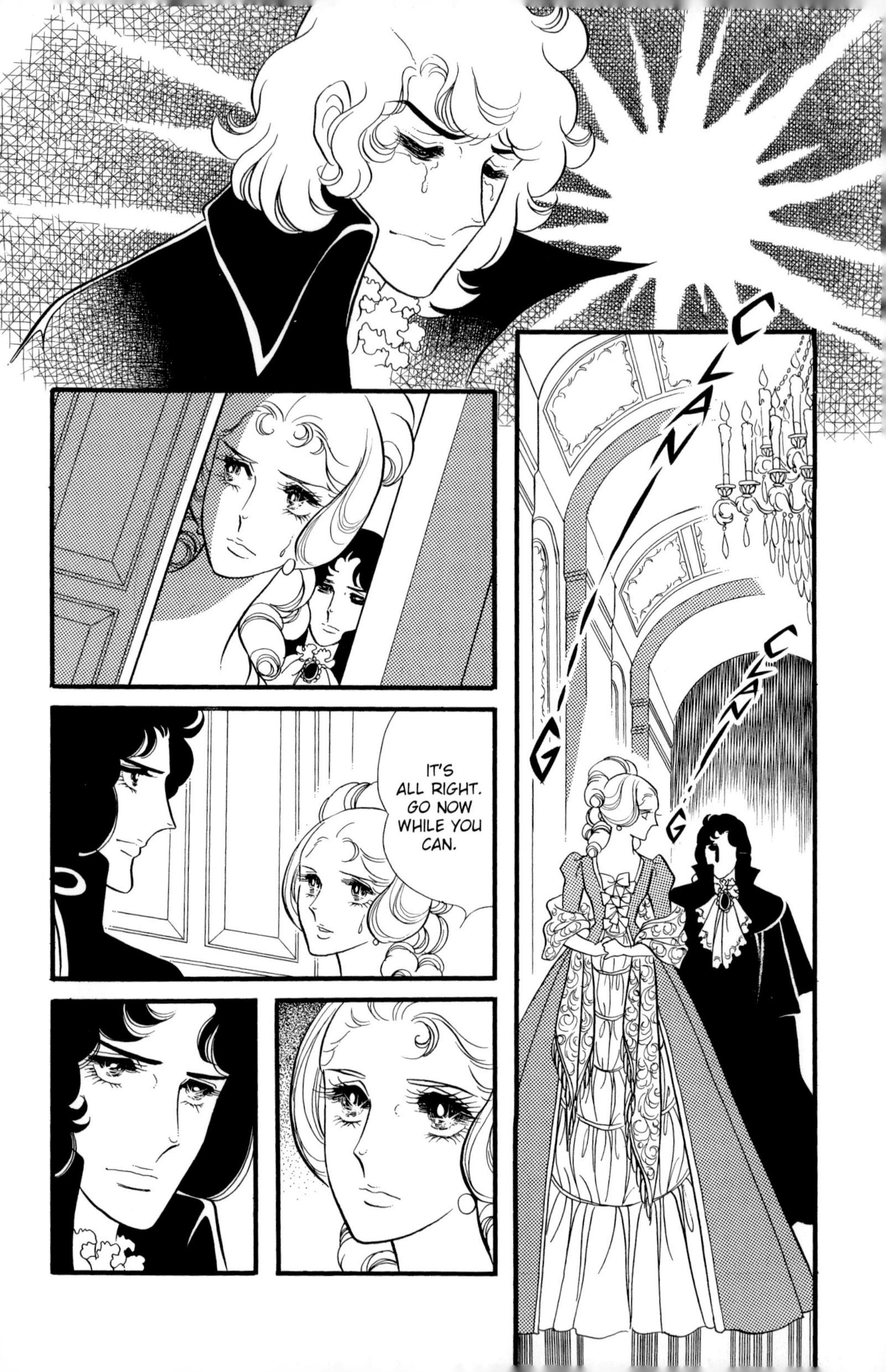
CLAN---G
CLAN...G
IT'S ALL RIGHT. GO NOW WHILE YOU CAN.

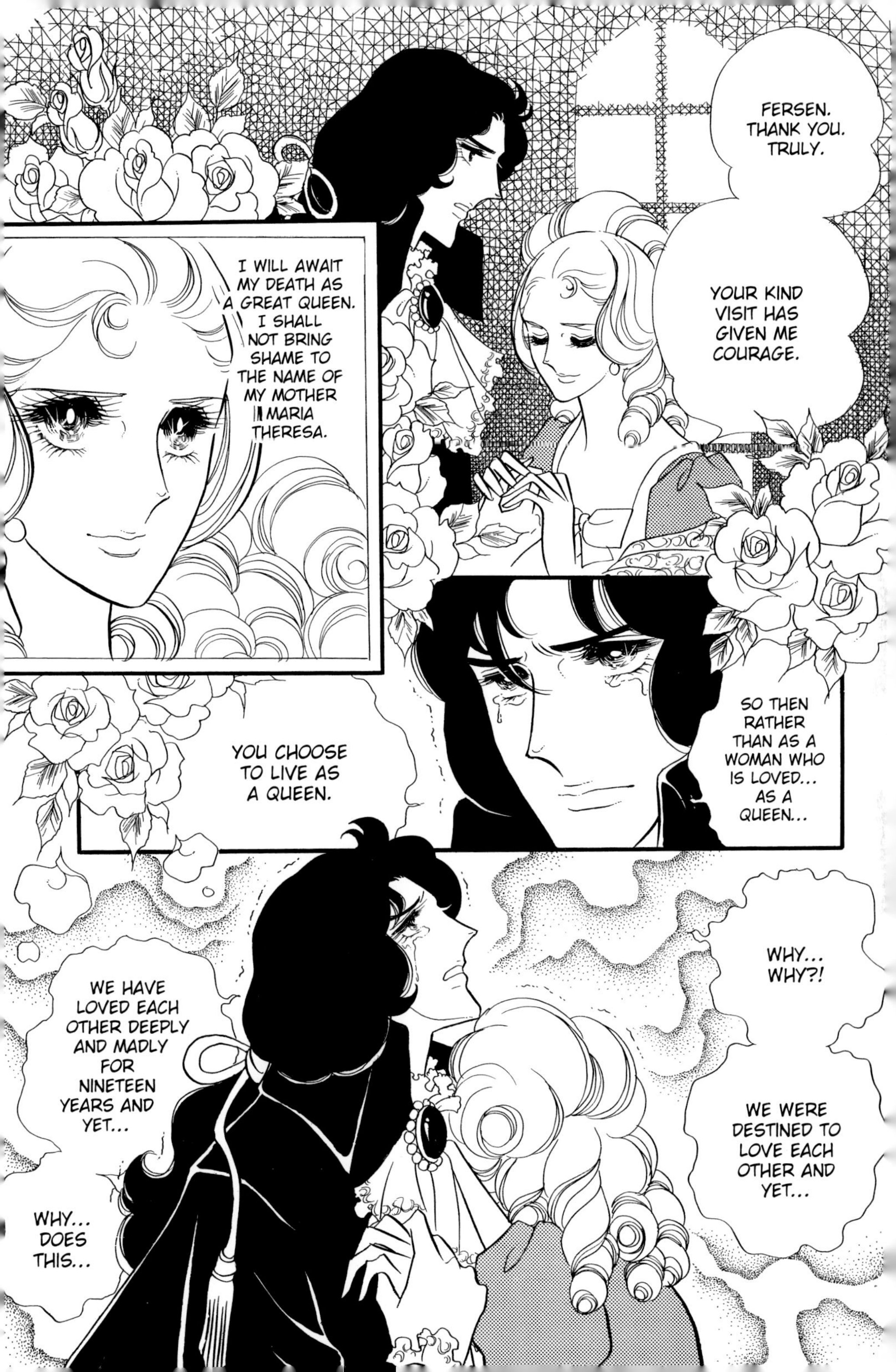
FERSEN. THANK YOU. TRULY.
YOUR KIND VISIT HAS GIVEN ME COURAGE.
I WILL AWAIT MY DEATH AS A GREAT QUEEN. I SHALL NOT BRING SHAME TO THE NAME OF MY MOTHER MARIA THERESA.
SO THEN RATHER THAN AS A WOMAN WHO IS LOVED... AS A QUEEN...
YOU CHOOSE TO LIVE AS A QUEEN.
WHY... WHY?!
WE WERE DESTINED TO LOVE EACH OTHER AND YET...
WE HAVE LOVED EACH OTHER DEEPLY AND MADLY FOR NINETEEN YEARS AND YET...
WHY... DOES THIS...

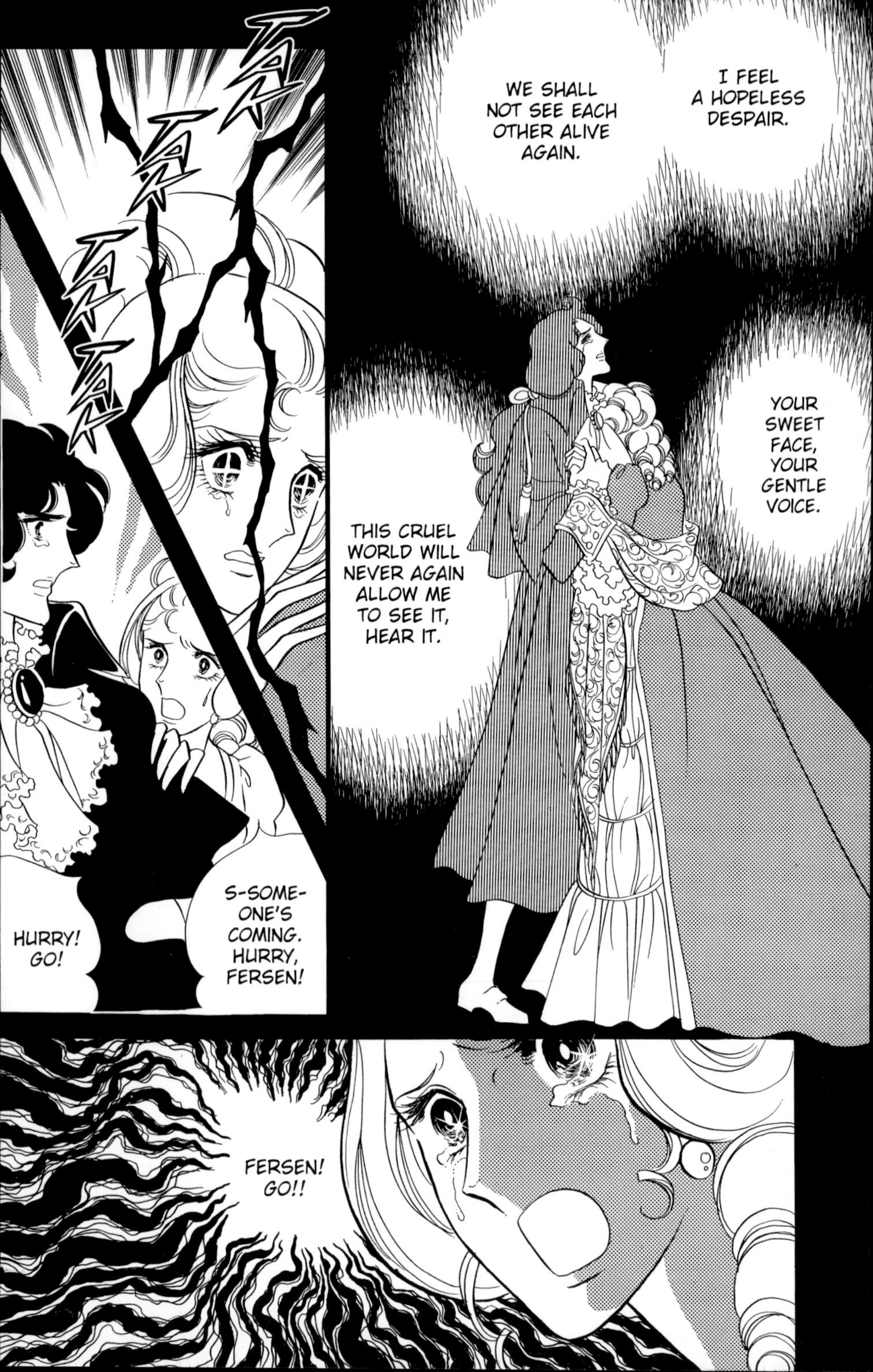
I FEEL A HOPELESS DESPAIR.
WE SHALL NOT SEE EACH OTHER ALIVE AGAIN.
YOUR SWEET FACE, YOUR GENTLE VOICE.
THIS CRUEL WORLD WILL NEVER AGAIN ALLOW ME TO SEE IT, HEAR IT.
TAK TAK TAK TAK TAK
S-SOME-ONE'S COMING. HURRY, FERSEN!
HURRY! GO!
FERSEN! GO!!

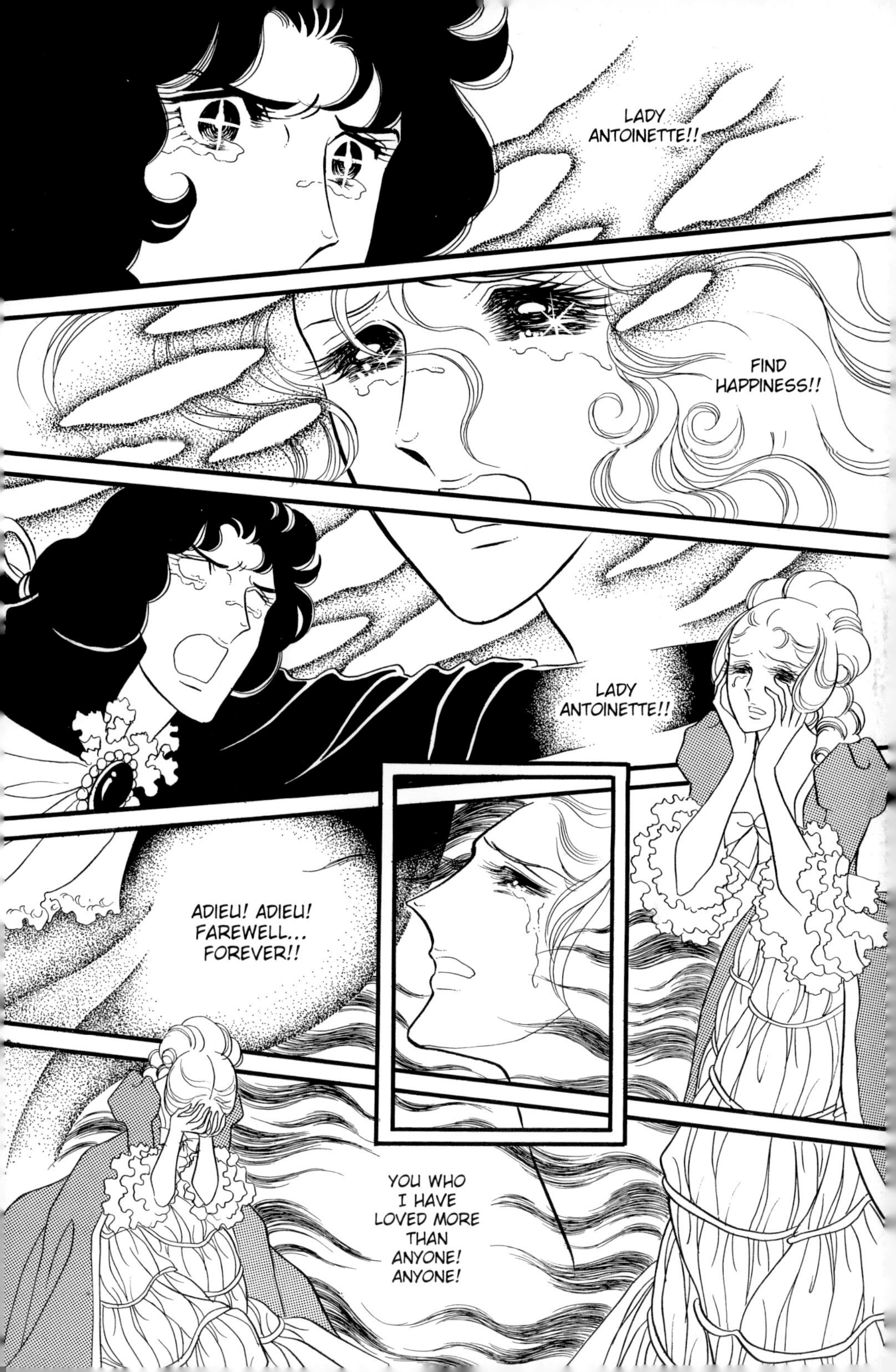
LADY ANTOINETTE!!
FIND HAPPINESS!!
LADY ANTOINETTE!!
ADIEU! ADIEU! FAREWELL... FOREVER!!
YOU WHO I HAVE LOVED MORE THAN ANYONE! ANYONE!

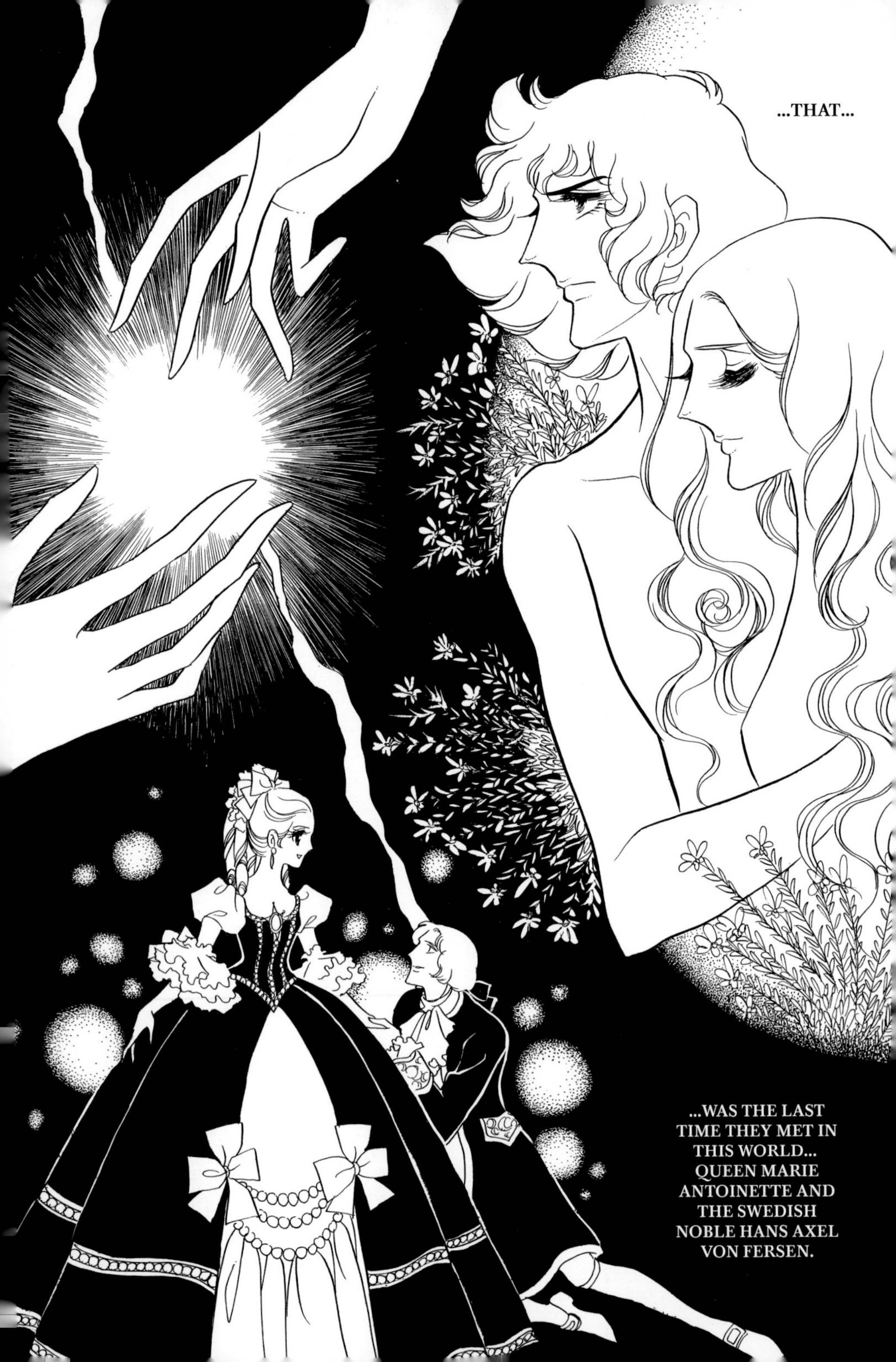
...THAT...
...WAS THE LAST TIME THEY MET IN THIS WORLD... QUEEN MARIE ANTOINETTE AND THE SWEDISH NOBLE HANS AXEL VON FERSEN.

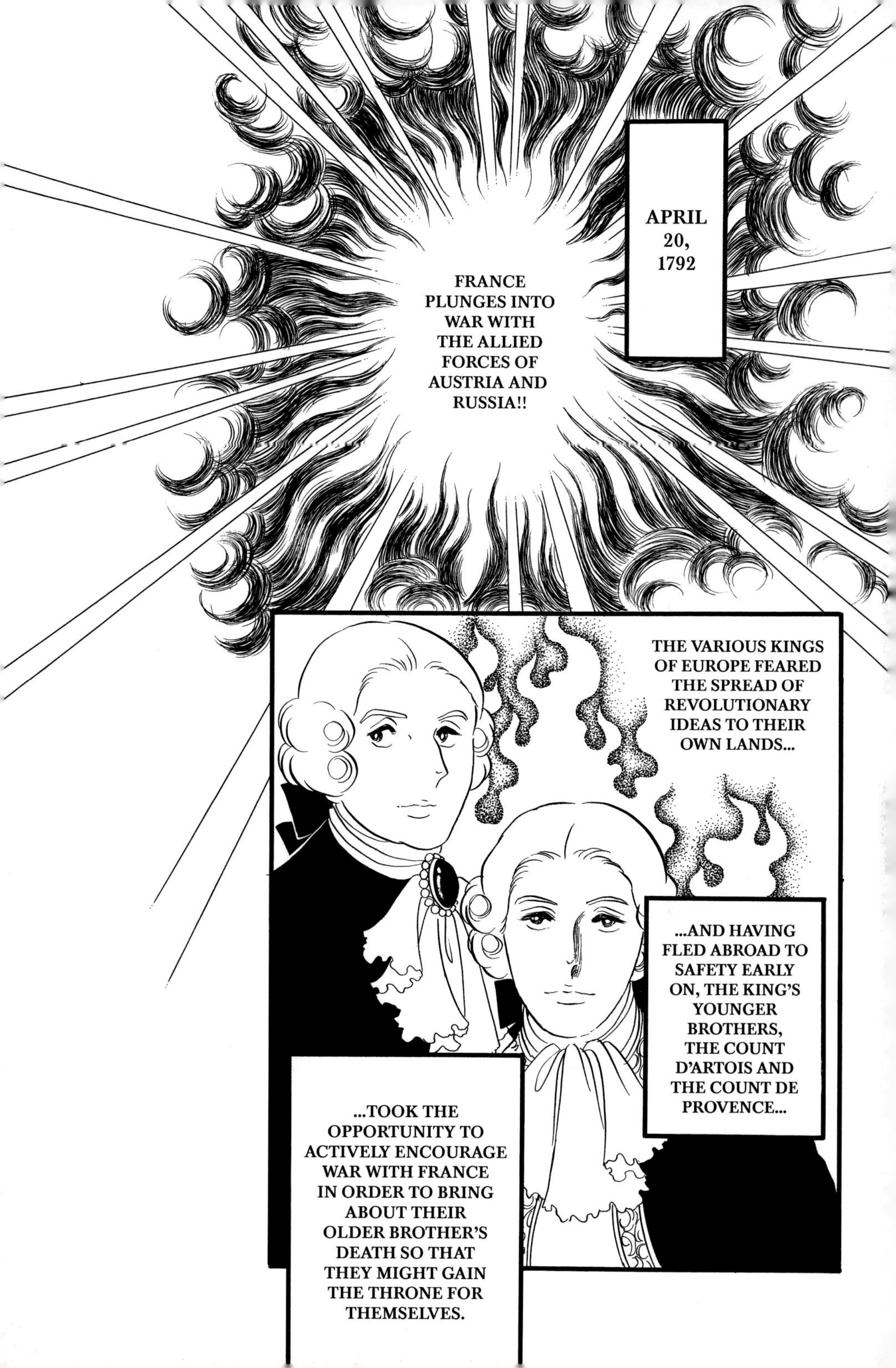
APRIL 20, 1792
FRANCE PLUNGES INTO WAR WITH THE ALLIED FORCES OF AUSTRIA AND RUSSIA!!
THE VARIOUS KINGS OF EUROPE FEARED THE SPREAD OF REVOLUTIONARY IDEAS TO THEIR OWN LANDS...
...AND HAVING FLED ABROAD TO SAFETY EARLY ON, THE KING'S YOUNGER BROTHERS, THE COUNT D'ARTOIS AND THE COUNT DE PROVENCE...
...TOOK THE OPPORTUNITY TO ACTIVELY ENCOURAGE WAR WITH FRANCE IN ORDER TO BRING ABOUT THEIR OLDER BROTHER'S DEATH SO THAT THEY MIGHT GAIN THE THRONE FOR THEMSELVES.

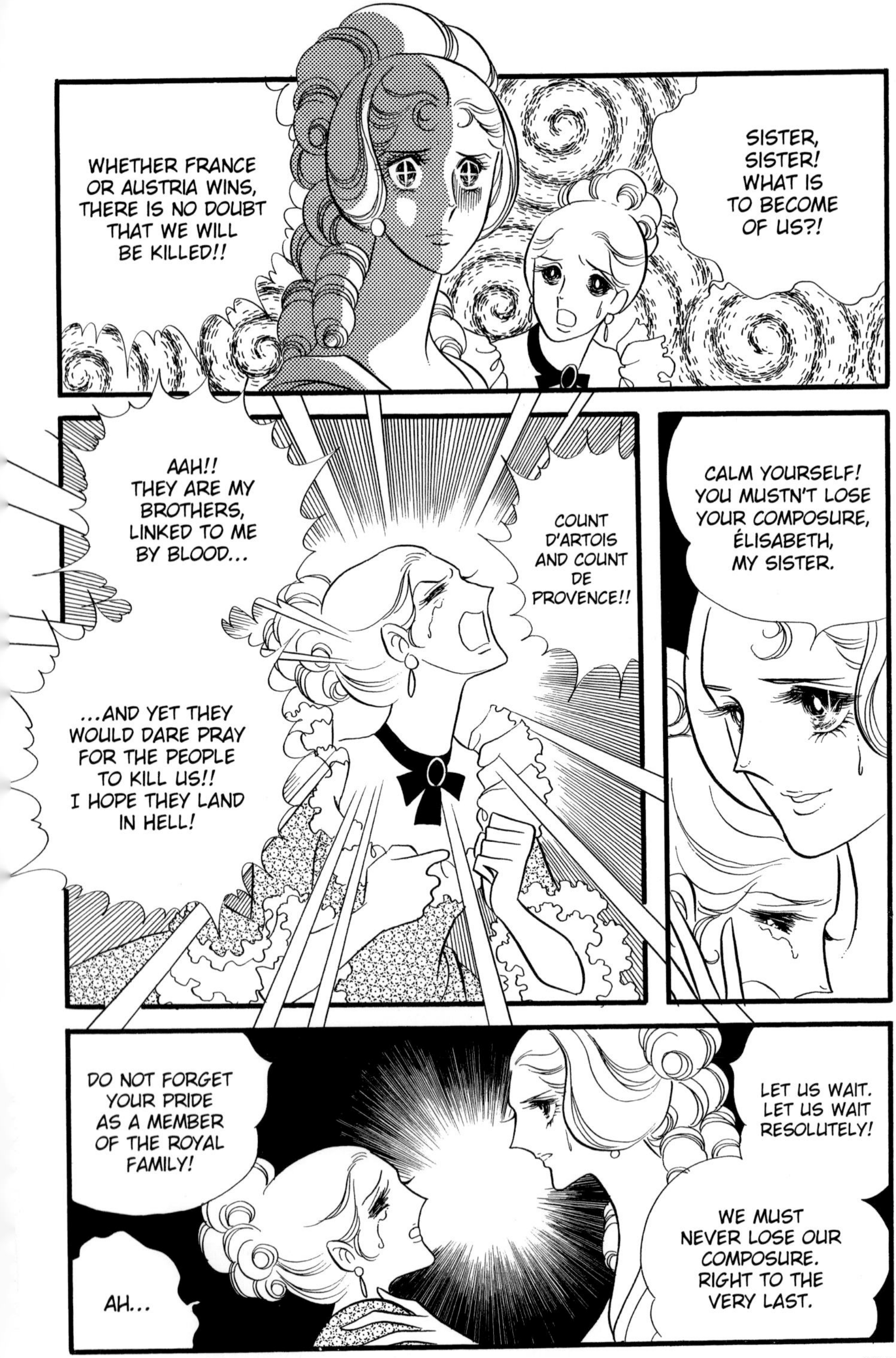
SISTER, SISTER! WHAT IS TO BECOME OF US?!
WHETHER FRANCE OR AUSTRIA WINS, THERE IS NO DOUBT THAT WE WILL BE KILLED!!
CALM YOURSELF! YOU MUSTN'T LOSE YOUR COMPOSURE, ÉLISABETH, MY SISTER.
COUNT D'ARTOIS AND COUNT DE PROVENCE!!
AAH!! THEY ARE MY BROTHERS, LINKED TO ME BY BLOOD...
...AND YET THEY WOULD DARE PRAY FOR THE PEOPLE TO KILL US!! I HOPE THEY LAND IN HELL!
LET US WAIT. LET US WAIT RESOLUTELY!
WE MUST NEVER LOSE OUR COMPOSURE. RIGHT TO THE VERY LAST.
DO NOT FORGET YOUR PRIDE AS A MEMBER OF THE ROYAL FAMILY!
AH...

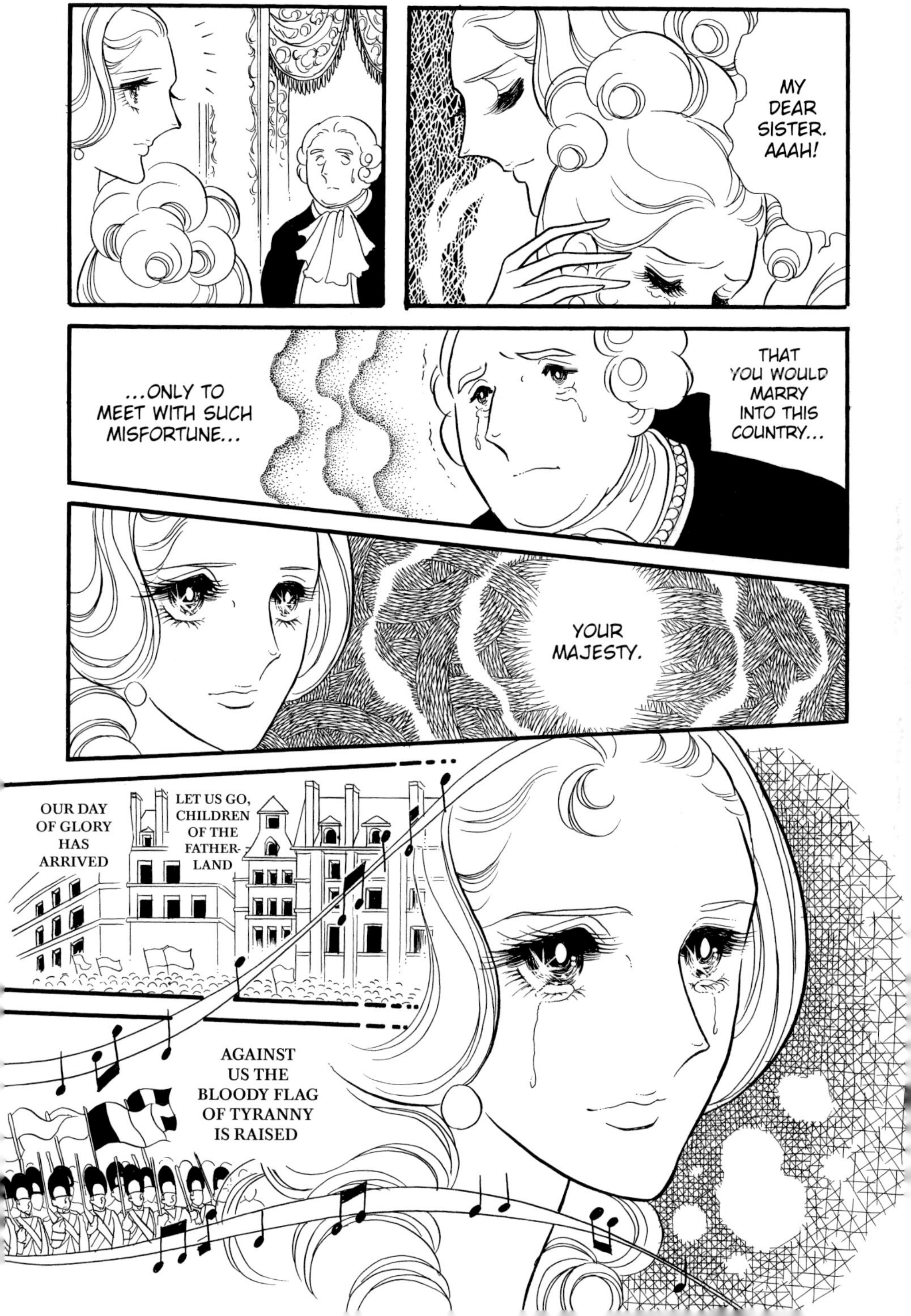
MY DEAR SISTER. AAAH!
THAT YOU WOULD MARRY INTO THIS COUNTRY...
...ONLY TO MEET WITH SUCH MISFORTUNE...
YOUR MAJESTY.
LET US GO, CHILDREN OF THE FATHER-LAND
OUR DAY OF GLORY HAS ARRIVED
AGAINST US THE BLOODY FLAG OF TYRANNY IS RAISED

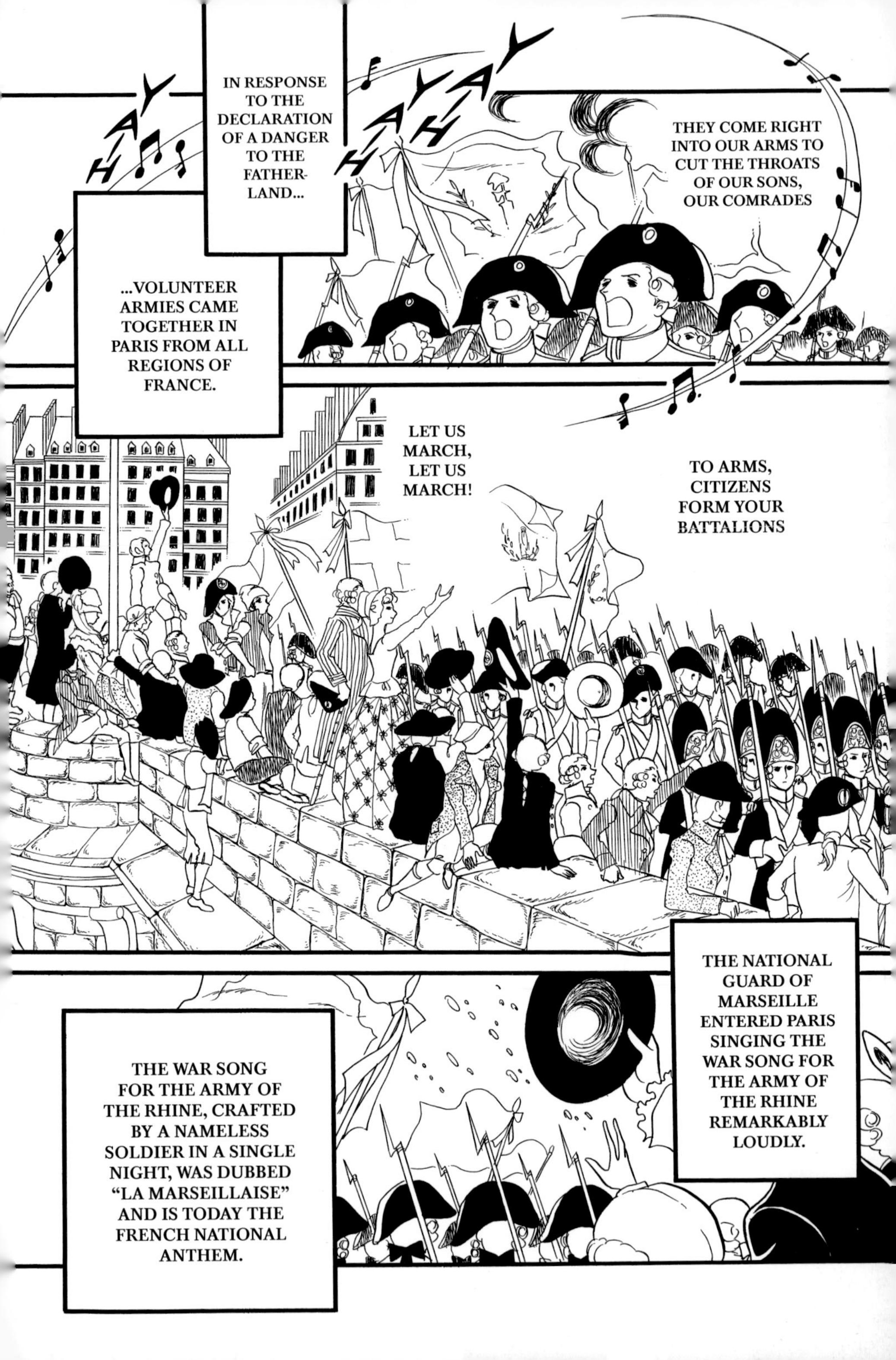

THEY COME RIGHT INTO OUR ARMS TO CUT THE THROATS OF OUR SONS, OUR COMRADES
IN RESPONSE TO THE DECLARATION OF A DANGER TO THE FATHER-LAND...
...VOLUNTEER ARMIES CAME TOGETHER IN PARIS FROM ALL REGIONS OF FRANCE.
TO ARMS, CITIZENS FORM YOUR BATTALIONS
LET US MARCH, LET US MARCH!
THE NATIONAL GUARD OF MARSEILLE ENTERED PARIS SINGING THE WAR SONG FOR THE ARMY OF THE RHINE REMARKABLY LOUDLY.
THE WAR SONG FOR THE ARMY OF THE RHINE, CRAFTED BY A NAMELESS SOLDIER IN A SINGLE NIGHT, WAS DUBBED "LA MARSEILLAISE" AND IS TODAY THE FRENCH NATIONAL ANTHEM.

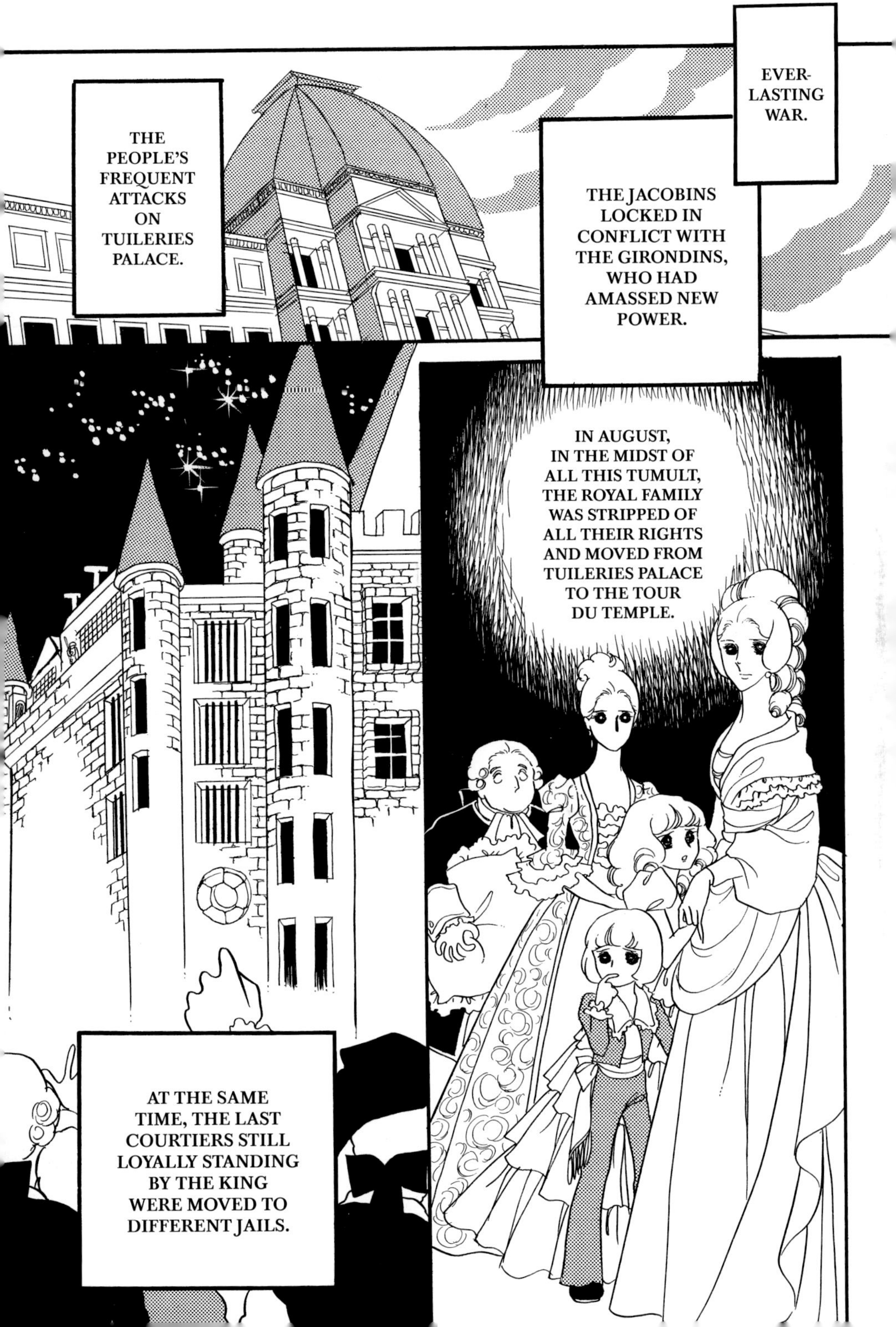
EVER-LASTING WAR.
THE JACOBINS LOCKED IN CONFLICT WITH THE GIRONDINS, WHO HAD AMASSED NEW POWER.
THE PEOPLE'S FREQUENT ATTACKS ON TUILERIES PALACE.
IN AUGUST, IN THE MIDST OF ALL THIS TUMULT, THE ROYAL FAMILY WAS STRIPPED OF ALL THEIR RIGHTS AND MOVED FROM TUILERIES PALACE TO THE TOUR DU TEMPLE.
AT THE SAME TIME, THE LAST COURTIERS STILL LOYALLY STANDING BY THE KING WERE MOVED TO DIFFERENT JAILS.

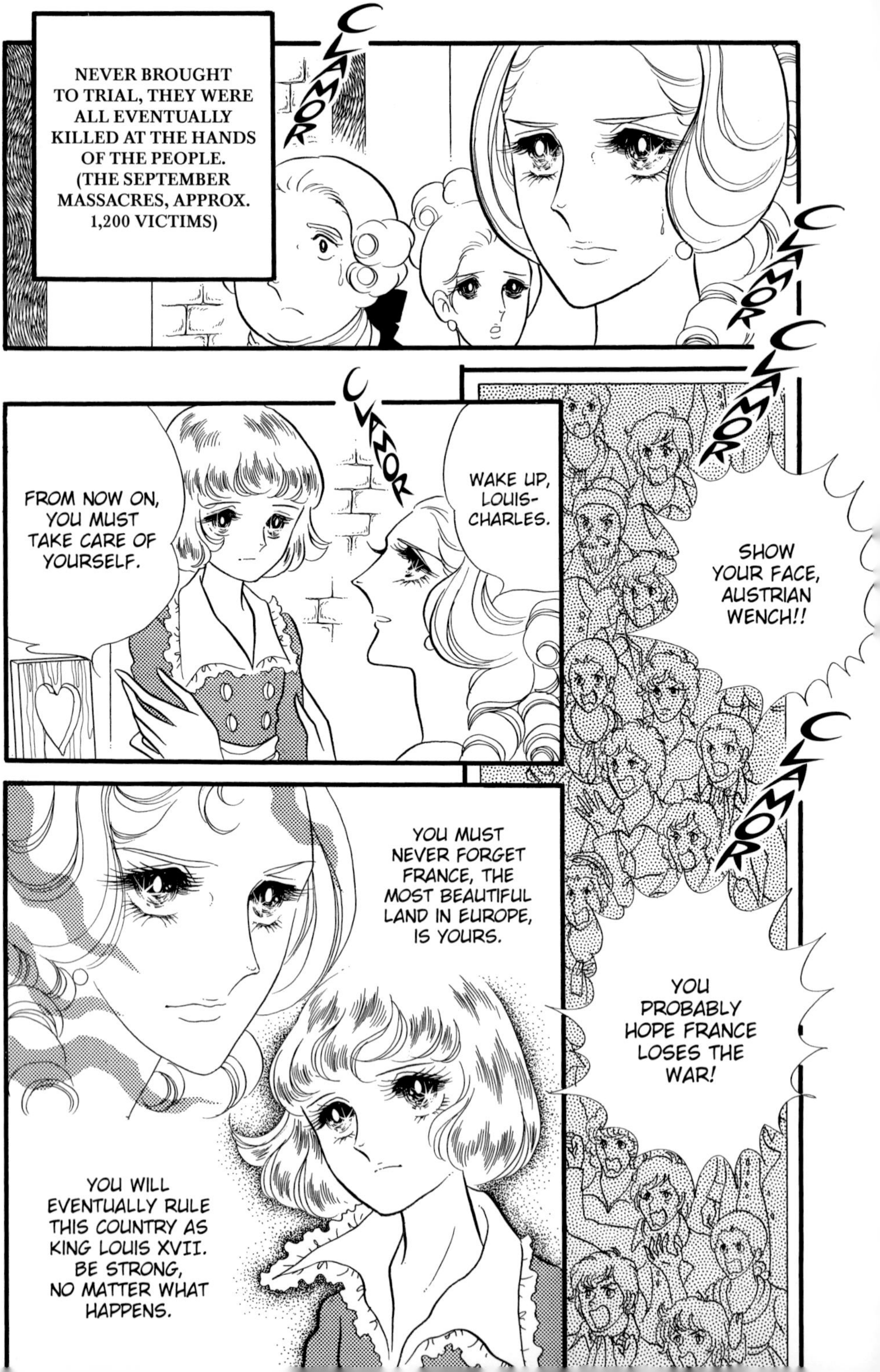
NEVER BROUGHT TO TRIAL, THEY WERE ALL EVENTUALLY KILLED AT THE HANDS OF THE PEOPLE. (THE SEPTEMBER MASSACRES, APPROX. 1,200 VICTIMS)
CLAMOR
CLAMOR
CLAMOR
SHOW YOUR FACE, AUSTRIAN WENCH!!
CLAMOR
YOU PROBABLY HOPE FRANCE LOSES THE WAR!
WAKE UP, LOUIS-CHARLES.
CLAMOR
FROM NOW ON, YOU MUST TAKE CARE OF YOURSELF.
YOU MUST NEVER FORGET FRANCE, THE MOST BEAUTIFUL LAND IN EUROPE, IS YOURS.
YOU WILL EVENTUALLY RULE THIS COUNTRY AS KING LOUIS XVII. BE STRONG, NO MATTER WHAT HAPPENS.

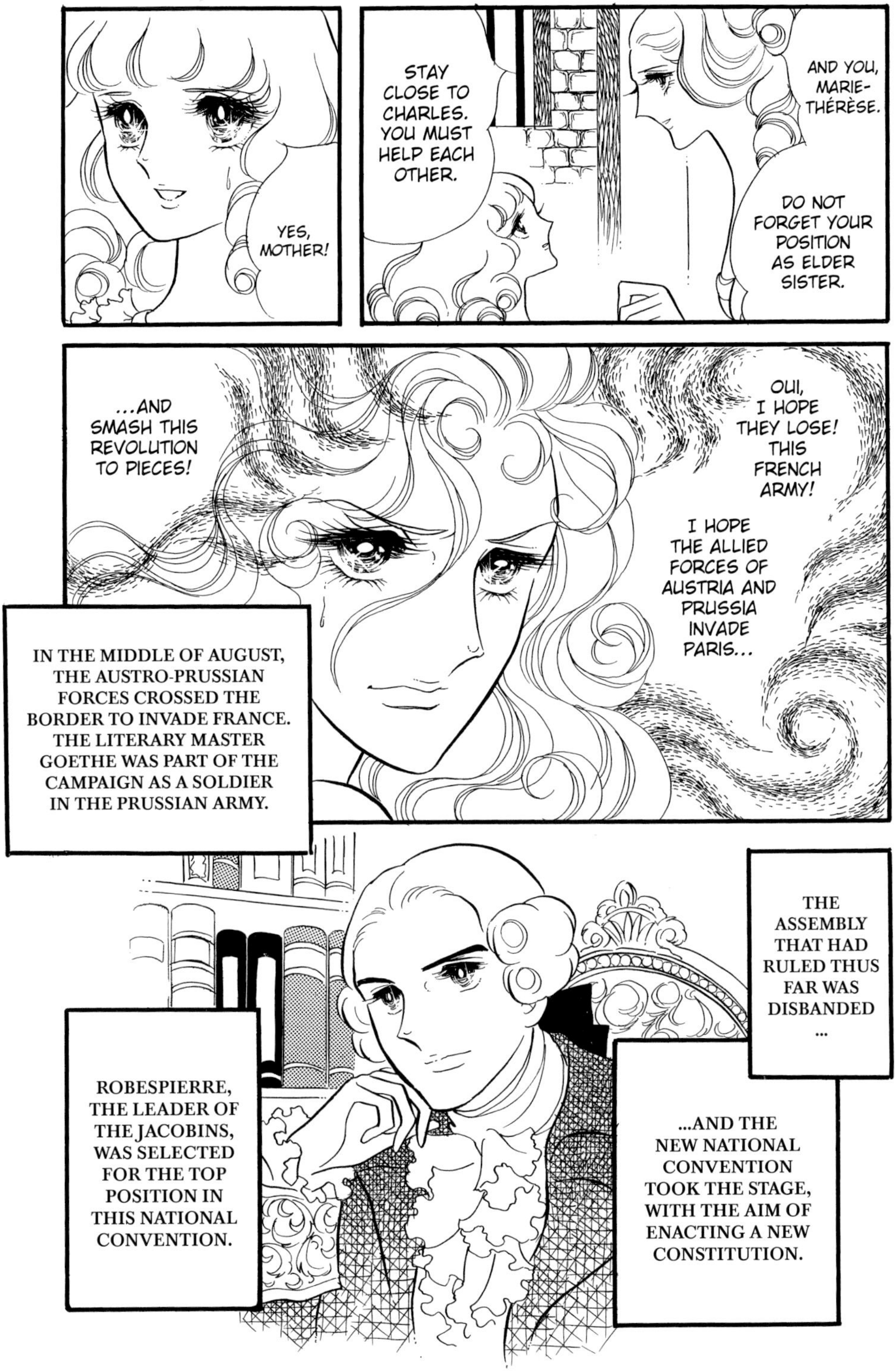
AND YOU, MARIE-THÉRÈSE.
DO NOT FORGET YOUR POSITION AS ELDER SISTER.
STAY CLOSE TO CHARLES. YOU MUST HELP EACH OTHER.
YES, MOTHER!
OUI, I HOPE THEY LOSE! THIS FRENCH ARMY!
I HOPE THE ALLIED FORCES OF AUSTRIA AND PRUSSIA INVADE PARIS...
...AND SMASH THIS REVOLUTION TO PIECES!
IN THE MIDDLE OF AUGUST, THE AUSTRO-PRUSSIAN FORCES CROSSED THE BORDER TO INVADE FRANCE. THE LITERARY MASTER GOETHE WAS PART OF THE CAMPAIGN AS A SOLDIER IN THE PRUSSIAN ARMY.
THE ASSEMBLY THAT HAD RULED THUS FAR WAS DISBANDED ...
...AND THE NEW NATIONAL CONVENTION TOOK THE STAGE, WITH THE AIM OF ENACTING A NEW CONSTITUTION.
ROBESPIERRE, THE LEADER OF THE JACOBINS, WAS SELECTED FOR THE TOP POSITION IN THIS NATIONAL CONVENTION.

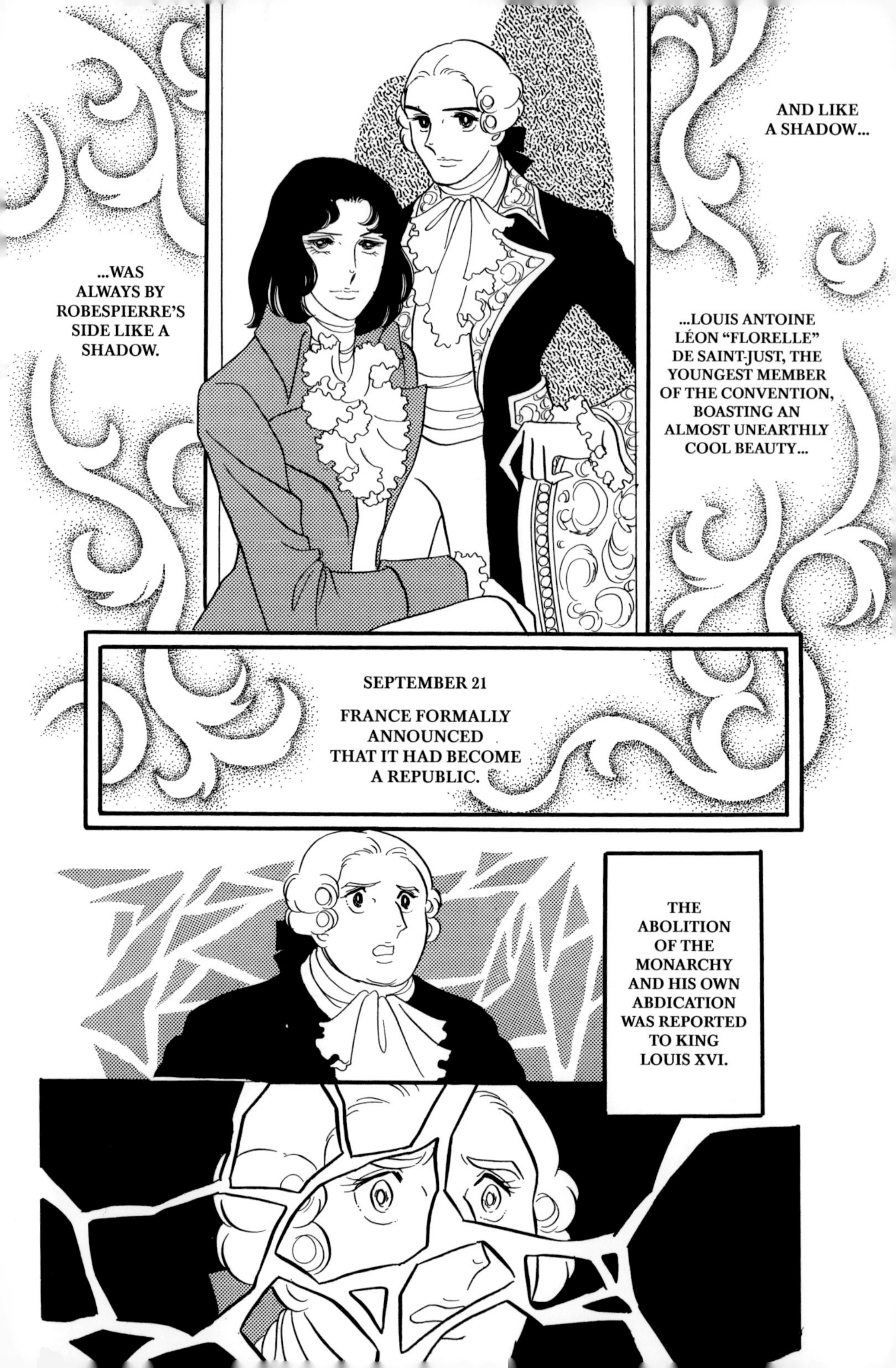
AND LIKE A SHADOW...
...LOUIS ANTOINE LÉON "FLORELLE" DE SAINT-JUST, THE YOUNGEST MEMBER OF THE CONVENTION, BOASTING AN ALMOST UNEARTHLY COOL BEAUTY...
...WAS ALWAYS BY ROBESPIERRE'S SIDE LIKE A SHADOW.
SEPTEMBER 21
FRANCE FORMALLY ANNOUNCED THAT IT HAD BECOME A REPUBLIC.
THE ABOLITION OF THE MONARCHY AND HIS OWN ABDICATION WAS REPORTED TO KING LOUIS XVI.

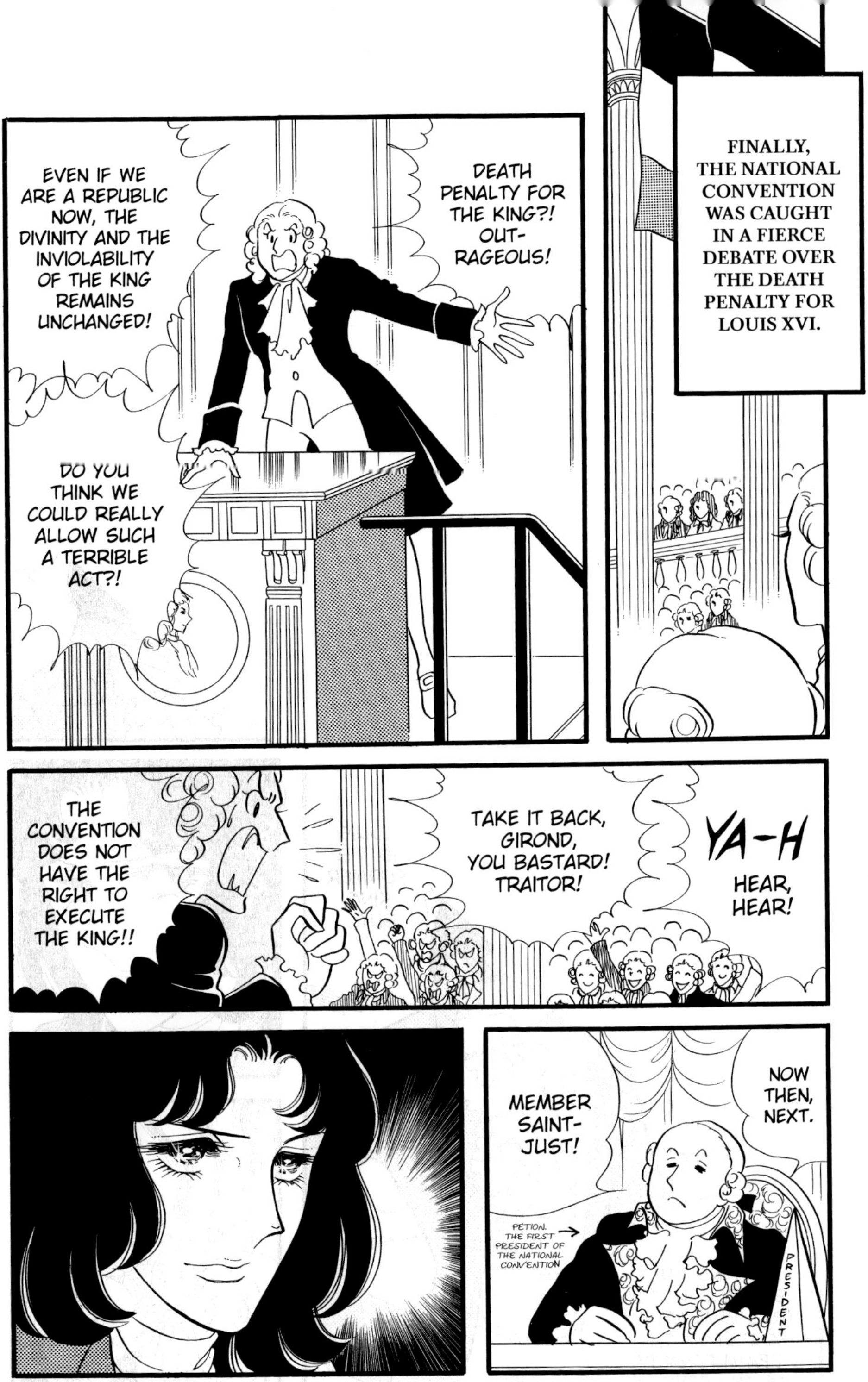
FINALLY, THE NATIONAL CONVENTION WAS CAUGHT IN A FIERCE DEBATE OVER THE DEATH PENALTY FOR LOUIS XVI.
DEATH PENALTY FOR THE KING?! OUT-RAGEOUS!
EVEN IF WE ARE A REPUBLIC NOW, THE DIVINITY AND THE INVIOLABILITY OF THE KING REMAINS UNCHANGED!
DO YOU THINK WE COULD REALLY ALLOW SUCH A TERRIBLE ACT?!
YA-H
HEAR, HEAR!
TAKE IT BACK, GIROND, YOU BASTARD! TRAITOR!
THE CONVENTION DOES NOT HAVE THE RIGHT TO EXECUTE THE KING!!
NOW THEN, NEXT.
MEMBER SAINT-JUST!
PÉTION. THE FIRST PRESIDENT OF THE NATIONAL CONVENTION
PRESIDENT

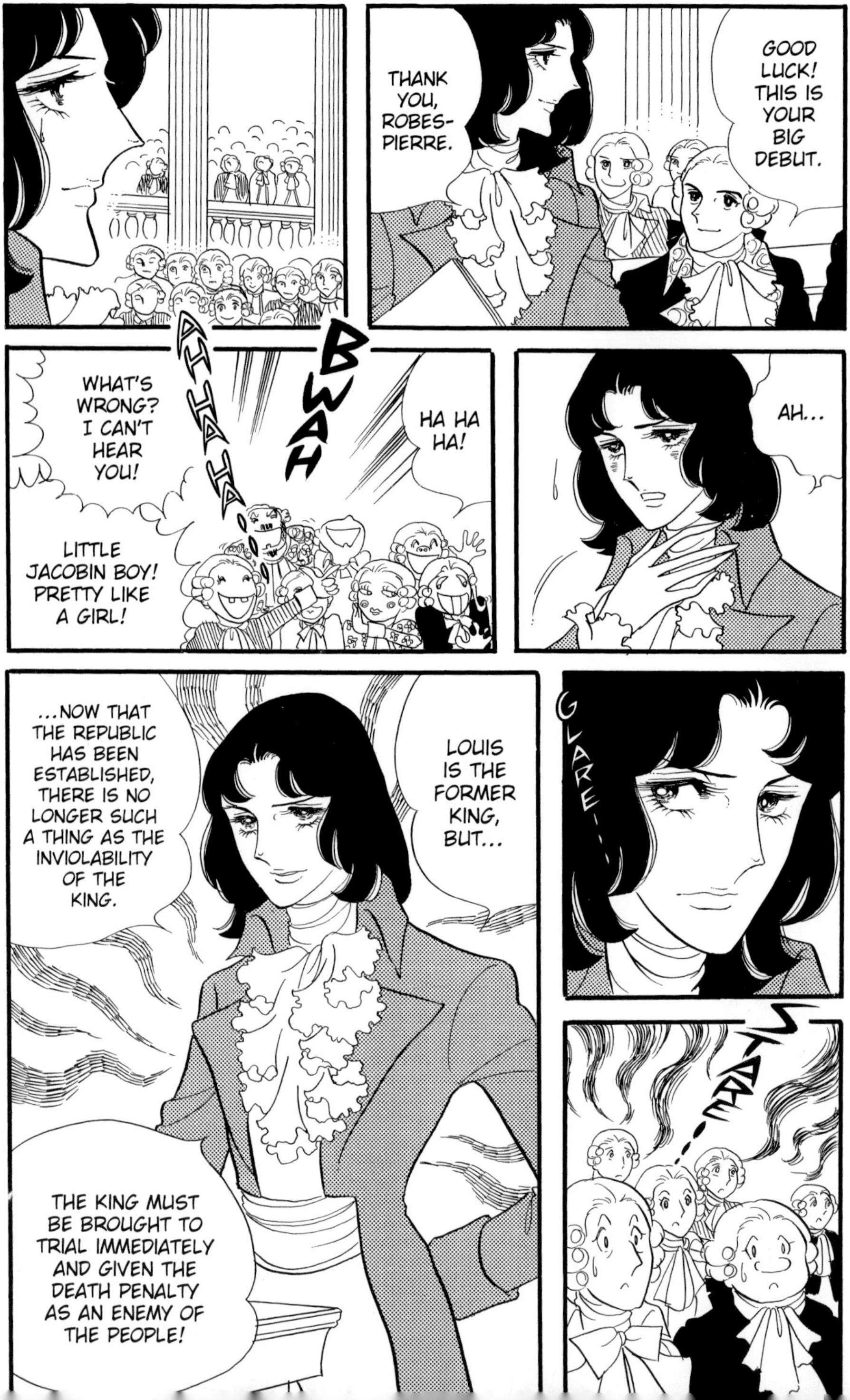
GOOD LUCK! THIS IS YOUR BIG DEBUT.
THANK YOU, ROBES-PIERRE.
AH...
HA HA HA!
BWAH
WHAT'S WRONG? I CAN'T HEAR YOU!
AHAHAHA!!
LITTLE JACOBIN BOY! PRETTY LIKE A GIRL!
GLARE...
STARE...
LOUIS IS THE FORMER KING, BUT...
...NOW THAT THE REPUBLIC HAS BEEN ESTABLISHED, THERE IS NO LONGER SUCH A THING AS THE INVIOLABILITY OF THE KING.
THE KING MUST BE BROUGHT TO TRIAL IMMEDIATELY AND GIVEN THE DEATH PENALTY AS AN ENEMY OF THE PEOPLE!

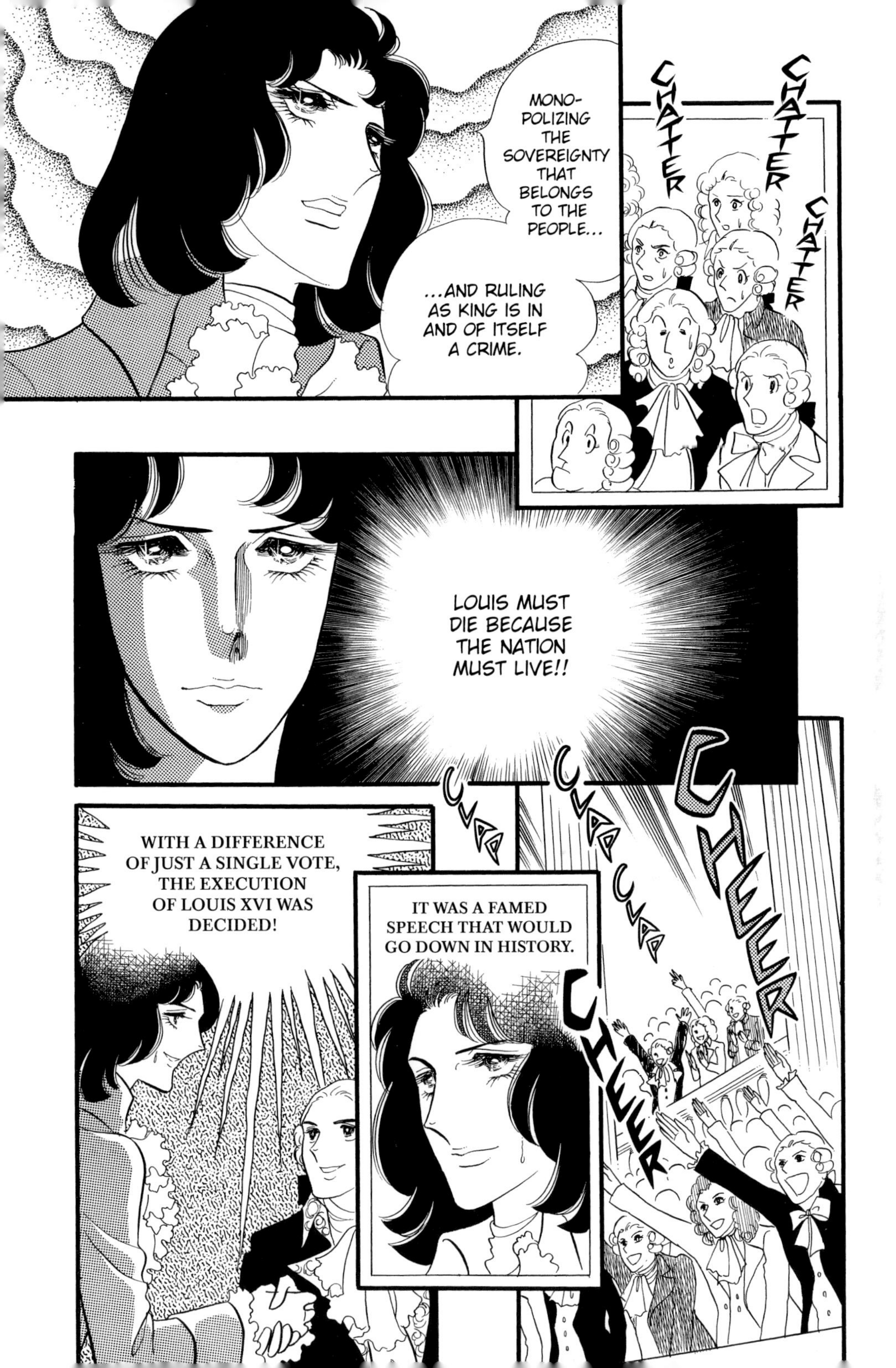
CHATTER
CHATTER
CHATTER
MONO-POLIZING THE SOVEREIGNTY THAT BELONGS TO THE PEOPLE...
...AND RULING AS KING IS IN AND OF ITSELF A CRIME.
LOUIS MUST DIE BECAUSE THE NATION MUST LIVE!!
CHEER
CLAP
CLAP CLAP
CLAP
CHEER
IT WAS A FAMED SPEECH THAT WOULD GO DOWN IN HISTORY.
WITH A DIFFERENCE OF JUST A SINGLE VOTE, THE EXECUTION OF LOUIS XVI WAS DECIDED!

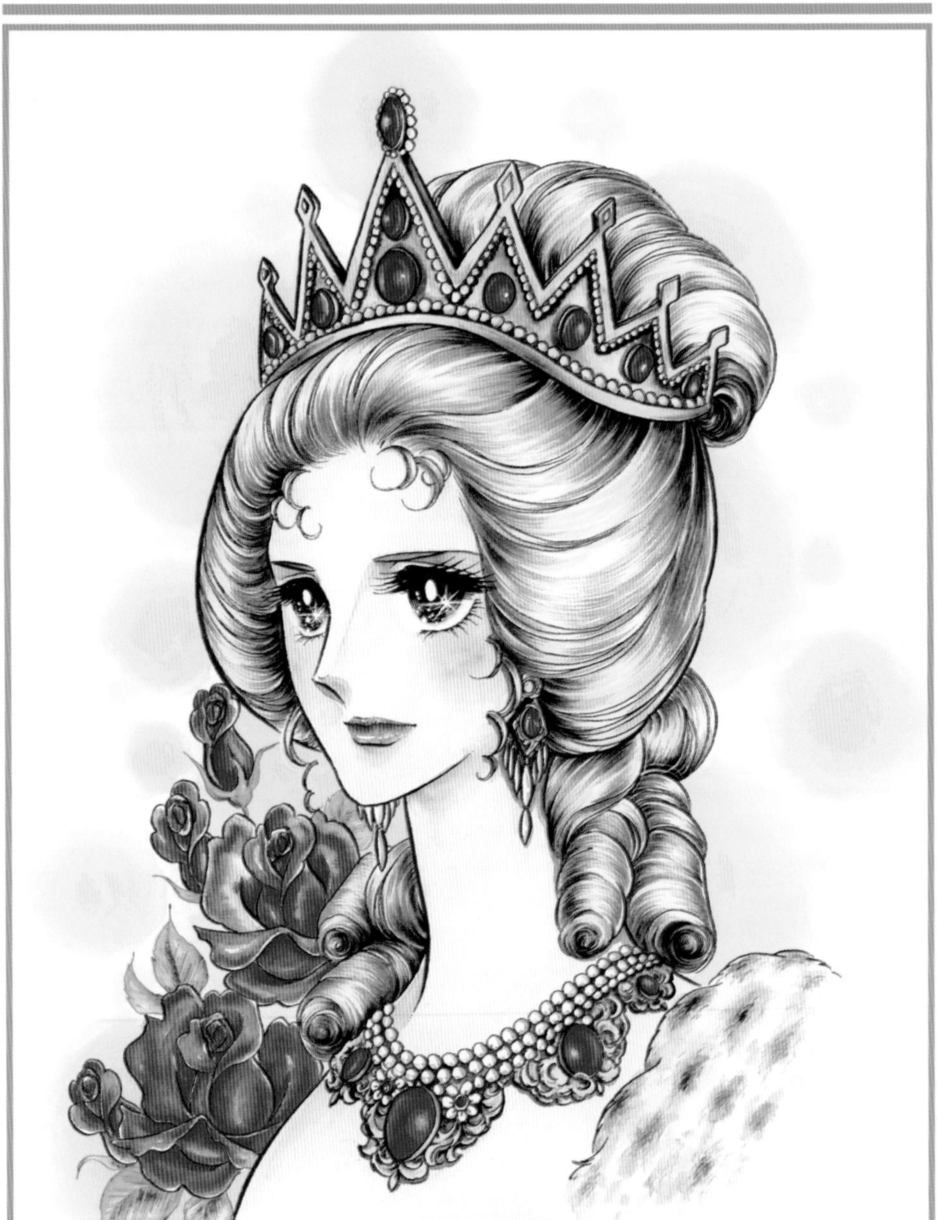

1973 WEEKLY MARGARET MAGAZINE ISSUE 49 COVER PAGE
(SPECIAL COLORIZED VERSION)

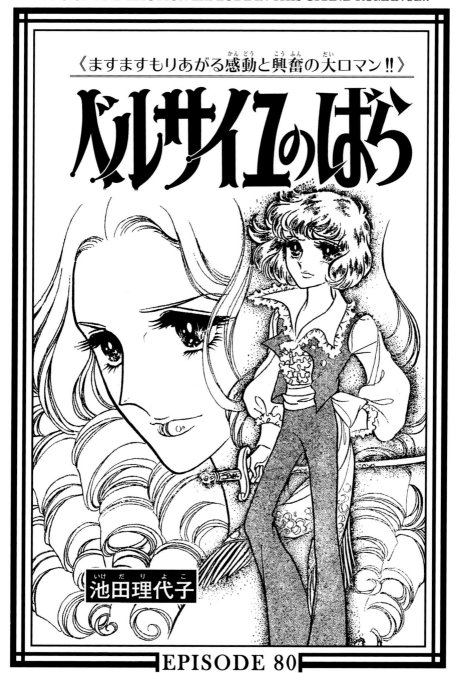

TENSION AND EMOTION EXPLODE IN THIS GRAND ROMANCE!!

《ますますもりあがる感動と興奮の大ロマン!!》

バルサイユのばら

池田理代子

EPISODE 80

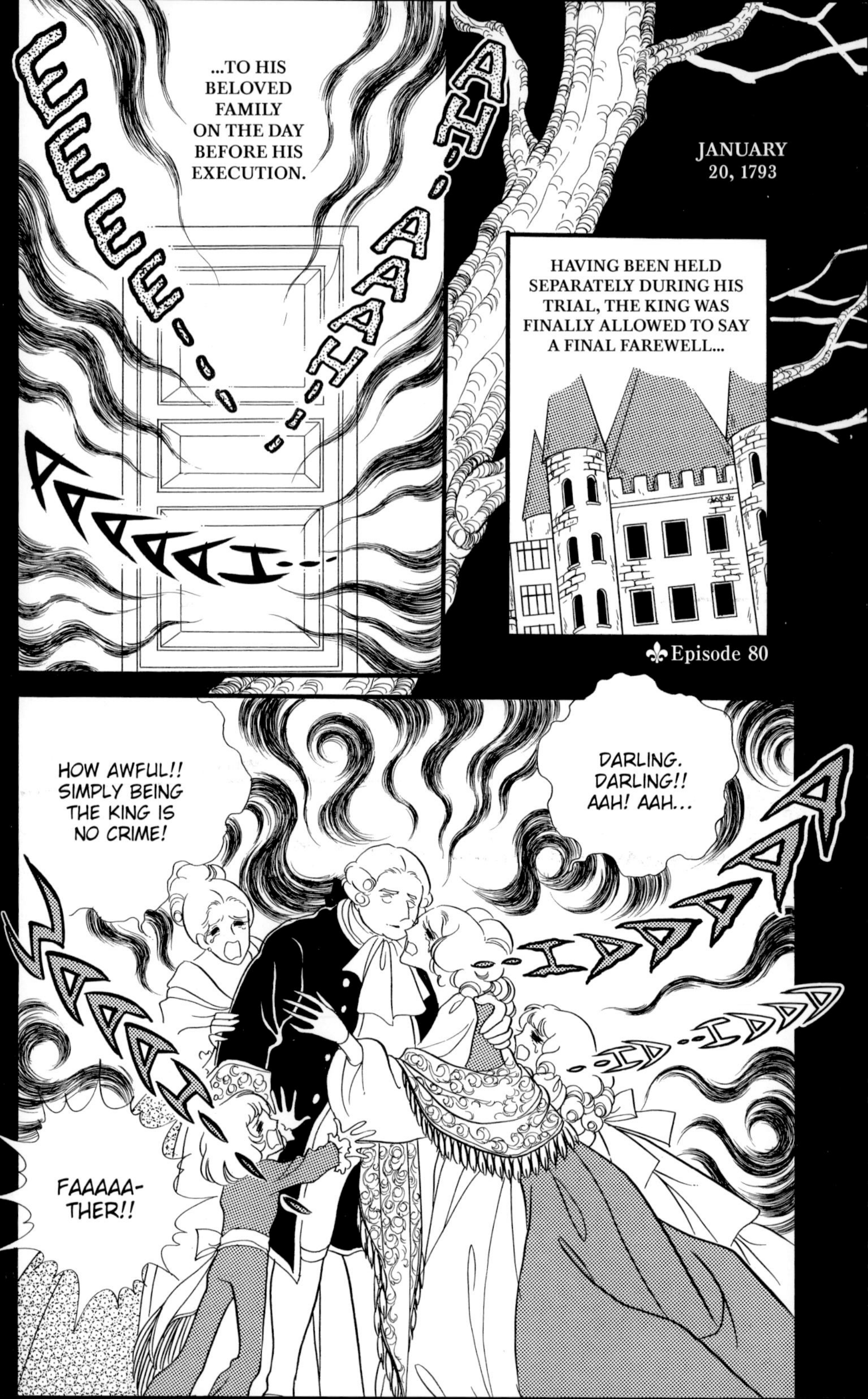
JANUARY 20, 1793
HAVING BEEN HELD SEPARATELY DURING HIS TRIAL, THE KING WAS FINALLY ALLOWED TO SAY A FINAL FAREWELL...
Episode 80
...TO HIS BELOVED FAMILY ON THE DAY BEFORE HIS EXECUTION.
DARLING. DARLING!! AAH! AAH...
HOW AWFUL!! SIMPLY BEING THE KING IS NO CRIME!
FAAAAA-THER!!

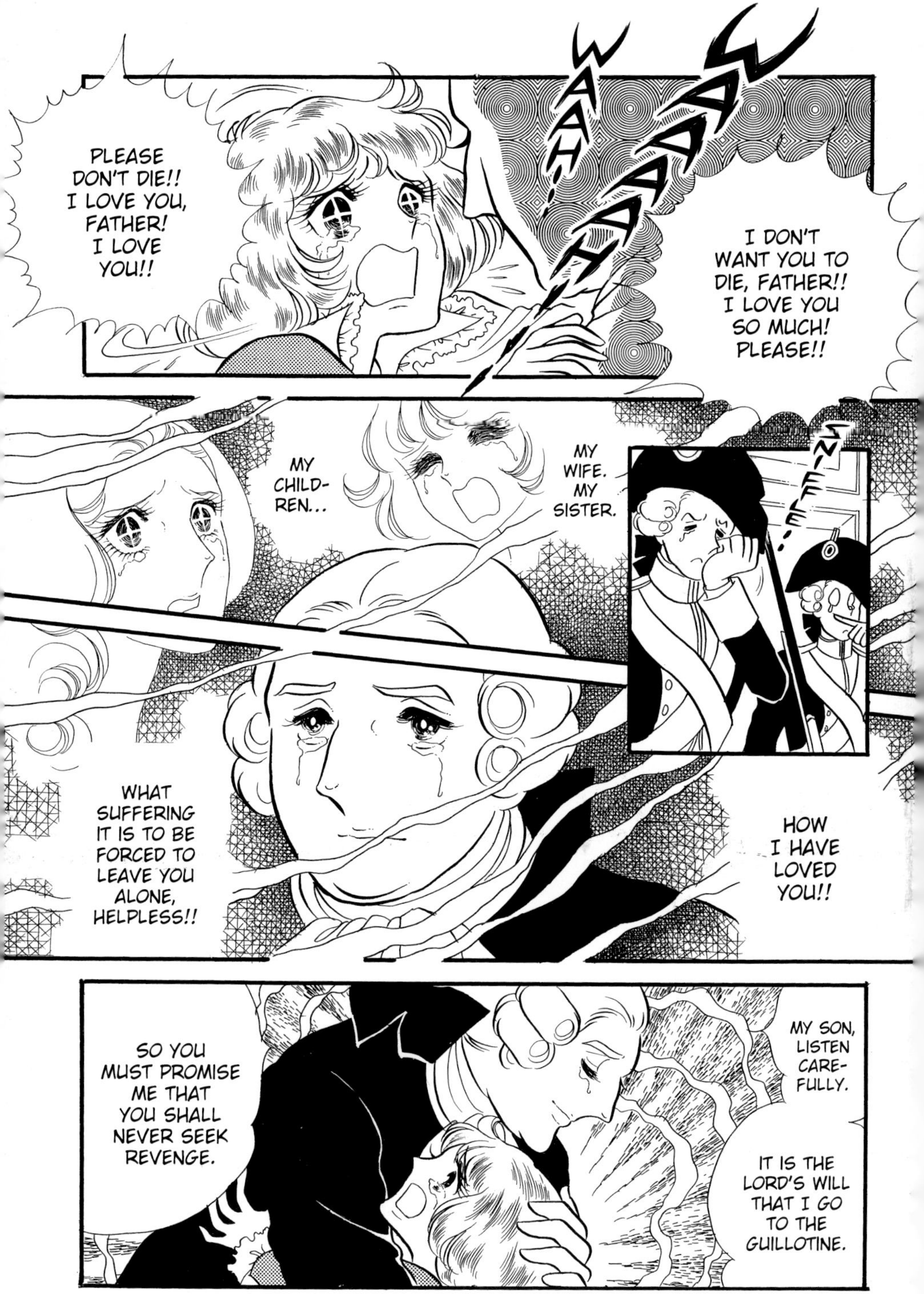
I DON'T WANT YOU TO DIE, FATHER!! I LOVE YOU SO MUCH! PLEASE!!
WAAAAH!!
WAAH!!
PLEASE DON'T DIE!! I LOVE YOU, FATHER! I LOVE YOU!!
SNIFFLE!!
MY WIFE. MY SISTER.
MY CHILDREN...
HOW I HAVE LOVED YOU!!
WHAT SUFFERING IT IS TO BE FORCED TO LEAVE YOU ALONE, HELPLESS!!
MY SON, LISTEN CAREFULLY.
IT IS THE LORD'S WILL THAT I GO TO THE GUILLOTINE.
SO YOU MUST PROMISE ME THAT YOU SHALL NEVER SEEK REVENGE.

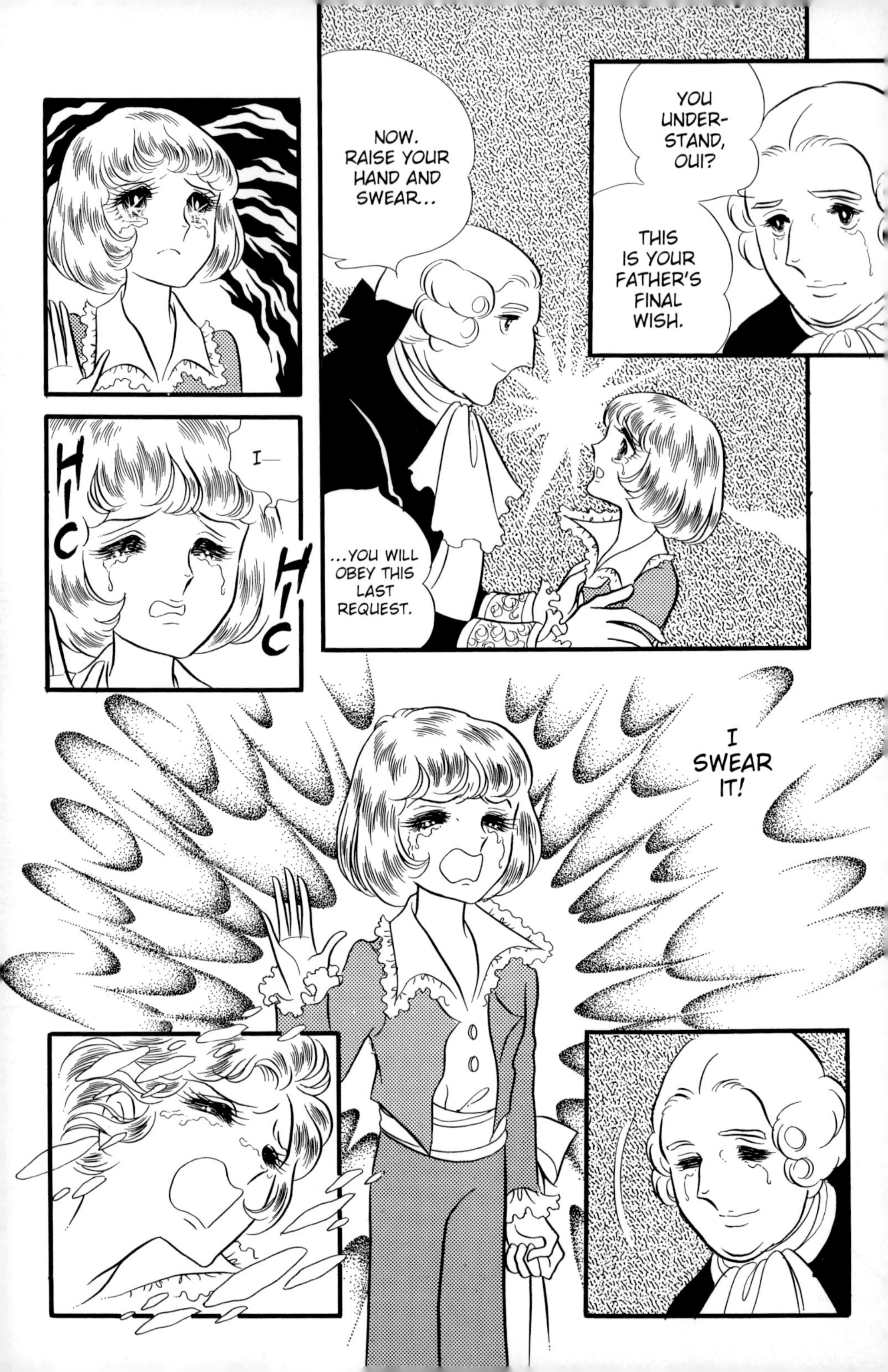
YOU UNDER-STAND, OUI?
THIS IS YOUR FATHER'S FINAL WISH.
NOW. RAISE YOUR HAND AND SWEAR...
...YOU WILL OBEY THIS LAST REQUEST.
I—
HIC
HIC
I SWEAR IT!

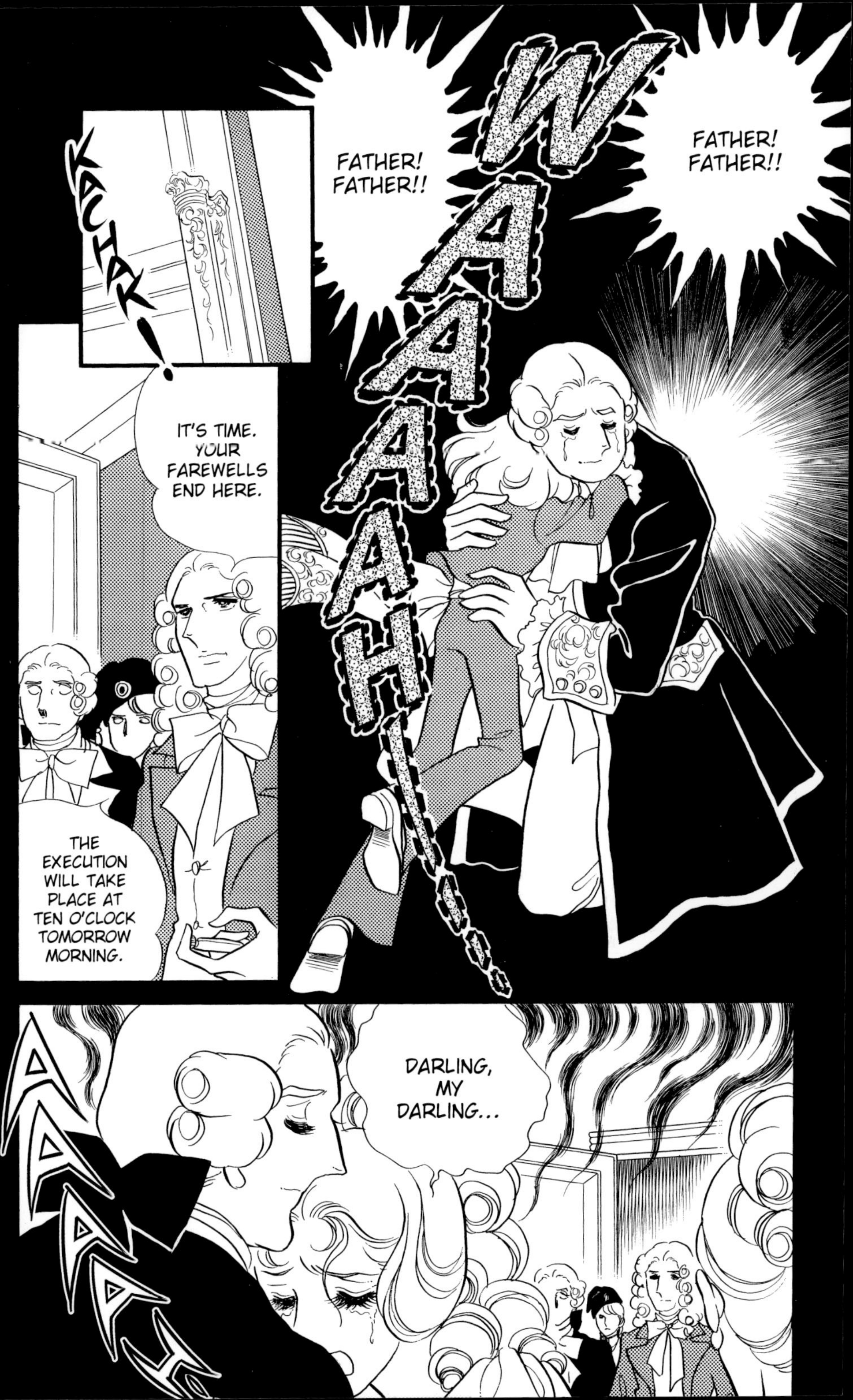
FATHER! FATHER!!
WAAAAH!!
FATHER! FATHER!!
KACHAK!
IT'S TIME. YOUR FAREWELLS END HERE.
THE EXECUTION WILL TAKE PLACE AT TEN O'CLOCK TOMORROW MORNING.
DARLING, MY DARLING...
AAAAAH

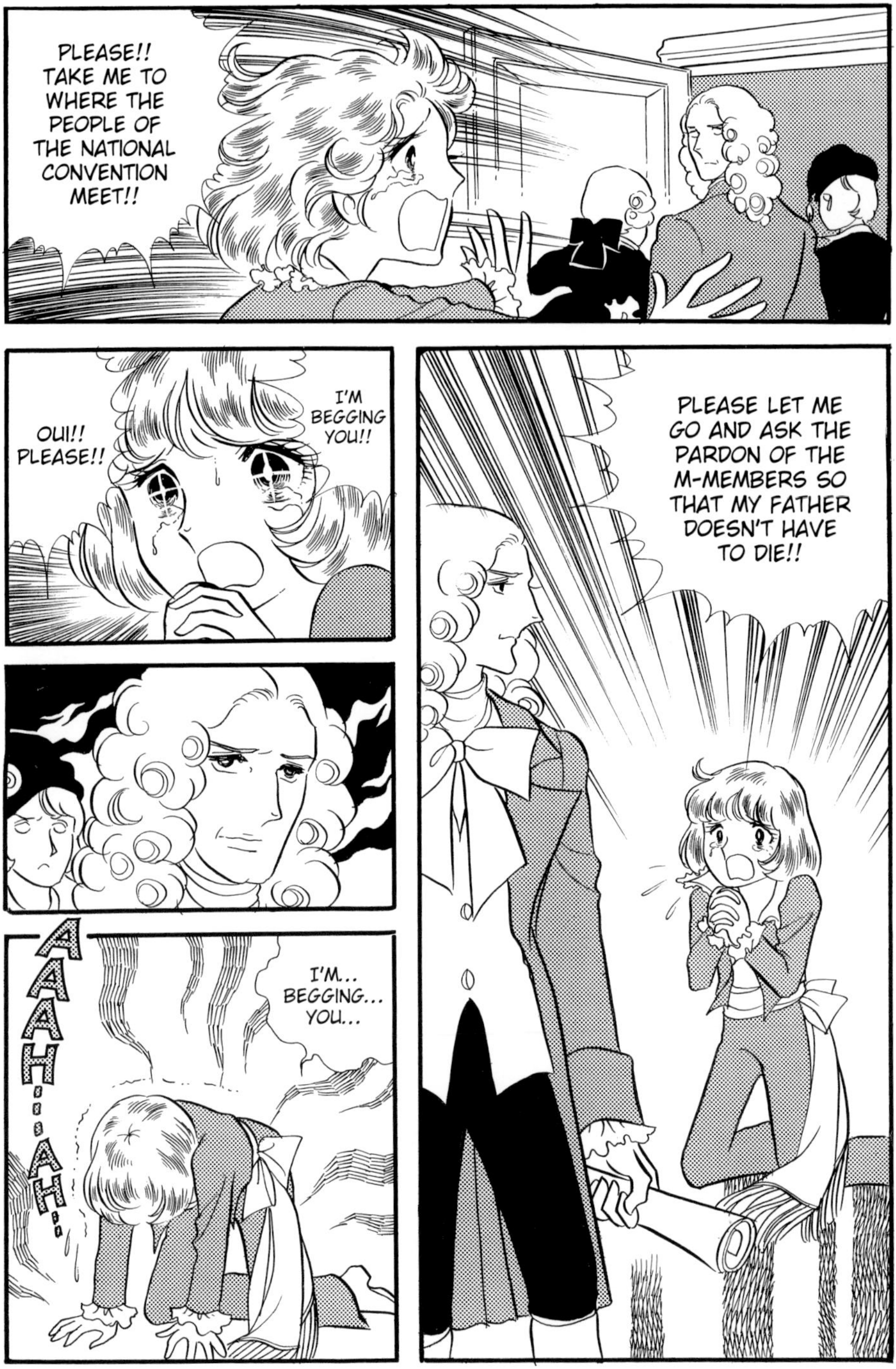
PLEASE!! TAKE ME TO WHERE THE PEOPLE OF THE NATIONAL CONVENTION MEET!!
PLEASE LET ME GO AND ASK THE PARDON OF THE M-MEMBERS SO THAT MY FATHER DOESN'T HAVE TO DIE!!
I'M BEGGING YOU!!
OUI!! PLEASE!!
I'M... BEGGING... YOU...
AAAAH...AH...

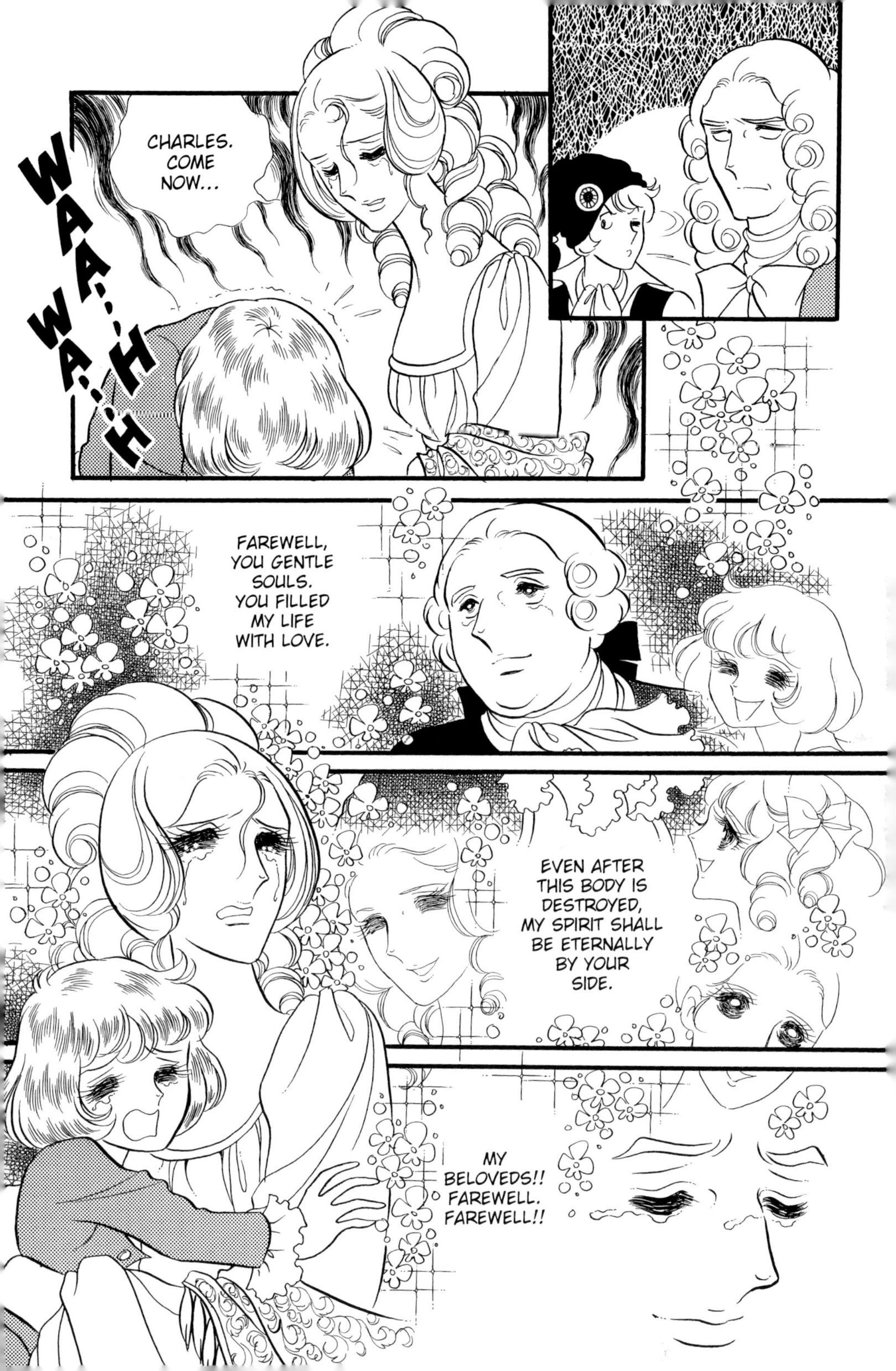
CHARLES. COME NOW...
WAA...H
WA...H
FAREWELL, YOU GENTLE SOULS. YOU FILLED MY LIFE WITH LOVE.
EVEN AFTER THIS BODY IS DESTROYED, MY SPIRIT SHALL BE ETERNALLY BY YOUR SIDE.
MY BELOVEDS!! FAREWELL. FAREWELL!!

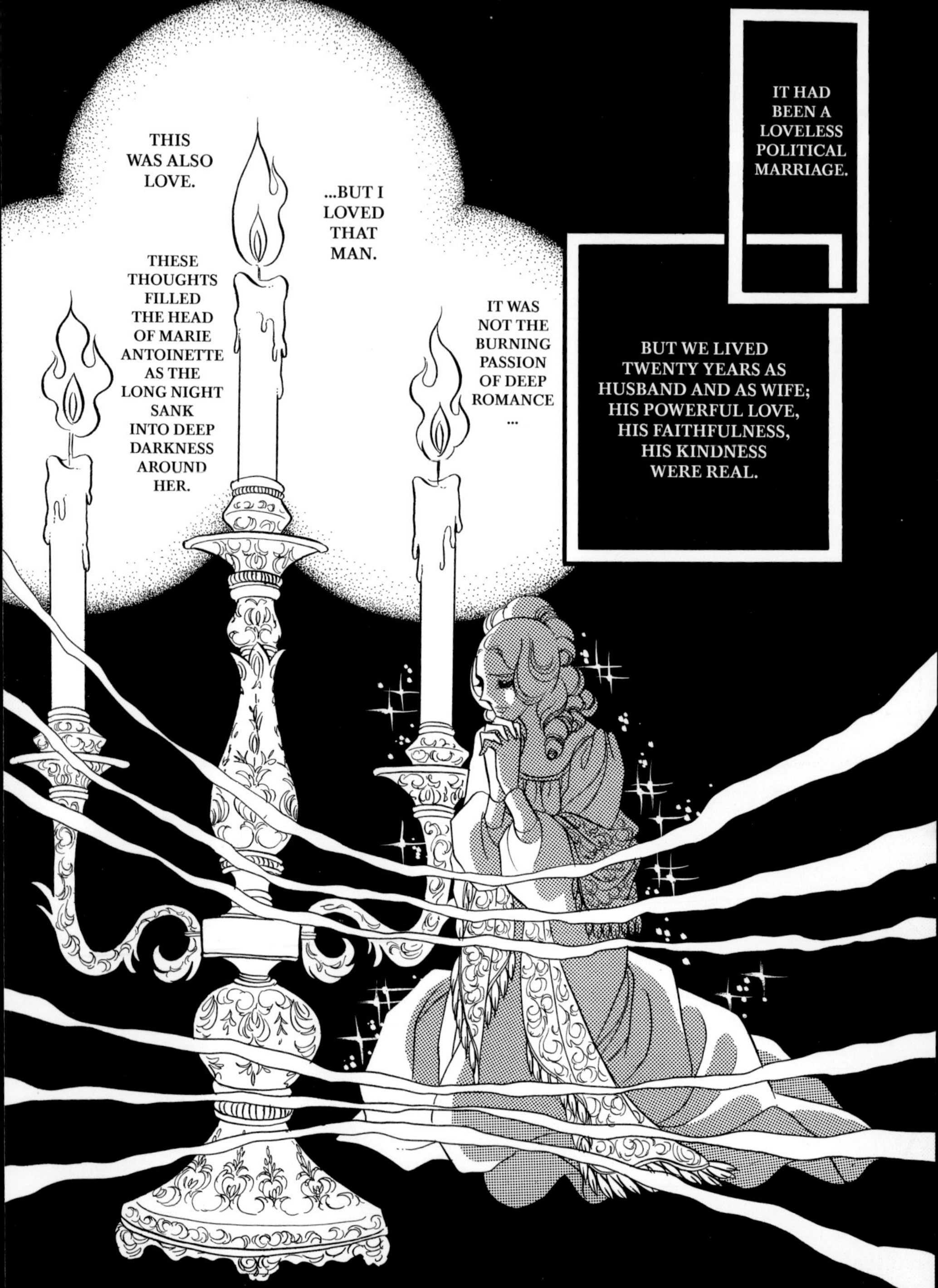
IT HAD BEEN A LOVELESS POLITICAL MARRIAGE.
BUT WE LIVED TWENTY YEARS AS HUSBAND AND AS WIFE; HIS POWERFUL LOVE, HIS FAITHFULNESS, HIS KINDNESS WERE REAL.
IT WAS NOT THE BURNING PASSION OF DEEP ROMANCE ...
...BUT I LOVED THAT MAN.
THIS WAS ALSO LOVE.
THESE THOUGHTS FILLED THE HEAD OF MARIE ANTOINETTE AS THE LONG NIGHT SANK INTO DEEP DARKNESS AROUND HER.

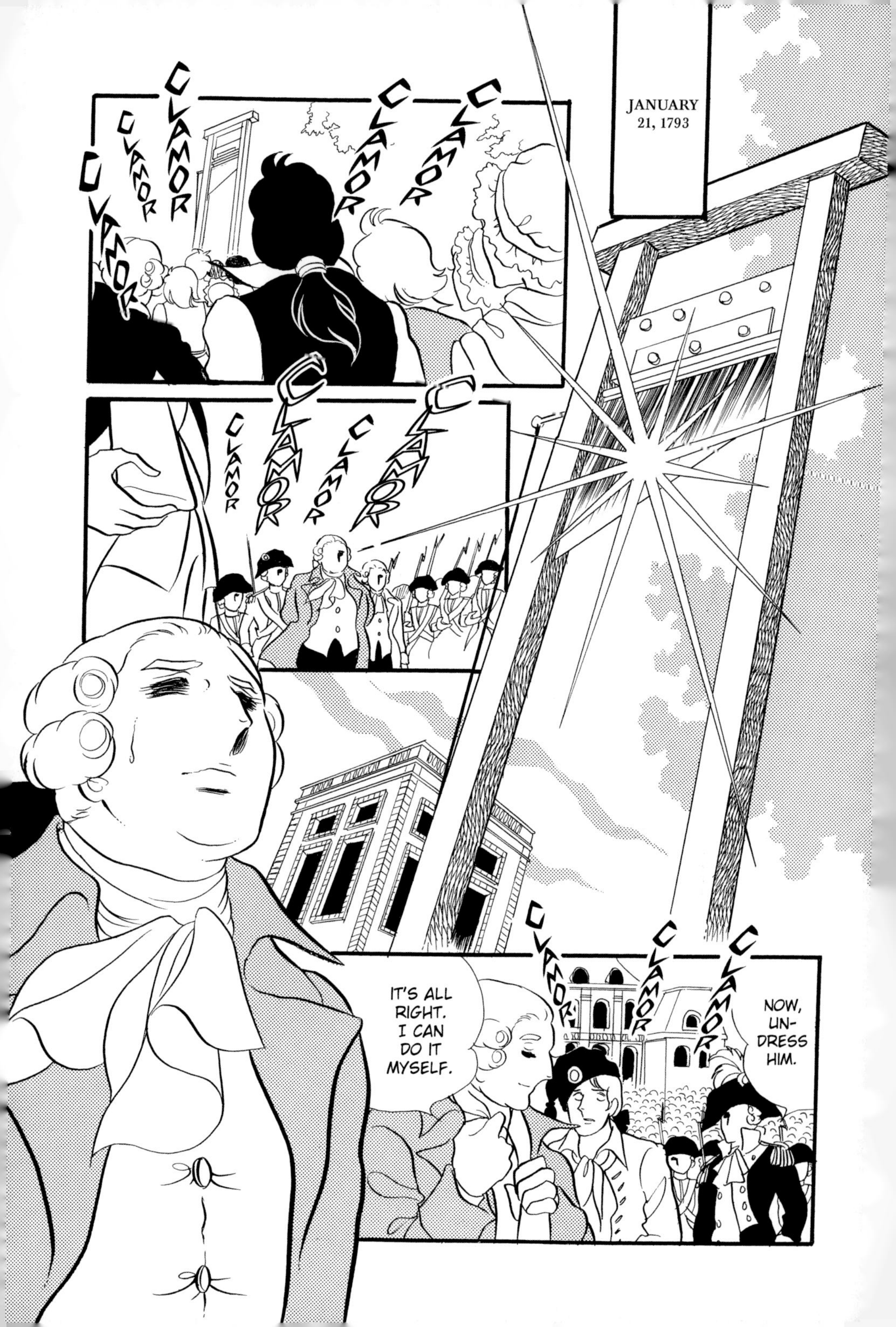
JANUARY 21, 1793
CLAMOR
CLAMOR
CLAMOR
CLAMOR
CLAMOR
CLAMOR
CLAMOR
CLAMOR
CLAMOR
CLAMOR
CLAMOR
CLAMOR
NOW, UN-DRESS HIM.
IT'S ALL RIGHT. I CAN DO IT MYSELF.

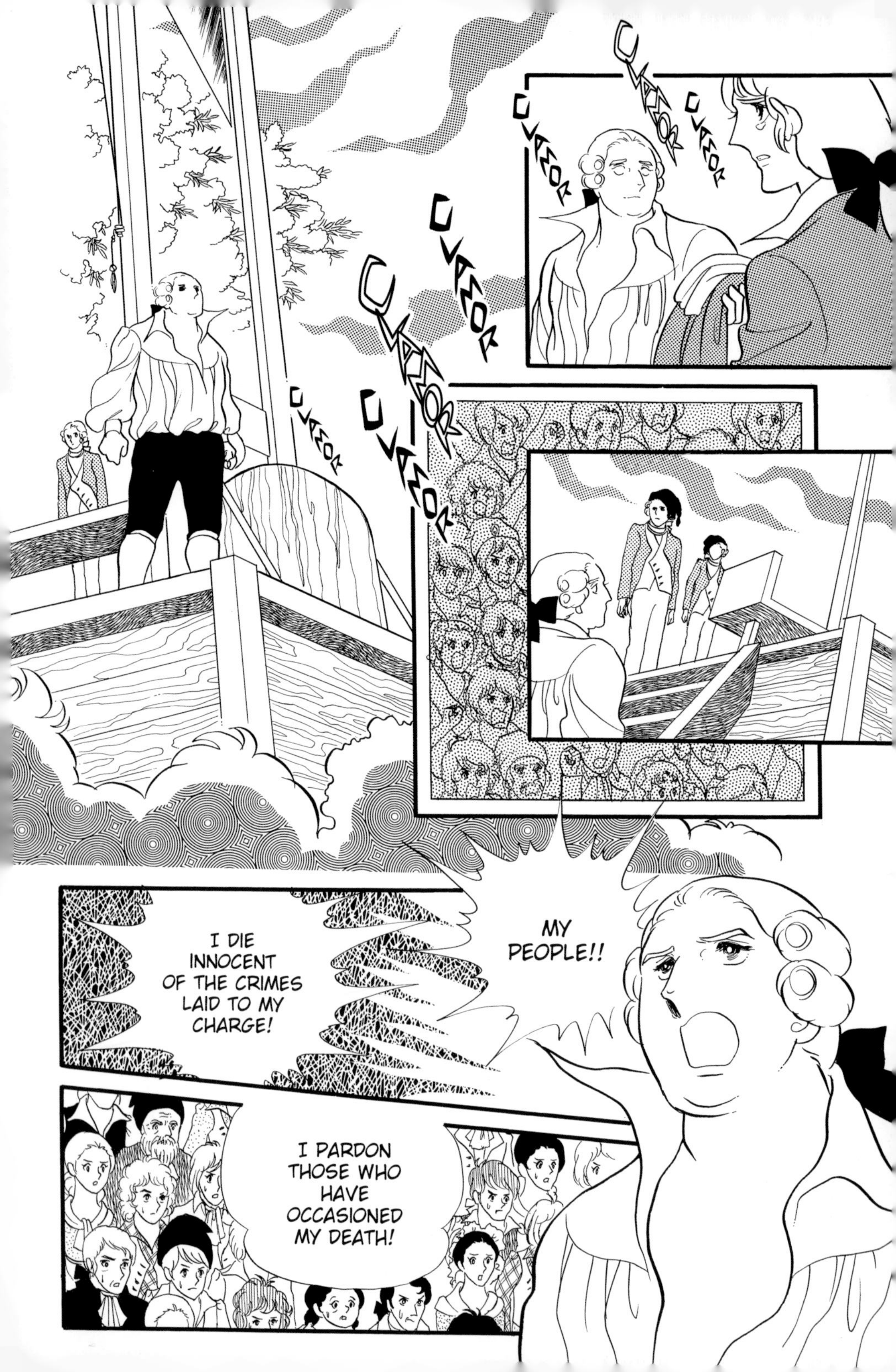
MY PEOPLE!!
I DIE INNOCENT OF THE CRIMES LAID TO MY CHARGE!
I PARDON THOSE WHO HAVE OCCASIONED MY DEATH!

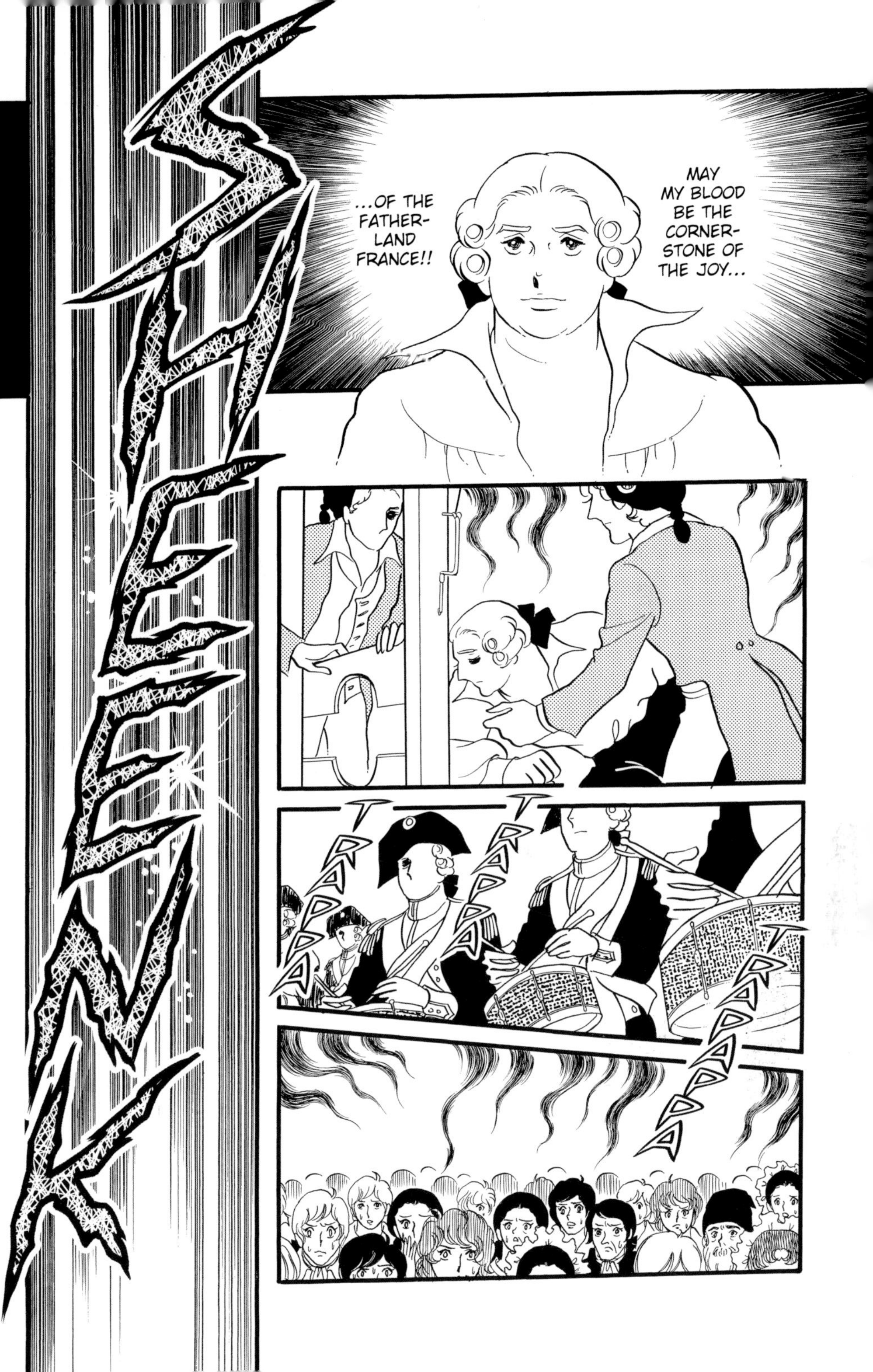
MAY MY BLOOD BE THE CORNER-STONE OF THE JOY...
...OF THE FATHER-LAND FRANCE!!

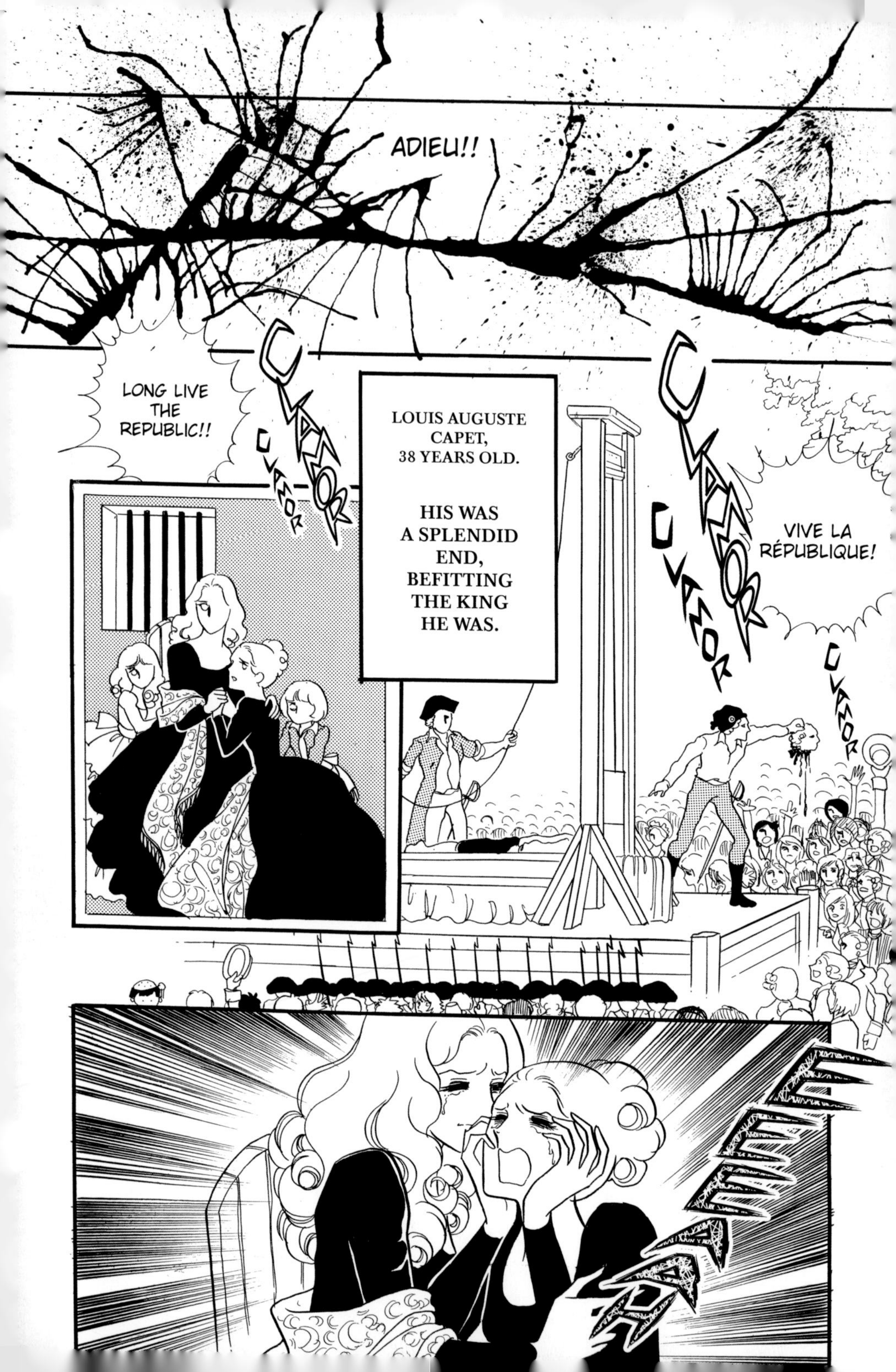
ADIEU!!
VIVE LA RÉPUBLIQUE!
LOUIS AUGUSTE CAPET, 38 YEARS OLD.
HIS WAS A SPLENDID END, BEFITTING THE KING HE WAS.
LONG LIVE THE REPUBLIC!!

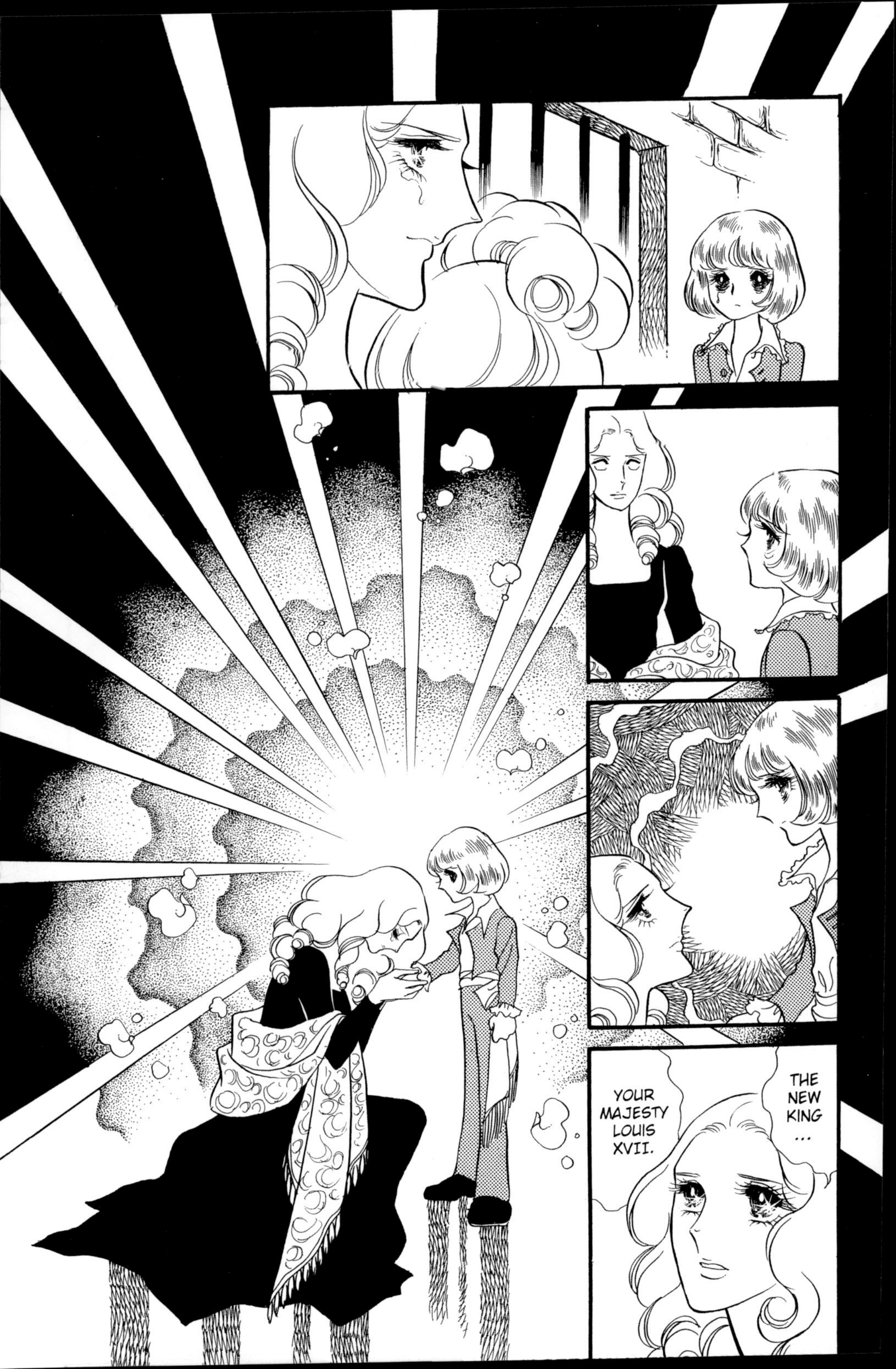
THE NEW KING ...
YOUR MAJESTY LOUIS XVII.

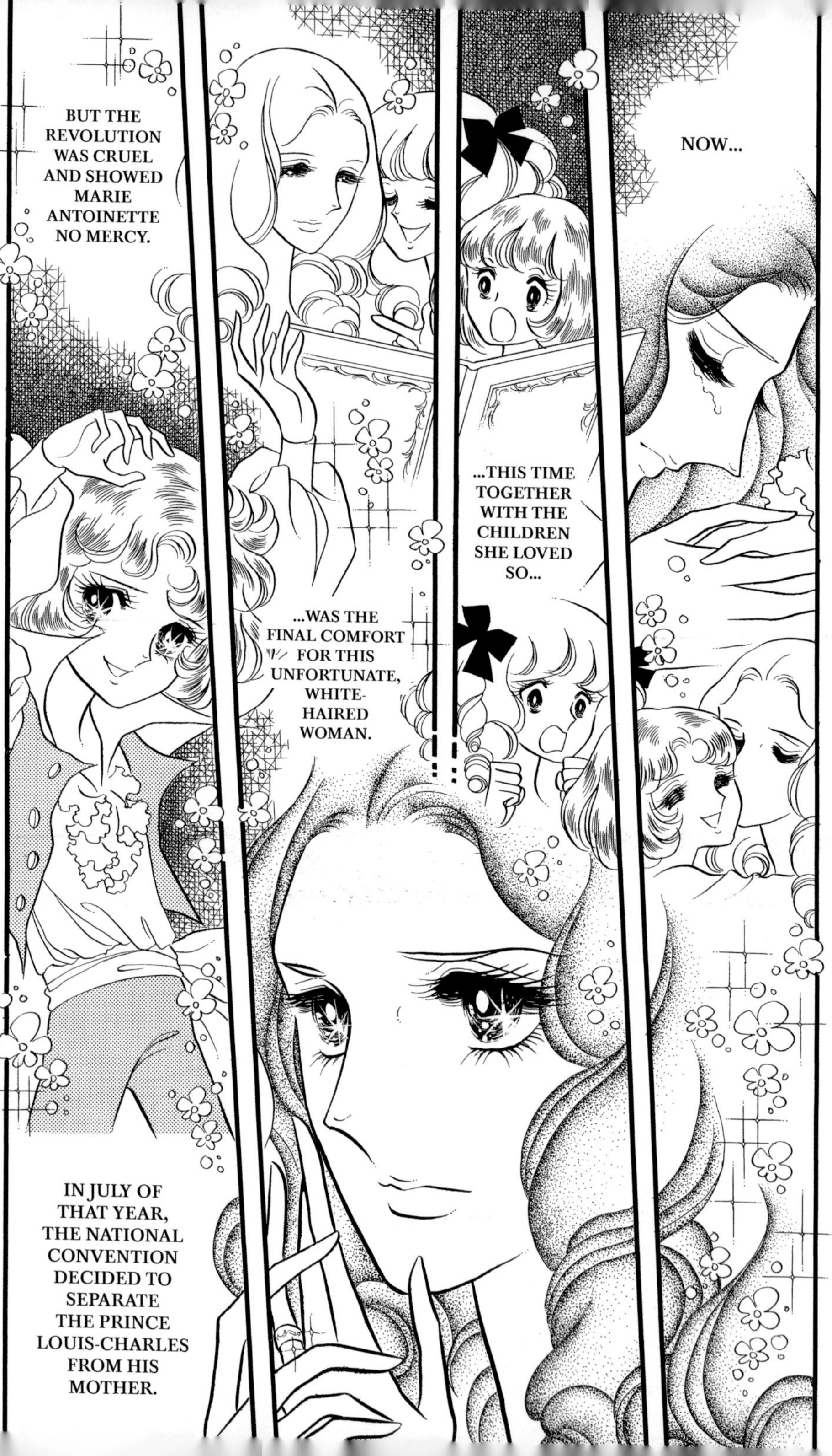
NOW...
...THIS TIME TOGETHER WITH THE CHILDREN SHE LOVED SO...
...WAS THE FINAL COMFORT FOR THIS UNFORTUNATE, WHITE-HAIRED WOMAN.
BUT THE REVOLUTION WAS CRUEL AND SHOWED MARIE ANTOINETTE NO MERCY.
IN JULY OF THAT YEAR, THE NATIONAL CONVENTION DECIDED TO SEPARATE THE PRINCE LOUIS-CHARLES FROM HIS MOTHER.

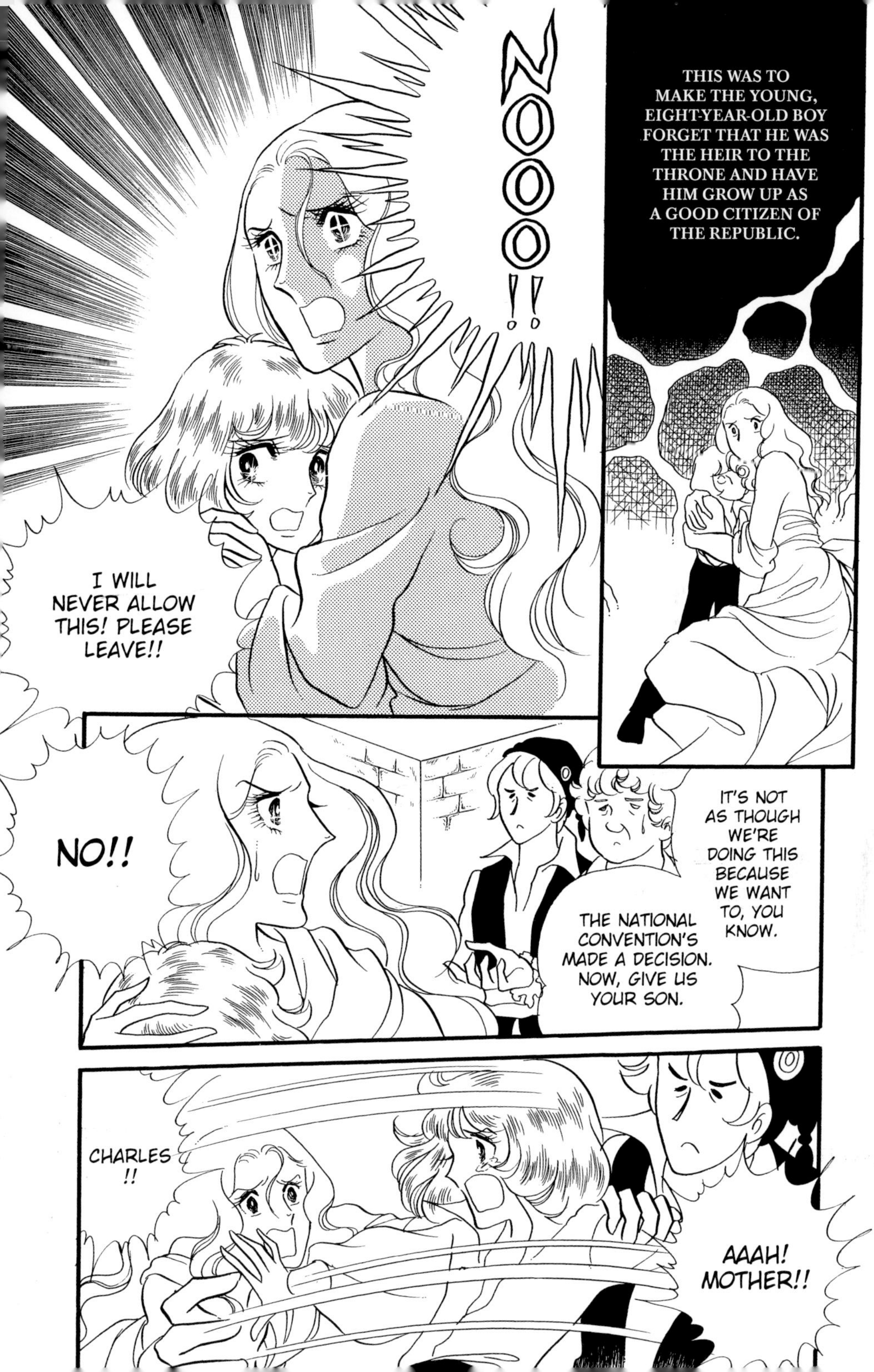
THIS WAS TO MAKE THE YOUNG, EIGHT-YEAR-OLD BOY FORGET THAT HE WAS THE HEIR TO THE THRONE AND HAVE HIM GROW UP AS A GOOD CITIZEN OF THE REPUBLIC.
NOOOO!!
I WILL NEVER ALLOW THIS! PLEASE LEAVE!!
NO!!
IT'S NOT AS THOUGH WE'RE DOING THIS BECAUSE WE WANT TO, YOU KNOW.
THE NATIONAL CONVENTION'S MADE A DECISION. NOW, GIVE US YOUR SON.
AAAH! MOTHER!!
CHARLES!!

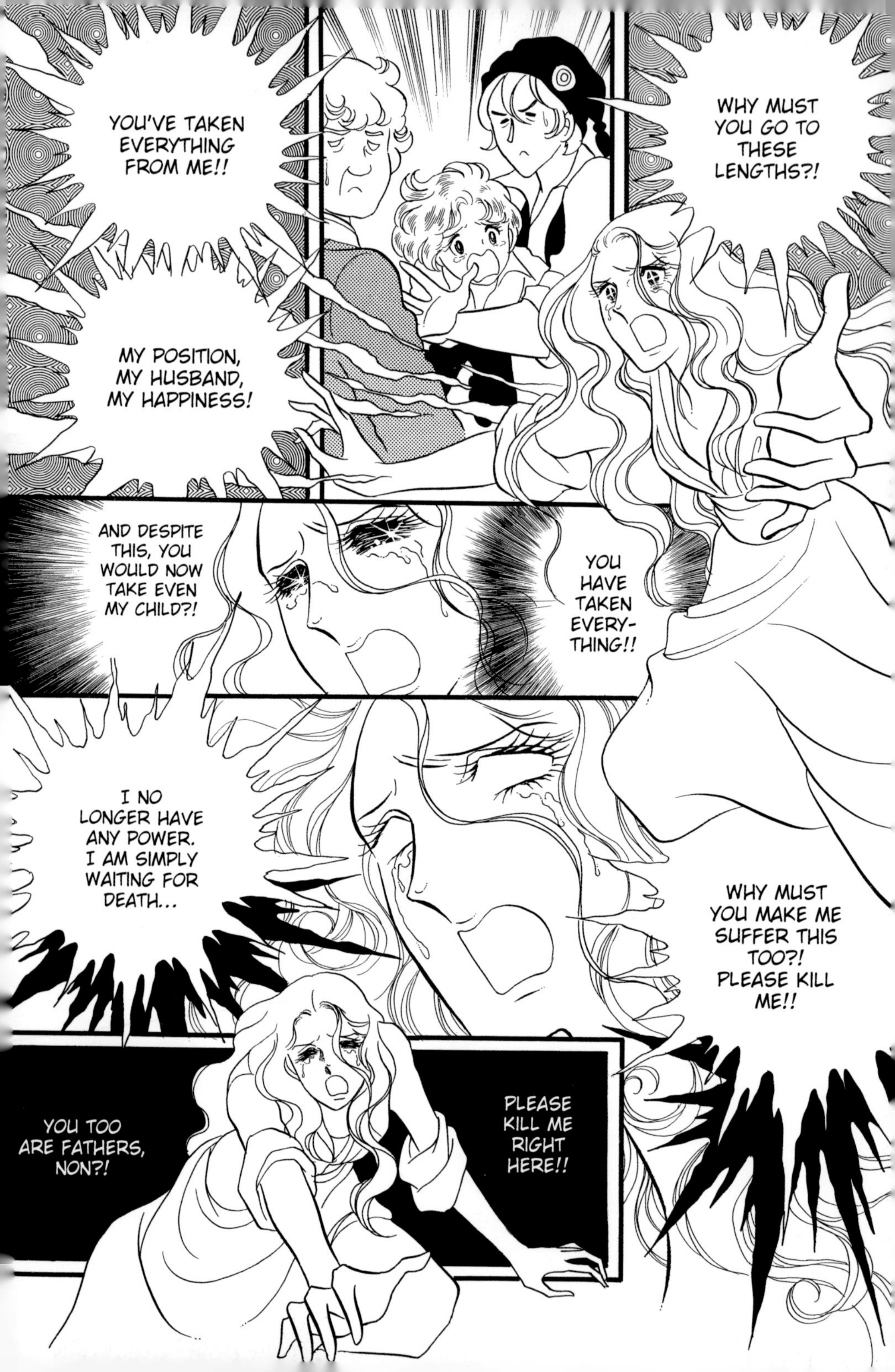
WHY MUST YOU GO TO THESE LENGTHS?!
YOU'VE TAKEN EVERYTHING FROM ME!!
MY POSITION, MY HUSBAND, MY HAPPINESS!
YOU HAVE TAKEN EVERY-THING!!
AND DESPITE THIS, YOU WOULD NOW TAKE EVEN MY CHILD?!
WHY MUST YOU MAKE ME SUFFER THIS TOO?! PLEASE KILL ME!!
I NO LONGER HAVE ANY POWER. I AM SIMPLY WAITING FOR DEATH...
PLEASE KILL ME RIGHT HERE!!
YOU TOO ARE FATHERS, NON?!

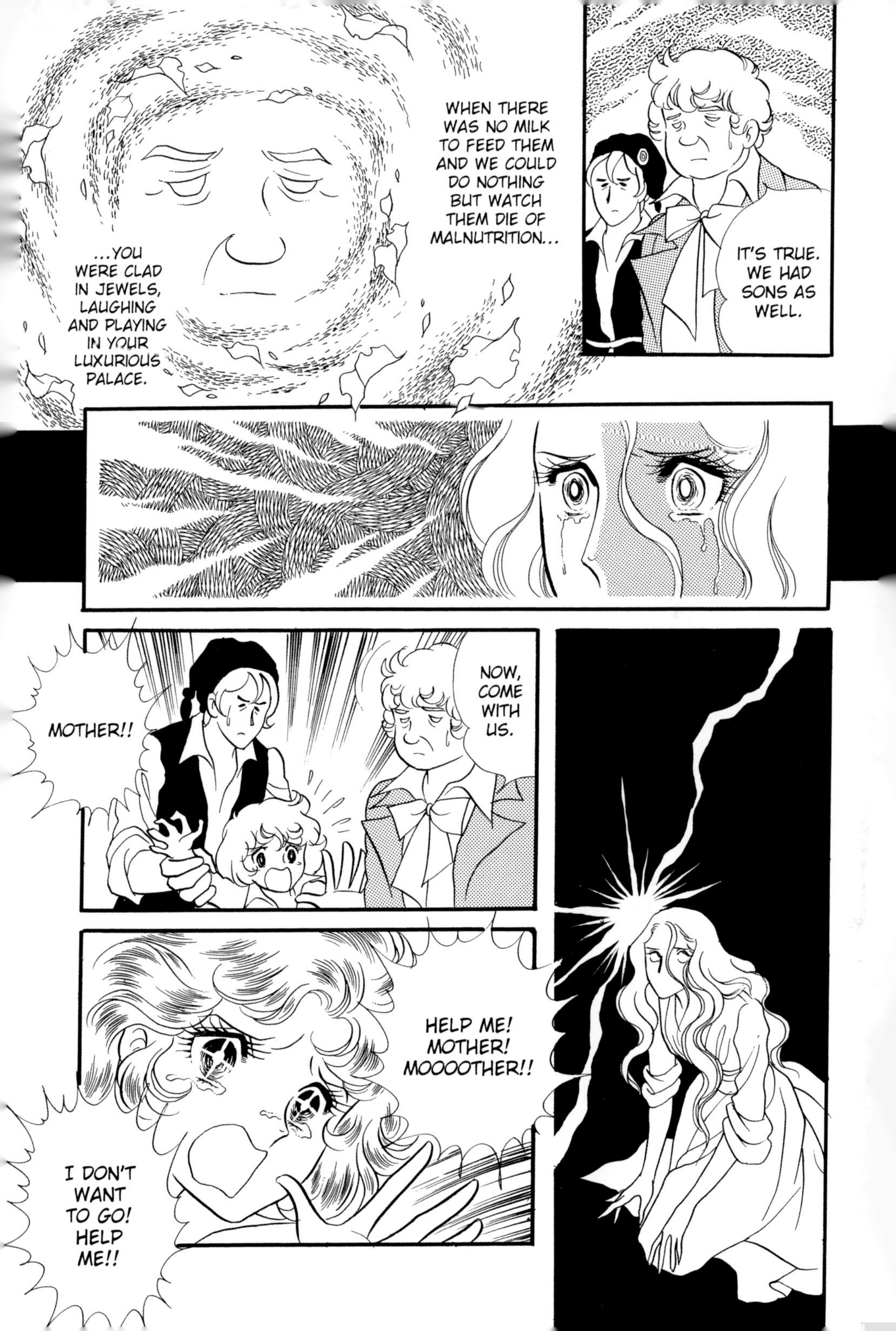
IT'S TRUE. WE HAD SONS AS WELL.
WHEN THERE WAS NO MILK TO FEED THEM AND WE COULD DO NOTHING BUT WATCH THEM DIE OF MALNUTRITION...
...YOU WERE CLAD IN JEWELS, LAUGHING AND PLAYING IN YOUR LUXURIOUS PALACE.
NOW, COME WITH US.
MOTHER!!
HELP ME! MOTHER! MOOOOTHER!!
I DON'T WANT TO GO! HELP ME!!

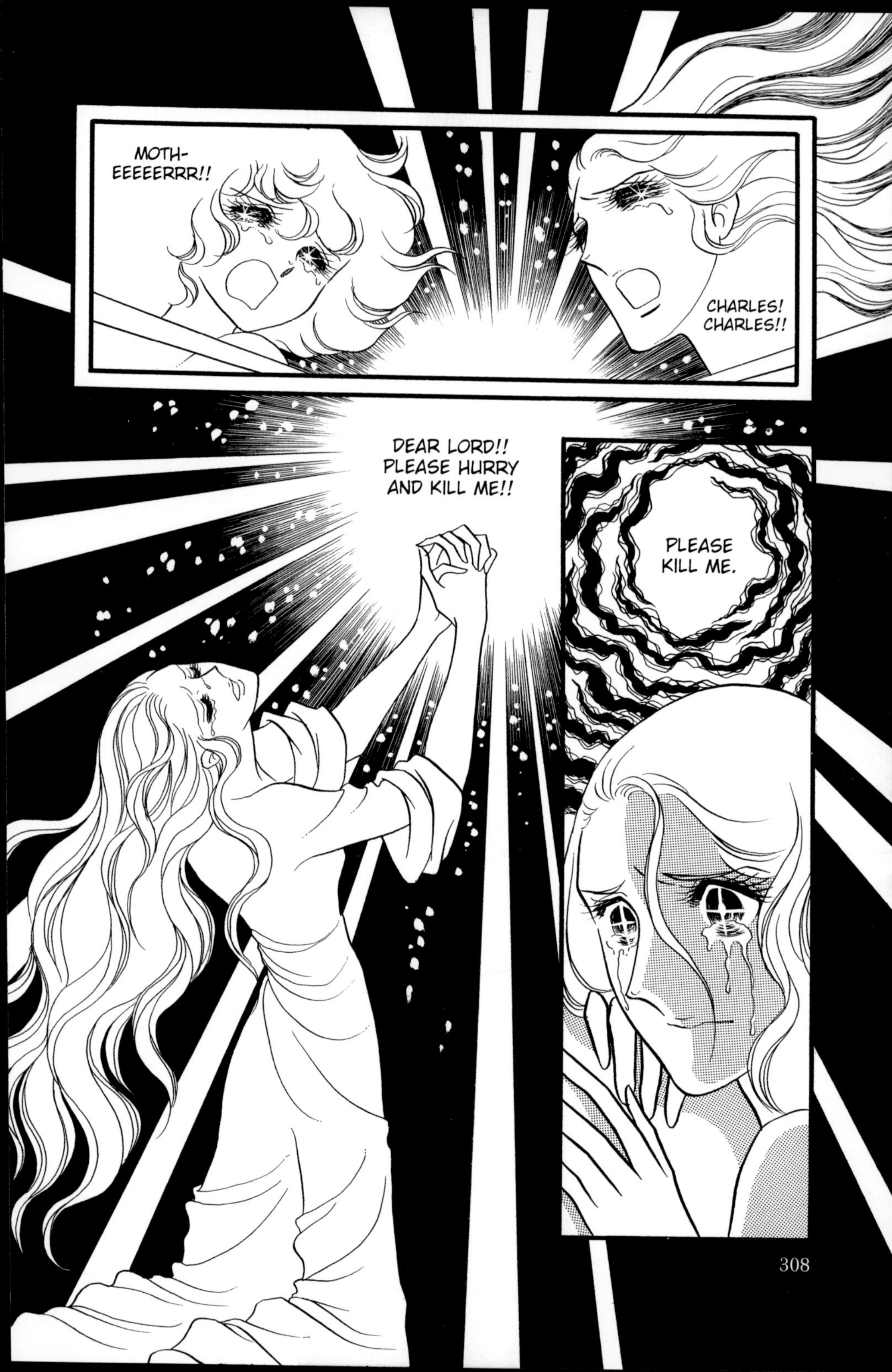
CHARLES! CHARLES!!
MOTH-EEEEERRR!!
PLEASE KILL ME.
DEAR LORD!! PLEASE HURRY AND KILL ME!!

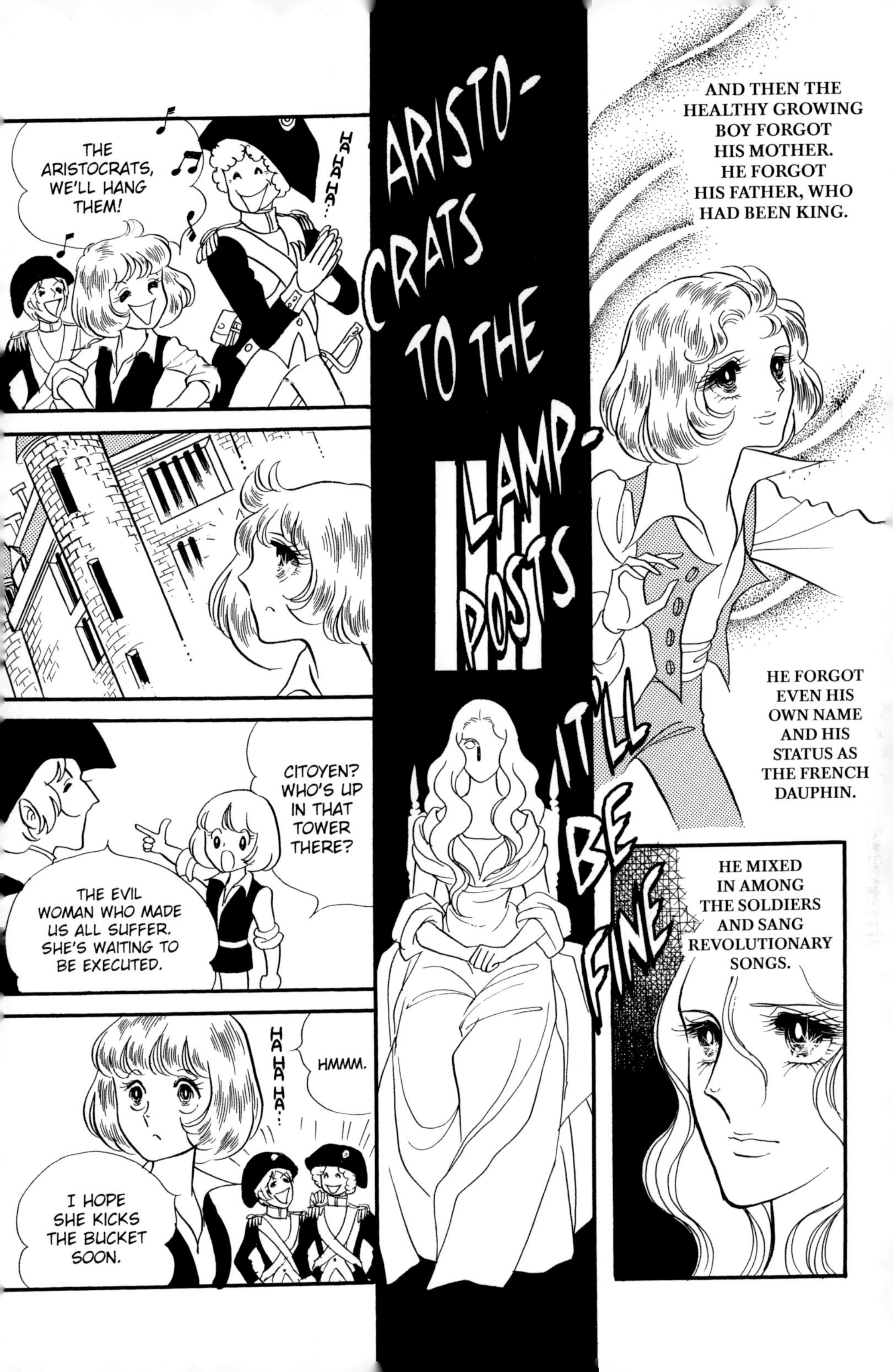
AND THEN THE HEALTHY GROWING BOY FORGOT HIS MOTHER. HE FORGOT HIS FATHER, WHO HAD BEEN KING.
HE FORGOT EVEN HIS OWN NAME AND HIS STATUS AS THE FRENCH DAUPHIN.
HE MIXED IN AMONG THE SOLDIERS AND SANG REVOLUTIONARY SONGS.
ARISTO-CRATS TO THE LAMP-POSTS
IT'LL BE FINE
HA HA HA HA...
THE ARISTOCRATS, WE'LL HANG THEM!
CITOYEN? WHO'S UP IN THAT TOWER THERE?
THE EVIL WOMAN WHO MADE US ALL SUFFER. SHE'S WAITING TO BE EXECUTED.
HMMM.
HA HA HA HA...
I HOPE SHE KICKS THE BUCKET SOON.

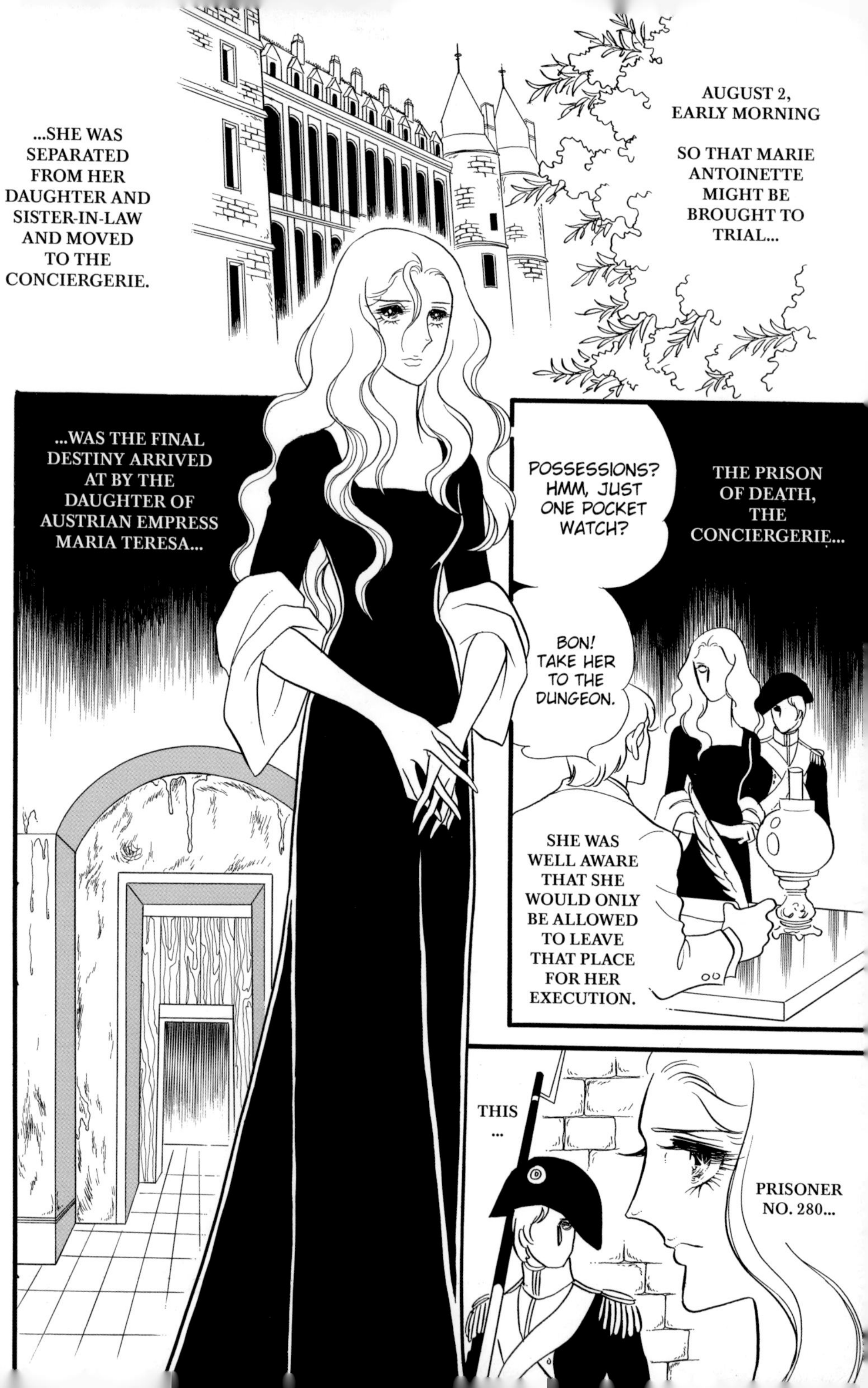
AUGUST 2, EARLY MORNING
SO THAT MARIE ANTOINETTE MIGHT BE BROUGHT TO TRIAL...
...SHE WAS SEPARATED FROM HER DAUGHTER AND SISTER-IN-LAW AND MOVED TO THE CONCIERGERIE.
THE PRISON OF DEATH, THE CONCIERGERIE...
POSSESSIONS? HMM, JUST ONE POCKET WATCH?
BON! TAKE HER TO THE DUNGEON.
SHE WAS WELL AWARE THAT SHE WOULD ONLY BE ALLOWED TO LEAVE THAT PLACE FOR HER EXECUTION.
PRISONER NO. 280...
THIS ...
...WAS THE FINAL DESTINY ARRIVED AT BY THE DAUGHTER OF AUSTRIAN EMPRESS MARIA TERESA...

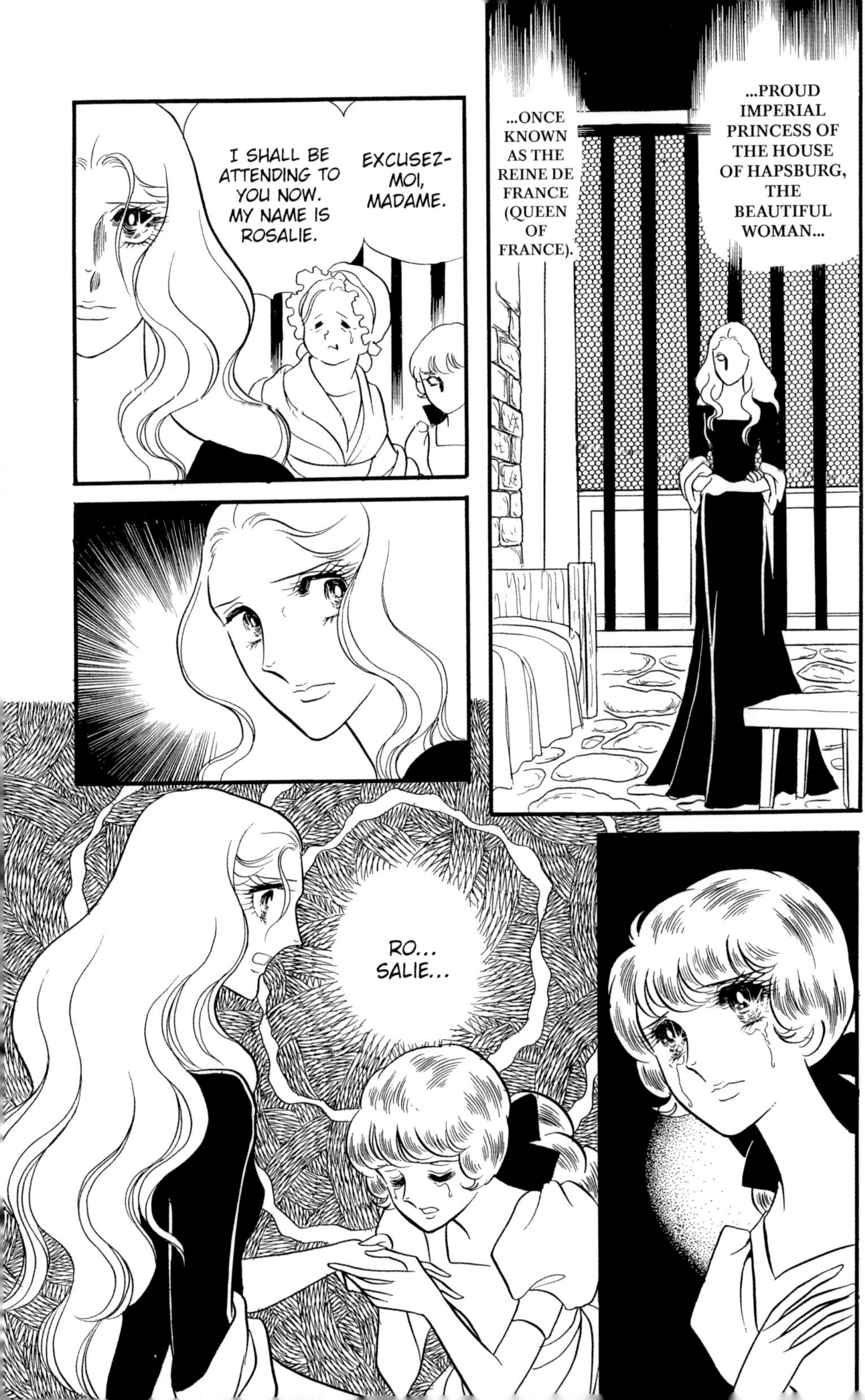
...PROUD IMPERIAL PRINCESS OF THE HOUSE OF HAPSBURG, THE BEAUTIFUL WOMAN...
...ONCE KNOWN AS THE REINE DE FRANCE (QUEEN OF FRANCE).
EXCUSEZ-MOI, MADAME.
I SHALL BE ATTENDING TO YOU NOW. MY NAME IS ROSALIE.
RO... SALIE...

**1974 WEEKLY MARGARET MAGAZINE
ISSUE 50-52 GIFT PROMOTION
[ROSE OF VERSAILLES NOTEBOOK] COVER**

FINALLY! THE THRILLING AND MOVING CLIMAX OF THIS GRAND ROMANCE!!

《いよいよもりあがる興奮と感動の大ロマン!!》

ベルサイユのばら

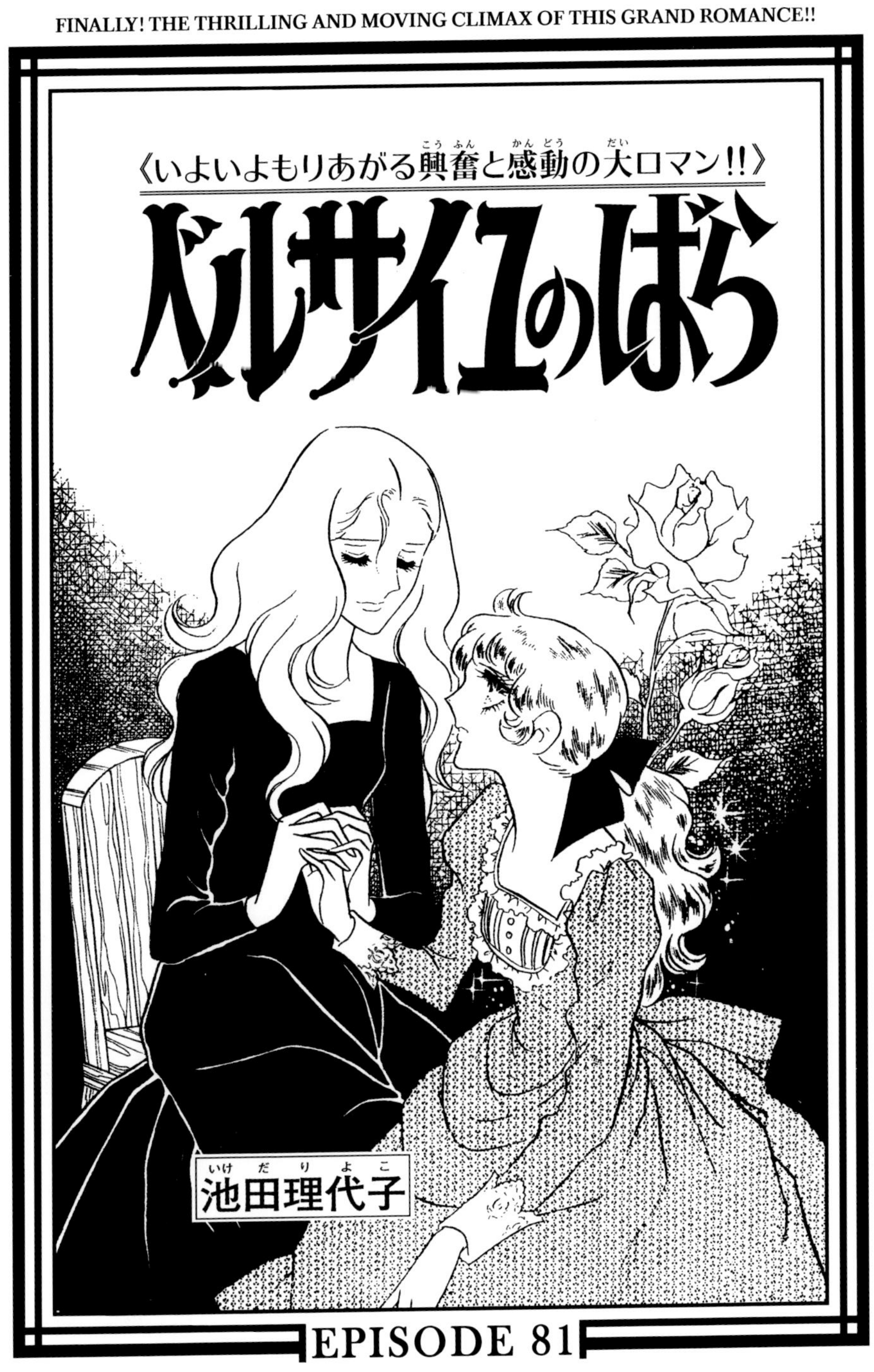

池田理代子

EPISODE 81

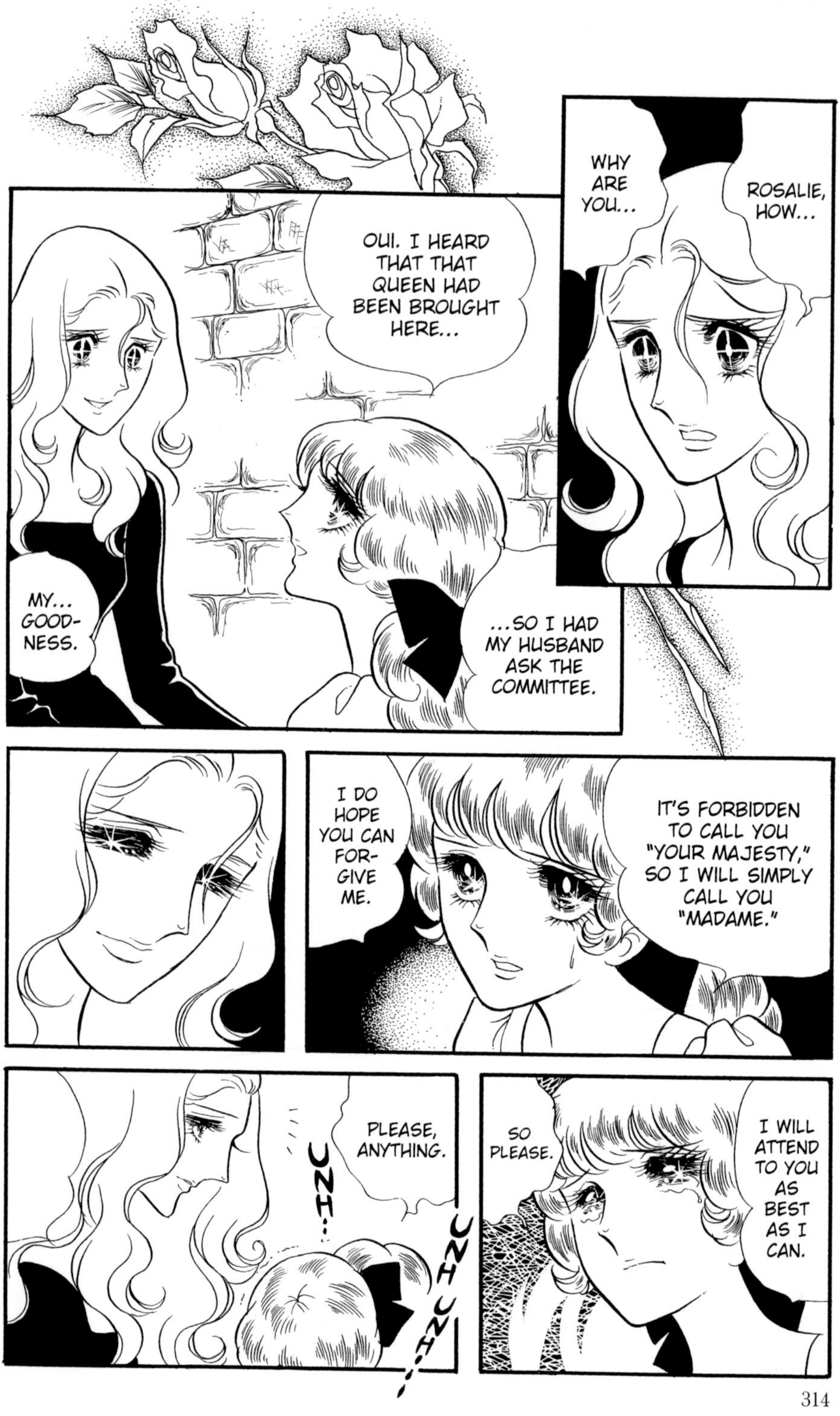
ROSALIE, HOW...
WHY ARE YOU...
OUI. I HEARD THAT THAT QUEEN HAD BEEN BROUGHT HERE...
...SO I HAD MY HUSBAND ASK THE COMMITTEE.
MY... GOODNESS.
IT'S FORBIDDEN TO CALL YOU "YOUR MAJESTY," SO I WILL SIMPLY CALL YOU "MADAME."
I DO HOPE YOU CAN FORGIVE ME.
I WILL ATTEND TO YOU AS BEST AS I CAN.
SO PLEASE.
PLEASE, ANYTHING.
UNH...
UNH UNH...

Episode 81

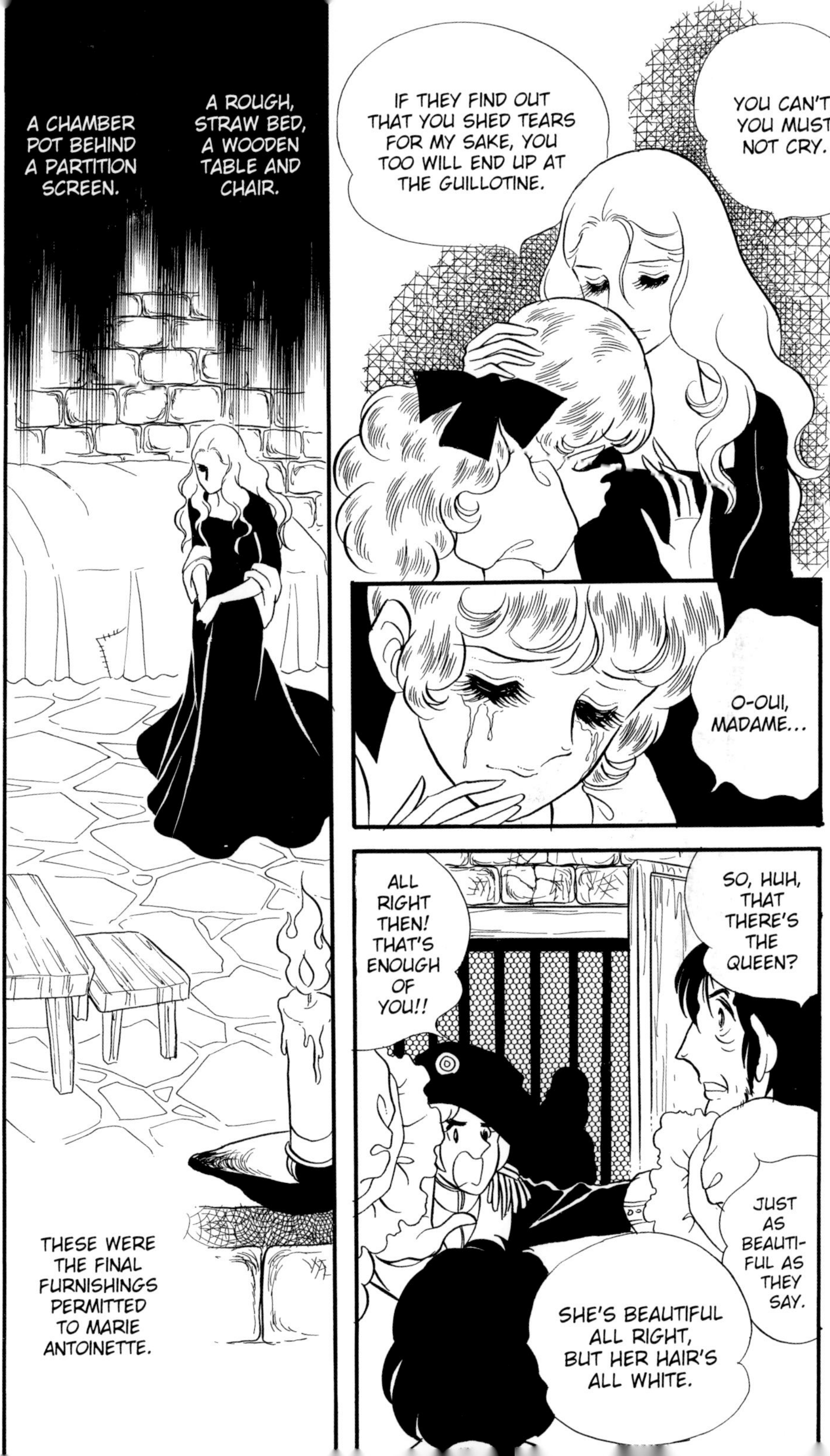
YOU CAN'T. YOU MUST NOT CRY.
IF THEY FIND OUT THAT YOU SHED TEARS FOR MY SAKE, YOU TOO WILL END UP AT THE GUILLOTINE.
O-OUI, MADAME...
SO, HUH, THAT THERE'S THE QUEEN?
JUST AS BEAUTI-FUL AS THEY SAY.
SHE'S BEAUTIFUL ALL RIGHT, BUT HER HAIR'S ALL WHITE.
ALL RIGHT THEN! THAT'S ENOUGH OF YOU!!
A ROUGH, STRAW BED, A WOODEN TABLE AND CHAIR.
A CHAMBER POT BEHIND A PARTITION SCREEN.
THESE WERE THE FINAL FURNISHINGS PERMITTED TO MARIE ANTOINETTE.

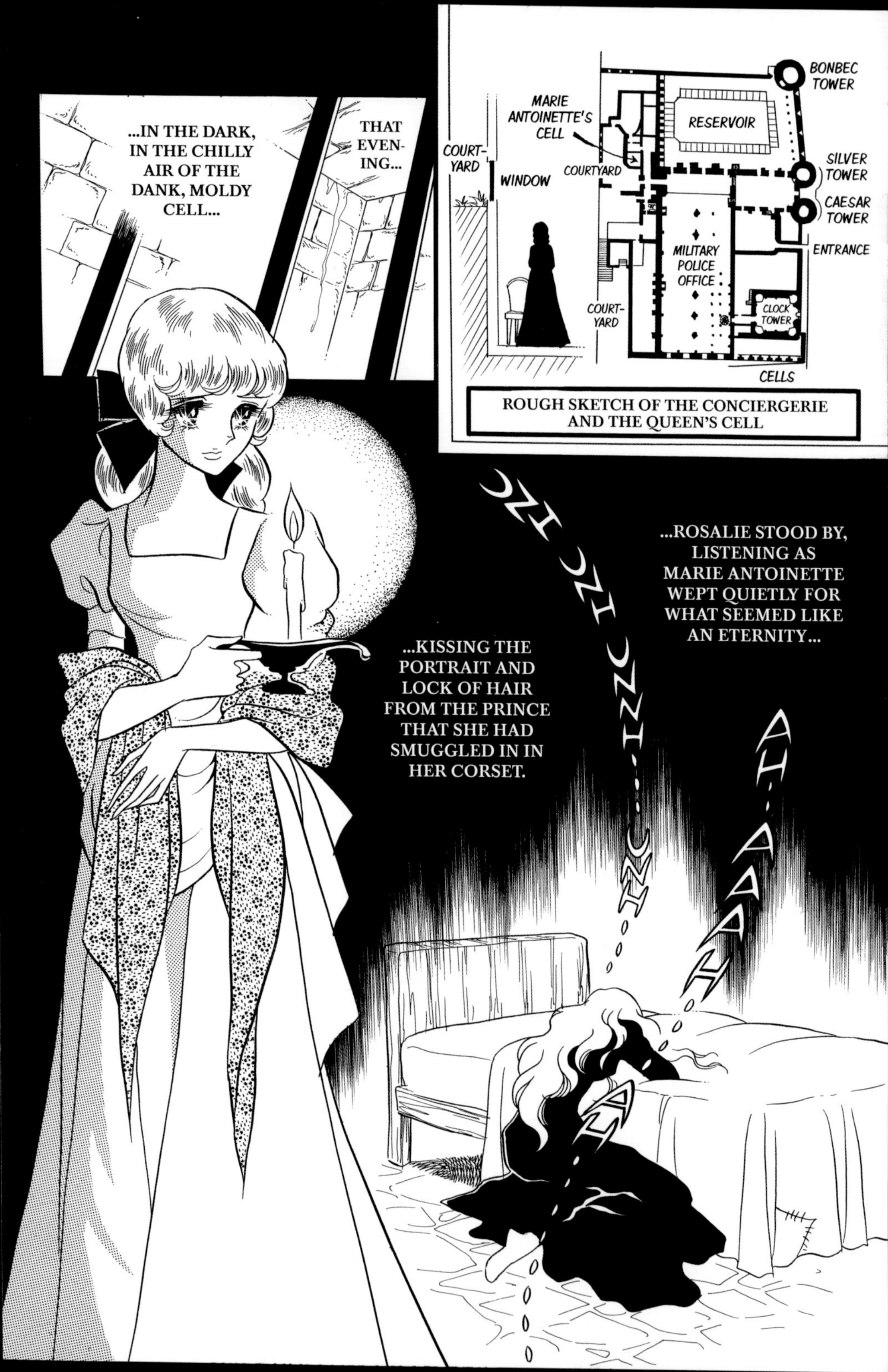
BONBEC TOWER
MARIE ANTOINETTE'S CELL
RESERVOIR
COURT-YARD
COURTYARD
WINDOW
SILVER TOWER
CAESAR TOWER
ENTRANCE
MILITARY POLICE OFFICE
COURT-YARD
CLOCK TOWER
CELLS
ROUGH SKETCH OF THE CONCIERGERIE AND THE QUEEN'S CELL
THAT EVENING...
...IN THE DARK, IN THE CHILLY AIR OF THE DANK, MOLDY CELL...
...ROSALIE STOOD BY, LISTENING AS MARIE ANTOINETTE WEPT QUIETLY FOR WHAT SEEMED LIKE AN ETERNITY...
...KISSING THE PORTRAIT AND LOCK OF HAIR FROM THE PRINCE THAT SHE HAD SMUGGLED IN IN HER CORSET.
AH...AAAAH

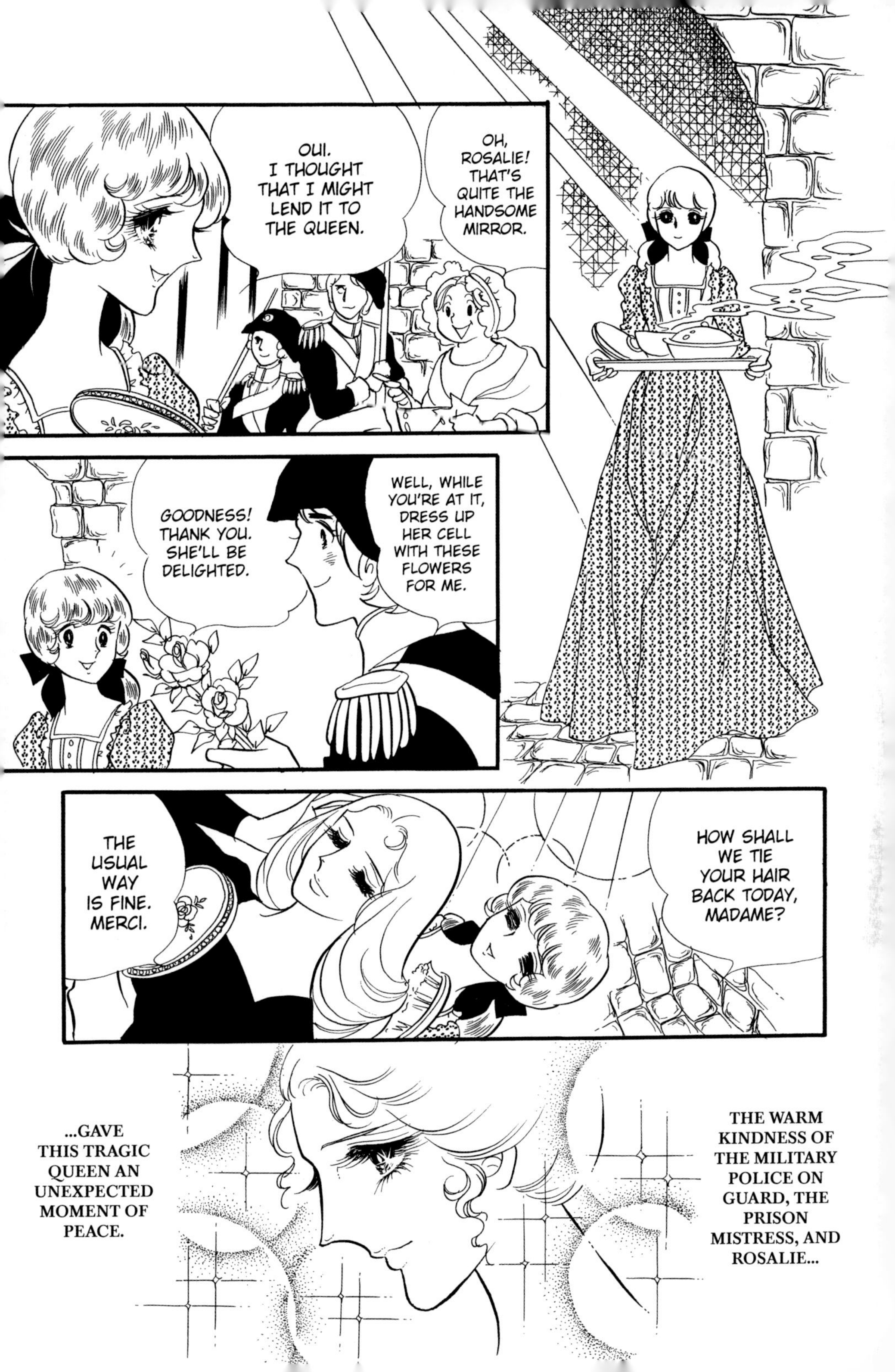
OH, ROSALIE! THAT'S QUITE THE HANDSOME MIRROR.
OUI. I THOUGHT THAT I MIGHT LEND IT TO THE QUEEN.
WELL, WHILE YOU'RE AT IT, DRESS UP HER CELL WITH THESE FLOWERS FOR ME.
GOODNESS! THANK YOU. SHE'LL BE DELIGHTED.
HOW SHALL WE TIE YOUR HAIR BACK TODAY, MADAME?
THE USUAL WAY IS FINE. MERCI.
THE WARM KINDNESS OF THE MILITARY POLICE ON GUARD, THE PRISON MISTRESS, AND ROSALIE...
...GAVE THIS TRAGIC QUEEN AN UNEXPECTED MOMENT OF PEACE.

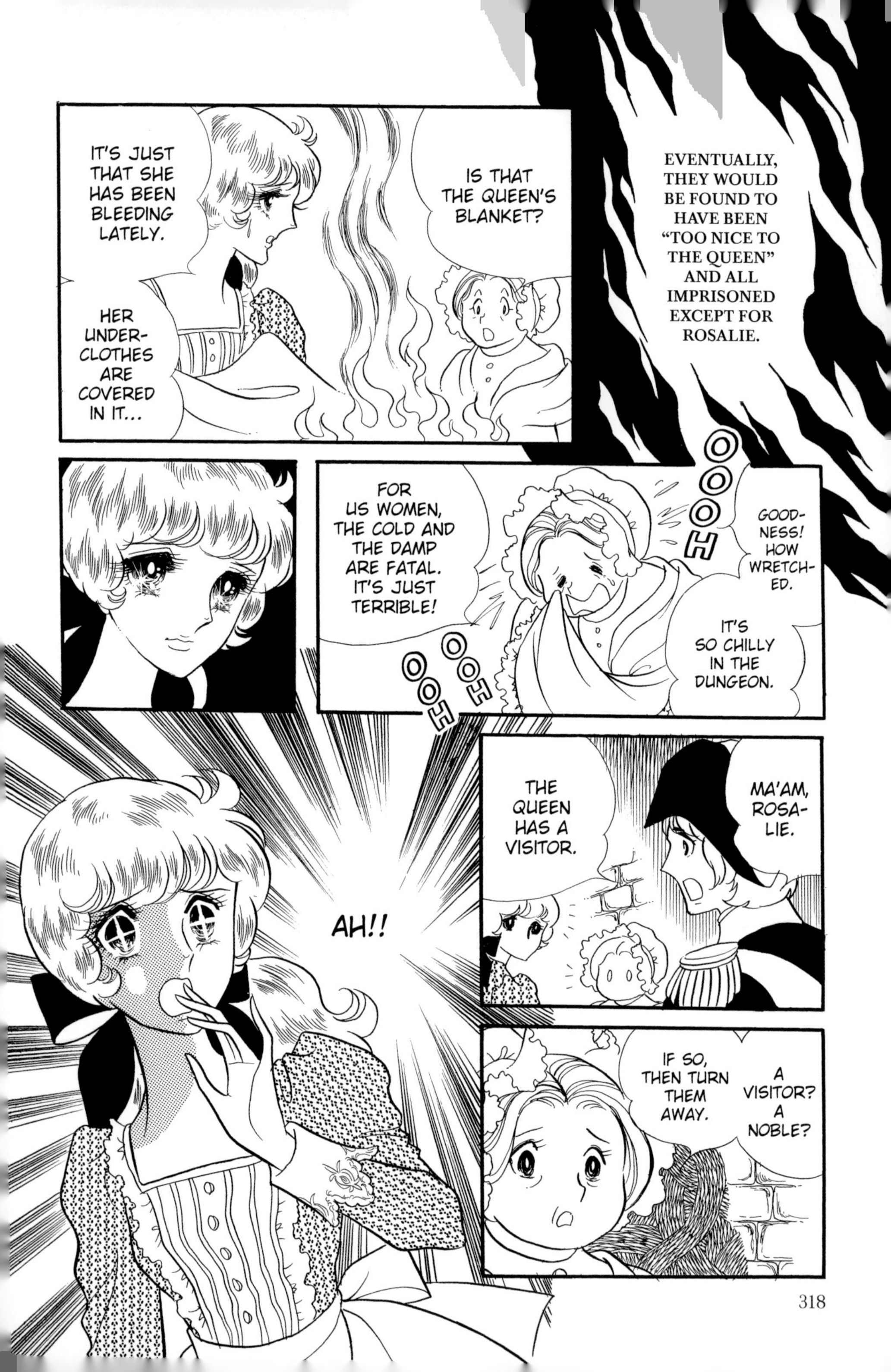
EVENTUALLY, THEY WOULD BE FOUND TO HAVE BEEN "TOO NICE TO THE QUEEN" AND ALL IMPRISONED EXCEPT FOR ROSALIE.
IS THAT THE QUEEN'S BLANKET?
IT'S JUST THAT SHE HAS BEEN BLEEDING LATELY.
HER UNDER-CLOTHES ARE COVERED IN IT...
OOOH
GOOD-NESS! HOW WRETCH-ED.
IT'S SO CHILLY IN THE DUNGEON.
FOR US WOMEN, THE COLD AND THE DAMP ARE FATAL. IT'S JUST TERRIBLE!
OOH
OOH
MA'AM, ROSA-LIE.
THE QUEEN HAS A VISITOR.
A VISITOR? A NOBLE?
IF SO, THEN TURN THEM AWAY.
AH!!

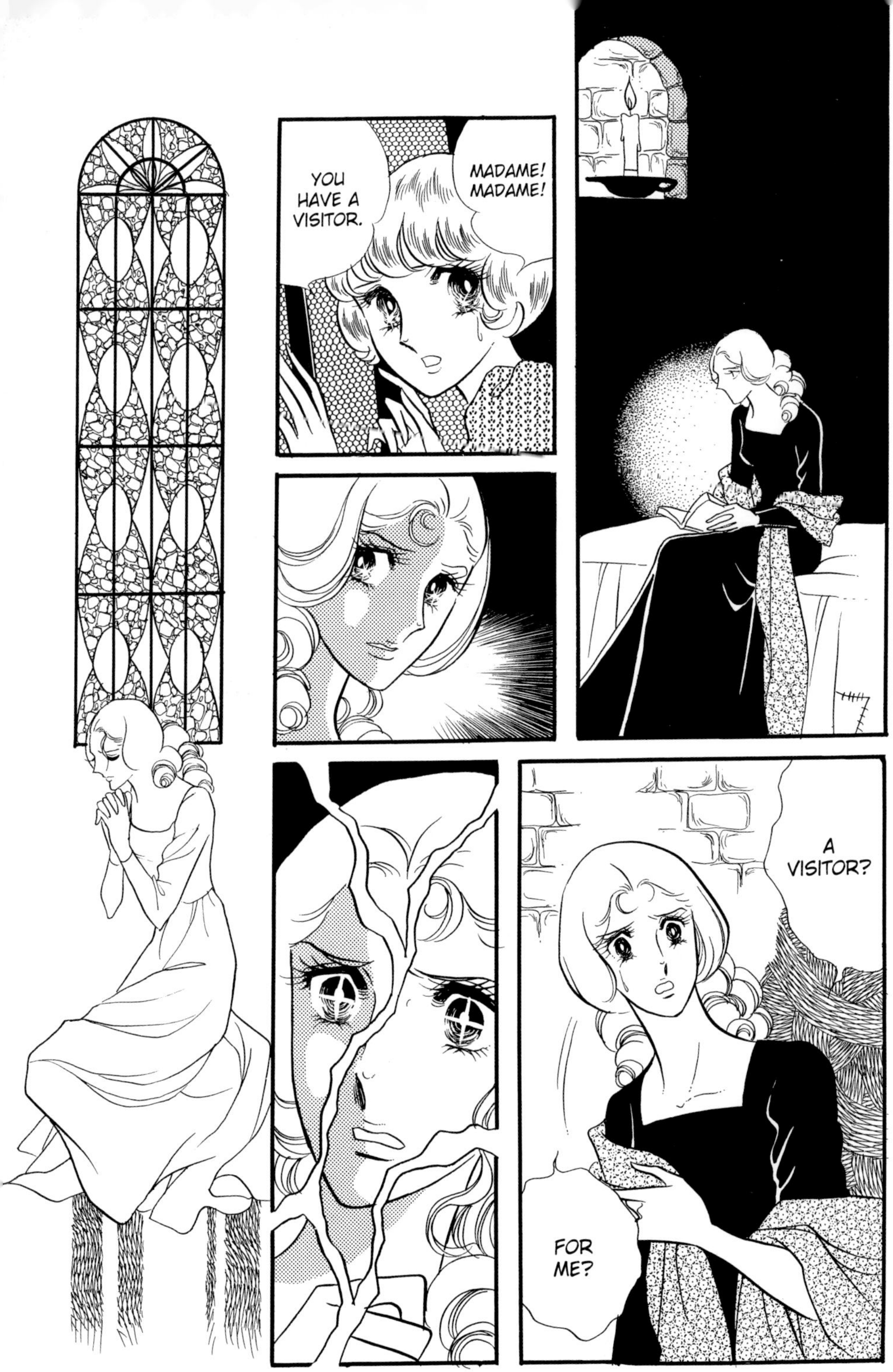
MADAME! MADAME!
YOU HAVE A VISITOR.
A VISITOR?
FOR ME?

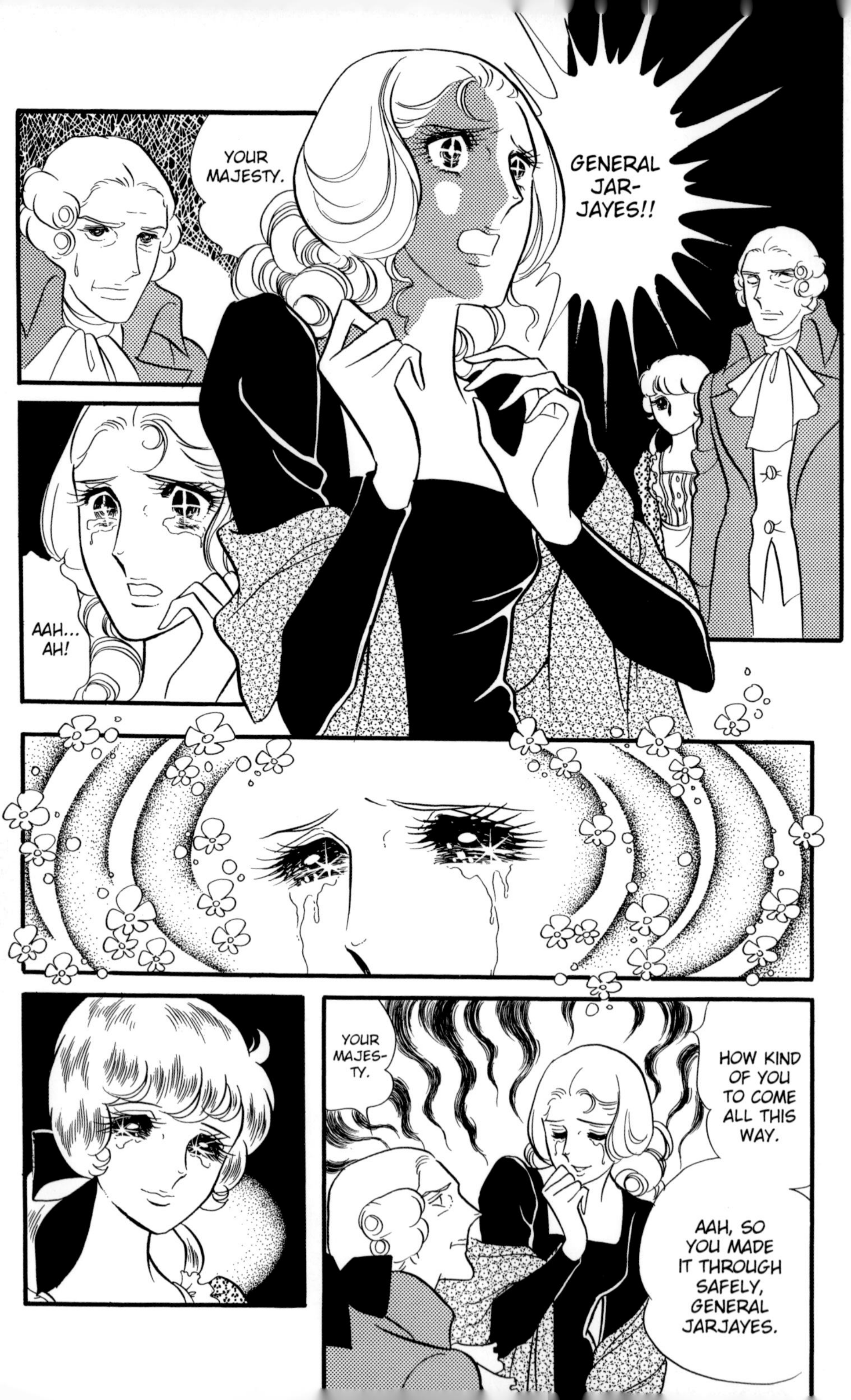

GENERAL JAR-JAYES!!
YOUR MAJESTY.
AAH... AH!
HOW KIND OF YOU TO COME ALL THIS WAY.
YOUR MAJES-TY.
AAH, SO YOU MADE IT THROUGH SAFELY, GENERAL JARJAYES.

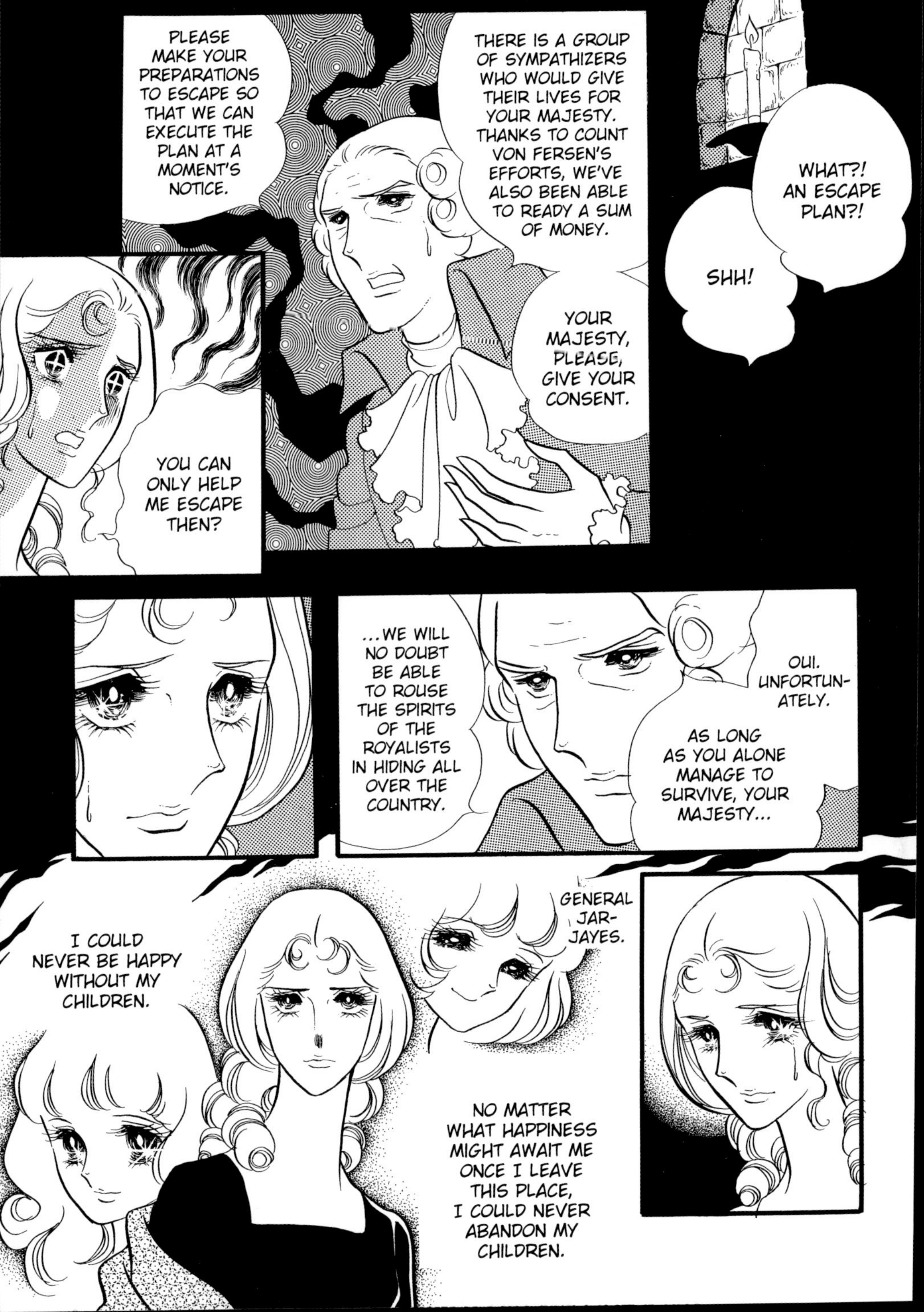
WHAT?! AN ESCAPE PLAN?!
SHH!
THERE IS A GROUP OF SYMPATHIZERS WHO WOULD GIVE THEIR LIVES FOR YOUR MAJESTY. THANKS TO COUNT VON FERSEN'S EFFORTS, WE'VE ALSO BEEN ABLE TO READY A SUM OF MONEY.
PLEASE MAKE YOUR PREPARATIONS TO ESCAPE SO THAT WE CAN EXECUTE THE PLAN AT A MOMENT'S NOTICE.
YOUR MAJESTY, PLEASE, GIVE YOUR CONSENT.
YOU CAN ONLY HELP ME ESCAPE THEN?
OUI. UNFORTUNATELY.
AS LONG AS YOU ALONE MANAGE TO SURVIVE, YOUR MAJESTY...
...WE WILL NO DOUBT BE ABLE TO ROUSE THE SPIRITS OF THE ROYALISTS IN HIDING ALL OVER THE COUNTRY.
GENERAL JARJAYES.
I COULD NEVER BE HAPPY WITHOUT MY CHILDREN.
NO MATTER WHAT HAPPINESS MIGHT AWAIT ME ONCE I LEAVE THIS PLACE, I COULD NEVER ABANDON MY CHILDREN.

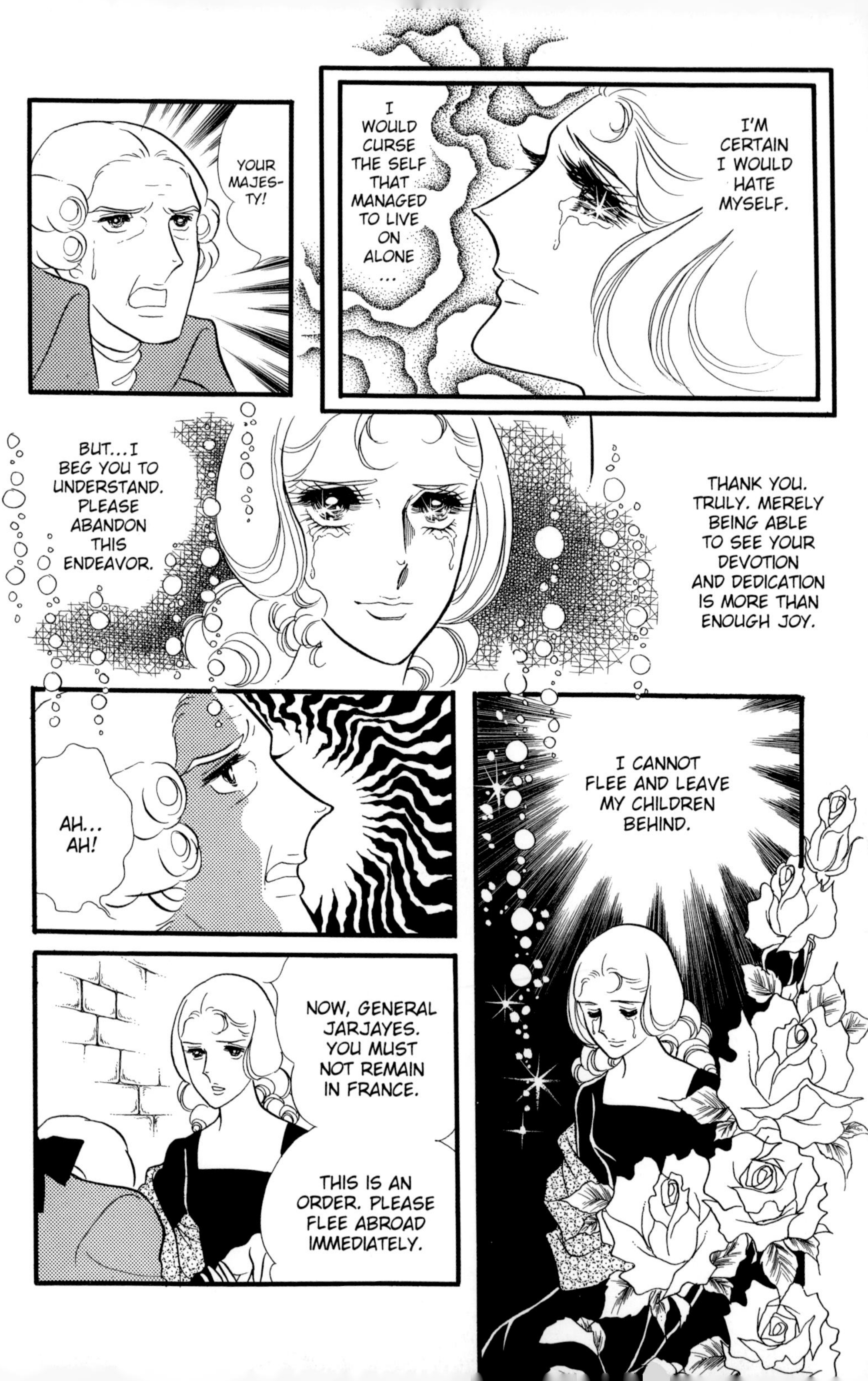
I'M CERTAIN I WOULD HATE MYSELF.
I WOULD CURSE THE SELF THAT MANAGED TO LIVE ON ALONE ...
YOUR MAJES-TY!
THANK YOU. TRULY. MERELY BEING ABLE TO SEE YOUR DEVOTION AND DEDICATION IS MORE THAN ENOUGH JOY.
BUT...I BEG YOU TO UNDERSTAND. PLEASE ABANDON THIS ENDEAVOR.
I CANNOT FLEE AND LEAVE MY CHILDREN BEHIND.
AH... AH!
NOW, GENERAL JARJAYES. YOU MUST NOT REMAIN IN FRANCE.
THIS IS AN ORDER. PLEASE FLEE ABROAD IMMEDIATELY.

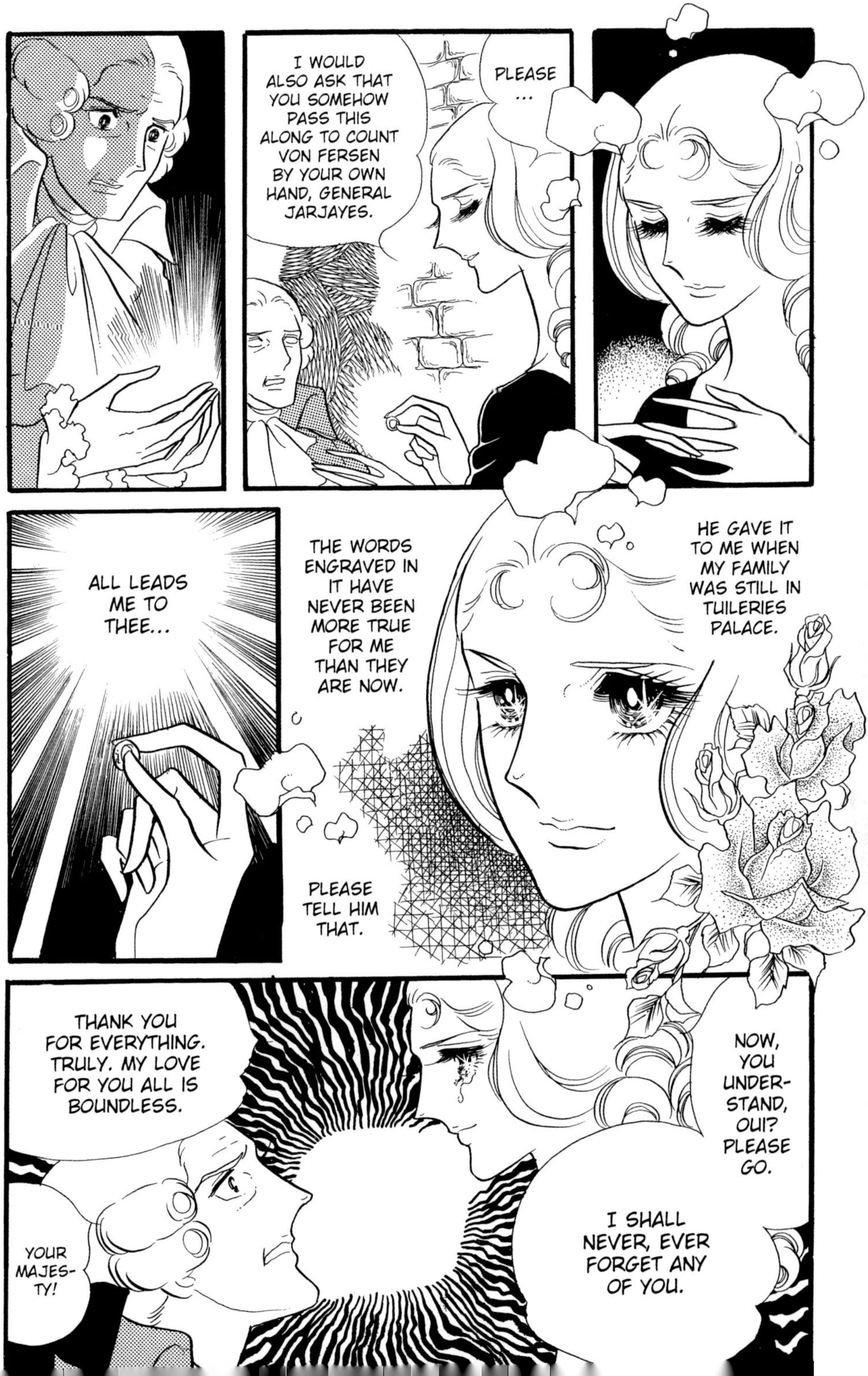
PLEASE ...
I WOULD ALSO ASK THAT YOU SOMEHOW PASS THIS ALONG TO COUNT VON FERSEN BY YOUR OWN HAND, GENERAL JARJAYES.
HE GAVE IT TO ME WHEN MY FAMILY WAS STILL IN TUILERIES PALACE.
THE WORDS ENGRAVED IN IT HAVE NEVER BEEN MORE TRUE FOR ME THAN THEY ARE NOW.
PLEASE TELL HIM THAT.
ALL LEADS ME TO THEE...
NOW, YOU UNDER-STAND, OUI? PLEASE GO.
I SHALL NEVER, EVER FORGET ANY OF YOU.
THANK YOU FOR EVERYTHING. TRULY. MY LOVE FOR YOU ALL IS BOUNDLESS.
YOUR MAJES-TY!

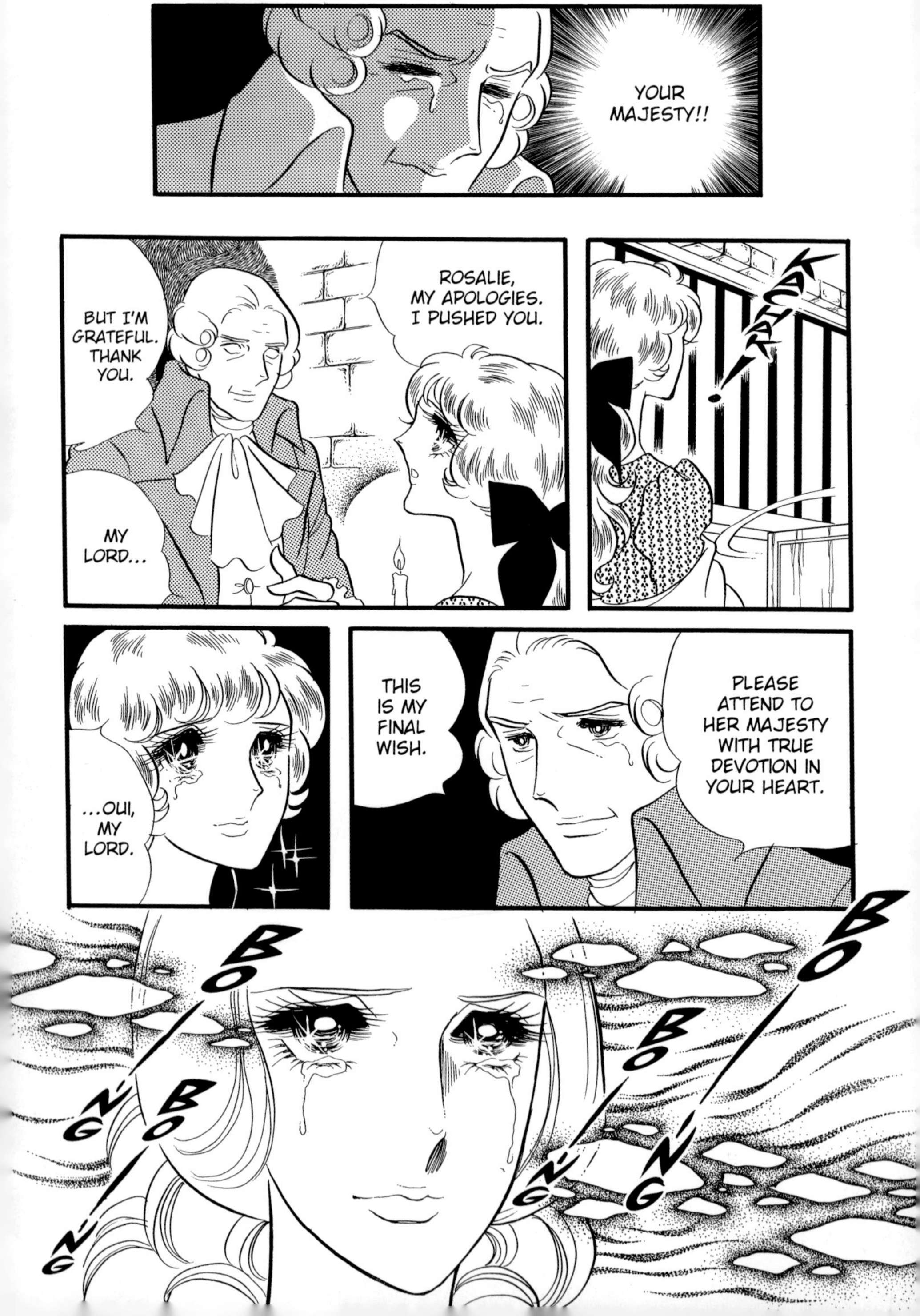
YOUR MAJESTY!!
KACHAK!
ROSALIE, MY APOLOGIES. I PUSHED YOU.
BUT I'M GRATEFUL. THANK YOU.
MY LORD...
PLEASE ATTEND TO HER MAJESTY WITH TRUE DEVOTION IN YOUR HEART.
THIS IS MY FINAL WISH.
...OUI, MY LORD.
BO—'NG
BO—'NG
BO—'NG
BO—'NG

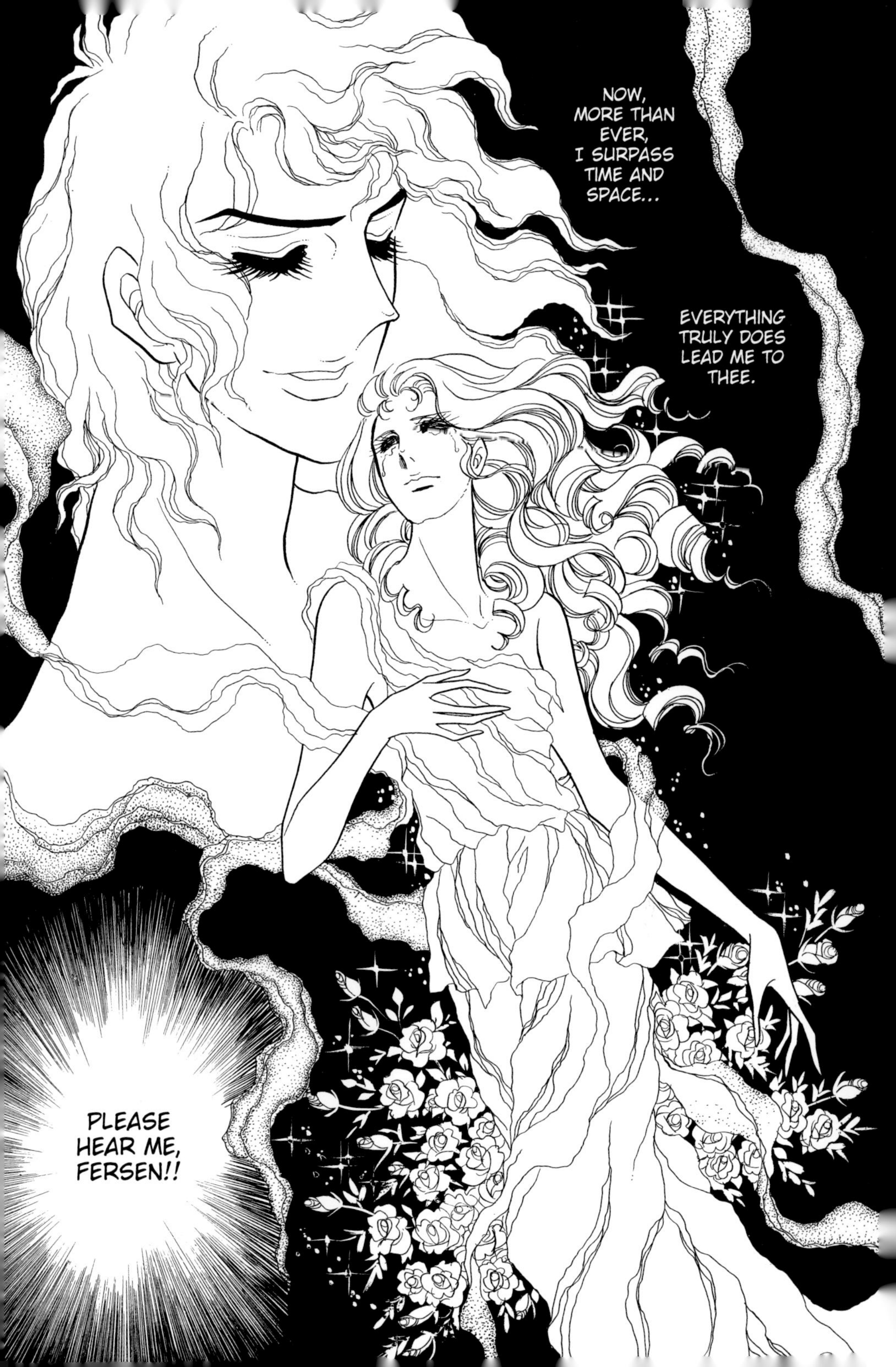
NOW, MORE THAN EVER, I SURPASS TIME AND SPACE...
EVERYTHING TRULY DOES LEAD ME TO THEE.
PLEASE HEAR ME, FERSEN!!

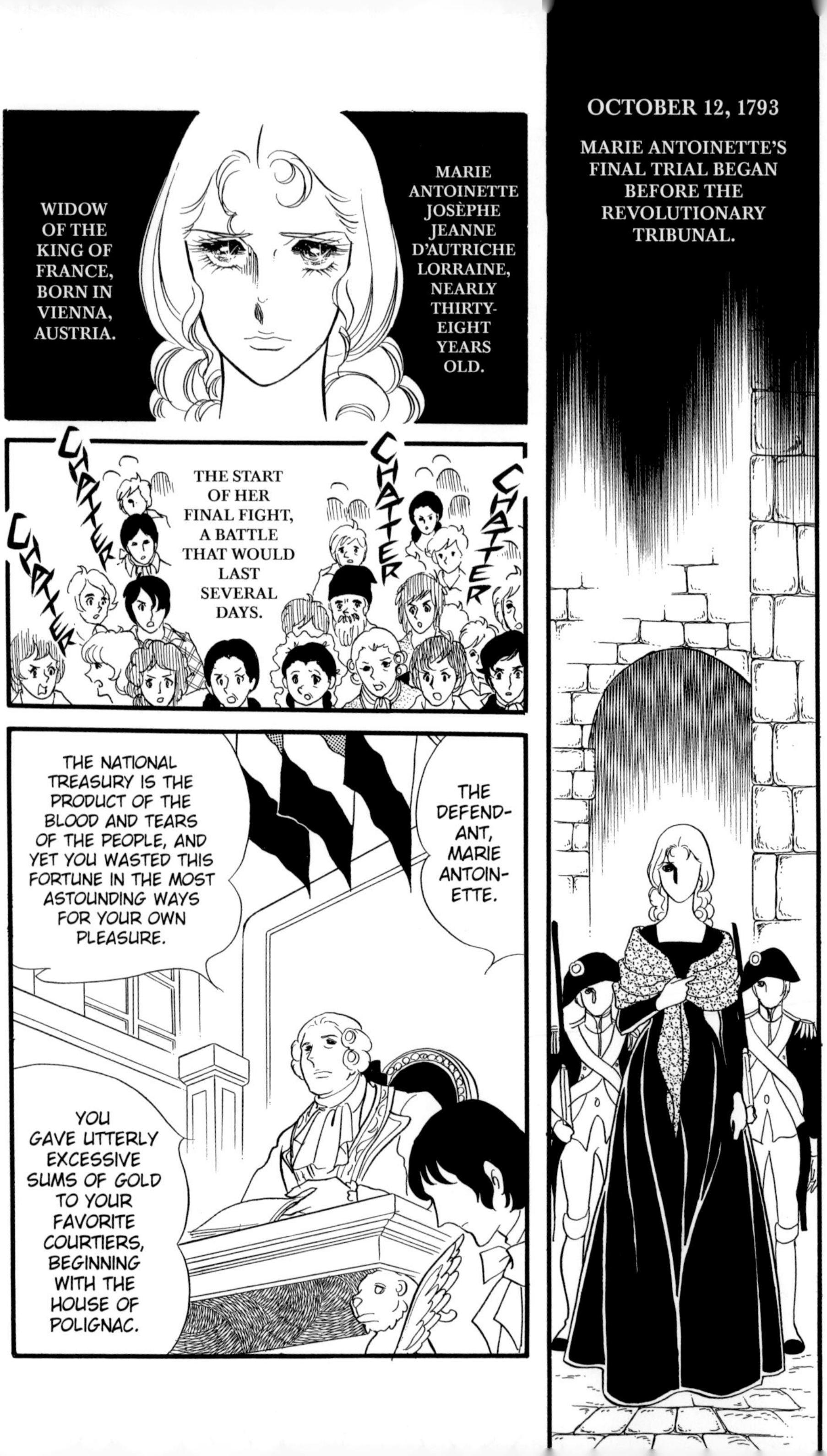
OCTOBER 12, 1793
MARIE ANTOINETTE'S FINAL TRIAL BEGAN BEFORE THE REVOLUTIONARY TRIBUNAL.
MARIE ANTOINETTE JOSÈPHE JEANNE D'AUTRICHE LORRAINE, NEARLY THIRTY-EIGHT YEARS OLD.
WIDOW OF THE KING OF FRANCE, BORN IN VIENNA, AUSTRIA.
CHATTER
CHATTER
THE START OF HER FINAL FIGHT, A BATTLE THAT WOULD LAST SEVERAL DAYS.
CHATTER
CHATTER
THE DEFENDANT, MARIE ANTOINETTE.
THE NATIONAL TREASURY IS THE PRODUCT OF THE BLOOD AND TEARS OF THE PEOPLE, AND YET YOU WASTED THIS FORTUNE IN THE MOST ASTOUNDING WAYS FOR YOUR OWN PLEASURE.
YOU GAVE UTTERLY EXCESSIVE SUMS OF GOLD TO YOUR FAVORITE COURTIERS, BEGINNING WITH THE HOUSE OF POLIGNAC.

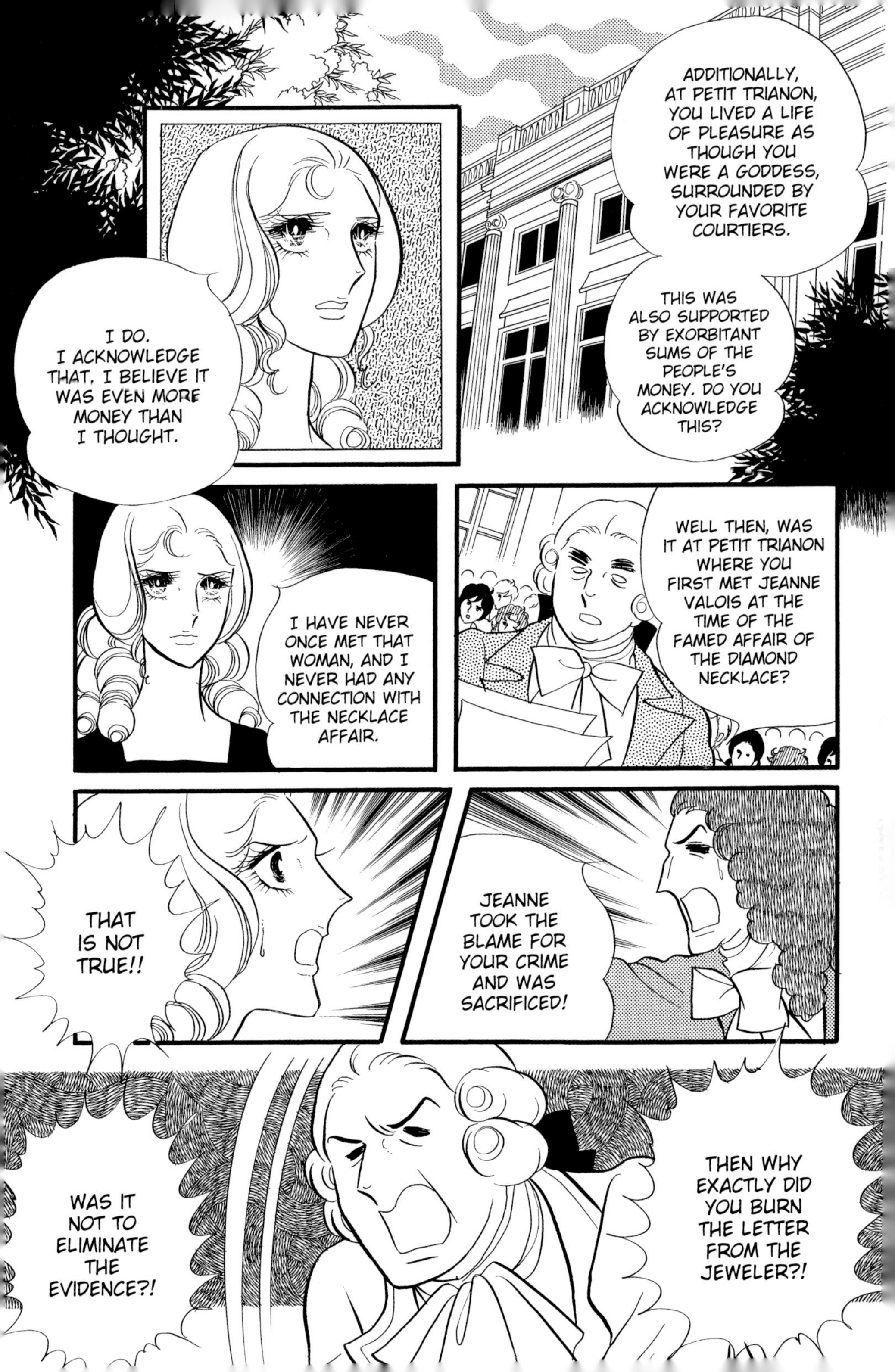

ADDITIONALLY, AT PETIT TRIANON, YOU LIVED A LIFE OF PLEASURE AS THOUGH YOU WERE A GODDESS, SURROUNDED BY YOUR FAVORITE COURTIERS.
THIS WAS ALSO SUPPORTED BY EXORBITANT SUMS OF THE PEOPLE'S MONEY. DO YOU ACKNOWLEDGE THIS?
I DO. I ACKNOWLEDGE THAT. I BELIEVE IT WAS EVEN MORE MONEY THAN I THOUGHT.
WELL THEN, WAS IT AT PETIT TRIANON WHERE YOU FIRST MET JEANNE VALOIS AT THE TIME OF THE FAMED AFFAIR OF THE DIAMOND NECKLACE?
I HAVE NEVER ONCE MET THAT WOMAN, AND I NEVER HAD ANY CONNECTION WITH THE NECKLACE AFFAIR.
JEANNE TOOK THE BLAME FOR YOUR CRIME AND WAS SACRIFICED!
THAT IS NOT TRUE!!
THEN WHY EXACTLY DID YOU BURN THE LETTER FROM THE JEWELER?!
WAS IT NOT TO ELIMINATE THE EVIDENCE?!

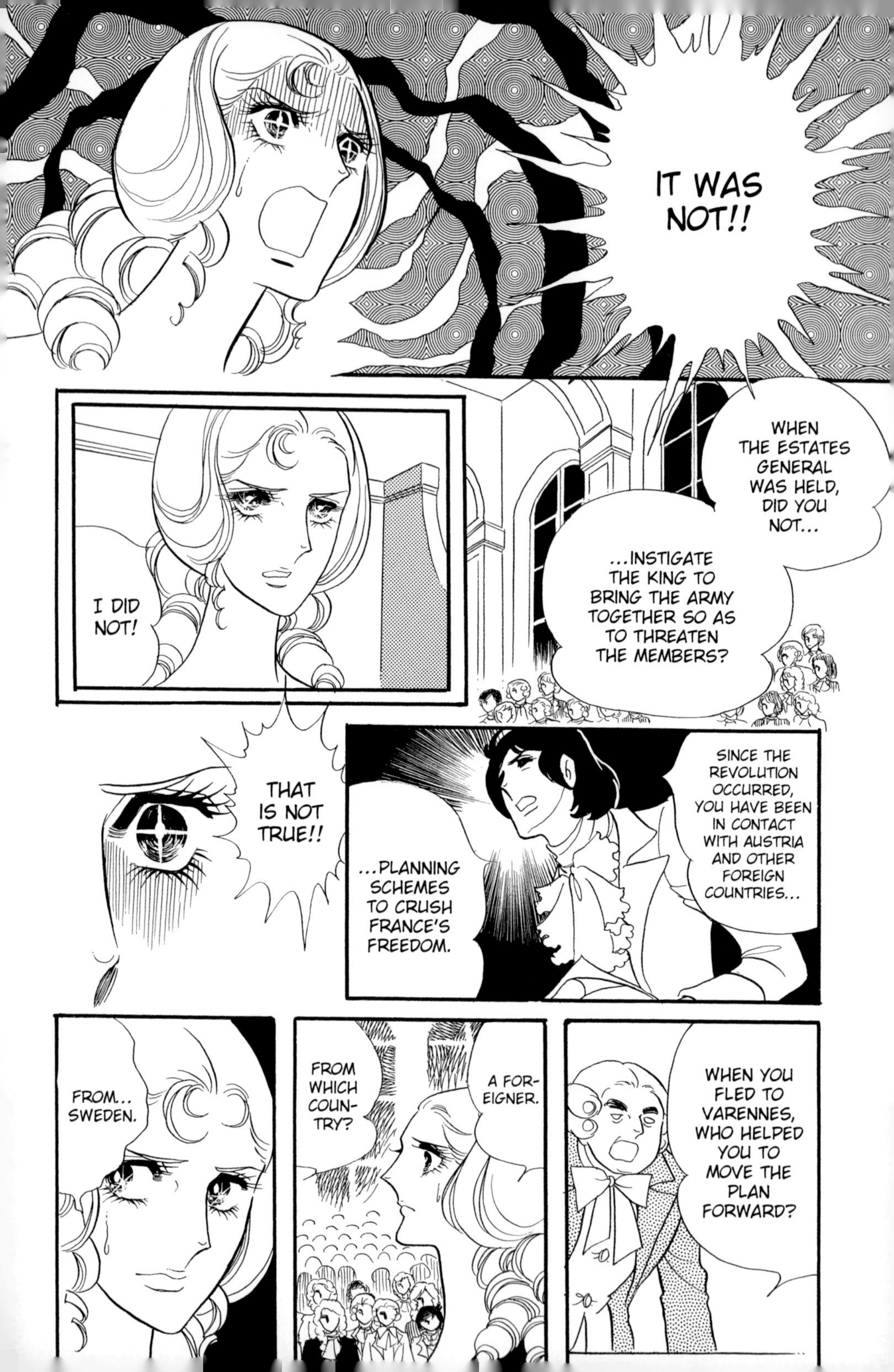
IT WAS NOT!!
WHEN THE ESTATES GENERAL WAS HELD, DID YOU NOT...
...INSTIGATE THE KING TO BRING THE ARMY TOGETHER SO AS TO THREATEN THE MEMBERS?
I DID NOT!
SINCE THE REVOLUTION OCCURRED, YOU HAVE BEEN IN CONTACT WITH AUSTRIA AND OTHER FOREIGN COUNTRIES...
...PLANNING SCHEMES TO CRUSH FRANCE'S FREEDOM.
THAT IS NOT TRUE!!
WHEN YOU FLED TO VARENNES, WHO HELPED YOU TO MOVE THE PLAN FORWARD?
A FOR-EIGNER.
FROM WHICH COUN-TRY?
FROM... SWEDEN.

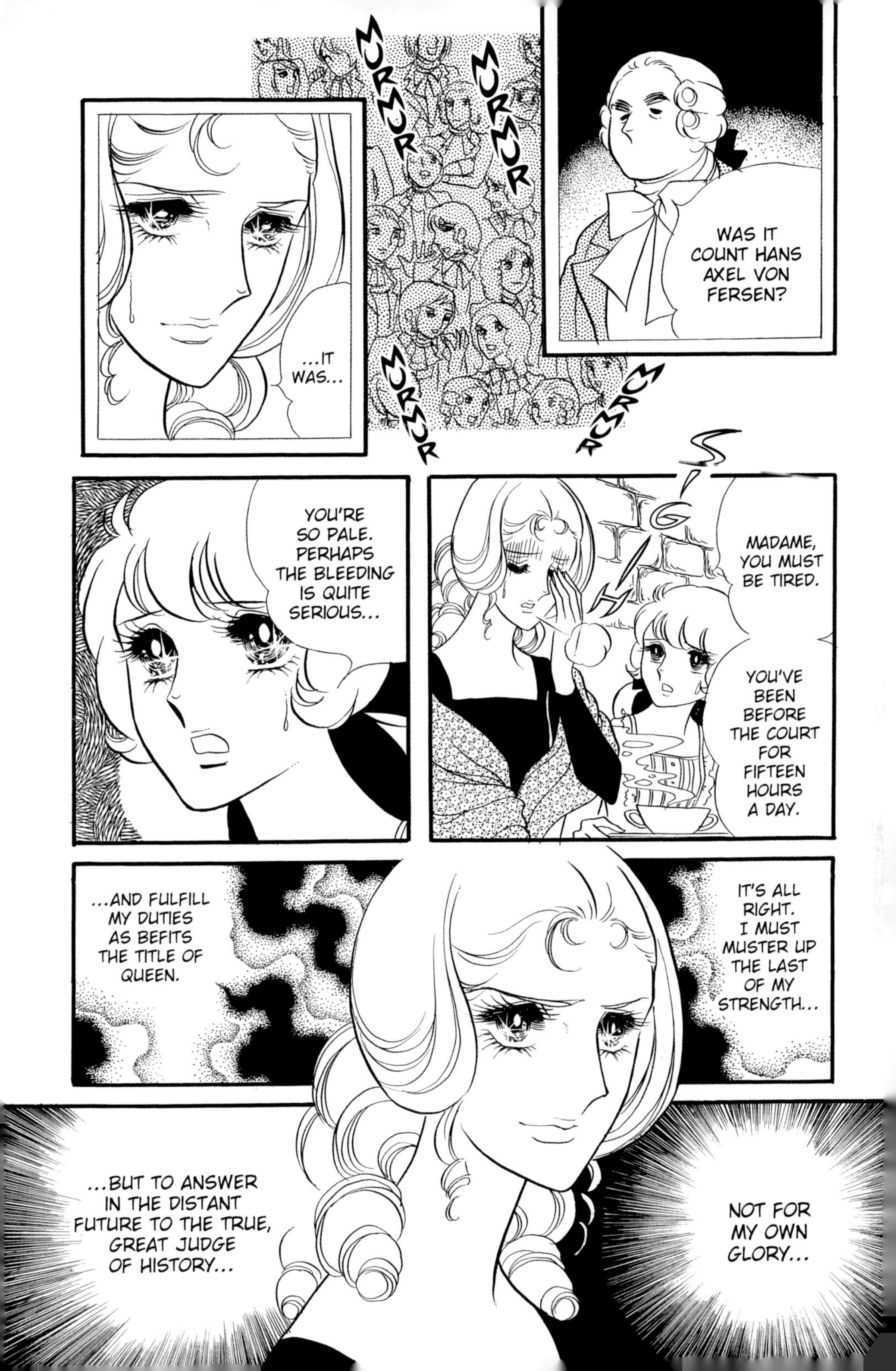
WAS IT COUNT HANS AXEL VON FERSEN?
MURMUR
MURMUR
MURMUR
MURMUR
...IT WAS...
SIGH
MADAME, YOU MUST BE TIRED.
YOU'VE BEEN BEFORE THE COURT FOR FIFTEEN HOURS A DAY.
YOU'RE SO PALE. PERHAPS THE BLEEDING IS QUITE SERIOUS...
IT'S ALL RIGHT. I MUST MUSTER UP THE LAST OF MY STRENGTH...
...AND FULFILL MY DUTIES AS BEFITS THE TITLE OF QUEEN.
NOT FOR MY OWN GLORY...
...BUT TO ANSWER IN THE DISTANT FUTURE TO THE TRUE, GREAT JUDGE OF HISTORY...

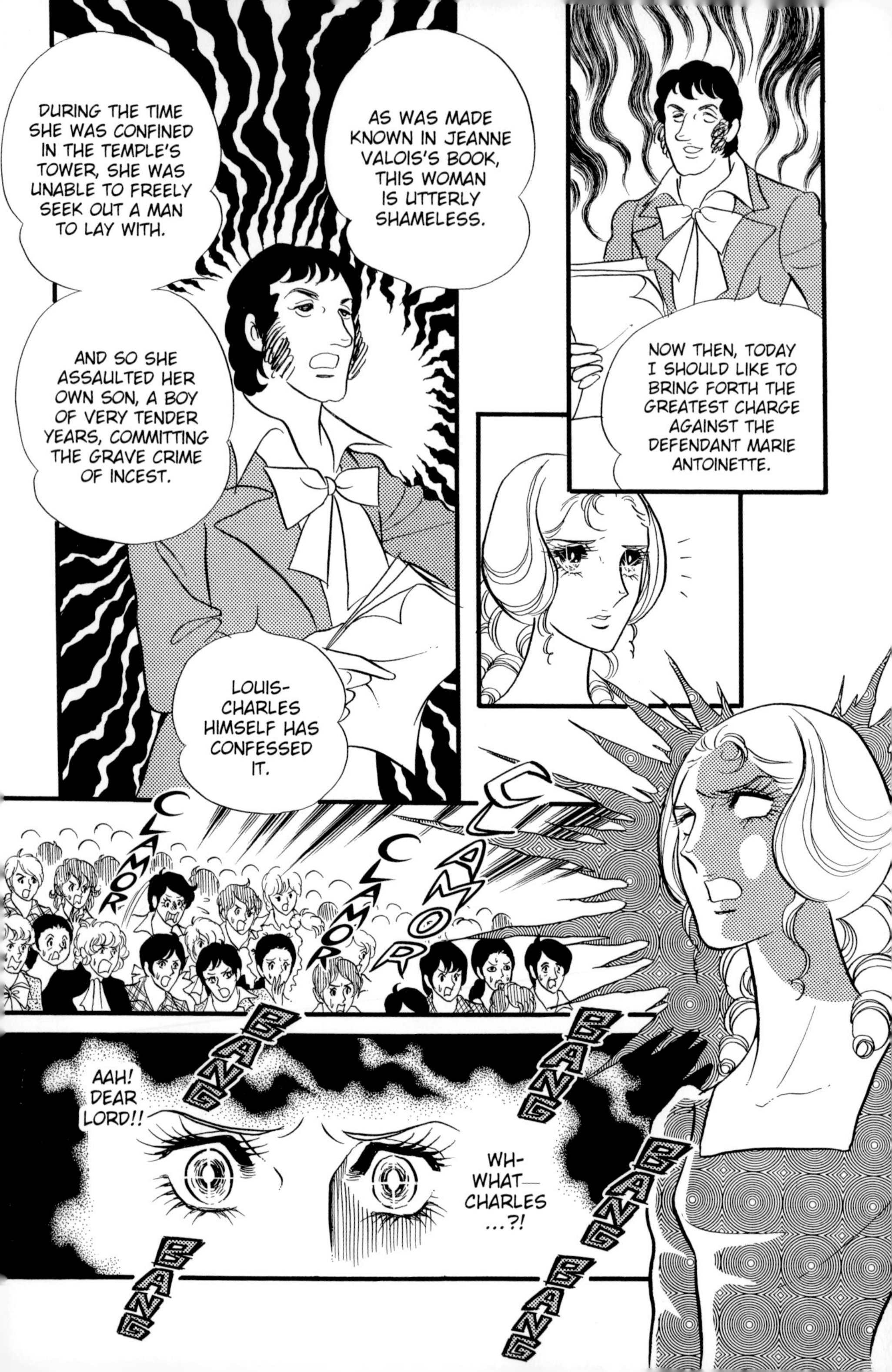
NOW THEN, TODAY I SHOULD LIKE TO BRING FORTH THE GREATEST CHARGE AGAINST THE DEFENDANT MARIE ANTOINETTE.
AS WAS MADE KNOWN IN JEANNE VALOIS'S BOOK, THIS WOMAN IS UTTERLY SHAMELESS.
DURING THE TIME SHE WAS CONFINED IN THE TEMPLE'S TOWER, SHE WAS UNABLE TO FREELY SEEK OUT A MAN TO LAY WITH.
AND SO SHE ASSAULTED HER OWN SON, A BOY OF VERY TENDER YEARS, COMMITTING THE GRAVE CRIME OF INCEST.
LOUIS-CHARLES HIMSELF HAS CONFESSED IT.
CLAMOR
CLAMOR
CLAMOR
CLAMOR
BANG
BANG
BANG
BANG
BANG
WH-WHAT— CHARLES ...?!
AAH! DEAR LORD!!

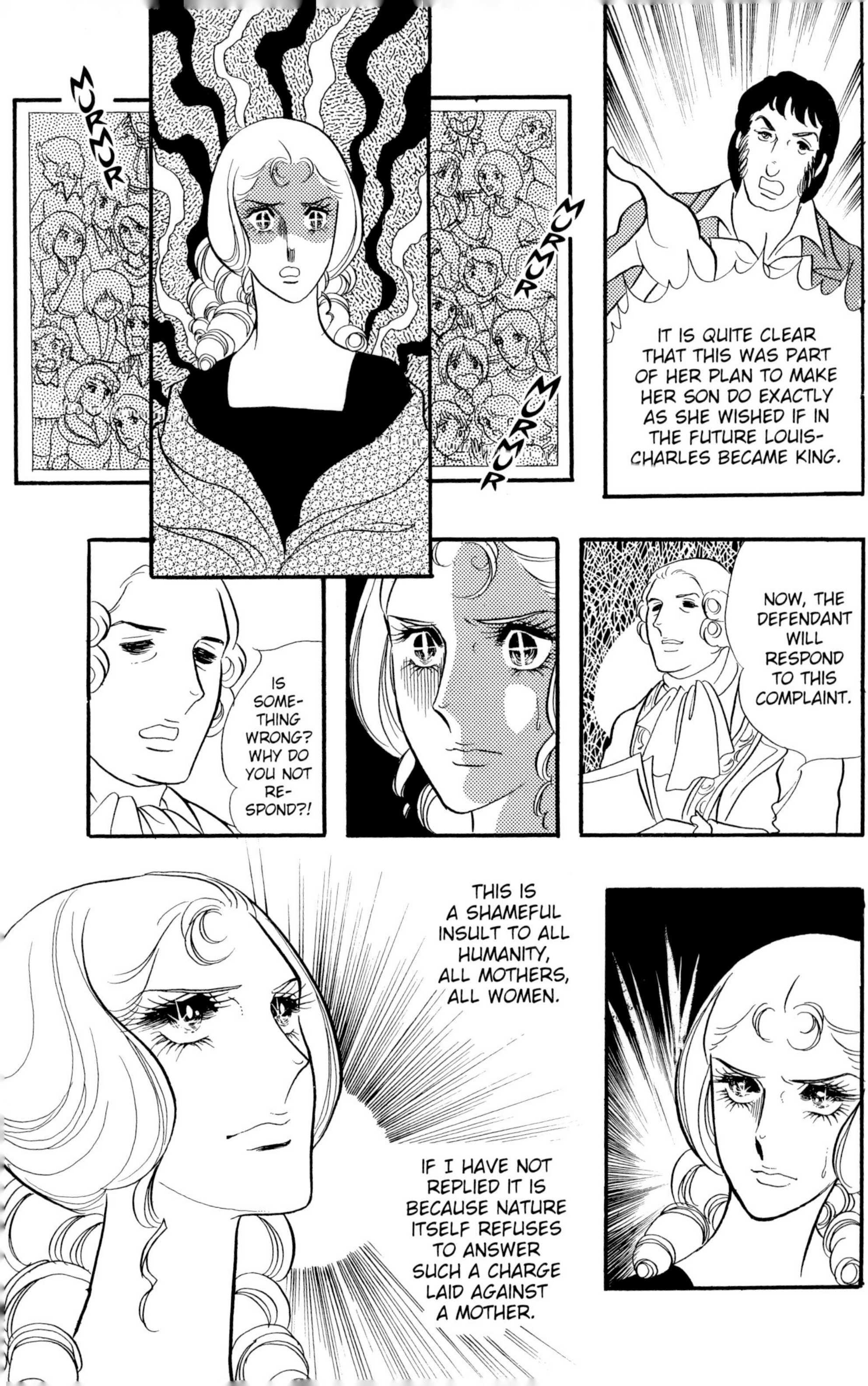
IT IS QUITE CLEAR THAT THIS WAS PART OF HER PLAN TO MAKE HER SON DO EXACTLY AS SHE WISHED IF IN THE FUTURE LOUIS-CHARLES BECAME KING.
MURMUR
MURMUR
MURMUR
NOW, THE DEFENDANT WILL RESPOND TO THIS COMPLAINT.
IS SOME-THING WRONG? WHY DO YOU NOT RE-SPOND?!
THIS IS A SHAMEFUL INSULT TO ALL HUMANITY, ALL MOTHERS, ALL WOMEN.
IF I HAVE NOT REPLIED IT IS BECAUSE NATURE ITSELF REFUSES TO ANSWER SUCH A CHARGE LAID AGAINST A MOTHER.

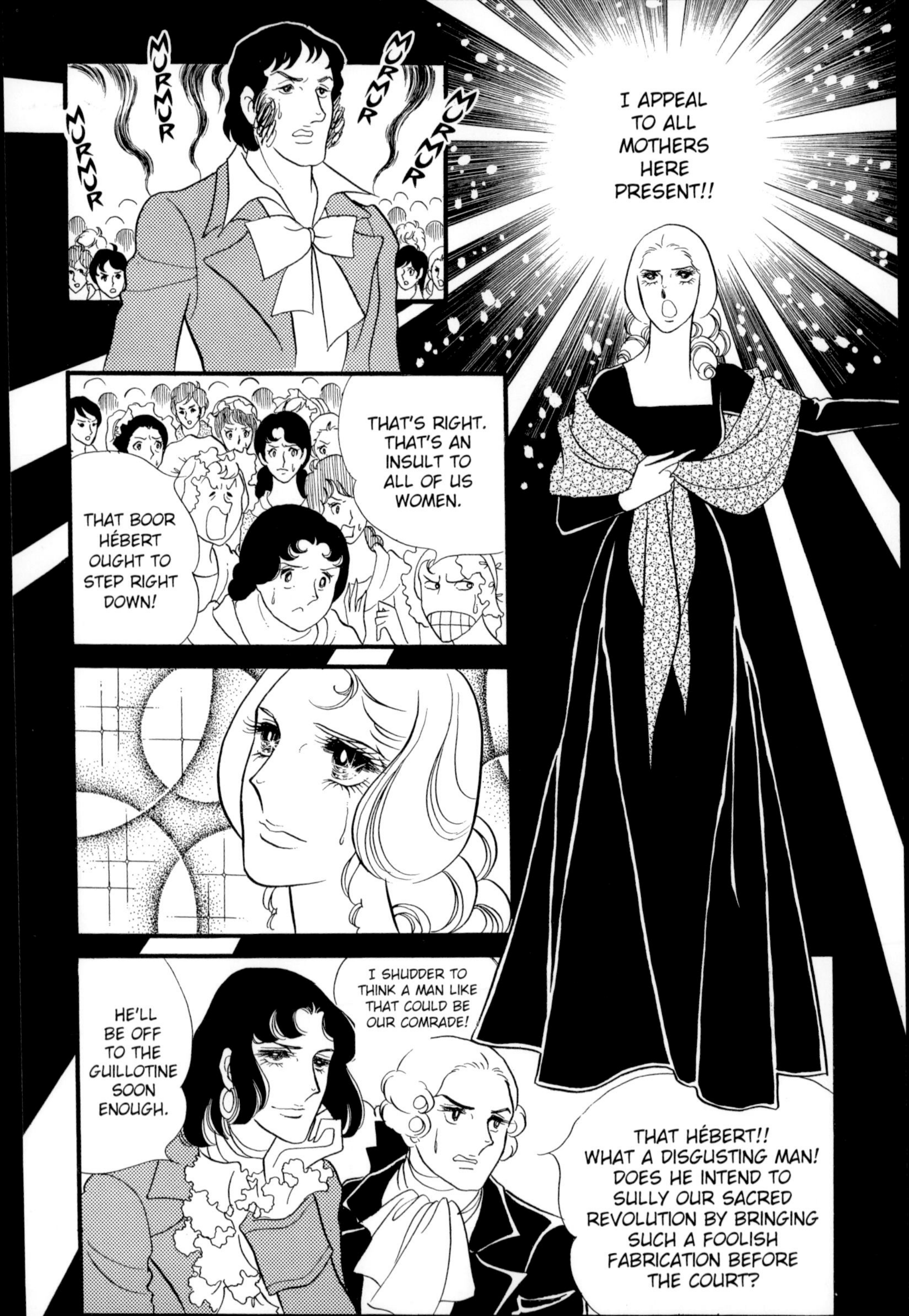
I APPEAL TO ALL MOTHERS HERE PRESENT!!
MURMUR
MURMUR
MURMUR
MURMUR
THAT'S RIGHT. THAT'S AN INSULT TO ALL OF US WOMEN.
THAT BOOR HÉBERT OUGHT TO STEP RIGHT DOWN!
THAT HÉBERT!! WHAT A DISGUSTING MAN! DOES HE INTEND TO SULLY OUR SACRED REVOLUTION BY BRINGING SUCH A FOOLISH FABRICATION BEFORE THE COURT?
I SHUDDER TO THINK A MAN LIKE THAT COULD BE OUR COMRADE!
HE'LL BE OFF TO THE GUILLOTINE SOON ENOUGH.

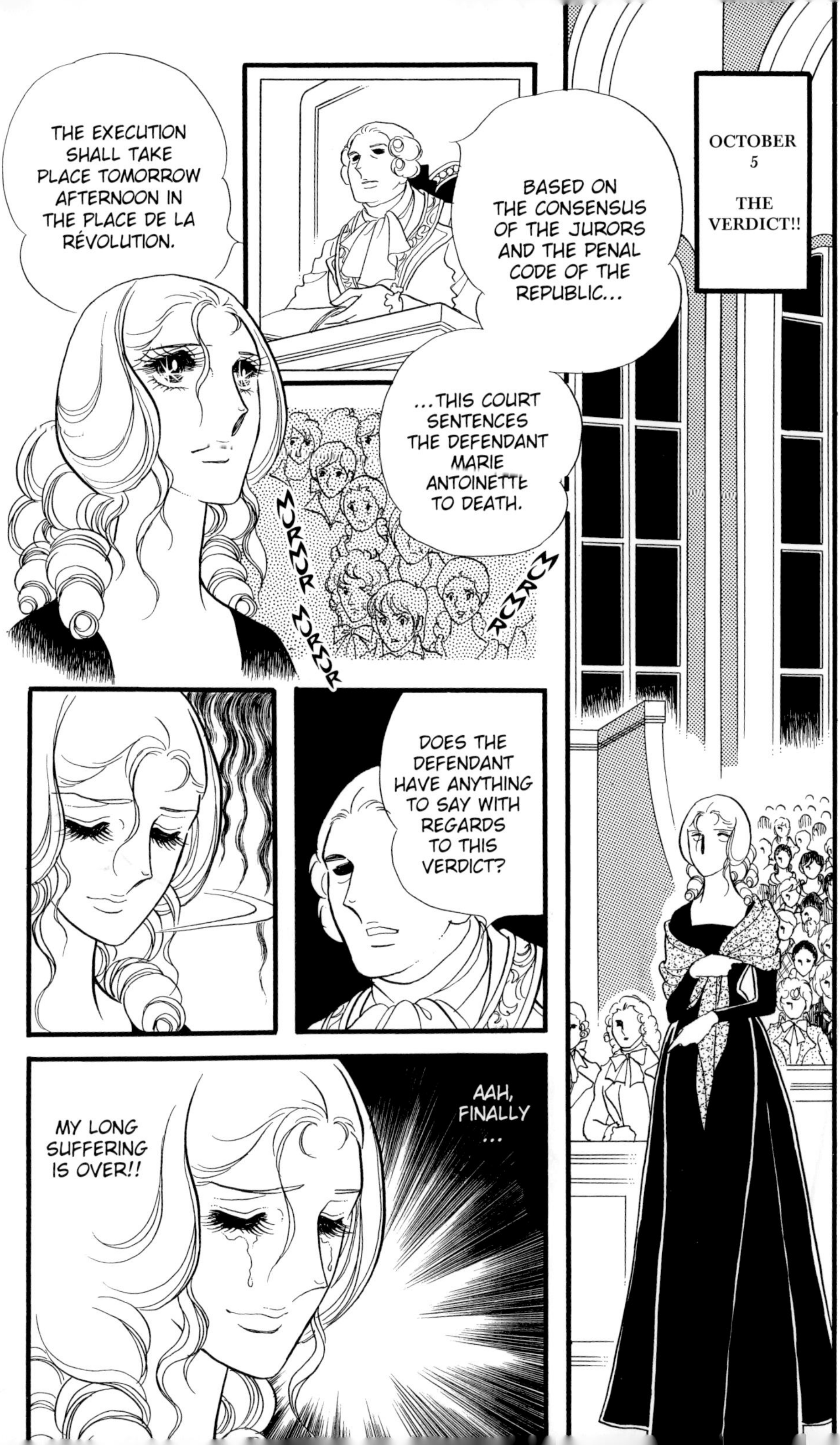

OCTOBER 5 THE VERDICT!!
BASED ON THE CONSENSUS OF THE JURORS AND THE PENAL CODE OF THE REPUBLIC...
...THIS COURT SENTENCES THE DEFENDANT MARIE ANTOINETTE TO DEATH.
MURMUR
MURMUR MURMUR
THE EXECUTION SHALL TAKE PLACE TOMORROW AFTERNOON IN THE PLACE DE LA RÉVOLUTION.
DOES THE DEFENDANT HAVE ANYTHING TO SAY WITH REGARDS TO THIS VERDICT?
AAH, FINALLY ...
MY LONG SUFFERING IS OVER!!

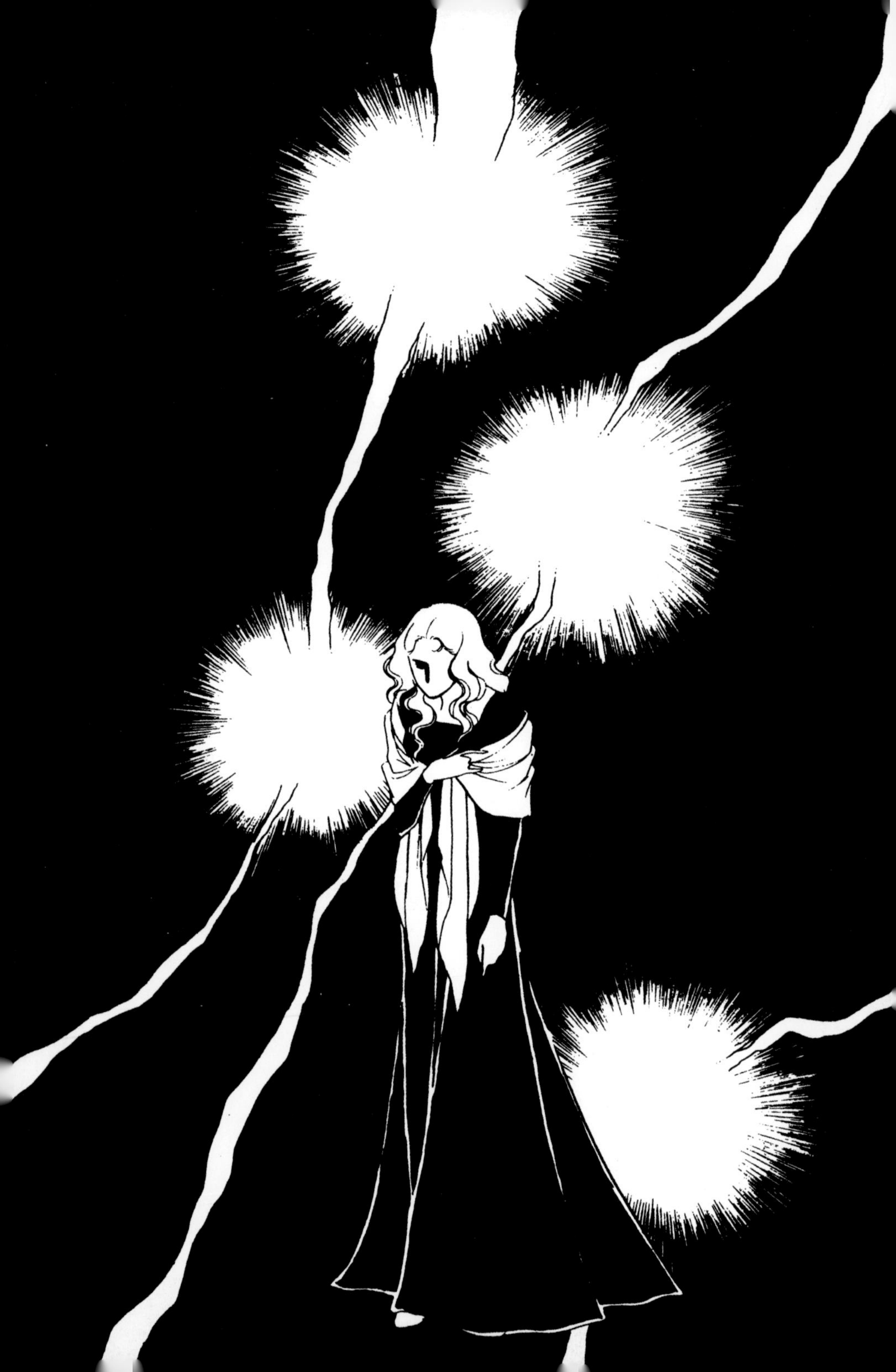

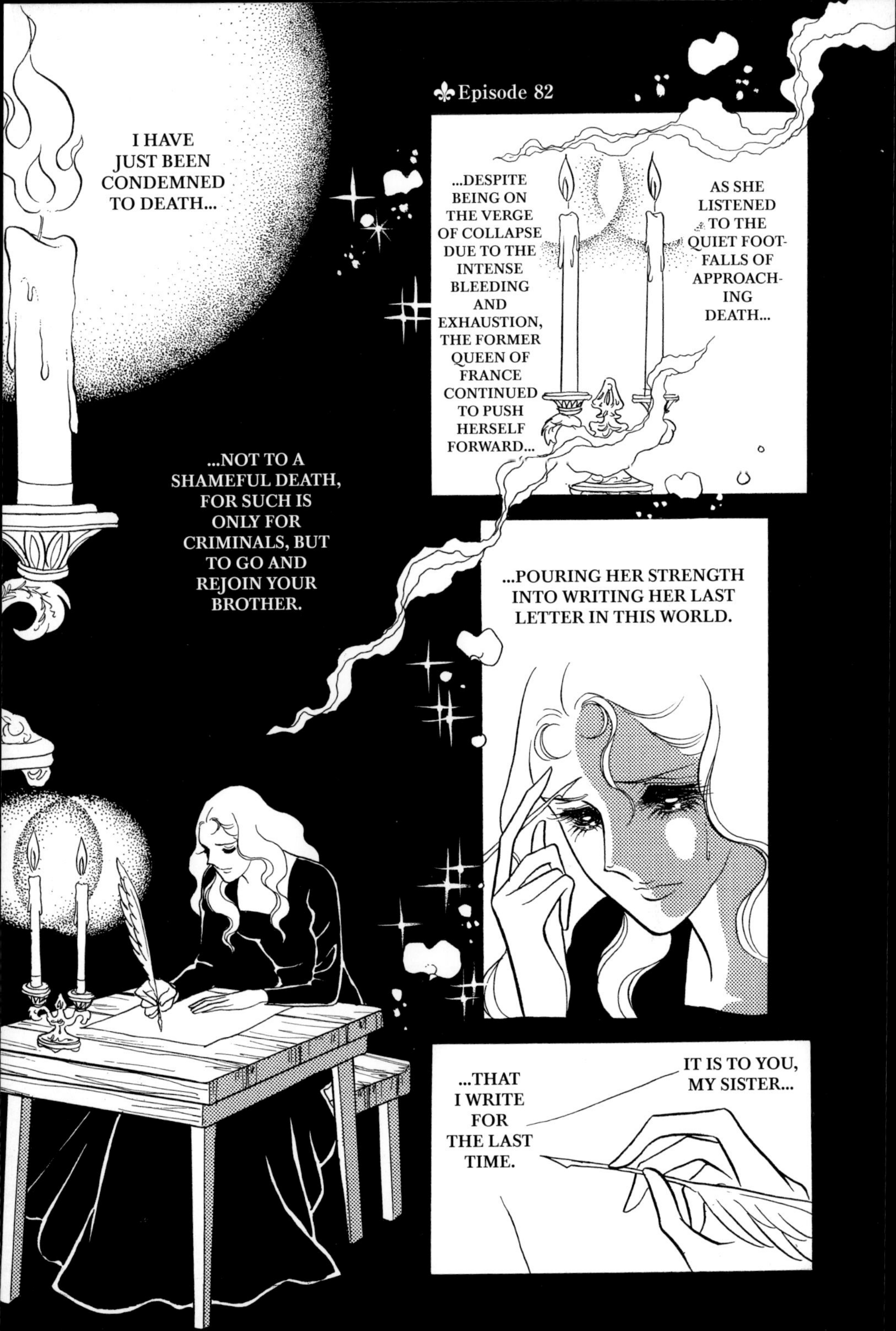
Episode 82
AS SHE LISTENED TO THE QUIET FOOT-FALLS OF APPROACH-ING DEATH...
...DESPITE BEING ON THE VERGE OF COLLAPSE DUE TO THE INTENSE BLEEDING AND EXHAUSTION, THE FORMER QUEEN OF FRANCE CONTINUED TO PUSH HERSELF FORWARD...
...POURING HER STRENGTH INTO WRITING HER LAST LETTER IN THIS WORLD.
IT IS TO YOU, MY SISTER...
...THAT I WRITE FOR THE LAST TIME.
I HAVE JUST BEEN CONDEMNED TO DEATH...
...NOT TO A SHAMEFUL DEATH, FOR SUCH IS ONLY FOR CRIMINALS, BUT TO GO AND REJOIN YOUR BROTHER.

INNOCENT LIKE HIM,
I HOPE TO SHOW THE
SAME FIRMNESS IN
MY LAST MOMENTS.
I AM CALM, AS ONE IS
WHEN ONE'S CONSCIENCE
REPROACHES ONE
WITH NOTHING.

I FEEL PROFOUND SORROW
IN LEAVING MY POOR CHILDREN:
YOU KNOW THAT I ONLY LIVED
FOR THEM AND FOR YOU,
MY GOOD AND TENDER SISTER.
YOU WHO OUT OF LOVE HAVE
SACRIFICED EVERYTHING TO BE WITH US,
IN WHAT A POSITION DO I LEAVE YOU! ...
IN OUR OWN MISFORTUNES HOW
MUCH COMFORT HAS OUR AFFECTION
FOR ONE ANOTHER AFFORDED
US! AND, IN TIMES OF HAPPINESS,
WE HAVE ENJOYED THAT DOUBLY
FROM BEING ABLE TO SHARE IT
WITH A FRIEND. ...

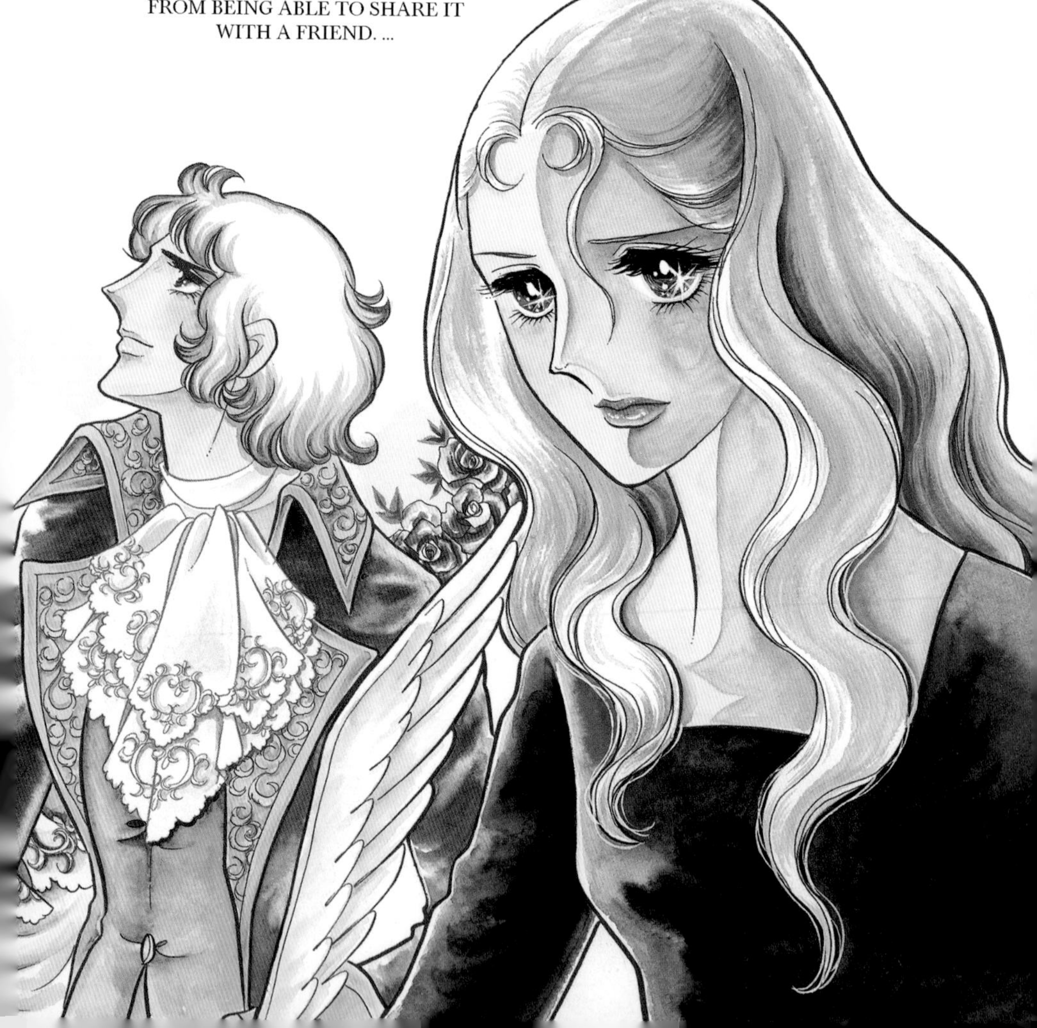

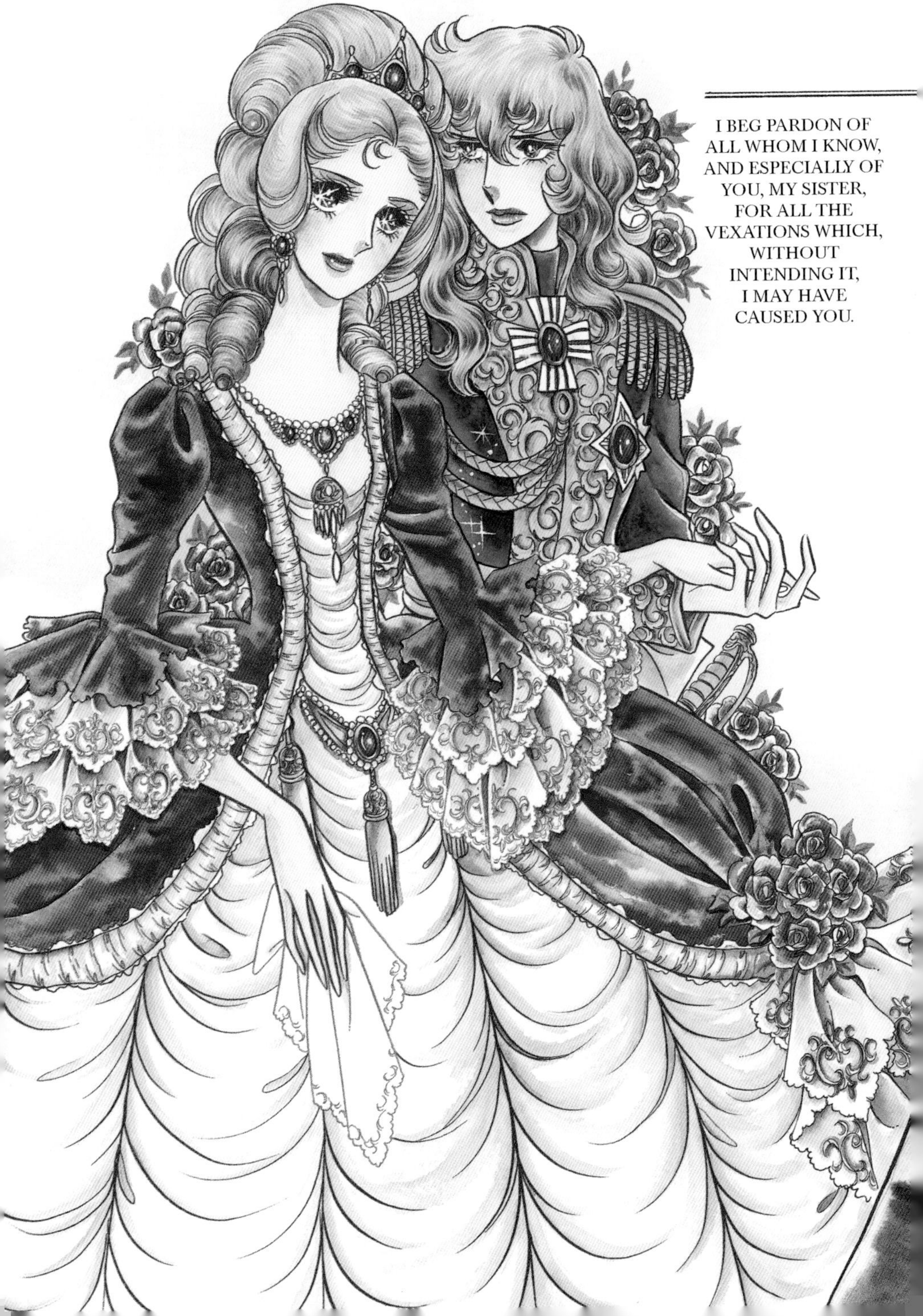
I BEG PARDON OF ALL WHOM I KNOW, AND ESPECIALLY OF YOU, MY SISTER, FOR ALL THE VEXATIONS WHICH, WITHOUT INTENDING IT, I MAY HAVE CAUSED YOU.

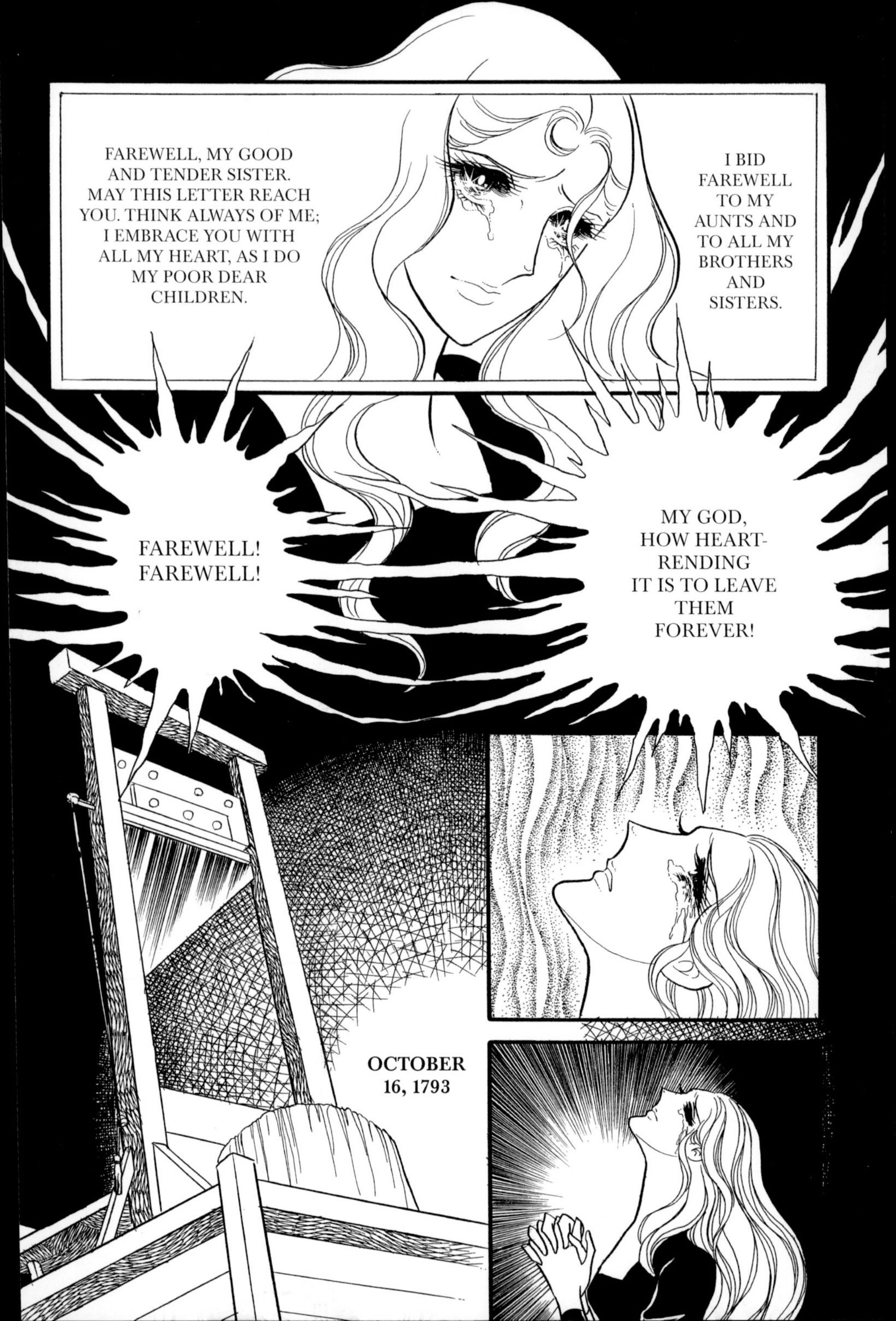
I BID FAREWELL TO MY AUNTS AND TO ALL MY BROTHERS AND SISTERS.
FAREWELL, MY GOOD AND TENDER SISTER. MAY THIS LETTER REACH YOU. THINK ALWAYS OF ME; I EMBRACE YOU WITH ALL MY HEART, AS I DO MY POOR DEAR CHILDREN.
MY GOD, HOW HEART-RENDING IT IS TO LEAVE THEM FOREVER!
FAREWELL! FAREWELL!
OCTOBER 16, 1793

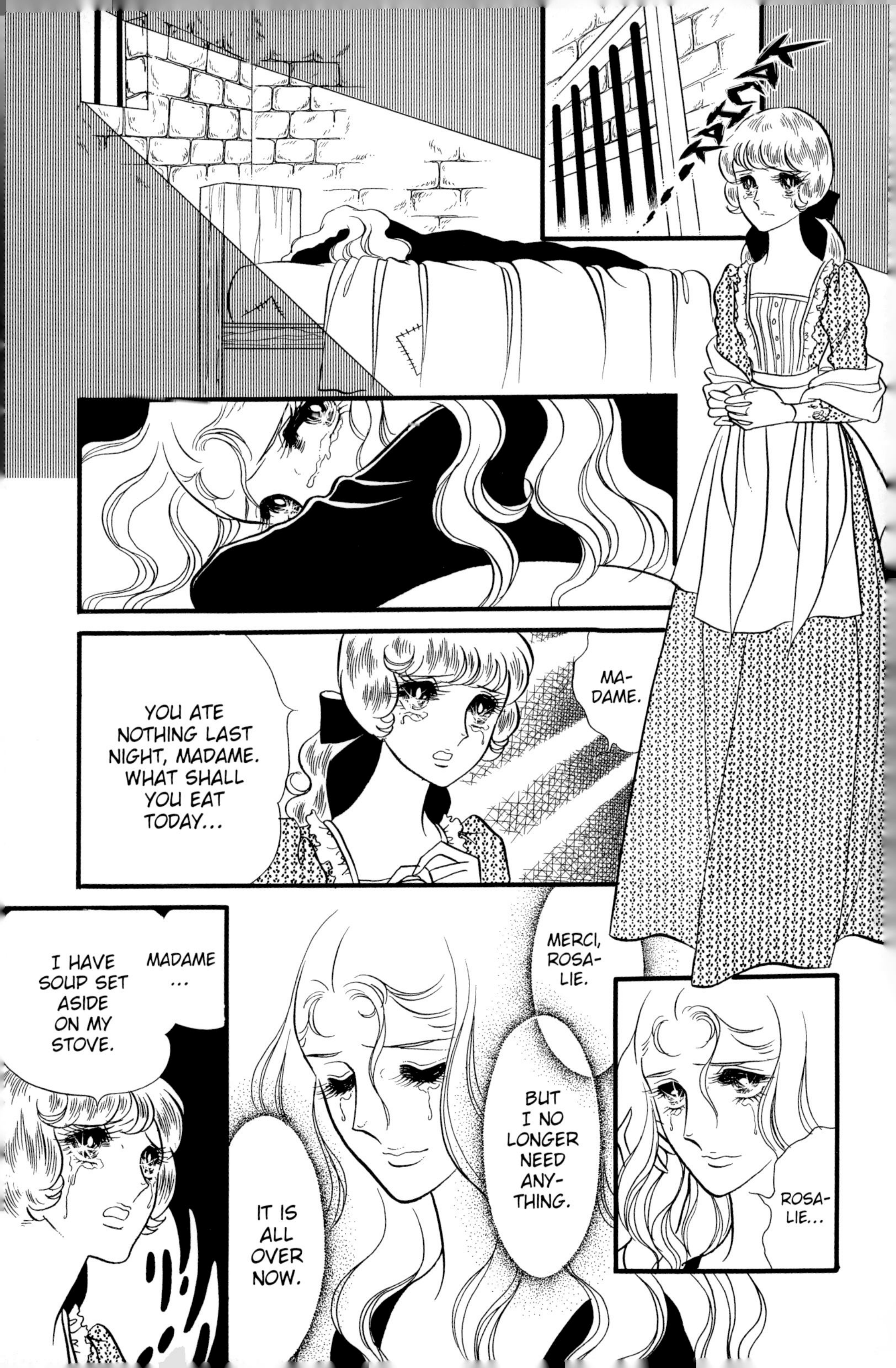
MA-DAME.
YOU ATE NOTHING LAST NIGHT, MADAME. WHAT SHALL YOU EAT TODAY...
ROSA-LIE...
MERCI, ROSA-LIE.
BUT I NO LONGER NEED ANY-THING.
IT IS ALL OVER NOW.
MADAME ...
I HAVE SOUP SET ASIDE ON MY STOVE.

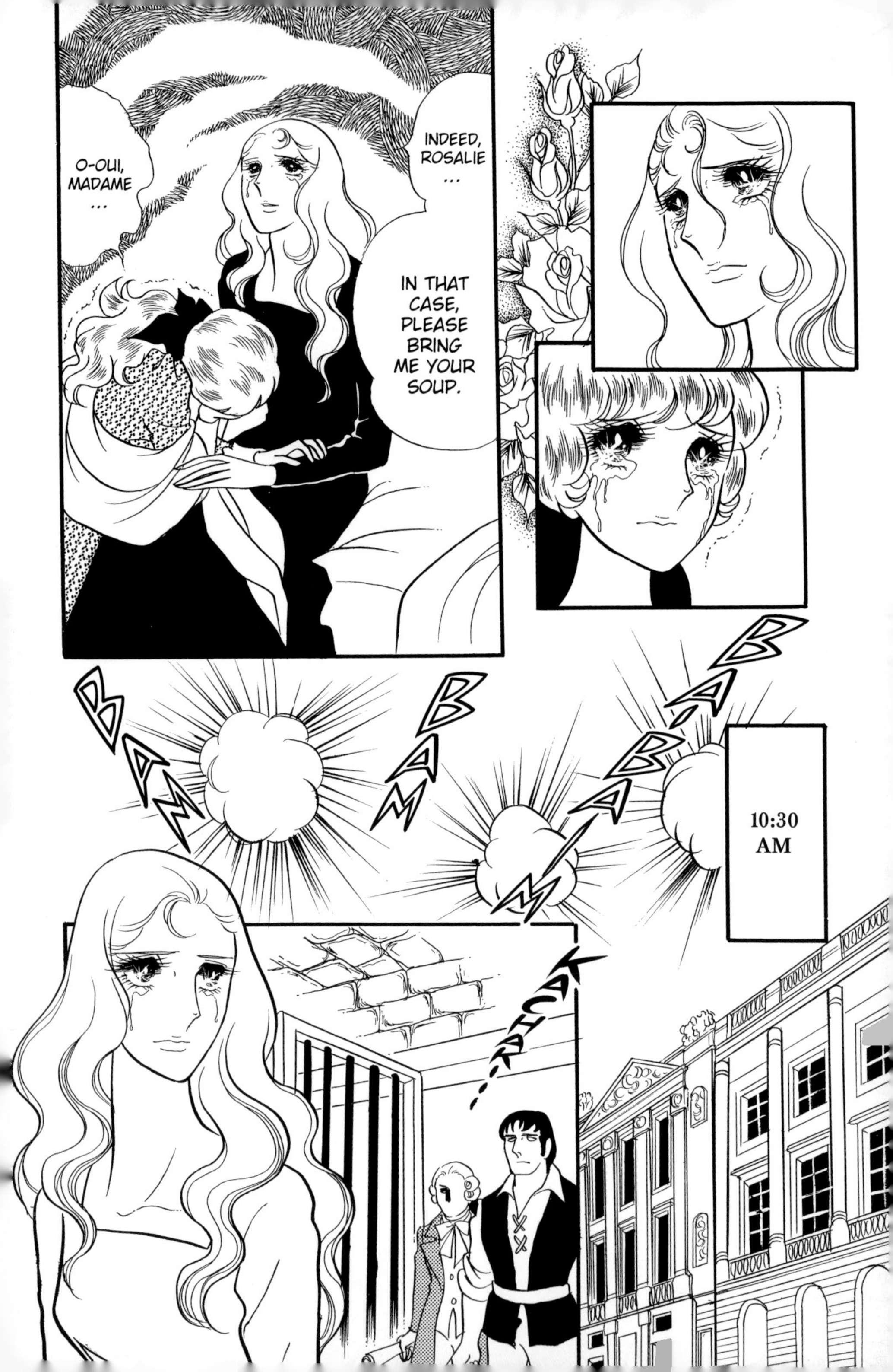
INDEED, ROSALIE ...
IN THAT CASE, PLEASE BRING ME YOUR SOUP.
O-OUI, MADAME ...
10:30 AM
BABAM
BAM
BAM
KACHAK...

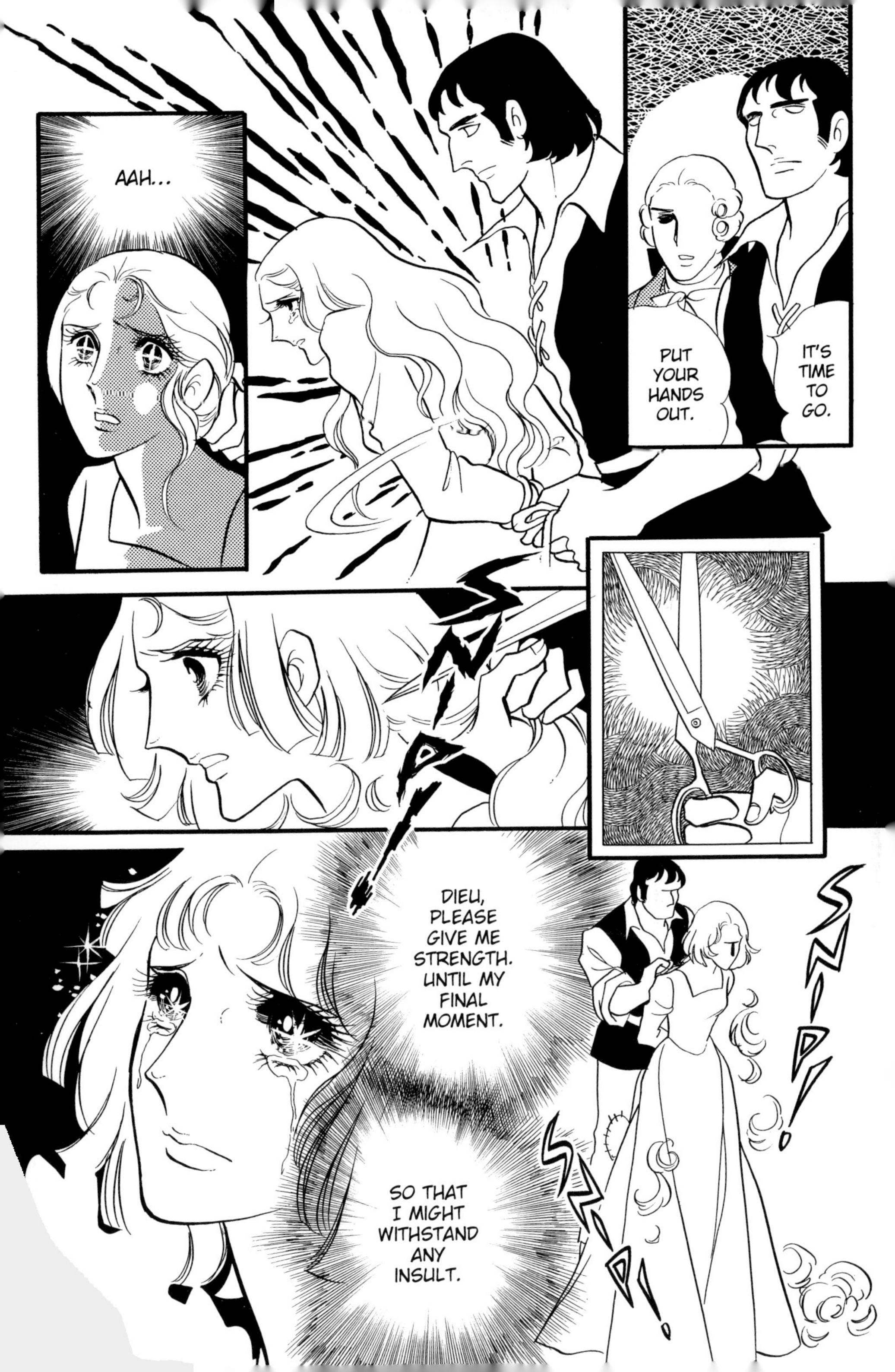

IT'S TIME TO GO.
PUT YOUR HANDS OUT.
AAH...
SNAP
SNIP!
SNIP!
DIEU, PLEASE GIVE ME STRENGTH. UNTIL MY FINAL MOMENT.
SO THAT I MIGHT WITHSTAND ANY INSULT.

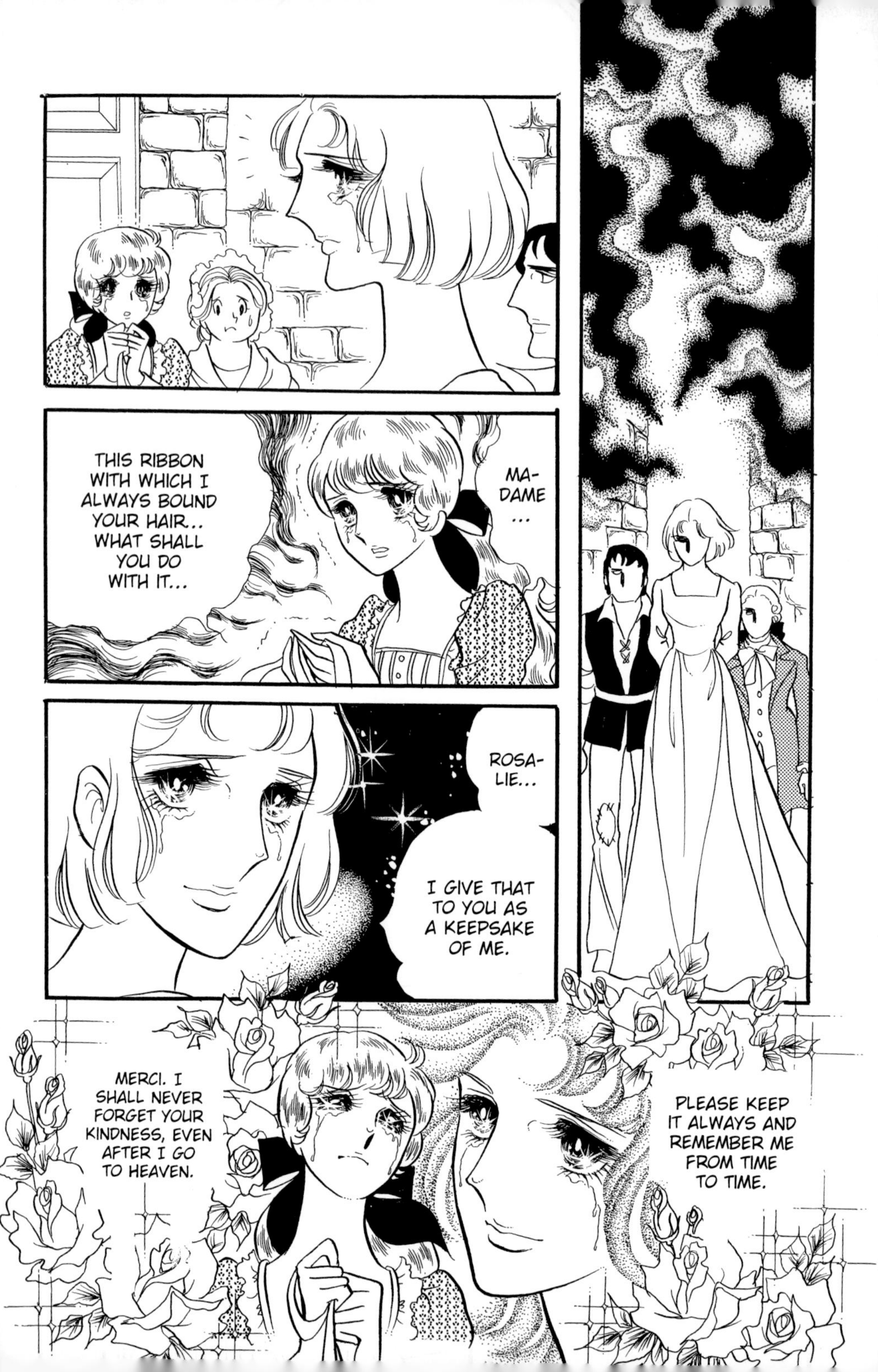
MA-DAME...
THIS RIBBON WITH WHICH I ALWAYS BOUND YOUR HAIR... WHAT SHALL YOU DO WITH IT...
ROSA-LIE...
I GIVE THAT TO YOU AS A KEEPSAKE OF ME.
PLEASE KEEP IT ALWAYS AND REMEMBER ME FROM TIME TO TIME.
MERCI. I SHALL NEVER FORGET YOUR KINDNESS, EVEN AFTER I GO TO HEAVEN.

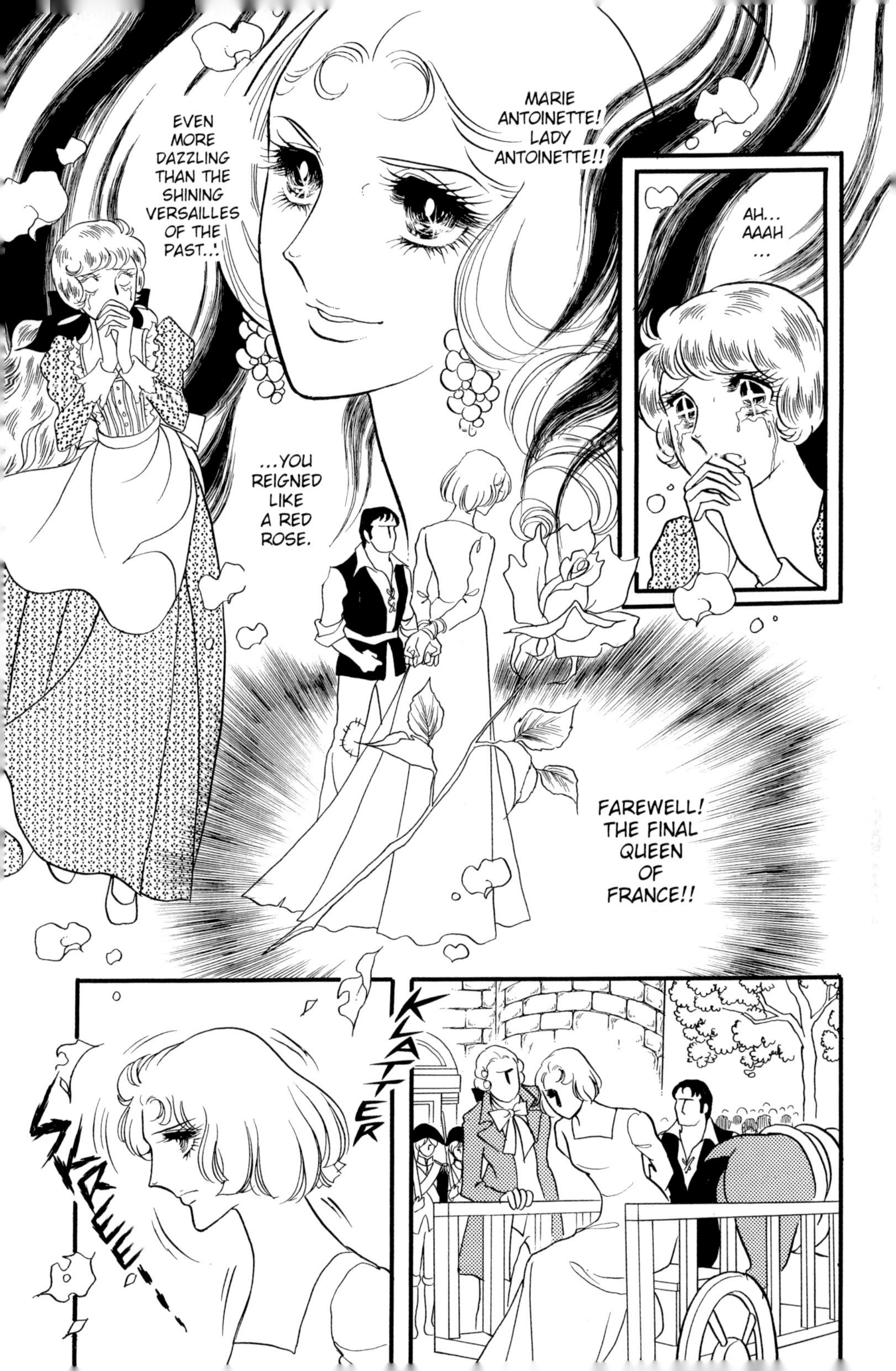
MARIE ANTOINETTE! LADY ANTOINETTE!!
AH... AAAH ...
EVEN MORE DAZZLING THAN THE SHINING VERSAILLES OF THE PAST..!
...YOU REIGNED LIKE A RED ROSE.
FAREWELL! THE FINAL QUEEN OF FRANCE!!
KLATTER
SKREEE...

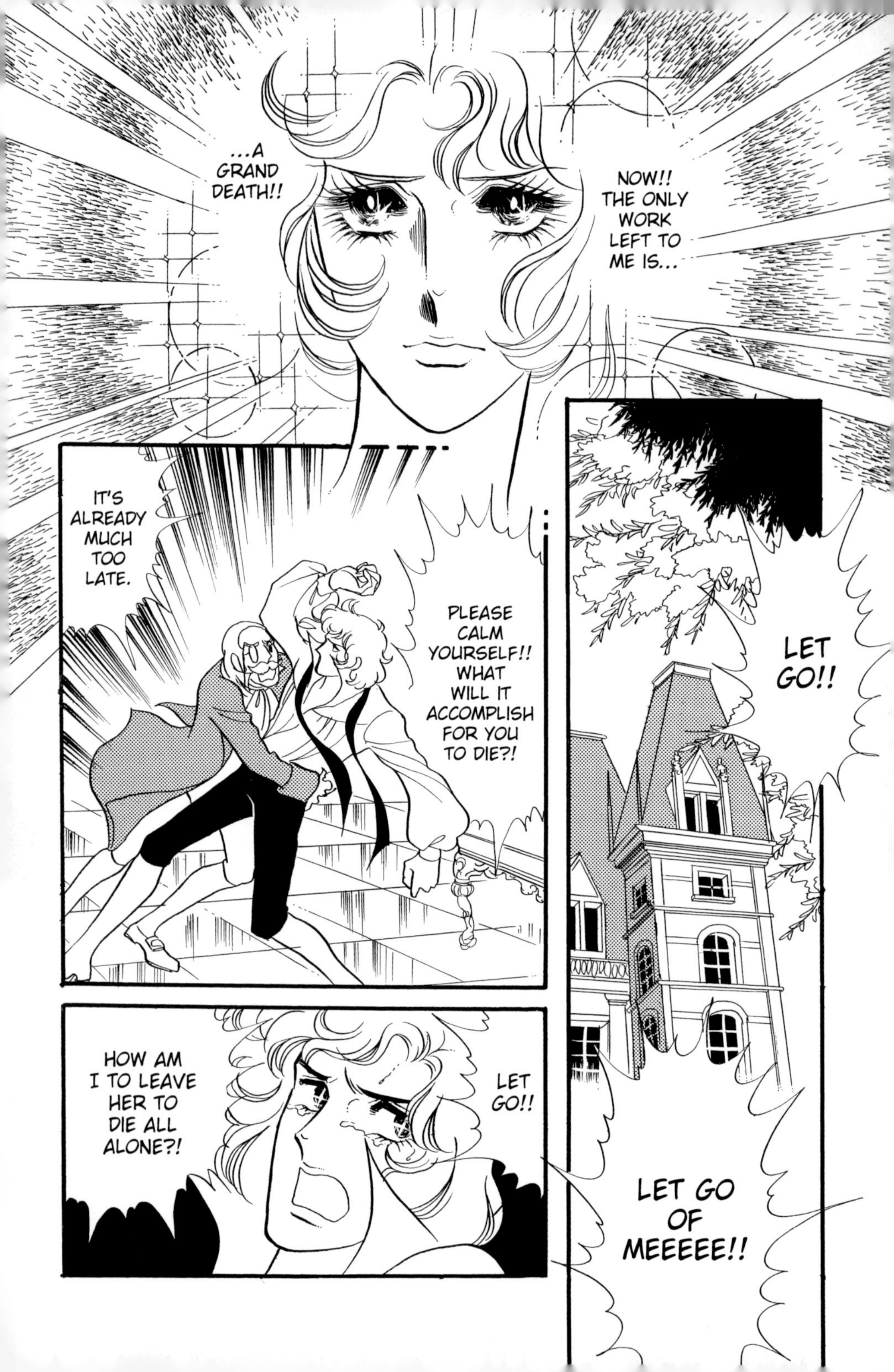
NOW!! THE ONLY WORK LEFT TO ME IS...
...A GRAND DEATH!!
LET GO!!
LET GO OF MEEEEE!!
PLEASE CALM YOURSELF!! WHAT WILL IT ACCOMPLISH FOR YOU TO DIE?!
IT'S ALREADY MUCH TOO LATE.
LET GO!!
HOW AM I TO LEAVE HER TO DIE ALL ALONE?!

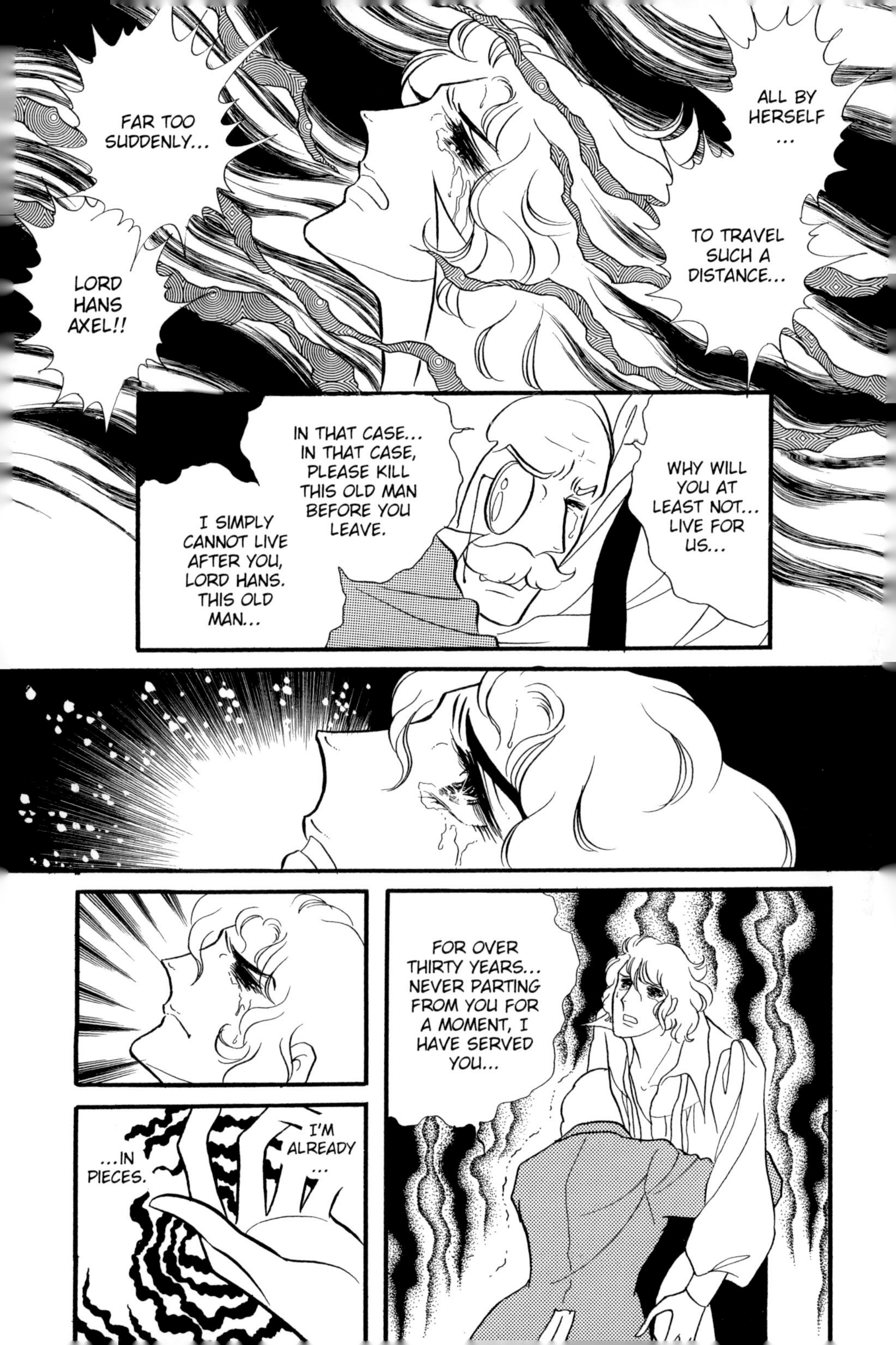
ALL BY HERSELF ...
TO TRAVEL SUCH A DISTANCE...
FAR TOO SUDDENLY...
LORD HANS AXEL!!
WHY WILL YOU AT LEAST NOT... LIVE FOR US...
IN THAT CASE... IN THAT CASE, PLEASE KILL THIS OLD MAN BEFORE YOU LEAVE.
I SIMPLY CANNOT LIVE AFTER YOU, LORD HANS. THIS OLD MAN...
FOR OVER THIRTY YEARS... NEVER PARTING FROM YOU FOR A MOMENT, I HAVE SERVED YOU...
I'M ALREADY ...
...IN PIECES.

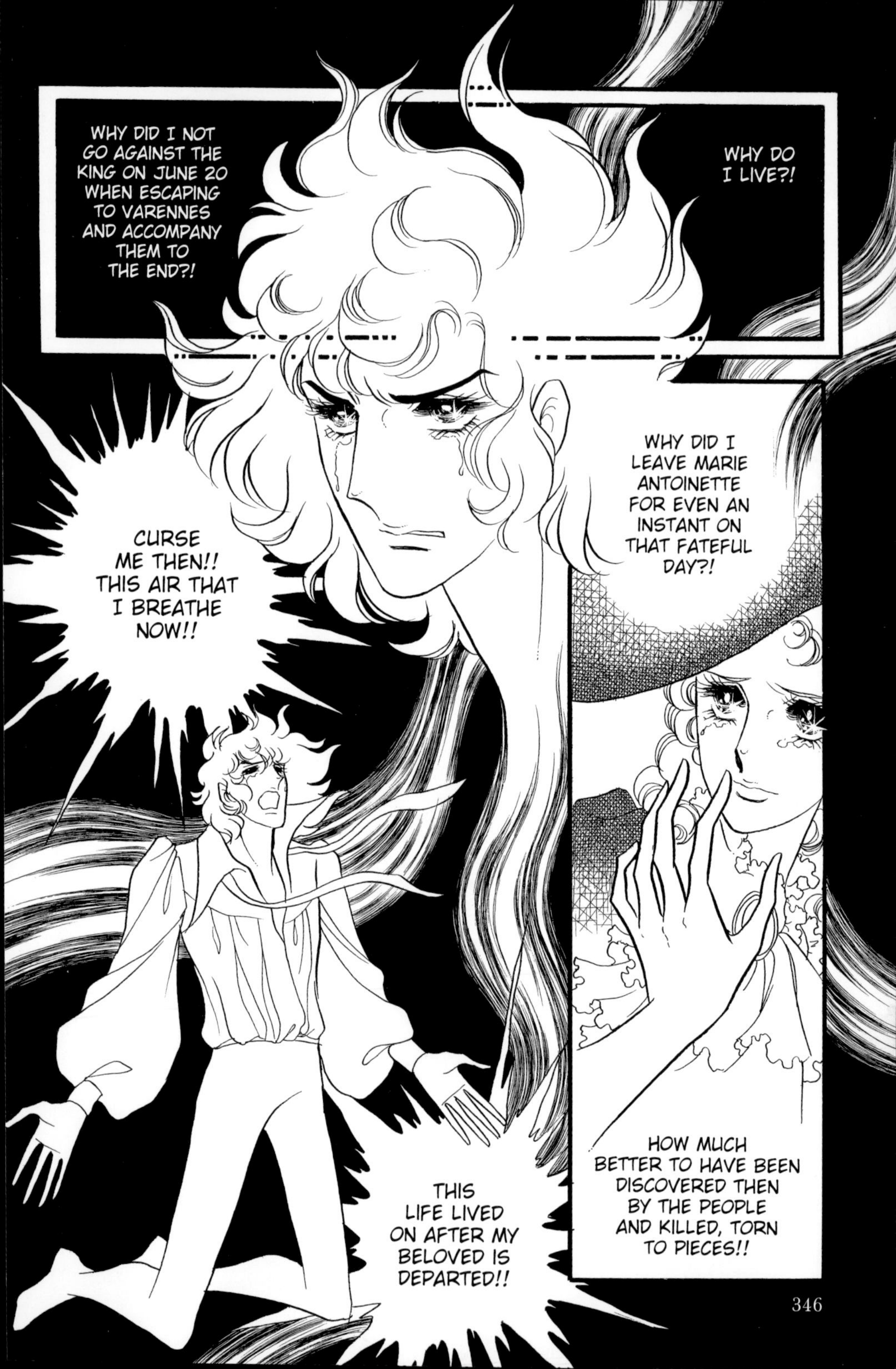
WHY DO I LIVE?!
WHY DID I NOT GO AGAINST THE KING ON JUNE 20 WHEN ESCAPING TO VARENNES AND ACCOMPANY THEM TO THE END?!
WHY DID I LEAVE MARIE ANTOINETTE FOR EVEN AN INSTANT ON THAT FATEFUL DAY?!
HOW MUCH BETTER TO HAVE BEEN DISCOVERED THEN BY THE PEOPLE AND KILLED, TORN TO PIECES!!
CURSE ME THEN!! THIS AIR THAT I BREATHE NOW!!
THIS LIFE LIVED ON AFTER MY BELOVED IS DEPARTED!!

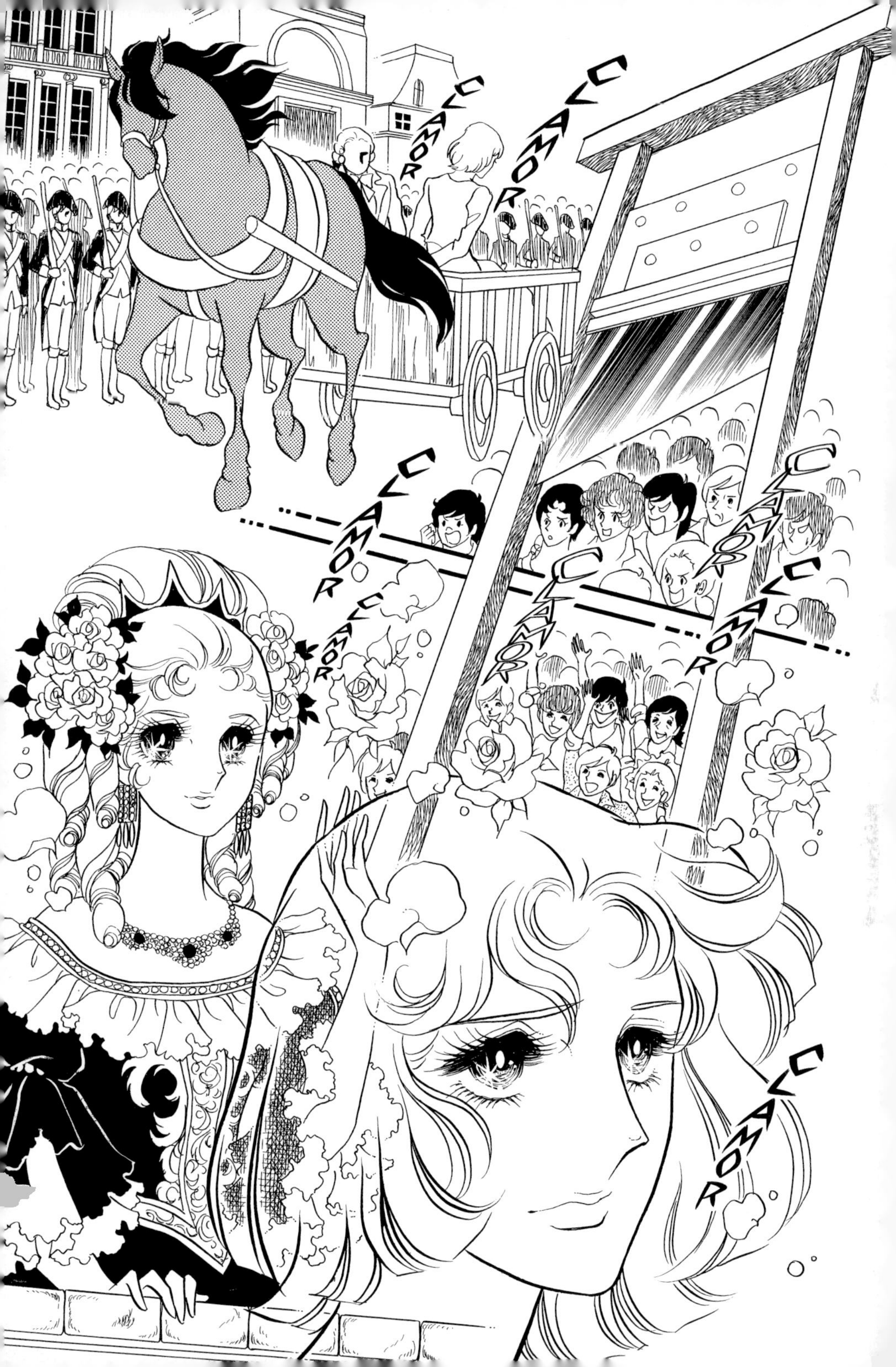

CLAMOR
CLAMOR
CLAMOR
CLAMOR
CLAMOR
CLAMOR
CLAMOR
CLAMOR

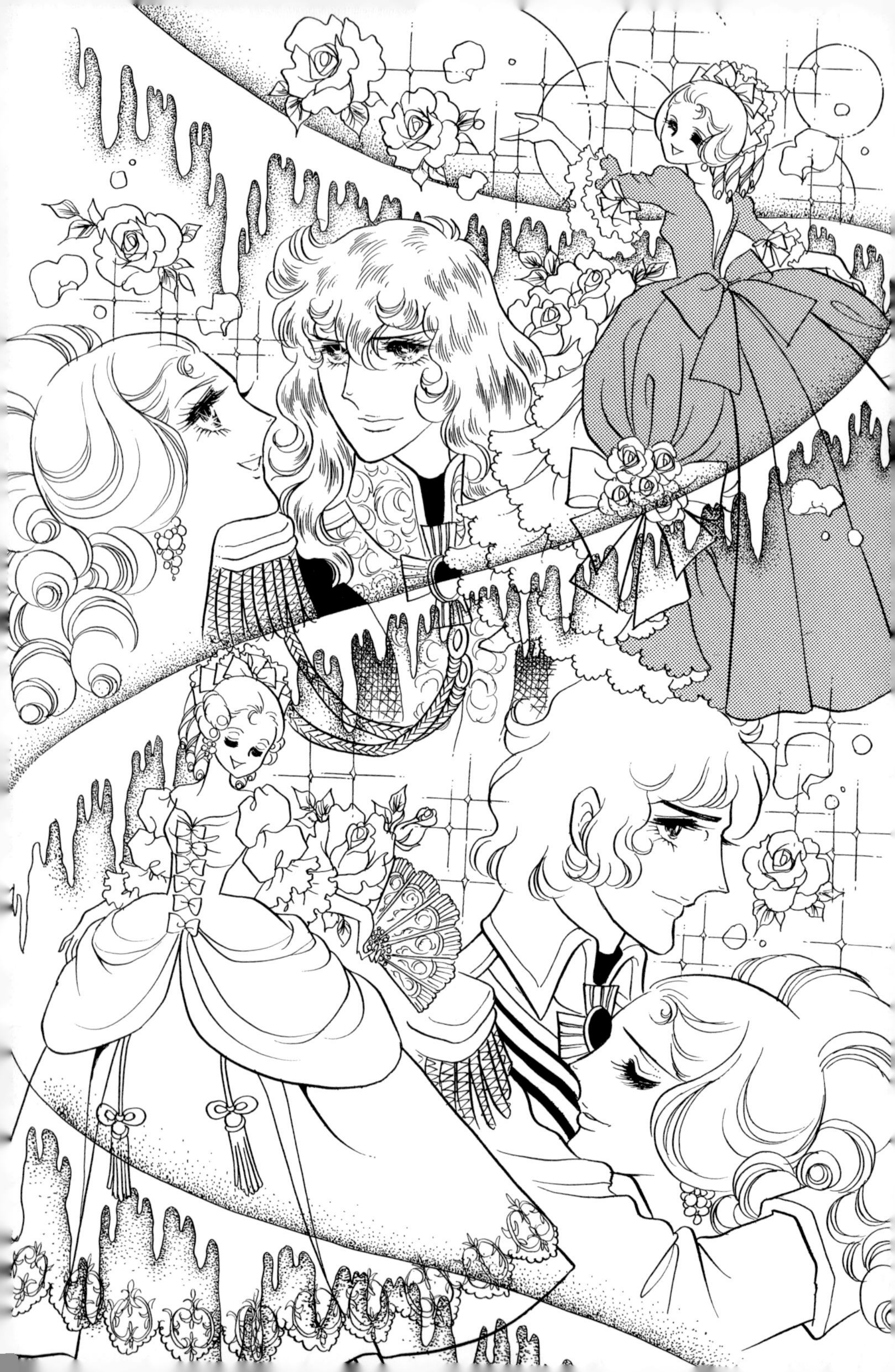

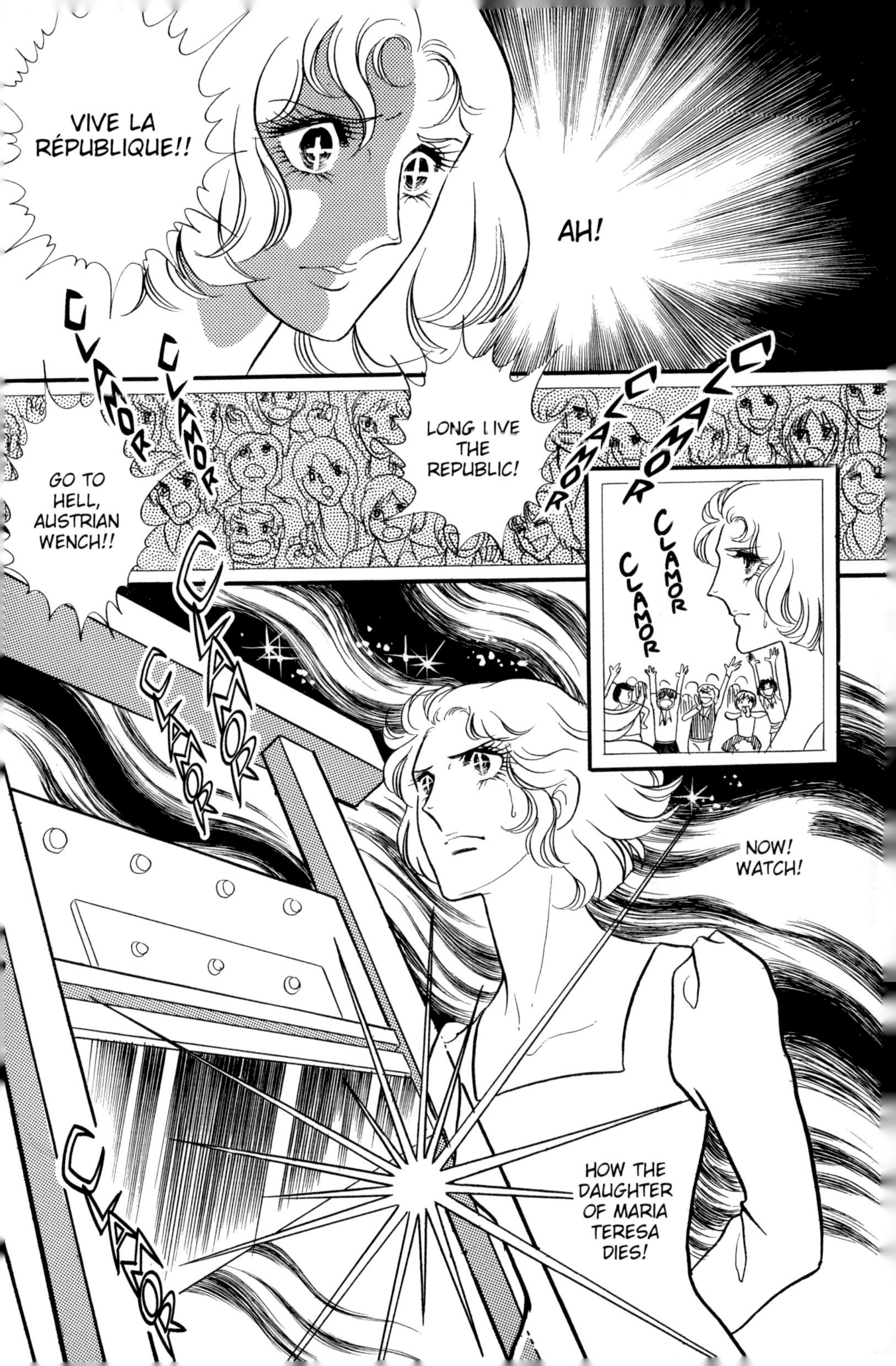
VIVE LA RÉPUBLIQUE!!
AH!
CLAMOR CLAMOR
LONG LIVE THE REPUBLIC!
CLAMOR CLAMOR
GO TO HELL, AUSTRIAN WENCH!!
CLAMOR CLAMOR
NOW! WATCH!
HOW THE DAUGHTER OF MARIA TERESA DIES!
CLAMOR CLAMOR
CLAMOR

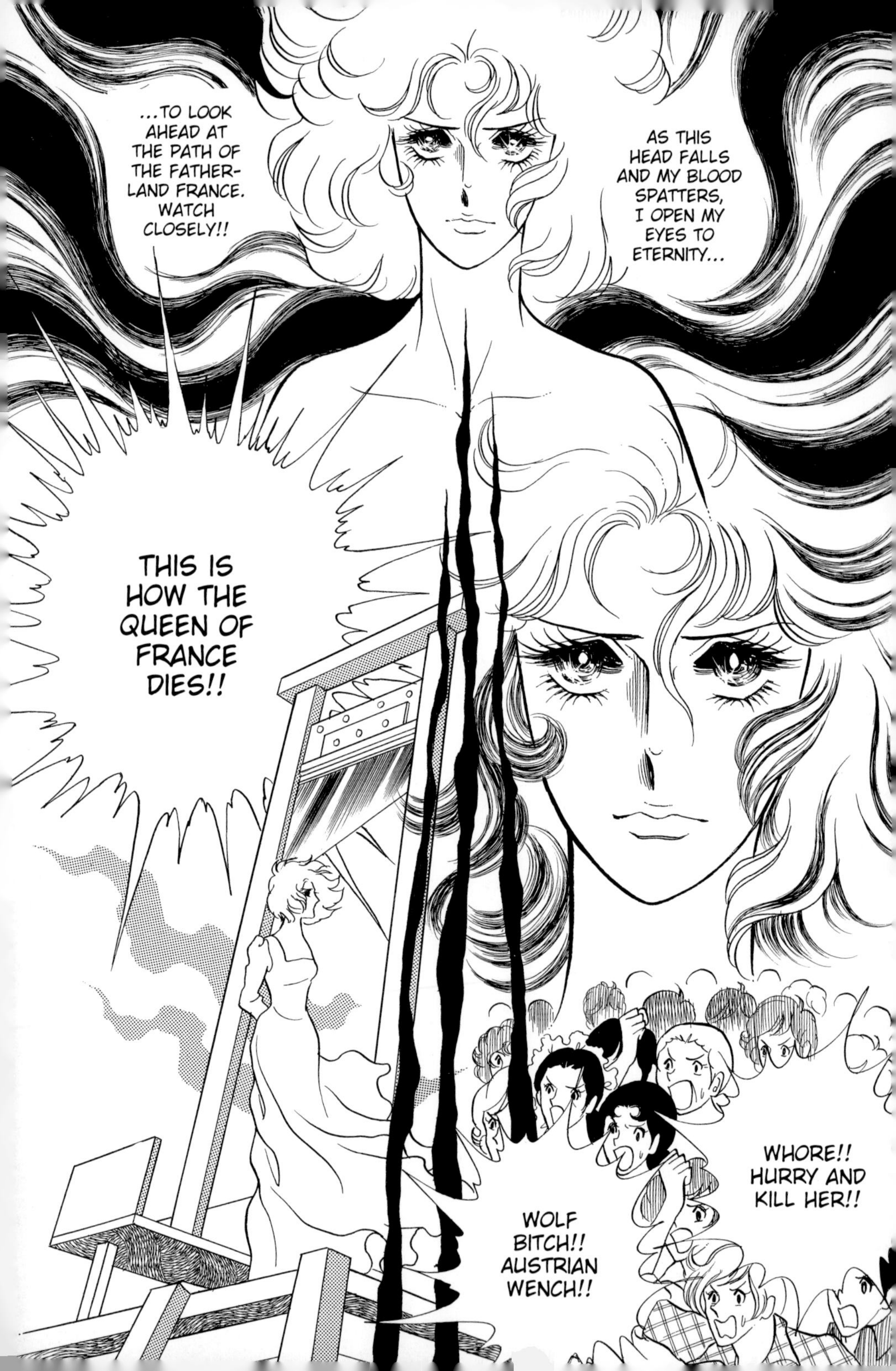
AS THIS HEAD FALLS AND MY BLOOD SPATTERS, I OPEN MY EYES TO ETERNITY...
...TO LOOK AHEAD AT THE PATH OF THE FATHER-LAND FRANCE. WATCH CLOSELY!!
THIS IS HOW THE QUEEN OF FRANCE DIES!!
WHORE!! HURRY AND KILL HER!!
WOLF BITCH!! AUSTRIAN WENCH!!

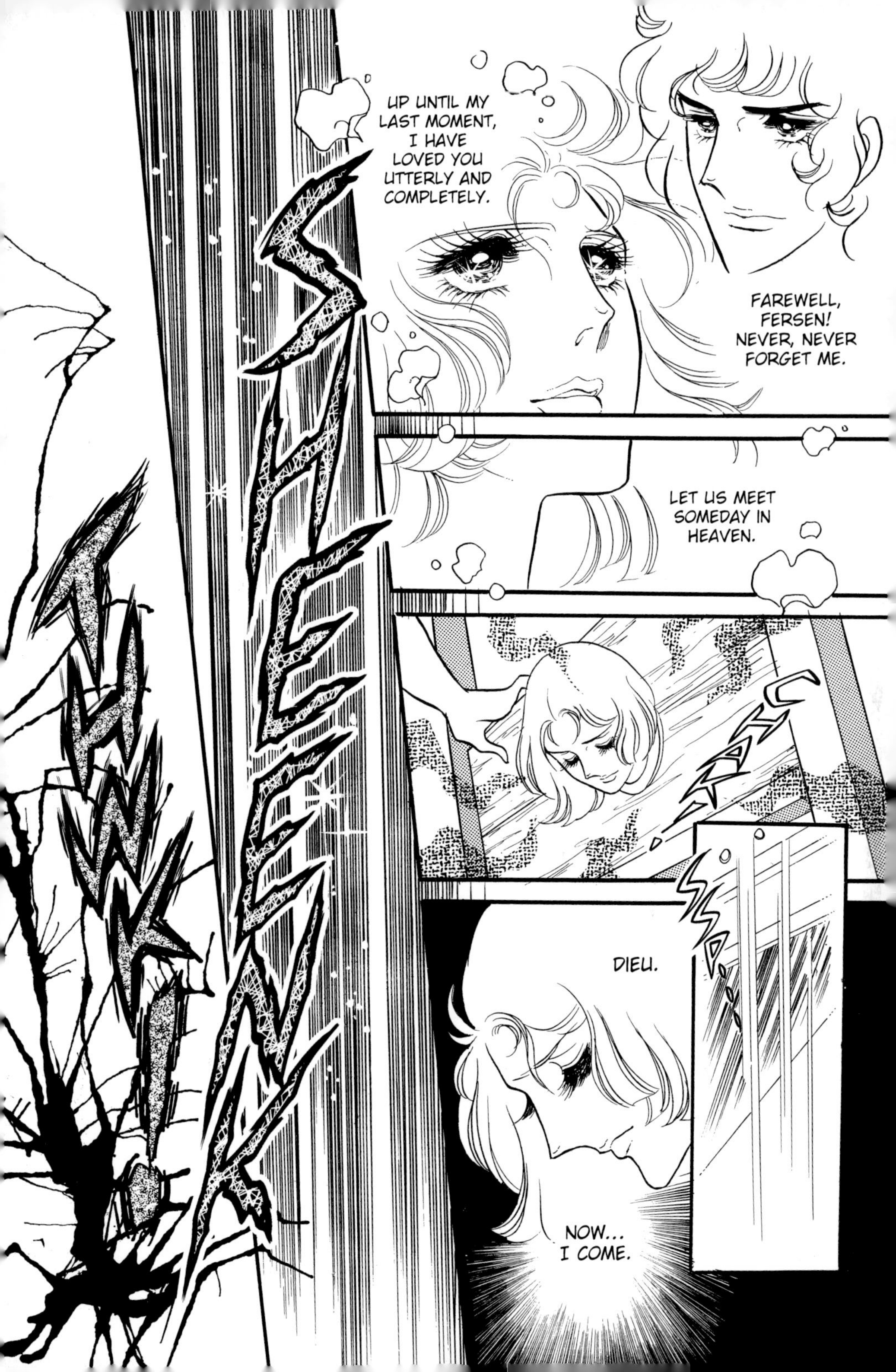
UP UNTIL MY LAST MOMENT, I HAVE LOVED YOU UTTERLY AND COMPLETELY.
FAREWELL, FERSEN! NEVER, NEVER FORGET ME.
LET US MEET SOMEDAY IN HEAVEN.
DIEU.
NOW... I COME.

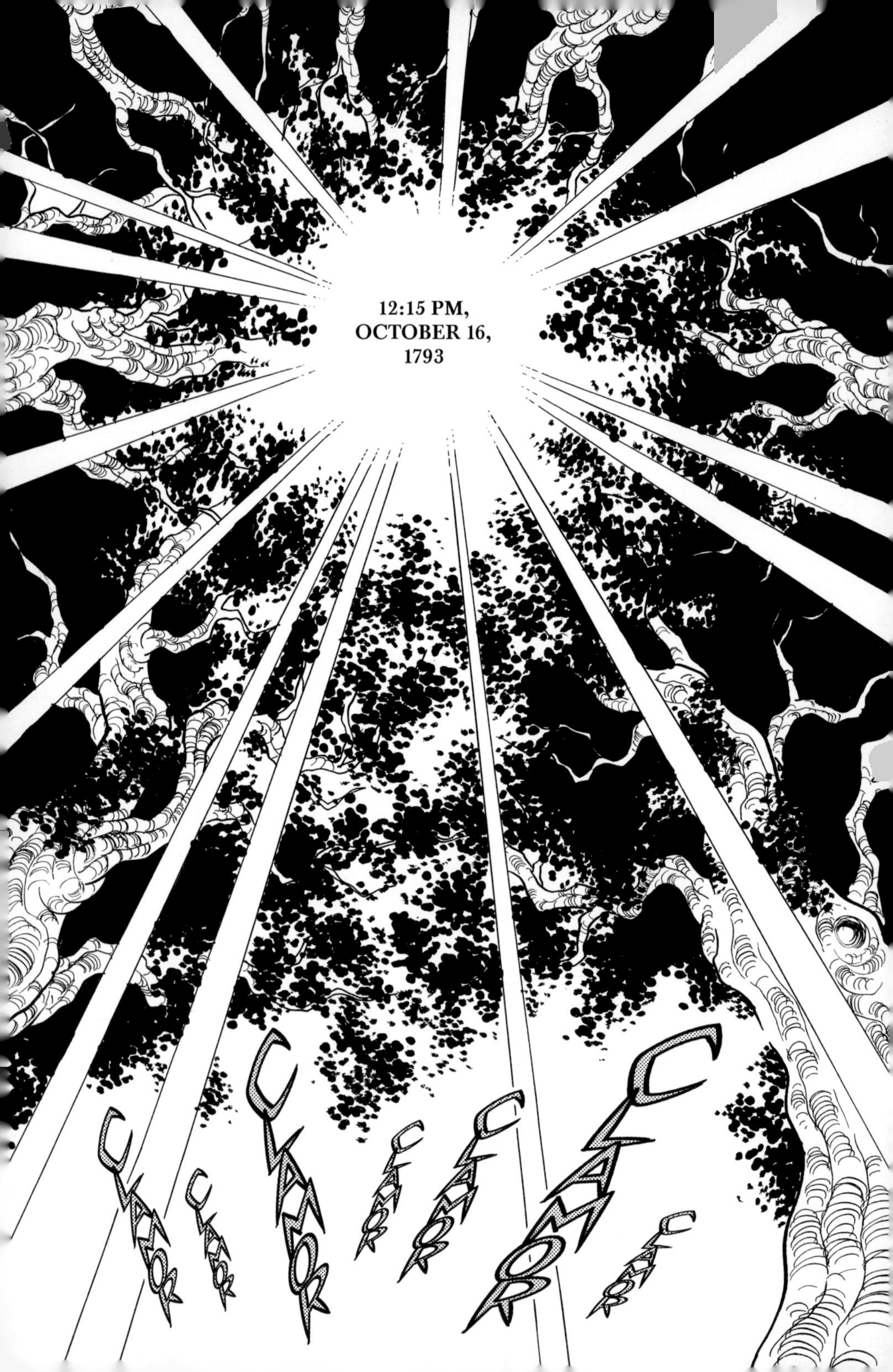
12:15 PM,
OCTOBER 16,
1793

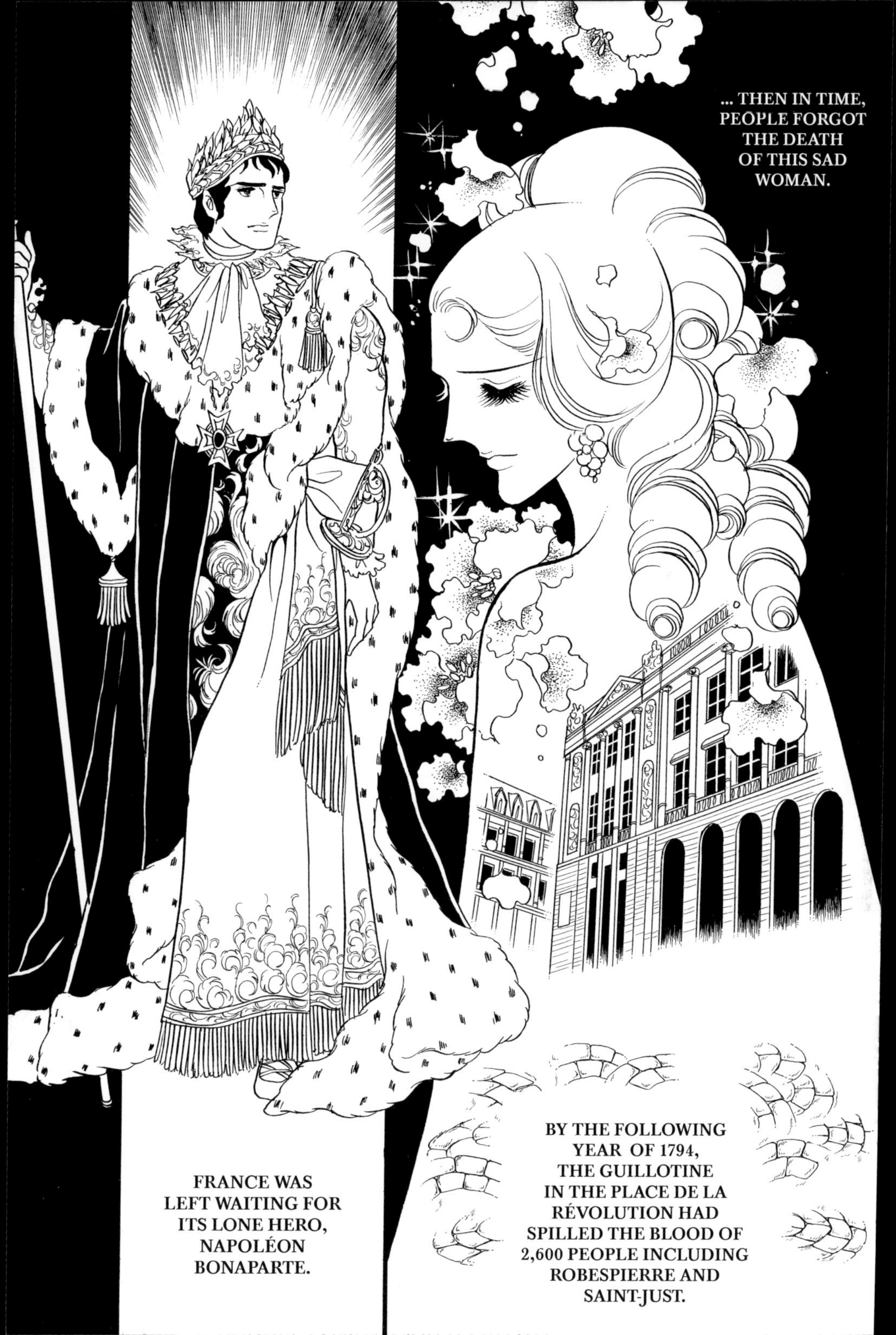
... THEN IN TIME, PEOPLE FORGOT THE DEATH OF THIS SAD WOMAN.
BY THE FOLLOWING YEAR OF 1794, THE GUILLOTINE IN THE PLACE DE LA RÉVOLUTION HAD SPILLED THE BLOOD OF 2,600 PEOPLE INCLUDING ROBESPIERRE AND SAINT-JUST.
FRANCE WAS LEFT WAITING FOR ITS LONE HERO, NAPOLÉON BONAPARTE.

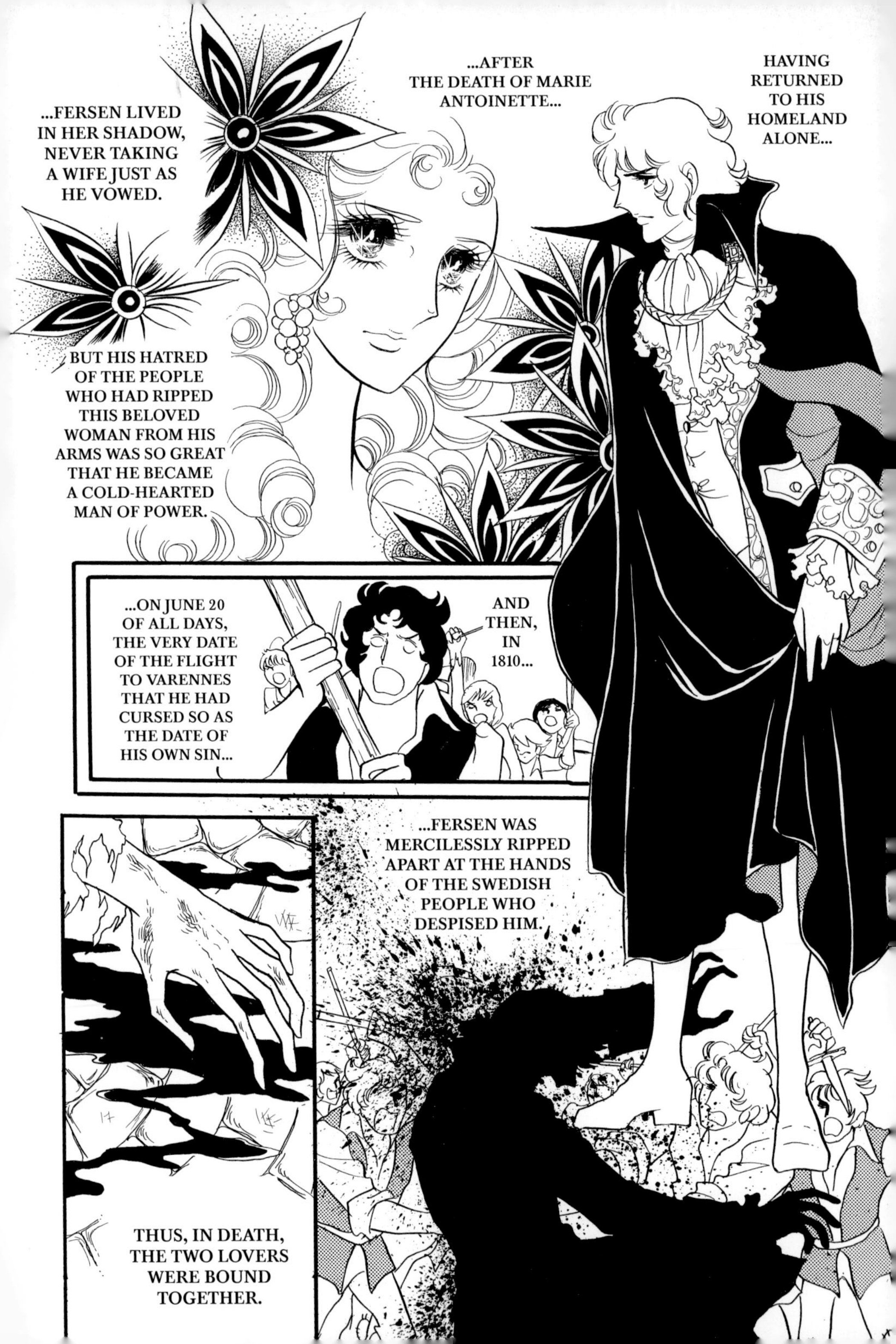
HAVING RETURNED TO HIS HOMELAND ALONE...
...AFTER THE DEATH OF MARIE ANTOINETTE...
...FERSEN LIVED IN HER SHADOW, NEVER TAKING A WIFE JUST AS HE VOWED.
BUT HIS HATRED OF THE PEOPLE WHO HAD RIPPED THIS BELOVED WOMAN FROM HIS ARMS WAS SO GREAT THAT HE BECAME A COLD-HEARTED MAN OF POWER.
AND THEN, IN 1810...
...ON JUNE 20 OF ALL DAYS, THE VERY DATE OF THE FLIGHT TO VARENNES THAT HE HAD CURSED SO AS THE DATE OF HIS OWN SIN...
...FERSEN WAS MERCILESSLY RIPPED APART AT THE HANDS OF THE SWEDISH PEOPLE WHO DESPISED HIM.
THUS, IN DEATH, THE TWO LOVERS WERE BOUND TOGETHER.

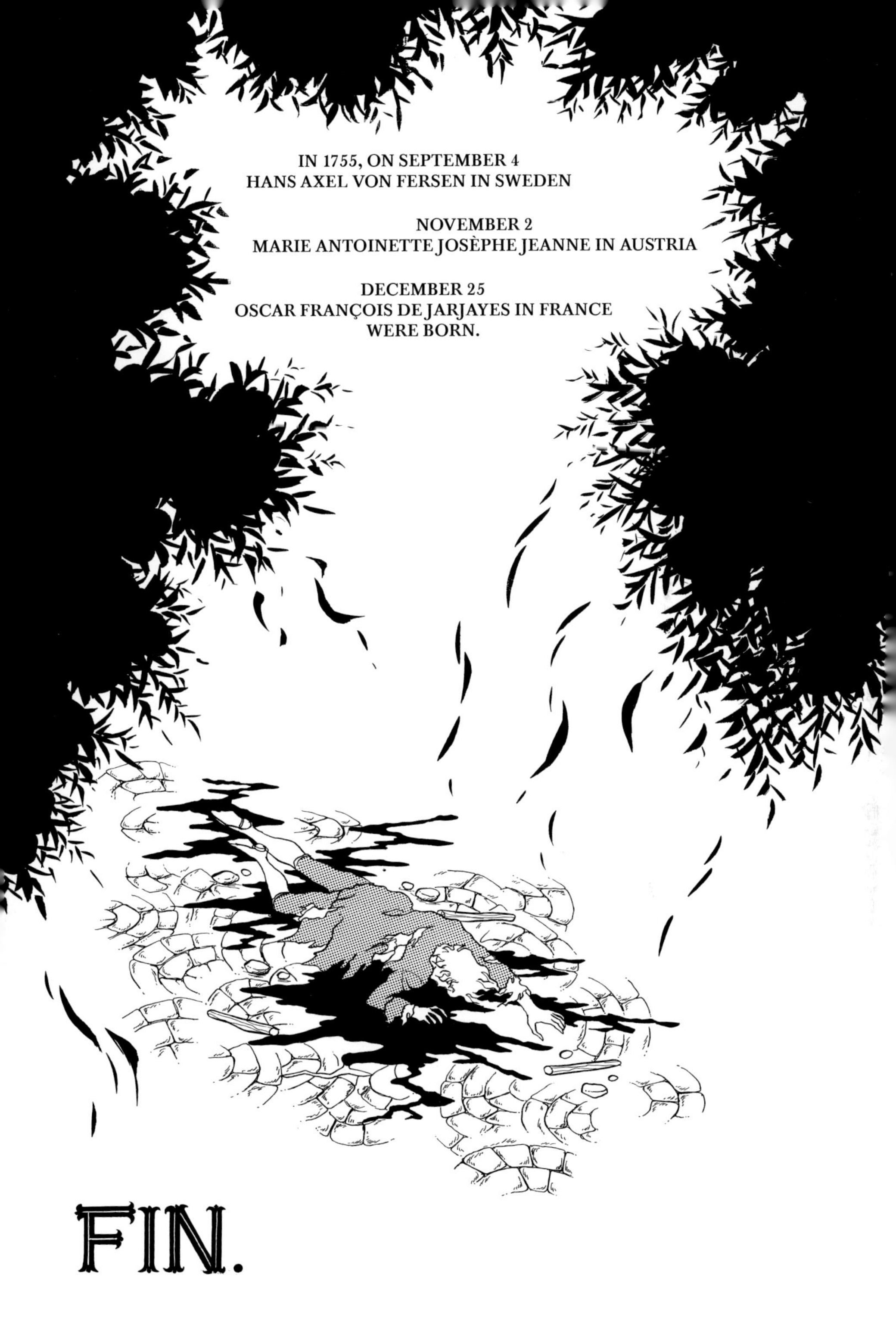
IN 1755, ON SEPTEMBER 4
HANS AXEL VON FERSEN IN SWEDEN
NOVEMBER 2
MARIE ANTOINETTE JOSÈPHE JEANNE IN AUSTRIA
DECEMBER 25
OSCAR FRANÇOIS DE JARJAYES IN FRANCE
WERE BORN.
FIN.

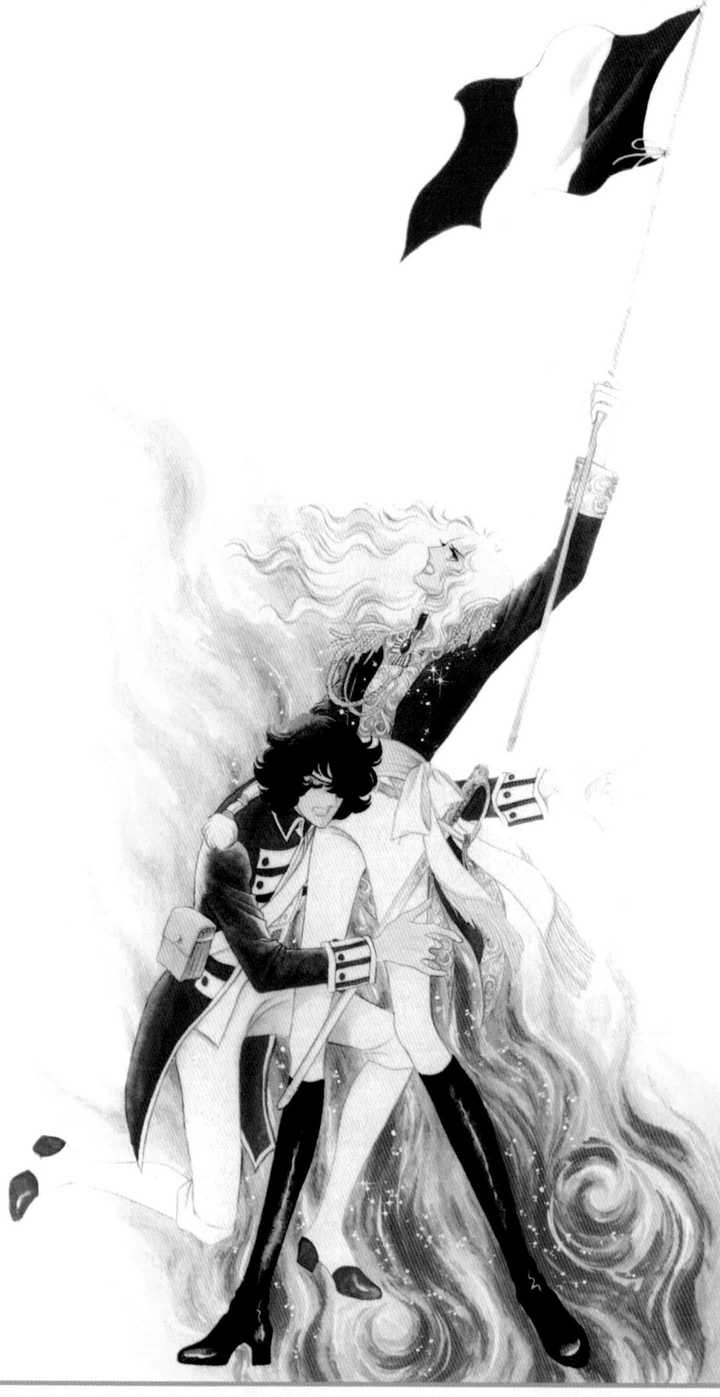

1976 DEFINITIVE EDITION: THE ROSE OF VERSAILLES MAGAZINE INSERT POSTER ART

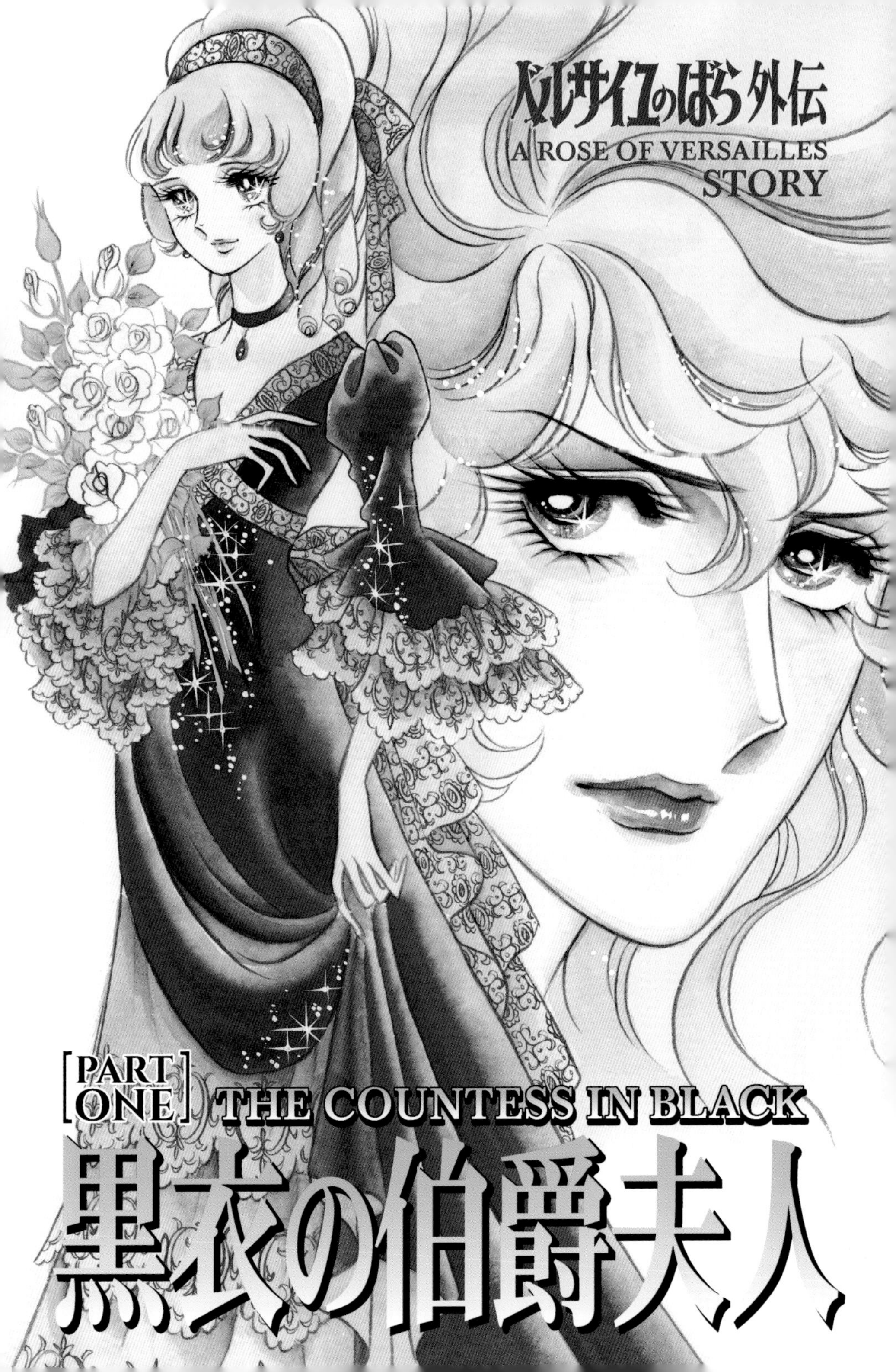
ベルサイユのばら外伝
A ROSE OF VERSAILLES
STORY
[PART ONE] THE COUNTESS IN BLACK
黒衣の伯爵夫人

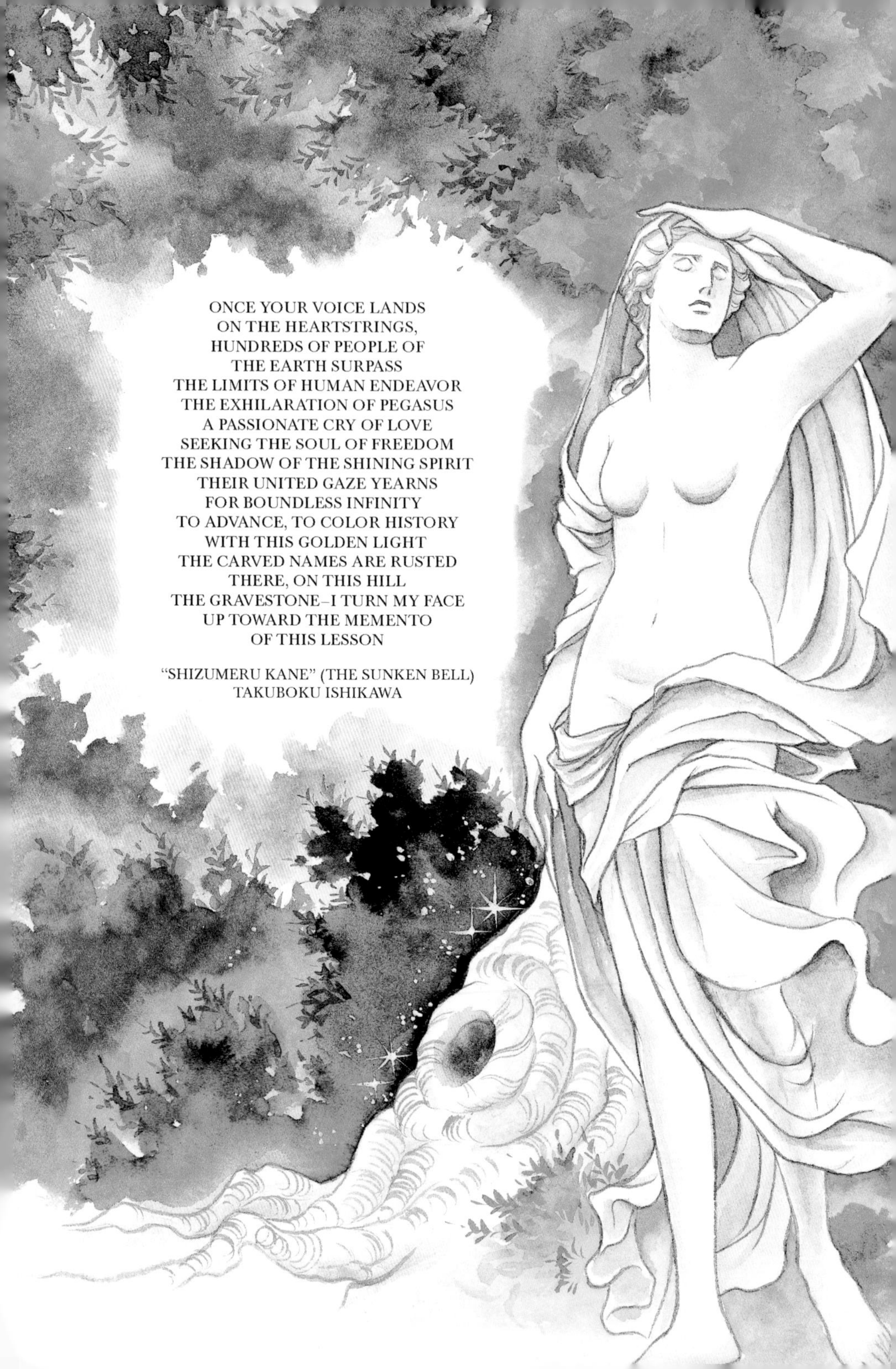

ONCE YOUR VOICE LANDS
ON THE HEARTSTRINGS,
HUNDREDS OF PEOPLE OF
THE EARTH SURPASS
THE LIMITS OF HUMAN ENDEAVOR
THE EXHILARATION OF PEGASUS
A PASSIONATE CRY OF LOVE
SEEKING THE SOUL OF FREEDOM
THE SHADOW OF THE SHINING SPIRIT
THEIR UNITED GAZE YEARNS
FOR BOUNDLESS INFINITY
TO ADVANCE, TO COLOR HISTORY
WITH THIS GOLDEN LIGHT
THE CARVED NAMES ARE RUSTED
THERE, ON THIS HILL
THE GRAVESTONE–I TURN MY FACE
UP TOWARD THE MEMENTO
OF THIS LESSON

"SHIZUMERU KANE" (THE SUNKEN BELL)
TAKUBOKU ISHIKAWA

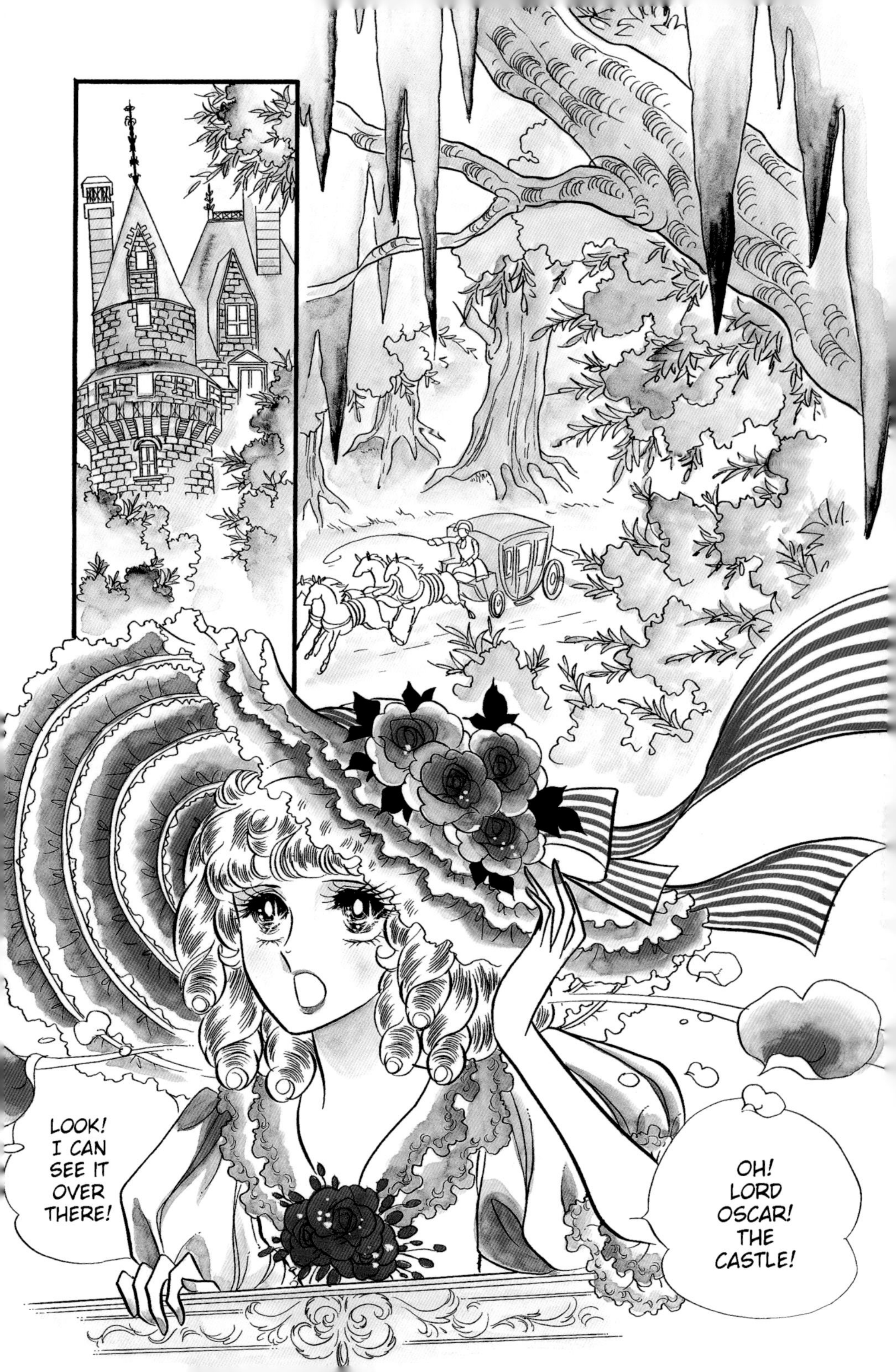
OH! LORD OSCAR! THE CASTLE!
LOOK! I CAN SEE IT OVER THERE!

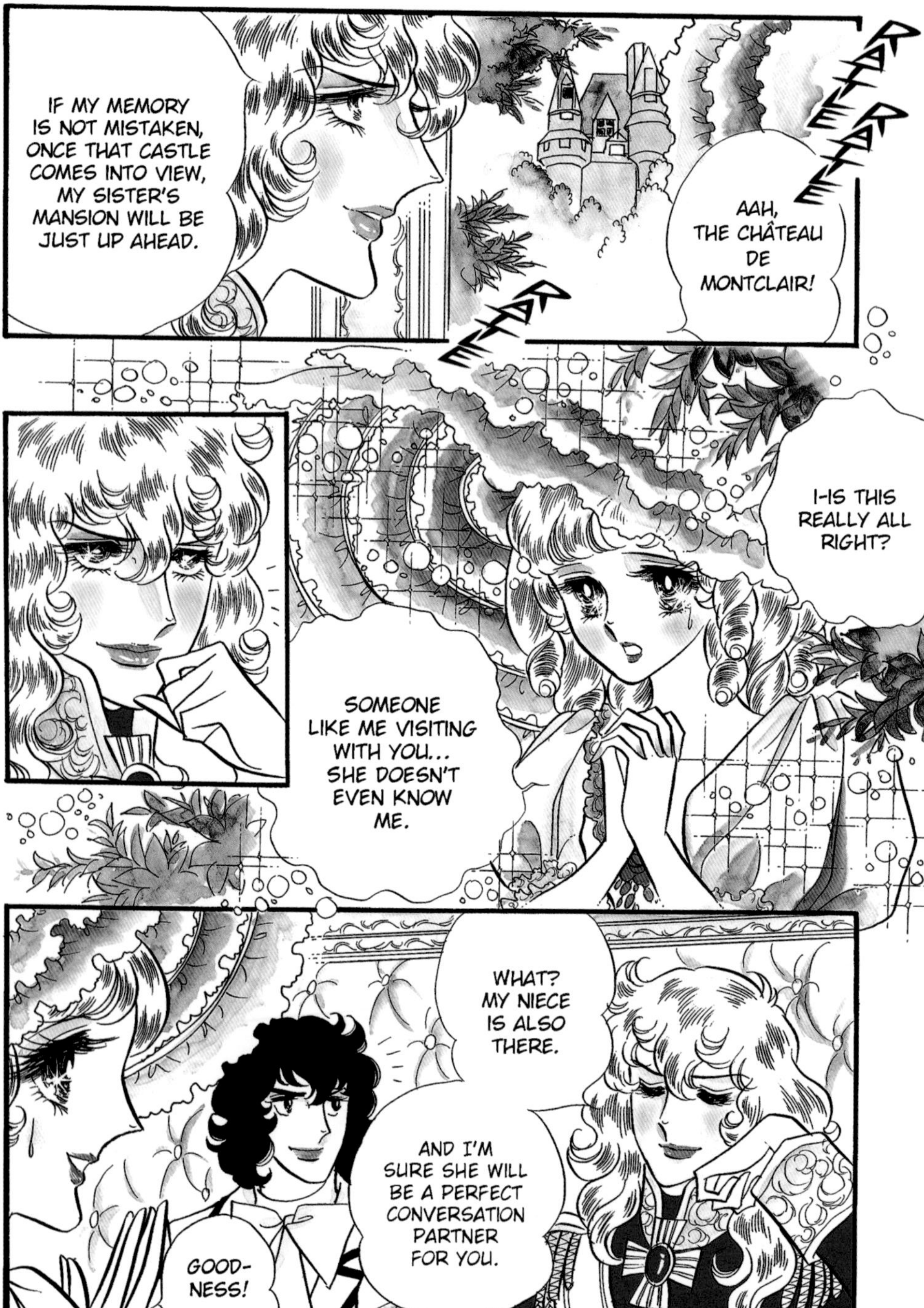
RATTLE RATTLE
AAH, THE CHÂTEAU DE MONTCLAIR!
RATTLE
IF MY MEMORY IS NOT MISTAKEN, ONCE THAT CASTLE COMES INTO VIEW, MY SISTER'S MANSION WILL BE JUST UP AHEAD.
I-IS THIS REALLY ALL RIGHT?
SOMEONE LIKE ME VISITING WITH YOU... SHE DOESN'T EVEN KNOW ME.
WHAT? MY NIECE IS ALSO THERE.
AND I'M SURE SHE WILL BE A PERFECT CONVERSATION PARTNER FOR YOU.
GOOD-NESS!

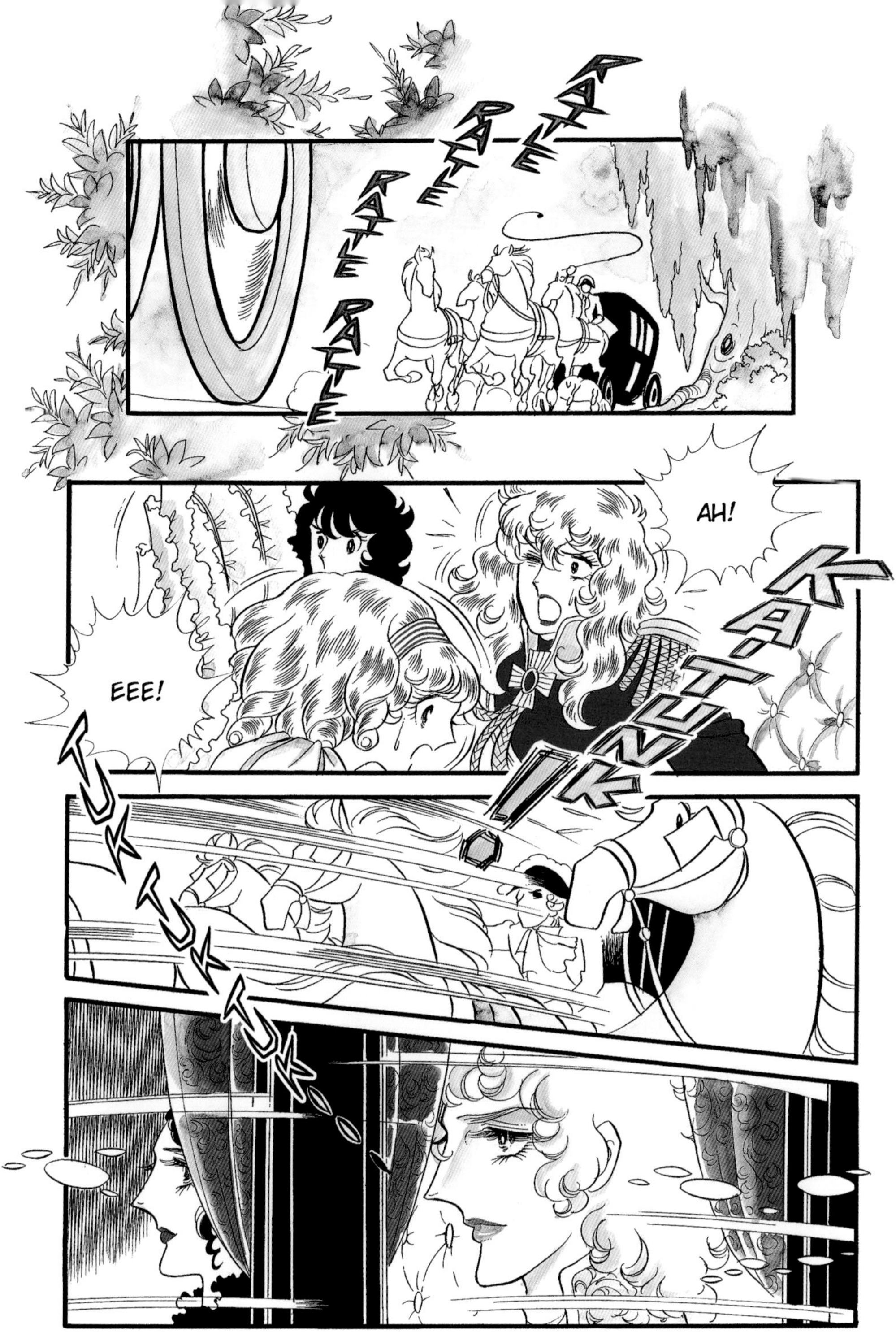
RATTLE
RATTLE
RATTLE
RATTLE
AH!
KATUNK!
EEE!
TUK TUK TUK

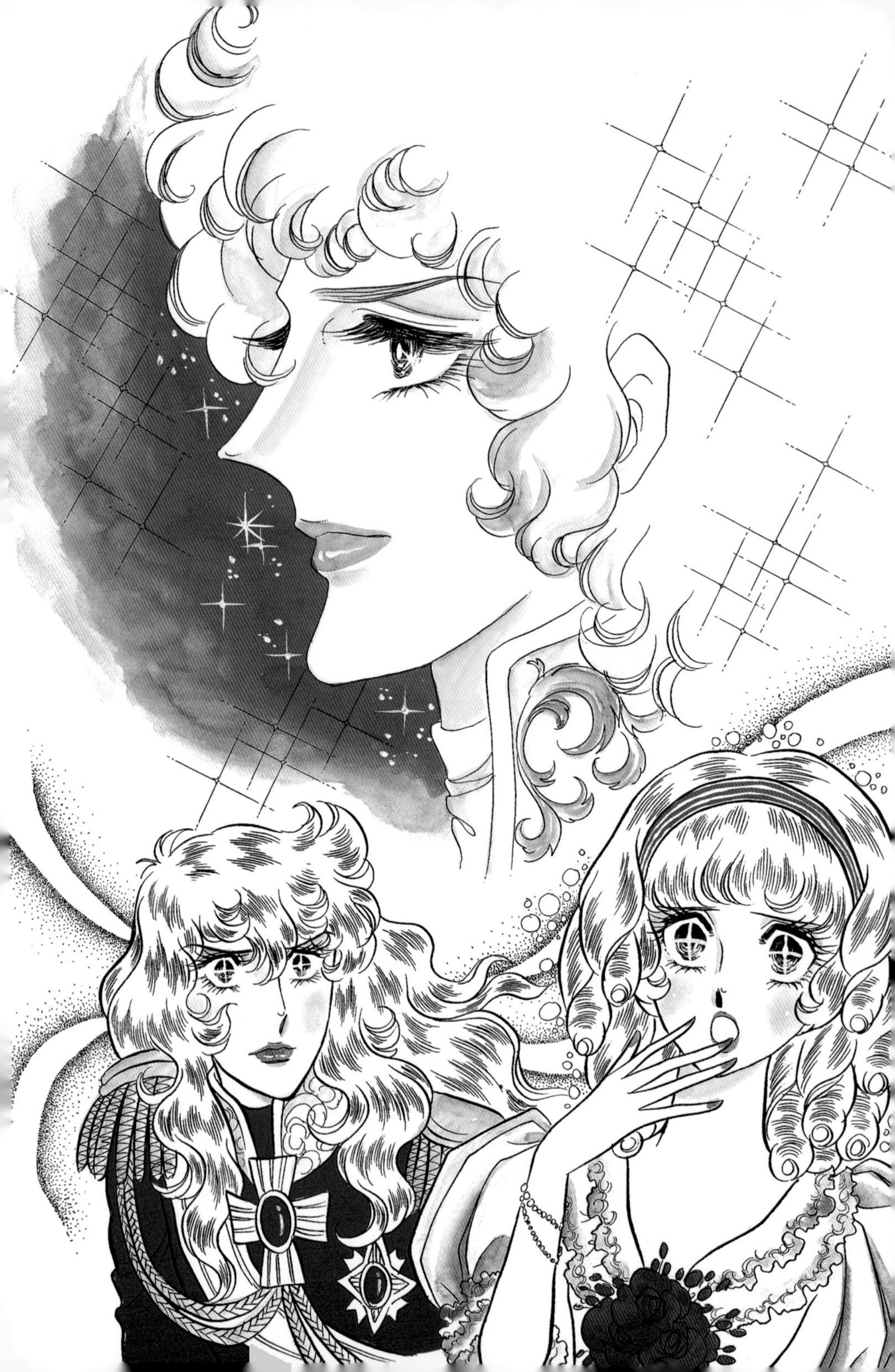

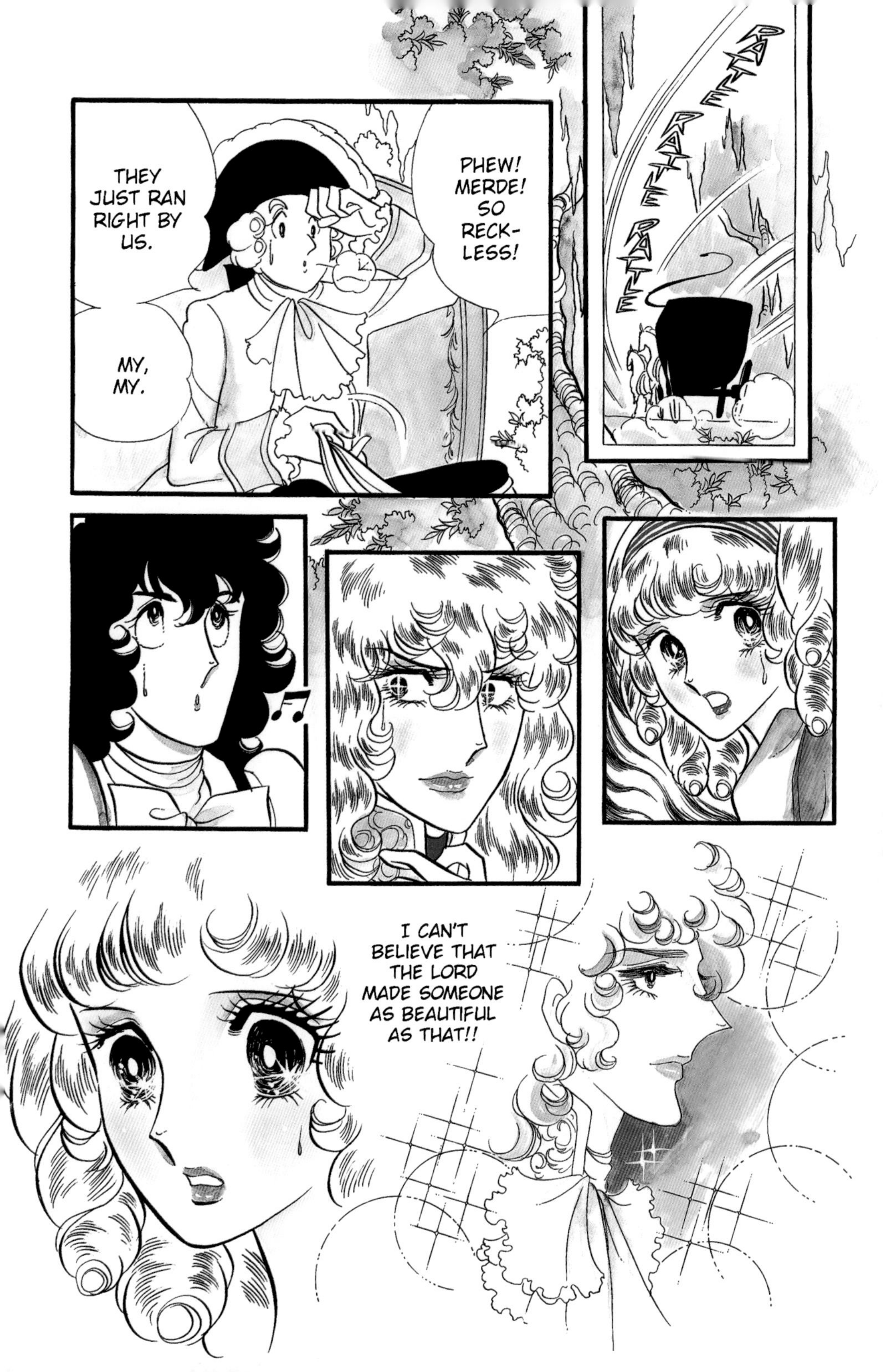
RATTLE RATTLE RATTLE
PHEW! MERDE! SO RECK-LESS!
THEY JUST RAN RIGHT BY US.
MY, MY.
I CAN'T BELIEVE THAT THE LORD MADE SOMEONE AS BEAUTIFUL AS THAT!!

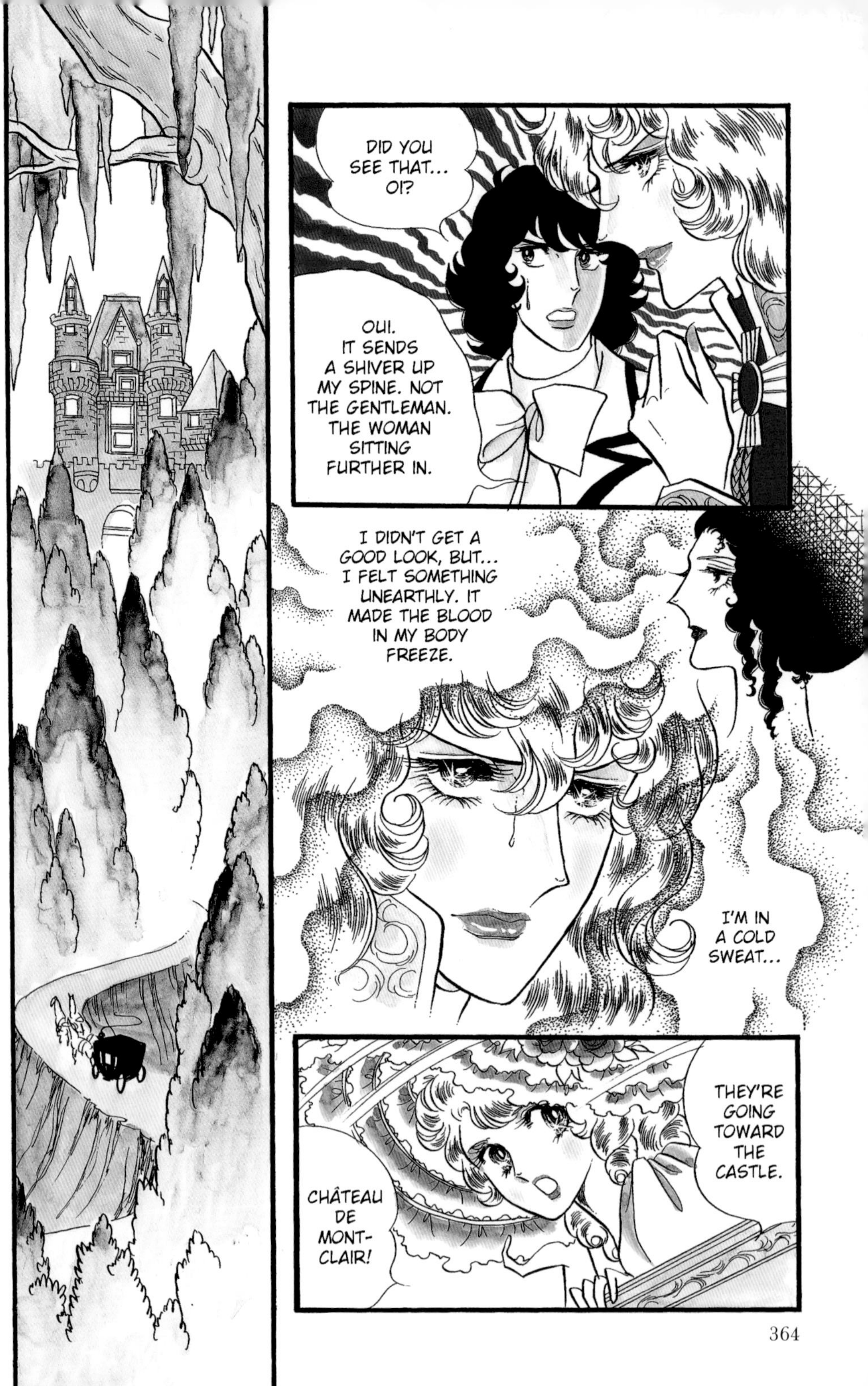
DID YOU SEE THAT... OI?
OUI. IT SENDS A SHIVER UP MY SPINE. NOT THE GENTLEMAN. THE WOMAN SITTING FURTHER IN.
I DIDN'T GET A GOOD LOOK, BUT... I FELT SOMETHING UNEARTHLY. IT MADE THE BLOOD IN MY BODY FREEZE.
I'M IN A COLD SWEAT...
THEY'RE GOING TOWARD THE CASTLE.
CHÂTEAU DE MONT-CLAIR!

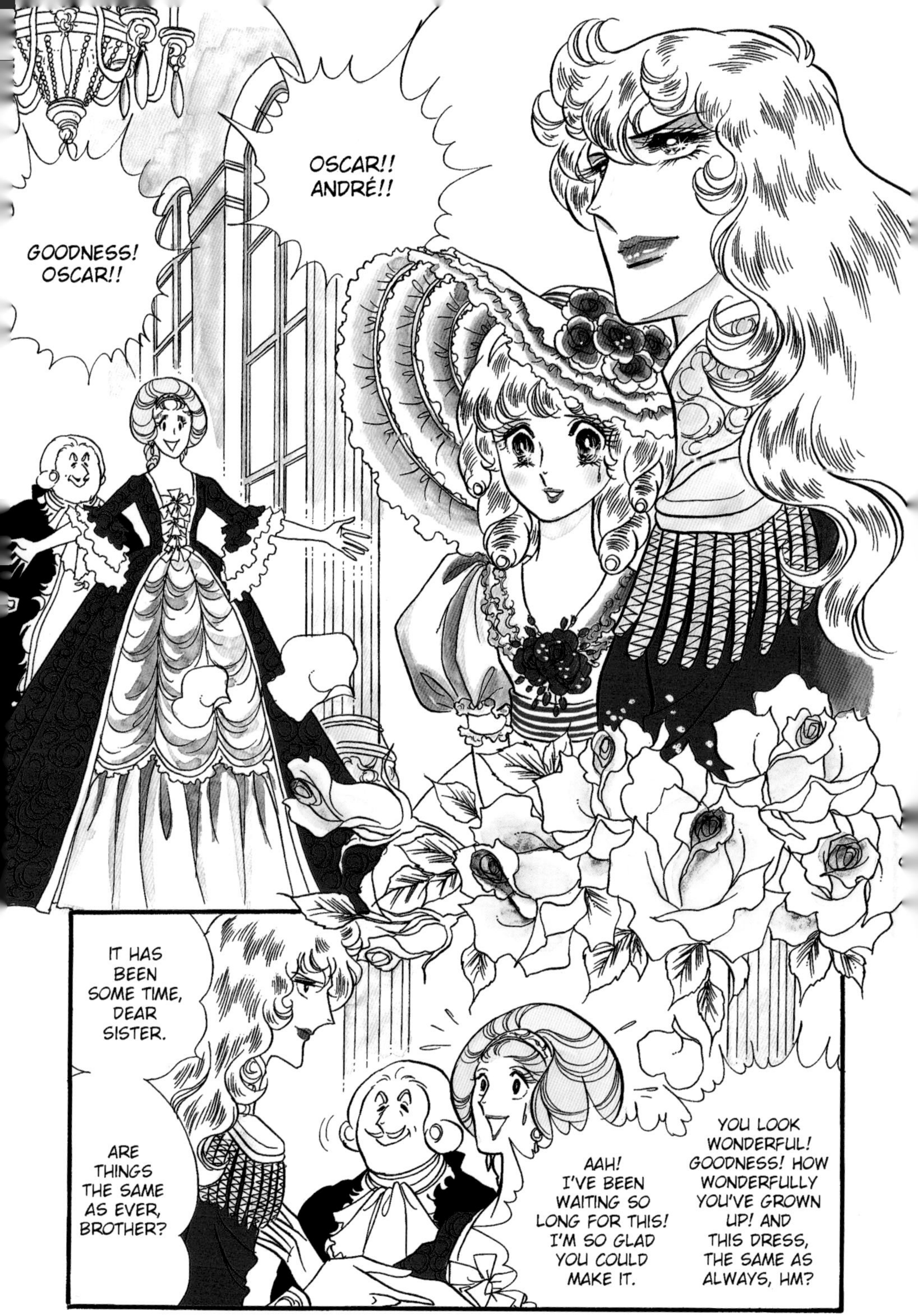
OSCAR!! ANDRÉ!!
GOODNESS! OSCAR!!
YOU LOOK WONDERFUL! GOODNESS! HOW WONDERFULLY YOU'VE GROWN UP! AND THIS DRESS, THE SAME AS ALWAYS, HM?
AAH! I'VE BEEN WAITING SO LONG FOR THIS! I'M SO GLAD YOU COULD MAKE IT.
IT HAS BEEN SOME TIME, DEAR SISTER.
ARE THINGS THE SAME AS EVER, BROTHER?

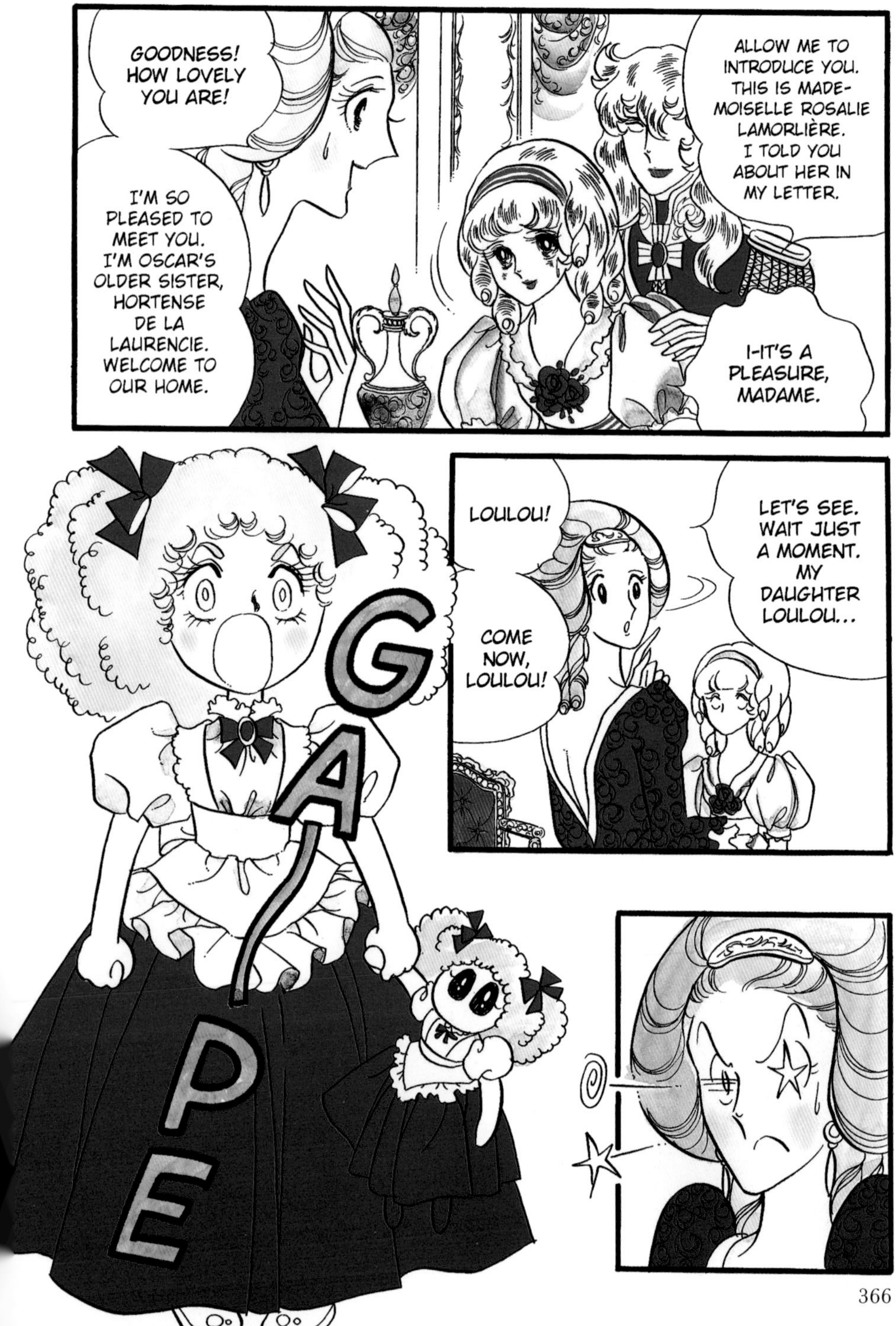
ALLOW ME TO INTRODUCE YOU. THIS IS MADE-MOISELLE ROSALIE LAMORLIÈRE. I TOLD YOU ABOUT HER IN MY LETTER.
GOODNESS! HOW LOVELY YOU ARE!
I'M SO PLEASED TO MEET YOU. I'M OSCAR'S OLDER SISTER, HORTENSE DE LA LAURENCIE. WELCOME TO OUR HOME.
I-IT'S A PLEASURE, MADAME.
LET'S SEE. WAIT JUST A MOMENT. MY DAUGHTER LOULOU...
LOULOU!
COME NOW, LOULOU!
GAPE

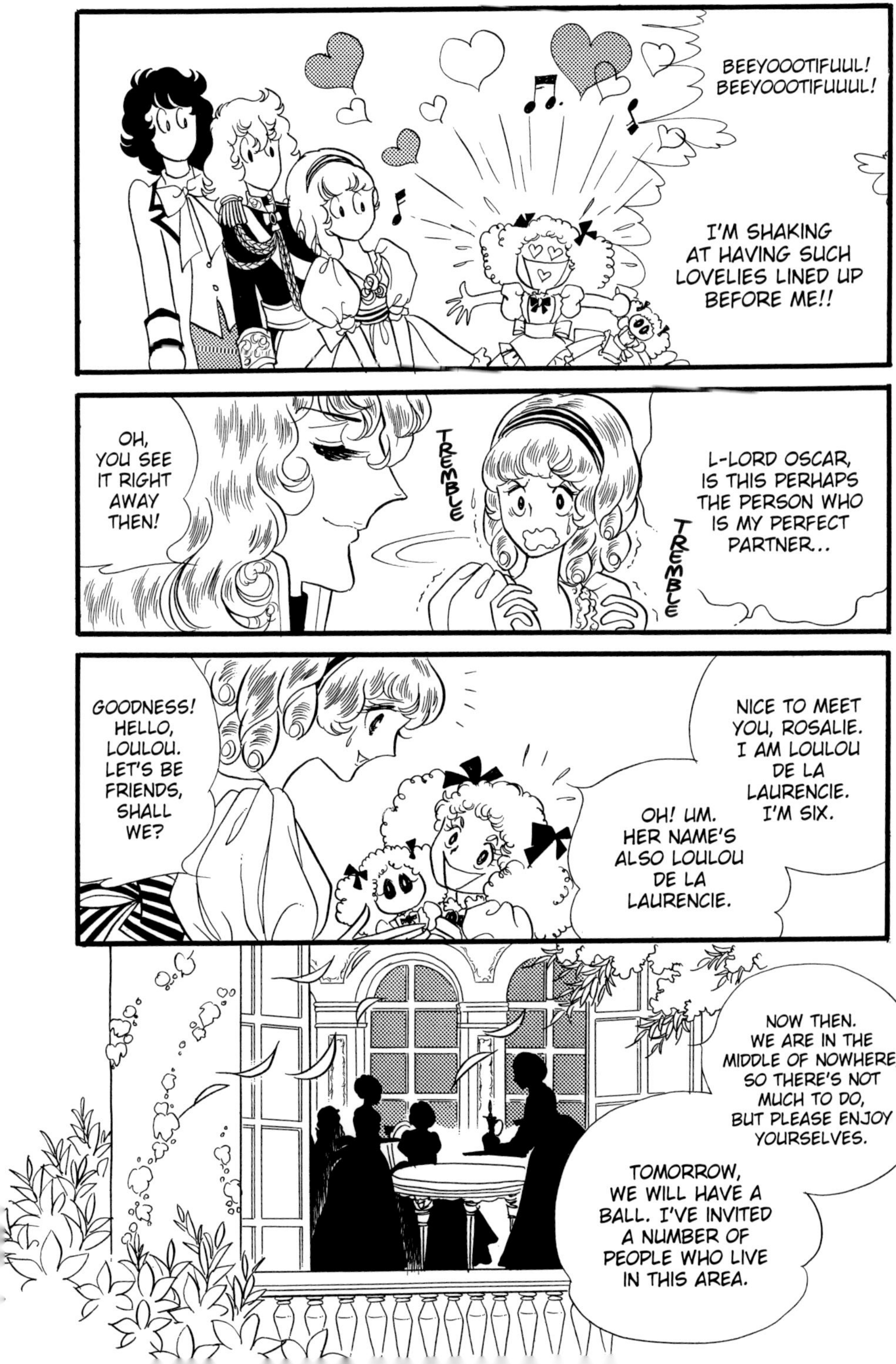
BEEYOOOTIFULL! BEEYOOOTIFUUUL!
I'M SHAKING AT HAVING SUCH LOVELIES LINED UP BEFORE ME!!
L-LORD OSCAR, IS THIS PERHAPS THE PERSON WHO IS MY PERFECT PARTNER...
TREMBLE
TREMBLE
OH, YOU SEE IT RIGHT AWAY THEN!
NICE TO MEET YOU, ROSALIE. I AM LOULOU DE LA LAURENCIE. I'M SIX.
OH! UM. HER NAME'S ALSO LOULOU DE LA LAURENCIE.
GOODNESS! HELLO, LOULOU. LET'S BE FRIENDS, SHALL WE?
NOW THEN. WE ARE IN THE MIDDLE OF NOWHERE, SO THERE'S NOT MUCH TO DO, BUT PLEASE ENJOY YOURSELVES.
TOMORROW, WE WILL HAVE A BALL. I'VE INVITED A NUMBER OF PEOPLE WHO LIVE IN THIS AREA.

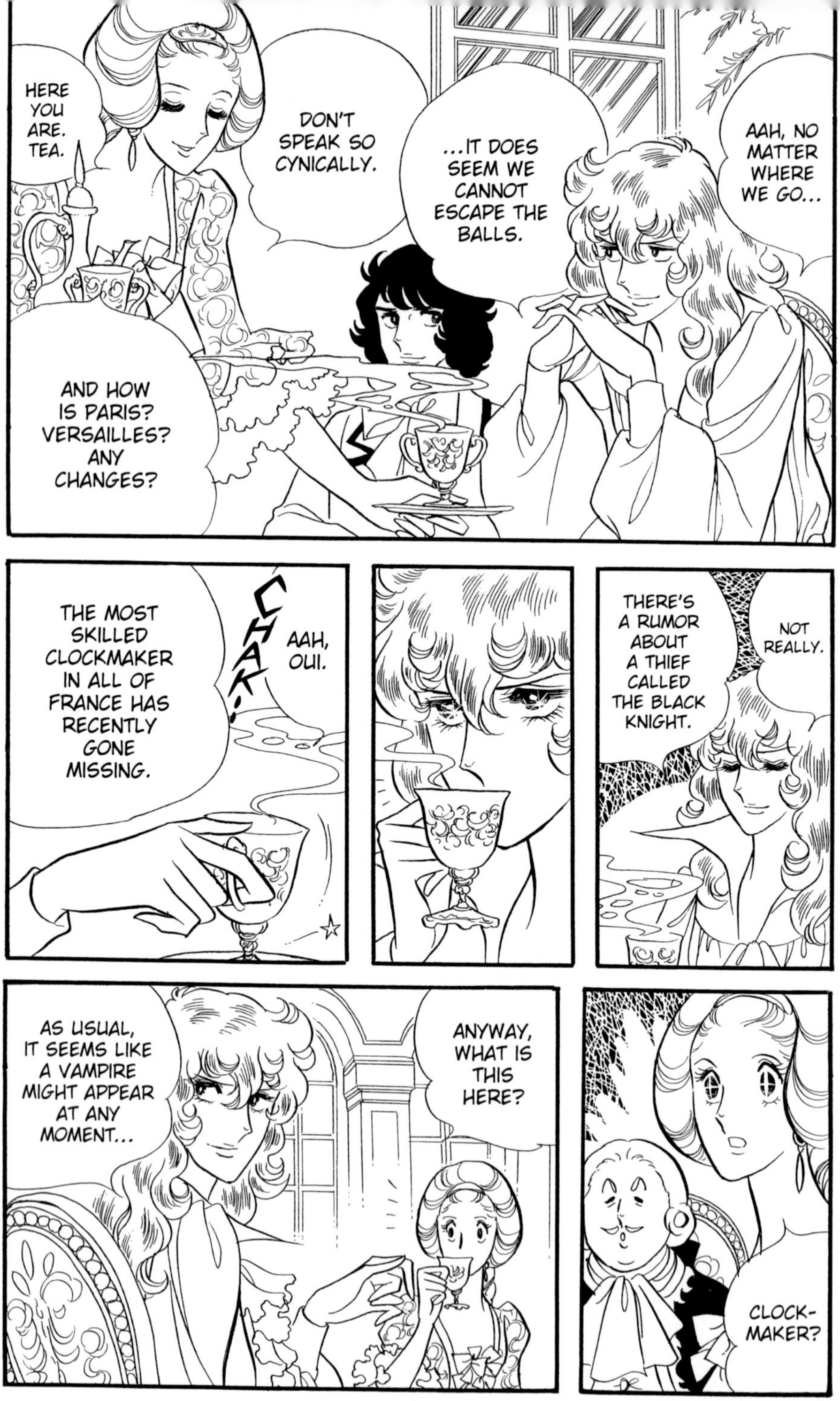
AAH, NO MATTER WHERE WE GO...
...IT DOES SEEM WE CANNOT ESCAPE THE BALLS.
DON'T SPEAK SO CYNICALLY.
HERE YOU ARE. TEA.
AND HOW IS PARIS? VERSAILLES? ANY CHANGES?
NOT REALLY.
THERE'S A RUMOR ABOUT A THIEF CALLED THE BLACK KNIGHT.
AAH, OUI.
CHAK!
THE MOST SKILLED CLOCKMAKER IN ALL OF FRANCE HAS RECENTLY GONE MISSING.
CLOCK-MAKER?
ANYWAY, WHAT IS THIS HERE?
AS USUAL, IT SEEMS LIKE A VAMPIRE MIGHT APPEAR AT ANY MOMENT...

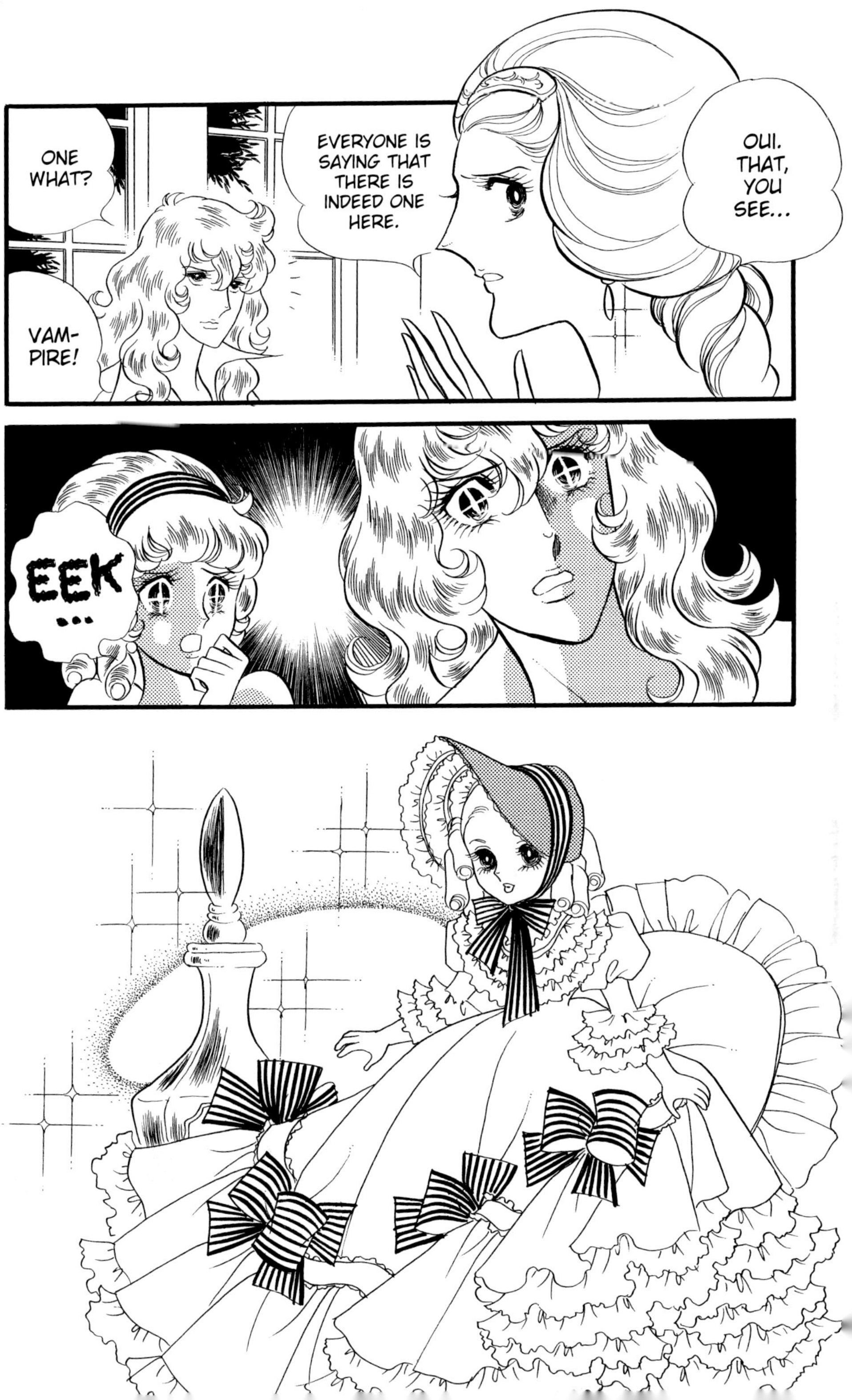
OUI. THAT, YOU SEE...
EVERYONE IS SAYING THAT THERE IS INDEED ONE HERE.
ONE WHAT?
VAMPIRE!
EEK ...

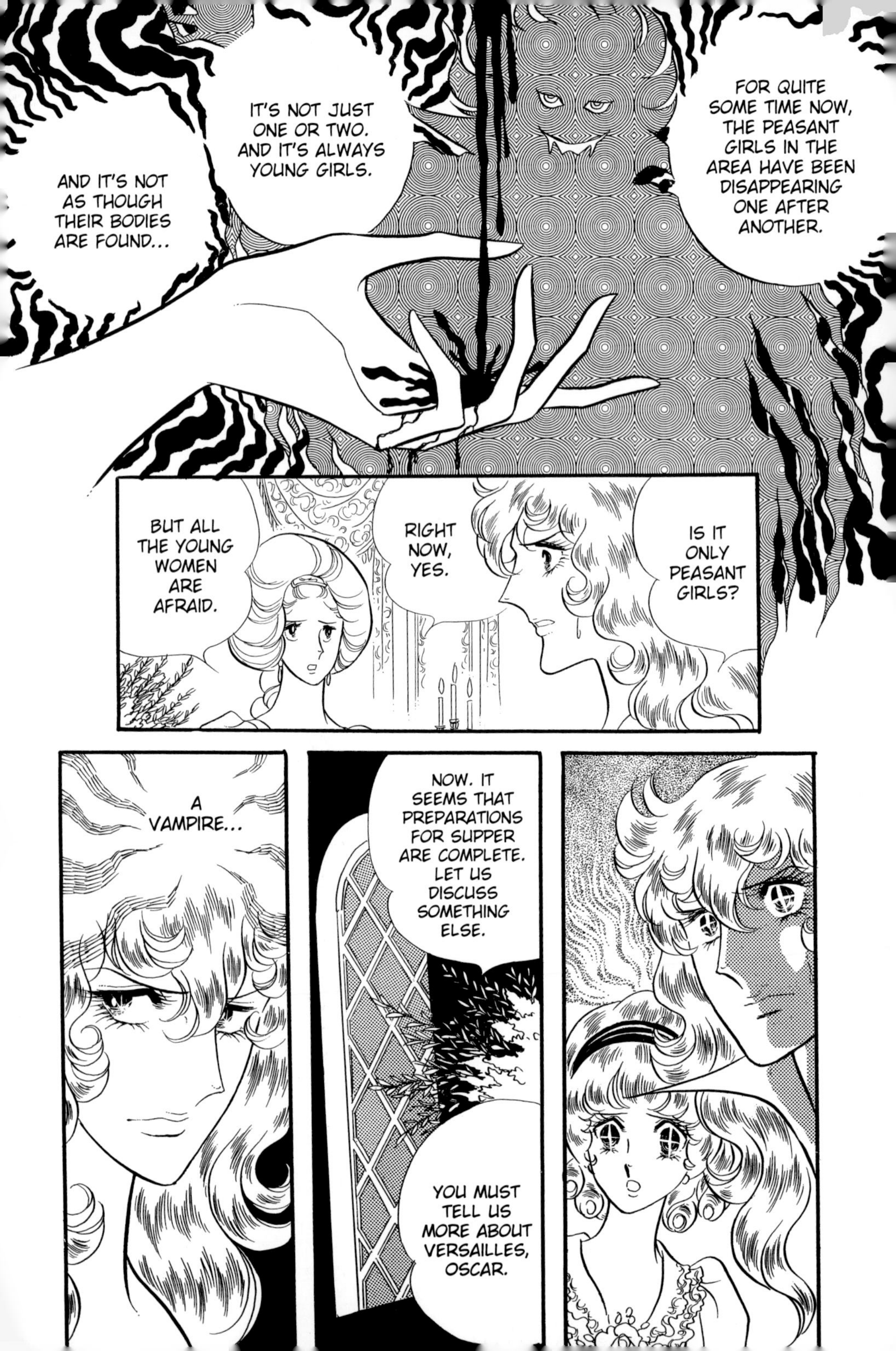
FOR QUITE SOME TIME NOW, THE PEASANT GIRLS IN THE AREA HAVE BEEN DISAPPEARING ONE AFTER ANOTHER.
IT'S NOT JUST ONE OR TWO. AND IT'S ALWAYS YOUNG GIRLS.
AND IT'S NOT AS THOUGH THEIR BODIES ARE FOUND...
IS IT ONLY PEASANT GIRLS?
RIGHT NOW, YES.
BUT ALL THE YOUNG WOMEN ARE AFRAID.
NOW. IT SEEMS THAT PREPARATIONS FOR SUPPER ARE COMPLETE. LET US DISCUSS SOMETHING ELSE.
YOU MUST TELL US MORE ABOUT VERSAILLES, OSCAR.
A VAMPIRE...

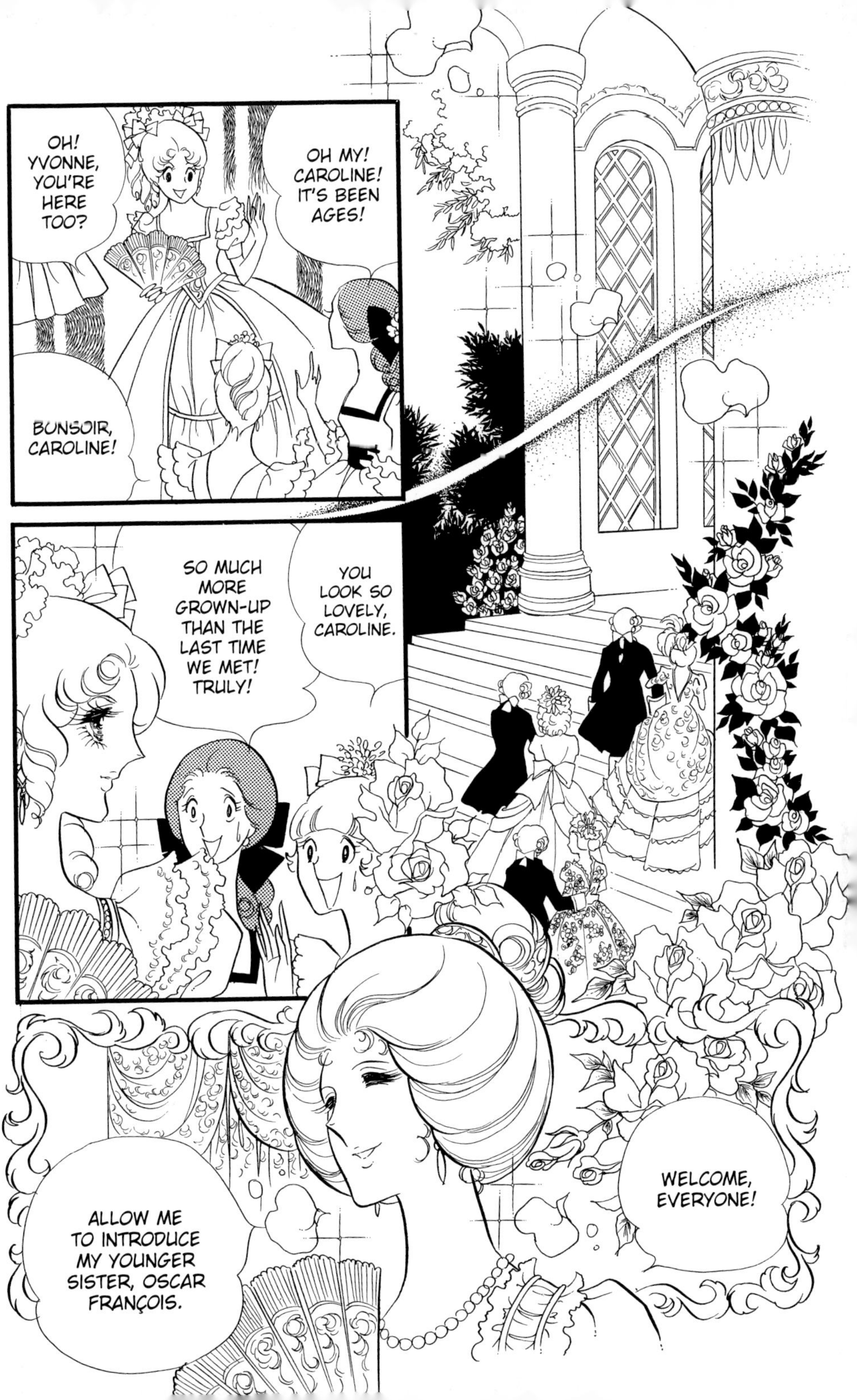
OH MY! CAROLINE! IT'S BEEN AGES!
OH! YVONNE, YOU'RE HERE TOO?
BONSOIR, CAROLINE!
YOU LOOK SO LOVELY, CAROLINE.
SO MUCH MORE GROWN-UP THAN THE LAST TIME WE MET! TRULY!
WELCOME, EVERYONE!
ALLOW ME TO INTRODUCE MY YOUNGER SISTER, OSCAR FRANÇOIS.

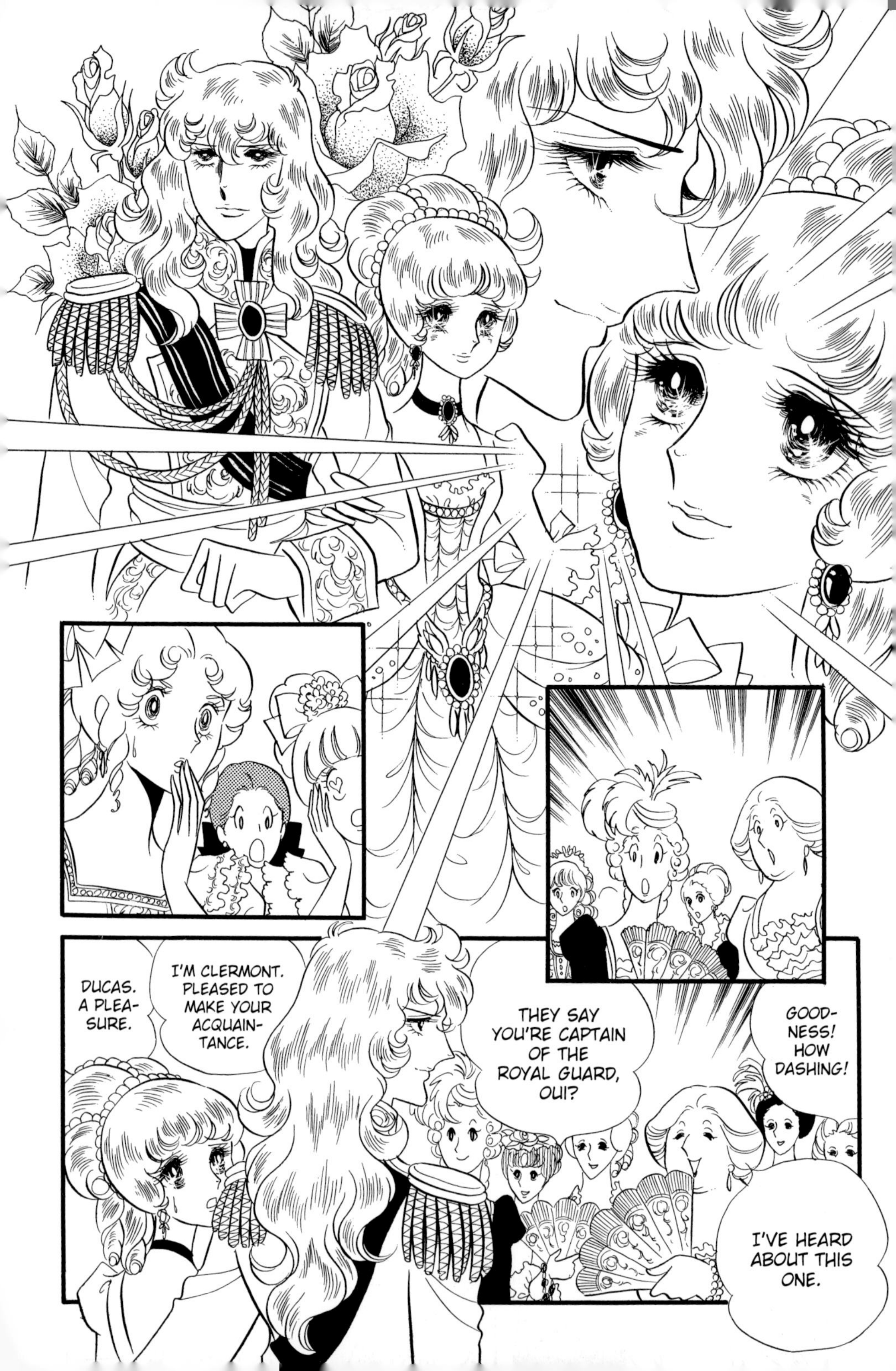
GOOD-NESS! HOW DASHING!
THEY SAY YOU'RE CAPTAIN OF THE ROYAL GUARD, OUI?
I'M CLERMONT. PLEASED TO MAKE YOUR ACQUAIN-TANCE.
DUCAS. A PLEA-SURE.
I'VE HEARD ABOUT THIS ONE.

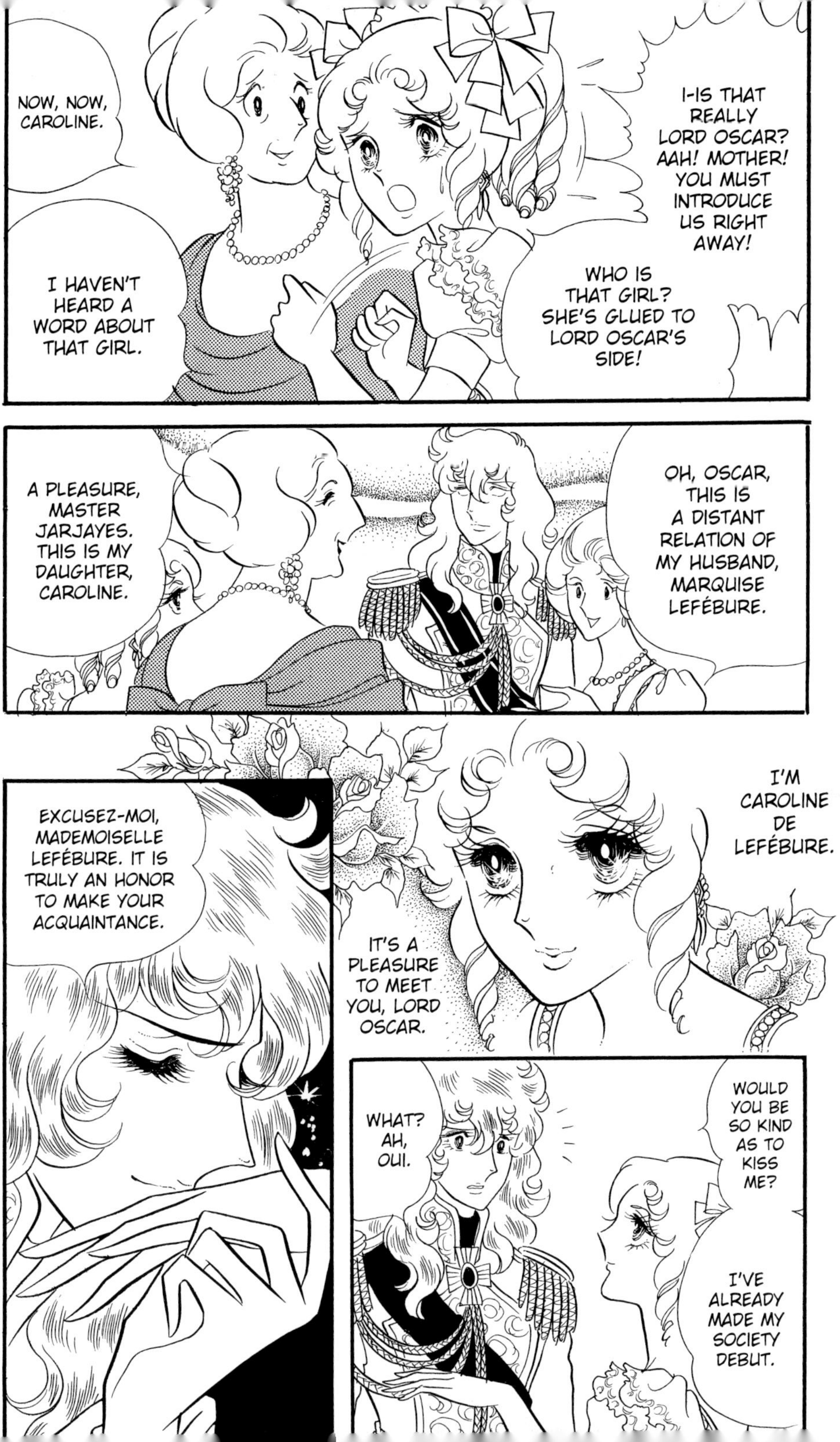
I-IS THAT REALLY LORD OSCAR? AAH! MOTHER! YOU MUST INTRODUCE US RIGHT AWAY!
WHO IS THAT GIRL? SHE'S GLUED TO LORD OSCAR'S SIDE!
NOW, NOW, CAROLINE.
I HAVEN'T HEARD A WORD ABOUT THAT GIRL.
OH, OSCAR, THIS IS A DISTANT RELATION OF MY HUSBAND, MARQUISE LEFÉBURE.
A PLEASURE, MASTER JARJAYES. THIS IS MY DAUGHTER, CAROLINE.
I'M CAROLINE DE LEFÉBURE.
IT'S A PLEASURE TO MEET YOU, LORD OSCAR.
WOULD YOU BE SO KIND AS TO KISS ME?
I'VE ALREADY MADE MY SOCIETY DEBUT.
WHAT? AH, OUI.
EXCUSEZ-MOI, MADEMOISELLE LEFÉBURE. IT IS TRULY AN HONOR TO MAKE YOUR ACQUAINTANCE.

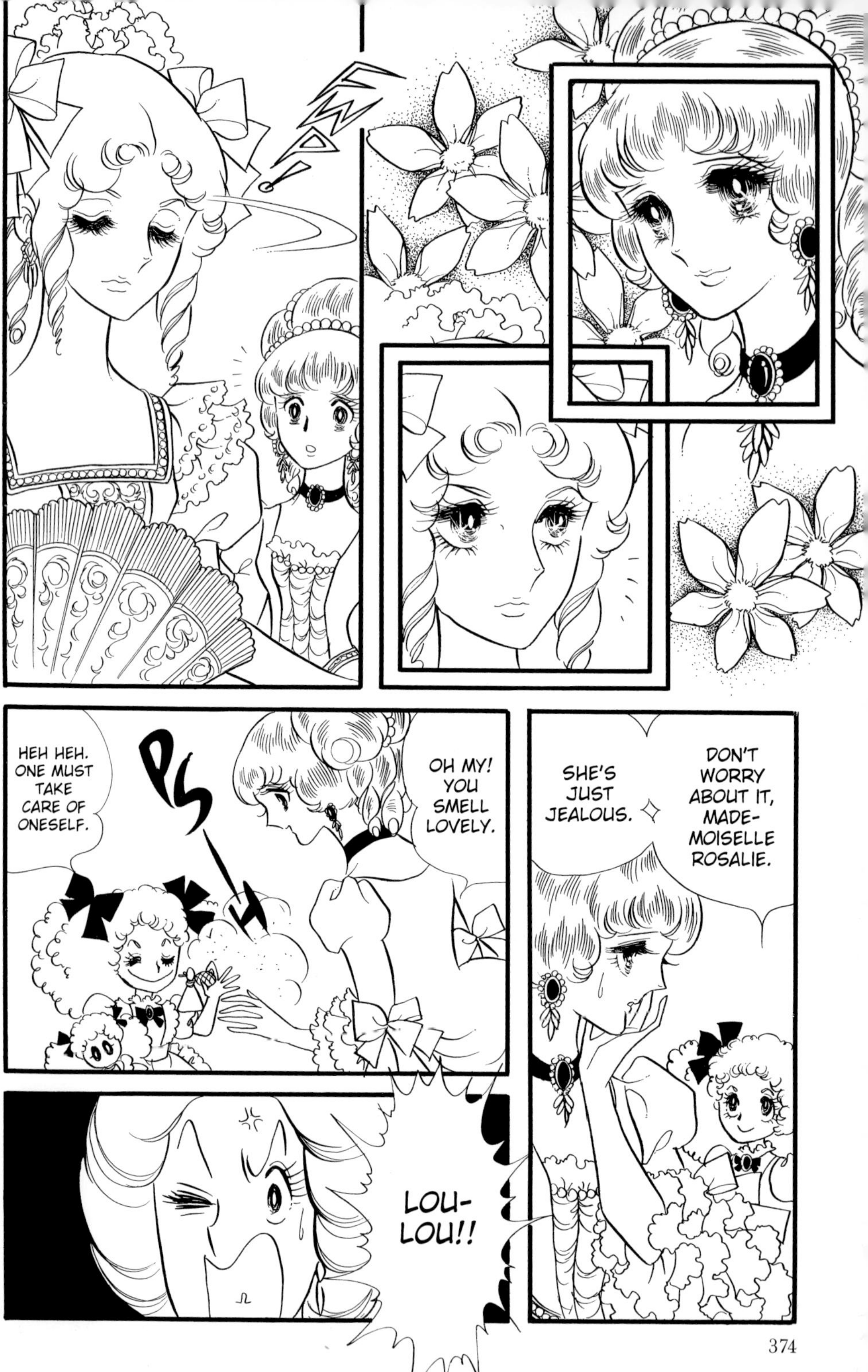
DON'T WORRY ABOUT IT, MADEMOISELLE ROSALIE.
SHE'S JUST JEALOUS.
OH MY! YOU SMELL LOVELY.
HEH HEH. ONE MUST TAKE CARE OF ONESELF.
PSH
LOU-LOU!!

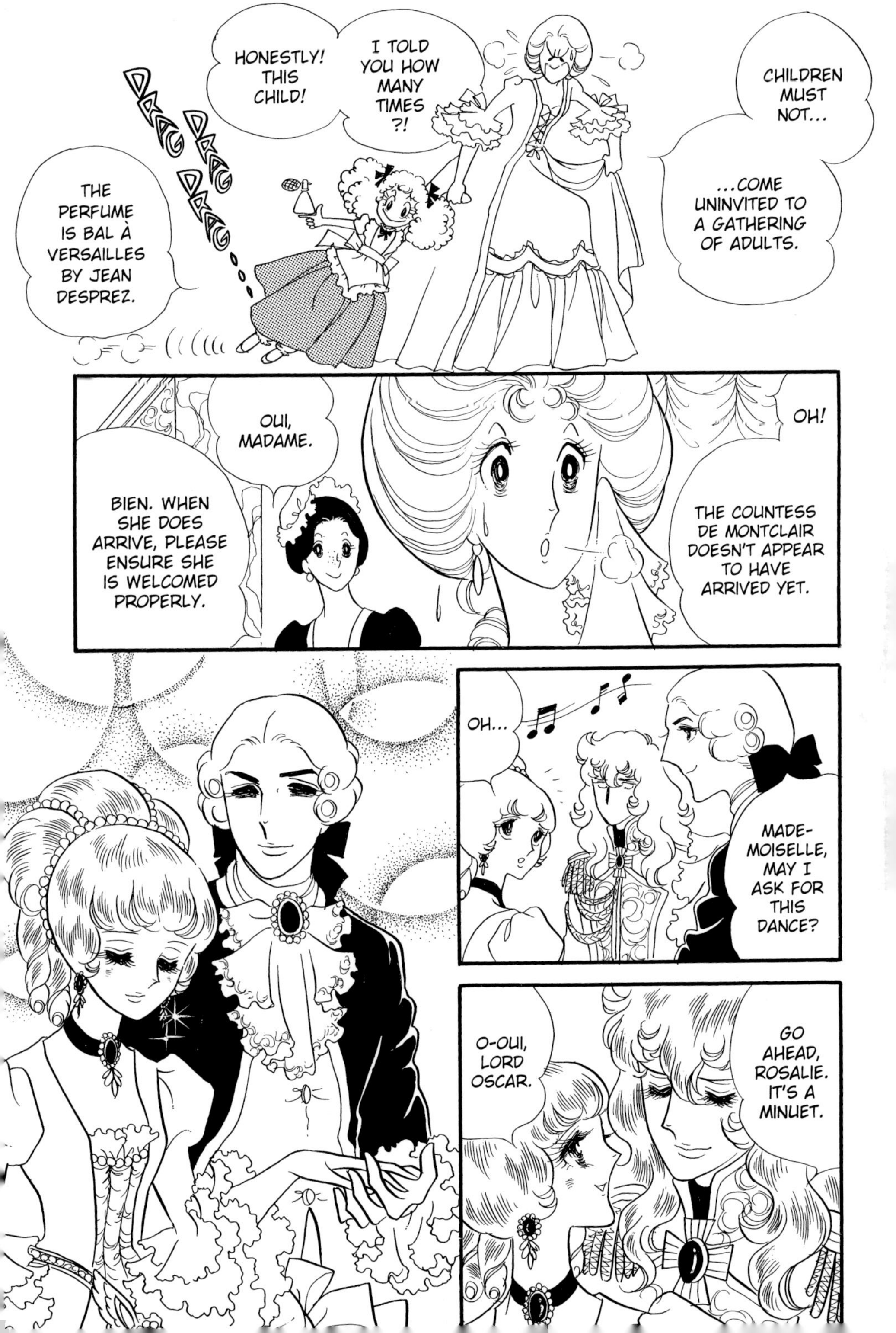
CHILDREN MUST NOT...
...COME UNINVITED TO A GATHERING OF ADULTS.
I TOLD YOU HOW MANY TIMES?!
HONESTLY! THIS CHILD!
DRAG DRAG DRAG...
THE PERFUME IS BAL À VERSAILLES BY JEAN DESPREZ.
OH!
THE COUNTESS DE MONTCLAIR DOESN'T APPEAR TO HAVE ARRIVED YET.
BIEN. WHEN SHE DOES ARRIVE, PLEASE ENSURE SHE IS WELCOMED PROPERLY.
OUI, MADAME.
MADEMOISELLE, MAY I ASK FOR THIS DANCE?
OH...
GO AHEAD, ROSALIE. IT'S A MINUET.
O-OUI, LORD OSCAR.

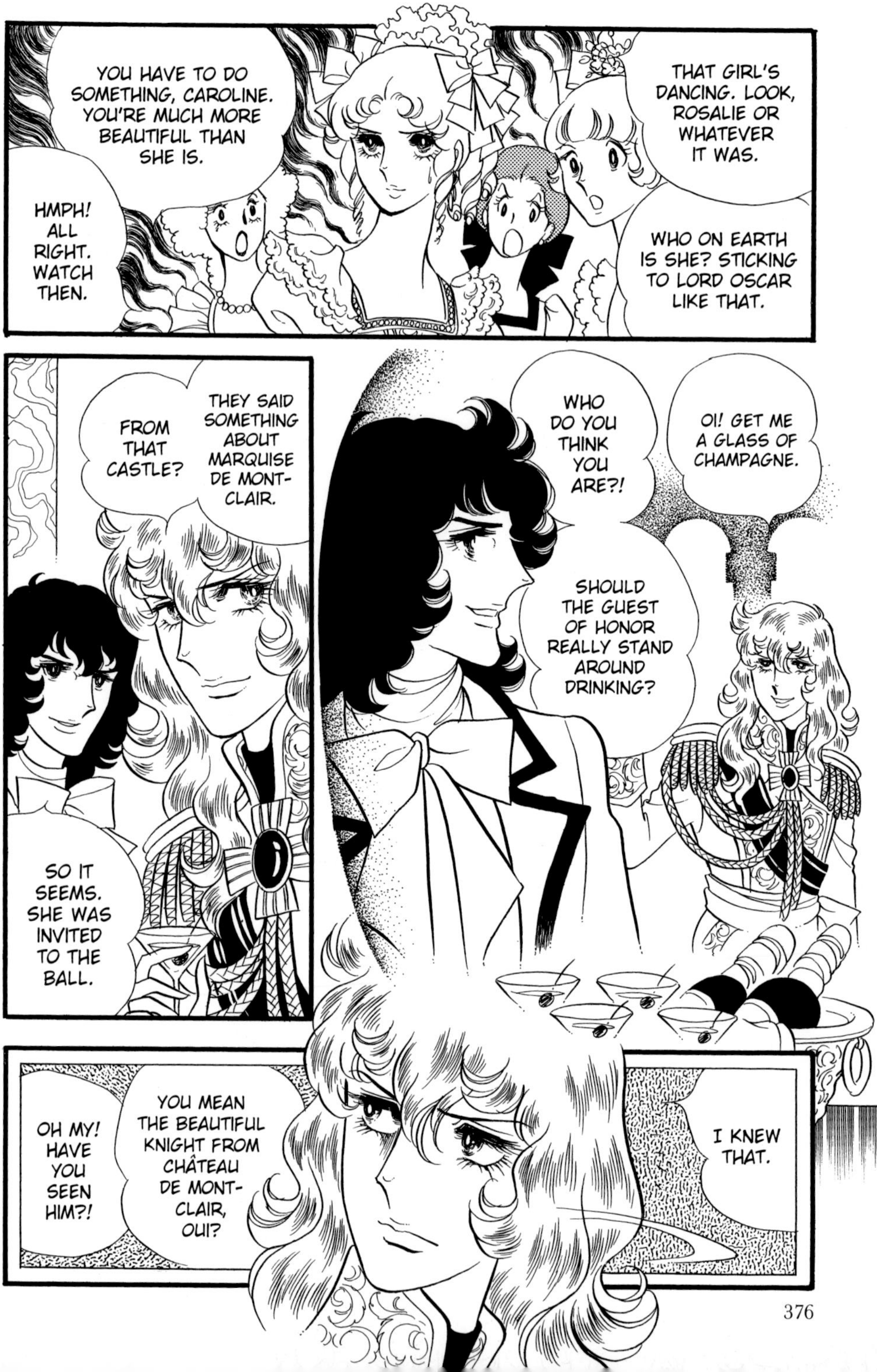
THAT GIRL'S DANCING. LOOK, ROSALIE OR WHATEVER IT WAS.
WHO ON EARTH IS SHE? STICKING TO LORD OSCAR LIKE THAT.
YOU HAVE TO DO SOMETHING, CAROLINE. YOU'RE MUCH MORE BEAUTIFUL THAN SHE IS.
HMPH! ALL RIGHT. WATCH THEN.
OI! GET ME A GLASS OF CHAMPAGNE.
WHO DO YOU THINK YOU ARE?!
SHOULD THE GUEST OF HONOR REALLY STAND AROUND DRINKING?
THEY SAID SOMETHING ABOUT MARQUISE DE MONT-CLAIR.
FROM THAT CASTLE?
SO IT SEEMS. SHE WAS INVITED TO THE BALL.
I KNEW THAT.
YOU MEAN THE BEAUTIFUL KNIGHT FROM CHÂTEAU DE MONT-CLAIR, OUI?
OH MY! HAVE YOU SEEN HIM?!

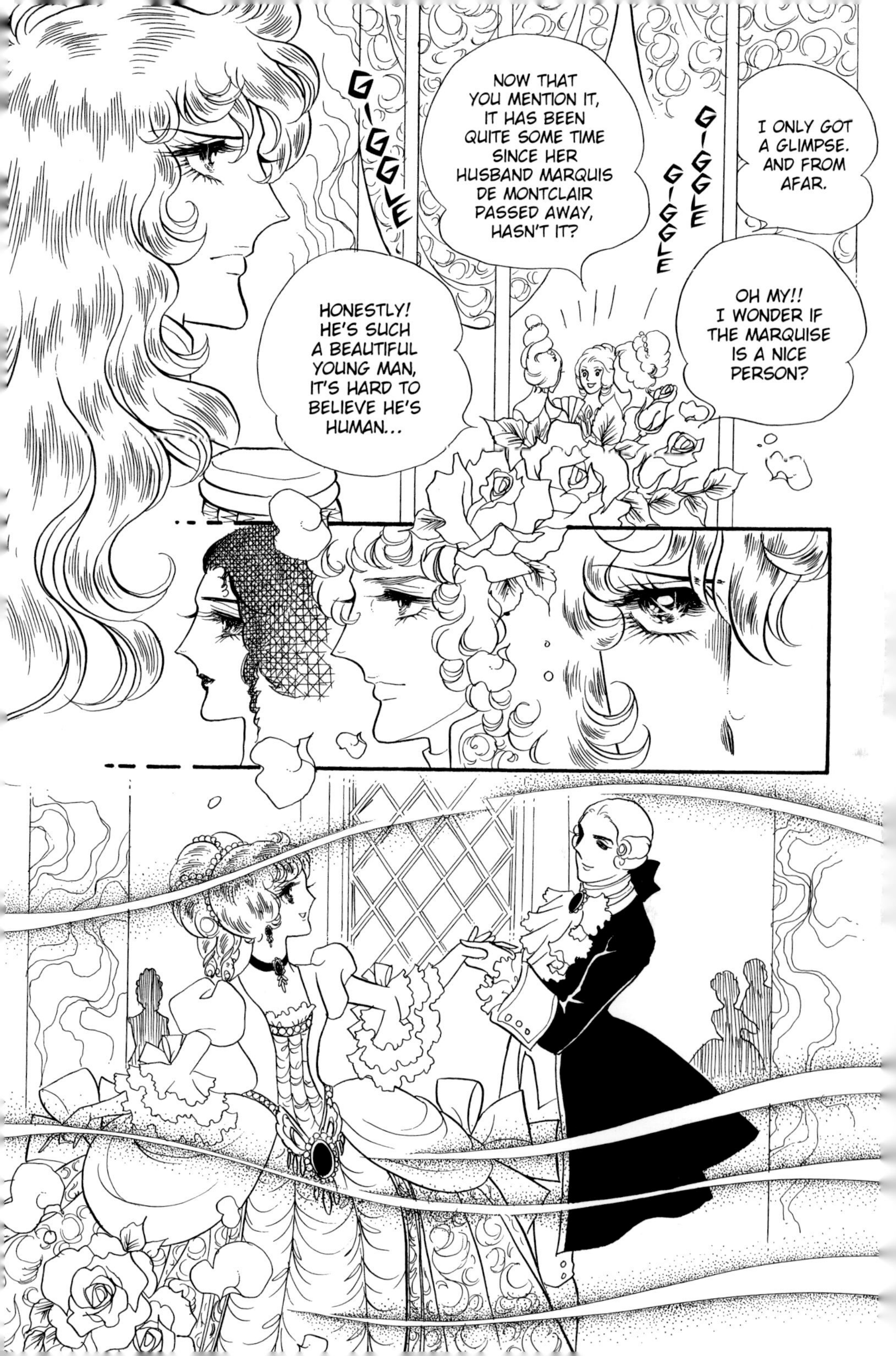

I ONLY GOT A GLIMPSE. AND FROM AFAR.
GIGGLE GIGGLE
NOW THAT YOU MENTION IT, IT HAS BEEN QUITE SOME TIME SINCE HER HUSBAND MARQUIS DE MONTCLAIR PASSED AWAY, HASN'T IT?
GIGGLE
OH MY!! I WONDER IF THE MARQUISE IS A NICE PERSON?
HONESTLY! HE'S SUCH A BEAUTIFUL YOUNG MAN, IT'S HARD TO BELIEVE HE'S HUMAN...

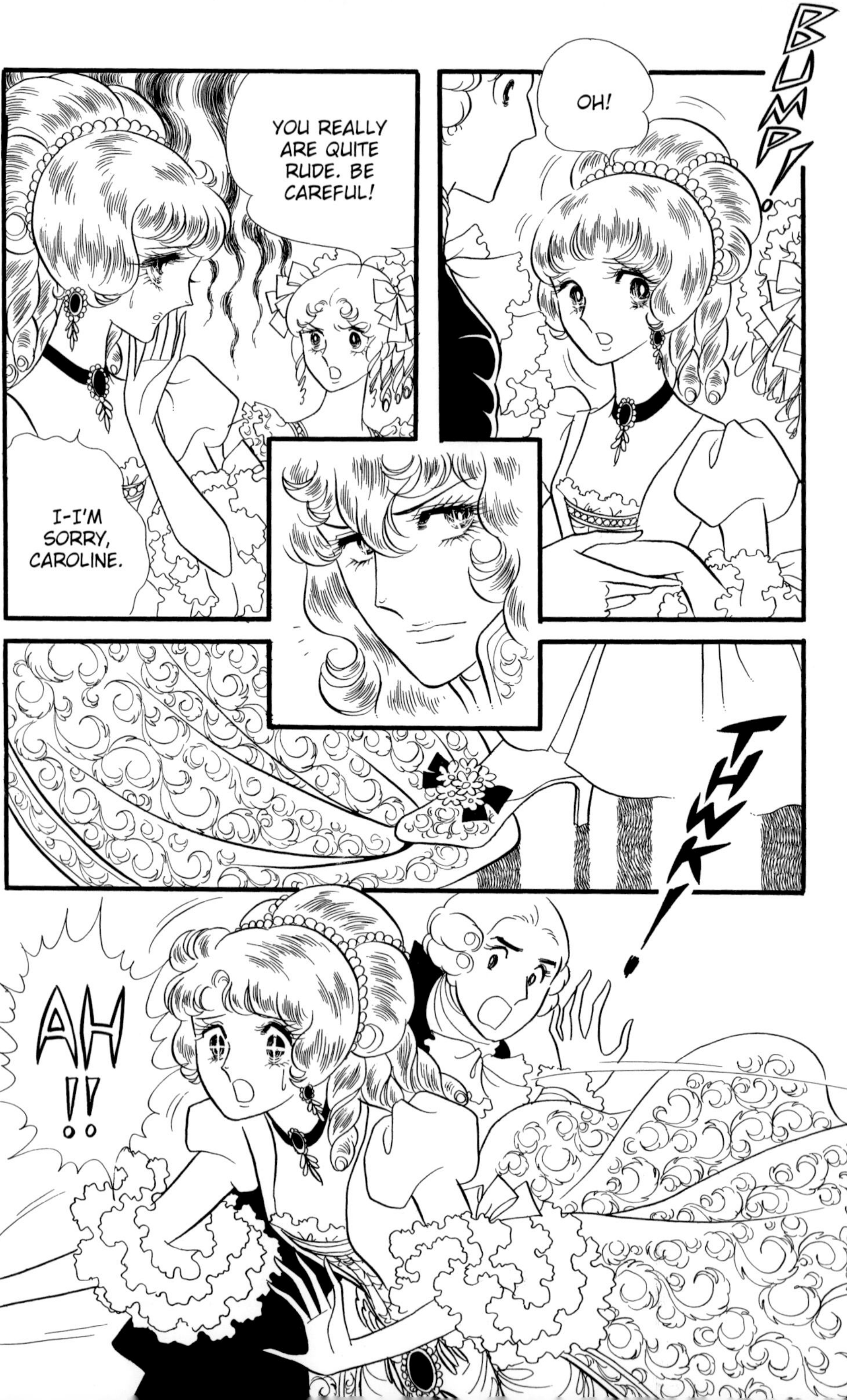
BUMP!
OH!
YOU REALLY ARE QUITE RUDE. BE CAREFUL!
I-I'M SORRY, CAROLINE.
THWK!
AH!!

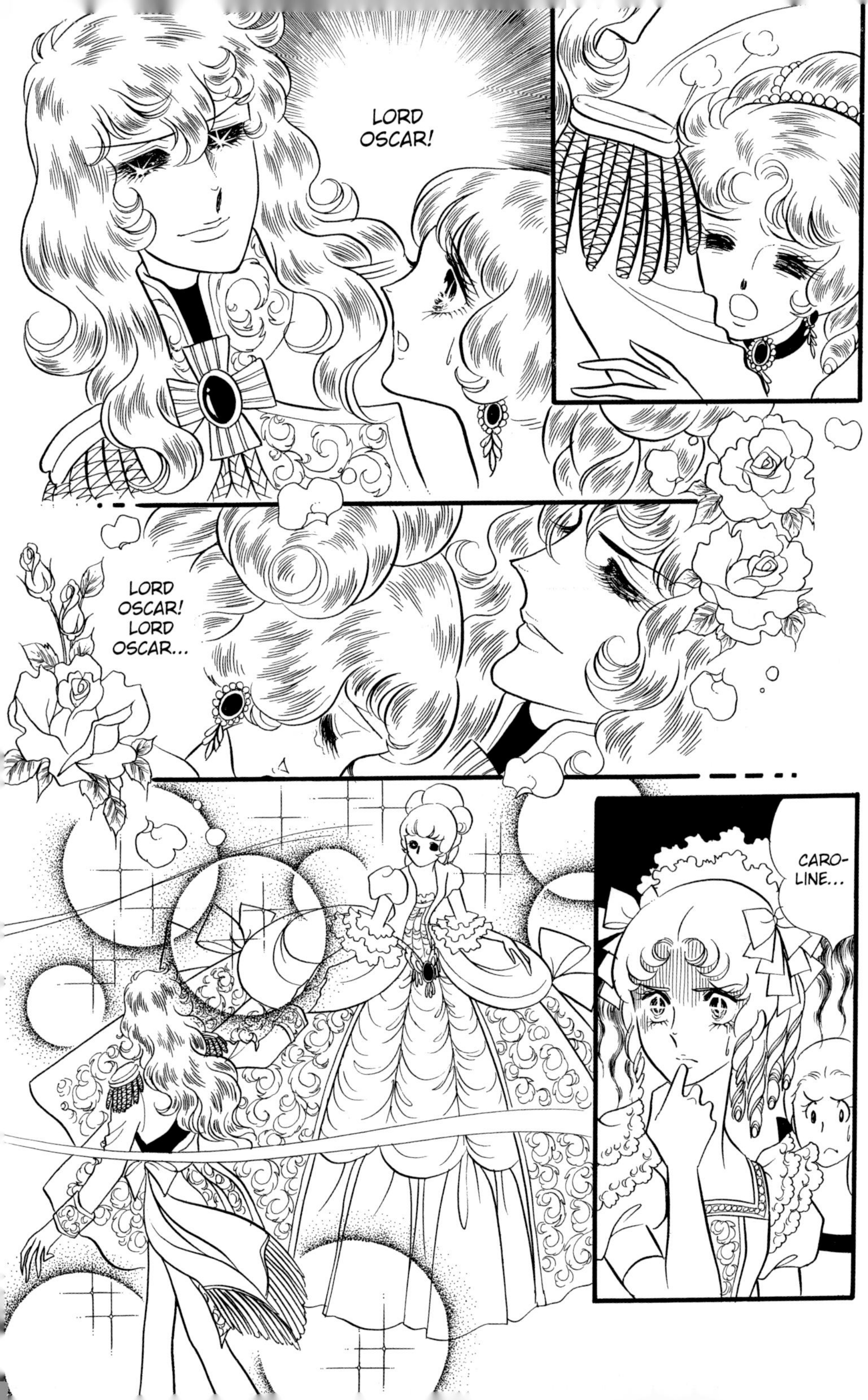
LORD OSCAR!
LORD OSCAR! LORD OSCAR...
CARO-LINE...

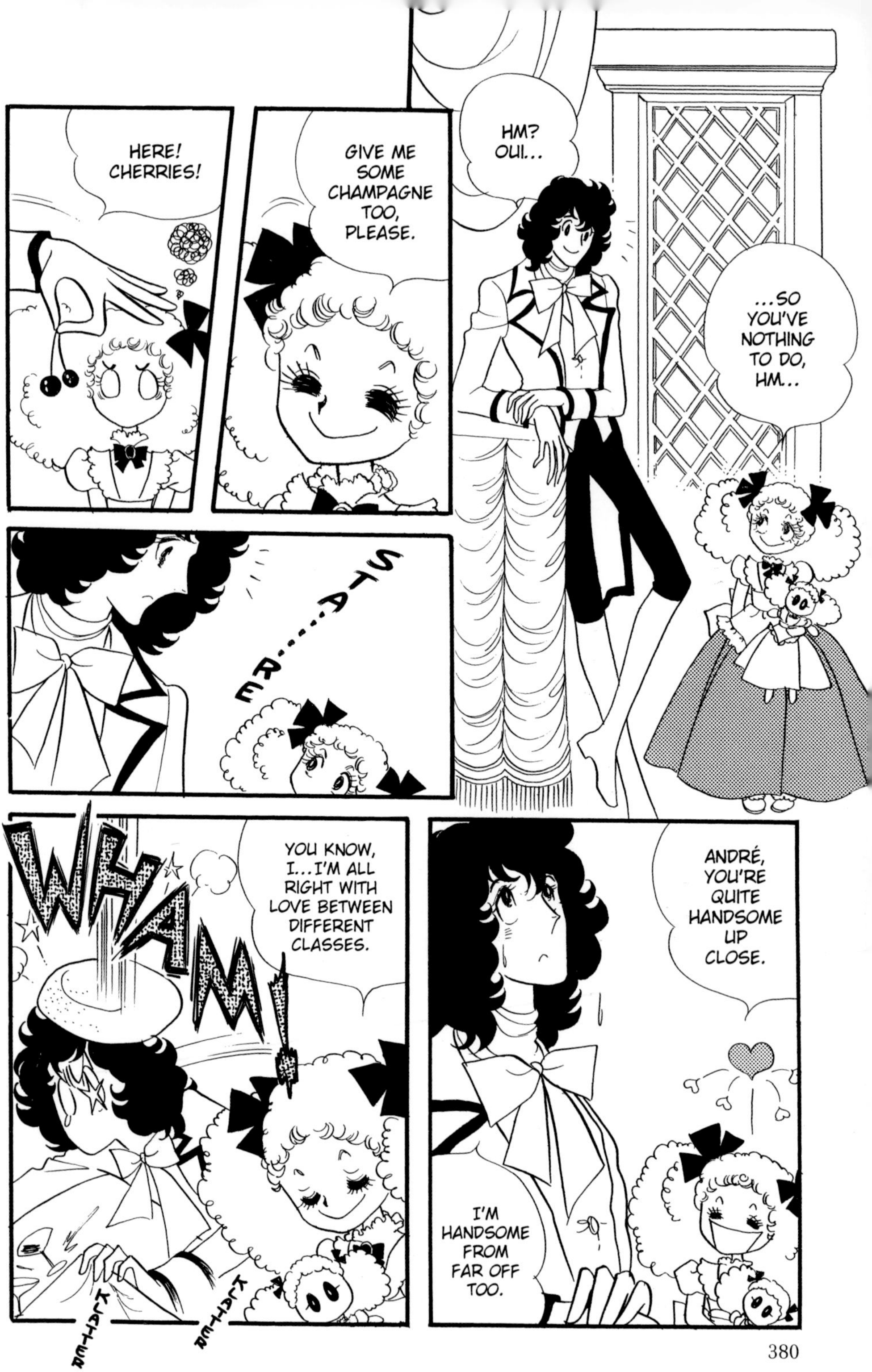
...SO YOU'VE NOTHING TO DO, HM...
HM? OUI...
GIVE ME SOME CHAMPAGNE TOO, PLEASE.
HERE! CHERRIES!
STA...RE
ANDRÉ, YOU'RE QUITE HANDSOME UP CLOSE.
I'M HANDSOME FROM FAR OFF TOO.
WHAM!
YOU KNOW, I... I'M ALL RIGHT WITH LOVE BETWEEN DIFFERENT CLASSES.
KLATTER
KLATTER

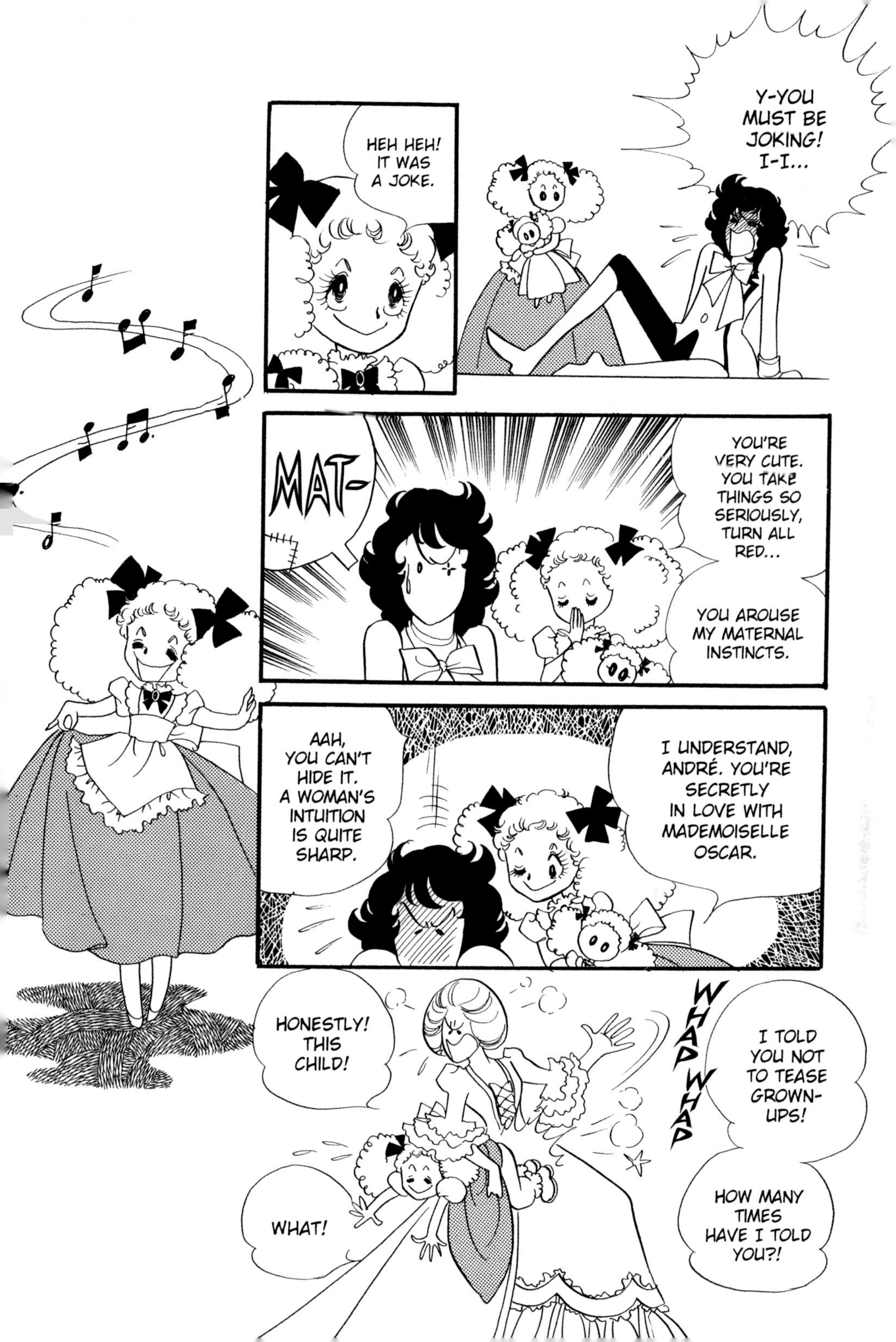

Y-YOU MUST BE JOKING! I-I...
HEH HEH! IT WAS A JOKE.
YOU'RE VERY CUTE. YOU TAKE THINGS SO SERIOUSLY, TURN ALL RED...
YOU AROUSE MY MATERNAL INSTINCTS.
MAT-
I UNDERSTAND, ANDRÉ. YOU'RE SECRETLY IN LOVE WITH MADEMOISELLE OSCAR.
AAH, YOU CAN'T HIDE IT. A WOMAN'S INTUITION IS QUITE SHARP.
I TOLD YOU NOT TO TEASE GROWN-UPS!
WHAP WHAP
HOW MANY TIMES HAVE I TOLD YOU?!
HONESTLY! THIS CHILD!
WHAT!

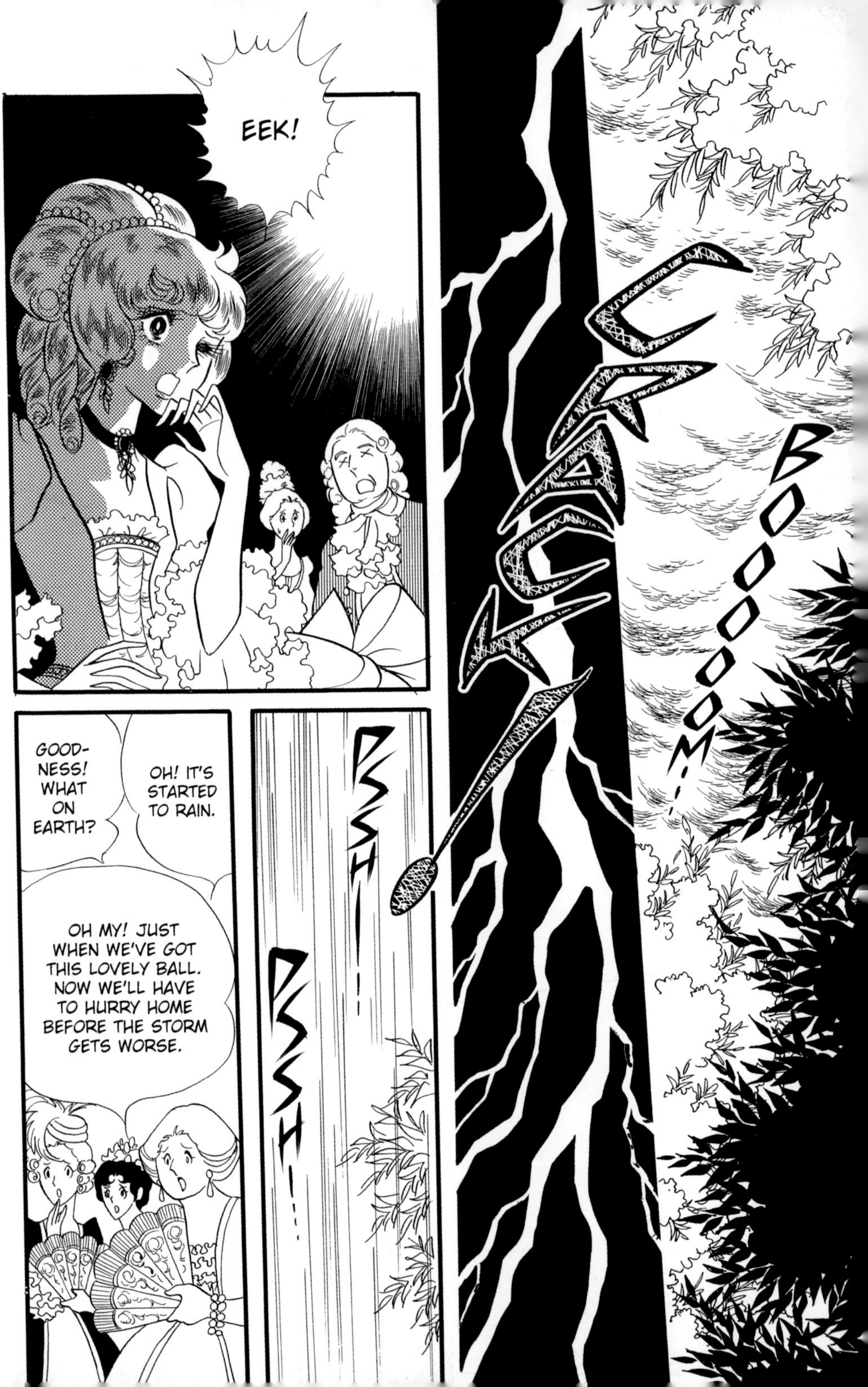
CRACK
BOOOOOM...
EEK!
PSSH!!!
PSSH!!...
GOOD-NESS! WHAT ON EARTH?
OH! IT'S STARTED TO RAIN.
OH MY! JUST WHEN WE'VE GOT THIS LOVELY BALL. NOW WE'LL HAVE TO HURRY HOME BEFORE THE STORM GETS WORSE.

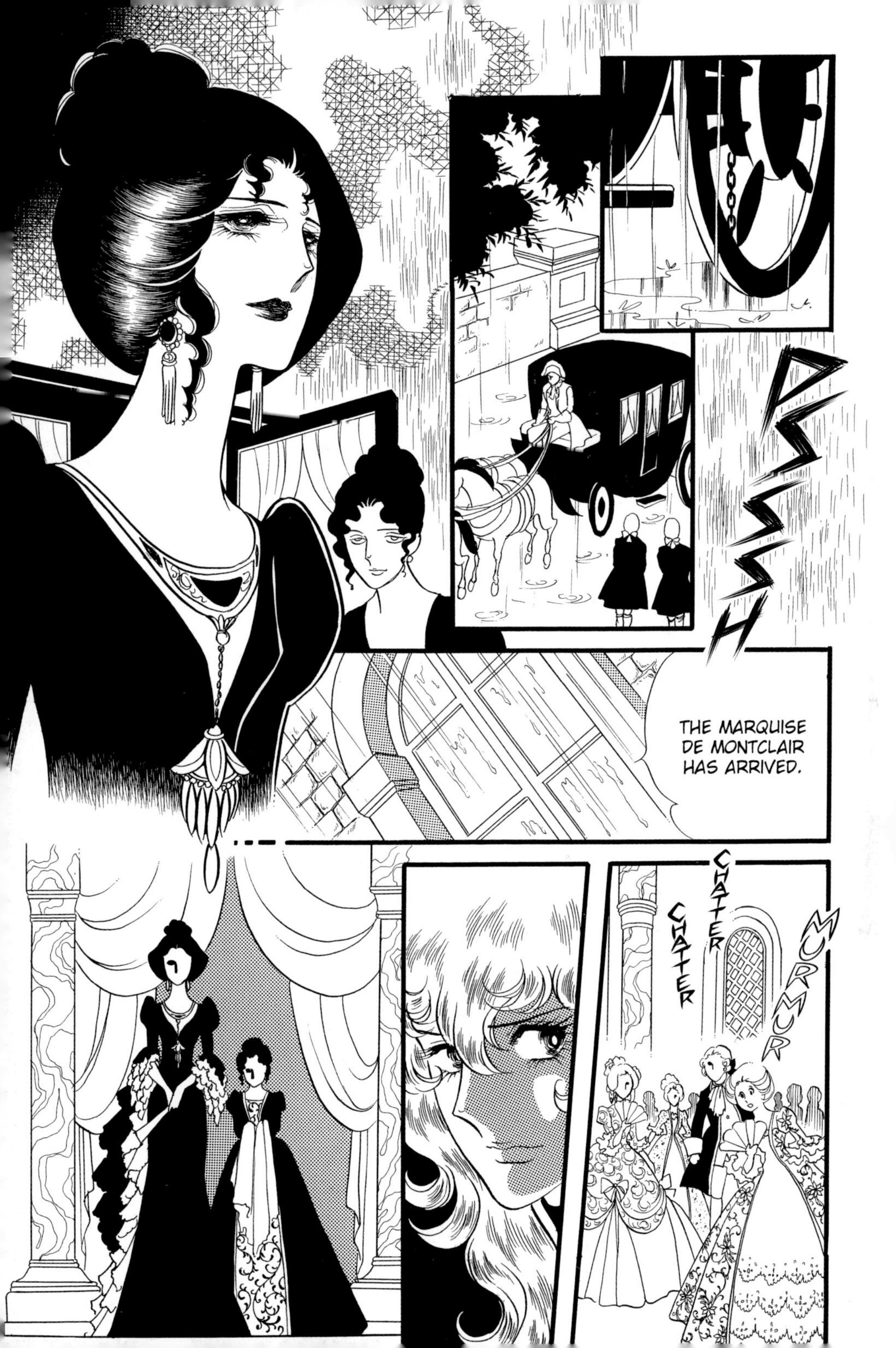
PSSSH
THE MARQUISE DE MONTCLAIR HAS ARRIVED.
MURMUR
CHATTER
CHATTER

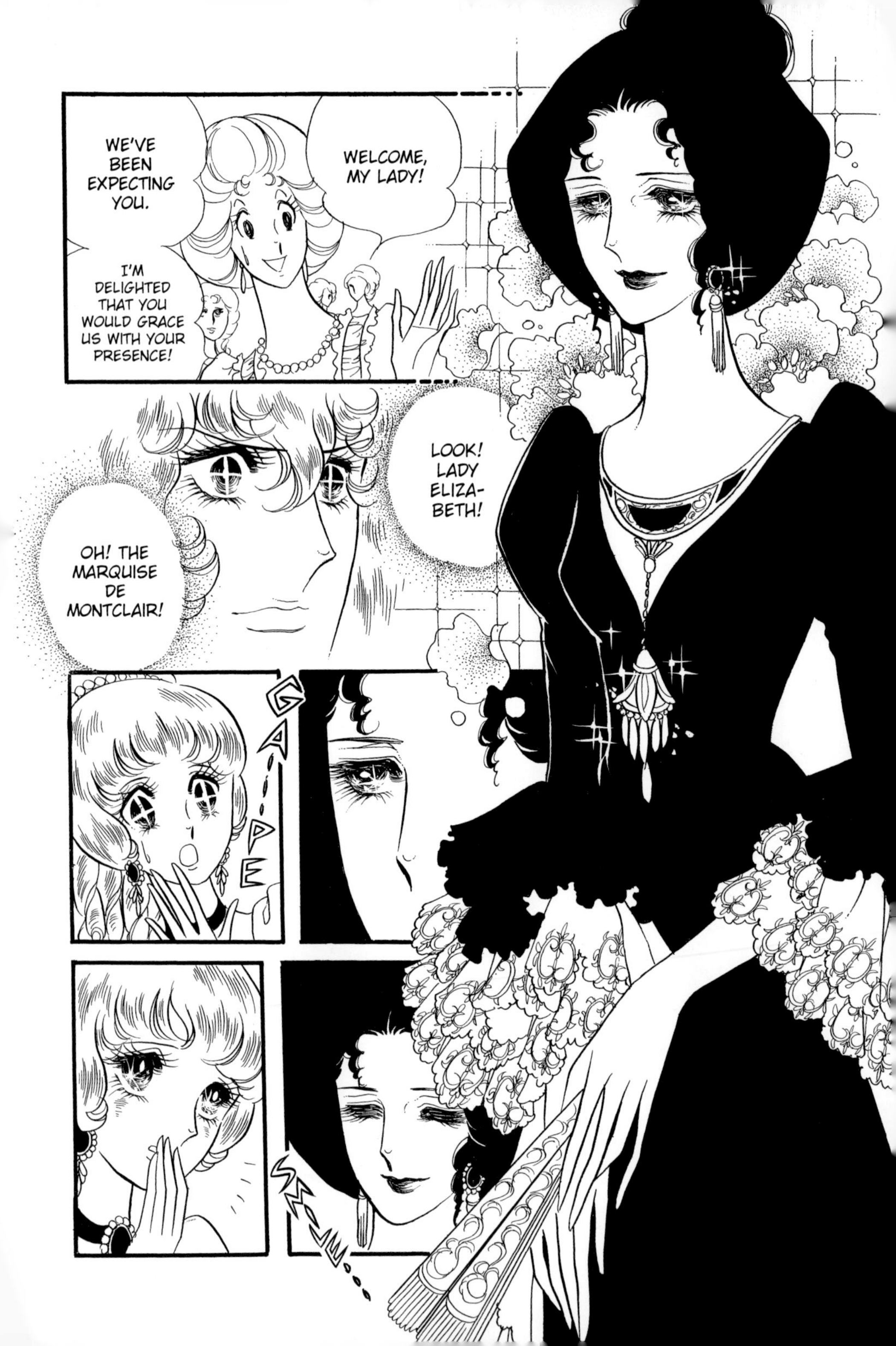
WELCOME, MY LADY!
WE'VE BEEN EXPECTING YOU.
I'M DELIGHTED THAT YOU WOULD GRACE US WITH YOUR PRESENCE!
LOOK! LADY ELIZA-BETH!
OH! THE MARQUISE DE MONTCLAIR!
GA-PE
SMILE...

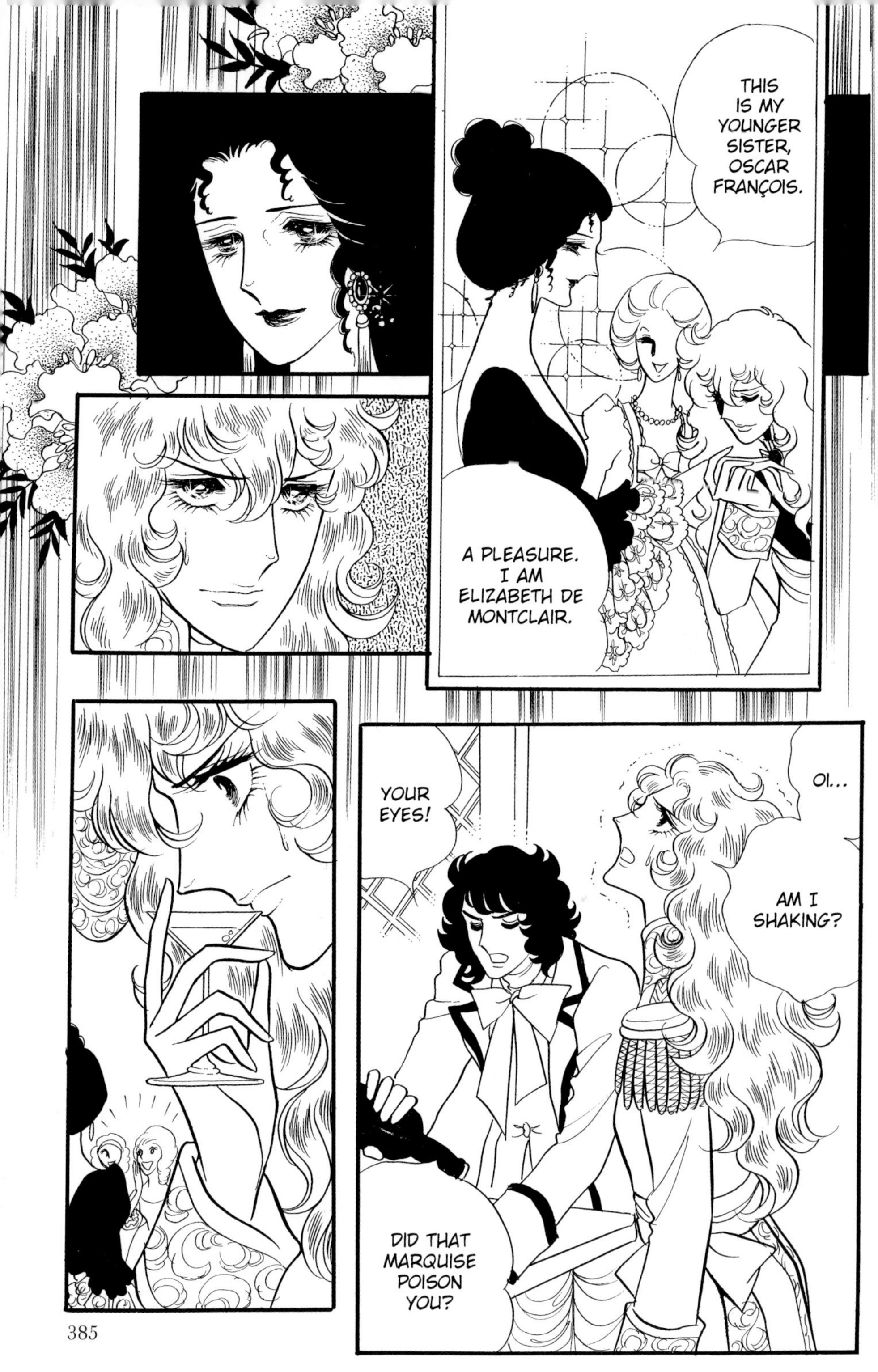
THIS IS MY YOUNGER SISTER, OSCAR FRANÇOIS.
A PLEASURE. I AM ELIZABETH DE MONTCLAIR.
OI...
AM I SHAKING?
YOUR EYES!
DID THAT MARQUISE POISON YOU?

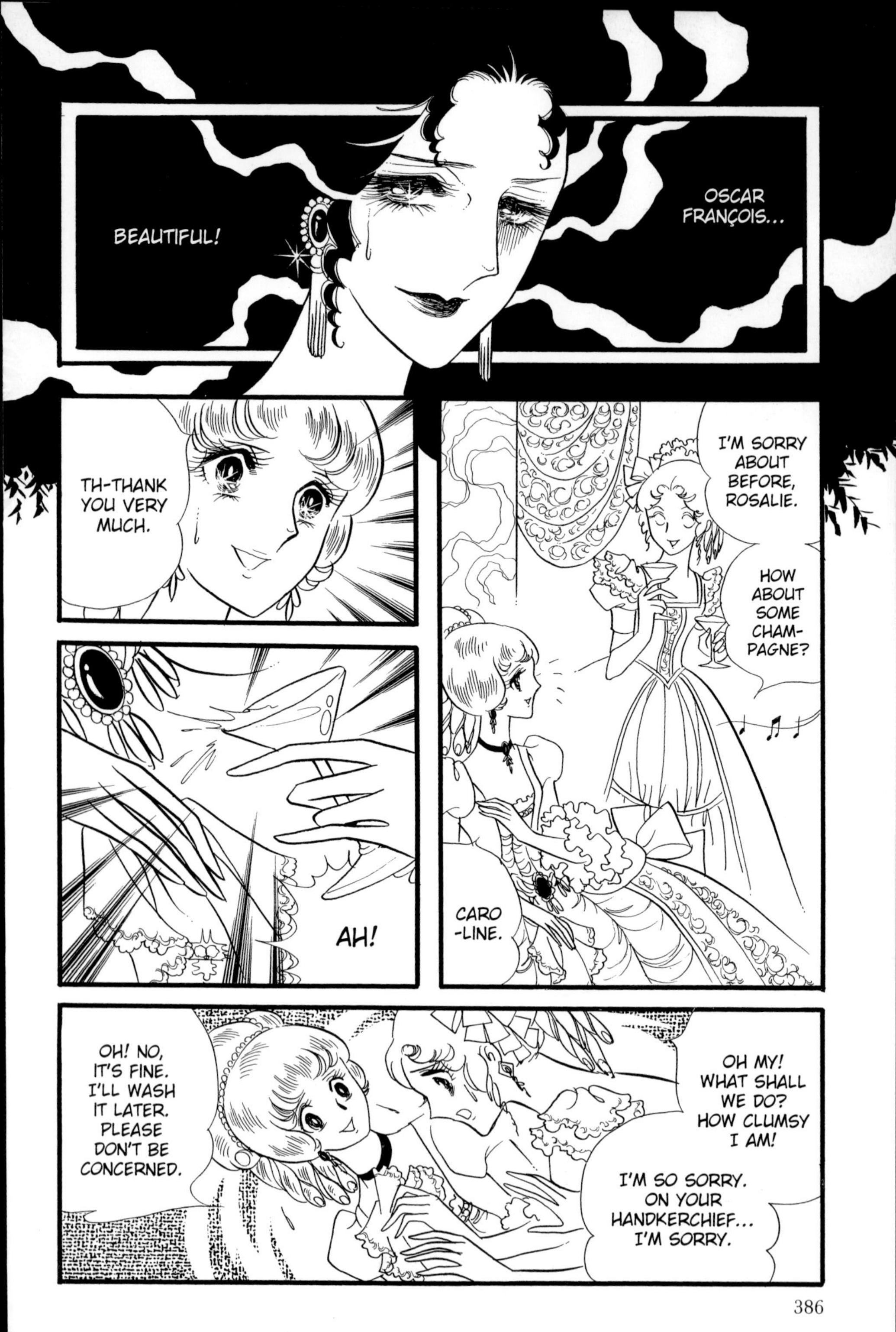

OSCAR FRANÇOIS...
BEAUTIFUL!
I'M SORRY ABOUT BEFORE, ROSALIE.
HOW ABOUT SOME CHAM-PAGNE?
CARO-LINE.
TH-THANK YOU VERY MUCH.
AH!
OH MY! WHAT SHALL WE DO? HOW CLUMSY I AM!
I'M SO SORRY. ON YOUR HANDKERCHIEF... I'M SORRY.
OH! NO, IT'S FINE. I'LL WASH IT LATER. PLEASE DON'T BE CONCERNED.

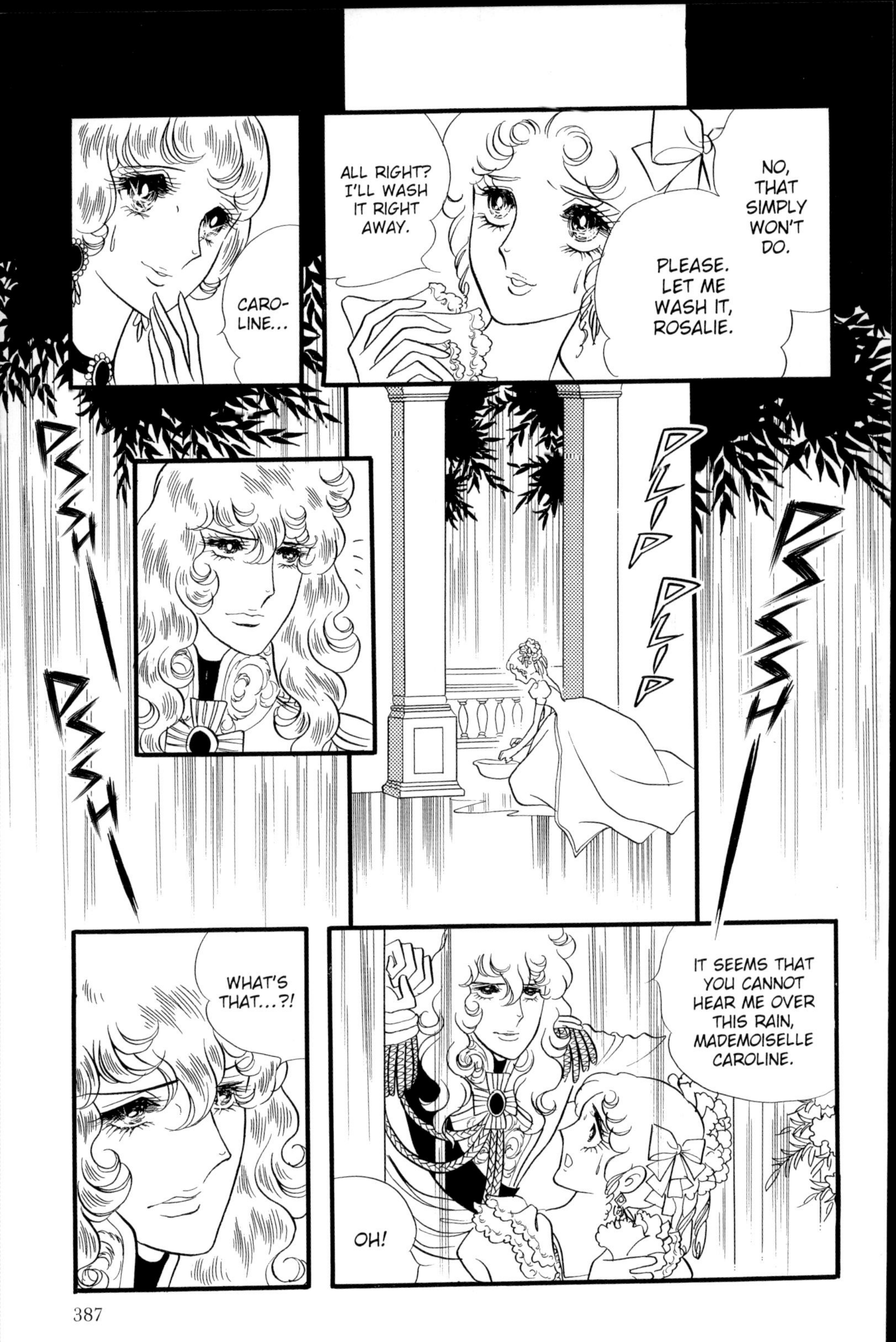
NO, THAT SIMPLY WON'T DO.
ALL RIGHT? I'LL WASH IT RIGHT AWAY.
PLEASE. LET ME WASH IT, ROSALIE.
CARO-LINE...
PLIP PLIP
IT SEEMS THAT YOU CANNOT HEAR ME OVER THIS RAIN, MADEMOISELLE CAROLINE.
OH!
WHAT'S THAT...?!

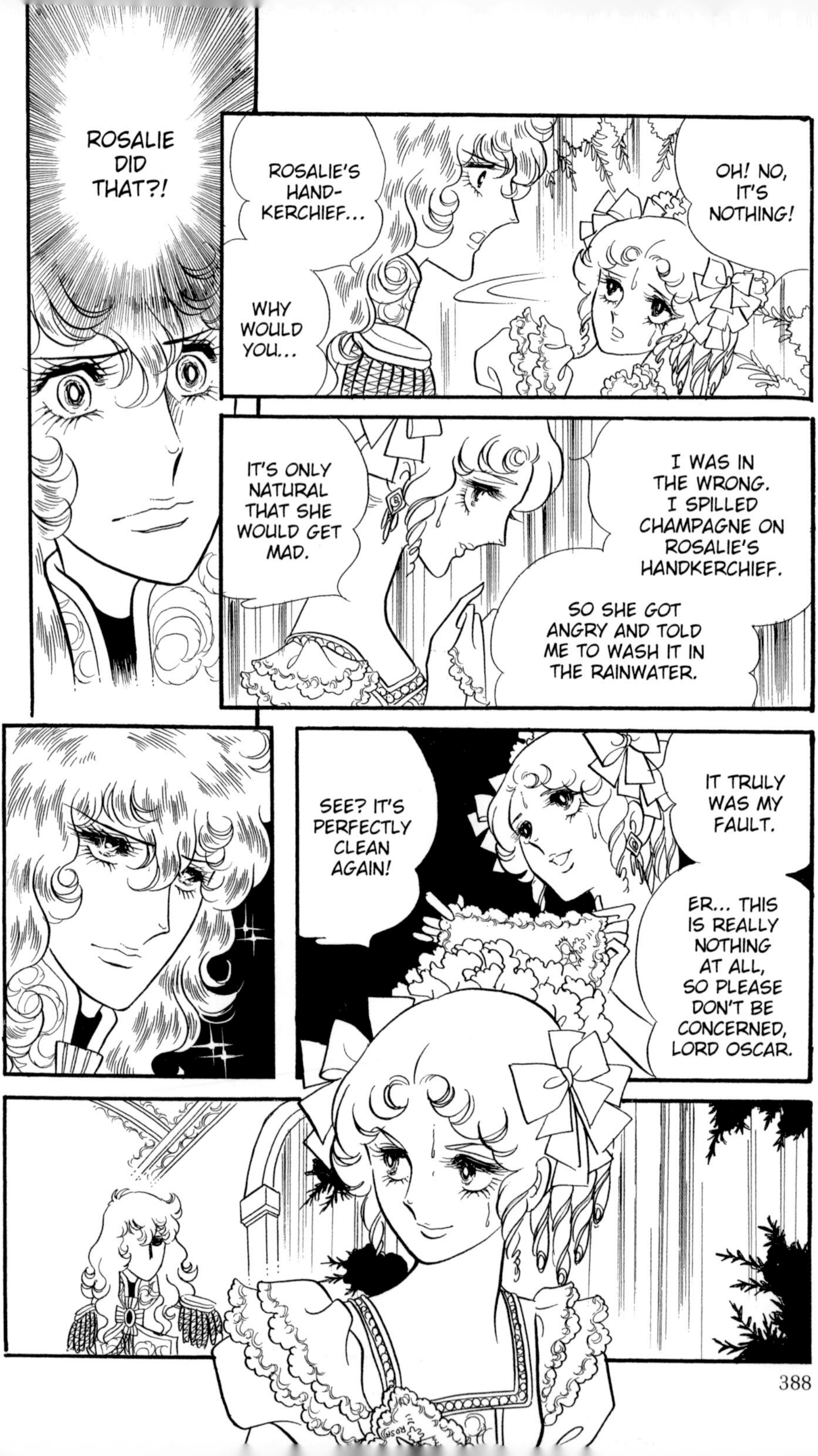
OH! NO, IT'S NOTHING!
ROSALIE'S HANDKERCHIEF...
WHY WOULD YOU...
I WAS IN THE WRONG. I SPILLED CHAMPAGNE ON ROSALIE'S HANDKERCHIEF.
SO SHE GOT ANGRY AND TOLD ME TO WASH IT IN THE RAINWATER.
IT'S ONLY NATURAL THAT SHE WOULD GET MAD.
ROSALIE DID THAT?!
IT TRULY WAS MY FAULT.
ER... THIS IS REALLY NOTHING AT ALL, SO PLEASE DON'T BE CONCERNED, LORD OSCAR.
SEE? IT'S PERFECTLY CLEAN AGAIN!

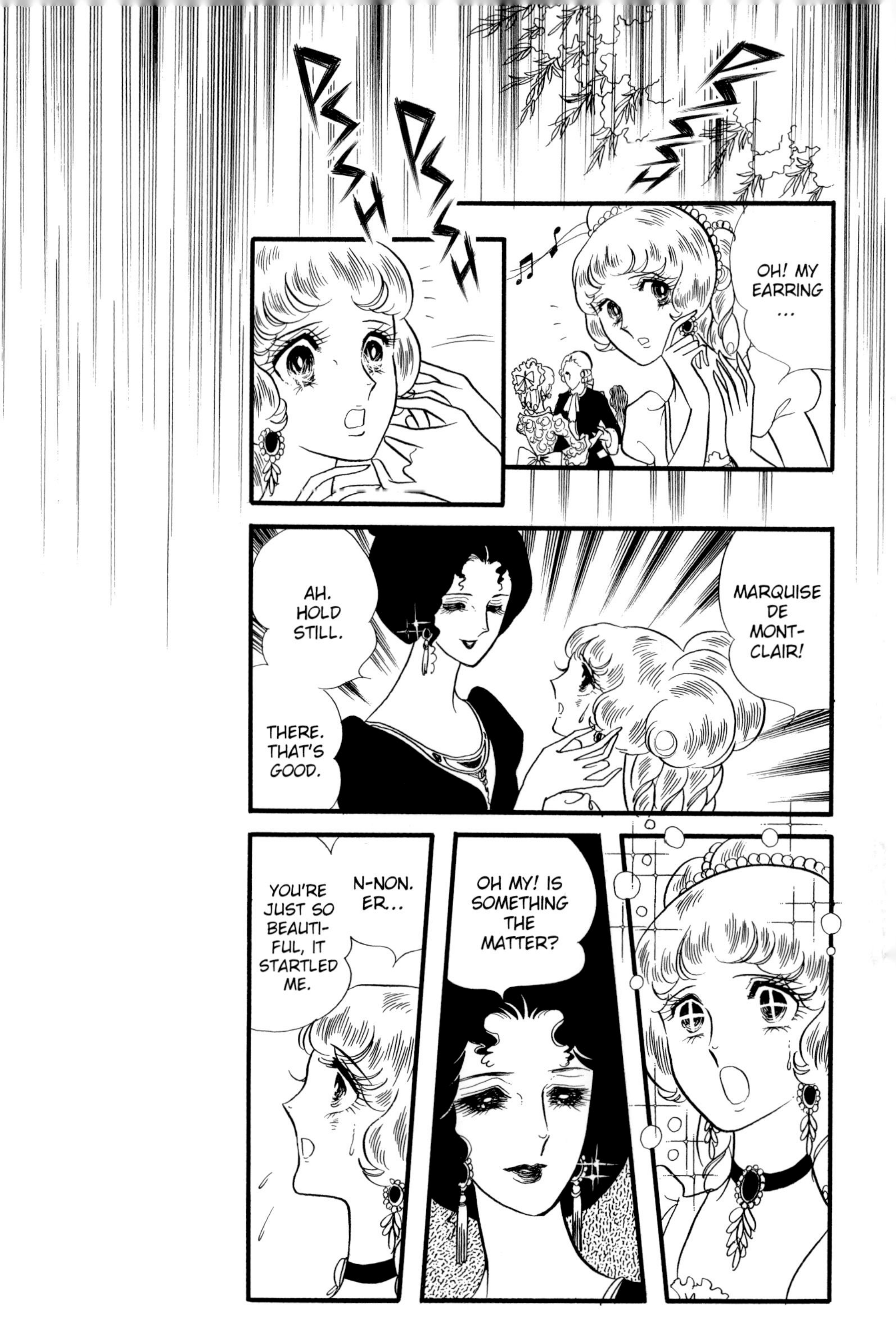
PSSH
PSSH PSSH
OH! MY EARRING ...
MARQUISE DE MONT-CLAIR!
AH. HOLD STILL.
THERE. THAT'S GOOD.
OH MY! IS SOMETHING THE MATTER?
N-NON. ER...
YOU'RE JUST SO BEAUTIFUL, IT STARTLED ME.

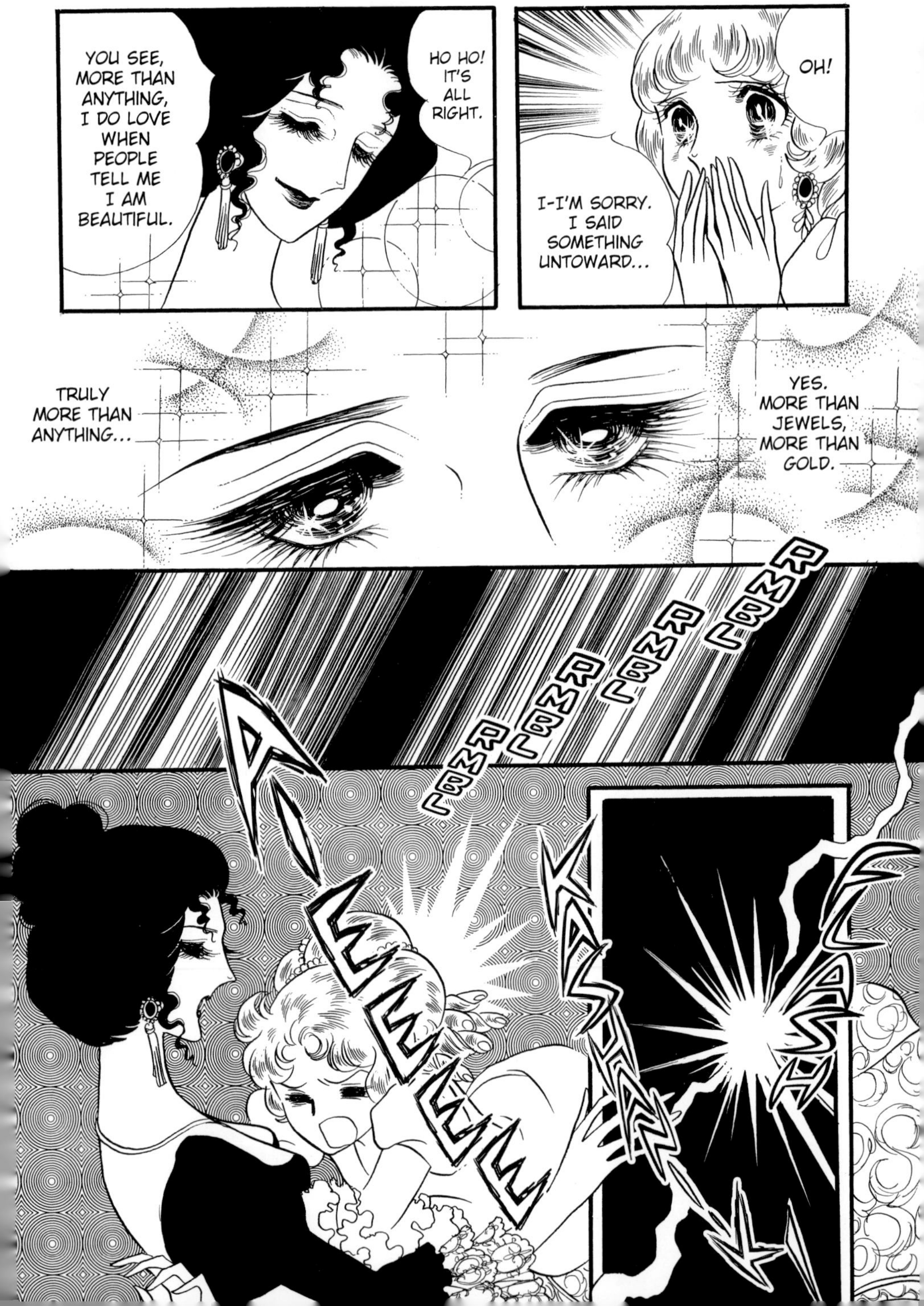
OH!
I-I'M SORRY. I SAID SOMETHING UNTOWARD...
HO HO! IT'S ALL RIGHT.
YOU SEE, MORE THAN ANYTHING, I DO LOVE WHEN PEOPLE TELL ME I AM BEAUTIFUL.
YES. MORE THAN JEWELS, MORE THAN GOLD.
TRULY MORE THAN ANYTHING...
RMMBL RMMBL RMMBL RMMBL
FLASH
KASHAK
AEEEEEE

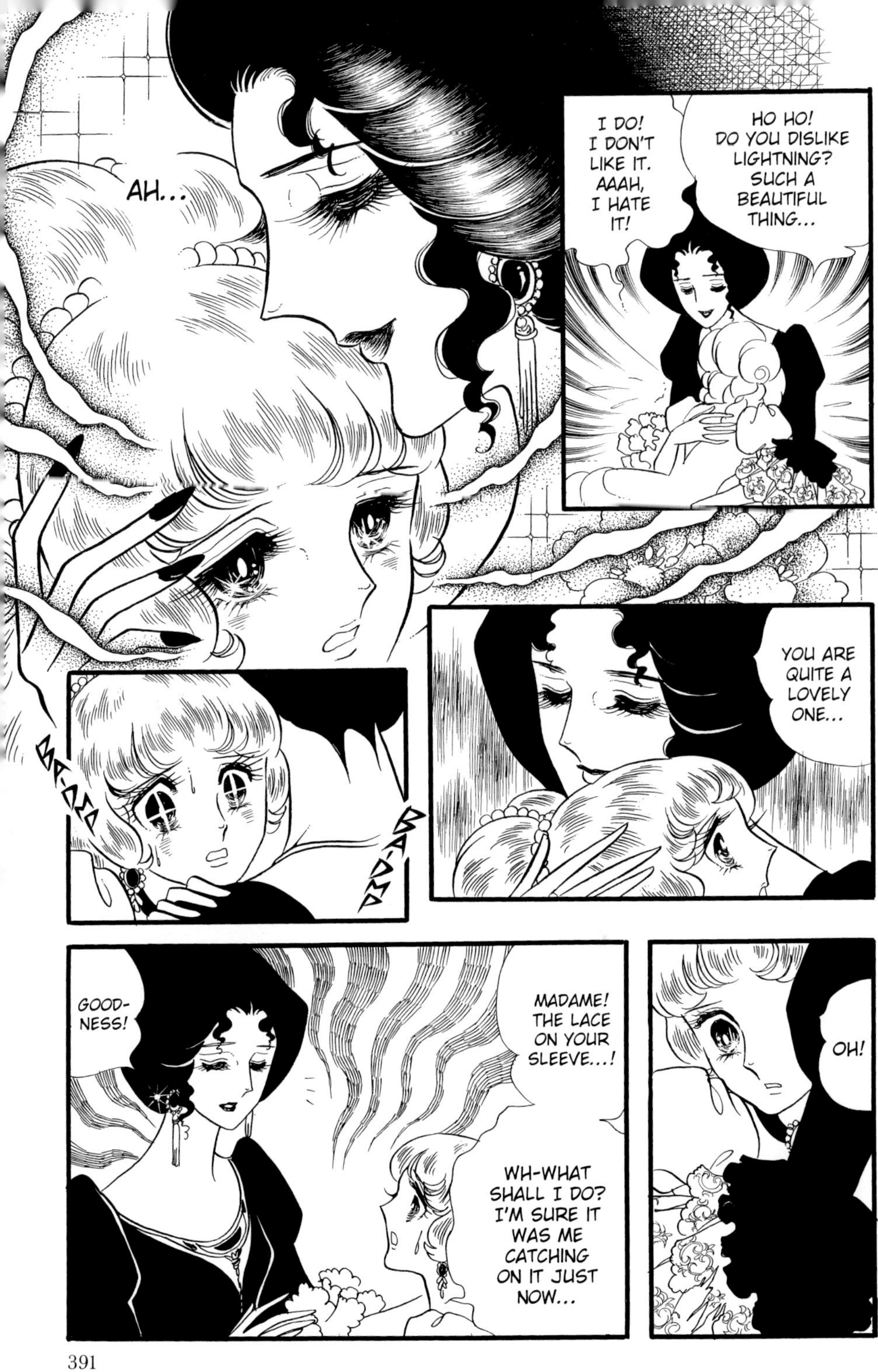
HO HO! DO YOU DISLIKE LIGHTNING? SUCH A BEAUTIFUL THING...
I DO! I DON'T LIKE IT. AAAH, I HATE IT!
AH...
YOU ARE QUITE A LOVELY ONE...
BA-DMP
BA-DMP
OH!
MADAME! THE LACE ON YOUR SLEEVE...!
GOOD-NESS!
WH-WHAT SHALL I DO? I'M SURE IT WAS ME CATCHING ON IT JUST NOW...

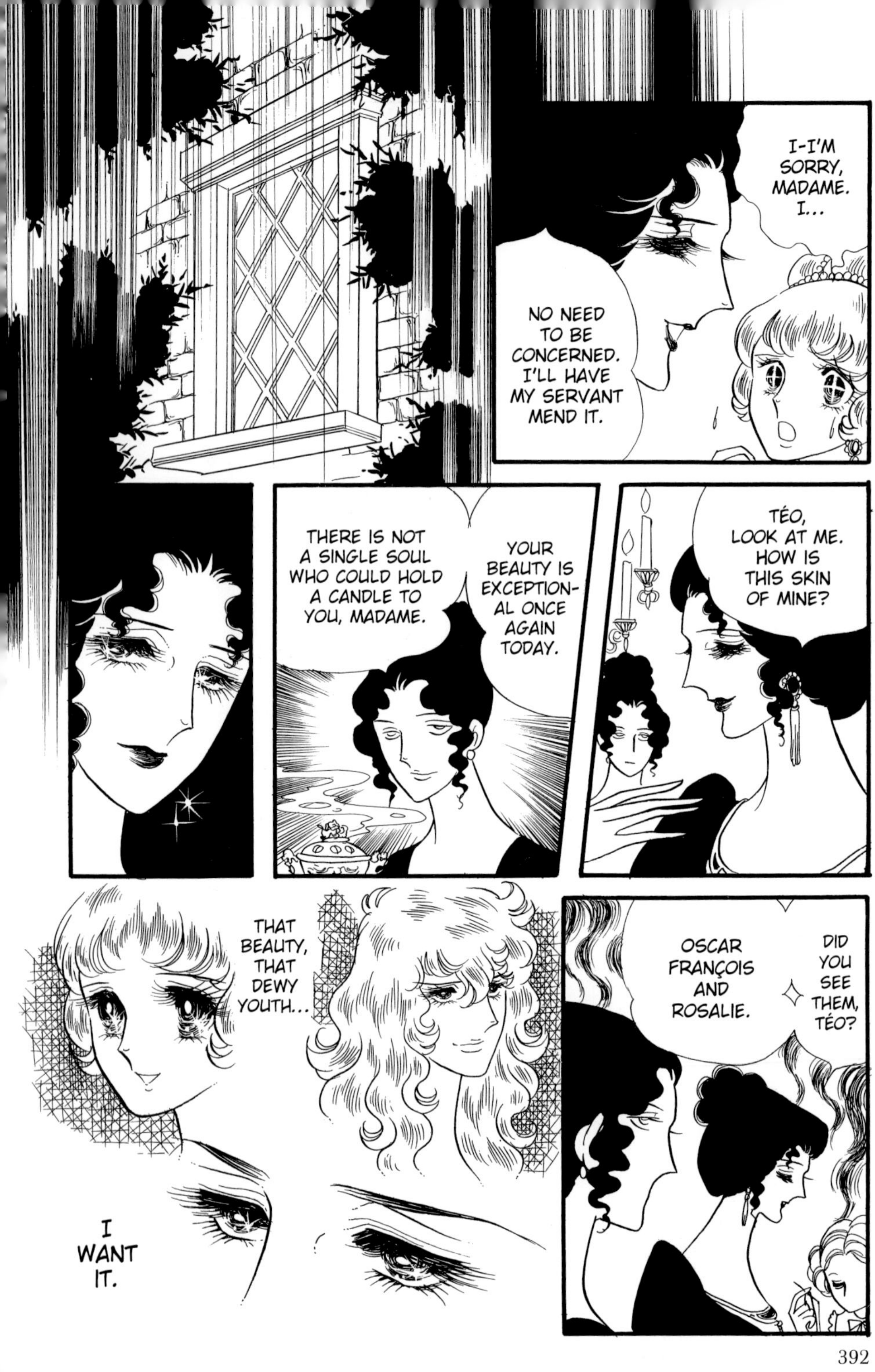
I-I'M SORRY, MADAME. I...
NO NEED TO BE CONCERNED. I'LL HAVE MY SERVANT MEND IT.
TÉO, LOOK AT ME. HOW IS THIS SKIN OF MINE?
YOUR BEAUTY IS EXCEPTION-AL ONCE AGAIN TODAY.
THERE IS NOT A SINGLE SOUL WHO COULD HOLD A CANDLE TO YOU, MADAME.
DID YOU SEE THEM, TÉO?
OSCAR FRANÇOIS AND ROSALIE.
THAT BEAUTY, THAT DEWY YOUTH...
I WANT IT.

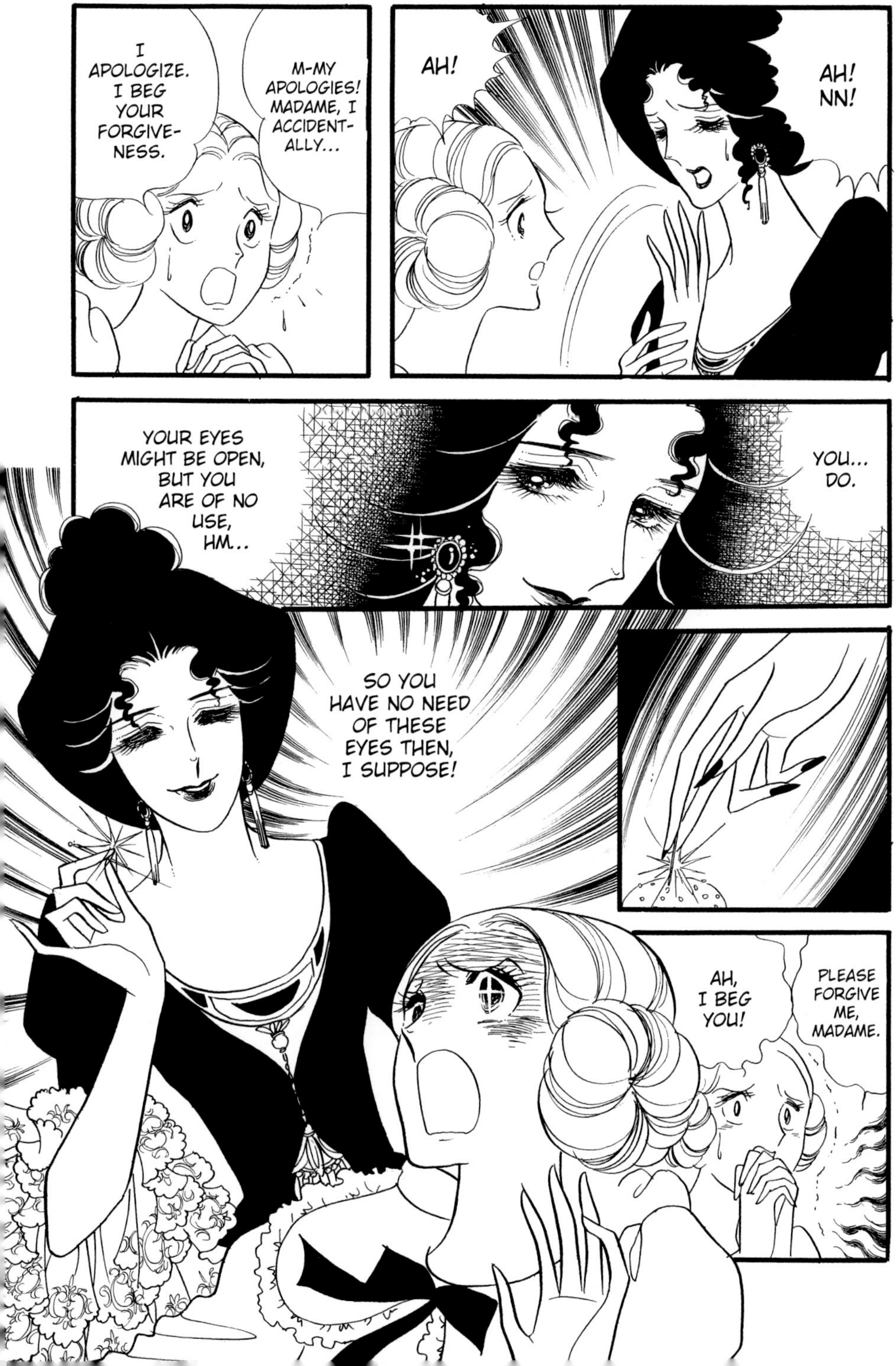
AH! NN!
AH!
M-MY APOLOGIES! MADAME, I ACCIDENT-ALLY...
I APOLOGIZE. I BEG YOUR FORGIVE-NESS.
YOU... DO.
YOUR EYES MIGHT BE OPEN, BUT YOU ARE OF NO USE, HM...
PLEASE FORGIVE ME, MADAME.
AH, I BEG YOU!
SO YOU HAVE NO NEED OF THESE EYES THEN, I SUPPOSE!

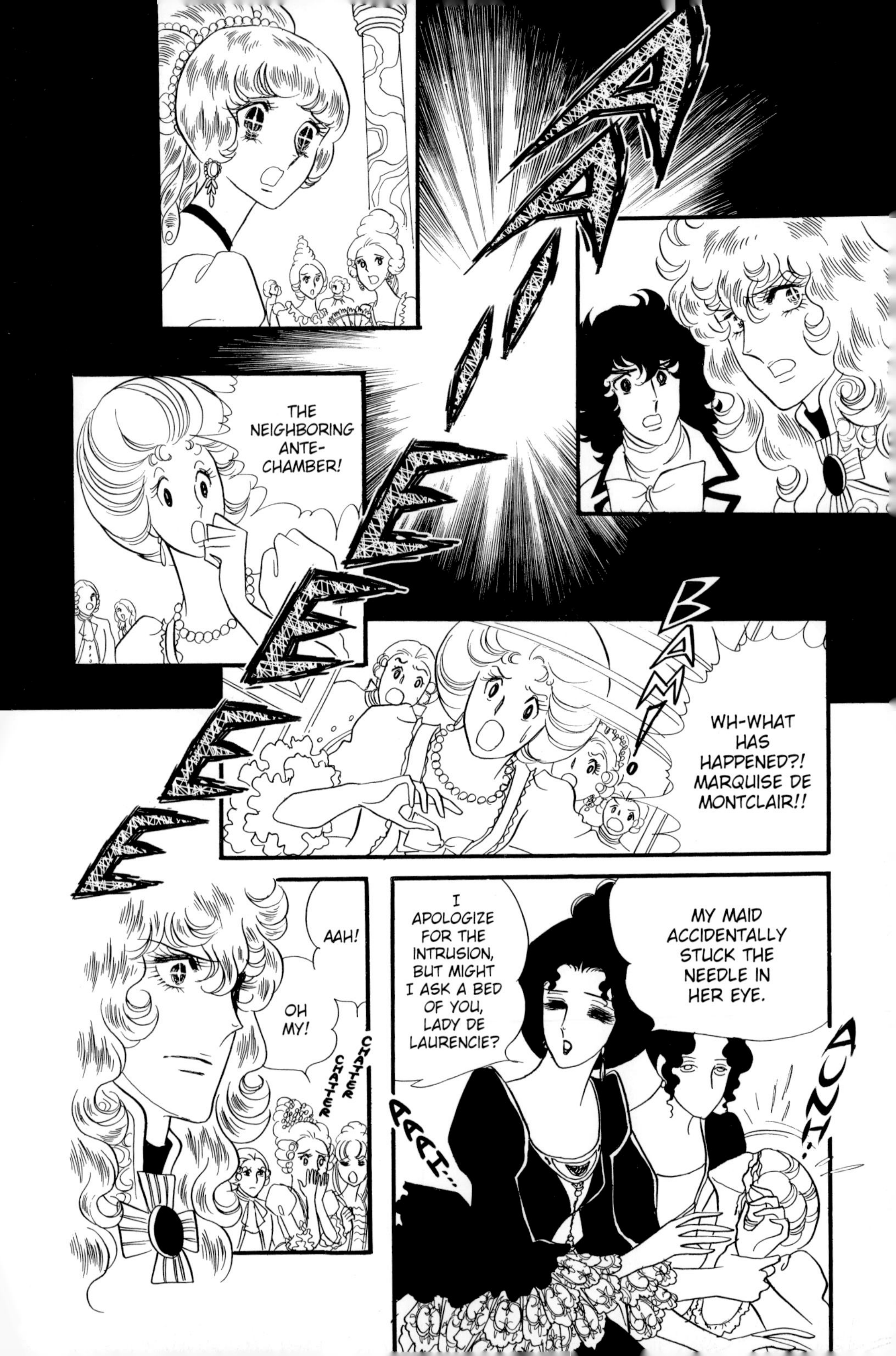
THE NEIGHBORING ANTE-CHAMBER!
BAM!
WH-WHAT HAS HAPPENED?! MARQUISE DE MONTCLAIR!!
MY MAID ACCIDENTALLY STUCK THE NEEDLE IN HER EYE.
I APOLOGIZE FOR THE INTRUSION, BUT MIGHT I ASK A BED OF YOU, LADY DE LAURENCIE?
AUHH!
AAAH...
AAH!
OH MY!
CHATTER CHATTER

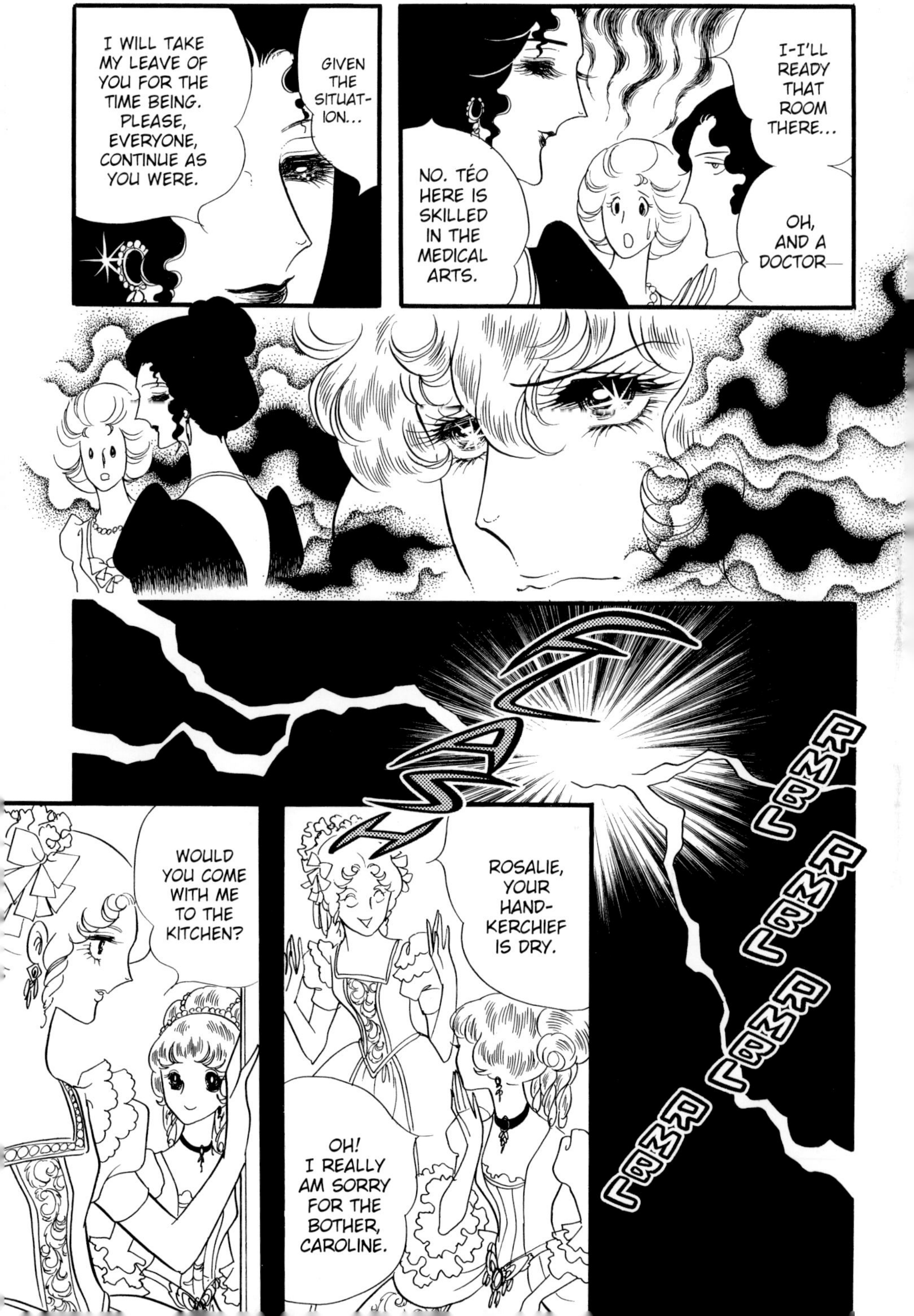
I-I'LL READY THAT ROOM THERE...
OH, AND A DOCTOR—
NO. TÉO HERE IS SKILLED IN THE MEDICAL ARTS.
GIVEN THE SITUATION...
I WILL TAKE MY LEAVE OF YOU FOR THE TIME BEING. PLEASE, EVERYONE, CONTINUE AS YOU WERE.
FLASH
RMBL RMBL RMBL RMBL
ROSALIE, YOUR HANDKERCHIEF IS DRY.
OH! I REALLY AM SORRY FOR THE BOTHER, CAROLINE.
WOULD YOU COME WITH ME TO THE KITCHEN?

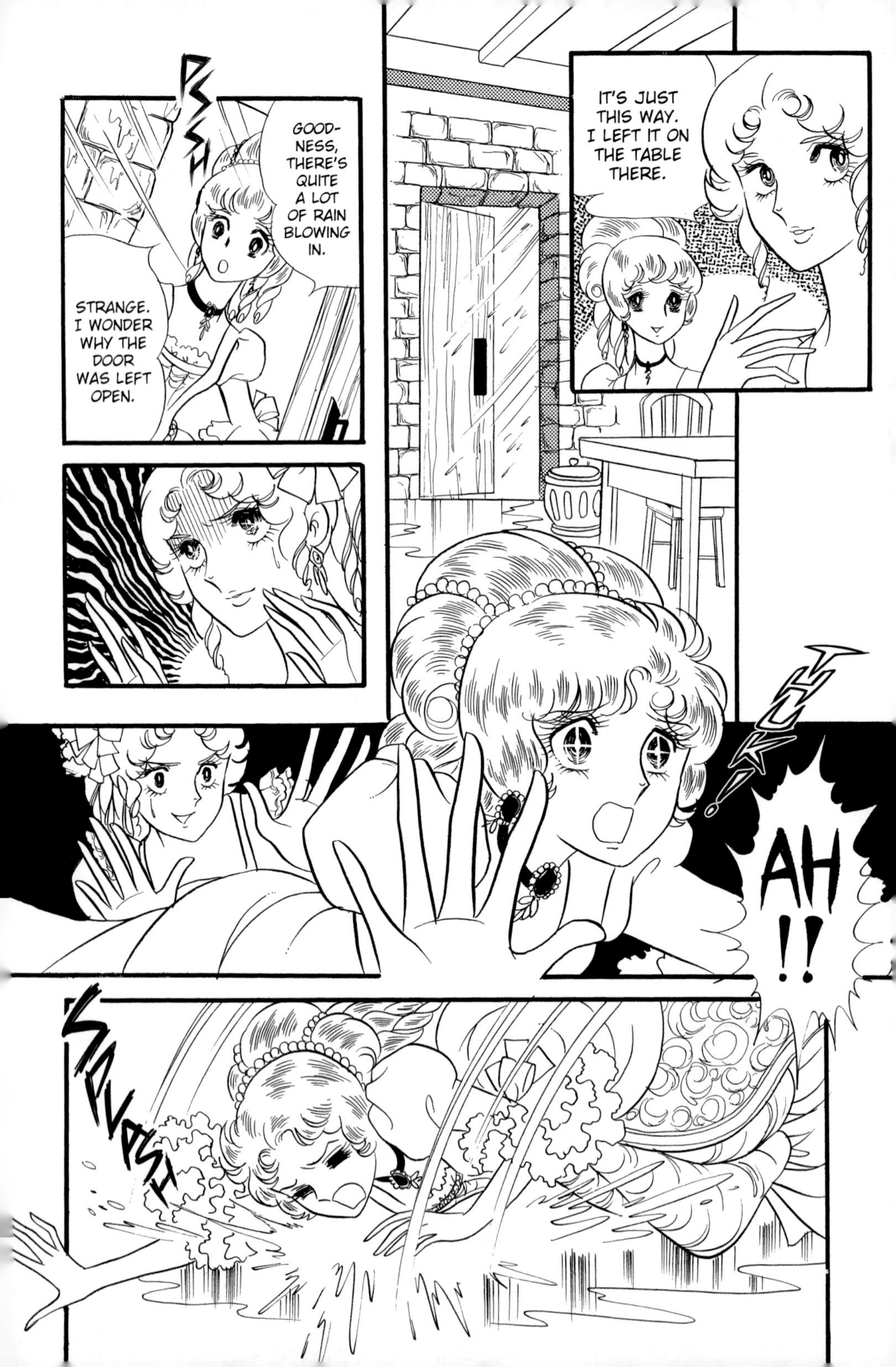
IT'S JUST THIS WAY. I LEFT IT ON THE TABLE THERE.
PSSH
GOODNESS, THERE'S QUITE A LOT OF RAIN BLOWING IN.
STRANGE. I WONDER WHY THE DOOR WAS LEFT OPEN.
HUK!
AH!!
SPLASH

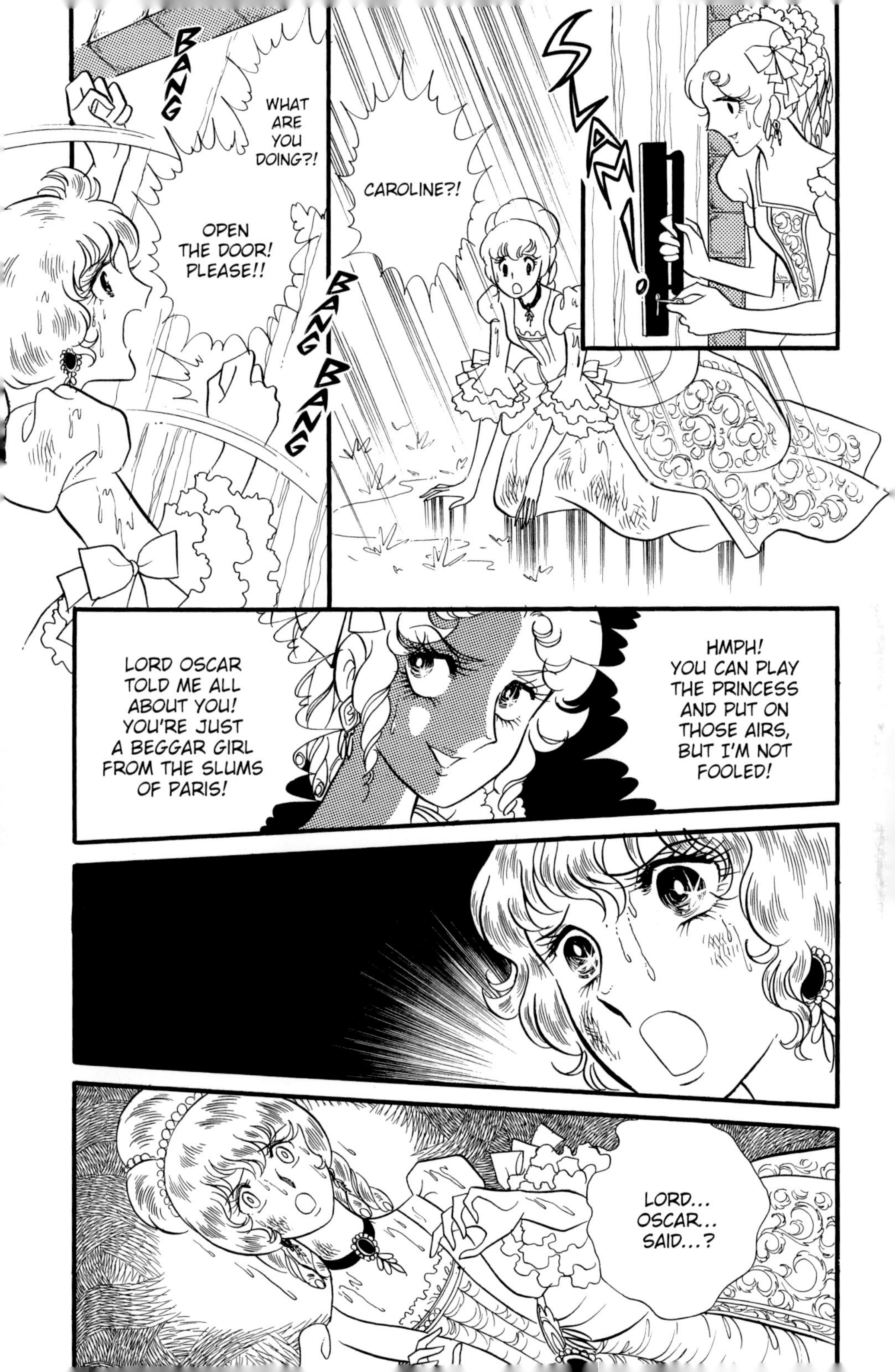

SLAM!!
CAROLINE?!
BANG
WHAT ARE YOU DOING?!
OPEN THE DOOR! PLEASE!!
BANG BANG
HMPH! YOU CAN PLAY THE PRINCESS AND PUT ON THOSE AIRS, BUT I'M NOT FOOLED!
LORD OSCAR TOLD ME ALL ABOUT YOU! YOU'RE JUST A BEGGAR GIRL FROM THE SLUMS OF PARIS!
LORD... OSCAR... SAID...?

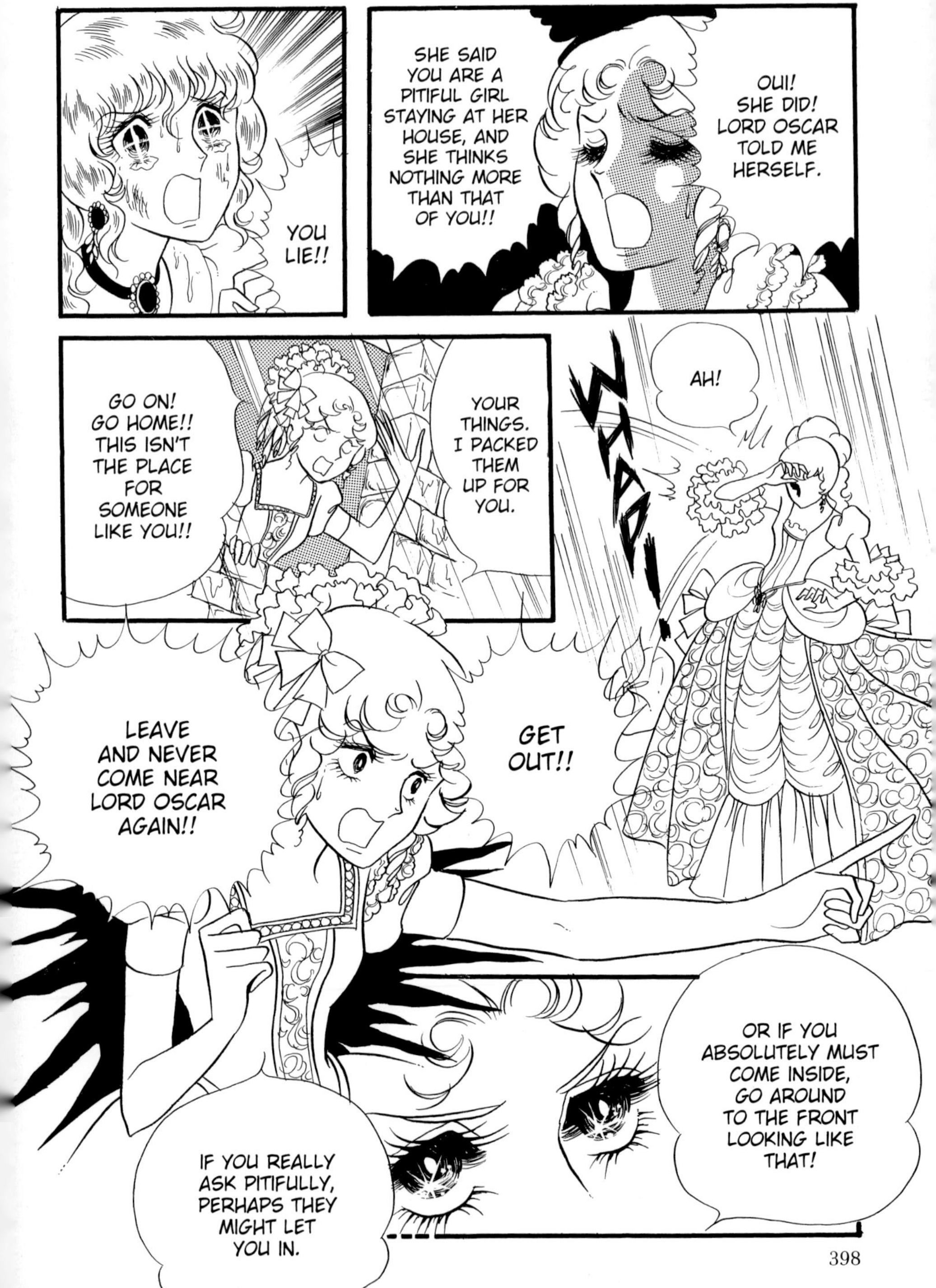
OUI! SHE DID! LORD OSCAR TOLD ME HERSELF.
SHE SAID YOU ARE A PITIFUL GIRL STAYING AT HER HOUSE, AND SHE THINKS NOTHING MORE THAN THAT OF YOU!!
YOU LIE!!
AH!
YOUR THINGS. I PACKED THEM UP FOR YOU.
GO ON! GO HOME!! THIS ISN'T THE PLACE FOR SOMEONE LIKE YOU!!
GET OUT!!
LEAVE AND NEVER COME NEAR LORD OSCAR AGAIN!!
OR IF YOU ABSOLUTELY MUST COME INSIDE, GO AROUND TO THE FRONT LOOKING LIKE THAT!
IF YOU REALLY ASK PITIFULLY, PERHAPS THEY MIGHT LET YOU IN.

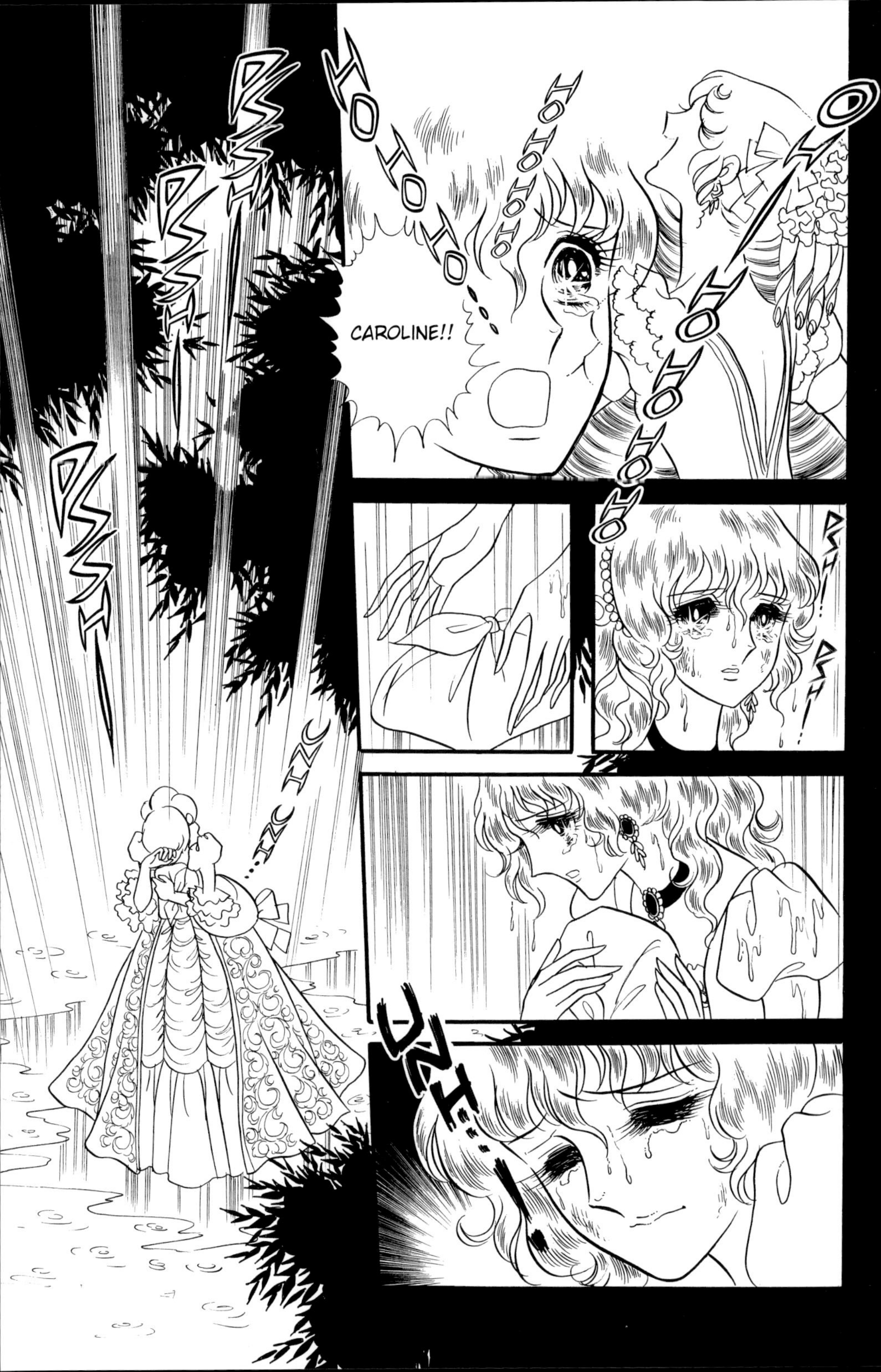

HOHOHOHO...
HOHOHOHO
CAROLINE!!
HOHOHOHOHOHO
PSH! PSH!
UNH...!
PSSSH!
PSSSH!
PSSSH!
HIC HIC...

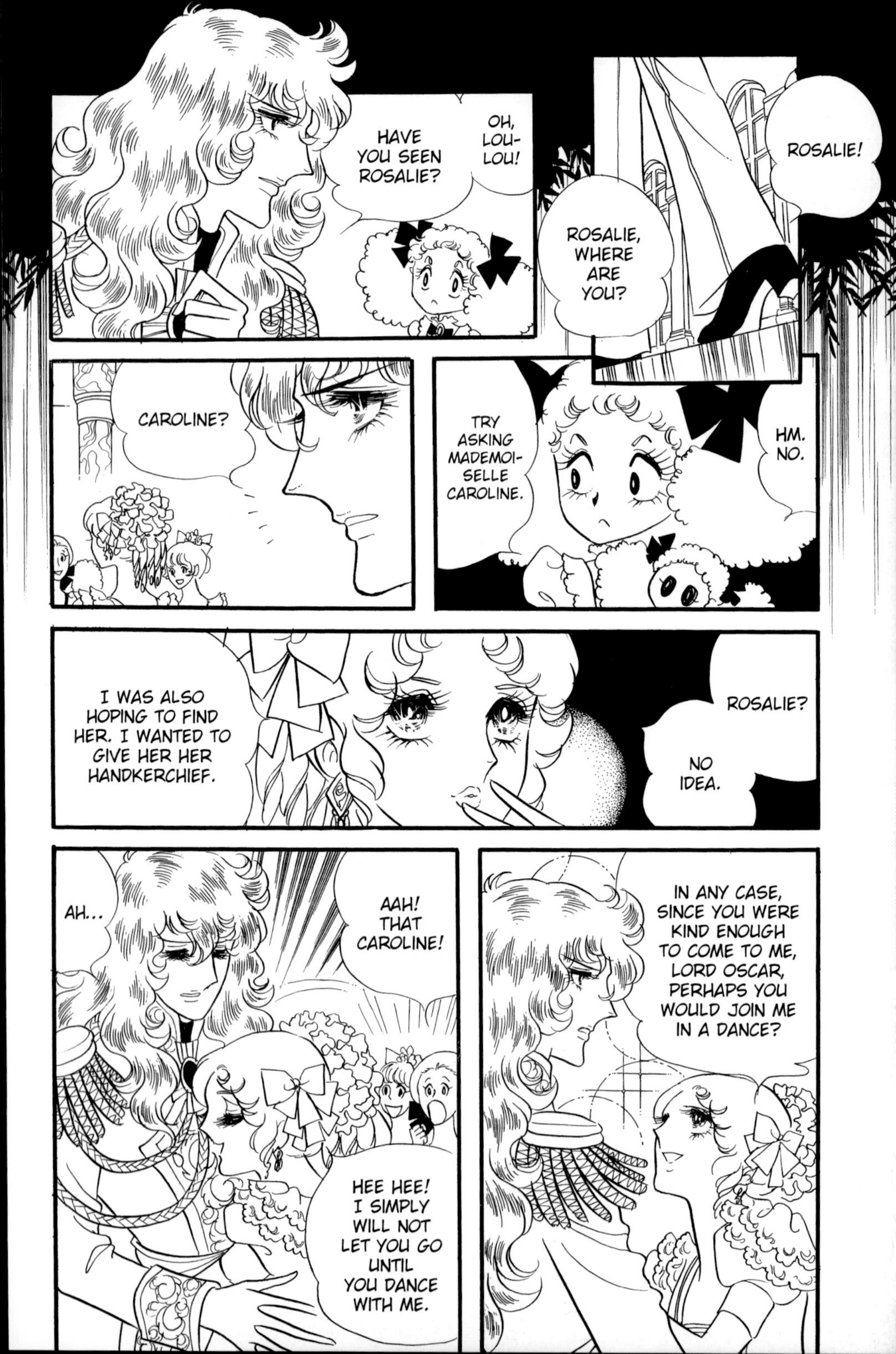
ROSALIE!
ROSALIE, WHERE ARE YOU?
OH, LOU-LOU!
HAVE YOU SEEN ROSALIE?
HM. NO.
TRY ASKING MADEMOISELLE CAROLINE.
CAROLINE?
ROSALIE?
NO IDEA.
I WAS ALSO HOPING TO FIND HER. I WANTED TO GIVE HER HER HANDKERCHIEF.
IN ANY CASE, SINCE YOU WERE KIND ENOUGH TO COME TO ME, LORD OSCAR, PERHAPS YOU WOULD JOIN ME IN A DANCE?
AAH! THAT CAROLINE!
AH...
HEE HEE! I SIMPLY WILL NOT LET YOU GO UNTIL YOU DANCE WITH ME.

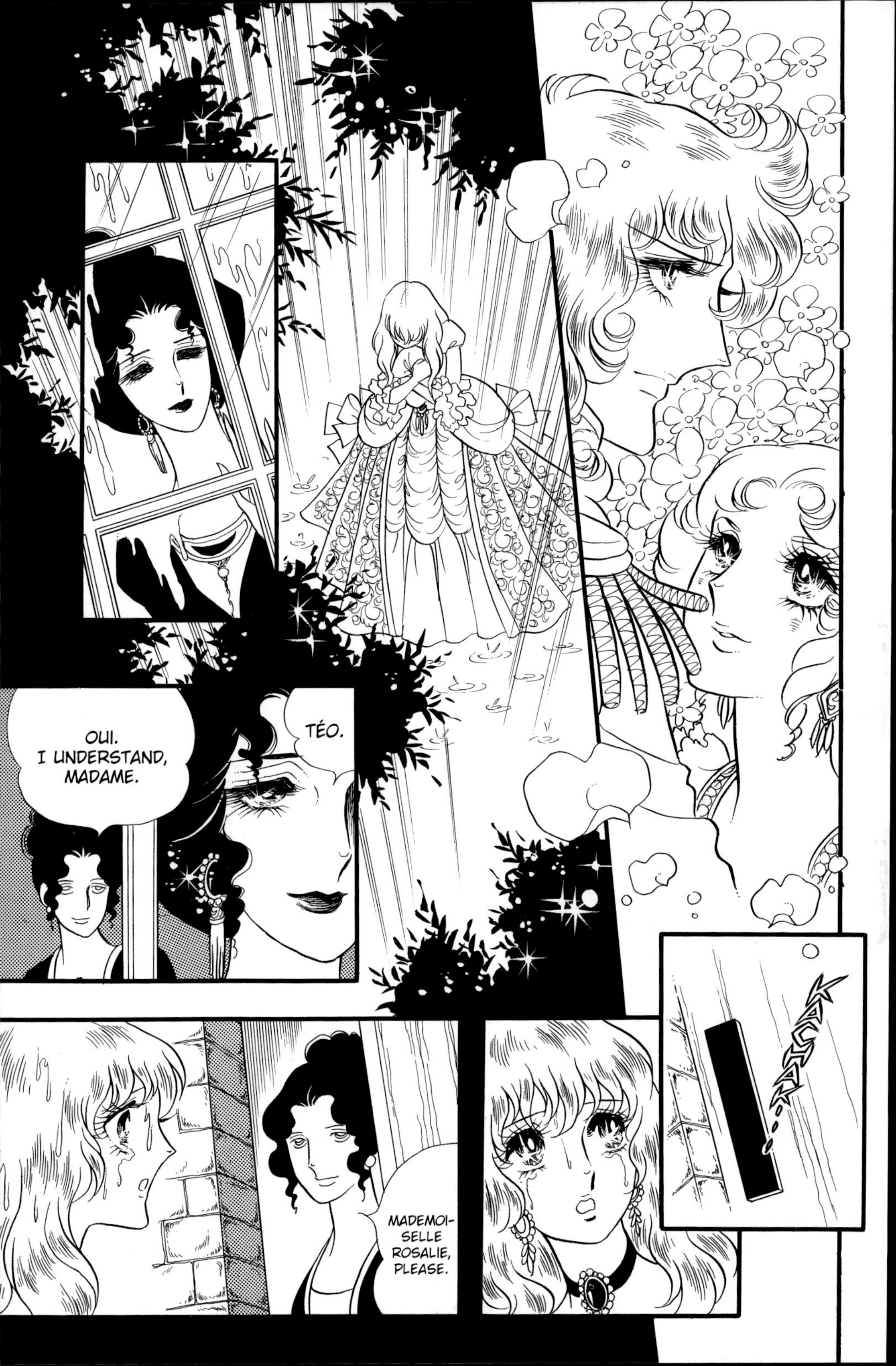
TÉO.
OUI. I UNDERSTAND, MADAME.
KACHAK...
MADEMOISELLE ROSALIE, PLEASE.

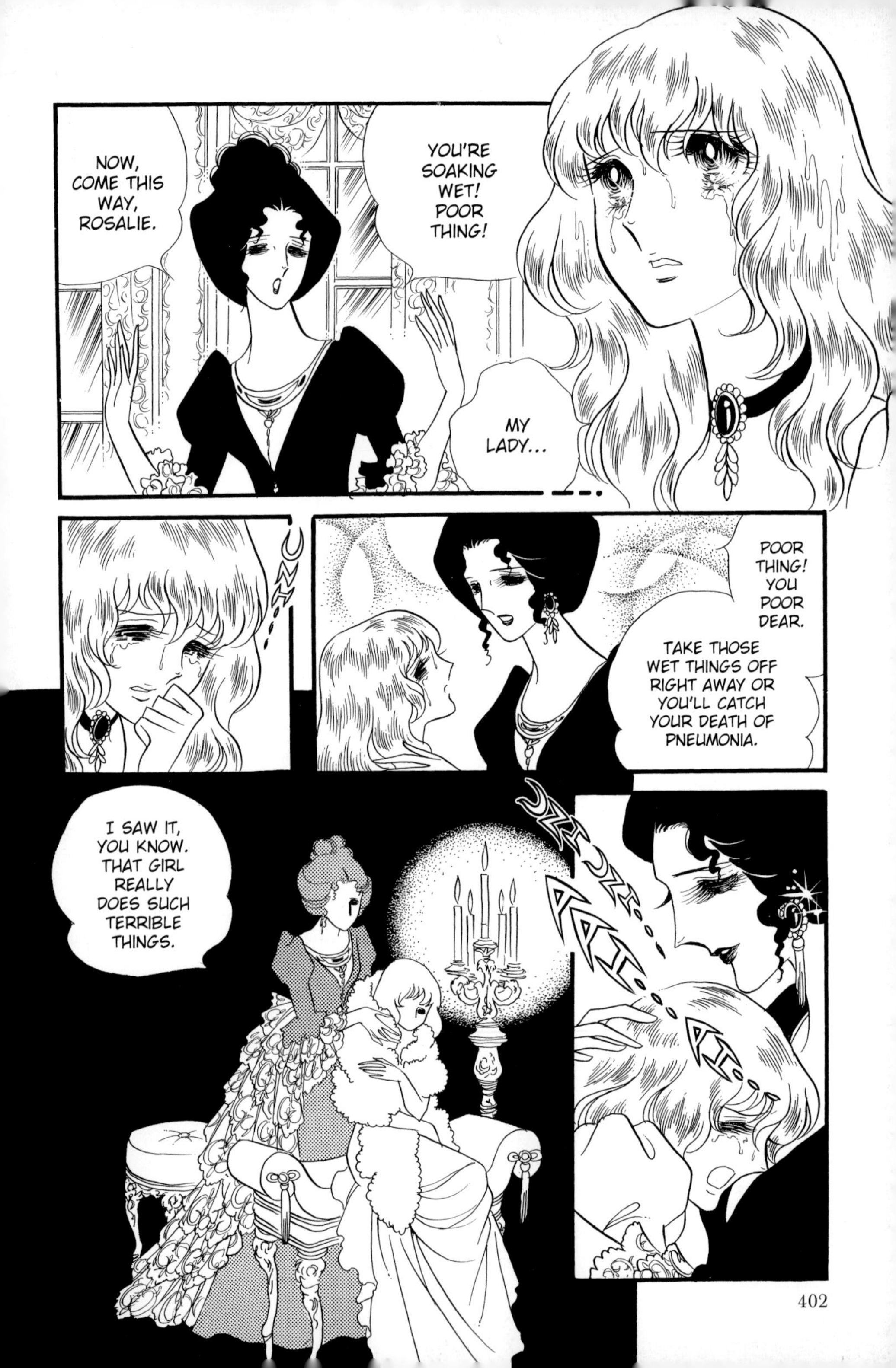
MY LADY...
YOU'RE SOAKING WET! POOR THING!
NOW, COME THIS WAY, ROSALIE.
POOR THING! YOU POOR DEAR.
TAKE THOSE WET THINGS OFF RIGHT AWAY OR YOU'LL CATCH YOUR DEATH OF PNEUMONIA.
I SAW IT, YOU KNOW. THAT GIRL REALLY DOES SUCH TERRIBLE THINGS.

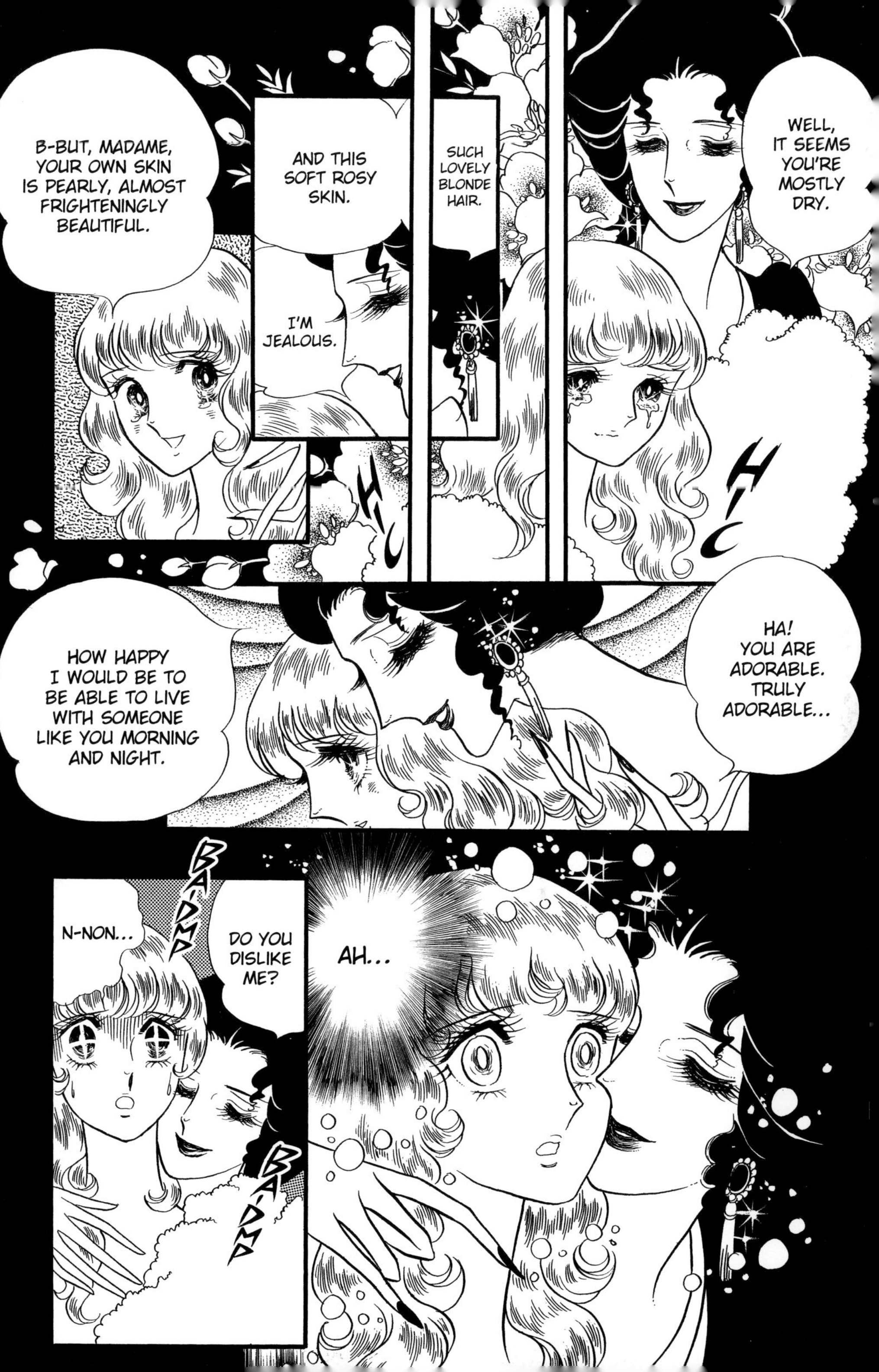
WELL, IT SEEMS YOU'RE MOSTLY DRY.
HIC
SUCH LOVELY BLONDE HAIR.
AND THIS SOFT ROSY SKIN.
I'M JEALOUS.
HIC
B-BUT, MADAME, YOUR OWN SKIN IS PEARLY, ALMOST FRIGHTENINGLY BEAUTIFUL.
HA! YOU ARE ADORABLE. TRULY ADORABLE...
HOW HAPPY I WOULD BE TO BE ABLE TO LIVE WITH SOMEONE LIKE YOU MORNING AND NIGHT.
AH...
DO YOU DISLIKE ME?
N-NON...
BA-DMP
BA-DMP

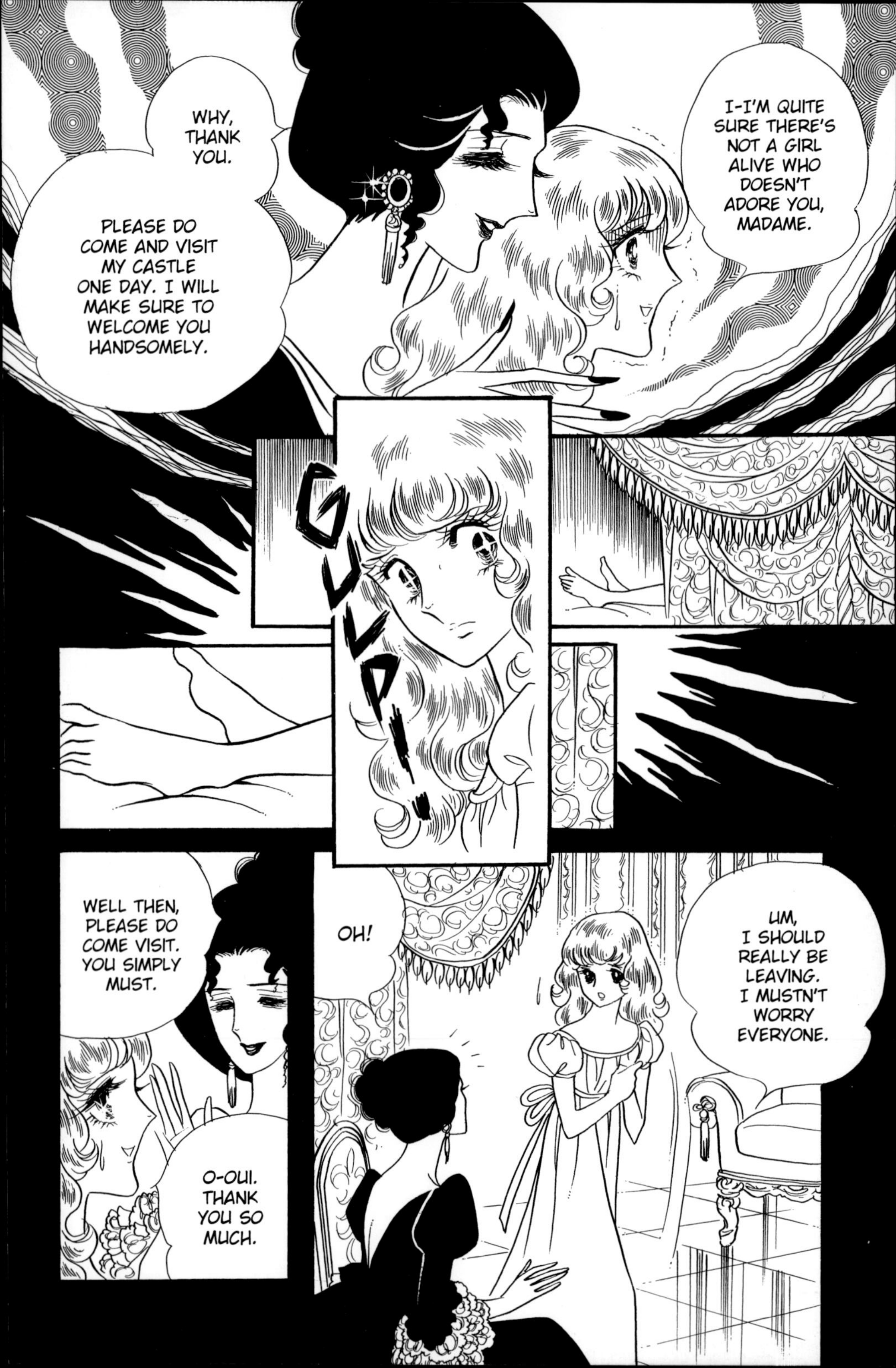
I-I'M QUITE SURE THERE'S NOT A GIRL ALIVE WHO DOESN'T ADORE YOU, MADAME.
WHY, THANK YOU.
PLEASE DO COME AND VISIT MY CASTLE ONE DAY. I WILL MAKE SURE TO WELCOME YOU HANDSOMELY.
GULP!!
UM, I SHOULD REALLY BE LEAVING. I MUSTN'T WORRY EVERYONE.
OH!
WELL THEN, PLEASE DO COME VISIT. YOU SIMPLY MUST.
O-OUI. THANK YOU SO MUCH.

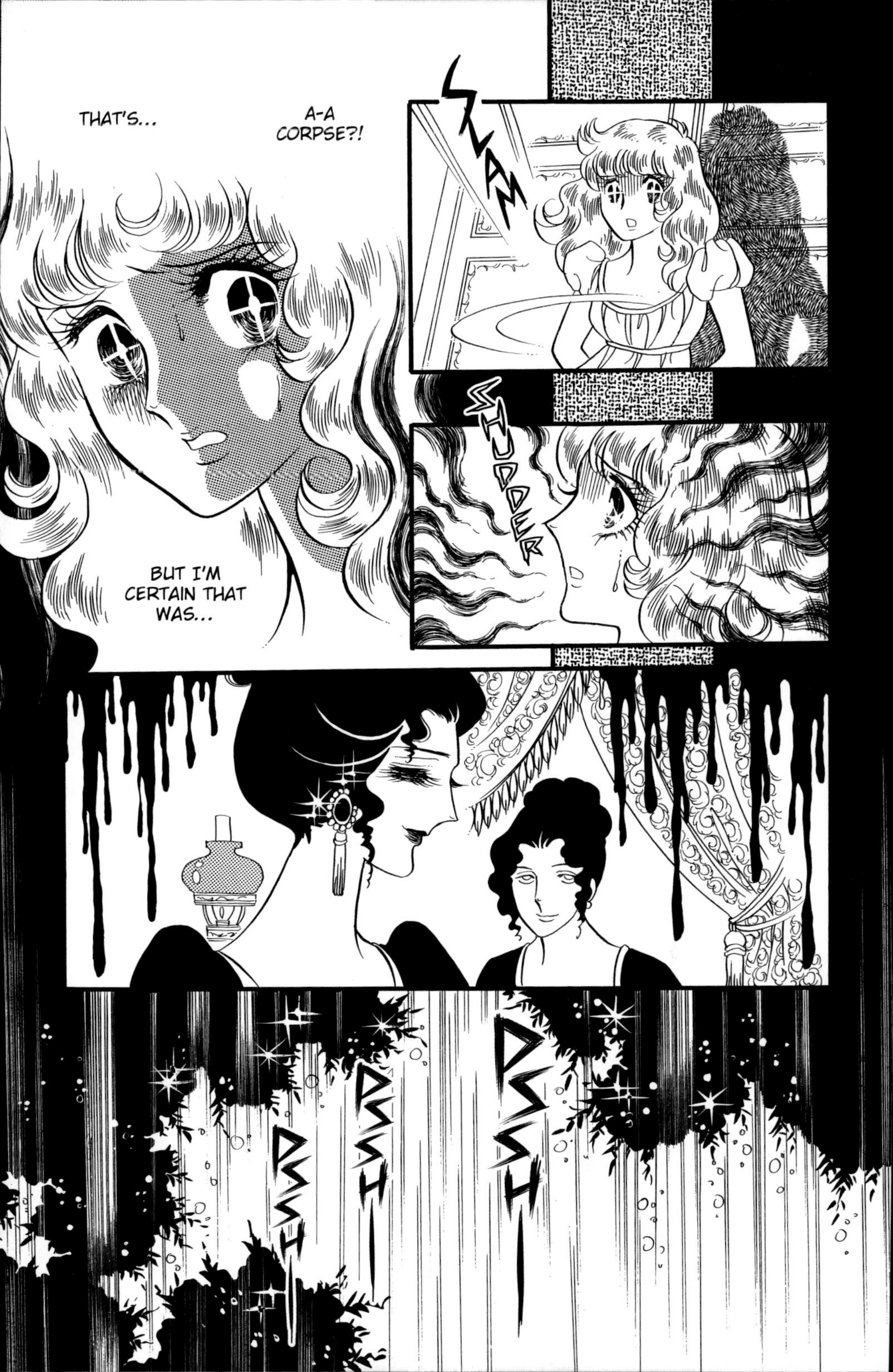

SLAM
SHUDDER
THAT'S...
A-A CORPSE?!
BUT I'M CERTAIN THAT WAS...
PSSH—
PSSH
PSSH

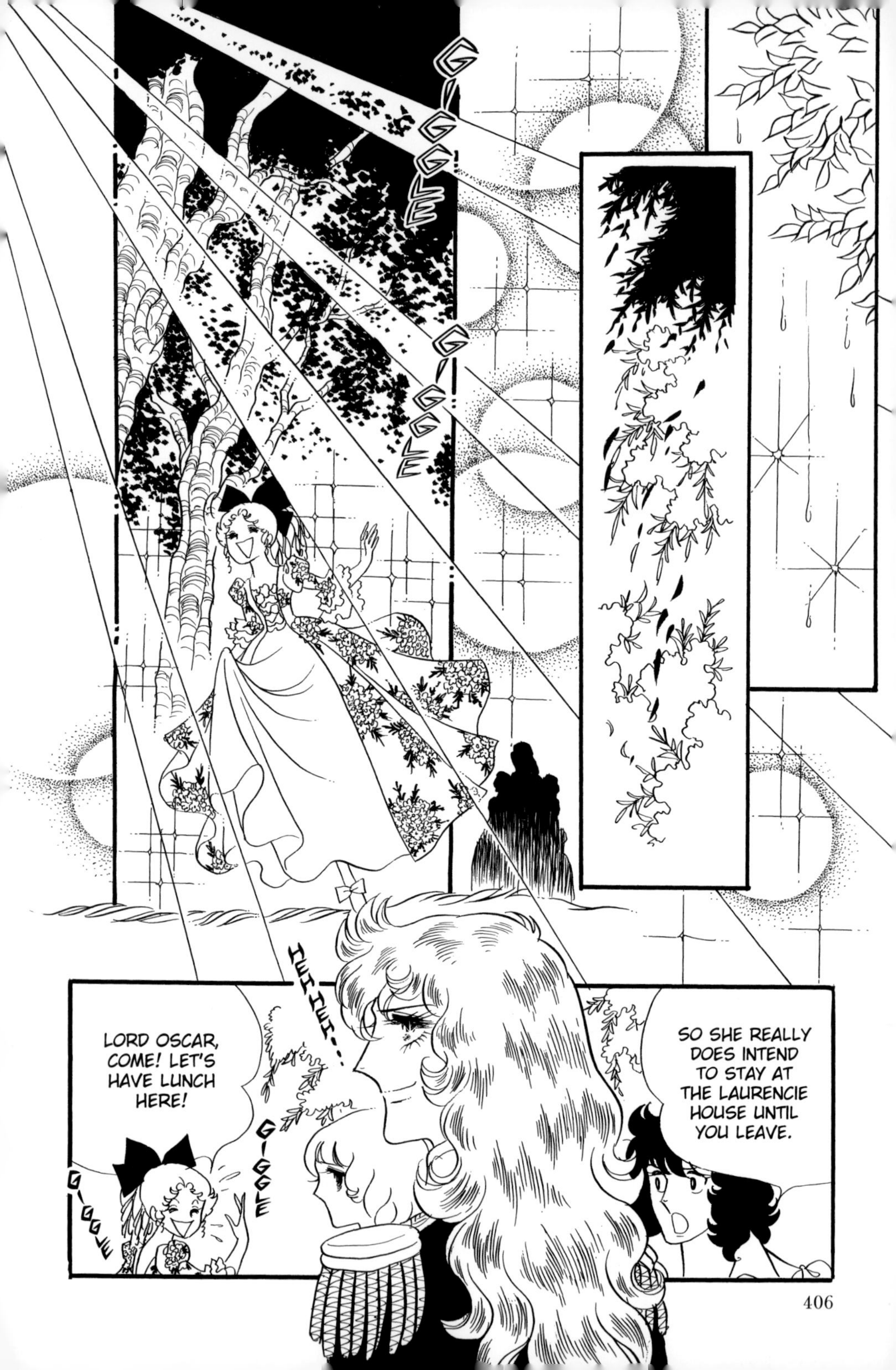
GIGGLE
GIGGLE
SO SHE REALLY DOES INTEND TO STAY AT THE LAURENCIE HOUSE UNTIL YOU LEAVE.
HEH HEH...
LORD OSCAR, COME! LET'S HAVE LUNCH HERE!
GIGGLE
GIGGLE

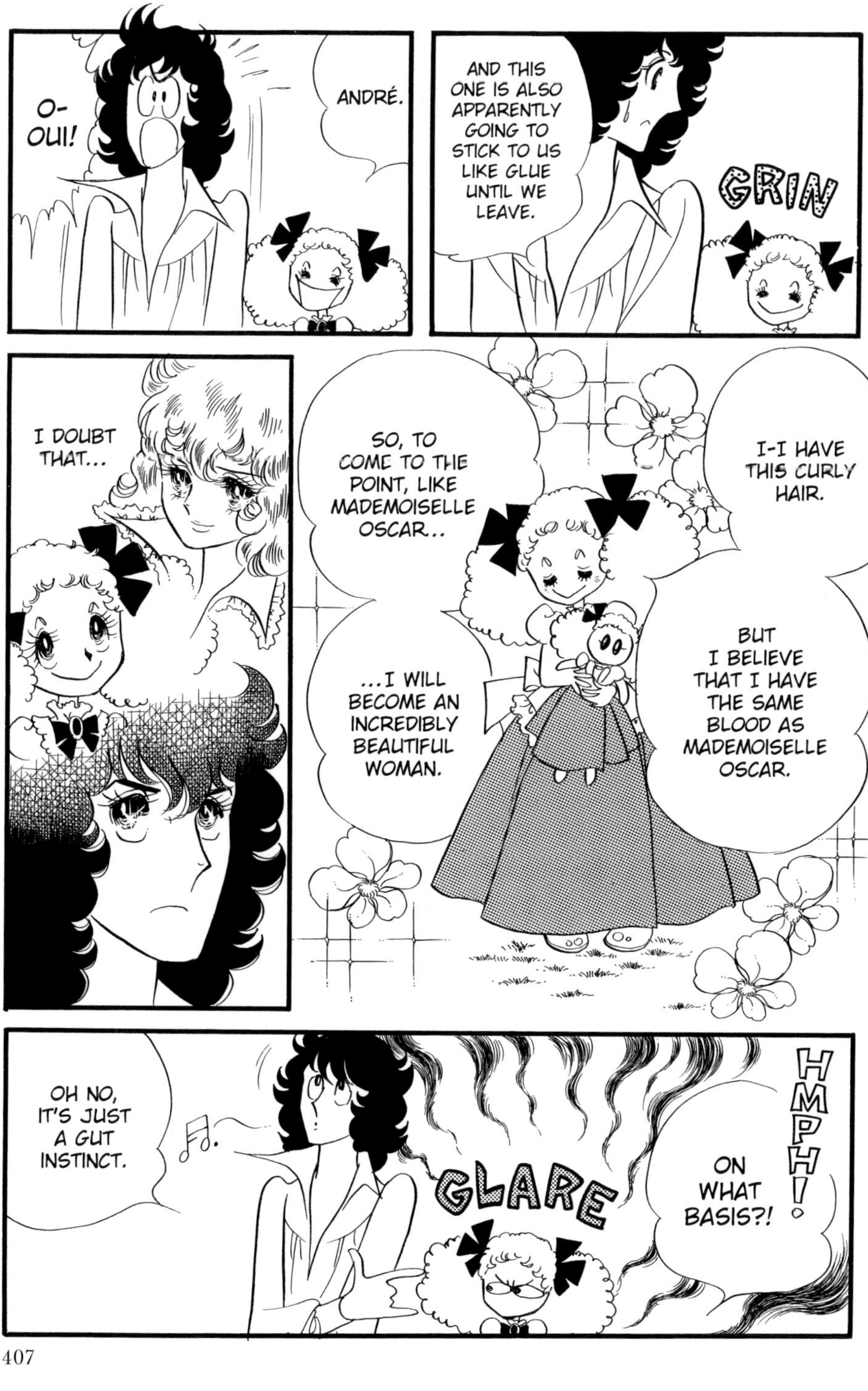

AND THIS ONE IS ALSO APPARENTLY GOING TO STICK TO US LIKE GLUE UNTIL WE LEAVE.
GRIN
ANDRÉ.
O-OUI!
I-I HAVE THIS CURLY HAIR.
BUT I BELIEVE THAT I HAVE THE SAME BLOOD AS MADEMOISELLE OSCAR.
SO, TO COME TO THE POINT, LIKE MADEMOISELLE OSCAR...
...I WILL BECOME AN INCREDIBLY BEAUTIFUL WOMAN.
I DOUBT THAT...
HMPH!
ON WHAT BASIS?!
GLARE
OH NO, IT'S JUST A GUT INSTINCT.

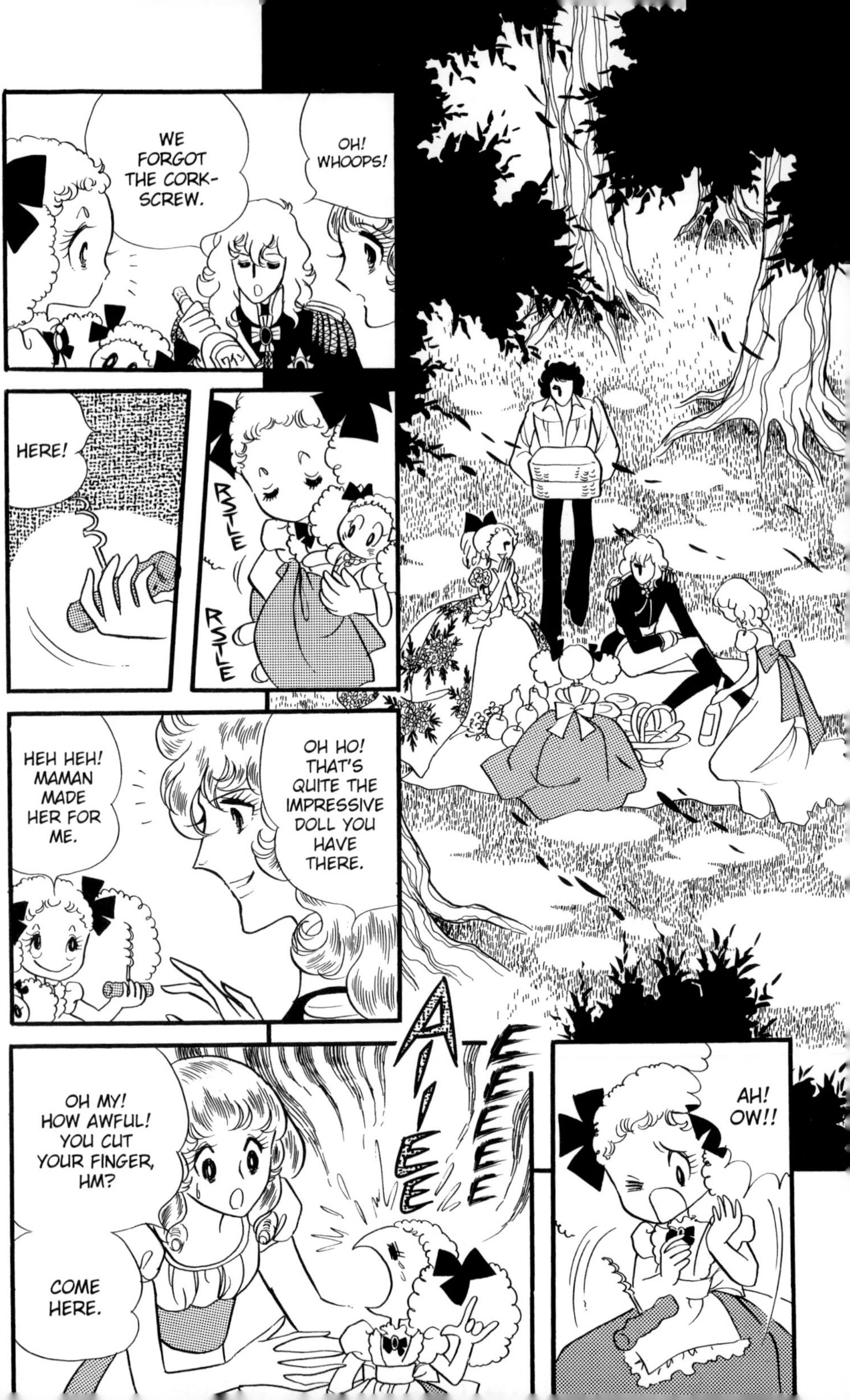
OH! WHOOPS!
WE FORGOT THE CORK-SCREW.
RSTLE
RSTLE
HERE!
OH HO! THAT'S QUITE THE IMPRESSIVE DOLL YOU HAVE THERE.
HEH HEH! MAMAN MADE HER FOR ME.
AH! OW!!
AIEEEEE
OH MY! HOW AWFUL! YOU CUT YOUR FINGER, HM?
COME HERE.

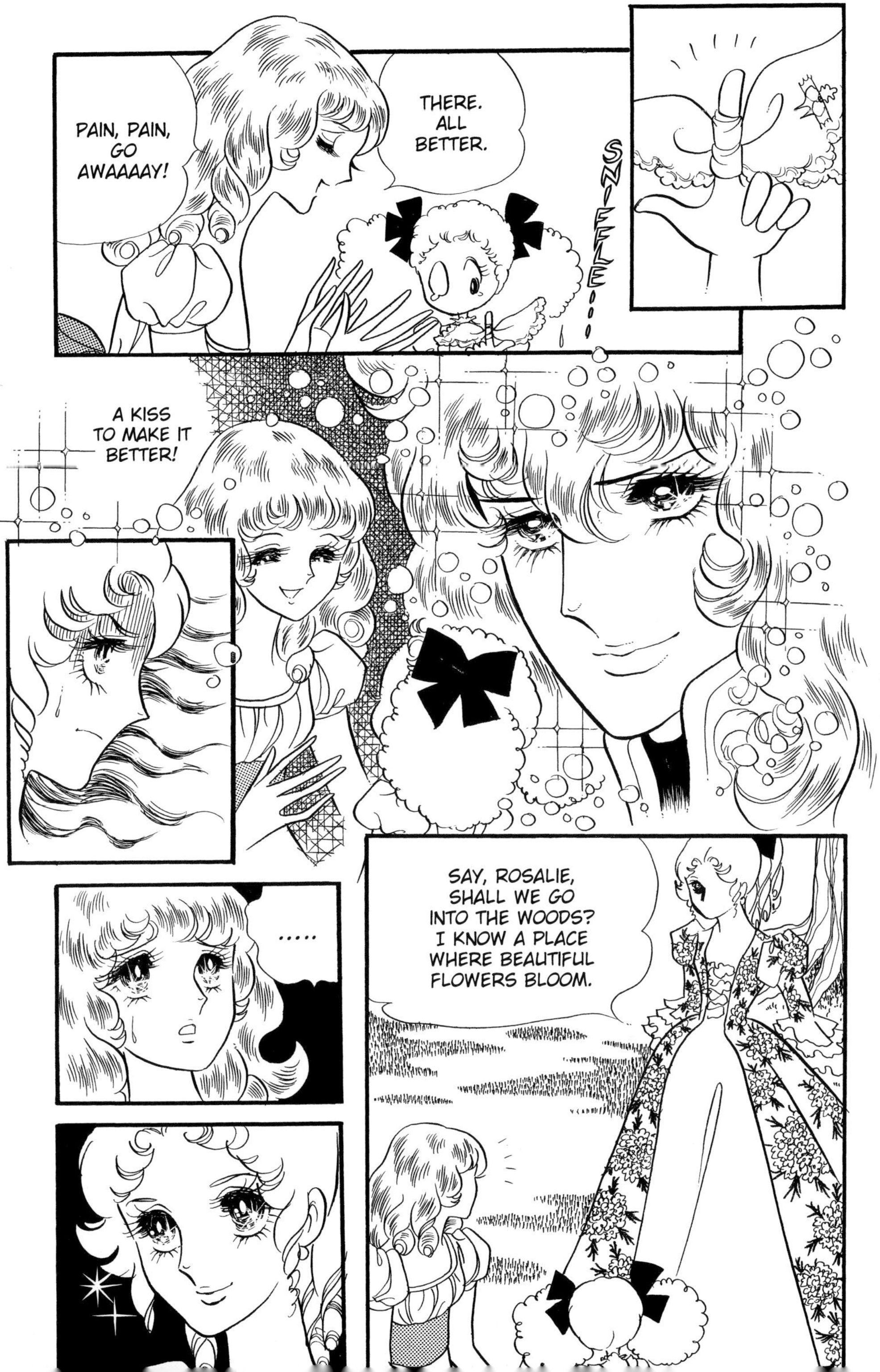
SNIFFLE...
THERE. ALL BETTER.
PAIN, PAIN, GO AWAAAAY!
A KISS TO MAKE IT BETTER!
SAY, ROSALIE, SHALL WE GO INTO THE WOODS? I KNOW A PLACE WHERE BEAUTIFUL FLOWERS BLOOM.
.....

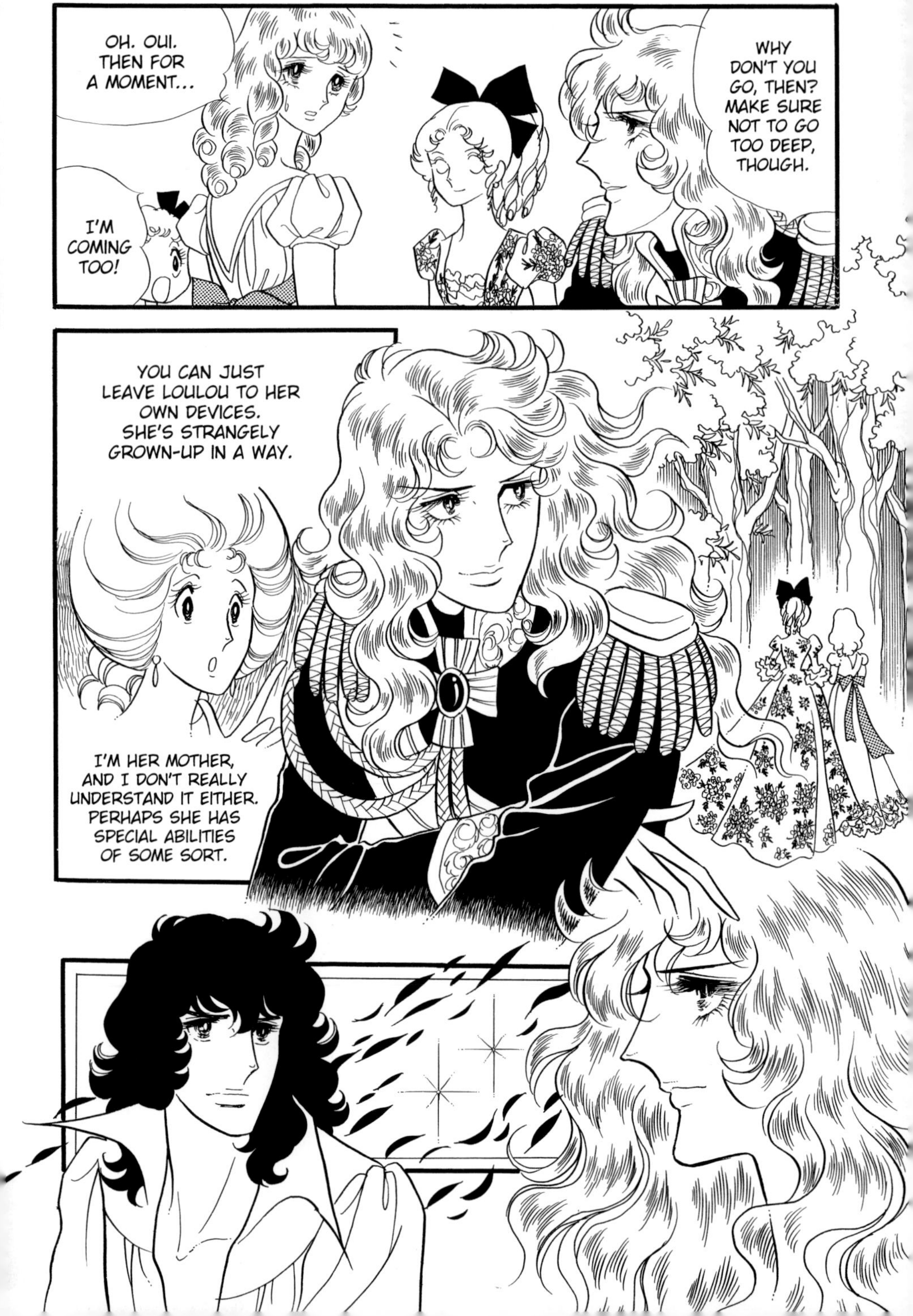
WHY DON'T YOU GO, THEN? MAKE SURE NOT TO GO TOO DEEP, THOUGH.
OH. OUI. THEN FOR A MOMENT...
I'M COMING TOO!
YOU CAN JUST LEAVE LOULOU TO HER OWN DEVICES. SHE'S STRANGELY GROWN-UP IN A WAY.
I'M HER MOTHER, AND I DON'T REALLY UNDERSTAND IT EITHER. PERHAPS SHE HAS SPECIAL ABILITIES OF SOME SORT.

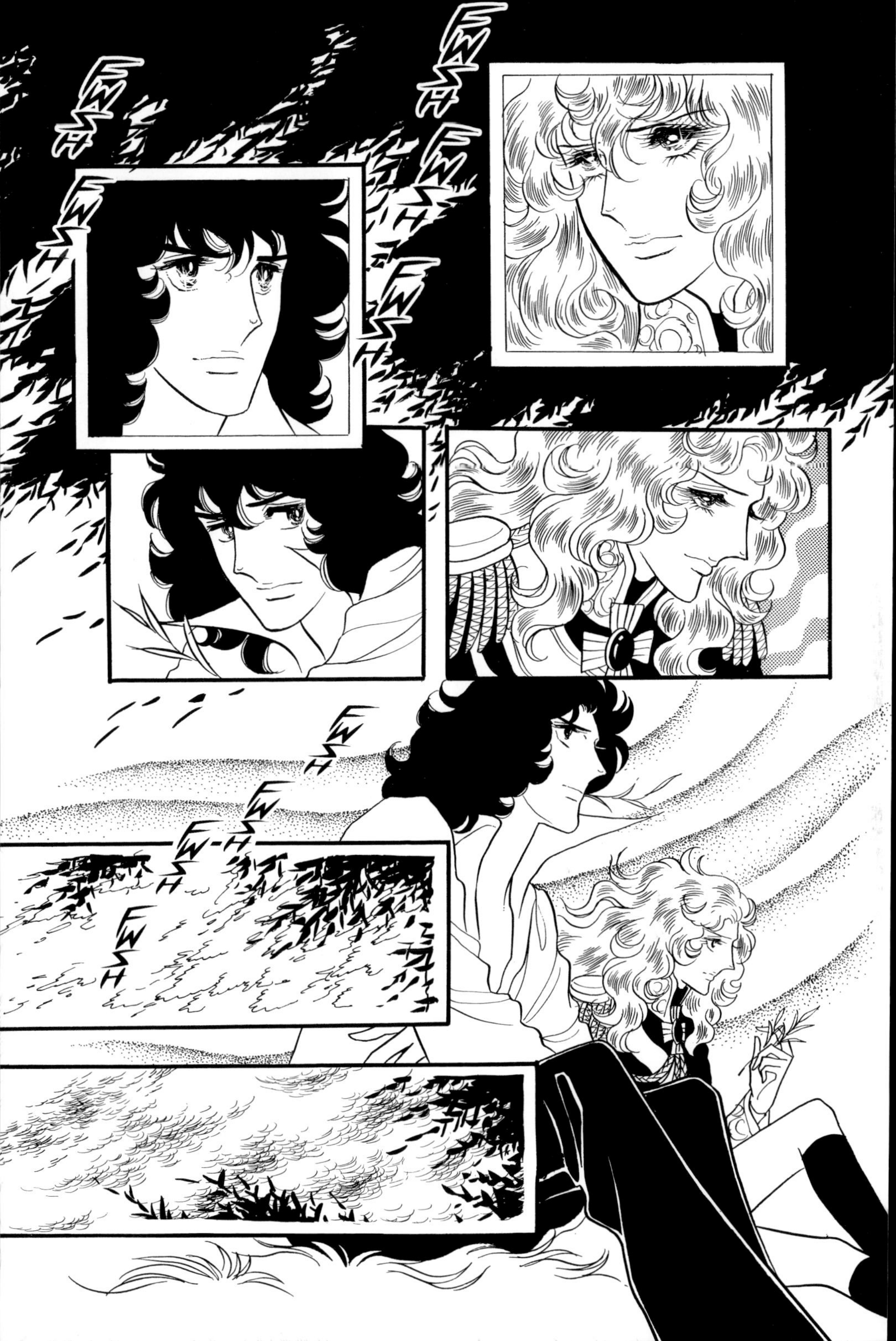
FWSH
FWSH
FWSH
FWSH
FWSH
FWSH
FWSH
FW-
FWSH
FWSH

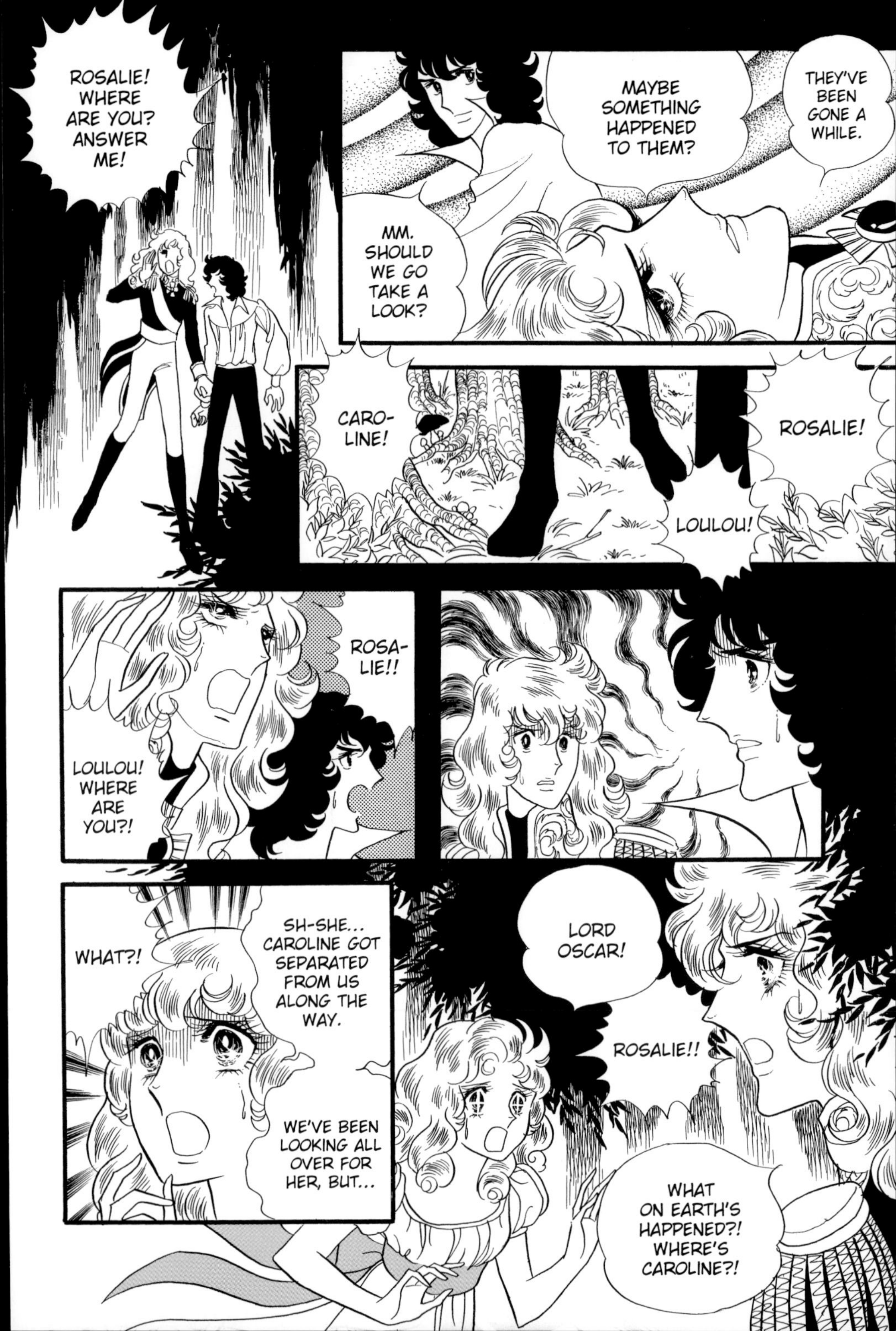
THEY'VE BEEN GONE A WHILE.
MAYBE SOMETHING HAPPENED TO THEM?
MM. SHOULD WE GO TAKE A LOOK?
ROSALIE!
LOULOU!
CARO-LINE!
ROSALIE! WHERE ARE YOU? ANSWER ME!
ROSA-LIE!!
LOULOU! WHERE ARE YOU?!
LORD OSCAR!
ROSALIE!!
WHAT ON EARTH'S HAPPENED?! WHERE'S CAROLINE?!
SH-SHE... CAROLINE GOT SEPARATED FROM US ALONG THE WAY.
WE'VE BEEN LOOKING ALL OVER FOR HER, BUT...
WHAT?!

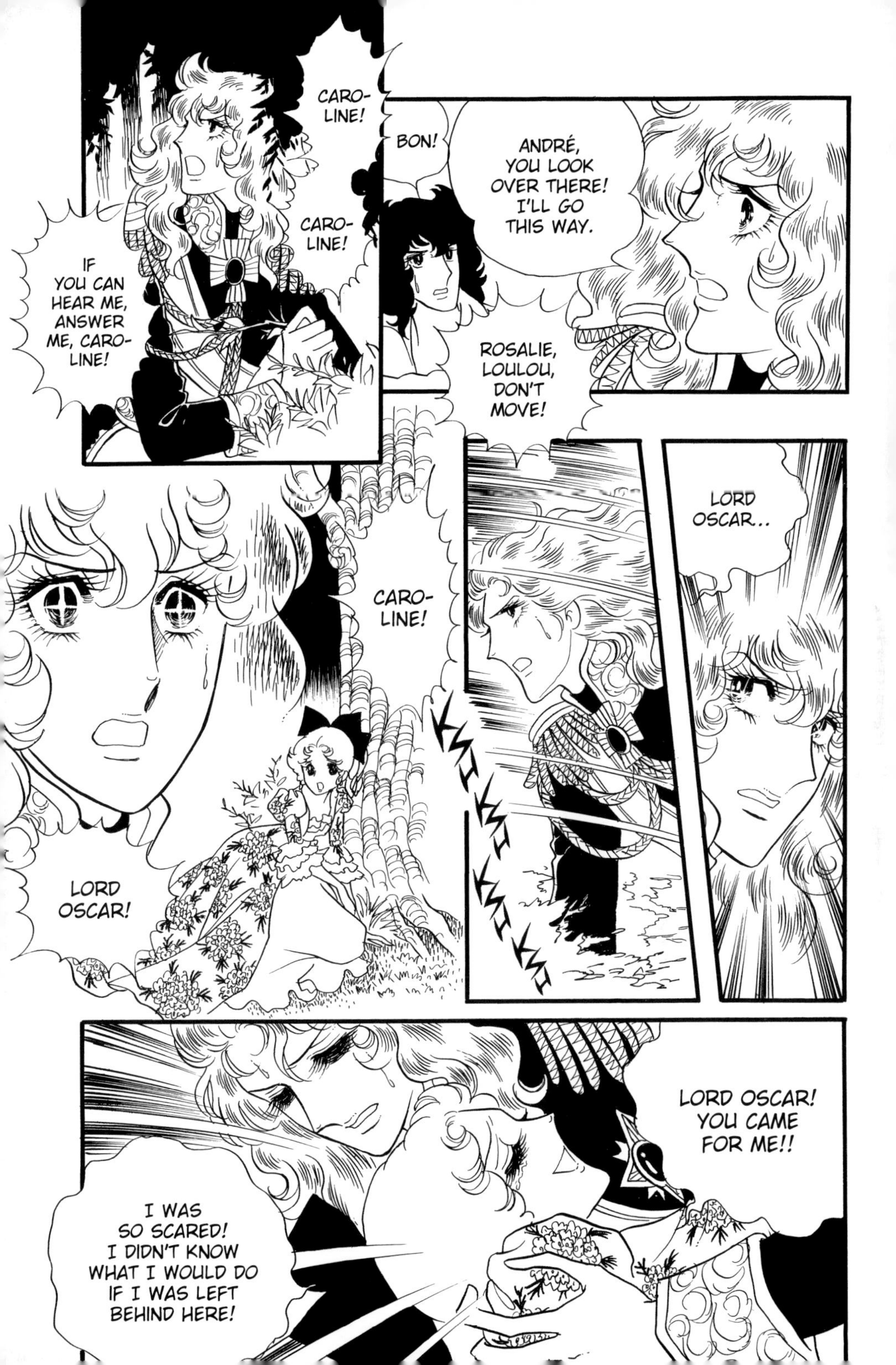

ANDRÉ, YOU LOOK OVER THERE! I'LL GO THIS WAY.
BON!
ROSALIE, LOULOU, DON'T MOVE!
CARO-LINE!
CARO-LINE!
IF YOU CAN HEAR ME, ANSWER ME, CARO-LINE!
LORD OSCAR...
KWI KWI KWI KWI
CARO-LINE!
LORD OSCAR!
LORD OSCAR! YOU CAME FOR ME!!
I WAS SO SCARED! I DIDN'T KNOW WHAT I WOULD DO IF I WAS LEFT BEHIND HERE!

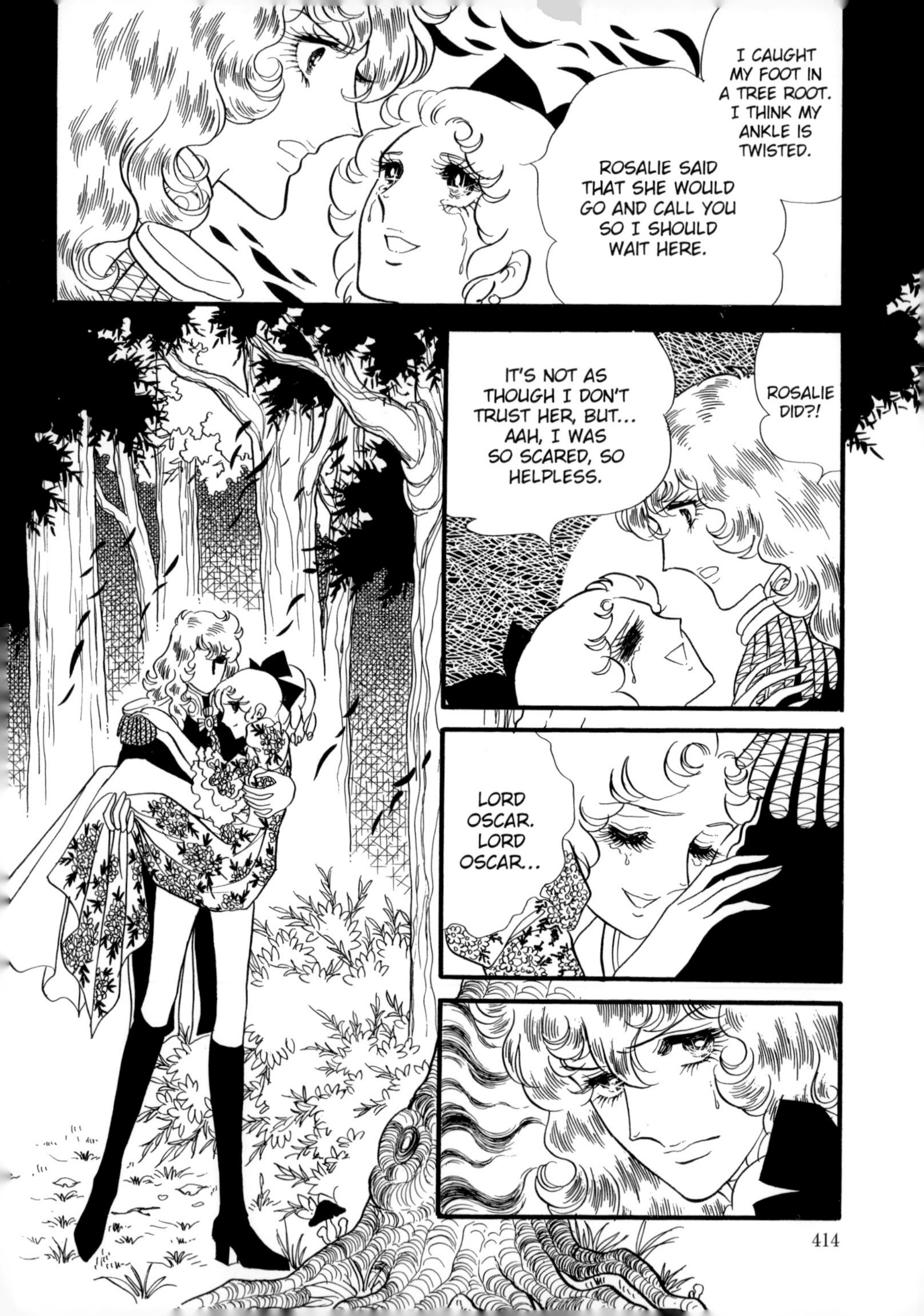
I CAUGHT MY FOOT IN A TREE ROOT. I THINK MY ANKLE IS TWISTED.
ROSALIE SAID THAT SHE WOULD GO AND CALL YOU SO I SHOULD WAIT HERE.
ROSALIE DID?!
IT'S NOT AS THOUGH I DON'T TRUST HER, BUT... AAH, I WAS SO SCARED, SO HELPLESS.
LORD OSCAR. LORD OSCAR...

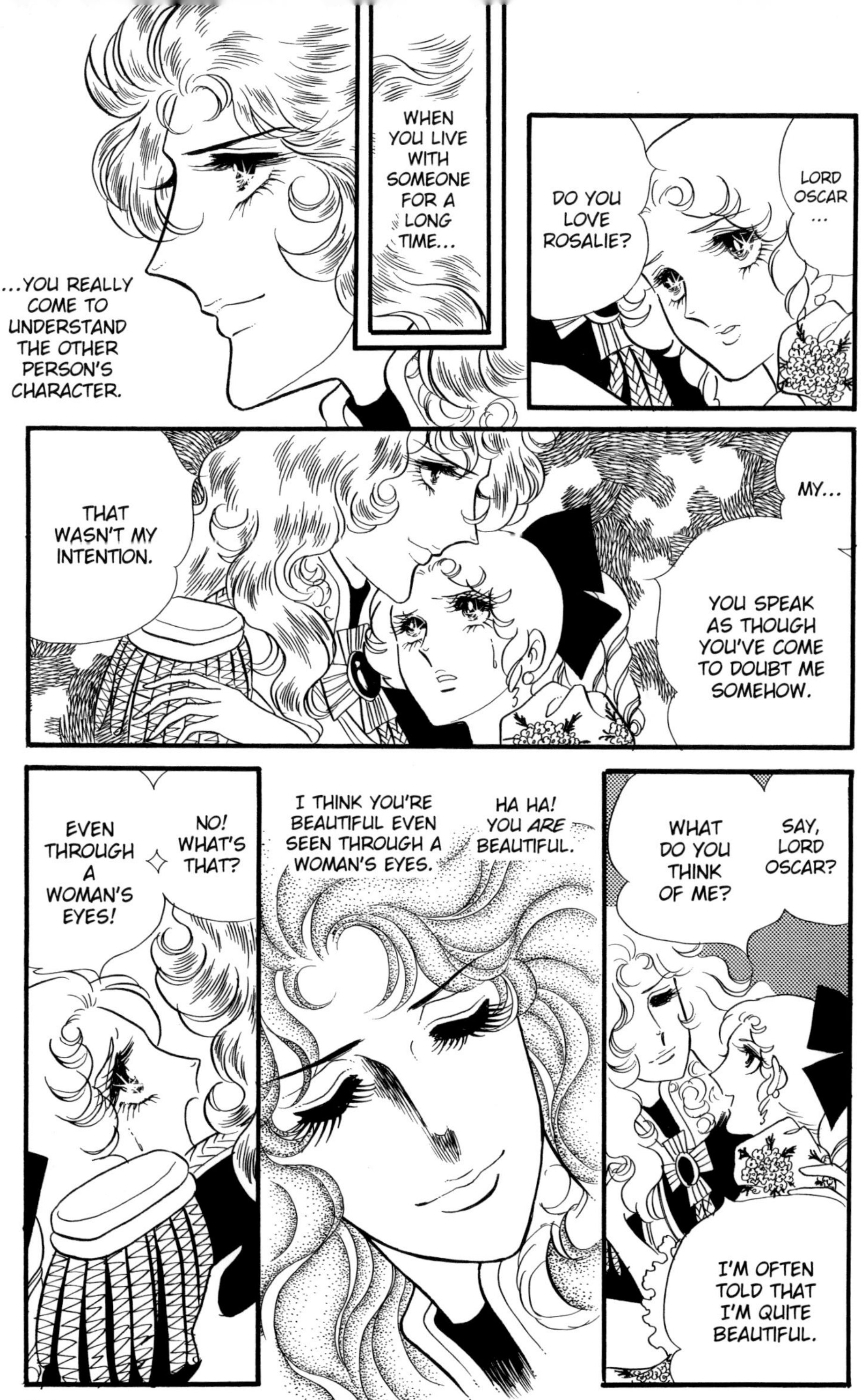

LORD OSCAR...
DO YOU LOVE ROSALIE?
WHEN YOU LIVE WITH SOMEONE FOR A LONG TIME...
...YOU REALLY COME TO UNDERSTAND THE OTHER PERSON'S CHARACTER.
MY...
YOU SPEAK AS THOUGH YOU'VE COME TO DOUBT ME SOMEHOW.
THAT WASN'T MY INTENTION.
SAY, LORD OSCAR?
WHAT DO YOU THINK OF ME?
I'M OFTEN TOLD THAT I'M QUITE BEAUTIFUL.
HA HA! YOU *ARE* BEAUTIFUL.
I THINK YOU'RE BEAUTIFUL EVEN SEEN THROUGH A WOMAN'S EYES.
NO! WHAT'S THAT?
EVEN THROUGH A WOMAN'S EYES!

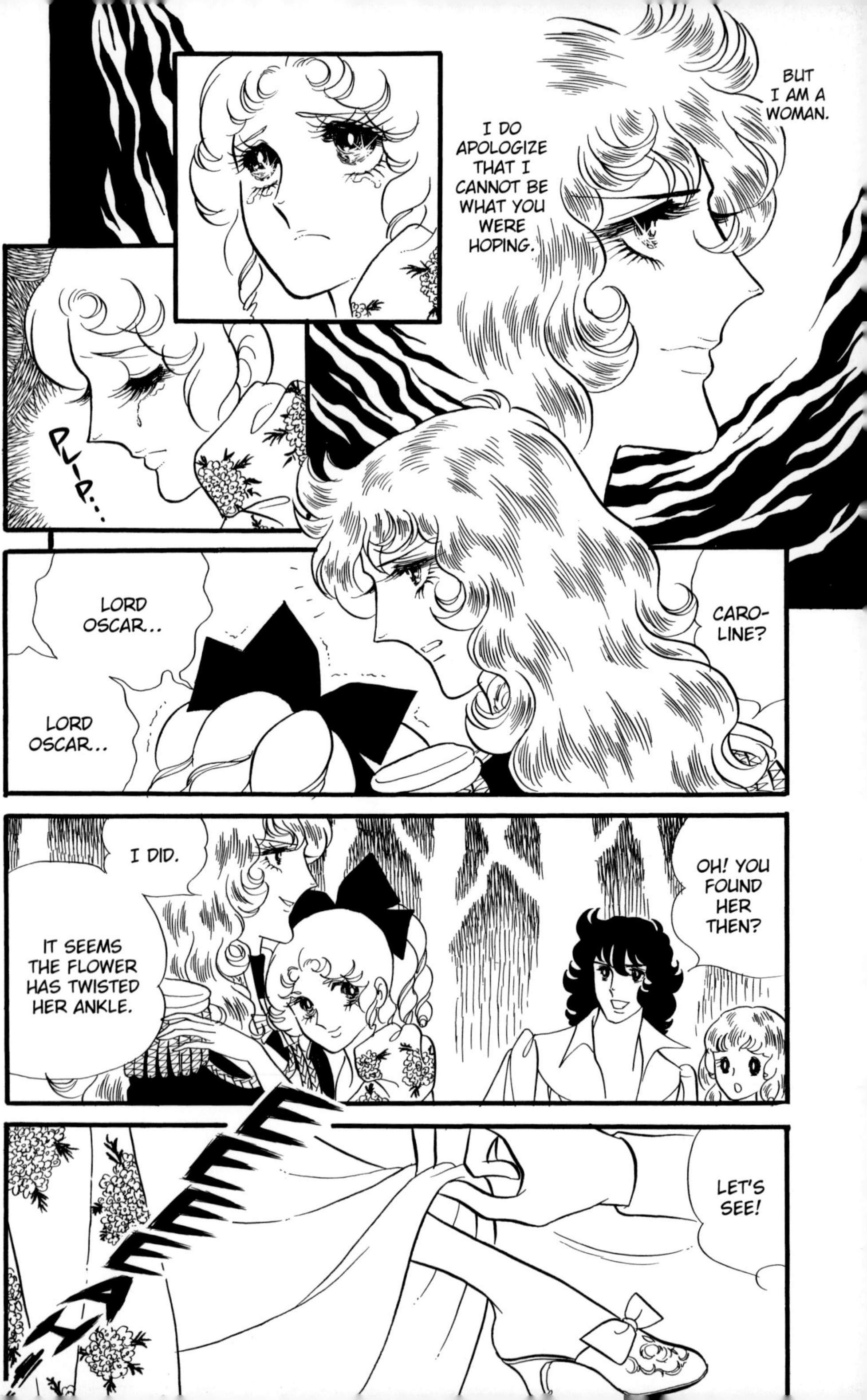
BUT I AM A WOMAN.
I DO APOLOGIZE THAT I CANNOT BE WHAT YOU WERE HOPING.
PLIP...
CARO-LINE?
LORD OSCAR...
LORD OSCAR...
OH! YOU FOUND HER THEN?
I DID.
IT SEEMS THE FLOWER HAS TWISTED HER ANKLE.
LET'S SEE!
HAEEEEEE

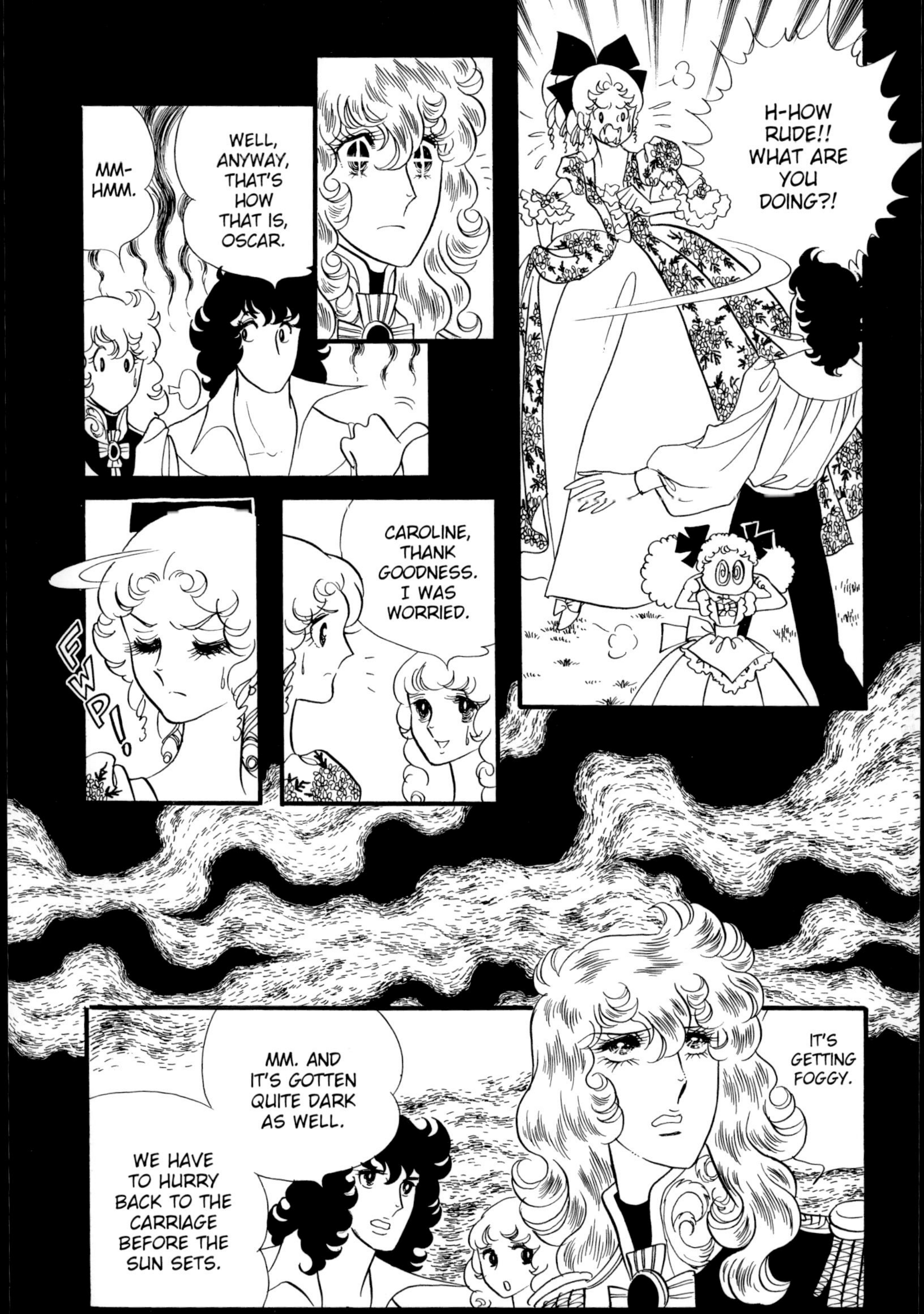
H-HOW RUDE!! WHAT ARE YOU DOING?!
WELL, ANYWAY, THAT'S HOW THAT IS, OSCAR.
MM-HMM.
CAROLINE, THANK GOODNESS. I WAS WORRIED.
FWP!
IT'S GETTING FOGGY.
MM. AND IT'S GOTTEN QUITE DARK AS WELL.
WE HAVE TO HURRY BACK TO THE CARRIAGE BEFORE THE SUN SETS.

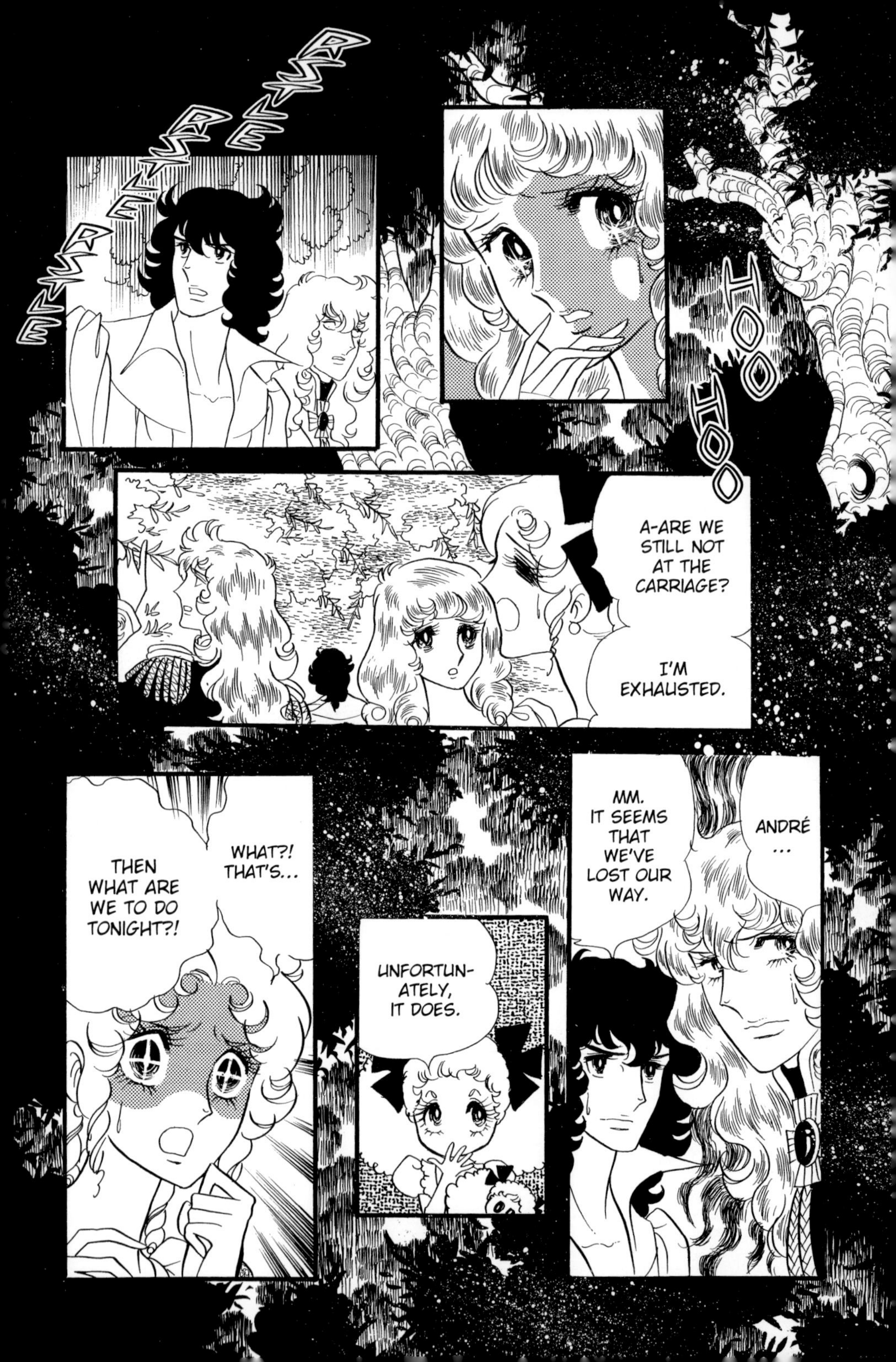
HOO HOO
RSTLE RSTLE RSTLE
A-ARE WE STILL NOT AT THE CARRIAGE?
I'M EXHAUSTED.
ANDRÉ...
MM. IT SEEMS THAT WE'VE LOST OUR WAY.
UNFORTUN-ATELY, IT DOES.
WHAT?! THAT'S...
THEN WHAT ARE WE TO DO TONIGHT?!

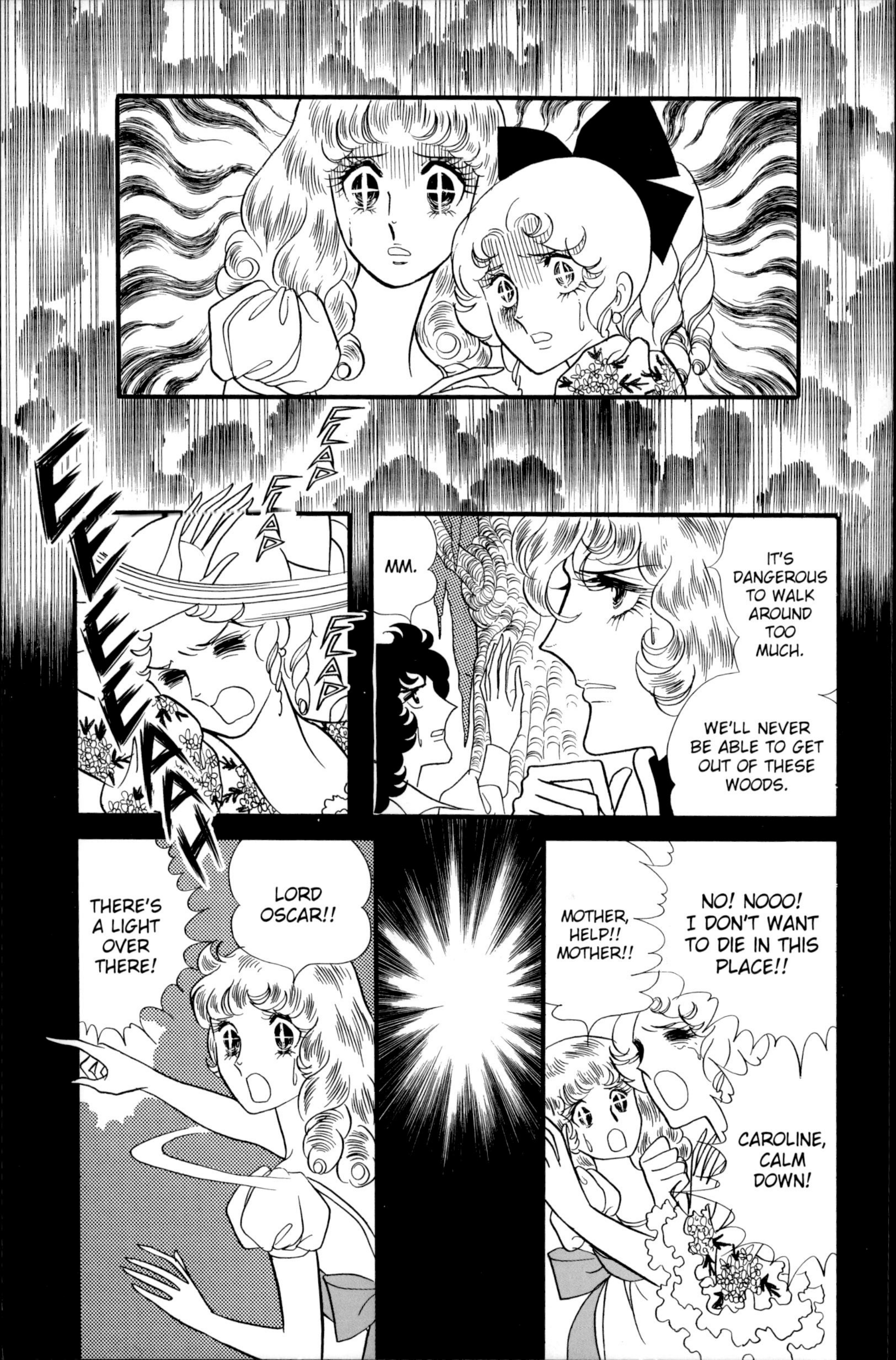

IT'S DANGEROUS TO WALK AROUND TOO MUCH.
MM.
WE'LL NEVER BE ABLE TO GET OUT OF THESE WOODS.
FLAP FLAP FLAP
EEEEAAH
NO! NOOO! I DON'T WANT TO DIE IN THIS PLACE!!
MOTHER, HELP!! MOTHER!!
CAROLINE, CALM DOWN!
LORD OSCAR!!
THERE'S A LIGHT OVER THERE!

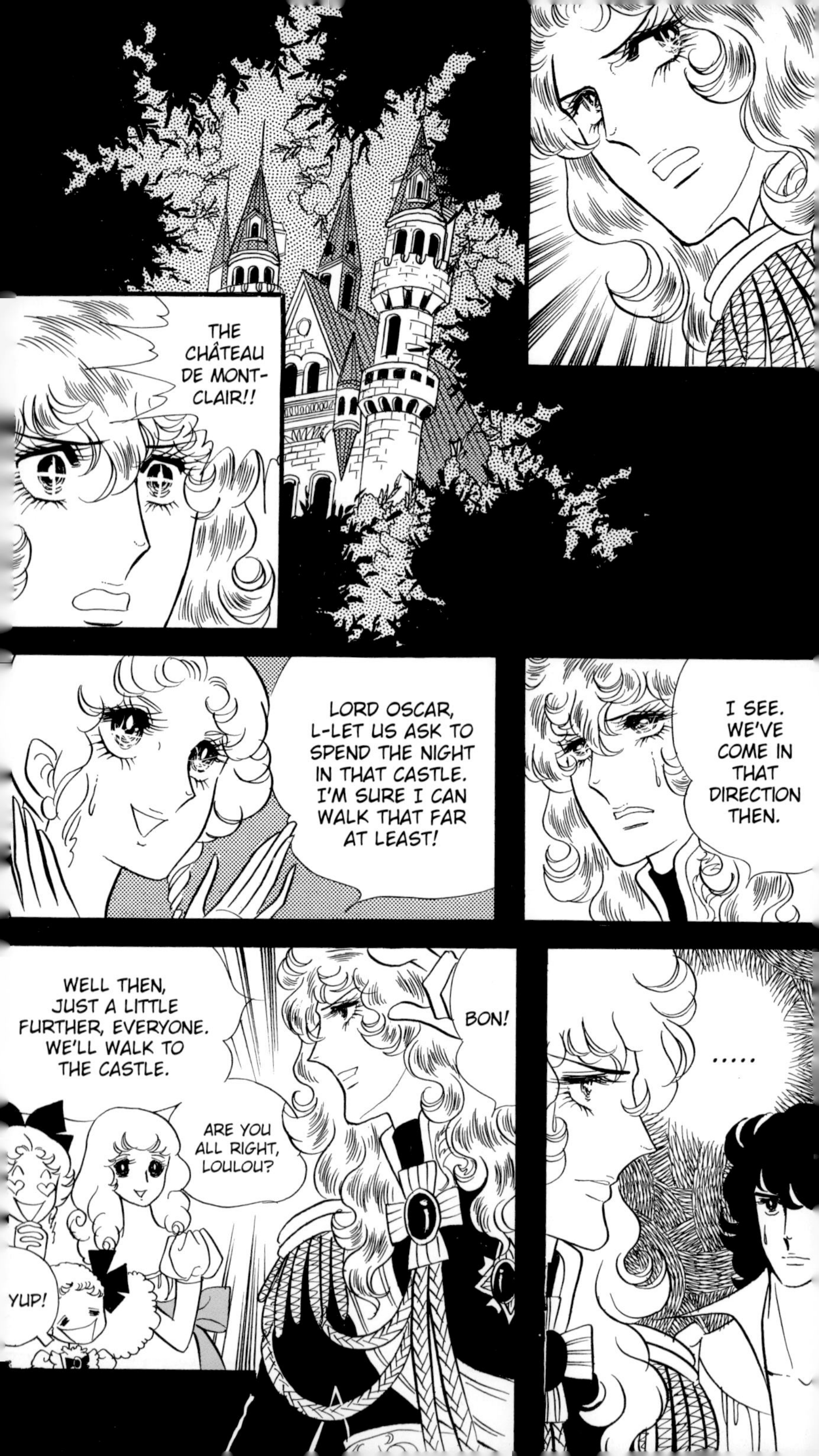
THE CHÂTEAU DE MONT-CLAIR!!
I SEE. WE'VE COME IN THAT DIRECTION THEN.
LORD OSCAR, L-LET US ASK TO SPEND THE NIGHT IN THAT CASTLE. I'M SURE I CAN WALK THAT FAR AT LEAST!
.....
BON!
WELL THEN, JUST A LITTLE FURTHER, EVERYONE. WE'LL WALK TO THE CASTLE.
ARE YOU ALL RIGHT, LOULOU?
YUP!

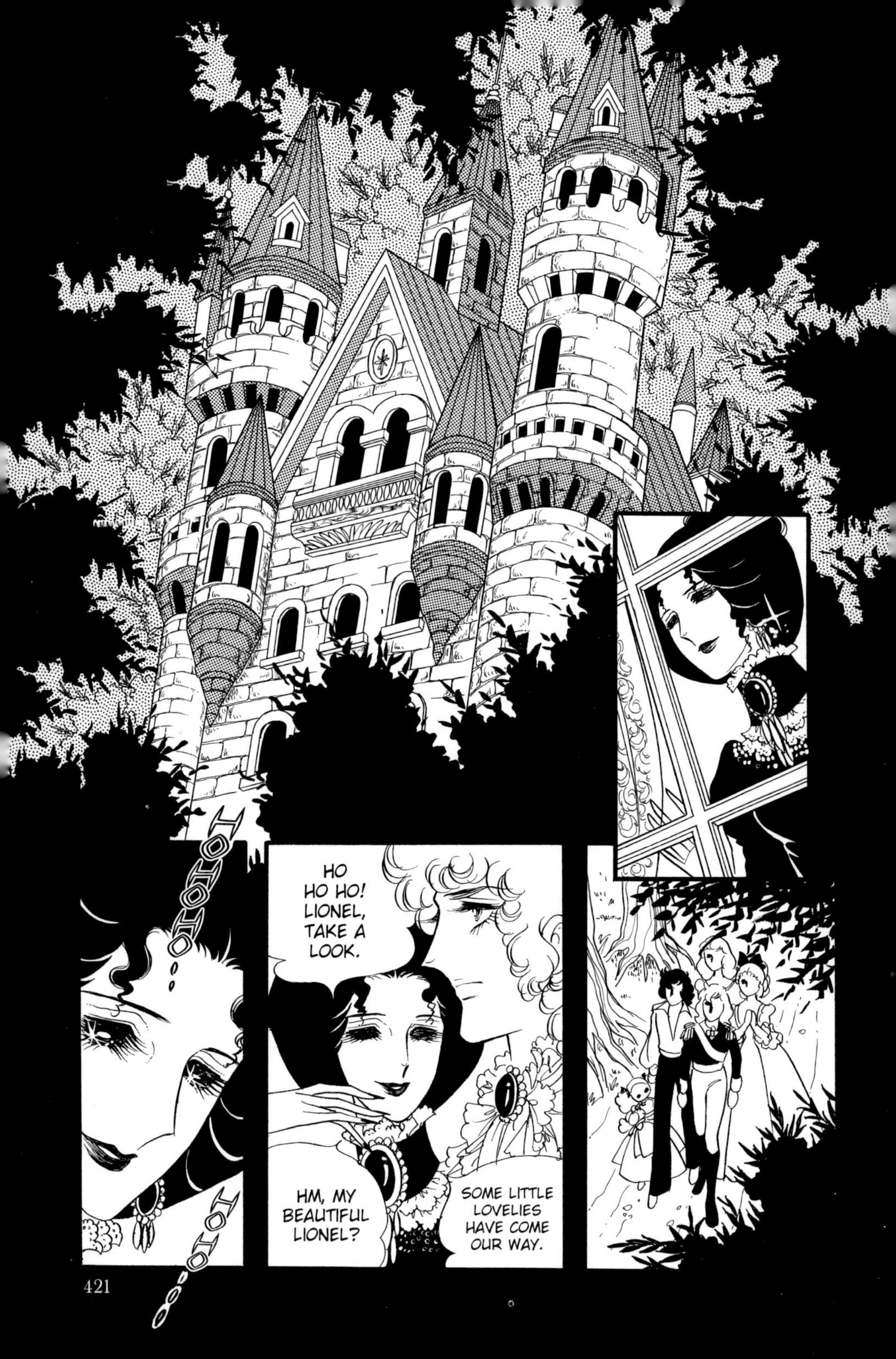
HO HO HO! LIONEL, TAKE A LOOK.
SOME LITTLE LOVELIES HAVE COME OUR WAY.
HM, MY BEAUTIFUL LIONEL?
HOHOHOHO...
HOHOHO...

1974 MARGARET MAGAZINE
COMBINED ISSUE 02-03 PREVIEW ART

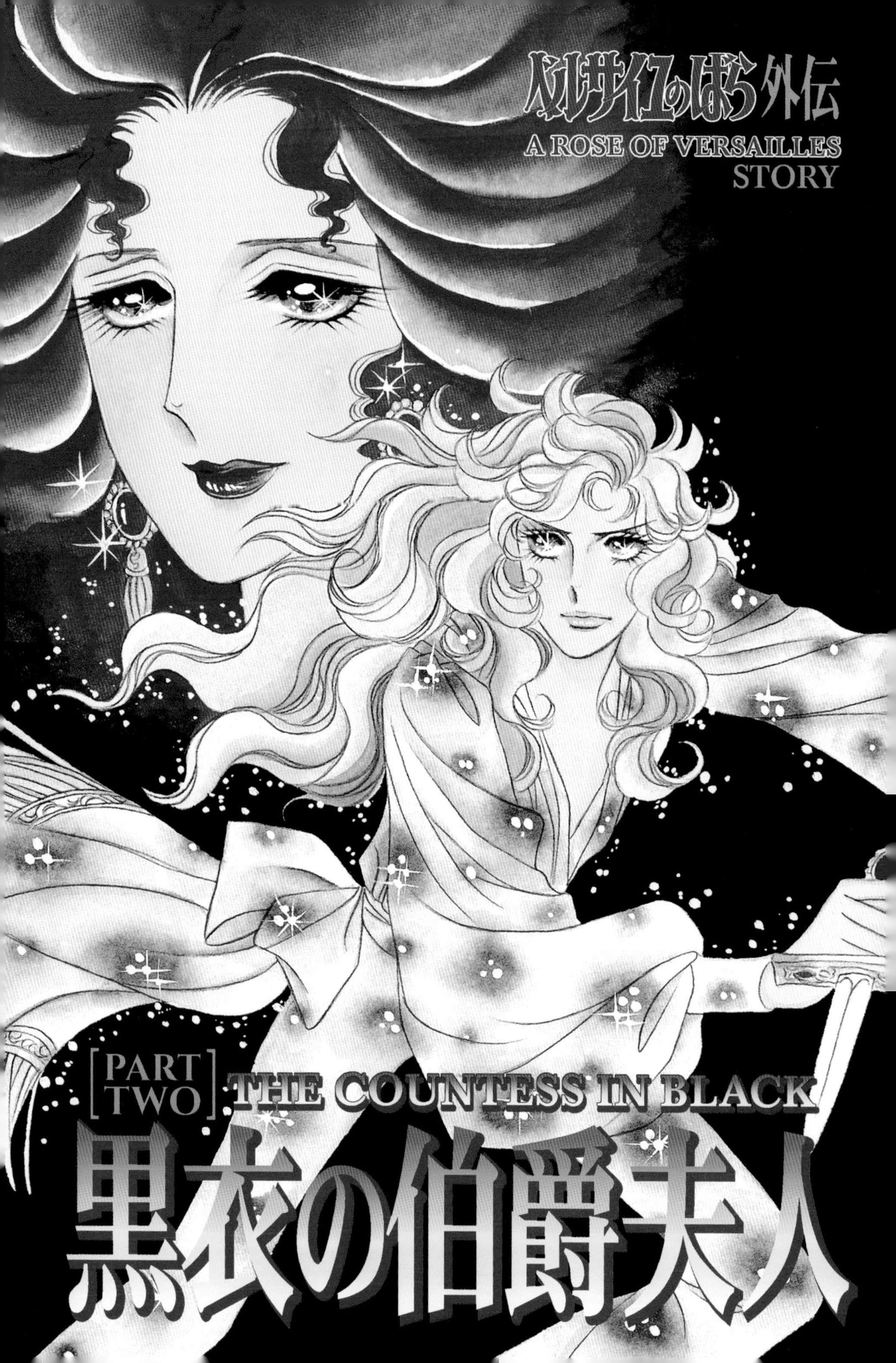
ベルサイユのばら外伝
A ROSE OF VERSAILLES STORY
[PART TWO] THE COUNTESS IN BLACK
黒衣の伯爵夫人

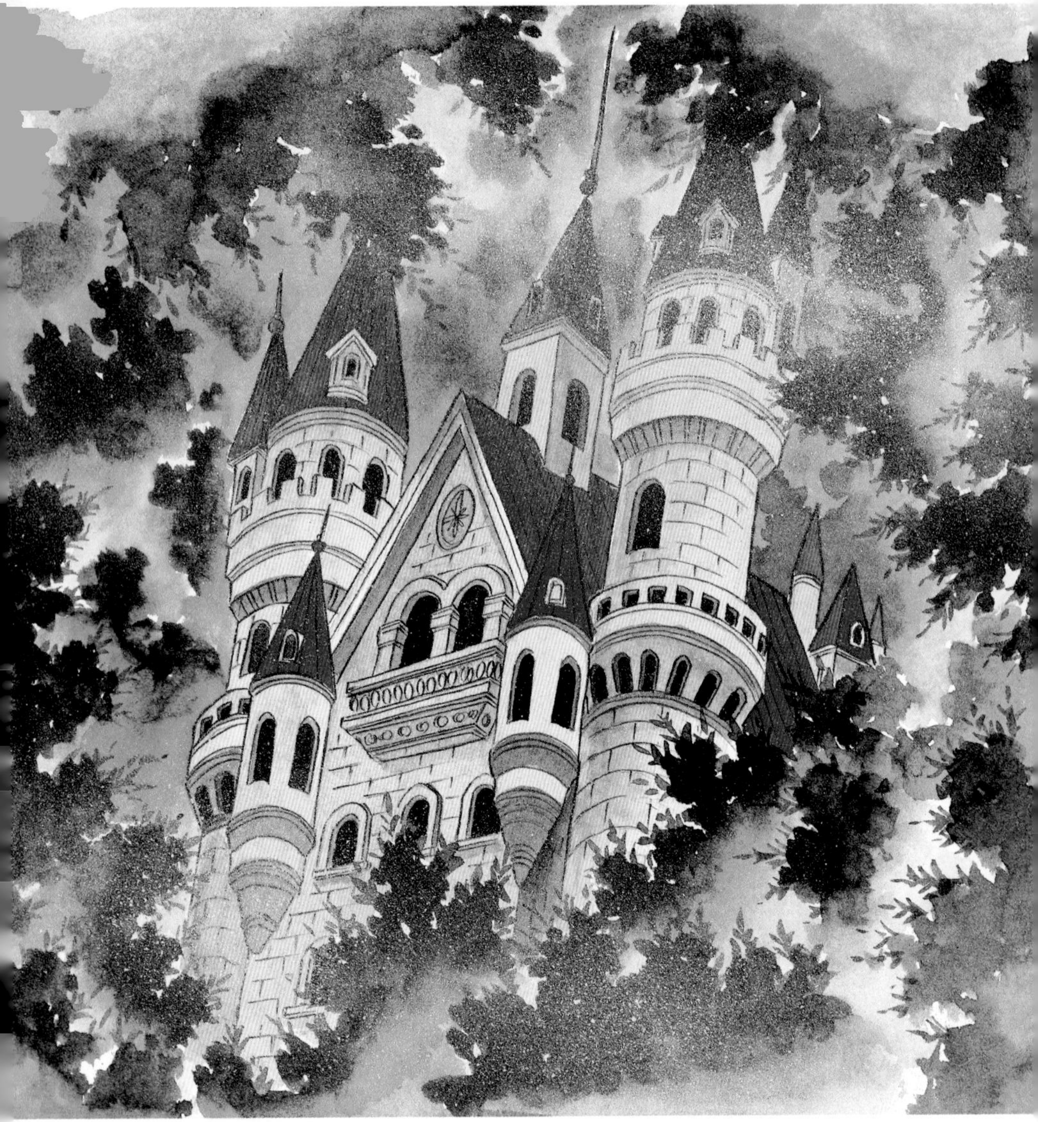

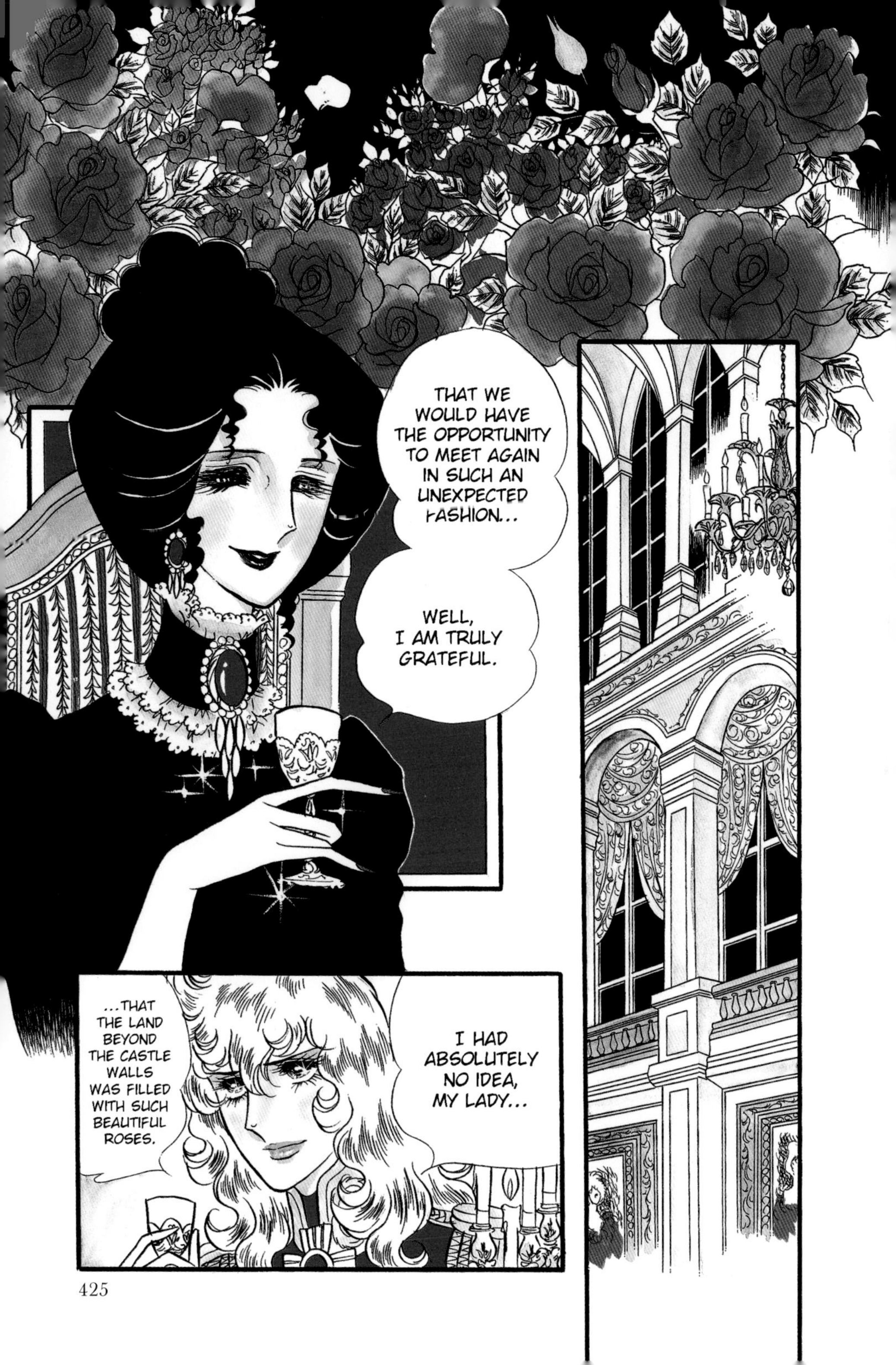
THAT WE WOULD HAVE THE OPPORTUNITY TO MEET AGAIN IN SUCH AN UNEXPECTED FASHION...
WELL, I AM TRULY GRATEFUL.
I HAD ABSOLUTELY NO IDEA, MY LADY...
...THAT THE LAND BEYOND THE CASTLE WALLS WAS FILLED WITH SUCH BEAUTIFUL ROSES.

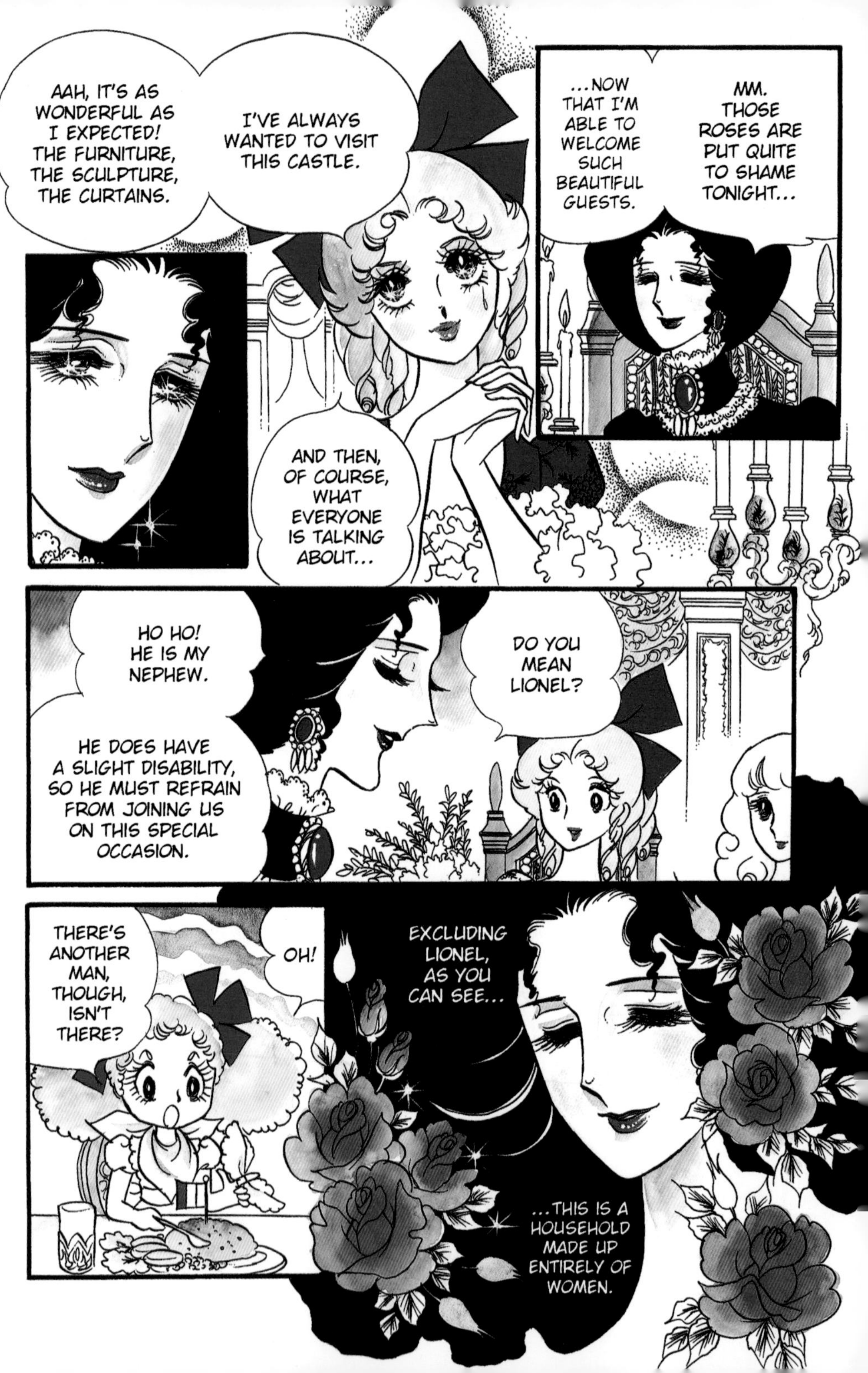
MM. THOSE ROSES ARE PUT QUITE TO SHAME TONIGHT...
...NOW THAT I'M ABLE TO WELCOME SUCH BEAUTIFUL GUESTS.
I'VE ALWAYS WANTED TO VISIT THIS CASTLE.
AAH, IT'S AS WONDERFUL AS I EXPECTED! THE FURNITURE, THE SCULPTURE, THE CURTAINS.
AND THEN, OF COURSE, WHAT EVERYONE IS TALKING ABOUT...
DO YOU MEAN LIONEL?
HO HO! HE IS MY NEPHEW.
HE DOES HAVE A SLIGHT DISABILITY, SO HE MUST REFRAIN FROM JOINING US ON THIS SPECIAL OCCASION.
EXCLUDING LIONEL, AS YOU CAN SEE...
...THIS IS A HOUSEHOLD MADE UP ENTIRELY OF WOMEN.
OH!
THERE'S ANOTHER MAN, THOUGH, ISN'T THERE?

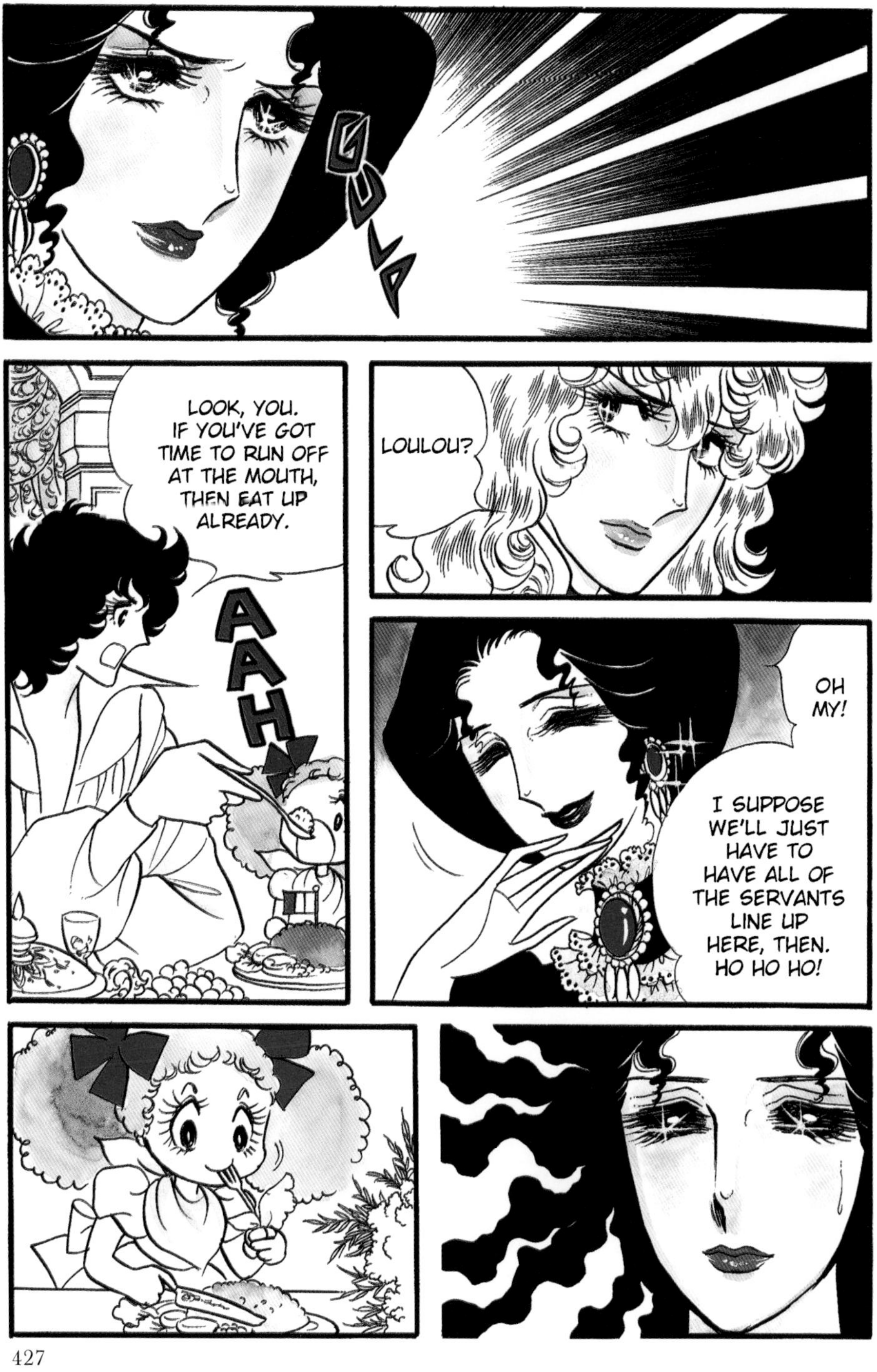
GULP
LOULOU?
OH MY!
I SUPPOSE WE'LL JUST HAVE TO HAVE ALL OF THE SERVANTS LINE UP HERE, THEN. HO HO HO!
LOOK, YOU. IF YOU'VE GOT TIME TO RUN OFF AT THE MOUTH, THEN EAT UP ALREADY.
AAH

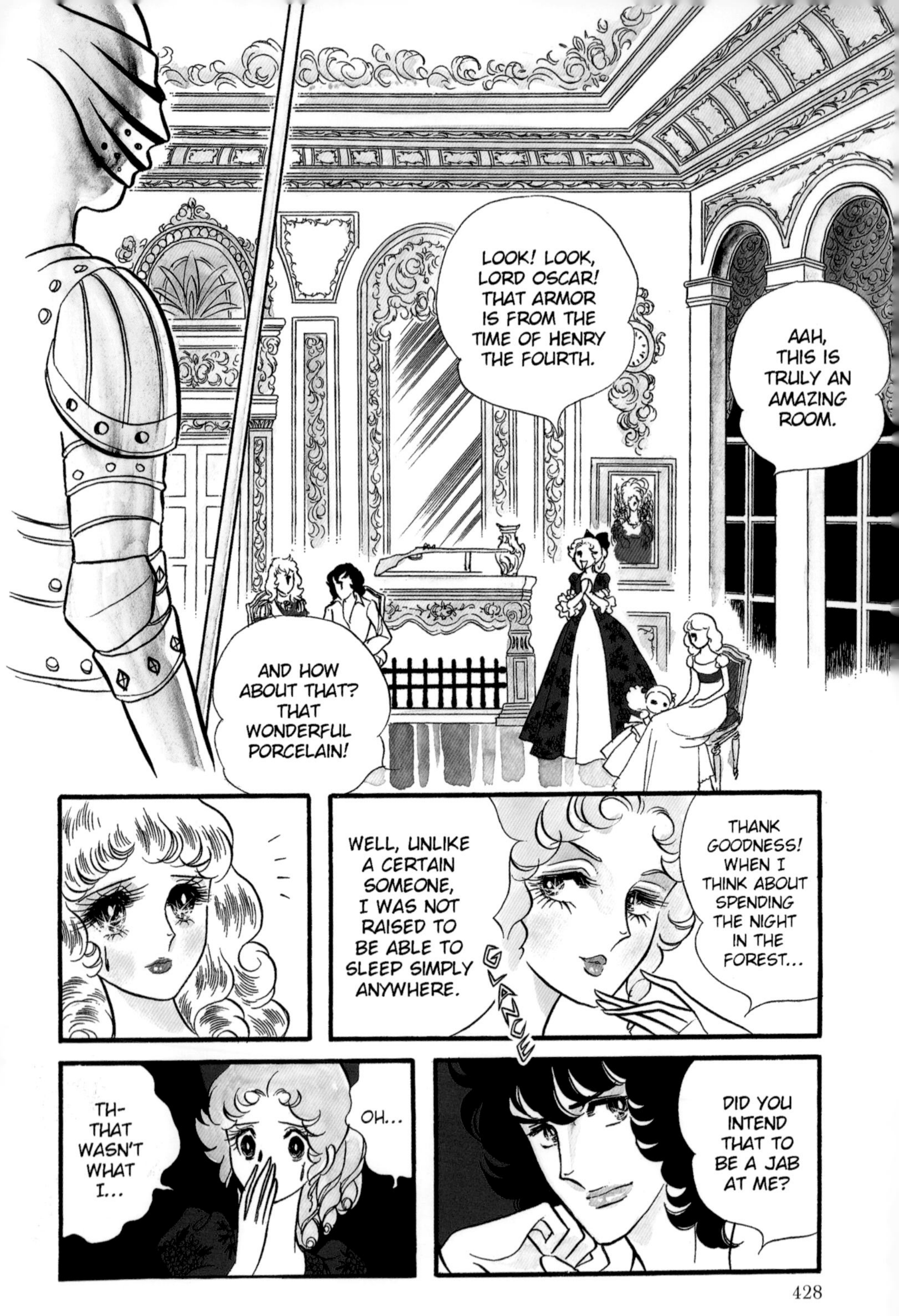
AAH, THIS IS TRULY AN AMAZING ROOM.
LOOK! LOOK, LORD OSCAR! THAT ARMOR IS FROM THE TIME OF HENRY THE FOURTH.
AND HOW ABOUT THAT? THAT WONDERFUL PORCELAIN!
THANK GOODNESS! WHEN I THINK ABOUT SPENDING THE NIGHT IN THE FOREST...
WELL, UNLIKE A CERTAIN SOMEONE, I WAS NOT RAISED TO BE ABLE TO SLEEP SIMPLY ANYWHERE.
GLANCE
DID YOU INTEND THAT TO BE A JAB AT ME?
OH...
TH- THAT WASN'T WHAT I...

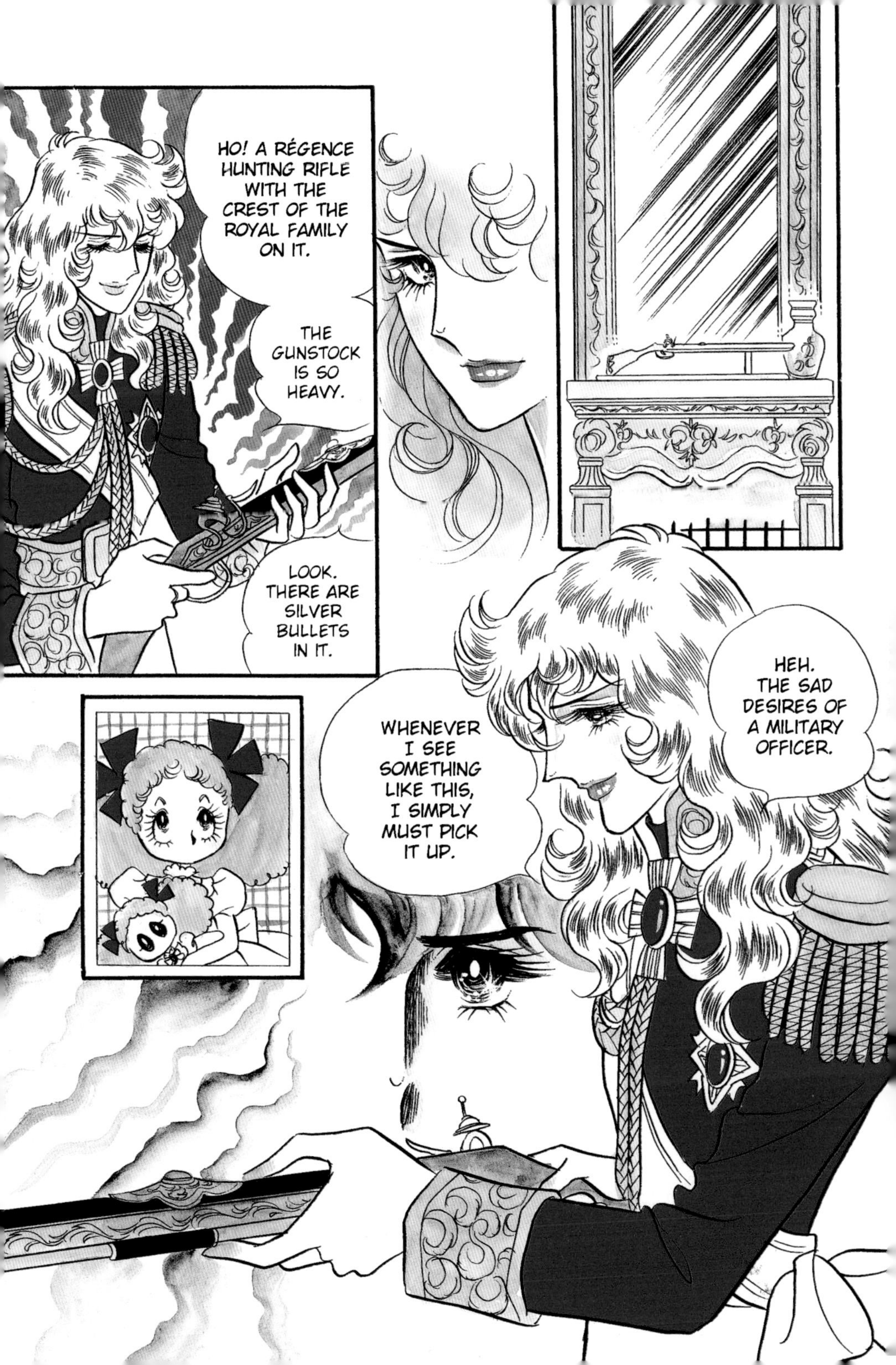
HO! A RÉGENCE HUNTING RIFLE WITH THE CREST OF THE ROYAL FAMILY ON IT.
THE GUNSTOCK IS SO HEAVY.
LOOK. THERE ARE SILVER BULLETS IN IT.
HEH. THE SAD DESIRES OF A MILITARY OFFICER.
WHENEVER I SEE SOMETHING LIKE THIS, I SIMPLY MUST PICK IT UP.

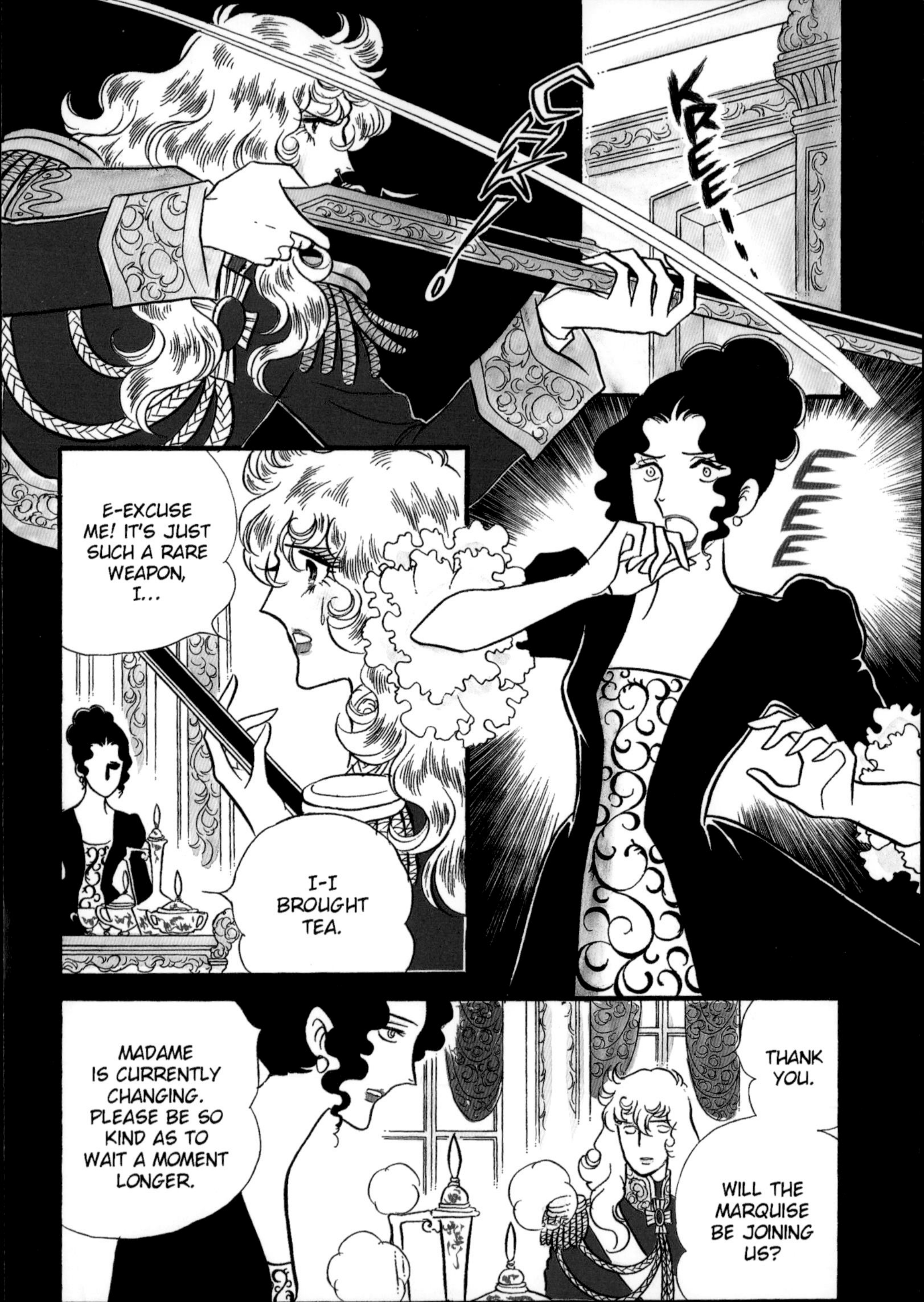
KREE...
CHK!
EEEE
E-EXCUSE ME! IT'S JUST SUCH A RARE WEAPON, I...
I-I BROUGHT TEA.
THANK YOU.
WILL THE MARQUISE BE JOINING US?
MADAME IS CURRENTLY CHANGING. PLEASE BE SO KIND AS TO WAIT A MOMENT LONGER.

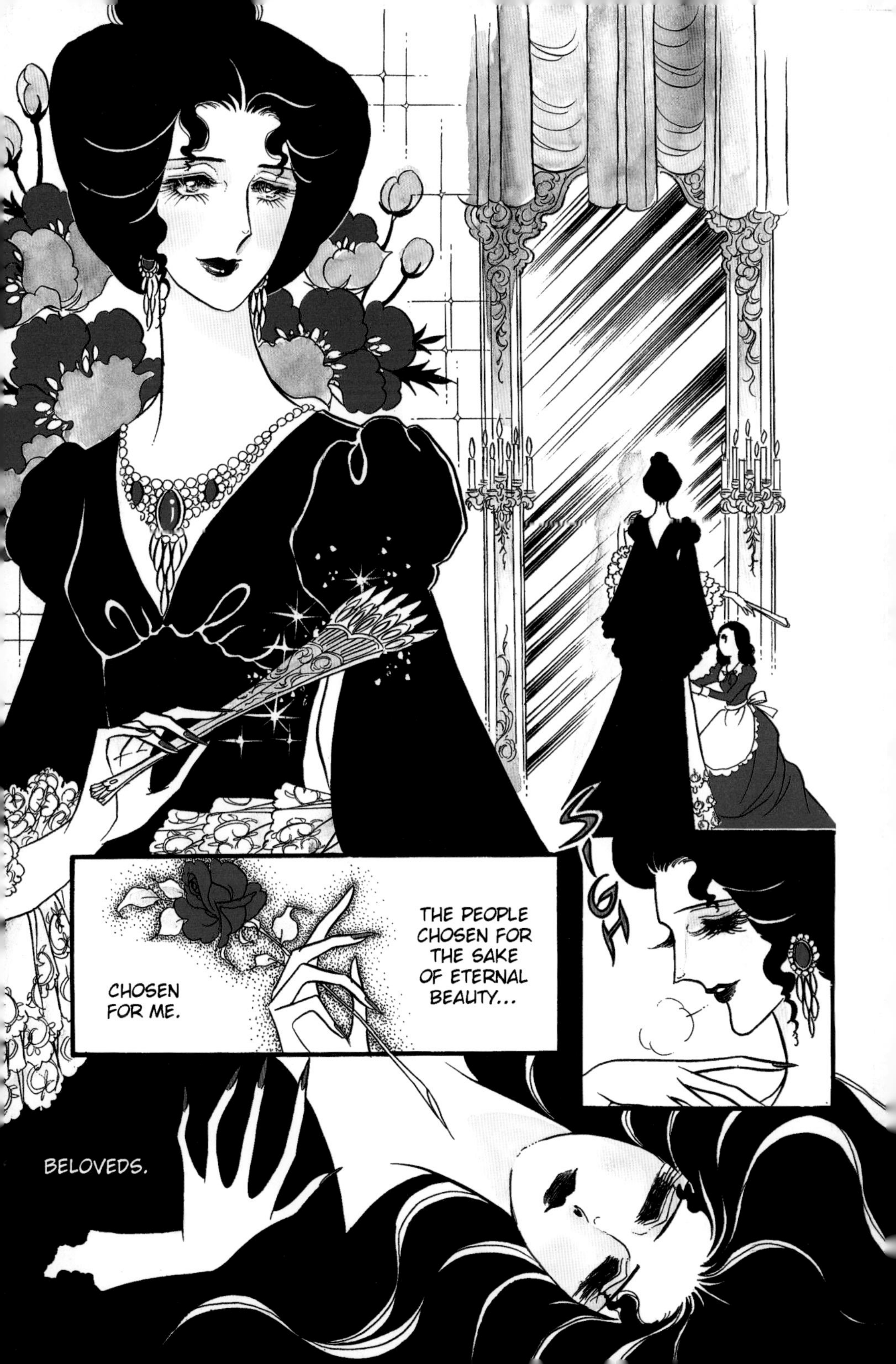
SIGH
THE PEOPLE CHOSEN FOR THE SAKE OF ETERNAL BEAUTY...
CHOSEN FOR ME.
BELOVEDS.

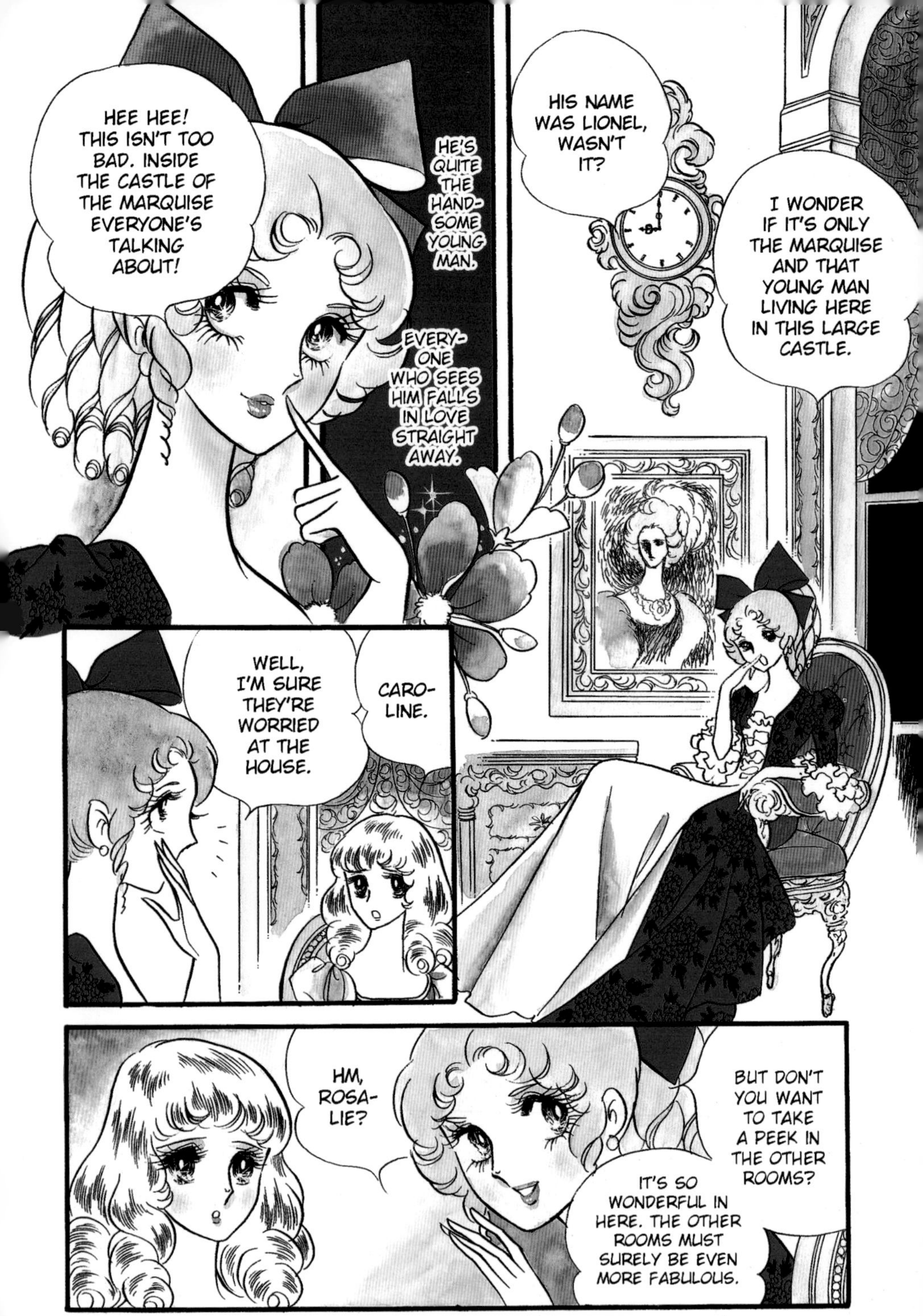
HIS NAME WAS LIONEL, WASN'T IT?
I WONDER IF IT'S ONLY THE MARQUISE AND THAT YOUNG MAN LIVING HERE IN THIS LARGE CASTLE.
HEE HEE! THIS ISN'T TOO BAD. INSIDE THE CASTLE OF THE MARQUISE EVERYONE'S TALKING ABOUT!
HE'S QUITE THE HAND-SOME YOUNG MAN.
EVERY-ONE WHO SEES HIM FALLS IN LOVE STRAIGHT AWAY.
CARO-LINE.
WELL, I'M SURE THEY'RE WORRIED AT THE HOUSE.
BUT DON'T YOU WANT TO TAKE A PEEK IN THE OTHER ROOMS?
IT'S SO WONDERFUL IN HERE. THE OTHER ROOMS MUST SURELY BE EVEN MORE FABULOUS.
HM, ROSA-LIE?

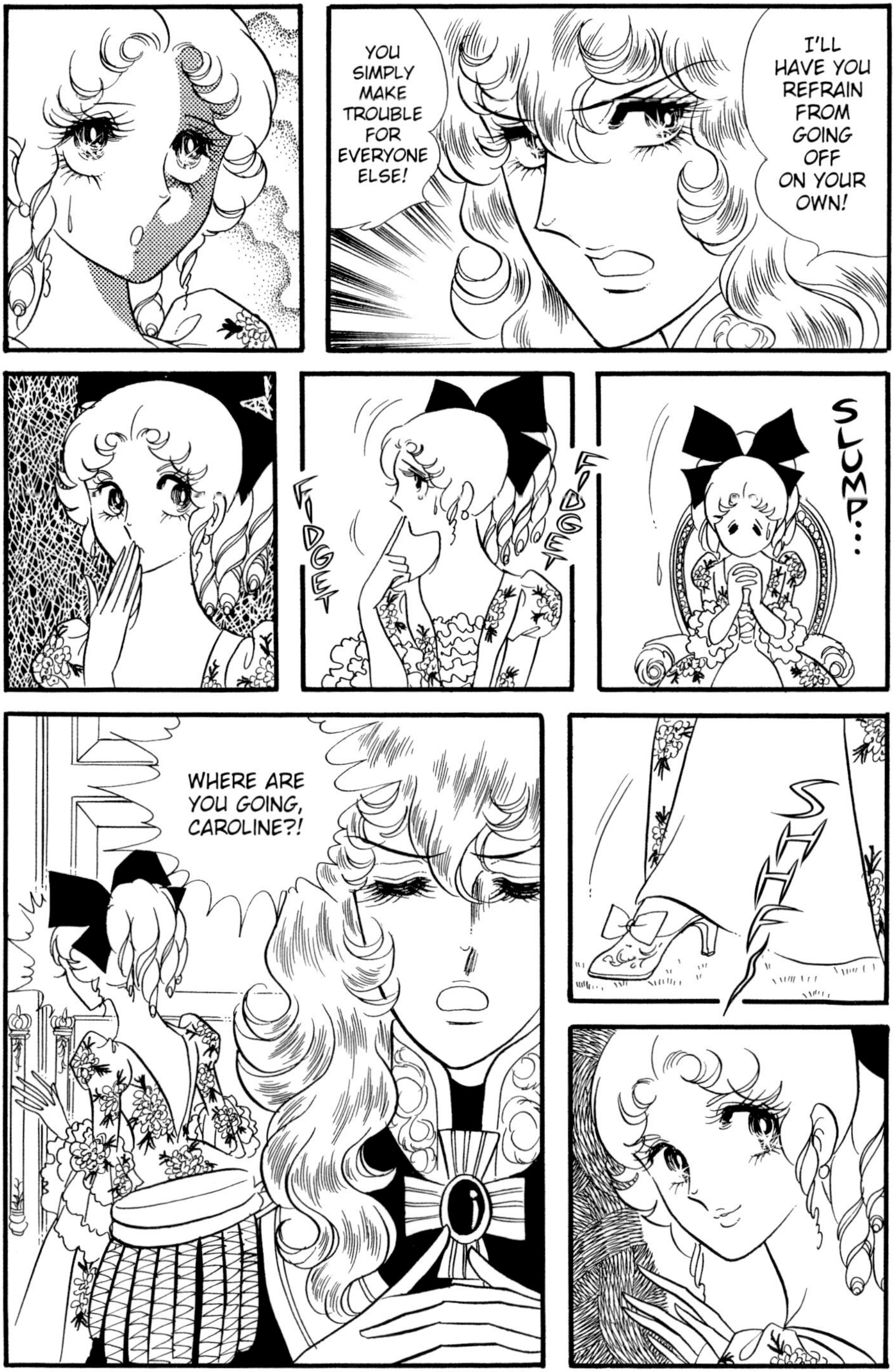
I'LL HAVE YOU REFRAIN FROM GOING OFF ON YOUR OWN!
YOU SIMPLY MAKE TROUBLE FOR EVERYONE ELSE!
SLUMP...
FIDGET
FIDGET
SHHF
WHERE ARE YOU GOING, CAROLINE?!

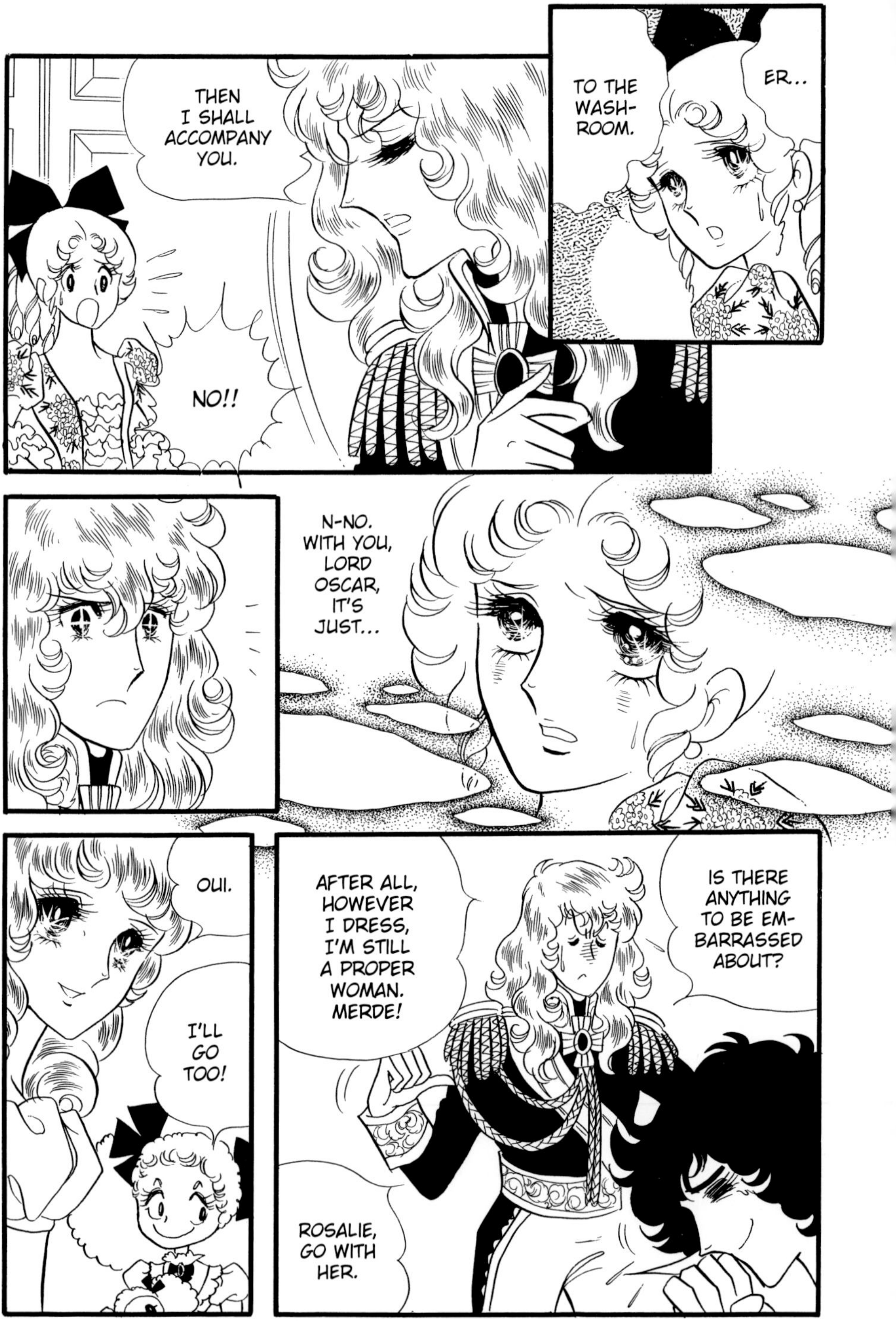
ER...
TO THE WASH-ROOM.
THEN I SHALL ACCOMPANY YOU.
NO!!
N-NO. WITH YOU, LORD OSCAR, IT'S JUST...
IS THERE ANYTHING TO BE EM-BARRASSED ABOUT?
AFTER ALL, HOWEVER I DRESS, I'M STILL A PROPER WOMAN. MERDE!
ROSALIE, GO WITH HER.
OUI.
I'LL GO TOO!

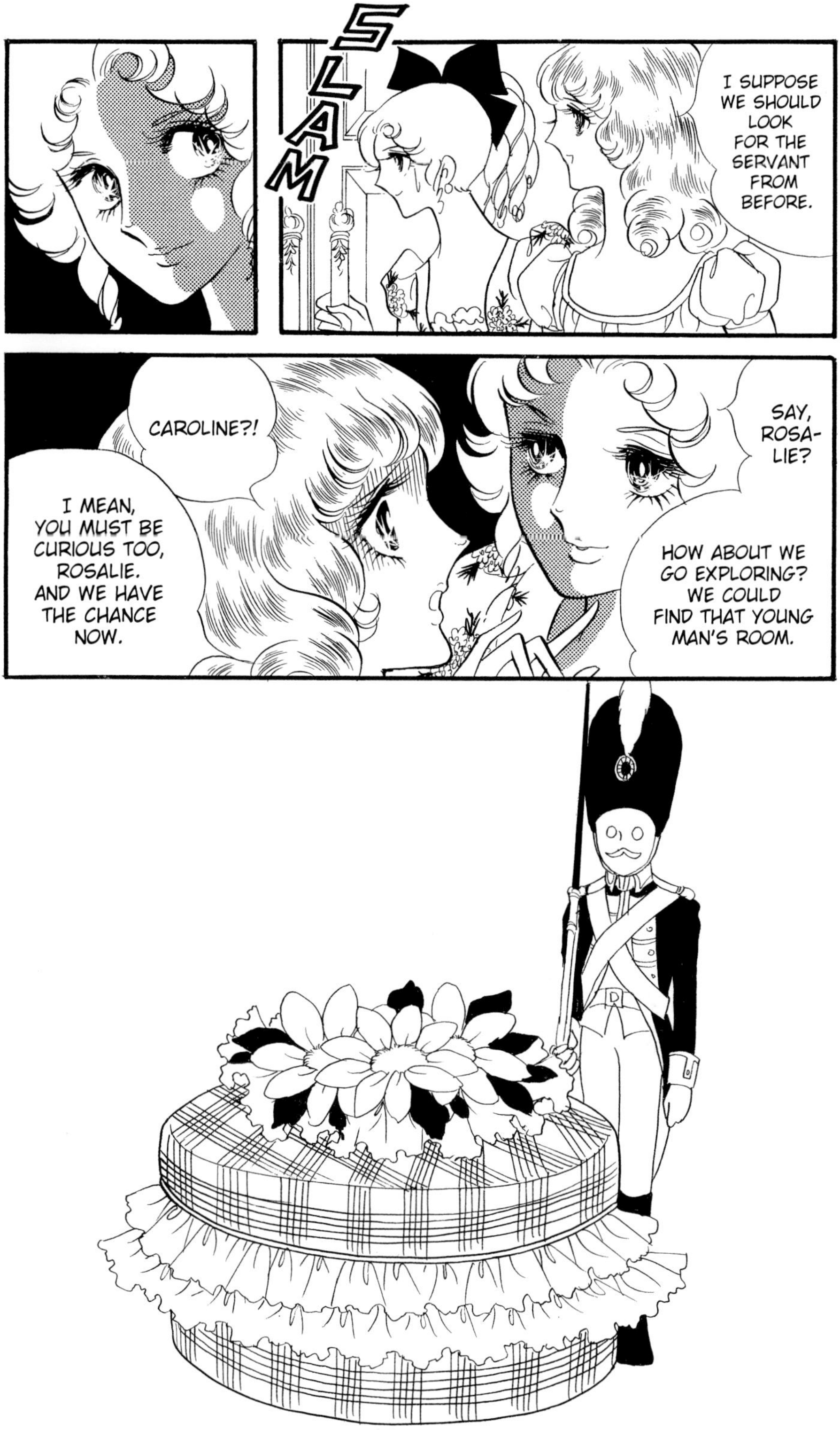
SLAM
I SUPPOSE WE SHOULD LOOK FOR THE SERVANT FROM BEFORE.
SAY, ROSA-LIE?
HOW ABOUT WE GO EXPLORING? WE COULD FIND THAT YOUNG MAN'S ROOM.
CAROLINE?!
I MEAN, YOU MUST BE CURIOUS TOO, ROSALIE. AND WE HAVE THE CHANCE NOW.

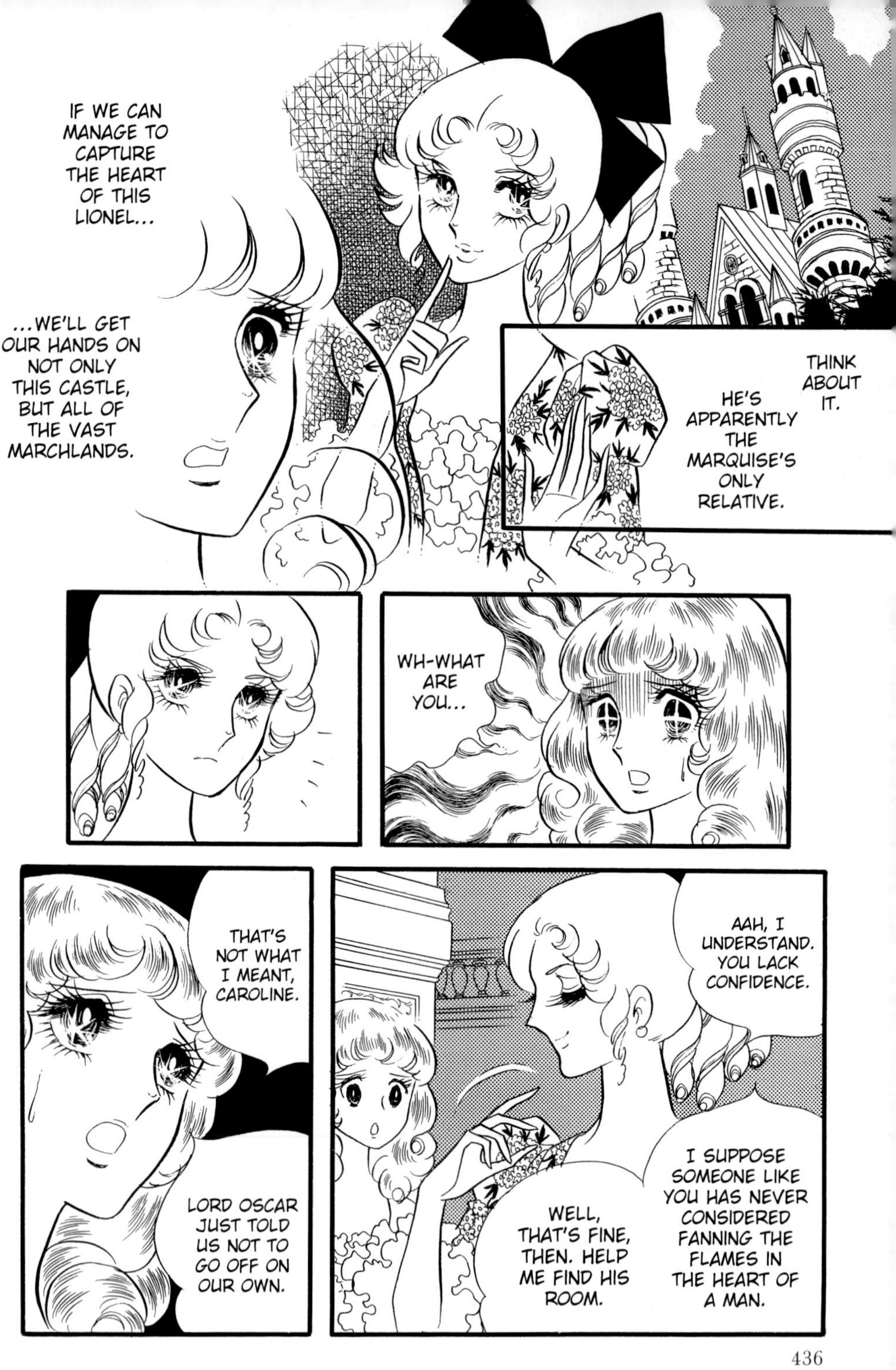
THINK ABOUT IT.
HE'S APPARENTLY THE MARQUISE'S ONLY RELATIVE.
IF WE CAN MANAGE TO CAPTURE THE HEART OF THIS LIONEL...
...WE'LL GET OUR HANDS ON NOT ONLY THIS CASTLE, BUT ALL OF THE VAST MARCHLANDS.
WH-WHAT ARE YOU...
AAH, I UNDERSTAND. YOU LACK CONFIDENCE.
I SUPPOSE SOMEONE LIKE YOU HAS NEVER CONSIDERED FANNING THE FLAMES IN THE HEART OF A MAN.
WELL, THAT'S FINE, THEN. HELP ME FIND HIS ROOM.
THAT'S NOT WHAT I MEANT, CAROLINE.
LORD OSCAR JUST TOLD US NOT TO GO OFF ON OUR OWN.

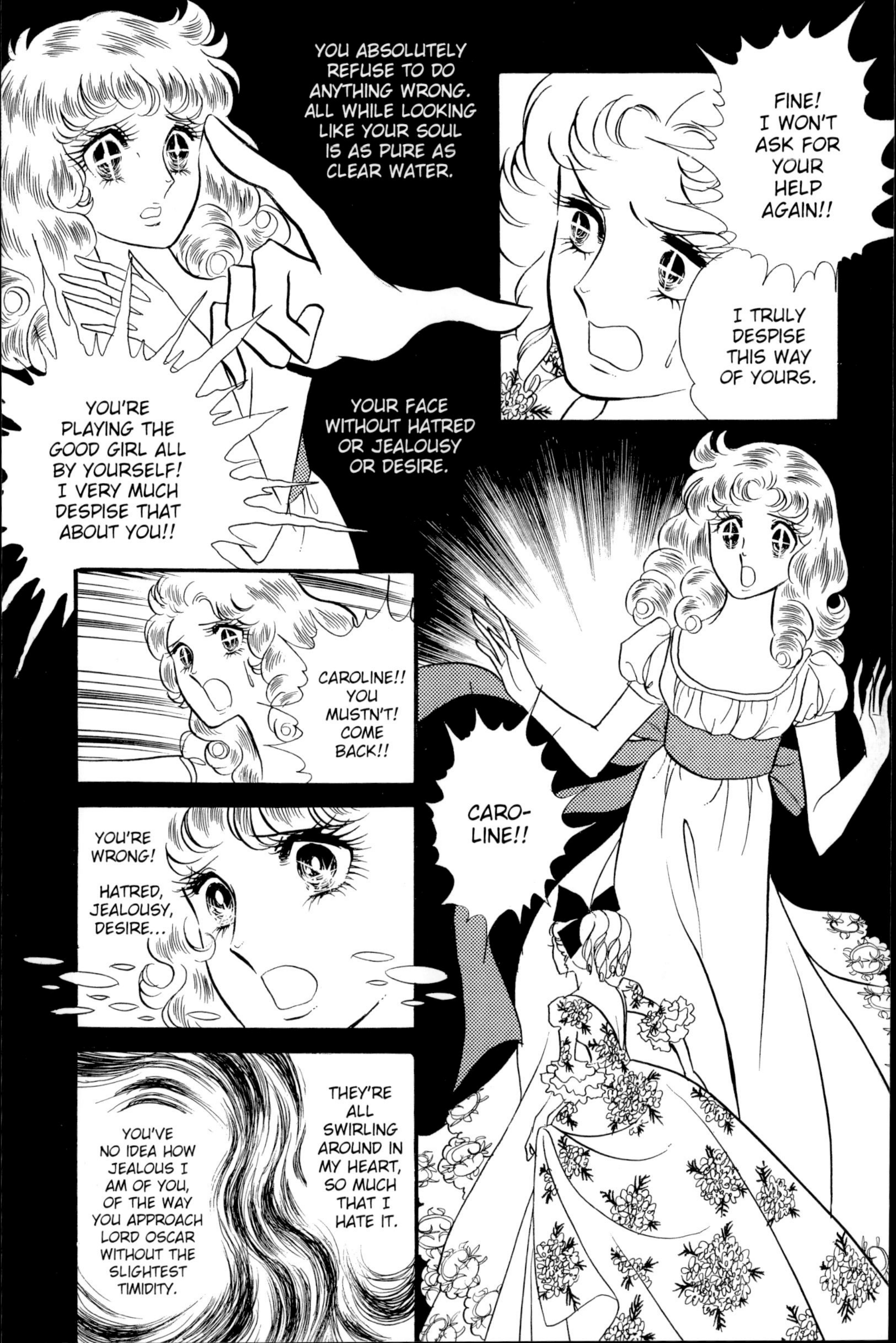
FINE! I WON'T ASK FOR YOUR HELP AGAIN!!
I TRULY DESPISE THIS WAY OF YOURS.
YOU ABSOLUTELY REFUSE TO DO ANYTHING WRONG. ALL WHILE LOOKING LIKE YOUR SOUL IS AS PURE AS CLEAR WATER.
YOUR FACE WITHOUT HATRED OR JEALOUSY OR DESIRE.
YOU'RE PLAYING THE GOOD GIRL ALL BY YOURSELF! I VERY MUCH DESPISE THAT ABOUT YOU!!
CARO-LINE!!
CAROLINE!! YOU MUSTN'T! COME BACK!!
YOU'RE WRONG!
HATRED, JEALOUSY, DESIRE...
THEY'RE ALL SWIRLING AROUND IN MY HEART, SO MUCH THAT I HATE IT.
YOU'VE NO IDEA HOW JEALOUS I AM OF YOU, OF THE WAY YOU APPROACH LORD OSCAR WITHOUT THE SLIGHTEST TIMIDITY.

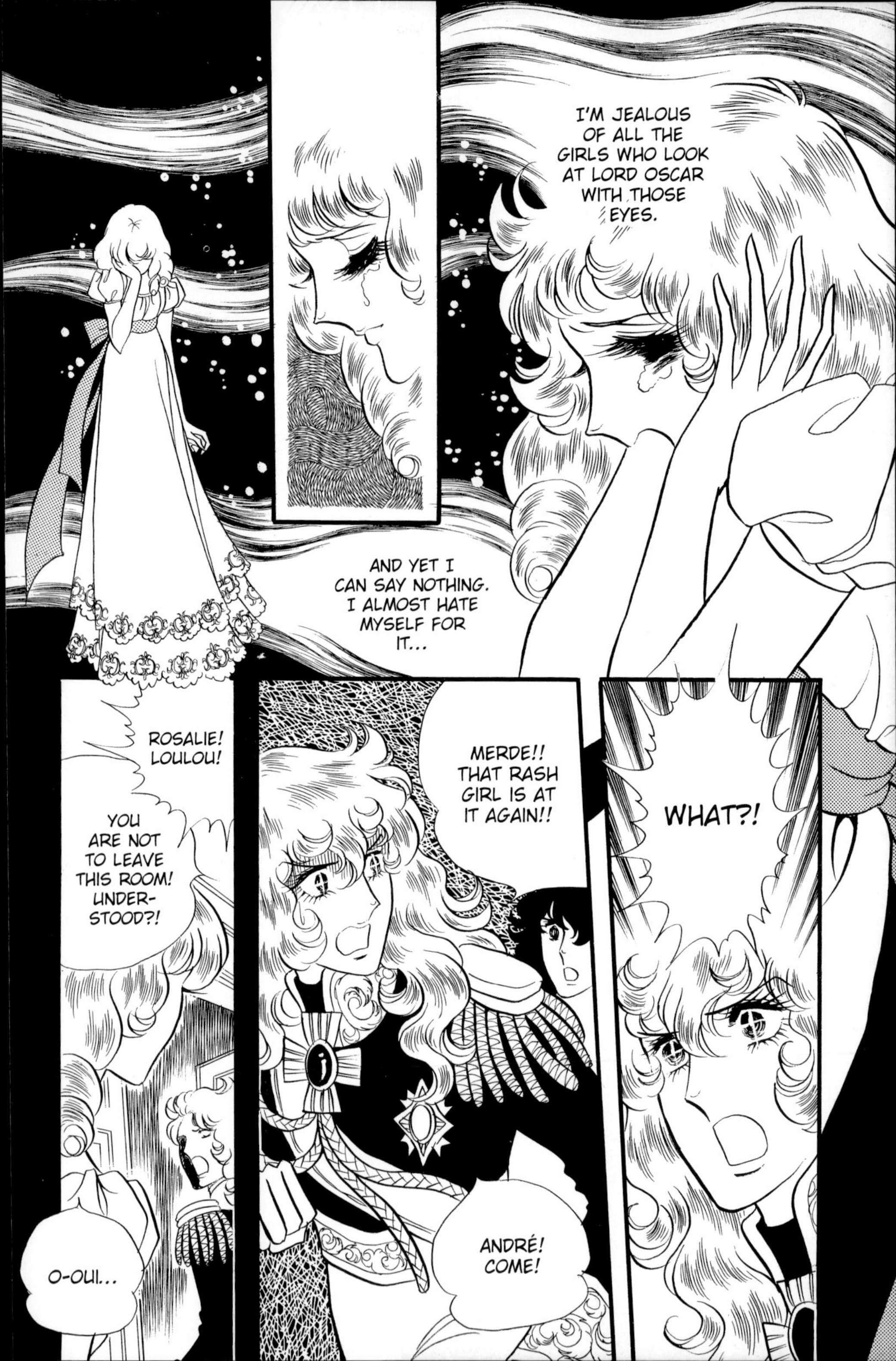
I'M JEALOUS OF ALL THE GIRLS WHO LOOK AT LORD OSCAR WITH THOSE EYES.
AND YET I CAN SAY NOTHING. I ALMOST HATE MYSELF FOR IT...
WHAT?!
MERDE!! THAT RASH GIRL IS AT IT AGAIN!!
ANDRÉ! COME!
ROSALIE! LOULOU!
YOU ARE NOT TO LEAVE THIS ROOM! UNDER-STOOD?!
O-OUI...

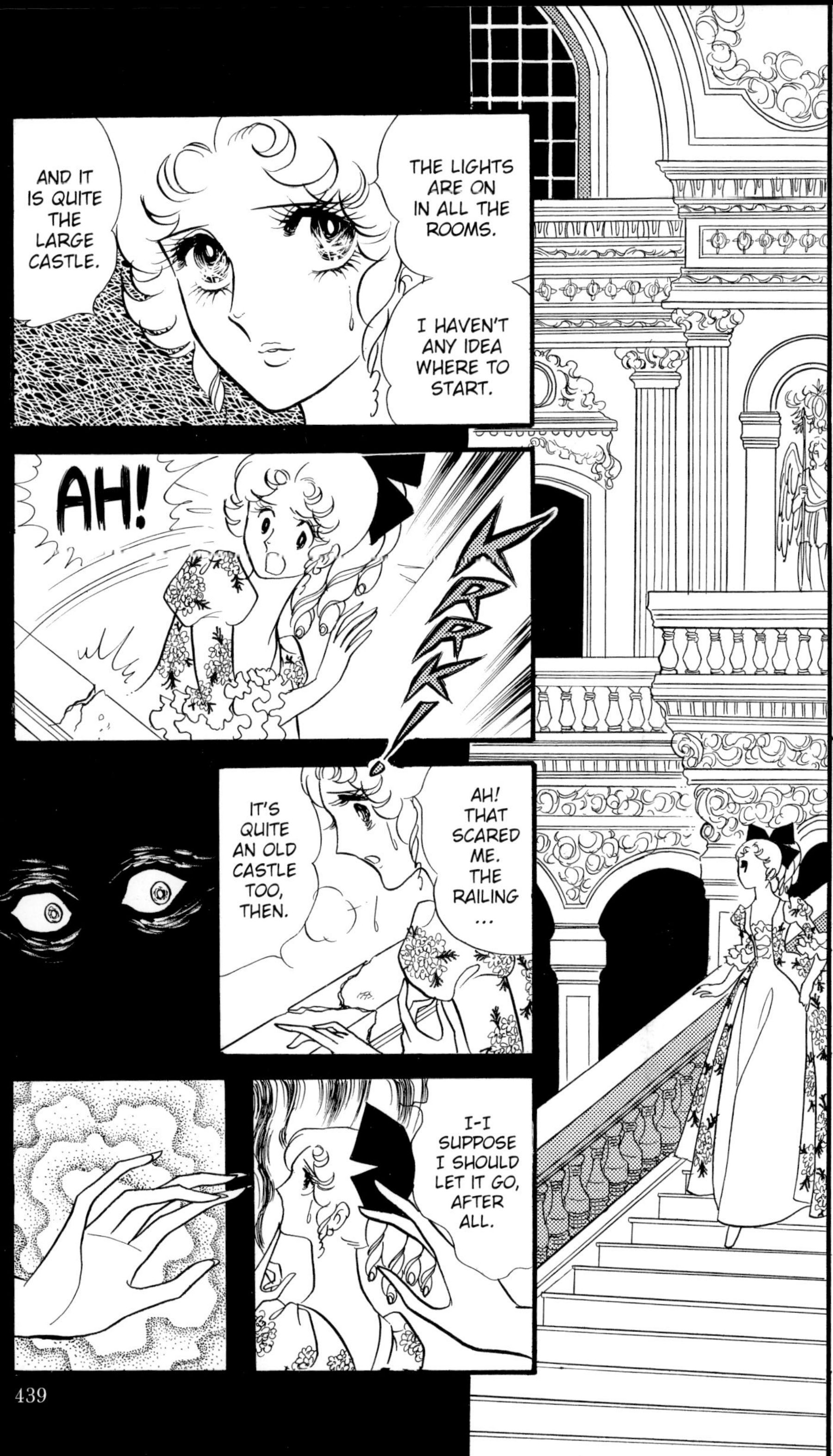
THE LIGHTS ARE ON IN ALL THE ROOMS.
I HAVEN'T ANY IDEA WHERE TO START.
AND IT IS QUITE THE LARGE CASTLE.
KRRRK
AH!
AH! THAT SCARED ME. THE RAILING ...
IT'S QUITE AN OLD CASTLE TOO, THEN.
I-I SUPPOSE I SHOULD LET IT GO, AFTER ALL.

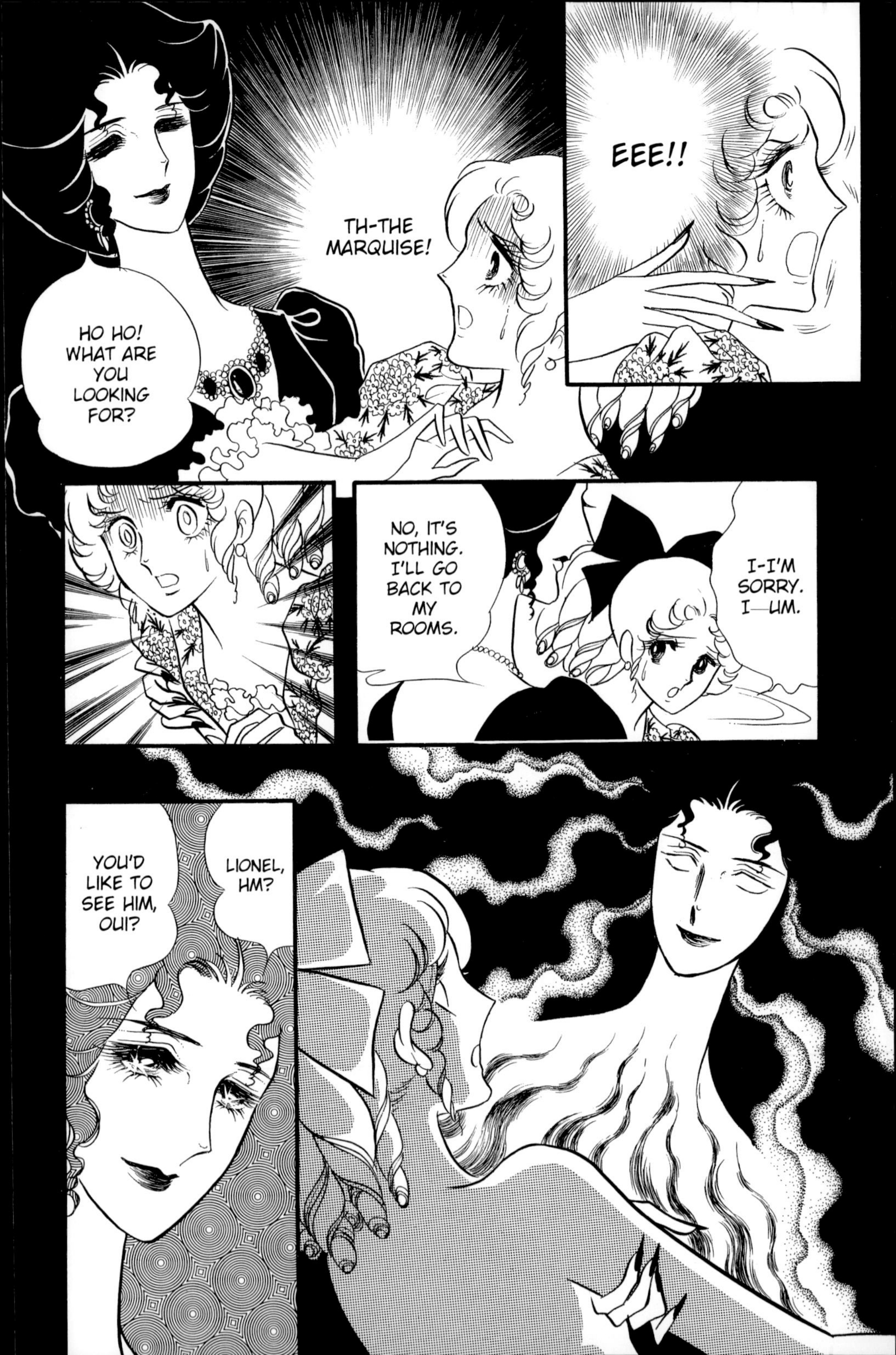
EEE!!
TH-THE MARQUISE!
HO HO! WHAT ARE YOU LOOKING FOR?
I-I'M SORRY. I—UM.
NO, IT'S NOTHING. I'LL GO BACK TO MY ROOMS.
LIONEL, HM?
YOU'D LIKE TO SEE HIM, OUI?

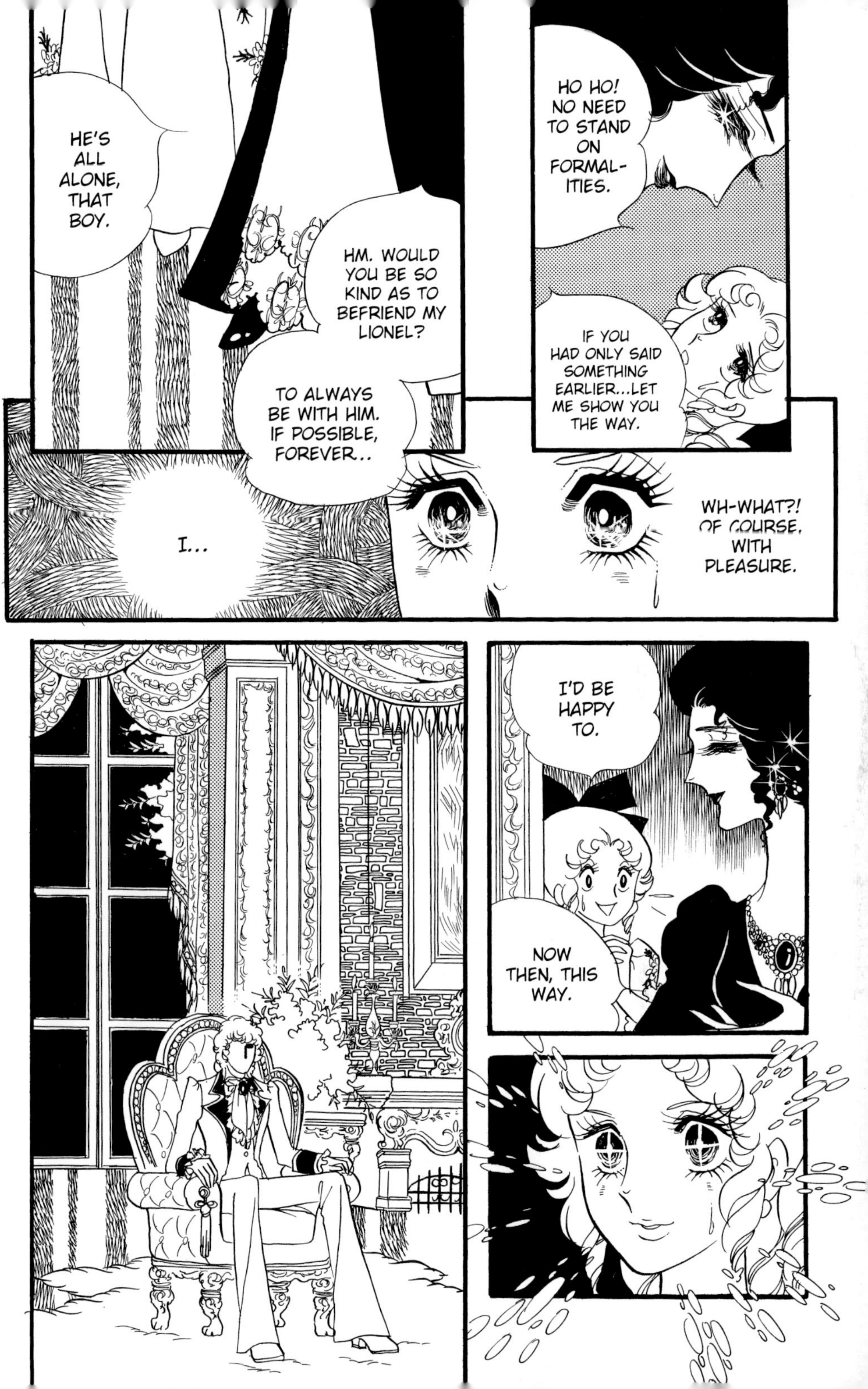
HO HO! NO NEED TO STAND ON FORMAL-ITIES.
IF YOU HAD ONLY SAID SOMETHING EARLIER...LET ME SHOW YOU THE WAY.
HE'S ALL ALONE, THAT BOY.
HM. WOULD YOU BE SO KIND AS TO BEFRIEND MY LIONEL?
TO ALWAYS BE WITH HIM. IF POSSIBLE, FOREVER...
WH-WHAT?! OF COURSE. WITH PLEASURE.
I...
I'D BE HAPPY TO.
NOW THEN, THIS WAY.

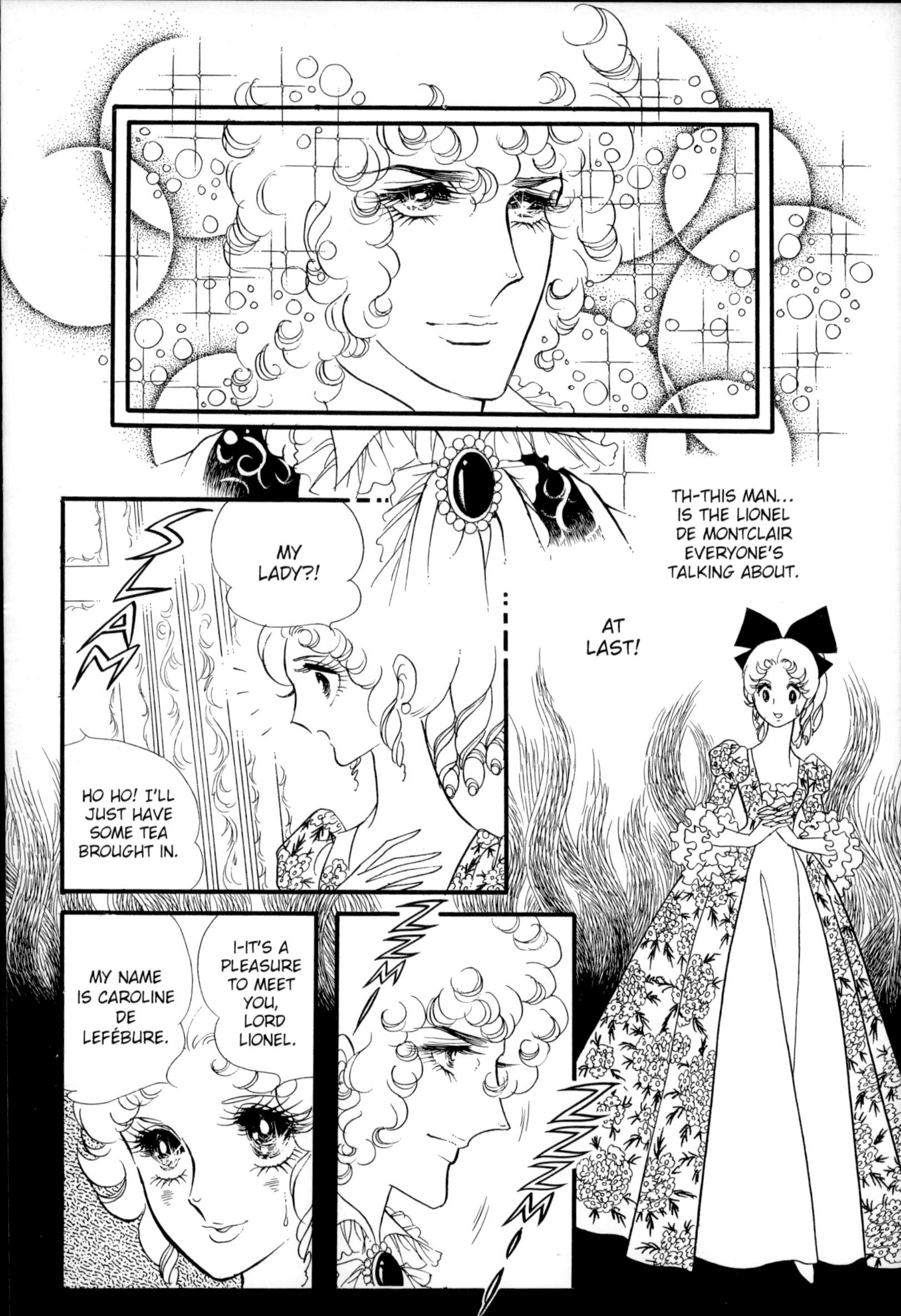
TH-THIS MAN... IS THE LIONEL DE MONTCLAIR EVERYONE'S TALKING ABOUT.
AT LAST!
MY LADY?!
SLAM
HO HO! I'LL JUST HAVE SOME TEA BROUGHT IN.
I-IT'S A PLEASURE TO MEET YOU, LORD LIONEL.
MY NAME IS CAROLINE DE LEFÉBURE.

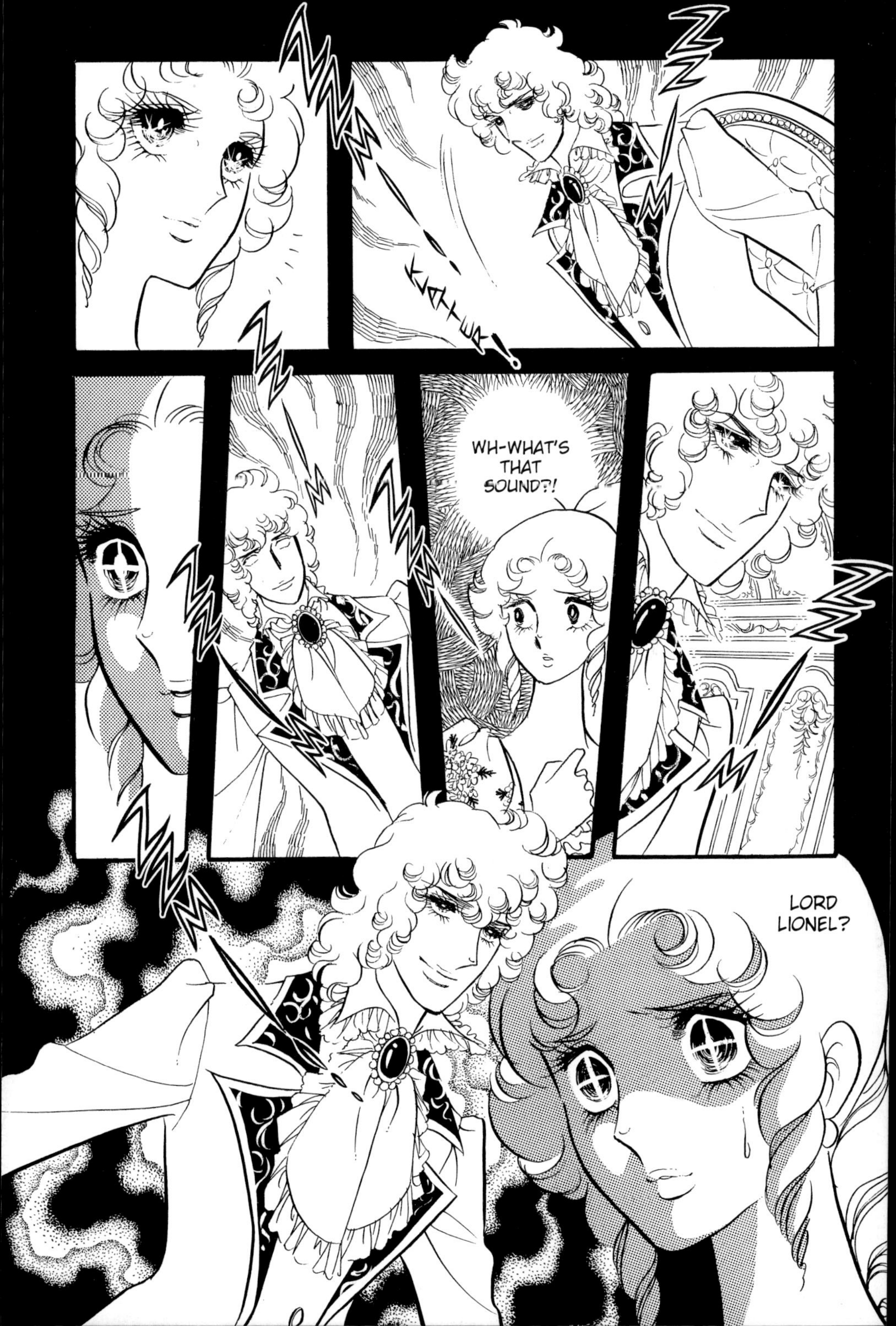
KLATTER!
WH-WHAT'S THAT SOUND?!
LORD LIONEL?

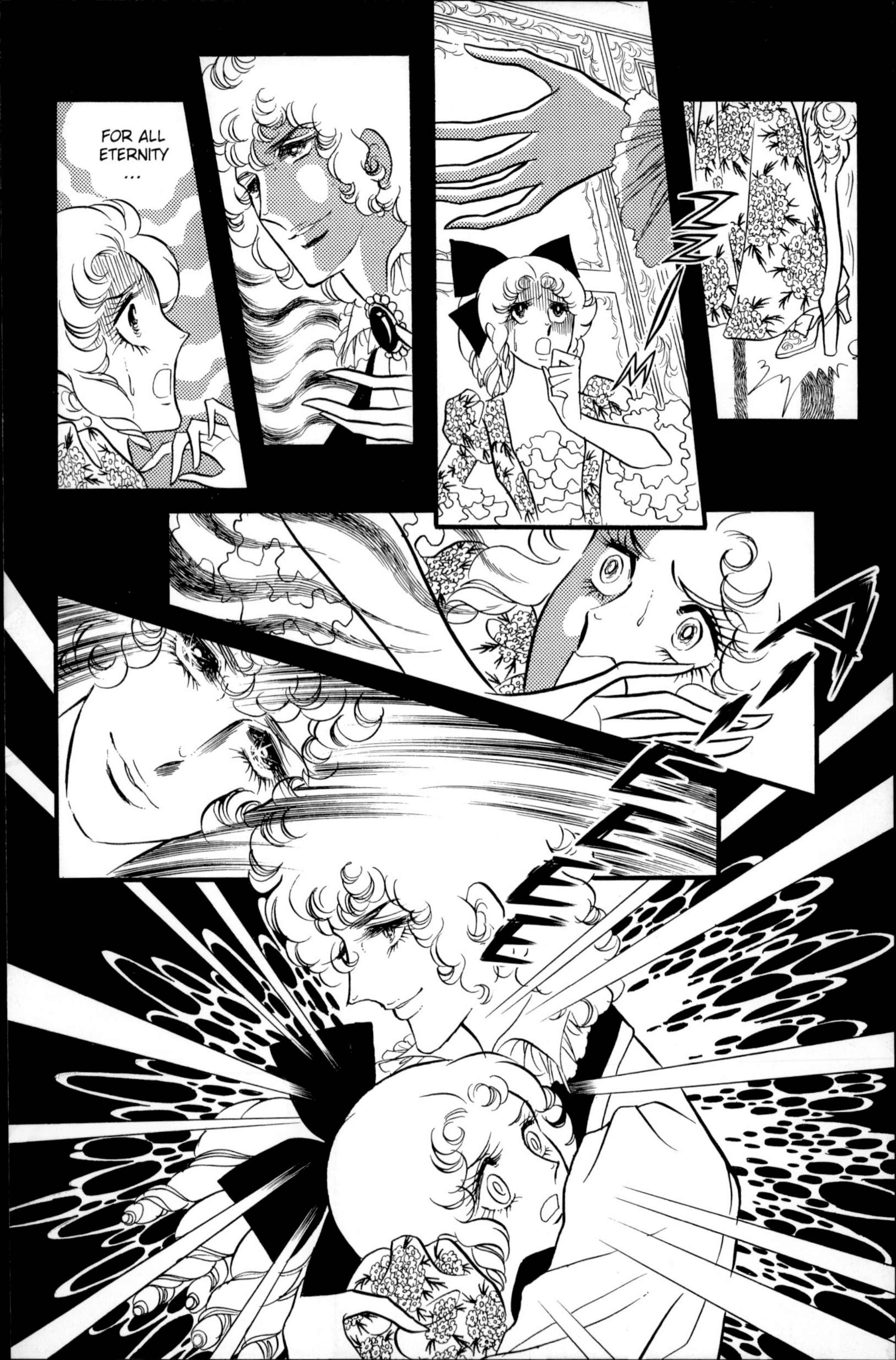
FOR ALL ETERNITY ...

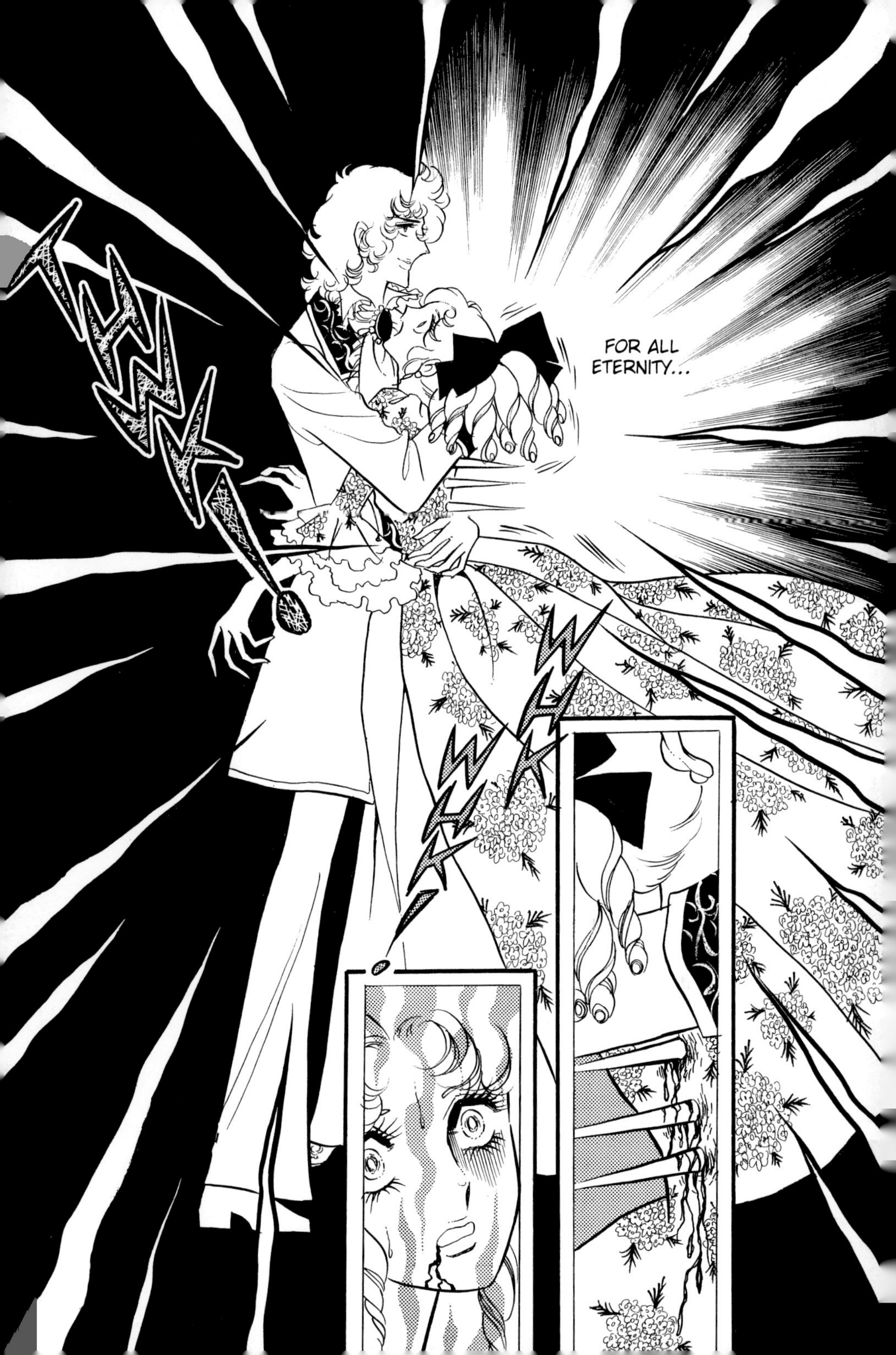
FOR ALL ETERNITY...
WHK
WHK!
THWK!

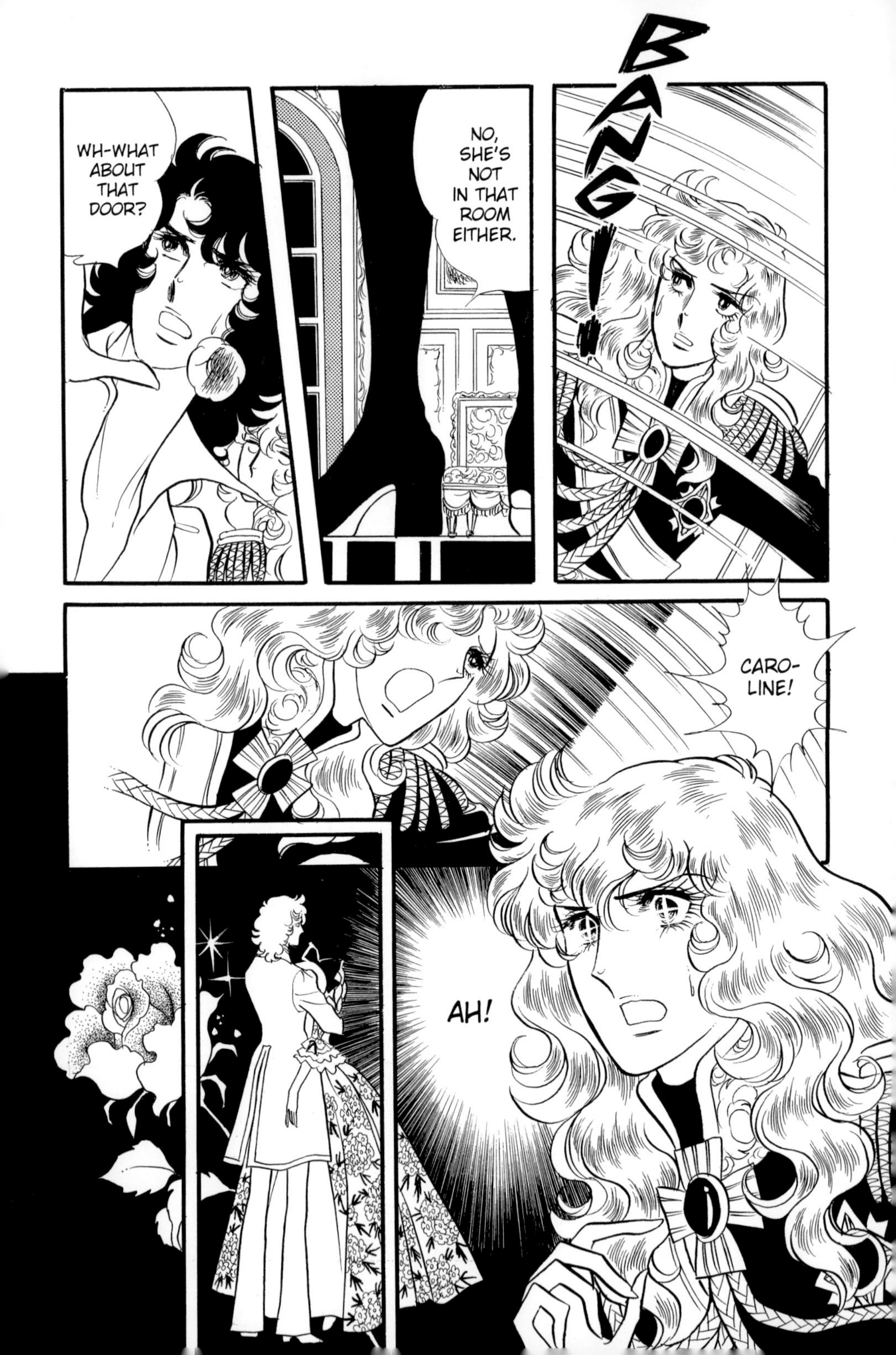
BANG
NO, SHE'S NOT IN THAT ROOM EITHER.
WH-WHAT ABOUT THAT DOOR?
CARO-LINE!
AH!

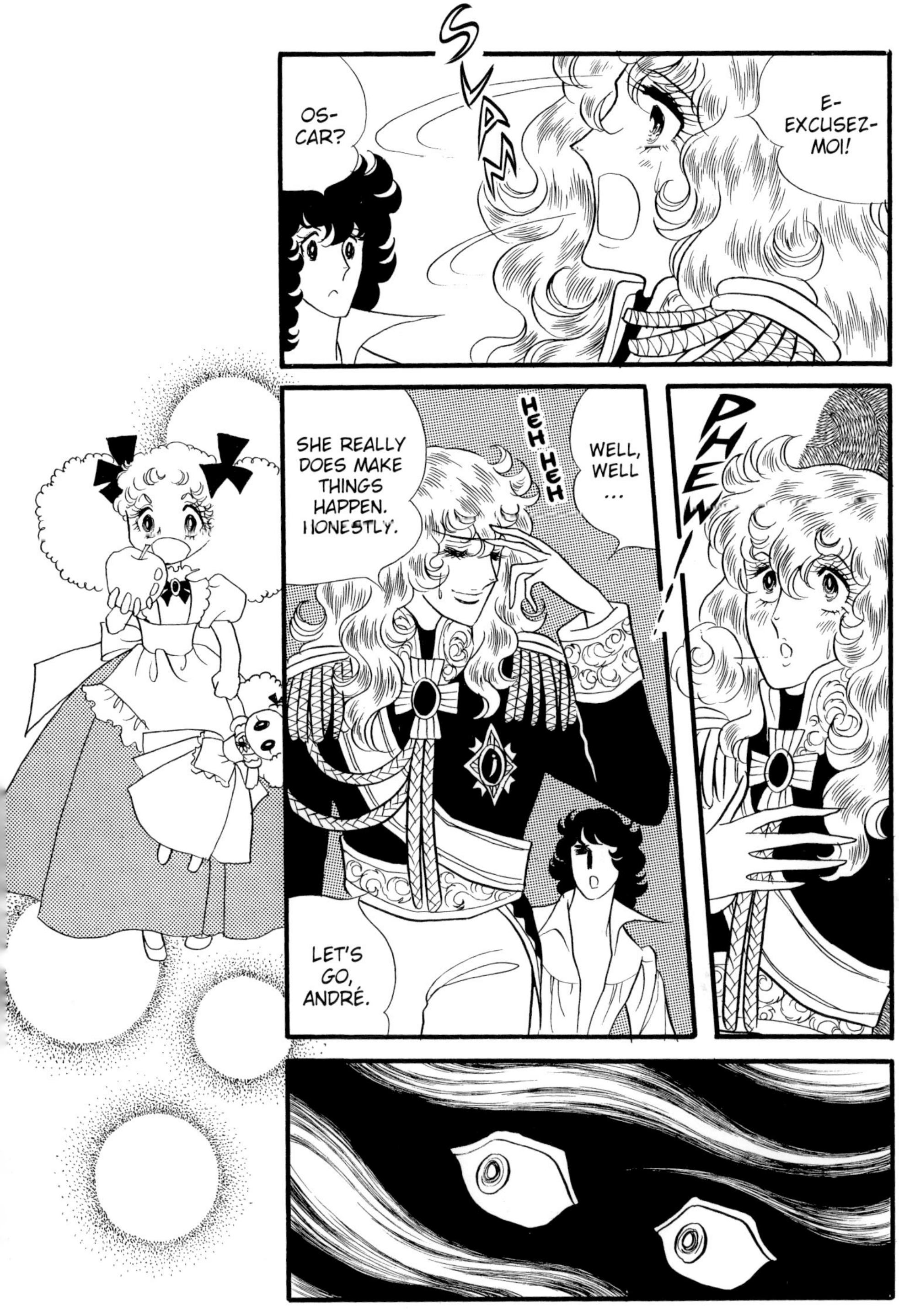
E-EXCUSEZ-MOI!
SLAM
OS-CAR?
PHEW!
WELL, WELL ...
HEH HEH
SHE REALLY DOES MAKE THINGS HAPPEN. HONESTLY.
LET'S GO, ANDRÉ.

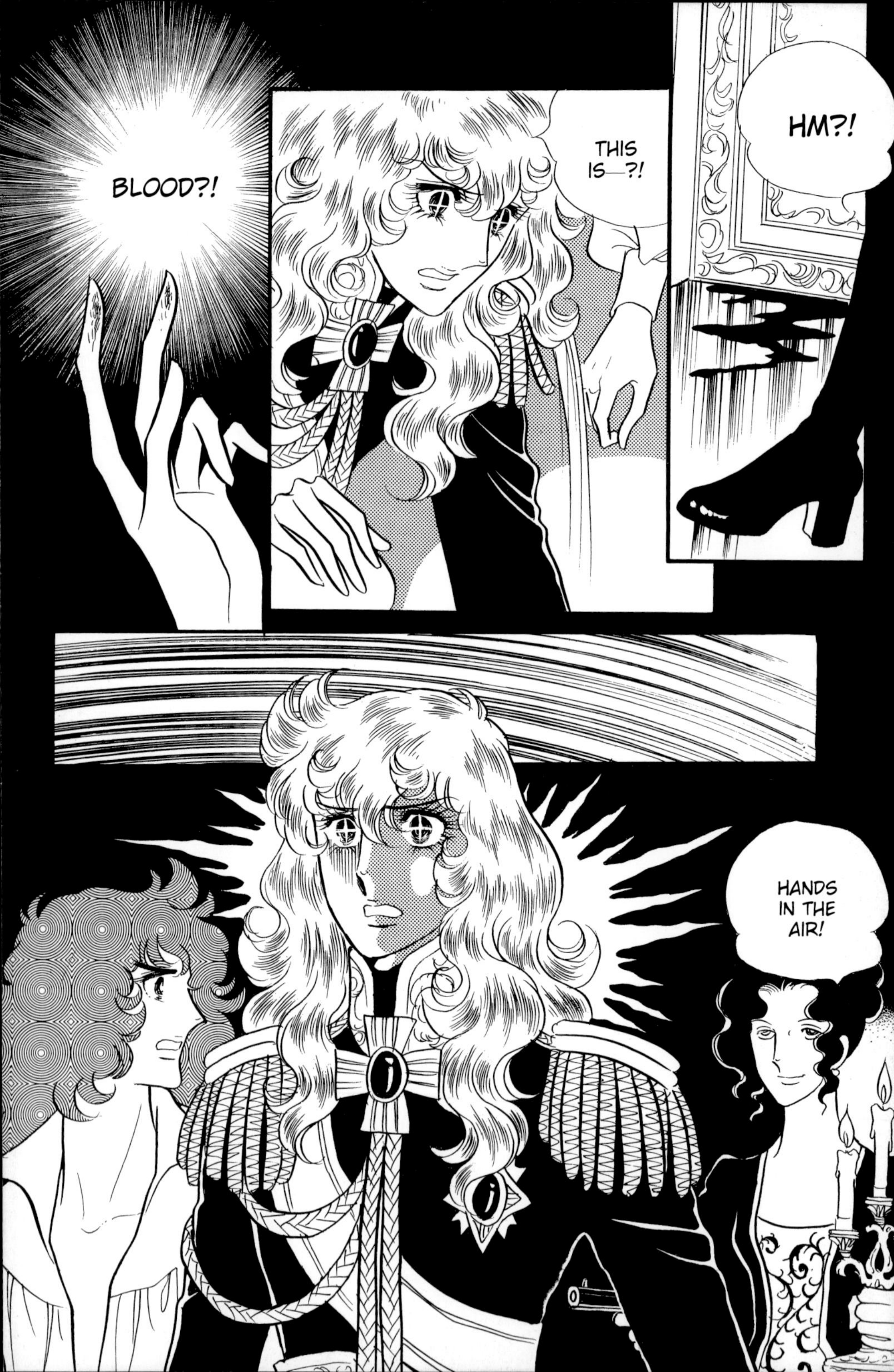
HM?!
THIS IS—?!
BLOOD?!
HANDS IN THE AIR!

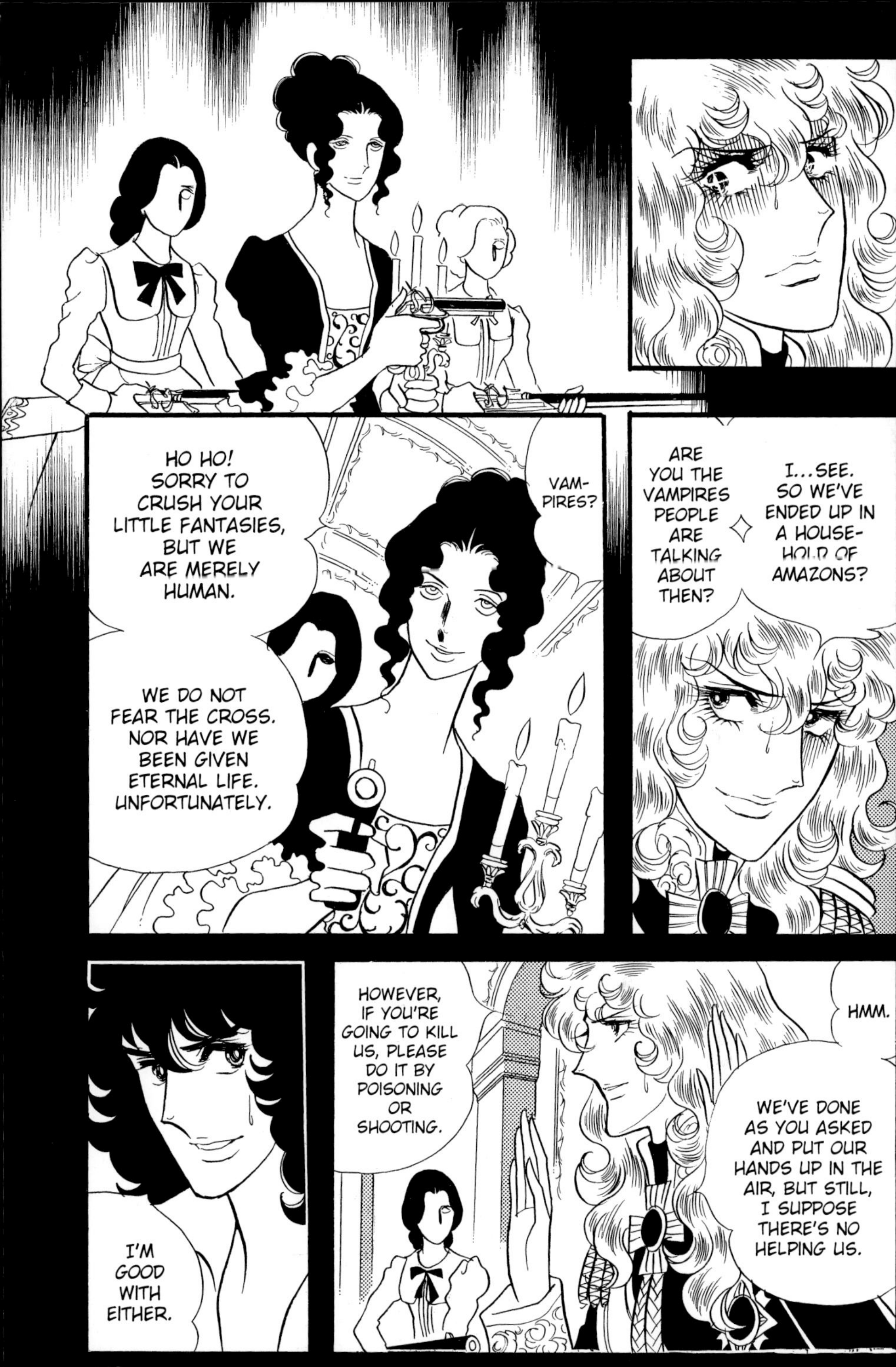

I...SEE. SO WE'VE ENDED UP IN A HOUSE-HOLD OF AMAZONS?
ARE YOU THE VAMPIRES PEOPLE ARE TALKING ABOUT THEN?
VAM-PIRES?
HO HO! SORRY TO CRUSH YOUR LITTLE FANTASIES, BUT WE ARE MERELY HUMAN.
WE DO NOT FEAR THE CROSS. NOR HAVE WE BEEN GIVEN ETERNAL LIFE. UNFORTUNATELY.
HMM.
WE'VE DONE AS YOU ASKED AND PUT OUR HANDS UP IN THE AIR, BUT STILL, I SUPPOSE THERE'S NO HELPING US.
HOWEVER, IF YOU'RE GOING TO KILL US, PLEASE DO IT BY POISONING OR SHOOTING.
I'M GOOD WITH EITHER.

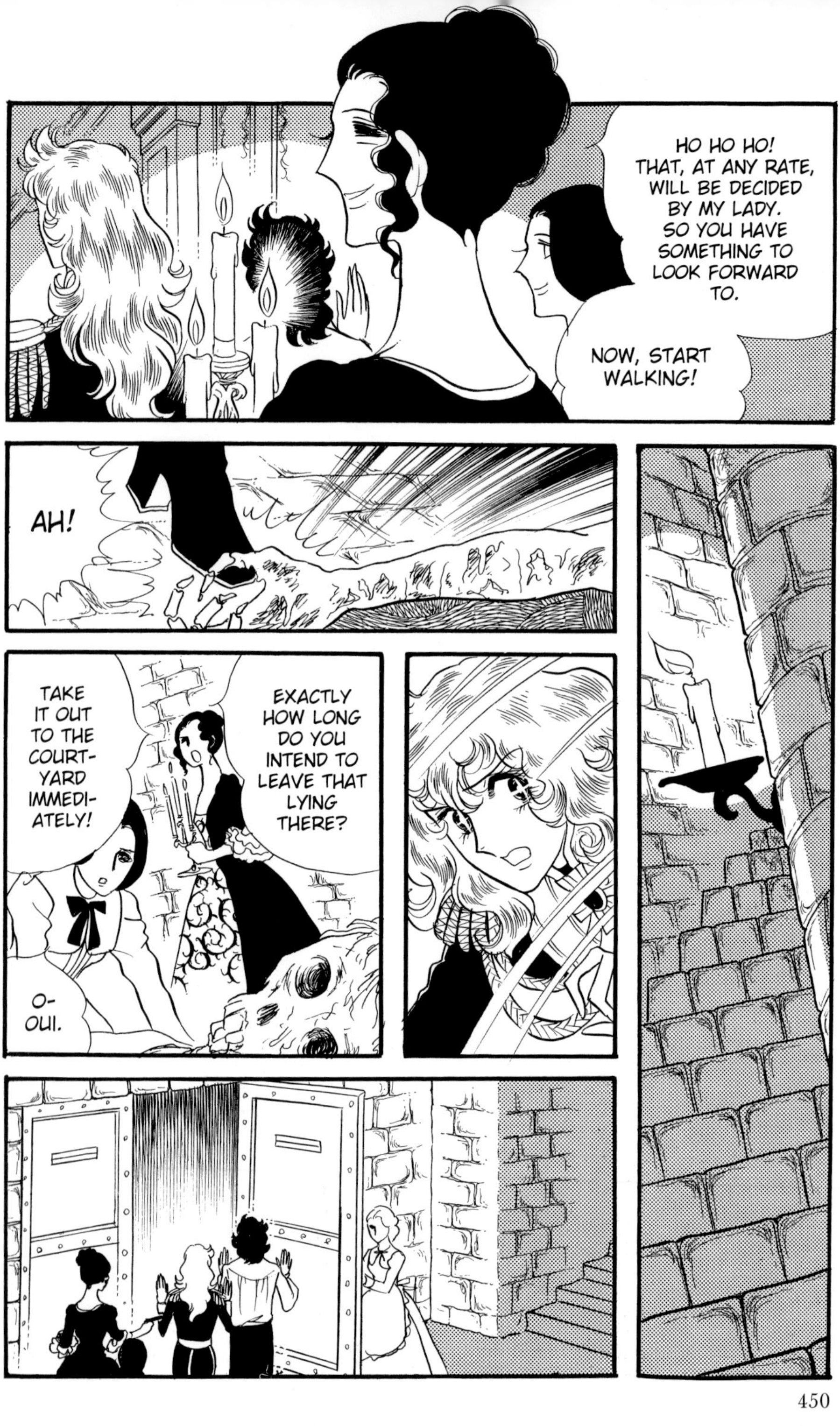
HO HO HO! THAT, AT ANY RATE, WILL BE DECIDED BY MY LADY. SO YOU HAVE SOMETHING TO LOOK FORWARD TO.
NOW, START WALKING!
AH!
EXACTLY HOW LONG DO YOU INTEND TO LEAVE THAT LYING THERE?
TAKE IT OUT TO THE COURT-YARD IMMEDI-ATELY!
O-OUI.

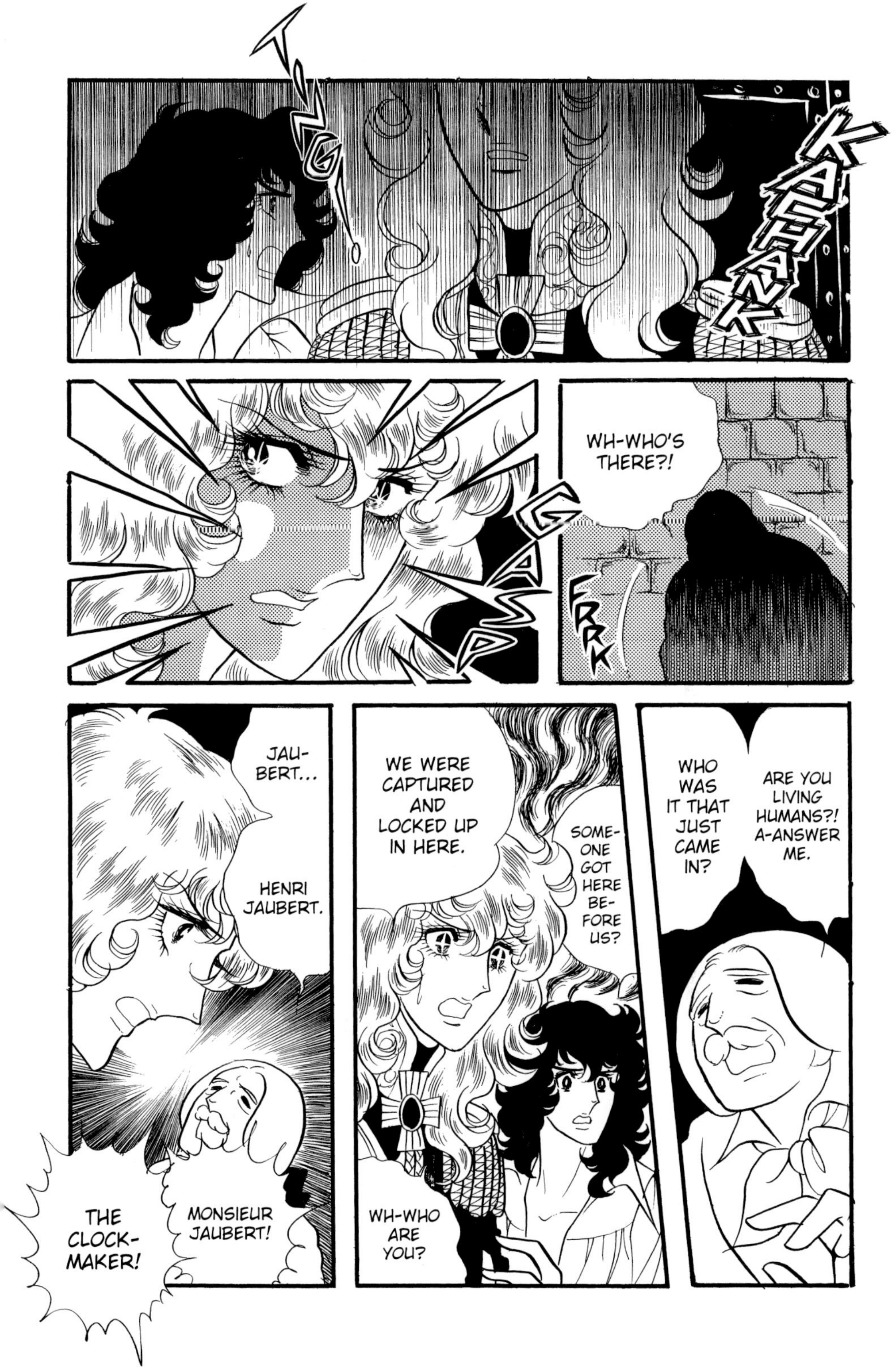
KACHANK
TING
WH-WHO'S THERE?!
FRRK
GASP
ARE YOU LIVING HUMANS?! A-ANSWER ME.
WHO WAS IT THAT JUST CAME IN?
SOME-ONE GOT HERE BEFORE US?
WE WERE CAPTURED AND LOCKED UP IN HERE.
WH-WHO ARE YOU?
JAU-BERT...
HENRI JAUBERT.
MONSIEUR JAUBERT!
THE CLOCK-MAKER!

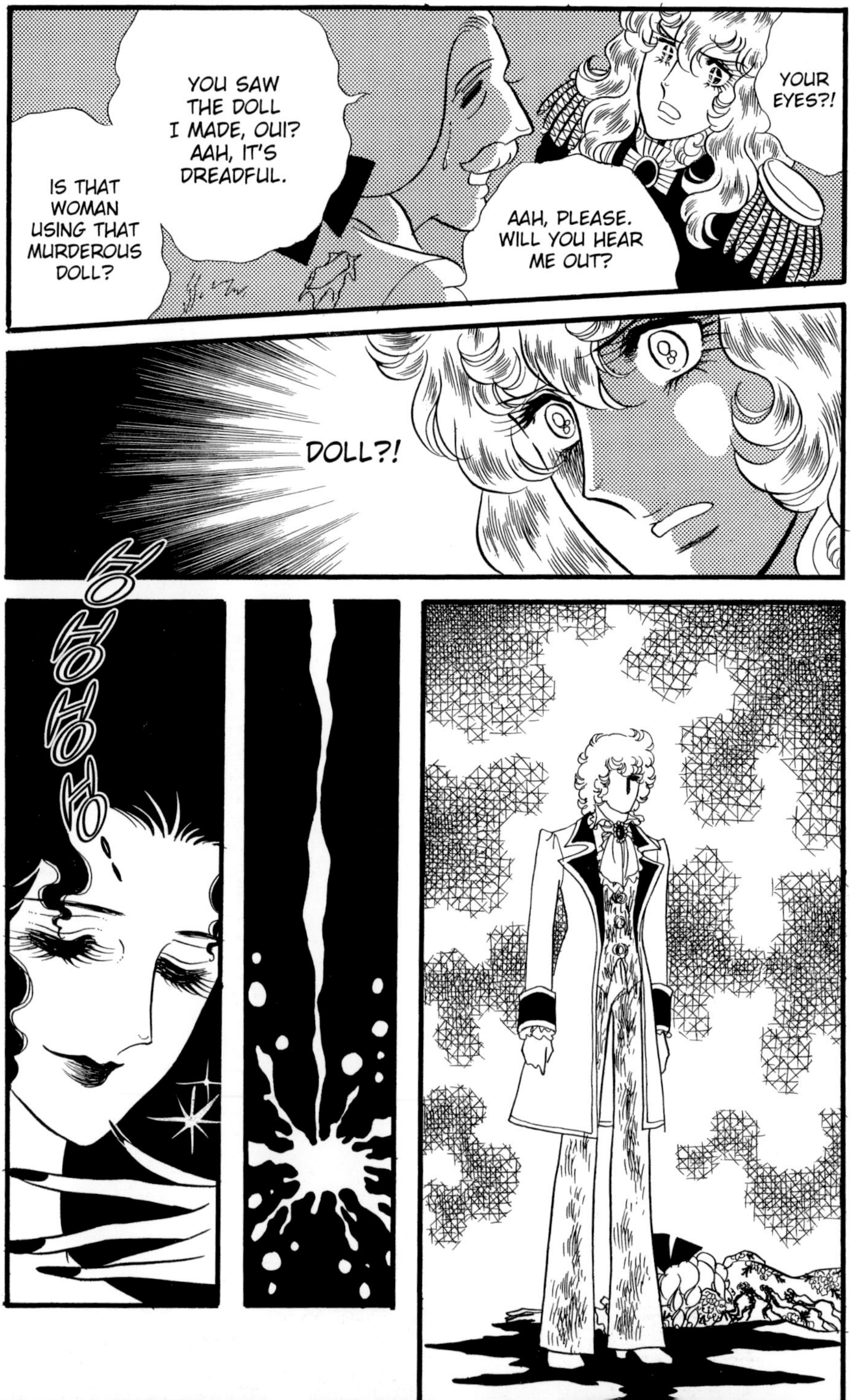
YOUR EYES?!
AAH, PLEASE. WILL YOU HEAR ME OUT?
YOU SAW THE DOLL I MADE, OUI? AAH, IT'S DREADFUL.
IS THAT WOMAN USING THAT MURDEROUS DOLL?
DOLL?!
HOHOHOHO

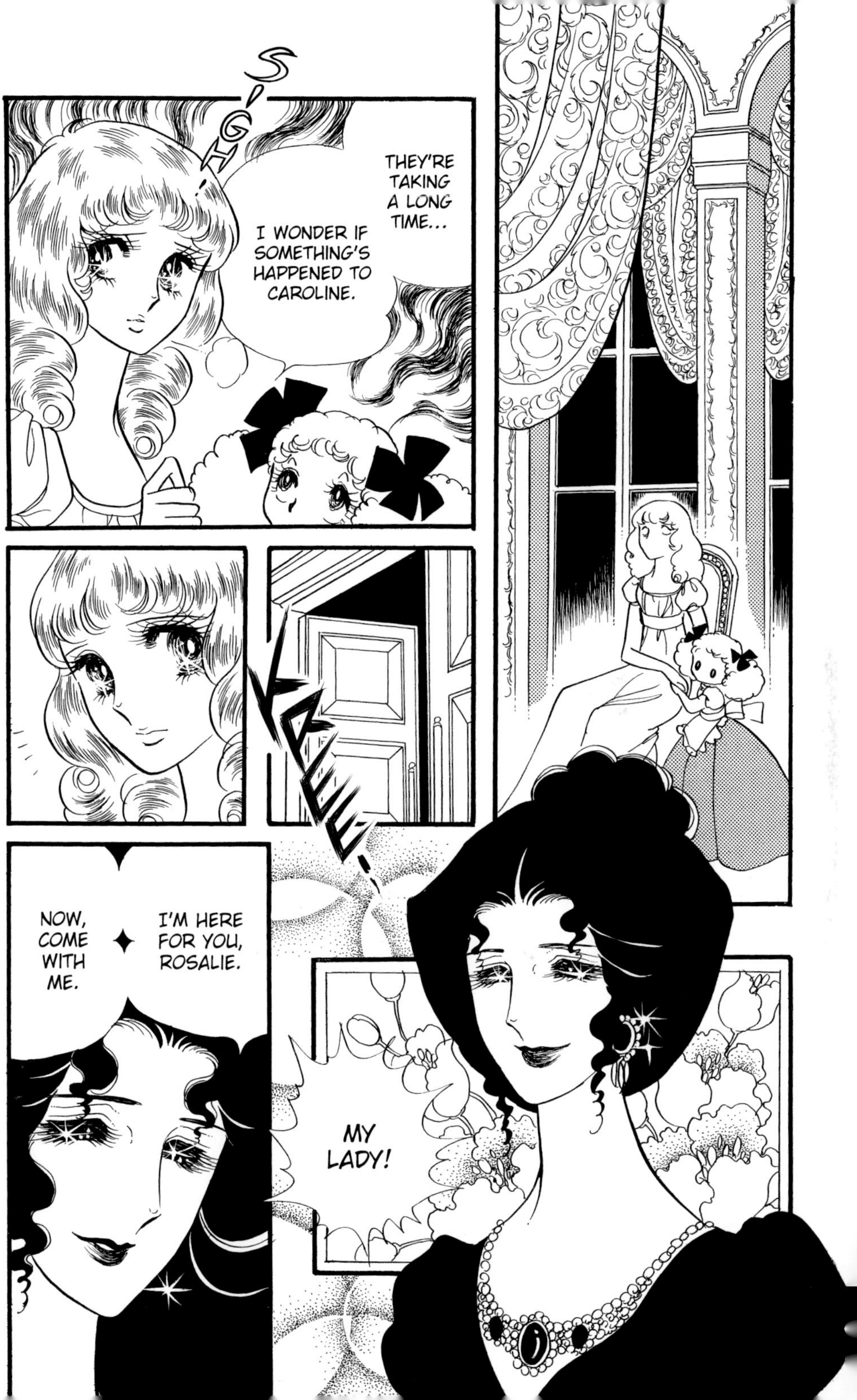
SIGH!
THEY'RE TAKING A LONG TIME...
I WONDER IF SOMETHING'S HAPPENED TO CAROLINE.
KREEE...
MY LADY!
I'M HERE FOR YOU, ROSALIE.
NOW, COME WITH ME.

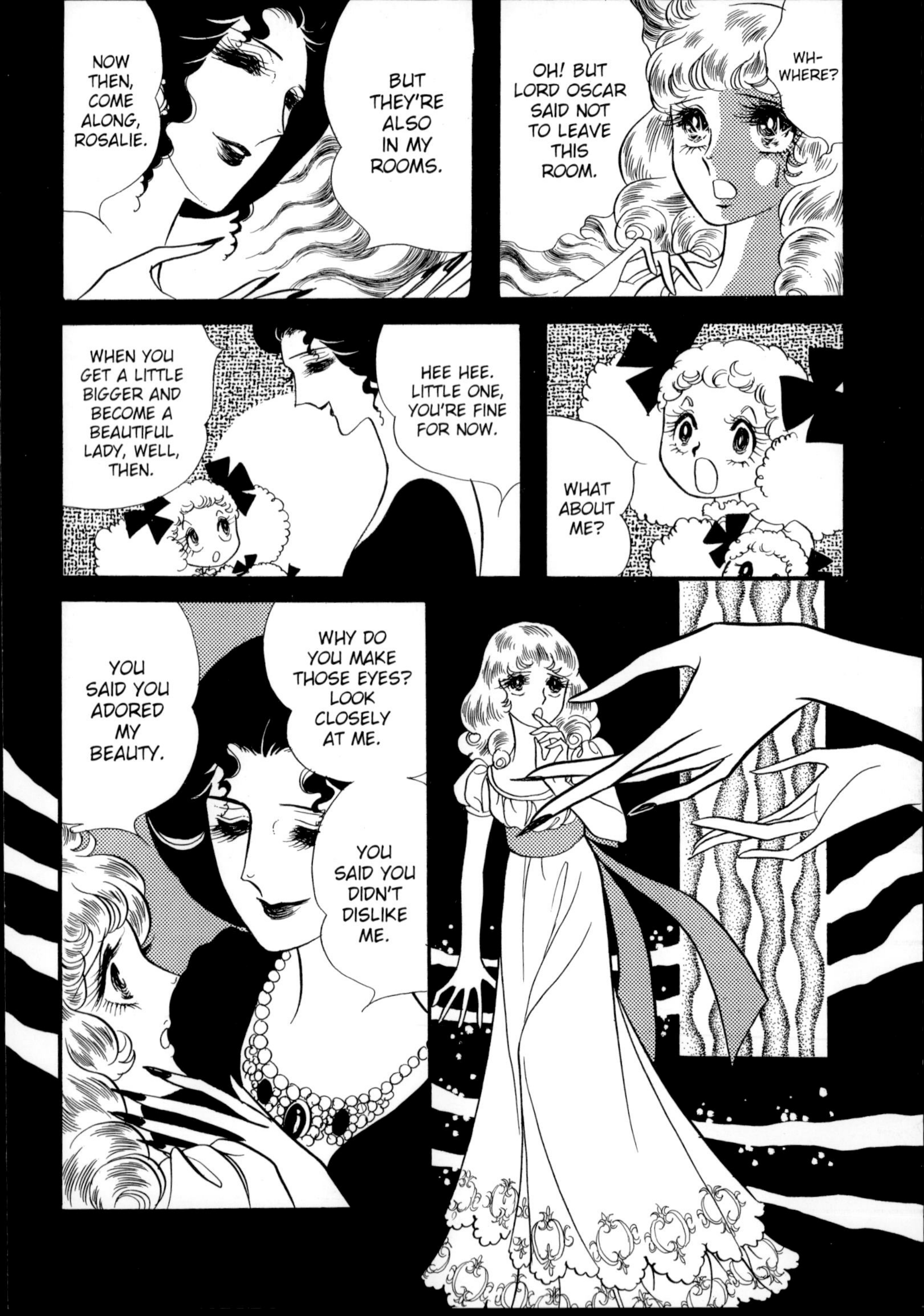
WH- WHERE?
OH! BUT LORD OSCAR SAID NOT TO LEAVE THIS ROOM.
BUT THEY'RE ALSO IN MY ROOMS.
NOW THEN, COME ALONG, ROSALIE.
WHAT ABOUT ME?
HEE HEE. LITTLE ONE, YOU'RE FINE FOR NOW.
WHEN YOU GET A LITTLE BIGGER AND BECOME A BEAUTIFUL LADY, WELL, THEN.
WHY DO YOU MAKE THOSE EYES? LOOK CLOSELY AT ME.
YOU SAID YOU DIDN'T DISLIKE ME.
YOU SAID YOU ADORED MY BEAUTY.

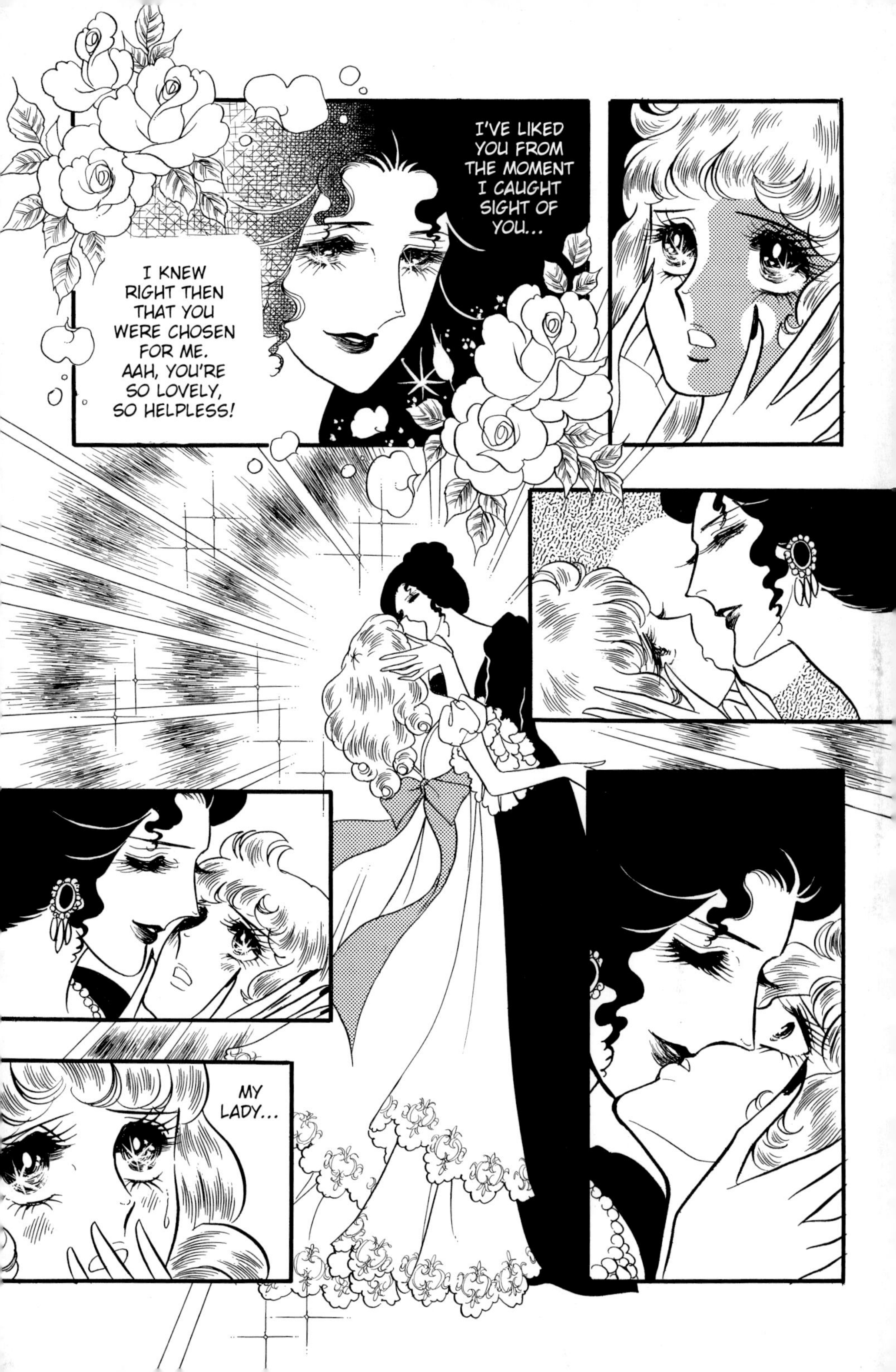
I'VE LIKED YOU FROM THE MOMENT I CAUGHT SIGHT OF YOU...
I KNEW RIGHT THEN THAT YOU WERE CHOSEN FOR ME. AAH, YOU'RE SO LOVELY, SO HELPLESS!
MY LADY...

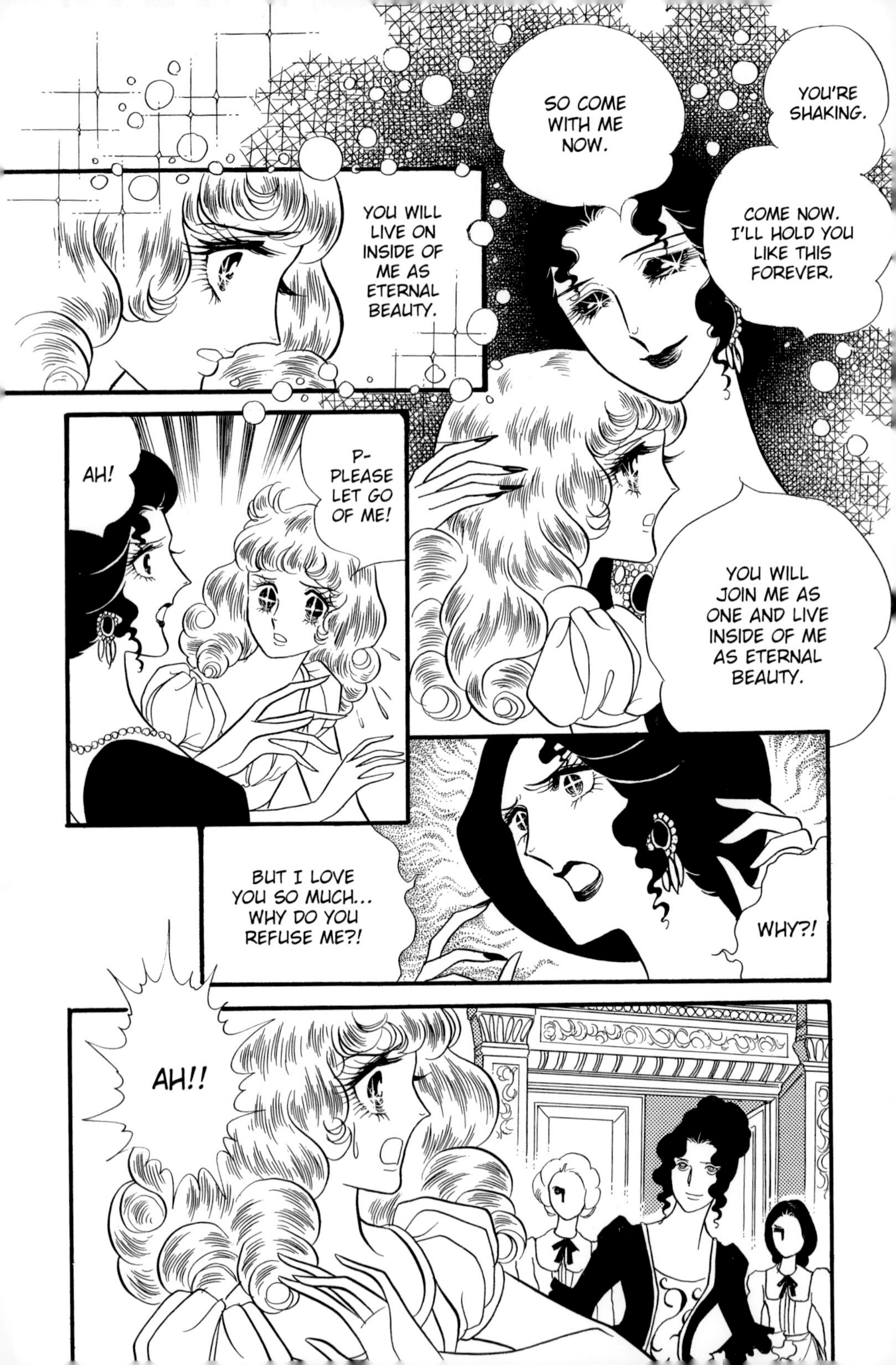
YOU'RE SHAKING.
SO COME WITH ME NOW.
COME NOW. I'LL HOLD YOU LIKE THIS FOREVER.
YOU WILL JOIN ME AS ONE AND LIVE INSIDE OF ME AS ETERNAL BEAUTY.
YOU WILL LIVE ON INSIDE OF ME AS ETERNAL BEAUTY.
P-PLEASE LET GO OF ME!
AH!
WHY?!
BUT I LOVE YOU SO MUCH... WHY DO YOU REFUSE ME?!
AH!!

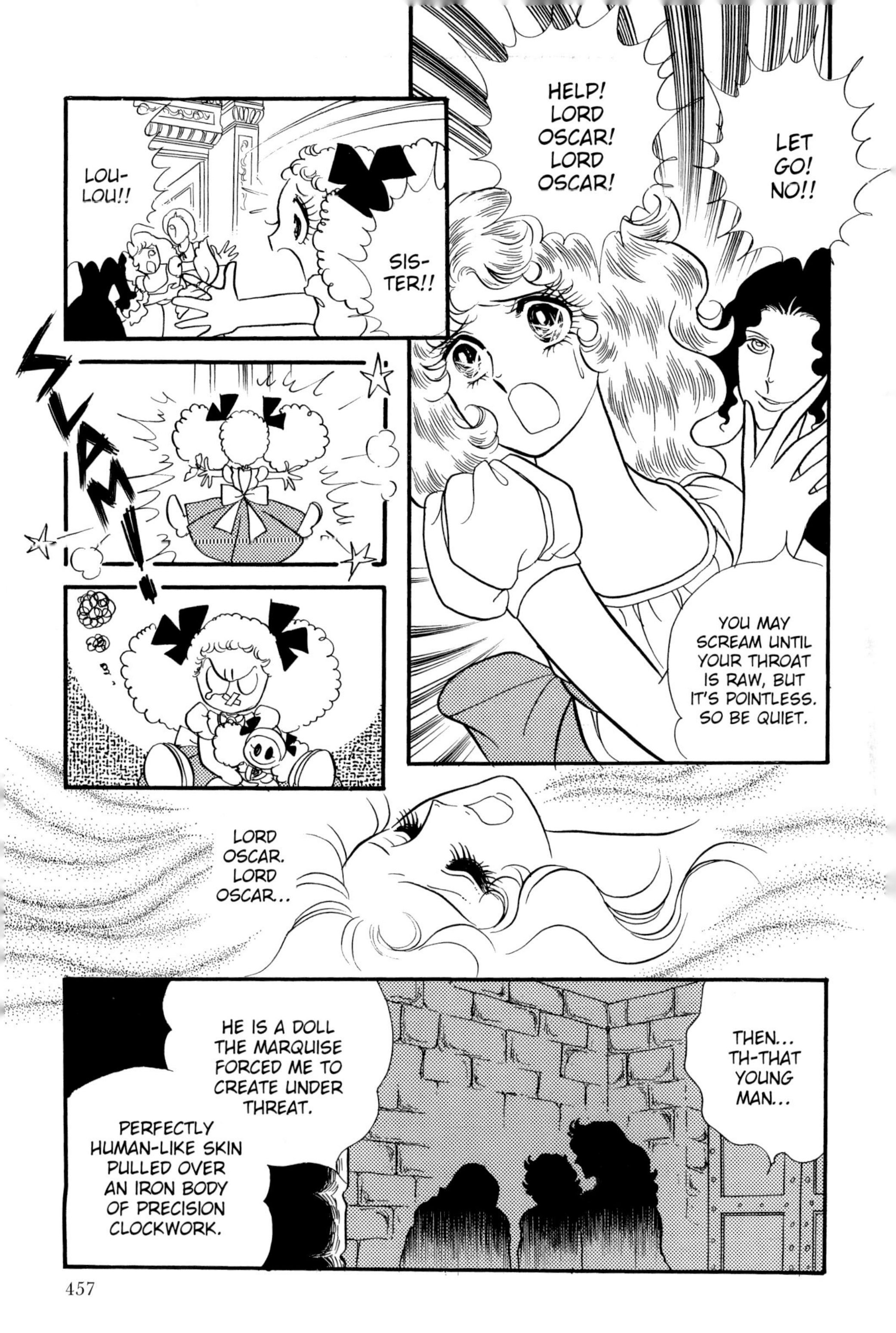
LET GO! NO!!
HELP! LORD OSCAR! LORD OSCAR!
YOU MAY SCREAM UNTIL YOUR THROAT IS RAW, BUT IT'S POINTLESS. SO BE QUIET.
SIS-TER!!
LOU-LOU!!
SLAM!!
LORD OSCAR. LORD OSCAR...
THEN... TH-THAT YOUNG MAN...
HE IS A DOLL THE MARQUISE FORCED ME TO CREATE UNDER THREAT.
PERFECTLY HUMAN-LIKE SKIN PULLED OVER AN IRON BODY OF PRECISION CLOCKWORK.

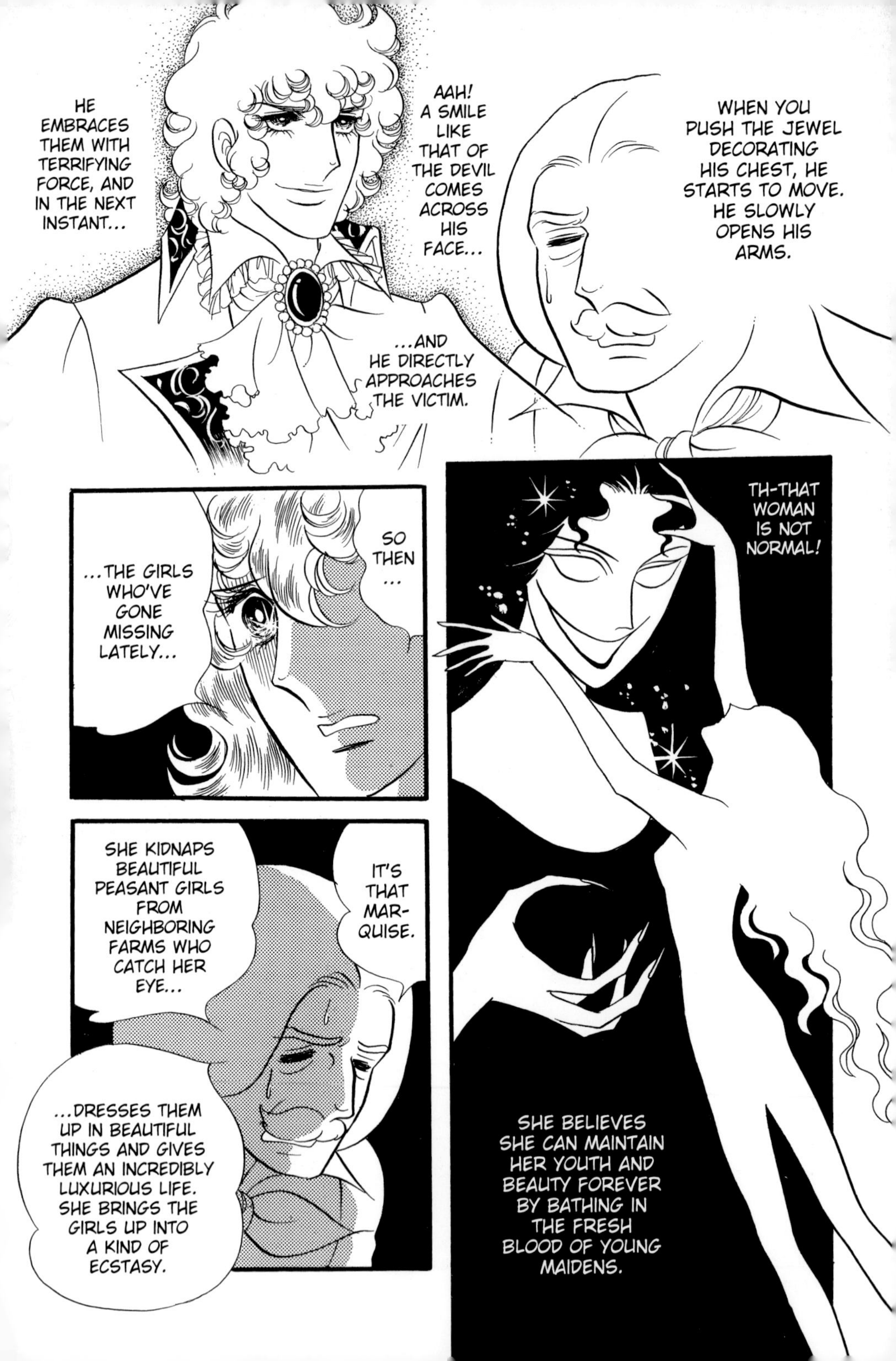
WHEN YOU PUSH THE JEWEL DECORATING HIS CHEST, HE STARTS TO MOVE. HE SLOWLY OPENS HIS ARMS.
AAH! A SMILE LIKE THAT OF THE DEVIL COMES ACROSS HIS FACE...
HE EMBRACES THEM WITH TERRIFYING FORCE, AND IN THE NEXT INSTANT...
...AND HE DIRECTLY APPROACHES THE VICTIM.
TH-THAT WOMAN IS NOT NORMAL!
SHE BELIEVES SHE CAN MAINTAIN HER YOUTH AND BEAUTY FOREVER BY BATHING IN THE FRESH BLOOD OF YOUNG MAIDENS.
SO THEN ...
...THE GIRLS WHO'VE GONE MISSING LATELY...
IT'S THAT MAR-QUISE.
SHE KIDNAPS BEAUTIFUL PEASANT GIRLS FROM NEIGHBORING FARMS WHO CATCH HER EYE...
...DRESSES THEM UP IN BEAUTIFUL THINGS AND GIVES THEM AN INCREDIBLY LUXURIOUS LIFE. SHE BRINGS THE GIRLS UP INTO A KIND OF ECSTASY.

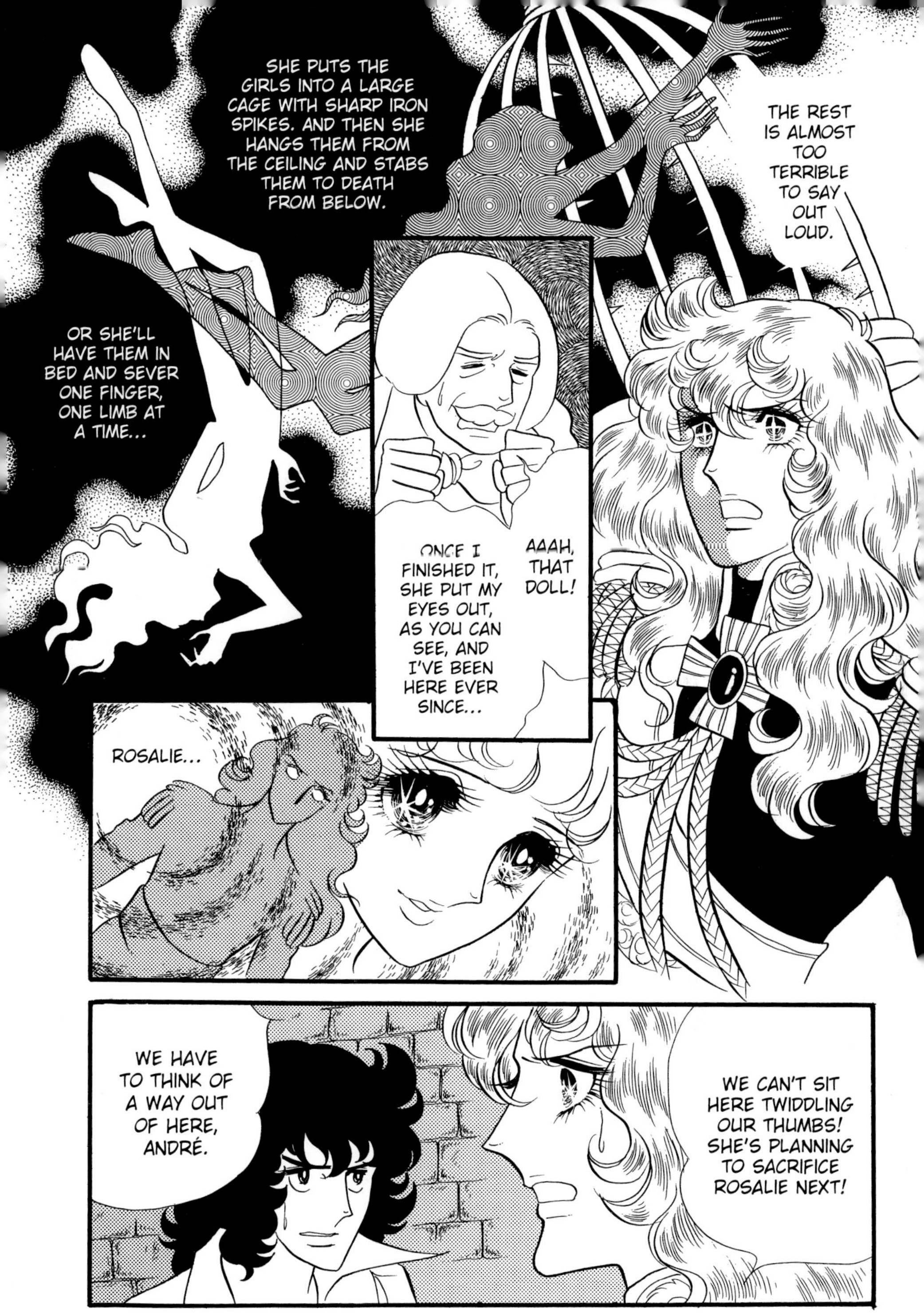
THE REST IS ALMOST TOO TERRIBLE TO SAY OUT LOUD.
SHE PUTS THE GIRLS INTO A LARGE CAGE WITH SHARP IRON SPIKES. AND THEN SHE HANGS THEM FROM THE CEILING AND STABS THEM TO DEATH FROM BELOW.
OR SHE'LL HAVE THEM IN BED AND SEVER ONE FINGER, ONE LIMB AT A TIME...
AAAH, THAT DOLL!
ONCE I FINISHED IT, SHE PUT MY EYES OUT, AS YOU CAN SEE, AND I'VE BEEN HERE EVER SINCE...
ROSALIE...
WE CAN'T SIT HERE TWIDDLING OUR THUMBS! SHE'S PLANNING TO SACRIFICE ROSALIE NEXT!
WE HAVE TO THINK OF A WAY OUT OF HERE, ANDRÉ.

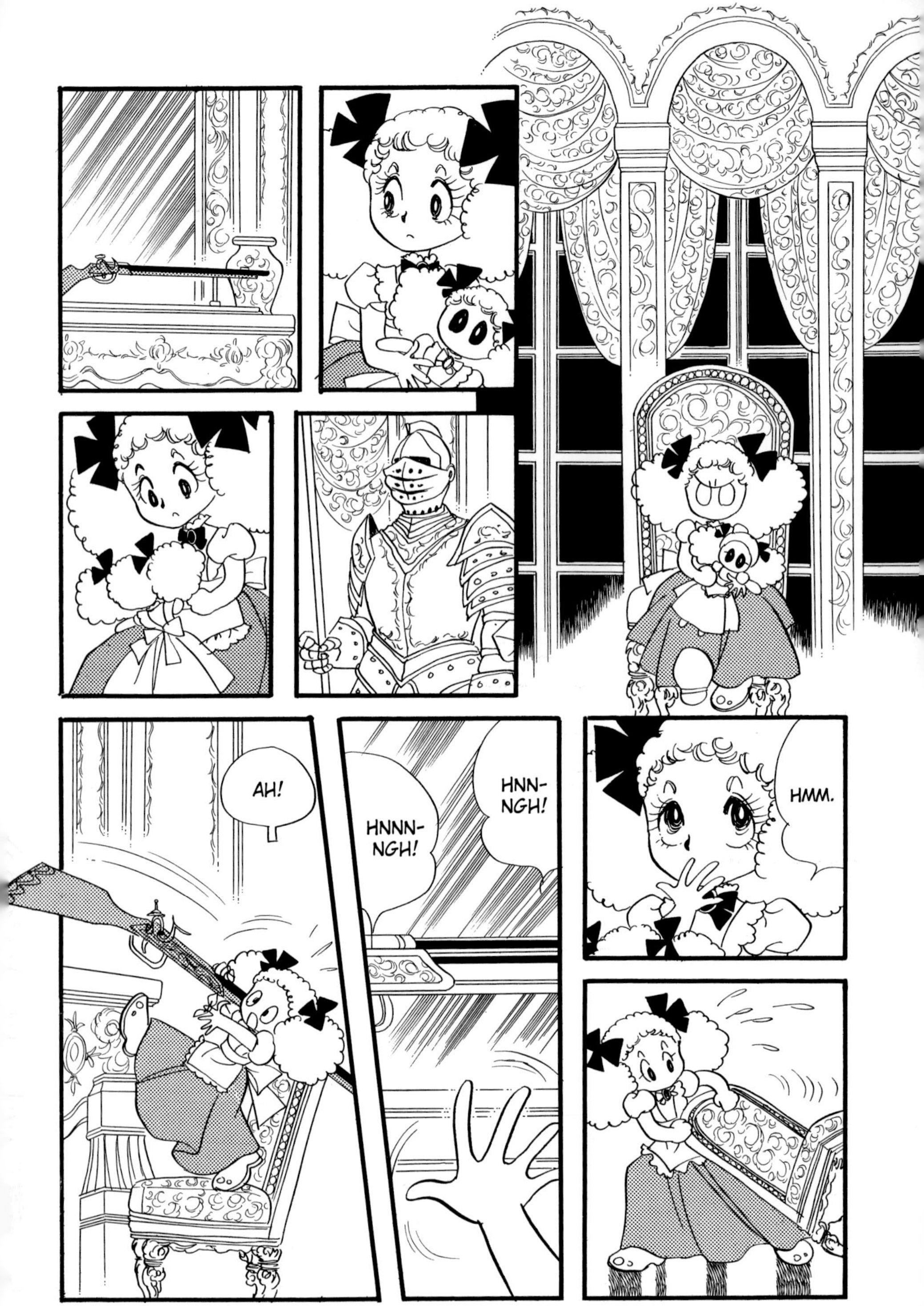
HMM.
HNN-NGH!
HNNN-NGH!
AH!

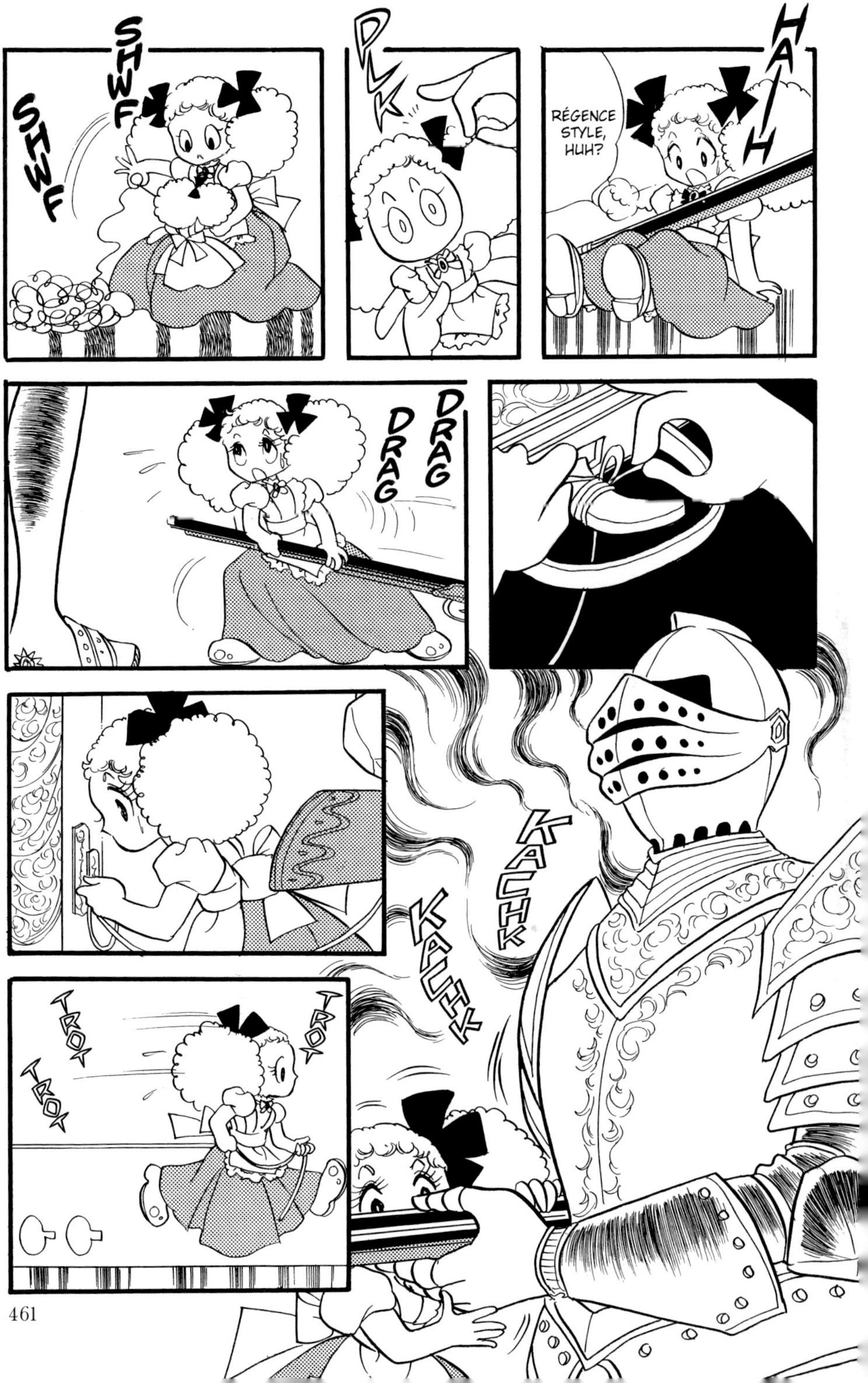
HAH
RÉGENCE STYLE, HUH?
DLLK
SHWF
SHWF
DRAG
DRAG
KACHK
KACHK
TROT
TROT
TROT

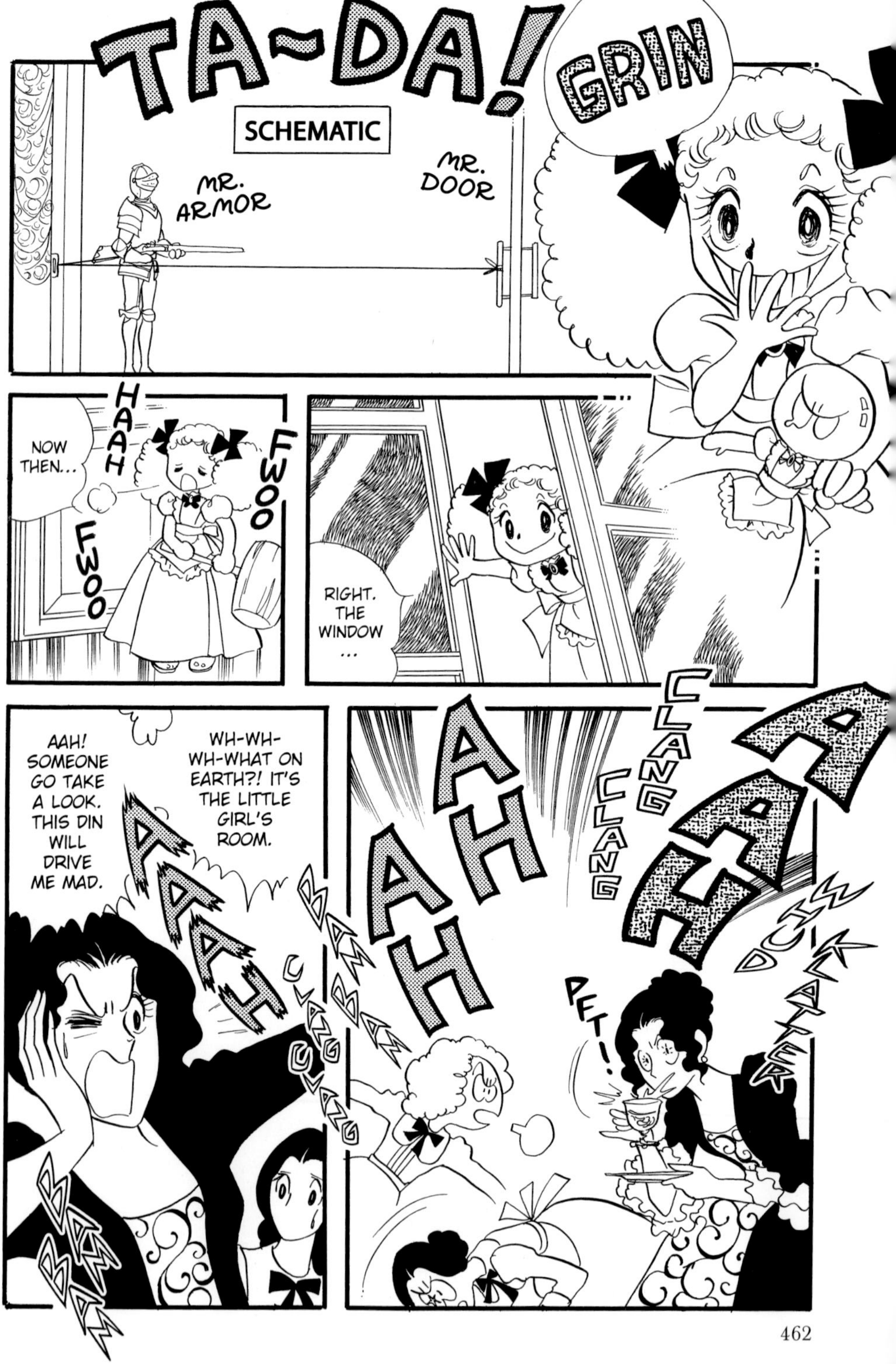
GRIN
TA-DA!
SCHEMATIC
MR. DOOR
MR. ARMOR
RIGHT. THE WINDOW ...
NOW THEN...
HAAH
FWOO
FWOO
CLANG
CLANG
PFT!
CLATTER
WH-WH-WH-WHAT ON EARTH?! IT'S THE LITTLE GIRL'S ROOM.
AAH! SOMEONE GO TAKE A LOOK. THIS DIN WILL DRIVE ME MAD.
AAAH

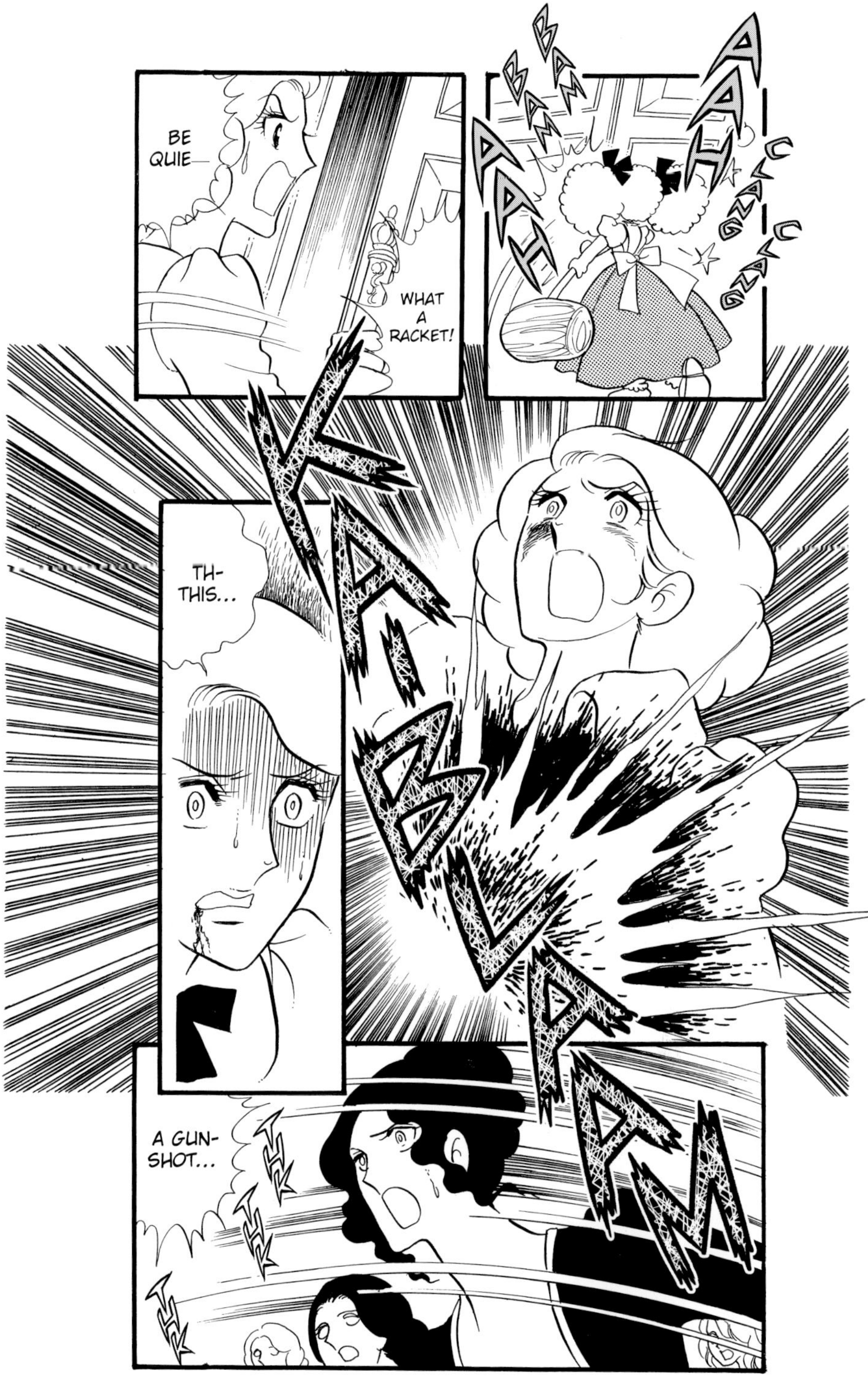
AAH
AAH
BAM
BAM
CLANG
CLANG
BE QUIE—
WHAT A RACKET!
KABLAM
TH- THIS...
A GUN-SHOT...
THK
THK
THK

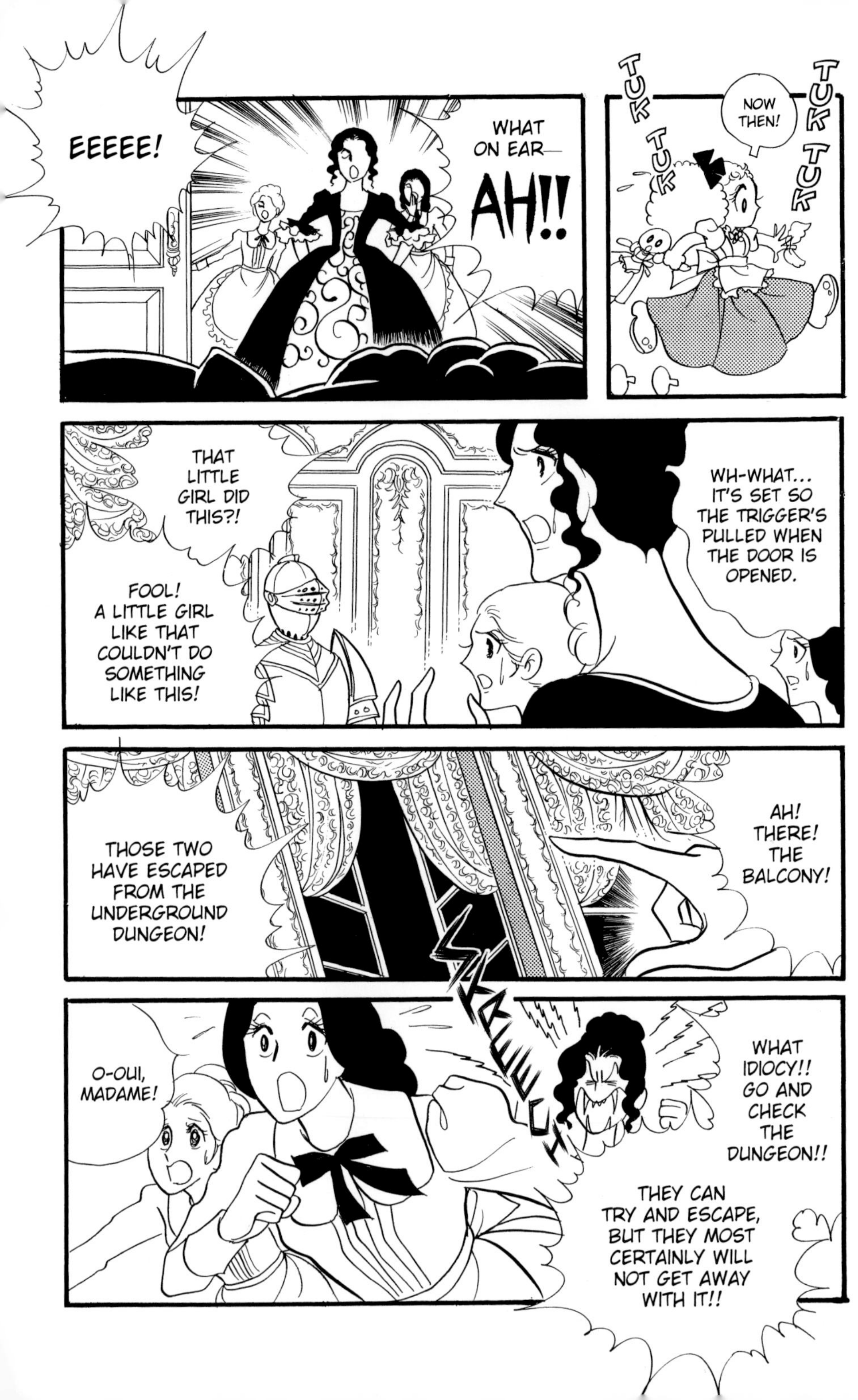

TUK TUK
NOW THEN!
TUK TUK
WHAT ON EAR—
AH!!
EEEEE!
WH-WHAT... IT'S SET SO THE TRIGGER'S PULLED WHEN THE DOOR IS OPENED.
THAT LITTLE GIRL DID THIS?!
FOOL! A LITTLE GIRL LIKE THAT COULDN'T DO SOMETHING LIKE THIS!
AH! THERE! THE BALCONY!
THOSE TWO HAVE ESCAPED FROM THE UNDERGROUND DUNGEON!
SKREEEECH
WHAT IDIOCY!! GO AND CHECK THE DUNGEON!!
THEY CAN TRY AND ESCAPE, BUT THEY MOST CERTAINLY WILL NOT GET AWAY WITH IT!!
O-OUI, MADAME!

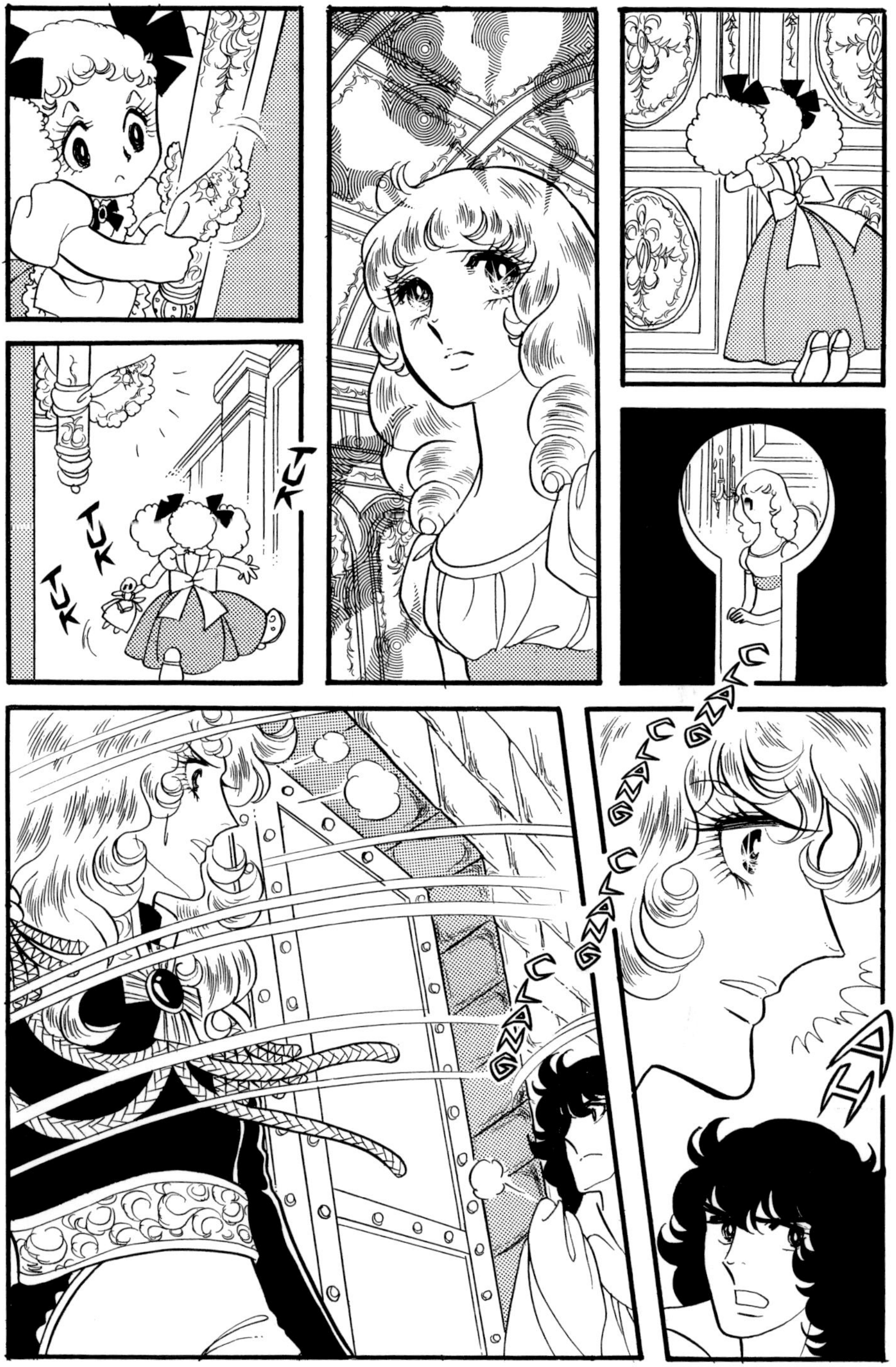
TUK
TUK
TUK
CLANG
CLANG
CLANG
CLANG
HA

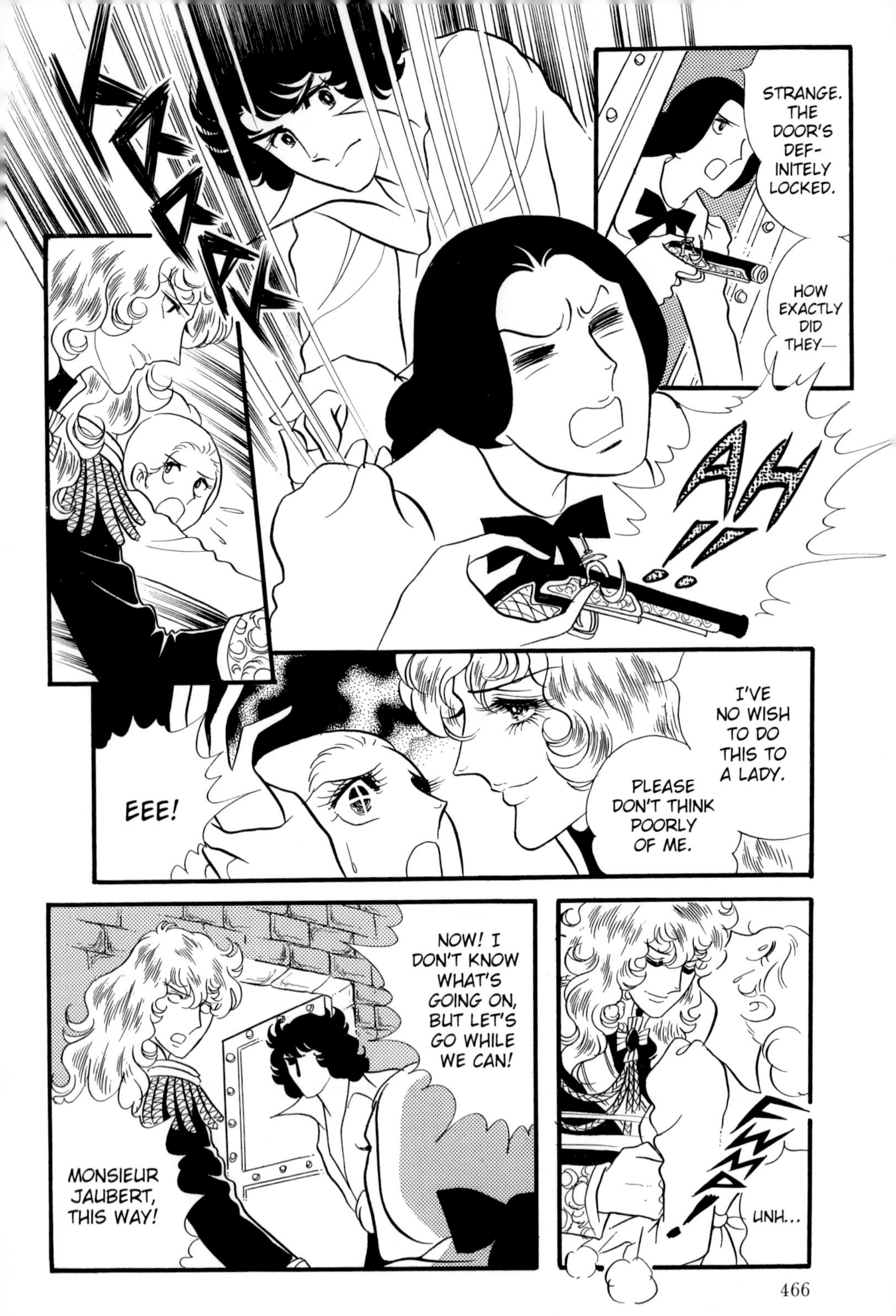
STRANGE. THE DOOR'S DEF- INITELY LOCKED.
HOW EXACTLY DID THEY—
I'VE NO WISH TO DO THIS TO A LADY.
PLEASE DON'T THINK POORLY OF ME.
EEE!
UNH...
NOW! I DON'T KNOW WHAT'S GOING ON, BUT LET'S GO WHILE WE CAN!
MONSIEUR JAUBERT, THIS WAY!

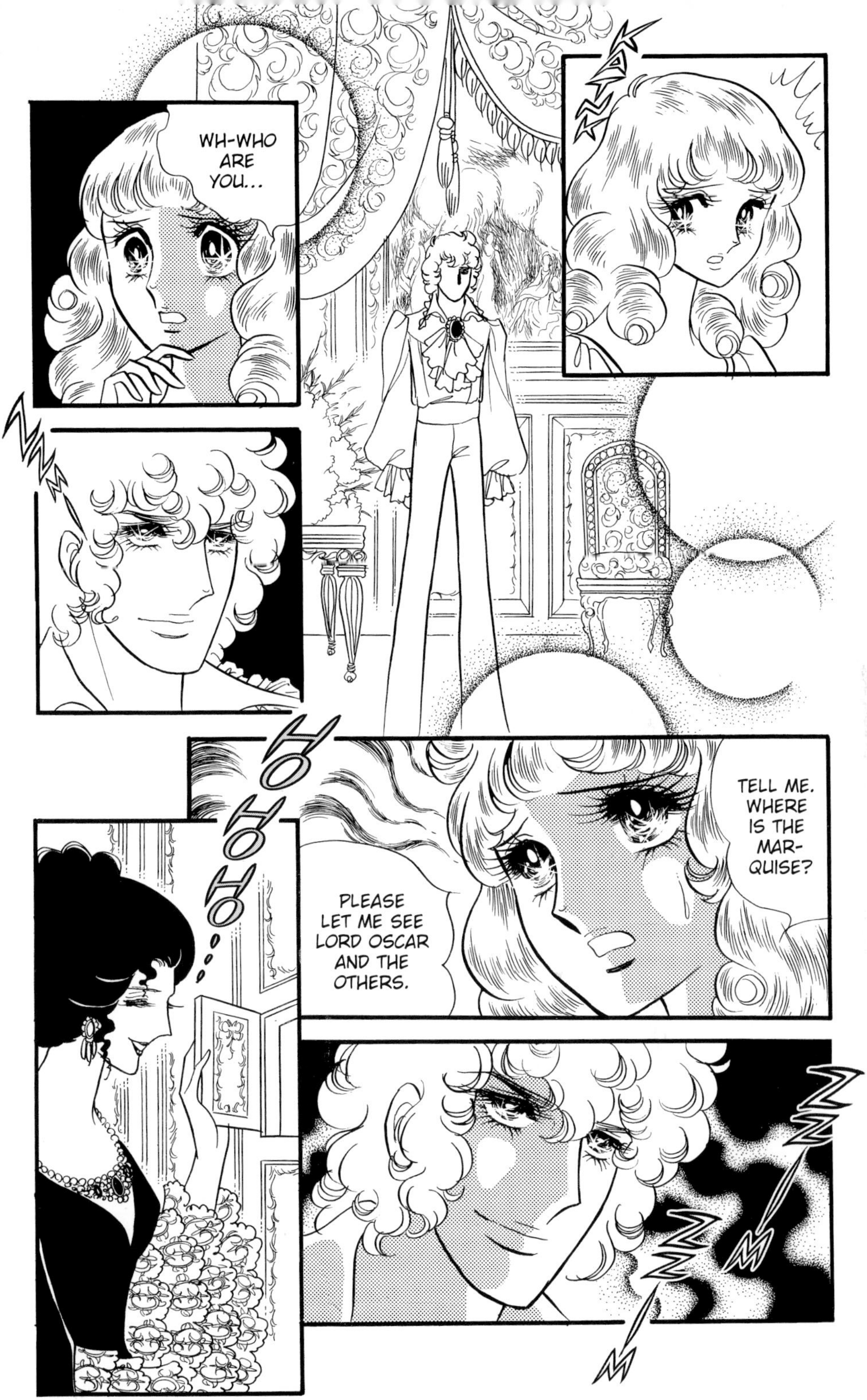
WH-WHO ARE YOU...
TELL ME. WHERE IS THE MARQUISE?
PLEASE LET ME SEE LORD OSCAR AND THE OTHERS.
HO HO HO HO...

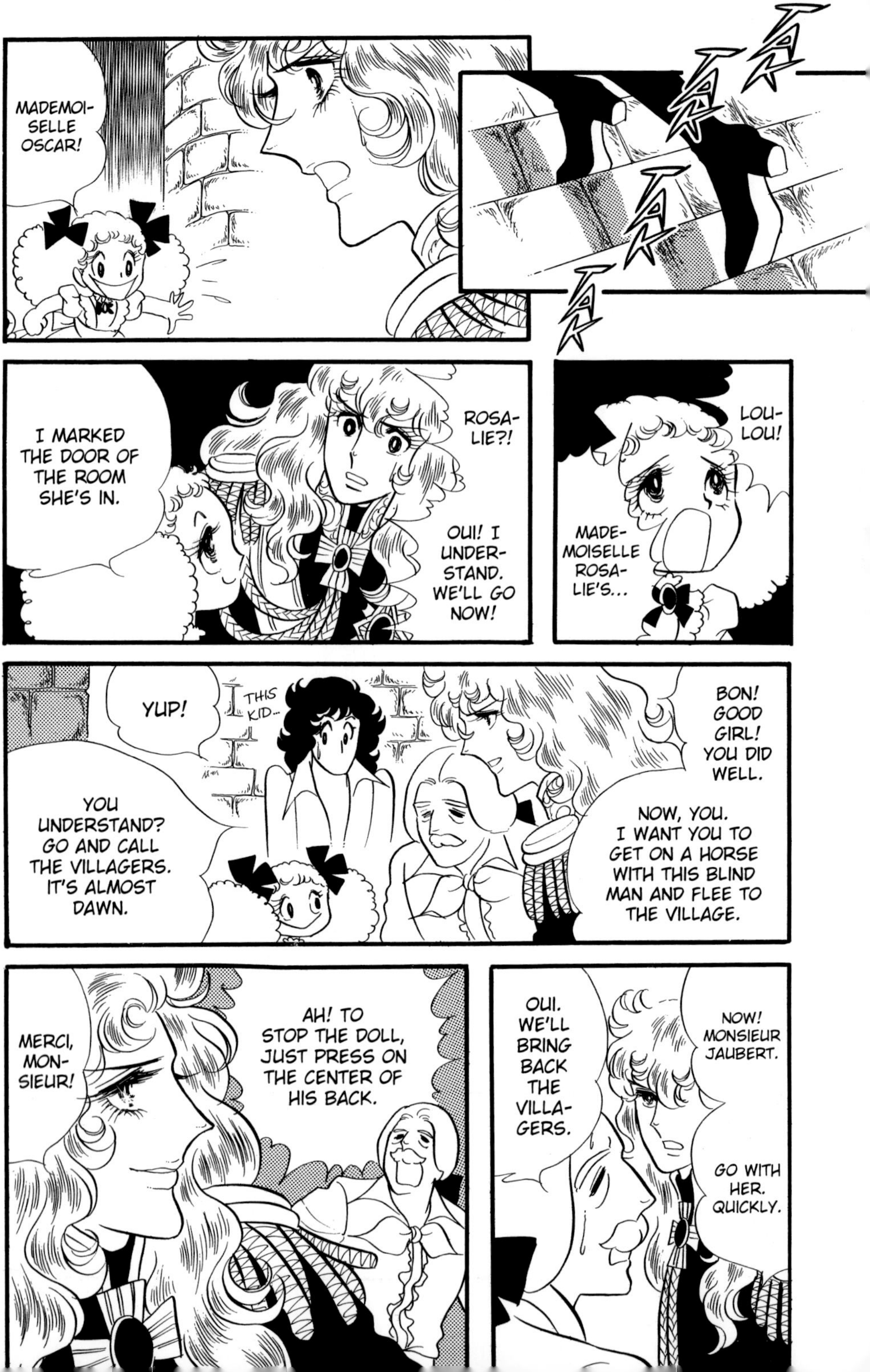
TAK TAK TAK TAK
MADEMOISELLE OSCAR!
LOU-LOU!
MADEMOISELLE ROSALIE'S...
ROSALIE?!
I MARKED THE DOOR OF THE ROOM SHE'S IN.
OUI! I UNDERSTAND. WE'LL GO NOW!
BON! GOOD GIRL! YOU DID WELL.
YUP!
THIS KID...
NOW, YOU. I WANT YOU TO GET ON A HORSE WITH THIS BLIND MAN AND FLEE TO THE VILLAGE.
YOU UNDERSTAND? GO AND CALL THE VILLAGERS. IT'S ALMOST DAWN.
NOW! MONSIEUR JAUBERT.
OUI. WE'LL BRING BACK THE VILLAGERS.
GO WITH HER. QUICKLY.
AH! TO STOP THE DOLL, JUST PRESS ON THE CENTER OF HIS BACK.
MERCI, MONSIEUR!

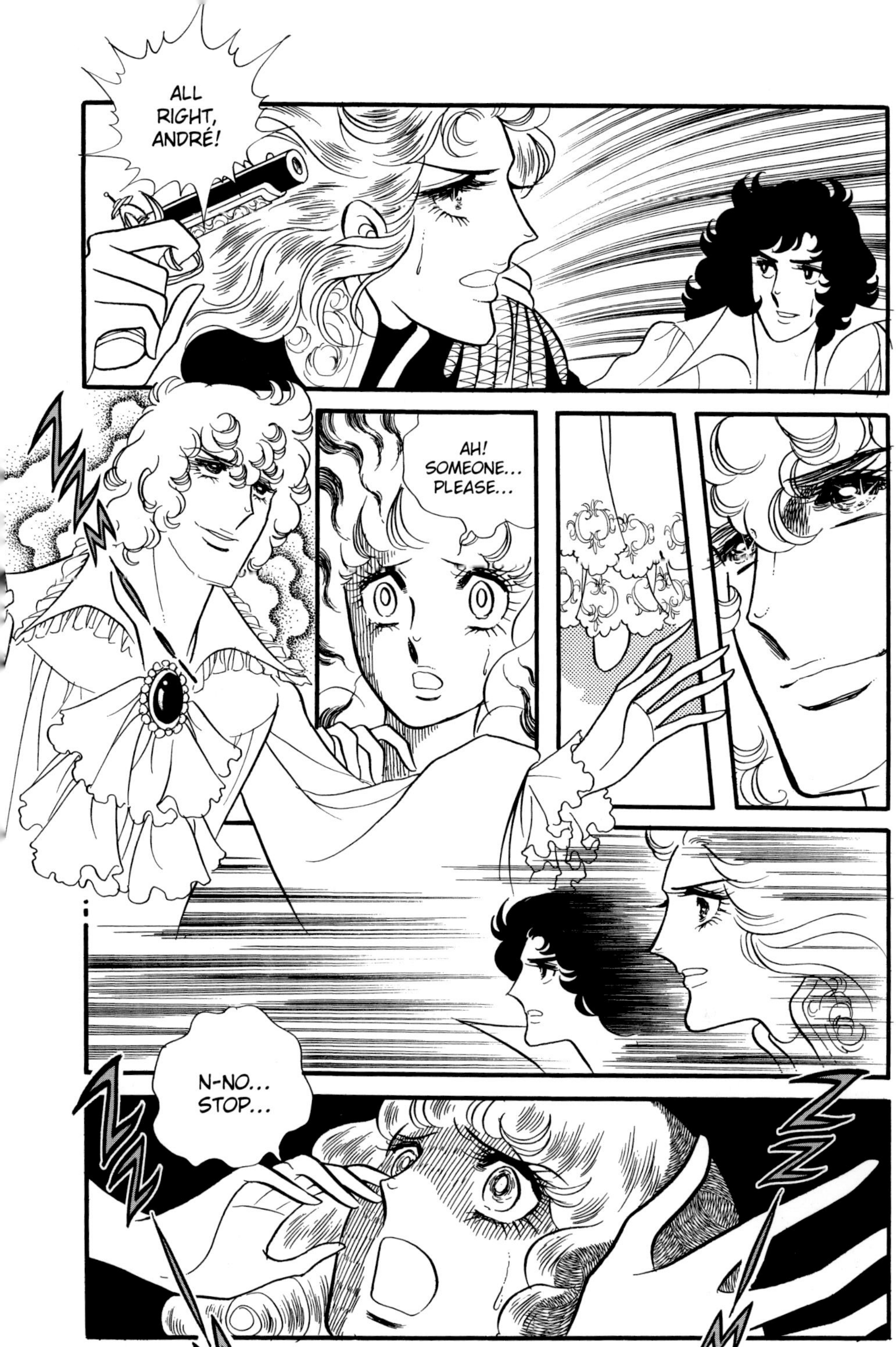
ALL RIGHT, ANDRÉ!
AH! SOMEONE... PLEASE...
N-NO... STOP...

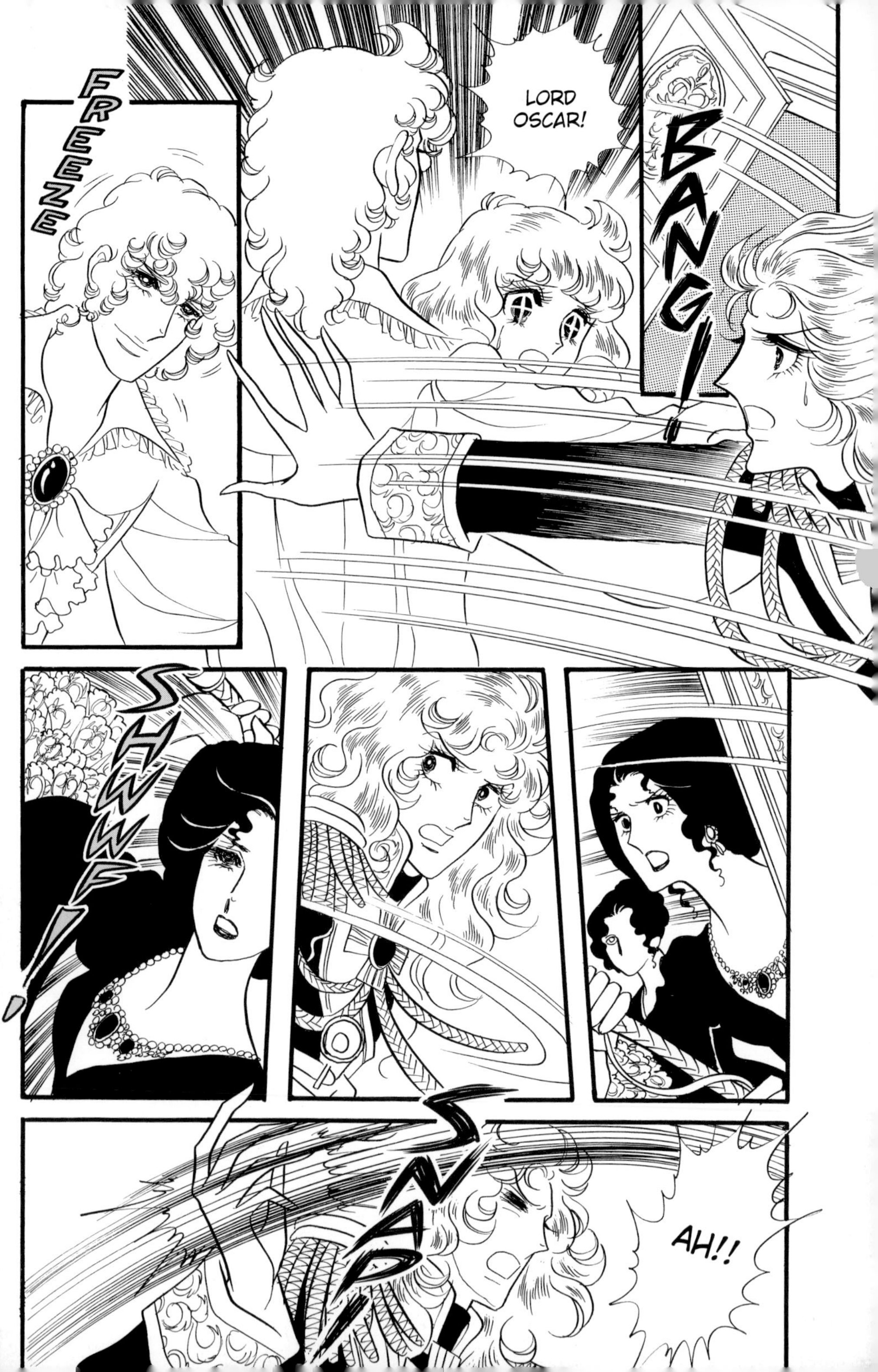
BANG!
LORD OSCAR!
FREEZE
SHWWF
AH!!
SNAP

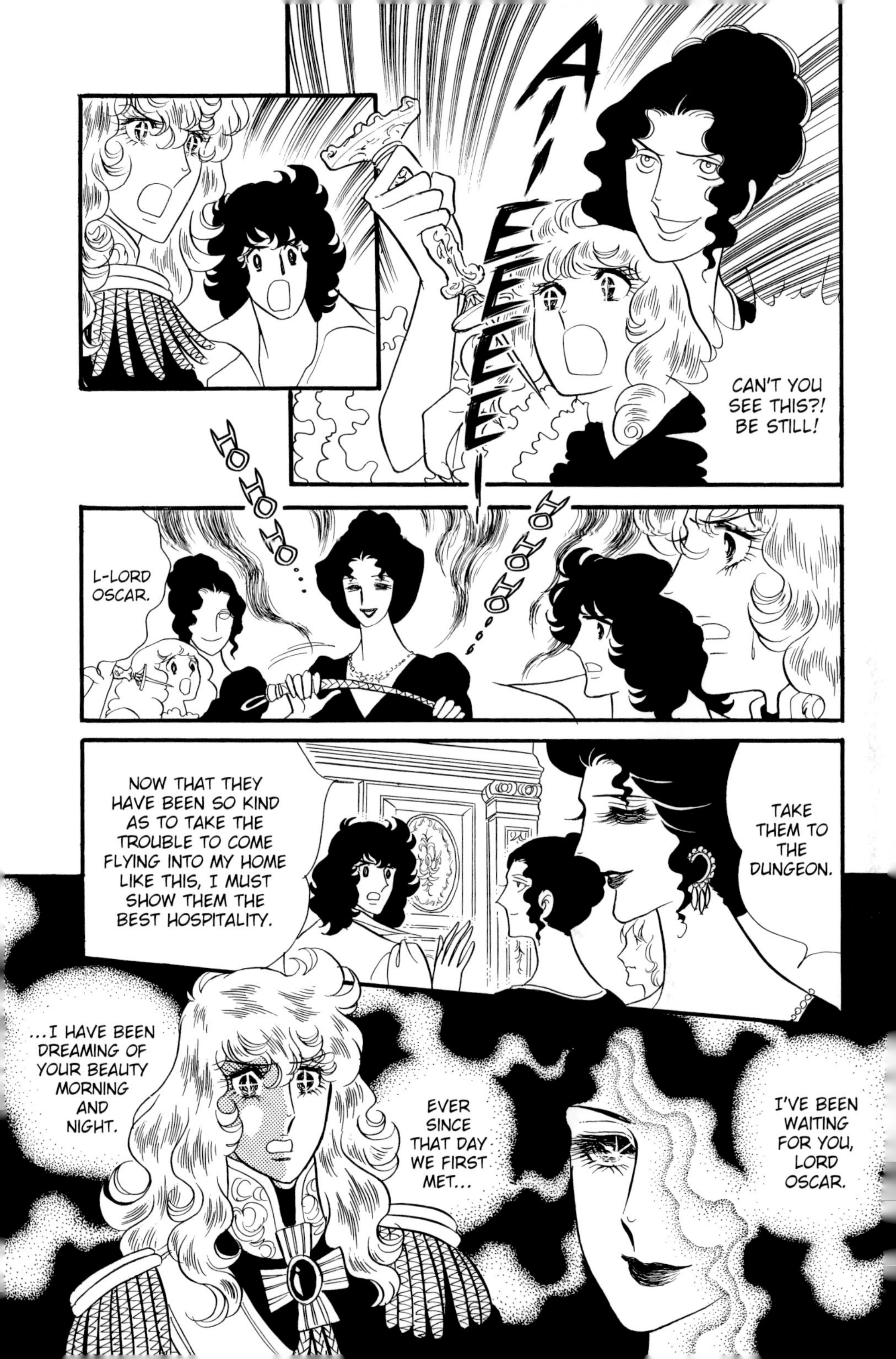
AIIEEEEEEEE
CAN'T YOU SEE THIS?! BE STILL!
HOHOHOHO...
HOHOHO...
L-LORD OSCAR.
TAKE THEM TO THE DUNGEON.
NOW THAT THEY HAVE BEEN SO KIND AS TO TAKE THE TROUBLE TO COME FLYING INTO MY HOME LIKE THIS, I MUST SHOW THEM THE BEST HOSPITALITY.
I'VE BEEN WAITING FOR YOU, LORD OSCAR.
EVER SINCE THAT DAY WE FIRST MET...
...I HAVE BEEN DREAMING OF YOUR BEAUTY MORNING AND NIGHT.

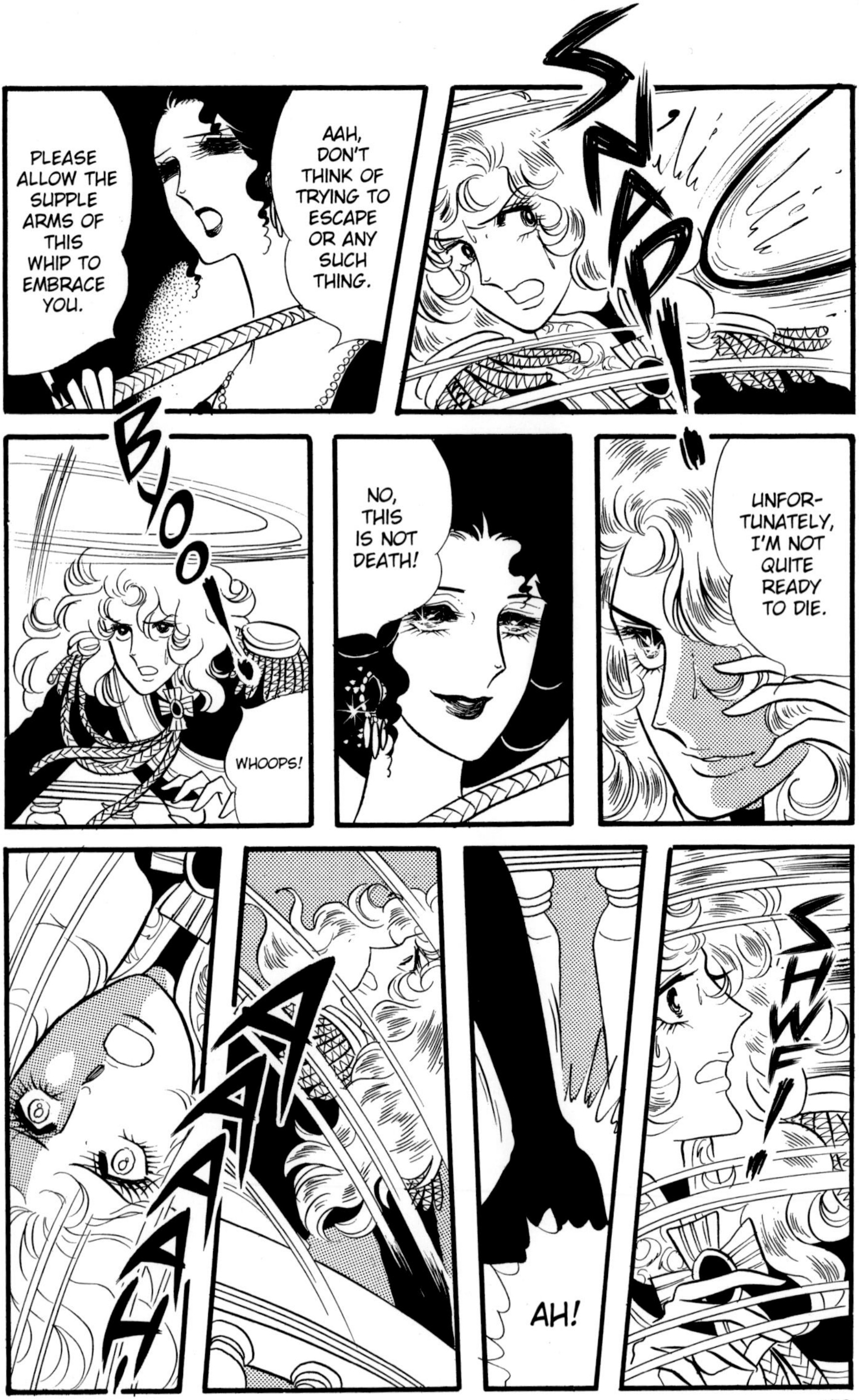
SNAP!
AAH, DON'T THINK OF TRYING TO ESCAPE OR ANY SUCH THING.
PLEASE ALLOW THE SUPPLE ARMS OF THIS WHIP TO EMBRACE YOU.
UNFORTUNATELY, I'M NOT QUITE READY TO DIE.
NO, THIS IS NOT DEATH!
BYOO!
WHOOPS!
SHWF!
AH!
AAAAAH!

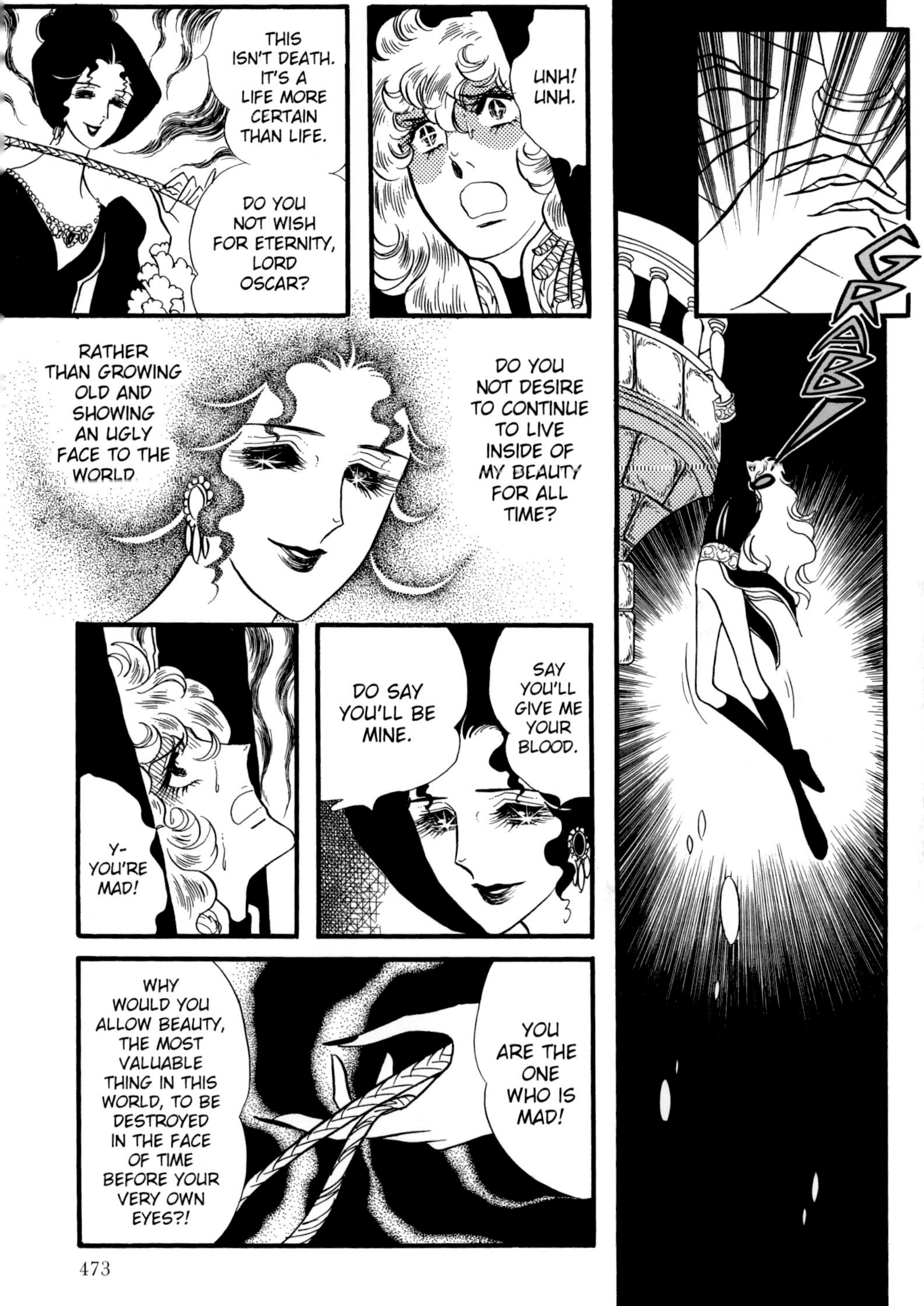
GRAB
UNH! UNH.
THIS ISN'T DEATH. IT'S A LIFE MORE CERTAIN THAN LIFE.
DO YOU NOT WISH FOR ETERNITY, LORD OSCAR?
DO YOU NOT DESIRE TO CONTINUE TO LIVE INSIDE OF MY BEAUTY FOR ALL TIME?
RATHER THAN GROWING OLD AND SHOWING AN UGLY FACE TO THE WORLD.
SAY YOU'LL GIVE ME YOUR BLOOD.
DO SAY YOU'LL BE MINE.
Y-YOU'RE MAD!
YOU ARE THE ONE WHO IS MAD!
WHY WOULD YOU ALLOW BEAUTY, THE MOST VALUABLE THING IN THIS WORLD, TO BE DESTROYED IN THE FACE OF TIME BEFORE YOUR VERY OWN EYES?!

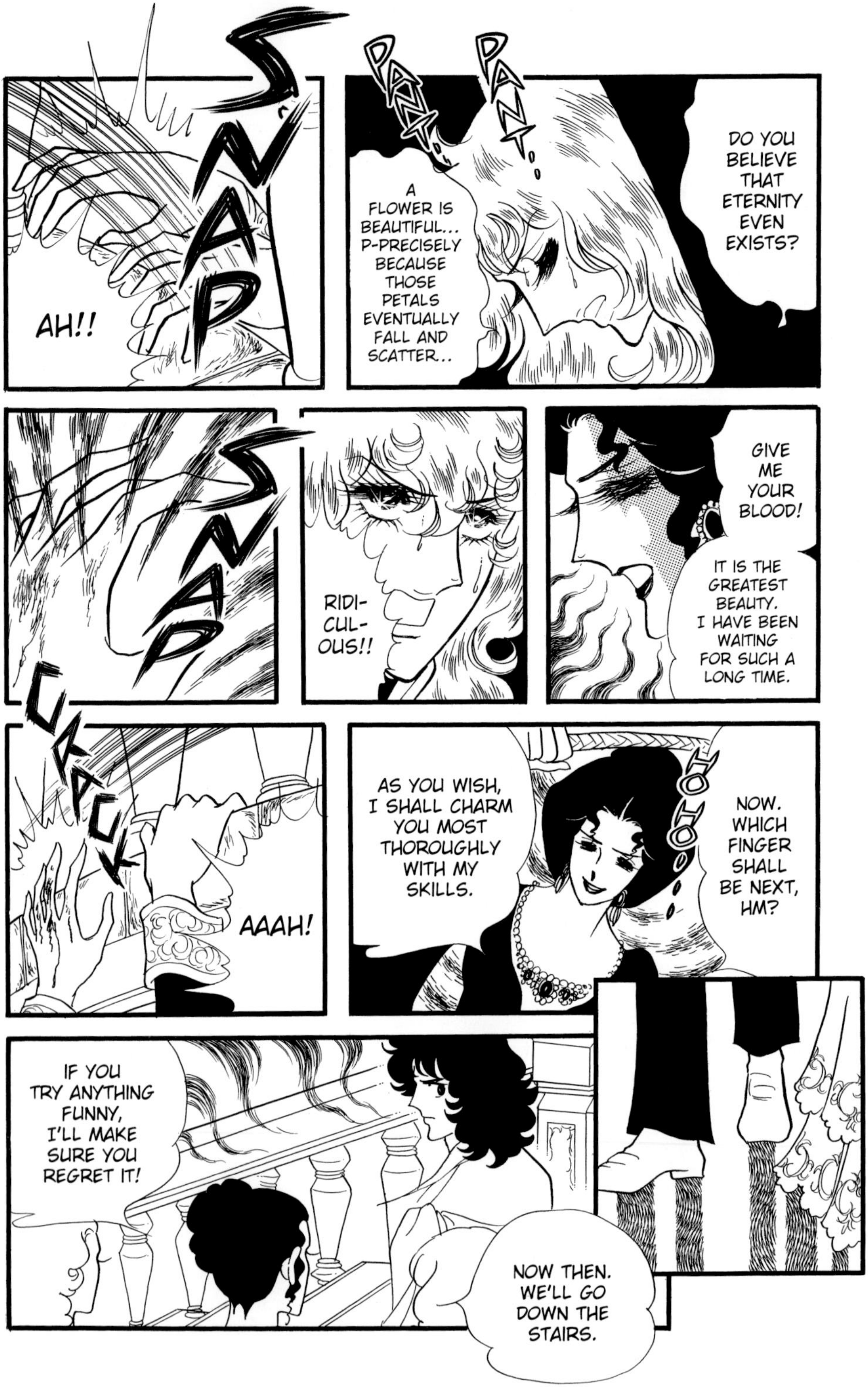
DO YOU BELIEVE THAT ETERNITY EVEN EXISTS?
PANT...
PANT...
A FLOWER IS BEAUTIFUL... P-PRECISELY BECAUSE THOSE PETALS EVENTUALLY FALL AND SCATTER...
SNAP
AH!!
GIVE ME YOUR BLOOD!
IT IS THE GREATEST BEAUTY. I HAVE BEEN WAITING FOR SUCH A LONG TIME.
RIDI-CUL-OUS!!
SNAP
CRACK
NOW. WHICH FINGER SHALL BE NEXT, HM?
HOHO...
AS YOU WISH, I SHALL CHARM YOU MOST THOROUGHLY WITH MY SKILLS.
AAAH!
IF YOU TRY ANYTHING FUNNY, I'LL MAKE SURE YOU REGRET IT!
NOW THEN. WE'LL GO DOWN THE STAIRS.

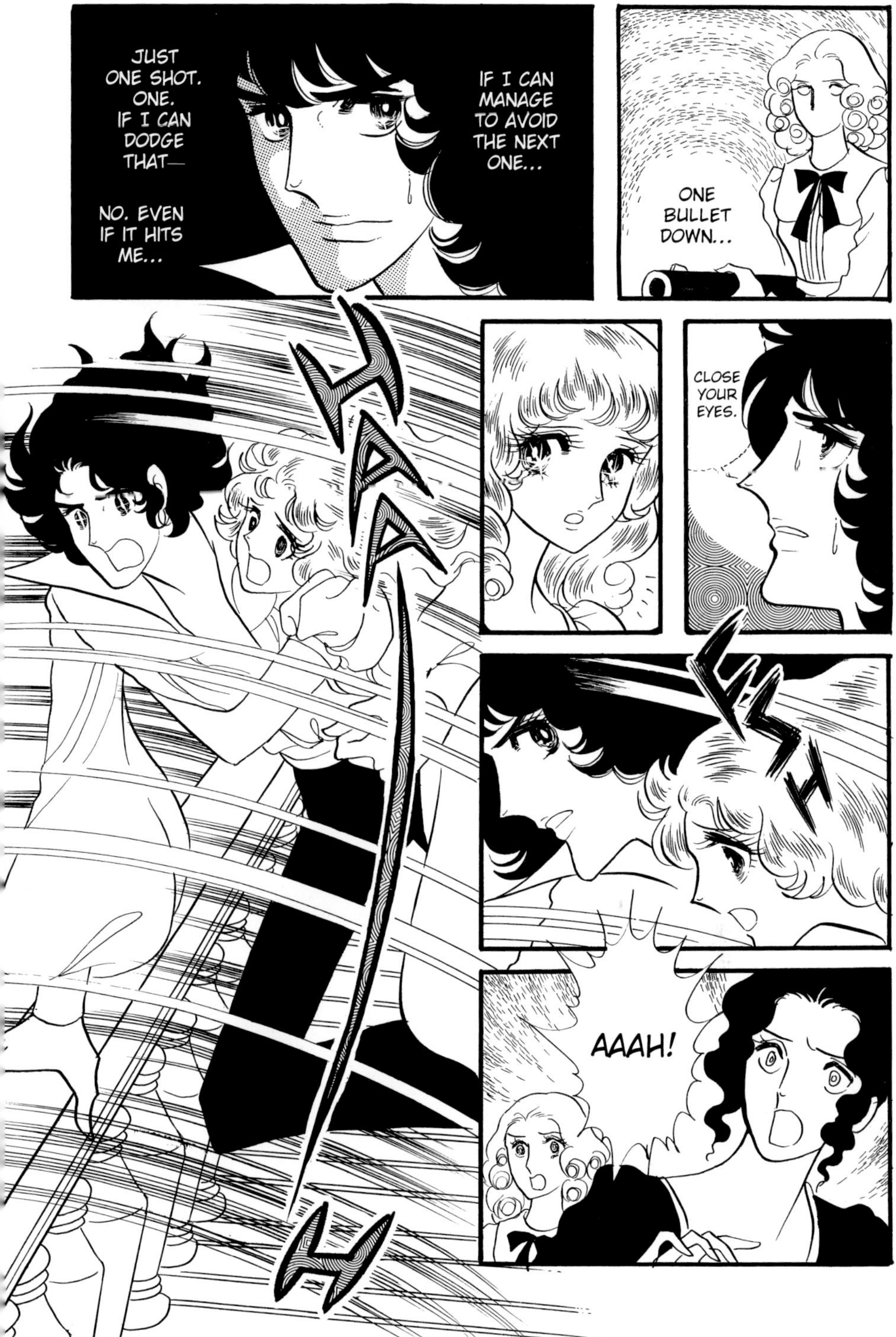
ONE BULLET DOWN...
JUST ONE SHOT. ONE. IF I CAN DODGE THAT—
NO. EVEN IF IT HITS ME...
IF I CAN MANAGE TO AVOID THE NEXT ONE...
CLOSE YOUR EYES.
AAAH!

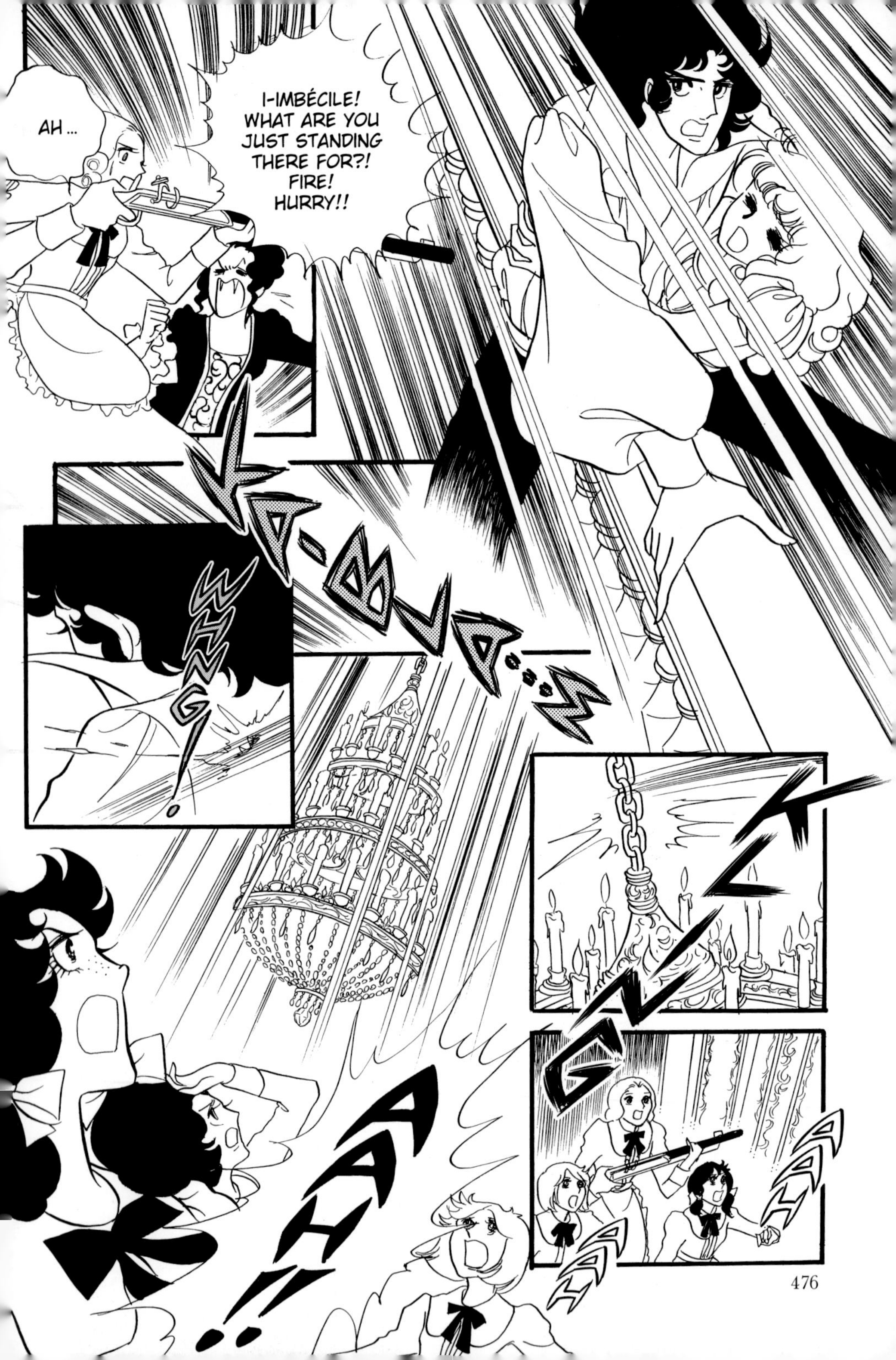
I-IMBÉCILE! WHAT ARE YOU JUST STANDING THERE FOR?! FIRE! HURRY!!
AH ...
KA-BLA...M
WHNG!
AAAH!!

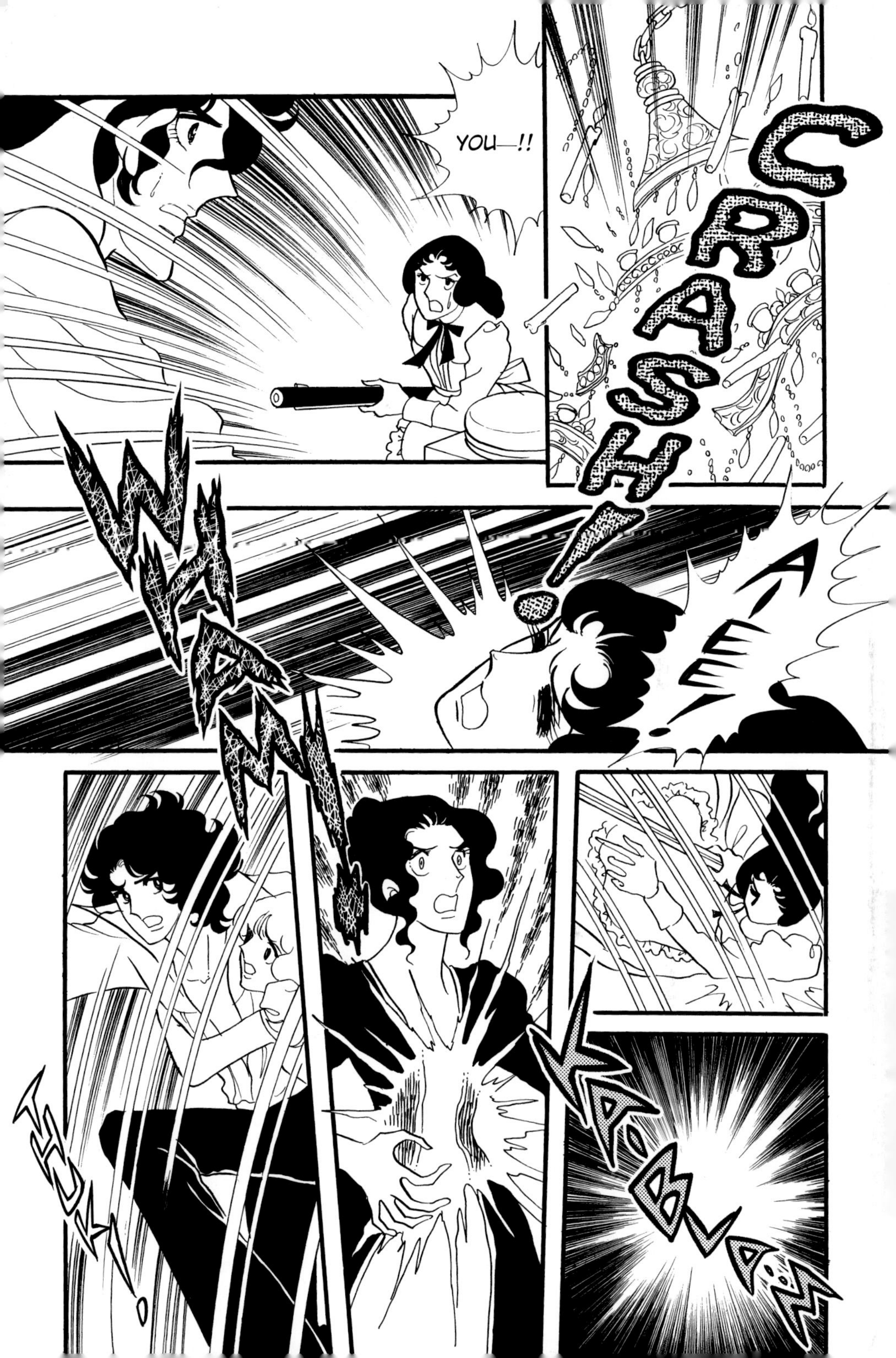
CRASH!
YOU—!!
AIEE!
WHAM
KABLAM
THUNK!

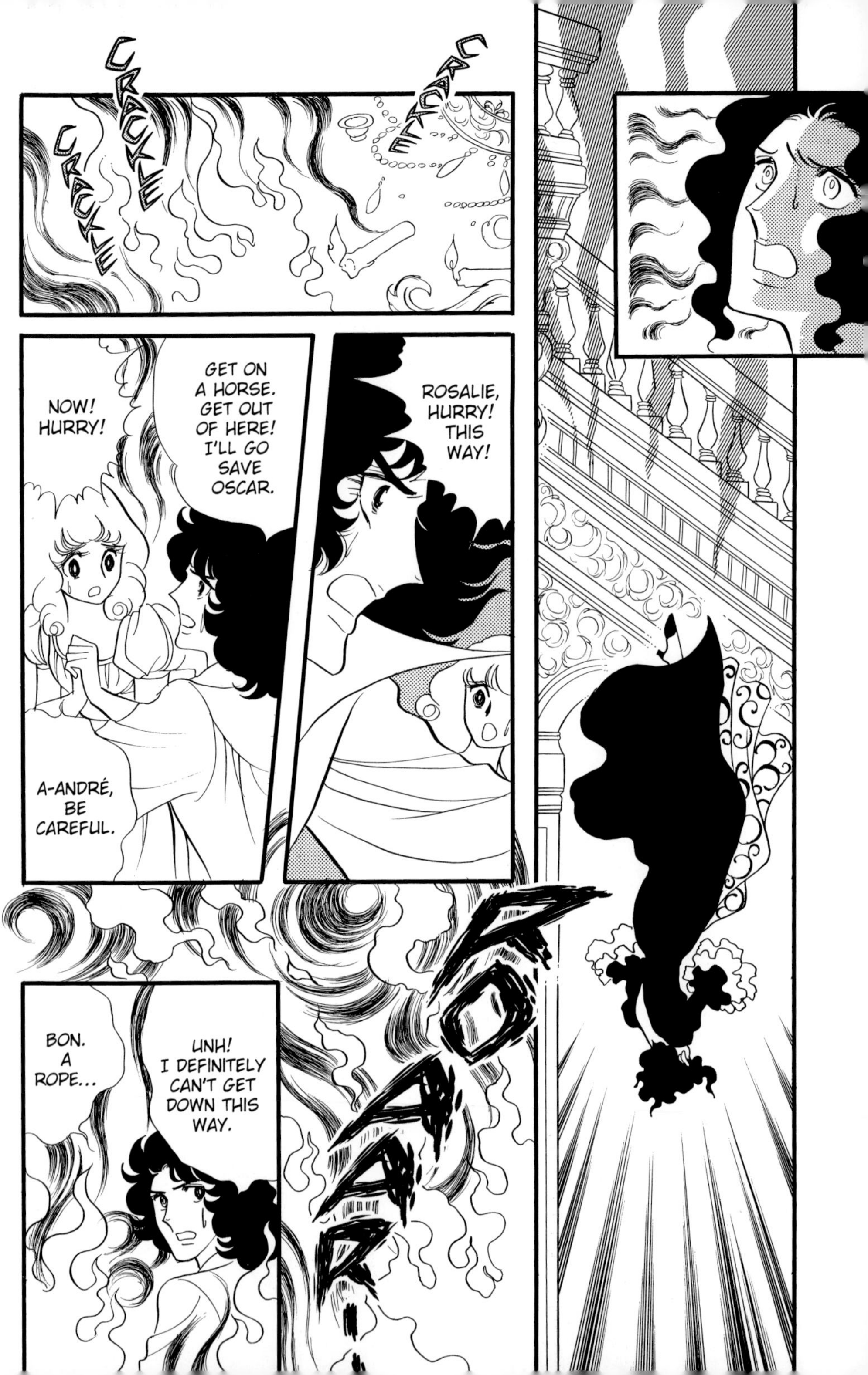
CRACKLE
CRACKLE
CRACKLE
ROSALIE, HURRY! THIS WAY!
NOW! HURRY!
GET ON A HORSE. GET OUT OF HERE! I'LL GO SAVE OSCAR.
A-ANDRÉ, BE CAREFUL.
UNH! I DEFINITELY CAN'T GET DOWN THIS WAY.
BON. A ROPE...

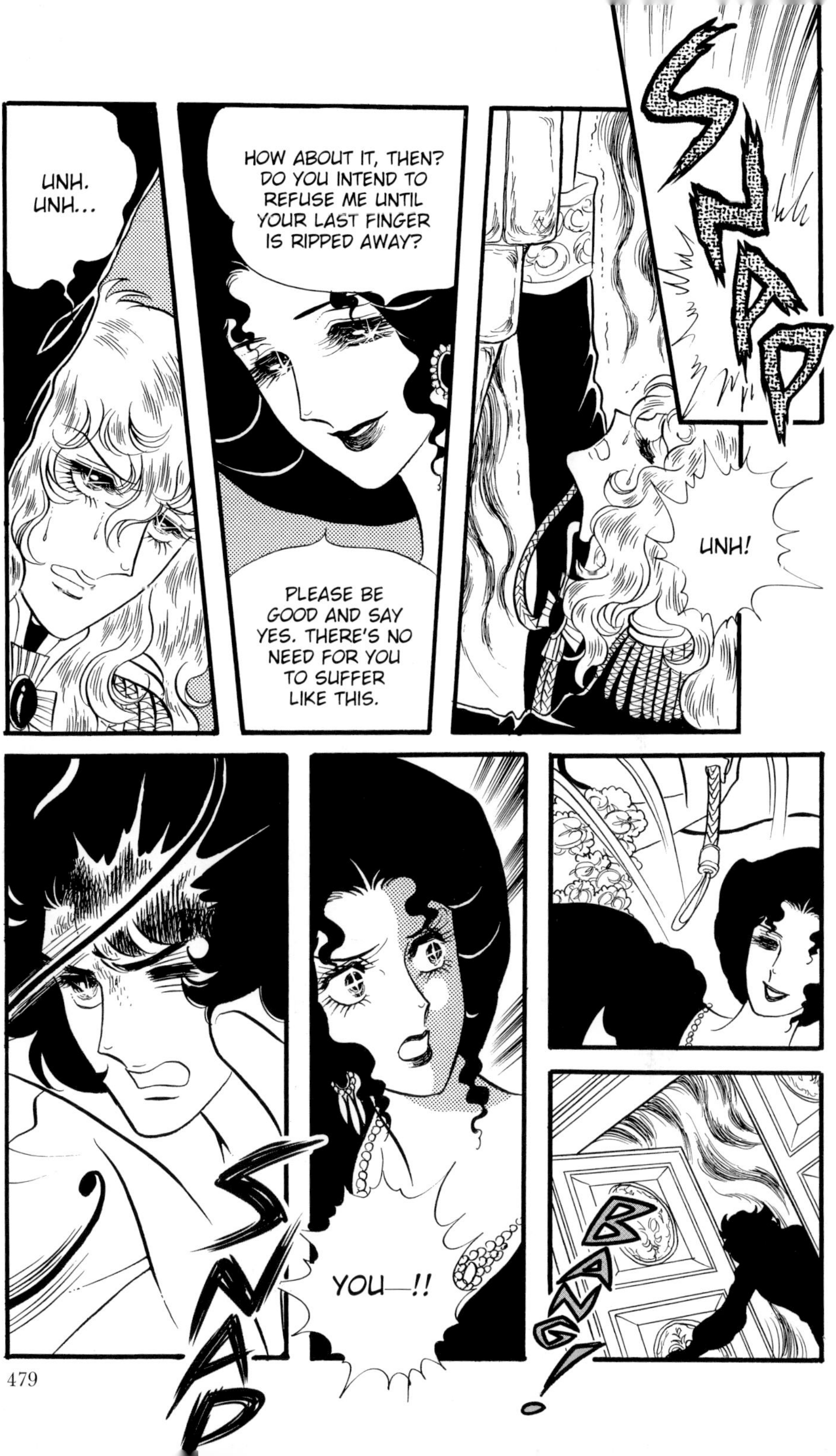
SNAP
UNH!
HOW ABOUT IT, THEN? DO YOU INTEND TO REFUSE ME UNTIL YOUR LAST FINGER IS RIPPED AWAY?
PLEASE BE GOOD AND SAY YES. THERE'S NO NEED FOR YOU TO SUFFER LIKE THIS.
UNH. UNH...
BANG!
YOU—!!
SNAP

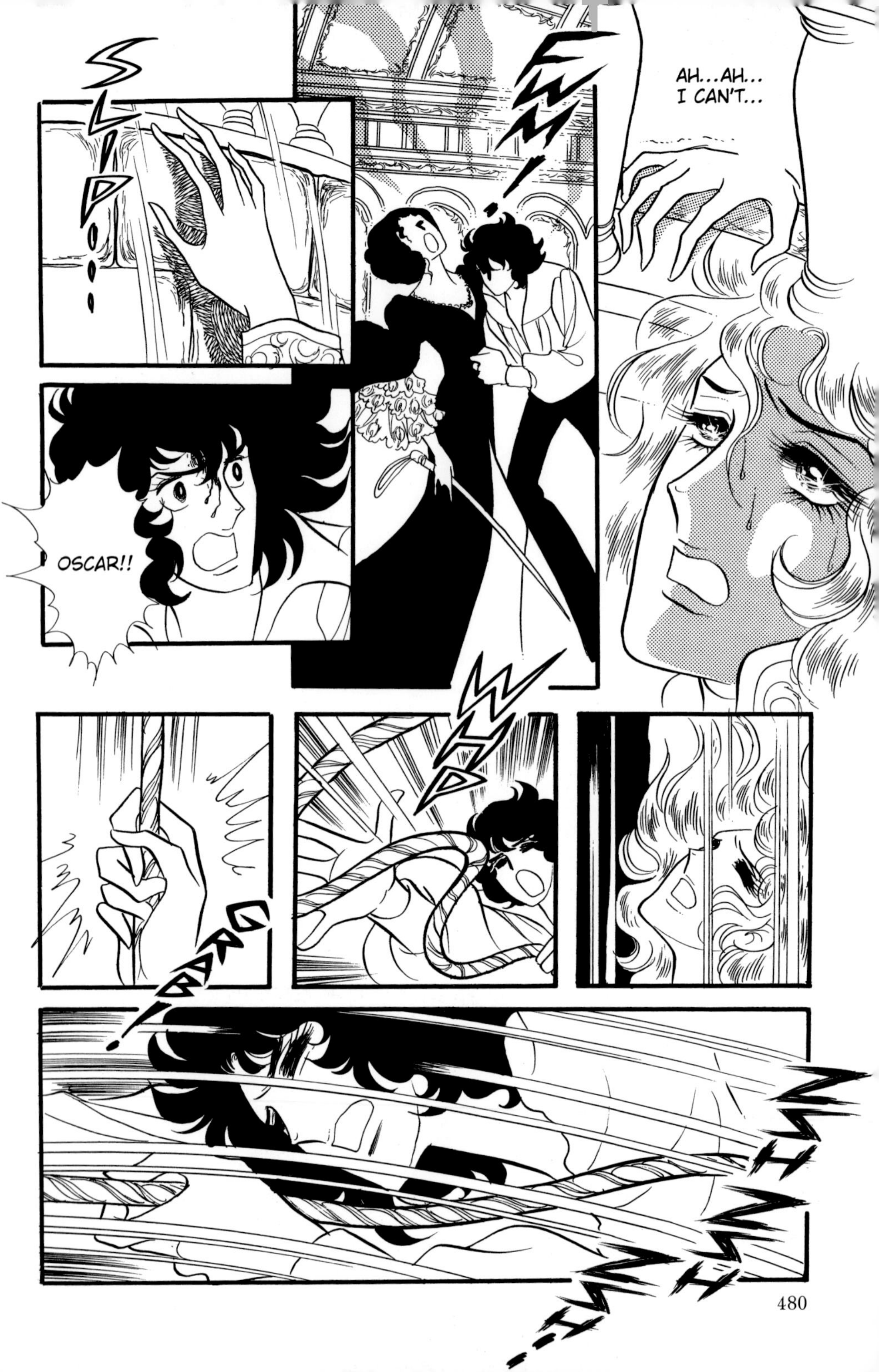
AH...AH... I CAN'T...
FWM!.
SLID...
OSCAR!!
GRAB!

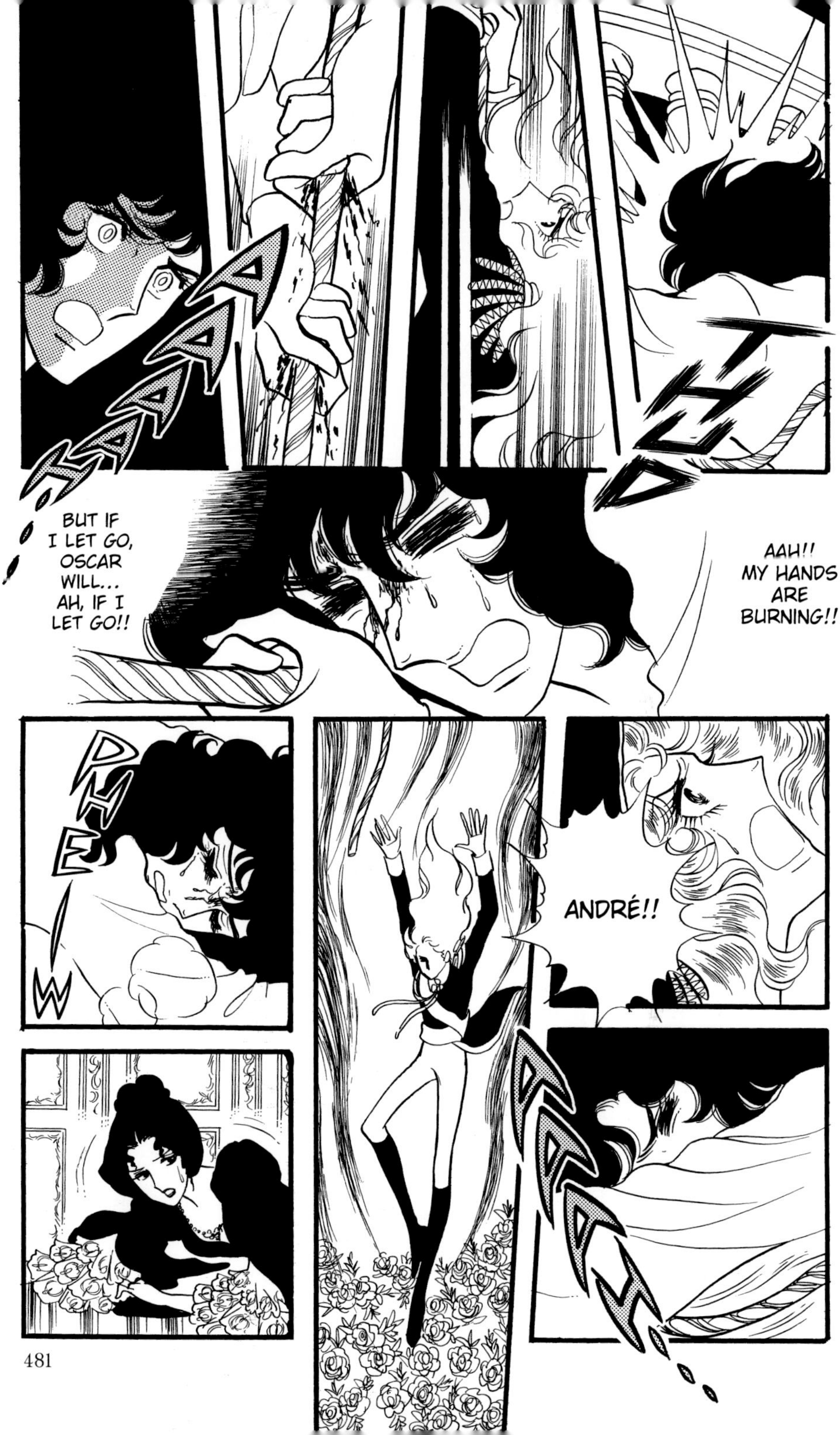
THUD
AAAAAH...
AAH!! MY HANDS ARE BURNING!!
BUT IF I LET GO, OSCAR WILL... AH, IF I LET GO!!
ANDRÉ!!
AAAAH...
PHEW!

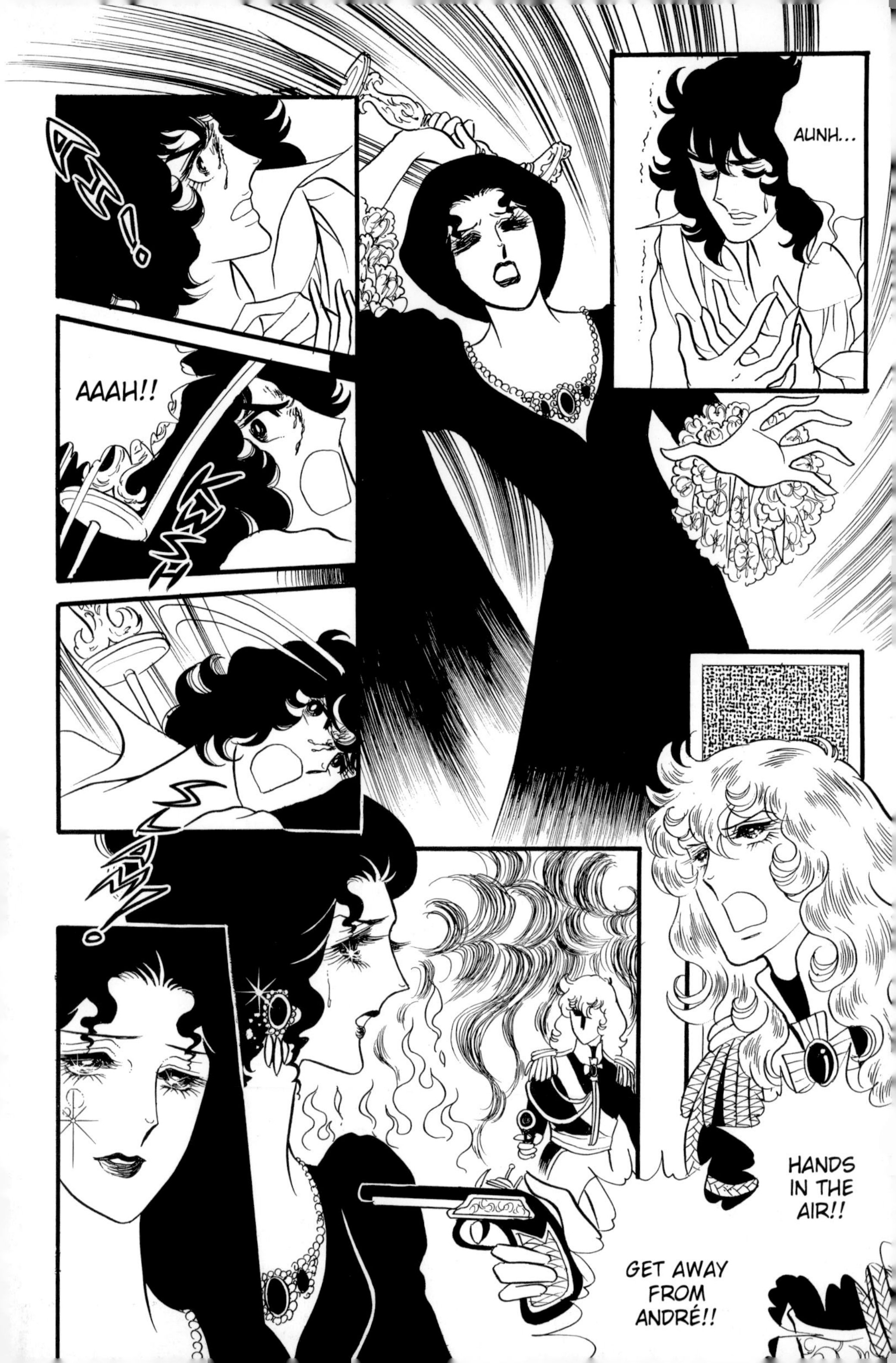

AUNH...
AAAH!!
HANDS IN THE AIR!!
GET AWAY FROM ANDRÉ!!

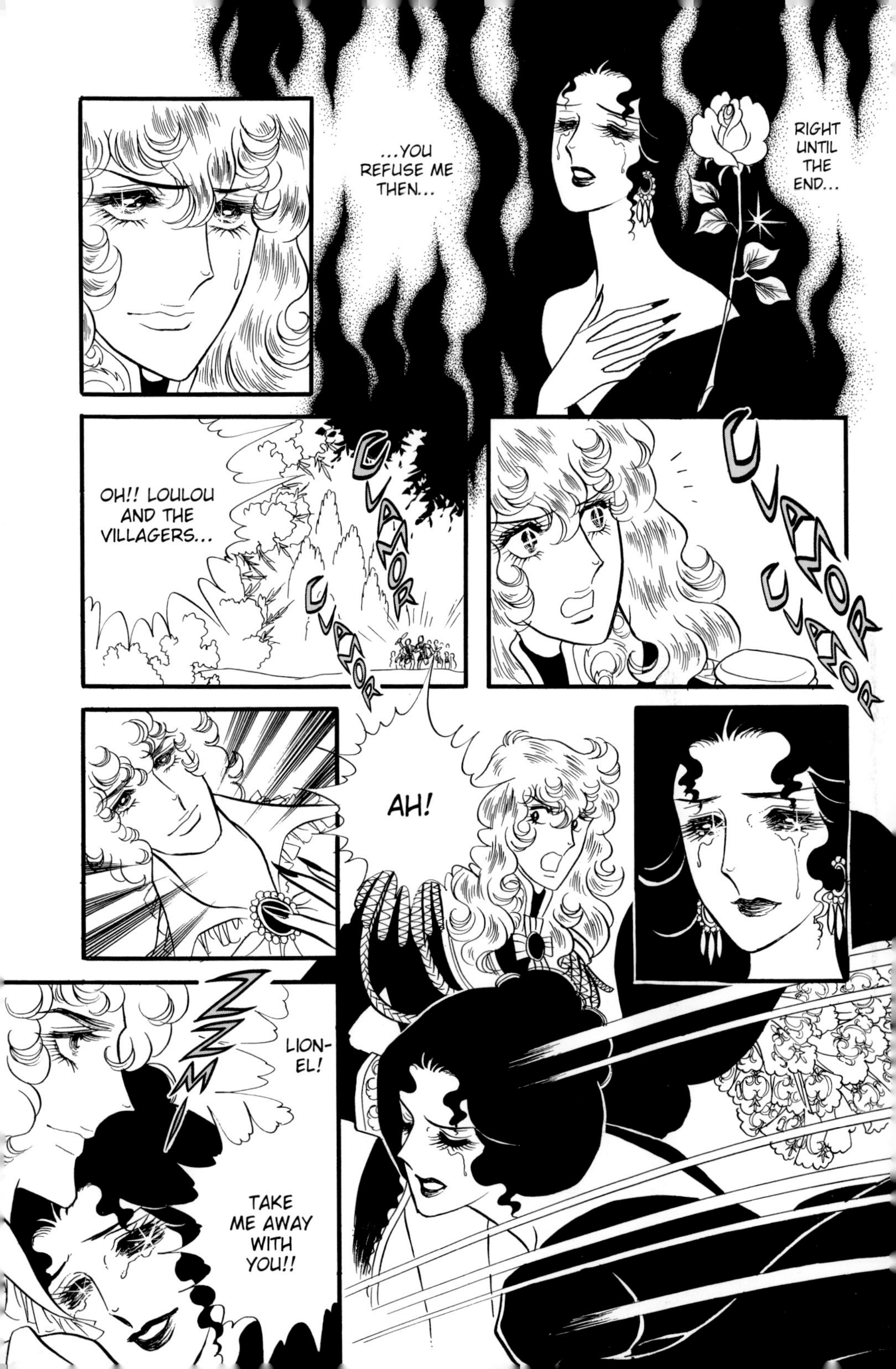
RIGHT UNTIL THE END...
...YOU REFUSE ME THEN...
CLAMOR
CLAMOR
CLAMOR
CLAMOR
OH!! LOULOU AND THE VILLAGERS...
AH!
LION-EL!
TAKE ME AWAY WITH YOU!!

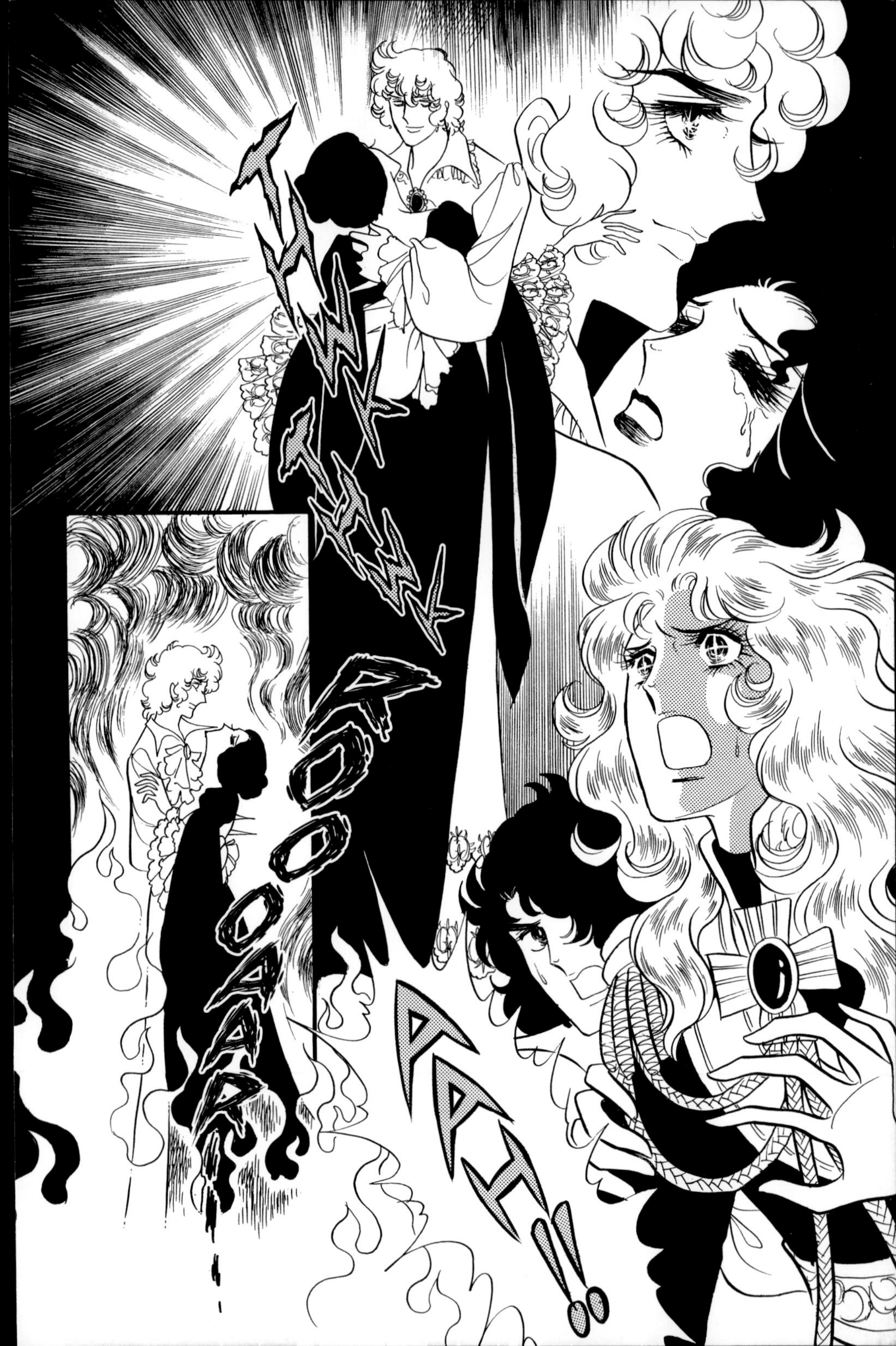
TWK
TWK
AOOOAAAA
AAH!!

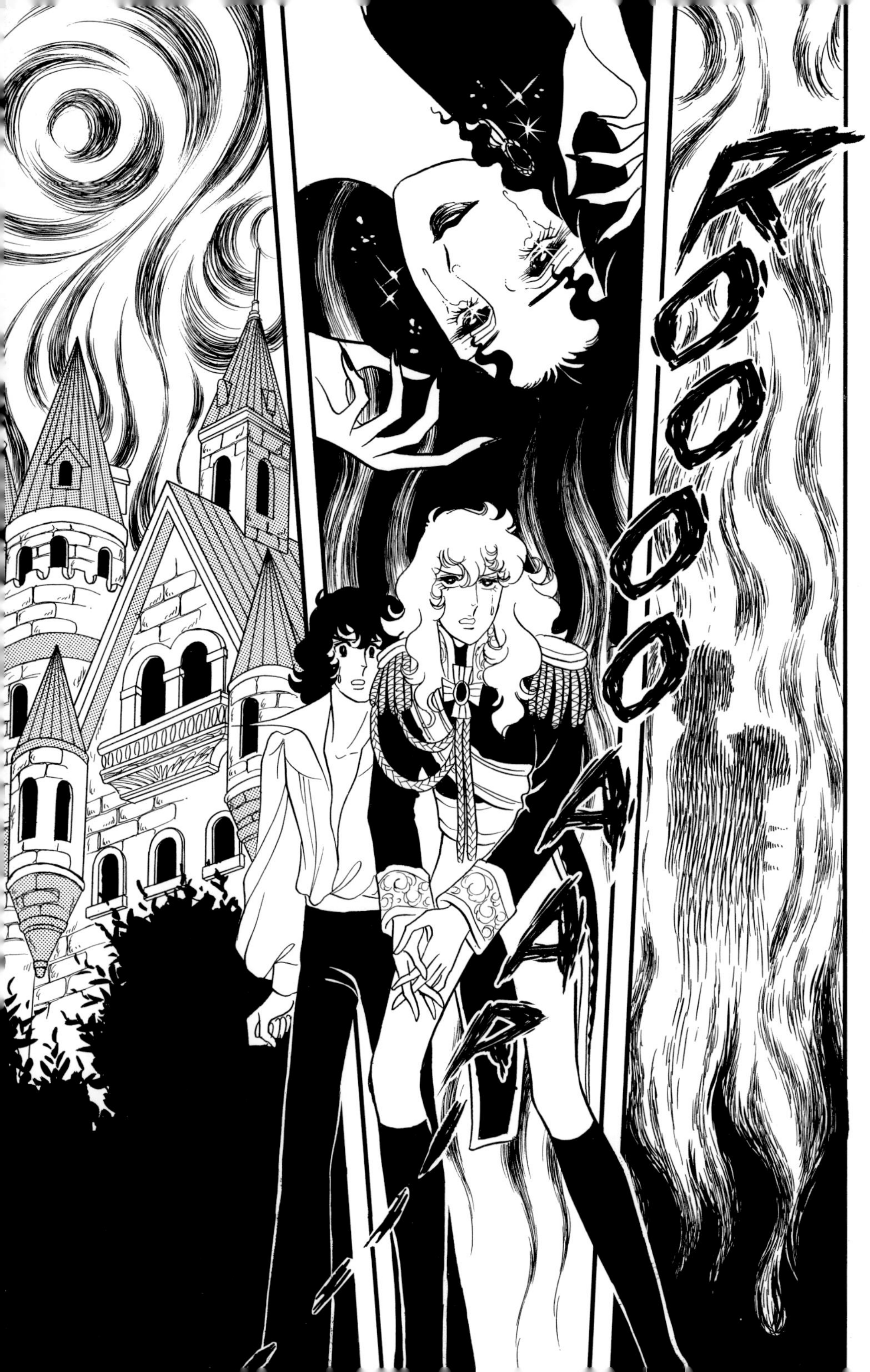
AOOOOAAA

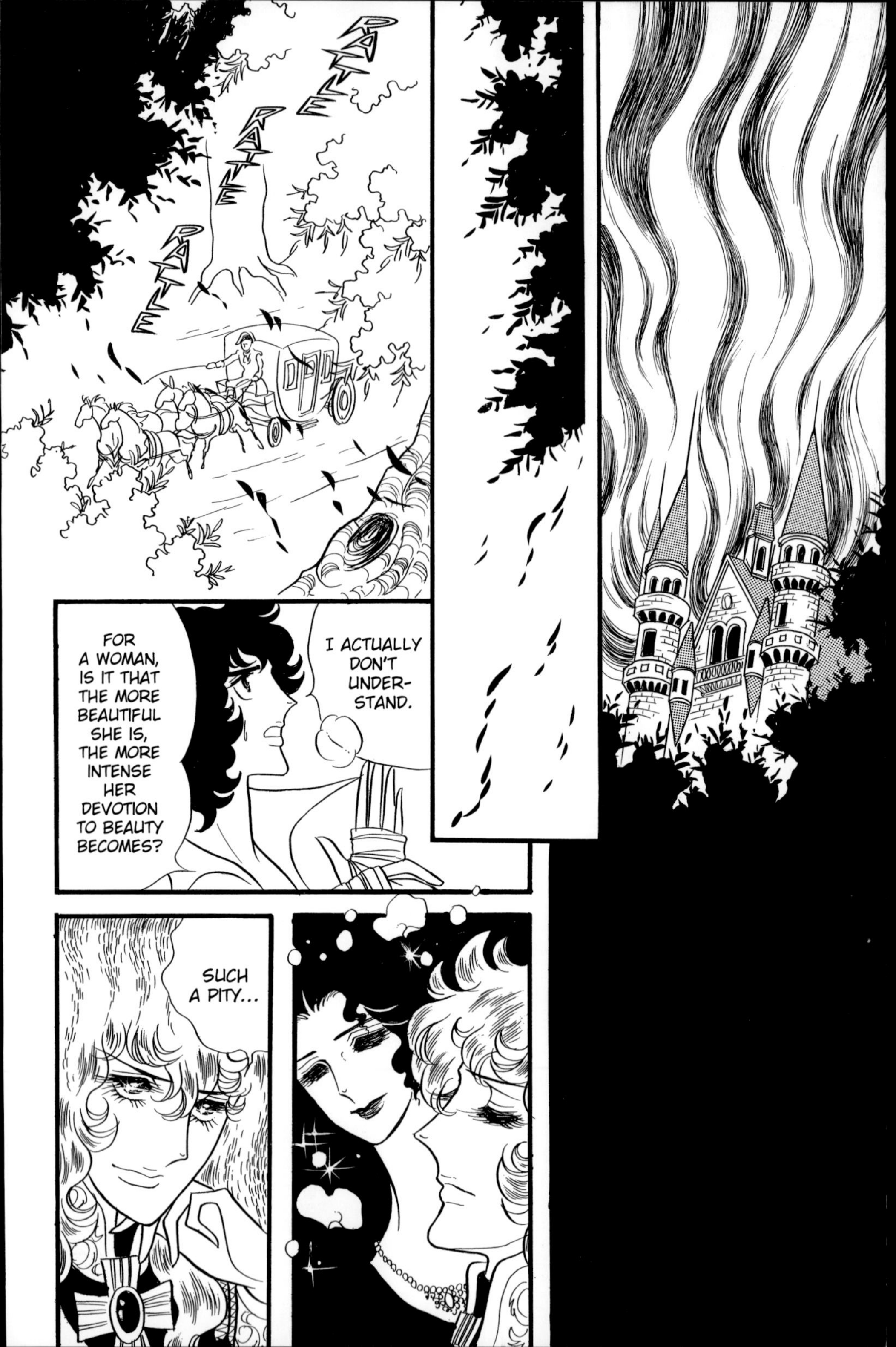
RATTLE
RATTLE
RATTLE
I ACTUALLY DON'T UNDER-STAND.
FOR A WOMAN, IS IT THAT THE MORE BEAUTIFUL SHE IS, THE MORE INTENSE HER DEVOTION TO BEAUTY BECOMES?
SUCH A PITY...

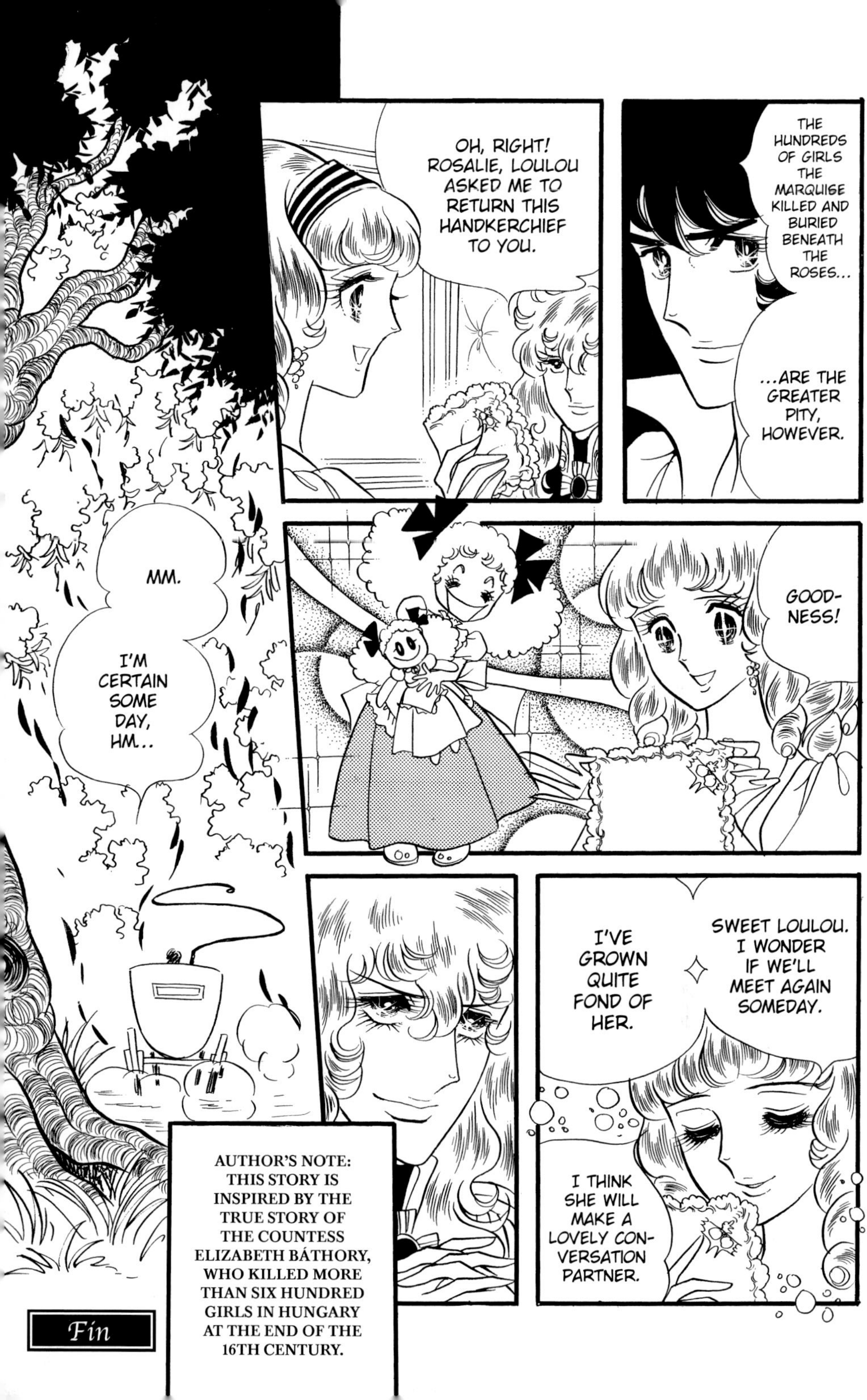
THE HUNDREDS OF GIRLS THE MARQUISE KILLED AND BURIED BENEATH THE ROSES...
...ARE THE GREATER PITY, HOWEVER.
OH, RIGHT! ROSALIE, LOULOU ASKED ME TO RETURN THIS HANDKERCHIEF TO YOU.
GOODNESS!
SWEET LOULOU. I WONDER IF WE'LL MEET AGAIN SOMEDAY.
I'VE GROWN QUITE FOND OF HER.
I THINK SHE WILL MAKE A LOVELY CONVERSATION PARTNER.
MM.
I'M CERTAIN SOME DAY, HM..
AUTHOR'S NOTE: THIS STORY IS INSPIRED BY THE TRUE STORY OF THE COUNTESS ELIZABETH BÁTHORY, WHO KILLED MORE THAN SIX HUNDRED GIRLS IN HUNGARY AT THE END OF THE 16TH CENTURY.
Fin

THE ROSE OF VERSAILLES

**1974 MARGARET COMICS TRADE PAPERBACK
VOLUME 10 COVER**

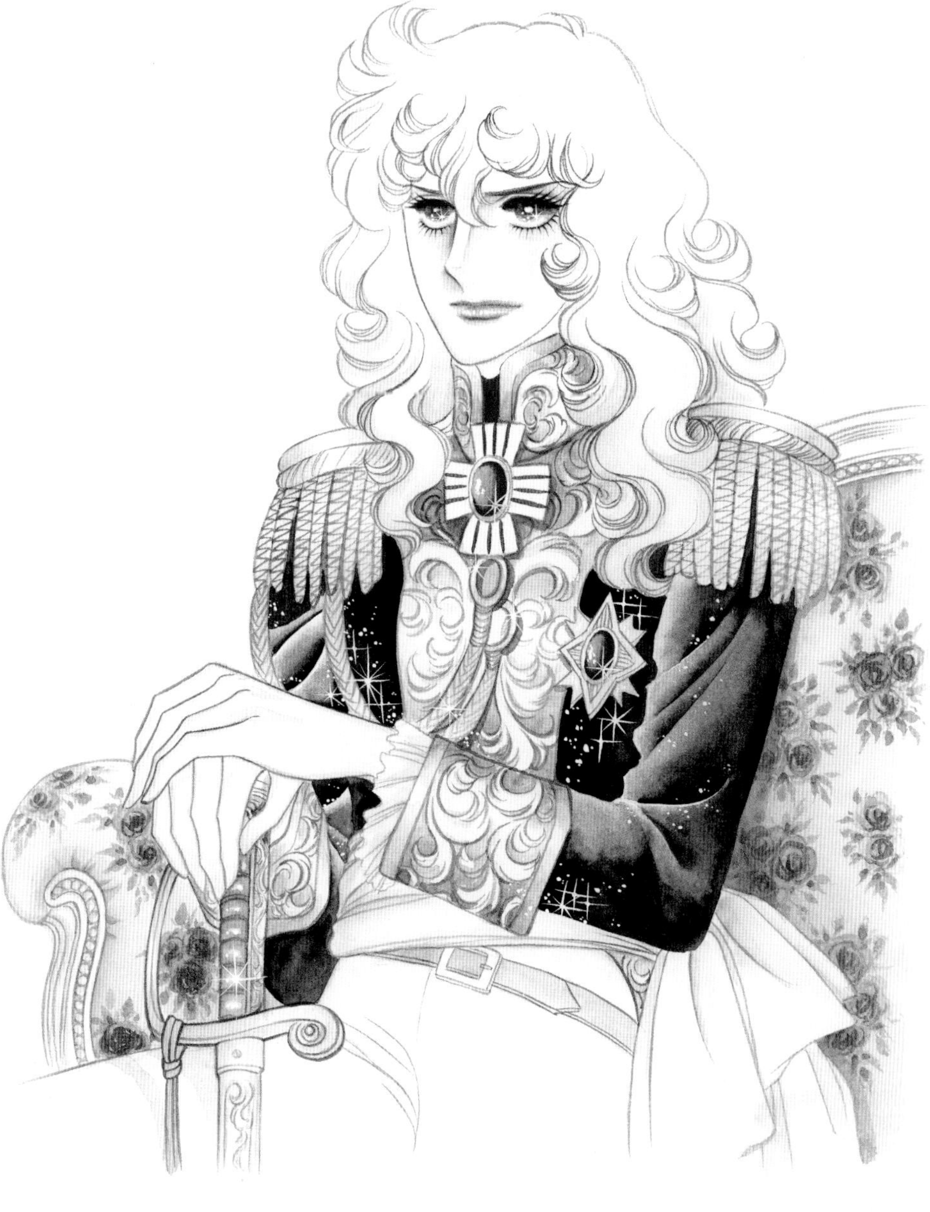

1974 ALL COLOR ILLUSTRATIONS ARTBOOK COVER

Oscar's Famous Scenes

White Rose Forever...

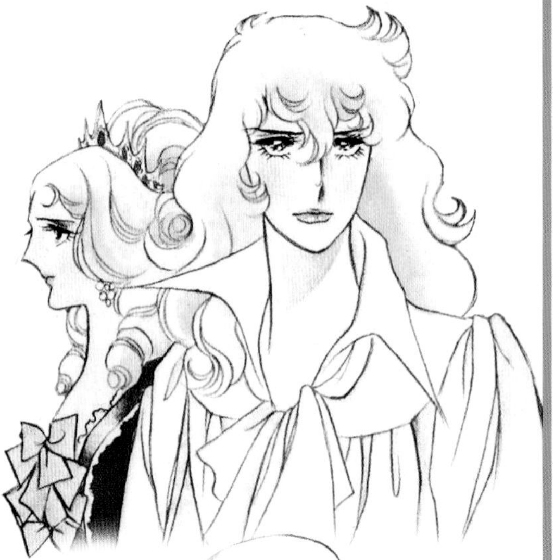

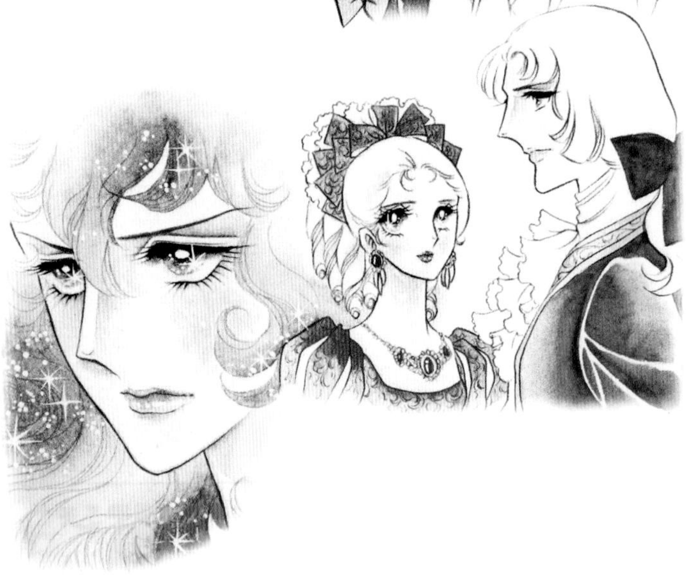

1974 WEEKLY MARGARET MAGAZINE ISSUE 01
OSCAR'S FAMOUS SCENES IN COLOR: [WHITE ROSE - FOREVER...] ILLUSTRATIONS

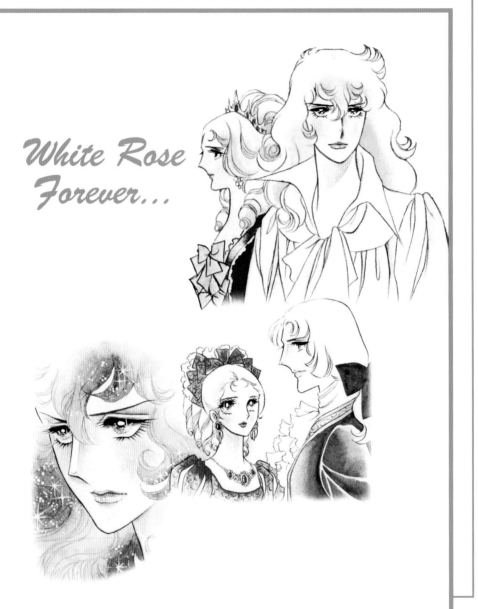

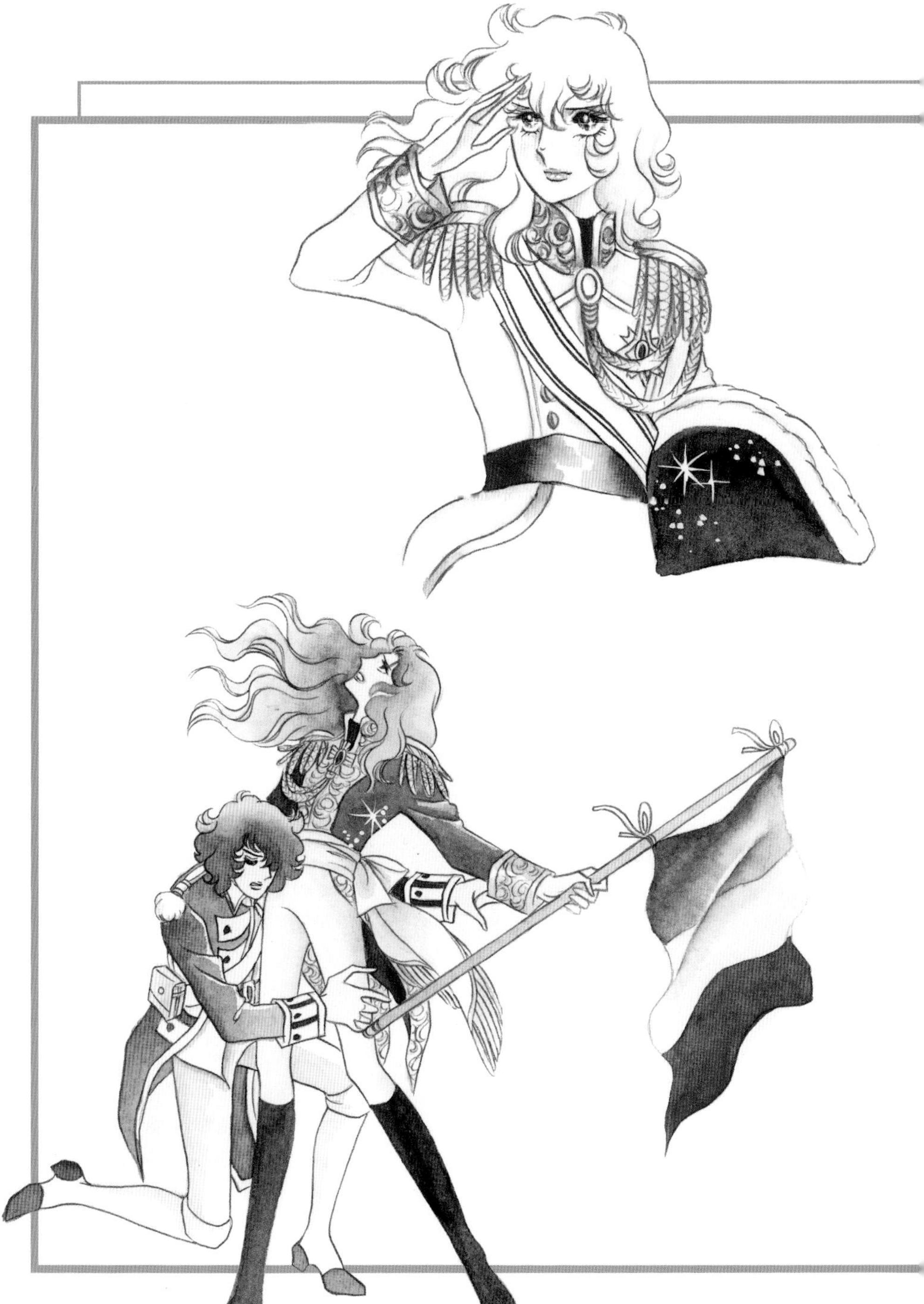

Poster Art Gallery

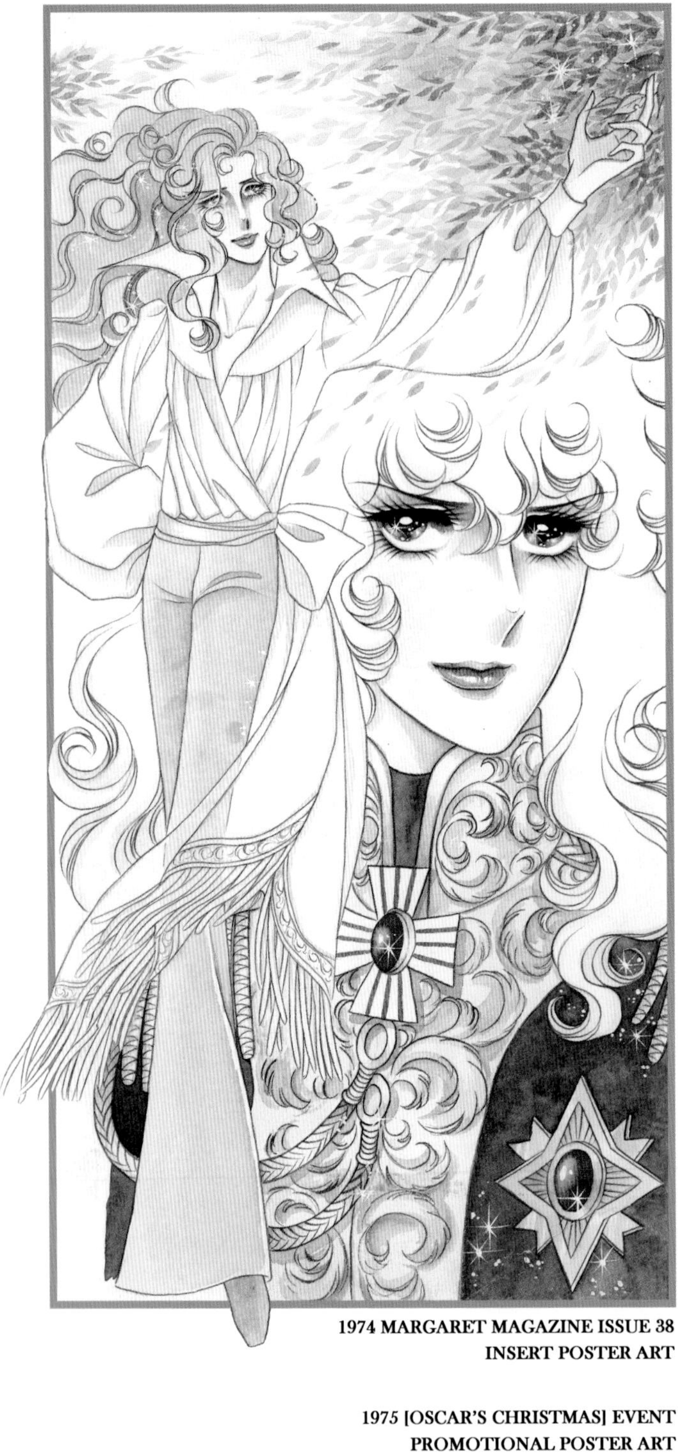

1974 MARGARET MAGAZINE ISSUE 38
INSERT POSTER ART

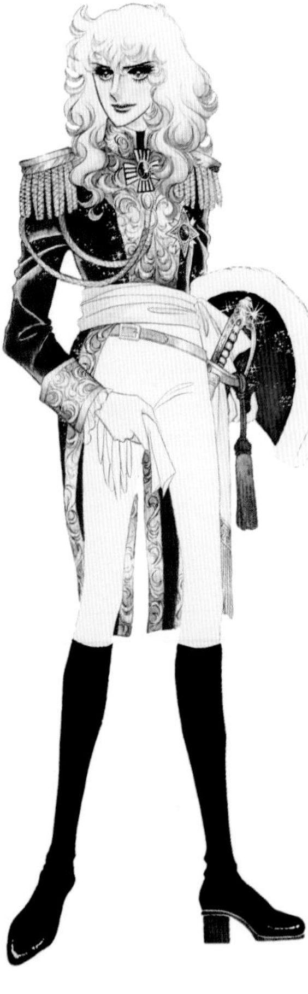

1975 [OSCAR'S CHRISTMAS] EVENT
PROMOTIONAL POSTER ART

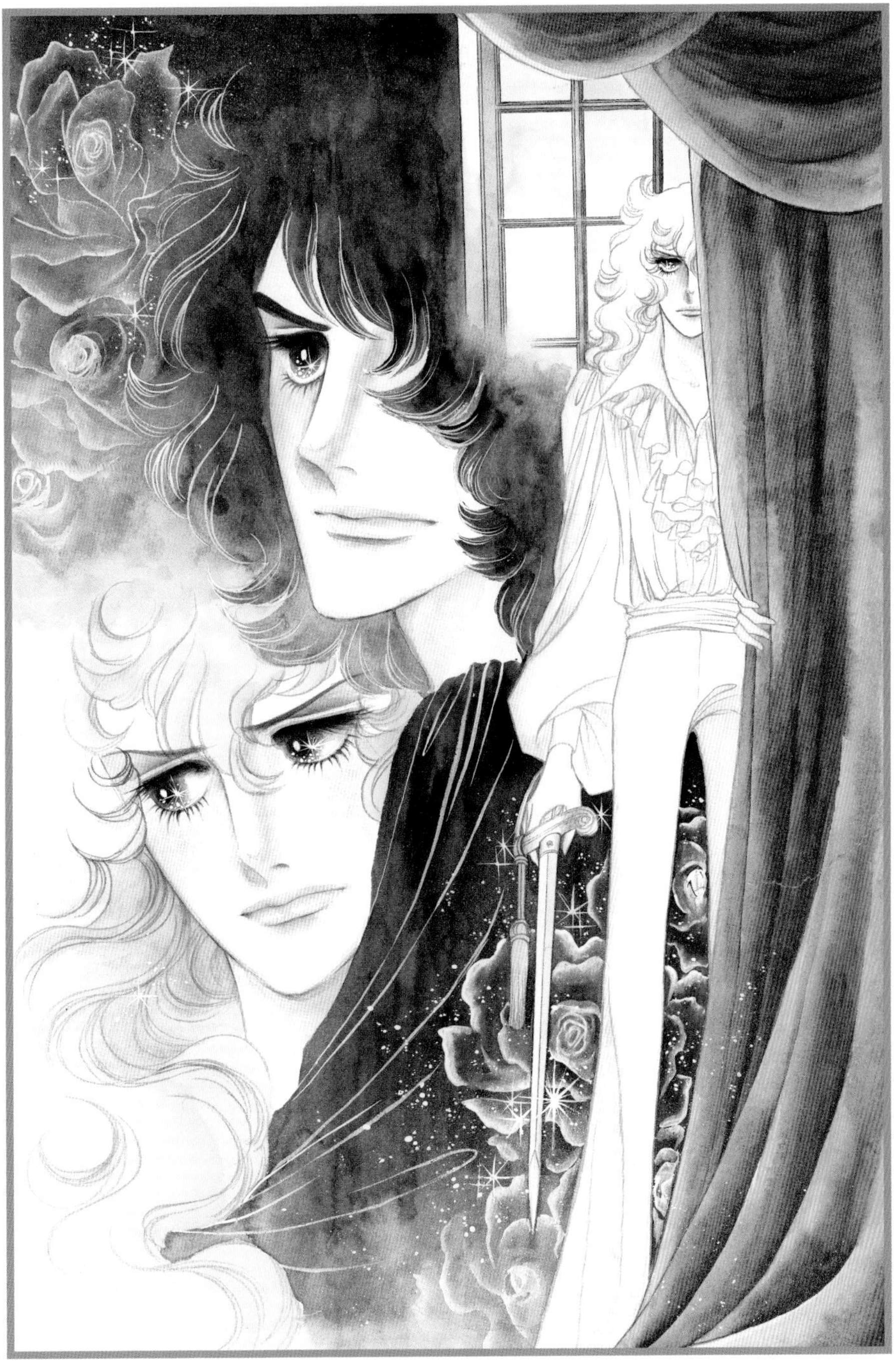

1974 ALL COLOR ILLUSTRATIONS ARTBOOK POSTER ART

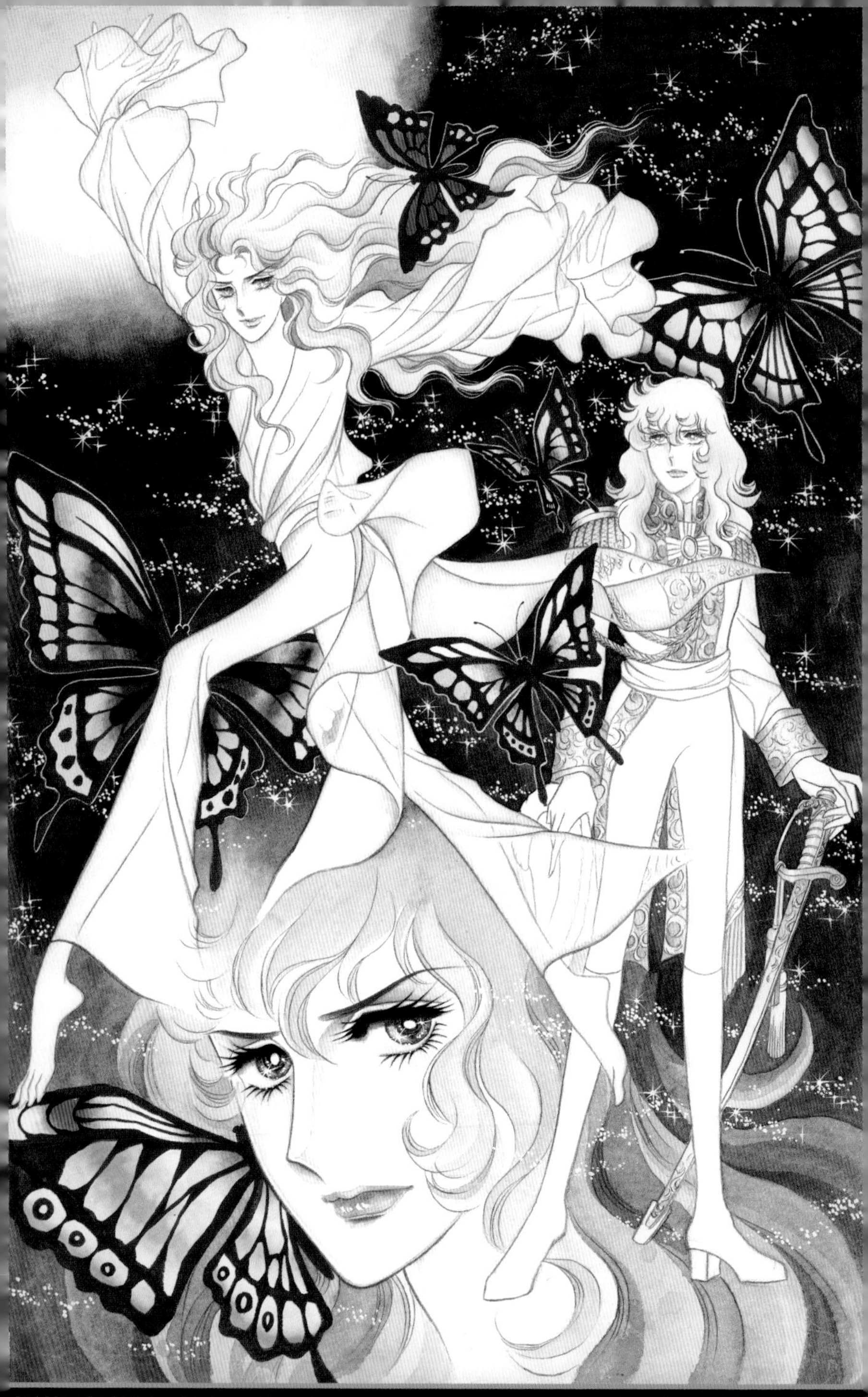

974 MARGARET MAGAZINE ISSUE 42

1973 MARGARET MAGAZINE ISSUE 4

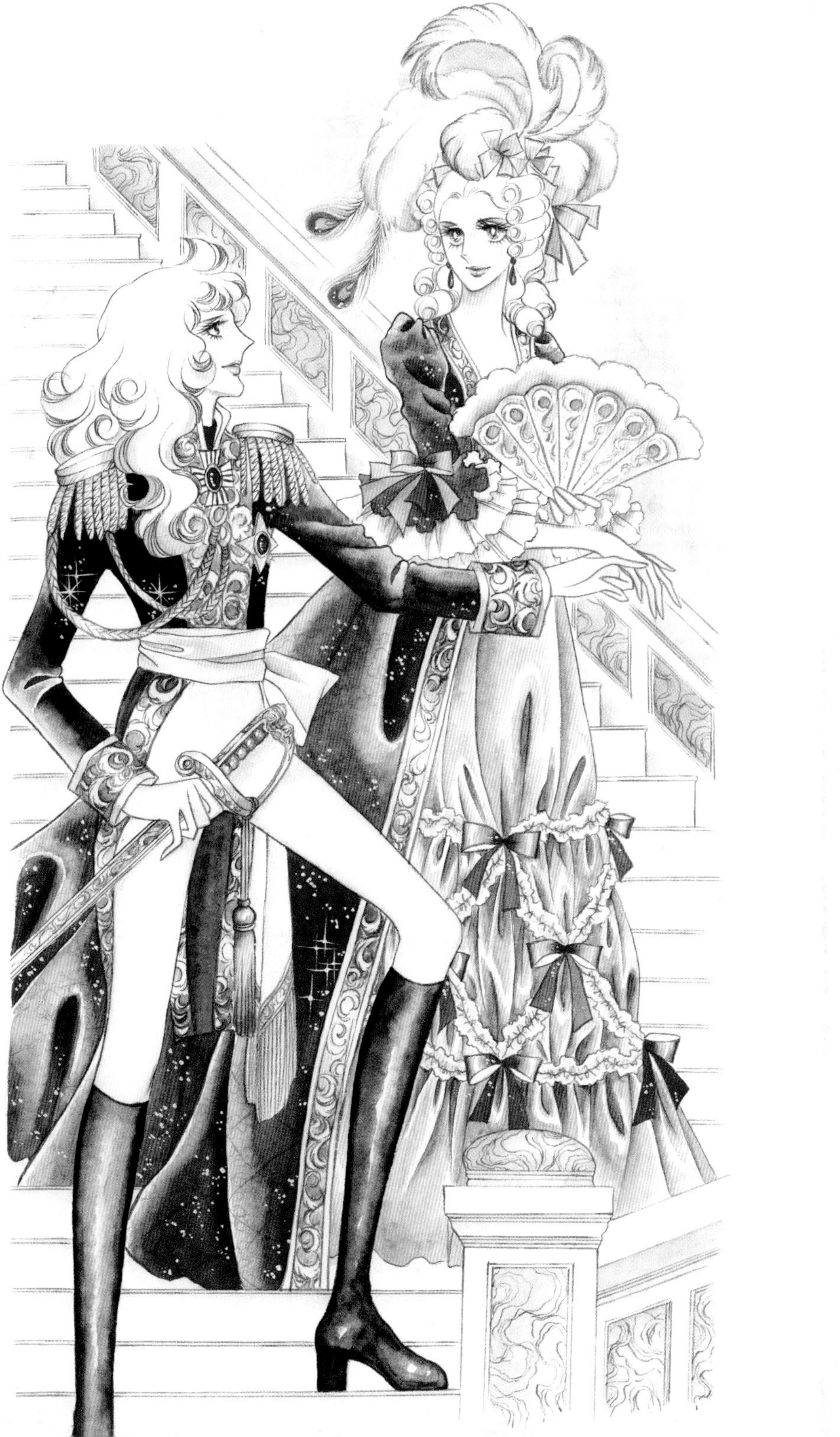

Special Treasured Gallery

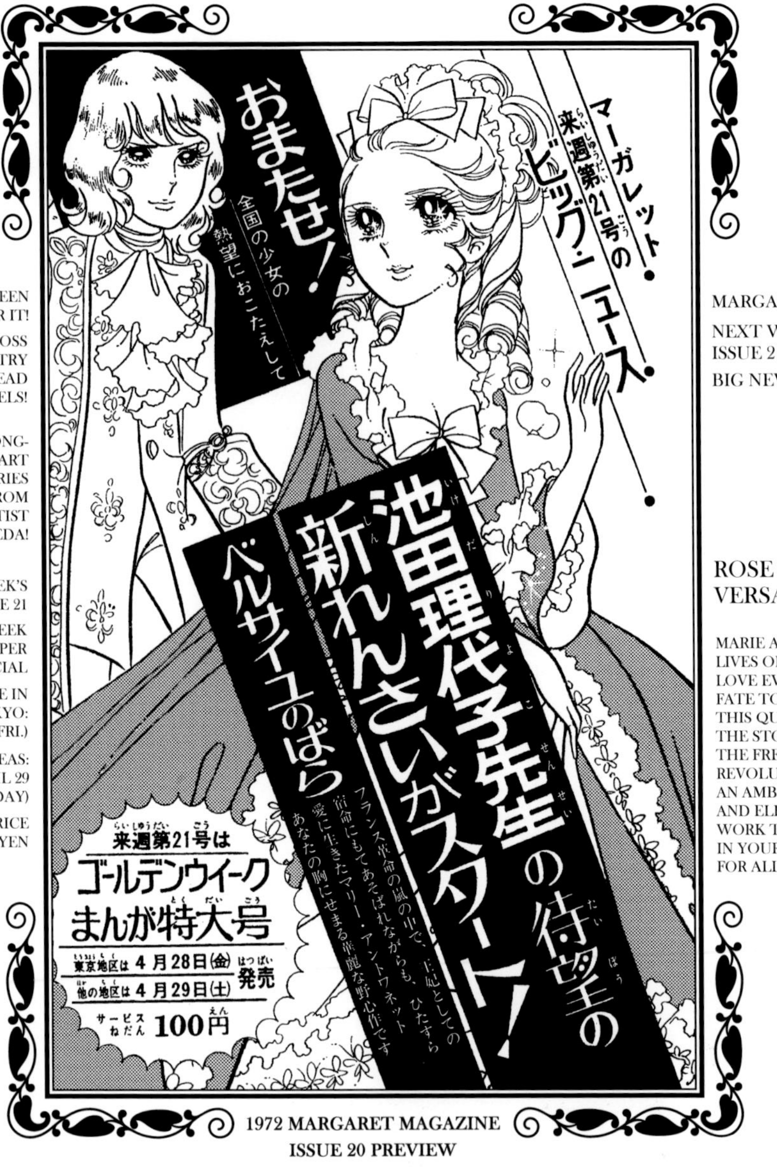
マーガレット・
来週第21号のビッグ・ニュース・
おまたせ！
全国の少女の熱望におこたえして
池田理代子先生の待望の
新れんさいがスタート！
ベルサイユのばら
フランス革命の嵐の中で、王妃としての宿命にもてあそばれながらも、ひたすら愛に生きたマリー・アントワネット あなたの胸にせまる華麗な野心作です
来週第21号は
ゴールデンウイーク
まんが特大号
東京地区は 4月28日(金)
他の地区は 4月29日(土)
発売
サービスねだん 100円

YOU'VE BEEN WAITING FOR IT!

GIRLS ACROSS THE COUNTRY ARE HEAD OVER HEELS!

THE LONG-AWAITED START OF A NEW SERIES FROM MASTER ARTIST RIYOKO IKEDA!

IN NEXT WEEK'S ISSUE 21

GOLDEN WEEK MANGA SUPER SPECIAL

ON SALE IN TOKYO: APRIL 28 (FRI.)

IN OTHER AREAS: APRIL 29 (SATURDAY)

SPECIAL PRICE 100 YEN

MARGARET

NEXT WEEK'S ISSUE 21

BIG NEWS

ROSE OF VERSAILLES

MARIE ANTOINETTE LIVES ONLY FOR LOVE EVEN AS FATE TOYS WITH THIS QUEEN IN THE STORM OF THE FRENCH REVOLUTION. AN AMBITIOUS AND ELEGANT WORK TO LIVE IN YOUR HEART FOR ALL TIME!

1972 MARGARET MAGAZINE
ISSUE 20 PREVIEW

5,665名

ベルばらファンにプレゼント

5,665
WINNERS

ROSE OF
VERSAILLES
GIFT

1973 WEEKLY
MARGARET
MAGAZINE
ISSUE 47
PRIZE
ANNOUNCEMENT
INSET

RIYOKO IKEDA

Manga artist, author, essayist, vocalist. Born 1947 in Osaka.

Started drawing graphic novels while enrolled at Tokyo University of Education
(now University of Tsukuba), Department of Philosophy.

This work, **The Rose of Versailles**, which began serialization in **Weekly Margaret** in 1972,
became the rage across near all of society, a smash hit that was adapted for the stage by
the Takarazuka Revue and into anime and feature films, crossing media barriers
and changing the history of shojo manga.

Since then, she has continued drawing manga works based on her deep perception of history and
humankind, and written essays and critiques full of insight, to the present day.

Other representative works include **Orpheus no Mado** (**The Window of Orpheus**),
which was awarded the 9th Japan Cartoonists Association Award in 1980, **Eikô no Napoleon – Eroika**
(**Eroica – The Glory of Napoleon**), and **Shôtoku Taishi** (**Prince Shôtoku**).

Ms. Ikeda entered Tokyo College of Music, Voice Department, in 1995,
and graduated the same institution in 1999.

In 2006, she was active as a soprano in theatrical and musical performances.

In addition, her 4-panel color comic strip **Berubara Kids** (**Rose of Versailles Kids**),
serialized in the **Asahi News** Saturday edition, is drawing the interest of fans new and old.

Official webpage: http://www.ikeda-riyoko-pro.com/

VERSAILLES NO BARA Volume 4
© 1973, 1974 IKEDA RIYOKO PRODUCTION
All rights reserved.
Engish translation rights arranged with IKEDA RIYOKO PRODUCTION
through Tuttle-Mori Agency, Inc. Tokyo.

AGE: Young Adult (13+)
BISAC: CGN004050 CGN004140 CGN004130 CGN009000
LIBRARY SUBJECT: Manga, Graphic Novel, Historic Fiction, LGBTQ

www.udonentertainment.com

First Printing September 2020
Second Printing November 2021
ISBN 10: 1-927925-96-7
ISBN 13: 978-1-927925-96-6
Printed in China